Keith, with all my ?
Thanks for all you[r] ...
Jan

1-114.

THE LOCAL HISTORY SERIES

This series of books is being published in order to satisfy the ever increasing interest in the history of Galloway, especially the county of Wigtownshire.

It is our intention to continue to publish further titles indefinitely as and when they are ready for printing.

Some of the books will be previously unpublished material. As such they will be in great demand by local historians, educationalists and libraries along with the "man in the street".

Published by G.C.Book Publishers Ltd.,
17 North Main Street,
Wigtown. Scotland. DG8 9HL
Tel/fax 01988 402499

e mail: gcbooks.demon.co.uk

1997

ALBANICH

A History of the Galloway Rifle Volunteers

by
Ian Devlin
editor
John Carter

(1) GRV Cap Badge surmounted by Queen's Crown 1899 - 1901

ISBN 1 872350 07 0

This first edition is limited to 500 signed and numbered copies

Number 21 */500*

Author .... *Ian Devlin* ....

Ian Devlin

Editor .... *John Carter* ....

John Carter

Published by G. C. Book Publishers Ltd
17 North Main Street,
Wigtown,
Scotland.   DG8 9HL
Tel/fax 01988 402499

Authentic history begins with the Battle of the Standard 1129 AD.

"The Scots of Galloway, a fierce ungovernable race, who fought half naked, had already distinguished themselves in King David's advance. They demanded the right to lead the van. In the second line came the Borderers and men at arms led by the young and gallant Prince Henry. In support were the men of the Lothians and Highlanders.

The enemy consisted of a solid phalanx of Barons and their retainers, clad in full armour, with quantities of Archers in reserve. The men of Galloway, shouting *"Albanich"* charged, and during two hours wrought such slaughter amongst the English spearmen that these latter began to yield."

War History of the 5th Battalion K.O.S.B.
G.F. Scott Elliot, M.A F.R.G.S. (1927).

(2) GRV Cap Badge surmounted by King's Crown and bearing legend "South Africa 1900-02"
Issued 1905 - 1908

Contents

List of Illustrations

There are few books written on the history of the Volunteer Movement, 1859 - 1908, and there is no written history of a particular Volunteer Regiment. The volunteers were very much the forgotten army, who nevertheless played an important part in the defence of the Country when Louis Napoleon III, had similar territorial aims as these of his infamous uncle, Napoleon Bonaparte, in the invasion of Britain and the conquest of Europe.

To write a history of a Territorial Regiment was by no means an easy task, the Volunteer Force existed purely as a defensive force, with their training being composed of drill and rifle shooting, later to embrace camps of exercise. Apart from the Boer War, 1899 - 1902, when members of the Volunteer Movement offered their services in South Africa, there was to be no active service.

From the outset, it was realised that very few records of the Volunteer Movement exist in the archives of the Public Records Office. On the inception of the Volunteer Movement it was the wish of Government that the Volunteer Movement should be raised and maintained by public subscription and be administered on a Regional basis by local committees, under the check approval of the Lord Lieutenant of the County, and as such all records were held locally with very few of the records ever finding their way to some central records office.

Initially, the Senior Officer ranks, within the Volunteer Movement, were held by the landed gentry, with the Junior Officer ranks being held by the legal and medical professions, and it was to these Junior Officers ranks, and invariably to the legal profession that the keeping of the Volunteer records was to fall. In 1897, the then Commanding Officer of the Galloway Rifle Volunteers, Colonel Kennedy, was to write that most of the early Regimental records had been destroyed. In an effort to find any surviving records it was necessary to trace through the Officer ranks, placing the Officers to a particular firm of solicitors and bring them forward to the present day. Major McLellan of Kirkudbright, was a partner in the firm of "McLellan and McKenzie", who in turn were taken over by "Gibson and Montgomery" and who were themselves to be superseded by the current firm of solicitors, "Williamson and Henry". Despite many years of such search, despite pleas for information of such records through the columns of the local press, searches through reference sections of local libraries, archive centres and Museums, very few Company or Regimental records of the Galloway Rifle Volunteers have been traced. During the course of such search and enquiry, however, it was found that the local press, throughout Galloway, contained a wealth of information on the Galloway Rifle Volunteers, 1859 - 1908, and particularly with there being no form of press censorship, on such delicate matters, during that period, I have been able to piece together, what I now consider to be a very full and comprehensive history of the Regiment. It should, however, be stressed that this history, is not the history of the Volunteer Movement in general but is in fact the history of a Regiment, the Galloway Rifle Volunteers. I trust that this history will now fill the void which has existed in Galloway between the Militia and the formation of the Territorial Forces of Galloway, the 5th (Dumfries and Galloway) Battalion of the King's Own Scottish Borderers and the 5th (South Ayrshire) Battalion of the Royal Scots Fusiliers, and perhaps give an insight into the formation and existence of other Regiments, who formed the Volunteer Movement.

My own fascination with the Volunteer Movement, manifested itself when I fell heir to my Great Grandfather, Michael Crossan's, war medals. A former stable boy, at the age of 15 years, he enlisted in a Sabre Regiment, the 11th Hussars, taking part in the Egyptian campaigns and the relief of General Gordon of Khartoum, holding the Nile expedition medal and the Khedive Star. On leaving the army he enlisted in the Galloway Rifle Volunteers, and at 34 years of age, with the Volunteers, he saw service in South Africa, receiving the Boer War medal with bars, Johannesburg, Orange Free State and Cape Colony, together with a local Boer War Tribute Medal, presented by the former Provost of Kirkcudbright.

In 1914, on the outbreak of World War 1 at the age of 48 years, he enlisted as a Sergeant in the 3/5th Battalion of the King's Own Scottish Borderers and was sent to France to train Officers in the use of horse on active service. In 1916, he was shot in the head but survived having a steel plate inserted in his skull and invalided home. He suffered severe pains, being frequently found lying, with his head in some cold stream. He became a recluse, living by himself, in an old wooden caravan, on the edge of the town gardens and drank heavily, frequently clearing the bar of the local hostelry with his imaginary sabre charges. He, however, lived to a ripe old age, dying in 1943, a very much unappreciated and misunderstood, "Old Soldier".

It is to my Great Grandfather, Michael Crossan, and to my mentor in this task, the late Alexander (Sandy) Bowick, Kirkhouse, Kirkcudbright, who died in 1993, during my writing of this history, that I dedicate my work.

I would also like to take this opportunity to record my eternal and grateful thanks to all the people who have contributed in some measure to the successful compilation of this history. My record of thanks is produced purely at random and does not in any way reflect the degree of assistance given.

Firstly I would like to thank my wife, Marion who not only supported me fully in this project but who accompanied and actively assisted me in the research and compilation of the history.

The Editor and Staff, Galloway News Office, Castle Douglas.

The Editor and Staff, Galloway Gazette Offices, Newton Stewart and Stranraer.

The Editor and Staff, Wigtownshire Free Press Offices, Stranraer.

The Editor and Staff, Dumfries and Galloway Standard Offices, Dumfries.

The Staff of the Reference and Historical Section of the Ewart Library, Dumfries.

Marion Stewart, M.A.M.Litt. F.S.A. (Scot) Regional Archivist, Archive Centre, Dumfries.

Dr. David Devereux and Staff, Stewartry District Museum, Kirkcudbright.

Alistair Penman L.B.P.A F.S.A Scot., Castle Douglas.

Donnie Nelson, Stranraer.

Miss Drew and Colleagues, Newton Stewart Museum.

John Picken B.A AM.A, District Museum, Stranraer and Wigtown.

Tommy Henderson and Colleagues, Dalbeattie Museum.

Bill Kerr, Stanraer.

Major (Retd.) W. Shaw, M.B.E. Assistant Regimental Secretary, Regimental Headquarters, the Royal Highland Fusiliers (Princess Margaret's Own Glasgow and Ayrshire Regiment), Glasgow.

Lieutenant Colonel C.G.O. Hogg, Regimental Secretary; D.C.R. Ward, Archivist; Mr. T. Gallagher, all of Regimental Headquarters, The King's Own Scottish Borderers, Berwick-on -Tweed.

Brigadier K.A Timbers, Historical Secretary, The Royal Artillery.

Historical Trust, Old Royal Military Academy, Woolwich, London.

Siobhan Ratchford, Museums Officer, Dumfries Museum.

Lieut. Colonel C.C.C. Cheshire, O.B.E. Chief Executive, National Rifle Ass., Bisley Camp, Surrey.

Colin R. Aitken, Hon. Secretary, Scottish Rifle Association, Edinburgh.

Leslie, Sue and Felicity, Kirkcudbright Library.

The Staff, Stanraer Library.

The Staff, Newton Stewart Library.

Christine, Dalbeattie Library.

The Staff, Castle Douglas Library.

"Copycats", The Vennel, Dumfries.

Lieutenant Colonel Clark-Kennedy, Knockgray, Dalry.

John Thomson, Grove Street, Edinburgh.

Ernie Smith, Broomlands Drive, Dumfries.

David Henderson, Kirkcudbright.

Neil Paterson, Kirkcudbright.

"Mac" Fennessy, Kirkcudbright.

Geoff Keating, Gatehouse.

Jim Allan, Librarian, Broughton House, Kirkcudbright.

George W. Simpson, Whithorn.

Tom Murchie, Newton Stewart.

Holly MacNish Porter, Phillips Scotland, International Fine Art Auctioneers and Valuers.

Ian Steele, Kirkcudbright.

Lexa Sloan, Stoke Bishop, Bristol.

Grace Livingstone Pope, Bognor Regis, Sussex.

Joe Rafferty, Stranraer.
Mrs. D. Alcorn, Company Secretary, Queen of the South F.C. Ltd., Dumfries.
Donald McLennan, Kirkcudbright.
Douglas Swan, Kirkcudright.
Ray Taylor, Queen Street, Newton Stewart.
John McQueen, Dumfries.
Rev. Gordon Savage, M.A, B.D., Maxwellton West Church, Dumfries.
Mrs Sproat, Plunton House, Borgue.
Biddy Melville, Monreith, Port William.
Ian Armour, Kirkcudbright.
Norman J. Hunter, Stranraer.
Sandy Sproat, Brighouse, Borgue.
Bryan Byrne, R.S.M. Retd., Kirkcudbright.
Arlene Henderson, Castle Douglas.
Carol Gillard, New Zealand

Kirkcudbright, 1996......Ian Devlin.

CHAPTER 1

GALLOWAY RIFLES MILITIA - "PRINCE REGENT'S ROYAL REGIMENT OF AYR AND WIGTOWN MILITIA" - "SCOTTISH BORDERERS MILITIA" - ROYAL DUMFRIES VOLUNTEERS , VOLUNTEER FORCE OF 1798 - THE GALLOWAY RANGERS - KIRKCUDBRIGHT GENTLEMEN AND YEOMANRY CAVALRY.

By Act of Parliament (17 and 18 Vict., Cap.,13), issued on the the 12th May, 1854, the Government granted authority to Her Majesty Queen Victoria to call out, or embody the Militia in the event of war with another country. Prior to this Act being passed the Militia could only be embodied if the shores of the United Kingdom were threatened by invasion or in the event of some real civil disorder.

This policy change in Militia service was created to counter the absence of regular troops, called from Britain to the Crimea in the war with Russia A further Act was passed on the 11th August, 1854, four months after the declaration of war, requiring a force of 10,000 Militia to be raised in Scotland. A force was raised throughout Galloway under, Sir William Maxwell, Bart., of Monreith, Commanding Officer of the Galloway Rifles Militia and on 1st May, 1855, a force was raised in Dumfries under the Marquis of Queensberry. These Militia Forces, although offering to serve overseas, remained within the United Kingdom until the cessation of hostilities in 1856, when they were disembodied or stood down.

"Who were the Militia?" The origins of the Militia dated in various forms from the ancient "Saxon Fyord", which was a compulsory levy of manpower raised for coastal defence. The Militia evolved through this old Constitutional force to its present form and were charged, not only with the duty of defending their particular coastline but were also charged with the preservation of peace and good order within that region, thereby freeing valuable military resources which were particularly stretched by the threatening menaces of a Republican France. Within the Galloway region, the Militia could be considered the forerunners of the Galloway Rifle Volunteers, who were in turn the forerunners of the 5th Battalion of the King's Own Scottish Borderers.

The 'Militia Bill' - Act, (37 George 111. Cap., 103), was issued by Government in July, 1797, authorising a force of 6,000 Militia to be raised in Scotland by ballot, to combat the ever present menace of French invasion. To the populace of Scotland this was a totally new and alien concept and was to be met, initially, with much resistance.

By the provisions of this Act, the local Schoolmaster was required to draw up and publish in some prominent position a list of all eligible men between the ages of 18 and 45 years. Exceptions being regular forces, schoolmasters, clergy, apprentices and those with two or more children, this was, however, changed in 1802 to no longer grant exemption to those with two children or more. Applications for exemption to the ballot were heard by a travelling Deputy Lieutenant of that particular County.

When the required quotas of Militia were fixed by the authorities a ballot was held amongst those considered eligible and the names of these men drawn were ordered into Militia service. Initially the Militia were only required to serve during the course of threatened invasion, filling the gap left by the Regular Army called to serve overseas and were required to be disembodied one month after hostilities or the threat of invasion had ceased. However, this was very soon altered to the Militia being enlisted for a period of 5 years with the further proviso that should their Regiment be embodied during the 5 year period then they were required to serve until the reason for their emodiment had ceased. Initially the Militia could not be ordered to serve outwith the boundaries of Scotland nor could they be required to serve in the Regular Army but by 1799, once the Militia Bill had been accepted, the Militia had volunteered to serve anywhere within the United

Kingdom. The period of annual training was fixed at 21 days.

Some strange and additional exemptions to the Militia Bill were to become recognised by the authorities, who, at the end of the day were purely concerned that the required Militia quotas were being met. In the event of an eligible man being drawn in the ballot he was quite at liberty to provide a substitute to take his place in the Militia service. This was similar to the old, prestigious, 16th Century, position in Scotland of Town Constable, invariably held by a person of some rank. In the event of hostilities or insurrection, the Town Constable could be called to arms or name a substitute. The substitute was a man of much lower rank paid by the Constable to fulfil his duties in the call to arms.

The person balloted could also be excused Militia service on the payment of £10. It was felt by the authorities that a substitute could be procured for that sum. With this cash payment being an exemption to Militia service, Insurance Companies were to spring up offering coverage to those eligible men wishing to avoid service. For the payment of an agreed sum of money, reportedly in the region of 3 guineas, the Insurance Company would provide a substitute or pay the £10 exemption fee should their policy holder be balloted. This worked very well in the event of the policy holder being drawn in the ballot but should his name not be drawn, he had lost 3 guineas, a sum, the working class man could ill-afford to lose. It was no wonder that resentment was felt with the introduction of the Bill.

Opposition to the Militia Bill was to build up leading eventually to rioting throughout Scotland. Groups of young men were to go on the rampage destroying Militia lists, breaking into the schools and churches destroying the Parish and Schoolmaster's records. In the August of 1797, a meeting of the Deputy Lieutenants of Galloway, being held in Wigtown, was broken up by a violent mob. However, this unrest was to die down very quickly, the populace of Scotland accepting the patriotic pleas of Government to the ever present threat of French invasion. We find that by 1798, all hostilities to the Militia Bill had stopped and a feeling of pride in their new Regiments was beginning to emerge.

The following extracts were to appear in the *Weekly Journal,* "On the 24th April, 1798, a Court of Lieutenancy was held in Castle Douglas, agreeable to public Acts and Orders of the Privy Council, when the meeting appointed balloting for the different Parishes to proceed at certain times and places."

The day fixed for the Glenkens, which included the Parish of Parton, was on the 8th May, 1798. "There breakfasted at Kenmure Castle, on the green, in a tent before the house, eighty-four persons. On this occasion several toasts were drunk under a salute of five cannon each. The Company was as under, 50 Privates, 5 Sergeants, 3 Officers, one Surgeon, one Drummer, one Fifer, 3 Servants, in all sixty-four."

The Militia in Scotland was divided into 10 Regiments. The following Counties formed as one Regiment, to be called the 4th North British Militia, under the Command of the Earl of Dalkeith, later to succeed as the 4th Duke of Buccleuch.

Counties referred to:- Peebles - Selkirk - Roxburgh - Kirkcudbrightshire - Wigtownshire - Dumfries-shire.

In 1802, by Act of Parliament, Dumfriesshire - Roxburgh and Selkirk, were to form as one Regiment, with Kirkcudbrightshire and Wigtownshire, forming as a separate Regiment. In 1803, Dumfriesshire - Roxburgh and Selkirk, were to be designated the 70th Regiment of Militia, with Kirkcudbrightshire and Wigtownshire, forming as the 21st Regiment of Militia and for the first time to bear the title of the "Galloway Rifles Militia"

The most serious threat of French invasion was to take place in 1803, when Napoleon Bonaparte began to assemble a large fleet of flat-bottomed boats at Boulogne for the immediate invasion of England. Throughout 1803 and 1804, Napoleon was to further assemble, at Boulogne, an invasion force of upwards of 100,000 men. The Militia were embodied throughout Britain to counter this menace. The following extracts were to appear in the *Dumfries Weekly Journal.*

Galloway Militia

His Majefty having been gracioufly pleafed to direct that the Militia Force of the Stewartry of Kirkcudbright shall be called out and embodied with the fmalleft poffible delay, the Convener of the Lieutenancy of the Stewartry in abfence of his Majefty's Lieutenant hereby directs, in conformity to the Act of 42d of the King, intitled, "An Act for raifing a Militia Force in that part of Great Britain, called Scotland," that a GENERAL MEETING of the Lieutenancy of the Stewartry of Kirkcudbright aforefaid be held at Caftle Douglas, on Tuefday the fifth of April next, at ten forenoon for the purpofe of iffuing the neceffary orders for calling out and embodying the Militia Force of the faid Stewartry.

(Signed) AND. WRIGHT. D Lt and Conv.

19.3.1803.

Dumfriesshire Militia

Notice is hereby given, that in confequence of his Majefty's Warrant, dated the 12th current, a GENERAL MEETING of Lieutenancy of the County of Dumfries appointed the Dumfriesshire Militia to be embodied at Dumfries, on Tuefday the fifth day of April next - And all the men enrolled af Principals, or Subftitutes, in the faid Regiment, are therefore hereby directed to repair to Dumfries, the Headquarters on the above day, for the purpofe of being muftered trained and exercifed; and thofe who shall neglect to appear time and place aforefaid, will be confidered af deferters, and punished accordingly - All in terms of the Militia Acts of Parliament. THOS. GOLDIE CLERK GM.
Dumfries 21ft March, 1803.

With the defeat of the French Fleet by Admiral Lord Nelson at Trafalgar in 1805 the immediate threat of invasion was to subside and the Militia in Scotland were reduced to a force of 8,000 men. However Napoleon was still to continue his domination of Europe with victories at Austerlitz (1805) and Jena (1806).

In 1808, the Spanish rebelled against Napoleon and assisted by a British Force under the Duke of Wellington, they met with some measure of success. This encouraged Russia to join the war against Napoleon resulting in his disastrous invasion of Russia in 1812 when 600,000 French troops were lost to the severe Russian winter.

With this unrest continuing in Europe the Militia were to remain embodied, the following extracts from the *Edinburgh Courant* chronicle the movements of the Galloway Rifles Militia during their period of embodiment from the immediate threat of invasion in 1803 until disembodied in August, 1814:-

"Friday, 3rd May, 1805, colours were presented in the Square of the Citadel, Leith, to the Galloway Militia"

"Friday, 29th May, 1807, the Galloway Militia were reviewed at Leith Links. This morning they marched into the Castle."

"Wednesday, 12th October, 1808, the Galloway Militia were reviewed at Port Seton."

"Saturday, 25th March, 1809, the Galloway Militia were inspected at Port Seton."

"Thursday, 18th May, 1809, the Galloway Militia marched into quarters at Leith."

"Saturday, 2nd February, 1811, a detachment of Galloway Militia marched to Penicuik to guard prisoners in that neighbourhood."

"Monday, 25th February, 1811, the Galloway Militia marched from Dalkeith to Penicuik and adjacent villages to guard prisoners at Esk Mills, after nearly two years at Dalkeith."

"Tuesday, 9th July, 1811, the Galloway Militia left Penicuik for Glasgow. The Militia were to remain in Glasgow from 10th July, 1811, to 27th July, 1812, when they marched to Dumbarton."

"July, 1813, the Galloway Militia marched from Glasgow to Dumbarton where they were to remain until, 9th August, 1813, when they marched to Port Seton."

"Monday, 8th August, 1814, the Galloway Militia marched from Penicuik to Kirkcudbright." (The prisoners referred to were French prisoners of war taken during the Napoleonic Wars.)

In the Kirkcudbright Town Council Minutes of 1814, it is reported that the Galloway Rifles Militia, had never been quartered in the district since their embodiment 12 years previous in 1803, and later that year we find Sir Alexander Gordon, Lieutenant Colonel, Commandant of the Galloway Rifles Militia writing to the Provost of Kirkcudbright, asking for the use of the Assembly Rooms in Kirkcudbright, for clothing and stores and the use of the Court House as a depot for their arms.

At a meeting of the Kirkcudbright Town Council of 8th August, 1814, Bailie Burnie was to inform the Council that the Militia would arrive in Kirkcudbright on the 15th August, 1814, to be quartered prior to their being disembodied, in Kirkcudbright.

Encouraged by Napoleon's disastrous foray into Russia, the combined Forces of Britain, Prussia, Russia, Austria and Sweden, were to move against Napoleon. News of the Napoleonic Wars, it was reported, generally took about 3 months to reach Galloway, and it was not until the beginning of September, 1815, that we find news of Napoleon's defeat at Waterloo had in fact reached Galloway, when it was reported that subscription lists were opened for "The Relief of the Widows and Orphans of Waterloo." It is recorded that Kirkcudbright Town Council were to subscribe £54, a church collection was to raise £15, and the Galloway Rifles Militia, quartered in Kirkcudbright, subscribed £15.7s.6d.

With this time lapse in mind, we find that a further call for the Militia to be embodied, no doubt in readiness for the final conflict with the French resulting in the battle of Waterloo, was to take place on the

1st July, 1815, when the following call, for the embodiment of the Stewartry Militia, was to appear in the *Dumfries Courier*.

For Embodying the Militia
of the Stewartry of Kirkcudbright.
In terms of His Royal Highness the Prince Regent.
Warrant, dated the 16th day of June last and an order by the Lieutenancy in consequence thereof, the MILITIA of the said Stewartry are ordered and directed to be drawn out and embodied at Kirkcudbright upon Friday the 14th July current, at noon; of which all concerned are hereby warned to take notice or abide the consequences.

DAd. Miller Dpy C.G.Lt.
Kirkcudbright 1st July, 1815.

The following extracts from the *Edinburgh Courant* once again chronicle the movements of the Galloway Rifles Militia.

"Friday, 15th September, 1815, the Galloway Militia march to Ayr from Kirkcudbright. Arrived Ayr, 19th September."

"Saturday, 25th March, 1816, the Galloway Militia are disbanded."

In 1795, 2 years prior to the introduction of the Militia Bill of July, 1797, a Territorial Force was raised in Dumfries under the title of the Royal Dumfries Volunteers. This force comprised of 100 Gentlemen Volunteers who were raised to maintain the internal peace of their area as well as the defence of their town. They were not, however, obliged to serve more than 5 miles from the Burgh of Dumfries. Robert Burns was a member of this force from its inception in 1795 until his death the following year in 1796. It was reported that he frequently offended his comrades in arms by his after dinner toast of, "May we never see the French nor the French see us."

In April, of 1795, Burns was to publish the following song, in the *Dumfries Weekly Journal,* which was later to become a valuable patriotic rallying call by Government to have their Militia Bill of 1797 accepted in Scotland, particularly with its reference to French invasion, "Does haughty Gaul invasion threat?" This song, entitled the "Dumfries Volunteer" was to prove popular, not only in Scotland, but was adopted by the Volunteer Regiments throughout Britain and we find almost a century later the same song being used to inspire the Galloway men yet again when the threat of Republican France was once again to threaten British shores.

The Dumfries Volunteer.

Does haughty Gaul invasion threat?
Then let the loons beware, Sir;
There's wooden walls upon our seas,
And Volunteers on shore, Sir.
The Nith shall run to Corsincan,
And Criffel sink in Solway,
Ere we permit a foreign foe,
On British ground to rally.

O let us not, like snarling tykes,
In wrangling be divided;
Till, slap, in comes a foreign loon,
And with a gun decides it.
Be Britain still to Britain true,
Among ourselves united;
For never but by British hands
Must British wrongs be righted.

The union of the Church and State,
Perhaps will need some patching.
But never will a foreign rogue,
Ever knock a nail in't.
Our father's blood the Union bought,
And who would dare to spoil it,
By Heavens a sacrilegious dog,
Will never come to foil it.

The wretch who would a tyrant own,
And the wretch, his true born brother,
Who's set the mob upon the throne,
May they be damned together
Who will not sing 'God save the King'.
Shall hang as high's the steeple,
But while we sing 'God save the King',
We'll not forget the people.

On the introduction of the Militia Bill in 1797, a second Corps of the Royal Dumfries Volunteers was raised, this Corps was to become, the Dumfries Militia.

With the acceptance of the Militia Bill in 1798, and the ever present threat of French invasion, everyone was to become a Volunteer of some sort or another. It was loudly proclaimed that the enemy was in full possession and sight of the heights across the Channel and his intention to invade was imminent. The demand therefore, on the patriotism of the populace was immediate and the Government pleas were to be answered accordingly. The Volunteer was to go through his own peculiar species of initiation by which he was considered to be a soldier. It was only requisite to join a Corps, to don a uniform, to acquire the first rudiments of the manual exercise and to march in a tolerable manner on the occasion of Inspection or Review. The end result was an enormous force of Volunteers, clothed in their own inimitable, red-coat, but animated with sufficient vigour and spirit beyond that insepable from the natural courage of the "True Brit".

As in times past, Galloway was to heed the calls of Government and rally to the cause, and in a very short period of time Volunteer Companies had sprung up in every town and village in Galloway, with their services being offered to Major Drummond, the Officer Commanding the Western District, by the July of 1798. The Volunteer services were offered subject to the immediate threat of, or in the event of invasion.

Subscription lists were opened with subscriptions coming from every Parish of the county, reported under the heading, "Voluntary contributions over and above assessed taxes, in aid of the exertions of Government against the enemies of this County".

"26th June, 1798, subscriptions for the **Parish of Borgue** for the defence of the County - David Blair of Borgue, £10.10s.; Adam Thomson, Lieutenant Loyal Borgue Volunteers, £10.10s.; Mrs Thomson of Ingleston, £5.5s.; William Grierson, Mary Sproat, Mary Tait, Susan Edwards - servants to Mr Thomson, 5s.; long list of smaller subscribers ending with. Alexander Sproat, tenant in Concheton, £1.0s; John Campbell, tenant in Sproats - Plunton, 10s. 6d. Total of £36.6d. from this Parish.

Parish of Kirkbean. D. Hamilton Craik Esq., of Arbigland, £31.10s; John McKenne in Dumbar, £1.1s; Mrs. McKenne in Dumbar, 10s.6d; Theodore Corrie, Paoliment, £1.1s; Mark Louden, Carsethorn, £2.0s; long list of subscribers ending with, David Bewly, South Carse, 2s. 6d; Andrew Taylor, Laglee, 2s.6d. Total of £61.9s.6d from this Parish.

Troqueer. James Maxwell of Kirkconnell, £40; Mrs. Maxwell of Kirkconnell, £5.5s; James Stothart of Cargen, £40; George Maxwell of Carruchan, £10.10s; John Maxwell of Terraughtie, £10.10s; Mrs. Maxwell of Terraughtie, £10.10s; Commisary Goldie, £20; John McGhie of Castlehill, £15.15s ; John Syme of Ryedale, £20; The Rev. John Ewart, £8; Mrs.Milligan of Dalscairth; long list of subscribers.

Rerrick. Thomas Cairns of Dundrennan; Large list of subscribers concluding with Rev. James Thomson £5.5s; his servants 3s; Thomas Kirkpatrick 2s.6d; Isaac Carson, 2s.6d; making a total of £350.3s.6d from this Parish alone.

Balmaghie. £300 from Thomas Gordon Esq., of Balmaghie; Gordon of Cambellton gives 50 guineas in Tongland.

Kells. Honourable John Gordon of Kenmure £50; Mrs. Gordon, £5; Mrs. Gordon's Servants, £1.17s.6d; Rev. J. Gillespie £3; Mr. Grierson of Garroch, £3.3s; W. Newal Esq., £2.2s; Mr. Baillie Murray, Junior, £1.1s; Mrs. Livingstone, £1.1s; Sundry inhabitants £5.15s.6d; Mr. Kennedy of Knocknailling, £1.1s; Anthony McMillan of Barlae, £1.1s.

Balmaclellan. Mr. McCan, £10 ; James Carson Esq., £2.2s; Mr. J. Thompson, £1.1s; Mr. Gibson, £1.1s; Mr. Anderson, £1.1s; Mr. Moffat, 25s; Sundry inhabitants, £3.14s.6d.

Dalry. Rev. Mr. McGowan, £1.1s; Mr. Alexander of Mackilston, £2.2s; Robert McMillan of Fingland, £2. 2s. Mr Barbour of Bogue, £2.2s; Mr. Donaldson of Duchrae, £1.1s; Mr. McGaw, £2; Sundry inhabitants, £3.14s.6d.

Carsphairn. Rev. Mr. Gordon, £3.3s; Mr. McMillan of Holm, £5.5s; Mr. Wallace of Knockgray, £3.3s. etc.

Parton. Mr. William Glendonwyn of Glendonwyn, £31; Servants, £1.15s; Rev. Mr. Donaldson; Mr. Mitchell of Barwhillanty. Mr. Gillespie, of Borland; Mr. Shaw of Drumrash; Mr. Crosbie of Merkland £1.1s. each, etc.

The following extracts from the *Dumfries Weekly Journal* give an interesting insight into the 'happy-go-lucky' atmosphere which was to be enjoyed by the members of the various Companies of the Galloway Volunteers. This was indeed a far cry from only the year previous, when rioting had taken place throughout Scotland, on the introduction of the Militia Bill. Perhaps the men of Scotland and Galloway were quite willing to Volunteer their services for the defence of their Country but did not want to be dictated to by Act of Parliament, no doubt, the Inspecting Officers, Colonel Nicholson and Colonel Ferrier, had this very much in mind when their glowing remarks were reported to the several Companies.

"On Saturday 28th March, 1799 New Galloway Volunteers, commanded by Mr. Gordon, Kenmure, after a very handsome compliment to the loyalty and soldier-like appearance of the Corps, Mrs. Gordon of Kenmure, presented them with an elegant pair of colours. They were then addressed in a short complimentary speech by the Captain. The Chaplain, Mr. William Gillespie, concluded the evening with a very suitable discourse and prayer."

"On Thursday, 2nd April, 1799, the loyal Castle Douglas Volunteers were inspected by Colonel Nicholson, who after seeing them perform the Manual and Platoon exercises, expressed himself highly satisfied with their regularity, steadiness and military appearance and was pleased to add, "Without flattering you, I must say you march astonishingly well, and fire like good old soldiers."

"On Friday, 3rd April, 1799, a discharge of cannon from Kenmure Castle, having announced the arrival of Colonel Nicholson, the New Galloway Volunteers, commanded by Mr. Gordon of Kenmure, were drawn up in order, to be inspected. Colonel Nicholson was pleased to express in a very handsome manner his perfect approbation of their appearance and the correctness of their firings and evolutions. A great crowd of spectators were assembled on the occasion. It was pleasant to observe that a part of the country so thinly inhabited should send down, from their native mountains, so many brave young fellows. In the words of a Caledonian Bard,

"with hearts resolved, and hands prepared
The blessings they enjoy to guard."

The Corps, immediately after partook of a cold repast, which their Comandant had prepared for them, after which the Officers, having drunk several loyal toasts with the men, were entertained at Kenmure Castle, the enjoyment which true friendship and loyalty never fail to impose."

"On Monday, 23rd March, 1800, the loyal Borgue Volunteers were inspected by Colonel Ferrier, when they performed their various evolutions and firings with their usual exactness and precision. Colonel Ferrier was so well pleased with their discipline that he readily granted a certificate relieving them from a stated attendance on drill. After the inspection the Company sat down to an elegant dinner prepared for them by their Captain, where in the midst of conviviality and harmony they expressed their attachment to his Majesty's person and Government, by the warmest effusions of loyalty."

"On Monday, 23rd March, 1800, the loyal Gatehouse of Fleet Volunteers, commanded by Captain Birtwhistle, were inspected by Colonel Ferrier. The correct and steady manner in which the Company performed the different parts of the military evolutions were such as to meet the Colonel's entire approbation, who readily granted them a certificate excepting them from duty in terms of the Regulations of the War Office. The Company was entertained with an elegant Ball by their Captain. The evening was spent with that social order and unanimity which has always distinguished this Corps."

"On Tuesday, 31st March, 1800, the New Galloway Volunteers, commanded by Captain John Gordon of Kenmure, were reviewed by Colonel Ferrier on the green before Kenmure Castle, when they went through a variety of evolutions and firings, much to the satisfaction of the Colonel, who desired Captain Gordon to convey to the Company his entire approbation on the appearance they made."

"On Thursday, 2nd April, 1800, the loyal Portpatrick Volunteers, commanded by Captain Adam Gordon, were reviewed by Colonel Ferrier. Their appearance gave him such satisfaction and he was particularly pleased with their firings."

Very little and in most cases no history has survived of these many and varied Galloway Volunteer Infantry Companies and it must therefore be assumed that with the defeat of the French Navy, by Admiral Nelson, (1805) and the immediate threat of invasion lifted, these Infantry Companies were to disband, leaving only their once proud titles to cast but a faint shadow on Galloway's glorious past.

In addition to the numerous Companies of Volunteer Infantrymen, there was also raised in Wigtownshire,

(1797) and Kirkcudbrightshire, (1803), Troops of Yeomanry Cavalry. The Wigtownshire Troop, bearing the title, the "Galloway Rangers" was raised by Colonel McDowall, of Logan, and comprised of three Cavalry Troops - Stranraer - Newton Stewart - Wigtown. Colonel McDowall was to become the Troop's first Commanding Officer .

Once again little history has survived of this once fine Regiment and the following extracts chronicle its brief reported history.

"26th June, 1798, Colonel McDowall, has volunteered the Galloway Rangers for service in Ireland."

"Wednesday, 25th July, 1798, Colonel Ferrier inspected the Wigtownshire Troop of Cavalry in the presence of a vast crowd of spectators attracted by the novelty of the scene and the good sense of the weather. The fine appearance of the Company, the exact uniformity of their dress and the good taste of their arms, attracted the notice of the Colonel and every spectator. From the manner in which they performed the field manoeuvres and the firing, the Colonel said he had no difficulty in reporting the Company in so complete a state of efficiency and discipline and to make a further attendance of a Drill Sergeant unnecessary."

The following figures refer to the strengths of Volunteers 1804.

Statistical Statements.

Dumfriesshire Cavalry	84 -Infantry 1875.
Kirkcudbrightshire Cavalry	200 - Infantry 748.
(Kirkcudbright Gentlemen and Yeomanry Cavalry.)	
Wigtownshire Cavalry (Galloway Rangers)	105 - Infantry 623.

"*Dumfries Courier,* 21st August, 1821. The Wigtownshire Cavalry went into quarters, for a period of six days drill, at Stranraer, on the 23rd of last month. This County musters three troops of Cavalry, under the command of Major Sir William Maxwell, which in point of military appearance and zeal in the service, can only be equalled by the unexampled precision and rapidity of their evolutions, acquired under the discipline of an energetic and able commander. His care and assiduity while the Corps were in quarters, could not fail to excite and gain the esteem and respect, not only of every one who had occasion to mark his conduct, but must at the same time, have secured the entire venerations and services of those under his command. The proficiency of the Corps, in its appearance, and in all its movements procured the eulogiums of one well qualified to judge, Colonel Cathcart of Genoch one of the Deputy Lieutenants of the County, who reviewed it on Saturday the 26th ult. The steadiness and rapidity of the movements may be attributed to the skill and management of the riders, and in great measure to the breed of horses introduced into the Corps, from the well known studs of Sir William Maxwell and Sir James D. Hay. The town of Stranraer, every evening presented a scene of festivity, carried on in the utmost good humour, and the races by the horses in the Corps, during the week, afforded such good sport."

The Wigtownshire Troop of Cavalry appears to have survived until the mid 1820's when it was disbanded and in 1831 we find a brief report that two of the former "Galloway Rangers" troops, Wigtown and Stranraer, had been reformed. It can only be assumed that this was to be of a short duration with no report of their activities surviving. In the May of 1860 an unsuccesful attempt was made to reinstate a Wigtownshire troop of Cavalry by Sir William Maxwell, Bart., of Monreith, ex. Commanding Officer of the Galloway Rifles Militia.

Returning to the Kirkcudbrightshire Yeomanry Cavalry (1803). This force was to far outlive that of its Wigtownshire counterpart, the Galloway Rangers, and the other Volunteer Companies of the period, and as such, various records have survived, which give an interesting insight and indication as to the workings and duties in which the troop was employed.

The Force was raised initially in the Spring of 1803, as four independent troops, Kirkcudbright - Castle Douglas - Glenkens - Gatehouse. Gatehouse being the last to offer their services to the Crown in June, 1803. In August, 1803, the four independent troops were to join as the "Kirkcudbright Gentlemen and Yeomanry Cavalry," under the Command of Lieutenant Colonel James Gordon of Greenlaw, Crossmichael, with Headquarters at the Court House, Kirkcudbright.

The new Force comprised as under:-

St. Mary's Troop, Kirkcudbright - under the Command of Captain William Mure.
Castle Douglas troop under the Command of Captain Smith.
Glenkens Troop - under the Command of Captain Robert Johnstone.
Cally Troop, Gatehouse - under the Command of Captain H. Stewart, of Gategill.

On the formation of this Regiment, in August, 1803, it reported an establishment of 19 Officers and Staff Officers; 1 Sergeant Major; 10 Sergeants; 10 Corporals; 5 Trumpeters; 170 Troopers. This establishment was to remain fairly constant throughout the existence of the Regiment.

On the 7th August, 1803, Ordnance was to supply the Regiment with 50 pistols and 50 sabres, but by 5th October, 1803, the Regimental returns show them to be in possession of 150 pistols and 150 sabres. However, quantity does not necessarily mean quality and pencilled in the margin of the returns is the legend, "The swords and pistols were not new when issued and as they have been in use for 16 years are much worn and could never be kept in the order they ought to be from their having been rusted in previous issues."

In keeping with many such Regiments of the day, the Officer ranks were filled by landed gentry and gentlemen farmers with the Regiment being very much an upper and middle class domain. As its title suggests it was indeed a 'Gentleman's Yeomanry Cavalry." Needless to say the most prevalent and detailed records to survive of this Regiment are the Officers "Mess Bills."

The duties of the Regiment were as those of the Militia, the preservation of internal peace and the good order and defence of their particular coastline. In 1797, on the introduction of the Militia Bill to Scotland, the Jedburgh Yeomanry were called out to surpress a civil disorder, within their area, instigated by the introduction of this Bill. No evidence exists to show that the Kirkcudbright Gentlemen Yeomanry Cavalry were ever embodied or called to serve, either within, or, outwith their area.

The following circular was issued by the War Office on the 10th December, 1807, "The number of days for which Corps of Yeomanry Cavalry are permitted to assemble for the purpose of being trained and exercised is limited by Act of Parliament to 14 in the year for which payment is received on the authority of the Secretary of War." Members of the Regiment were to receive the statutory rates of Regular Army pay whilst undergoing training on "Permanent Pay and Duty Service."

After the defeat of Napoleon at Waterloo in 1815, with the relative calm throughout Europe, Government were obviously intent on cost cutting and we find in a further Government circular, "Corps of Yeomanry Cavalry are allowed under the new Regulations to assemble as Permanent Pay and Duty Service for a period not exceeding 6 successive days in the present year, exclusive of the days of marching to and from the place of assembly."

Despite Government attempts to cut cost, we find that on the 1st August, 1823, on account of Permanent Pay and Duty Service, for the Kirkcudbright Corps of Gentlemen and Yeomanry Cavalry, for the year 1823, the Lieutenant Colonel James Gordon, was to submit an account of £510.10s.0d. to the Secretary of War, in respect of their annual training Camp of 6 days at Castle Douglas.

By 1810, the Glenkens troop had disbanded and the Urr Troop from Dalbeattie was to join with the Regiment. However, by 1824, only St. Mary's, Castle Douglas and Cally Troops formed the Regiment. In 1826, the Kenmure Troop, New Galloway, was to join with the Regiment.

The continued peace in Europe was to sound the death knell for many Volunteer Regiments and by 1831, Castle Douglas, Cally and Kenmure Troops had disbanded, leaving St. Mary's Troop to continue alone, with the new title of the "Kirkcudbright Independent Troop of Yeomanry Cavalry," under the command of Captain William Maxwell. 10 years later, in 1841, this Troop was also to disband with the Regiment taking its final resting place in the annals of Galloway history.

A determined attempt was made to resurrect this Yeomanry Cavalry Regiment during the earlier months of the Boer War conflict, in 1900, but despite a large number of signed pledges from many of the landed and farming community, it failed to materialise.

Galloway in keeping with the rest of Europe was to settle to a period of relative calm and with the threat of invasion temporarily removed, the Militia, were to become a 'Paper Regiment', existing on paper for 11 months of the year and coming together once a year for annual training. In the first instance this was a period of 21 days but after the Indian Mutiny of 1857, the period of training was reduced to 14 days. However, in 1870, the training period was to be again raised, to 28 days per year. Initially recruits paraded 2 weeks prior to the embodiment of their Regiment, for additional training, this being changed in 1870, to 28 days additional training, making their initial commitment to the Regiment of 2 months.

Under an Act of 1852 the Militia were envisaged as an army of Home Defence and recruiting to the Militia was to become by voluntary enlistment, with a bounty being paid, this was later changed to Regular Army rates of pay being paid to Militia whilst undergoing training or in the event of their being embodied.

The Militia, with its now massive source of semi-trained manpower, was seen by the army authorities, not only for its public order and defensive role but also as an untapped source of recruits to the Regular Army. The Militia now comprised, those who had joined for monetary gain, those under age, those who did not meet the statutory medical requirements for the Regular Army through size or health and those who wished to try the army life before making a permanent commitment. We now find regular reports of recruiting staff, in attendance at the final days of the Militia annual training, waiting to sign up Militiamen for the Regular Army. The following extract was issued by Govenment in a General Order to encourage recruits to the Regular Army:-

> *"Wages in the Army - Infantry of the Line -*
> *Including Militia in training - 13s 3¾d. per week.*
> *The necessary outgoings to provide groceries and vegetables in addition to the*
> *rations provided and to pay for washing, haircutting and library subscriptions - It*
> *has been calculated that a prudent soldier could save 2/- per week and on termination*
> *of 6 years service become master of a capital of £50."*

Under the pressure of the Crimean War of 1854 - 1856 and the implementation of the Act of Parliament of 12th May, 1854 the role of the Militia had been greatly transformed. They were now a self-sufficient and independent body. They had been embodied when there was no threat of invasion to the United Kingdom and they were now acting as a regular supplier of recruits to the Regular Army. Over 70,000 men were to pass from the Militia to the Regiments of the Line during the Crimean conflict.

The Militia were once again to be embodied during the period of the Indian uprising, the 'Indian Mutiny' (1857) but were not to serve overseas, serving only to fill the gap left by the regular troops sent to India to quell the mutiny. The Militia were disembodied the following year in 1858.

In 1859, with a renewed threat of invasion of Britain by the French Emperor, Louis Napoleon III a nephew of Napoleon Bonaparte, the insurrection within the Colonies and the pressing need to further expand and protect the Empire, the Secretary of State for War, felt it necessary to greatly increase army strengths and to form many new Battalions.

It was the intention of Government to form 50 new Battalions of some 42,000 men, with the proposal that all the Regiments of Foot, from 1st to 25th be given 2nd Battalions. However, it was found impossible to fill these new Battalions whilst maintaining the current reserve force.

A plan, which was to prove extremely costly, was devised, whereby the Militia Regiments, again embodied (1859) were to be dis-embodied in the Spring of 1860, with the Officers, non-commissioned officers, and rank and file being paid compensation. In return high tariff bounties and allowances were to be offered to the Militiamen to have them re-enlist, as permanent soldiers, in the newly formed Battalions.

History records that this plan was to be met with a great deal of success and the new Battalions were very quickly brought to their required strengths, with the Militiamen heeding Government calls and offering their services in full time service with the new Battalions.

However, with the depletion of the Militia Regiments much re-structuring of the Militia Force was to take place resulting in only one Militia base surviving within the Dumfries and Galloway Region, that of the Dumfries Militia, with their Headquarters at Barracks Yard, English Street, Dumfries. We still find the Rhins of Galloway a favoured recruiting ground for the Ayr Militia and can only assume that some sort of recruiting presence was to continue in Stranraer.

In October, 1860, the Galloway Rifles Militia, comprising of four Companies, which had been raised in Kirkcudbrightshire and Wigtownshire, was broken up. The two Kirkcudbrightshire Companies joining with the Dumfries Militia, whilst the two Wigtownshire Companies were incorporated with the Royal Ayrshire Regiment of Militia Rifles, later in 1866 to be renamed the 'Prince Regent's Royal Regiment of Ayr and Wigtown Militia', under the Command of Lieutenant Colonel, the Earl of Galloway, with an establishment of upwards of 1,000 men. This Regiment assembled each year for their annual training at the Racecourse, Ayr.

The Dumfries Militia were now recruited from Kirkcudbrightshire, Dumfriesshire, Jedburgh, Kelso, Galashiels, Selkirk, Roxburgh, Hawick, Peebles and a small proportion of English recruits from Longtown. The designation of the Dumfries Militia was hardly representative of the various areas comprising the Corps and in 1863, on the application of the Commanding Officer, Lieutenant Colonel McMurdo, the title was altered to that of the 'Scottish Borderers'. In 1864, the reported strength of the Scottish Borderers was a total of 677 men.

In 1869, the Estate of Kingholm fell to the Crown as 'Ultima Haeres' and was given over to the War Office. Hannahfield, Kingholm Merse, was thereafter, to become the training and camping ground of the Scottish Borderers Militia

From 1873, the King's Own Borderers, the present King's Own Scottish Borderers, the 25th of Foot and itself the former Sussex Regiment which traced its roots to the Edinburgh Regiment founded in 1689, had been localised in York. The Regiment still maintained its full Scottish traditions and as such much influential movement was under way to have the Regiment returned to its Scottish origins.

Originally it had been intended to locate the King's Own Borderers in Ayr, with Militia from Ayrshire, Wigtownshire, Kirkcudbrightshire, Dumfriesshire, Peebles, Selkirk and Roxburgh and accordingly in 1873, the Scottish Borderers Militia were attached to the 61st Sub-District with their headquarters in Ayr, along with the Volunteer Regiments, the two Battalions and Depot of the 21st Royal Scots. Once again the Scottish Borderers were to join with their former comrades of the Prince Regent's Royal Regiment of Ayr and Wigtown Militia, in readiness for the King's Own Borderers move. It was intended that the 21st (Royal Scots Fusiliers) would be transferred to Edinburgh. However, on the 30th June, 1881, the following telegram was received at the King's Own Borderers Depot at York. "It has been decided to locate the 25th (King's Own Borderers) at Berwick-on-Tweed, as the King's Own Borderers with no Militia or Volunteer Battalions." The Depot Companies of the King's Own Borderers were to move to Berwick-upon-Tweed on the 29th July, 1881.

In consequence of the new Army Regulations of August, 1881, requiring Militia Regiments to adopt the names of the Regiments of the Line with which they chanced to be linked, the Scottish Borderers Militia were to become the 3rd (Militia) Battalion of the 21st or Royal Scots Fusiliers, and the Prince Regent's Royal Regiment of Ayr and Wigtown Militia, the 4th (Militia) Battalion of the Royal Scots Fusiliers.

In 1886, the King's Own Borderers laid claim to the Scottish Borderers Militia as its natural Militia Battalion, and in June, 1887, the Jubilee year, by General Order issued by H.R.H. The Field Marshal Commanding in Chief, the Scottish Borderers Militia, late 3rd (Militia) Battalion Royal Scots Fusiliers became the 3rd (Militia) Battalion King's Own Borderers, and on the removal from the Northern English to the Scottish District their titles were to be interwoven to form the "King's Own Scottish Borderers."

The two former Wigtownshire Companies of the Galloway Rifles Militia were to continue as an integral part of the Prince Regent's Royal Regiment of Ayr and Wigtown Militia, being re-designated as the 3rd (Militia) Battalion Royal Scots Fusiliers, the title vacated by the Scottish Borderers.

On the 8th February, 1889, the following order was to appear in the local Press:- "The Militia annual training scheme." The dates as follows, 3rd Battalion Royal Scots Fusiliers (Prince Regent's Royal Regiment of Ayr and Wigtown) preliminary drill (recruits) May 13th 1889, at Ayr Racecourse Camp. Full training 8th July, 1889, to 3rd August, 1889. 3rd Battalion King's Own Scottish Borderers (Scottish Borderers Militia) preliminary drill (recruits) 6th May, 1889. Full training 1st July, 1889, to 27th July, 1889, at Hannahfield, Kingholm Merse."

With the outbreak of the Boer War in South Africa in 1899, the Militia were once again embodied, this time many of the Militia Regiments volunteering and being accepted for overseas service. The 3rd (Prince Regent's Royal Regiment of Ayr and Wigtown Militia) Battalion Royal Scots Fusiliers, were embodied on the 1st December, 1899, and numbered on the 8th December, 1899, a strength of 500 men with an additional 200 recruits, under the Command of Colonel W.H. Campbell. The 3rd (Scottish Borderers Militia) Battalion King's Own Scottish Borderers were embodied on the 25th January, 1900. The Regiments sailed for South Africa some 6 weeks later where they were to remain and see service at the seat of the war for the next two years, returning home in April, 1902.

In 1907, Mr Haldane, the Secretary of State for War, introduced a series of reforms of the existing Militia, Yeomanry and other Territorial forces, throughout the United Kingdom. These units, despite sharing a common patriotism, had too many varying and individual characteristics to fit them for assimilation into a general force, particularly in the terms of modern European warfare. Wide differences were found in the terms of service, type and length of training, use of arms and proficiency therein and, moreover, the purpose of each force varied greatly. Haldane proposed to channel the best of these separate forces into one specialised and highly trained body which could be linked and integrated, when the need arose, with the Regular Army. Gone were the days of embodiment on the threat of invasion or war with another country. Haldane proposed that with modern needs the new Territorial Forces would be liable for foreign service and proposed new and additional training periods.

With these changes in mind, by Army Order of 23rd December, 1907, the King's Own Scottish Borderer's Militia were transferred from Dumfries to Berwick, leading to a public outcry, which led the Dumfries Member of Parliament, John W. Gulland to write in the following terms to the Right Honourable Mr. Haldane, M.P., Secretary of State for War, of which the following is a part extract:-

8 Claremont Terrace,
Edinburgh. 6th January, 1908.

"The Militia has been connected with Dumfries for over a century; the Staff buildings were erected by the liberality of the district and belong to the local authorities; the camping ground at Kingholm is the property of the War Office. The annual muster of the Militia has been a popular feature which has brought interest and business to the area. The large district of the South West of Scotland would be left without any kind of military centre and the curious anomaly would arise that the Scottish Borderers would be quartered outside Scotland. I do not need at present to press strongly the many arguments that can be urged against this change: if the order is anything more than a provisional suggestion, that will be done by the local authorities more qualified to speak than I am. But I am very hopeful that in your plan, Dumfries may become more of a military centre rather than less. It might well become the Headquarters of the King's Own Scottish Borderers Militia instead of Berwick, or indeed a more comprehensive scheme might well be devised whereby so suitable a district might be chosen for the promised Cavalry Depot for Scotland. I do not at the present trouble you with arguments in favour of either of these courses, but I trust that you will soon be able to make some announcement that will relieve the fears of my constituents.
Yours Faithfully,
John W. Gulland."

The following reply was received by Mr. Gulland, from the Secretary of State for War and is produced in its entirety."

War Office 11th January, 1908.

My Dear Mr. Gulland, - I have had letters from the Lord Chancellor and the Duke of Buccleuch about the Dumfries question, and I much regret that the sense of hardship should have arisen and must sympathise with the dislike to change. But this change was the inevitable outcome of the deliberate decision made by Parliament last summer to reorganise the Militia. One hundred and one Battalions recruited on new terms, which involved liability for foreign service and a much longer recruit training, were to supersede the old 124 Militia Battalions, and the old Militia Battalion of each regular regiment was to go to and merge the Depot. In no other way could efficiency and economy be combined. To move the Depot from Berwick to Dumfries would (1). inflict far more hardship on Berwick than Dumfries has suffered, and (2). involve the building of a new Depot and Barracks with costly mobilization stores. I dare not propose it even if, from a military point of view, it were advantageous. I am sorry that you should have this troublesome question in your Burghs and I wish I could have written some thing more comforting. However, the new Territorial units will really take the place of the old Militia in each locality. Moreover, if it is any comfort to know it. English Boroughs and Counties have been more heavily hit by far than Scotland in the Militia reorganisation.
Yours very truly.
R.B. Haldane."

This was to signal the end of Militia involvement in the Dumfries and Galloway Region after a period of 111 years, a far cry from its early days when the populace had risen in confrontation against the introduction of the first Militia Bill of 1797.

After 1908, the Militia Battalions were to be re-designated as a Special Reserve Battalion, serving only to supply regular drafts to the regular battalions. They were to continue in this vein throughout the 1st Great War, being finally disbanded in 1918.

CHAPTER 2

THE WAR FEELING IN FRANCE -
THE ESTABLISHMENT OF THE VOLUNTEER FORCE 12th MAY 1859

England's first and Major line of defence against its long standing and natural enemy, France, was through the Cinque Ports of Sandwich, Dover, Romney, Hythe, Rye, and Winchelsea, which ran from Seaford in East Sussex to Birchington in Kent. From the earliest times, these ports were required to supply a total of 57 vessels, each fully laden with armed Marines, to suppress the threat of invasion by preventing the enemy from ever setting foot on English soil, it being reported.

"Not to let him land at all should be our aim and desire, because, if he once set foot on our shores he might before being repelled or annihilated commit irreparable ravages. In trying to stop the would-be invader on the threshold of his enterprise, we would have mainly to depend on the Channel Fleet and only on coastal defences thereafter."

However, following the Crimean War of 1854 - 56, the Wooden Walls of England's defences were finally shown to be extremely vulnerable to modern warfare and the consequent danger of foreign invasion was made fairly evident. During the Crimean conflict, in which Britain and France had been allied against a common Russian enemy, the French had deployed floating ironclad batteries to counter the Russian armament. Following the end of the war, the French continued to produce a fleet of such vessels, with this action being interpreted as a direct threat to the continuation of English naval supremacy and mastery of the Seas.

With the advent of these ironclad vessels and the transfer of steam power to ships, it was felt, by the authorities, that the 20 mile stretch of Channel, between France and England, could be easily breached in one hour and in the course of a single night, a force of some 100,000 Frenchmen might be landed on shore. Many of the gun-boats, forming an important part of the French Navy, were of light draught and could run up most of Britain's Firths and Rivers with the greatest of ease, and it was to this end that the principal towns and ports, along exposed coastal plains were to increase their defences through direct Government aid. Again it was considered that in the event of invasion the Cinque Ports would now be unable to fulfil their obligations and contingency plans were drawn up for the defence of the Capital along the Medway, at Chatham.

It was publicly stated that no dependence could be placed on the profession of the French Emperor, that the reliance between England and France could remain in the close and friendly state it had so recently enjoyed. The threat of Louis Napoleon III, to carry out the ambitious schemes of his uncle. He was to annexe the Provinces of Savoy and Nice and was expected to move against Switzerland, Belgium and the Rhemish Provinces of Prussia It was feared that he would seek an alliance with his recent enemy, Russia, and his ultimate ambition, the domination of Europe, would be achieved. It was only a mere question of time before these aims would be effected, after which England would be invaded and the victory at Waterloo and the humiliation of St. Helena, would be avenged.

The following Editorial which appeared in the *Saturday Review* of October, 1859, under the heading of "The War Feeling in France" fully outlined Britain's fears.

"On this side of the Channel we are all so heartily anxious to keep out of war, and are so utterly without any intention of quarrelling with France if we can possibly avoid it, that we can scarcely believe that at this very moment, Frenchmen of all ranks and callings speak of an expedition against England as a thing as certain to come soon as the winter to follow autumn. The most cool and wary do no more than urge that sufficient preparation can scarcely be made under 18 months. All agree that war will be declared directly the Government is ready, and that the Government is getting ready as fast as possible.

We can appeal to the experience of an Englishman who has passed through France or stayed in Paris during the last few weeks, and who is sufficently acquainted with the people and their language to understand what is passing. An attack on England is the regular theme of conversation in all public conveyances and public places. The army naturally takes the lead, but it is singular how many classes of persons echo the opinions and wishes of the army. The clergy are almost to a man in favour of an attack on the foster-mother of heresy and the *Universe* speaks of an expedition to pillage the Bank of England in much the same language as a hermit of the middle ages might have used when exhorting Christendom to enter on a crusade for the recovery of the Holy Sepulchre.

The Legitimist Party, which still commands a certain amount of provincial influence, raves against England, and urges an attack on her with a bitterness proportioned to the benefits which its chief received from her so many years ago. Even the monied classes begin to say that anything would be better than the state of utter stagnation to which they are now condemned by the suspense in which they are kept. Persons, also, who are acquainted with the working classes of Paris and the large towns, assert that there is now running through them one of those strange upheavings of vague, uneasy emotion which from time to time stir their depths, and that this uneasiness takes the shape of a senseless animosity against England.

In the navy there is, of course, a wish to see whether the Channel has really been bridged over by steam, and along the coast fronting the English shores, the population is occupied with no other thought than that of estimating its perils in case of war, and longing for an expedition which, it is hoped, may cripple England for years. There remain no friends to England except those who think this proposed outbreak of unprovoked hate either wicked or likely to be prejudicial to the future liberties of France. Such men are few, indeed, and it is not too much to say generally that the French nation is determined on attacking England."

However, as in the past Britain was to take up the gauntlet and the respective editorials of the *Galloway Gazette* and the *Kirkcudbrightshire Advertiser,* take up the patriotic fervour which was to be nurtured and to grow until a Force of some proportion was raised to once again thwart the threat of French invasion.

"The bellicose nations of the Continent may "harry" each other as they please but if ever they hazard a hostile approach to this "tight little island" they will find a mustacho and breakers ahead, but before they reach that point, they may also meet with certain obstacles which will not be easily overcome, for our iron-sheathed navy may render a good service to the Nation in the future as the old wooden ship did in the past."

"We are in a very isolated position and must make up for our weaknesses by being prepared. Nothing like an alliance exists between us and any of the great European Powers, except, perhaps between Prussia and Britain and so long as these two Powers are joined in a friendly alliance, we may never expect to see Louis Napoleon exhibit the same aggressive tendencies that marred the career of the first Napoleon."

With this threat of European domination and the reported, imminent invasion of England by the French, a Royal Commission was appointed to consider the defences of the Country. This report was to make evident the necessity for even greater and more extensive works to be carried out on the more vulnerable parts of the coast, together with increased defences for many of the Major towns and cities. However, the Commission were to recommend a less costly and more effectual measure, the formation of a Volunteer Force.

With these increased costs in mind and the Government spending already strained through the insurrection of the Indian Mutiny (1857) and the raising of new Battalions to the Line, by the payment of compensation and bounties to the militia, this recommendation was welcomed and readily accepted by the Government of the then, Lord Derby, and in a Government circular, dated the 12th May, 1859, the Secretary of War, Mr Sidney Herbert, sanctioned the establishment of a Volunteer Force. This Force was seen as a Territorial Force for the defence of the Country and was described by Government as "The true Peace League", it was said, "The very object of our present armament is to render invasion impossible, and, as for any aggressive movement on our part, the known sentiments of the entire nation on the subject of war are sufficent to forbid suspicion. We are thinking of self-defence and of that only."

At present, it was understood that, by volunteering to join these forces, members would be liable for service at home, in case of invasion or insurrection and overseas, in those special circumstances where Colonies or Dependancies were in danger. Subject to these conditions, the Volunteer Regiments would appear as available on the Army List. It was not until The Volunteers (Military Service Act) of 1895, that Volunteers could offer their services for duty which did not amount to invasion or insurrection.

This Volunteer Force was seen not only as a means of replacing the depleted Militia Regiments but as an army of defence with a large portion of the population skilful riflemen, making the rifle a national weapon, and to have in the Country a reserve of men fully trained to fill the Volunteer ranks to capacity in the event of an emergency.

The Episcopal Motto of the Volunteers was to be *"Pro aris et facis"*, "For our altars and firesides".

The Civil Motto translating to become the Volunteers rallying cry of, "Defence not Defiance".

In a letter to the Lords Lieutenant of 13th July, 1859, Mr Sydney Herbert, Secretary of War, while stressing that the very essence of the Volunteer Force consisted in their undertaking themselves to bear without any cost to the public, the whole charges for their training and practice, previous to being called out for actual service, authorised the issue of rifles at Government expense to 25% of it members. This issue was made subject to certain conditions, the possession of a suitable rifle range and the willingness to submit to periodic inspection. However, by January, 1860, Government had undertaken to supply all the rifles to the Volunteer Force.

It was the wish of Government that the Volunteer Movement should be raised and maintained by public subscription with no cost whatsoever to the Government. The Force was to be administered on a regional basis, by local committees, with the Act empowering Lord Lieutenants to submit proposals for the raising of such a Force. No Volunteers were to be enrolled who were not able, from their own funds to provide their clothing and accoutrements and to serve without pay. In a letter of 2nd December, 1859, to the Chairmen of Volunteer Committees, the Earl of Selkirk, Lord Lieutenant for the Stewartry, was to write, "None in my opinion should be enrolled who cannot afford to serve without any pecuniary assistance, whether in the way of pay or bounty, and they should also be liable to provide their uniforms and accoutrements."

These restrictions prompted a public appeal for financial assistance and support, townsmen were encouraged to show their approval and countenance by co-operating and giving substantial support to the Volunteer Movement. It was to this end that subscription lists were opened in every city, town and village, throughout the Country.

On the 13th May, 1859, a circular was sent from General Peel to the Lords Lieutenants of Counties, inviting them to raise Corps of Volunteers. This circular was not only seen as being in harmony with the wishes of the people, being hailed with great enthusiasm, but was also met with the firm approval of the Press, the following extract from the *Spectator*, of 20th May, 1859. "This is what we have so long desired, and so long looked for. We trust that the Government have recognised that a nation unaccustomed to the use of arms is never safe, that a reliance upon the Militia, is reliance upon a rotton prop, that a good rifleman, in tens of thousands, would enable the country to laugh at the idea of an invasion. We are glad they have given a distinct and emphatic sanction to the national desire for an adequate and truly national defensive force. Far more fruitful of solid results to the nation will be the raising of efficient Corps of Volunteer marksmen than the adding of fifty battalions to the Line, not because marksmen would be more effective than the regulars but because they will be more numerous and, we hope, more permanent than those sudden additions to the Regular Army and those sudden subtractions from that army to which Governments are prone."

However, many members of Government, among them Lord Palmerston, were to remain sceptical of such a Force and privately nursed grave doubts of the usefulness of the Volunteers. It was reported: "the want of discipline of such troops; the danger they might occasion in time of peace to the internal security; and the probability that their irregular efforts would produce confusion at a time when strict order, method and unity of purpose were of great importance." Nevertheless Lord Derby's Government were compelled to put themselves at the head of the movement and await with a certain amount of trepidation the fruits of the seed sown by them.

General Sir William Napier, a visionary of his day was to make the following comments on the subject of the Volunteer Rifle Corps and offered the following advice in a written report to Government; "An invading enemy's column must generally march and examine all the roads leading through the country and generally take the main roads. It will therefore be well for Volunteer Officers, either singly or with their companies, to look upon London or any other great town, and thus ascertain all the points of advantage for hiding behind sticks and stones, and to trees and bushes should be added, railroads, banks, houses, private or public, bridges etc., from whence their rifle balls will pitch into the enemy's columns. The longest range is best here, because it will give time for the riflemen to retire from the enemy's sharpshooters, and to find a new stick or stone for hiding. In examining the county, our Volunteers should also look well to the line of their retreat, choosing that which will be the most difficult country for the enemy's riflemen to follow, or that which will lead the enemy towards the rear of his line of march, and that also, which will enable the Volunteer most readily to join other Volunteer Corps acting in the same way. Accumulation in this case will be most efficacious, but the forming of large bodies of riflemen to move about in masses, under the command of one man, cannot be too strongly depecated. It is not meant that there should not be commanding officers of large bodies, for that will be essential to concert and combination, but in the actual fighting and minor movements small bodies only should be employed."

It was to be General Napier's contention that by use of such a system, Britain could be successfully defended against any number of foreign invaders.

With this advice firmly in mind, the War Office was to issue a second circular, dated 25th May, 1859, which stated, "The main emphasis of a Volunteer should be not on drill but on rifle firing in small units composed of individuals having a knowledge of and a thorough dependence upon each other personally." The following day, 26th May, 1859, a further circular was issued laying down the standards the Volunteers were expected to attain.

The Volunteer movement was seen initially as a middle class organisation and the Commander-in-Chief was to speak of the desirability of enlisting as much middle class education and intelligence as possible for the service of the Country. "On the whole volunteering promotes ambition, intelligence, perseverence, wealth and a variety of many other advantages in life."

The story was told of a Volunteer Rifle Corps who attended a brief course of training at the Musketry School at Hythe and attained higher proficience in their shooting than troops of the Regular Army, on account of their superior intelligence.

This middle class vision was amply shown by the exemptions given to the Volunteers to encourage their services in the movement. They were to be exempt from being drawn to serve as Militiamen, in the event of the ballot again coming into operation and the somewhat anomalous distinction of Volunteers being allowed to use hair-powder without paying tax. (This was the "Hair-Powder Tax of 1795 - 1869, which was one of the many ways employed by the Government, in the raising of funds for the Anglo-French Wars).

This superior intelligence and middle class imagery was to remain with the Volunteers throughout the service of the movement, although very soon after its inception, the Volunteer Force was recruiting from all spheres of the social spectrum and in particular from the working class.

The potential financial consequences of volunteering was by no means a small matter to the "Citizen Soldier". The drain on personal resources ranged from, joining fees, annual subscription fees, the purchase of uniform and all travel expenses, to the possibility of Court proceedings for non-payment of Company fines. Attendance at meetings or drills of the Company could necessitate in the loss of wages and indeed in many cases with the very real threat of losing his job. However, throughout 1859, the Volunteer Movement was met with a phenomenal display of national patriotism and by the unanimous voice of the public man. The youth and valour of the country were to come forward in an uncompromising and unabashed display of loyalty to Queen and Country.

In the *Times* of 5th August, 1859, it was reported, "The progress of the Volunteer Movement has been characteristic of our national temper, and must be productive of the very best results. No sudden burst of transitory, though fervent enthusiasm has roused the country to arms, on the contrary, the scheme seemed to hang fire for a time, and was only fairly taken up after sober consideration and deliberate approval. When this stage of opinion, however, had once been passed the impulse became irresistable, and at this moment Companies are being formed, exercising, grounds with adequate ranges are being obtained, the men being sworn in, and the institution may be considered now as fairly established."

On the 19th August, 1859, Mr Sydney Herbert, Secretary of War, was to tell the House of Commons, "That at present no fewer than 90 Volunteer Corps are at present in the course of formation, and many others are in contemplation regarding which the Government has not as yet received any official information. Nor is this all. Not only in zeal and patriotism have the middle classes fully answered our expectations, but in efficency and intelligence they have amply justified our predictions, and compelled the approbation even of the martinet politicians who are always ready to sneer at any departure from the beaten track of official rule and precedent. Lord Palmerston himself has seen the propriety of explaing away the disparaging expression he applied to the Volunteer movement some weeks ago, when he spoke of the "Rifle Corps Fever" and he has now paid a handsome tribute to the importance of having some organisation of that kind for our permanent national defence, not in substitution for, but in addition to, our other forces."

In November, 1859, the following regulations and instructions were issued for the guidance of Volunteers concerned in the formation of Corps, by the authority of the War Office;

RULES, REGULATIONS, INSTRUCTIONS.
The Rifleman's Oath.

The following is the prescribed oath administered to Volunteers:-

"I (AB.) do make oath that I will be faithful, and bear true allegiance to Her Majesty, her heirs and successors, that I will, as in duty bound, honestly and faithfully defend Her Majesty, her heirs and successors, in person, crown and dignity, against all enemies, and will observe and obey all orders of Her Majesty, her heirs and successors, and of the generals and officers set over me. So help me God."

Duties and Etiquette of Volunteer Corps.

When Volunteers do duty in brigade, the commanding officer, whose commission bears prior date, takes the right and command of the whole brigade, unless a line officer of equal military rank be appointed for the purpose. Should Volunteers and Militia be brigaded with troops of the line for duty, the commanding officer of the line will, as a matter of course, take the command, without reference to the date of his commission, if Volunteers and Militia only are brigaded for duty, the Commanding Officer of the Militia will take command without reference to the date of commission, but should either the line officer or the Militia officer be of an inferior grade, the Volunteer officer is entitled to take command.

No officer holding a commission in a Volunteer Corps has the power of resigning the same without Her Majesty's permission. He is entitled to all the privileges, advantages and exemptions of a Military officer, during Her Majesty's pleasure, and entitled to appear at Court, and all State ceremonies, in uniform, when in order of precedence, he comes immediately after militia officers of the same grade and before line officers of a grade under.

Volunteer officers do not take rank in the army, but while on duty or in uniform, are entitled to the military salute, not from Volunteers only, but from non commissioned officers and privates of all military services.

Non commissioned officers and privates of Volunteer Corps cannot resign without giving regular notice of their intention, neither can they absent themselves from duty without leave, or reasonable excuse, such as sudden illness etc. They are bound whilst on military duty to deport themselves in every respect consonant with military form and etiquette.

Officers, non commissioned officers and privates of Volunteer Corps, are bound to conform in every respect to the uniform and outward arrangements of their Corps, and to observe the strictest care and neatness, as regards their dress, arms and accoutrements.

Officers holding commissions in Volunteer Corps are liable to trial by Court Martial for any breach of military duty, and non commissioned officers and privates are subject to the provisions of the Mutiny Act, excepting that which relates to any punishment affecting life or limb, for which they are exempt.

Rules generally observed in the formation of a Volunteer Corps.

(1) That candidates for admission must be either persons of well known position, or present unexceptional recommendations as to character etc. In Corps formed according to Act of Parliament, candidates are not chosen by ballot.

(2) The entrance fee in most Corps is ten and sixpence, or one guinea, and an annual subscription of one guinea, the same to be paid into the hands of the treasurer immediately on a new member receiving notice of election.

(3) Members are compelled, under penalty of a fine, to attend such meetings for drill and exercise, as may be specified in the rules for the Corps on their joining it.

(4) Each member is to provide himself with a rifle-shell jacket and forage cap, together with the necessary arms and accoutrements of a rifleman, wherewith to attend meetings for drill and exercise. He is also to provide himself with a full dress rifle tunic, and a shako or helmet, for full dress meetings.

(5) According to existing regulations, each member is to provide ammunition at his own expense. Two afternoons in the month to be set apart for target practice.

(6) Extra expenses for ornamental purposes, such as bands etc., are not to be entered on without the question having been put to the vote, unless the commanding officer should wish to furnish a band at his own expense, or unless the regular subscription should be sufficient to defray the same.

(7) Whenever a proposal is made for the Corps to have a few days field practice out of town, or at any of the large military encampments, it will be optional for members to go or not, as the expense of such an arrangement is to be borne by such member individually.

(8) The same laws and regulations apply to all Corps, irrespectively of their strengths.

In consequence of the circular of 12th May, 1859, which sanctioned the establishment of a Volunteer Force, it was the duty of the Lords Lieutenant of the County, in the Stewartry, the Earl of Selkirk, and in Wigtownshire, the Earl of Stair, to submit proposals for the formation of Volunteer Corps.

Meetings were called and committees were formed. In the main the members of these committees were elderly retired gentlemen who, with little or no knowledge of military affairs, were responsible for the selection of the officers and awarded ranks commensurate with the applicant's personal wealth. Once selected, officers, were in effect expected to subsidise the very existence of the Corps and could well disburse in excess of £50 per annum on such varied expenses as uniform purchase, payment of subscription fees, these increasing dependent to his rank, Corps entertainment and cash prizes to encourage his men in rifle practice. The appointment of officers was vested by Act of Parliament in the Lords Lieutenant, subject to the Queen's approval and on the selection of an officer by the Committee, the Lord Lieutenant would normally grant the commission subject to such approval. By the Regulation of the Forces Act, 1871, the Lords Lieutenant were to lose the privilege of granting commissions and the power of selecting officers was to be transferred to the Commanding Officer of the Regiment.

The election of non-commissioned officers was by the vote of the Corps members. The most popular, but not necessarily the best suited for the purpose, being selected for these ranks. As in the case of the selection of Volunteer Officers, by War Office order dated, 18th September, 1873, the selection and appointment of non-commissioned officers was to transfer to the Commanding Officer.

Sub-committees were formed being responsible for the day to day running of the Corps; raising funds by subscription, bazaars, fairs, and balls. These fund raising events were received with amazing public enthusiasm from the highest in the land to the humblest servant. These committees were further responsible for the selection of uniforms, arms, suitable rifle ranges, store-rooms and the appointment of drill instructors.

Lists of enrolled members were then prepared and when the Corps was considered to be on a firm footing, the services of the Corps were offered to the Lord Lieutenant for Her Majesty's approval. When accepted the Corps was given a number, in a particular Regiment, subject to the order of precedence in which its services had been offered to the Lord Lieutenant.

A Company comprised a minimum of 60 men, which entitled the officer of that Company to the rank of Captain. A Sub-Division was less than 60 men but more than 27, which entitled, the officer to hold the rank of Lieutenant. A Section was expected to comprise of more than 20 men but less than 27, being referred to as a detachment should its numbers fall below 20 men.

Company rules and regulations were drawn up, which instituted fines for various Company misde-meanours. These fines and annual subscriptions were recoverable, in default, through the civil courts. Initially a Volunteer was normally eligible for service between the ages of 18 and 60 years, but no hard and fast rules of age were applied to potential recruits. An enrolled Volunteer could leave the Corps on his giving 14 days notice to his Company officer, however, by 21st July, 1863, when limited Government assistance was being given, a Volunteer was expected to give a written guarantee that he would make himself efficient for a period of three years. In theory the Volunteer could still quit the force after a period of 14 days notice but he was then responsible for the payment to the Corps, recoverable through the Courts, of the 3 years Government grant he would have failed to earn. A Volunteer could be dismissed, immediately, by his Company Officer, but the same grant rules applied.

The Volunteer Force was only subject to Martial Law whilst on active service or after, the Regulation of the Forces Act, 1871, whilst training with the Militia or Regular Army, this was later to encompass, whilst in training or attending Brigade camps.

The Volunteer year ran from 1st May to 30th November, changing in October, 1872, by War Office circular to end on 31st October. It was during these mainly summer months that the Companies engaged in rifle shooting, attended Company and Battalion drills, Inspections and also, to later include Camps of Exercise. However, the Company was seen by its members more in the lines of a social club, with the members organising football matches, cricket, quoiting, curling, dancing clubs, smoking evenings, annual balls and Company rifle clubs. It was considered to be part of the Sergeant Instructors duty to encourage the men in these activities, particularly during the winter months, where they engaged in 'Winter Drills', Company shooting matches, with the highlight of the close season being the New Year's Day shoot.

No Company Rule Books of the Galloway Rifle Volunteers, for this early period, appear to have survived, but the following rules refer to the 6th Kircudbright Rifle Volunteers - Dalbeatie, who did not join the Regiment until the 23rd June, 1869. Nevertheless, the rules would be very similar to those of the other earlier Corps and give an interesting insight into the formation and discipline of the Corps. The term 'Efficient', refers to the Royal Commission of 14th August, 1862, on the Volunteer Force, which recommended a grant of 20/- to every Volunteer who made himself 'efficient' by attending 9 drills in the year, of which 6, in the case of Consolidated, and 3 in Administrative Battalions, (as was the case of the Galloway Rifle Volunteers) should be Battalion drills, and who had gone through a course of Musketry Instruction and attended the Inspection of the Corps. A further grant of 10/- was also paid to those firing a prescribed quantity of ball cartridge in the course of a year.

In the case of recruits, 30 drills and a short course of Musketry Instruction was held as qualification. However, should the Inspecting officer find a member non-effective his grant would be disallowed.

An additional 4/- per annum, was given for the conveyance of effectives, the Headquarters of whose Corps was more than 5 miles from that of the Administrative Battalion, to which they belonged.

The total cost to the Government in the implementation of this grant to the Volunteers was half a million pounds.

Rules of the
6th Kirkcudbright Rifle Volunteer Corps.

The Corps serving under the Volunteer Act, 1863, the members are consequently subject to the provisions of that Act, and of any other Act, by which it shall be ammended, and to all regulations which have been or shall be issued under the authority of the Secretary of State for War.

II.

The Corps shall consist of two Classes - (1). Enrolled Members, consisting of Efficients and Non-Efficients, and of - (2). Honorary Members, the latter contributing to the funds of the Corps, but not being enrolled for service.

III.

All subcriptions shall fall due on the 1st of the month succeding that in which the Queen shall have signified her acceptance of the Corps.

IV.

The Commanding Officer will propose Gentlemen to the Lord Lieutenant for Commissions as Officers, but the Commissioning of all Officers is vested by Act of Parliament in the Lord Lieutenant, subject to the Queen's approval.

V.

The Non-Commissioed Officers shall be appointed by the Commanding Officer.

VI.

After the acceptance of the services of the Corps, no person shall be admitted as a Member unless with the approval; of the Commanding Officer, on the proposal of three Gentlemen, two of whom at least must be Members of the Corps.

VII.

Each Member must be provided with Uniform and Accoutrements of the pattern approved by the Lord Lieutenant of the Stewartry.

VIII.

Each member shall be responsible for the due preservation of all articles issued to him, which are the property of Her Majesty's Government or of the Corps, fair wear and tear only excepted.

IX.

The expression "Property of the Corps" shall include all articles which have been purchased out of the General Funds of the Corps, or presented to the Corps.

X.

When the Corps is not assembled for actual service, the Commanding Officer is, by the general provision of the Act of Parliament, solely responsibnle for the discipline of the Corps, but he may at any time assemble a Courts of Enquiry, consisting of three or five members of the Corps (one of whom, at least, is to be an Officer), to be appointed by rollster, for the purpose of investigating any irregularity, and assisting him in coming to a conclusion upon it. But an enquiry in reference to a Commissioned Officer shall be made by a Court composed of Officers of the Volunteer Establishment within the County, convened under the authority of the Lord Lieutenant.

XI.

The Commanding Officer shall fix the time and place for parades, drills, and rifle practice.

XII.

The Senior Officer in Command shall have power, subject to the approval of the Commanding Officer, to inflict the following Fines, viz:-

For absence from each special parade, drill, or rifle practice, fixed by the Commanding Officer...1s.0d.

For being late therat, that is after roll-call but within a quarter of an hour of the time fixed, if later than this is to be considered absent....................................0s.6d.

For appearing thereat without Uniform, Arms and Accoutrements, in proper order...0s.6d.

For not observing proper silence in the ranks...1s.0d.

For any disorderly or insubordinate conduct or appearance, besides being liable to expulsion, at the discretion of the Commanding Officer...............................2s.6d.

The Senior Officer in Command at each parade or drill to have power to excuse absence, lateness or incomplete uniform, on cause shown to his satisfaction.

For leaving the ranks without the consent of the Senior Officer in Command..........1s.0d.

And a fine of 5s. may be inflicted upon all Members who fail to make themselves efficient during the year.

XIII.

For loading contrary to orders, or shooting out of turn...2s.6d.

For discharging the rifle accidently...5s.0d.

For pointing the same, loaded or unloaded, at any person without orders.................5s.0d.

XIV.

All fines imposed on Members of the Corps shall be entered in a book kept by the Commanding Officer for that purpose.

XV.

All fines shall become due on the first day of every month succeeding that in which they have been incurred, and shall be collected by one of the Sergeants, and paid by him to the Commanding Officer.

XVI.

The property of the Corps is by Act of Parliament legally vested in the Commanding Officer, but a Committee to aid him in the management of its finances shall be appointed yearly. The Committee shall consist of the Commissioned Officers, and five members of the Corps, and shall be convened under the direction of the Commanding Officer.

XVII.

The Commanding Officer shall cause an abstract of the accounts to be annually prepared, for the information of every Member of the Corps.

XVIII.

Honorary Members may, if they wish it, wear the Uniform of the Corps, but they are not in any way to interfere with the military duties of the Corps.

XIX.

Honorary Members will be permitted to use the Practice Ground when it is not required by the Enrolled Members.

XX.

Honorary Members shall severally pay a donation of Five Pounds or Annual Subscription of Five Shillings.

XXI.

The system of Musketry Instruction prescribed in the Musketry Regulations for the Army, must be adhered to.

XXII.

Every Member is expected to provide himself with a copy of the Rules of the Corps.

The terms of service of a Volunteer were for service at home, in the event of invasion or insurrection, with certain previously explained provisos. The defensive role of the Volunteer movement was well understood but confusion was to arise as to what constituted insurrection and to what extent the Volunteers could be utilised in the event of civil disorder. It does help to clarify the Volunteers official role from the outset, although the circular, clarifying the position, was not finally issued until 1867.

Volunteer Circular No. 31. War Office.

3rd June, 1867.

Memorandum in respect of the employment of the Volunteers in aid of the Civil Power.

(1) Questions having arisen as to the power of the Civil Authority to call upon the Volunteer Force to act in aid of the civil power in suppression of riot or public commotion, and as to the duty of the members of the Volunteer Force, if so called upon, the following circular is issued for the general information of that Force, in accordance with the opinion of the Law Officers of the Crown.

(2) Her Majesty's subjects are bound, in the case of the existence of riots to use all reasonable endeavours, according to the necessity of the occasion, to suppress and quell such riots, and members of the Volunteer Force are not exempted from this general obligation, and they may, in common with all other of Her Majesty's subjects, be required by the civil authority to act as special constables for such purposes, but they must not, when so active appear in their military dress.

(3) The civil authority is not in any case entitled to call upon or order Volunteers to act as a military body in the preservation of peace.

(4) In cases of riots and disturbances, not amounting to insurrection, and not having for their object the commission of felonious acts or the subversion of the civil government, special constables, whether members of the Volunteer Force or others, should be armed with the ordinary Constable's staff.

(5) In cases of serious and dangerous riots and disturbances, the civil authority may require Her Majesty's subjects generally, including members of the Volunteer Force to arm themselves with and use other weapons suitable for the occasion, and such other weapons may be used accordingly by members of the Volunteer Force, according to the necessity of the occasion.

(6) In the event of an attack upon their storehouses or armouries, members of the Volunteer Force may combine and avail themselves of their organisation to repel such an attack, and to defend such storehouses and armouries, and for such purposes may, if the necessity of the occasion requires, use arms.

Longford.

War Office.

On the 23rd June, 1860, a Royal Review was to take place in Hyde Park, London, before Her Majesty Queen Victoria, when 21,000 enrolled and efficient Volunteers from all over England took part. On the 7th August, 1860, 21,500 of their Scottish counterparts paraded before Queen Victoria, in a Royal Review, in Queen's Park, Holyrood, Edinburgh.

The authorities at the War Office were determined that enrolled Volunteers should not be permitted to relax in any of the essentials to bring them up to and maintain them in, a proper state of efficiency, and on the 12th November, 1860, the following circular, from the War Office, was issued to Commanding Officers.

"The form accompanying this document is of a very elaborate character and calls upon the Adjutant of the Regiments to make correctly the following returns, viz:-

The designation of each Corps, Station of Headquarters, distance from Headquarters of Battalion establishments, Companies, Sub-divisions, Sections, Enrolled strengths, Field Officers, Captains, Subalterns, Staff Sergeants, Buglers, rank and file - Total.

Daily distribution of duties, with date, where employed, how employed, the description of parade or drill and the nature of instruction imparted, present on parade, Field Officers etc., (as before to rank and file), employed, how employed, the description of parade or drill and the nature of instruction imparted. Present on parade, Field Officers etc., (as before to rank and file).

It will be therefore seen that this return will not only embrace the numerical strength at which the Volunteer Corps muster from day to day but it will also form a guide to the War Office authorities of how the Officers who have been honoured with Her Majesty's Commission perform the duties presented to them."

By the end of the Volunteer year in 1861, 150,000 Volunteers, throughout Britain had been drilled and equipped. This figure did not include, Artillery Volunteers, 40,666, Volunteer Engineers, 6580.

Very quickly the new Volunteer Regiments were to forge within their ranks a strong sense of union and comradeship, whilst acting together for common purpose in drill and discipline. Faced with the phenomenal pace at which the Volunteer Movement had come to the fore, the Government felt it necessary to produce a drill book especially shortened and simplified to standardise the necessary training of the Volunteer. The drill book was referred to as the "Green Manual" from the colour of its cover and cost sixpence. This specially shortened and simplified version was quickly outgrown by the Volunteer who, was then to adopt the drill book as used by the Regular Army.

The question as to the suitability of incompetent officers was soon raised and quickly dealt with. The following part extract coming from the *Volunteer's Service Gazette* of 5th October, 1861.

"Inefficient Officers are of two kinds, those who strive hard to do their work well, and fail, and those who, from want either of time or inclination, have never really applied themselves to learn their duties.

It is not uncommon to see a Captain or covering Sergeant, who we know to be a perfect master of the Red Book, make the grossest blunders in the simplest movements on the parade ground.

We should be glad to see it a universal role that a Volunteer Officer should drill his men himself for a portion of the time allotted to Company Drill.

In considering the other class of incompetant Officers, we must advert to the circumstances which attended the original raising of the Force. It was impossible to predict whether a man would turn out to have the necessary qualifications for an Officer, or if he had, whether his ardour would not cool after a short trial. In many cases to, men were nominated who, from their social position were almost necesssary to the fostering of the young Force, but who from occupation, previous habits or years, were not those best adapted to make efficient Officers. Many of these have seen that we can now walk alone and have gracefully stepped aside.

As to the remainder, with whom we class, those who accepted commissions through vanity, and those who care for nothing but the braided tunic and the trailing sword, we believe that the evil will cure itself."

Volunteers had already begun policing their own ranks, which in time was to lead to the creation of a formidable and highly trained military defensive force, on a level with and indeed, in many cases, superior to comparable Regular Army units of the day.

Sir Edward Bulver Lytton, was to say of the Volunteers in 1861, "Volunteers who have sprung up, not mere raw undisciplined, unskilled pretenders, but patiently learning the use of their weapons, so that a wasp could not more safely enter a bee-hive than an invader could brave all the stings of the rifles in Britain."

With the ground rules firmly established, Grey Galloway was to show as it had in times gone past, its true warlike and patriotic spirit, the very flower of Galloway manhood coming early, and well to the fore, in the formation of this, the 'Citizen Army' or Volunteer Force - The Galloway Rifle Volunteers.

CHAPTER 3

THE FORMATION OF THE VARIOUS COMPANIES FORMING THE GALLOWAY RIFLE VOLUNTEERS - KIRKCUDBRIGHT - CASTLE DOUGLAS - GLENKENS - GATEHOUSE - MAXWELLTON - DALBEATTIE - WIGTOWN - STRANRAER - NEWTON STEWART - WHITHORN - MONREITH - KIRKMAIDEN

KIRKCUDBRIGHT.

In terms of a numerously signed requisition to the Provost of Kirkcudbright, to call a meeting for the purpose of taking into consideration the expediency of forming a Rifle Corps in the district, a meeting was held in the Court-room, on Friday, 2nd December, 1859, which proved to be most successful and enthusiastic.

Provost Shand opened the meeting. Mr. R.M. Gordon of Rattra, moved that the Provost retain the chair and spoke at some length of the position in which Great Britain stood and the threatening affairs accross the Channel. Louis Napoleon, he said, might not after all deem it prudent to invade our shores but it was nevertheless advisable to be prepared for his reception. Numerous Rifle Corps were formed and were still being organised over the whole of Great Britain and the movement, Kirkcudbright was making in the matter was proof that they were not meaning to be behind in their patriotism (cheers). He wished the movement every success and said that a number of resolutions would be proposed, afterwards parties wishing to enrol themselves should be good enough to come forward and subscribe the lists. (cheers).

Various proposals were put before the meeting and considered as to which service of the Volunteers, Kirkcudbright should subscribe. The Earl of Selkirk and Dr. Shand, coming out heavily in favour of an Artillery Corps. However, Mr. Laurie of Woodhall (Laurieston Hall), proposed the first resolution, that it was highly expedient that a Volunteer Rifle Corps should be formed in the Stewartry, "What good would a handful of isolated artillerymen do, unassisted as they would be by a Company like themselves, were the French to enter the Dee? The Rifle Corps of the district aided by those of the other surrounding places would prove far more effective in repelling any invading force and on the whole he considered that kind of Corps was best (cheers).

Mr. Maitland of Compstone, seconded the motion which was carried unanimously. (An Artillery Corps however, was to be later formed in Kirkcudbright, through the efforts of the Earl of Selkirk and Dr. Shand).

The following gentlemen were thereafter, appointed as a committee to carry out the previous resolution, viz ; The Magistrates and Town Council of Kirkcudbright. Mr W.H. McLellan, Kirkcudbright; Mr. Laurie of Woodhall, Laurieston; Mr. D. H. Gordon, Kirkcudbright; Mr. R.M. Gordon of Rattra; Mr. Neilson of Queenshill; Mr. D. McLellan, Kirkcudbright; Major Irving of Barwhinnock; Mr. Hamilton; with power to add to their numbers. (Major Irving was to later withdraw from the committee on a point of order). Lists were then prepared for the enrolment of Volunteers and the acceptance of subscriptions. A considerable number of gentlemen were to come forward, Mr. David Gordon, Procurator Fiscal, Kirkcudbright, being the first to subscribe his name to the list of enrolled Volunteers. The Messrs. McCulloch of Ardwell, subscribing £30, to be divided between the Corps of Kirkcudbright, Castle Douglas and Gatehouse of Fleet.

On Friday, 13th January, 1860 a meeting of Volunteers and others, was held in the Town Hall, Kirkcudbright, presided over by Mr. Maitland of Barcaple. Mr. Hamilton, one of the committee, read over the names of those enrolled as members of the Corps, numbering 80, sufficient to warrant them in forwarding the list to the Lord Lieutenant of the County, for the approval of Her Majesty. He also stated that the subscription list now amounted to £180.

The Chairman said that the main object now, when matters stood so satisfactorily was to get started drilling with the least possible delay and that it would be their duty to propose a Captain, whom they would recommend to Her Majesty. Mr. W.K. Laurie of Woodhall, was proposed, seconded and approved. No other candidate was proposed.

Mr. Laurie, thanked the meeting for the honour done him and stated that he would do his utmost to render himself as effective as possible. He mentioned that he already knew something of military matters, but that it would be necessary for him to practice at a military school to rub off the rust he had contracted from want of practice. (Mr. Laurie, had previously held a commission in the 'Duke of Brunswick's Rifle Corps' the famous 'Death's head and Cross Bones.') The Chairman next stated that various matters still required their attention and some arrangements should be made to have them attended to. After some discussion, the former committee was appointed. Various other matters were then dealt with, such as, arms, uniforms, etc. The meeting was closed with a vote of thanks to the chair.

An editorial of the *Dumfries and Galloway Standard* dated, 18th January, 1860. "In the report of a contemporary, it is stated that the greater number of the Kirkcudbright Rifle Volunteers are under age, but this is incorrect. The Rifle Corps is made up of stout, hardy young men, the most suitable in the place, while the Artillery Corps is mainly composed of parties far beyond the age specified by the War Office. (This arch rivalry between the two Corps was to continue throughout their existence. A report of 25th January, 1900, on the departure of Volunteers to the Boer War, stated, that it was the first time in over 30 years that the two Companies had sat down together).

The first General meeting of the Rifle Corps was held in the store room at the Cross (Tolbooth) on Friday, 3rd February, 1860, called by Mr. Maitland of Barcaple, Convener. The roll was called with 50 men answering their names. Mr. Maitland told the meeting that the Earl of Selkirk had kindly given a practice ground at Lochfergus and the Magistrates, a store-room at the old jail, as an Armoury. A room in the old jail was being fitted that it might be used for indoor drill.

A committee was formed to arrange dress, times of drill and other matters. The rules would be similar to those of other Rifle Corps in the Stewartry as would be the uniforms. The committee selected was, Mr. Laurie; Mr. Hamilton; Mr. Tennant; Mr. Corrie; Mr. Wallace.

A few days later, the services of a Drill Instructor, Sergeant White, were obtained and soldiering begun. A report of 22nd February, 1860, was to report, "This body is being regularly drilled at such hours of the day as best suit the convenience of members. There is a morning drill from eight to nine o'clock, well attended, and at which all the forms of marching are gone through. This constitutes a most pleasant exercise and imparts vigour to the bodily system. The members have not yet got their uniforms but it is expected they will soon be obtained."

From the minutes of the meeting of the Corps on the 3rd February, 1860, and the following letters which appeared in the local press, it was quite obvious that some discussion had taken place throughout the town as to suitable accommodation for the Volunteers. They were plainly in need of a drill hall but this was not to materialise until 1878.

Kirkcudbright. 20th December, 1859.

"Sir. As we are to have Artillery after all, a friend of mine, who has seen many lands, who has seen Fort Hamilton, commanding the entrance to New York, suggests, what a splendid locality there is at Torrs Point for forming a fort, which would command the whole entrance to the river. What a fine field the fort and ground around, having ample and verge enough, would afford for practice, far removed from harms way. Again for our Rifles, can they not manage to get part of our fine old Castle reinstated for a store? Indeed there is an apartment in it which would admit of the Riflemen drilling.

No great amount of money would be required to make the necessary repairs and to prevent accidents from stones falling from the chimney heads and gable tops, for these are in a very caduciary state.

A. Subscriber."

A number of years were to pass before a seconder was found to this proposal.

Kirkcudbright. 11th June, 1875.

"The letter of a number of years previous suggested that some parts of the Castle might be made available for the Artillery and Rifle Volunteers, and that the appearance of members of the force occasionally looking out of the window framed in ivy would have a fine effect and recall the days of the fortalices of old. Nothing, however, came of the idea, thrown out, the Volunteers stick to the ugly Old Tolbooth, where if the stock of powder was to explode, the once west end of the Burgh would be blown-up."

The services of the Corps were accepted by Her Majesty Queen Victoria on the 2nd March, 1860, being formed as one Company and bearing the title the 1st Kirkcudbright Rifle Volunteers.

Friday, 18th April, 1860, was the day fixed for the swearing in of the Corps and at 3pm all along the High Street from the Bank of Scotland to the drill ground at the Academy swarmed vast crowds of interested spectators. At the appointed hour, Sergeant White gave the appropriate order and a variety of evolutions were gone through for the benefit of the onlookers, right and left wheeling, falling into double file and telling-off, wheeling in double-file, marching in file, forming company of new, extending from the halt in skirmishing order, changing front on the right, left and centre, which demonstration called forth the enthusistic cheers of the crowds.

Headed by Captain Laurie, who was present in his new uniform, Lieutenant Hamilton and Ensign Tennant, commissioned on 16th March, 1860, the Company formed four deep and marched up the Wynd, along High Street and into the Court House. The Court House could scarcely afford standing accommodation for the Corps, all the seats being previously taken, the jury box being packed with ladies. Lord Selkirk, the Lord Lieutenant of the County took his seat as the representative of Her Majesty. Mr. Sandford, the Principal Steward of the Stewartry on his right and Provost Shand on his left. The members of the Corps formed four deep around the bar, the Lord Lieutenant briefly explained the nature of the oath and requested each member of the Corps to hold up his right hand while he read it over, and they to repeat the concluding words. This was done with the greatest solemnity. Sheriff Sandford in addressing the gentlemen of the Kirkcudbright Rifle Corps, said, "You have taken the oath of allegiance to the Queen and although I do not know that it required that ceremony, either to give greater warmth to your loyalty or to increase your patriotism, still it does bind you to your Sovereign." Sheriff Sandford was to continue at some length concluding by saying, "You are not going to move in a war of aggression but in a work of defence and recollect that when you don that uniform, which my friend Captain Laurie so well graces, (cheers) you will have put on your working dress. You will have work to do, you will have to drill regularly, to master your manoeuvres and have to hit a mark although you may often miss it, (laughter). The fattest of you must learn to run and Captain Laurie will no doubt show you how (laughter). For, gentlemen, if you are well drilled you will be ready, in the hour of conflict, if that comes, and come it may, you have resolved and vowed here today to defend your homes and your altars, your wives, your daughters, your sisters and your dear fatherland and I know if that conflict does arise where the men of Galloway will be found. They will be found among the foremost."

The Lord Lieutenant briefly addressed the assembled Company thus terminating that portion of the proceedings. The word of command was given and the Corps marched out with a number of friends, to the Armoury, where an enjoyable and convivial evening was spent.

That same evening, 18th April, 1860, a juvenile Corps of the Rifle Volunteers, formed by the boys attending the Academy were reviewed on the School Green in the presence of a numerous crowd. They were put through various movements and thence marched to the quay, where they went through many intricate evolutions to the delight of the spectators.

A section of the 1st Kirkcudbright Rifle Volunteers was raised in Ringford with a further Section being raised at Dundrennan on 25th November, 1878. Twynholm and Borgue were to supply detachments to the Kirkcudbright Artillery Volunteers. On 17th August, 1866, Gatehouse Rifle Corps, ex-4th Kirkcudbright Rifle Volunteers, were disbanded, joining as a Section of the Kirkcudbright Company.

By the year 1883, 1,240 Rifle Volunteers had passed through the ranks, the strength of the Company then being 92, with the then, Captain Craig, being the only member surviving of those enrolled in 1860.

CASTLE DOUGLAS.

In accordance with a numerously and influentially signed requisition from the community of Castle Douglas, on Monday, 5th December, 1859, a meeting was held in the Court House, for the purpose of taking measures for the formation of a Volunteer Rifle Corps, in the district. The Court House was crowded with a large number being unable to gain admission. Provost Nicholson was called to the chair and briefly outlined the purpose for which the meeting was being held.

Mr. Mackie of Bargaly and Ernespie, M.P. for the Stewartry, in moving the first resolution expressed his gratification at so large and influential a turnout, to show that the people of Castle Douglas were prepared to join in the movement taking place, for the formation of a Rifle Corps by way of supplementing the national defences. He continued, "I say not, that the Emperor of the French is about to change his policy towards this country, far from it, for I, for one, do not believe that such is his intention, I do not say that even if war between

France and Great Britain should break out tomorrow that our regular forces of the army and navy would be found insufficient for the national defence, but I do say that by forming Rifle Corps it is possible to prevent war and continue to this country the blessings of a permanent peace,"(cheers). He was to continue, "It is a precautionary movement, and what we may call a domestic one, a movement, indeed, which has not been inaptly designated the true peace league, and then, in a secondary point of view, supposing that war should unhappily arise between France and this country and bring with it the contingencies of a possible invasion, then what better resources than those Volunteer Corps has this country to fall back upon to punish and repel the invaders, whose insolent foot should venture to desecrate the shore of our island home, (loud cheers).

He continued, "In Wigtownshire they have been beforehand with us in promoting the movement and gentlemen, should it be said that in the Stewartry we are to sit with our arms folded, as if we had no interest in the matter? Are we to be the drones who are to enjoy the labour of the working bees around us? Shall we remain above in our apathy and singular in our inertness, so that if ever the question should be asked,

"Lives there a man with soul so dead
Who never to himself has said
This is my own, my native land?"

The answer be given 'Yes', in the Stewartry you will find such men (loud cheers).

He continued, "It appeared necessary, for the purpose of rifle practising and drill, that the County should be divided into districts, and that with regards to the Corps itself about 60 men will be required". He continued, "I now beg to lay on the table a list containing the names of 25 Volunteers, all obtained in one day (cheers). The financial department of the question to equip 60 riflemen, about £500 would be needed at a calculation of 8 guineas per man, but I do not think, judging from the results of the movement in other Counties that more than half would find their own equipments." He continued, "the subscriptions already laid on the table show that £205 has been raised and I would be insulting the head and heart of every one in this meeting should I think that for one moment they would hesitate to forward the movement, either by purse or person or by both (great cheers). He continued in this vein at some length, concluding by saying, "That it is expedient to raise a Rifle Corps in this district to form a portion of a force to be called, "the Kirkcudbrightshire Volunteers." The motion was seconded by Mr. Maitland Kirwan, Gelston Castle.

Mr. Laurie, Woodhall, moved the second resolution "That the following gentlemen be appointed as a committee to carry out the first resolution; Provost Nicholson; Messrs. Kirwan, Gelston Castle; Laurie, Woodhall; Renny, Danevale; Mackie, Ernespie; Grierson, Caigton; Thompson, Chapleton; Bell, Hillowton; Skirving, Croys; Hunter, Leaths; Grierson, Breoch; with power to add to their number.

Mr. Hewat, banker, briefly seconded the resolution which, like the first was put to the meeting and carried amidst enthusiastic applause.

Speeches were to continue in a patriotic manner at some length, concluding with Mr. Maitland of Barcaple, "The sight now presented by this country would make any despot think twice before he invaded. He alluded to the rifle as the weapon, which in the practised hands of Volunteers gave victory to the Americans in the great revolutionary war against this country, and he doubted not that it would do equally good service in our own hands should there be an invasion. It was with great pride that he saw a revival of the spirit which pervaded the country in 1804, and he hoped that this feeling would take deep root, so that our country might no longer be said to be destitute of military spirit (cheers). Mr. Mackie moved a vote of thanks to the Chairman and the meeting closed.

An advertisement was to appear in the *Kirkcudbrightshire Advertiser*, of 9th December, 1859, signed by Mr. Renny, Convener of the Castle Douglas Rifle Corps, announcing that meetings would be held every Monday for the purpose of enrolling Volunteers. The first man to subscribe his name to the list being Mr. Adam Skirving of Croys.

On Tuesday 26th January 1860, a numerously attended meeting was held in the Town Hall of members of the Castle Douglas Rifle Corps.

Mr. Renny in introducing the business of the meeting said he was glad to be able to inform the members of the Corps that their funds had now accumulated to upwards of £420 which was enough to warrant them in at once proceeding with the embodiment of the Corps. They had secured an excellent practising ground at Corra, belonging to Mr. Grierson of Caigton and they had secured a store for their arms, Major-General Johnston of Carnsalloch, Honorary Member, having placed an empty house at their disposal. Application had been made to the Lord Lieutenant, requesting that he secure the services of a Drill Sergeant for the Corps. He had only further to add that rules and regulations would be drawn up for the guidance of the members and the regulation of the Corps.

Mr. James Mackie, M.P. Bargaly, addressed the meeting and said, "he was not assuming too much when he said that it was intended that he should have the honour of being Captain of the Castle Douglas Rifle Corps. He might state that his own wish was, and still is, that he should simply have acted as one of the rank and file, a full private, in which capacity he would have endeavoured to have done his duty, but circumstances had occurred which had induced the Lord Lieutenant to recommend him as Captain. He was going, as they were aware, in a few days to London and he thought it desirable that the nominations of the Subaltern Officers should take place before he left.

Mr. J. Renny Esq., of Danevale and John Bell Esq., of Hillowton, were proposed and seconded for the position of Lieutenant in the Corps. Mr. Mackie suggested it might be the more agreeable course, the gentlemen themselves consenting, to draw lots for the higher of the two offices, the loser to be elected Ensign. By trusting to the blind goddess, it would, he was sure, give satisfaction to all parties. Messrs. Bell and Renny agreeing to this suggestion, two slips of paper, one bearing Lieutenant, the other Ensign, were placed in a hat and Mr. Bell's name being first called, a gentleman in the body of the hall drew a slip of paper from the hat in which was written Lieutenant.

The nomination was therefore in favour of Mr. Bell. Mr. Renny accepting the nomination of Ensign. The result created some amusement and to none more than the two candidates themselves, who accepted their respective honours.

Mr. Mackie told the meeting that they had at present only 67 members and he expressed the hope that an energetic effort would be made to increase the number of effective members. He continued, "There would be no difficulty with arms, as the Government would supply to each Corps. With regards accoutrements, the large number of subscriptions they had secured would enable them to help those who could not help themselves.

A vote of thanks having been proposed the meeting closed.

Before the meeting of the Corps on Monday, 6th February, 1860, was a letter from the Earl of Selkirk, stating that he had been unable to secure the services of a drill Sergeant from the Militia of the Castle Douglas Corps. (Apparently no Castle Douglas Militia drill instructor, would offer his services to the new Volunteer Corps in consequence of the Galloway Rifles Militia being broken up and transferred to Dumfries.) A suggestion was made that the services of a drill Sergeant be obtained and the cost be divided between Kirkcudbright and Castle Douglas, this was dismissed. Mr. Mackie saying they should have a drill Sergeant of their own and he would look one up in Aldershot. The rate of pay was 18/- per week with free lodgings. The committee considered this too dear and sent to Edinburgh to procure the services of a drill Sergeant from the Militia quartered there.

The Corps was however, to commence drill immediately, Mr. R.J. Congrieve, Esq., of Mollance. consenting to do drill duty until the services of a regular Drill Sergeant could be obtained. The services of a Drill Sergeant were finally obtained on the 5th March, 1860.

On the 14th February, 1860, Captain Lloyd of the West Yorkshire Rifles visited Castle Douglas, for the purpose of inspecting the ground fixed for rifle practice, the farms of Corra and Caigton. Captain Lloyd expressed himself highly satisfied with the nature of the ground and considered it perfectly adapted for the purpose to which it had been devoted. The store for arms, donated by Major-General Johnstone did not meet with the approval of Captain Lloyd, however, the committee were to be relieved from their dilemma when Mr. James Gordon, cabinet-maker placed one of the stores in connection with his own business at the disposal of the committee, which met with the approval of the Captain. The problem in obtaining a store-room was to prompt the following editorial in the *Advertiser*, "As it is probable that in a very short time the arrangements for the erection of a Police Station in Castle Douglas will be finally agreed upon, we may be permitted to hint that a few pounds would not be thrown away in making the building sufficiently commodious so as to accommodate the resident Police Officer and the arms used by the members of the Rifle Corps. In such a place they could not fail to be well cared for and the mere fact the Police station being a depot for a Government military store, would impact to it a dignity which it otherwise would not possess."

On the 2nd March, 1860, the services of the Corps were accepted by Her Majesty Queen Victoria, being formed as one Company and bearing the title the 2nd Kirkcudbright Rifle Volunteers.

On 5th March, 1860, Mr. Mackie, writing from Ernespie, addressed the following letter to the members of the Castle Douglas Rifle Corps, "Gentlemen, I am happy to inform you that the Queen has been graciously pleased to accept of the services of our Corps, the Officers being myself, Captain, John Bell, Esq., Lieutenant, and William John Renny Esq., Ensign. I need not impress upon you the necessity of making the Corps as effective as possible, nor need I say that this desired efficiency will depend upon the energy and zeal of each individual, each in his place, and all of us together, co-operating in promoting that united and patriotic action which is the basis of the Volunteer movement."

On Thursday, 22nd March, 1860, the members of the 2nd Kirkcudbright Rifle Volunteers, assembled in the Court House, Castle Douglas, for the purpose of taking the oath of allegiance. Captain Clark of Dunmuir, J.P. attended to administer the oath. He said, "Gentlemen, some nights back when the rules of the Company were under consideration, the principal sections of the Acts of Parliament under which you were enrolled were explained, and I will now take the liberty of reading the clause relative to the oath which I am in Her Majesty's name, about to administer." Captain Clark read the clause and administered the oath, he continued, "You will perceive gentlemen, although the words of the oath are few in number still they are significant. The Lord Lieutenant has been pleased to approve of the Officers of your choice, they have been gazetted and are now vested with the authority of the Sovereign."   In all 34 members took the oath.

On Friday, 13th April, 1860, the Company felt confident enough to make their first public appearance in a field owned by Captain Clark, Dunmuir, when 30 members performed their drill evolutions for upwards of one hour in a creditable manner. The story is told however, that one member of the Corps was to take part in only this one drill, he being so corpulant that when the order was given to receive cavalry, he had much difficulty in getting into position and much pain in getting out, that in the circumstances he considered discretion the better part of valour and deserted the ranks.

Up to the year 1883, a total of 523 men had passed through the ranks, the strength of the Company then being 76 with no members, who had enrolled in 1860, still serving in the Corps.

The following is a part list of subscriptions towards the formation of the Volunteer Rifle Corps in Castle Douglas:

The Dowager Lady Abercrombie (per Captain Clarke, Dunmuir)	25.0.0.
James Mackie, M.P., Bargaly and Ernespie	20.0.0.
C.L. Kirwan, Gelston Castle	10.0.0.
W. Kennedy Laurie. Woodhall	10.0.0.
R.. J. Congreve, Mollance	10.0.0.
Adam Skirving, Croys	10.0.0.
S. C. Maitland, Compston.	10.0.0.
Walter McCulloch. Ardwell	10.0.0.
Major-General Johnston, Carnsalloch	10.0.0.
A Murray Dunlop, M.P. Corsock	10.0.0.
Ivie Mackie. Nutwood.	10.0.0.
Dr. Cowan, Dildawn.	10.0.0.
John Hall, Mollance	10.0.0.
Wellwood H. Maxwell, Munches	10.0.0.
The Hon. Marmaduke C. Maxwell, Terregles	10.0.0.
J. Cunninghame, Hensol.	10.0.0.
William J. Renny, Danevale.	5.0.0.
John Bell, Dunjop	5.0.0.
W.G. Lawrence, Larhnean	5.0.0.
H, G. Murray-Stewart, Cally	5.0.0.
Patrick Dudgeon, Cargen	5.0.0.
Robert Comrie, Largs	5.0.0.
David Maitland, Barcaple	5.0.0.
James Moffat, Glaisters	5.0.0.
Captain Sanderson, Glenlaggan	5.0.0.
A. Young Herries, Spottes	5.0.0.
James Clarke, Dunmuir	5.0.0.
W.Y. Herries. Spottes	5.0.0.
T.W. Campbell, Walton Park	5.0.0.
J. Fergusson, Kilwhanity	5.0.0.
Alexander McKnight, Barlochan	5.0.0.
R.Glendonwyn Gordon, Cogarth	5.0.0.
Colonel Johnston, Balcary	5.0.0.
Major-General McHaffie. Torhousemuir	5.0.0.
Joseph Bowstead, Hyde House, Stroud	5.0.0.
Sir George Abercrombie, Bart	5.0.0.
J, Clark Maxwell, Glenlair	5.0.0.
Mrs, Maitland, Gelston Castle	3.0.0.
Robert Johnston, Netherhall	3.0.0.
Rev. Thomas Stevenson, Balmaghie Manse	3.0.0.

William Barbour, Kelton Hill	2.10.0.
James W. Stuart, Erncrogo (Culgruff)	2.10.0.
Donald Ross, Boreland.	2. 2.0.
Samuel Simpson, King's Grange	2. 2.0.
Thomas Biggar, Chapelton, King's Grange	2. 2.0.
Rev. S. Cowan, Kelton Manse	2. 0.0.
Rev. J. R. Grant, Buittle Manse	2. 0.0.
Rev. Richard A. Gillespie, Crossmichael Manse	1. 0.0.

The list continued at some length with numerous donations of £1; 10/-; 5/-; 2/6d; making the total at that date 29th December, 1859 - £361.10s.6d.

To now clear up a misunderstanding of 100 years ago. In the *Regimental Gazette* of the Galloway Rifle Volunteers, for the year 1897, Mr. Adam Skirving of Croys was to write "a considerable sum was subscribed for the purpose of equipping and raising the force, Castle Douglas had the honour of leading the way, but when the town of Kirkcudbright also proposed to raise a Company some of the subscriptions were transferred to it being the county town." However, at the meeting of the Castle Douglas Rifle Corps on 5th December, 1859, Mr. Mackie informed the meeting that Volunteer Corps would be raised in different parts of the Stewartry, drilling separately coming together as a Battalion for only a few days of the year. Mr. Neilson of Queenshill asked of Mr. Mackie, "are the funds to be raised for each district separately?" Mr. Mackie was to answer, "Yes" and referred to the sum already raised saying, "he saw several names on the list who might now naturally prefer that their subscriptions be transferred to the Kirkcudbright subscription list." Accordingly on 30th December, 1859, the sum of £10 was transferred from Castle Douglas to Kirkcudbright.

Haugh of Urr was to raise a Section of Rifle Volunteers attached to the Castle Douglas Company.

On Friday, 5th February, 1864, Captain Clark of Dunmuir administered the oath of allegiance to men from Dalbeattie who joined the Castle Douglas Company as a Dalbeattie Section, drills were held in both Castle Douglas and Dalbeattie.

On 23rd June, 1869, Dalbeattie were to form a Company of Volunteers in their own right.

In July,1897, Colour Sergeant Horsley, retired from the regular service of the King's Own Scottish Borderers taking over as sub-postmaster at Springholm where he became active in the Volunteer movement. On Saturday 13th November, 1897, at the request of Sergeant Horsley the band and members of the Castle Douglas Rifle Corps travelled to Springholm and Kirkpatrick Durham in a recruiting drive. Altogether 18 men subscribed their names to the formation of a Section with a further 12 signifying their like intention. The oath of allegiance was administered that evening by Mr. Hyslop, Knockwalloch J.P., the ceremony taking place in the Oddfellow's Hall, Kirkpatrick Durham. Corsock were also to join as a detachment to the Castle Douglas Company under the Command of H.B.Wilkinson, later to become Lieutenant in the Castle Douglas Company.

The yearning for his former army life proved too strong for Colour Sergeant Horsley, however, and on the 9th December, 1898, we find he has left the Post Office and re-enlisted as a Sergeant Instructor to the Earlston Volunteers - Border Rifles, Berwick.

In the Rhonehouse Public Hall on Wednesday, 4th October, 1905, a large audience gathered to consider a proposal to form a Volunteer detachment in the Village and district, Mr. J.H. McDill presided.

Brigadier-General Gordon of Threave said that he had much pleasure in coming there to support the Volunteer force, which of course was capable of being improved and its numbers largely increased. This depended chiefly on the amount of local support it received, which he did not consider was at present sufficient. People who did not pay in person should pay with their purse. He continued by saying he himself had joined the force as a Private 41 years ago, and was now a Brigadier-General and therefore spoke with some knowledge of the movement. He would not hesitate to go on service with the battalion of his own Brigade. He continued, the village of Rhonehouse gave some admirable recruits to the Regular Army and it ought not to be behind with regard to the Volunteers, there was plenty of raw material. He hoped that the pilgrimage of Captain Forde and Colour Sergeant McIlroy from Castle Douglas Rifle Corps would not be in vain.

A Rhonehouse Section of Rifle Volunteers was finally added to the Castle Douglas Company on the 11th October, 1906.

In December, 1867, the death occurred of Captain James Mackie, M.P., Bargaly, 2nd Kirkcudbright Rifle Volunteers, Castle Douglas, when the Chaplain to the Company, the Rev. R.A Gillespie, preached the funeral sermon to a large congregation in the Town Hall, Castle Douglas.

On the 29th January, 1879, Major Renny, Danevale, of the 2nd Kirkcudbright Rifle Volunteers, Castle Douglas died and was buried, on the 30th January, 1879, in Crossmichael Cemetary, with full military honours. The following were the strengths of the various Companies in attendance.

Kirkcudbright -	Captain Craig, Acting Surgeon Johnstone, 2 Sergeants and 7 Privates.
Castle Douglas -	2 Sergeants, 39 Privates, including the Band.
New Galloway -	Captain Millman, Lieutenants Craig and Dalziel, 4 Sergeants 1 Corporal and 4 Privates.
Maxwellton -	Lieutenants Lennox and Symons, 2 Sergeants and 13 Privates.
Dalbeattie -	Lieutenant Kerr, 3 Sergeants and 7 Privates.
Newton Stewart -	Captain Picken, 4 Sergeants and 3 Privates.

The members of the Castle Douglas Company, under the command of Lieutenant Lennox, Maxwellton, fired three volleys over the grave.

The following is an extract from Battalion Orders dated 30th January, 1879.

(1). Lieutenant Colonel Gordon Maitland has with the deepest regret to announce to the Galloway Battalion of Rifle Volunteers, the death of Major Renny.

(2). As a zealous Officer and a truly kind hearted person, he will long be remembered in the Battalion.

(3). As a mark of respect to the late Major Renny, the Lieutenant Colonel Commanding desires all Officers in the Battalion, when in uniform to appear in mourning for the space of one month."

* * * *

Mr. Adam Skirving, Croys, Castle Douglas, a founder member of, and the first enrolled member of, the 2nd Kirkcudbright Rifle Volunteers, died on the 23rd December, 1903, aged 83 years. He was buried on the 26th December, 1903, at Kirkpatrick Durham Cemetary, with full military honours by members of the Castle Douglas Rifle Company,

GLENKENS ,

The following requisition was addressed to the Provost of New Galloway:-

New Galloway, 21st July, 1859,

"Sir, We the undersigned request you to call a public meeting of the inhabitants of the Glenkens to consider the propriety of raising a Rifle Corps in the district. We are respectfully yours,
Signed, J. Maitland; Wellwood Maxwell; George Murray; James Carruthers; William Alexander; William Scot; William Barbour; Thomas Barbour; Alfred McKinlay Millman; W. Dickson; Robert McKay. "

As a result of this influentially signed requisition, on Thursday, 11th August, 1859, a numerously attended meeting of the inhabitants of the Glenkens was held in the Town Hall, New Galloway for the purpose of considering measures for raising a Rifle Corps in that district.

A very large number of the gentry, farmers, and inhabitants of the district were present, among them, Rev. Dr. Maitland, Kells; Rev. George Murray, Balmaclellan; Wellwood Maxwell Esq., of Glenlee; Gordon Maitland Esq., of the Hon. East India Company; W. Barbour Esq., of Barlae; T. Barbour of Dalshangen; James Carruthers Esq., of Craig; Provost Muir; Messrs O. Brown; Shaw; Lee; McKay etc. Provost Muir was called to the chair.

Dr. Maitland proposed, "That this meeting is of the opinion that steps should be taken for the formation of a Rifle Corps in the Glenkens," He humorously referred to the threatened invasion by the French, 50 years ago and then said, "Let us ever be on the watch and always prepared for any contingency. When we consider that our native island is separated from France by only 20 miles of sea, which is only about an hours sail, and when we contemplate how easily an army of some 50,000 men could be wafted across the waters, it is certainly a duty of the greatest importance for everyone who has the interest of his Country at heart to defend it. I think, too, the exercise of the Rifle Corps, will form an excellent amusement for our young men, some of whom are at a loss to occupy their time, and what can be a more legitimate, healthy or better exercise and occupation than that of learning the use of arms with which they may defend their hearths and homesteads?"

Mr. T. Barbour of Dalshangen, seconded the motion.

Mr. Wellwood Maxwell of Glenlee moved that the following parties be requested to promote the formation of a Rifle Corps in their respective Parishes: Messrs. McKay, and P. Muir for New Galloway; Messrs. John E. Spalding, L. Cowan and Thomas Smith, Dalry; Messrs. W. Barbour and Carruthers, Balmaclellan; Messrs. Jamieson, Thomas Barbour and Patterson, Carsphairn. Mr. Maxwell then proceeded to inform the assembled meeting the steps necessary to take for the formation of a Rifle Corps and continued, "All these matters can however, be more definitely arranged by a Committee. We cannot expect to accomplish everything at our present meeting which is the first that has been held on this subject in the Stewartry, but the sooner we can arrive at some sort of organisation the better. There can be no doubt, I am sure, in the mind of any one individual as to the necessity of being efficiently prepared for any aggression, not only of France but of any nation in Europe or in the world. We are in a very isolated position and therefore it behoves to make up for our weakness by being thoroughly prepared to meet any foe, (cheers). He was to continue in this patriotic vein at some length, concluding by saying, "I may also mention that the English invasion fever ran so high some time ago in France, that some of Louis Napoleon's adherents or as I might appropriately call them, his creatures, proposed that every man in the Country should subscribe a shilling if he would invade England, but I have no doubt that every individual in these realms would subscribe not only a shilling but would drain his coffers to the very last farthing to keep him out of it, (cheers)."

Mr. Gordon-Maitland proposed and Mr. William Barbour seconded, that the above named parties, mentioned in Mr. Maxwell's resolution form a General Committee and that Mr. McKay be requested to act as Secretary - agreed to. Mr. Maxwell proposed the vote of thanks to the chair and the meeting closed.

On Saturday, 7th January, 1860, a public meeting was held in the Town Hall, New Galloway, for the purpose of promoting the Rifle movement in the Glenkens. Those present; Rev. Dr. Maitland; Rev. George Murray, Troquhain; Mr Maxwell; Mr W. Barbour; Mr T. Barbour; Mr. Carruthers; Mr. Dalziel, Waterside; Mr. McMichael of Fallow-wheat; Mr. Grierson, Balmaclellan, and over 30 enrolled Volunteers.

Mr. Maxwell told the chair that since the last meeting 35 effective members and 10 honorary members had been enrolled on the Secretary's list and that subscriptions amounted to £106. He showed the importance of the movement and gave an explanation of the duties which the members would be called on to undertake. He urged the members of the different Parish committees to use all their influence to increase the numbers of effectives up to that required to form a Company. A canvas of the various Parishes was agreed upon and meetings fixed to be held in Balmaclellan and Dalry. The Secretary read the list of subscribers to the fund and after the usual formalities the meeting separated.

The following is a part list of, "donations towards the founding of a Volunteer Rifle Corps in the district of the Glenkens." dated, 1st February, 1860.

Amount of donations formerly advertised	£106.2s.0d.
Mrs. Grierson, Youretoun of Garroch	5.5s.0d.
James Carruthers of Craig	2.2s.0d.
Peter Dalziel of Waterside	2.2s.0d,
Robert McKay, New Galloway	2.2s.0d.
George McMichael, Fallow-Wheat	2.2s.0d.
Davie Cowan, Dalry	1.1s.0d.
James Good, Bridgemark	1.1s.0d.
John Thomson, Thornhill	1.0s.0d.
William Rooke, Kenmuir Arms	10s.6d.

Subscriptions for the above object will be received by Mr. Maxwell of Glenlee; Mr, Barbour, Union Bank, Dalry; Mr. Corrie, Clydesdale Bank, New Galloway; or the Secretary, Robert McKay, New Galloway.

A General meeting of the effective members of the Corps was held in the Town Hall, New Galloway, on Friday, 10th February, 1860, for the purpose of nominating Officers and considering any other business connected with the Corps.

About 60 members were present, Mr. Maxwell of Glenlee presiding. The minutes of the former meeting having been read by the Secreatary, the rules to be submitted to the Lord Lieutenant, for the government of the Corps were considered and agreed to.

The nominations of Officers was then proceeded with, Mr. Dalziel, Waterside proposed Mr. Maxwell of Glenlee as Captain. Mr. Muir, Balmaclellan proposed Mr. Carruthers of Craig as Lieutenant and Mr. John Robb, New Galloway; proposed Mr. Dalziel Waterside, as Ensign, all of which motions were unanimously approved. Mr. Maxwell, Mr. Carruthers and Mr. Dalziel respectfully returned thanks for the honour the Corps had conferred on them. Their commissions were received on the 28th March, 1860,

It was then announced to the meeting that the Secretary had engaged, subject to their approval, Sergeant Brown, late of the New Galloway Militia, as Drill Instructor to the Corps. This arrangement was approved and it was resolved to commence drill forthwith. On Mondays and Tuesdays at New Galloway, on

Wednesdays and Thursdays at Dalry and Fridays and Saturdays, at Balmaclellan.

It was stated that a storeroom for arms etc., had been rented in New Galloway and that Mr. Maxwell had kindly agreed the use of a field with a range of over 300 yards for rifle practice. It was also agreed to offer the services of the Corps to the Lord Lieutenant.

On Monday 13th and Tuesday 14th February, 1860, the New Galloway members of the Corps, numbering 30, assembled for drill in the Town Hall, at 8 pm and received their first lesson. The number of New Galloway Volunteers represented 7% of the entire population of New Galloway.

The services of the Corps were accepted by Her Majesty on the 28th March, 1860, being formed as one Company in New Galloway, as the 3rd Kirkcudbright Rifle Volunteers, comprising of a Section from Dalry with detachments being supplied from Mossdale, Laurieston, Parton, Balmaclellan and Carsphairn,

In October, 1866, Wellwood Maxwell Esq., of Glenlee, Captain of the 3rd Kirkcudbright Rifle Volunteers died at an early age, and was succeeded in the Corps, on the 9th November, 1866, by Captain John Gordon Maitland. The following lines were composed on the death of Captain Maxwell by the Rev. George Murray, Chaplain to the Corps and Minister of Balmaclellan.

Our Captain.

Our Captain sleeps!
What is it that keeps
Our Chief from the field away?
Each Volunteer
In the ranks is here
What aileth Glenlee today?

Our Captain sleeps!
Death comes and reaps
The green and the stately corn:
To his lonely grave
The young and the brave
Is slowly and sadly borne.

Our Captain sleeps!
And his widow weeps
For the gift gone to the Giver:
Each Volunteer
Sheds the bitter tear
That his Chief has gone for ever.

For ever? not so:
The trump, shall blow
Arousing the good and true:
And the Chief and his men
Shall meet again
At the last The Grand Review.

GATEHOUSE-OF-FLEET.

Very little history exists as to the formation of this Corps but from the information contained herein, it gives a most interesting insight into how the early survival of a Corps was very much dependent on their having a Commanding Officer of some wealth.

At a meeting held of the members of this Corps within the Mason's Lodge, Gatehouse, on Saturday, the 10th March, 1860, Major Rainsford-Hanney of Kirkdale in the chair, it was agreed that the services of the Corps be offered to Her Majesty's Government. The Chairman was also unanimously elected to be Captain of the Corps, subject to the approval of the Lord Lieutenant. The Honourable Secretary, Mr. D.J.Ewart, was instructed to communicate the result to his Lordship, and to request that a Drill Sergeant should be sent as soon as possible.

The rules and style of uniform of the Kirkcudbright and Castle Douglas Corps were to be adopted at Gatehouse.

The services of the Corps were accepted by Her Majesty on the 19th May, 1860, forming as a Sub-Division and bearing the title, the 4th Kirkcudbright Rifle Volunteers.

A report of the 10th September, 1860, "the 4th Kirkcudbright Rifles, Gatehouse, enjoyed an excursion to Kirkdale the seat of Major Rainsford-Hanney, Commanding Officer of the Corps. They left Gatehouse preceded by their Fife and Drum Band, where they performed a few evolutions on the lawn."

On 17th August, 1866, the 4th Kirkcudbright Rifle Volunteers, Gatehouse were disbanded for the want of a suitable Officer. They were transferred as a Section to the 1st Kirkcudbright Rifle Volunteers, Kirkcudbright.

The following letters were to appear in the *Dumfries and Galloway Standard*, some years later:

Gatehouse, 2nd July, 1879.

"Sir. The appearance of Mr. H.G. Murray-Stewart of Broughton at the Galloway Rifle Volunteers Association meeting at New Galloway range on Tuesday last may well make one explain with Horatio in Hamlet, 'O day and night, but this is wondrous strange.' Why this new-born affection for the Volunteers, after allowing one of the best little Corps in the County to become extinct for the want of an Officer. I refer to the 4th Kirkcudbright or Gatehouse Corps which was at his very door, and in which Corps he was gazetted Lieutenant, got a uniform, and appeared on parade, once, and the said Corps became defunct for want of Officers. It does not require either a prophet or the son of a prophet to predict that his sudden affection for the Volunteers in view of the forthcoming election, will, like his permission to his tenants to trap rabbits on the eve of last election, quietly disappear after having served its purpose.

'Marksman.'

Gatehouse. 9th July, 1879.

"Sir, As Marksman in your issue of the 2nd instant has apparently got his rifle wrongly sighted, kindly allow me to resort to the old custom of 'Coaching' which is now disallowed at rifle competitions, but may still be brought into use in the range he has saw fit to use, and I will now point out where he is in error. Mr. Murray-Stewart has on frequent past occasions witnessed the contests at the Galloway battalion meeting so that his appearance at New Galloway on the 24th ultimo was no matter of surprise to anyone acquainted with his previous conduct in this respect. All along he has taken the liveliest interest in the Volunteer movement, and given very tangible support to various Companies of the battalion, besides being a subscribing member to the Galloway Rifle Association. As I always like to see a Marksman shoot fair, and as an old Volunteer, who knows Mr. Murray-Stewart's very friendly feeling to the Volunteer Movement. I hope you will permit me this correction.

'Bulls-eye.'

No doubt, partly prompted, by the strong feeling expressed in the letter of 'Marksman' of 2nd July, 1879, on the 21st July, 1879, W.F. Maxwell, younger, of Cardoness, through the Commanding Officer of the Galloway battalion of Volunteers, made application to the War Office for permission to reform the 4th Kirkcudbright Rifle Volunteer Corps in Gatehouse. Permission was refused, no doubt the War Office bearing in mind their forthcoming consolidation of the Galloway Administrative Battalion of Rifle Volunteers, when the control of capitation grants and all finances, concerned with the battalion, were to pass to the direct control of the Colonel Commanding the Regiment. Gatehouse were to continue their roll as a section of the 1st Kirkcudbright Rifle Volunteers,

MAXWELLTON.

On the evening of 17th January, 1860, a meeting was held in the Court-House, Maxwellton, for the purpose of organising a Company of Rifle Volunteers in that district, Mr. D.C. Pagan occupied the chair and made suitable observations. A resolution was duly put and carried, pledging the meeting to take steps for raising a Rifle Corps.

It was also resolved that 5/- entry money be paid by every member, that the uniforms and equipment be provided out of a general fund, and that honorary members be admitted on subscribing £2.2s. to the general fund.

Mr. A Crackston moved and Mr. John Baillie seconded that the following gentlemen be appointed as a general committee to carry into effect the views of the meeting and to report progress to a meeting of Volunteers to be held in two weeks. D.C. Pagan; J.B.A, McKinnel; John Dewar; Joseph Walsh; G.W. Irving; A. Crackston; John Davidson; F.S. Allan; W. Welsh; T. McMutrie and Captain Smith, with power to add to their number. W. F. S. Allan to be honourable secretary.

By the close of the meeting 23 gentlemen had subscribed their names to the list of effective enrolled members.

A further meeting was held on 1st February, 1860, in the Court-House, Mr. Allan, the secretary, reported that subscriptions had been received since the last meeting amounting to £80, and that the number of effective members was now 42. It was agreed, after some discussion to empower the committee to make arrangements with the Dumfries Corps, for the use of their practising ground at Conhuith, which has already been approved by the Government Inspector. The committee were also instructed to rent a store for the arms and accoutrements, and to appoint a store-keeper.

A sub-committee; Messrs. Walsh, Pagan, McKinnel and Allan, was appointed to make arrangements for commencing drill, the secretary to call a meeting when such arrangements have been completed,

The following is a list of subscriptions towards the formation of a Rifle Volunteer Corps for the Maxwellton District of the Stewartry;

James Mackie of Bargaly, M.P.	5.0s.0d.
William Ewart M.P;	5.0s.0d.
Major Walker of Crawfordton	5.0s.0d.
Patrick Dudgeon of Cargen	5.0s.0d.
Walter McCulloch of Ardwell	5.0s.0d.
H.G. Stewart of Cally	5.0s.0d.
Wellwood Maxwell of the Grove	5.0s.0d.
Alexander Maxwell of Glengaber	5.0s.0d.
William K. Laurie of Woodhall	5.0s.0d.
James B. Neilson of Queenshill	5.0s.0d.
Colonel Hyslop of Lotus	5.0s.0d.
Alexander Harley of Portrack	5.0s.0d.
James Davidson of Summerville	4.4s.0d.
Phillip Forsyth of Nithside	3.3s.0d.
David C. Pagan, Maxwellton	3.3s.0d.
James B.A McKinnel, Maxwellton	3.3s.0d.
George W. Irving, Maxwellton	3.3s.0d.
J.W. Hutchinson, Maxwellton	3.3s.0d
Francis S. Allan Maxwellton	3.3s.0d.
James Caldow, Maxwellton	2.2s.0d
John Sproat of Landis	2.2s.0d.
Robert K.Walker, Maxwellton	2.2s.0d.
Peter Murray, Portland Place	2.0s.0d.
John McKenzie, Barnhill	1.0s.0d.
Robert McLellan, Maxwellton	1.0s.0d.
Thomas Costine, Maxwellon	1.0s.0d.
W. C. McKay, Maxwellton	1.0s.0d
John McNae, Flatts of Cargen	1.0s.0d.

The number of effective members requisite to form a Company being now enrolled, further subscriptions will be received at the various banks in Dumfries, at the Stamp Office, Maxwellton, and by the Honourable Secretary,

On the evening of 16th March, 1860, a further meeting was held in the Court-House, Maxwellton, for the purpose of electing three officers. The meeting was informed that the Corps now numbered 63 effective members and for the last six weeks they had been drilling in the Court-House. The attendance had been good and the men had made rapid progress in both the manual and the platoon exercises,

Mr. James Bairden Affleck McKinnel of Macmurdiston was chosen as Captain. Mr. D. Pagan was chosen Lieutenant and Mr. Francis S. Allan, was chosen Ensign. The Secretary was then instructed to write to the Lord Lieutenant, offering the services of the Corps.

The services of the Corps were accepted by Her Majesty on the 1st June, 1860, as one Company, and bearing the title, the 5th Kirkcudbright Rifle Volunteers,

On Tuesday, 5th June, 1860, a meeting of the Corps was held in the Court House, Maxwellton, for the purpose of qualifying themselves by taking the oath of allegiance. Phillip Forsyth Esq., of Nithside, Steward-Substitute, officiated on the occasion and administered the oath, to upwards of 60 members.

It was reported that "with the exception of one or two, old enough for active duty, they were a body of as fine athletic young men as could be desired." Captain McKinnel wore the uniform which had been selected by the Corps. After the business of the meeting had been disposed of the Company enjoyed 'a treat' liberally provided by Mr.McKinnel.

Mr. Forsyth then addressed the members, "It had afforded him much pleasure in having this evening administered the oath of allegiance to so many respectable inhabitants of this Burgh who have nobly volunteered their services in defence of their country from foreign invasion, should that course of providence be necessary (cheers). Every man has rights to defend, his life, his fireside, his property, his liberty. These, if not destroyed by the invasion of a foreign foe, would, if we were unprepared to resist, be seriously injured. It therefore becomes every true patriot to be at all times fully prepared to defend them. Let your motto therefore be, *Pro aris et focis*, For our altars and our firesides," (cheers). He continued, "I doubt not you will be trained to become, in a short time efficient riflemen, and that you are sensible of the duties devolving upon you by the oath which you have this night taken. The first duty, you are doubtless aware, is obedience to your Officers, for without obedience there can be no discipline and without either or both, soldiers cannot show a successful resistance in warfare. It is also gratifying to see that, with one or two exceptions, the Company is composed of young men, few of you having yet attained the meridian of life. As in all other professions, youth is the period for learning military tactics. I hope that this movement on the part of the young men of this Country will lead very soon to the introduction of a system of military training of boys in our schools. He continued, "I consider therefore, that when a boy receives military training he will be, in some measure at least, prepared to join a military Corps." He continued, "the man who is trained has undoubtedy a more dignified appearance, instead of lounging as he goes along, he walks erect, his body is a machine, every joint of which is at command in a moment, and if attacked, will, with a single motion, defend himself." Mr. Forsyth then concluded amidst great applause.

Captain McKinnel then briefly addressed the assembled Corps. From what he had observed that night, the general appearance of the members the zeal with which they seem to be animated, and knowing, the character of the Officers whom they had chosen, he had no doubt, as he had said already, they would soon be an efficient Corps. It is related of the Laird of Logan, that having gone from Cumnock, where he resided, to Ayr, at the time of the last threatened invasion, when Volunteers were being raised in every district, a warlike bailie met him and asked why they were not raising Volunteers in Cumnock, 'Ne'er fash your thumb, bailie', said the Laird, 'there will be nae scarcity of Volunteers, for if the French was ance landed at Ayr, we'll hae you and maer of your Volunteers amang us than we'll ken up how to gie hidings tae" (great laughter). This was only the Laird's opinion of the day. Mercenary and conscript soldiers may fly but Volunteers do not, cannot, should they, their destruction is imminent and their cause is best. He felt confident therefore, that should an enemy appear on the shore of the Solway. Captain McKinnel would turn his back upon Cumnock and gallantly lead his men down to oppose the invaders. (great cheering).

Many fine words were thus spoken on the formation of this Corps, but after the initial euphoria had died down it is well to remember the words from the *Volunteer Gazette* of 1861, "those who accepted commissions through vanity and those who care for nothing but the braided tunic and the trailing swords." After a few short months Mr. D. Pagan was to resign his commission, with Francis Allan being promoted Lieutenant, J.G. Starke was to succeed as Ensign but again after a few months was to resign his commission. The Company was on the brink of disbanding or at the very least being reduced to a Sub-Division. By 1862, Captain McKinnel had resigned his commission leaving Lieutenant F. Allan as the sole Officer in the Corps. The very basis for the formation of a Rifle Corps, shooting, was being neglected and no officer, non-commissioned officer nor rifleman was to attend the 'Blue Riband' event of the Galloway Volunteer Assosciation shooting competition at New Galloway in 1862. However, in March, 1863, Captain Howat of Mabie was to assume command of the 5th Kirkcudbright Rifle Volunteers, and by June of that year he had increased the membership to 63, thus consolidating the Corps at Company strength. By the December of 1863, he had increased the membership to 93 effective members and in 1865, the membership was increased sufficiently to warrant the 5th Kirkcudbright Rifle Volunteers forming as one and a half Companies. Recruiting was to continue on the increase and in 1871, a Section of the 5th was raised in the village of Lochfoot and the district of Lochrutton, enabling the Corps on the 10th January, 1872, to increase its strength to two Companies of 198 enrolled Volunteers, 193 being efficient, entitling them to £311.10s. of Government capitation grants.

DALBEATTIE ,

On Thursday, 2nd March, 1860, a meeting of the inhabitants of Dalbeattie was held in the Commercial Hotel ballroom for the purpose of forming a Volunteer Corps in the district.

Those present were Wellwood Maxwell Esq., of the Munches; Francis Maxwell Esq., of Breoch; Messrs Stewart, Dudgeon and Gordon; Dr. McKnight; Mr. Grieve Esq., Banker; James Welsh Esq., of Firthhead; Thomas Maxwell, Chief Magistrate; Messrs. McMurtrie, Carsewell, Backett and McLaurie.

On the motion of Dr. McKnight, Wellwood Maxwell was called to the chair, He said, "the reason they had been called together that evening was to ascertain whether it was possible to form a body of Volunteers for the district of Dalbeattie. He thought he was the worst man they could have picked as chairman as he had the least knowledge of Military matters. He had thought the day had come when swords should be turned into pruning hooks and that wars were at an end. He thought that now they could hold converse with the wild places of Russia and soon hopefully with the backwoods of America, they had put an end to wars but that had been found to be a great mistake and so long as the world remained in its present state, wars must prevail and although they had been called a nation of shopkeepers, they must not fail to show that they were determined to uphold their dignity and position among the nations of the earth. Their armies had never been behind and they had always been able to meet any emergency. It might be desirable that we in the Kingdom should follow something like the course observed in other nations, but in connection with meetings such as this unfortunate tone of argument had prevailed which he could not too strongly appreciate and that was speaking wholly and unjustifiable of the Emperor of the French, who had certainly proved himself to be one of the most wonderful men of the present age, despite what was reported in the press of calls to 'avenge Waterloo'. They could not look into the breast of that man and ascertain what were his feelings. They were on the best of terms with him and it was only a few months since we were fighting side by side with his armies in the Crimea and just at this very moment he was preparing to share our battles in China. They had no right to dictate to France and the French people. In electing Louis Napoleon they had appointed a man who had shown himself capable of governing that country in the most wonderful style. They should not as a meeting make their feelings of illusion and anger, towards the Emperor of the French for they were surrounded by dangers from other powers equally great, if not greater. They should have an eye to all countries and while doing so, try if they could not at moderate expense arm this country, so that they would at all times have a ready and determined force to protect and defend their hearths and their homes.

The object of the Volunteer movement was to place this country in a similar position to other great military powers. They had already a standing army but it was not in point of numbers sufficient to cope with other military countries. They should have men so trained as to be able to handle a rifle in case of need. The support which this movement had received was quite astonishing and it had tended much to the esteem in relations with other countries. Its success had been greatest in the large towns and it was these towns from which the expected support was to be looked for but small districts might materially further the cause. If therefore the people of Dalbeattie considered they were in a position to form a Corps, he thought they would act rightly in doing so but if they thought the thing was to be a failure and that they could not make a good muster, he would have nothing to do with it. Do not run into anything that was likely to prove a failure. He was willing to give the movement his heartiest support if they so desired, but he was now too old and too grey in the head to sport a uniform, (cries of 'no' from the meeting).

Mr. Maxwell of Breoch regretted the absence of any military man who might aid them with his advice. Mr. Maxwell said he had been in touch with Dr. Shand of the Kirkcudbright Artillery Corps and had since received a reply which gave a full description of how a Corps should be organised, the expense of equipment and their relative value over bodies of riflemen. The drill of the riflemen Mr. Maxwell said, appeared to him so intricate that he would prefer studying it to performing it but it was not so with Artillerymen, for one efficient man could work a gun although, the other nine were inefficient. The distances of the district were so convenient that members of the Corps might assemble from Buittle, Kirkgunzeon and Colvend for practice and they were permitted to enrol in Sections of 20 upwards, which riflemen could not do.

Mr. Welsh deprecated the formation of an Artillery Corps as it was not needed in this particular district, French ships of War could never get beyond the De'ils Reach and could only destroy a few small wherries (crab apple trees) or act as a means of defence to the new house at Munches, (laughter).

After further remarks a committee was formed to ascertain the feeling in the district whether it was expedient to form a Corps in Dalbeattie.

With these strong pro-French feelings, held by the influential Mr. Maxwell of Munches, and perhaps with an educated and enlightened foresight into the French Emperor's plans and ambitions, and the lack of professional militiary guidance, Dalbeattie was to fall out of step with the rest of the Stewartry and did not at this stage form a Volunteer Rifle Corps. The neighbouring village of Haugh of Urr however, was to form a Section of Castle Douglas Rifle Corps and on the 5th February, 1864, 30 men from Dalbeattie were to enrol as a Section of the Castle Douglas Company.

In the old minute book of the Dalbeattie Section dated, 15th February, 1868, it was agreed that, "we demand our discharges from the Castle Douglas Company". This was to enable the men to join with a new Company being formed in Dalbeattie by Mr. W.W. Platt of Kirkennan. In due course the discharges were granted and the men were enrolled in the new Company bearing the title, the Battalion of Rifle Reserve Volunteers.

The services of this Company were offered to Her Majesty and were accepted on the 9th July, 1868, being formed as one Company and bearing the new title of the 6th Kirkcudbright Rifle Volunteers, under the command of Captain W.W. Platt. Captain Platt's reign was short lived, however, dying on the 9th July 1869, exactly one year to the day of the acceptance of his new Company. He was to be succeeded by his Lieutenant, James Grieve, who took over the Captaincy of the Company.

The prosperity of Dalbeattie was bound by the granite trade and the strength of the Company was a fair indication whether the trade was prosperous or not. The Majority of the Dalbeattie Company of Volunteers were employed in the granite trade. During the spring, when trade was brisk, the numbers on the roll could exceed 100 but before the end of the Volunteer year, the numbers could drop dramatically and the Volunteers were unable to therefore make themselves efficient thereby depriving the Company of valuable capitation grants,

By 30th November, 1869, Haugh of Urr Section had joined with Dalbeattie, the full strength now numbering, 88, and by 30th November, 1871, the strength of the 6th Kirkcudbright Rifle Volunteers was reported as 100 of which 97 were efficient.

In 1883, a slump in the granite trade resulted in 400 men leaving Dalbeattie for the American granite market, It was reported that 'To Let" signs had been erected all around the Burgh. A total of 43 members resigned from the Dalbeatie Rifle Volunteers leaving 66 on the roll, and by the end of 1888, 138 members had retired from the ranks. Notwithstanding this migratory factor by 30th November, 1889, the Corps was to still comprise a comfortable Company of 74 members,

On the 28th June, 1860, a meeting was held in Kirkbean Parish School, to consider the propriety of forming a Volunteer Corps for that district, Mr. Stewart of Southwick was in the chair. A deputation from Dalbeattie, was in attendance, Mr. Maxwell of Munches; Mr. Welsh of Meikle Firthhead; Dr. McKnight and Mr. Muir. Mr. Maxwell offered to the meeting a few observations respecting the Volunteer movement, and then proceeded to say that the district between the Nith and the Urr had in this respect fallen rather behind the rest of the country. He could not for a moment attribute this to any want of patriotic spirit but was sure that they would embrace this opportunity of placing themselves on a par with the rest of the country. There might be difficulties to surmount from the thinness of the population but sure he was that these were by no means insurmountable. While he anxiously desired that something would come out of this meeting, he hoped that none would join who were not really Volunteers prepared to co-operate heartily, and to give both time and trouble in their endeavours to promote the efficiency of the Corps.

Several other gentlemen were to address the meeting, all of the same desire to organise a Corps of either Artillery or Riflemen and Messrs. McIntosh and Gibson were appointed a committee to ascertain the feeling in the district and to those disposed to concur in the movement.

However, as with Dalbeattie, and no doubt the lack of interest on the part of the influential Mr. Maxwell of the Munches, Kirkbean was not to form, nor indeed ever did form, either a Company or Section of Dalbeattie. This prompted the following reply to the editor of the *Kirkcudbrightshire Advertiser,* dated 25th October, 1861,

"Sir, Permit me to draw attention to the fact that in the large tract of country extending from Auchencairn to Maxwellton there is not a single Company of Volunteers, whereas the corresponding range of country on the opposite side of the Firth, there are several of both Rifles and Artillery. I think it a great pity that we should be surpassed by our neighbours in this movement, so much in keeping with the Scottish character, and I feel convinced that there are many young men who would come forward and feel proud in being called on to share in the grand cause, provided they get a little assistance in equipping themselves, New Abbey, Kirkbean and Southwick, might make one district and Colvend and Urr another. If a few loyal hearts in each Parish would form a deputation to wait on the leading influential gentlemen of the district and solicit their aid and support in the matter, there would be little fear of success, and we would retrieve that good name which we are rather losing,

Signed 'A Willing Volunteer."

On 21st October, 1904, a Section of the Dalbeattie Company was raised at Beeswing and New Abbey, under the command of Lieutenant Gillies, a doctor from New Abbey.

WIGTOWN.

On Wednesday, 12th October, 1859, in terms of a requisition by R.Vans Agnew Esq., of Sheuchan and Barnbarroch, a meeting of influential gentlemen was held in the Court House, Wigtown, for the purpose of forming a Volunteer Rifle Corps. Among those present was, Lord Garlies; Sir William Maxwell, Baronet; Stair Hawthorne Stewart Esq., of Glasserton and Physgill; Henry Stuart Esq., of Bellvue; Major P. Stewart; John Fletcher Hawthorne Esq., of Castlewigg; W.J. McHaffie Esq., Younger of Torhousemuir. Thomas Murray Esq,, and John Graham Esq., Bailies of Wigtown; George C. Black and Ebenezer S. Black, Bankers, Wigtown; Rev. Irving Beattie, Wigtown, etc.

Sir William Maxwell, Baronet, Chairman, addressed the meeting and said, he for one, was strongly in favour of the movement, for he felt, as surely as that sun now shining upon them would relight the sky of tomorrow that, sooner or later, he would not be so presumptuous as to name a date, the Volunteer Rifle Corps now gathering over the length and breadth of the land would be called upon, in serious conflict, to defend their common country.

R. Vans Agnew Esq., thanked all present for their attendance in compliance with the requisition and for the prompt manner in which almost all of them had intimated their willingness to serve as Volunteers. He then alluded to the great efforts made by the country in 1804, when there were enrolled and trained 800,000 men, regulars, militiamen and Volunteers, all in arms for its defence. Now, he grieved to say, there were not 50,000 of the old defensive force, while the population had infinitely increased. He continued, we had all seen but lately how lightly and easily the peace of Europe had been broken and that battles had been fought, in which there had been more men engaged, and there was greater slaughter than at Waterloo, the conflict which decided the Empire of the world. He continued, no one in his senses can doubt that it is for the interest of both England and France to remain at peace. We know this and so does the intelligent portion of the French population, but somehow there was a sad, 'cat and mouse' feeling between some portions of the two populations. Mr. Agnew then read extracts from the circulars issued by the War Office, explanatory of the terms on which Government was ready to accept the service of such Volunteer Rifle Corps as that now to be enrolled. He was glad to say that he now had about 60 men down on the list, who had expressed their willingness to act as Riflemen. Some of his friends, to whom he had submitted the list, declared he had got the pick of the County already enrolled. The following motion was then proposed by Mr. Agnew and seconded by Lord Garlies.

(1) That a Volunteer Rifle Corps be formed in the lower district of Wigtownshire.

(2) That the following gentlemen be appointed to carry the resolutions into effect, A Vans Agnew Esq; Henry Stuart Esq; William J. McHaffie Esq; James Caird Esq., M.P; Messrs. James Erskine; Alex. McCredie; Thomas Murray; Samuel Clanahan; Thomas Limond and John Fraser; with power to add to their number.

(3). That the said committee be hereby instructed to request the Lord Lieutenant of the County to forward their application to be enrolled, to the Secretary of State for War.

The resolutions having been unanimously carried the meeting broke up. The following noblemen and gentlemen had already entered their names as honorary members of the Corps; The Right Honourable the Earl of Galloway; Lord Garlies; Stair H. Stewart Esq; E. Stopford-Blair Esq; Sir William Maxwell, Baronet; Henry Stuart Esq; W.C.S. Hamilton Esq; General McHaffie; J.F. Hawthorne Esq; Captain James Reid; John McGuffie Esq., Provost of Wigtown. By the rules, each Honorary Member paid £5 or upwards of enrolling money and £1 annual subscription, Effective Members paid £1 of annual subscription.

At a meeting of the proposed Sub-Division of the Wigtown Volunteer Rifle Corps, on 30th November, 1859, it was proposed by Mr. Caird, M.P. and seconded by Mr. Henry, that the following gentlemen be recommended to the Lord Lieutenant as officers, Robert Vans Agnew Esq., and William McHaffie. It was proposed that Ebenezer Black be requested to act as Secretary. It was also resolved that in aid of funds a subscription list be entered into.

On the 24th February, 1860, the services of the Corps were accepted by Her Majesty and numbered the first in the County, bearing the title the 1st Wigtown Rifle Volunteers, and being formed as a Subdivision.

At a meeting of the 1st Wigtown Volunteers on the 1st March, 1860, Bailie Murray in the chair, the

Secretary, Mr. E.S. Black was to inform the meeting that the services of a Drill Sergeant had been obtained and his rate of pay was to be agreed upon. It was also agreed that a store-keeper be appointed to clean and take care of the arms.

It was further arranged that the hours of drill should be from 7.30am to 8.30am and from 7.30pm to 9.30pm daily and that each member of the Corps should attend one of the drills per day at least. The following evening, 2nd March, the members met for their first drill in the Assembly Rooms at Wigtown,

On the evening of Tuesday, 27th March, 1860, the election of the Sergeants and Corporals of the Corps took place in the Assembly Rooms;

Sergeants - Messrs. E.S. Black; K. Henry; William McKie.

Corporals - Messrs. P.B. Kevan; T. Martin; William McNarney.

In keeping with many of the Volunteer Rifle Corps of the day, after the initial burst of patriotic fever, the threat of invasion had passed and the appeal of the 'braided uniform and trailing sword' had gone, there was a dearth of Gentlemen in the Wigtown district prepared to give of both their time and money and in consequence of no gentlemen being prepared to take command of the Corps, on the 20th June, 1873, the Wigtown Sub-Division was to disband.

On the 11th July, 1873, at a farewell presentation to their former Drill Instructor, Sergeant Lock, the members of the ex-Wigtown Sub-Division presented Sergeant Lock with a purse of sovereigns. In addressing the assembled Company, he was to say that in his 11 years in charge of the Wigtown Corps, 250 members had passed through the ranks.

However, through the efforts of an accountant from Wigtown, George Coupland, on the 9th February, 1891, Wigtown was to re-form and join as a Section of the Newton Stewart Company, under the command of Corporal G. Coupland.

STRANRAER.

On Tuesday, 29th November, 1859, a large and influential meeting was held in the Town Hall, Stranraer, convened by the Provost of the Burgh to take into consideration the propriety of forming a Volunteer Rifle or Artillery Corps for the district. Amongst those present were: The Viscount Dalrymple; Sir James D. Hay, Bart., of Park Place; N. Taylor of Belmont; Charles Kerr Esq., Banker; M. Cole Esq., Ivy House; Captain Hawes R.N. Portpatrick; Rev. W.M Simpson; Rev. G. Sherwood, Sheuchan; Provost Guthrie; Bailies McDowall and Dalrymple; Alex. Ingram Esq; Alex. Guthrie Esq; Charles Brown Esq; Charles Hunter Esq; Hugh Adair Esq; Hugh McLean Esq; James Allison Esq; F. Garrick Esq; John Forsyth Esq., of Valleyfield; John McClew Esq., of Dinvin; John McBryde Esq., of Balker; A McLean Esq., of Auchneel; Drs. Orgill and Fleming, Stranraer. Provost Guthrie was elected to the chair, and addressed the meeting;

"My Lord and gentlemen to one whose existence, or even whose memory, stretches not back to the last French war, so gloriously terminated at Waterloo, or to the alarm which then filled the country, it is somewhat difficult to realise our present circumstances, or the object of our present meeting. Gentlemen, I am no alarmist, and even, it is not long since, in one of our civic meetings, I expressed myself, some said, if not coldly, at least equivocally, in regard to our Volunteer movement, that movement which is now so deeply stirring the hearts of the people of this country, from Lands End to John O'Groats, stirring the hearts, not only of the young and the excitable but of old and experienced, of the Peer and the peasant, the calculating merchant and the still more calculating, the sober Judge, the learned Professor and even the peaceful Missionary of the Cross, and indeed any who have anything to lose or anything to defend in this great country, (cheers). Yes, Gentlemen, the Volunteer movement has now become a great fact. The Government is aroused and anxiously seeks to promote it. Our gracious Queen, with her excellent Consort, encourage it, and shall we longer hesitate to join it, to enrol ourselves as Volunteers in that Corps, that embodiment of patriotism, as I may call it, (cheers) which has for its object certainly nothing aggressive or offensive but simply the response to an invasion threat and the defence of all we cherish and hold dear (loud cheers). Gentlemen, I have convened this meeting and it seems, I must undertake the duty of explaining the object of enforcing its canvas. Gentlemen, I must tell you in the first place, how I came to call this meeting. I received a letter from our excellent Country Member, Sir Andrew Agnew, M.P. which I will take the liberty of reading,

21, Upper Grosvenor Street, London,
16th November, 1859.

"My dear Provost, I am not surprised at hearing that the Volunteer enthusiasm is spreading towards Stranraer, for we do not require to be reminded that the men of Galloway have always been ready and able to defend their liberty and freedom. I have a hearty sympathy with the movement, when the Volunteering is bona fide as tending to keep up amongst the most valuable part of our population, manly habits of thought and self reliance, as well as to give to the commercial community a feeling of greater security, but when it degenerates into a mere excuse for convivial meetings and for ordering a uniform, or when it arises from the mere act of a few richer men subscribing a set of bad soldiers to gratify a vanity for command it becomes absurd.

It behoves all who are placed in responsible positions to consider well at this moment how they can take advantage of the present excitement so as to turn the strong current of popular feeling into that course which may ensure permanent advantage to their fellow citizens.

Now it must surely be admitted that in a strategical point of view, nothing is less probable than an invading army should march through Wigtownshire but in the event of war, an enterprising Captain of the John Paul Jones stamp might run into Lochryan, shell Stranraer and plunder at his leisure. A Rifle Company could offer no effective resistance to anything in the shape of a man-of-war, whereas a well served battery could put well paid to his plans.

With this idea in mind I went the other day to the War Office and represented the importance of Stranraer and Lochryan, the increasing prospects of traffic which a railway opens to us, and the defenceless state of the town and harbour and I now beg to give you semi-officially the result of my representations.

Her Majesty's Government will send down a Government Inspector to report on the circumstances of the case immediately on being apprised that 30 gentlemen are willing to enrol themselves as Coast Artillery Volunteers. Government will provide at once two heavy guns, they will send regular instructors and supply ammunition all gratis, and further, if an entire Company of 80 can be raised or even a minimum of 50 they would authorise the appointment of a Captain and Lieutenant and erect a battery on the most suitable spot.

As a matter of courtesy it appears to me the most proper course to address these suggestions to yourself as the Chief Magistrate of Stranraer, which is the place requiring the most fortification in the Rhins, is in order that you may consider whether you are disposed to take the lead in raising Volunteers. You will no doubt consult with Lord Dalrymple as our Lord Lieutenant on the subject and if you decide to follow up the idea I will be happy to assist you by all means in my power.

Yours etc.,
Andrew Agnew."

On receiving this letter, I communicated with our much beloved Lord Lieutenant, now beside me, and also with many of my fellow townsmen and having done so, I with their concurrence convened the present meeting, calling together my fellow citizens and the attendance of the proprietors and farmers in the adjoining districts."

Provost Guthrie continued his address in a patriotic theme at great length, but before sitting down he read a letter of apology from the ardent Volunteer, Robert Vans Agnew of Barnbarroch and Sheuchan, begging to be enrolled as an honorary member, he being an effective member at Wigtown, and enclosing a £10 subscription, and also laid, before the meeting, a further 2nd letter from Andrew Agnew M P..

21, Upper Grosvenor Street, London.
25th November, 1859.

"*My Dear Provost,*

I was much gratified in receiving your letter of the 23rd and findling that you had replied to my last one by calling a public meeting to take into consideration the subject of our defences.

As I shall be unable to be present at your meeting I am not unnaturally anxious to state my own opinion which has been the result of much consideration, but if, in the compass of a letter, I find it impossible to do so without the appearance of writing dogmatically. I hope you will believe that on the contrary, I merely venture to advance these suggestions as my private views and as thus taking part in the discussion and that I do so with a feeling of the greatest deferrence to your long and extended local experience.

I think it probable, as a matter of taste a Rifle Corps is likely to be more popular than an Artillery one but the very essence of the Volunteer principle is self-denial. The question for a meeting representing the property and intelligence of the district to determine is, 'How can the Town and Harbour of Stranraer be defended?' and if you admit that a Privateer, with a large traversing gun, might run up Lochryan, and laying a mile or two off, place you all at its mercy, and that Rifle Companies would give you no adequate security, then the only practical answer to your query appears to be, to man a Battery. Surely if an appeal is made to our young men, the response will be in the affirmative. The question I would put to our youths is not would you rather be an Artilleryman or a Rifleman but will you enrol yourself in a Corps of Volunteers which will form an integral part of the Volunteer Force of Great Britain and secondly, are you willing to sacrifice a little of your money and a good deal of your spare time?

It would be a great pity if two Corps were formed with advantage to one with a disadvantage to the more useful. I spent all morning at the War Office in order to supply you with authentic and official information. If a Rifle Corps is formed Government will supply 50% of arms and will issue ammunition as required at cost price, this however, must be paid for out of their own pockets, they must also procure as they can, their own ground as well as Instructors. In the case of an Artillery Company, practising ground, guns, Instructors and ammunition are all presented gratis, besides which 50% smooth bored carbines will at once be issued and side arms if wished for and as soon as possible.

I proceeded to the War Department and saw the Inspector of Fortifications and looked at the plans and report on our Coasts.

He recommends a battery at the Cairn to protect the anchorage but says it would be impossible for it to be manned by regular artillery. He says if a Company was organised in Stranraer, he would recommend the immediate construction of a practising ground close to Stranraer, and send guns and Instructors. Should a war break out the Stranraer Corps would then be expected to go out on permanent duty and would as a matter of certainty receive full pay whilst so employed.

Yours etc.,

Andrew Agnew."

Viscount Dalrymple, and various other influential personages were to address the meeting at some length, in a patriotic manner, some in favour of the Rifle Corps, others favouring the Artillery. Committees were appointed and the Chairman then called upon all present to come forward and enrol, stating their preference as to Rifleman, Artillery or Honorary member. He then informed the meeting that funds would be required to assist Volunteers who were not able fully to equip themselves with all requisites of uniform, weapons, etc., and a subscription list was handed round, headed by Lord Dalrymple who subscribed £25 to the Artillery Corps. Sir James D. Hay signified his intention to convene a meeting at Glenluce and Mr. John McBryde, Balker and Mr. James Brown of Damhouse, agreed to take charge of their respective Parishes of Inch and Kirkcolm, a similar duty also to be undertaken in Kirkmaiden. The meeting then separated.

The youth of the day conceived the role of the Rifleman to be much more exciting and glamorous by outflanking and harrassing the enemy than the role of the more mundane and static Artillery Volunteer who was perceived as a sitting target, to be shot at by the enemy. To counter this romanticised but firmly held notion, the Government conceded free guns, ammunition, instructors and practice grounds to encourage the formation of Artillery Batteries for coastal defence in the more exposed and vulnerable regions.

On Tuesday, 13th December, 1859, the various committees of the Stranraer Volunteer Corps met in the Town Hall, Provost Guthrie in the chair. He reported the lists of enrollment they had attained; 39 effectives had enrolled for Artillery, that 47 effectives in Stranraer had enrolled for Rifles and Mr. Brown, Damhouse, reported that 26 effectives had enrolled at Kirkcolm. It was also reported that 42 honorary members had enrolled and the subscriptions had amounted to £144. Lord Stair was to subscribe £100, to be divided as follows; Stranraer Artillery, £35; Stranraer Rifles, £30; Whithorn Rifles, £15; Newton Stewart and Wigtown Rifles, £10 each.

It was agreed to report to the Lord Lieutenant that upwards of a Sub-Division of 30 effective members had volunteered to enrol themselves as Artillerymen, that upwards of 60 effective members had volunteered to enrol as Riflemen and that their services should be offered to Her Majesty,

It was resolved that a special appeal be made to the landed proprietors in the district for subscriptions in aid of the funds, which at present were quite inadequate to meet the requirements of the Corps.

On Friday, 20th January, 1860, a meeting of the enrolled members of both services of the Volunteer Corps was held in the Town Hall. The meeting was very crowded with Lord Dalrymple seated beside the Chairman, Provost Guthrie. The Chairman was to address the meeting and said that he had been at meetings of the Corps in Kirkcolm and Inch and spoke favourably of the spirit of the members in these districts, The Volunteer Movement was also taking hold in Stoneykirk and Kirkmaiden. The Artillery Volunteers now had 64 effective members and the Stranraer Volunteers, alone, had 54 effective members. Provost Guthrie then moved that the Rifles and Artillery should be formed as two distinct companies, this resolution was unanimously agreed to and the two Corps separated. Lord Dalrymple going with the Artillery Volunteers, later to be elected their Captain and Provost Guthrie, being a Rifleman, went with the Rifle Volunteers.

On the departure of the Artillery Volunteers, referred to in Stranraer as the Senior Service, the Rifle Corps proceeded with business. A committee was appointed to arrange the running of the Corps consisting of Messrs. John McBryde; William Miller; S.H. Taylor; E. Fleming; D. Guthrie; D.W. Shaw; James Jones; James Meikle; Alex. Ingram; A Bennoch, Sheuchan; P. Constan and J. Wylie.

An election of officers was then to take place with Provost Guthrie being elected Captain, Alexander Ingram elected Lieutenant and John McBryde elected Ensign. Ebenezer Fleming was appointed Hon. Surgeon. The following were elected Sergeants:- William Miller; S.H. Taylor; W.J. McBryde.

The hours of drill were fixed from seven to nine morning and evenings, the committee to arrange with Mr. Holding or any other Drill Sergeant as to drilling the Corps. The committee was instructed to obtain information as to uniform and to report to the next meeting. The rules and regulations having been read over were remitted to the committee for consideration,

On the 16th March, 1860, the services of the Corps were accepted by Her Majesty, forming as one Company, bearing the title, the 2nd Wigtown Rifle Volunteers with Sections being formed at Kirkcolm and Kirkmaiden, with detachments later being formed at, Cairnryan, Castle Kennedy, Lochans and Leswalt. Portpatrick, Stoneykirk and Sandhead were to form as Corps of Artillery. Glenluce was to play no part in the Volunteer movement.

The ranks of the two Volunteer Companies from Stranraer Burgh, excluding the Rhins, constituted 20 effective Volunteers to every 1,000 of its population, a statistic well to the fore in the newly formed movement,

On 22nd March, 1860, a junior branch of the Rifle Volunteers was started in Stranraer and to enable them to learn the drill they raised a sum sufficient to engage a Drill Sergeant, George Young, for that purpose. They were to meet in the Academy three nights a week.

On the 23rd November, 1860, Kirkmaiden was to separate from, Stranraer, the 2nd Wigtown Rifle Volunteers, offering their services to Her Majesty, through the offices of the Lord Lieutenant and forming as a Sub-Division, in their own right, and bearing the title the 5th Wigtown Rifle Volunteers.

On Thursday 23rd May, 1860, the day chosen for the parade and enrolment of the 2nd Wigtown Rifle Corps of Stranraer Volunteers was also the day of the Queen's birthday and what a splendid day it was, the sun shone with barely a cloud in the sky. From early morning the streets and houses were bedecked in bunting, An air of excitement and awareness, completely unprecedented was taking place in Stranraer. At 10am the Rifle Volunteers mustered outside the Town Hall, under the command of Lieutenant Ingram and Ensign McBryde, where they were joined by their Provost and Captain Guthrie. Headed by their band they then proceeded to march through the principal streets of the Town cheered on every corner and from every window by crowds of patriotic and loyal citizens. They arrived at Castle Kennedy at noon where they were formed in front of the Castle which had been brightly decorated with flags and were there met by excited crowds not only from Stranraer but from the whole of the Rhins, from the Mull to Corsewall. They were there joined by deputations of Rifle Volunteers from Wigtown and Newton Stewart, Militiamen and the Stranraer Artillery Corps who had all been invited to add their number to the spectacle.

The Rifles, under the command of Lieutenant Ingram, Captain Guthrie acting for the day as Reviewing Officer, went through their much practised drill to the delight of the onlookers. The evolutions being over, the Corps was formed into a close column of Section and Sheriff Rhind, placing himself to the front, proceeded to administer the oath which was afterwards subscribed by the Corps in the face of the assembled thousands.

The Viscount Dalrymple, The Lord Lieutenant, addressed the now embodied Volunteers as follows, "Sheriff Rhind said he had come, with pleasure, to administer the oath of allegiance to their Sovereign. At any time the duty would have been an agreeable one but that day had been well selected as the birthday of the Queen, of her, who ever since she was born, and more especially since she ascended the throne of these realms, had been at once the source of pride and of blessings to her people (cheers). While the day had been thus auspiciously chosen, he thought that the place for the ceremony and for their parade had been appropriately fixed to take place beside the ancient walls of Castle Kennedy (cheers). He continued in this vein at some length concluding by saying, he congratulated Captain Guthrie and the Corps on the precision and efficiency of their evolutions which were admired and most creditable considering the short time they had been drilled. He saw present deputations from Wigtown and Newton Stewart who would, he hoped, carry home such an account of the Stranraer Companies as would stimulate the military practice of the other end of the county (cheers).

After the cheering had subsided, Captain Guthrie addressed his comrades in the following terms, "Brother Volunteers, I congratulate, heartily congratulate you, on the appearance you have this day made, on the step you have just taken, You have now formally enrolled yourselves among the defenders of your Country, that great Country we are proud to call our own (cheers). When I look around you upon this present scene, need I tell you how rich it is in beauty, animate and inanimate, need I remind you of its vast extent and enormous resources, of what a treasury it is of arts and science, what a sanctuary of home and social endearments, or tell you of the glories which its annals present, or of its rich charter of liberties which your forefathers have transmitted to you to cherish and defend (cheers). Captain Guthrie continued in this patriotic manner for some time, giving a history of the great empires of Greece, Rome and Carthage, likening their services to their Country as did the Spartans and Romans before. He finally concluded by saying, "I have now only to congratulate you on the presence of your brethern of the Artillery, who grace and gladden the scene, and I am sure it affords us all very much pleasure to see them here today. I have heard of jealousies existing between members of the Corps, surely this cannot, must not be for each Corps cannot but rejoice in the success and fullest efficiency of the other. There must be no jealousies between us save for the honour of our respective Corps (cheers). No rivalries, but who shall exhibit the greatest proficiency in drill, and the best behaviour out of it (cheers), and if war should unhappily come, who shall best defend our common Country or carry furthest into the enemy's ranks those standards with which I have no doubt, if we deserve them, our fair friends, the ladies will some day present us (great applause).

Captain Guthrie then asked three cheers for Lieutenant Stuart and the other deputations of Militia and Volunteers which were heartily given. Three cheers were given for Captain Guthrie when he gave the word of command 'to the Ladies and Luncheon'.

The Volunteers dispersed with their ladies to a picnic on the terrace amphitheatre facing the lake. More than 500 sat down to the meal. Speeches were to continue during and after the meal, in the same patriotic vein, for some time, with many toasts being drunk, until Captain Guthrie was once again to issue the order 'Quick march' when the whole assemblage adjourned to the esplanade of the Castle, where dancing was kept for some considerable time. Eventually the bugle was to sound the retreat and the Corps of Volunteers, under the command of Captain Guthrie, preceded by their band, marched to Stranraer and were disbanded.

A concert was held in the Town Hall that evening for the Volunteers, and afterwards an impromptu dance was continued, with great spirit, until the early hours of the morning, the whole grand affair being summarised in one eloquent sentiment, 'and thus began, continued and ended the grandest festival in Galloway'.

NEWTON STEWART.

Little history appears to exist as to the influential personages involved in raising the Newton Stewart Corps of Rifle Volunteers, but there is no doubt that Mr. R. Vans Agnew, an ardent supporter of the Volunteer movement was very much to the fore in the raising of this Corps, together with Henry Stuart Esq., of Corsbie West and Bellvue, Edward Stopford-Blair Esq., of Penninghame, Snowden Henry Esq., of Kirroughtree, and Mr. Alexander McCutcheon, Banker, who was to act as Honourable Secretary to the Corps.

The first reference of the Newton Stewart Rifle Corps is on Friday, 20th January, 1860, when at a meeting held in Newton Stewart, it was requested that the names of the enrolled Volunteers be forwarded to the Lord Lieutenant, for the approval of Her Majesty. It was further reported that the services of a Drill Instructor had been obtained, Sergeant-Major Ireland, formerly of the Galloway Rifles Militia, and it was agreed that drill should take place three times a week, at the 'Race' ground, Kirroughtree, to begin immediately. An election of Officers was to take place with Henry Stuart Esq., and Edward Stopford-Blair, the younger, being respectively chosen as Captain and Lieutenant.

On Wednesday, 23rd February, 1860, a meeting of the Corps was called for the purpose of electing the non-commissioned Officers. The following names were chosen as under,:-
Sergeants; Messrs. R. McConchie; Craik and Carson.
Corporals; Messrs. Scott; Picken and Dickson.

The services of the Corps were accepted and approved by Her Majesty, being formed on the 21st March, 1860, as the 3rd Wigtown Rifle Volunteers. However, the Lord Lieutenant intimated to the Corps that the establishment necessary to form a Company was 60 men, excluding officers and as they had only 59 enrolled members then they must form as a Sub-Division, authorising Henry Stuart Esq., to the rank of Lieutenant and Edward Stopford-Blair Esq., the rank of Ensign.

On the evening of Wednesday, 5th July, 1860, the members of the 3rd Wigtown Rifle Volunteers, under the command of Lt. Henry Stuart, assembled at the 'Angle', where they were joined by a section of the 1st Wigtown Rifle Volunteers, under the command of Lieutenant R. Vans Agnew and a large number of the 2nd Wigtown Rifle Volunteers, under the command of Captain Guthrie, for the purpose of the members of the Newton Stewart Corps swearing the oath of allegiance. The Volunteers were inspected and marched through the town, to a field at Bellvue House, the home of Lieutenant Stuart, where a large crowd of fashionable assemblage had been invited to be present at the ceremony. The oath was administered to 32 members of the Newton Stewart Corps by Mr. James Stewart of Cairnsmore.

The Corps were thereafter invited to partake of the hospitality of Lieutenant Stuart, where many toasts were drunk and the National Anthem sung. Lieutenant Stuart was to address the assembled company saying that he felt a pride in the position he held and that his efforts had been so nobly seconded by so many respectable men around him, coming at the call of duty and devoting themselves to the use of arms, which makes them beloved at home and feared abroad, and the very name of Volunteers effected a good deal in quelling the boasting indulged in some quarters. The Corps was then marched to the Town Hall where they were dismissed,

Arrangements having been made to finish the evening with a ball, the men assembled, in full uniform, at the New Assembly Rooms, accompanied by the elite of the Town, where dancing was kept with great spirit until two in the morning,

The Newton Stewart Company were obviously stretched to capacity, in that they were unable to raise the further Volunteer, necessary to form as a Company and in any event the roll was very quickly to fall to 40 enrolled Volunteers. Lieutenant Stopford-Blair, in keeping with many other Officers of the day was soon to resign his commission, with Robert Picken Esq., of Barnkirk, being elected Ensign to fill the vacancy. However, through the energetic efforts of these two officers, the members were soon to increase until more than the requisite number of 60 enrolled members had been achieved and on the 31st March, 1864, the 3rd Wigtown Rifle Volunteers formed as one Company, entitling Henry Stuart Esq; to the rank of Captain and Robert Picken Esq., to the rank of Lieutenant, with David Stroyan Esq., Banker being elected Ensign. (David Stroyan was later sentenced to 6 years penal servitude for embezzlement from his employers at the British Linen Bank, Newton Stewart).

It is difficult now to judge, just exactly, what were the 'energetic efforts' employed by Captain Stuart and Lieutenant Picken in increasing their Corps to Company strength and thus securing their promotion, but one must now ask the question, have they been caught out? The following letter appeared in the local press dated, 9th March, 1864.

'The Volunteers versus Total Abstinence.'

"Sir, I am glad to learn that the Volunteer movement is making such progress here this season. Already 25 young men, principally of the working class, have been enrolled. I was very sorry, however, to be informed that no sooner had they been sworn in than they were treated by the Captain, in a public house, to as much drink as they were inclined to take. Now Sir, the Total Abstinence Society have been doing their utmost to induce young men to abandon these drinking habits, which are acknowledged in all hands to be so ruinous to them and the success which has attended their efforts has been gratifying, and it was surely imprudent for anyone in the Captain's position to act in a manner which all must admit had a tendency to undo the good which has been done. Ten of these young men were abstainers and if they did not break through their resolution, the Captain is not to be thanked for it. Had a quarrel arisen amongst them and the case been brought to the J.P. Court here, I am sure his seat on the bench must have been empty. While wishing the Volunteer movement every success, I hope it will not in future be associated with the public house.

A Teetotaller."

On the 20th June, 1873, the Wigtown Sub-Division were to disband. On the 9th February, 1891, Wigtown was to reform as a Section of the Newton Stewart Company, under the command of Corporal George Coupland. Wigtown, was later to become No. 4 Section of the Newton Stewart Company.

On the 7th May, 1880, a Section of the Newton Stewart Company was raised in Kirkcowan, later to become No.1 Section of that Company.

On the 5th August, 1898, a Section of the Newton Stewart Company was raised in Creetown and Carsluith, later to become No. 2 and 3 Sections, respectively.

WHITHORN.

On Monday, 12th December, 1859, a public meeting, called by Provost Main, was held in the Town Hall, Whithorn, to take into consideration a proposal for the formation of a Rifle Corps. On the motion of the Right Honourable, the Earl of Galloway, Provost Main was called to the chair.

Provost Main introduced the business of the meeting by enforcing the claims of the Volunteer movement upon all who have it in their power to do so either by money or their personal service. The first resolution was moved by Lord Galloway who said in support of his resolution, "it is wise and politic for this Country to be well prepared for all contingencies at a time like the present, when the continent of Europe, especially the French, are dailly increasing their armaments, particularly their Fleet. It is wise and prudent for us as a nation to be prepared for all eventualities."

The second resolution was moved by Robert Vans Agnew Esq., of Barnbarroch, who gave in support of his motion valuable information as to constitution and practical operation of a Rifle Corps and the rules for this new arm of defence. In speaking of the alliance with England and France, he thought the best thing between them was the Channel. The third resolution was moved by Provost Main.

The following are the resolutions

(1) That this meeting being convinced that the surest means of averting the danger of war and preserving to our country the blessings of peace, is a thorough and complete system of national defence, and considering that the formation of a Volunteer force would be a safe and effective auxilliary to any system of defence which may be adopted, resolve to organise a Volunteer Corps for this district.

(2) That a subscription list be opened to provide funds in furtherence of this movement, and in supplement of the aid given by Government, in order to encourage all classes to enrol, and to render the organisation more complete and efficient.

(3) That a committee be appointed to carry out the above resolutions to consist of, Hugh D. Stewart Esq., of Tonderghie; Messrs. J. Nicholson, Physgill; R. Gourlay, Arbrick; D. McMonnies, Drumoral; J. Dounan, Boyach; H. Stewart, Balsmith; S. Clanahan, Austan; J. McGuffie, Balteer; J. Waldie, Millisle; Thomas Limond, Drumgin; J. McConnell Chapelharron; J. McMonies, Skiddoch; J. Drew, Whithorn; George A Main, Whithorn; with power to add to their number. Provost Main to be Convener, and five to be a quorum.

Lord Galloway intimated that should a division of about 30 Volunteers, or upwards, be formed in Whithorn, he was willing to subscribe £100, towards the outfits of Newton Stewart, Wigtown and Whithorn, in equal proportions, according to their relative numbers.

A vote of thanks was given to Lord Galloway and to Provost Main for his conduct in the chair. A subscription list was then entered into, when several handsome sums were inhibited.

On Wednesday, 4th January, 1860, a meeting of the Committee of the Whithorn Rifle Volunteers were met by the effective members of the Corps, who ratified their consent to become members by signing an initiatory document. The required number of the Corps being almost complete the names were to be sent to the Lord Lieutenant for representation to Her Majesty. The Company was to consist of independent and professional gentlemen, farmers, artisans and agricultural servants. The subscription list was upwards of £150 with many contributions still to be received.

On Friday 15th January, 1860, the Committee responsible for choosing a location for drill and shooting selected a range of upwards of a mile on the farm of Claymaddie on the estate of Stair H. Stewart of Physgill and Glasserton. However by July, 1860, they had moved to a range on the Coonan shore.

On Friday, 17th February, 1860, a meeting of the Whithorn Volunteers was convened for the election of Officers and other business, Hugh D. Stewart of Tonderghie was elected Lieutenant. James Drew Esq., Solicitor, was elected Ensign. It was further agreed that the uniform to be worn should be of the same colour and pattern as the other Companies in the County. The Corps now numbered 34 effective members, with ample funds at their disposal, and the names of the effectives were therefore transmitted to the Lord Lieutenant. An announcement was made that drill would commence on the 20th February, 1860, and until the services of a Drill Sergeant could be procured the recruits were to receive instruction from Thomas Broadfoot, a young man from the Isle of Whithorn who fought at the heights of Alma and closed his military career at the fall of Lucknow where he was twice wounded. Sergeant Major Locke, was appointed Drill Sergeant to the Corps shortly after.

On the 11th April, 1860, the services of the Corps were accepted by Her Majesty and formed as a Sub-division, bearing the title of the 4th Wigtown Rifle Volunteers.

The following song was published on the 31st May, 1860, by Alexander Blain, Whithorn, the author of "Flowers of the Wayside", entitled

"The Rifle Volunteers - A Patriotic Song", Air - "The Garb of Old Gaul".

"Brittania, the home of the brave and the free,
With our guards on the land and our ships on the sea,
Should the proud daring foe on our island appear
We will give them a treat of our true British cheer.
Such is our love of liberty, our country and our cause,
Defenders of our native land - we stand for Brittania's laws;
When joined in one united band our country has no fears,
Protected by our patriotic bands - The Rifle Volunteers.

Caledonia, the land to our fore fathers so dear,
With our Campbells and Stewarts we have nothing to fear;
From the north to the south it should never be said
That the foot of a foe on our thistle shall tread,
With our red blooming heath on our mountains and glens,
And our blue Scottish bells on our woodland and plains;
To guard our homes and native land if danger e'er appears
We have our true and patriot bands - The Rifle Volunteers.

Should the standard of Britain again be unfurled
The glory and pride of the wandering world.
With our Generals on the land and our sons on the wave
We never will strike to the tyrant or slave,
Then one British cheer for Victoria we crave,
May her banner long waive o'er the free and the brave,
And let the wondering world see that Britain has no fears
While guarded by our patriot bands - The Rifle Volunteers."

On the 6th July, 1860, 40 members of the Whithorn Rifle Corps mustered at the Town Hall at 3pm under the command of Lt. H. D. Stewart and Ensign Drew, where the oath of allegience was administered by George A Main Esq., Provost of the Burgh. The Volunteers, then headed by their band, marched through the principal streets to the delight of the large number of onlookers.

The 4th Wigtown Rifle Corps were to play a full role in the Administrative Battalion of the Galloway Rifle Volunteers, attending the Wing and Battalion drills, the Company and Battalion rifle shooting competitions, the annual inspections, the Royal and other Reviews, their members becoming efficient, thereby ensuring the existence of the Corps both financially and according to the rules and regulations of the War Office. On the evening of Monday 5th, and Tuesday 6th June, 1873, the Whithorn Volunteers were inspected by their Adjutant Singleton, when the existence of the Corps seemed to be assured, the Adjutant reporting, "There was a good muster of the Corps in full uniform. The Company continues in a prosperous condition both numerically and financially." However, within a very short time the Corps was to fall into decline and by the 1st January, 1874, they reluctantly had to terminate the services of their Instructor, Sergeant Major Locke, who was to join with the Stranraer Rifle Corps. Without the services of an Instructor the Corps could not hope to continue efficiently and on the 11th July, 1874, the Corps was to finally disband. It was reported, "the Whithorn Volunteers had endured until all apprehension of their services being required had passed away."

An interesting ceremony was to take place on the dissolution of the Corps. The members whose names were on the roll when it broke up received, according to an arrangement come to by their financial committee, the uniform and a sum of money at the rate of 6/8d for each year they had been in the Corps, four, who had been members all the time of its duration received £4.13s.4d. The remainder of the cash was donated for charitable purposes. The targets were delivered to the Galloway Artillery and Rifle Volunteers Association and the guns and ammunition returned to the Government stores.

MONREITH.

A Corps of Rifle Volunteers was raised at Monreith on the 7th May, 1860, under the patronage of Sir William Maxwell, Bart., Monreith, (Ex Lieutenant Colonel and Commanding Officer of the Galloway Rifles Militia, who was made redundant in 1860, on the break up of the Galloway Rifles Militia) Mr. Fraser, Banker; Mr. J. Brown; Garrerie; Mr. Routledge, Accountant; Mr. William McCormick, and others formed a committee

The services of a Drill Instructor, Colour Sergeant Brown, late of the Coldstream Guards, were obtained and drill commenced preparatory to the services of the Corps being offered to the Lord Lieutenant, with the object of forming as a Sub-Division in their own right, subject to Her Majesty's approval. However, the services of the Corps were never offered to the Lord Lieutenant, Sir William Maxwell, switching his attentions to the more upmarket and gentlemanly Corps of Mounted Rifles. To quote Sir William, "let it be the boast of Wigtownshire that she has got a Troop of Mounted Volunteers". Without the support of the influential patronage, the proposed Monreith Sub-Division of Rifle Volunteers was to disband.

On the 25th October, 1860, a meeting was called by Sir William Maxwell, with the purpose of forming a Mounted Rifle Corps of Volunteers. The following committee was appointed, Sir William Maxwell; Messrs, Hugh Wright; James Gilchrist, Killantrae; James Peacock, Whithorn; P. Anderson, Gillespie; J. Anderson, Airies; R. McCulloch, Kirkland; W. Heron., Airyhassen; B. Hendrie, Boreland; John Fraser, Portwilliam. Sir William, was to tell the meeting that equipment would not cost more than £8 for each effective. He produced a parchment roll executed by Lady Maxwell, containing the Royal Arms of Scotland and those of Galloway and Monreith, with columns for the signatures of those inclined to join the movement, 27 names were immediately subscribed, along with 10 Honorary Members. This number constituted a minimun Sub-Division, permitting of a Lieutenant and Coronet. It was hoped that this would be increased to a Troop of 41 effectives, permitting of a Captain.

A further meeting took place, on the 31st October, 1860, when it was stated that 33 members had subscribed their names, but unless 50 effectives and 20 honorary members, could be obtained it would be impossible to meet the large expense attending the movement. It was agreed that the uniform be blue with scarlet facings, wellington boots with spurs attached, felt helmet with plume, the men to supply their own saddles, a uniform bridle, head collar and chain, total cost £6. The annual subscriptions for effective members was £1, with Honorary members paying £2 annual subscriptions. Sir William intimated that he would supply horses and horse's keep for a Sergeant Major, Sergeant Farrier and Trumpeter, with an allowance of £5 to be paid to the Trumpeter, from Company funds. Sergeant Major Lincoln of the 13th Light Dragoons had been approached to join the Troop and it was proposed that drill would take place in different parts of the district on such days as would suit each of the district squads.

On 29th December, 1861, following derisory cries of "where are the Mounted Volunteers?", the local population obviously aggrieved at the disbanding of their Rifle Corps, Sir William was to write, in some length, to the Editor of the *Wigtownshire Free Press*, "that 44 men had enrolled in the Troop, but the committee's decision was that unless 50 effective members had been enrolled their services should not be offered to the Lord Lieutenant. Sergeant Major Lincoln had agreed to offer his services for a limited period but he had now been approached by a Troop in England and Sir William felt that they should now close with him. He made a plea that all who felt inclined to join should make up their minds at once, so that the Troop could either proceed or be given up."

The Troop was indeed to be given up with neither a Mounted Rifle nor a Rifle Volunteer Corps being formed in the district, despite the obvious wealth of willing Volunteers, which was to continue, judging by the following letter which was written to the Editor of the *Galloway Gazette*, dated 10th May, 1902:

"Sir, I should like very much to see a Company of Volunteers formed in this district, with Portwilliam as headquarters, There are plenty of young men in the district, and if the movement was properly gone about, I am certain we could muster from 40 to 50 easily, It would be a great advantage to our young lads, and give them something to take up their attention in the long summer nights. We have a hall here which on wet nights would be suitable for drill. A shooting range can be had most convenient and I am of the opinion that a movement of this kind could be started at once if gone about in the proper way. What think the young men of Mochrum?

Signed,
Drill."

KIRKMAIDEN

Very little history appears to exist of this Corps who were noted, not only for their remarkable size, but also for their reported manly appearance, being referred to as the "Grenadier Guards" of the Galloway Rifle Battalion.

The Corps was formed through the patronage of Colonel MacDouall of the House of Logan, who was himself, to enlist as a Private in the Corps, and the endeavours of two brothers named Anderson from Drummore, who were instrumental, not only in the formation of the Section but on its later elevation to Sub-Division status.

On the 7th February, 1860, a meeting of the Kirkmaiden Volunteer Riflemen, was held in the Schoolhouse, Drummore, to arrange as to the future proceedings. The roll then consisted of 27 effective members and two honorary members.

On the 16th March, Kirkmaiden Rifle Volunteers were to form as a Section of the 2nd Wigtown Rifle Volunteers - Stranraer, and were to attend the Royal Review of 7th August, 1860, in Edinburgh, as such a Section. However, with Her Majesty's approval, on the 23rd November, 1860, the Kirkmaiden Rifle Volunteers were to separate from the Stranraer Company, forming in Drummore, as a Sub-Division, in their own right and bearing the title, the 5th Wigtown Rifle Volunteers. Lieutenant Watson was elected to take charge of the Company, with one of the Anderson brothers being elected Ensign, as a suitable reward for his endeavours.

An interesting anecdote is told of the annual inspection of the Kirkmaiden Volunteers, in October, 1861, by Major Young, Volunteer Inspector for the South Western district of Scotland, who asked Private MacDouall how he held so many medals. Private MacDouall was to reply that he had been a Colonel in command of the Household Troop of Her Majesty. The Inspecting officer replied saying, "it should be you taking the parade, not me!"

The 5th Wigtown Rifle Volunteers were to disband in 1866. There is no reported reason as to the demise of this once fine Corps and we can only now surmise that after the initial euphoria of the Volunteer movement had passed, with the threat of French invasion removed, and the familiar lack of suitable Officer material, interest was to diminish, with the Corps disbanding, leaving but little trace on Galloway's rich and colourful past.

COMPANIES AND SECTIONS - PEACE WITH FRANCE

On the issue of the circular dated, 12th May, 1859, which sanctioned the establishment of the Volunteer Force, it was the duty of the Lord Liutenant of the County to submit proposals for the formation of a Volunteer Corps, in his particular County. When a particular Corps within the County had been established on a firm footing, the services of the Corps were offered, by the Lord Lieutenant, for the approval of the Crown and once the services of the Corps had been accepted it was numbered in order of precedence within that particular County, i.e. 1, 2, 3, Wigtownshire Rifle Corps.

With the Rifle Corps being formed from within a particular County, each County was considered to be, in fact, a separate Force and was given, by the Crown, a Regimental number, in order of precedence of that County's acceptance. Wigtownshire and Kirkcudbrightshire, being two separate Counties were given the Regimental numbers, "65" and "77", respectively. It was not until the 30th June, 1860, that Wigtownshire and Kirkcudbrightshire were united to form as an Administrative Battalion of Rifle Volunteers, with its Headquarters at Newton Stewart. The Galloway Battalion of Rifle Volunteers - The Galloway Rifles - was renumbered as an Administrative Battalion and given the order of precedence and Regimental number, "202".

On the same date, 30th June, 1860, the following appointment was to appear in the *London Gazette,* "By the Lord Lieutenant and High Steward of the Stewartry of Kirkcudbright, Captain William Kennedy Laurie, Esq., ex - 1st Kirkcudbright Rifle Volunteers, to be Lieutenant-Colonel and Commanding Officer of the 1st Battalion of Galloway Rifle Volunteers".

On its formation the following Corps, together with those subsequently formed, were attached to the Battalion:-

1st Kirkcudbright Rifle Volunteers. formed at Kirkcudbright, as a Company,
on the 2nd March, 1860.
Officers:- Captain William Kennedy Laurie, (Captain George Hamilton taking command on the 30th June, 1860); Ensign Tennant. Sections raised at Ringford, 1860; Gatehouse-of-Fleet. ex-4th Kirkcudbright Rifle Volunteers, on the 17th August, 1866; Dundrennan, on the 25th November, 1878.
Juvenile Corps formed at Kirkcudbright Academy on the 2nd March, 1860.

2nd Kirkcudbright Rifle Volunteers. formed at Castle Douglas, as a Company,
on the 2nd March,1860.
Officers:- Captain James Mackie M.P; Lieutenant John Bell; Ensign J. Renny.
Sections raised at Haugh of Urr, 1860. Dalbeattie, on the 5th February, 1864; Springholm - Kirkpatrick Durham. on the 13th November, 1897. Rhonehouse, on the 11th October, 1906.
Detachment formed at Corsock, 1897.

3rd Kirkcudbright Rifle Volunteers. formed at New Galloway, as a Company,
on the 28th March, 1860.
Officers:- Captain Wellwood Maxwell; Lieutenant James Carruthers; Ensign Peter Dalziel.
Section raised at Dalry. 1860, with detachments being raised in 1860, at Mossdale, Laurieston, Parton, Balmaclellan and Carsphairn.

4th Kirkcudbright Rifle Volunteers. formed at Gatehouse-of-Fleet, as a Sub-Division
on the 19th May, 1860. Disbanded on the 17th August, 1866 and becoming a Section of the 1st Kirkcudbright Rifle Volunteers.
Officers: - Lieutenant Frederick Rainsford-Hanney; Ensign David James Ewart.

5th Kirkcudbright Rifle Volunteers. formed at Maxwellton, as a Company on the 1st June, 1860. Increased to 1½ Companies in 1865, and to two Companies on 10th January, 1872.
Officers:- Captain James Bairden Affleck McKinnel; Lieutenant David Pagan; Ensign Francis S. Allan.
Section raised at Lochrutton on the 10th January, 1872.

6th Kirkcudbright Rifle Volunteers. formed at Dalbeattie, as a Company on the 9th July, 1868. Previously, from 5th February, 1864, to 15th February, 1868, as a Section of the 2nd Kirkcudbright Rifle Volunteers, thereafter, becoming the Battalion of Rifle Reserve Volunteers until accepted into the Galloway Battalion of Rifle Volunteers.
Officers:- Captain W.W Platt; Lieutenant James Grieve.
Section at Haugh of Urr. raised 30th November, 1869, ex- Section of 2nd Kirkcudbright Rifle Volunteers. Section raised at Beeswing, New Abbey. on the 21st October, 1904,

1st Wigtown Rifle Volunteers. formed at Wigtown as a Sub-Division, on the 24th February, 1860. Disbanded on the 20th June, 1873. Reformed as a Section of the 3rd Wigtown Rifle Volunteers on the 9th February, 1891.
Officers: - Lieutenant Robert Vans Agnew; Ensign William McHaffie.

2nd Wigtown Rifle Volunteers. formed at Stranraer, as a Company on the 16th March, 1860.
Officers:- Captain David Guthrie, Provost; Lieutenant Alexander Ingram; Ensign John McBryde.
Sections raised at Kirkcolm and Kirkmaiden, 1860, with Kirkmaiden separating from the 2nd Wigtown Rifle Volunteers on the 23rd November, 1860, and forming as a Sub-Division in their own right.
Detachments raised at Cairnryan, Castle Kennedy, Lochans and Leswalt. 1860.
Juvenile Corps formed at Stranraer on the 22nd March, 1860.

3rd Wigtown Rifle Volunteers. formed at Newton Stewart, as a Sub-Division on the 21st March, 1860.
Increased to Company strength on the 31st March, 1864.
Officers:- Lieutenant Henry Stuart; Ensign Edward Stopford-Blair.
Sections raised at Kirkcowan on the 7th May, 1880, Wigtown. ex-1st Wigtown Rifle Volunteers, on the 9th February, 1891, and Creetown - Carsluith on the 5th August, 1898.

4th Wigtown Rifle Volunteers. formed at Whithorn, as a Sub-Division on the 11th April, 1860.
Disbanded on the 11th July, 1874.
Officers:- Lieutenant Hugh D. Stewart; Ensign James Drew.

5th Wigtown Rifle Volunteers. formed at Drummore, as a Sub-Division on the 23rd November, 1860. From the 16th March, 1860, until its formation as a Sub-Division served as a Section of the 2nd Wigtown Rifle Volunteers, Disbanded in 1866.
Officers:- Lieutenant Watson; Ensign Anderson.

Monreith Rifle Volunteers. formed as a Corps on the 7th May, 1860, but were disbanded prior to their services being offered to Her Majesty the Queen.

The purpose or design of an Administrative Battalion, as was the case of the Galloway Rifle Volunteers, was that each Company or Sub-Division acted quite independently of one another, electing their own officers, under the check approval of the Lord Lieutenant, and non-commisioned officers, responsible for managing or mismanaging their Government grants, to be partially introduced on the 1st August, 1861, and fully introduced as a capitation grant on the 21st July, 1863, and other funds subscribed to the Corps, coming together once a year for Inspection or Battalion drills. Owing to the fluctuating supply of monies, the Companies were frequently led to spend more on band entertainments, expeditions and prizes, than they found themselves able to pay, as the funds from private sources soon decreased after the first burst of enthusiasm in favour of the Volunteers. It was reported in 1877 that one Company of the Galloway Rifles was £800 in debt.

Although the power to grant Commissions was to pass from the Lord Lieutenant to the Commanding Officer of the Regiment, by the Regulation of the Forces Act, 1871, and the selection of non-commissioned officers to be passed to the Commanding Officer by War Office Order, dated, 18th September, 1873, it was not until the 26th May, 1880, that the Galloway Battalion was to be consolidated, that is brought together as one body, under the direct control of the Commanding Officer of the Regiment, with more Government influence, who assisted by his officers, was to become responsible for the centralisation and administration of the Battalion,

The first Adjutant, Captain W. Munro, late 79th Foot and late Captain of the Galloway Rifles Militia was appointed to the Battalion on the 16th July, 1860, and was to remain so attached until his retiral on the 31st July, 1871. It was reported that, "in the early days of the Battalion it was quite usual for the Adjutants to drill the Companies in plain clothes, but Captain Munro always did so in tall hat and frock coat. So that he never set a bad example of slackness or easy going carelessness."

By 1860, France and in particular, Napoleon III, was openly distressed at the pressure which conscription was to exercise upon the industry of his Country and the expense involved in the maintainance of a large standing army of some 700,000 men.

France was embroiled, not only politically but actively in the continued unrest of Europe. Napoleon's recent war with Austria (1859) where he was forced to make peace before the intervention of the German Confederation of States. Garibaldi (1860) was involved in the conquest of Scicily and Naples and the unification of Italy. He wished to attack the Papal States and make Rome the capital of Italy, however the Papal States were garrisoned by the French thus threatening to drag the French into further conflict. France and Russia stood accused by Turkey of interfering in its internal affairs and there was the ever continuing threat of the invasion of England.

With this continued drain on French resources, Napoleon was to discontinue his dream of European domination and embark on a policy of economic expansion. He sought the opening of new ways to increase commerce and fresh outlets for his exports overseas. He intensified the expansion of French Colonial power in Indochina and West Africa. He supported the building of the Suez Canal and stamped his French influence throughout the Middle East. He was to sign a commercial treaty (1860) with Great Britain, based on free trade across national borders with international monetary agreements.

With the implementation of these new economic policies, France, like Britain was to emerge as one of the world's great Colonial Powers, much wealthier and wielding more power than through their previous policy of domination through conflict and conquest.

With the introduction of these policies and the recent trade agreements between France and Britain, the fear of invasion by Napoleon III was to rapidly disappear but not so the movement which it had called into being. Volunteers were first seen under arms by the Queen at the Hyde Park Review of the 23rd June, 1860, when 21,000 Volunteers from all over England paraded before Her Majesty, and on the 7th August, 1860, when 21,500 of their Scottish counterparts paraded before Her Majesty at Queen's Park, Holyrood, Edinburgh. The Galloway Rifle Volunteers paraded a total of 279 Volunteers that day, comprising of 140 effective members from the Kirkcudbright Volunteer Companies with 139 effective members from the Wigtown Volunteer Companies. The Kirkcudbrightshire and Wigtownshire Volunteer Artillery Companies paraded a total of 70 effective members. By the end of 1861, 150,000 Rifle Volunteers throughout Great Britain had been drilled and equipped. The earliest available returns of the Galloway Rifle Volunteers showed a strength of 559 effective members at the end of the Volunteer year 1863.

However, once the threat of invasion had passed, the Volunteer Movement, was to settle to a less romantic and more mundane existence of drill and rifle shooting. The fervour of the day which had initially swelled the ranks with the wealthier and more affluent upper and middle class was to pass and the ranks were soon filled with the less financially secure artisan, shopkeeper and working class. Government, therefore had a duty to arm and equip these men who had, not only given of their time but who now had a clearly defined role to play in the future defence of their Country.

Note: Napoleon III was to later lead his Country to defeat in the Franco-Prussian War of 1870-71, and in consequence he was deposed and fled to England with his Empress Eugenie. He died in 1873 and was buried at Chislehurst in Kent. His son, Napoleon Eugene Louis Bonaparte, was killed in the Zulu Wars of 1879 whilst serving with the British Army.

(3) Medal presented to the men of the Galloway Rifle Volunteers who attended the Royal Review, Queen's Park, Holyrood, Edinburgh, on the 7th August, 1860.

CHAPTER 4

THE UNIFORMS OF THE GALLOWAY RIFLE VOLUNTEERS
- THE VOLUNTEER DEFENCE MEDAL -
THE VOLUNTEER LONG SERVICE MEDAL -
CAP BADGES OF THE GALLOWAY RIFLE VOLUNTEERS

In a Government circular of May, 1859, it was recommended by the War Office that the new Volunteer uniform should be of the "Simplest possible design." It was further recommended that the uniform of each Company, within that particular County, be of a similar design and colour.

Little attention was paid to the order, leading one well-known Major-General of the day to comment, "In the matter of uniform, the earliest Volunteer Riflemen frequently indulged their fancy or their taste in the wildest flights.

One such instance of the breach of this order is given, that when the 16 Companies of the newly formed 1st Lanarkshire Volunteer Rifle Corps attended their first Battalion drill, each Company was wearing a different uniform. This was very often found to be the case throughout the Volunteer movement. However, a certain amount of uniformity was attained in the colour of the uniforms with grey being the favoured colour of the Scottish Regiments, whereas the darker shades of green, of the Rifle Brigade, were much favoured by their English counterparts. Few Regiments were to adopt the scarlet of the line infantry.

With the formation of these new Regiments taking place, it was desired that some sort of uniformity in dress and design be attained. With this in mind, the then War Secretary, Mr. Sidney Herbert, was to set up a committee to consider suitable dress for Volunteer uniforms.

One such suggestion was to come from Lord Elcho, Commanding Officer to the London Scottish Volunteers, who in writing from St. James's Palace, on 20th November, 1859, to Mr Fairbairn of the Manchester Volunteers, stated, "I should recommend for Volunteers, the two things we ought all to study, economy and efficiency, for I believe without the one we shall never attain the other. Be economical in dress, and what you save in braid and useless ornament, spend it on Instructors and on the best arms you can obtain.

Now, my experience at Hythe has shown me that a Volunteer may be neatly, comfortably and efficiently clothed for 28/-, i.e. cap, blouse and peg-top trousers, to which must be added 8/- or 10/- for belt or pouch. This was the cost of my Hythe equipment of which the *Times* expressed a favourable opinion.

The material was grey woollen serge, strong and wiry, with green collar and cuffs, and green piping down the sides of the trousers. The blouse being loose, is as easy as a shirt, there is plenty of room for pockets, and as it does not close to the figure, one can put on as much underclothing, knitted waistcoats, as may be necessary in winter, and in summer one might under strip to the skin without affecting the external appearance of this blouse tunic.

I took the pattern from one which had been designed for the army and militia, in lieu of the "shell-jacket", but I have, I think, improved upon it since I left Hythe. I am sure of one thing, that when once a man has enjoyed the freedom of the blouse, he will never submit to the comparative imprisionment of a regular military tunic."

The Secretary of State for War was favourably impressed, not only by the colour of Lord Elcho's dress, later to be known as Elcho grey, but also with the shape and pattern along with the grey woollen serge which he said would stand a great deal of wear and tear. "The best pattern of a Rifleman's uniform deserves careful consideration as well as the best colour. My first impressions were favourable to the comfortable, capacious looking grey uniform of the London Scottish Volunteers but many of the Corps in both England and Scotland have adopted the green uniform of the Rifle Brigade which is less roomy and comfortable but is better adapted for skirmishing and contact with bushes and briars."

Many irreverant Volunteers in green, at Hythe, had been heard to comment, "that if it came to a question of scrambling through quickset hedges, Lord Elcho, would be caught by his "peg-tops", like a ram in a thicket."

The Secretary of State for War was to continue, "I cannot doubt that the committee of Officers will consider the subject of the Volunteer's uniform with calm and unprejudiced minds, and trust that the decision will commend itself to the candour and good sense of the Volunteer Corps by the strength and cogency of facts and arguments on which it is founded."

On the 11th February, 1860, Mr Herbert, Secretary of State for War, on the recommendation of his committee, was to release the following Government circular from the War Office. "The enclosed specification for Volunteer uniforms are those recommended by the Committee recently assembled at this office to consider the question. I am to add that suits are deposited for general inspection in the waiting room at this office and that coloured drawings may be obtained from Mr. Ackerman of Regent Street, London.

Specification for patterns of Rifle Volunteer clothing - Recommended by Committee.

Tunic - Brown and grey mixture, single-breasted, with fly one inch and three quarters broad on the inside; collar of the same material, one inch and three quarters high, rounded off in front; the sleeve to have an Austrian knot, the braid or cord to form a pointed cuff, three inches deep, the knot nine inches and three quarters long and four inches in width, the edges trimmed with the same cord, to be of such colour as the Corps may decide on; the skirt ten and a half inches deep, for an Officer or Private, with a variation of half an inch longer or shorter for every inch in height; the back and skirt to be cut whole, and not to open; nine bronzed buttons in front and two behind.

Trousers - cut so as to be sewn into a band round the waist, large from hip to ankle, and 17 inches round the bottom, trimmed with square cord down the side seam, of the same colour as that used on the tunic.

Cap - To be made of the same material as tunic, three and a quarter inches high in front and four and a half inches at the back, with band of the same material round the head; the trimming to consist of two pieces of cord, same as on tunic, round top and bottom of band, and round edge of crown; small rosette on the left side, of the same colour as braid; round peak, slightly drooping.

Belts - Of dark brown leather, with pouch to contain 30 rounds of ammunition, and a ball bag to slide on the waist belt, to contain 10 rounds of ammunition, caps, and an oil bottle, bayonet frog on left side; on the large pouch a shoulder-belt is fixed, so as to be perfectly level on the waist, passing under the right arm and over the left shoulder, fastening on the breast with a buckle.

Leather Gaiters - To be made of sheep-skin, to match in colour with the pouch and belts; black enamelled facing at bottom, cut with a point behind to form a continuation of boots; buttons of the same material.

Cloak - To be made from the same material as tunic, cut two inches below the knee, forming a plain double-breasted coat, buttoning close to the neck, with stand or fall collar, having tabs buttoned over to protect the neck. A cape, fifteen inches deep, fits on the shoulder, attached or detached at pleasure, and formed of double material, the inward part expanding and, when reversed, forming a hood to protect the head.

However, the question as to uniformity in colour and design of Volunteer dress was never to be resolved and the Regiments were to continue in their numerous forms of dress until the Haldane reforms of 1908. The Elcho style of uniform, of the London Scottish Volunteers, was very much a favoured and popular style of dress and was adopted, with some form of variation, by a large number of the Volunteer Regiments.

On the 1st December, 1859, the Volunteers handbook was issued giving rules and instructions to the Volunteers. Rule No. 4 was to state, "Each member is to provide himself with a rifle-shell jacket and forage cap, together with the necessary arms and accroutrements of a rifleman, wherewith to attend meetings for drill and exercise. He is also to provide himself with a full dress rifle tunic and a Shako or helmet, for full dress meetings."

Initially, each volunteer was expected to pay for his own uniform, supply his own rifle, later he was given half the cost of the rifle from Government funding. Pay for his share in a drill and practice ground and for the services of a Sergeant instructor. Subscription lists were opened to defray the costs to the volunteers but after the initial euphoria of the formation of the various companies had died down many of the Volunteers found themselves once again having to meet their own expenses.

At a meeting in Stranraer on the 15th December, 1859, Lord Dalrymple was to say of the Volunteers, "The rifleman has to pay for his uniform, for half of his weapon, for his teaching, for his practice ground. The artilleryman has to pay for nothing but his dress, which may be as cheap as he pleases. Everything else, guns, small arms, teaching, practice ground all will be gladly and instantly furnished by the Government."

The Artillery volunteers were the favoured means of protecting large, open tracts of coastline and it was considered that every town and village in the Rhins of Galloway was susceptible to attack by a man-of-war, therefore incentives were given to have the Artillery Volunteer ranks filled before that of the Rifle Volunteers.

Over the years many myths have arisen as to the early dress of the Galloway Rifle Volunteers. No doubt many informed sources, with reference to the following excerpt from Volume 1 of the *Regimental Gazette* of 1897, have perpetuated these myths. "The changes of dress have been slight but the head-gear has undergone several changes, not always for the better. At first feathers in a French cap and fancies of all kinds, such as varieties in trimmings were worn. The French cap was very comfortable in some ways, as the leather pique kept the sun out of the eyes.

On the 5th December, 1873, the Shako was adopted and continued to our great discomfort, both in wind and rain, till 9th May, 1883, when Glengarry caps and badges were substituted. Even they are not much good at all times, certainly not when shooting in bright sun."

The early history of the Corps uniform is fairly sketchy up to 1873 and most sources gloss over these early years by sweeping generalisations of the dress. "Original uniforms of the Corps were steel or dark grey and varied not only between each Company but also within the Company from year to year. One year with plumes of cock feathers and the next with Shakos of the Highland Light Infantry."

Colonel Kennedy, in his address of 1897, did clarify this position by saying, "Unfortunately the Regimental Book containing the records of some of the earlier years has been destroyed."

Initially the Galloway Rifle Volunteers were an Administrative Battalion, each Company or Sub-Division acting quite independently of the other. Each Company was responsible, not only for the election of their own officers but for the administration of expenses, grants and the supply of rifles and uniforms. Committees were formed to administer each aspect of the Company and the uniform was dealt with by one such committee.

I will deal first with the formation of Wigtownshire, who, from the outset, through the offices of their Lord Lieutenant, the Earl of Stair, found uniformity of dress almost immediately. This was not to last, however, and although variations in the style and design over the years were slight, many colour changes were to take place.

The first mention is of the 30th November, 1859, at a meeting of the proposed Wigtown Sub-Division of the Wigtownshire Rifle Corps - Robert Vans Agnew; Esq., Chairman. It was moved by Mr. Caird and seconded by Mr. Graham, that the uniform of the Corps should consist of, blouse, trousers and caps. Waist belt and leggings. The committee is to fix upon a colour and quality of cloth for the uniform to be submitted to the Lord Lieutenant for his approval.

15th March, 1860, - Stranraer. The uniform which has been decided upon and approved by the Lord Lieutenant, is a very handsome one of dark grey with red facings.

22nd March, 1860, - Newton Stewart. The uniform is a handsome dark grey with red facings and black belts.

Drummore, which was initially formed as a Section of Stranraer, adopted the uniform design and colour of it's parent Company.

Whithorn was also to fall into line with the other Companies of Wigtownshire, and through the offices of the Lord Lieutenant, the Government circular was honoured in that a standard uniform was created throughout Wigtownshire, of blouse, trousers, French cap, all of dark Oxford Grey, with red facings on the collars and cuffs and red piping down the trousers, with leggings and black waist belts.

It was originally intended that the Volunteers of the Battalion were to be issued with a knapsack of the pattern of the Swiss Light Infantry with a short waterproof cape, however, by July, 1889, the Volunteers were still awaiting the issue of some sort of waterproof coat.

Complete uniformity, in Wigtownshire, was achieved when the contract to supply the five Wigtownshire Companies was awarded to "A. Gibb and Co., Clothiers and Tailors, Cloth Hall, Stanraer". The following advert was to appear on the front page of the *Wigtownshire Free Press* of 15th March, 1860. "A Gibb and Co., beg to intimate that the Rifle suit made and exhibited by them has been approved by the Stranraer and other Rifle Corps and sanctioned by the Lord Lieutenant, as a uniform for the Rifle Volunteers of Wigtownshire: and they are now prepared to supply suits and accoutrements on the best terms."

Moving on to the Stewartry. On Tuesday, 3rd February, 1860, in the store room at the Cross, (Tolbooth) a sub-committee was formed to arrange dress, drill and other like matters of the Kirkcudbright Rifle Corps. The committee comprised, Mr. Laurie; Mr. Hamilton; Mr. Tennent; Mr. Corrie and Mr. Wallace. The committee agreed that the rules and dress of the Rifle Corps should be similar to those of the other Rifle Corps in the Stewartry.

On Monday, 13th February, 1860, Mr. Tennant, representing the Kirkcudbright uniform committee, met with his Castle Douglas counterparts, in the Town Hall, Castle Douglas, in an effort to reach some sort of agreement as to uniformity of dress.

Mr. Tennent exhibited a cloth of dark grey, already approved by his Kirkcudbright committee and this was accepted by the Castle Douglas committee. They, however, agreed that a superior quality of cloth than that exhibited, should be procured.

It was agreed that the coat should be in the form of a tunic and of the regular military cut and length. The tunic was to have black braid on the breast and black cord on the collar and cuffs. It was decided by the two committees that both a waist and shoulder belt of black should be adopted, as being calculated to give the Volunteer a more soldier-like appearance. Accoutrements and decorations were to be at the discretion of the officers commanding their respective Companies. The French Cap was to be adopted.

Mr. Tennent stated that the Kirkcudbright Corps were desirous of adopting the peg-top trousers and gaitors of Elcho design but the Castle Douglas committee preferred the ordinary loose trouser of the Rifle Brigade. It was agreed that in these matters, whichever design gave the greatest satisfaction to the individual member of the Corps then that design would be adopted.

However, the final decision was to become apparent when at the Royal Review in Edinburgh of the Scottish Volunteers, of 10th August, 1860, a correspondant was to write, "The Company under the command of Lieutenant Bell, comprising Volunteers from Kirkcudbright and Castle Douglas, was much admired for its steadiness and soldier-like bearing; the detachments from these Towns and a Company from Lanarkshire Volunteers being the only parties present who wore leggings or knickerbockers, as they are commonly styled."

At a meeting of 10th March, 1860, Gatehouse Sub-Division was to adopt the uniform of the Kirkcudbright and Castle Douglas Companies.

Neither New Galloway nor Maxwellton Companies were to adopt the trouser of "peg-top" or "knickerbocker" design, preferring the straight trouser of the Rifle Brigade. New Galloway Committee were to choose a uniform similar to the design of the other Companies of the Stewartry, the only real distinction being that their uniform was of a medium grey woollen serge. However, as was often to be the case, Maxwellton were to go it alone, choosing a uniform of dark grey woollen serge with the blouse braided in green with green piping running down the trouser leg. This was very much in keeping with the uniform of the London Scottish Volunteers, designed by Lord Elcho and exhibited at Hythe in 1859. In keeping with the other Companies of Galloway both New Galloway and Maxwellton were to adopt the French cap as their head-gear.

Uniform designs in the Stewartry were submitted through the Offices of the Lord Lieutenant, the Earl of Selkirk and although there were slight variations in colour and trouser design, he was to approve the uniforms in that the criteria of the Government circular of 1859 had been met in that they were of a similar design and colour to the other Companies in the County.

Returning to the myths which have surrounded the early uniforms of the Corps. "At first feathers in a French Cap and fancies of all kinds." Each Company was to form an instrumental band to give their marching a more measured and military gait. Ideally each company hoped to form their own band but in the earlier years of the movement many of the Companies formed the much simpler, "Fife and Drum bands." It was common practice to have the bandsmen stand out by embellishing the service dress with various fancies of braid and colour, as in the account of the new Fife and Drum band of the Stranraer Rifle Corps, of 4th April, 1861. "The uniform is the same as the Company of, dark grey and French Cap, which has been fitted with a gold band and red feathers." The feathers in a French Cap and fancies of all kinds?

In common with Officers of the Regular Army, Volunteer Officers sought to create their own individuality by the embellishment of their uniforms. It was reported, "that some Officers had been fixing the "hemming material" from a ladies dress around their hats and the bonnets were covered in ostrich plumes, or in reality cock's feathers."

This form of embellishment appeared to be tolerated but when it was reported that some Officers were wearing gloves of different colour whilst on parade, "Some were wearing white gloves, some brown, some of no particular colour and others none at all", Colonel Laurie called the offending Officers before him and put paid to any such further embellishments. "Varieties in trimmings were worn?"

A further story was related on the early volunteering days by Major Maxwell, 'H' Company Dalbeattie, at a smoking evening in 1889, when he said, "The pattern of the tunic and the colours of cloth were many, and the men were in the habit of packing the space between the collar and the neck with cravat". He remembered one inspection at Castle Douglas, the Inspecting officer was very cynical and on looking down the line he saw one Company heavy in cravat, "This Company I suppose" said he, "comes from somewhere near the North Pole" and this was on a sweltering day.

On the 1st August, 1861, a supplemental estimate was issued to Parliament from the War Office of the sum required to be voted towards defraying charges on account of the Volunteer Corps. The total amount was £30,000. £10,000 for pay and allowances and contingencies of Adjutants and £20,000 for pay of Drill Instructors. No provision was made for defraying the cost of Volunteer uniforms. There was a country wide outcry of uniforms wearing out and on the 13th March, 1862, the Government sanctioned the supply of Volunteer Companies with cloth at cost price. This was intended as the first step in clothing the entire Volunteer Force in the same uniform. It was said that with the present varied forms of Volunteer uniforms, if they were called out in active service, it would be very difficult for them to distinguish, friend from enemy. Despite pleas from Lord Elcho and other like personages the Volunteer Force was never to achieve any form of uniformity in dress.

With this generous offer of Government to supply cloth at cost price, the Volunteers of Galloway were to embark on a myraid of colour changes. The uniform style was to remain much the same apart from minor pattern changes. It was estimated that the life of a Volunteer uniform was 2 to 3 years and with the supply of cheap cloth, every time they changed their uniform, they would change the colour.

Now that the Companies were able to obtain this cheap cloth they began to shop around to find the best deal in cash as well as a Tailor who would make a uniform best suited to the Companies individual needs or requirements.

On the 16th January, 1863, Mr. James, Clothier and Tailor, Stanraer, was to obtain the sole rights to supply the uniforms of the Stranraer Rifle Corps. At the same time an advert was to appear in the *Kirkcudbrightshire Advertiser.* "Whithorn, 4th WRV, much wanted by the public, a qualified Tailor. One who would and could make Volunteer uniforms".

By 16th June, 1863, Kirkcudbright, Castle Douglas, Gatehouse and New Galloway, had changed their uniforms to that of the green and style of the Rifle Brigade. Maxwellton were to once again fall out of step with the rest of the Stewartry and adopt the scarlet of the line infantry, thus, falling into line with the uniform of their counterparts in the Dumfries Volunteer Rifle Corps.

Throughout 1863, Wigtownshire Rifle Corps were to retain the original uniform of dark Oxford grey blouse and trousers but by the 10th March, 1864, Stranraer Rifle Corps had adopted the scarlet of the line infantry. Pressure through the press was brought to bear for the other Wigtownshire Companies to follow suit but no record now exists as to whether or not they were to fall into line.

On 25th April, 1868, Maxwellton Rifle Corps, the 5th K.R.V. were to appear in their new uniforms, the scarlet jacket had been discarded and a blue tunic with red facings had been adopted. However, this change was to be of a very short duration as by August, 1868, at the Volunteer Review in Carlisle, for the first time, uniformity in dress was reached, when the whole Battalion was finally clothed in the dark green uniform of the Rifle Brigade.

This uniformity was not to last and in the next five years, many of the Companies, particularly in Wigtownshire, were to revert to their old and favoured Oxford grey uniform. Kirkcudbright, Gatehouse and Castle Douglas were once again to change, this time to the earlier uniform favoured by Maxwellton Corps, of dark blue with red facings. It would be interesting to know if Maxwellton were to have taken their old, short used uniforms, from their moth-balls and if in fact uniformity was once again achieved within the Stewartry with this dark blue uniform. No record of this stage exists as to the uniform of Maxwellton or New Galloway.

On the 10th January, 1873, an Order was issued, from the Home Office, directing Commanding Officers of Volunteer Corps, to postpone, for the present, the equipment of recruits, in consequence of the alterations to be made in the uniform of the auxilliary Forces. "It has generally been admitted that assimilation either to the Regular Army, with certain distinctions, or among the Volunteer Force generally is a necessity, now that the Force has established its right to permanency, but it need hardly be said that while there are a great number of advocates of the dark green uniform of the Rifles or the scarlet of the line, an almost equal number prefer the less soldier-like but more serviceable grey, the colour which has been adopted by most Rifle Regiments since the institution of the movement".

This further attempt to obtain uniformity in the dress of the Volunteer movement was once again to fail, however, this order may have been in the mind of Colonel Macbean, Commanding the 61st Sub-District, on his inspection of the Galloway Rifle Battalion of Volunteers at Castle Douglas, on the 12th January, 1873. His scathing remarks were issued in the following Battalion Order;

"The appearance of the Regiment was satisfactory. It would have been more so had there been a greater uniformity in dress: each Corps was different from the other. By Corps this is not so much observed as it is in Battalion, as it was on this occasion. Some steps ought to be taken to remedy this. The marching past was indifferent and the movements generally were not well or steadily performed. More attention ought to be paid to Company Drill. With reference to Battalion drill, the light infantry drill was only elementary. Company Officers ought to be able to throw out skirmishers in any direction, re-inforce them, intermix them and call them in and restore order rapidly and without noise or talking."

For a moment, stepping forward a few years. When Colonel Maitland was to announce his retiral on the 31st July, 1887, he said. "When he took commmand of the Battalion on 31st July, 1871, they made a very different appearance in parade then, than they did now. The regulations were absurd that enabled Officers to fix and order their own uniforms regardless of orders from Headquarters. The result was every Company was in uniform of varying colour and design and he knew for certain that some wore "top-boots" (laughter). From the moment he took command, he endeavoured to get some sort of similarity throughout the whole of the Companies and he thought he had succeeded."

Returning to 1873, no doubt a culmination of many things, the Home Office Order, of January, 1873, the remarks of Colonel Macbean a few days later and the desire of Colonel Maitland to stamp his authority on the Regiment, led to complete uniformity in dress being attained on the 5th December, 1873. The whole Battalion was clothed in dark Oxford grey tunics and trousers with scarlet cuffs and collars, piping and Austrian knot, (later with black tracing all around), dark grey Shakos with black ball tuft and black belts.

On Saturday, 26th August, 1876, Colonel Macbean was once again to inspect the Galloway Battalion at Castle Douglas. On this occasion he was to remark. "There was now uniformity in the clothing of the Battalion and they were a remarkable fine body of men."

Once again an unsuccessful attempt was made to achieve uniformity in the dress of the Volunteer movement and by Reserve Forces circular No. 38(April) and No. 64 (July) of 1874, the Secretary of State for War, Mr. Hardy in his first Military budget intimated a desire that Volunteers of the line should be clad in scarlet. However, he was to continue, "the colour of the Volunteer Corps, other than new Regiments is still at their own option but if they voluntarily change their existing grey or drab, they are then and then only to be forced to adopt scarlet."

On the 1st July, 1881, a change of uniform and colour was decided on for the Battalion. The tunic of scarlet with dark blue cuffs and collar and with white cord facings, dark blue trousers with very broad/red stripe, dark blue helmet with gilt spike. The whole being similar to that of the former 25th Lanark. An order was issued that all Companies were to receive their new uniforms by January, 1882, however the implications of the Reserve Forces circular of 1874, were suddenly realised and a week later, on the 8th July, 1881, a further order was issued from the Headquarters of the Galloway Battalion which said. "With regards to the new uniform to be issued, it has now been decided that the "Cockney Tartan" would have to be the pattern of the trousers, it has therefore been decided to make no change to the present uniform."

A report of 25th August, 1881, on the Royal Review at Holyrood, Edinburgh (Wet Review) made comparisons between the uniforms and in particular comparisons between the headgear of the 1860 and 1881 Royal Reviews. "At the Review of 1860, almost every conceivable description of head-gear was on show. Now-a-days so far as head covering is concerned, many Corps have gone to the opposite extreme and content themselves with the simple Glengarry; few still retain the Shako, while a number have the helmet."

The official returns of the Review Strengths Part 1, refers to the uniforms;
Galloway Rifles.
Headquarters - Newton Stewart
Uniform and Head-dress - Dark Oxford grey with Shako.

As seen in the above report many of the Volunteer Companies had gone over to the Glengarry and in keeping with the other Volunteer Regiments, on the 9th May, 1883, the Shako of the Galloway Battalion was replaced by a plain Glengarry, the whole cost of the change of head-gear being borne personally by the Commander, Lieutenant Colonel Gordon Maitland.

At the Battalion inspection of the Galloway Rifle Volunteers on Saturday, 14th July, 1883, the following report appeared, "For the first time the Battalion appeared in the Glengarry bonnets, the new Regimental Head-dress, we cannot say that the change is a great improvement so far as appearances are concerned but for comfort there is no comparison between it and the heavy Shako and on Saturday, when some of the Companies were under arms for 15 hours, the bonnet relieved to a considerable extent the irksomeness of the day's work. The bonnet is entirely black with the exception of a scarlet fringe round the badge, which is in the form of a shield, displaying the Galloway Lion, with the letters GRV, (Galloway Rifle Volunteers) above it, surmounted by a crown and the old gaelic word, "ALBANICH" - Albion of Scotland - the war cry of the ancient Gallovidians, being placed on a scroll underneath it, the whole being surmounted by a wreath of thistles.

The design is by Quarter-Master Major Harper, a Staff Officer of the Regiment and formerly a member of 'B' Company, Castle Douglas".

The uniform style of 1873 was to remain and indeed did so until the final change of dress in 1905. The 1873 uniform was to remain the standard regulation for officers in full dress until 1908.

In 1881, the Galloway Rifle Volunteers joined with the 21st (Royal Scots Fusiliers) Regimental District as one of their allotted Volunteer Battalions, and from that date many attempts were made to have the uniform changed to that of the Royal Scots Fusiliers. Quarter-Master Major Harper, the designer of the cap badge, was also a member of the Regimental clothing committee and at a speech to his old Company, on the evening of 10th February, 1888, he said. "The Galloway Battalion was now in the new scheme as a Volunteer Battalion of the Royal Scots Fusiliers. In thus forming a part of that Regiment, it would be a wise policy in the War Office to insist in this Battalion being put into the uniform of the Territorial Regiment. This he was sure would lead to more interest and pride being taken by Officers and men in their connection with the Regular Army and identify them more with their comrades if ever called upon to do active service with the army."

He continued, "he had long been convinced that their present uniform, though somewhat serviceable was so unattractive as to be no inducement, but the reverse to recruits to join the ranks and if they were to adopt the scarlet uniform of the Regiment a stimulus would be given to the movement in Galloway."

He considered their present uniform to be very unsoldier-like, and continued, "this was demonstrated many years ago when attending a rifle competition just outside Glasgow, I was then a Sergeant and we had to spend many hours in the City in uniform and what do you think we were taken for or rather mistaken for? members of the Post Office Letter Carriers. Since then I have always thought that it would be well to adopt a uniform so distant from the Post Office that such a mistake could not again be made."

In March, 1888, permission was given for the Galloway Battalion to adopt the uniform of their Line Battalion, however, a request that Officers be allowed to adopt the dirk and plaid and for the Claymore to be slung from the shoulder was turned down, as these distinctions for Officers had already been refused to the Officers of the Line Battalion.

Despite the pleas of many rank and file and previous authority from the War Office for the Galloway Battalion to adopt the scarlet uniform of the Territorial Regiment of the Royal Scots Fusiliers, many of the Senior ranks of the Galloway Battalion and Line Regiment, favoured the current grey dress of the Volunteers. Colonel Bainbridge, Commanding the 21st Regimental District, on his annual inspection of the Galloway Rifles at Castle Douglas on the 12th July, 1890, commented, that he liked the grey drape of the Volunteers, better than the scarlet, although many Regiments of Volunteers had adopted the latter. The object of the War Office was not to allow the enemy to know that the lesser trained Volunteers were at a particular point in a defence line and as far as possible to have the different forces uniformly clothed. Still, he continued, he liked to see the dark grey uniforms of the Volunteers.

With these strong views held by the Senior ranks no change was to take place in uniform, in the Galloway Battalion until 1905, even though the Battalion was transferred to the King's Own Scottish Borderers, as one of their allotted Volunteer Battalions, in 1899.

Despite the earlier promises that the Regiment was to be provided with a waterproof cape, as early as 1860, no over-garment of any description was to be issued to the Volunteers until 1895.

After the infamous "Wet Review" of 1881, promises were again made that the Battalion would be supplied with over-garments but no such garment was issued.

On the 25th February, 1887, the War Office increased capitation grants and offered Volunteer Battalions financial assistance for the provision of great-coats and valise equipment. No great-coats were received.

On the 5th July, 1889, the Inspecting officer of the Galloway Rifles, was to comment that he hoped to see the men in camp next year properly equipped for any active service with great-coats, leggings and good boots, however, it was not until the Brigade Camp at Hawick of 24th June, 1895, that the men of the Galloway Battalion were issued with "Patrol Jackets" for wearing off-parade. It was reported that it was a coat more in keeping with regulation army dress for Volunteers, and it was not until July, 1900, that we find the first reports that the Galloway Rifles have at last been issued with their long awaited great-coats.

On Saturday, 15th December, 1900, a Regimental Brass Band was formed, along with a Regimental Pipe Band. Regimental Orders were issued which stated that the Pipers were to be dressed in kilts but the drummers and the Regimental Band were to wear the ordinary uniform of the Corps with the exception of the Bandmaster and the Pipers who would wear silver-plated badges on their caps, the same as the Sergeants wore.

On 12th August, 1904, a movement was afoot to have the uniform of the Galloway Rifles changed to a khaki tunic with tartan trousers, but by the 19th of May, 1905, a new uniform was issued comprising:- drab serviceable khaki with scarlet piping on the trousers and drab putties, along with a blue glengarry with Regimental badge and red, white and blue diced border, brown leather equipment with bandolier.

Initially it was intended, in view of the cost that the change to the new "service khaki" should be done gradually, two Companies per year, taking four years in all to bring the entire Battalion into line. 'A' and 'H' Companies, Kirkcudbright and Dalbeattie respectively were the first two Companies to be issued with the new uniform. However, the whole economics of the scheme were thrown into dis-array when it was announced that a Royal Review was to take place in September of that year, before the King, in Edinburgh, and it was thought prudent that the entire Battalion should be dressed in the new uniform. On the 22nd July, 1905, application was made to the authorities for permission to make the changes in uniform immediately.

Permission to have the Battalion uniformly dressed was obviously received as on the 22nd September, 1905, the following report was to appear in the *Times* relating to the 1905 Review. "The latter, (Galloway Rifle Volunteers) who were in the Scottish Border Brigade furnished, in spite of their dull khaki kit, the best set-up unit that marched past in the day. The average physique would have done credit to the foot guards."

On the 7th July, 1905, authority was granted to the Galloway Rifle Volunteers, in recognition of their having supplied contingents to South Africa, to wear the South African honours, 1900-02 on the Officer's buttons and on cap badges of the Regiment. In rifle battalions not having colours this was a recognised practice.

On the 2nd January, 1908, the War Office notified that all Volunteer Corps should be conducted as economically as possible up to the end of the financial year when Commanding Officers would be relieved of financial responsibility especially, economy was to be observed in respect of expenditure in uniform, in consideration of the possibility of some men who were now serving, quitting the ranks, on the transfer of the Corps to the new Territorial Army.

The Galloway Rifle Volunteer Battalion was to cease to exist on the 31st March, 1908. A week earlier it was reported that their successors in the Territorial Army were to adopt the uniform of the King's Own Scottish Borderers, namely, red-coat and tartan trews. They were also to be issued with a suit of khaki.

VOLUNTEER DEFENCE AND LONG SERVICE MEDALS. - THE CAP BADGES.

Volunteer Defence Medal - Officers.

In 1892, Her Majesty Queen Victoria, introduced the Volunteer Officer's Decoration, (V.D.) for Officers of the Volunteer Force, who had served as an Officer in the Volunteer Force for a period of 20 years. In the event of an Officer having risen from the ranks, half of his service in the ranks was to be counted towards the requirement.

The Volunteer Decoration, to be worn on the left breast, together with any awarded war medals, was silver, being of a gilt wreath with a Crown and V.R. in the centre, with the head of Queen Victoria on the reverse. The medal was suspended by a green ribbon.

On the 1st August, 1892, the Adjutant General, issued the following instruction referring to the Volunteer Officer's Decoration.

"Applications for the decoration are to be made through the Commanding Officer of the Corps, who, in the case of Officers still serving, will certify that the applicant holds a Commission, that he has completed the qualifying 20 years of service, and he is an efficient and thoroughly capable Officer, and he is in every way deserving of the decoration.

In the case of retired Officers, the certificate must state that the applicant has completed the 20 years, and has been granted the priviledge of honorary rank on retirement.

Though 20 years commissioned service or its equivalent as previously laid down, are required, the service need not be consecutive and Honorary Colonels of Corps, who have qualifying service will be eligible.

The letters "V.D.", Volunteer Decorations will be inserted in the Army List before the name of each Officer to whom the decoration is granted."

On the afternoon of Saturday, 22nd January, 1893, the Officers of the Dumfriesshire Rifle Volunteers and the Galloway Rifle Volunteers, who were then, entitled to the new Volunteer Decoration for long service, were presented with their medals in the Drill Hall, Dumfries, by Brigadier the Earl of Minto, Commander of the South of Scotland Brigade. The Galloway Riflemen honoured with the Volunteer Defence Medal, were:-

Colonel J.M. Kennedy, Commander of the Galloway Rifles -	30 years service.
Lieutenant-Colonel Maxwell, Staff Officer -	23 years service.
Major Harper, 'B' Company, Castle Douglas -	28 years service.
Major McLellan, 'A' Company, Kirkcudbright -	25 years service.
Surgeon Lieutenant-Colonel Lorraine, 'B' Company -	25 years service.
Colonel Maitland (Retired) former Commander of the Galloway Rifles	26 years service.
Major Kerr, 'H' Company, Dalbeattie -	24 years service.

Volunteer Long Service Medal.

On the 1st June, 1894, Army Order 85, was issued to the Volunteer Force formally announcing that Her Majesty Queen Victoria was pleased to.institute a new decoration, to be known as the "Volunteer Long Service Medal". The medal was to be granted to all men, including Officers, who had not qualified for the Officer's decoration, on completion of 20 years service in the Volunteer Force, provided they were actually serving on the 1st January, 1893, and were recommended by the former or present Commanding Officer. Retired Volunteers who qualified for the medal were required to apply to the Officer Commanding the Regiment in which they served. The decision of the General Officer Commanding the District, upon the validity or otherwise of any claim, would be final.

It was further provided that the service of the Volunteer, whether Officer, or non-commissioned officer or private, must have been consecutive and that any Officer, who was subsequently awarded the Volunteer Officer's Decoration, would be required to surrender his prior decoration.

The medal, of silver, bore the head of Queen Victoria, with the reverse showing the inscription, "For Long Service in the Volunteer Force," suspended by a green ribbon. The medal to be worn on the tunic, on the left breast, along with other war medals.

The names of all qualified recipients were promulgated quarterly by Army Orders.

CAP BADGES

All Cap Badges of the Galloway Rifle Volunteers are in the form of a shield, displaying the Galloway Lion, with the letters "G.R.V." above it, surmounted by a Crown and the old gaelic word "ALBANICH" on a scroll beneath it, the whole being surrounded by a wreath of thistles. Prior to the 9th May, 1883, all Corps distinctions were worn on the tunic buttons and belt buckles.

(1) Black coloured metal badge,	surmounted by the Queen's Crown. Issued 9th May, 1883-1899.
(2) Silver coloured metal badge,	surmounted by the Queen's Crown 1899-1901.
(3) Silver coloured metal badge,	surmounted by the King's Crown. 1902-1905.

(4) Silver coloured metal badge,   surmounted by King's Crown and bearing the
legend "South Africa 1900-02"
7th July, 1905-31st March, 1908.

(5) Silver badge,   surmounted by either Queen or King's Crown.
          These were cap badge embellishments often worn by the Officers.

(6) Silver plated badge,   surmounted by Queen or King's Crown.
          These were issued to Sergeants.

Note: On the formation of the Regimental Brass and Pipe Bands on the 15th December, 1900, the Pipers and Bandmaster only, were also issued with the silver plated cap badge. The drummers and members of the brass band were to wear their normal service uniform and therefore did not qualify for the silver plated cap badge.

(4) Medal presented to the men of the Galloway Rifle Volunteers who attended the Royal Review, Queen's Park, Holyrood, Edinburgh, on the 25th August, 1881.

CHAPTER 5

COMPANY - ADJUTANT - BATTALION - BRIGADE - DRILLS - ANNUAL IN-SPECTIONS - CONSOLIDATION OF BATTALION - TRANSFER OF TERITORIAL DISTRICTS.

Initially hours of drill were allocated by the Volunteer Committtee of a particular Corps. In the case of the 3rd Wigtownshire Rifle Volunteers, Newton Stewart, drill was fixed at three times a week and in the case of the 1st Wigtownshire Rifle Volunteers, Wigtown drill was fixed as 7.30am to 8.30am and 7.30pm to 9.30pm daily, with the proviso that the Volunteer should attend at least one of the drills per day.

However, in consequence of the report of the Royal Commission of the 14th Augustt, 1862, which recommended a grant of 20/- to every Volunteer who attended 9 drills in the year, of which 6 in the case of Consolidated and 3 in Administrative Battalions (as was the case of the Galloway Battalion) shall have been Battalion drills; who has gone through a course of Musketry Instruction and who attended the Inspection of the Corps. A further grant of 10/- was recommended for each Volunteer who fired a prescribed quantity of ball-cartridge in a year. In the case of recruits 30 drills and a short course of Musketry Instructions was held as qualification, the drill quota of Company drills was to become less stringent. With drills being set to accommodate the new Regulations during the Volunteer year of 1st May to 30th November, changing to 31st October, in 1872. The drill plan of the 2nd Kirkcudbrightshire Rifles, Castle Douglas, as was to be practiced in amended form by the other Corps forming the Battalion was, every Friday and alternate Wednesday during the season, suitably accommodating the drill requirements of both the established Volunteer and recruit and thus enabling him to earn the newly introduced capitation grant.

Lord Elcho, writing in the *Pall Mall Gazette* was to say. "Every Field day the Volunteers have had necessarily originated with themselves, since no authority in the Kingdom has power to call them out for a field day or any other given day, save for repelling invasion."

The first Battalion drills were held in the Stewartry on Tuesday, 21st October, 1862, when 121 of all ranks were present. In Wigtownshire the following day, Wednesday, 22nd October, 1862, an unspecified but unsatisfactory total of all ranks were present. These parade strengths, together with the annual inspection and Battalion drill, for 1863, are fully reported on page 291 of Chapter 11.

To fulfil the obligations of Battalion drill, it was necessary that at least four Companies of the Battalion were present and paraded a minimum of 128 members of all ranks, later changing, by Regulation of the Forces Act, 1871, "To constitute a Battalion drill at least 100 of all ranks must be present, this total to include a minimum of 16 officers and Sergeants. "If the Volunteer was absent from Inspection he was required to perform 2 extra drills to make himself 'efficient'. Rifle Corps were required to attend with at least half of their strength one Brigade Drill in the year of two hours duration under a regular officer.

In a further circular from the War Office, dated 21st April, 1874, "the attendance at 3 Battalion drills only is required, amongst other qualifications, to render a Rifle Volunteer efficient and that attendance at the Annual Inspection, as well as Brigade Drill, is allowed to count towards the completion of 3 Battalion drills.

Moving forward at pace, and at present slightly out of context. On the 1st November, 1880, a further War Office Order dispensed with the necessity of Battalion drills should a Rifle Corps go into Camp, but later clarified their somehat ambiguous Order by stating that. "In cases where Volunteers are unable to go into Camp for Battalion drill, they may be permitted to substitute Company for Battalion drills."

The Drill Order of the Volunteer to earn that part of his capitation grant was that of Company, Battalion and Brigade Drills, with an annual inspection of the Corps by an appointed officer. In the Regulations issued under the Volunteer Act, 1863, it clearly stated. "Where the Inspecting Officer at the Annual Inspection, reports that a Corps is not proficient in drill or Instruction, to the Secretary of State, he shall have the power to direct the withholding of the certificates from all members of the Corps. The Inspecting Officer may also direct the withholding of a certificate from any Volunteer who does not appear to him to be proficient." i.e. thus debarring the Volunteer from attaining the Government Grant.

To ensure this proficiency each Company was subject to an annual inspection, by a suitably appointed Inspecting Officer, not only was the Volunteer to be inspected in drill and arms, but the Company was also inspected as to its Stores and Ranges. This was to be the case, on the evening of Wednesday, 18th November, 1863, when the annual inspection of the 2nd Wigtownshire Rifle Volunteers, Stranraer, took place in the Town Hall, Stranraer. The Inspecting Officer was Colonel Roney. who was accompanied by Colonel Laurie, Commanding the Galloway Rifles and Captain Munro, Adjutant.

Captain Guthrie put the Company through their manual exercises and Ensign Taylor, through the Platoon, of which exercises, the Company acquitted themselves in a very creditable manner. Company drill was then gone through under the command of Captain Guthrie, in an efficient and satisfactory manner, the Corps fully maintaining their previous position of discipline. On the whole the Inspection was quite up to mark, the Company receiving the commendations of the Inspecting officer. Colonel Roney was however, to recommend the Officers to attend well to their duties and learn a clear, quick and sharp word of command, to which alone the men might move more steadily. He also recommended the habit of saluting Officers when passing them, should be adopted, nothing being more soldier-like. For his part he felt aggrieved when a Volunteer passed him without saluting and rather than allow him to pass he would salute himself. Colonel Roney further recommended the Volunteer to attend steadily to drill in the winter months, instead of having merely a 'bout' of drilling, now and again, when an Inspection was expected, and thus becoming confident, instead of a feeling of dread of coming under the notice of a sharp Inspecting officer.

Further to ensure a high standard of efficiency, each Corps was subject to an Adjutant's drill and inspection on a fairly regular basis and if found to be lacking in that requirement the Adjutant could order additional drills, as was the case, on the 15th June, 1866, when the 1st Kirkcudbrightshire Rifle Volunteers, Kirkcudbright, were ordered by Captain Hamilton, to attend, every night for a week of intensive drill, by their Captain and Adjutant Munro, in order that the efficiency of the Corps might be improved. Captain Hamilton was to address his men in the hope that they would forego cricket and bowling for the week. On the first evening there was a good attendance at Adjutant's drill, but on the second evening, three members of the Corps were found at cricket on the next field. The men refused, on being summoned to come to drill, and they were there and then, in front of the Company, dismissed from the Corps and their names expunged. The following week the 2nd Kirkcudbrightshire Rifles, Castle Douglas, were to be subjected to a weeks' intensive drill by Adjutant Munro, with an Editorial in the *Advertiser* warning their members to be on their guard.

****

In April, 1871, the members of the 2nd Kirkcudbrightshire Rifles, Castle Douglas, were ordered to attend Adjutant's drill, every Wednesday and Friday, in order to improve the proficiency of the Corps.

****

A full Battalion drill was held at the Race Green, Kirroughtree, Newton Stewart, on the 8th October, 1864. with the following being present:-
Colonel Roney - Inspecting Officer.
Earl of Selkirk, Lord Lieutenant of the Stewartry.
Lord Garlies: Sir William Dunbar M.P; Mr Dunbar; Hon, Mr. Rollo; Sheriff and Mrs. Rhind; Mr. Snowdon Henry, Kirroughtree; Lieutenant Colonel Laurie, Woodhall:; Captain Du Barre Cunninghame, 2nd Life Guards, of Hensol; Captain Clark of Dunmuir; Mr. McMillan, Factor for the Earl of Galloway; Henry Stuart Esq., of Corsbie West; Mrs. Stopford-Blair of Penninghame House and party; together with a large gathering of Ladies and Gentlemen from the Town.
The parade state was as follows:-

1st Kirkcudbright -	46 rank and file and non-commissioned officers, Captain Hamilton and Ensign Craig.
2nd Castle Douglas -	89 rank and file, Captain Mackie, M.P. and Ensign Renny.
3rd New Galloway -	44 rank and file. Captain Maxwell and Ensign Dalziel.
4th Gatehouse -	20 rank and file. Corporal Gibson.
5th Maxwellton -	98 rank and file. Captain Howat; Lieutenants Allan and Howat.

Total 297 rank and file and 9 Officers.

1st Wigtown -	33 rank and file. Lieutenant Vans Agnew.
2nd Stranraer -	89 rank and file. Captain Guthrie; Lieutenant Taylor; Ensign Andrews.
3rd Newton Stewart -	70 rank and file. Lieutenant Picken and Ensign Stroyan.
4th Whithorn -	21 rank and file. Ensign Drew.
5th Drummore -	20 rank and file. Lieutenant Watson.

Total 233 rank and file and 9 officers.

Total of 548 of all ranks on parade.

A Battalion drill of the Galloway Battalion of Rifle Volunteers was held at Barnkirk, Newton Stewart. owned by Lieutenant Picken, on 1st October, 1865.

The Parade state was as follows:-

1st Kirkcudbright -	4 Sergeants. 41 rank and file. 22 absent with leave. 8 absent without leave. Captain Hamilton and Ensign Craig.
2nd Castle Douglas -	7 Sergeants. 64 rank and file. Captain Mackie M.P. and Ensign Renny.
3rd New Galloway -	3 Sergeants. 51 rank and file. Captain Maxwell and Ensign Dalziel.
4th Gatehouse -	Sergeant Cairns. 19 rank and file.
5th Maxwellton -	9 Sergeants. 94 rank and file. Captain Howat and Ensign Starke.
1st Wigtown -	2 Sergeants. 25 rank and file. Lieutenant Agnew and Ensign McHaffie.
2nd Stranraer -	4 Sergeants. 48 rank and file. Captain Guthrie and Lieutenant Taylor.
3rd Newton Stewart -	10 Sergeants. 60 rank and file. Captain Stewart and Lieutenant Picken.
4th Whithorn -	2 Sergeants. 13 rank and file. No officer.
5th Drummore -	No record.

****

The annual drill and inspection of the Galloway Battalion took place at Barnkirk, Newton Stewart, on 22nd September, 1866, under Colonel Erskine. Inspector General of Volunteers in Great Britain. There was a total parade strength of 447 of all ranks.

****

On the 22nd March, 1867, Captain Mackie, 2nd Kirkcudbrightshire Rifle Volunteers, Castle Douglas, on addressing 16 new members of the Dalbeattie Section was to say, "It was important that they should attend the requisite number of drills, as the public in general, had no idea how large the sums of money that Captains and other Officers of Volunteers had to supply from their private purses to keep matters straight. He trusted they would be diligent in their attendance at drill so that they might pass as efficient and be entitled to a capitation grant of 30/- each."

With the requirement of 6 Battalion drills, per year, in the case of a Consolidated Battalion and 3 in the case of an Administrative Battalion to earn the capitation grant. Wing Battalion drills were introduced. which comprised of the minimum requirements for the attendance of Battalion drills, a minimum of four Companies, parading a minimum strength of all ranks of 128, thus designed to accommodate the Volunteer in his attendance at Battalion drill and thereby fulfill his obligations to earn the Government grant.

The Wigtownshire Companies of the Galloway Administrative Battalion, 1st to 5th, to the number of 200, assembled at Newton Stewart, on the 30th June, 1866, for Wing drill, under Captain and Adjutant Munro.

****

On the 12th June, 1869 a Wing drill of the Kirkcudbrightshire Companies of the Galloway Administrative Battalion of Rifle Volunteers, met at Castle Douglas. No recorded parade strength.

****

It was in the October of this year, 1869, that Ensign Taylor, 2nd Wigtownshire Rifle Volunteers, Stranraer, together with other fellow Volunteer officers from throughout the United Kingdom, travelled to Belgium to extol the virtues of the Volunteer Movement. On his return to Ostend, from Brussels, on the 5th October, he, along with another three Volunteers, chartered a carriage, from the railway to the boat. There was a race among the various Flymen (Drivers) to get to the boat first. The driver of Ensign Taylor's coach, who was drunk, instead of driving along the Quay, drove over the side into the harbour basin. The workers on the Lugger boats nearby swam to their aid and succeeded in dragging the four men and the driver to safety. Ensign Taylor was removed to hospital and remained there that and the whole of the next day, suffering from severe bruising to the head, but happily he was thereafter to continue his journey home.

To further encourage the Volunteer in their drill, cash prizes were offered by the Company officers, for best attendance at drill during the season. In December, 1871, the cash prizes were reported as 1st £1; 2nd 12/6d; 3rd 7/6d, a substantial sum of money in those days.

At the conclusion of Brigade drill in Dumfries on the 13th July, 1878, to further encourage the Volunteers of the other Companies in their drill attendance, Captain Craig, Kirkcudbright, presented cash prizes to members of his Company for best attendance at drill. Each of the successful competitors had attended all drills, both Company and Battalion: -

1st equal, - Sergeant D. M. Farrell; Corporal A. Rain; Private P. Collins; Lance Corporal J. Green; Private R.Livingstone; Private J. Osborne; Corporal W. Phillips, (Bandmaster); Private S. Stevenson; Private A. Walker; Private W. Ramage.
Gatehouse Section, - Private J. McDill.
2nd Equal, - Lance Corporal J. Campbell; Private J. Kirkpatrick; Private Hannay.

Cash prizes were also to be offered to members who introduced the most recruits, together with bounties being paid. by the officers, for each recruit enrolled.

On the 12th May, 1899, Private Neil McDonald, 'H' Company, Dalbeattie, was presented with a silver badge for having brought in the largest number of recruits in a season.

****

With the vast Majority of the members of the Galloway Rifle Volunteers coming from a working class background, and many of its members being employed on the land, the summer drill months were to be their busiest time of the year and in consequence many of its members were to experience difficulty in fulfilling their commitment to Battalion or Wing drill. To alleviate this problem special drills were called, usually towards the end of the Volunteer Season, to allow the members to attend the necessary drills and thus earn the full capitation grant for their Company.

On Saturday, 2nd September, 1882, a drill took place for the special benefit of those members of the Battalion, who had not made themselves 'efficient.' The officers present were: Captain and Adjutant Bovill; Captain Lennox:; Lieutenant Phyn and Chaplain, the Reverend Wm. Graham, Maxwellton, together with a full muster of the Maxwellton Companies, and Captain Taylor and Lieutenant Garrick, Stranraer.

****

An Inspection and Battalion drill of the Galloway Battalion of Rifle Volunteers took place at Newton Stewart on Saturday, 6th August, 1870, by Colonel Gordon, Assistant-General of Reserve Forces.
The Parade state was as follows:-

1st Kirkcudbright -	Captain Craig; Lieutenant McLellan.
2nd Castle Douglas -	Captain Skirving (joined as a Private in 1860, and has now risen to Captain in place of Captain Mackie, M.P. who died); Ensign Crosbie.
3rd New Galloway -	Captain Maitland; Lieutenant J.M. Kennedy.
5th Maxwellton -	Captain Howat:; Lieutenant Rennie; Ensign Harkness.
6th Dalbeattie -	Captain Grieve; Lieutenant Burnie; Ensign Maxwell.
1st Wigtown -	Lieutenant R. Vans Agnew; Ensign McHaffie.
2nd Stranraer -	Captain Taylor; Lieutenant Millar.
3rd Newton Stewart -	Captain Stroyan; Lieutenant Picken.
4th Whithorn -	Lieutenant Stewart; Ensign Hughan.

	Officers.	Sergeants.	Band.	Rank & File.	Total.
1st Kirkcudbright	2	3	-	54	59
2nd Castle Douglas	2	4	-	50	56
3rd New Galloway	2	4	-	48	54
5th Maxwellton	4	6	32	70	112
6th Dalbeattie	3	5	-	70	78
1st Wigtown	2	2	-	30	34
2nd Stranraer	2	4	20	50	76
3rd Newton Stewart	4	6	16	64	90
4th Whithorn	2	2	-	41	45

The Companies were put through their drill exercises by Colonel Laurie and the manual and platoon exercises by Captain and Adjutant Munro, followed by the Skirmishing and Volley firing. Colonel Gordon was to express his satisfaction as to the appearance of the men and the manner in which their exercises were executed, however, he observed that there was far too much talking in the ranks, otherwise he would be submitting a favourable report.

****

From its inception the Galloway Battalion of Rifle Volunteers formed within the 'James Regimental District', as did the Scottish Borderers Militia and the Dumfriesshire Battalion of Rifle Volunteers. However, the Volunteers were not subject to Martial Law, excepting when called to Active Service, and therefore could not be permitted to Brigade with the Militia who were, unlike the Volunteers, subject to the Mutiny Acts. Under the Regulation of the Forces Act, 1871, the scope of the Mutiny Act was enlarged to embrace the Volunteers and make them subject to Martial Law when in training with the Militia or the Regular Army, later to encompass, whilst in training or attending Brigade camps. With both Volunteers and Militia now subject to Martial Law, the Galloway Battalion was to Brigade yearly with the Scottish Borderers Militia and the Dumfriesshire Battalion of Rifle Volunteers, on the final day of the Militias annual embodiment for training, at Hannahfield, Kingholm Merse, Dumfries. Interestingly, it appears that although the riflemen could now Brigade with the Militia, they were unable to drill with their comrades of the Artillery Volunteers.

On Saturday, 4th July, 1876, a Wing drill of the 1st (Kirkcudbright), 2nd (Castle Douglas), 3rd (New Galloway), 6th (Dalbeattie), Kirkcudbrightshire Rifle Volunteers, took place at Kirkcudbright. They were joined in the parade field by the members of the 1st Kirkcudbright Artillery Volunteers under Captain Shand. The officers of the Rifle Volunteers pointed out that under a War Office circular the Rifle Volunteers were disallowed from drilling with the Artillery Volunteers. The Artillery Volunteers were very upset at the petty-mindedness of the Rifle officers and left the field, returning to their battery.

****

On the 22nd July, 1876, a Brigade Field Day of the Scottish Borderers Militia was held on the Kingholm Merse. The Dumfriesshire Volunteers were represented by all their Corps, the Galloways being represented by the 1st, 2nd, 5th and 6th Kirkcudbrightshire Companies only. The Dumfriesshire Battalion wore their new uniforms of bright scarlet tunics and 'Busby' hats.

The Galloway Rifle Volunteers were to continue to Brigade annually with the Scottish Borderers Militia until May, 1887, when the Scottish Borderers Militia and the Dumfriesshire Rifle Volunteers, were removed from the 21st to the 25th Regimental District. In August, 1888, however, all Volunteer Corps were to become part of a Brigade, the Galloways forming as part of the South of Scotland Volunteer brigade, which comprised the Volunteer Battalions of Galloway, Roxburgh, Selkirk, Berwick, Dumfriesshire and the two Highland Regiments of the Black Watch.

****

The following Regimental Orders were issued by Colonel John Gordon Maitland, Officer Commanding the Galloway Rifle Volunteers:-

Newton Stewart, 22nd May, 1872.

"Colonel Gordon, C.B. Assistant Adjutant-General at Glasgow will inspect the Battalion, by separate Corps, as follows, commencing on Monday, 5th August:

> 1st Kirkcudbright Rifle Volunteers, at Kirkcudbright, at 6pm on the 5th August.
> 2nd Kirkcudbright Rifle Volunteers, at Castle Douglas, at 8pm on the 5th August.
> 3rd Kirkcudbright Rifle Volunteers, at New Galloway, at 7.30pm on the 6th August.
> 1st and 4th Wigtownshire Rifle Volunteers, at Wigtown, at 4.30pm on the 7th August.
> 3rd Wigtownshire Rifle Volunteers, at Newton Stewart, at 7.30pm on the 7th August.
> 2nd Wigtownshire Rifle Volunteers, at Stranraer, at 1.30pm on the 8th August.
> 6th Kirkcudbright Rifle Volunteers, at Dalbeattie, at 6.30pm on the 8th August.
> 5th Kirkcudbright Rifle Volunteers, at Maxwellton, at 6pm on the 9th August.

The Assistant Adjutant-General will visit the Armouries and inspect the Corps' books, either before or after the parade, on the days on which he arrives at each station.

The Lieutenant Colonel trusts that every effort will be made by the officers in command of each Corps to procure as good musters as possible at their respective inspection and that the arms and accoutrements will be in the best possible order.

By Order,   D. C. Singleton. Adjutant, Galloway Rifle Volunteers."

There was an Adjutant's drill and inspection of the Whithorn Company of the Rifle Volunteers, on the evenings of Monday, 5th and Tuesday, 6th June, 1873, by Adjutant Singleton. There was a good muster of the Corps, who continued to prosper both numerically and financially.

* * * *

In consequence of a report of 'The Localisation Committee of 1872' by General Regulations and Instructions dated 24th July, 1873, the Volunteer Force was to be closer linked with the Militia and the Regular Army.

The United Kingdom was to be drawn into 70 Infantry Sub-Districts and for recruiting purposes each Sub-District was to be given, two Line Battalions; two Militia Battalions; and the Volunteer Units from that area. Of the two Line Battalions, generally one was stationed abroad and the other at home, however, two Companies of each were required to be permanently stationed at Sub-District Headquarters, to form the Brigade Depot. The Depot, the Militia and the Volunteer Battalions, together with the Army Reserve, were to form the Sub-district Brigade, and become subject to the command of the Lieutenant-Colonel Commanding the Sub-District Brigade, who himself was to become responsible for the training and inspection of the Territorial Forces, which was to include the Volunteers.

The Infantry Sub-district of the North British District, which encompassed the Counties of Ayr, Wigtown, Kirkcudbright, Dumfries, Selkirk and Roxburgh, was numbered '61', with its Depot at Ayr.

Regular Battalion -21st Foot (2 Battalions)

Militia - Scottish Borderers and Prince Regent's Royal Regiment of Ayr and Wigtown Militia.

Volunteers - 1st Administrative Battalion Roxburgh and Selkirk; 1st and 2nd Administrative Battalions, Ayr; 1st Administrative Battalion Dumfries, and 1st Administrative Battalion Galloway.

By this Order the 'James Regimental District' ceased to exist and for the first time the Galloway Battalion of Rifle Volunteers was to come under the direct control and influence of a Line Regiment.

* * * *

A Wing drill of the Galloway Rifle Volunteers was held at Castle Douglas, on 19th July, 1873. Only Stewartry members of the Corps were present.

The Parade state was as follows:-

Lieutenant Colonel Maitland, Commanding; Captain Singleton, Adjutant; Captain Craig and Lieutenant McLellan, Kirkcudbright; Lieutenant McGuffog; Ensign Gordon, Castle Douglas; Acting Major Rennie; Captain Barrie; Lieutenants Finlay and Smith, Maxwellton; Captain Grieve; Ensign McKercher, Dalbeattie.

	Officers	Sergeants	Buglers	Rank & File.	Total.
1st Kirkcudbright	2	3	1	27	33
2nd Castle Douglas	2	5	2	34	43
5th Maxwellton	4	9	2	86	101
6th Dalbeattie	2	3	1	34	40

* * * *

On the 12th September, 1873, Colonel Macbean, Commanding the 61st Sub-District, inspected the Galloway Battalion for the first time and issued a scathing Battalion Order, criticising both the dress and the drill of the Volunteers and the ability of their Company officers in their handling of their men whilst at drill and once again, the age old problem of talking in the ranks.

The following remarks were written by an Acting Adjutant of a Sheffield Volunteer Corps, "the talking in the ranks is I fear a general failing with Volunteers but I always try to stop it as they cannot attend to words of command or instruction." Colonel Macbean was to conclude his remarks however by saying that it was satisfactory to find so many officers had presented themselves for examination and with regards to the men it was evident that they were actuated by the best possible spirit. The attendance at the inspection was most satisfactory. The individual bearing was excellent and their arms were clean and in good order.

* * * *

On Saturday, 18th October, 1873, the closing drill of the season of the Galloway Rifle Volunteers, took place in a field near to the railway station at Castle Douglas, under the command of Lieutenant Colonel Maitland and Captain Singleton, Adjutant.

The Parade state was as follows:-

	Officers	Sergeants	Buglers	Rank & File	Total
1st Kirkcudbright	2	1	1	15	19
2nd Castle Douglas	3	4	2	42	51
3rd New Galloway	1	3	-	21	25
5th Maxwellton	4	6	2	69	81
6th Dalbeattie	1	-	-	37	38
2nd Stranraer	-	2	1	14	17
4th Whithorn	2	2	-	10	14

Total - 245.

The Volunteer returns for year ended 31st October, 1873, were shown as: -

1st Kirkcudbright Rifle Volunteers	Kirkcudbright. 77 efficient; 11 non efficient -	total 88
2nd	Castle Douglas. 88 efficient; 2 non efficient -	total 90
3rd	New Galloway. 59 efficient; 9 non efficient -	total 68
5th	1st Battalion, Maxwellton. 93 efficient; 6 non efficients -	total 99
	2nd Battalion, Maxwellton. 92 efficients; 5 non efficients -	total 97
6th	Dalbeattie. 80 efficients - 8 non efficients. -	total 88

The Volunteer returns for Wigtownshire for year ended 31st October, 1873, were not to be reported singly:

Wigtownshire - enrolled 488. Efficient 324. Non-efficient 64.

* * * *

On Saturday, 16th May, 1874, there was a muster of the 2nd Wigtownshire Rifle Volunteers, Stranraer, and the 3rd Wigtownshire Rifle Volunteers, Newton Stewart, for the first drill of the season and inspection. Staff Officers present, Lieutenant Colonel Maitland, Commanding, Major Renny, Captain Singleton, Adjutant. The Stranraer Corps were represented by Captain Taylor and Lieutenant Kerr, four Sergeants, and 48 rank and file. Newton Stewart Corps were represented by Captain Picken, Lieutenant Agnew, 7 Sergeants and 59 rank and file.

* * * *

The annual inspection of the Galloway Battalion of Rifle Volunteers took place in a field of Torrs Farm, Castle Douglas, on Saturday, 10th October, 1874. In previous years the inspection had taken place at Newton Stewart but it was felt that Castle Douglas was more central for the greater majority of the Volunteers, who lived in the Stewartry.

The parade was ordered at 2pm after which time one line was formed and Colonel Macbean, Inspecting Officer and Officer Commanding the 61st Sub-District took the field and received the general salute. The Battalion was afterwards broken into column to the right and marched past in Company distance and in quarter column and on again being formed into line the manual and firing exercises were gone through, with Major Renny in command, column was again formed and each Company was severally inspected by Colonel Macbean. Other Battalion movements were gone through under the command of Lieutenant Colonel Maitland, assisted by Adjutant Singleton. Skirmishing was then proceeded with by two Companies going forward to skirmish, two others remaining in support and the remainder forming the reserve. After several advances and retirals, the ensemble was sounded and on the Column being formed, Colonel Macbean, in a few remarks expressed himself highly satisfied with the way the Battalion had worked. The Battalion had a very fine appearance, all the Companies being handsomely dressed, in fact he had never seen a finer body of men. He still, however, had to complain of the habit of talking in the ranks which he hoped would be given up, otherwise he was well satisfied with the efficiency of the Battalion.

The Parade state was as follows:

lst K.R.V.	Captain Craig, Lieutenant McLellan
2nd K.R.V.	Captain Skirving, Lieutenants McGuffog and Gordon.
3rd K.R.V.	Lieutenants Millman and Craig.
5th K.R.V.	Captains Rennie and Barrie, Lieutenants Smith and McGowan.
6th K.R.V.	Captain Grieve, Lieutenants Maxwell and Kerr.
2nd W.R.V.	Captain Taylor and Lieutenant Kerr.
3rd W.R.V.	Captain Picken, Lieutenant Agnew.

	Offrs.	Sgts.	Buglers.	Band.	Rank& File.	Total
1st K.R.V. (Kirkcudbright)	2	4	2	0	55	63
2nd K.R.V. (Castle Douglas)	3	5	2	3	61	74
3rd K.R.V. (New Galloway)	2	6	0	0	48	56
5th K.R.V. (Maxwellton)	4	10	0	10	111	135
6th K.R.V. (Dalbeattie)	3	5	2	2	60	72
2nd W.R.V. (Stranaer)	2	5	2	2	39	50
3rd W.R.V. (Newton Stewart)	2	6	2	0	50	60

Total - 510

After having taken the field for three hours, the Companies were marched from the field. The 2nd Kirkcudbright Rifles, Castle Douglas were, however, retained, in order to allow Colonel Macbean the opportunity of testing the capabilities, in Company drill of, Lieutenant William Kerr, 6th; Lieutenant McGowan, 5th; Lieutenant Kerr, 2nd. Earlier that week they had each undergone a four hour oral and written examination by Colonel Macbean. The three Officers passed and received their certificates of Proficiency thereby gaining an additional grant of 50/- for their Company.

* * * *

On the 16th May, 1875, at a Wing drill in Castle Douglas, Adjutant Singleton was to make the following remarks regarding the age old Volunteer problem of talking in the ranks, "I wish also to draw most particular attention to the constant talking in the ranks. Every Inspecting Officer, ever since I had the honour to belong to the Battalion has complained of this. We constantly hear it stated in this Country, that the superior intelligence of the Volunteer should make up for want of discipline or drill. If there be the slightest foundation for this statement surely I may appeal to you, Volunteers of Galloway, to retain silence whilst on parade, for perhaps not much more than one hour."

* * * *

On the afternoon of 7th July, 1875, the 2nd Wigtownshire Rifle Volunteers, Stranraer, were inspected on the Academy Green, Stranraer, by Colonel McBean, who was accompanied by Colonel Maitland, Commanding the Galloway Battalion, and Captain Singleton, Adjutant. Colonel McBean also inspected the Armoury and the accounts of the Corps.

The parade state was:-

Captain Taylor, in Command, Lieutenant Taylor, with 65 other ranks. The full Company strength was 76.

On the evening of the 7th July, 1875, Colonel McBean, together with the other staff officers, inspected the 3rd Wigtownshire Rifle Volunteers, in the Market Field, Newton Stewart. There were 52 of all ranks on parade. The total strength of the Company was, 2 officers; 6 Sergeants; 2 buglers; 10 bandsmen; 60 rank and file.

* * * *

A Wing drill was held at Castle Douglas, on Saturday, 3rd October, 1875, between the 2nd, 3rd, 6th Kirkcudbrightshire Rifle Volunteers and the 2nd, and 3rd, Wigtownshire Rifle Volunteers. There were 154 present on parade. The staff officers present were, Colonel Maitland, Major Renny, Captain and Adjutant Singleton.

A further Wing drill was held in Dalbeattie, on the 10th October, 1875, between the 1st, 5th and 6th Kirkcudbrightshire Rifle Volunteers.

* * * *

On the afternoon of Saturday, 26th August, 1876, the Inspection of the Galloway Battalion of Rifle Volunteers, was made at Castle Douglas, by Colonel McBean, Her Majesty's Inspector of the 61st Sub-District. The Battalion was Commanded by Lieutenant-Colonel Gordon Maitland, the other staff officers present being, Major Renny, Captain and Adjutant Singleton and Quartermaster Harper.

The officers in charge of the Companies were:

1st K.R.V (Kirkcudbright) - Captain Craig, Lieutenant McLellan, and Assistant Surgeon Johnstone.
2nd K.R.V. (Castle Douglas) - Captain Gordon, Lieutenant McGuffog.
3rd K.R.V. (New Galloway) - Captain Kennedy, Lieutenant's Millman and Craig.
5th K.R.V. (Maxwellton) - Captains Barrie and Smith.
6th K.R.V. (Dalbeattie) - Lieutenants Maxwell and Kerr.
2nd W.R.V. (Stranraer) - Lieutenant Kerr.
3rd W.R.V. (Newton Stewart) - Captain Picken, Lieutenant Agnew.

	Officers.	Sgts.	Band & Buglers.	Rank & File.	Total.
1st K.R.V. (Kirkcudbright)	3	5	2	55	65
2nd K.R.V. (Castle Douglas)	2	6	5	46	59
3rd K.R.V. (New Galloway)	3	6	0	39	48
5th K.R.V. (Maxwellton)	2	10	20	116	148
6th K.R.V. (Dalbeattie)	2	6	4	52	64
2nd W.R.V. (Stranraer)	1	4	2	58	65
3rd W.R.V. (Newton Stewart)	2	5	2	58	67
	----	----	----	----	----
	15	42	35	424	516

Staff - 4

Total of all Ranks - 520.

At the conclusion of the inspection, Colonel McBean briefly addressed the regiment, expressing himself highly satisfied with the various movements. They had drilled very well that day, though occasionally there was a little unsteadiness in the ranks, but that was no doubt owing to the few opportunities they had of attending Battalion drill. Some of the Companies were rather weak-on Company. Having only one more than the requisite two-thirds, others having four, but that was no doubt owing to the number of men being engaged in the harvest. It was necessary, however, for each Company to have two-thirds of its enrolled strength on parade, or they would be required to be inspected over again, or else lose the capitation grant. There was now a uniformity in the clothing of the Battalion and they were a remarkably fine body of men. He would have much pleasure in reporting favourably of their appearance.

* * * *

The annual inspection of the Galloway Battalion of Rifle Volunteers, took place in a field near to the railway station, Castle Douglas. on Saturday, 4th August, 1877. The Companies paraded at 2pm and were put through various drills by Major Renny. At 3pm Colonel McBean, Her Majesty's Inspector of the 61st Sub-District, arrived with Colonel Maitland, who then put them through a variety of field movements. Colonel McBean expressed himself highly satisfied with their appearance and drill manoeuvres but once again he was extremely critical of the Volunteers constant talking whilst on parade. He was now pleased to see that the men were getting into the habit of saluting their officers. On previous occasions he himself had not been saluted but if he had stopped to correct each and every soldier it would have taken all day. They should remember that it is not the man they are saluting but the Queen's Commission.

The Parade State was as follows:

	Offrs.	Surgeons.	Sgts.	Band & Buglers.	Rank & File.	Total.
Field Officers and Staff	5	-	7	-	-	12
1st K.R.V. (Kirkcudbright)	3	1	4	2	58	68
2nd K.R.V. (Castle Douglas)	1	1	6	3	63	74
3rd K.R.V. (New Galloway)	2	-	6	-	47	55
5th K.R.V. (Maxwellton)	3	1	9	19	122	154
6th K.R.V. (Dalbeattie)	2	-	6	5	74	87
2nd W.R.V. (Stranraer)	2	-	3	-	50	55
3rd W.R.V. (Newton Stewart)	1	-	4	2	50	57

Total of all ranks - 562

On the 11th May, 1878, the first Battalion drill of the season was held in Castle Douglas.

* * * *

On the 15th June, 1878, a Wing drill of the Galloway Battalion of Rifle Volunteers was held in Kirkcudbright.

* * * *

On Saturday, 10th May, 1879, the first Wing drill of the season was held in Castle Douglas, those Companies present being the 2nd (Castle Douglas), 3rd (New Galloway), 2nd (Stranraer), 3rd (Newton Stewart).

There was a total of 209 all ranks on parade.

* * * *

On the 21st June, 1879, a Battalion drill of the Galloway Rifle Volunteers was held in Kirkcudbright, those present being, 1st, 2nd, 3rd, 5th Kirkcudbrightshire Rifle Volunteers, and the 2nd and 3rd Wigtownshire Rifle Volunteers.

Total of all ranks on parade including Staff - 346.

* * * *

On Saturday, 5th July, 1879, a Wing drill was held at Maxwellton, with the 1st, 2nd 5th and 6th Kirkcudbrightshire Rifle Volunteers and the 2nd and 3rd Wigtownshire Rifle Volunteers, being present.

* * * *

On Saturday, 18th July, 1879, a Brigade Drill was held at Kingholm Merse, between the Dumfriesshire Battalion of Rifle Volunteers and the Galloway Battalion of Rifle Volunteers. The Scottish Borderers Militia were excluded from this drill owing to their short training season.

* * * *

On Saturday, 9th August, 1879, the Galloway Battalion of Rifle Volunteers was inspected in a field at Airds Farm, Castle Douglas, by Lieutenant-Colonel Leech of the 50th Regiment. Staff officers present, Lieutenant-Colonel Maitland; Major J. M. Kennedy. Captain and Adjutant Farrer; Quartermaster Harper.

1st K.R.V. (Kirkcudbright) - Captain Craig, Lieutenant McLellan, and 76 of other ranks.
2nd K.R.V. (Castle Douglas) - Lieutenant Moffat. 64 of other ranks.
3rd K.R.V. (New Galloway) - Captain Millman, Lieutenant Craig, Lieutenant Dalziel. 60 other ranks.
5th K.R.V. (Maxwellton) - Captains Lennox and Symons. 151 of other ranks.
6th K.R.V. (Dalbeattie) - Captain Maxwell, Lieutenant Kerr. 83 of other ranks.
2nd W.R.V, (Stranraer) - Captain Picken, Lieutenant Agnew. 56 of other ranks.
3rd W.R.V. (Newton Stewart) - Captain Taylor, Lieutenant Anderson. 82 of other ranks.

Total of all ranks on parade - 598.

* * * *

On Saturday, 22nd May, 1880, a Wing drill was held at Castle Douglas, between the 1st, 2nd, 3rd Kirkcudbrightshire Rifle Volunteers and the 2nd and 3rd Wigtownshire Rifle Volunteers. There was a total of 256 of all ranks on parade.

* * * *

On Saturday, 29th May, 1880, there was a Wing drill of the Galloway Battalion of Rifle Volunteers, on the Cannee Home Farm, Kirkcudbright, between the 1st, 5th, 6th Kirkcudbrightshire Rifle Volunteers. There were only 67 of all ranks on parade.

* * * *

On Saturday, 19th June, 1880, a Wing drill of the Galloway Rifles was held in Dalbeattie, between the 1st, 2nd, 5th and 6th Kirkcudbrightshire Rifle Volunteers. There was a total of 287 of all ranks on parade.

* * * *

On Saturday, 26th June, 1880, there was a Wing drill of the Galloway Battalion of Rifle Volunteers, held at Newton Stewart, between the 2nd and 3rd Wigtownshire Rifle Volunteers, (Stranraer), (Newton Stewart) and the 3rd Kirkcudbrightshire Rifle Volunteers, (New Galloway). There was a total of 214 of all ranks on parade.

The annual inspection of the Galloway Battalion of Rifle Volunteers took place on Saturday, 24th July, 1880, at Airds Farm, Castle Douglas. The Inspecting officer was Colonel Herbert of the 61st Sub-District.

Staff Officers - Colonel Maitland, Commanding; Major Maxwell; Captain and Adjutant Farrer; Quartermaster M.M. Harper.

Company Officers -

        1st K.R.V. (Kirkcudbright) -   Captain Craig; Lieutenants McLellan and Muir.

        2nd K.R.V. (Castle Douglas) - Lieutenant McKie.

(It had been reported on numerous occasions that the gentlemen from Castle Douglas, were not coming forward to fill the vacancies of officers in this Company. The same problem led to the disbanding of the 4th (Gatehouse) Rifle Volunteers.

Note. Eventually Castle Douglas were to finish up with no officers but Quartermaster M.M. Harper, a staff officer (Bank Manager of the British Linen Bank, Castle Douglas) was to assume the duties of Commanding Officer until suitable gentlemen were to come forward.)

        3rd K.R.V. (New Galloway) -   Lieutenants Craig and Dalziel,.

        5th K.R.V. (Maxwellton) -   Captain Lennox and Symons.

        6th K.R.V. (Dalbeattie) -   Lieutenant Kerr.

        2nd W.R.V. (Stranraer) -   Captain Taylor; Lieutenant Garrick.

        3rd W.R.V. (Newton Stewart) -   Captain Picken; Lieutenant Agnew.

The Parade State was as follows:

	Officers.	Sgts.	Buglers & Band.	Rank & File.	Total.
1st K.RV. (Kirkcudbright)	3	5	2	65	75
2nd K.R.V. (Castle Douglas)	1	6	2	48	57
3rd K.R.V. (New Galloway)	2	6	-	47	55
5th K.R.V. (Maxwellton)	2	13	21	115	151
6th K.R.V. (Dalbeattie)	1	7	-	60	68
2nd W.R.V. (Stranraer)	2	6	2	79	89
3rd W.R.V. (Newton Stewart)	2	6	2	68	78

Total - 573

Total strength of Regiment 705

In 1879, a Committee was appointed by the War Office to report on the efficiency and organisation of the Volunteer Force. This report, released in December, 1879, was to recognise the growth of the Volunteer Movement from 162,935 enrolled members in 1863, to a total of 203,213 enrolled members in 1878. With the Volunteer Movement responding well to calls for increased efficiency by a proportional increase of almost 26% of efficients to enrolled members, between the years 1863 - 1878.

The Committee whilst accepting the efficiency and organisation of the Force in general did not propose any sweeping changes but was to suggest several alterations so as to secure higher efficiency and easier manipulation. The report was to recommend closer links with the auxilliary forces of the Sub-Districts and to the consolidation of the various Administrative Battalions, and thus, while lessening the work of the Department, bringing the Force more under command of a Line Regiment.

When the Volunteer Movement began in 1859, each Corps managed or as was often the case, mis-managed their own funds and affairs and appointed its own officers, with the check approval of the Lord Lieutenant. This popularisation of the Movement had no small effect upon the success which attended the efforts of the promotors and it had the effect of strengthening and consolidating it. By degrees the popular element was eliminated and after the Lord's Lieutenant were deprived of the issue of commissions to the Force, in 1871, and that power kept in the hands of the Government, the qualifications of efficiency were much increased. This gradually extended through all the grades of the Force until 1880, when Government had removed most of the old elements of popularisation and while the Volunteers had been placed more under the command of the Department, they had gained in efficiency. Indeed it was now said that the Force had grown and prospered to such an extent that Government had been forced to acknowledge the importance and benefit of the Force to the country.

This latest exposition of the Department was now the consolidation of the various Battalions throughout the Country. Under the old nomenclature a small county, though attached to another for administrative purposes, never lost its individuality and continued prominantly as it had done before. Under the new system several small counties, from a military aspect were to be blotted from the map. In relation to the Rifle Volunteers - Bute was to be swallowed up in Renfrew; Orkney and Caithness into Sutherland; whilst Kirkcudbright and Wigtown were to disappear as two separate entities, into Galloway.

Note. Kirkcudbright and Wigtown had formed as an Administrative Battalion on the 30th June, 1860, and had then assumed the title of the Galloway Administrative Battalion of Rifle Volunteers - "Galloway Rifles". Whilst the title of each Company, relative to its County, Kirkcudbrightshire or Wigtownshire Rifle Volunteers, was to disappear, there was to be no real change in relation to the Galloway Battalion and this change was readily accepted by its members.

These apparently radical changes in the composition of the Force were to come into being on the 26th May, 1880, when the control of the finances were also to pass to the Commanding Officer of the Battalion, but the new designations were not to be finally published by the War Office until the November of 1880.

The Battalion was to be consolidated under the title of the Galloway Rifle Volunteer Corps. The former Administrative Battalion Headquarters, at Newton Stewart, were to be retained, and the eight Companies were re-organised as follows:

'A' Company - Kirkcudbright, late, 1st Kirkcudbright Rifle Volunteers.
'B' Company - Castle Douglas, late, 2nd Kirkcudbright Rifle Volunteers.
'C' Company - Stranraer, late, 2nd Wigtown Rifle Volunteers.
'D' Company - Newton Stewart, late, 3rd Wigtown Rifle Volunteers
'E' Company - New Galloway, late, 3rd Kirkcudbright Rifle Volunteers,
'F' & 'G' Companies - Maxwellton, late, 1st and 2nd Companies of the 5th Kirkcudbright Rifle Volunteers.
'H' Company - Dalbeattie, late, 6th Kirkcudbright Rifle Volunteers.

On the 4th February, 1881, the 5th Kirkcudbrightshire Rifle Volunteers, Maxwellton, took part in their first drill of the season. After drill, as was the custom of the Volunteers, they marched through the streets of Dumfries, headed by their band, and as a result 20 recruits joined the Corps.

* * * *

On the afternoon of Saturday, 28th May, 1881, the first Wing drill of the season was held in a field at Dalbeattie. The mounted Staff Officers present were, Major Kennedy; Major Maxwell; Captain and Adjutant Farrer.

The Company officers present were:

'A' Company, Kirkcudbright - Lieutenant William McLellan; Lieutenant J. Muir;
Act. Surgeon W. Johnston.
'B' Company. Castle Douglas - Quartermaster Harper; Staff Officer Commanding Pro-temp.
(An appeal to the gentlemen of Castle Douglas to come forward and fill the officer vacancies was still outstanding.)
'F' & 'G' Companies - Maxwellton - Captain Lennox; Hon. Chaplain Rev. William Graham.
'H' Company, Dalbeattie - Lieutenant William Kerr; Rev John Mackie M. A.

	Officers.	Sgts.	Buglers.	Rank & File.	Total.
'A' Kirkcudbright	2	4	2	63	71
'B' Castle Douglas	1	1	2	41	48
'F' & 'G' Maxwellton	1	8	4	80	93
'H' Dalbeattie	1	7	2	73	83

Staff Officers and Sergeants - 10

305

* * * *

On the 4th June, 1881, a Wing drill of the Galloway Battalion of Rifle Volunteers, was held in Stranraer. Major J.M. Kennedy was Officer in Command, with Lieutenant-Colonel Maitland absent through illness. Major Maxwell; Captain and Adjutant Farrer - Staff.
Company Officers;

'C' Company, Stranraer - Lieutenant Anderson; Lieutenant Garrick.
'D' Company, Newton Stewart - Captain Picken: Lieutenant Agnew.
'E' Company, New Galloway - Captain Millman; Lieutenants Craig and Dalziel.

	Officers.	Sgts.	Rank & File.	Total.
'C' Stranraer	2	5	85	92
'D' Newton Stewart	2	5	63	70
'E' New Galloway	3	6	58	67
Staff	3	3	-	6

235.

* * * *

In consequence of the report of a committee convened in 1876, under Colonel Stanley, to consider the formation of Territorial Regiments in 1881, the labours of that committee were to reach fruition, with sweeping changes taking place in the formation of the Territorial Districts. The two Line Battalions and the Militia Battalions of the Sub-District Brigade were formed into Territorial Regiments, bearing the name of the Regular Battalion and to be continued as the Regimental District. The Regular Battalion would form as the 1st and 2nd Battalions, with the Militia continuing in numerical sequence, i.e. 3rd. 4th. etc. The Volunteer Battalions were to be numbered in separate order, commencing once again as 1. 2. 3. etc. By General Order 70, on 1st July, 1881, the re-organisation of the Regimental Districts came into force, the 61st Sub-District being re-grouped as a Regiment of the Scottish Infantry

Royal Scots Fusiliers.
Regimental District No. 21 - Ayr.
1st and 2nd Battalions of the 21st Foot .
Scottish Borderers; Prince Regent's Royal Regiment of Ayr and Wigtown Militia.
Volunteers: - 1st Roxburgh and Selkirk; 1st and 2nd Ayr; 1st Dumfries; Galloway Rifles.

In consequence of these new Army Regulations, the Militia were required to adopt the name of the Regiment of the Line, with which they chanced to be linked, the Scottish Borderers Militia became the 3rd Battalion of the 21st Royal Scots Fusiliers and the Prince Regent's Royal Regiment of Ayr and Wigtown Militia, the 4th Battalion of the 21st or Royal Scots Fusiliers.

The Dumfriesshire and Galloway Volunteers were to be designated the 3rd and 4th Volunteer Battalions of the Royal Scots Fusiliers, but owing to influential and widespread pressure from within Galloway, the Galloway Rifles were to remain as one of the Royal Scots Fusiliers allotted Volunteer Battalions but without change in title. This constant struggle to retain the title of the 'Galloway Rifles' was to continue throughout the final life of the Regiment until the demise of the Volunteers in 1908.

By this same General Order of the 1st July, 1881, the King's Own Borderers were to become the Territorial Regiment of Berwick-on-Tweed, Berwick being the Headquarters of the 25th Regimental District, and on the 29th July, 1881, the Depot Companies of the King's Own Borderers moved to Berwick with no Militia nor Volunteer Battalions.

* * * *

On the evening of the 5th October, 1881. an Adjutant's drill was held in Castle Douglas, this was to be the last drill of the season.

* * * *

On the 20th May, 1882, the first Wing drill of the season was held at Dalbeattie. The staff Officers present were Major W. J. Maxwell, in Command; Captain F.H. Bovill, Adjutant; Quartermaster Harper.
Company Officers:-

'A' Company, Kirkcudbright - Captain D. Craig; Lieutenants McLellan and Muir; Surgeon Johnston.
'B' Company, Castle Douglas - No officers.
'F' & 'G' Companies, Maxwellton - Captain J. Lennox: Lieutenant Phyn.
'H' Company. Dalbeattie - Lieutenant William Kerr.

	Officers.	Sgts.	Band.	Rank & File.	Total.
'A' Kirkcudbright	4	2	2	55	63
'B' Castle Douglas	-	4	2	38	44
'F' & 'G' Maxwellton	2	13	4	101	120
'H' Dalbeattie	1	5	19	48	73
				Staff -	7

307

The annual Inspection of the Galloway Rifle Volunteers, took place at Castle Douglas, on the afternoon of Saturday, 30th July, 1882, in a field given for the occasion by Mr. Samuel Moffat. The Inspecting Officer was Colonel Herbert, Commanding the 21st Regimental District, who on entering the field was received with the general salute. The Companies were then subjected to a searching inspection after which the march past took place. This movement was creditably performed especially in quarter column, though owing to the long grass, thistles and rushes which clothed the field, the step was not quite what it would have been. Line was then formed on the rear Company, when Major Kennedy took command and put the Regiment through the manual and firing exercises, the former being done in a manner seldom seen in County Battalions, while the latter, with the exception of one Volley, the success of which was marred by some of the men on the extreme right of the line, firing before the order was given; met with the approbation of the Inspecting Officer. Major Maxwell was thereafter called to Command and exercised the Regiment in a variety of movements. Colonel Maitland resumed command when 'F' Company, under Captain Lennox was sent out in skirmishing order to feel for a supposed enemy, the remainder of the Regiment advancing in line of half Battalion. The extension of 'F' Company was worthy of special notice as being rapidly and correctly executed, the requisite distances being calculated to a nicety, while the men walked with a quiet steadiness. The Regiment was next formed in quarter columns and addressed by the Inspecting Officer.

"Colonel Maitland, officers, non-commissioned officers, and men of the Galloway Rifles. I expected great things of this Battalion after its most admirable conduct at the Royal Review, in Edinbugh last year (The Wet Review of 1881). No Battalion could have done better. No Battalion there was subjected to such a severe test, for none was jammed, as you were in that terrible crowd and no Battalion could have extricated itself and formed up more quickly than you did and I assure you it was with peculiar satisfaction that I saw you in your places and going so steadily on the march past. I have noted today the willing manner in which you have obeyed the commands of your Officers and the clean and tidy appearance you present. Your arms, accoutrements, and clothing are clean and neat, while your hair is cut short, as soldiers wear it. This is very satisfactory to me, for as Volunteers are recruited from the most respectable classes of society, they ought to be, and people expect them to be clean and soldier-like. I have noted with satisfaction the entire absence of that talking which is too frequently observed at Volunteer Parades, and I shall have much pleasure in reporting most favourably on what I have seen today." The men then marched from the field.

The following was the Parade State: -

	Officers.	Sgts.	Band.	Rank & File.	Total.
'A' Kirkcudbright	3	3	2	69	77
'B' Castle Douglas	-	5	2	53	60
'C' Stranraer	2	4	2	69	77
'D' Newton Stewart	1	4	1	56	62
'E' New Galloway	1	6	1	56	64
'F' Maxwellton	3	6	3	64	76
'G' Maxwellton	-	5	15	57	77
'H' Dalbeattie	1	6	2	64	73
Total of all ranks present -					578
Absent with Leave -					94
				Strength of Regiment	672

* * * *

The following Regimental Order was issued by Lieutenant-Colonel Maitland. Officer Commanding the Galloway Rifle Volunteers:-

(1). The Officer Commanding the 21st Regimental District has intimated his intention of inspecting the Battalion at Dumfries on the 14th July, 1883, and of holding a Brigade drill the same day, at which the 3rd Battalion, the Royal Scots Fusiliers (Scottish Borderers Militia), the Galloway Rifle Volunteers and the Dumfriesshire Rifle Volunteers will attend.

(2). The Battalion drills of the season as follows : -

(a) 'A' Kirkcudbright. 'B' Castle Douglas; 'F' & 'G' Maxwellton, and 'H' Dalbeattie, on the 2nd June, 1883. at Dalbeattie.

(b) 'E' New Galloway; 'C' Stranraer; 'D' Newton Stewart, on the 9th June, 1883, at Newton Stewart.

(c) 'B'; 'F'; 'G', and 'H' Companies, on the 23rd June, 1883, at Maxwellton .

(d) 'A', 'B', 'E' and 'H' Companies, on the 30th June, 1883, at Castle Douglas.

At 11.30am on the 14th July, 1883, the Dumfriesshire and the Galloway Battalions of Rifle Volunteers were inspected at their drill field, Palmerston Park. Maxwellton, and at 3.15pm the two Battalions marched to the Kingholm Merse where they took part in a Brigade Drill with the 3rd (Militia) Battalion Royal Scots Fusiliers, under the Command of Colonel Sir George Walker, A.D.C., K.C.B.

* * * *

The following are the list of Battalion drills to be held during the 1884 season:-
31st May, at Maxwellton for 'B'; 'H'; 'F' and 'G' Companies;.
7th June, at Newton Stewart for 'C'; 'D'; and 'E' Companies.
14th June, at Dalbeattie for 'A'; 'B'; 'F'; 'G' and 'H' Companies .
21st June, at Stranraer for 'C' and 'D' Companies.
28th June, at Castle Douglas for 'A'; 'B'; 'H' and 'E' Companies.
The Officer Commanding has instructed his intention of inspecting the Regiment on either the 12th or 19th July, 1884, at Castle Douglas.

* * * *

A Wing drill was held on the 31st May, 1884, in the drill field at Maxwellton, under the command of Major Bovill. Adjutant. 'B'; 'F'; 'G' and 'H' Companies were represented.

* * * *

A Wing drill of the Galloway Rifles took place on Saturday, 7th June, 1884, in a field at Holm Park.
The Officers in Command were Colonel Maitland; Major Kennedy and Major and Adjutant Bovill. The following was the muster:-

'C' Company Stranraer - Major Taylor; Lieutenant Garrick; 6 Sergeants; 1 staff Sergeant; 1 bugler; 70 rank and file.
Total of 78 on parade.
'D' Company Newton Stewart -Lieutenant Agnew; 4 Sergeants; 2 buglers; 9 band; 57 rank and file.
Total of 73 on parade.
'E' Company New Galloway - Lieutenant Craig; 4 Sergeants; 2 Buglers; 58 rank and file.
Total of 63 on parade.

The men were equalised into four Companies, being officered by Major Taylor; Lieutenant Agnew; Lieutenant Craig and Lieutenant Garrick. The Battalion was put through a variety of movements lasting in total 2½ hours.

* * * *

A Battalion drill took place at Dalbeattie on the afternoon of Saturday, 14th June, 1884. Major Kennedy was in command, assisted by Major and Adjutant Bovill. The following officers were on parade:-

'A' Company, Kirkcudbright -   Major Craig. Lieutenants McLellan and Muir, Surgeon Johnstone.
'B' Company. Castle Douglas -   Captain Harper, Lieutenants Dunn and Hewat.
'F' & 'G' Companies, Maxwellton - Captains Lennox, and Phyn.
'H' Company, Dalbeattie -   Captain Kerr. Chaplain Rev. J. Mackie.

Major Kennedy exercised the Battalion in a variety of movements which, considering the uneven state of the ground, were pretty well executed. In the latter part, Major Bovill exercised the Companies in the 'attack' which appeared to be intelligently carried out, though there was a little disposition on the part of the younger members, to treat the final charge, with fixed bayonets, as a huge joke. The Battalion was dismissed at 5.30pm.

The Parade State was as follows:-

	Officers.	Sgts.	Rank & File.	Total.
Staff	2	4	-	6
'A' Company Kirkcudbright	4	5	66	75
'B' Company Castle Douglas	3	5	34	42
'F' & 'G,' Companies, Maxwellton	2	11	98	111
'H' Company, Dalbeattie	2	5	41	48
	---	---	----	-----

At a Wing Drill of 'C' Stranraer and 'D' Newton Stewart, Companies, held at Stranraer, on the 22nd June, 1884, under Major and Adjutant Bovill, 'C' Company had a total of 80 of all ranks on parade, whilst 'D' Company had a total of 65 of all ranks on parade.

* * * *

A Wing Drill Was held at Castle Douglas, on Saturday, 28th June, 1884, for 'A', 'B', 'E', 'F', 'G ', and 'H' Companies, there was a total of 390 of all ranks on parade.

****

On the 19th July, 1884, the annual Inspection of the Galloway Battalion of Rifle Volunteers, took place at Blackpark, Castle Douglas, by Colonel Allan, Commanding the 21st Regimental District. This was the largest turnout ever held, to that date, the total of all ranks being 556, this was only 87 less than the total enrolled strength. Staff Officers were, Colonel Maitland, Commanding the Galloway Rifle Volunteers; Majors Kennedy, Maxwell and Adjutant Bovill.

The Company Officers were as follows:-

'A' Company,	Kirkcudbright -	Major Craig, Lieutenants McLellan and Muir.
'B'	Castle Douglas -	Captain Harper, Lieutenants Hewat and Dunn.
'C'	Stranraer -	Major Taylor, Lieutenant Garrick.
'D'	Newton Stewart -	Lieutenant Agnew.
'E'	New Galloway -	Lieutenant Craig.
'F' & 'G'	Maxwellton -	Captain Phyn
'H'	Dalbeattie -	Captain Kerr.

The parade state was:-

	Officers	Sgts.	Band	Rank & File	Total
'A' Kirkcudbright	3	5	1	60	69
'B' Castle Douglas	3	6	12	48	69
'C' Stranraer	2	5	2	65	74
'D' Newton Stewart	1	4	2	63	70
'E' New Galloway	1	4	1	53	59
'F' & 'G' Maxwellton	1	11	16	128	156
'H' Dalbeattie	1	5	2	40	48
Staff	4	7	-	-	11
	----	----	----	-----	-----
	16	47	36	457	556

****

On the 21st March, 1885, the Galloway Rifle Headquarters, were transferred to Castle Douglas, with its more central location. However in reality, it was often whispered but never said, that the transfer of the Headquarters took place because the vast majority of the Volunteers, who formed the Battalion, lived in the East of Galloway.

On the 27th June, 1885, a Wing Drill of 'C', 'D', and 'E' Companies, took place in a field of Machermore Farm, Newton Stewart.

'C' Company, Stranraer - Major Taylor, Lieutenant Garrick, 5 Sergeants, 2 buglers, 66 rank and file.
Total 75 of all ranks.
'D' Company, Newton Stewart - Captain Thomas Agnew, 5 Sergeants, 2 buglers, 58 rank and file.
Total 75 of all ranks.
'E' Company, New Galloway - Lieutenants Craig and Jamieson, 7 Sergeants, 1 bugler, 40 rank and file.
Total 50 of all ranks.
The Staff Officers were Majors Kennedy and Maxwell. Major Douglas, Adjutant. Total of all ranks on parade - 207

****

A Wing Drill of 'A', 'B', 'F', 'G', and 'H' Companies took place at Dalbeattie on the 4th July, 1885.

****

The annual inspection of the Galloway Battalion of Rifle Volunteers took place on Saturday, 18th July, 1885, in the forenoon, in a field beyond the Naptha Works, Greenbrae, Dumfries. The weather was of the most miserable description, rain falling most of the day, but this had no effect on the turn out, as it was, to that date, the largest muster that had ever taken place, the total of all ranks numbering 619, from a total enrolled strength of 740.

The Officers present were, Major Kennedy in Command, Colonel Maitland having been granted leave by the authorities on a medical certificate. Major Maxwell, Major and Adjutant Douglas, and the following Company Officers:-

'A' Company, Kirkcudbright -	Major Craig, Lieutenant McLellan, Surgeon Johnstone.
'B' Company, Castle Douglas -	Captain Harper, Lieutenant Dunn.
'C' Company, Stranraer -	Major Taylor, Lieutenant Stewart.
'D' Company, Newton Stewart -	Captain Agnew
'E' Company, New Galloway -	Lieutenants Craig and Jamieson.
'F' & 'G' Companies, Maxwellton -	Captain Phyn, Rev. W.V. Graham, Chaplain, Surgeon Lorraine.
'H' Company, Dalbeattie -	Captain Kerr.

The Inspecting Officer, Colonel Allan, Commanding the 21st Regimental District, having previously examined the books of the different Companies at their Armouries, proceeded to the field and was received by the General Salute, after which Colonel Allan rode along the lines. The ranks were then closed and the Battalion broke into column to the right, when the Colonel dismounted and made a careful inspection of all the Companies, except Maxwellton, whom he had previously inspected at their Drill Hall. Major W.J. Maxwell then assumed command and put the Battalion through the manual and firing exercises. The Battalion was then taken in hand by Major Kennedy and under him the men marched past in column and twice in quarter column. A variety of other field movements were gone through when Colonel Allan addressed the men.

The march past in columns, he said was well done, so far as the men were concerned, but the distances were very badly kept, only one Company, the rear one, having anything like enough distance. The saluting by the Officers was generally speaking, bad, and he wished more attention to be paid to this in future. In quarter column the distances were fairly kept, and the dressing was good, and he was also satisfied with the manual and firing exercises.

Owing to the miserable weather which showed no signs of clearing up he ordered the abandonment of the Brigade Drill but said as they were a country Corps they had little opportunity of drilling in large numbers and he would therefore have another drill at 3.30pm, when he would test them further in Battalion movements. The Battalion was dismissed but reconvened at the appointed hour, when Colonel Allan took command himself and put the Battalion through a most constructive drill, at the close of which he referred to the occasional outbursts of talking in the ranks, which he was convinced were mainly caused by the officers and N.C.O's endeavouring to set the men right. Now while this was well meant and quite right at their own Company Drills it was altogether out of place at such a time as a Brigade drill, and he would prefer to see the men left to themselves. Officers he would like to see take advantage of such schools of instruction as Aldershot and Wellington Barracks and he was sure they would feel greatly benefited by attending them. The men were then marched to the Station where they were dismissed. The music for the day was provided by the combined bands of the Castle Douglas and Maxwellton Companies.

The following was the parade state:-

	Officers	Sgts.	Band	Rank&File	Total
Staff	3	7	-	-	10
'A' Company, Kirkcudbright	3	5	1	61	78
'B' Company, Castle Douglas	2	6	14	49	71
'C' Company, Stranraer	2	5	2	66	75
'D' Company, Newton Stewart	1	5	2	77	85
'E' Company, New Galloway	2	5	2	60	69
'F'&'G' Companies, Maxwellton	4	-	24	133	170
'H' Company, Dalbeattie	1	5	2	53	61
	----	----	----	-----	-----
	18	47	47	507	619

There were 119 absent with leave and 2 without leave. There were also on parade, attached by authority, 2 men, one belonging to the 10th Lanarkshire and one to the 1st Northumberland.

On Saturday, 19th June, 1886, a Wing Drill was held in Stranraer between 'C' Company, Stranraer and 'D' Company, Newton Stewart. 'C' Company paraded a total of 68, of all ranks, under Major Taylor and

Lieutenant Stewart. 'D' Company paraded a total of 88 of all ranks under Captain Agnew.

The annual inspection of the Galloway Battalion of Rifle Volunteers took place at Torrs Farm, Castle Douglas, on the 30th July, 1886.

Despite basing the 25th Regimental District Headquarters at Berwick, the King's Own Borderers, who had no county connections and therefore no Militia or Volunteer Regiments, were unable to function effectively. In the event of mobilisation, the Regiment would find it impossible to achieve their required complement to complete their home based Battalion to the required authorised strengths. In view of the fact that the recruiting area of the 25th Regimental District was clearly ill defined, and indeed covered both sides of the Border within a small radius of Berwick, the King's Own Borderers, who drew their recruits, chiefly from the Scottish side of the Border, laid claim to the Scottish Borderers Militia, as its own and effectively secured its future.

In May, 1887, H.R.H. The Field Marshal, Commanding-in-Chief, issued a General Order, whereby the Scottish Borderers Militia, the 3rd (Militia) Battalion Royal Scots Fusiliers, were transferred to the 25th Regimental District, becoming the 3rd (Militia) Battalion the King's Own Borderers and at the same time the 1st Roxburgh and Selkirk, 1st Berwick and the 1st Dumfriesshire Rifle Volunteers were transferred to the 25th Regimental District, as the King's Own Borderers allotted Volunteer Battalions. Kirkcudbrightshire was to be removed from the 21st Regimental District and added to that of the 25th (King's Own Borderers) but the Kirkcudbright and Wigtown, or Galloway Rifle Volunteers were to remain affiliated to the Royal Scots Fusiliers, until the King's Own Borderers were removed from the Northern (English) to the Scottish District.

1st Volunteer Battalion (King's Own Scottish Borderers) - 1st Roxburgh and Selkirk, (The Border Rifles).
2nd Volunteer Battalion (King's Own Scottish Borderers) - 1st Berwickshire.
3rd Volunteer Battalion (King's Own Scottish Borderers) - Dumfriesshire.

By General Order 65 of the 1st April, 1899, the Galloway Battalion of Rifle Volunteers, now incorporating Wigtownshire, were removed from the 21st Regimental District of the Royal Scots Fusiliers and transferred to the 25th Regimental District of the King's Own Scottish Borderers, with once again no change in designation, retaining its now distinctive title of simply, the Galloway Rifle Volunteers.

****

On Saturday, 11th June, 1887, a Wing drill took place in a field near to the railway station at Newton Stewart, Majors Kennedy, Maxwell and Adjutant Douglas in Command. Whilst drill was in progress, the Battalion was in line, Major Douglas, Adjutant, rode to the rear of the line at a smart pace but had to make an abrupt turn to clear the line, by which the horse was thrown from its feet, falling heavily on the Major's legs. He was carried to the railway station where he received medical aid. He was taken by the evening train to his home in Castle Douglas where he was attended by Dr. Lorraine, Castle Douglas. The Major, although not severely injured was not to return to his duties for some months, Captain Carr, 2nd Ayrshire, being appointed temporary Adjutant in his absence.

****

The annual inspection of the Galloway Battalion of Rifle Volunteers took place at Castle Douglas, on the 13th July, 1888.

The previously mentioned War Office Order of the 1st November, 1880, dispensed with the necessity of Battalion drills when a Rifle Corps went into camp, and allowed those Volunteers who did not go into camp for Battalion drills to substitute Company for Battalion drills. The first camp attended by the Galloway Rifle Volunteers was not to be held until 1891, by which time the Battalions were attached to the Line Territorial Regiment, i.e. Royal Scots Fusiliers (1881) and the King's Own Scottish Borderers (1899) and had been Brigaded (1888). From 1891 all annual inspections of the Galloway Rifle Volunteers were held whilst in camp, the Galloway Battalion going into camp every alternate year until the issue of an Army Order of 4th November, 1901, which made for the holding of annual Volunteer Camps compulsory with attendance by the Volunteer, compulsory every second year.

****

On the 5th July, 1889, the annual inspection of the Galloway Battalion of Rifle Volunteers took place at Castle Douglas, with a total of 640 of all ranks on parade.

On the afternoon of Saturday, 21st June, 1890, the Regiment of the Galloway Rifle Volunteers, paraded at the Market Hill, Castle Douglas, where they marched, preceded by the combined bands of Castle Douglas and Maxwellton, to a field on the farm of Blackpark, where they were exercised for upwards of two hours, the latter part of the drill being occupied in practising the attack. The Staff, mounted Officers were; Colonel Kennedy; Lt.-Colonel Maxwell and Major Spurgeon, Adjutant.

Company Officers:-

'A' Company, Kirkcudbright -	Major McLellan, Lieutenant Muir.
'B' Company, Castle Douglas -	Major Harper, Lieutenant Dunn, Lieutenant Hewat, Surgeon Major Lorraine, Rev. G. Walker.
'C' Company, Stranraer -	Lieutenants Stewart and McLellan.
'D' Company, Newton Stewart -	Captain Agnew, Lieutenants McPhater and Kelly.
'E' Company, New Galloway -	Captain Jamieson, Lieutenant Stewart.
'F' & 'G' Companies, Maxwellton -	Captains Lennox and Phyn; Rev. W. Graham, Chaplain.
'H' Company, Dalbeattie -	Major Kerr.

The Parade state was as follows:-

	Officers	Sgts	Band & Bugler	Rank & File	Total
Staff	3	7	-	-	10
'A' Kirkcudbright	2	4	-	42	48
'B' Castle Douglas	5	6	13	42	66
'C' Stranraer	2	4	-	72	78
'D' Newton Stewart	3	3	2	53	61
'E' New Galloway	2	5	1	54	62
'F' Maxwellton	2	4	13	48	68
'G' Maxwellton	1	4	10	42	56
'H' Dalbeattie	1	5	2	40	48
	21	42	41	393	497

On Saturday, 5th July, 1890, a Battalion Drill of the Galloway Rifle Volunteers was held in Blairmount Park, Newton Stewart. This was the first full Battalion Drill held in Newton Stewart for 15 years.

The annual inspection of the Galloway Battalion of Rifle Volunteers was held at Castle Douglas, on the afternoon of Saturday, 12th July, 1890. The Inspecting Officer was Colonel Bainbridge, Commanding the 21st Regimental District, who addressed the Battalion in the following terms on the completion of their drill and inspection. "They had marched very well and the firing and manual exercises were exceedingly well done. The Column movements had been done with tolerable precision. In the formation by file they were in the habit of jumbling up a good deal, and this would require some attention. However, in the form of attack he did not like to hear commands of "Go on, go on." There was no such command as "Go on, go on.", the command should be "Advance".

'A', 'B', 'F' & 'G' Companies were inspected in the week commencing 19th July, 1891, by Colonel Jackson, Commanding the 21st Regimental District. 'F' & 'G' Companies were inspected at their drill field at Palmerston.

The annual inspection of the Galloway Rifle Volunteers took place at Castle Douglas, on Saturday, 4th June, 1892, when there was the largest muster in the history of the Regiment. The Companies, on their arrival from their respective trains, mustered on the Market Hill, where they were joined by the Castle Douglas Company. Preceded by the Cycling Section of 'D' Company and the combined Castle Douglas and Maxwellton Regimental Bands, the Battalion marched to a field on the farm of Torrs, given for the occasion by Mr Gibson, farmer. Unfortunately heavy showers fell during most of the afternoon somewhat diminishing the spectacle of the occasion.

The Inspecting Officer was Colonel Jackson, Commanding the 21st Regimental District. The Staff Officers - mounted - were, Colonel Kennedy, Lieutenant Colonel Maxwell, Major and Adjutant Spurgin and Quartermaster Harper.

The Company Officers were as follows:-

| 'A' Kirkcudbright - | Major McLellan, Lieutenant Muir, Lieutenant Clark, Surgeon Major   Johnstone. |
| 'B' Castle Douglas - | Captain Dunn, Lieutenant Hewat, Surgeon Colonel W. Lorraine, Surgeon Lieutenant R.T. Lorraine and Rev. G. Walker, Chaplain. |

'C' Stranraer -   Captain Stewart, Lieutenant McLellan, Lieutenant McLean, Lieutenant Watson.
'D' Newton Stewart -   Captain Agnew, Lieutenant McPhater, Lieutenant Kelly, Surgeon Lieutenant McKie.
'E' New Galloway -   Lieutenant Stewart, Rev. Mr. Cuthill, Chaplain.
'F' & 'G' Maxwellton - Captain Lennox, Captain Phyn, Surgeon Captain R.B. Lorraine, Rev. Mr. Graham, Chaplain.
'H' Dalbeattie -   Captain Maxwell, Rev. Mr. Kirkpatrick, Chaplain.

The Parade State was as follows:-

	Officers	Sgts.	Band& Buglers	Rank& File	Total
Staff	4	7	-	-	11
'A' Kirkcudbright	4	4	1	66	75
'B' Castle Douglas	5	5	17	71	96
'C' Stranraer	4	4	2	63	73
'D' Newton Stewart	4	4	1	84	93
'E' New Galloway	2	6	3	51	62
'F' Maxwellton	2	6	14	56	78
'G' Maxwellton	2	5	13	54	74
'H' Dalbeattie	2	5	2	64	73
	---	---	---	----	----
	29	46	53	509	637

Absent with leave   96
Absent without leave   5
Battalion strength   738

The Inspecting Officer arrived on the field shortly after 3pm and was received in open order with a general salute. Accompanied by the Commanding Officer, he passed up and down the ranks, the band played a slow march. The Battalion was then put through a number of movements, after which Colonel Maxwell put the Battalion through the manual and firing exercises. The attack having been performed.

Colonel Jackson then addressed the Battalion. He said he was exceedingly well pleased with the way their accoutrements were put on, and he was rather surprised to see how well they performed the manual exercises with the accoutrements on. He knew they were not accustomed to it and he was therefore very much pleased to find that it was so creditably done. At the same time there was room for improvement in the cutting away of the hands in the manual exercises. They should make a decided pause between each motion, then cut away the hand sharply, and when they had done, stand perfectly still and look to the front. Some of the youngsters had a way of looking round and making confidential communications with their neighbours (still talking in the ranks.) This was not right on parade. Considering the short time they had been practising the new drill he considered it was performed in a very creditable manner. Their volley firing was especially steady. He had only heard one indifferent volley out of the whole lot, and no bad ones. Their physique, he thought was very good. He hoped that the following year they would have a camp and he trusted that he would be there for a day or two to see them. He felt sure by that time they would have perfectly mastered the new drill in all its details. The Ambulance Corps performed their duties very creditably, and he was very much pleased with the Cyclists, who seemed to him to have sprung very suddenly into a very respectable Corps. The marching of the men was steady but it required a little more decision. For instance when moving into quarter column he should like to see each section to continue to move at a sharp pace until they were halted. They should not hang fire and walk a little slower expecting the word halt.

He thought they were a very smart Battalion and very well dressed, and as he had said before, he was exceedingly well pleased with their accoutrements. It showed that both the officers and non-commissioned officers had taken pains with them. It had been a very wet day, and they had not had so much drill as they might have, however, they had sufficient to show that they were in a good position, and he would have much pleasure in reporting favourably on them.

The Battalion was then marched off the ground and dismissed.

A close of the season drill was held on the afternoon of Saturday, 6th August, 1892, in the drill field at Palmerston, Maxwellton, when an opportunity was given to those few members who required a Battalion Drill to complete their efficiency requirements. There were only two small Companies on parade, mainly comprising of Maxwellton men. The Officers on Parade were, Major Spurgin, Adjutant; Major Lennox; and Captain Phyn. After an hours smart drill the men were dismissed.

On the 3rd April, 1896, Orders were issued from Headquarters to the various Companies of the Galloway Rifle Volunteers, calling for a return of the number of men willing to take part in a route march, not to exceed 4 days, about the end of June, beginning of July. The men would be required to march in full order with tents and kit-bags being carried by wagons which would accompany them. No definite route had been decided upon but it would probably take place from Maxwellton to Ayr, a distance of some 60 miles. The return journey would be by train.

This suggestion the first of its kind was also to be the last of its kind and did not meet with the approval of the rank and file. On the 5th June, 1896, a further Order was issued from Headquarters stating that the route march had been cancelled.

A Battalion drill of the Galloway Rifle Volunteers was held in Stranraer, on Saturday, 6th June, 1896. A special train was run from Dumfries, conveying the Maxwellton Companies and picking up the other Companies en-route. There was a large turnout, notwithstanding the unfavourable weather. The Companies assembled at the railway station and marched 2 miles to the parade field at Innermessan. The Staff Officers present were; Colonel Kennedy; Captain R.W.M. Blake, Adjutant, Quartermaster Major Harper.

The Company Officers were:-

'A' Company, Kirkcudbright -	Major McLellan.
'B' Company, Castle Douglas -	Captain Dunn.
'C' Company, Stranraer -	Captain Stewart, Lieutenant McLelland, Lieutenant McLean, Lieutenant Watson, Surgeon Lt. Munro.
'D' Company, Newton Stewart -	Captain McPhater, Lieutenants McLean and Kelly.
'E' Company, New Galloway -	Captain Timms, Lieutenant Stewart, Surgeon Lieutenant Cavan.
'F' & 'G' Companies, Maxwellton -	Captain Phyn.
'H' Company, Dalbeattie -	Captain Maxwell.

The men were exercised for well over two hours after which Captain Stewart and Private Gracie, Stranraer, were presented with their Long Service Medals by Colonel Kennedy. The Battalion was then marched back to town and dismissed.

The Parade State was as follows:-

	Officers.	Sgt. Inst.	Sgts.	Band& Buglers.	Rank& File.	Total.
Staff	4	-	-	-	-	4
'A' Kirkcudbright	1	1	5	1	77	85
'B' Castle Douglas	1	1	9	21	52	84
'C' Stranraer	5	1	3	2	70	81
'D' Newton Stewart	3	1	3	2	63	72
'E' New Galloway	3	1	5	5	52	66
'F' & 'G' Maxwellton	1	1	8	23	135	168
'H' Dalbeattie	1	1	5	1	70	78
	---	---	---	---	----	----
	19	7	38	55	519	638

The following advice regarding "Drill" and "Class Firing" was offered by "Mack", writing in the *Regimental Gazette* of the Galloway Rifle Volunteers, in a letter dated 9th December, 1896. This letter shows all to well the difficulties then being experienced in the Volunteer Movement, whilst the Regular Army was moving forward at pace, both in ideas and weaponry, into the 20th Century:

"Now that the attack movement is one of the principal parts of our military education, one requires special training. All non-commissioned officers particularly should devote as much time as possible to learn their duties as commanders of their respective sections, and Officer in command of companies should see that they get as much practice as possible, as the section leader is a very important factor in the attack. A section commander to gain the confidence of his section must be able to give his words of command in a clear and distinct voice, giving the cautionary words slowly and distinctly, and the executive word sharply and quickly, and without hesitation. When the least hesitation is shown the men hesitate and consequently the drill is not gone through with precision. Section commanders should meet at least once a week, and practice words of command. They require to train their voices as much as a singer has to train his voice. If this suggestion was carried out they would be more at home when on parade. There are a great many details which they would do well to study if they wish to become proficient. I would suggest that a trophy should be given for competition between the different sections of the Corps, each section to consist of say 16 men, the best drilled and most efficient section in the Battalion to be declared the winner for that year. I am certain that

this would help to improve the drill and give the members of the different Companies encouragement to attend drill. It would also give section commanders confidence and practice as well as the men. Possibly our Colonel will move in this direction.

Another matter of importance is how to use the rifle with effect. The great secret of success with the rifle is practice, and every opportunity is being given to the members of the Battalion for this, if they will only embrace the opportunity, but some men show a great lack of spirit in going to the ranges, even to do their Class Firing. They put off going until time compels them to go. This always keeps the Instructor back, while a little thoughtful consideration on the part of the Volunteer might have taken him up to the ranges to get his class fired much earlier. It is the case that the Instructor has asked a man half a dozen times to go out the following Saturday to class fire, and each time he will seriously say to the Instructor, "Oh, yes, Sergeant, I'll be there on Saturday", but when Saturday comes John or Tom forgets all about his promises until the Instructor meets him, when he makes a humble apology, and again promises "faithfully" but possibly with the same result. Now to improve the state of matters, I think, if on a Saturday, a Company parade might be ordered, and the Company marched to the ranges for musketry training, say 50 men were present with the increased target accommodation, which the Galloway Rifles now have, the 3rd class could very easily be completed in the afternoon when volley firing and field firing could be carried out by the different section commanders. Of course some little encouragement might require to be given, possibly some small prizes. I would advise all members to go to the targets as early in the season as possible, and not to forget that, "the early bird gets the worm", and I would say to all Volunteers, "Early at the targets, early done". One other matter which I think would foster rifle shooting is occasional matches on the range with teams drawn from the sections or half Companies. This would be a very good way of bringing up young shots to the front. On the Kirkcudbright range for the last four years there has been a competition of this kind, the first two years by sections, the last two by half Companies. On the last two occasions over 40 members took part in each match, and took a great interest in the competition. At the conclusion of the matches, the members have sat down to an excellent supper and fight their matches over again."

"Mack"

Kirkcudbright, 9th December, 1896.

Again the following advice was offered by, "Silver Sand" in a letter to the *Regimental Gazette* of the Galloway Rifles, dated, 31st December, 1896. The reasons were becoming all too obvious, why reforms within the Volunteer Movement were now becoming necessary. This had been partially rectified by the encouragement of annual camps of exercise which were later, in 1901, to become compulsory, with a total reform of the Volunteer Movement taking place in 1908.

"I have for years felt that our summer drill season is spread over too long a time. Our system has been to have outdoor drill every week from the time that it is clear enough to do so right on to the inspection. Roughly speaking, it extends over a period of three months. The consequence is that there is no life in it, only during the last month is there interest taken to get drills put in for inspection. There is nothing more damaging to anything than a lingering existence.

I am firmly of the opinion that if field exercise was confined to say four weeks prior to the inspection there would be a better attendance, and a better efficiency would be obtained. Much of what is learned is lost by long intervals.

Our last inspection showed that Section work was much at fault, but under our present system section drill is impossible. How can the section commander know his men thoroughly, and how can the men know him and confine their movements to his commands, when he has this week 10 of his section, next week 4, the following week 2? This is no exaggeration. Dividing a Company into four equal sections some men are certain not to be under their own commander at any drill during the season. By adopting the above suggestion this would be considerably improved. The Companies would also come to the inspection fresh from the course of training, and give a better account of themselves before the Inspecting Officer.

This system is adopted by the city regiments. They have drill every night for a month before the inspection. The men can thus keep themselves free from engagements for a sufficient period to make themselves efficient, and I am certain they would not get the same good results by adopting our system.

Everyone who has to do with Companies knows how disheartening it is to appear on parade week after week with a handful of men. Besides the men don't like to march through the street when there is a small number on parade. Many of those who would be better attenders have stated that they have repeatedly absented themselves from drill, being disgusted at the small turnout.

Of course a scattered Company like New Galloway could not have sufficient winter drills to make themselves efficient, but all the other Companies of the Battalion could.

The suggestion would work thus. During the winter months, Company drill could be taken up and the necessity pointed out to the men of each putting in so many drills in the hall before going outside. For four weeks prior to the inspection let each Company have two nights a week for field practice outside.

The matter is worth the consideration of our gallant Colonel and his Staff, to whom this epistle is respectfully submitted."

"Silver Sand"
Galloway, 31st December, 1896.

****

On the 23rd July, 1897, a Wing drill was held at Maxwellton.

****

The first Battalion drill of the season of the Galloway Rifle Volunteers was held at Dalbeattie on Saturday, 7th May, 1898. The Battalion paraded at 3pm, the several Companies having been conveyed to Dalbeattie by special train. The drill was to take place in a field on the Haugh Road.

The Staff Officers on parade were:- Colonel John Murray Kennedy in Command, Captain Blake, Adjutant, Quartermaster Major Harper.

The Company Officers present on parade were:-

'A' Company,	Kirkcudbright -	Captain Comrie.
'B'	Castle Douglas -	Captain Dunn, Surgeon Lieutenant Lorraine.
'C'	Stranraer -	Major Stewart, Lieutenants McLean and Watson.
'D'	Newton Stewart -	Captain McPhater, Lieutenants Kelly, Brand and McLean.
'E'	New Galloway -	Captain Timms, Lieutenant Stewart, Surgeon Captain Cowan.
'F'&'G'	Maxwellton -	Majors Lennox and Phyn, Lieutenants Blacklock, Shortridge and Grierson.
'H'	Dalbeattie -	Captain Maxwell, Lieutenant Anderson.

Arriving at the field the Battalion was formed up in column, afterwards wheeling and forming quarter column on number one. The Battalion next moved in fours to the right, wheeled to the left and marched past in column and quarter column. They then reformed line and advanced in review order. The Battalion was next put through the manual exercises by Major Lennox, Colonel Kennedy being in command during the firing exercises, by half Companies from the right, after which it changed front to the right and formed square on the two centre Companies. Other Battalion movements were to follow, including forming column of half Battalion and forming square on each half Battalion. The men were dismissed at 5.30pm.

The Parade State was as follows:-

	Officers	Sgt. Insts.	Sgt.	Compy. Clerks.	Band & Buglers	Rank & File	Total.
Staff	3	-	-	-	-	-	3
'A' Kirkcudbright	1	1	4	-	2	78	85
'B' Castle Douglas	2	1	9	-	19	64	95
'C' Stranraer	4	1	5	-	-	50	60
'D' Newton Stewart	3	1	5	-	-	75	84
'E' New Galloway	3	1	4	-	-	50	58
'F' & 'G' Maxwellton	5	1	12	3	19	89	129
'H' Dalbeattie	3	1	5	-	12	64	85
	24	7	44	3	52	479	609

****

The second Battalion Drill of the Galloway Rifle Volunteers took place at Newton Stewart, on the 21st May, 1898.

****

The annual inspection of the Galloway Battalion took place at Castle Douglas on the 17th June, 1898.

****

The local Volunteer season of the Galloway Rifle Volunteers was brought to a close on Saturday, 15th July, 1899, with a Battalion drill at Dalbeattie. The weather was dry and warm and a large turnout of spectators witnessed the proceedings.

On their arrival at Dalbeattie the Companies paraded in Station Road, and preceded by the massed bands of the Dalbeattie, Castle Douglas and Maxwellton Companies, under Bandmaster Keane, Castle Douglas, the Battalion marched to a field on the farm of Redweel.

The Staff Officers present were Colonel Kennedy and Adjutant Blake.

The Company Officers were as follows:-

'A' Company, Kirkcudbright -	Captain Comrie.
'B' Company, Castle Douglas -	Lieutenant Hewat.
'C' Company, Stranraer -	Captain McLean, Lieutenants Watson and McLauchlan.
'D' Company, Newton Stewart -	Lieutenants Brand and McLean.
'E' Company, New Galloway -	Captain Timms, Lieutenant Stewart.
'F' & 'G' Companies, Maxwellton -	Majors Lennox and Phyn, Lieutenants Shortridge and Blacklock.
'H' Company, Dalbeattie -	Captain Maxwell, Chaplain Wilson.

The usual manoeuvres were gone through and Colonel Kennedy then read the following telegram on parade, from Captain Kelly at Bisley, containing an account of the Galloway Rifles successes at that event. "Westminster", 2nd £5; "Whitehead" 1st no money; "Mullens" 2nd £30; "Brinsmead" 7th £3; "Mappin", 7th nothing. No other team shoots until next Friday. Men well; good spirits, flukey winds. The reading of the telegram was received with great cheering for Captain Kelly and his team. Colonel Kennedy then presented long service medals to - Colour-Sergeant Peattie and Sergeant Angus McDonald 'D' Company. Privates W. Law and Armstrong, 'F' Company.

The Parade state was as follows:-

	Staff Officers	Company Officers	Per'nt Staff	Sgts	Band & Buglers	Rank & File	Total
'A' Kirkcudbright	-	1	1	3	4	59	68
'B' Castle Douglas	2	1	1	5	17	36	62
'C' Stranraer	-	3	1	3	-	23	30
'D' Newton Stewart	-	2	-	3	2	75	82
'E' New Galloway	-	2	1	2	-	27	32
'F' & 'G' Maxwellton	-	4	1	8	15	73	101
'H' Dalbeattie	-	2	1	5	13	58	79
	2	15	6	29	51	351	454

At the close of the drill the Battalion was marched back into Dalbeattie and dismissed.

****

The Galloway Rifle Volunteers had their first Battalion drill of the season in the park at Newton Stewart, on the afternoon of Saturday, 8th June, 1901. The Staff Officers present were Colonel J. M. Kennedy, Commanding, Acting Adjutant Major Lennox, Maxwellton, Major Dunn, Quartermaster, Castle Douglas. The Company Officers present were:-

'A' Company, Kirkcudbright -	Captain Comrie. Lieutenant Nicholson.
'B' Company, Castle Douglas -	Captain Hewat, Lieutenants Biggar and Gifford.
'C' Company, Stranraer -	Captain McLean, Lieutenant McLauchlan, Surgeon Captain Munro.
'D' Company, Newton Stewart -	Captain McLean, Surgeon Lieutenant Douglas, Chaplain Rev. J. Mc D. Inglis.
'E' Company, New Galloway -	Lieutenant Ford, Surgeon Captain Cowan.
'F' & 'G' Companies, Maxwellton -	Major Phyn, Lieutenant Grierson.
'H' Company, Dalbeattie -	Captain Maxwell.

There was to be no ceremonial drill. Three Companies were thrown out as a skeleton enemy and five Companies went through the attack formation. The enemy was skilfully concealed and repulsed the attack.

The following was the parade state:-

	Officers	Sergeants	Pipes, Band & Buglers	Rank & File	Total
'A Kirkcudbright	2	6	8	75	91
'B' Castle Douglas	6	5	1	84	96
'C' Stranraer	3	5	3	68	79
'D Newton Stewart	3	7	2	95	107
'E' New Galloway	2	5	2	45	54
'F' & 'G' Maxwellton	2	8	24	110	144
'H' Dalbeattie	1	5	6	71	91
	---	----	---	----	----
	19	41	46	556	662

On the 27 th July, 1901, the Galloway Rifle Volunteers were inspected on the Market Hill, Castle Douglas. The Parade State was as follows:-

	Officers	Sergeants	Pipers & Buglers	Rank & File	Total
'A' Kirkcudbright	2	6	2	83	93
'B' Castle Douglas	7	7	1	87	102
'C' Stranraer	3	4	1	79	87
'D' Newton Stewart	4	6	1	103	114
'E' New Galloway	3	2	2	53	60
'F' & 'G' Maxwellton	2	11	-	142	155
'H' Dalbeattie	3	6	3	84	96
	---	---	---	----	----
	24	42	10	631	707

****

A joint Battalion drill of the 3rd Volunteer Battalion, King's Own Scottish Borderers, Dumfriesshire, and the Galloway Rifle Volunteers, took place on Saturday, 31st August, 1901, Colonel Dudgeon, 3rd V.B. (K.O.S.B.) in Command. The drill was held in order to enable those previously unable to make the requisite number of drills to become efficient before the close of the season. For two hours the men were exercised and at the close, Colonel Dudgeon made a few remarks expressing his pleasure at being in command of a joint parade.

****

With the issue of Army Order of the 4th November, 1901, which made the holding of annual Volunteer camps compulsory, on the 3rd April, 1902, Colonel J. M. Kennedy, Commanding the Galloway Rifle Volunteers, was to issue an Order which stated that there were to be no further Battalion drills, exepting those to be held during the Brigade camps. It would appear that this Order was also to include the annual inspection of the Battalion, with there being no further Inspections reported, save for those held at the Brigade camp. However, this did not dispense with the necessity of the required Company drills to fulfil the requirements of the capitation grant, nor did it dispense with the necessity of Adjutant's drills or of Company Inspections.

On the 7th August, 1902, Lieutenant-Colonel Lennox, Maxwellton, was to offer the following advice to the aspiring Volunteer, at the close of the annual camp at Dingleton Common, Melrose; "All that was required of a Volunteer, was one hour, for one night, for three summer months, with Volunteering being a safeguard against conscription."

On the 6th September, 1904, the Headquarters of the Galloway Battalion of Rifle Volunteers, were once again moved, this time to the 'Brig'en, Maxwellton, (West side of the Nith, by the Old Bridge) where it was to remain until the Force ceased to exist in 1908.

CHAPTER 6

*RIFLES - RULES & REGULATIONS PERTAINING TO RIFLES, RANGES,
AND THE VOLUNTEER COMPANY - INTER-COMPANY AND REGIMENTAL
COMPETITIONS - MUSKETRY RETURNS*

"In the Crimea, a Cavalry Picket, detached from a crack Regiment, and consisting of from 30/40 men, skirmished one day with a Cossack Picket. The distance between the two parties was some 80 yards. Both bodies fired away upwards of 200 rounds and the net result was the wounding of one man. How could this be otherwise, when we hear of a Regiment in which the men have in 2 years actually been once engaged in target practice? On that occasion many of the men had never loaded and fired with ball in their life."

The following Editorial was to appear in the *Kirkcudbrightshire Advertiser* dated 25th November, 1859. "We are happy to believe that the formation of Rifle Corps bids fair to be a great movement, valuable for the immediate defence of the country, and still more valuable as restoring to the population that self dependence and those manly habits which a nation can never lose with impunity.

The Rifle Corps are in their infancy, a strong and healthy one, but still in infancy. It requires a national sympathy and national activity to bring them to a happy and useful maturity. Now, if there were any signs that the members of these Corps had joined them in a spirit of caprice or affection, if they were what certain similar institutions have too much been, mere appendages to the station of country gentleman or means of gaining a mock military uniform to be worn three or four times a year as a fancy dress, we should not think it worth while to urge perseverance or improvement.

The Rifle Corps, which are being established are in no way akin to the old apparatus for nominal soldiering. They have sprung into being because every man of common judgement is convinced that the Country is on the point of being exposed to very great dangers. All classes may have occasion for the exercise of courage, self denial and public spirit until the clouds which threaten Europe are overpast. It is this conviction which has made the Volunteer Movement successful at its outset, and as circumstances tend to show that particular disquiet must endure for some time to come, the stimulus to activity will not be wanting. All who believe that the Volunteers are actuated by really earnest motives, and that their Corps are likely to contain before long many thousand effective men, must be desirous that the system adopted should be a good one, and that the Corps at the outset should adopt such a model as will make them really useful to the country.

The naturalisation of the rifle among us, is an object as much to be sought after as the formation of any definite body for service in case of a particular event. But the two things may be accomplished by the same method. If in the course of the next 12 months, the Volunteer Corps of this Country succeed in making the practice of rifle shooting popular; if in addition to the strength derived from their actual numbers, the country has the benefit of their example, and finds that the youth from one end of the land to the other are taking to the use of the rifle, and are anxious for the formation of fresh association, then we may congratulate ourselves on having not only a present but prospective defence against all dangers.

The truth is, that habitual use of weapons is nine-tenths of a soldier's trade. In the present state of warfare even the usefulness of a private in a Line Regiment must depend much more on his proficiency with the highly finished weapon in his hands than on the mechanical drill to which he has been subjected. We cannot conceive any plan more likely to hinder the usefulness of this motive, than the attempt to turn Volunteers into Linesmen and waste the time which should be spent on rifle practice than producing a bad imitation of the Regular Army.

To obtain the best marksmen and the best weapons should be the object of every Corps. Meeting for practice will naturally bring with them a certain and a sufficient amount of military science. The gentlemen of the higher and middling classes are not ignorant rustics who do not know their right hand from their left, and whose walk is a roll or a shuffle. They have already a great deal of the soldier in them. They are quick, intelligent, hold themselves well and have quite as much of a military appearance as the troops of our formidable neighbour, France.

For the present every means should be used to obtain a sufficient supply of men and weapons, and places of exercise. On the first point we can say no more. If the present state of Europe does not call forth the patriotism of our young men, then it is needless for the Press to exert itself. With respect to the supply of rifles, it seems to us the "National Association for the Encouragement of Volunteer Rifle Corps and the Promotion of rifle shooting throughout Great Britain", among many excellent objects which it proposes to itself, makes a mistake in proposing to offer prizes for rifles. The care of the Government and the competition of the manufacturers will supply the nation with all that is necessary and the Association will do well to direct its energies to encouraging the formation of Corps or clubs and inducing men of every condition to join."

This was to be the whole essence of the Volunteer movement, a means of making a large portion of the populace skilful in the use of the rifle, with the rifle the national weapon and the exercise in the use of the weapon, a national exercise, in order that the failings recently attributed to the Crimean War, would not be repeated.

In his circular to Lord's Lieutenant dated 13th July, 1859, Mr. Sidney Herbert, Secretary of War, stressed that the Volunteer Force should be raised and maintained by public subscription with no cost to Government whatsoever. The Government had insufficient clothing, arms and ammunition, in store, with which to supply the Volunteer Force. Mr Herbert was, however, to announce that Government was in the position to supply 25% of the weapons to the several Volunteer Corps, the remainder having to be supplied by the Corps or by the individual member. He did, however, undertake that in the event of a national crisis the Government would at once supply all the Volunteer's needs. However, Government re-armament was to move forward with some pace and in a Government Circular dated 20th December, 1859, Mr Herbert was to sanction the supply of the Long Enfield Rifle, by Government, to all the Volunteer Corps, commencing after the 1st January, 1860, at 50% of cost, providing the Corps had a suitable range of at least 200 yards with a recommendation that the range should extend to 900 yards, and a suitable lockfast store or armoury, in which to keep the weapons.

The following is an extract from an Act passed in June, 1860, to facilitate the acquisition of grounds for rifle practice by a rifle Volunteer Corps; "Any Rifle Volunteer Corps may purchase or acquire by such grants as are hereinafter mentioned, any land for rifle practice, and for the erection of butts and other accommodation for the use of the Corps, when practising with rifles, subject to the following restrictions:- The assent of Her Majesty's Principal Secretary of State for the War Department, for the time being hereinafter called the said Principal Secretary, shall be obtained to the purchase of any land under the powers of this Act, or to the grant of any land by any person or body of persons, in pursuance of the powers, hereinafter given; that, in addition to such assent, the sanction of Parliament, shall be obtained in manner hereinafter mentioned, before it shall be lawful for any Volunteer Corps to put in force such provisions of the Acts hereinafter incorporated as relate to the purchase and taking of lands otherwise than by agreement."

Initially the Volunteer purchased his own ammunition from Government, through his Corps Commanding Officer, at cost price, 4d for 10 rounds, but on the 7th February, 1861, a circular was issued from the War Office intimating the quantities of ammunition to be issued free to the Rifle Volunteer:-

"110 rounds ball and 20 blank cartridge per man the 1st year issued gratis, with liberty to purchase 110 more of ball and 100 more of blank cartridge; and 90 ball and 50 blank cartridge in every succeeding year, with liberty to purchase 130 ball and 60 blank cartridges."

A Volunteer Corps was not authorised to fire blank or ball ammunition in military formation unless it had its own Adjutant or was authorised through the Inspector of Musketry for that particular District.

Although the Government rifles were not received at the Headquarters of the Galloway Rifle Volunteers until the end of April, 1860, by the 6th January, 1860, Castle Douglas Volunteer Rifle Corps had become sufficiently organised to announce that for the purpose of encouraging proficiency in rifle practice, a subscription list was opened with a view to giving a prize to the best shot in the Corps, after it had been organised and sufficiently practiced. The prize was to be a rifle to the value of £10.

On the 15th March, 1860, in Stranraer, Provost Guthrie, Captain of the Stranraer Volunteer Rifle Corps, offered prizes of £5, £3 and £2 respectively, to be awarded to the three best marksmen in his Company at the end of the year.

On the 20th April, 1860, the first 75 rifles for use by the Galloway Rifle Volunteers were received at their armoury. The Companies being required to pay half the cost of the rifle. This charge was to be of short duration as by the end of 1860, Government had undertaken to supply all rifles to the Volunteers, free of cost.

The rifle was the Long Enfield Rifled Musket, of 1852 pattern, .577 calibre, muzzle-loading, single shot, percussion, which used the Pritchett expanding bullet. This muzzle-loading rifle was the last of its type to be issued to British troops.

This musket was a pretty fearsome weapon, and although with a killing distance of only 250 yards or thereby it was almost identical to the Springfield Musket, firing the 'Minie Ball', used by both sides in the American Civil War with such devastating effect.

The bullet was a conical cylindrical lead shot with an iron cap in the base and when this was fired, the pressure forced the base of the lead shot to expand, thereby gripping the rifling within the barrel. The bullet, which was approximately ½" in diameter and 1" in length, weighed about 1¼ ounces. It was made of soft lead and with the bullet being partially hollow, it produced a 'dumdum' effect, exploding on impact causing horrendous injuries resulting in death or amputation of the whole limb in most cases.

The loading of this musket was fairly involved and entailed a number of set drill manoeuvres. The musket was held upright with the butt to the ground. The Volunteer then had to take a cartridge, which was a paper cylinder, wrapped around a bullet and a charge of powder. He would tear this open with his teeth, pour the powder down the barrel and insert the bullet. Using the rod, he would ram the bullet home. The hammer was cocked and a percussion cap inserted. He was then ready to fire.

In conjunction with the issue of the new Long Enfield Rifled Musket, the following *'Hints on Shooting to Rifle Volunteers'* were to be published, with the recommendation that the Volunteer avail himself of a copy of the requisite Table 'A'. Perhaps this imagery of a well educated, middle class Volunteer was to be seriously underestimated when considering the complexities involved in rifle shooting:-

(1). Every Rifleman ought to possess a copy of a Table 'A' this day published: it shows the fall by gravity as modified by the resistance of the atmosphere, together with the velocity resulting from such a fall.

(2). It is to be procured from Edmonston and Douglas, or Mr. Bryson, of No. 60 Princes Street, Edinburgh: its price is 6d, the profits of the sale to be given as a purse to be shot for by Scottish Rifle Volunteers.

(3). It is only by using a table of this description that it is possible for any Rifleman to calculate the initial velocity of his bullet and to determine its trajectory or path in air.

(4). Mr. Bryson shall be enabled to show an instrument by the use of which the exact elevation of the direction given to the ball may be measured: it is from this elevation, together with the measured horizontal range in feet, that the velocity can be found.

(5). We work thus: Multiply the range by the secant of the elevation. The product is the oblique ascent of the ball in the time of flight "t", multiply the range by the tangent of the elevation, the product is the vertical descent of the ball in the same time "t", these two simultaneous motions must be compounded together, in order to obtain the actual motion of the ball.

(6). The vertical descent is nothing but the fall by gravity: therefore we find in table 'A' the value of "t", to the tenth of a second, which we can further reduce to the hundredth part of a second. We find the time of flight "t", from the known vertical descent or fall by gravity.

(7). Divide the magnitude of the oblique ascent by the time, "t", the quotient is the 'mean velocity' of the ascent. Divide the magnitude of the vertical descent by the same time "t", the quotient is the 'mean velocity' of the descent.

(8). Find in table 'A' the time in which a ball, suffered to fall freely from a state of rest will require velocity equal to the 'mean velocity' of the ascent: call this time "a".

(9). Find also the time in which the same ball would require the velocity equal to the 'mean velocity' of the descent: call it "b".

(10). Now add together these two times, "a" and "b", turn once more to table 'A': the velocity acquired in the time "a" and "b", is the initial velocity for the given range and elevation, and the portion of table 'A' which precedes the time "a" and "b" is the graduation of the ascent inverted. We can therefore now compound the simultaneous ascent and descent to obtain the actual motion of the ball.

(11). Printed examples of the working of this rule may be obtained, and any explanation required shall be most readily available.

P. Anstruther, Major-General
of Thirdpart, Fife.

The following Editorial appeared in the *Kirkcudbrightshire Advertiser* of May, 1860: "The Volunteer Regiments are receiving from Government the Long Enfield Rifles of the same pattern as those issued to the Regular Army. It is stated that the weapons now delivered are to be exchanged in due course of time for the Short Enfield Rifle, but it may be safely calculated that the exchange cannot be effected in much less than 2 years and long before that time elapses, we should expect that the Volunteer will have become so used to the Long Rifles and will like them so well that they will not wish to part with them. It is perhaps an open question whether the Long or the Short Rifles, are on the whole, the more efficient weapon but it is a matter of fact the Volunteers have got the Long Rifle and therefore they ought to make the best of it.

We would therefore urge upon them that they should diligently practice under competent Instructors, some simple system of bayonet practice resembling in principle those so much adapted by the French Army. It will be found that they will thus obtain an agreeable variety of drill, which may be carried on either indoors or outdoors and without any of the danger to the neighbours and spectators which may be apprehended from the earliest efforts of inexperience and careless marksmen. It is not easy to exaggerate the advantages which would result from steady perseverance in such an exercise. It would give the Volunteers a command of their weapons and a confidence in using them which nothing else could give. The exercise which is intended to give the necessary skill ought to be practised regularly until the Volunteer has ceased to be conscious of the weight and has become fully alive to the capabilities of his rifle and fixed bayonet."

In due course the Long Enfield Rifled Musket was replaced by the Short Enfield Rifled Musket, which as the name suggests, had a shorter barrel and was considered more appropriate for use by Light Infantry. However, with the longer barrel of the Long Enfield, it was considered much more accurate and better suited to target shooting and we find that at the annual gold medal shooting match of the 1st Kirkcudbrightshire Rifles, on the 10th October, 1868, an objection was raised to the eventual winner, Sergeant John Osborne, who won the event by an unprecedented 10 clear points. The objection being that Sergeant Osborne had shot with the superior Long Enfield Musket. As a matter of interest, the objection was not upheld.

On Friday, 8th June, 1860, Drill Sergeant Roberts, Castle Douglas, gave the first of four lessons on practical Musketry, in the Free Church School Room, Castle Douglas. Before a Volunteer was allowed to practice at the targets or in any military formation he was required to undergo these courses of instruction. There were upwards of 40 Volunteers present, together with Lieutenant Bell and Ensign Renny. The first lesson, which was considered to be the most important was, "Lock Instruction".

Sergeant Roberts took off the lock and named each of the springs in rotation, after which he gave a description of the construction of the rifle barrel. The outside, he said, was a conical cylinder thicker at the breech and tapering down gradually to the muzzle, the weight being 4lbs. 2ozs. and the length 3' 3". He then explained what is termed the line of fire. A bullet discharged from one of their rifles went 1,200 feet the first second and if there was nothing to interfere with its progress it would continue at that rate but the instant the ball left the muzzle of the rifle it began to leave the line of fire. The first element it had to contend with was air and the next gravity, the consequence being that the ball took a curved direction downwards after travelling a certain distance. When they knew the law which acted on the ball, they measured the distance which the ball fell below the object aimed at. That distance was 1' 5" on the first 100 yards travelled and to enable them to hit the mark they must aim the same distance above the object as the ball fell below it. To aim with accuracy it was necessary to keep the sight mark on the rifle between the eye and the object aimed at. They must however, aim lower when firing at a near object as the ball rose on short distances. Sergeant Roberts then continued his instruction on how to clean the lock and rifle, with the Volunteers taking part in this practical exercise at some length. The following Friday night was fixed for the next lesson.

Despite these careful instructions to the Volunteer and the following news report on the "Power of the Rifle Bullet". "During the firing this week the power of the conical rifle bullet was shown in a remarkable manner. Just under the butts were some planks of wood to steady them. A ball fired from 400 yards penetrated a spar 4" thick and then striking the side of a plank 18" wide and 2½" thick, drilled a hole in it from side to side, or in other words through 22" of timber." The following Editorial was to appear in the *Wigtownshire Free Press*:- "We understand a ball was fired into the small wooden house at the Battery at Lochryan and the flag staff has been shattered by bullets. This dastardly and reckless conduct should be reported to the P.F. and if the culprits are discovered, should be severely punished. Those entrusted with rifles should know how to use them with discretion and officers cannot too strongly warn the men of the great danger of shooting with ball, excepting at the regular butts."

This did not, however, appear to placate an "Anxious Volunteer", who wrote in the following terms to the *Kirkcudbrightshire Advertiser* on the 31st August, 1860; I declare I have been in the ranks and heard going on behind me, on one occasion with my own rear-rank man, matter that would quail the stoutest heart.

What can be more unnerving, than to know, as I did, that my rear-rank man was capping with his rifle at full cock, at the same time the muzzle wandering playfully about the small of my back and the region of my short ribs, the rifle all the time only requiring a touch or an extra shake to cause it to explode and so injure me for life, if not kill me on the spot.

I would suggest that the Commander-in-Chief should issue a circular memorandum to all Commanding Officers of all Volunteer Corps, making it a *sine qua non,* that every man, before having a rifle entrusted to him, should go through a certain number of drills and receive a certificate of competency."

The "Anxious Volunteers" fears were to be completely unfounded with only one reported shooting accident taking place in the complete history of the Galloway Rifle Volunteers, 1859 - 1908, which unhappily was to prove fatal; "On Friday night, 22nd February, 1901, in the Drill Hall, Laurieknowe, Maxwellton, while some members of the Galloway Rifles were engaged in practice with the Morris Tube, Charles Harper, a Painter, 23 years of age, was acting as marker, when one of the Company, Alfred Hannah, a Plasterer, accidentally touched the trigger of his rifle and the bullet hit Harper on the chest near to his lungs. Private Harper, who lived in Glasgow Street, with his widowed mother, had gone towards the targets to see the result of the last shot and was in the act of returning when the accident happened. He did not fall, and though suffering severely he walked home accompanied by some of his comrades, and Dr. Robson was summoned. Harper passed a restless night, coughing up clotted blood. In the morning he was removed to the Dumfries Infirmary, where he was found to be too weak to be operated on. At 6pm. on Friday, 1st March, 1901, Private Harper, died from his wounds.

His funeral took place on Tuesday, 5th March, 1901, in Troqueer Churchyard. It was attended by a large contingent of both Dumfriesshire and Maxwellton Volunteers. His coffin was carried shoulder high by a party of his comrades and at the Churchyard three volleys were fired and the "Last Post" sounded."

Very quickly practice grounds were acquired, by various Rifle Corps, together with suitable ranges, with the Sergeant instructors imparting, to the Volunteers, the instruction necessary in the use of firearm and in August, 1860, it was reported that many rifle contests had been taking place throughout Galloway.

The first recorded contest was that of the 2nd Kirkcudbrightshire Rifle Corps - Castle Douglas, when on Wednesday, 14th/15th October, 1860, on the range at Corra, a contest took place, for a rifle, presented by Captain Mackie. Such was the entry that the contest had to be continued on to the Friday, 16th/Saturday, 17th. The final result being that Corporal McVane was to draw the competition with a Short Enfield, in distances of 150, 200, 250, and 350 yards, with a score of 26 points, with Mr. Gordon of Castle Douglas, but in a shoot-out Corporal McVane was to win by 4 hits to 2. On presenting the rifle, Captain Mackie was to say that the Armoury in Queen Street would be a rallying point from whence would come some of the best shots in the Stewartry.

On 4th January, 1861, Captain Munro, on inspecting the 2nd Wigtownshire Rifle Corps - Stranraer, was to say, that he hoped to be able to have a silver cup and various prizes arranged to be offered in competition by the various Companies in Galloway. No one would be allowed to compete who did not attend regular drills.

On the 7th January, 1861, the following order was issued to Lords Lieutenant, of their respective Counties, by Sidney Herbert, Secretary of War, in an effort to bring some sort of uniformity into the arms borne by the Volunteers. Although Government had now undertaken to supply all arms to the Volunteers, free of charge, and Mr. Herbert now required that all Volunteer Corps use only the arms issued to them by Government, this did not refer to rifles used in competition, with most marksmen supplying and using their own rifles for competition.

War Office, Pall Mall,
7th January, 1861.

My Lord,

Having had under my consideration the whole subject of the arming of Corps of Rifle Volunteers, and the measures which appear to be necessary in order to ensure an uniform system, as well in accounting for the arms in possession of the Volunteers, as in providing for their due preservation and efficiency. I have the honour to recall to your recollection that, at the period when the greatest number of Corps offered their services, the state of the stores did not permit the Government to arm the Volunteers completely. At first, therefore, they were required to provide their own rifles, under prescribed conditions as to sizes of bore and nipple: then a certain number were issued percent to them by the Government: and afterwards the arms were supplied for all enrolled members.

Thus two systems of arming Volunteers came into operation, and recent inspections have shown that not infrequently two descriptions of rifle are in use in the same Corps, some the property of the Government, and some of the Volunteers themselves, who have provided them at their own expense.

As it is desirable that the supply of rifles should for the future be made from one source only, and that these Corps which have purchased their own arms, should be relieved as far as possible from the expenses which they have incurred in this respect, beyond those now thrown upon the more recently formed Corps. Her Majesty's Government are prepared to purchase all such rifles as are now the property of Corps or individual Volunteers, at the price paid for arms of similar pattern under the Government contract, namely £3.2s.6d., and in cases where Volunteers object to part with their own rifles upon those terms, it is to be understood that Government arms will be issued for their use in the Corps.

I have, therefore, requested that you will make known this decision to the various Rifle Volunteer Corps in the County under your charge, and will cause a return to be made to me of the number and description of arms, not the property of the Government, which are now in use by them.

The Volunteers will be allowed the continued use of the arms thus purchased, on the conditions in force with respect to the arms issued by the Government, except in cases where there are two descriptions of arms in one Corps, and where it may be necessary, for the sake of uniformity, to issue the Enfield Rifle to all the Volunteers.

For the future, however, all Rifle Volunteer Corps will be required to use the arms issued to them by Government, and no new Corps will be sanctioned in which it is intended that the members should be armed in any other manner.

I have also to impress upon you the importance of maintaining the Regulation which requires that all the rifles should be invariably deposited in the armouries of the Corps. I am aware, however, that certain Corps would be subjected to much inconvenience were a rigid adherence to the regulations enforced in these cases, and I shall be prepared, therefore, upon receiving a recommendation from you to that effect, to sanction a relaxation of this regulation in cases of such rural or scattered Corps as you may consider from their local distribution to require it; and in such cases to permit the arms to remain in the charge, and be retained at the houses of the members of the Corps, provided always, that every rifle is subject to the inspection of the Officers Commanding Companies, once a week: and of the Assistant Inspector of the Division, and in the cases of Administrative Battalions, of the Field Officer Commanding, as often as they may deem necessary, on the understanding, that in all instances where the arms are neglected, the privilege shall be withdrawn.

I am also disposed to extend this privilege to such members of Corps existing in cities and large towns as may, from residing at a distance from their Headquarters, be unable to conveniently deposit their rifle daily in the armoury. In such cases written permission may be given, at the discretion of the Commanding Officer to individual members, but the privilege is to be judiciously exercised, and strictly under the provisions already prescribed for Rural Corps, and the Commanding Officers will be required to cause the number of members to whom, he has granted permission to retain their arms to be inserted in the periodical return furnished by the Adjutant.

Having thus considered the convenience of the Volunteers by affording them the greatest possible latitude which a due regard for the public interests will permit. I have to urge the necessity of strictly adhering to the Regulations in all other cases. It has been found that arms not kept in the store are often subject to rapid deterioration from want of careful and proper treatment, and there is no doubt that the habitual return of the arms to the store after use is important to the efficiency of the Corps, and I have to express my hope that these Regulations will be strictly obeyed, and I beg that you will intimate to the Volunteers serving in your County that I feel it my duty strictly to enforce them.

I have the honour to be
MY LORD
Your most obedient servant,
SIDNEY HERBERT.

Her Majesty's Lieutenant,
for the County of Wigtown,
Culhorn House, Stranraer,
Wigtownshire.

The first recorded Wigtownshire meeting was that of the 1st Wigtownshire Rifle Volunteers, Wigtown, on the 8th May, 1861. Lieutenant Agnew and Ensign McHaffie, donated £5 to be shot for as three prizes, in competition at 150, 200, 250, and 300 yards. It was a condition that unless the winner scored a total of at least 25 points, 2nd 23 points, 3rd 21 points, then the prize money would be halved. The first score was 22 points, 2nd 18 points. It was, however, mentioned that of the entry, not one, man had fired more than 50 shots in practice.

The competition for prizes given by Captain Guthrie, to be shot for by members of the 2nd Wigtownshire Rifle Volunteers, Stranraer, took place on their rifle range at Aird Cottage, on Saturday, the 10th August, 1861. The weather was rather unfavourable by strong winds blowing across the range, accompanied at intervals by thick rain. The shooting was pretty good considering their want of practice, but the more accustomed they got the more excited they became. The following results are those of the 11 men who finished highest:-

Sergeant McBryde	24 points	Sergeant Taylor	12 points
Sergeant Miller	15	Wingate R. Mann	12
John Dornan	14	John Gourlay	12
W.C. Inglis	13	John McLean	11
William Grey	13	W. Patterson	11
John Williamson	13		

On the 10th August, 1861, the first recorded friendly competition was to take place between two Companies of the Galloway Rifle Volunteers, the 1st and 2nd Kirkcudbrightshire Rifle Volunteer Corps - Kirkcudbright and Castle Douglas, at Caigton. Kirkcudbright was to win the match. It was then arranged for the winner of this match to meet the 3rd Kirkcudbrightshire Rifles - New Galloway, at Mossdale the following week.

Thursday, 22nd August, 1861, was the day fixed for shooting of the 5th Wigtownshire Rifle Volunteers - Kirkmaiden, for prizes donated by the Ladies of the Parish. The weather was fine and early in the day numerous gaily dressed parties were seen to be wending their way to the range of the Corps on the shore at Killiness. The Corps under Lieutenant Watson mustered at 11am and moved out to meet the Stranraer Rifle Volunteers who had brought their Fife and Drum Band to add colour to the occasion. They marched to the range where the shooting was at 150, 200, and 300 yards, 5 rounds at each. The result being as follows:-

1st Prize -	Field Glasses and a silver medal -	Private John McBryde - 18 pts.
2nd Prize -	Walnut Dressing Case -	Private John Bickford - 16 pts.
3rd Prize -	Walnut Writing Desk -	Private John McLurg - 16 pts.

The Companies were then drawn up in line and marched forward to a splendid array of Ladies who were seated on a beautiful bank looking upon the bold promontory of the Mull. The Corps halted in front of the Ladies and presented arms. The successful competitors were then marched to the front and presented with their prizes, by Misses Anderson, Graham and Hardie.

In his closing speech Captain Guthrie congratulated the Volunteers on their excellent shooting pointing out the necessity for Company drill. He referred to the warlike force at "Bull's Run" (American Civil War then taking place), as illustrating the necessity of the Company being properly drilled. "For although the Americans were generally excellent rifle shots, they were no sooner engaged with the enemy than they got into confusion and ran helter-skelter to the rear."

On Saturday, 18th October, 1861, the 1st, 3rd and 4th Wigtown Rifle Volunteers - Wigtown, Newton Stewart and Whithorn Corps, met at Kirwaugh, Wigtown, to compete for a Whitworth Rifle, value £25, presented by the Earl of Galloway. The day was dull but favourable for the contest. There was a large turnout of spectators. The Volunteers competing, numbered 67. The conditions of the competition were 5 rounds at 200 yards, with those scoring 5 points, which numbered 33 going on to the 400 yards and 600 yards range, which were also 5 rounds at each. The contest began at 9am, and at mid-day the Earl and Countess of Galloway and family appeared on the field. The contest finished at 3pm with the following results:-

	200yds.	400yds.	600yds.	Total.
George Christison, Wigtown Corps.	7	5	6	18
Thomas Stewart, Newton Stewart Corps.	8	5	4	17
James Christison, Wigtown Corps.	8	5	3	16
Ensign McHaffie, Wigtown Corps.	9	4	2	15
James Erkskine, Newton Stewart Corps.	5	5	5	15
Sergeant Mackie, Wigtown Corps.	11	2	1	14
Thomas Rea, Whithorn Corps.	9	5	0	14
Sergeant Limmond, Whithorn Corps.	7	6	1	14

	200yds.	400yds.	600yds.	Total.
George Paton, Wigtown Corps.	6	5	2	13
Corporal McConnell, Whithorn Corps.	7	4	2	13
W. McNaught, ...	7	3	3	13
James Young, ...	5	5	3	13
Sergeant Candlish, ...	7	4	2	13

At 5pm the Earl of Galloway presented Private Christison with the rifle when 40 of the Volunteers retired to the Queen's Arms for a dinner and social evening.

7th September, 1861, the members of the 2nd Kirkcudbrightshire Rifle Volunteers, were shooting for a marble time piece and 55 rounds of ammunition.

In consequence of the report of the Royal commission of the 14th August, 1862, and subsequent Regulations, under the Volunteer Act, 1863, issued on the 21st July, 1863, which recommended a grant of 20/- to every Volunteer who made himself efficient by attending 9 drills in a year of which 6, in the case of Consolidated and 3 in Administrative Battalions should be Battalion drills, and have gone through a course of Musketry. A grant of 10/- was also paid to riflemen who fired a prescribed quantity of ball cartridge in the course of a year. The Act was to be quite specific in the first stage. "No Volunteer will be considered efficient unless his Commanding Officer can certify that he has attained a competent knowledge of Squad and Company drills, including the Manual and Platoon exercises and Skirmishing as a Company. He must also possess a competent knowledge of the theory and practice of Musketry and fire 20 rounds of ball ammunition. This will constitute the 1st stage of efficiency and will enable the Corps to draw from Government 20/- for every man who is thus efficient.

The next stage will be entirely a Musketry affair and the 2nd part of the grant of 10/- per man will only be given for men who have fired 60 rounds of ball ammunition, and who make 15 points in 3rd Class firing - that is in 20 rounds firing from 150 to 300 yards."

Pressure from the Volunteer Corps was to result in the requirement for the firing of 20 rounds of ball ammunition to be dropped as a condition of the 1st stage.

By 1869, the Government demanded a greater degree of skill from the Volunteer and whereas he could still earn the 2nd stage of the capitation grant by firing 60 rounds of ball ammunition and scoring 15 points in 3rd Class firing, he would now lose the capitation grant if he failed to achieve 2nd Class Musketry in three consecutive years.

In consequence of a further War Office circular in August, 1870, relative to formation of Volunteer Camps of Exercise and for the first time Government were to authorise grants for proficiency by officers and Sergeants who undertook courses of instruction and a written examination in front of their Adjutant, the Government were to add the proviso that, after 1871, no Volunteer would be passed as efficient unless his rifle had been inspected and found to be in good order.

The following are the rules for rifle practice for the Volunteers, issued on the 13th January, 1864, in a circular from the School of Musketry, Hythe, and which outlined the various classes of firing which were required and which could be attained by the Volunteer.

(1) The number of targets and the dimensions of bulls-eyes and centres for the several classes to be as follows.
Dimensions of:-

Classes	No. of Targets	Centre		Bulls-eye	
		Height	Breadth	Height	Breadth
From 150 to 300 yards, inclusive, or for 3rd Class.	2	4'	1'	1'	6"
From 400 to 600 yards, inclusive, or for 2nd Class.	3	4'	2'	1'	1'
From 600 to 900 yards, inclusive, or for 1st Class.	4	4'	3'	1'	2'
File and Volley firing.	6	-	-	1'	12'
Skirmishing	1	-	-	1'	2'

(2) Shots hitting the target to be valued for all classes as follows:-
Bulls-eyes - 4 points; centres - 3 points; outers - 2 points.
All shots hitting the horizontal black line, in file, volley and skirmishing practice, to count 4.

(3) The points to be obtained as a qualification to pass into a higher class, and to establish a claim for extra

pay as marksman, are as follows - number of points to be obtained with Enfield in 3rd class to pass into 2nd class - 30 points; with small bore - 40 points. In 2nd class to pass into 1st class with Enfield - 30 points; with small bore 40 points. In 1st class to be 'marksman' with Enfield - 30 points; with small bore 32 points.

(4) In executing the volley practice a man whose rifle misses fire in the volley is not to be allowed to fire at the target singly but his round is to be counted as having been expended.

(5) The order of merit regulating the issue of extra pay to men who become marksmen to be determined by the greatest number of points obtained in shooting in the 1st and 2nd classes, i.e. 40 rounds.

(6) The best shot of the Battalion will be that man who having attained in the 1st class upwards of 30 points with the Enfield rifle or 32 points with the small bore, scores the highest number of points in the 1st and 2nd classes, i.e. in 40 rounds and is in the first class judging distance at the final classification.

]****

On the 4th September, 1862, the 2nd Wigtownshire Rifle Corps - Stranraer, and the 5th Wigtownshire Rifle Volunteers - Drummore, met at the Craigcaffie range, Stranraer, for a shoot for prizes. Conditions 5 rounds at 400 and 600 yards. The result was as follows:-

1st pair of Field Glasses won by Private Crawford, Stranraer.
2nd No prize   Private Fleming, Stranraer.
3rd No prize   Captain Guthrie, Stranraer.
    Sweepstake. Conditions - 5 rounds at 200 yards.
1st Ensign Anderson, Drummore.
2nd Mr. McClurg.   ..

****

The following Company competition took place at Newton Stewart on the 16th September, 1862. 1st Prize - donated of a Silver Cup.

	200 yds.	400yds	600yds.	Total
1. William Picken	15	16	11	42
2. Robert Picken	12	15	10	37
3. Joseph Hewetson	14	13	8	35
4. James Erskine	12	16	5	33
5. Thomas Stewart	9	14	9	32
6. Alex. McConchie	12	11	7	30
7. Lieutenant Stewart	13	10	6	29

On the 16th October, 1862, a match at rifle shooting took place amongst the 4th Wigtownshire Rifle Volunteers - Whithorn, on their range at the Coonan Shore, of a sweepstake of 2/6d each, with a subscription of £2 added. Invitations had been sent to Wigtown and Newton Stewart. The weather was rather windy for good shooting at the longer distances. The conditions were 5 shots at 400, 500 and 600 yards. The prizes being:- £1.12s.6d; £1.2s; 15/-; 8/-. The results as follows:-

1. Private James Christison, Wigtown	36 points and hits
2. Private Joseph Jibb, Whithorn	29
3. Private G. Christison, Wigtown	21
4. Private Thomas Rae, Whithorn	19
5. Sergeant James Young, Whithorn	14
6. Private James Henderson, Wigtown	14
7. Sergeant Stair Connel, Whithorn	13
8. Private Agnew, Wigtown	12

A friendly shooting match took place on Wednesday, 26th November, 1862, between 5 members of the Gatehouse, 4th Kirkcudbrightshire Rifle Volunteers and Kirkcudbright, 1st Kirkcudbrightshire Rifle Volunteers, at the range belonging to the Gatehouse Company. The conditions were 5 rounds at 150, 200, 400 and 500 yards.

Kirkcudbright		Gatehouse	
Sergeant Payne	38 points	Ensign Ewart	47 points
Sergeant Thomson	42	Sergeant Waugh	50
Private Williamson	52	Corporal McBride	39
Private Grierson	46	Private Cairns	50
Private Lightbody	33	Private McLean	44
	----		----
	211 points		230 points

Gatehouse Majority 19 points.

****

The shooting season of the Volunteer Corps generally took place during the course of the Volunteer year, 1st May until the 30th November, later changing in 1872, to 31st October. However, in 1863, a novelty New Year shoot was to take place by members of the 1st Kirkcudbrightshire and the 2nd Kirkcudbrightshire Rifle Volunteers - Kirkcudbright and Castle Douglas. These shoots were to prove of such a success to both Volunteers and public alike, who came forward in great numbers to support the events, that the other Kirkcudbrightshire and Wigtownshire Companies were to follow suit with New Year's rifle meetings. The tradition was carried on annually by most Companies of the Galloway Rifles, until the demise of the volunteers in 1908.

On Thursday, 1st January, 1863, 30 members of the Kirkcudbright Rifle Volunteers, marched to the practice ground at Lochfergus. The contest lasted from 9am till dark. The 1st three prizes were gained as follows:-

1st Mr Grierson, Campbelton.
2nd Mr Campbell, Culcrae.
3rd Mr. Brown, Kirkcudbright.

The 2nd Class prizes were won by Mr. Blacklock and Mr Thomas Martin. The prizes for those who had not yet got out of 3rd class were won by Mr. McSkimming and Mr. A. Williamson of Sypland.

****

On New Year's day, 1st January, 1863, the members of the 2nd Kirkcudbright Rifles, Castle Douglas, met for a competition for a rifle presented by Captain Mackie, M.P. and a six barrelled revolver presented by Mr. Samuel Gordon, and a volume of books presented by Sergeant Skirving. The following were the results at 200 and 400 yards.

	Points	Hits	Total
Sergeant Robertson	16	9	25
A. Kirk	13	9	22
J. Murdoch	14	8	22
J. Henderson	14	7	21
Robert Grierson	11	8	19
B. Rae	11	7	18
James Murdoch	10	8	18
Sergeant McVane	10	7	17
Sergeant R. C. Thomson	10	7	17
J.Mitchell	10	7	17
Corporal Boreland	9	7	16
Joseph Grierson	10	6	16
Joseph Pearson	10	6	16
James Pearson	10	6	16
Sergeant J. Thomson	8	7	15

The 3rd annual competition of the 5th Wigtown Rifles, Drummore, took place on the range at Killiness on Wednesday, 27th August, 1863. The medal was won by Private William Watson, for the 2nd time, who was the son of the Commanding Officer. 5 rounds at 500 and 600 yards;.

1st Private William Watson	21 points
2nd Lieutenant Watson (father)	20
3rd Ensign Anderson	19

A friendly competition took place between the 1st Wigtown and the 3rd Kirkcudbright, New Galloway, on the ranges at Newton Stewart, on Saturday, 21st November, 1863. 11 Competitors on each side. 7 shots at 200 and 600 yards. Hythe position. Wimbledon scoring.

3rd Kirkcudbrightshire (New Galloway)	200 yds	600 yds	Total
Hon. Surgeon Millman	15	9	24
Sergeant Muir	17	5	22
Sergeant Henderson	16	2	18
Privates Craig	16	12	28
Bruce	15	21	36
Milroy	13	11	24
Wilson	18	11	29
Kerr	16	12	28
Stevenson	6	8	14
Geddes	11	18	29
Kinna	14	16	30
	-----	-----	-----
	157	125	282
1st Wigtownshire (Wigtown)			
Ensign McHaffie	11	5	16
Sergeant McCulloch	13	5	18
Privates Anderson	11	3	14
Christison	11	10	21
D. Henderson	8	6	14
McDonald	14	4	18
McAnally	12	5	17
McBean	16	8	24
W. Wilson	13	5	18
Paton	11	2	13
J. McCulloch	14	9	23
	-----	----	-----
	134	62	196

New Galloway won by a Majority of 86.

****

A friendly match took place between 10 members of the 2nd Kirkcudbright Rifles, Castle Douglas, and the 3rd Wigtownshire Rifles, Newton Stewart, on Thursday, 24th March, 1864, at the Newton Stewart ranges. Conditions 5 rounds at 200, 500 and 600 yards, with Wimbledon scoring.

Newton Stewart.	200yds.	500yds.	600yds	Total	
Privates Joseph Hewitson	16	13	11	40	
James Dargie	12	14	13	39	
A. McConchie	14	12	11	37	
James Picken	12	11	14	37	
Sergeant McConchie	15	11	10	36	
Privates James Erskine	14	14	6	34	
Wm. Agnew	14	13	7	34	
W. Picken	15	10	6	31	
Sergeant Picken	8	12	8	28	
Private Thomas Stewart	12	13	3	28	
					344
Castle Douglas					
Sergeant Robertson	13	14	13	40	
Sergeant Skirving	13	13	11	37	
Corporal McGuffog	12	12	10	34	
Kirk	14	10	10	34	
Privates Papple	11	12	10	33	
Joseph Grierson	12	8	10	30	
John Murdoch	14	10	2	26	
Corporal Aitken	14	6	5	25	
Private James Mitchell	12	5	5	22	
James Henderson	13	7	2	22	
					303

Newton Stewart won by a Majority of 41 points.

A friendly competition between 12 members of the 1st Dumfries Rifle Volunteer Corps, Dumfries and the 5th Kirkcudbrightshire Rifle Volunteers, Maxwellton, came off at the ranges of the Dumfries Corps, at Mabie, on 26th September, 1864. Conditions 5 rounds each at 150, 300, 500 and 650 yards.

Maxwellton	Points & hits	Dumfries	Points & hits
Lieutenant Allan	15	Ensign Dunbar	30
Sergeants Crackston	32	Colour Sergeant McNeillie	34
Kirk	26	Sergeant Alder	29
Rae	24	Corporal Aikman	40
Private Tait	37	Privates Calderwood	21
Corporal MacMillan	33	Crichton	18
Privates Gordon	19	D. Gourlay	32
Walker	31	Hutchison	34
Holmes	33	Johnstone	34
McGeorge	40	Maxwell	25
Corrie	21	Mens	45
Anderson	26	Jardine	40
	337		382

Majority for Dumfries, 1st D.R.V. 45 points.

On 10th November, 1864, the members of the 2nd Wigtownshire - Stranraer, shot for a gold medal presented by Captain Guthrie, with £2 added. The medal was won by Captain Guthrie but as he had presented it, he let it be given to the runner-up.

On the 11th August, 1865, the last shoot of the season for the 5th Kirkcudbrightshire Rifles, Maxwellton, monthly medal, was held.

On the 30th December, 1865, the 3rd Kirkcudbrightshire Rifles, New Galloway, shot for a gold medal.

On New Year's day, 1st January, 1866, the members of the 3rd Wigtownshire Rifles, Newton Stewart, held a Company sweepstake on their Barrhill ranges. The conditions being 200, 400 and 500 yards. 7 rounds at each distance. Hythe position throughout. The following were the principal scores:-

	200yds	400yds	500yds	Total
1st Private James Picken	17	26	12	55
2nd Sergeant William Agnew	19	21	14	54
3rd Senior Sgt. Thomas Stewart	16	19	17	52
4th Corporal James Hinds	18	15	19	52

The first inter Stewartry v Wigtownshire Meeting took place at the Caigton Ranges, Castle Douglas, on the 24th May, 1866, but unfortunately without result.

On Thursday, 24th May, 1866, a friendly match took place between the 2nd Kirkcudbrightshire Rifle Volunteer Corps and the 3rd Wigtownshire Rifle Volunteer Corps, Newton Stewart, at the Caigton Ranges, Castle Douglas. The conditions were 7 rounds at 200, 400 and 500 yards. Wimbledon scoring.

Newton Stewart	200yds	400yds	500yds	Total	
Corporal W. Picken	23	17	14	54	
Sergeant Hewetson	18	22	13	53	
Corporal James Picken	17	13	18	48	
Sergeant Agnew	17	17	2	36	
Sergeant Stewart	11	17	10	33	
					224
Castle Douglas					
Corporal Kirk	19	21	12	52	
Sergeant Robertson	17	13	19	49	
Corporal McGuffog	18	20	10	48	
Sergeant R. C. Thomson	18	18	9	45	
Private Joseph Grierson	18	21	5	44	
					238

Castle Douglas won by a Majority of 14 points.

On the 26th May, 1866, the Whithorn Volunteers mustered at their range for a sweepstake at 150 and 200 yards, 5 rounds at each distance.

Sergeant McConnell	31 points		
Sergeant Hughan	25	Corporal Rae	22 points
Private H..D. Stewart	23	Private H. Dickey	21
Private Hewitson	23	Private J. Mathews	20

****

On Friday, 15th June, 1866, the Whithorn Volunteers met in a contest for a pair of Field Glasses and money prizes. Results:-

1st Private Hewitson	4th Corporal Jibb
2nd Private Webster	5th Private Halliday
3rd Private Dickie	6th Private McAdam

****

The 1st of the meetings between the Dumfriesshire Rifle Volunteer Battalion and the Galloway Rifle Volunteer Battalion, was to take place on Thursday, 26th July, 1866, at the ranges of Conhuith, Maxwellton, having been arranged between Ensign Skirving of the Galloway Battalion and Lieutenant Anderson of Moffat and the Dumfriesshire Battalion. The Dumfriesshire team comprised of 3 x 1st Dumfries; 2 x 2nd Thornhill; 2 x 3rd Sanquhar; 3 x 4th Penpont; 2 x 5th Annan; 2 x 6th Moffat; 2 x 7th Langholm; 2 x 8th Lockerbie; 2 x 9th Lochmaben. The Galloway team comprised 3 x 1st Kirkcudbright; 4 x 2nd Castle Douglas; 3 x 3rd New Galloway; 3 x 1st Wigtown; 5 x 3rd Wigtown, Newton Stewart; 1 x 2nd Wigtown, Stranraer; 1 x 4th Wigtown, Whithorn. The conditions were 20 men a-side with 5 shots at 200, 500 and 600 yards. One sighting shot at each distance.

Dumfriesshire		Total	Galloway Rifles		Total
Colour Sergeant Lindsay	3Dfs.	45	T. R. Bruce	3 Kbt.	51 points
W. T. Noake	2	44	Corporal Kirk	2Kbt.	43
Alex. Jardine	8	40	Corporal McGuffog	2Kbt	41
Captain J. Mitchell	4	38	Ensign Craig	1 Kbt.	41
W. Davey	7	38	Sergeant W. Agnew	3Wgn.	40
Captain J. Jardine	1	36	Corporal J. Picken	3Wgn.	38
Captain A. Hutchison	1	36	Sergeant Muir	3Kbt	38
G. Byers	7	36	Corporal W. Picken	3 Wgn.	38
Sergeant S. Halliday	6	36	Sergeant W. Wilson	1Wgn.	37
P. Waugh	9	35	Sergeant Cairns	3Wgn.	37
Sergeant C. Howitt	2	35	John Watret	3Kbt	37
James Broadfoot	3	31	Sergeant Waugh	1 Kbt.	36
C. Craike	9	30	J. Grierson	2Kbt.	36
R. Maxwell	1	29	Jas. McCulloch	1 Wgn.	35
Ensign Morrison	5	29	Sergeant Caird	1Kbt.	34
Sergeant Kennedy	4	28	Sergeant Robertson	2 Kbt.	34
Corporal J. Schoolar	8	27	Corporal J. Hewitson	3Wgn.	33
W. Anderson	6	26	Sergeant J. McConnell	4Wgn.	32
J. Milligan	4	23	G. Geddes	3Kbt.	26
Sergeant Thomson	5	22	Corporal J. Christison	1Wgn.	22
		-----			-----
		665			729

The Galloway Battalion won by 64 points. The contest was said to have been decided at the 200 yard range where the Galloway men, out of their 100 shots never missed the target. Mr. T. R. Bruce alone made 51 points, with a maximum at the 200 yard range, scoring 5 bulls-eyes, 14 points at the 500 and 17 points at the 600 yard range.

****

The annual competition among the Officers and men of the 2nd Wigtownshire Rifle Volunteers, Stranraer, for the gold medal given by Captain Guthrie and other prizes, took place on the Stranraer ranges, on Saturday, 13th October, 1866. The conditions being 5 rounds at 200 and 400 yards.

1st Private W. Watson - gold medal & £3	24 points
2nd Private J. Watson - £2.10s.	24
3rd Private G. Wither - £1	22

4th Private J. Warren - 15/-	22	
5th Private W. Paterson - 15/-	19	
6th Private A. Crawford -5/-	19	

The role of the Rifle Volunteer was seen first and foremost as being that of a rifleman as opposed to that, of a line infantryman, his whole training being geared towards his affinity to and use of, the rifle, and it was to this end that every effort was made by, Government and officers alike, to promulgate the rifleman image and encourage the Volunteer in his every step, in the Movement's infancy. The stimulus, to the early Volunteer, in the use of the rifle, was to be very much that of inducement through cash and kind. It was only in later years, when the Volunteer Movement was seen to be fully established that merely to be a member of a Volunteer Corps was in itself sufficient stimulus, with cups, badges and medals and small cash prizes, being the trappings of a successful Rifle Volunteer.

It will be noted throughout the history of the Galloway Rifle Volunteer's various competitions, both at Company and at county level, that, in the early years fairly high cash prizes of many pounds were on offer but in the later years, the cash prizes were to become much smaller and spread over a wider placement. Further to encourage the early Volunteer, prizes in kind were to be offered, as was seen in the rifle meeting of the Kirkmaiden Volunteers, and on the 22nd August, 1861, when field glasses, dressing table and writing desk, were to be won. An extremely interesting "Subscription Shooting" match was to take place on the 14th September, 1872, the result being lovingly recorded in the Company shooting records, of the 7th Dumfriesshire Rifle Volunteers - Langholm. These prizes were donated by local townsmen and businessmen:-

	200yds	500yds	Total
1. R. MacVittie - A Rifle by A. Reid	17	17	34
2. Jas. Bell - Gold Locket by Jas. Hogg	15	18	33
3. W. Little - Waterproof by R. Smellie	14	17	31
4. Thos. Winhope - Trouser Piece by J. Bell & Sons	15	15	30
5. S. Hounam - Trouser Piece by W. Millar	15	15	30
6. A. Pearson - Courier Bag by A. & H. Sanders	16	14	30
7. A. Rae - Half dozen pairs of socks by N. McLeary	13	16	29
8. W. Bell - 4 stones of flour by Wm. Easton	11	16	27
9. Thos. Thornburn - Meerschaum Pipe by Jas. Graham	13	15	28
10. W. Scott - Pocket Knife by Jas. Glendinning	13	15	28
11. Jno. Beattie - Water Colour by	15	13	28
12. G. Byers - Pocket Knife by J. Harkness	15	12	27
13. A. Scott - 2lbs Tea by W. Mepser	11	15	26
14. W. Murray - Thompson's Poems by R. Scott	11	15	26
15. J. Pearson - Keg of Herring by G. Balfour	12	14	26
16. W. Little - Tobacco by J. Church	13	13	26
17. Jas. Beattie - Shirt by W. Elliot	13	13	26
18. T. Bell - Burns Poems by W. Wilson	14	12	26
19. J. Cowan - 2lbs Tea by J. J. Thompson	13	12	25
20. A. Moses - Box of Cigars by R. M. Rome	16	9	25
21. J. Glendinning - Photographs (local) by C. Carruthers	13	11	24
22. T. A. Bowman - Pocket Knife by J. Knowx	14	10	24

This "Subscription Shooting" or "Prize Shooting" was very much reflected in the humour of the day - "Friend (to Private Butts of the Mumbleton Fallbacks) - Are you going in for the "Queen's Prize"? Private B - "Queen's Prize" be hanged! I always enter for the usual competitions. Already I've won a sewing machine, three dozen of Scotch Whisky, a package of sardines in oil, a miniature organ, and a box of compressed soups. And I've got a very good chance of getting a case of champagne and a revolver tomorrow, Old Boy!"

To appeal to the Volunteer's competitive nature and maintain his interest, as well as Company meetings, competitions between the varying Companies of the Galloway Rifles were introduced. These Inter-Company meetings, together with the County Association meetings were to prove to be the mainstay of the rifle shooting within the Volunteer Movement and were to gather in popularity as the Movement progressed. Many other successful events were introduced, which remained popular, in one form or another, many novelties being added to maintain the Volunteer's interest. Surprisingly no Inter-Company league was ever formed within the Galloway Rifle Volunteers.

We have already mentioned New Year's shoots which proved most successful. The monthly medal was a successful Company event but in April, 1867, the 2nd Kirkcudbrightshire Rifles, Castle Douglas, introduced a rule that the distance at which the next competition would take place should be chosen by the current holder of the monthly medal. Gold medals were presented by various dignitaries and Officers, Captain Guthrie to the 2nd Wigtownshire Rifle Volunteers and Viscountess Kenmure to the 3rd Kirkcudbrightshire Rifles, New Galloway.

To promote friendly rivalry, the officers of the Artillery and Rifle Volunteers in Kirkcudbright, gave a gold medal to be competed for between the two Companies. It was arranged that whichever Corps won the medal, was thereafter, to have amongst its own members, a competition to decide who was to have the honour of wearing the medal for the ensuing year. The first competition took place on Saturday, 13th October, 1866. 5 rounds at 100, 200 and 300 yards, at Lochfergus. The competition was quite comfortably won by the Galloway Rifle Volunteers, with a margin of 72 points. On Thursday, 18th October, 1866, at Lochfergus Range, the medal was gained by Ensign Craig. The medal was manufactured by Mr McSkimming, Jeweller, Kirkcudbright.

Note. In the annual competitions between the Kirkcudbright Rifles and the Kirkcudbright Garrison Artillery, these were held alternately at their own ranges. 1st Kirkcudbright Rifles at Lochfergus and the 1st Kirkcudbright Garrison Artillery at the Shore Park. The 1st Kirkcudbright Artillery range was closed at the Shore Park on the 26th April, 1890, owing to the danger of the bullets from the Martini-Henry rifle. The targets at Lochfergus were altered to accommodate the Artillery Canvas targets, the only problem being apparently that the markers could not now see the splash of the shell as they could at the Shore Park.

On Saturday, 20th October, 1866, the 3rd Wigtownshire Rifles, Newton Stewart, competed at the Barrhill Range, for two Silver Cups presented by Captain Stroyan and Ensign McConchie. These cups were to become known as the Captain's Cup and the Ensign Cup, and were to be shot for annually. The winning of the Ensign Cup was to decide the winning of a match for a dinner, between 'The Benedicts and the Bachelors'. On this occasion the 'Benedicts' won the dinner. This type of competition was to become very popular among the Volunteers, and we find that on the 17th November, 1866, a contest was to take place at Castle Douglas, between the Married Men and the Unmarried Men, of the 2nd Kirkcudbright Rifles. The Married Men won on this occasion.

An unusual event took place in Dalbeattie, which also happened to be the first recorded shooting competition of the 6th Kirkcudbrightshire Rifle Volunteers. On the 21st January, 1869, the members of the Dalbeattie Corps, held a belated New Year's Ball, which finished at 3am Later that morning, at 9am a shoot took place on their ranges for prizes donated by the Merchants of the Burgh. Scoring was said to be very average, notwithstanding the fatigue and excitement which most of the shooters underwent the previous night. 17 Prizes were on offer with the following result:-

	200yds.	400yds.	Total.		200yds.	400yds.	Total.
Corporal Kerr	18	16	34	Private Glendinning	17	9	26
Private Shearer	14	14	28	Private Allan	14	12	26
Sergeant Graham	16	12	28	Private McLaghlan	15	10	25
Sergeant Hume	18	10	28	Private Gillespie	12	12	24
Corporal McGregor	13	13	26	Sergeant Clark	13	10	23
Private Craig	13	13	26	Private Marchbank	8	15	23
Private McMullen	15	11	26	Private Gilbertson	14	8	22
Private Wilson	14	12	26	Private Birss	9	10	19
				Private James Hume	10	9	19

By October, 1869, weekly shoots during the Volunteer Year were taking place in all Companies of the Galloway Rifles, together with the inter-Company shoots, both home and away. The Movement was now fairly established. However a further novelty was noted in a competition between men who joined on the inception of the Movement in 1860 and those who had recently joined. A later variation on this theme was competitions between retired and present numbers of the various Companies.

In July, 1871, members of the 5th Kirkcudbright Rifles, Maxwellton, held a competition of the Band v Rank and File.

On the 4th September, 1871, subscription shooting took place on the ranges of the 2nd Kirkcudbrightshire Rifle Volunteers, for prizes donated by the townspeople.

On 3rd October, 1871, the 3rd Kirkcudbrightshire Rifle Volunteers, held a shoot between the non-commissioned officers and privates.

By 1870, we were to find that annual competitions were now taking place between Ayrshire and Galloway, both at Company and at County level. The earliest trace of an inter-county shoot at Company level was on the 12th August, 1864, when the 2nd Kirkcudbrightshire Rifle Volunteers, Castle Douglas, met a team from Kilmarnock. There was no result recorded.

In June, 1888, Captain Kerr 'H' Company, Dalbeattie, presented his Company with a Silver Cup, for half yearly competition. It was at the presentation of this cup some three years later, on 18th September, 1891, that Captain now Major Kerr, intimated his intention to retire from the Company. He was to be succeeded by Captain Maxwell, Kirkennan.

A single sweepstake was suffice on occasions to keep the Volunteer's interest alive, as on the 2nd September, 1892, when Gatehouse Section of 'A' Company met for a sweepstake and a few prizes donated by friends of the Movement. The competition took place at the Disdow Ranges. The squad was under the Command of Corporal Kirkpatrick, and the result of the day's shooting was as follows:-

1.	James Bertram	8.	N. M. Hughan
2.	William Cairns	9.	W. Crawford
3.	E. Ewan	10.	W. Dalrymple
4.	Thos. Dalrymple	11.	W. Carson
5.	J. Ewan	12.	John Veitch
6.	R. McCourty	13.	A. Nelson
7.	J. R. Kirkpatrick	14.	D. Y. Veitch

The final and probably the most bizarre incentive for competition was on the 12th October, 1901, when the Ladies of Kirkcudbright presented to the Bachelors of 'A' Company, Kirkcudbright, for annual competition, a plain gold marriage ring, inscribed 'Ladies Prize 1901'. The condition being that should the winner get married in the year he held the ring, it became his property. No record exists as to whether the purpose of the ring was ever attained.

On Thursday, 26th September, 1867, a shoot took place on the Mabie Estate, between members of the 5th Kirkcudbright Rifles, Maxwellton.

1st Competition a silver medal presented by Lieutenant Starke. Conditions 5 rounds at 200 and 400 yards.

1st	Private Mitchell (silver medal and 5/-)	28 points
2nd	Sergeant Gillum (books to the value of 5/-)	27

2nd Competition a Snider Rifle. Conditions 5 rounds at 150, 200, 300, and 500 yards.

1st	Sergeant McGeorge (Rifle)	46 points
2nd	Corporal Forteith (£1 cash)	39
3rd	Private Wemyss (10/- cash)	37
4th	Private Brown (5/- cash)	36

3rd Competition Gold Medal and 10/-.

1st	Corporal Anderson	35 points
2nd	Private McLellan (7/6d cash)	31
3rd	Sergeant McGeorge (2/6d cash)	30

****

All comers Enfield Rifle Meeting. In the early season of 1868, the first of these competitions was held at the Caigton Ranges, Castle Douglas. This experimental meeting proved to be such a success that it was decided to hold a similar meeting but on a larger scale. A Council was appointed of Captain Howat, Maxwellton, Lieutenant McGuffog, Castle Douglas, Ensign Stewart, New Galloway, Mr. Joseph Grierson, Breoch, Mr. R. C. Thompson, National Bank and Mr. M. M. Harper, British Linen Bank, both Castle Douglas, who acted as secretaries. Subscriptions were received to such an extent to enable them to issue a programme so attractive as to bring together most of the marksmen of Galloway and competitors from Dumfriesshire, Edinburgh, Cumberland and Lancashire etc.

The meeting took place on Tuesday, 13th July, 1869, Mr. J. Renny, of Danevale, acted as Umpire. The 200 yard range on the farm of Breoch and the 500 yard range on the farm of Caigton.

The conditions of the contest were 200 and 500 yards with 7 rounds at each distance. Wimbledon Targets and disc marking, position Hythe. Entry money 5/-. From an entry of 70 the following were the successful prize winners:-

1. Private Agnew, Newton Stewart (£7)	46 points.	
2. Sergeant Picken, Newton Stewart (£5)	44	
3. Private McCaull, Newton Stewart (£4)	44	
4. Corporal Christison, Wigtown (£3)	42	
5. Sergeant Wilson, New Galloway (£3)	41	
6. Private John Grierson, Castle Douglas (£2)	39	
7. Sergeant R. C. Thomson, Castle Douglas (£2)	37	
8. Col-Sergeant Muir, New Galloway (£2)	36	
9. Corporal Henderson, Castle Douglas (£1)	36	
10. Sergeant Watret, New Galloway (£1)	36	
11. Private Jos. Grierson, Castle Douglas (£1)	35	
12. Private Ritchie, Dalbeattie (£1)	35	
13. Corporal Picken, New Galloway (£1)	35	
14. Private Whinney, 7th Cumberland (10/-)	35	
15. Private Hannay, Newton Stewart (10/-)	35	

A special prize of £5 was donated by Mr. Gordon of Argrennan, which was divided into two prizes of £3 and £2 and shot for over 600 yards, 5 rounds each.

1. Private John Grierson, Castle Douglas (£3)	15 points.
2. Sergeant John Watret, New Galloway (£2)	12

It was hoped, by the organisers to repeat this competition the following year and so make it an annual competition, however, no further report was ever recorded of this competition and we can only assume that this was the first and the last of its kind.

By War Office Circular issued August, 1870. "The issue of Snider Rifles, to the Volunteers, will be first made to the Battalions which have the highest percentage of Efficients."

It was at first hoped to have the Snider Rifle issued to the Galloway Rifle Volunteers by the end of October of that year but they were not finally received into the Armouries of the Battalion until the end of December, 1870. The Snider Rifle was to replace the Short Enfield Rifled Musket.

The new Snider Rifle was the Snider-Enfield conversion of 1867. It was considered that the breech loading rifle was the weapon of the future and a conversion was produced by Jacob Snider, which was applied to the British Enfield Rifled Musket. The calibre of .577 was as before but the bullet was now produced in cartridge form relieving the Volunteer from the arduous necessity of the muzzle-loading drill. It was still however, basically the same fearsome weapon, throwing out this large lump of lead.

The Snider Rifle was to be the only weapon, to be used at the Wimbledon meeting of 1871.

With the issue of the Snider Rifle, a new drill was evolved infusing both spirit and interest in the Volunteer Movement, not only within Galloway but throughout the Country as a whole. The membership of the Galloway Rifle Volunteers was to increase by 62 members in the years ended 1870-71.

From the establishment of the 5th Kirkcudbrightshire Rifle Volunteers, Maxwellton, it had been customary to have Company competitions on the Thursday of the Rood Fair for some small prizes restricted to the Corps. For the year 1872, something more pretentious was attempted. It was resolved to have numerous and more valuable prizes, as well as "All Comer's Prizes". An appeal was made to the local Members of Parliament, to the Officers of the Battalion and to Principle Gentry of the District. The result being that the committee were enabled to offer some very fair prizes.

From what I note the "Fair Prizes" were kept to the Corps. Competitions 1-4 were confined to members of the 5th Kirkcudbright Rifles. The All Comers being made sweepstakes, with only £1 being added by the Corps.

The shooting took place at Conhuith ranges on Thursday, the 3rd October, 1872, commencing at 10am, with a large entry. Sergeant John Ferguson acted as Secretary, Scorer and Range Officer. Sergeant Murdoch was in charge of the targets. The first four competitions were confined to members of the Maxwellton Corps. Competition No.1 200 yards, 5 rounds standing. 1st Prize a vest and trousers presented by Messrs. A. Stewart & Son.

1. W. Stewart (1st Prize)	16 points
2. S. McAlister (15/-)	16
3. R. Armstrong (12/6d)	15
4. James Beck (7/6d)	14
5. D. Cameron (7/6d)	13
6. S. McLellan (5/-)	13
7. W. Wright (5/-)	13
8. W. Dobie (3/-)	13
9. Sergeant Coltart (2/6d)	12
10. T. Newlands (2/6d)	12

Competition No.2 - at 400 yards, 5 rounds any position. 1st Prize a Waterproof Coat presented by Mr. Tweedie, Hatter.

1. James Beck (1st Prize)	18 points
2. James Little (15/-)	17
3. Corporal R. Armstrong (10/-)	16
4. G. Armstrong (7/6d)	16
5. D. Johnstone (5/-)	16
6. W. Gardiner (2/6d)	15

Competition No.3. - at 500 yards, 5 rounds any position.

1. A. McLelland (25/-)	15points
2. W. Gardiner (15/-)	15
3. J. Murray (10/-)	14
4. Corporal R. Armstrong (7/6d)	14
5. W. Jardine (5/-)	12
6. G. Armstrong (3/-)	12
7. W. Murray (2/6d)	11

Competition No.4. - at 600 yards, 5 rounds any position. 1st Prize a Silver Cup presented by J. J. Fryer.

1. R. Johnstone (The Cup)	13 points
2. T. Newlands (20/-)	13
3. G. Armstrong (10/-)	12
4. W. Lockerby (5/-)	9
5. W. Gardiner (2/6d)	9
6. Corporal R. Armstrong (2/6d)	9

Competition No.5. - All Comers Sweepstake prize, with £1 added. 500 yards, 5 rounds any position.

1. Sergeant McAulay, Dumfries (£2)	18 points
2. J. Murray, Maxwellton (£1)	18
3. W. Dobie, Maxwellton (10/-)	16
4. Sergeant Henderson, Castle Douglas (10/-)	15

Competition No.6. - All Comers Sweepstake at 200 yards, 5 rounds standing. Two Divisions. 1st at 1pm 2nd at the conclusion of the tournament. Winners from 1pm Division disallowed from 2nd. Division. 47 entries to the 1st Division. 30 in the 2nd Division.

1st Division.

1. Sergeant McGhie, Dumfries (8/-)	13 points
2. D. Cameron, Maxwellton (5/3d)	13
3. John M. Gunn, Dumfries (4/-)	12

2nd Division.

1. John Murray, Maxwellton (5/-)	No scores recorded
2. R. Service, Dumfries (3/-)	.. ..
3. R. McNaught (2/-)	.. ..

On Saturday, 8th July, 1876, a friendly match took place between the 2nd Kirkcudbrightshire Rifle Volunteers, Castle Douglas, and the 3rd Kirkcudbrightshire Rifle Volunteers, New Galloway, at the Airie ranges, New Galloway. The conditions were 15 men a-side, 7 shots at 200 and 500 yards, one sighting shot at each distance, any position. The New Galloway Team were under the Command of Lieutenant Millman and the Castle Douglas Team were under the Command of Captain Gordon. Castle Douglas were to win the match by 6 points.

Castle Douglas Team.	200yds.	500yds.	Total.
Corporal W. McCaw	24	20	44
Corporal T. Myers	21	21	42
Corporal H. Murdoch	23	19	42
Corporal R. McAdam	23	18	41
Quartermaster Harper	21	19	40
Corporal J. McAdam	19	20	39
Private Bell	19	20	39
Private Campbell	22	16	38
Lieutenant McGuffog	20	17	37
Sergeant P. McKinna	22	15	37
Private T. Myers	21	16	37
Captain Gordon	20	16	36
Private T. Riddick	21	15	36
Sergeant J. Hyslop	21	14	35
Private J. Henderson	15	12	27
	312	258	570

New Galloway Team	200yds.	500yds.	Total
Private Anderson	24	20	44
Private Hogg	23	19	42
Corporal Dalziel	19	21	40
Private Coskrie	21	18	39
Sergeant Stewart	20	18	38
Corporal Johnstone	20	18	38
Private Kerr	22	16	38
Sergeant Milligan	22	15	37
Private R. McGill	19	18	37
Lieutenant Craig	21	15	36
Corporal Milligan	22	14	36
Private Turner	24	12	36
Private Gardiner	20	16	36
Private J. McGill	20	15	35
Private Barton	21	11	32
	318	246	564

On Friday, 12th May, 1876, the Volunteer Inter-Regimental shooting match was to take place on the ranges of the Battalions entered throughout England and Scotland. The idea was to encourage good shooting amongst all the Volunteer Regiments in England and Scotland. A large committee was formed and based in London to co-ordinate all the arrangements and scores. The entry money was £5, made up into prizes of large amounts, to be given to the Battalion whose team of 20 men made the highest score. The prize money offered was as follows: 1st £80; 2nd £60; 3rd £50; 4th £40; 5th £30; 6th £25; 7th £20.

The Queen's Prize Regulations as to targets, number of shots and scoring were observed and Officers from competing Regiments checked the marking of the opposing teams. All returns were forwarded to London. The Galloway Battalion shot at the Dalbeattie ranges. Captain and Adjutant Singleton was Officer in Charge of the team. Lieutenant Kerr, Dalbeattie, was check marker. Captain Gordon, Castle Douglas kept the register and Lieutenant Gun, 1st Dumfries, was checking Officer.

The Galloway Team was selected by the Top 8 shots of the Regiment gaining automatic selection: Sergeant M. M. L. Harper, Castle Douglas; Lieutenant McGuffog, Castle Douglas; Sergeant Osborne, Kirkcudbright; Sergeant J. Agnew, Newton Stewart; Sergeant T. Agnew, Newton Stewart; Corporal T. Myers, Castle Douglas; Corporal Agnew, Newton Stewart; Private Bell, Dalbeattie. The other 12 places were competed for by shooting matches throughout the Battalion. The following were the Galloway Battalion scores:-

	200yds	500yds	600yds	Total
Sergeant M. M. L. Harper, Castle Douglas	29	25	24	78
Corporal T. Myers, Castle Douglas	28	25	24	77
Private Anderson, New Galloway	26	29	22	77
Private G. Legg, Dalbeattie	28	30	19	77
Sergeant J. Agnew, Newton Stewart	27	32	18	77
Sergeant T. Agnew, Newton Stewart	28	21	27	76
Private Bell, Dalbeattie	28	29	17	74

Private Craig, Dalbeattie	27	29	17	73
Private Beattie, Maxwellton	24	27	21	72
Private G. Coutts, Dalbeattie	26	26	19	71
Corporal Service, Maxwellton	27	25	18	70
Sergeant Armstrong, Maxwellton	30	22	17	69
Lieutenant McGuffog, Castle Douglas	22	19	26	67
Corporal H. Murdoch, Castle Douglas	29	22	15	66
Private T. Myers, Castle Douglas	23	22	20	65
Sergeant Osborne, Kirkcudbright	31	15	13	59
Sergeant Douglas, Kirkcudbright	23	27	9	59
Corporal Agnew, Newton Stewart	24	22	13	59
Corporal McGeorge, Dalbeattie	24	22	11	57
Private T. Campbell, Castle Douglas	20	22	11	53
	-----	-----	-----	-----
	524	491	361	1376

On the Thursday of 18th May, 1876, the seven top places were declared as follows:-

1st	1st Batt. Queens Edinburgh Vol. Rifle Brigade (£80)	1443 points
2nd	1st Batt. 1st Lanarkshire (£60)	1432
3rd	Robin Hoods (£50)	1419
4th	2nd Batt. Queens Edinburgh Vol. Rifle Brigade (£40)	1411
5th	19th Lanark (£30)	1403
6th	Dumfriesshire Rifle Volunteers (£25)	1401
7th	Galloway Rifle Volunteers (£10)	1376
7th	47th Lancashire (St. Helens) (£10)	1376

The annual shooting match between the 5th Kirkcudbrightshire Rifle Volunteers and the 6th Kirkcudbrightshire Rifle Volunteers, Maxwellton and Dalbeattie respectively, took place on the afternoon of Saturday, 2nd September, 1877, at the Dalbeattie Ranges. The conditions were 10 men a-side. 5 rounds at 200, 500 and 600 yards. No sighting shots. Wimbledon 1877 targets and scoring. Captain Barrie was in charge of the Maxwellton team with Captain Maxwell in charge of the Dalbeattie team. Lieutenant Lennox, Maxwellton, was in attendance.

Dalbeattie		Maxwellton	
Sergeant Brown	55	Sergeant Armstrong	62
Lieutenant Kerr	52	Corporal Chalmers	51
Private Legg	51	Private Beattie	46
Sergeant Wilson	47	Corporal Taylor	45
Lance Corporal Robinson	47	Private Briggs	45
Corporal Craig	46	Private Sharpe	42
Private Coskrie	46	Private Welsh	40
Private Graham	45	Sergeant Cameron	39
Lance Corporal Coutts	40	Sergeant Newlands	35
Private Millburn	40	Lance Corporal Roberts	33
	469		438

Dalbeattie won by a Majority of 31 points.

The 3rd annual Inter-Regimental Volunteer shooting match took place on Wednesday, 22nd May, 1878, on the shooting ranges of the several Battalions entered. There were 56 Battalions represented - 36 English - 20 Scottish.

The number of competitors entered from each Battalion was 2% of the efficient strength according to the preceding annual returns, each incomplete 100 men counting as a full 100, providing that no team be less than 10 or more than 20. Thus a Battalion with less than 500 efficients would have a team of 10 men. A Battalion of 750 efficients, a team of 16 men, and a Battalion with more than 902 men a team of 20 men.

The distances were 200, 500 and 600 yards. 7 rounds at each distance with no sighting shot. The size of the targets were:-

200 yard target 4' square; bulls-eye 8" diameter - 5 points; inner 12" diameter - 4 points; Magpie (outer ring) 24" diameter - 3 points. Outer remainder of target - 2 points.

500 and 600 yards target 6' square; bulls-eye 24" diameter; inner 36" diameter; Magpie 48" diameter; outer remainder of target.

The Galloway Battalion shooting took place on the ranges at Dalbeattie. Captain and Adjutant Farrer, was the officer in charge of the team. Quartermaster Harper was Register Keeper. Lieutenants Gun and Brown, 1st Dumfriesshire Rifle Volunteers were Check Register Keepers. Sergeant Millar, Dalbeattie acted as Umpire, with Sergeant Major Murdoch, Maxwellton being check marker.

The team of the Galloway Rifle Volunteers selected was as follows;
Lieutenant Muir; Colour-Sergeant Osborne, Kirkcudbright.
Sergeant McAdam, Corporal Myers, Corporal Murdoch, Private Grierson, Castle Douglas.
Private Anderson, New Galloway.
Sergeant Armstrong, Private Lawson, Private Beattie, Maxwellton.
Lieutenant Kerr, Corporal Coutts, Dalbeattie.
Sergeant J. Agnew, Sergeant T. Agnew, Newton Stewart.
Reserves:- Privates Riddick and Blackwood, Castle Douglas.
Of the 56 teams entered the following were to be the top 8 results:-

		Men	200yds	500yds	600yds	Total	Average
1	3rd A. B. West Yorkshire (£60)	12	335	328	312	975	81.25
2	47th Lancashire (£45)	12	325	321	322	968	80.66
3	1st Batt. 1st Lancashire (£35)	14	419	390	308	1117	79.78
4	2nd Batt. 1st Lancashire (£30)	10	274	268	232	774	77.4
5	1st Devon (£25)	10	292	245	227	765	76.5
6	1st A. B. Clackmananshire (£20)	14	383	373	307	1063	75.92
7	London Rifle Brigade (£20)	14	396	362	301	1059	75.64
8	1st A. B. Galloway Rifles (£15)	14	370	370	318	1058	75.57

This was to be the second time in the three annual competitions of this event that the Galloway team were placed on the prize list. In 1879 the Galloway team were placed 13th in the competition but unfortunately not in the money list.

On the 1st January, 1879, the annual New Year's competition of the Gatehouse sub-division of the Kirkcudbright Rifles, took place on the Cally ranges, Gatehouse. 7 rounds at 200 yards. The following were the successful competitors:-

1. Private J. R. Kirkpatrick	23 points	8. Private R. Brackenridge	17 points
2. Private J. Campbell	21	9. Sergeant W. Wylie	17
3. Private C. McNeillie	20	10. Private J. Riddick	17
4. Private J. McDill	20	11. Private S. Leitch	16
5. Private J. McMichael	20	12. Private J. Gibson	14
6. Private J. Biggam	19	13. Private J. Welsh	11
7. Private A. Hughan	18	14. Private W. Hay	10

A match was also held between 6 members - Married and 6 members - Bachelors. The match resulted in a tie.

On Saturday, 31st July, 1880, the annual match between 'A' Company Kirkcudbright and 'B' Company, Castle Douglas, took place on the ranges at Lochfergus, Kirkcudbright. The conditions were 11 men a-side, distances 200, 500 and 600 yards, 7 rounds at each distance with one sighting shot at each distance. The competition began at 3pm and finished in virtual darkness at 9pm

Kirkcudbright		Castle Douglas	
Sergeant Osborne	87 points	Private J. McGaw	86 points
Private Hughan	85	Corporal H. Murdoch	84
Private H. Paterson	83	Corporal T. Myers	81
Lieutenant Muir	82	Private J. Turner	77
Corporal Logan	75	Private Blackwood	77
Sergeant Douglas	72	Corporal W. McCaw	75
Private W. Paterson	71	Private J. Grierson	74
Private J. Hogg	71	Private T. Riddick	72
Corporal Murray	70	Private D. McKinna	68
Private Campbell	63	Sergeant Myers	65
Private A. Hogg	61	Private A. Baldenoch	59
	-----		-----
	820		818

Kirkcudbright 'A' Company won by a Majority of 2 points.

The annual match between 'F' & 'G' Companies, Maxwellton and 'H' Company, Dalbeattie, took place on the Maxwellton ranges of Conhuith, on Saturday, 31st July, 1880. The distances 200, 500 and 600 yards, 7 rounds at each distance, one sighting shot at each distance. 10 men a-side.

Maxwellton	200yds.	500yds.	600yds.	Total
Sergeant Service	25	27	20	72
Sergeant Armstrong	25	26	18	69
Sergeant Cameron	25	28	15	68
Corporal Beattie	23	23	18	64
Corporal Lawson	22	15	22	59
Corporal Hanlon	23	22	15	58
Sergeant Chalmers	21	24	10	55
Private J. Briggs	21	17	16	54
Sergeant Johnstone	17	17	10	44
Private Armstrong	22	5	0	29
	-----	-----	-----	-----
	224	204	142	570
Dalbeattie				
Sergeant Coutts	27	26	20	73
Private McGowan	25	21	21	67
Sergeant Craig	22	17	20	59
Private Carson	23	16	18	57
Private Grant	21	21	15	57
Private Kirk	26	21	9	56
Private Sturgeon	22	13	14	49
Private Wyness	17	20	12	49
Corporal Legg	16	18	12	46
Private Black	19	8	6	33
	-----	-----	-----	-----
	218	181	147	546

Maxwellton won by a Majority of 24 points.

The 9th annual Competition of the 'F' & 'G' Companies, Maxwellton, took place on the ranges at Conhuith, on Saturday, 14th August, 1880. 70 competitors took part. Captain Symons was in Charge. Lieutenant Junner, of the Queens Edinburgh Brigade, acted as Umpire. Sergeant J. Ferguson acted as Secretary.

1st Competition - 200 yards, 7 rounds, any position. 12 prizes.

1. Private A. Walker	28 points	7. Sergeant Major Murdoch	24 points
2. Sergeant Cameron	25	8. Private T. Johnstone	24
3. Private R. J. Walker	24	9. Corporal Hanlon	24
4. Private Andrew Geddes	24	10. Sergeant Armstrong	23
5. Private S. Callender	24	11. Sergeant J. Service	23
6. Corporal J. Beattie	24	12. Private G. Armstrong	22

2nd Competition - 500 yards, 7 rounds, any position. 12 prizes.

1. Private A. Walker	31 points	5. Private A. Geddes	28 points
2. Private S. Callender	31	6. Corporal J. Beattie	28
3. Private John McMillan	31	7. Corporal J. Hanlon	27
4. Private G. V. Smith	29	8. Sergeant Cameron	27

3rd Competition - 600 yards, 7 rounds, any position. 12 prizes.

1. Private J. Briggs	26 points	5. Private A. Walker	20 points
2. Private John McMillan	23	6. Sergeant J. Service	19
3. Corporal A. Roberts	23	7. Corporal J. Hanlon	19
4. Private R. J. Walker	23	8. Sergeant Cameron	18

4th Competition - Officers Prize, to be shot for at 200 and 500 yards. 30 prizes

1. Private A. Walker	59 points	5. Corporal J. Beattie	52 points
2. Private S. Callender	55	6. Sergeant Cameron	52
3. Private John McMillan	53	7. Corporal J. Hanlon	51
4. Private A. Geddes	52	8. Sergeant Armstrong	49

5th Competition - Highest Aggregate in competitions 1, 2, and 3. 52 prizes.

1. Private A. Walker	79 points		7. Private R. J. Walker	64 points
2. Private John McMillan	75		8. Private G. Armstrong	64
3. Corporal Hanlon	70		9. Sergeant J. Service	63
4. Corporal A. Roberts	68		10. Corporal J. Beattie	62
5. Private John Briggs	67		11. Sergeant Cameron	61
6. Private S. Callender	65			

6th Competition - Recruit's Prizes. 200 yards, any position. 5 prizes.

1. Peter Candlish	22 points
2. James Walker	21
3. William Jeffs	21
4. John E. Hill	20
5. William Shortridge	20

7th Competition - All Comers' Competition. 200 yards, 5 rounds, any position.

1. Private R. J. Walker	23 points
2. Private John Welsh	21
3. Private A. Walker	20

8th Competition - All Comers' Sweepstake at 500 yards, 5 rounds any position.

1. Sergeant Cameron	21 points
2. Corporal Hanlon	21
3. Private W. Law	20
4. Sergeant McAulay, 1DRV.	19

The annual competition of 'H' Company, Dalbeattie, was held at the Dalbeattie ranges, on Saturday, 4th September, 1880. Major Maxwell, was Officer in Command at the Firing Point. Lieutenant Kerr assisted. Sergeant Instructor Flynn who was Officer in Charge of the range and targets. A prize fund was subscribed by the local gentlemen and townspeople, with cash prizes ranging from £1 downwards, in addition to prizes in kind.

The Silver Cup, presented by Miss Weems, for the highest score at 200 yards and 500 yards was won by Lieutenant Kerr. The money prize of £1 for highest score at 200, 500 and 600 yards was also won by Lieutenant Kerr.

The Silver medal presented by the late Captain Grieve for the highest scores at 200 and 600 yards was won by Lance Sergeant Gordon Coutts, with 17/6d cash and goods to the value of 7/6d.

The complete prize list was as follows:-

	200 yards	500 yards	600 yards	Total
1. Lieutenant Kerr	20	22	16	58
2. Sergeant Coutts	20	15	20	55
3. Private S. Gourlay	17	15	19	51
4. Lance Corporal McGowan	19	18	13	50
5. Private G. Grant	20	15	14	49
6. Sergeant Craig	22	15	12	49
7. Lance Corporal Wyness	15	16	15	46
8. Private Thomas Black	13	24	8	45
9. Sergeant Instructor Flynn	17	16	11	44
10. Private J. Carson	19	16	9	44
11. Corporal J. Legg	18	10	15	43
12. Private R. Kirk	18	15	10	43
13. Private A. Sturgeon	17	20	6	43
14. Sergeant J. Clark	17	14	9	40
15. Private S. Milroy	20	15	5	40
16. Corporal J. Kimm	15	18	4	37
17. Private J. McKie	16	11	6	33
18. Quartermaster Sergeant Clark	13	18	1	32
19. Sergeant Crosbie	14	13	5	32
20. Private Gibson	14	8	6	28

Recruits Prizes.

	200 yards	500 yards	600 yards	Total
1. Privates D. McKnight	18	16	7	41
2. T. Wood	12	13	11	35
3. Theo. Black	12	16	6	34

		200 yards	500 yards	600 yards	Total
4.	J. Campbell	14	9	7	30
5.	E. Crocket	18	6	6	30
6.	W. Craig	12	9	6	27
7.	J. McMillan	10	14	2	26
8.	C. Clark	16	7	0	23
9.	R. Watson	10	5	2	17
10.	J. Stewart	4	5	2	11

Drill Competition.
1. Robert Watson.
2. Ebenezer Crocket.

The Annual competition of 'D' Company, Newton Stewart, took place at the Knockbrex ranges, on Saturday, 2nd October, 1880. The prizes were more numerous and of greater value than any previous year.

(1) 7 rounds at 200 yards. 30 money prizes. The leading scores were:-
1. Private G. Hinds 29 points 4. Private J. Hannah 26 points
2. Corporal J. Agnew 26 5. Private W. Love 26
3. Sergeant T. Agnew 26 6. Sergeant McFarlane 26

(2) 7 rounds at 500 yards. 30 prizes of goods. The leading scores were:-
1. Private G. Hinds 28 points 4. Corporal J. Agnew 22 points
2. Sergeant T. Agnew 27 5. Sergeant Anderson 21
3. Private G. McNeillie 23 6. Sergeant McFarlane 18

(3) 7 rounds at 600 yards. 30 prizes of goods. The leading scores were:-
1. Corporal J. Agnew 29 points 4. Private A. McDonald 20 points
2. Private J. Thomson 22 5. Lieutenant Agnew 19
3. Private R. Erskine 20 6. Private J. Owen 19

(4) Highest Aggregate in competitions (1), (2), and (3).
1. Corporal J. Agnew 77 points 4. Private J. Thomson 60 points
2. Sergeant T. Agnew 69 5. Private W. Love 59
3. Private G. Hinds 61 6. Private G. McNeillie 59

(5) Recruit's Prizes.
1. Private G. Findlay 25 points 3. Private J. Rennie 21 points
2. Private S. Crawford 25 4. Private J. Murchie 21

'B' Company, Castle Douglas, held their annual competition for prizes on Saturday, 2nd October, 1880, at the Caigton ranges.

(1) 7 rounds at 200 yards. 7 prizes.
1. Corporal Murdoch 32 points 5. Private McGaw 26 points
2. Sergeant McAdam 30 6. Private D. McKinna 26
3. Private McGregor 29 7. Sergeant Myers 26
4. Corporal McAdam 27

(2) 7 rounds at 500 yards. 4 prizes.
1. Private D. McKinna 31 points 3. Private Grierson 27 points
2. Sergeant Dick 28 4. Corporal MacMurray 27

(3) Highest Aggregate at 200 and 500 yards. 13 prizes.

	200 yards.	500 yards.	Total.
1. Private D. McKinna	26	31	57
2. Sergeant McAdam	30	27	57
3. Sergeant Myers	26	26	52
4. Private Grierson	23	28	51
5. Private McGaw	26	25	51
6. Corporal McAdam	27	24	51
7. Corporal Murdoch	31	19	50
8. Sergeant Dick	22	28	50

9. Corporal Myers

	200 yards.	500 yards.	Total.
10. Corporal MacMurray	21	27	48
11. Private Blackwood	25	23	48
12. Private Badenoch	23	24	47
13. Corporal McGaw	23	24	47

(4) Recruit's Prizes. 7 rounds at 200 yards. 4 prizes.

1. Private McCreath	26 points	3. Private Donnelly	22 points
2. Private T. Kirk	23	4. Private McQueen	21

(5) Men who were efficient Volunteers in 1860. 3 prizes. 7 rounds at 200 and 500 yards.

	200 yards	500 yards	Total
1. Mr. Skirving of Croys	25	18	43
2. Mr. McGuffog	22	20	42
3. Mr. Henderson	25	15	40

The annual competition of the members of 'C' Company, Stranraer, took place at Stranraer, on Saturday, 1st October, 1881. The first prize was a silver challenge medal, there being 11 other prizes. Conditions 5 rounds at 200 yards. The following were the prize winners:-

1. Private Joseph Harold	21 points
2. Quartermaster Sergeant Watson	20
3. Private J. McKie	19
4. Bugler D. Gordon	18
5. Private J. McQuistan	16
6. Private A. Douglas	16
7. Sergeant W. Watson	15
8. Private D. Harold	15
9. Private H. Lock	15
10. Private W. Boe	14
11. Private James Rankine	14
12. Private T. Donnan	13

Recruit's Prizes
1. Private J. Caldwell
2. Private J. G. Murray
3. Private J. Keenan

The first Inter-County match between teams of 20 men, representing the Dumfriesshire and the Galloway Rifle Volunteers, was held at Conhuith, on Saturday, 30th August, 1884, using the Martini-Henry rifle. The idea of instituting a county match had been in the minds of some of the more enthusiastic shots of the two Battalions for some time, but it was only now that the match had been brought to fruition, under the notice of Colonel Malcolm, Dumfriesshire and Colonel Maitland, Galloway, who responded to the match. Neither of the Colonels were in attendance at the match but the arrangements were placed in the hands of Captain Sharpe, Dumfries and Captain Harper, Castle Douglas, who discharged their duties with credit.

It may be said, that scarcely any, except men who had been in the habit of shooting at Wimbledon, had ever shot with the Martini-Henry and here rose a difficulty of raising teams of 20. Only 3 of the Galloway team had never competed at Wimbledon, whereas, only 7 of the Dumfriesshire team had ever shot at Wimbledon. However, notwithstanding, everything in connection with the match passed off satisfactorily and it was the wish that the match should be made an annual one.

On the whole the weather was favourable for good scoring, although the wind was rather variable. The conditions of the match were 7 rounds at 200, 500 and 600 yards, with one sighting shot at each distance.

At 200 yards, where, the now orthodox kneeling position had been adopted, the Galloway men led their opponents by 30 points, with a score of 571 as against 541.

At 500 yards, they scored 592 as against 558, and increased their lead by a further 34 points.

At the long distance, which was of course the more difficult of the three, the Dumfriesshire men, with a total of 543, as against 513 for Galloway, beat their own records at the 1st range and almost reached their 500 yards score. Here as has already been indicated, the Gallovidians lost 50 points but left them victors overall by a score of 34 points.

The highest individual score in the match was made by Corporal McCaw, Castle Douglas, who made a splendid score of 95 points.

Any score under 80 points with the Martini-Henry was scarcely considered passable but in the circumstances already explained the Galloway average of 83.8 was very creditable, only four men making lower than 80. Nine Dumfriesshire men scored 86 and over, while not one of the remaining 11 reached a higher figure than 80. The following were the scores:-

Galloway

	200yds	500yds	600yds	Total
Corporal W. McCaw, Castle Douglas	30	34	31	95
Sergeant Geddes, New Galloway	30	31	31	92
Private Bruce, New Galloway	29	33	30	92
Corporal J. McGaw, Castle Douglas	31	31	29	91
Corporal Murdoch, Castle Douglas	33	31	26	90
Corporal Ferguson, New Galloway	29	32	27	88
Corporal Law, Maxwellton	29	30	28	87
Private Turner, Castle Douglas	28	32	26	86
Private Henderson, Maxwellton	28	28	28	84
Sergeant Osborne, Kirkcudbright	27	30	27	84
Captain Kerr, Dalbeattie	30	25	28	83
Sergeant Johnstone, New Galloway	29	26	27	82
Private W. Cairns, Gatehouse	27	29	26	82
Sergeant Service, Maxwellton	27	27	27	81
Bugler Blackstock, Maxwellton	29	27	25	81
Private Callendar, Maxwellton	21	30	21	81
Lieutenant Muir, Kirkcudbright	27	30	21	78
Sergeant Lawson, Maxwellton	27	27	23	77
Private Badenoch, Castle Douglas	27	33	15	75
Corporal Agnew, Newton Stewart	27	26	14	67
	571	592	513	1676

Dumfriesshire

	200yds	500yds	600yds	Total
Private McVittie, Langholm	29	33	31	93
Corporal Cunningham, Sanquhar	30	32	29	91
Sergeant Cumming, Dumfries	30	32	28	90
Corporal McLaurie, Langholm	29	28	32	89
Sergeant Macaulay, Dumfries	28	30	31	89
Corporal Robson, Dumfries	30	29	30	89
Private J. Young, Sanquhar	28	29	31	88
Sergeant Dods, Dumfries	29	31	27	87
Private Weatherstone, Langholm	28	30	28	86
Private Bryden, Thornhill	23	27	30	80
Sergeant McNeil, Dumfries	27	27	26	80
Qtr. Mstr. Sergeant Beattie, Dumfries	28	21	30	79
Corporal Halliday, Lochmaben	26	28	25	79
Sergeant Blyth, Lockerbie	30	22	26	78
Private Murchie, Lockerbie	22	26	27	75
Corporal Hounan, Langholm	26	27	22	75
Private W. Rae, Lockerbie	27	27	21	75
Private McCubbing, Thornhill	23	27	24	74
Lieutenant Brown, Dumfries	23	28	23	74
Private Chapman, Lockerbie	25	24	22	71
	541	558	543	1642

At the close of the match the rival teams were supplied with refreshments and Captain Sharpe, as Captain of the losing team, in intimating the result, expressed the pleasure it had given his team to meet their Galloway opponents and admitted he had been beaten - not very heavily - but fairly beaten in a fair stand-up fight. He hoped the match might become an annual one. He was sure the Dumfriesshire men would make a supreme effort to turn the tide of victory on the next occasion and concluded by calling on the members of his team to give three hearty cheers for their opponents.

Captain Harper in thanking Captain Sharpe and his team for the compliment said the Galloway men were undoubtedly proud of their victory and as anxious as their opponents that the match should be an annual one. Three cheers were given for Corporal McCaw, the highest scorer, and for the Queen.

Note. Although the first meeting of the two Battalions of the Dumfriesshire and Galloway Rifles, actually took place on the 26th July, 1866, it did not then go onto become an annual event. After the meeting of 30th August, 1884, the event was to become an annual fixture, only to be discontinued in 1908, when the Volunteers were disbanded.

****

In January, 1885, the Secretary of State for War, with the concurrence of His Royal Highness, the Field Marshal Commanding in Chief, decided to withdraw the Snider rifle, and issue the Volunteers with the Martini-Henry rifle. The Martini-Henry rifle had been issued to the Regular Army as early as 1871. The Snider rifles were to be sent to the Army Stores at Weedon where they would be sold by public auction. At the previous sale of military rifles, the price paid was 3/8d per rifle.

On the 12th March, 1885, the Martin-Henry rifles were received at the Armouries of the Galloway Rifle Volunteers. The Martini-Henry was a rifle of .45 calibre, using the Martini Breech Action, with a barrel designed by Alexander Henry.

Note. On the 24th February, 1871, Mr Alexander Henry, of Martini-Henry fame, was the honoured guest, at the Masonic Provincial Grand Lodge Ball, held in the Public Rooms, Kirkcudbright.

Although the Martini-Henry was only issued to the Galloway Battalion in 1885, many of the Regiment's "top-shots" had been using their own Martini-Henry rifles in competition, as early as 1875. The National Rifle Association, was to accept the Martini-Henry, as a competition rifle, as early as 1872.

With the introduction of the .303 calibre cartridge and the issue of the new Lee-Metford rifle to the Regular Army, many of the Martini-Henry rifles were re-barrelled with a .303 calibre, for use by the Militia and Volunteer Forces. These modifications became the Enfield-Martini rifle and the Martini-Metford rifle. On the 19th July, 1885, it was reported that the Galloway Rifle Battalion was to receive the first of these modifications, The Enfield-Martini, and on the 20th September, 1895, it was reported that they were to receive the more up to date of these modifications, the Martini-Metford rifle. In reality, neither of these modifications were ever received by the Battalion.

****

The two Companies, 'F' and 'G' of Maxwellton Rifle Volunteers, engaged in a friendly competition, 10 men a-side, at the Conhuith ranges, on Saturday, 29th June, 1886. The weather was of the worst description. Captains Lennox and Phyn were in charge of their respective Companies. Captain Lennox, 'F' Company and Captain Phyn in command of 'G' Company. Ultimately success crowned the efforts of Captain Lennox, defeating Captain Phyn's team by 17 points.

'F' Company		'G' Company	
Corporal Law	88 points	Corporal Walker	88 points
Sergeant Wallace	87	Sergeant Welsh	86
Private Henderson	82	Sergeant Briggs	84
Sergeant Beattie	79	Private Caven	84
Corporal McMechan	79	Sergeant Blackstock	79
Captain Lennox	77	Captain Phyn	75
Sergeant Service	77	Private W Henderson	75
Private Harper	76	Sergeant Hanlon	67
Private Carruthers	72	Private Jackson	65
Private J. Walker	64	Sgt. Major Murdoch	61
	----		----
	781		764

In consequence of a meeting held in the House of Commons, on the 1st March, 1886, and a committee appointed under Lord Harris, to consider the question of Volunteer Grants and the subsequent report of the 25th February, 1887, which recommended an increase of the capitation grant of 5/-, the payment of this increase to be made dependant upon an improved standard of musketry. The terms then in formation were said to be quite within the ability of the Volunteer to perform, even in more difficult cases, where rifle ranges were not so easy to access.

The exact terms of what constituted an improved standard of musketry were to be issued under the Volunteer Act, of October, 1886, and was 35/- payable on the attendance of the previously prescribed number of drills and the Volunteer to pass into the 2nd Class of Musketry. "Every man, with the exception of the officers and instructors must fire 20 rounds and make 45 points in the 3rd Class." i.e. Therefore passing into 2nd Class. The officers capitation grants were based purely on his attending the prescribed number of drills with no musketry qualification required.

For the Volunteer who failed to pass into the 2nd Class of Musketry, the Company received only 10/- capitation grant for him. For this grant of 10/-, he was expected to fire 60 rounds and hit the target 12 times. The same conditions applied in the second year, but if he failed in the 3rd year to pass into 2nd Class, the grant was withheld altogether. The Volunteer might then be held personally responsible for his failing to qualify for the full grant of 35/- and the Company could then seek recompense, from the Volunteer, through the Court of Law, if necessary.

Problems had obviously arisen in the case of some less able Volunteers, as on the 13th June, 1890, Government was to issue the following circular. "It has now been decided that in the case of those Corps whose Commanding Officer certify that more than 75 rounds are required to ensure a high standard of efficiency in their Corps, the allowance may be increased to 90 rounds."

In March of 1890, Captain J. Lennox, 'F' Company, Maxwellton, (later Commander of the Galloway Rifle Volunteers) was Gazetted as having qualified from the School of Musketry, Aldershot, as Instructor of Musketry to the Galloway Battalion of Rifle Volunteers. However, Captain Lennox was to find the duties of this post too demanding, his duties conflicting severely with his own private business, and on the 27th November, 1891, he resigned his appointment. He was to continue as unofficial Instructor of Musketry to the Battalion, as his duties permitted. In 1896, Captain Lennox, then Major, writing in the *Regimental Gazette* of the Galloway Rifle Volunteers was to offer the following advice in the Art of Musketry:-

"All drill tactics and strategy can do is to put the soldier into position to use his weapon, and to make the enemies use as little effective as possible. So far, to the rank and file, musketry is of paramount importance. In Regiments like ours the chief, I might almost say the only, weapon is the rifle, and it behoves all officers, non-commissioned officers and privates to pay attention to the minutest details in connection with musketry instruction which naturally falls into two parts - (1) What can be learned on the parade ground or in the drill hall; and (2) what can be learned on the ranges fixed and temporary. We can only place them in this order, because it is waste of ammunition and dangerous to the public to go to the range till theoretical principles are mastered.

What can be learned on parade is handling the rifle sharply and in such a way as to make it feel light in our hands. The method of loading, taking position, adjusting the sights, and how to take aim. I found when I was musketry instructor to the regiment that almost every man knew how to load or to take aim and how to allow for light or wind to some extent, but that not 10% knew how to adjust their sights correctly. That this is the cause of poor shooting I believe by what I have seen at large rifle meetings like Wimbledon, Bisley or Darnley, where good scores are spoiled through the carelessness of the men, most of them good shots, not adjusting their sights properly and constant practice in seeing that they are correctly adjusted is an absolute necessity. Now, the only remedy I can suggest is, that all officers, non-commissioned officers in command of any parade should devote some time of that parade to the firing exercise; examining every sight at first, and later as large a proportion as they find necessary, to see that it is not only understood but done, and I feel sure that the figure of merit of the Battalion would be increased 20 points by this method alone. One of the other points that can be learned on parade is correcting the position, standing and kneeling when practising the firing exercise, and kneeling and lying when on the attack. In standing, bringing the right toe well to the front, in kneeling the right knee turned to the front thus bringing the right shoulder into the correct position to make a bed for the butt. In lying turn the body off at an angle of 45 degrees to the line of fire, relieving the collar bone, and thus preventing bruising the shoulder, which makes so many men nervous.

As all effective fire is by volleys for reasons indicated below, and will in most cases be in sections, it is most essential that all non-commissioned officers should be trained in the right method of giving words of command, and that their sections should know and have confidence in them.

What can be learned at the range?   (a) Individual firing.
                                               (b) Volley firing.
                                             (c) Field firing.

(a) Individual - The utility of which, as a preliminary, is so self-evident to any one who wished to become proficient that it requires no word of commendation; the objections to individual firing in the field are that no control can be kept of the ammunition, men fire in the smoke, and do not see what they are firing at. If proof of this assertion is required by any one, I would ask him to observe what takes place at a prize meeting. No shot who hopes to win a prize will pull a trigger when a puff of smoke is crossing his line of sight.

(b) Volleys - Among the advantages of volleys in addition to those indicated in the objections to individual firing are the variation of wind, light and the fact that the object is moving are overcome, and that if the volley falls short or goes beyond the object of attack through faulty gauging of distance, the dust raised assists in estimating the amount of correction necessary if the commander takes up his position to windward.

The moral effect is so much greater as a lot of bullets whizzing past your ear has a far greater effect on the nerves, and consequent steadiness of any man or body of men.

The most perfect method I know of training men in this practice is after they are made good individual shots is to take a squad of men and place every one opposite a separate target, and have the result of each round accurately signalled then after that, training to fire in close formations at one target to accustom men to more trying conditions. The objections to this method are the want of target accommodation, the expense of the ammunition, and the amount of time it requires from each individual member. The objection of target accommodation, I believe, will be overcome gradually in a province like Galloway where the population is scattered and the natural backgrounds - i.e. hills - are good; the second is one of expense, and would I venture to think be the best way of spending money in the Corps; i.e. the tax on men's time, I feel sure will not be a stumbling block when men recognise its utility. One thing can be done to improve volleys, and that is if company officers will see that their half company and section commander acquire the proper method of giving the word of command, and gaining the confidence of their section thereby.

(c) Field Firing - This, of course, is the nearest approach to the actual conditions of warfare we can have in peace, and if the time and ground were at the disposal of the Colonel and his commanders, I know he would not be long in trying a tactical march winding up with field firing. This is the object every man in the regiment should aim at, and is possible, as if all wished for it a way would be found of carrying it out. Having been asked, as your old musketry instructor, to give my opinions on how to improve the shooting of the regiment, I have done so believing that some of my comrades would like to have them. Of every one I would ask not to accept these ideas as gospel, but to think how to improve the musketry of the regiment, and if we all try to, we will succeed. In conclusion, do not forget to help the bad shots.

John Lennox, Captain and Hon. Major,

lately Musketry Instructor, G.R.V.

****

On Saturday, 13th August, 1887, 'E' Company , New Galloway and 'G' Company, Maxwellton, met on the Conhuith ranges for their first friendly match. Conditions 10 men a-side, 7 rounds at 200, 500 and 600 yards. Lieutenant Jamieson was in command of the New Galloway team, while Captain Phyn laid aside the sword for the day and assisted his men with the rifle. The result was a win for New Galloway by a majority of 23 points. The match which throughout was of the most pleasant and friendly nature, was brought to a close by speeches from the officers. The results were as follows:-

New Galloway	200yds	500yds	600yds	Total
Sergeant Ferguson	33	32	24	89
Sergeant Geddes	28	26	30	84
Privates J. Coltart	32	29	20	81
Byers	30	28	20	78
J. McGill	29	21	25	75
R. Coltart	25	20	29	74
D. Brown	28	24	20	72
Harley	23	21	14	58
D. Mackenzie	25	11	22	58
McGinnes	14	19	24	57
	----	-----	-----	-----
	267	231	228	726
Maxwellton				
Sergeant Briggs	33	31	24	88
Corporal Walker	29	25	26	80
Private Henderson	31	26	22	79
Private Jackson	29	26	23	78
Bugler Blackstock	29	25	23	77
Captain Phyn	28	28	15	71
Corporal Shortridge	27	18	18	63
Sergeant Wallace	29	25	9	63
Private McKay	26	19	14	59
Private Irving	26	13	6	45
	-----	----	----	----
	287	236	180	703

The annual match between teams of 20 men selected from the Dumfriesshire and the Galloway Battalion of Rifle Volunteers, was shot on Saturday 27th August, 1887, at the ranges of Conhuith, Maxwellton. Captain Sharpe was in charge of the Dumfriesshire team and Captain Lennox that of the Galloway team. Among the officers present during the day was Colonel Dudgeon, Captain and Adjutant Hewitt, Captain Browne, Captain McLaurin, Captain Junner, Lieutenant Robson, Lieutenant McPhater. The weather on the whole was hardly shooting weather, the light being bad and the wind blowing straight across the range. Firing commenced shortly after mid-day and concluded at 4.30pm. As will be seen from the subjoined scores, the contest which was very close throughout, resulted in favour of Galloway by 3 points.

Dumfriesshire

	200yds	500yds	600yds	Total
Sergeant Ferguson, Penpont	31	33	28	92
Sergeant Moodie, Dumfries	32	26	30	88
Private G. Cowan, Langholm	31	31	25	87
Private T. Hounam, Langholm	29	29	27	85
Sergeant Macaulay, Dumfries	29	30	26	85
Private Bryden, Thornhill	30	30	25	85
Sergeant McNeil, Dumfries	29	28	26	83
Private McVittie, Langholm	30	29	24	83
Private F. Reid, Langholm	28	32	23	83
Sergeant Dods, Dumfries	32	27	23	82
Private Wright, Thornhill	28	21	32	81
Sergeant Beattie, Lochmaben	30	28	23	81
Corporal Blyth, Moffat	30	31	20	81
Corporal Thom, Dumfries	27	25	27	79
Corporal Young, Sanquhar	25	25	27	77
Sergeant Tweedie, Annan	26	25	24	75
Sergeant J. Cowan,Langholm	27	27	19	73
Corporal Cunningham, Sanquhar	29	21	20	70
Private Harris, Sanquhar	26	25	19	70
Sergeant Hinde, Dumfries	26	19	24	69
	575	542	492	1609

Galloway

	200yds	500yds	600yds	Total
Lieutenant McPhater, Newton Stewart	29	30	32	91
Col. Sgt. Osborne, Kirkcudbright	30	28	29	87
Sergeant Myers, Castle Douglas	29	28	29	86
Private Callender, Maxwellton	27	34	25	86
Sergeant Watson, Stranraer	29	35	22	86
Sergeant G. Geddes, New Galloway	30	26	29	85
Sergeant Ferguson, New Galloway	30	26	28	84
Sergeant Briggs, Maxwellton	29	32	23	84
Corporal Law, Maxwellton	31	32	19	82
Corporal Murdoch, Castle Douglas	30	31	20	81
Private Coltart, New Galloway	29	29	21	79
Private W. Paterson, Kirkcudbright	28	31	20	79
Corporal W. McCaw, Castle Douglas	30	29	20	79
Private Miller, Kirkcudbright	26	25	26	77
Corporal J. McGaw, Castle Douglas	29	23	25	77
Private Carruthers, Maxwellton	30	24	23	77
Private Turner, Castle Douglas	30	21	25	76
Sergeant Service, Maxwellton	26	29	21	76
Private Henderson, Maxwellton	29	23	21	73
Corporal Walker, Maxwellton	27	24	16	67
	578	560	474	1612

****

The "Captain's Cup", a silver challenge cup presented by Captain Kerr 'H' Company, Dalbeattie, in June, 1888, for half yearly competition and the monthly medal presented by the Chaplain of the Corps, Rev. R. S. Kirkpatrick, took place on Saturday, 9th June, 1888, when Private Sturgeon proved to be the winner.

The following were the leading scores:-

	200yds	500yds	600yds	Total
Private Andrew Sturgeon	26	30	29	85
Lance Corporal Robertson	32	24	28	84
Col. Sgt. Thomas Craig	30	26	26	82
Private Michael Clark	24	24	31	79
Private Thomas McGregor	29	25	24	78
Private Thomas Laing	30	25	11	66
Private William McGhee	20	19	26	65
Bugler John McKenzie	26	23	16	65
Private John Riley	24	20	13	57

****

The annual shooting competition of 'D' Company, Newton Stewart, for Company prizes, took place at Knockbrex ranges on Saturday, 8th September, 1888, in fine weather. There were 7 different competitions on the programme and the following were the principal prize winners:-

Competition No.1. - For prizes presented by the nobility and gentry.   7 rounds at 200 yards.

1.	Private Dods	32 points
2.	Private Smith	32
3.	Private Murchie	31
4.	Corporal Agnew	30

Competition No. 2. - Non-Commissioned Officer's prizes.   7 rounds at 500 yards.

1.	Private Davidson	32 points
2.	Captain Agnew	31
3.	Lieutenant McPhater	31
4.	Corporal Agnew	28

Competition No. 3. - Merchant's Prizes.   7 rounds at 600 yards.

1.	Private Murchie	28 points
2.	Corporal Agnew	25
3.	Private Dods	25
4.	Captain Agnew	23

Competition No. 4. - Officer's Prizes. Aggregate of competitions 1, 2, & 3.

1.	Captain Agnew	84 points
2.	Private Dods	83
3.	Corporal Agnew	83
4.	Lieutenant McPhater	81

Competition No. 5. - Recruit's Prizes.   7 rounds at 200 yards.

1.	Private Carter	27 points
2.	Private Currie	26
3.	Private Vernon	26
4.	Private Thomas Agnew	25

****

The annual match between 10 men of 'E' Company, New Galloway and 'F' & 'G' Companies, Maxwellton, took place at the Airie Ranges, New Galloway, on Friday, 26th October, 1888. The day was very unfavourable, a strong wind and a heavy mist at the long distances making scoring almost impossible, especially to those acquainted with the exposed range.
The distances were 200, 500 and 600 yards. 7 shots at each distance. The following were the scores:-

New Galloway		Maxwellton	
Sergeant R. Ferguson	81 points	Sergeant Law	81 points
Sergeant R. Johnstone	79	Corporal Carruthers	72
Sergeant G. Geddes	78	Captain Phyn	67
Bugler J. Bell	77	Sergeant D. Johnston	66
Private D. Brown	75	Private N. Henderson	65
Private J. Ferguson	72	Private W. Hope	61
Private W. Byers	70	Private Hall	59
Private P. Shaw	68	Sergeant Briggs	54
Private J. Coltart	68	Private Wallace	47
Private Harley	67	Private Grierson	37
	----		-----
	725		609

New Galloway won by a Majority of 116 points.

On Saturday, 20th July, 1889, the annual match between the Maxwellton and Dalbeattie Volunteers was shot off at the Richorn ranges, Dalbeattie. The day was unfavourable for high scoring, as the smoke from the rifles hung in front of the firing point and partially obscured the view of the targets. The conditions of the match were 10 men a-side. 7 rounds at each distance, 200, 500 and 600 yards, one sighting shot at each distance. The result was a victory for Dalbeattie by 36 points. Captain Phyn on behalf of Maxwellton expressed the pleasure they had in meeting the Dalbeattie men and called for three cheers. Captain Kerr on behalf of the winning team made a suitable reply.

Dalbeattie

	200yds	500yds	600yds	Total
Corporal A. Sturgeon	33	30	25	88
Sergeant T. Craig	33	26	27	86
Sergeant Robertson	31	27	26	84
Captain Kerr	28	26	26	80
Private George Millburn	23	26	25	74
Private A. Burnie	24	18	21	63
Private T. Burnie	23	20	13	56
Private R. Sturgeon	29	20	6	55
Corporal M. Clark	25	16	13	54
Private T. McGregor	25	22	5	50
	-----	----	----	----
	272	231	187	690

Maxwellton

	200yds	500yds	600yds	Total
Sergeant Beattie	26	31	26	83
Corporal Carruthers	27	32	20	79
Corporal Walker	31	17	25	73
Sergeant Walsh	27	19	24	70
Private Black	29	32	9	70
Private McKay	27	24	18	69
Private Hope	28	15	20	63
Captain Phyn	18	14	22	54
Sergeant Wallace	23	22	4	49
Private Souter	13	16	15	44
	----	----	----	----
	249	222	183	654

The annual match between 'F' Company, Maxwellton and 'A' Company, Kirkcudbright, took place on the Conhuith ranges, Maxwellton, on Saturday, 28th July, 1889. The day though fine from a holiday point of view, was against good scoring, some of the best shots having to be content with very small totals. The light was bad with a rather troublesome wind from the right. The conditions were 12 men a-side, the highest 10 scores to count. Distances 200, 500 and 600 yards, 7 rounds at each distance with one sighting shot. Kirkcudbright had to shoot 11 men, one of their Company being unable to attend. The match resulted in a victory for 'F' Company by 2 points. The scores were as follows:-

'F' Company, Maxwellton

	200yds	500yds	600yds	Total
Private Coupland	31	31	28	90
Corporal J. Henderson	34	21	25	90
Corporal W. Henderson	32	32	24	88
Captain Lennox	28	19	32	79
Sergeant Armstrong	25	23	29	77
Sergeant Service	28	21	25	74
Sergeant Beattie	28	24	18	70
Corporal Carruthers	20	16	27	69
Private J. Hall	26	20	22	68
Col. Sgt. D. Johnstone	25	17	23	65
	----	----	----	----
	283	234	253	770

	200yds	500yds	600yds	Total
'A' Company, Kirkcudbright				
Private E. Patterson	28	33	30	91
Col. Sgt. Osborne	28	29	26	83
Corporal W. Patterson	26	25	31	82
Private H. Patterson	27	28	24	79
Private A. Heughan	31	24	24	79
Private J. Hogg	28	29	22	78
Private W. Miller	29	15	27	71
Private. W. D. Douglas	30	21	19	70
Sergeant W. R. Murray	28	18	23	69
Private. W. C. Howitt	23	22	21	66
	----	----	----	----
	278	243	247	768

****

The annual match between 'E' Company, New Galloway, and 'G' Company, Maxwellton, took place on the Conhuith ranges, Maxwellton, on the same day as 'F' and 'A' Companies. The conditions were the same, with the exceptions of it being 10 men a-side. The following were the scores:-

	200 yds.	500 yds.	600 yds.	Total
'E' Company, New Galloway.				
Corporal Coltart	29	27	26	82
Corporal Byers	31	18	28	77
Col. Sgt. Gallacher	28	21	26	75
Private J. Ferguson	30	26	19	75
Private McGinnies	27	21	23	71
Bugler Bell	28	26	17	71
Sergeant Geddes	30	25	16	71
Sergeant Fergusson	29	27	14	70
Captain Jamieson	25	24	20	69
Sergeant Shaw	29	17	12	58
	----	----	----	----
	286	232	201	719
'G' Company, Maxwellton.				
Sergeant Law	30	29	26	85
Sergeant Walker	29	25	25	79
Private Mackay	26	23	22	71
Private Gallacher	26	26	15	67
Sergeant Welsh	23	23	16	62
Private Hope	23	23	16	62
Sergeant Briggs	27	23	10	60
Private Black	28	23	4	55
Private Moffat	23	11	20	54
Sergeant Wallace	27	7	2	36
	----	----	----	----
	263	213	156	631

New Galloway won by a Majority of 88 points.

****

There was little doubt that the Galloway Rifles finest years were in the late 1890's through to the early 1900's, when the Battalion was possessed of its finest athletes and marksmen, culminating in the heroic adventures of its members in volunteering and proudly serving in South Africa, during the Boer War conflict. The following Musketry returns mark the Galloway Rifle Volunteers prowess with the rifle, during these 'heady' years, in conjunction with other Volunteer units of the North British District, together with their national positions where available. These official Musketry returns are still as true today as they were in these far off days, being now practised and published under the 'Skill at Arms'.

The financial year of the Volunteer Force ended on 31st October, 1889, and the following tabulated statement gives the total strength of the different Companies forming the Galloway Battalion, and the number of efficients, non-efficients and proficients in each, for that year:-

	Effs	Non-Effs	Total enrolled Strength	Proficient Offcrs	Sgts	Officers passed in Tactics
'A' Kirkcudbright	79	-	79	3	5	-
'B' Castle Douglas	90	-	90	4	6	-
'C' Stranraer	79	-	79	3	5	-
'D' Newton Stewart	86	4	90	3	5	-
'E' New Galloway	65	3	68	1	6	-
'F' Maxwellton	89	-	89	1	6	1
'G' Maxwellton	85	-	85	2	5	-
'H' Dalbeattie	57	4	61	1	5	-
Staff	10	-	10	2	-	-
	----	----	----	----	----	----
	640	11	651	20	43	1

The following were the Musketry returns for the year ended 31st October, 1889:-

	Number exercised	Figure of Merit	Marksman	Classification 1	2	3
'A' Kirkcudbright	71	140.40	-	37	35	-
'B' Castle Douglas	70	211.55	11	32	27	-
'C' Stranraer	66	118.03	-	18	48	-
'D' Newton Stewart	65	227.24	17	4	44	-
'E' New Galloway	52	205.15	15	19	18	-
'F' Maxwellton	79	235.43	2	58	19	-
'G' Maxwellton	74	241.17	4	60	10	-
'H' Dalbeattie	41	166.78	3	12	26	-

The Battalion figure of merit was 193.18 with 518 men exercised. The Battalion was placed 7th in order of merit for the North British District, for the year ended, 31st October, 1889.

On the 16th January, 1891, the results of the Musketry training for the North British District for year ended 31st October, 1890 were published. The report stated that the order of merit should be considered in conjunction with the fact that the Corps do not compete under the same conditions, some having had greater advantage than others in regards to range accommodation, weather etc. The number of men trained was 28,280, as compared with 28,878 in 1889. Of these, 3,179 or 11.26% were classified as marksmen, being an increase of 1.72%; 7,783 or 27.59% were classified as 1st class shots, an increase of 7.50%; 16,908 or 59.89% were classified as 2nd class shots, a decrease of 9.49%; 360 or 1.27% were classified as 3rd class shots, a slight increase of .27%.

Notice was taken, in the report of the increased attention paid to the class firing; field practices and judging distances. The great advantage to be derived from having Musketry Instructors attached to each Battalion was also commented upon, a practical result of this being observed that the two Maxwellton Companies, Captain Phyn's 1st and Captain Lennox's 2nd, being the best shooting Companies in Scotland.

The following is a tabulated statement which accompanied the report; giving the results of the first 28 Battalions figure of merit, along with the lowest. The Galloway Rifle Volunteers had the honoured position on the list.

Order of Merit.	Battalion.	Figure of Merit.
1.	Galloway Rifle Volunteers (459 exercised)	233.28
2.	5th V.B. A. & S. Highlanders	217.68
3.	2nd Royal Scots Fusiliers	216.49
4.	2nd K.O.S.B.	215.49
5.	3rd K.O.S.B.	213.32
6.	2nd Gordon Highlanders	212.46
7.	7th Royal Scots	211.88
8.	1st Royal Scots Fusiliers	203.14
9.	3rd Gordon Highlanders	198.50
10.	5th Royal Highlanders	197.86
11.	1st Roxburgh and Selkirk	195.45
12.	Queen's Edinburgh Volunteer brigade	188.60
13.	3rd V.B. A. & S. Highlanders	188.31
14.	4th Royal Scots	187.44
15.	6th Royal Scots	186.31
16.	4th A. & S. Highlanders	185.75

Order of Merit.	Battalion.	Figure of Merit.
17.	9th Lanark Rifle Volunteers	183.19
18.	6th V.B. Gordon Highlanders	182.86
19.	3rd Seaforth Highlanders	178.72
20.	1st A. & S. Highlanders	178.21
21.	7th A. & S. Highlanders	177.81
22.	6th Royal Highlanders	177.56
23.	1st Sutherland Rifle Volunteers	177.50
24.	2nd V.B. Scottish Rifles	175.81
25.	8th Royal Scots	175.79
26.	5th Highland Light Infantry	175.10
27.	2nd A. & S. Highlanders	174.27
28.	1st Cameron Highlanders	173.61
29. - 44.	*********	
45.	3rd Highland Light Infantry	129.37

The Musketry returns for year ended 31st October, 1891, of the North British District were to show the Galloway Rifle battalion as occupying 3rd position, with a figure of merit of 223.77. The breakdown of the men exercised in the Galloway Battalion was as follows: 67 were classified as Marksmen; 311 as 1st Class Shots; 135 as 2nd Class Shots; and 2 as 3rd Class Shots.

The Musketry return for the Scottish Infantry Volunteers for the year ended 31st October, 1892, were as follows, with the Galloway Battalion once again gaining a prominent position in the table :

	Figure of Merit.	Marksmen.	1st Class.	2nd Class.	3rd Class.
5th A. & S. Highlanders	238.88	329	223	81	-
Galloway Rifle Volunteers	234.78	90	385	78	1
2nd K.O.S.B..	228.09	144	345	100	1
5th R. Highlanders	221.09	54	281	262	2
1st Royal Scots Fusiliers	219.96	93	265	184	6
3rd K.O.S.B.	219.40	96	254	200	4
7th Royal Scots	215.14	58	118	132	5
2nd Royal Scots Fusiliers	212.80	197	168	310	-
3rd Gordon Highlanders	210.16	107	191	171	-
2nd Gordon Highlanders	207.47	75	105	167	1
8th Royal Scots	205.39	84	178	158	-
1st Roxburgh and Selkirk	205.30	164	159	295	2
3rd Seaforth Highlanders	200.18	114	318	362	1
1st Seaforth Highlanders	197.83	68	200	376	7
6th Royal Highlanders	195.08	50	320	306	2
6th Royal Scots	190.29	153	183	336	1
4th A. & S. Highlanders	189.67	187	134	340	10
4th Gordon Highlanders	188.93	54	100	238	4
6th Gordon Highlanders	188.87	82	97	270	3
4th Royal Scots	188.07	73	95	273	6
1st Cameron Highlanders	186.41	85	226	487	2
4th Royal Highlanders	185.70	33	140	290	6
9th Lanark	185.44	13	163	215	2
5th Royal Scots	183.56	92	95	315	2
1st A. & S. Highlanders	181.73	140	131	516	12
1st Dumbarton	180.24	139	265	543	1
7th A. & S. Highlanders	177.18	84	73	343	3
3rd A. & S. Highlanders	176.63	85	162	373	-
1st Sutherland	175.43	29	233	455	3
5th Gordon Highlanders	175.31	26	101	344	2
4th Scottish Rifles	174.65	83	91	393	3
2nd Royal Highlanders	174.62	64	168	340	24
2nd Scottish Rifles	173.08	52	134	473	6
2nd A. & S. Highlanders	172.62	75	131	324	18
5th Scottish Rifles	170.90	54	157	387	3
3rd Lanark	169.95	85	138	667	2
5th Highland Light Infantry	169.79	103	86	477	6
Queen's Edinburgh Brigade	168.41	133	269	1025	35
3rd Highland Light Infantry	165.74	55	69	502	7

	Figure of Merit.	Marksmen.	Classification		
			1st Class.	2nd Class.	3rd Class.
1st Lanark	158.90	102	115	835	7
1st Highland Light Infantry	158.50	63	46	559	-
1st Gordon Highlanders	158.13	69	67	410	8
2nd Highland Light Infantry	147.58	57	64	651	5
1st Royal Highlanders	142.42	46	19	374	24
3rd Royal Highlanders	130.74	10	53	358	10

For year ended 31st October, 1892, Maxwellton was the best shooting Company of the Galloway Rifles with Private W. Hetherington, 'B' Company, Castle Douglas being the best shot in the Battalion with 218 points.

In the Musketry returns for year ended 1893, the Galloway Battalion of Rifle Volunteers, exercised 621 men, attaining a figure of merit of 232.96, and an order of merit of 3rd best shooting Regiment In England, Scotland and Wales. 'B' Company, Castle Douglas, was the best shooting Company, with Colour-Sergeant Osborne, 'A' Company, Kirkcudbright, the best shot in the Regiment with 220 points.

The following year, 1894, the Galloway Battalion was once again to figure in a prominent position in the order of merit for England, Scotland and Wales, with a position of 8th best shooting Regiment. 601 members were exercised gaining a figure of merit of 170.89. 'G' Company, Maxwellton, was the best shooting Company in the Battalion, with Private J. Ferguson, 'E' Company, New Galloway, the best shot in the Battalion, with a score of 215 points.

In 1895, 624 members of the Galloway Battalion were exercised, attaining a figure of merit of 142.52 and an order of merit of 5th best shooting Regiment in the Scottish Infantry Volunteers. 'E' Company, New Galloway, was the best shooting Company in the battalion, with Private W. Hetherington, 'B' Company, Castle Douglas, being the best shot in the Battalion with a score of 174 points.

The Musketry returns for the Companies of the Galloway Battalion of Rifle Volunteers, for year ended 31st October, 1895, was as follows:-

'A' Company, Kirkcudbright -	117.54
'B' Company, Castle Douglas -	149.49
'C' Company, Stranraer -	118.48
'D' Company, Newton Stewart -	102.26
'E' Company, New Galloway -	186.43
'F' Company, Maxwellton -	170.85
'G' Company, Maxwellton -	167.88
'H' Company, Dalbeattie -	127.81

It would appear that the Galloway Battalion of Rifle Volunteers were not to feature in any further prominent position in the Order of Merit, after 1895. The 1896 figures showed 639 men exercised, with a figure of merit of 151, however, no order of merit was given. The best shooting Company for year ended 1896, was 'E' Company, New Galloway, once again with Sergeant R. Ferguson of 'E' Company being the best shot in the Regiment.

The annual returns for financial year ended 31st October, 1900, were as follows:

	Proficient.				Total
	Officers.	Sgts.	Effts.	Non-Effts.	Strength.
'A' Company, Kirkcudbright	2	5	96	-	103
'B' Castle Douglas	5	6	110	2	123
'C' Stranraer	4	5	78	-	87
'D' Newton Stewart	4	5	122	2	133
'E' New Galloway	2	5	69	2	78
'F' Maxwellton	2	8	74	5	89
'G' Maxwellton	2	4	78	3	87
'H' Dalbeattie	3	6	108	-	117
	---	---	-----	---	-----
	24	44	735	14	817.

The Best Shot in the Regiment, 1900, was Sergeant Thomas McGregor, 'H' Company, Dalbeattie.
The Best Shot in the Regiment, 1901, was Corporal John McGaw, 'B' Company, Castle Douglas.

The Best Shot in the Regiment, 1903, was Private Dougan 'B' Company, Castle Douglas.
The Best Shot in the Companies for year ended 31st October, 1905, were:-

'A' Kirkcudbright -	Sergeant Reid.
'B' Castle Douglas -	Colour-Sergeant Wright.
'C' Stranraer -	Sergeant McGeoch.
'D' Newton Stewart -	Private William McCreadie.
'E' New Galloway -	Private George Geddes.
'F' Maxwellton -	Lance Corporal T. Graham.
'G' Maxwellton -	Sergeant Moffat.
'H' Dalbeattie -	Colour-Sergeant Thomas McGregor.

The Best Shot in the Battalion was Private George Geddes, 'E' Company, New Galloway.

The following Musketry returns were published for the Galloway Battalion of Rifle Volunteers, for year ended, 31st October, 1906.

Musketry .

	Trained & Exercised.	Marksmen.	1st Class Shots.	2nd Class Shots.	3rd Class Shots.
'A' Kirkcudbright	87	31	53	3	-
'B' Castle Douglas	99	25	60	14	-
'C' Stranraer	73	9	28	36	-
'D' Newton Stewart	100	34	46	16	4
'E' New Galloway	35	29	6	-	-
'F' Maxwellton	92	11	72	9	-
'G' Maxwellton	96	14	77	5	-
'H' Dalbeattie	63	21	40	2	-

	Recruits. Number exercised.	Best Shots per Company	
'A' Kirkcudbright	18	'A' Kirkcudbright -	Corporal Gourlay
'B' Castle Douglas	31	'B' Castle Douglas -	Corporal McGaw
'C' Stranraer	13	'C' Stranraer -	Sergeant McGeoch
'D' Newton Stewart	24	'D' Newton Stewart -	Private William McCreadie
'E' New Galloway	17	'E' New Galloway -	Sergeant Bell
'F' Maxwellton	14	'F' Maxwellton -	Sergeant Coupland
'G' Maxwellton	11	'G' Maxwellton -	Sergeant Henderson
'H' Dalbeattie	16	'H' Dalbeattie -	Sergeant Seggie

The Best Shot in the battalion was Sergeant James Bell 'E' Company, New Galloway.

The final figures for the year ended, 31st October, 1907, were purely those of Best Shots in the Battalion being reported as:

'A' Kirkcudbright -	Corporal McGowan.
'B' Castle Douglas -	Private J. Turner.
'C' Stranraer -	Armourer - Sergeant McHaffie.
'D' Newton Stewart -	Private William McCreadie.
'E' New Galloway -	Sergeant James Bell.
'F' Maxwellton -	Sergeant Coupland.
'G' Maxwellton -	Sergeant Ferguson.
'H' Dalbeattie -	Private Clingan.

The Best Shot in the battalion was Armourer-Sergeant McHaffie, 'C' Company, Stranraer.

The annual match between 'B' Company, Castle Douglas, and 'D' Company, Newton Stewart, took place on Saturday, 28th May, 1893, at the Newton Stewart ranges of Knockbrex. The distances were, 200, 500, and 600 yards. 7 rounds at each distance. There being a scorching sun and a slightly rear wind, the scoring was not up to the average. Castle Douglas, led at all distances and ultimately won by 40 points.

Lieutenant Hewat, was in command of the Castle Douglas team, and Captain Agnew, was in command of the Newton Stewart team.

Castle Douglas.		200yds.	500yds.	600yds.	Total.
	Corporal W. McCaw	28	28	28	84
	Corporal Hetherington	30	26	21	77
	Mus. Sergeant Murdoch	27	24	25	76
	Private J. McAdam	26	24	24	74
	Corporal J. McGaw	30	24	20	74
	Lance Sergeant Wilson	27	27	20	74
	Sergeant Gordon	24	26	22	72
	Corporal Kirk	21	28	22	71
	Quartermaster Sergeant Myers	26	29	16	71
	Private Ireland	22	21	24	67
		-----	-----	-----	-----
		261	257	222	740

Newton Stewart.		200yds.	500yds.	600yds.	Total.
	Private W. McCreadie	25	32	27	84
	Lieutenant McPhater	28	23	24	75
	Private Drysdale	26	25	23	74
	Private Davidson	27	25	20	72
	Corporal J. Agnew	20	24	27	71
	Lance Corporal Murchie	25	25	19	69
	Lance Sergeant Love	25	23	17	65
	Captain Agnew	23	27	15	65
	Sergeant Peattie	24	26	14	64
	Private McMurray	20	16	22	61
		----	----	-----	-----
		243	249	208	700

*****

A match between 'A' Company, Kirkcudbright, and 'E' Company, New Galloway, took place on Saturday, 5th August, 1893, on the New Galloway ranges. The conditions were 10 men a-side. 7 rounds at 200, 500 and 600 yards. The day was fine and the sun shone brightly but the scoring was not quite up to the average. Ultimately New Galloway won by 3 points.

New Galloway.		200yds.	500yds.	600yds.	Total.
	Private G. Anderson	29	29	29	87
	Private J. Fergusson	29	25	29	83
	Private G. Geddes	28	25	29	82
	Sergeant G. Geddes	27	24	29	80
	Private A. Geddes	30	25	23	78
	Sergeant R. Fergusson	30	24	23	77
	Corporal J. Bell	29	30	15	74
	Colour-Sergeant Farrell	29	20	21	70
	Sergeant W. Turner	24	21	19	64
	Private J. McKie	21	19	9	49
		----	-----	----	----
		276	242	226	744

Kirkcudbright.					
	Private Patterson	31	31	26	88
	Colour-Sergeant Osborne	29	26	27	82
	Colour-Sergeant Tuck	28	27	25	80
	Private Miller	30	27	21	78
	Private Douglas	26	28	22	76
	Sergeant Murray	27	15	28	70
	Sergeant McGregor	30	23	17	70
	Major Campbell (Artillery)	28	19	21	68
	Private Bowie	29	22	15	66
	Lieutenant Muir	22	19	22	63
		-----	-----	-----	----
		280	237	224	141

****

A match took place on Saturday, 5th August, 1893, between two teams of 'B' Company, Castle Douglas, chosen by Captain Dunn and Lieutenant Hewat. The match shot over 200 and 500 yards took place on the Caigton ranges.

Lieutenant Hewat's Team.	200yds.	500yds.	Total.
Quartermaster Sergeant Myers	29	31	60
Corporal T. Kirk	27	28	55
Sergeant J. Scott	26	28	54
Corporal W. McCaw	25	27	52
Sergeant Wright	26	26	52
Colour-Sergeant J. Dick	25	24	49
Private Dougan	20	28	48
Private Todd	29	19	48
Private R. Howard	24	23	47
	231	234	465

Captain Dunn's Team.	200yds.	500yds.	Total.
Corporal J. McGaw	31	31	62
Quartermaster Sergeant Hyslop	26	31	57
Corporal W. Hetherington	26	28	54
Private John Fergusson	29	23	52
Lance Corporal W. Haugh	19	31	50
Mus. Sergeant Instructor Murdoch	22	26	48
Sergeant R. W. Wilson	21	25	46
Sergeant McKinna	27	19	46
Sergeant S. R. Gordon	24	19	43
	225	233	458

Lieutenant Hewat's Team won by a Majority of 7 points.

The annual match between 'G' Company, Maxwellton, and 'H' Company, Dalbeattie, took place On the Richorn ranges, Dalbeattie, on Saturday afternoon, of 19th August, 1893. Conditions 12 men to shoot, 10 to count. Captain Maxwell Captained the Dalbeattie team, Major Lennox Captained the Maxwellton team in the absence of Captain Phyn. The day was very unfavourable for high scoring. The visitors gained a good lead at the short range and then losing a few points in the middle range, more than held their own at 600 yards, winning the match by a Majority of 30 points. At the close of the match Captain Maxwell entertained the teams to dinner in the King's Arms Hotel, where a couple of hours were spent very pleasantly with song and sentiment. The results of the match were as follows:-

'G' Company. Maxwellton.	200yds.	500yds.	600yds.	Total.
Sergeant W. Law	30	31	26	87
Private W. Hope	29	27	25	81
Private R. McMurdo	28	22	26	76
Colour-Sergeant Service	24	22	26	72
Private G. Black	22	28	22	72
Sergeant Campbell	23	24	22	69
Ambulance Sergeant Briggs	24	26	19	69
Corporal Moffat	29	22	15	66
Private H. Halliday	18	26	19	63
Private D. Simpson	25	17	18	60
Sergeant Wallace	24	12	16	52
Private R. Crosbie	18	23	10	51
	294	280	244	818
Two lowest scores off:-				103

Total - 715.

'H' Company. Dalbeattie.	200yds.	500yds.	600yds.	Total.
Private Millburn	27	26	28	81
Colour-Sergeant Craig	27	29	24	80
Sergeant Gallagher	27	27	25	79
Private Lynch	22	28	23	73
Sergeant M. Clark	25	25	17	67
Sergeant McGregor	23	22	19	64

	200yds.	500yds.	600yds.	Total
Sergeant Gillespie	20	22	20	62
Private J. Flynn	19	24	17	60
Corporal Sturgeon	22	17	17	56
Private Lawson	15	25	15	55
Private R. Halliday	21	22	10	53
Private Gourlay	21	16	14	51
	-----	-----	----	----
	269	283	229	781
	Two lowest scores off.-			104

Total -   677.

The annual match between teams representing 'A' Company, Kirkcudbright, and 'F' Company, Maxwellton, was held at the Conhuith ranges, Maxwellton, on Saturday, 26th August, 1893. The weather was good until mid-afternoon, when a strong unsteady wind from the right got up, necessitating an allowance of from 3 to 5 feet at the long ranges. The match was a very close one ending in favour of 'F' Company, by the narrow margin of 11 points. Lieutenant Muir and Major Lennox, Kirkcudbright and Maxwellton, respectively were in command of the teams.

'F' Company. Maxwellton.

	200yds.	500yds.	600yds.	Total.
Private G. Callender	25	28	29	82
Corporal D. Haining	25	31	24	80
Sergeant A. McKay	24	27	28	79
Corporal J. Coupland	24	31	21	76
Colour-Sergeant J. Beattie	26	30	20	76
Sergeant W. Kivlichan	22	28	25	75
Private Joseph McKenzie	28	22	23	73
Sergeant J. Carruthers	26	24	22	72
Private F. Armstrong	27	23	18	68
Private T. Dean	25	19	21	65
Sergeant A. Walker	24	22	17	63
Sergeant J. Welsh	21	20	14	55
	-----	-----	----	----
	297	305	262	864
	Two lowest scores off:-			118

Total -   746.

'A' Company. Kirkcudbright.

	200yds.	500yds.	600yds.	Total.
Private A. D. Bowie	30	32	23	85
Colour-Sergeant Osborne	26	31	20	77
Corporal A. Gourlay	25	28	22	75
Private J. Hogg	21	26	27	74
Private W. Patterson	24	29	20	73
Sergeant McGregor	24	25	23	72
Sergeant G. Tuck	24	33	15	72
Corporal E. Patterson	31	27	13	71
Private W. D. Douglas	26	22	20	68
Sergeant W. R. Murray	26	23	19	68
Corporal J. Swan	28	16	19	63
Private N. A. Miller	21	18	16	55
	----	-----	-----	----
	306	310	237	853
	Two lowest scores off:-			118

Total   735.

Lieutenant Muir in announcing the result, paid a high compliment to the Maxwellton men, remarking that winning or losing he always enjoyed this match with the Maxwellton men, they were such thoroughly pleasant and gentlemanly fellows and could give or take a beating with such good grace. Major Lennox referred to the good feeling which had long existed between the two Corps, and intimated his intention of increasing the number of the team for another season, so as to bring out as many young shots as possible. Three cheers were given for the highest scorer, Private Bowie, Kirkcudbright.

In 1894, the conditions of efficiency were made more stringent in respect of the Musketry qualification by the issue of the following War Office circular of 2nd November, 1894. "In consequence of the next issue of the Volunteer Regulations not being ready for the 1st November, (1894) when many of the Corps begin their shooting, the War Office has sanctioned the immediate announcement of the more important portions of the new scheme of Musketry Training which is to supersede that in use during the last few years.

The full capitation grant of 35/- is paid only for those Infantry Volunteers who pass out of the 3rd Class in each year, and the course in this has been greatly changed. The target reduced in height by 2 feet, will in future be 4 feet square, the bulls-eye remaining 1 foot in diameter, but the centre ring being 2 feet across instead of 3 feet, and the rest of the smaller target being the outer.

Shots in three divisions will continue to count 4, 3, and 2 points, but instead of firing at three ranges, from 100 to 300 yards, in this class, all the firing will be at 200 yards. 7 shots standing, 7 kneeling and 7 lying down. With the 21 shots it is possible to make 84 points, and those men who score 30 and upwards will pass out of the 3rd into the 2nd Class, and so far as musketry goes, will have earned the capitation grant. Those failing to do so must fire the class again and even a third time on a second failure.

In the 2nd Class the target and its divisions are to be left as before, but the 400 yard range will no longer be used, the practice in future being 7 rounds at 500 yards, kneeling and 7 rounds at 600 yards in any military position, and out of the possible 56 points a man must raise at least 30 to pass out of that class.

The 1st Class targets are also unaltered but at each of the ranges 700 and 800 yards, 7 shots instead of 5 have to be fired and men making 30 out of the possible 56 will be marksmen, the others, 1st Class shots.

* * * *

A new rifle range which had been acquired by the Stranraer Rifle and Artillery Volunteers, and which was situated on the farm of Innermessan, 2 miles from the town, was opened on Saturday, 17th August, 1895, by Master John Dalrymple, grandson of the Earl of Stair. A team of marksmen were present from the 3rd Lanark Rifle Volunteers, which included, Lieutenant Rennie, who had won the 'Queen's Prize' at Bisley, the previous year, Private Boyd, who had tied for the same prize a few weeks previous and Private Muirhead, and other renowned marksmen. Provost McRobert, the Commanding Officer of the Stranraer Artillery Corps, introduced Master Dalrymple. The Earl of Stair was also present. Master Dalrymple fired at the target from 500 yards and in a few sentences declared the range open. Thereafter shooting commenced. The teams were Captained by Lieutenant Rennie, 3rd Lanark, and Sergeant McHaffie of the Stranraer Artillery.

Lieutenant Rennie's Team.	200yds.	500yds.	600yds.	Total.
Private Muirhead, 3rd L.R.V.	31	28	32	91
Lieutenant Rennie.	30	32	27	89
Sergeant Yates	34	27	24	85
Lieutenant Watson, Str. R. V.	26	25	28	79
Sergeant Willoch, 3rd L.R.V.	25	27	27	79
Corporal Stewart, Str. R.V.	29	34	12	75
Lieutenant McLelland, ..	27	24	22	73
Surgeon Cochran, ..	24	24	20	68
Sergeant McIlroy ..	21	19	12	52
Corporal Craig, ..	29	18	5	52

				743
Sergeant McHaffie's Team.				
Corporal McDermott, 3rd L.R.V.	30	29	31	90
Private Boyd, ..	30	27	29	86
Sergeant McHaffie, Str. Artillery	30	24	28	82
Bombardier Torrance, ..	27	27	24	78
Lieutenant McLean, Str. R.V.	26	31	13	70
Sergeant Lock, ..	26	29	14	69
Corporal Devoy, ..	26	15	27	68
Private McGeoch, ..	27	24	12	63
Sergeant Stewart, ..	27	19	2	48
Private Caldwell, ..	16	18	9	43

				697

'C' Company, Stranraer v 'D' Company, Newton Stewart. This match took place on Saturday, 27th June, 1896, in a friendly competition between a team of 10 men from each Company on the ranges at Innermessan.

Newton Stewart			Stranraer.		
Private W. McCreadie	86 points.		Private McGeoch	79 points.	
Captain McPhater	83		Private McGill	78	
Corporal Malcolm	82		Corporal Stewart	73	
Corporal Agnew	79		Sergeant Devoy	72	
Private Priestly	78		Col. Sgt. McIlroy	71	
Sergeant Love	78		Lieutenant McLelland	67	
Sergeant Milne	76		Captain Stewart	66	
Col. Sgt. Peattie	65		Lieutenant McLean	63	
Private Davidson	59		Private Caldwell	61	
Private Sloan	30		Private McMillan	58	
	Total	716.		Total	688.

Newton Stewart won by a majority of 28 points.

The 13th annual inter-County shooting match between the Dumfriesshire and Galloway Rifle battalions, took place on Saturday, 22nd August, 1896, at the Conhuith ranges, Maxwellton. Major Carlyle commanded the Dumfriesshire Team while Colonel Maxwell was in command of the Galloway Team.

The afternoon was fairly favourable for shooting, but there was an unsteady breeze from the right front which required careful watching. The light was better than was generally experienced on the Conhuith ranges. The conditions were the usual 'Queen's Prizes', of 200, 500 and 600 yards. 7 rounds at each distance, with a sighting shot at each.

The Galloway Team was 7 points up at the 200 yard range but went down 48 points at the 500 yards and 7 points at the 600 yards, leaving Dumfriesshire with a majority of 48 points. The following is a record of the individual scores together with a comparative table of averages, made in the last four matches: -

Dumfriesshire.

Corporal Corrie, Dumfries	92 points	Sergeant Kean, Canonbie	84 points	
Captain Dods, Dumfries	92	Private Armstrong, Lockerbie	82	
Sergeant Thorburn, Ecclefechan	90	Corporal Cowan, Langholm	82	
Colour-Sergeant Tweedie, Annan	88	Private McKenzie, Thornhill	81	
Private F. Jardine, Lockerbie	88	Sergeant Irving, Canonbie	81	
Sergeant Cheyne, Lockerbie	88	Col. Sergeant Cowan, Langholm	80	
Sergeant Fergusson, Thornhill	86	Private Jackson, Langholm	78	
Sergeant McNae, Dumfries	86	Sergeant White, Dumfries	77	
Sergeant Beattie, Lockerbie	85	Corporal Wilson, Langholm	75	
Sergeant Jardine, Lockerbie	84	Sergeant McNeil, Dumfries	70	
			Total:	1669

		200yds.	500yds.	600yds.	
Average per man	(1893)	27.15	26.6	22.9	76.65
	(1894)	28.40	27.30	22.95	78.65
	(1895)	28.8	28.25	24.1	81.15
	(1896)	29.45	28.2	25.8	83.45

Galloway.

Private Carnochan, Kirkcudbright	90 points.	Private Patterson, Kirkcudbright	81 points	
Corporal J. McGaw, Castle Douglas	89	Corporal McCaw, Castle Douglas	81	
Corporal Coupland, Maxwellton	87	Private McCreadie, Newton Stewart	80	
Qrtr/master Sgt Myers, Castle Douglas	86	L/Corp Hetherington, Castle Douglas	79	
Private Law, Maxwellton	86	Sergeant Carruthers, Maxwellton	78	
Private Urquhart, Maxwellton	85	Corporal Haining, Maxwellton	78	
Captain McPhater, Newton Stewart	85	Private Deans, Maxwellton	75	
Private Fergusson, New Galloway	83	Private Callender, Maxwellton	73	
Lance-Sergeant Clingan, Castle Douglas	82	Arm/Sgt Geddes, New Galloway	72	
Corporal Bell, New Galloway	82	Pay/mstr. Sgt Osborne, Kirkcudbright	69	
			Total:	1621

		200yds.	500yds.	600yds.	
Average per man	(1893)	26.65	27.15	24.3	78.1
	(1894)	29.85	26.75	21.8	77.9
	(1895)	28.7	28.6	24.9	82.2
	(1896)	29.8	25.8	25.45	81.5

In the 13 annual inter-county competitions between Dumfriesshire and Galloway Rifle Battalions, held from 1884, Dumfriesshire had won 7 while Galloway had won 6. The following table shows the points difference gained by each Team from 1884:

Year.	Winner.	Dumfries.	Galloway.
1884	Galloway	-	34
1885	Dumfries	13	-
1886	Dumfries	38	-
1887	Galloway	-	3
1888	Galloway	-	30
1889	Dumfries	38	-
1890	Dumfries	10	-
1891	Galloway	-	18
1892	Dumfries	21	-
1893	Galloway	-	29
1894	Dumfries	15	-
1895	Galloway	-	21
1896	Dumfries	48	-

The Company Competitions of 'H' Company, Dalbeattie, were shot for at the Richorn ranges, Dalbeattie, on the 1st Saturday, in September, 1896. It was worthy of note that the prize for the Aggregate, was won by a 2nd year recruit, Private Derry, with a score of 88, after shooting off a tie with Private Smith, a 3rd year man.

The winner of the other principal prizes were:- Miss Weem's Cup Lance-Sergeant M. Clark; Captain Grieve's Medal - Private Derry.,

Mr. Kerr's Medal - Lance-Corporal Melburn; Lieutenant Armstrong's Medal Colour-Sergeant Craig; Mr Newall's Medal - Sergeant Instructor Gallagher. Sergeant Craig's Medal - Private Derry.

Recruits. - Captain's Medal - Private Toon; Morris Tube Prize - Private Toon; Sectional Field Practice - 1st (No. 3 Section), Sergeant McGregor. 2nd (No.2 Section), Lance-Sergeant M. Clark.

Prizes were given to the 'Marksmen'; for their scores at 700 and 800 yards. - 1st Private R. Flynn, 42 points; 2nd Lance Corporal Melburn 40 points; 3rd Sergeant T. McGregor, 39 points; 4th Private Tait, 37 points; 5th Lance Corporal Burnie, 35 points; 6th Private Derry, 34 points.

The statistical Musketry returns for 'H' Company, Dalbeattie, for year ended, 31st October, 1896, were, Class Firing - 11 Marksmen; 60 1st Class Shots; 8 2nd Class Shots; with no 3rd Class Shots. Sergeant T. McGregor was best shot in the Battalion with a score of 146. Private Toon was the best recruit with a score of 111.

* * * *

The next rifle to be issued to the Galloway Rifle Battalion, replacing the Martini-Henry, was in the February of 1897, when the Battalion was issued with the Lee-Metford. a .303 calibre, bolt action, which had already seen service, of a short duration, with the Regular Army. Apparently, with the introduction of a new cordite propellant, for the cartridge, it was found to be wearing out the rifling of the barrel. However, notwithstanding, the members of the Galloway Rifle Volunteers, were to report that from the introduction of the Lee-Metford Rifle, scores, over the long distances, had gone through the roof.

* * * *

The Competition for Company Prizes of 'E' Company, New Galloway, were shot for at the Aird ranges, on Saturday, 8th October, 1898, with the following results:

Competition (a). 200 yards.		Competition (b) 500 yards.	
Private G. Geddes	33 points.	Private G. Geddes	33 points
Sergeant J. Lawson	32	Lance Corporal H. Mitchell	33
Sergeant R. Fergusson	32	Corporal W. Coltart	32
Private G. Caldow	31	Private S. Fergusson	32
Corporal J. Bell	31	Private S. Kennedy	32
Corporal A. Murdoch	30	Corporal J. Bell	32
Armourer-Sgt G. Geddes	30	Private R. Knocker	31
Surgeon-Captain J. Cowan	29	Sergeant R. Fergusson	31
Sergeant R. Grierson	29	Surgeon-Captain J. Cowan	30
Lance Corporal P. Johnstone	29	Sergeant R. Grierson	30

Competition (c).   600 yards.

Surgeon-Captain J. Cowan	30 points.
Corporal J. Bell	29
Corporal H. Mitchell	28
Private S. Fergusson	27
Private G. Geddes	26
Sergeant R. Fergusson	26
Sergeant J. Lawson	26
Armourer-Sgt G. Geddes	26
Sergeant W. Coltart	26
Sergeant G. Dargaval	24

Competition (d). Aggregate of (a). (b). (c).

	200yds.	500yds.	600yds.	Aggregate.
Corporal J. Bell	31	32	29	92
Private G. Geddes	33	33	26	92
Lance Corporal H. Mitchell	29	33	28	90
Surgeon-Captain J. Cowan	29	30	30	89
Sergeant R. Fergusson	29	31	26	89
Private S. Fergusson	29	32	27	88
Sergeant J. Lawson	32	29	26	87
Armourer-Sergeant G. Geddes	30	27	26	83
Private R. Knocker	29	31	23	83
Sergeant W. Coltart	24	32	26	82
Private G. Caldow	31	27	24	82
Sergeant R. Grierson	29	30	23	82
Corporal A. Murdoch	30	29	20	79
Private S. Kennedy	27	32	17	76
Private J. Turner	22	28	20	70
Private R. Cochrane	20	27	20	67
Lance Corporal J. McAdam	26	22	19	67
Sergeant G. Dargaval	22	20	24	66
Private F. Aitken	18	23	23	64
Corporal H. Tool	23	25	16	64
Private J. Murray	36	16	20	62
Lance Corporal P. Johnston	29	17	16	62
Private W. Spark	22	19	17	58
Private J. Campbell	27	17	12	56
Private M. Donaldson	20	24	12	56
Private J. Hyslop	20	25	9	54
Private J. McCulloch	24	16	13	53
Sergeant J. Bell	24	15	11	50
Private A. Milligan	19	3	25	47
Private J. McKie	23	11	13	47
Private W. Murray	24	17	4	45

Competition (e). 200 and 500 yards.
(Recruits).

Private S. Fergusson	61 points.
Private R. Knocker	60
Private G. Caldow	58
Private R. Cochrane	47
Private J. Hyslop	45
Private J. Campbell	44
Private J. Murray	42
Private F. Aitken	41
Private J. McKie	34

Competition (f) 200, 500 and 600 yards
(Veterans)

Sergeant W. Coltart	82 points
Corporal H. Toul	64
Sergeant J. Bell	50
Private W. McKie	46
Col. Sgt W. McCulloch	36

Choice of prize in order of merit

Competition (g). 500 yards.
All Comers.

Private G. Geddes	33 points.
Lance Corporal H. Mitchell	33
Sergeant W. Coltart	32
Private S. Fergusson	32
Private S. Kennedy	32
Corporal J. Bell	32
Private R. Knocker	31

All Comers Sweepstake - 5 shots, 200 yds.
lying - no sighter.

Private G. Geddes	24 points
Private S. Ferguson	24
Arm/Sgt. G. Geddes	24
Corporal J. Bell	23
Sergeant J. Lawson	23
Corporal H. Toul	23

Special Prizes.

Kenmure Gold Medal for Highest Aggregate at 200, 500, and 600 yards.
Winner, Corporal James Bell.   Score 92.
Knocknalling Silver Cup for Highest Aggregate at 200 and 500 yards.
Winner Private G. Geddes.   Score 66.
Bruce Silver Cross for Highest Aggregate at 200 and 600 yards.
Winner Corporal James Bell.   Score 60.
Rowatt Medal for best score at 500 yards.
Winner Private G. Geddes.   Score 33.

* * * *

In August, 1899, the final and long awaited amendments to the Musketry Training Scheme for Volunteers were issued, from the War Office, and were to become obligatory from the beginning of the next official Volunteer year, on November, 1st (1899), making once again the earning of the capitation grant more stringent by added Musketry qualification.

"For recruits it is directed that the course shall consist of deliberate individual firing from 200 up to 600 yards, instead of from 100 up to 500 yards, as at present. At 200 yards, the 21 rounds are to be fired by sevens - kneeling and standing; at 300 and 400 yards, seven rounds at each kneeling - 2nd Class targets, instead of 3rd Class, being used at 200 yards. At 500 and 600 yards, 7 shots at each distance, are to be fired, lying, as at 1st Class targets.

Those recruits who with the 49 rounds obtain 100 points and upwards, will be rated as 1st Class; 50 points and less than 100 points, 2nd Class; and less than 50 points, 3rd Class.

There are modifications for cases where the range does not extend to 500 yards, but the former recruits course with 'reduced charge' is abolished.

In the next 'trained men's course', instead of Volunteers earning the capitation grant merely by firing 21 rounds in the 3rd Class (200 yards and obtaining 30 points, as hitherto, individual firing up to 600 yards is made compulsory. Seven deliberate volleys at 500 yards are made, obligatory, taking the place of the former 'optional volleys' at 500 or 300 yards; and 7 rounds of rapid independent fire at 500 yards, are also made compulsory.

In the individual practice, 7 rounds kneeling and 7 standing must be fired at 200 yards at a 3rd Class target, and other 7's at 500 and 600 yards lying, at a 2nd Class target. The volleys and rapid independent fire must be from the knee. The classification is to be:

Those who obtain 70 points and upwards -   'Marksman'.
40 points and less than 70 -   '2nd Class shots'.
Less than 40 points -   '3rd Class Shots'.

To earn the full grant of 35/- a Volunteer must not only pass out of the 3rd Class, with 40 points or more, but must also fire in the collective practices, or in the case of Sergeants, must have commanded sections in these practices.

As in the case of recruits there are modifications of the Scheme to suit ranges which do not admit of 500 and 600 yards firing and the, reduced charges, course is abolished.

* * * *

On Saturday, 23rd September, 1899, a four way competition took place on the Conhuith ranges, Maxwellton, between 'F' Company, and 'G' Company, Maxwellton, 'D' Company, Newton Stewart and 'H' Company, Dalbeattie. This again was a variation on a theme, with triangular matches of three Companies regularly taking place, however this was the first recorded four-way competition. Despite the most disagreeable weather, Newton Stewart proved victorious, the scoring being as follows:

Newton Stewart. 'D' Company.	200yds.	500yds.	Total.
Private William McCreadie	29	29	58
Private P. Priestly	28	29	57
Private T. Hanlon	27	28	55
Sergeant W. Love	28	27	55
Private J. McAllister	28	26	54
Private J. Coulter	26	26	52
Colour-Sergeant G. R. Peattie	23	28	51
Corporal J. McKeand	25	26	51
Sergeant R. Agnew	25	25	50

	200yds.	500yds.	Total.
Private J. McConchie	23	26	49
Sergeant J. Malcolm	23	24	47
Corporal J. Murchie	28	18	46
Private T. McMurray	26	18	44
Private J. L. Davidson	18	25	43
	-----	-----	-----
	357	355	712

Maxwellton. 'F' Company	200yds.	500yds.	Total.
Sergeant D. Haining	30	30	60
Sergeant W. Kivlichan	24	34	58
Private S. Carson	26	29	55
Sergeant J. Carruthers	26	28	54
Colour-Sergeant J. Beattie	25	27	52
Private P. Dunn	26	26	52
Sergeant J. Coupland	23	28	51
Corporal J. McKenzie	26	25	51
Corporal W. Hope	27	23	50
Sergeant A. McKay	26	22	48
Private F. Armstrong	25	21	46
Corporal T. Grierson	26	15	41
Major Lennox	19	19	38
Private Dalziel	25	13	38
	-----	-----	----
	354	340	694

Maxwellton 'G' Company.	200yds.	500yds.	Total.
Private R. McMurdo	29	31	60
Private J. Henderson	27	31	58
Corporal J. Moffat	29	29	58
Private D. Ferguson	25	27	52
Colour-Sergeant Service	27	23	50
Corporal R. Crosbie	21	28	49
Private W. Law	22	26	48
Private Bendall	25	22	47
Private Black	17	26	43
Private J. Taora	24	18	42
Private J. Johnstone	24	15	39
Lieutenant Shortridge	20	14	34
Average for two men short	48	48	96
	----	-----	-----
	338	338	676

Dalbeattie. 'H' Company.	200yds.	500yds.	Total.
Private A. Burnie	25	35	60
Private Halliday	30	27	57
Private H. Sturgeon	24	32	56
Sergeant G. Melbourne	25	30	55
Private Clark	28	26	54
Colour-Sergeant Craig	28	21	49
Private R. Tait	20	28	48
Private D. Brown	25	23	48
Private C. Irving	23	24	47
Private T. Craig	26	19	45
Colour-Sergeant Gallagher	21	23	44
Private A. Brown	21	20	41
Private A. Millburn	7	26	33
Private Hume	17	7	24
	----	----	----
	320	341	661.

At the annual distribution of prizes to the Dumfries Volunteers, on Wednesday evening of 27th September, 1899, Captain J. W. Dods, Dumfries, sought to explain away, how the Galloway Rifles ware much more talked about on the occasion of National Competitions, than their Dumfriesshire brothers in arms. It may have been believed, he said, that the reason was that the Galloway men secured higher places, and were more successful than the 3rd V.B. K.O.S.B., Dumfriesshire, but that was a delusion, the true reason being that the Galloway Rifles, when they went forth were accompanied by a Reporter whose special job was to sing their praises.

* * * *

The Gatehouse Section of 'A' Company, of the Galloway Rifles, held a shooting competition at the Disdow ranges, on Saturday, 4th November, 1899. Conditions, 5 shots at 200 and 500 yards. The results were announced at a social evening, held by the Gatehouse Section, on Tuesday, 8th November, 1899, when Sergeant J. R. Kirkpatrick presented the prizes to the successful competitors.

Aggregate Winners ;

1st. Corporal W. Dalrymple.   6th. Private T. Dalrymple.
2nd. Private A. D. Reid.   7th. Private W. Carson.
3rd Private N. M. Hughan.   8th. Private W. Murray.
4th. Private A. Murray.   9th Private W. McGaw.
5th. Private John Ramsay.

Recruits.

1st. Private R. Jardine.   3rd. Private W. Thomson.
2nd. Private W. Dalrymple.   4th Private W. McKnight.

* * * *

'E' Company. The Stewart Cup was shot for on Saturday, 18th May, 1901, on the Waterside Ranges, by the Dalry Section of 'E' Company. Conditions 10 rounds, 9 to count, at 200 and 500 yards. Lieutenant E. S. Forde, (a doctor from Dalry) gave the money prizes. 1st the Cup and 10/-; 2nd 7/6d; 3rd 2/6d. There were 19 entries, the following being the prize-winners:

1st. Private William Kirk   44 - 36 - 80.
2nd Private William Turner   42 - 36 - 78.
3rd. Private William Murray   40 - 34 - 74.

A friendly match was to take place between 'B' Company, Castle Douglas and 'C' Company, Stranraer, at the Caigton Ranges, Castle Douglas, on Saturday, 6th July, 1901. From the inception of the Volunteer movement some 41 years previous, this was to be the first time that these two Companies had ever met in a shooting competition. The original conditions were 15 men a-side, all to count, with 7 rounds at 200, 500 and 600 yards. However, as 'C' Company only totalled 12 men, it was decided to give the absentees an average.

There was no wind of any consequence but the light was variable and required careful watching. Notwithstanding this, however, some very good scores were made, notably that of Cyclist McHaffie, Stranraer, who was the top scorer in the match with 100 points. Lieutenant Gifford was in charge of the Castle Douglas team, whilst Captain McLean was in charge of the Stranraer team. The results of the scoring was as follows:

Castle Douglas. 'B' Company.	200yds.	500yds.	600yds.	Total.
Quartermaster Sergeant T. Myers	32	32	28	92
Cyclist Ewen	24	31	26	91
Private Turner	26	32	30	88
Private Ireland	31	28	29	88
Sergeant Gordon	31	32	25	88
Corporal Todd	32	28	26	86
Corporal W. McCaw	33	28	21	82
Corporal J. McGaw	34	19	27	80
Private Dougan	33	23	24	80
Private Haugh	28	29	22	79
Corporal Hetherington	25	28	24	77
Corporal Connolly	24	27	22	73
Corporal McKeand	25	28	20	73
Colour-Sergeant Dick	24	24	22	70
Lieutenant Gifford	21	21	26	68
	-----	-----	-----	-----
	433	410	372	1215

Average for 15 men - 81.

Stranraer 'C' Company.	200yds.	500yds.	600yds.	Total.
Cyclist McHaffie	33	33	34	100
Sergeant Derry	27	31	26	84
Corporal Shaw	27	31	25	83
Corporal McGeoch	32	28	22	82
Colour-Sergeant McIlroy	26	24	28	78
Corporal Martin	28	23	25	76
Private Miller	27	24	24	75
Corporal Miller	26	30	18	74
Private McMillan	26	28	19	73
Captain McLean	26	26	20	72
Sergeant Stewart	27	25	18	70
Lieutenant McLauchlan	20	24	3	47
	-----	-----	-----	----
	328	327	579	914

Average for 3 men - 228

1142.

Castle Douglas won by a majority of 173 points.

* * * *

The Kirkpatrick Durham and Corsock Sections of 'B' Company, held their annual competition for a medal, presented by Miss Skirving, Croys, and money prizes presented by gentlemen of the neighbourhood, on the Brockloch ranges, on Saturday, 20th July, 1901. The conditions were 7 rounds each at 200, 500 and 600 yards. The aggregate scores of the prize-takers was as follows:

l. Corporal J. McPhee, Corsock	76 points.
2. Private R. Roxburgh, Kirkpatrick Durham	66
3. Private W. Glover, Kirkpatrick Durham	62
4. Private S. Rae, Kirkpatrick Durham	60
5. Lieutenant Biggar, Kirkpatrick Durham	58
6. Corporal W. Sloan, Kirkpatrick Durham	55
7. Private A. Harris, Corsock	55
8. Private J. McCormick, Corsock	53
9. Private W. Landsborough, Kirkpatrick Durham	52.
10. Corporal Mathieson, Kirkpatrick Durham	52
11. Private A. Ewing, Corsock	52
12. Private J. Marrine, Corsock	49
13. Private J. Johnstone, Kirkpatrick Durham	48
14. Private J. Haggart, Corsock	45

* * * *

The Creetown Section of 'D' Company, held their annual competition on their range at Souter Croft, on Saturday, 22nd September, 1901. A strong wind blew in from the sea making for extremely difficult conditions, it was said that the competitors who failed with their first shots at the 500 and 600 yards were 'all at sea', there being only breakers for a background. Owing to the wet sand, the kneeling position was adopted at the 200 yard range.

Annexed are the resulting scores:

1. Cyclist Wm. Birrell	88 points.	9. Corporal Wm. Henry	46 points,
2. Cyclist P. Birrell	75	10. Private J. Cuthbertson	45
3. Private R. Wilson	68	11. L/Corporal H. McDavid	45
4. Cyclist R. Halliday	64	12. Private D. McDowall	33
5. Sergeant A. Birell	58	13. Private J. Garroch	32
6. Private P. Garroch	58	14. Private J. Innes	26
7. Private A. Scott	54	15. Private T. Topping	18
8. Private T. Gordon.	52		

On the 14th March, 1902, a Maxim Automatic Machine Gun was received at the Armoury of the Galloway Rifle Volunteers. The Machine Gun was a .303 calibre, belt fed and water cooled. It was first introduced to the British Army in 1889. Many of the Companies of the Battalion were to make application for the gun to be placed with them but in the end the Commanding Officer, Colonel J. M. Kennedy, decided that in view of a Regimental Order of December, 1900, reducing the number of Company Brass Bands, 'H'

Company, Dalbeattie, and 'B' Company, Castle Douglas, were to be disbanded, and Maxwellton were to provide the Regimental Band. 'B' Company, however continued their Brass Band at their own expense but 'H' Company had to disband, and that as Dalbeattie had lost their Band, the Commanding Officer felt that they should have the honour of possessing the Maxim Gun, to make amends. In December, 1904, the Maxim gun, was transferred to 'E' Company, New Galloway.

* * * *

A shooting match between Wigtown and Creetown Section of 'D' Company, took place on the Wigtown ranges, on Saturday, 22nd August, 1903. Notwithstanding the stormy weather a very pleasant match ended in a win for Wigtown by 27 points. The following were the scores:

Wigtown.

	200yds.	500yds.	Total.
Private Edwards	25	28	53
Private R. Drynan	25	24	49
Private McClure	23	25	48
Sergeant Coupland	22	24	46
Private D. Boyd	28	16	44
Private W. Boyd	21	22	43
Corporal Russell	23	20	43
Private Kerr	23	19	42
Private McCubbin	24	18	42
Private Tait	26	15	41
Private J. Drynan	19	16	35
Private Gardner	15	4	19
	276	229	505

Creetown.

	200yds.	500yds.	Total.
Private Halliday	26	28	54
Private W. Birrell	26	23	49
Sergeant Birrell	24	21	45
Private Cuthbertson	24	20	44
Private Wilson	22	21	43
Private P. Birrell	28	12	40
Private Collin	21	16	37
Private Beattie	24	12	36
Private McCleary	21	14	35
Private Hall	23	12	35
Private McClelland	18	13	31
Private W. Brown	19	10	29
	276	202	478

* * * *

Parker-Jarvis Cup.

The annual competition for the custody of the Parker-Jarvis Cup took place on Saturday, 1st October, 1904, on the ranges at Souter Croft, Creetown. The competition was confined to the members of 'D' Company, Newton Stewart, and the Sections of 'D' Company, Kirkcowan No.1 Section, Creetown No. 2 Section, Carsluith No.3 Section and Wigtown No.4 Section.

The Companies under the command of Sergeant Axon, assembled at the Waverly Hotel, Creetown, and headed by Pipers Watson, Newton Stewart, and Edwards, Wigtown, playing stirring airs, marched out to the range. The appearance of the men brought forth much favourable comment from the many onlookers.

Arriving at the range, the Sections drew for places with Newton Stewart being the first to the targets, but whether from excitement or light they only managed to score 15 points. Kirkcowan followed and scored 28 points. Creetown were next and it was early seen that they would easily beat both, who had gone before. This was borne out when 43 points were signalled as their score.

Wigtown the previous year's holders, then lined up and much excitement was evinced among the spectators. The shooting was steady and the general opinion was that scoring was good. The signallers soon appeared and set all doubts to rest by returning the score of the holders at 50 points. The result was received by loud cheering.

The conditions of the competition were 10 men a-side with 7 rounds each.

The Cup was presented to the winners, by Colonel Rainsford-Hannay, of Kirkdale, in the Waverly Hotel, that evening, at a social gathering of the competing teams.

* * * *

It must be said that without the dedication of the Volunteer, the Movement might never have progressed from its infancy, leading to the much maligned alternative of conscription. In reality much truth may have been drawn from the old adage of one Volunteer being much more preferable than 10 pressed men. This dedication by the Volunteer was shown in its extreme, on Friday, 18th August, 1905, in Stranraer by the plucky George McHaffie of 'C' Company.

The Rifle range at Stranraer was a good walk from the town and only gave of the accommodation of up to and including 600 yards, but this did not deter McHaffie from having practice at the long range. Set into the sand at 90 yards below the high water mark, he placed a few stones, and there lying on the wet sand and stones, he extended the range to 1,000 yards.

In April, 1907, the Galloway Rifle Volunteers were issued with the Long Rifle Lee-Enfield. which had been adopted by the Regular Army in 1895. Once again the weapon was of .303 calibre, bolt action and was distinct from the Short Rifle Lee-Enfield, supplied in 1903, to the Regular Army, as being, as was the case in 1860, more appropriate for use by the Light Infantry.

RIFLES AND RANGES USED BY THE GALLOWAY RIFLE VOLUNTEERS

Rifles issued to the several Companies forming the Galloway Battalion of Rifle Volunteers. 1860 - 1908.

(1). Long Enfield Rifled Musket. .577 calibre. 20th April, 1860 until 1862/63.
(2). Short Enfield Rifled Musket. .577 calibre. 1862/63, until December, 1870.
(3). Snider Rifle. .577 calibre. December, 1870, until 12th March, 1885.
(4). Martini-Henry, .45 calibre. 12th March, 1885, until February, 1897.
(5). Lee-Metford. .303 calibre. February, 1897, April, 1907.
(6). Long Rifle Lee-Enfield. .303 calibre. April, 1907, until disbanded, in 1908.
(7). Maxim Automatic Machine Gun. .303 calibre. 14th March, 1902, until disbanded in 1908.

Rifle Ranges of the various Companies of the Galloway Rifle Volunteers.

1st Kirkcudbright Rifle Volunteers; range at Lochfergus 1860 -1908 .
> Kirkcudbright Garrison Artillery - range at Shore Park until 26th April, 1890, when they moved to Lochfergus where the range was modified for Artillery use and shared with the Rifle Volunteers.

2nd Kirkcudbright Rifle Volunteers; 1860 range on the Corra Farm; 1861, moved to Caigton Farm;
> (When the Castle Douglas ranges were used in connection with the Galloway Artillery and Rifle Volunteer annual shooting competition, the ranges were spread over Corra, Breoch and Caigton Farms).
> Kirkpatrick Durham and Springholm Sections; range on the Brockloch Farm opened on the 19th October, 1900.

3rd Kirkcudbright Rifle Volunteers; range at Airie Farm; Private Range on Slogarie, owned by Mr.
> T. R. Bruce, which gave the longer ranges of 800; 900; and 1000 yards.
> Laurieston Section range on Crue Farm.
> Dalry Section. opened a range at Waterside Hill on the 1st September,1900.

4th Kirkcudbright Rifle Volunteers; 1860, range at Cairn Moor. 1870, moved to Disdow Farm; also
> used ranges at Kirkdale and Blackloch.

5th Kirkcudbright Rifle Volunteers; range at Conhuith. 1860 - 1908. Lochrutton Section. range at Bourick.

6th Kirkcudbright Rifle Volunteers; range at Cuil Farm, later moving to the Richorn ranges.

1st Wigtown Rifle Volunteers; ranges at Kirwaugh and Maidland Farms.

2nd Wigtown Rifle Volunteers; 1860, Aird ranges, jointly shared with the Stranraer Garrison Artillery. On the 11th August, 1883, opened their own range at Marks Farm. on the 17th August, 1895, moved to a new range at Innermessan, which they shared with the Stranraer Artillery.

3rd Wigtown Rifle Volunteers; 1860, ranges at Barrhill. Knockbrex, and Culbratten, 1897, moved to their new ranges at Barquhion Farm,

4thWigtown Rifle Volunteers; On the 18th January, 1860, opened a range at Claymaddie, but by the July, 1860, had moved to their new ranges on the Coonan Shore.

5th Wigtown Rifle Volunteers; range on the shore at Killiness.

CHAPTER 7

1ST AYRSHIRE AND GALLOWAY ROYAL GARRISON ARTILLERY (VOLUNTEERS) - AYR, WIGTOWN AND KIRKCUDBRIGHT.

With the advent of the ironclad and steam-powered ships, the ever present threat of French invasion, in the latter part of the 1850's, and the considered vulnerability of Britain's major towns and ports, along with the many exposed coastal regions, the War Office was to increase their defences by direct Government aid, and in a later report of a Royal Commission, appointed to consider the Country's defences, made it clear the necessity of even greater and more extensive works to be carried out on the more vulnerable parts of the coast.

With the creation of the Volunteer Movement, by War Office circular of the 12th May, 1859, the Secretary for War, Mr. Sidney Herbert, sanctioned the establishment of the Volunteer Force, with their undertaking themselves to bear, without any cost to the public, the charges for their training and practice grounds. However, Government, with funds already allocated for the fortification of their coastal defences, were in a position to offer inducements to the Volunteers for the formation of the much more required Artillery Volunteer Corps, as part of that coastal defence plan. The role of the Rifleman was seen by the masses to be far more glamorous and exciting than that of the Artillery Volunteers and accordingly the youth of the day were to favour the creation of the Volunteer Rifle Corps. However, with funds readily available, Government were able to offer to supply the complete needs of the Artillery Volunteer Force on its formation, the heavy guns, the practice and drill grounds, the Instructors, and all their ammunition, together with 50% smooth-bored carbines, to the Corps, and side arms if required. The Rifle Volunteer on the other hand was required to pay for his own dress, 50% of his arms, his ammunition at cost price, the cost of his drill and practice ground, as well as his Drill Instructor.

On the formation of the Volunteer Force in Galloway, much discussion was to take place amongst the influential personages of the day, as to whether a Rifle or Artillery Force was best suited to their particular area, the following advice being offered through the columns of the local press;

"As a rule, there should be Artillery Corps for all towns on the coast, and Rifle Corps for towns and districts in the interior. If a coastal town can get up a Rifle Company in addition to an Artillery Company, good and well, but if not, the latter should be preferred. Places on the coast that will either be particularly tempting to an enemy on account of their wealth or easily reached on account of their proximity and the nature of their seaboard, may be expected to need little stimulus to attend to their defences in addition to the danger which would be the penalty of their neglect, but insignificant out of the way kind of places need not plume themselves on the idea of being safe and therefore exempt from the duty and necessity of taking part in the defence movement, since these are the very places which the enemy, would be the first to pay his respects to. The besieger of fortress does not waste ball and powder against its impregnable towers if there be a weak, ill defended wall in it anywhere, and so a French or Russian invading force would scarcely chose to assail us in the teeth of a Battery bristling with Whitworth Guns, but would rather go a few miles round about, to some part on the Solway Coast, perhaps, if they were sure of thus being able to effect their descent unopposed, however, the Volunteer Artillery men might just be of incalculable service in making the crews pay dearly for their visit. This is just the sort of work for which they ought to be provided, in view of possible invasion, to attack gun-boats that might show themselves in assailable bays or estuaries and if they kept them in play till supported by other forces on land or water, they would do much to render the hostile expedition a failure.

There is scarcely such a thing as an Artillery Corps to be seen in any part of the South of Scotland, washed by the sea, it is a phenomenon rarely to be met with, while Riflemen abound, though in some places such as Dumfries, they are not flourishing as well as we could wish. Kirkcudbright to the credit of the venerable Burgh, has an Artillery Company, the visit of the "roving vagabond" who carried off, Lord

Selkirk's plate, having left in the town a traditional terror of invaders and we believe there is no other similar Corps nearer to us than Whitehaven. This state of matters should be mended, and the sooner the better."

Kirkcudbright might never have produced the two arms of the Volunteer Force, the Artillery and Rifle Volunteer Corps, had it not been for a disagreement between the Earl of Selkirk, Dr. Shand, Mr. Laurie of Woodhall, Provost Shand and other influential gentlemen of the district. At a meeting convened on the 2nd December, 1859, to discuss the formation of a Volunteer Service in Kirkcudbright, the Earl of Selkirk, did not attend, but sent a letter apologising for his absence, in which he expressed his hearty concurrence in the Volunteer Movement and suggested that as Kirkcudbright was a seaport town an Artillery Corps would be much more preferrable to a Rifle Corps. However, the meeting, through the efforts of Mr. Laurie, carried the resolution that a Rifle Corps should be formed in their district, and to this end a Committee was formed.

Dr. Shand, arrived after the resolution had been passed but addressed the meeting and began to advert whether an Artillery or a Rifle Corps should be formed. Mr. Laurie objected that the Dr. was entirely out of order, the question of a Rifle Corps had already been settled and that it was improper to raise the matter again. Dr. Shand expressed his regret that a professional appointment had kept him from being present at the commencement of the meeting and began to dilate at some length as to whether the meeting had the authority to make the decision. Several gentlemen interposed saying the Dr. was entirely out of order. Major Irving of Barwhinnock, however, insisted that the Dr. should be heard and called on the meeting to apologise to the Dr. A considerable commotion arose resulting in Major Irving withdrawing his name from the newly formed committee. The meeting was brought to a close amid uproar but the resolution to form a Rifle Corps was to remain.

Through the efforts of the Earl of Selkirk and Dr. Shand, an Artillery Corps was formed in Kirkcudbright, in addition to the Rifle Corps, the committee being, Messrs. Barber, Torrs, Riggs and Banks; Grierson, Bishopton; Sproat, Jnr., Brighouse; Gordon, Jnr., Culraven; McWhae, Kirkcastle; Mitchel, Barjesky; J. Hannah, Secretary; A.B. Rae; and Dr. John Shand, Convener.

At a meeting of the Corps on the 4th January, 1860, a despatch from the War Office was read which signified that Her Majesty had been graciously pleased to approve and accept the services of the 1st Kirkcudbright Artillery Volunteer Corps and was given the Order of Precedence number "34" in the Artillery Force of the United Kingdom. Dr. John Shand was commended to the Artillery Corps by the Lord Lieutenant, the Earl of Selkirk, as their first Commandant. The Corps was to consist of, Captain, (Dr. Shand), first and second Lieutenants and 80 men. The Corps which was filled, with scarely an exception, by members of the sea-going and kindred trades, was named, in the November, 1860, by the Earl of Selkirk as the, "St. Mary's Battery".

Twynholm and Borgue were to become very much the favoured recruiting grounds for the Kirkcudbright Artillery Volunteer Corps but it was not until the May of 1892, that a detachment was finally formed in Twynholm, which was then provided with a 32 pounder, smooth bored gun. Borgue was to form their own detachment four years later in 1896, also being supplied with their own 32 pounder gun. Their Instructor was to be Sergeant Sach, Royal Artillery, who travelled from Kirkcudbright to take gun drill at each detachment, twice a week.

There was to be no such problem in Stranraer, the formation of both an Artillery Volunteer Corps and a Rifle Corps, being dealt with in a more dignified and democratic manner. On the 29th November, 1859, a meeting was held in Stranraer to consider the propriety of forming either an Artillery or Rifle Corps. Provost Guthrie, an old rifleman, was to speak in favour of the Rifle Corps, whereas Viscount Dalrymple favoured the War Office line that in coastal regions an Artillery Corps should be raised. On the conclusion of the meeting, the Chairman, called on all persons present to enrol in the Volunteer Force, and at the same time state their preference as to Riflemen or Artillery.

By the 13th December, 1859, sufficient effective members had enrolled in both arms of the service to report to the Lord Lieutenant that upwards of a Sub-Division of 30 effective members had volunteered to enroll as Artillerymen and that upwards of 60 effective members had volunteered to enroll as Riflemen, and that their services should be offered to Her Majesty.

In due course the following letter was received by Viscount Dalrymple in relation to the Artillery Volunteer Corps.

War Office.
9th January, 1860.

My Lord. With reference to your Lordship's letter of the 26th ult., offering for the Queen's acceptance the service of a Company of Artillery Volunteers, at Stranraer, under the Act 44 Geo. III Cap. 54., I have the honour to inform you that Her Majesty has been graciously pleased to approve and accept the same. The maximum establishment of the Company will consist of one Captain, one first Lieutenant, one second Lieutenant and 80 men of all ranks.

The County of Wigtown hold the 38th place in the Artillery Force of Great Britain (Order of Precedence number) and this Company is numbered as the 1st in the County of Wigtown.

I have the honour to be,
My Lord,
Your Lordship's Obedient Servant,
(signed) S. Herbert.

By the 20th January, 1860, the Stranraer Artillery Corps had 64 effective members and the Stranraer Rifle Corps alone had 54 effective members, with Stoneykirk and Kirkmaiden showing a great deal of interest in the Volunteer Movement. Stoneykirk and Sandhead were to become the favoured recruiting ground of the Stranraer Artillery Corps, whereas Kirkmaiden was to form as a Section of the Stranraer Rifle Corps. Sandhead and Stoneykirk were to later form as an Artillery Corps in their own right as was to be the case of the Kirkmaiden Rifle Volunteers.

The following were appointed a committee of management of the 1st Wigtown Artillery Volunteer Corps, Stranraer. The Commanding Officers; the Surgeon; the Chaplain; Messrs. H. Adair; T. Dalrymple, Jnr.; Alex. Adair; W. Bruce, Jnr.; C.M. Hunter; J. McMillan; Robert Morland, Jnr., and C. Brown.

On the 9th February, 1860, a letter was received from the War Office indicating the approval of the election of the following Officers; Viscount Dalrymple, Captain; John Campbell, 1st Lieutenant; Alexander Guthrie, 2nd Lieutenant; and John Orgill, Hon. Surgeon.

The uniform of the Corps was dark blue with red facings, white belts and silver accoutrements. However, in a report of May, 1866, in honour of the Queen's Birthday, the members of the Stranraer and Portpatrick Artillery Volunteers, in their new "Busby Hats", marched through the town, along the London Road, to their Battery at Airds Cottage, where they fired a 21 gun salute.

The following, however, was the favoured uniform of the Artillery Companies as recommended by the War Office, in a letter of the 11th February, 1860.

Tunic - Blue cloth, tweed or serge. Single-breasted with fly one inch and three-quarters broad on the inside, collar and cuffs of the same material, the collar one inch and three-quarters high, rounded off in front and corner of skirts also. The sleeves to have an Austrian knot, to form a cuff three inches deep at the point, the knots to be eight inches in depth, three inches and three-quarters in width, formed with black square cord, and traced round with scarlet tracing braid, the collar edged with square cord, and traced inside with scarlet braid, the tunic to be edged with scarlet cloth, one quarter of an inch in width, nine buttons in front and two behind the skirt, without opening behind, buttons of white metal, with raised pattern of a gun in centre.

Trousers. - Blue cloth, cut to fit a band round the waist, with side pockets, large from hip to knee, small over the foot, edged down the side-seams with black square cord and scarlet tracing braid, similar to collar and sleeve of the coat.

Gaiters - Made from black enamelled leather, 13 inches deep, six buttons down side, with side strap and buckle on the top.

Cap - Of blue cloth, having scarlet cord round top and bottom, of oak-leaf band, and round instead of sunk crown, knot in centre of crown, black leather peak and chin strap.

Belt - Plain black leather, with frog for sword, snake-hook fastening.

Great Coat - Of blue cloth, similar in pattern to the Rifle Volunteers.

In 1880/81, the 'Busby Hat' as worn by the Royal Artillery and adopted in the 1860's by the Artillery Volunteer, was replaced by a helmet and spike but this again was to be later superseded by the forage cap.

The Portpatrick Volunteers were to form two years later, in 1862, taking the title of the 2nd Wigtown Artillery Volunteer Corps. Very little history appears to have been published on this Corps but a surviving booklet entitled 'Auld Lang Syne in the Rhins of Galloway', written by Professor Charles McNeil, gives a short but extremely interesting account of the Portpatrick Artillery Volunteers.

"About sixty years ago on these platforms stood two cannon on their carriage. I stood by, a young lad, watching with fascinated interest, the artillery men at firing practice. Their uniform was dark blue, with red facings and pipings, and with helmets.

The Volunteers were big husky tanned men, nearly all fishermen, but I recognised also one or two farmers of gigantic size, and they filled their uniforms to bursting point.

Their side-arms were stacked alongside, and looked puny. But the great gunners handled long cleaners and ramrods, filled the muzzle with powder and a heavy ball, and trained the gun through the Creampot on the target, a barrel, which lay moored in the channel 600 yards away, bobbing in the evening sunshine.

All was ready, a gunner stood with his match at the touch-hole. Fire! flame and smoke at the cannon mouth, and the deep crack of the explosion. Then beside the target the shot struck a white splash, skipped on once or twice, and disappeared.

Several shots were fired and then the men marched back to the Drill Hall. They emerged as civilian fishermen, only the Drill Sergeant remaining in his spick-and-span uniform, and looking every inch a soldier.

These Drill Sergeants were men of authority, exacting the obedience of their men on duty. But a story is told in which one of these Sergeants, long before my day, had the worst of an encounter in the village with a fisherman's wife. Her name was Sarah, and one day when she was the worse of drink, but with all her wits at command, the Sergeant came up, stopped and hailed her. The two probably knew one another already.

The Sergeant was a Plymouth Brother, and he felt he must do his duty in rebuking and warning the sinner. So he opened fire.

Sergeant - Sarah! Flee from the wrath to come!

Sarah - Flee yersel'

Sergeant - But I have already flown.

Sarah - Weel then! ye can juist tak anither wee bit flutter.

With the last word the action was broken off."

On the 4th May, 1867, the detachments of the Stranraer Artillery Corps, from Stoneykirk and Sandhead, formed as an Artillery Volunteer Corps in their own right, taking the title of the 3rd Wigtown Artillery Volunteer Corps. The Commissions signed by the Lord Lieutenant were John Maitland to be Captain; William Cockran to be 1st Lieutenant; Thomas Frederick to be 2nd Lieutenant; Instructor to be Sergeant Major Murray from Ayr. The Company on their formation was to number 70 effective members.

The 1st Administrative Brigade of Ayrshire Volunteers was formed on the 19th December, 1860, with Headquarters at Irvine and to it was attached the following Artillery Volunteer Corps, then in existence within the County of Ayr:-

1st Ayrshire Artillery Volunteers - formed at Irvine on the 22nd December, 1859, as one and a half batteries but reduced to one battery in 1862.

2nd Ayrshire Artillery Volunteers - formed at Ayr on the 30th January, 1860, as one and a half batteries, increased to 2 batteries in 1874.

3rd Ayrshire Artillery Volunteers - formed at Largs on the 1st March, 1860, as one battery.

4th Ayrshire Artillery Volunteers - formed at Ardrossan on the 3rd March, 1860, as one battery.

5th Ayrshire Artillery Volunteers - formed at Kilmarnock on the 12th July, 1860, as one battery; increased to one and a half batteries in 1864.

In 1863, the 1st and 2nd Wigtown Artillery Corps, along with the 1st Kirkcudbright Artillery Corps, joined with the 1st Administrative Brigade of Ayr Artillery Volunteers, with the 3rd Wigtown Corps joining with the Brigade on its formation, and at this time the Brigade Headquarters were transferred from Irvine to Ayr.

1st Kirkcudbright Artillery Volunteers - formed at Kirkcudbright on the 2nd February, 1860, as one battery.

1st Wigtown Artillery Volunteers - formed at Stranraer on the 20th February, 1860, as one battery.

2nd Wigtown Artillery Volunteers - formed at Portpatrick on the 22nd February, 1860, as one battery.

3rd Wigtown Artillery Volunteers - formed at Sandhead/Stoneykirk on the 4th May, 1867, as one battery.

The following returns refer to the strengths of the Galloway Artillery Corps for the year 1873/74:-
1st Kirkcudbright Artillery Volunteers - Maximum establishment 80. Enrolled 80.
Wigtownshire Artillery Volunteers - Maximum establishment 240. Enrolled 164.

For the year 1876, the 1st Kirkcudbright Artillery Volunteers authorised strength was 80 with 51 efficients actually enrolled. The Wigtownshire Artillery Volunteers authorised strengths were 240 with 151 efficients actually enrolled.

In May, 1880, the Brigade was consolidated as the 1st (Ayr, Wigtown, and Kirkcudbright) Artillery Volunteer Corps, but the title was changed shortly after, on an application, by the Brigade, to the Commander in Chief Armed Forces to that of the 1st Ayrshire and Galloway Artillery Volunteer Corps with headquarters at Ayr. The Brigade was affectionately referred to as "The Hairy Galloways".

In 1880, the Brigade consisted of 1 Lieutenant-Colonel; 2 Majors; 11 Captains; 11 Lieutenants; 6 2nd Lieutenants; Adjutant; 1 Quartermaster; 1 Surgeon; 880 of all other ranks, exclusive of 9 Sergeant instructors.

The Corps was divided into 11 batteries as follows:-

No. 1 Garrison Battery	- Irvine. Late 1st Ayrshire Artillery Volunteers.
No. 2	- Ayr. Late 2nd Ayrshire Artillery Volunteers.
No. 3	- Ayr. .. ..
No. 4	- Largs. Late 3rd Ayrshire Artillery Volunteers
No. 5	- Ardrossan. Late 4th Ayrshire Artillery Volunteers.
No. 6	- Kilmarnock. Late 5th Ayrshire Artillery Volunteers.
No. 7	- Kilmarnock. .. ..
No. 8	- Kirkcudbright. Late 1st Kirkcudbright Artillery Volunteers
No. 9	- Stranraer. Late 1st Wigtown Artillery Volunteers.
No. 10	- Portpatrick. Late 2nd Wigtown Artillery Volunteers.
No. 11	- Sandhead/Stoneykirk (Section at Ardwell).
	Late 3rd Wigtown Artillery Volunteers.

In 1882, all Scottish Artillery Volunteer Corps were affiliated, without change in title to the Scottish Division, Royal Artillery.

In 1889, a positional battery of 16 pounder R.M.L. guns were issued to the Corps and manned by the two Kilmarnock batteries, with Corps Headquarters being moved to Kilmarnock.

By Army Order 166 of August, 1891, the Corps were termed "Volunteer Artillery Corps" and affiliated to the Southern Division, Royal Artillery, but were not required to add the later designation to the County Titles. This affiliation to Division was discontinued in 1901.

Note. From 1860, the "Companies" of Volunteer Artillery were designated, "batteries", retaining this title until, November, 1891, when by Army Order 234, they were termed "Companies".

In 1892, the existing positional battery No. 1, absorbing the 6th and 7th Companies, was amalgamated, as the 1st Positional Battery, Kilmarnock, and in 1901, two more batteries of 9 pounder R.M.L. guns were issued to the Corps, which took the numbers: 2nd and 3rd Positional Batteries, and absorbed the 1st Irvine and the 2nd and 3rd Ayr Companies and extra personnel formed as a 6th Company at Kilmarnock. The 8th to 11th Companies were reformed as follows:-

7th Garrison Company	- Kirkcudbright, late 8th battery.
8th	- Stranraer, late 9th battery.
9th	- Portpatrick, late 10th battery.
10th	- Sandhead, late 11th battery.

By Army Order 27 of February, 1902, the Corps were designated the 1st Ayr and Galloway Royal Garrison Artillery (Volunteers).

In 1903, 4.7 inch guns replaced the R.M.L. armament of all three heavy batteries with the formation of the Corps, until 1908, being, three heavy batteries - No. 1 Kilmarnock; Nos. 2 and 3 at Ayr, and 6 Garrison Companies, Nos. 4, 5, 7, 8, 9, and 10, with No. 6 being vacant with the extra personnel being transferred to the heavy batteries.

Note. The former positional batteries were designated heavy batteries by Army Order 120 of May, 1902. The Corps carried out their gun practice at Irvine, but the 7th to 10th Companies, Kirkcudbright, Stranraer, Portpatrick and Sandhead, had their own independent ranges.

In 1900, over 600 of the Corps volunteered their services for the Boer War, 26 alone coming from Kirkcudbright. Their services were not to be called upon. However, many of the members of the Corps volunteered their services in other arms of the forces serving in South Africa. One such member of No. 7 Garrison Company, Kircudbright, being Thomas Bruce Campbell, 24 years, who enlisted as a Farrier Sergeant in the 2nd Company of the Imperial Yeomanry, Glasgow. Sergeant Campbell was killed in action near to Harrismith, South Africa, on the 10th June, 1901.

Following the Haldane reforms of the Auxiliary Forces in general, in 1908, the Artillery Companies were to form as part of the 2nd Lowland Brigade of Royal Field Artillery, their future designations being fully outlined on page 391 chapter 14.

The following is a complete list of the Corps Commanding Officers from its inception in 1860, until its reorganisation in 1908:-

> Major Sir E. Hunter-Blair, Bart. May 8th, 1861.
> Lieutenant-Colonel Hon. G. R. Vernon, July 17th, 1863.
> Lieutenant-Colonel Sir E. Hunter-Blair, Bart. (re-appointed), September 4th, 1866.
> (Vacant in 1872 and 1873.)
> Lieutenant-Colonel John Shand, Kirkcudbright, May 6th, 1874.
> Lieutenant-Colonel Sir Mark J. Stewart, Bart., V.D., February 5th, 1879.
> Lieutenant-Colonel John G. Sturrock, V.D., (Hon. Col.) December 22nd, 1888.
> Lieutenant-Colonel T. R. Stuart, April 5th, 1905.

(5) Table Snuff Mull, made from a Ram's head, which was used to adorn the Officer's Mess of the 1st Ayrshire and Galloway Volunteer Artillery.

CHAPTER 8

THE REVIEWS AND ROYAL REVIEWS OF THE GALLOWAY RIFLE VOLUNTEERS

Royal Review of 1860

With the establishment of the Volunteer Force by Government circular of 12th May,1859, the Crown was to associate itself to the aims of the then Lord Derby's Government in the promulgation of the Volunteer movement and to this end, on the 7th March, 1860, at St. James Palace, Westminster, Queen Victoria was to publicly fete upwards of 3,000 Volunteer officers from throughout the country. To further encourage recruitment to the Volunteer movement and to honour the rank and file, Queen Victoria was to hold a Royal Review of the English Volunteers, on Saturday, 23rd June, 1860, at Hyde Park, London, which was attended by some 21,000 enrolled and efficient Volunteers. To honour their Scottish counterparts in their own country, Queen Victoria, was to announce a Royal Review of the Scottish Volunteers, to take place in Holyrood Park, Edinburgh.

This Royal Review, which had been looked forward to by all classes of the community in Scotland, was to take place on Tuesday, 7th August, 1860, in the Queen's Park, Holyrood, Edinburgh, in the presence of Her Majesty Queen Victoria, The Prince Consort, several members of the Royal Family, the elite of the rank of the country and innumerable thousands of the people, estimated from 200,000 to some 400,000.

The spot chosen for the unsurpassed spectacle was at the base of the hill forming part of Arthur's Seat and afforded a distinct view of the whole proceedings to those who took possession of the elevations. Opposite the Review ground was St. Anthony's Loch, while to the front of the hill, in a most commanding position stood the ancient ruin of St. Anthony's Chapel surrounded by hills which accommodated the greater mass of the people. The view of the assemblage of Volunteers and spectators was indescribable, the glittering steel of the bayonets and the varied dresses of the Volunteers gave striking effect to the display, while towards the south nothing was visible of the hills, so densely packed were the human faces. The weather proved all that could have been desired and in short, the Review was a great success.

Before the Review.

If Edwin the Northumbrian King who prefixed his name to the Burgh and which now constituted the metropolis of Scotland, could have been permitted on Tuesday, 7th August, 1860, to have re-visited the scenes of his former triumphs, he may well have been inclined to have used the words of the 'Waking High Drover', "Lads Ye've wakened the wrong man".

On Saturday, the City began to be frightened from its propriety by sundry arrivals of patches of Volunteers and civilians who secured for themselves comfortable quarters as speedily as possible. Sunday was passed over with its wanton and necessary decorum, but on the Monday, from an early hour, trains began to disgorge their loads and as the day progressed and evening drew on repeated crowds were added to the already heaving populace, the thoroughfares swelled into some great human rivers.

During the whole evening the City was in a harmonious uproar with a more heterogeneous mass of people who traversed the thoroughfares than could have been imagined, the mellow, lazy, intonations of the English, mingled with the sounds of the Irishman, with intonations from Newcastle, Aberdeen, Inverness and Glasgow, the whole being relieved by the greetings of the gaelic.

Various bands patrolled the streets discoursing their wonderful music to the teeming crowds, one party declaring with musical might, 'That all the blue bonnets were over the Border', whilst another avowed to die for 'Annie Laurie', as averse to his Queen and Country. By midnight the crowds subsided to their various resting places as fates had afforded them.

Arrival of Her Majesty.

At daybreak on Tuesday morning - the great day - thousands of window blinds were hastily wound aside. The anxious faces turned to view the heavens. Some of the Edinburgh Officials, took it for granted that the day would be brilliant and despatched 16 water-carts, at 2am to lay the dust on the hard surface of Queen's Park, where the great spectacle was to take place, alas! for their pains by 5am it was as dry and powdery as ever it had been.

At 8am the royal train arrived at St. Margaret's Station. The 13th Light Dragoons and an assemblage of Officers occupied the platform. The carriage door opened and the Queen made her appearance, scattering her benevolent smiles all around her. Her Majesty made her first steps upon highland heather, two large mats composed of the national flower having been placed on the platform. She ascended the staircase which had been laid with Stuart tartan and on entering the royal carriage was driven leisurely to Holyrood. The Dragoons, whose band stirred up the national anthem, formed the escort and at the Palace she was received by the Lucknow heroes, the gallant 78th Highlanders.

Decoration of the City

Edinburgh was a scene of complete gaiety, wreaths of evergreens had been entwined around every suitable column, bands of shrubs and flowers waved gracefully in the breeze, while flags and banners were in great profusion, with preparations in hand for the illumination of the City at night. The Bank of Scotland, which occupied a prominent position on the mound appeared in rare feather, in her respected and lusty old age, with almost every building being tastefully decorated.

To and fro along the whole of Prince's Street, the gay crowds passed, the character being vastly improved by the profuse mixture of Volunteer uniforms. The riflemen in their countless hues of green and grey, the artillerymen in blue and the engineers in scarlet. Mounted officers in superb uniforms continually galloped up and down, the streets filled with endless lines of Volunteers who marched steadily in high spirits, enlivened by the music of their bands. Officials of every description hurried about in all directions.

By noon the whole city had flowed towards the Queen's Park. On the north side stood the grand-stand, nearly 1000 feet in length, which was composed of 5 gradually elevated rows of seats, the woodwork being covered in red cloth and the front with Stuart tartan. The whole was canopied, the beams being hung with flowers and foliage, and 50 flags fluttered in the wind. By 1pm over 4000 of the honour, beauty, rank and gentility of Scotland, were seated upon the stand, among them the Steward of Kirkcudbrightshire, Mr. D. G. Sandford, with the Volunteers rapidly arriving headed by their splendid bands, playing such tunes as "Campbells are Coming", "Up with the Bonnets of Bonnie Dundee", and taking up their allotted positions on the field.

From 1pm to 3pm the muster went on, when the firing of a battery of Royal Artillery, stationed at the Queen's Drive, announced the approach of Her Majesty. The ground was kept by the Dragoons and Highlanders, and formed at the Royal Standard, was a guard of honour of the Royal Scottish Archers, commanded by Viscount Melville.

At 3.45pm the Royal procession entered the grounds, the improved aspect of the whole scene disturbed only by the tremendous clouds of dust which for a few moments buried the whole landscape. Her Majesty covered her face with a white veil which formed a protection for her, although, some would later insist that the dust turned aside from the royal carriage. The Princes and Princesses formed part of the procession, the Prince Consort rode in uniform by the side of Her Majesty. The order had been given that when Her Majesty passed along the line, as well as when the Volunteers passed before Her Majesty, the men would keep their eyes fixed upon a certain invisible front point, but patriotism and human nature prevailed when it was noted that various side-long glances, of the most lovable nature, were directed at Her Majesty.

The Review

Many Volunteers had made a point of proceeding to Edinburgh on the Monday evening and on the Tuesday, as each train arrived, the men were formed in their Companies and inspected by their officers prior to joining with their appointed rendezvous of the Battalion. An order had been given, that none but complete Battalions should enter the Park. The Battalions began to assemble in the Park about mid-day, many preceded by military bands. They continued to arrive till after 3pm. The Review base was the wall of the Clockmill

House, along which the grandstand had been erected. When the last Battalion had entered the field, the total number of Volunteers on parade was a vast 21,500, imposing in the extreme. The Queen's Drive, from the Palace to Parson's Green was lined by the 13th Light Dragoons with detachments of the 79th, 42nd and 78th Highlanders.

The Royal Procession consisted of a detachment of the 13th Light Dragoons, (Troop) preceded by the Staff Adjutant, Her Majesty's Aides-de-Camp, officers acting as Deputy Adjutant's General, and Deputy Quartermasters General, with the Queen's Equerries in waiting, the Adjutant General, and the Quarter Master General. The Queen followed in a carriage and four, accompanied by H.R.H. The Duchess of Kent, the Princess Alice and Prince Arthur. On the right of the carriage, on horseback, was H.R.H. The Prince Consort. on the left His Grace the Duke of Buccleuch, Lord Lieutenant of the County and Captain of the bodyguard of Scottish Archers. The second Royal carriage and four, contained, H.R.H. Princess Helena, H.R.H. Princess Louisa, H.R.H. Prince Leopold and the Lady in Waiting. The third Royal carriage contained the Lady Augusta Bruce, Lady in Waiting to the Duchess of Kent, the Hon. Beatrice Byng, Maid of Honour to the Queen, the Rt. Hon. Sydney Herbert, Secretary of State for the War Department, Lord James Murray, Equerry in Waiting to Her Royal Highness the Duchess of Kent. Then followed the Lord Lieutenants of Counties, Assistant Adjutant Generals, Assistant Quartermaster Generals and a detachment of Light Cavalry Troop.

When the Royal cortege was first observed by the multitudes, on Salisbury Crag, a loud and prolonged cheer rang along the whole mass and was caught up and continued from each ridge. A salute from the Artillery on the heights to the east was fired when the procession stopped in front of the Standard and the whole Company of Volunteers saluted Her Majesty. The band of the Queen's Own Light Infantry Militia played the National Anthem.

Her Majesty then drove along the front of the lines and when the Royal Procession returned to its position in front of the Standard, the march past of the troops began. This was done by nearly all the Companies in a soldierly manner with cries of "Bravo, Bravo" and other tokens of commendation being elicited from the several officers of the 42nd, 93rd, 71st and 79th Highlanders. The march past was particularly striking and imposing and occupied 1 hour and 20 minutes. Before the march past was concluded, the whole line was put in order to advance and when General Wetherall gave the word of command, the whole army, simultaneously marched forward about 40 to 50 yards and when "Halt" was called the troops again saluted, and the band played the National Anthem. Then as before unanimous and enthusiastic cheers burst from the whole line, with caps and shakos waved vehemently in the air. At a quarter past six, Her Majesty left the Review ground, followed by the renewed acclamation of the entire multiude.

The Review state, under the command of Lieutenant General Sir G. A. Wetherall K.C.B., comprised as follows with the total of all ranks shown:-

<u>1st Division</u>
Commanding - Major General Lord Rokeby K.C.B.
1st Fife Mounted Rifle Volunteers - Commanding, Major the Earl of Rosslyn   84

<u>1st Artillery Brigade</u>
Commanding - Colonel Maclean R.A.
1st Battalion - Commanding - Lieutenant Colonel Morris R.A.
    1st City of Edinburgh (7 Companies); 1st and 2nd Northumberland (2 Companies);
    1st Haddington; 1st, 3rd and 4th (3 Companies) Durham; 1st Newcastle-on-Tyne;
    1st Berwick A.V.   869
2nd Battalion - Commanding - Lieutenant Colonel Sir J. G. Baird, 1st Midlothian A.V.
    1st (8 Companies) and 2nd (2 Companies) Mid-Lothian; 1st, 2nd, 3rd, and
    4th Cumberland; 1st Berwick-on-Tweed; 1st Kirkcudbright A.V.   714
3rd Battalion - Commanding Lieutenant Colonel Anderson C.B. R.A.
    1st, 2nd, 3rd, 4th, 5th, 6th and 7th Forfar; 1st Kincardine; 1st Caithness;
    4th Aberdeen A.V.   353

<u>2nd Artillery Brigade</u>
Commanding - Colonel Gardiner R.A.
1st Battalion - Commanding Captain A. Montgomery, 1st Ayr A.V.
    1st, 2nd and 3rd Renfrew; 1st, 2nd, 3rd and 5th Ayr; 1st and 3rd Argyll;
    1st Wigtown; 1st and 2nd Dumbarton A.V.   460

2nd Battalion - Commanding Captain W. H. Maitland Dougall R.A.
>1st, 2nd, 3rd, 4th, 5th, 6th and 8th Fife; 1st Inverness; 1st and 2nd Stirling;
>1st Nairn A.V.   652
3rd Battalion - Commanding Major J. Reid Stewart, Lanark A.V.
>1st, 2nd, 3rd, 4th, 5th, 6th, 7th, 8th, 9th, 10th and 11th Lanark A.V.   663
Engineers - Commanding Captain R. Johnstone, 1st Lanark E.V.
>1st and 2nd Lanark and 1st City of Edinburgh E.V.   198

Rifle Volunteers

1st Brigade -
Commanding Lieutenant Colonel D. Davidson, Edinburgh R.V.
1st Battalion - Commanding Captain E. S. Gordon, Edinburgh R.V.
>1st, 2nd, 3rd, 4th, 5th, 6th, 7th, 10th, 18th and 1st Highland Edinburgh R.V.   706
2nd Battalion - Commanding Captain Sir G. Home, Bt. Edinburgh R.V.
>8th, 9th, 11th, 12th, 13th, 14th, 15th, 16th, 17th and 2nd Highland Edinburgh R.V. 655
3rd Battalion - Commanding Major Arnaud, 1st Mid-Lothian R.V.
>1st (5 Companies), 2nd (2 Companies) and 3rd (2 Companies) Mid-Lothian;
>1st and 2nd Roxburgh; 1st Selkirk R.V.   715
4th Battalion - Commanding Captain Hon. A. F. Cathcart, Berwick R.V.
>1st, 2nd, 3rd, 4th and 5th Berwick; 1st, 2nd, 3rd, 4th, and 5th Haddington;
>1st, 2nd, 4th and 5th Kirkcudbright; 1st Berwick-on-Tweed R.V.   733

2nd Brigade
Commanding Lieutenant Colonel Gordon, C.B.
1st Battalion - Commanding Captain G.L.Alison. 1st Forfar R.V.
>1st (7 Companies), 2nd, 3rd, 4th, 5th, (2 Companies), 8th 9th and 10th Forfar R.V. 835
2nd Battalion - Commanding Captain Sir T. Erskine, Bt., 3rd Fife R.V.
>1st (2 Companies), 2nd, 3rd, 5th, 7th and 8th Fife R.V.   479
3rd Battalion - Commanding Major Potter, 1st Northumberland R.V.
>1st (4 Companies), 2nd, 3rd, and 5th Northumberland; 1st, 2nd, 4th, 5th, 6th
>and 7th Cumberland R.V.   674
4th Battalion - Commanding Lieutenant Colonel Sir J. Fyfe, 3rd Durham R.V.
>3rd (4 Companies), 6th, 7th (2 Companies), 8th (2 Companies),
>11th and 13th Durham and 1st Newcastle-on-Tyne (7 Companies) R.V.   820

3rd Brigade
Commanding Lieutenant Colonel N. T. Christie, late 38th Foot.
1st Battalion - Commanding Major Elton, 22nd Depot Battalion
>1st, 2nd, 3rd, 4th, 5th, 6th, 7th, 8th and 9th Stirling; 1st (2 Companies) and
>2nd Clackmannan R.V.   743
2nd Battalion - Commanding Major Pitcairn, 23rd Depot Battalion.
>1st (9 Companies) and 7th Aberdeen; 1st Inverness Administrative Battalion (1st,
>2nd, 3rd and 4th Corps); 1st, 2nd and 3rd Sutherland; 1st Nairn R.V.   901
3rd Battalion - CommandingMajor Sir A. Gordon Cumming Bt.. 1st Perth R.V.
>1st (2 Companies), 5th, 6th, 7th, 8th, 9th, 11th and 12th Perth; 4th Kincardine;
>1st 2nd 3rd and 4th Elgin R.V.   852
4th Battalion - Commanding Major the Marquis of Breadalbane, 3rd Perth R.V.
>3rd Perth (3 Companies); 2nd, 3rd, (2 Companies), 7th, 9th and 10th Argyll;
>1st, 2nd and 3rd Linlithgow R.V.   859

2nd Division
Commanding Major General Cameron, C.B.
1st Brigade
Commanding Colonel Walter Hamilton, C.B.

1st Battalion - Commanding Major D. Latham, 1st A.B. Renfrew R.V. 1st A.B.
Renfrew R.V., comprising 1st (4 Companies), 5th, 10th, 11th and 22nd Corps   535
2nd Battalion - Commanding Lieutenant Colonel J. Graham, 3rd A.B. Renfrew.
2nd A.B. Renfrew, comprising 3rd, 6th, 9th, 14th, 15th, 17th and
24th Corps; 3rd A.B. Renfrew R.V. comprising of 4th, 7th, 8th, 16th, 19th,
21st and 23rd Corps   446
3rd Battalion - Commanding Captain Hay Boyd, 3rd Ayrshire R.V.
1st, 2nd, 3rd, 4th, 5th, 6th, 7th, and 8th Ayr R.V.   559

2nd Brigade
Commanding Lieutenant Colonel Sir A. Islay Campbell, 1st Lanark R.V.
1st Battalion - Commanding Major Robertson, 1st Lanark R.V. 1st Batt. 1st Lanark R.V.,
comprising of 1st, 9th, 11th, 15th, 17th, 33rd, 39th and 79th Corps   535
2nd Battalion - Commanding Major Macquorne Rankine, 1st Lanark R.V.
2nd Batt. 1st Lanark R.V. comprising of 2nd, 18th, 50th, 53rd,
63rd, 72nd, 76th and 77th Corps   517
3rd Battalion - Commanding Major D. Reid, 19th (2nd Glasgow Northern) L.R.V.
19th Lanark R.V. (7 Companies)   592
4th Battalion - Commanding Major D. B. Macbrayne, (3rd Glasgow Northern) L.R.V.
3rd Glasgow Northern, comprising of 51st, 67th, 74th, 80th, 81st,
83rd, 89th and 91st Lanark R.V., and 1st Bute R.V.   583

3rd Brigade
Commanding Lieutenant Colonel J. Tennant, 4th Lanark R.V.
1st Battalion - Commanding Major J. F. Jamieson, 1st Glasgow Northern L.R.V.,
4th Lanark(1st Glasgow Northern) (6 Companies); 60th and 61st
Lanark R.V.   562
2nd Battalion - Commanding Lieutenant Colonel W. Stirling,
7th Battalion Lanark R.V. 5th, 21st, 34th, 35th, 49th, 58th, 59th, 64th, 65th,
66th and 90th L.R.V.   586
3rd Battalion - Commanding Major Rigby, 6th Battalion Lanark R.V.
25th, 26th, 27th, 40th, 43rd,48th, 68th, 69th, 70th and 71st Lanark R.V.   582
4th Battalion - Commanding Major A. Crum Ewing, 4th Battalion Lanark R.V.
29th, 30th, 31st, 32nd, 38th, 45th 46th, 47th, 54th, 75th, 84th and
86th Lanark R.V.   730

4th Brigade
Commanding Lieutenant Colonel J. M. Gartshore, 1st A.B. Dumbarton R.V.
1st Battalion - Commanding Major S. Simpson, 3rd Batt. Lanark R.V.
16th, 42nd, 44th, 52nd, 56th, 37th, 55th and 73rd Lanark R.V.   765
2nd Battalion - Commanding Major Dawson, 1st A.B. Dumbarton R.V.
1st A.B. Dumbarton R.V comprising 1st, 2nd, 3rd, 4th, 5th, 6th, 7th, 8th, 9th
and 10th Corps   649
3rd Battalion - Commanding Major Walker, Inspector of Musketry.
1st, 2nd, 3rd, 4th, 5th 7th and 8th Dumfries and 1st, 2nd, 3rd and
4th Wigtown R.V.   495
4th Battalion - Commanding Lieutenant Colonel the Hon. W. F. Scarlett,
Scots Fusilier Guards. 3rd, 10th, 14th, 22nd, 78th, 82nd and 87th Lanark R.V.   413

The total Review strength of all ranks was 21,514 from a total of 348 Companies.

The Kirkcudbrightshire Companies.

The Stewartry Volunteers, made up of detachments from the 1st, 2nd, 4th and 5th Kirkcudbright Rifles, to the number of 140 Volunteers, formed themselves into two Companies, under the command of Lieutenant Bell, 2nd Castle Douglas Company and Captain McKinnell, 5th Maxwellton Company, they were placed in the 4th Battalion of the 1st Division, 1st Brigade, under the command of Lieutenant Colonel D. Davidson, Edinburgh Rifle Volunteers.

The Artillery were divided into two Brigades of three Battalions each. The 1st Kirkcudbright Artillery Volunteers being placed in the 2nd Battalion, 1st Artillery Brigade, under the command of Captain Shand with the 1st Wigtown Artillery Volunteers being placed in the 1st Battalion, 2nd Artillery Brigade under the command of Lord Dalrymple.

A number of Volunteers from Gatehouse, Kirkcudbright and Castle Douglas, travelled to Edinburgh on the Monday night. The majority of the Corps left on the 6.15am train on the Tuesday morning, travelling via Dumfries and Gretna to Edinburgh. However, owing to the increased rail traffic, considerable time was lost between Dumfries and Edinburgh, the train arriving two hours later than scheduled at 2pm. Owing to the lateness of the hour there was nothing left to do but to repair to the Review ground as quickly as possible, without refreshment.

At the conclusion of the Review the Companies once again returned to the rail station and despite a half hour's grace from the Superintendant of the Caledonian Railway Company, the Volunteers were unable to obtain refreshments as the shops in the immediate vicinity were completely besieged with customers. This tended to mar the enjoyment of the trip and the Volunteers left Edinburgh both hungry and thirsty. The same delays were to be experienced on the return journey with the Volunteers still unrefreshed not reaching Castle Douglas until 5am the following morning.

Arrangements for the reception of the Stewartry Volunteers had been made at Stewart's Hospital, Dean Bridge, Edinburgh, but owing to the lateness of the arrival of the train the rendezvous could not be kept. This was also true of the return journey, as no certainty could be given as to the definite hour of the departure of the train, and the Volunteers were loathe to leave the vicinity of the rail station. However, even with this care many of the Stewartry Volunteers missed the train for home with it starting its journey some distance from the station concourse. To make amends the Caledonian, South Western and Castle Douglas Railway Companies conveyed the strayed Volunteers to their destinations, the following day, free of charge.

Much soul searching and debate was to take place as to the Commissariat Department's failure to fulfil its obligations to the Volunteers, and from the experience dearly bought, it was agreed that in future, instead of trading to chance in a strange town, the Volunteers should in future carry their stores in their haversacks. This was indeed to be the case in future Reviews.

The Wigtownshire Companies.

The Wigtownshire Companies were justly aggrieved as to their treatment at the Review, with their Companies and members names being omitted from the official printed programmes of the Review. They numbered 139 Rifle Volunteers and were combined with the Dumfriesshire Companies, forming the 3rd Battalion of the 4th Brigade, 2nd Division.

It should be borne in mind the hardships with which the Wigtownshire Companies endured in contributing to the success of the Review. 121 men from Stranraer travelled 50 miles by sea and almost 100 miles by land. The Kirkmaiden Volunteers travelled an additional 17 miles. The Volunteers from the lower district of Wigtownshire travelled still greater distances by land, without railway accommodation, until they reached Girvan. In consequence, the whole 198 men were obliged to spend three days away from home.

It is worthy of note that every man of the Stranraer Artillery were present at the Review and of the Stranraer Rifle Company, only 7 were absent, with the Volunteers in the lower districts coming forward in good force to the proportion of their numbers.

The Parade state was as follows:-

Stranraer Rifles (2nd Wigtownshire) - Captain Guthrie (Provost)	62
Kirkmaiden Rifles (2nd Wigtownshire) -	12
Wigtown Rifles (1st Wigtownshire) - Lieutenant Vans Agnew	26
Newton Stewart Rifles (3rd Wigtownshire) - Ensign Stopford-Blair	24
Whithorn Rifles (4th Wigtownshire)- Lieutenant Drew	15
Stranraer Artillery (1st Wigtownshire A.V.) Lord Dalrymple	59

PLAN OF THE GROUND

Showing the Positions of the

BRIGADES and BATTALIONS

at

The Royal Review of Scottish Volunteers

Holyrood Park, Edinburgh

7th August, 1860.

A   WIGTOWN RIFLE VOLUNTEERS

B   KIRKCUDBRIGHT RIFLE VOLUNTEERS

C   1st WIGTOWN ARTILLERY VOLUNTEERS

D   1st KIRKCUDBRIGHT ARTILLERY VOLUNTEERS

"ALBANICH"

The Wigtownshire Companies were accommodated in George Watson's Hospital, Edinburgh.

The following list of names of the Dumfriesshire and Kirkcudbrightshire Volunteer Companies appeared in the official prgrammes of the Review, as previously explained the Wigtownshire Companies were inadvertantly omitted from the programme.

Artillery.
Kirkcudbrightshire

Captain Jno. Shand	A Rankine
Lieutenant Jno. Grierson	W. Cairns
Sergeant Carnhan	R. Sibbald
Sergeant Wm. Rigg	W. Little
John Gordon (1)	S. Douglas
John Gordon (2)	J. Nicholson
J. Stevenson	J. Thompson
M. Shields	J. McWhae
J. Rae	A. Stratton
W. Connell	J. G. Ritchie
R. Fisher.	

Rifles
Dumfriesshire

From Dumfries

Captain P. Dudgeon	Andrew Henderson
Lieutenant J. Sloan	John Haining
Ensign H. Gordon	John Johnston
Sergeant McGowan	John Jones
Sergeant Smith	William Kempsall
Lance Sergeant Pike	George Kellock
Lance Sergeant Strachan	Robert Lewis
Corporal Dunbar	William Martin
Corporal MacNeillie	William Marshall
Corporal Hellon	W. S. Murdoch
Corporal Rae	A. Malam
S. Adamson	John Milligan
Robert Aitken	John Moodie
W. C. Bell	John Mitchell
James Barbour	James McGowan
Alexander Crombie	Thomas McClure
William Corson	James McGrigor
Robert Cowan	John McGeorge
A. H. Craw	James A. Oney
R. A. Dickson	Robert Osborne
J. Drummond	James Payne
John Dickson	J. A. Paterson
George Forsyth	William Primrose
Robert Fergusson	A. Stewart
John Forsyth	J. B. Sinclair
James Forsyth	George Stitt
William Gornall	William Smith
Bryce Gracie	Robert Scott
John Grierson	John Weir
William Gordon	Robert Watt
William Howat	John Watt
Alexander Harley	William Ward

From Thornhill

Captain W. Maxwell	Thomas Kellock
Lieutenant Thomas Dickson	William Rae
Ensign Wm. Smith	Edward Elton
Sergeant J. McCregie	William Love
Sergeant John Smith	James A. Amys
Sergeant Charles Howitt	William Hyslop
John Nivison	James Hastings
William Davidson	William Hunter
George Corson	William Scott
John Gillespie	Robert Pagan
Robert Gracie	William Milligan
James Little	Peter Brown

James Stevenson

John Milligan

William Carson

George Lorimer

Thomas Milligan

James Milligan

Geo. D. McLauchlan

Abram Kerr

John Coltart

John Tassie

Charles Craike

John McKinlay

Wm. D. Dickson

Adam Menzies

Robert Colvin

John Johnstone

James B. Johnstone

George McLauchlan

From Sanquhar

Captain J. Kennedy

Lieutenant H. D. B. Hyslop

Ensign W. O. McQueen

Sergeant Gavin Lindsay

Sergeant John Thomson

Sergeant J. Williamson

Sergeant J. Wightman

Corporal James Wilson

Corporal J. Broadfoot

Corporal Charles Scott

Corporal Thomas Stoddart

Thomas Waugh

David Borthwick

A. C. Bramwell

John Campbell

Thomas Campbell

George Clennell

Alex. Dalziel

James Drife

Robert Duff

John Ferguson

James Fingland

Alex. Freebairn

Arch. Gilmour

John Gilmour

Archibald Hair

John Hair

From Penpont

Lieutenant R. Kennedy

Ensign George Dalziel

Sergeant John Beattie

Sergeant Henry Smith

Sergeant Thom. McGeorge

Sergeant John Hope

Sergeant O. Crawford

Corporal Robert Currie

Corporal John Mitchell

Robert Anderson

John Black

Adam Brown

Alexander Brown

John Brown

Alexander Brydson

Henry Carson

Robert Colvin

James Corrie

Charles Dalrymple

William Austin

William Nivison

William Muirhead

Andrew Glendinning

Robert Hastings

John Brown

Henry Dinwoodie

A. C. Hislop

William Meggat

William Hastings

Thomas Megatt

William T. Noake

William Seaton

John Kerr

Hugh Dalziel

Andrew Hastings

John Kellock

John Wallace

Ballantine Howat

John Hyslop

William Hyslop

Andrew Harkness

James Ingram

John Kerr (1)

John Kerr (2)

Thomas Kerr

Robert Laurie

George Laurie

John Laurie

Gavin Lindsay

William Lorrimer

Thomas Moffat

James Moffat

James Murdoch

James McNaught

John Pearson

James Logan Rae

James Rigg

George Shankland

James Stodart

James Watson

David Wilson

John Weir

James Williamson

Samuel Whigam

James Hewetson

William Hunter(1)

William Hunter (2)

John Hyslop

Robert Hyslop

Samuel Hyslop

William Hyslop

William Kennedy (1)

William Kennedy (2)

Thomas Maxwell

James Milligan

Robert Moffat

Ewart Morrison

John Muirhead

William Muirhead

John McCheyne

Walter McKinnell

Thomas McLetchie

Thomas McMillan

Robert Dalziel
Robert Dempster
William Dempster
James Donaldson
John Donaldson
Andrew Douglas
John Douglas
Charles Ferguson
John Gracie
William Gracie
James Hair
James Haugh

David McMurray
John Pagan
James Proudfoot
Joseph Sharp
James Smith
William Smith (1)
William Smith(2)
Samuel Steel
John Tyre
John Wilson
William Wilson
John Wylie

From Annan

Captain F. McConnel
Lieutenant Wm. Dobie
Ensign W. Roxburgh
Sergeant D. Montgomery
Sergeant J. C. Morrison
Sergeant Johnstone
Sergeant A. Roxburgh
William Batty
Charles Baxter
David Beattie
John Bell
John Brown
George Carruthers
Peter Chalmers
William Cuthbertson
W. J. Cuthbertson
Hugh Davidson
J. F. Donald
William Ensor
Robert Irving
Nath. Irving

James Little
Robert McLean
Thomas McLellan
James Moffat
John Nelson
John Richardson
Thomas Stark
George Steele
John Thompson
Andrew Irvine
R. Beattie
Gilbert Tweedie
James Watt
David Watt
B. Wikely
John Williamson
John Currie
Thomas Foster
Bell
Irving
Allison

From Langhom

Captain W. E. Malcolm
Lieutenant Dobie
Ensign Carlyle
Sergeant Laurie
Sergeant Easton
Sergeant Cairns
Sergeant Wallace
Sergeant J. Glendinning
Sergeant W. Anderson
Corporal R Coulthard
Corporal R. M. Rome
Corporal James Palmer
Corporal John Moffat
Corporal Borthwick
Thomas Bell (1)
Andrew Dow
A. H. Tod
John Hounam
Samuel Hounam
Thomas Sanders
Arch. Glendinning
Adam Smith
R. K. Hurry
James Knox
Joseph Park
William Grieve
Gilbert Byers

John Cross
Wm. Common
Wm Armstrong
Simon Irving
W. Kirkpatrick
John Brownlees
Arthur Bell
Irvine Dunlop
Adam Tudhope
Robert Milligan
Thomas Bell (2)
Robert Latimer
Thomas Slack
Thomas Tedcastle
Andrew Beattie
James MacVittie
William Scott (1)
William Scott (2)
William Murray
James Veitch
John Cowan
Alex. Johnston
Andrew Irving
James Reid
John Brydone
Daniel Elliot

From Lockerbie

Captain O. de H. Stewart
Lieutenant Thom. Stodart
Ensign Wm Wallace

A Jardine
George Bell
R. Cowan

Sergeant Blacklaws
Sergeant Matheson
Sergeant Mackintosh
Sergeant Carruthers
Sergeant Halliday
Corporal Dobie
Corporal Schooler
Corporal Murray
Corporal Graham
Adamson
A. Baird
A. L. Dobie
J. Richardson
William Gray
Thomas Shankland
George Dinwoodie
F. Dobie
P. Gillespie
J. P. Douglas
J. Baird
G. Kirk
Wm. Jardine
J. Jardine
James Underwood
Wm Wright
J. Gardiner

J. Beattie
E. Beattie
John Donaldson
J. Johnstone
A. Gifford
J. Schoolar
Wm. Johnstone
R. Davidson
D. Stewart
G. Graham
F. Carruthers
R. Gardiner
H. Gardiner
R. Hay
William Hope
A. Graham
William Graham
William Little
J. Henderson
James Burnie
John Bell
J. Johnstone
G. McDougall
John Moffat
George Halliday
J. Gillespie

Kirkcudbrightshire

From Kirkcudbright

Lieutenant D. Tennant
Ensign T.R. McLellan
Sergeant J. Williamson
Sergeant A. Campbell
Sergeant Rob. Thomson
Sergeant David Craig
James Sproat
Robert Stevenson
William Martin
Robert G. Blair
Robert Broatch
William Brown
Alexander Beck
David Niven
Alex. Donald
Alex. Williamson
Douglas Williamson
Samuel Williamson
William McNaught
Robert Thomson
William Graham
A. Meggat

William Lightbody
Andrew Sproat
John Mitchell
David Bell
David Jenkins
Anthony Mackenzie
John Fergusson
James McSkimming
Andrew Hannah
Thomas Brown
Alex. Gourlay
James Rae
James Payne
David McLellan
Thomas Stevenson
Samuel Stevenson
Alex. Campbell
John Campbell
James Grierson
James Belford
William Reid
William White

From Castle Douglas

Lieutenant John Bell
Ensign W.J. Renny
Sergeant William Roberts
Sergeant Adam Skirving
Sergeant J.T. Blackley
Sergeant George Robertson
Sergeant Andrew Nairne
Corporal Robert McVane
Corporal J.R. McMaster
Corporal J.B. McMichan
William Affleck
Thomas Aitken
W.D. Borland
William Bell
William Broadfoot

George Henderson
Peter Hutton
James Johnston
David Jardine
John Jackson
James Kennan
George Kennan
Alexander Kirk
Robert McGuffog
William McKenzie
James McLearie
John McClure
David McGeorge
Malcolm McGregor
John McNairn

163

T.W. Campbell
James Comline
Thomas Crosbie
William Gray
Joseph Grierson
James Gordon
John Hewitson

John Murdoch
Bernard O'Neil
Joseph Pearson
James Pearson
Samuel Pauling
Benjamin Rae
John Shaw

From Gatehouse

Ensign D.J. Ewart
Sergeant Samuel Waugh
Sergeant John Spearing
Corporal James Wylie
John Hunter
John Drait

H.D. Glover
Alex.McCulloch
William McLean
John Hall
William Gordon
John Wood

From Maxwellton

Captain J.B.A. McKinnel
Lieutenant F.S. Allan
Ensign J.G. Starke
Sergeant John Roberts
Sergeant John Dewar
Sergeant Thomas Kirk
Sergeant A. Crackston
Sergeant James Murdoch
Corporal James Glover
Corporal George Watson
Corporal Alex. Walker
Corporal John Davidson
James Rae
John Grierson
Archd. Hastings
Anthony McMillan
Walter Blyth
Robert Hastings
John Paterson
John Davidson

Mathew Glover
T.E. Crackston
David Gourlay
Robert McKnight
Patrick Handlin
George Tait
John Hannah
James S. Rae
William Maxwell
James McConchie
David Wilson
James Hope
John West
Alex. C. Irving
Andrew Waugh
William Grindal
James Owens
William Wilson
Edward Moffat
Robert McKay

GRAND VOLUNTEER REVIEW AT CASTLE KENNEDY, 16th JUNE, 1863

Funds for the annual Galloway Rifles Association meeting to be held in the August of 1863, at New Galloway, were found to be extremely low, there being the sum of 2/9d in the kitty, and at the suggestion of Provost and Captain Guthrie, 2nd Wigtownshire Rifles, Stranraer, it was agreed to hold a Review of both Kirkcudbrightshire and Wigtownshire Volunteers, in the grounds of Castle Kennedy, on Tuesday 16th June, 1863. There would be a fete in the grounds for the public, with dancing and games on the grass. Businesses in Stranraer would be closed for the day. The Volunteer Inspection would take place at noon, with the Review and fete commencing at 1pm. There would be shooting competitions for the Volunteers. Admission was fixed at 1/- per male adult and 6d for ladies and children.

The gathering of the Volunteers was to take place by the kind permission of the Earl of Stair, in the grounds of Castle Kennedy. To the north the shadow of the ruined castle posed an interesting spectacle clad as it was from top to bottom with the evergreen ivy, which clings like an ancient friend to the old stone walls.

"A dainty plant is the ivy green,
Which creepeth o'er the ruins old."

The castle was originally a spacious, stately, square edifice, built in the reign of James VI and belonged to the Earls of Cassilis, but in the reign of Charles II, the castle and the estate passed to the ancestors of the Earl of Stair. The Castle was destroyed by fire in 1715. The grounds around the castle, planned by Marshall Stair, formed a beautiful and picturesque scene with turf steps leading from the upper to the lower grounds. Near to the centre was an ornamental pond. The castle itself was surrounded by natural lochs dotted with islands. On every side as far as the eye could see were clumps of luxuriant foliage, composed of rhododendrons and azaleas in magnificent bloom, while from every commanding position, flags of every description were flown. All in all a scene not easily described, but nevertheless a credit to the talented conservator, Mr. Fowler.

The directors of the Portpatrick Railway Company intimated that the public and Volunteers could travel at much reduced fares to attend the Review. Lieutenant Ingram, 2nd Wigtownshire Rifles, Stranraer, was a director of the Portpatrick Railway Company and no doubt used his influence to obtain such a concession. On the appointed day there was a large muster of Volunteers from all parts of the Stewartry, Wigtownshire and as far away as Dumfries. The 1st Kirkcudbrightshire Rifles travelled by omnibus arriving just before the south train which began its journey from Dumfries conveying the 5th Kirkcudbrightshire Rifles, Maxwellton and members of the public, along its way picking up large numbers of passengers - Crossmichael - Parton - New Galloway. It was regrettably noticed that there were no representatives from the 3rd Kirkcudbrightshire Rifles, New Galloway; nor the 1st Kirkcudbright Artillery Volunteers. At Dromore Station, the 4th Kirkcudbrightshire Rifles, Gatehouse joined the already filled train and at Newton Stewart five carriages, with their complement of passengers, were added to the engine, making in all a total of 22 carriages. Additional passengers, were added at Kirkcowan - Glenluce - Dunragit and by the time the train arrived at Castle Kennedy it was filled to overflowing. The special train from Stranraer arrived shortly afterwards, the total crowd now estimated to be well in excess of 3,000.

The Parade state of the Volunteers was as follows:-

Officers present - **Artillery Companies** -   Captains Lord Dalrymple and Wauchope; Lieutenants Campbell and McClear; 2nd Lieutenants Guthrie and Robertson; Hon. Surgeon Orgill.

Rifle Volunteers - Wigtownshire - Captain Guthrie; Lieutenants Vans Agnew, H. Stuart and Watson. Stewartry - Captains Hamilton and Howat and Ensign Renny. The Musketry Instructors of the Companies were also on parade.

1st Wigtownshire Rifle Volunteers,	Wigtown	35
2nd	Stranraer	68
3rd	Newton Stewart	39
1st Wigtownshire Artillery Volunteers	Stranraer	48
1st	(band)	16
2nd	Portpatrick	38
1st Kirkcudbrightshire Rifle Volunteers	Kirkcudbright	18
2nd	Castle Douglas	21
4th	Gatehouse	18
5th	Maxwellton	37
	Total	329

Shortly before 1pm the martial strains of the instrumental band of the 1st Wigtownshire Artillery Volunteers, led by Sergeant Morland, could be heard as the Volunteers took their appointed positions on the Review Ground. All was now in readiness and at 1pm precisely, a lone bugle sounded to receive Viscount Dalrymple as Lord Lieutenant of the County, in open order and presented arms. Several military evolutions were gone through under the Command of Captain and Adjutant Munro, when on a given signal, the Volunteers broke into column of Companies and marched past to the sounds of the band. The Companies were thereafter wheeled into line and complimented by the Lord Dalrymple on their marching and excellent appearance. Three cheers were given for the Lord Dalrymple, a firm favourite of the Volunteers who intimated that dinner was provided for the Volunteers in a tent, while the officers present, along with invited guests were entertained to luncheon in the old garden behind the castle.

Shortly after the Review, the rain which had been threatening, fell in torrents and the Volunteers and spectators retired to the shelter of the trees around the loch. Sums of money had been subscribed by the officers, to be given away in games and a number of youths stepped forward, entertaining the crowds in their skills at foot racing, long and short distances, hop-step and leap, throwing the stone, jumping and other athletic exercises. The rain, however, marred the enjoyment of the sports but this was compensated for by a very good string band, which played dance music to a large party which had taken refuge in Mr Meikle's refreshment tent and kept possession until time for the departure of the train.

The train to convey the public and Volunteers to their respective homes arrived at Castle Kennedy from Portpatrick at 6.30pm and after stopping at the various stations, reached Castle Douglas at 9.30pm, the Dumfries passengers being forwarded by the Irish Express at 10.30pm.

The required purpose of the Review would appear to have been a complete success, despite the unfavourable weather, when it was reported that a considerable sum had been realised and that the annual Rifle Association meeting went ahead as planned on the 15th August, 1863.

GRAND FETE AND REVIEW AT WOODHALL, 24th OCTOBER, 1863.

On Saturday, 24th October, 1863, there was a great gathering of the various Companies of the Galloway Rifle Volunteers, at Woodhall, Laurieston, the home of their Lieutenant Colonel W. K. Laurie. Besides an official inspection of Volunteers and subsequent battalion drill, there was to be competitions in rifle shooting and sports on the lawn, an additional interest being added by the presence of a large and distinguished party of guests, specially invited by Colonel Laurie.

The hour of gathering was 10.30am the Kirkcudbright and Castle Douglas Companies being the first to arrive, piled their arms on the lawn in front of the mansion house to await the arrival of the other Corps, who had to march the four miles from New Galloway station. The Maxwellton Company arrived at 11.30am but owing to hold-ups on trains from the west, it was mid-day before the Wigtownshire Companies reached the ground. The following is a record of the parade strength of those Companies and of the officers present:-

1st Kirkcudbright - Captain Hamilton and Ensign Craig
2nd Castle Douglas - Captain Mackie, Lieutenant Bell and Ensign Renny
3rd New Galloway - Captain Maxwell; Rev. George Murray of Troquain, Minister of Balmaclellan and Chaplain.
4th Gatehouse - No Officers.
5th Maxwellton - Captain Howat, Lieutenant Allan and Ensign Stark.
1st Kirkcudbright Artillery Volunteers - Captain Shand and Lieutenant Grierson.

	Officers	Sergeants	Rank & File	Total
1st Kirkcudbright	2	4	51	57
2nd Castle Douglas	3	6	68 (inc. band)	77
3rd New Galloway	2	4	38	44
4th Gatehouse	-	2	13	15
5th Maxwellton	3	5	60 (inc. band)	68
1st Kirkcudbright A.V.	2	1	27	30
Totals	12	22	257	291

1st Wigtown - Lieutenant Vans Agnew and Dr Snowdon.
2nd Stranraer - Captain Guthrie and Ensign Taylor.
3rd Newton Stewart - Lieutenant Stuart.
4th Whithorn - Lieutenant Stewart.
5th Drummore - Lieutenant Watson.

	Officers	Sergeants	Rank & File	Total
1st Wigtown	2	-	20	22
2nd Stranraer	2	5	66	73
3rd Newton Stewart	1	2	20	23
4th Whithorn	1	-	31	32
5th Drummore	1	3	22	26
Totals	7	10	159	176

In the morning the sky was grey with heavy dark clouds hanging over the hills of the Glenkens but by mid-day the sun was shining brilliantly, it being warm enough for a lazy day in August.

The mansion house of Woodhall had a fine southern exposure and was sheltered on all sides by wooded slopes. The muster of Volunteers took place on the extensive lawn in front of the house, on the northern side of which had been erected a spacious marquee, together with the flags of the British Ensign and the Union Jack. As the Volunteers reached the ground, Company after Company, piled arms and broke off into their various Companies which together with the parties of invited guests added to the colourful military spectacle.

It had been anticipated that the Battalion would be inspected by Lieutenant Colonel Roney, Inspecting Officer, but owing to illness his position was taken by Major Walker of Crawfordton, Inspector of Musketry.

Shortly after mid-day, the sound of the bugle called the Volunteers to 'fall-in', it also being the signal for the guests and spectators to attend the Review Ground. Lieutenant Colonel Laurie was in command of the Battalion but Captain and Adjutant Munro gave the words of command for the various movements. A large concourse of onlookers soon lined the avenues and carriage drives, with the fair sex who occupied the front rank forming a brilliant fringe of colour to the scene of the military display. The uniforms of the

Galloway Volunteers, though serviceable were a rather sombre shade but the glitter and sparkle of their accoutrements in the late sunshine made for a pleasant contrast.

Owing to the time likely to be entailed in the rifle shooting, it was found impossible to devote much time to the Inspection and Review. Some preliminary drills having been gone through, the Battalion was wheeled into line and on the arrival of Major Walker the general salute was given. The Companies were then reformed and marched past in quick time, a movement so well executed that the Inspecting Officer considered it worthy of an encore and it was accordingly done a second time. The marching past was steady and soldier-like and whereas all Companies did well, the appearance of the Maxwellton, Kirkcudbright, Castle Douglas and Stranraer Companies were especially commended by Major Walker, with Maxwellton Company being singled out for their general efficient appearance. The Battalion then broke up, the Review having lasted fully one hour. The Volunteers retired to luncheon, provided by Colonel Laurie, in the large marquee, in sittings of 100, with 20 minutes being allowed to each sitting. The luncheon was purveyed by Mr. Payne of the Douglas Arms, Castle Douglas. The Officers and invited guests were entertained in style, grace and elegance in the Mansion House at Woodhall.

Two targets had been erected on the south side of the lawn or Home Park, and at 2pm the rifle competitions were begun. On a neighbouring slope, two or three Pool and Aunt Sally Targets were sighted, proving a great draw to both Volunteers and spectators alike. A Miniature Range was created for the Ladies, who found great amusement with the "Pea Rifle", some of the Ladies proving to be quite deadly shots.

A series of sports were improvised, including jumping, running, sack and barrow races, for which cash prizes were awarded, all of which were productive of much amusement to the onlookers. Many of the spectators were to enjoy themselves by simply watching the various activities or taking part in the Pool and Aunt Sally target shooting, whilst others strolled in the garden, others were to be found deporting themselves in a boat over the waters of a pretty lake near to the house. All was motion and animation with the constant crack of the rifle adding an additional liveliness to the scene.

The following are the best scores made in competition for the five cash prizes presented by Captain and Adjutant Munro. For the best shot, a gold medal and £5 cash. Second prize, £4. Third prize, £3. Fourth prize, £2. Fifth prize, £1. The Competitors were required to have attended 25 Company drills between the 1st January and the 31st August, last. There were 150 entries. The contest was held over the 300 and 400 yard ranges, the 200 yard range being dispensed with owing to lack of time. The following are the highest scores made:-

Newton Stewart, Drummore, and Gatehouse Sections.	Points & Hits.	
Sergeant William Cairns, Gatehouse	3 3 3	-12
Privates A. McConchie, Newton Stewart	2 3 3	-11
J. Stewart, Newton Stewart	1 3 2	- 9
William M'Gavin, Drummore	1 3 2	- 9
Sergeants McCosh, Drummore	2 1 1	- 7
Waugh, Gatehouse	1 1 2	- 7

2nd Kirkcudbright Section (Castle Douglas)		
Corporal McGuffog	3 3 2	-11
Sergeant Skirving	2 3 3	-11
Privates Mitchell	3 3 2	-11
R. Turner	2 1 2	- 8
Sergeant Thomson	1 2 1	- 7
Private Papple	1 2 1	- 7
Corporal Aitken	0 3 2	- 7

1st Kirkcudbright Section (Kirkcudbright).		
Grierson	1 3 3	-10
J. McClurg	3 1 3	-10
J. Johnson	3 1 2	- 9
Caird	3 1 2	- 9
Payne	3 1 2	- 9
Williamson	2 2 1	- 8

	Points & Hits.

3rd Kirkcudbright Section (New Galloway)

Sergeant John Muir	3 2 2 -10
Privates G. Geddes	2 3 2 -10
Craig	2 3 2 -10
Robert Johnston	1 3 2 - 9
William Kiran	2 1 3 - 9
James Muir	2 2 1 - 8
A. Stevenson	2 2 1 - 8
Carsewell	2 1 2 - 8
J. McMath	2 0 3 - 7
A. Geddes	1 1 2 - 7
A. Anderson	2 1 1 - 7

5th Kirkcudbright Section (Maxwellton)

Corporal Douglas	1 3 3 -10

1st and 2nd Wigtownshire Sections (Stranraer & Wigtown).

Sergeant Inglis, Stranraer	3 3 2 -11
Privates D. Henderson, Wigtown	2 3 2 -10
W. Wilson, Wigtown	1 2 2 - 8

The highest score was made by Sergeant Cairns of Gatehouse, with a score of 12 points. A "shoot-off" to decide the subsequent prizes was to take place with the following result. 2nd prize, Sergeant Inglis, Stranraer. 3rd prize, Private McConchie, Newton Stewart. The 4th and 5th prizes to be divided between, Sergeant Skirving and Corporal McGuffog, Castle Douglas. The prizes were presented by Major-General Johnston of Carnsalloch.

Colonel Laurie then briefly addressed the Volunteers and thanked them for the honour they had done him in the manner in which they had responded to his invitation. He was now confident that the Battalion could come together at any time should the need ever arise. With regard to their appearance and Battalion drill, Major Walker had informed him that he would have no hesitation whatsoever in recommending them to the authorities. Three cheers were given for Major-General Johnston, Colonel Laurie, Captain and Adjutant Munro and the Queen.

CARLISLE REVIEW 1868

Friday, 28th August, 1868, was the date fixed for the annual Brigade Drill and Review of the Cumberland Volunteers to be held on the "Swifts", Carlisle, and to add additional colour and interest the Cumbrians invited and were reinforced by their local allies. This gathering, in the "Merrie City", proved to be the largest of its kind, in the City, from the inauguration of the Volunteer movement, some nine years earlier.

The following Regimental Orders were issued on the authority of Colonel W. K. Laurie, Officer Commanding the Galloway Rifle Volunteers:-

1. On the arrival of the Regiment at Carlisle, on the 28th inst., the Battalion will be formed in the open space near the Railway Station, and then marched to the Reviewing ground, where the arms will be piled and the men allowed to fall out.

2. After the Battalion has fallen in for parade, no Volunteer is on any account to fall out of the ranks except with permission of the Officer in Command of the Corps.

3. At the termination of the Review the men's pouches will be examined, and any blank cartridges collected by the Sergeant Instructors, after which the Battalion will be marched to the town and dismissed.

4. To prevent any confusion when leaving Carlisle, the Battalion will assemble in the open space near the Railway Station, at least 20 minutes before the hour named for starting and form a quarter distance column left in front, when the different Corps will be marched into the Railway Station to their different carriages.

By Order,
(Signed) W. Munro, Captain Adj.,
Galloway Rifle Vol. Battn.

Each arm of the service was to be represented at the Review. The Westmorland and Cumberland

Yeomanry represented the Cavalry. The Cumberland Brigade of Volunteer Artillery represented that branch of the service, while the infantry included the Cumberland and Westmorland, the Dumfriesshire and the Galloway Rifle Volunteers, and detachments of the 70th Regiment of Foot, then stationed at Carlisle.

The morning of the Review opened in a very threatening manner. Early in the forenoon heavy clouds hung over the City and showers fell, however, in the afternoon it proved much more favourable, although rather cold. The crowd was the largest ever gathered on the "Swifts" and it was estimated to be in the region of 25 to 30,000 strong.

Before one o'clock the Volunteers began to march to the ground and the air was filled with the sound of inspiring music, while the streets resounded with the 'martial tread of armed men'. The Whithaven Corps in their regulation grey with their scarlet coated band and the Galloway Corps dressed in dark green, making a fine compact Battalion of stalwart men, were the first to take possession of the field.

Gradually the patch of grey of the Cumberland Volunteers increased in size as the various Cumbrian Corps arrived. The Westmorland Battalion in bright scarlet constituted the next arrival, while the Yeomanry Cavalry, brilliant in scarlet and white, occupied a position in the rear.

Presently the Artillery Volunteers, with four field guns, arrived and the four Companies of the 70th Regiment of Foot, with that steadiness and regularity which belongs to the practised soldier, entered the "swifts" and took up the position assigned to them.

The whole of the arrivals having been completed the Parade State was as follows:-

Cumberland Battalion	962
Westmorland Battalion	405
Dumfriesshire Battalion	568
Galloway Rifles	515
Cumberland Artillery Brigade	192
Yeomanry Cavalry	120
70th Regiment of Foot	150
Total (Independent of Staff)	2912

General Staff

Colonel Roache - Commanding

Aides-de-Camp - Lt. Col. Sanderson R.C.M. - Lt. Col. Allhusen N.A.V. - Lt. Col. Gourlay S.R.V.

Major Provost, Staff Officer, Pensioners; Major Sir Rowland Errington, N.R.V.

Assistant Quartermaster-General; Major Cay, 70th Regiment.

Assistant Adjutant-General - Major Wolher, Dumfries Militia.

Cavalry and Field Batteries.

Lt. Col. Salkeld - Commanding.

Captain and Adjutant Wriford - Major of Brigade, Westmorland and Cumberland Yeomanry Cavalry, Cumberland Artillery Volunteers.

1st Infantry Brigade.

Major Ralston, 70th Regiment - Commanding.

Lt. Pearson, 70th Regiment - Aide-de-Camp.

Captain and Adjutant Nicholls, Sunderland R.V. - Major of Brigade.

70th Regiment - Captain Couper - Commanding.

1st Battalion Cumberland R.V. - Captain Thompson, Commanding.

1st Battalion Dumfriesshire R.V. - Major Clark, Commanding.

2nd Infantry Brigade.

Lt. Col. Thompson - Commanding.

Captain and Adjutant Walker, Northumberland - Major of Brigade.

1st Battalion Galloway R.V. - Captain and Adjutant Munro - Commanding.

2nd Battalion Cumberland R.V. - Lt. Col. Spedding, - Commanding.

1st Battalion Westmorland - Major Whitwell - Commanding.

Parade State of Local Companies.

Dumfriesshire Rifle Volunteers.

1st (Dumfries) - Captain Hope; Dr. Marshall	96
2nd (Thornhill) - Lieutenant Smith	44
3rd (Sanquhar) - Captain Kennedy; Lieutenant Hyslop; Ensign MacQueen.	60
4th (Penpoint) - Major Clark; Lieutenant Dalziel, Ensign Smith.	45
5th (Annan) - Lieutenant Roxburgh	57
6th (Moffat) - Captain Johnstone; Lieutenant Anderson; Ensign Gillespie.	67
7th (Langholm) - Major Malcolm; Lieutenant Dobie; Ensign Carlyle.	87
8th (Lockerbie) - Lieutenant Wallace.	64
9th (Lochmaben) - Captain Johnstone; Lieutenant Dinwoodie; Ensign Craike.	63

Kirkcudbrightshire Rifle Volunteers.

1st (Kirkcudbright) - Captain Hamilton	69
2nd (Castle Douglas) - Captain Skirving; Lieutenant McGuffog; Ensign Crosbie.	49
3rd (New Galloway) - Captain Maitland; Lieutenant Kennedy; Assistant Surgeon Milman.	46
5th (Maxwellton) - Captain Howat; Lieutenant J.G. Gibson-Starke; Lieutenant James Rennie; Assistant Surgeon Barrie	125
6th (Dalbeattie) - Captain Platt	20

Wigtownshire Rifle Volunteers.

1st (Wigtown) - Lieutenant Vans Agnew; Lieutenant Stewart; Ensign McHaffie; Ensign Hughan.	26
2nd (Stranraer) - Captain Guthrie; Lieutenant Watson; Ensign Taylor.	60
3rd (Newton Stewart) - Captain Stroyan; Lieutenant Picken; Ensign Stewart; Assistant Surgeon Clark.	97

When the Inspecting Officer, Colonel Roache arrived, the troops drawn up in line, gave the general salute. Having ridden round the lines, and inspected the whole force, preparations were made for the march past. When the troops were drawn up on the ground, the Yeomanry Cavalry were to the left of the saluting flag, the Artillery Volunteers with their ordnance, behind them, and then the other Corps, in the counties, in order of precedence, the extreme left being brought up by the Dumfriesshire and Galloway Corps. The Inspecting Officer and his staff took up position at the saluting flag and the troops proceeded to march past.

The Yeomanry led the way and passed the critical point with credit to themselves. They were followed by the Artillery, with their field guns, and without exception this branch of the Volunteer service acquitted themselves well, the most uniform of the Brigade, and its general good order calling forth warm encomiums. Next came the Infantry Volunteers, the "Belted Wills" wavered as they neared the Reviewing Officer, but gallantly closed up and passed like one man. The Dumfriesshire men, in their light uniform, won hearty praise not only for their steady marching but for their good soldierly appearance. The Galloway contingent were worthy representatives and "Well done Scotland" was the merited salute they received.

After the march past, the men were formed into open column of Companies in the flat opposite the grandstand, covered by four companies of the 70th Regiment, with four companies of Volunteers, as support, the remainder of the forces being deployed into line. Suddenly the enemy, who were behind the bank, near to the grandstand, and which was composed of a small number of Artillerymen and Riflemen, opened fire. The 70th Regiment were then formed into line, advanced by wings, and opened fire, but immediately reformed into skirmishing order, keeping up a continuous fire. After vainly endeavouring to force the enemy from its ambush, the whole of the defending forces retired in direct echelon (rank) of companies from the left. The line then formed squares and prepared to receive Cavalry, a troop of which advanced, but were immediately repelled. The enemy then shifted their position and took ambush behind the hill, near to the stile at the waterworks. This movement was observed by the defending party which immediately charged its front and opened fire. The whole army was now drawn up in line, but the entire breadth of the "Swifts" would not accommodate them, and nearly a full Battalion was kept in the background. The file-firing, while in this position was excellent. The Yeomanry next dashed in front in skirmishing order, and the whole army formed quarter-distance column in rear of right company of Battalions, after which a variety of marching and field manoeuvres were gone through. The force was then drawn up in squares and saluted. The Officers Commanding the Brigades were then called to the front.

Colonel Roache then addressed the Review and stated that upon the whole he was very much satisfied with the drill. Perhaps some Corps might have executed their movements rather better, but considering that the Battalions had never worked together before and the difficulties they had to contend with, he was well satisfied and would make a favourable report to the War Office.

Colonel Kennedy the 3rd Commander of the Galloway Rifles, then a Lieutenant in the 3rd Kirkcudbrightshire Rifles, was to later recall this review of which he wrote, "The Colonel and his Staff were very active on that occasion, making several descents or swoops down upon the auxiliaries to correct mistakes or irregularities which happened to catch the eye of the Commander. It was most alarming to see such a large distinguished body of fierce looking gentlemen charging right at us or our neighbours, and had not Volunteers been very staunch no doubt it would have been a complete rout".

On the conclusion of Colonel Roache's speech, the Volunteers were marched off the Ground with their progress through the streets keenly watched by an immense crowd of onlookers.

The Thornhill and Sanquhar Companies returned home by the 6.22pm train from Carlisle. The Dumfries, Maxwellton and other Stewartry and Wigtownshire Companies returned by special train, reaching Dumfries at 8.30pm and after changing engines, the train continued to Stranraer.

THE ROYAL OR "WET REVIEW" 1881

To honour the coming of age of the Volunteer movement, on the 9th July, 1881, at Windsor Great Park, London, Queen Victoria, reviewed upwards of 52,000 Officers and men of the English and Welsh Volunteers. It had been proposed that Queen Victoria would honour the Officers and men of the Scottish Volunteer movement, the year before, in the August of 1880, within the Queen's Park, Holyrood, Edinburgh, but at the last moment, on the 2nd July, 1880, an intimation was received from the Palace that the Queen's presence could not be guaranteed and the event was hastily cancelled. However, a further date was proposed by the Palace and readily accepted by the authorities, that of Thursday, 25th August, 1881, as being suitable for the Review of the Scottish Volunteers, within the Queen's Park, at Holyrood.

In July, 1881, the military authorities were to issue an order in which Volunteers taking part in the Royal Review should proceed, together with their anticipated parade strength.

1st number - number of Officers attending. 2nd number - number of men attending:-

1st Ayrshire and Galloway Artillery Volunteers;
    Irvine 1 - 59; Ayr 3 -128; Largs 2 - 49; Ardrossan 3 - 57; Kilmarnock 4 - 76; Kirkcudbright 2 - 48; Portpatrick 1 - 34; Stranraer 8 - 107; Combined total 24 Officers - 558 rank and file.

Galloway Rifle Volunteers;
    Stranraer 4 - 90; Kirkcowan 0 - 24; Newton Stewart 8 - 60; New Galloway 3 - 60; Maxwellton 4 -184; Kirkcudbright 4 - 80; Castle Douglas 2 - 62; Dalbeattie 3 - 88; Combined Total 28 Officers - 648 rank and file.

The whole to form under the 3rd Division, 1st Brigade.
Note. Although these figures were to represent the official parade state on the day of the Review, an amended return of the actual parade state of the 1st Ayr and Galloway Artillery and Galloway Rifle Volunteers, appears on pages 178 and 179.

In connection with the proposed Royal Review, the following Regimental Orders were issued by Lieutenant-Colonel Maitland:-

**Her Majesty the Queen's Review of Volunteers
at Edinburgh, 25th August, 1881.**

Regimental Orders
by Lt. Col. Gordon Maitland,
Commanding Galloway Rifle Volunteers.

i). The Galloway Rifle Volunteers will start for Edinburgh on the 25th August, from Stations as follows:-

'C' Company, from Stranraer, at 2am

'D' Company, from Newton Stewart, at 2.52 am.

'E' Company, from New Galloway, at 3.38am.

'F' & 'G' Companies, from Dumfries, at 5.15am.

The above Companies will form the right wing of the Battalion in charge of Major Murray Kennedy, who will take over command of them at 3.30am on 25th August, 1881.

'A' Company, from Kirkcudbright, at 3.45am

'B' Company, from Castle Douglas, at 4.15am

'H' Company, from Dalbeattie, at 4.25am

These Companies will form the left wing of the Battalion under Major Maxwell, who will take charge of them at Dumfries Station, at 5am on 25th August, 1881.

ii). Sergeant Instructor Harold of 'C' Company, will, with the permission of the Stationmaster, at any time, on the 24th inst., chalk the letter of Companies, as they will arrive at the various stations on the Portpatrick Line, beginning with 'C' Company nearest the engine, following with 'D' and 'E' Companies. ('D' Company will require 10 compartments, 'E' Company 8 compartments.) In the same way Assistant Sgt. Major Murdoch will mark the carriages of 'F' and 'G' Companies. Sgt. Instructor Gilmour will mark the carriages nearest the engine as 'A' Company, and afterwards 'E' and 'B' Companies. ('B' Company will require eight compartments. 'H' Company eleven). Officers Commanding Companies having arrived at the railway station will tell off their Companies into fours, fronting the train, and will march their sections with shouldered arms into the compartments.

iii) No one will be allowed to leave the train or fall out at any time during the day without permission from the Officer Commanding the Battalion. No bugles to be sounded except by his orders given direct, or through the Adjutant.

iv) The Maxwellton band only will march in front of the Regiment (when marching past in the ranks), and will not play except when ordered by the Officer Commanding the Battalion. Other bands will fall into the ranks.

v) In the march past with shouldered arms in quarter column, officers and men must look straight to the front. Mounted officers only will salute.

vi) Directing guides must look to their covering and distance remembering that six paces form the interval between Companies. All ranks must be careful to keep their arms from swinging. The butts to be well back when at shouldered arms. Officers to remember to keep hilts of their swords well back to the front, and hand inside.

vii) The strictest silence is to be maintained by all ranks, and should it be necessary on the part of Officers or N.C.Officers to make to make corrections, they must do so in a subdued tone of voice.

viii) Officers Commanding Companies will have made up in such hampers or boxes as will be easily carried by two men a sufficient quantity of sandwiches for two substantial meals at Edinburgh, in addition to anything that may be given before the arrival there, 2/6d should be expended on these two meals.

ix) Each hamper should have a cotton label fastened on and addressed with letter of the Company, Regiment and station. No 1 will be the morning meal on arrival at Edinburgh. No 2 will be the meal after march past. In addition to the above, labels must be brought to return the empties the day following, and addressed to each Company's headquarters.

The Quartermaster will be good enough to proceed to Edinburgh, on the evening of the 24th inst., to carry such instructions as may be issued by the Adjutant. All Quartermaster Sergeants of Companies will, on arrival at Morrison Street Station, report themselves to the Quartermaster. Two men per Company will be told off to assist the Quartermaster by the C.C. Companies, and they will be under the Quartermaster's orders, but they will march past with their Companies, and will, on return to Edinburgh, be under the orders of the Quartermasters until the departure of the train from Edinburgh.

x)Beer and lemonade will be provided regimentally.

xi) There will be no objections to Officers commanding Companies making arrangements on their own account for an extra meal on their return home.

xii) No liquor will be allowed to be supplied during the journey to and from Edinburgh, as beer will be provided on arrival at rendezvous, and before departure of train home.

xiii) No Volunteers will be allowed to proceed independently to the station.

xiv) It is incumbent on each one to carry out the above orders, so far as they relate to him, and not to forget that upon the conduct of each one will rest the credit of the Battalion.

By Order,

(signed) H. Farrer, Captain,

Adjutant, Galloway Rifle Volunteers.

Note. Captain Lennox of the Maxwellton Corps wrote to Messrs W. Younger and Co., of the Abbey and Holyrood Breweries, before the Review, as to the cost of furnishing his Company with ale. Messrs. W. Younger and Co., by return offered to supply, and in fact did supply, the entire Battalion of the Galloway Rifle Volunteers, some 600 men, with free ale.

The arrangements of the railway companies were made on a scale never before equalled in the country. The Caledonian Railway Company borrowed 500 carriages from the London and North Western Railway Company, these having to be conveyed from Lancashire the day before the Review. The smallest train to arrive in Edinburgh carried 16 carriages and the largest 26 carriages.

With regards to the local companies, the Kirkcudbright Artillery Volunteers, under the command of Captain Campbell left the county town at 5pm on Wednesday, 24th August, and travelled to Stranraer. This roundabout route being the subject of Regimental Orders. At 1.30am the Galloway Artillery Companies left Stranraer by the Girvan and Portpatrick line. At Kilwinning it was joined by the contingents from Kilmarnock, Irvine, Fairley and Ardrossan. At Irvine they were joined by the Cumnock Section, the whole passing through Shields junction at 7am and arriving at Morrison Street Station, Edinburgh at 8.55am.

The Rifle Volunteers under the command of Captain Craig left Kirkcudbright at 3.45am on the 25th and enroute took up the Stranraer, Newton Stewart, New Galloway and Castle Douglas Companies, at the latter place at 4.15am., picking up the Dalbeattie and Maxwellton Companies and proceeding to Edinburgh where they arrived at the Caledonia Railway Company's Coal Depot, in Morrison Street at 8.40am, the ordinary rail traffic having been suspended from 5am

Together with the 1st Cumberland Rifles, the 1st Lanarkshire Artillery, 1st Ayr and Galloway Artillery, the 1st Lanarkshire Engineers, the 1st Aberdeenshire Engineers and the 1st Dumfries Rifle Volunteers, the Galloway Rifles were marshalled outside the rail station by Lieutenant R. Wilson of the 10th Hussars and together they were marched to the Fountain-Head School Buildings where they were to partake of their refreshments.

Her Majesty Queen Victoria, accompanied by the Princess Beatrice, the Duke of Connaught and suite, later to be joined in Edinburgh by the Duke and Duchess of Edinburgh, left Osborne on the Tuesday night, 23rd August, crossed the Solent in the yacht "Alberta" and travelled by the North Western, Great Western, and London and North Western Railways arriving Carlisle at 5.30am on the Wednesday morning. The Royal Party then travelled by the North British Railway Company, arriving at St. Margaret Station near the Meadowbank entrance to the Queen's Park, Edinburgh at 9am This Station was reserved by the rail company solely for the patronage of the Queen on her visits to Edinburgh. The Queen then proceeded to the Palace by way of the Queen's Park which had been decorated for the occasion with bunting and flags and a large crowd gathered to cheer Her Majesty's arrival. The City bells were rung and a Royal Salute was fired from the Castle. In the afternoon Her Majesty visited the new Royal Infirmary and named two of the wards - The Albert and Victoria. Among the specially invited guests was Mrs. McLean of Penninghame.

On the morning of the Review everything at first gave great promise of success, the Volunteers were enthusiastic and admiring onlookers were flocking to the Capital in their tens of thousands and Royalty herself was to honour the scene with her gracious presence. One powerful potentate, however, had all the while been shaking his head, "Jupiter Pluvius" was in a surly mood and determined to withhold the Queen's weather. The summer had been poor and although the morning opened dry but dull, it soon turned to light rain and by 11am the heavens had opened to an absolute downpour which was to continue unabated, throughout the day and on into the night.

The last of the troops reached the City at 11am, with the whole being marched to their allotted positions in the Queen's Park. They were accompanied by admiring and cheering crowds. On leaving the West Meadows by the north-east gate for the Queen's Park, the 1st Division, numbering 12,901, marched by the Middle Meadow Walk, north side of George Square, Crichton Street, Chapel Street, West Nicholson Street, West and East Richmond Street, Pleasance, Brown Street, Hercules Street, Craigside Place and Arthur Street. Leaving the East Meadows by the South West Corner, the 3rd Division numbering 13,615, proceeded by Summerhall, Lord Russell Place, West and East Preston Street, Dalkeith Road and the Gibbet Loan, entering the Park by the Albert Gate. The 1st Division was arranged on the south and east sides of the Review Ground in two sides of a square. The Cavalry occupied the extreme north end of the line, a little to the east of the Grandstand, and beside, continuing the line towards Arthur's Seat was the 1st Brigade. The Line was then continued westwards in the order named, by the 2nd, 3rd, and 4th Brigades. The 1st Brigade of the 2nd Division contiued the Line to within a few yards of Holyrood Palace Gardens, the troops still occupying a position on the north side of the Queen's Drive. At this point there was a break, and the troops were stationed on the south side of the Drive, forming a continuous Line of Brigades, till the Line terminated opposite Heriot Mount by the 4th Brigade of the 3rd Division.

The Review Parade under the Command of Major-General A. McDonald, Commanding the Northern British District, was as follows:-

1st Division
Volunteer Cavalry Brigade.
Commanding - Colonel Hon. C.W. Thesiger, 1st Cavalry District.

Name of Corps	Officers.	N.C.O's & Men.	
1st Fife Light Horse	12	108	
1st Forfar Light Horse	2	38	
1st Roxburgh Mounted Rifles	5	45	
Total	19	191	

1st Brigade
Commanding - Colonel R.R. Jones, R.A., 1st North British Artillery Sub. District.

1st Forfar A.V.C.	31	838	
1st Renfrew and Dumbarton A.V.C.	18	434	
1st Argylle and Bute A.V.C.	16	385	
1st Caithness A.V.C.	6	147	
1st Aberdeen A.V.C.	18	482	
1st Inverness A.V.C.	19	490	
Total	108	2776	

2nd Brigade
Commanding - Colonel Madden C.B., 42nd Regimental District.

1st Forfar R.V.C.	22	600	
2nd Forfar R.V.C.	31	794	
3rd Forfar R.V.C.	14	336	
1st Perthshire R.V.C.	26	560	
2nd Perthshire R.V.C.	14	669	
Total	117	2959	

3rd Brigade
Commanding - Colonel D. MacPherson, C.B., 1st Battalion the Black watch (Royal Highlanders)

1st Stirlingshire R.V.C.	32	640	
1st Kincardineshire and Aberdeenshire RVC.	18	405	
1st Sutherland R.V.C	16	457	
1st Argylleshire R.V.C.	24	476	
1st Dumbarton R.V.C.	34	894	
1st Clackmannan and Kinross R.V.C.	29	573	
Total	153	3445	

4th Brigade
Commanding - Colonel Dalyell, 1st Regimental District.

6th Lanarkshire R.V.C.	23	610	
7th Lanarkshire R.V.C.	22	615	
1st Aberdeenshire R.V.C.	30	617	
1st Inverness R.V.C.	28	629	
1st Linlithgow R.V.C.	22	538	
Total	124	3009	

2nd Division
Commanding - Major-General W. G. Cameron, C.B.

1st Brigade
Commanding - Colonel Ingilby, C.B., R.A. Commanding North Britain.

1st Northumberland and Durham A.V.	22	480
2nd Northumberland A.V.	10	283
1st Berwick-on-Tweed A.V.	7	113
1st Edinburgh City A.V.	30	520
1st Berwickshire A.V.	3	37
1st Mid-Lothian A.V.	31	466
1st Haddington A.V.	2	50
2nd Berwickshire A.V.	2	48
3rd Durham A.V.	5	195
1st Newcastle-on-Tyne A.V.	20	342
Total	132	2534

2nd Brigade
Commanding - Colonel D. Baillie, 72nd Regimental District.

1st Fifeshire A.V.C.	30	716
1st Ross-shire R.V.C.	26	500
1st Elgin R.V.C.	22	550
1st Fifeshire R.V.C.	34	876
Total	112	2642

3rd Brigade

Commanding - Colonel Walker, 3rd Battalion, Royal Scots Fusiliers.

1st Newcastle and Durham R.V.C.	24	673
7th Middlesex (London Scottish) R.V.C.	20	330
1st Mid-Lothian R.V.C.	27	722
1st Cumberland R.V.C.	41	853
Total	112	2578

4th Brigade
Commanding - Colonel D. Davidson, C.B. 1st Edinburgh City R.V. Brigade

1st Edinburgh City R.V.C.	74	1726
2nd Edinburgh City R.V.C.	14	486
Cadet Corps	9	208
2nd Northumberland R.V.C.	15	355
1st Haddington R.V.C.	14	346
Total	126	3121

5th Brigade
Commanding Colonel Collingwood, C.M.G. 5th Regimental District.

1st Northumberland and Berwick-on-Tweed R.V.C.	13	370
2nd Mid-Lothian R.V.C.	25	755
1st Roxburgh and Selkirk R.V.C.	27	655
1st Berwickshire R.V.C.	22	501
1st Newcastle-on-Tyne R.V.C.	13	370
Total	100	2651

3rd Division
Major General Sir J. C. McLeod, K.C.B.

1st Brigade
Commanding - Colonel Herbert, 21st Regimental District.

1st Lanark A.V.C.	40	970
1st Ayrshire and Galloway A.V.C.	24	558
1st Lanarkshire E.V.C.	17	600
1st Aberdeenshire E.V.C.	5	115
1st Dumfries R.V.C.	31	614
The Galloway R.V.C.	28	644
Total	145	3501

2nd Brigade
Commanding - Colonel M. de la P. Beresford, 91st Regimental District.

1st Renfrewshire R.V.	30	770
2nd Renfrewshire R.V.	20	580
3rd Renfrewshire R.V.	23	624
1st Ayrshire R.V.	27	560
2nd Ayrshire R.V.	22	461
Total	122	2995

3rd Brigade
Commanding - Colonel Wiseman Clarke, 26th Regimental District.

1st Lanarkshire R.V.C.	50	1350
2nd Lanarkshire R.V.C.	25	791
5th Lanarkshire R.V.C.	22	700
9th Lanarkshire R.V.C.	16	471
Total	113	3312

4th Brigade
Commanding - Colonell A. Tisdall, 75th Regimental District.

3rd Lanarkshire R.V.C.	35	900
4th Lanarkshire R.V.C.	28	682
8th Lanarkshire R.V.C.	32	968
10th Lanarkshire R.V.C.	32	750
Total	127	3300

Summary

	Officers	Non.Com. Officers & Men	Total Divisions
Cavalry Brigade	19	191	
First Division			
1st Brigade	108	2776	
2nd Brigade	117	2959	
3rd Brigade	153	3445	
4th Brigade	124	3009	
			12,001
Second Division			
1st Brigade	132	2534	
2nd Brigade	112	2642	
3rd Brigade	112	2578	
4th Brigade	126	3121	
5th Brigade	100	2651	
			14,108
Third Division			
1st Brigade	145	3501	
2nd Brigade	122	2995	
3rd Brigade	113	3312	
4th Brigade	127	3300	
			13,615
Totals	1610	39,014	40,624

Of the above force about 36,000 were from Scotland itself, being about 76% of the whole number of efficient Volunteers in Scotland. The balance of the 40,600 was composed of Regiments from the English Border, and some 350 men of the London Scottish. Every Regiment of Volunteers in Scotland was represented except four. The English contingent was composed of the 1st Berwick-on-Tweed, the 3rd Durham, the 1st Newcastle, the 1st and 2nd Northumberland Artillery, the 1st Newcastle Engineers, !st Cumberland, the 7th Middlesex, the 1st Newcastle and the 1st and 2nd Northumberland Rifles - in all, upwards of 4,500 strong.

The 21st Hussars kept the ground and supplied the escort to Her Majesty, along with the 1st Battalion Royal Highlanders (42nd), the bands of the Royal Highlanders (42nd), Highland Light Infantry (71st), Royal Dublin Fusiliers (103rd) and the 2nd Battalion Iniskilling Fusiliers (108th), provided the music for the march past.

Uniforms:

The diversity of colour presented by the uniforms greatly enhanced the interest in the spectacle, of the 40,000 trops on parade nearly 8,000 artillerymen were dressed in blue, over 7,000 riflemen in grey, 3000 in green and more than 20,000 in scarlet. Of the 41 Scottish Battalions no less than 30 were dressed in scarlet, 5 were in green and the greys numbered six. Of the 5 English Battalion which took part in the Review, 3 were in scarlet and 2 in grey, one of the latter being the London Scottish Volunteers.

Medical Arrangements.

Three Field Hospitals were provided, each of them being thoroughly equipped for any emergency. Attached to each Brigade there was a "Stretcher Party" of Medical Officers equipped with a 'Field Companion' containing medicine for the treatment of 50 persons, and army medical haversacks filled with the requisite restoratives and appliances.

Grandstand

A grandstand was erected along the north of the Review Ground, with a space of 90 feet square in front of the middle of the stand which was reserved for Her Majesty and the Royal Party, while on each side sufficient ground was set apart for the accommodation of 25 carriages belonging to the Royal Party.

The following part extracts from the *Kirkcudbrightshire Advertiser*, 'Notes on an onlooker', describe the scene at Queen's Park prior to the Queen's arrival. "A scene presented itself on our arrival which we have no intention of trying to describe, for the splendid reality beggars description and cannot be anything like completely conceived by those who did not witness it. To say nothing of the 40,000 Volunteers upon the plain, or the crowds upon the Calton on the left, the whole range of the long hillside on the right was literally packed with people, thicker than any blackberries. A few were even perched upon the topmost peak of Arthur's Seat. Only here and there in some favoured hollow could the green-sward be detected. Every knoll was like a clump of trees and every sloping ridge quite a forest of umbrellas.

The waiting was somewhat weary, owing to the pelting rain, now become incessant of the catsand dogs description, but there were incidents that helped to pass the time. Staid old gentlemen or dainty dames, struggling up the hill, were seized suddenly with a tendency to slide and come to grief upon the slippery slopes. Many a grand new dress was crushed in most melancholy fashion. The crowd below broke through the barriers and excitement rose high, when a squadron of Hussars rode up and cleared the way.

When at last the signal was given a hub of expectation followed and then a tremendous volley of lusty cheers from some hundred thousand throats, as the Royal Carriages and mounted escort appeared. Thereupon the inspection began, necessarily a prolonged affair, and as can be imagined, not of surpassing interest to those at a distance on the hillside, but when the Queen, took up a position opposite the grandstand, the march past began, the chief event of the day."

The Troops had been in position, on the Review Ground, without great-coats (no allowance for these garments being paid until 1900), from 11am until the Queen's arrival at the Review Ground at 4pm

The 'Onlooker' continued, "Numerous were the expressions of sympathy for the luckless Volunteer, who were now drenched to the skin and in a very piteous sight. Talk of being under fire! What of being under a deluge of water, without even the protection of a cloak?"

Colonel J.M. Kennedy, 3rd Commander of the Galloway Rifles, then a Major at the Review, was later to recall the event:- "It began to rain hard about 11am, just after we had eaten our sandwiches at the Fountain-Head School, after the night in a train which managed to spend about 6 hours in going 90 miles. The rain fell all day, as well as large stones from the hillside behind us, of course, under these circumstances, added to the fact Her Majesty did not appear till about 4pm, when the water and mud were rising rapidly up our legs, there were some casualties, though we were all in the best of health.

The crowd broke through our lines, just as we were ordered to march on to the Reviewing Ground. If we had not taken great care and altered our formation to save the people from being crushed, many accidents would have happened.

We had to eat our second meal standing in deep mud, in a prefect deluge of rain, which was not at all pleasant. It was noticed that some of the Officers, in the grandest uniforms felt the inconvenience the most, but Galloway men can stand rough weather."

A correspondent of the *Times* was to write, "The square space in front of the grandstand, bare of grass, was one sea of mud, which recalled to mind the plateau of Sebastopol, in the winter of 1855. Though the Review, owing to the malice of the elements, was to a certain extent a failure, it was nevertheless an imposing sight and one not devoid of lessons. The best troops in the world could not have marched passed with precision through the sea of mud, in front of the saluting flag."

177

A correspondent in the *Daily News* was to write, "Scarce had the 1st Brigade passed, before trampling feet, and the increasing rain, had reduced the ground to a state in which all a man could do was to keep his feet. The men, themselves, chilled and stiff from the continued, standing in wet clothes, could move but indifferently. Time after time did battalions pass who made gallant efforts to keep step, to keep distances and keep dressing, but only to find that the inequality in the slippery ground battled their heartiest efforts."

The 'Onlooker' continued in his own inimitable way, "The Parade Ground, turfless to begin with, was a perfect puddle, or to quote the words of a simple country man, "It was desperately sloppy". Where it was not a quagmire, it was an extensive duck-pond, and through these, in duty to discipline, the rank and file had to splash and to splutter. Mounted men, like your Colonel and Major, had to do the "Tam O' Shanter" on his grey mare "Meg" and go "skelping on through dub and mire."

The men of Galloway and Dumfries were there and we compared them keenly with their counterparts of the different Counties. Those of Dumfries, we thought, were notably heavy and brawnily built. Those of Galloway, contrary to our fondest expectations, did not seem so big, for which the darkness of their uniform is partly to blame, but they were well-knit and had a hardy look. There was a Celtic seriousness and soldierly determination upon their countenance and it seemed to us to be particularly true that none were firmer and more manly in their steps, and as they marched along we thought of the lines of the great Minstrel, Glenkensian:-

> "And oh, loved warriors of the mounted land,
> Yonder your bonnets nod, your tartans wave.
> The rugged form may mark the mountain band,
> And harsher features, and a mien more grave,
> But ne'er in battlefield throbbed heart so brave
> As that which beats beneath the Scottish plaid;
> And when the pibroch bids the battle rave,
> And level to the charge your arms are laid,
> Where stands the desperate foe that for such onset stayed?"

When the Galloway Battalion marched past the Queen, every step taking them half-way to their knees in mud, the Duke of Cambridge, rising in the stirrups, was heard to exclaim, "Well Done! Very Well Done Indeed" No doubt the Commander-in-Chief expressed the sentiment to many other Battalions, but none more deserving than the men of Galloway."

As the troops left the Parade Ground, they were marched back to the places from which they had marched some hours earlier and were then compelled to wait around for some time after. This unquestionably was the most provoking part of the day's proceedings. The rain continued its downpour, the cutting east wind came right in upon the men, who were already wet to the skin and were now becoming chilled. The Galloway Rifle Battalion left Edinburgh, at 7.30pm that night, with a large number of the men taking off their wet tunics and travelling in their shirt sleeves. The train reached Dumfries at 1.30am on the Friday morning, Castle Douglas at 2.30am where the train divided, one part going to Kirkcudbright, and the other along the Portpatrick line. Stranraer was reached at 5am The Kirkcudbright Artillery, did not arrive home until 11.30am on the Friday morning, having been fully forty-two hours under arms.

OFFICIAL RETURN OF REVIEW STRENGTH.

An official return was issued, showing the actual number of Volunteers who attended the Review, and bringing out the numbers initially expected. The following is the summary, bringing out the gross results:-

	Officers	N.C.O&men	Total	
Numbers expected	1610	39,014	40,624	
Actual Numbers	1654	37,819	39,473	
		Deficiency		1,151

Total Present, 39,473 Officers and men.

The following is the Parade state of the local Corps:-

GALLOWAY RIFLES.

Headquarters- Newton Stewart.

Uniform and Head-Dress- Dark Oxford grey with Shako.
Field Officers- Lieutenant Colonel Gordon Maitland; Adjutant-Major H. Farrer, the Connaught Rangers.
Majors of Regiment- Major J. Murray Kennedy; Major W.F. Maxwell, Quartermaster Malcolm Mcl. Harper.
Officers of Companies-

Kirkcudbright- 'A'-	Captain Craig, Lieutenant McLellan; Lieutenant Muir; Dr. W. Johnstone.
Castle Douglas- 'B'-	Lieutenant Moffat; Dr. Lorraine.
Stranraer- 'C'-	Captain Taylor; Lieutenant Anderson; Lieutenant Garrick.
Newton Stewart- 'D'-	Captain Picken; Lieutenant Agnew.
New Galloway- 'E'-	Lieutenant Craig; Lieutenant Dalziel.
Maxwellton- 'F'-	Captain Lennox; Chaplain the Rev. Mr. Graham.
Maxwellton- 'G'-	Captain Symons.
Dalbeattie- 'H'-	Lieutenant Kerr.

	Officers	Rank and File.
Kirkcudbright 'A'	4	67
Castle Douglas 'B'	2	61
Stranraer 'C'	3	92
Newton Stewart 'D'	2	71
New Galloway 'E'	2	60
Maxwellton 'F' & 'G'	3	156
Dalbeattie 'H'	1	79
	---	----
Total	17	586

1st. Ayrshire and Galloway Artillery.

Lieutenant-Colonel Mark John Stewart, Commanding.

Officers of Companies:-
Captains William McGibbon, Stranraer; Thomas Campbell, Kirkcudbright.
Lieutenants John Milroy, Sandhead; Alexander McClymont, Portpatrick; James Dorman, Stranraer;
William Dunsmore, Stanraer; Alexander McNeillie, Sandhead; James Torrance, Stranraer;
Robert McConchie, Kirkcudbright; Surgeon Hugh Cochrane, Stranraer.

The Battalion of the 1st Ayrshire and Galloway Artillery numbered in all 626 of all ranks, including 7 Ayrshire Batteries, 3 Wigtownshire and 1 Kirkcudbright Battery, making a total of 11 Batteries in all.

	Officers.	Rank and File.
Kirkcudbright	2	48
Portpatrick	1	51
Stranraer	8	107
Sandhead and Ardwall	2	49
	---	----
Total	13	255

ISSUE OF GENERAL ORDER

The following General Order was issued by His Royal Highness the Duke of Cambridge, Field-Marshal Commanding-in Chief, through Sir Charles Ellice, Adjutant-General of the Forces:-

Edinburgh Castle, 26th August, 1881.

After an interval of twenty-one years the Queen has, for the second time, reviewed the Volunteers of Scotland, but the Corps which have now assembled for Her Majesty's inspection, including the Volunteers of the Border counties of England, have amounted in number to 40,000, or nearly double the forces brought together in 1860.

Although unhappily marred by continuous rain, the spectacle yesterday presented to Her Majesty was an admirable sequel to the great Review recently held at Windsor, and the Queen has observed with much gratification that the same soldierlike bearing, progress in discipline, and uniform good conduct which distinguished the Volunteers there assembled, were conspicuous in a like degree on the present occasion.

Yesterday's Review, and the avoidable discomfort attending the return of the troops to their homes, necessarily without change of clothing and after many hours of fatiguing delay, furnished a trial of endurance and discipline rarely called for, and Her Majesty, while deploring the cause has learned with satisfaction that the conduct of Her Volunteers had been all that could be desired.

The Field-Marshal Commanding-in-Chief has been Commanded by the Queen to express to the Volunteers of all ranks Her entire satisfaction with the appearance of the troops assembled, and His Royal Highness, in communicating Her Majesty's commands to the forces, desires on his own part to convey his thanks to Major-General Alastair MacDonald, on whom devolved the duty of organising the Review and Commanding the Force, as well as to the Army Corps, Divisional, Brigade, and Medical Staffs, through whose exertions this successful gathering of Corps, scattered throughout the Kingdom into one united force has been most successfully accomplished.

By command
C.H. Ellice, A.G.

The following Regimental Orders were issued by Colonel Gordon Maitland, Commanding the Galloway Battalion of Volunteers, relating to the Royal Review:-

Headquarters, Maxwellton,
26th August, 1881.

i). The following "gracious message" from H.M. the Queen, through Officer Commanding N.B. District, to Colonel Gordon Maitland, commanding Galloway Rifle Volunteers, is published for the information of all those of the Battalion who had the honour of marching past H.M. the Queen, viz:- 'Her Majesty desires me to express her congratulations and great satisfaction with the bearing and conduct of your men, and wishes to be informed as to their safe return'.

ii). The Lieutenant-Colonel also has much pleasure in stating that the Major-General Commanding N.B. District and the Earl of Galloway both congratulated him on the fine and fresh appearance of the men of the Battalion, notwithstanding all the fatigue they had gone through, also that Colonel Herbert, commanding Sub-District, telegraphed to express his high appreciation of the spirit and conduct of the Galloway Battalion of Rifle Volunteers.

iii). The Lieutenant-Colonel, on his own part, has both pride and pleasure in stating to Officers, N.C.O.'s and men of the Galloway Rifle Volunteers, his entire satisfaction as to the manner in which the various evolutions were gone through under the most difficult and trying circumstances. The Lieutenant-Colonel, would especially allude to what took place owing to the presence of the crowd before marching past, when the whole formation had to be changed. It was then that the soldier-like conduct of the Battalion was displayed, for the delay caused a gap of a quarter of a mile between this Battalion and the Battalion in front, to rectify which a long double in deep mud had to be made. During this movement not a man fell out, and the Regiment recovered its position close to the Dumfries Battalion in time to march past, but without a minute to prepare for the same. All, however, in the Battalion did their best, and if the marching of one or two of the Companies was not equal to some of the Regiments in front, it was through no fault of the Galloway Battalion, but owing to the adverse conditions with which they had to contend.

iv). The Lieutenant-Colonel has therefore much pleasure in thanking Majors Murray Kennedy and Maxwell, Officers, N.C.O.'s and men of this Battalion, not only for the manner in which they performed all duties required of them, but for their thoroughly soldier-like bearing, perfect discipline, and excellent conduct from the time they started for the Review up to the time they arrived at their several destinations, notwithstanding the great fatigue they had gone through in a drenching storm of wind and rain for nearly twelve hours.

v). To Captain Lennox and Quartermaster Harper, and Quartermaster-Sergeants of Companies and Assistants, especially to Quartermaster-Sergeant Myers, (who most unselfishly remained in charge of provisions at the redezvous, thereby depriving himself of the honour of marching past before Her Most Gracious Majesty), the Lieutenant-Colonel begs to tender his best wishes and thanks for the very efficient way in which they performed the duties allotted to them.

vi). To the whole of the permanent staff (especially to Major Farrer, Adjutant of the Galloway Rifles), he also begs to express his best thanks.

vii). To Messrs. W. Younger & Co., who supplied most handsomely the whole Regiment with beer, the Lieutenant-Colonel has given his best thanks on behalf of this Battalion.

viii). The Battalion is also indebted to Leiutenant Moffat for the trouble he took in obtaining the

Fountain-Head School, and the Lieutenant-Colonel begs that he will accept from him the thanks of the Battalion.

By Order,

(signed) H. Farrer, Captain,

Adjutant. Galloway Rifle Volunteers.

QUEEN VICTORIA'S DIAMOND JUBILEE CELEBRATIONS 1897
CORONATION OF KING EDWARD VII

Queen Victoria's Diamond Jubilee 1897.

In connection with the Queen's Diamond Jubilee, a detachment of the Galloway Rifle Volunteers went to London to assist in the lining of the streets. The detachment consisted of the following men, under the Command of Lieutenant Kelly, Newton Stewart. Privates W. Paterson and Carnochan, Kirkcudbright. Corporal J. McNaught, Privates Ireland, Clingan and Dunkeld, Castle Douglas. Privates Adair, Hunter and D. McCracken, Stranraer. Sergeant-Instructor Axon, Corporal Murchie, Privates W. McCreadie, Love, Priestly, Davidson and J. Murray, Newton Stewart. Corporal J. Bell and Private J. McCulloch, New Galloway. Corporals Haining and Coupland, Privates Law, Ferguson and Black, Maxwellton. Privates Derry, Tait and W. Grieve, Dalbeattie.

The party left on Monday, 28th June, 1897, for Carlisle, where they met with other detachments from the Border Brigade. They were taken under the command of Colonel Graham, the Brigade-Major.

The journey to London was uneventful but great interest was taken in the bonfires erected on the principal heights, with all the towns along the way gailly decorated with flags and bunting.

The Brigade reached St. Pancras at 9.30 pm and travelled by the underground railway to the 1st Surrey Drill Hall, the journey taking 2 hours, owing to the heavy volume of pedestrian traffic. Large numbers of the 1st Surrey Regiment turned out to greet the Border brigade and gave them a hearty reception. The men had supper and turned in the "last post" being sounded at 12.30am Sleeping accomodation had been provided at the Drill Hall, each man being provided with a waterproof sheet and blanket.

On the Tuesday morning, 29th June, the men were up early and watched the parade of the two Companies of the 1st Surrey Regiment, who had been detailed for duty along the route of the procession.

The Volunteers of the Border Brigade breakfasted at 7am and at 10.30am they marched to the Horse Guards where they were taken under the Command of the Earl of Minto, the Brigadier-General. They then marched along the Mall, taking up positions within 200 yards of Buckingham Palace, being greeted by cheers and cries of "Good Old Galloway", they being recognised as the current holders of the prestigious, Lord Wolseley's Cup, the Commander-in-Chief. Lord Wolseley himself was to recognise the "Galloways" and acknowledge their presence.

The Brigade were formed four deep along the north side of the Mall facing the English Volunteers who were formed along St. James Park. At 1pm the Royal procession reached the Mall and Lord Minto and his Staff, took up positions immediately opposite the "Galloways". The procession took a full hour to pass and a splendid view of the procession was obtained by every man of the detachment. Her Majesty looked in excellent health and a bystander was heard to remark that there was no reason why she should not see another Jubilee.

The Brigade remained in position until 3pm when they marched past Buckingham Palace, through Westminster, past the House of Commons, and along the Royal route on the south side, in order that the men might see the decorations.

Tuesday evening was spent in the West End admiring the illuminations and the men had all day on the Wednesday for sightseeing, leaving for home that evening.

Coronation of King Edward VII

The Galloway Rifle Volunteers were once more to be presented at the Coronation celebrations of King Edward VII, in London, on the 9th August, 1902, (originally fixed for the 26th June, 1902, but postponed as the future King took appendicitis) by the following members.

Officers- Lieutenant Colonel Lennox, Commanding; Lieutenant Forde, New Galloway.

'A' Company, Kirkcudbright -	Piper R. Goodwin; Private M. Crossan; Private R. Milligan.
'B' Company, Castle Douglas-	Sergeant W. Wright; Private A. Ewing; Private J.G. Rae.
'C' Company, Stranraer-	Sergeant H. Lock; Private J. Watson; Private R. McCracken.
'D' Company, Newton Stewart-	Private J. Harley; Private W. McCreadie; Private J. McIntyre.
'E' Company, New Galloway -	Private C. Taylor; Private John McKie.
'F' & 'G' Companies, Maxwellton -	Private Wm. Bell; Private R. Gunzeon; Private J. Wood; Private J. Brown; Private S. McMillan; Private T. Walker.
'H' Company, Dalbeattie -	Corporal J. Rae; Private R. Coupland; Private W. Tait.

ROYAL REVIEW 1905

The movement which led to the Royal Review of 1905, originated when the Lord Provost of Edinburgh, Sir Robert Cranston, who by his election to the Civic Chair, some two years earlier, was placed in the unprecedented position of being Hon. Colonel as well as Colonel Commandant of his own Brigade, the Queen's, the largest Regiment in the Kingdom. No sooner was he elected Lord Provost than he set in motion the scheme to hold a Review and the King was approached. His Majesty, however, intimated that his other engagements would not allow of his visiting Scotland at that time.

However, it was during this period, in consequence of deficiences found in both the Regular Army and the Territorial Forces, following the then recent Boer War conflict of 1899-1902, which resulted in the appointment of a Royal commission in April, 1903, to enquire into the terms and organisation of the Volunteer Movement, and their damning report of June, 1904, followed by Government reforms of July, 1905, which for the good or bad of the country would discourage the Volunteers and perhaps drive the country to compulsory conscription, that steps were taken to encourage recruitment to the Volunteer movement during this difficult transitional period.

In July, 1905, a somewhat unexpected announcement by Lord Knollys, intimated that the King, in consequence of the approach by Sir Robert Cranston, two years earlier, would Review the Volunteers in Holyrood, Edinburgh, on Monday, 18th September, 1905, the same ground previously selected for the Royal Reviews of 1860 and 1881.

This somewhat short notice was to lead at first to monetary difficulties, the Review arrangements having been made by the Lord Provost of Edinburgh, Sir Robert Cranston, and not through the War Office Authorities, who had made no cash provision for such a Review. Contributions from the municipalities of Edinburgh (£500), Glasgow (£750), other large towns and private contributions from those interested in the Volunteer movement, were made, but the benevolence of the War Office was sought by the local authorities in order that it might be possible to have the Review on a National scale. It was at first thought that only about 25,000 Volunteers would turn out for the Review, but so hearty was the response that the parade statement received by the Scottish millitary, Headquarters showed an estimate of 36,000 Volunteers, with later returns indicating a turnout of 38,000 Volunteers.

On Tuesday, 29th August, 1905, the following circular was issued by the War Office:- "In reference to the Scottish Volunteer Review by His Majesty the King, there appears to be considerable misapprehension in regard to the responsiblity for the arrangements. The War Office did not order, or in any way initiate the movement, but on being informed that His Majesty was pleased to review the Scottish Volunteers, made every effort to further the scheme. The precedents were, however, against making a grant of money towards the conveyance of troops to the place of review, and no money had been voted for the purpose. The Local Authorities, on being informed, then requested the Secretary of State to make this a special case, stating that the sum of £3,000 would be sufficient. The Army Council gave the case special consideration and eventually means were found by which the money could be provided, though at the expense of other services, the administration of the sum and the conduct of the review being placed at once in the hands of the General Officer Commanding. The Army Council has done all in its power to assist the Scottish Volunteers in carrying out a scheme which they themselves were unable, without assistance, to bring to a successful issue. This is the first occasion on which the War Office has provided funds to cover the travelling expenses of Volunteers to or from a Royal Review."

The War Office must have been feeling extremely benevolent, they were to eventually issue a grant of £4,000, to the Local Authorities, £1,000 above the sum initially requested.

When the announcement was made in July, 1905, that the King would review the Scottish Volunteers in the September of that year, it was found necessary that the question of uniform and equipment would have to be considered by the Commander of the Galloway Rifle Volunteers. Two Companies of the "Galloways",

'A' Company, Kirkcudbright, and 'H' Company, Dalbeattie, had already received their new khaki uniforms and its accompanying equipment. In order to prevent the peculiar appearance, which the Regiment would present by having two Companies in khaki and the remainder in dark grey, it was decided to complete the change at once. The contractors, fortunately, were able to forward the new uniforms in good time, and on Sunday, 17th September, the Regiment turned out for the first time in their new dress. One effect of the change of dress, together with the forthcoming Royal Review, by His Majesty, as was the hopes of the Authorities, was an immediate increase of over 130 members in the strength of the Galloway Regiment.

In consequence of the Review, ceremonial drill, which had not been practised, nor indeed, had been necessary for a long time was ordered by Colonel J. Kennedy, the men turning out to the parades in large numbers, not even the reflections of the effects of the disastrous "Review of 1881" could dampen the enthusiasm of the "Galloways".

The muster of the "Galloways", prior to their departure for the Royal Review by King Edward VII, at Edinburgh, on Monday, 18th September, 1905, was a total of 616 on parade. Maxwellton making the largest contribution, the return for that detachment numbering 200 rank and file, 99 members coming from 'F' Company and 101 members, coming from 'G' Company. The following is the Field State of the Regiment:-

	Officers	Sgts.	Band &Buglers.	Rank &File.	Total.	Total Enrolled.
'A' Kirkcudbright	3	8	5	76	92	112
'B' Castle Douglas	3	7	7	61	78	106
'C' Stranraer	-	6	6	50	62	83
'D' Newton Stewart	-	5	5	92	102	115
'E' New Galloway	1	5	2	24	31	37
'F '& 'G' Maxwellton	5	12	43	157	217	236
'H' Dalbeattie	2	3	9	49	63	90
	---	---	----	-----	----	----
	14	46	77	509	616	779

This Field State was to represent almost 83% of the strength of the Regiment.

The Review was totally national in its character and there were few towns throughout the country that did not add in greater or less proportions to swell the mighty host which descended upon the Capital. Indeed, it may well be said that for the day, all roads led to Edinburgh. It so happened that the Review date, 18th September, coincided with the autumn holiday, and the Railway Companies offered special facilities. There was a continuous influx into Edinburgh, from the Saturday, and it was estimated that the population of the Capital, on the Monday morning, was several hundred thousand above the normal.

The King's Park, Holyrood, the former Queen's Park, the title changed to accommodate the new Monarch, was once again the site chosen for the Review. The northern portion of the Park an admirable Review Ground, with Arthur's Seat, its cliffs and rocky projections and grassy slopes forming a magnificent amphitheatre from which to view the spectacle. From early morning the crowds passed through the park gateways to make sure of good vantage on the grassy slopes of Arthur's Seat. On the Northern margin of the park, to the east of Holyrood, a grandstand had been erected for the accommodation of priviliged visitors. It was a spacious and elaborately decorated structure, arranged gallery fashion in 5 bays, each seating about 1,000 people, the whole seating in excess of 5,000. The scheme of decoration was carried out in the national colours. The entire front was covered with crimson cloth, relieved with yellow, a band of evergreens and yellow tassels. From the eaves of the roof hung a valance in royal blue with a yellow fringe and to the summit of the dividing pillars were affixed heraldic shields and a gay array of flags floating overhead. The gables were draped in Stuart Tartan enriched with circular shields bearing the initials "E.R.", while in the centre was the Royal Scottish Coat of Arms.

Preparations were begun at 7am on the Monday morning to receive the King at Waverly Station. Lines of streamers stretched across the platform, with the bridge and the Station entrance decorated with evergreens, shields and banners. The passenger traffic was stopped at 7.35am with the crowds taking up their places behind the barricades on the west side of the platform. The guard of honour, which was from the Royal Artillery, under the Command of Captain Yates, was drawn up in front of the offices and opposite to where His Majesty would alight, the band of the Scottish Rifles. The travelling escort which was drawn from the Scots Greys was positioned at the foot of the Station entrance, under the Command of Lieutenant Palmer. In waiting was a carriage and pair, with the Royal outriders in scarlet uniforms.

Punctually to the hour of 8am the Royal Train steamed into the Station and on alighting from the train His Majesty was given the Royal salute and the National Anthem was played. The King was dressed in the uniform of a Field-Marshal, with a grey military overcoat. The King was greeted by Sir Robert Cranston, the Lord Provost, and introduced to Lieutenant-General Sir Charles Tucker. His Majesty then entered the carriage, accompanied by Colonel Arthur Davidson, and the Honourable John H. Ward, Equerries-in-waiting, amid the firing of guns from the Castle. In driving to Holyrood Palace, the King was cheered by huge gatherings which lined the streets en-route.

The time of the Review was fixed for 11am and about 9.30am the Battalions began the march into the King's Park, and took up their allotted positions. With the recollections of the last Great Review in the public mind it was only natural that the weather should be a source of anxiety, and to the thousands who witnessed the spectacle it was the first consideration when they awoke. The morning broke dull and cold, with a westerly wind and first appearances were not at all reassuring. At 6am the King's Park was shrouded in mist but as the morning wore on the sky cleared and by the time of the King's arrival, the weather was in all respects, most favourable.

The Parade State of the Troops to be Reviewed, under the Command of Lt.-Gen. Sir Charles Tucker K.C.B., Commanding-in-Chief Scotland, was as follows:-

	Officers	N.C.O's &Men	Guns
NAVAL TROOPS -			
Captain R.S.D. Cumming, R.N.			
R.N. Volunteer Reserve, Clyde & Tay-Commander			
The Marquess of Graham.	30	670	(3)
MOUNTED TROOPS -			
Colonel Sir W.J.G. Baird, Bart.			
Lothian and Berwick I.Y. Major Wauchope, D.S.O.	7	80	
Q.R.V.B. Mounted Infantry - Major G.G. Watson	4	63	
Total Mounted Troops	11	143	
ROYAL GARRISON ARTILLERY DIVISION -			
Brigadier-General Lord Playfair			
Heavy Battery Brigade- Colonel A.B. Grant V.D. 1st Lanark R.G.A.V.			
1st Mid-Lothian R.G.A.V.- Col. J.A. Dalmahoy, V.D.	12	98	(12)
1st Forfar R.G.A.V.- Col. J.A. Dalmahoy, V.D.	4	36	(4)
1st Lanark R.G.A.V. Lt. Col. J. Taylor, V.D.	19	151	(20)
1st R.G.A. Brigade - Col. T.W. Powles, R.G.A.			
1st Edinburgh City R.G.A.V. - Lt. Col. E. Campbell	16	460	(6)
1st Mid-Lothian R.G.A.V. - Mjr. C.L. Blaikie V.D.	8	227	
1st Berwick R.G.A.V. ..	2	34	
1st Fife R.G.A.V. ..	10	242	
1st Fife R.G.A.V.- Col. J.W. Johnston, V.D	16	458	
2nd R.G.A. Brigade - Col. A.B. Purvis R.G.A.			
1st Forfar R.G.A.V.- Col. T.G. Luis, V.D.	25	429	
1st Caithness R.G.A.V.- ..	17	210	
1st Aberdeen R.G.A.V. - Col. G. Milne, V.D. .	27	423	
1st Banff R.G.A.V. ..	17	257	
The Highland R.G.A.V. - Col. J.E. Baillie.	34	427	
1st Orkney R.G.A.V. ..	15	165	
3rd R.G.A. Brigade - Col. A. Powell, D.S.O. R.G.A.			
1st Renfrew and Dumbarton R.G.A. - Lt.Col. C.C. Scott, V.D.	15	340	
1st Argyll and Bute R.G.A.V. - ..	32	549	
1st Lanark R.G.A.V. - Lt. Col. A. M'I Shaw, V.D.	22	750	
1st Ayr and Galloway R.G.A.V. - Lt. Col. T. R. Stuart	23	581	
Total R.G.A. Division -	314	5837	(42)
ROYAL ENGINEER BRIGADE -			
Col. R.L. Hippisley, C.B. R.E.			
1st Lanark R.E.V. - Col. T.S. Park, V.D.	22	421	

1st Aberdeen R.E.V. - Col. W.S. Gill, V.D.	12	288
2nd Lanark R.E.V. - Lt. Col. A. Pearson	35	805
Clyde Division Submarine Miners - Col. D.F.D.Neill	10	175
Tay Division Submarine Miners - Lt. Col. F.S.Stephen	5	124
Forth Division Submarine Miners - Lt.Col. H.M.Cadell,V.D.	9	76
Total R.E. Brigade -	93	1889

1st INFANTRY DIVISION -
> Brigadier-General A. Broadwood.

1st Lothian Brigade - Col. Sir R. Cranston Kt., V.D.

1st Bn. Q.R.V.B. Royal Scots - Col. A.T.Hunter, V.D.	32	603
2nd Bn. Q.R.V.B. Royal Scots - Lt. Col. R.Clark, V.D.	32	633
3rd Bn. Q.R.V.B. Royal Scots - Col. J. Gibb, V.D.	31	663
4th V.B. Royal Scots - Lt. Col. G. McCrae, V.D.	27	822
9th V.B. (Highlanders) Royal Scots - Lt. Col. .J. Clark	23	517
Bearer Company - Captain A. Macdonald	3	53

2nd Lothian Brigade- Brigadier-General W. Cordon.

5th V.B. Royal Scots - Col. Sir J.M. Clark Bart., V.D.	20	1000
6th V.B. Royal Scots - Lt. Col. T. Rough, V.D.	18	515
7th .. .. - Col. R.M. Main, V.D.	16	374
8th .. .. - Lt. Col. C. Chalmers,V.D.	20	574
8th (Scottish) V.B. The King's (Liverpool Regt.) - Lt. Col. A.L. Macfie	20	480

Scottish Border Brigade - Col. J.H. Campbell.

1st V.B. Royal Scots Fusiliers - Lt. Col. J. Gow	20	610
2nd .. .. .. - Lt. Col. J.E. Shaw	22	501
1st Rox. and Selk. (Border) V.R.C. - Col.Sir R.J. Waldie-Griffith, Bart., V.D.	35	711
2nd V.B. K.O.S.B - Col. C. Hope	21	363
3rd .. .. - Col. R.F. Dudgeon, V.D.	21	407
Galloway V.R.C. - Col. J.M. Kennedy, V.D.	14	635
Bearer Company - Surgeon Captain G. R.Livingston	1	35
Total 1st Infantry Division -	376	9496

2nd INFANTRYDIVISION -
> Col. J.W. Hughes-Hallett. C .B., D.S.O.

Scottish Rifle Brigade - Brigadier-General E.C. Browne

1st Lanark V.R.C. - Col. J. Macfarlane, V.D.	49	833
2nd V.B. Scottish Rifles - Col. T.B. Ralston,V.D.	32	800
3rd Lanark V.R.C. - Col. J.B. Wilson, V.D.	40	610
4th V.B. Scottish Rifles - Col. F.J. Smith,V.D.	30	620

Highland Light Infantry Brigade - Col. J. Stevenson, C.B., A.D.C.

1st V.B. H.L.I. - Col. R.C. Mackenzie,V.D.	28	750
2nd .. .. - Col. J.D. Young, V.D.	25	500
3rd .. .. - Col. D.R. Graham, V.D.	30	700
9th Lanark V.R.C. - Major J. Lancaster, V.D.	14	344
5th (Glasgow Highland) V.B. H.L.I. - Lt.Col.P.W. Hendry, V.D.	30	770
Bearer Company - Surgeon-Major A.D. Moffat.	2	48

Argyll and Sutherland Brigade - Col. J.M.Hunt.

1st V.B. A.&S. Highlanders - Col. W.U. Park, V.D.	28	622
2nd V.B. .. .. - Col. J. Paton, V.D.	27	753
3rd V.B. .. .. - Lt. Col. J.M Campbell.	30	570
4th V.B. .. .. - Col. R. MortonV.D.	22	624
5th V.B. .. .. - Lt. Col.E.P. Campbell	27	583
1st Dumbarton V.R.C. - Lt. Col. H. Brock	50	1271
7th V.B. A. & S. Highlanders - Lt. Col.R. Haig.	23	477
Bearer Company - Captain J.A. Boyd.	3	47
Total 2nd Infantry Division -	490	10922

3rd INFANTRY DIVISION -
   Brigadier-General Forbes Macbean, C.B.

Black Watch Brigade - Col. E.G. Grogan,C.B.

1st V.B. Black Watch - Lt. Col. H. Hill, V.D.	19	581	
2nd .. .. .. - Col. J. Davidson V.D.	23	439	
3rd .. .. .. - Lt. Col. C. BatchelorV.D.	20	350	
4th .. .. .. - Col. Sir R.D.Moncrieffe, Bart., V.D.	24	434	
5th .. .. .. - Col. Marquis of Breadalbane, K.G. A.D.C.	25	478	
6th .. .. .. - Col. Sir R.W.Anstruther, Bart.	47	769	
Bearer Company - Surgeon-Major W. Kinnear	2	48	

Gordon Brigade - Brigadier-General P.D. Trotter,

1st V.B. Gordon Highlanders - Lt. Col. L.Mackinnon, V.D.	32	550	
3rd .. .. .. - Col. R.Robertson. V.D.	20	295	
4th .. .. .. - Lt. Col. W.A.Mellis, V.D.	27	328	
5th .. .. .. - Lt. Col. A.H. Farquharson	21	308	
6th .. .. .. - Col. J.G.Fleming, V.D.	16	271	
7th .. .. .. - Major J.C.C.Brown.	5	75	
London Scottish (7th Middlesex) V.R.C. Col. J.W. Greig, V.D.	20	240	

Seaforth and Cameron Brigade - Col. N. McLeod

1st V.B. Seaforth Highlanders - Col. A.R.B.Warrand	22	329	
1st Sutherland V.R.C. - Col. J. Morrison,V.D.	27	497	
3rd V.B. Seaforth Highlanders - Col. R.Urquhart, V.D.	24	446	
1st V.B. Cameron Highlanders - Col. D. Shaw,V.D.	19	453	
Bearer Company - Captain J. Macdonald	3	50	

Total 3rd Infantry Division -	396	6941	

ROYAL ARMY MEDICAL CORPS VOLUNTEERS -
   Lt. Col. Croly, R.A.M.C.

Aberdeen Companies R.A.M.C.V. - Captain F. Kelly	9	157	
Glasgow Companies R.A.M.C.V. - Lt. Col. G.T.Beatson V.D.	21	429	
6 War Ambulance Dogs - Major E.J. Richardson	-		
Detachment Motor Volunteer Corps (l0 Cars)	-		
Captain G. Macmillan.	-	10	

Keeping Ground

Detachment of 17th Lancers -	l	40	
Army Service Corps -	l	40	
Lothians and Berwick I.Y. -	2	65	

Grand Total of Force -	1744	36, 639	45

Grand Total of all Ranks - 38,383.   Total of Horses - 691.
Total of Guns - 45   Total of Motor Cars - 10

The Review Ground was kept by the 2nd Highland Light Infantry, with the music for the march past being supplied by the Band and Pipers of the 2nd Scottish Rifles, the 1st Black Watch, and the 2nd Highland Light Infantry. The Guard of Honour was supplied by the Royal Bodyguard of Scottish Archers, Commanded by the Captain-General the Duke of Buccleuch, K.T. Every Corps in the Country was represented with the exception of the 2nd Gordon Highlandes, this Corps being drawn from the north-east of Aberdeenshire.

The Army and Volunteer veterans did not attend in a body but were allotted their places by Major Boddie, of the Recruiting Department, Edinburgh. The military men numbered 120, with there being 1,830 Volunteers who had attended one or both of the last two Royal Reviews. The Officers were provided with seats in front of the Royal enclosure and the rank and file were disposed of on similar stands to the east and west. The Loch Katrine Volunteers, who were present in 1859, as a guard of honour to Queen Victoria, when Her Majesty, opened the Glasgow Waterworks, appeared with a sprig of white heather in their Glengarry bonnets and received a tumultous ovation as they took their places. The Old Soldiers of the Army presented a strong and healthy appearance showing that their vigorous constitutions had not been altogether shattered by the privations of the Crimea and Indian Mutiny. A large number of the Old Veterans appeared in uniform, many of the dresses worn, having long since passed from general usage. Among the Old Veterans, were a contingent of the north of England Volunteers, who attended the infamous 'Wet Review' of 1881, and who once again travelled north to show their support for the Citizen Soldiers, from across the Border.

Among the veterans present at the Review was Sergeant Robert Teesdale, from Dalbeattie, the compulsory officer of Urr School Board. Sergeant Teesdale, was a native of Lanarkshire, being born in Larkhall but at the age of 18 years, he enlisted in Glasgow as a gunner in the Royal Artillery in the year 1859. In January, 1860 he embarked for the Bermudas, the American Civil War then being in progress but before landing the problem was settled and Sergeant Teesdale served in the Bermudas, Nova Scotia, New Brunswick, Prince Edward Island and Gibraltar. During this period he received rapid promotion, being made Sergeant-Major with four stripes. He received his discharge with pension in 1880. In the same year he joined the Ayr and Galloway Artillery Volunteers, being made a Sergeant-Instructor at Kilmarnock. He attended the Royal Review of 1881. He remained 8 years at Kilmarnock before being transferred to Stranraer as Sergeant-Instructor. He retired at Stranraer where he was appointed School Board Officer, serving for 4 years, until 1892, when he received a similar position with the Urr School Board and continued to act as Drill Instructor to the pupils.

An interesting feature of the Review was a march past of the Motor Volunteer Corps, which for the first time in history appeared in a Review. The Headquarters of this Corps was in London and had a strength of 10 motorists under the Command of Captain George Macmillan, of Edinburgh. The Hon. Col. of the Corps, Sir John Macdonald, obtained permission from the authorities to ride at the head of the Corps, though not in Command, as they passed the saluting base.

The Motor Volunteer Corps was formed in 1903, by Colonel Mayhew, and Sir John Macdonald, a keen motorist and Volunteer, accepted from Col. Mayhew the rank of Hon. Col. in the Corps. The Motor Volunteer Corps, from their formation had taken part in many manoeuvres at Aldershot and their usefulness by the Military men of the day, was found to be of great value. The Scottish Section had been assisting the Inspector-General in his work in Scotland, and in Staff rides for the examination, for promotion of Regular Officers. Up to the date of the Review, the strength of the Corps had been confined to Edinburgh but it was hoped that before long the Corps would be recruiting in the west. However, questions were still unanswered as to their utility in the event of actual warfare.

The hour fixed for the arrival of the King at the Park was 10.45am and at 10.40am the Officers in Command took up their positions in front of the saluting base. The scene in the park was supremely striking and impressive. The sounds of command were stilled and upon the assembled multitudes a hush had fallen. The sun for a brief interval had broken through the filmy clouds bringing out in its full proportions the magnificence of the spectacle.

Precisely at the appointed hour on a signal from the Commanding Officer, the first round of the Royal Salute from the batteries stationed at Whinnyhill, on the lower spur of Arthur's Seat, announced that His Majesty had left the Palace and as he was seen emerging from the eastern gate, a ringing cheer, swelling in volume as it was taken up by the vast concourse was heard echoing and re-echoing amid the thunder of the guns. His Majesty, who once again, wore the uniform of a Field-Marshal, looked exceedingly well on a bay charger and was accompanied by Field-Marshal the Duke of Connaught and attended by the Marquis of Linlithgow, Secretary of Scotland, in the uniform of the Royal Archers; the Earl of Wemyss, in the uniform of the London Scottish; Lord Blythswood, in the uniform of the Highland Light Infantry. Lord Breadalbane in the uniform of the Black Watch; Major Sir John Maxwell, C.B.; Major Murray; Captain A. Davidson and Hon. John Ward. Riding slowly along, His Majesty graciously acknowledged the cheers and took up his position at the saluting base and at the command of General Tucker, the Royal Salute was given.

Preceded by General Tucker and the Officers of the Headquarters Staff of the Scottish District, His Majesty, proceeded to inspect the troops, assisted by Field-Marshal H.R.H. the Duke of Connaught, Inspector-General of the Forces. As His Majesty moved through each Brigade, one band from that Brigade played, and as the procession passed on this was continued till the end of the Parade was reached. On the completion of the Inspection, the King passed to the saluting base in front of the grandstand and took up a position under the Royal Standard .

The march past commenced at 11.40am The three bands of the 1st Battalion Black Watch, 2nd Battalion Highland Light Infantry and the 2nd Battalion Scottish Rifles, which were to provide the music during the ceremony, took up a position in front of the grandstand. The march past was led by the Royal Naval Volunteers, the Lothian and Berwickshire Yeomanry and the Mounted Infantry. Then followed the Artillery Brigades and the three Infantry Divisions. The sight was most impressive and as each Battalion succeeded another, they received a splendid ovation from the spectators. As the Border Brigade, which included the Galloway Rifles, passed, His Majesty was heard to remark of Colonel J.M. Kennedy, "Ah, there's an old hero now," and certainly the gallant Colonel in his service dress looked the beau ideal of a veteran soldier.

Note. In the *London Gazette* of 3rd October, 1905, an appointment appeared in which the King had been graciously pleased to announce that, John Murray Kennedy, Lieutenant-Colonel of the Galloway Rifle Volunteers, had been made a member of the Royal Victorian Order, 4th Class, in recognition of his involvement in the Review, of 18th September, 1905. This was one of only four similar awards in recognition of services at the Review.

The following report appeared in the *Times* dated 22nd September, 1905. "There was a roar of applause from the tribunes when the head of the 1st Infantry Division reached the saluting base, and it was seen that the popular Lord Provost of Edinburgh was commanding the 1st Lothian Brigade. The three Rifle Battalions went by in good state but Colonel James Clark's Battalion of Royal Scots Highlanders carried the honours in the Brigade. Their marching inspired one, and it was only rivalled in the Division by that of the 6th Royal Scots, the Liverpool Scottish and the Galloway Volunteer Rifle Corps. The latter, who are in the Scottish Border Brigade, furnished, in spite of their dull khaki kit, the best set-up unit that marched past in the day, their average physique would have done credit to the Foot Guards."

After the Review, the King returned to Holyrood and left Edinburgh at 2pm for Glenquoich, Inverness. A luncheon by the Edinburgh Corporation was given to the leading personages at the Review, along with a luncheon to the Indian and Crimean veterans and a dinner to distinguished visitors. Speaking at the Corporation luncheon, the Duke of Connaught, expressed the King's pleasure with the splendid arrangements made that day, stating that His Majesty told him to say that he would travel double the distance to see the very fine sight he had seen that day and he was thoroughly proud of the Scottish Volunteers who had shown what true patriotism there was in Scotland.

At the Lord Provost's dinner, His Lordship, the Duke of Connaught, read a telegram from Colonel Davidson, the King's Equerry, saying that His Majesty wished to convey to the citizens his appreciation of the loyalty displayed during his visit, which was a memorable one. He hoped that the extra-ordinarily fine appearance of the Volunteers that day would act as an incentive to others to join the force, whose patriotism was so greatly to be commended.

Local Companies.

Stranraer Company left home at 9.20pm on the Sunday night of 17th September, 1905, taking up the Newton Stewart and New Galloway Companies, joining with the Castle Douglas and Kirkcudbright Companies, at Castle Douglas, at 11.15pm, the whole coming together at Dumfries, at 11.50pm. The route travelled was via Gretna and Hawick, the train arriving at Leith Walk Goods Station at 4.8am. The men were promptly formed up and marched to the Maltings of William Younger and Sons Ltd., where most of the Brigade were quartered, together with the Regiment of the London Scottish Volunteers. Washing facilities were provided and breakfast, consisting of two substantial sandwiches, with coffee or tea, were available, purveyed by Messrs. Littlejohn and Son, Princes Street. Thereafter, the men occupied their time preparing for the big event of the day.

About 9.30am , the 'Galloways' took up their position in King's Park, as part of the Border Brigade, under the Command of Colonel J.H. Campbell. The Galloways had Dumfriesshire on their right and the Border Rifles on their left. By curious coincidence, the Galloways, were placed in almost the same position as their Regiment had occupied in the Royal Review of 1881. Though central, the Galloway's position was fraught with danger, with the enormous traffic of people ascending and descending the slopes of Salisbury Crag, above them, many large stones were dislodged and rolled down the hill with terrific force, only spending themselves when well within the Galloway's lines. Some of the spectators were badly injured whilst others had narrow escapes. All this however, lent excitement to the situation which helped to beguile the otherwise long and tedious wait.

After the march past, when the Regiments had passed the saluting post, the Volunteers were ordered to 'double' so as to clear the ground for those succeeding. The 'double' was continued until each Regiment was clear of the park gate, many of the older members of the Galloway Rifles, finding the reasons 'trying' rather than 'tiring.' The Regiments were thereafter, marched to their quarters, the Galloways returning to the Maltings of William Younger and Sons Ltd., where refreshments were once again supplied. The men were then allowed to go into Edinburgh for a couple of hours.

Shortly before 4pm the order came to 'fall-in' and before leaving Col. Kennedy called on the Battalion to give three cheers for Messrs Younger and Sons, for their kindness in allowing the use of their premises. The Galloways then marched off to the station. Some unavoidable confusion occurred on entraining and it was found impossible to then make the issue of a pie per man for the homeward journey as had been contemplated. Fortunately, the long distance Companies fared better, as food was distributed at Castle Douglas. Some delays occurred on the journey and Dumfries was not reached until 9.40pm. At Castle Douglas, the Kirkcudbright Company were detached and proceeded with their comrades of the Kirkcudbright Artillery Volunteers, who had arrived at Castle Douglas a quarter of an hour earlier. The Wigtownshire Companies then journeyed on their homeward way, the freely expressed opinion of the men being that the trip and Review had been most enjoyable and that they would not have missed it for the world.

Much hard work was occasioned by the Headquarters Staff in making all the arrangements, Captain Fraser, Adjutant, being ably assisted by Sergeant-Major Grierson, while Major Hewat, along with Master-Sergeant Myers had been responsible for the care of the 'inner-man'. The heartiest thanks of the Regiment were due to Messrs.W. Younger and Sons, not only for the kind use of their premises but once again for their supplying free beer to the entire Regiment, together with Messrs Duncan, Flockhart and Co., Chemists, for generously providing aerated waters, free of charges to the whole Regiment.

The following is a complete list of members of the Galloway Rifle Volunteers and Kirkcudbright Company of Artillery Volunteers, who attended the Royal Review at Edinburgh, on Monday, 18th September, 1905:-

STAFF .
Colonel J. Murray Kennedy of Knocknalling (Commanding)
Lieutenant-Colonel J. Lennox, Dumfries.
Captain A.G. Fraser (Adjutant).

'A' Company Kirkcudbright.
Captain W.L. Comrie.
Lieutenant E.S. Glover.
Second-Lieutenant H.B. Wilkinson.
Sergeants .

A. Cairns	H. Livingston	A. Reid.
J. Macgregor	W. McGaw	J.R. Kirkpatrick
J. Johnstone	E. Paterson	

Corporals.

A. Gourlay	J. Allan	J. McEwan

Privates.

R. Allan	W. Hay	John Milroy
J. Birnie	H. Henry	J.L. Murray
A. Blackhurst	F. Heron	J. Paterson
T. Blacklock	N.M Hughan	R. Patterson(1).
R. Branney	J. Hunter	R. Patterson(2)
T. Broadfoot	S. McBurnie	W. Patterson(1)
W. Caig	R. McClune	W. Patterson(2)
W. Campbell	T. McGaw	D.G. Rae
R. Clark	J. McGowan	J. Rae
J. Clarkson	D. McKay	J.G. Ramsay
T. Carnochan	A. McKinna	W. Rodgers
R. Clunie	J. McKenna	S. Ross
S. Dalrymple	G. McKie	D. Sharp
W. Dalrymple	A. McMillan	J. Sharp
W. Davenport	D. McMurray	J. Smith
E. Farmer	W. McMurray	A. Stevens
D. Fitzpatrick	R. McMonies	W. Stewart
F. Gallagher	S. McNeillie	T. Straiton
J. Gallagher	A. McQuarrie	J. Swan
A. Gilchrist	J. McSkimming	W. Tait
Adam Grant	C. Manson	G. Thompson
Allan Grant	A. Maxwell	J. Veitch
J. Halliday	A. Middleton	A. Walker
J. Hamilton	J. Middleton	R. Walker
W. Hannah	R. Milligan	S. Wilson
J. Hay	James Milroy	R. Young

'B' Company Castle Douglas

Major J.T. Hewat (acting Quartermaster of the Battalion.)

Sergeants.

T. McIlroy	P. Connolly	W. Haugh
T. Myers	S. Gordon	R. Todd
W. Wright		

Corporals.

A. Dougan	J. McGaw	J. McKeand
R. Howard	W. Sloan	J.C. Murray
W. McCaw	J.L. Baird	G. Veitch

Privates.

R. Johnston	J.M. Johnstone	A. Rae
R. McIlroy	D. Kay	S. Rae
J. Wright	T. Kirk	J. Robb
T. Anderson	A. Livingston	S.E. Robertson
W. Badenooh	N. Macadam	C.A. Roxburgh
J. Baxter	J. McAdam	J. Roxburgh
A. Boyle	R. McAdam	P. Roxburgh
S.H. Brodie	A. McDonald	J. Seaton
J. Clark	D. McFegan	G. Scott
John Ferguson	R. McGaw	W. Scott
W. Ferguson	G. McKay	R. Smith
W.H. Glover	H. McKie	J. Tait
J.W. Halliday	J. McKie	G. Thomson
John Halliday	R. McKie	R. Trollan
R. Hastie	J. McLelland	R. Wardhaugh
W. Haugh	John McNaught	A. White
J. Haugh	W.J. Morgan	W. Wood
G. Hogg	J. Myers	W. Wright
R. Hogg	W. O'Haire	J. Burns
J. Johnstone	R. Purdie	J. Hyslop

'C' Company Stranraer.

Sergeants.

P. Fennessey	T.D. Stewart	J. Watson
G. McHaffie	J. Kennedy	J. Brown
J. Devoy		

Corporals.

R. McEwen	J. Pirrie	E. Galloway
J. McGhee	D. Irons	R. McKie
J. Devoy	D. Morland	

Privates.

R. Biggam	Joseph Devoy	- McMurtrie
W. Pirrie	W. Devoy	W. McNeill
W. Johnstone	R. Emmerson	D. Miller
R. Watson	A. Findlay	James Miller
D. McVicar	- Gillon	John Miller
R. McCandlish	J. Gillespie	D. Murray
H. Watson	H. Hamilton	W. Nelson
R. Adair	J. Kelly	J. Parker
J. Arnott	D. Mackenzie	T. Pirrie
J. Berry	- McCall	W. Rennie
E. Burns	E. McCandlish	R. Rennie
J. Byers	- McClymont	A. McSkimming
M. Cook	J. McCulloch	J. Tweedie
J. Craig	H. McCutcheon	W. Welch
H. Crawford	- McEwen	L. Wheatley
W. Devlin	J. McKie	

'D' Company, Newton Stewart.

Sergeants.

J. Axon	J. Millan	J. Russell
A. Birrell	J. Malcolm	W.S. Gray

Corporals.

| W. Edwards | W. McMurray | J. Hall |
| H. McDavid | W. Watson | |

Privates.

H. Agnew	W. Gass	A. McDowell
J. Agnew	T. Goldie	R. McDowell
G. Armstrong	T. Gordon	J. McGhie
T. McBannister	W. Gordon	R. McGhie
T. Beattie	W. Haining	W. McGiviran
P. Birrell	W. Hall	T.A. Gibney
W. Birrell	J.S. Hannah	D. McGinis
J. Blain	J. Harding	J. McGinis
W. Boyd	J. Harley	J. McGowan
D.A. Boyd	J. Heron	D.S. McMurray
S. Brown	C. Hodgson	J.A. McNair
L. Brown	J. Innes	J. McNearnie
J. Bryden	A. Jardine	J.F. McWilliams
G. Bryden	W.J. Kelly	A. Marshall
J. Butler	J. Kerr	J.M. Matthews
J. T. Butler	A. Knowles	G. Moffat
A. Callender	J. Lavery	R.F.Muir
W. Carmont	W. Longridge	W. T.R. Nimmo
T.B. Cavan	D.J. Longridge	T. O'Hara
J.K. Christie	R. Lupton	J. Parker
T. Cochrane	J. McCleary	S. Rankine
O. Cosker	J. McClure	J. Ravey
W.H. Courtney	A. McClure	W. Ross
W. Cowell	J. McConchie	W. Scott
M. Cullen	R. McConchie	T. Smylie
J. Cuthbertson	W. McConchie	T. McD. Smylie
R. Drynan	D. McCulloch	H. Tait
A. Finningham	W. McCreadie	S. Varney
S. Fiskin	H. McDavid	W.C. Axon
J. Gardiner	W. McDavid	H. Carmont
J. Garrick		

'E' Company New Galloway.
Captain E.S. Forde.
Sergeants.

| J.W. Nelson | H. Tole | J. Bell |
| D. McNaught | A. Murdoch | |

Corporals.

| T. Corrie | J. McKie | W. Adamson |

Privates.

J. Dalziel	T.C. Martin	J. Peacock
S. Ferguson	J. McCulloch	W. Robertson
J. Geddes	G. McLauchlan	F. Stewart
D. Gibson	W. McMillan	W.T. Stewart
G. Hamilton	J. McKay	J. Wood
J. Johnstone	F.G. McQueen	J. Turner
W. Kirk	W.A. McTurk	W. McCulloch
A. Lee	J. Murray	

'F' Company Maxwellton.
Lieutenant G.F. Scott Elliot; Lieutenant W.F. Crombie
Sergeants.

R. Grierson	G. Bendall	W. Kivlichan
J. Johnstone	J. Coupland	J. McKinnell
J. Beattie	A. Edgar	J. Raphael
J. Johnstone		

Corporals.

W. Ritchie	T. Graham	F. Niven
G. Carson	J. Jardine	W. Law
S. Cowan	J .D. Moffat	

Privates.

T. Aitken	J. Cowan	J. Melbourne
J. Armstrong	J.W. Graham	J. Millar (1)
A. Anderson	W. Graham	J. Millar (2)
J. Bell	R. Grierson	J. Morrine
R. Bell	J. Hamilton	J. Newall
J. Brady	J. Harrison	T. Nicholson
G.R. Blount	J. Hastings	T. Potter
G. Carmichael	J. Inman	W. Pringle
D. Caskie	W. Inman	J. Paterson
W. Carnochan	R. Johnstone	J. Raphael
N. Cowan	H. Kirkpatrick	W. Richardson
W. Cowan	J. Kirkpatrick	T. Saddler
J. Craig	T. Lavens	G. Telford
W.D. Crichton	C. Loudon	D. Thom
J. Crossan	T. McAllister	J. Thom
D. Dickson	R. McCourty	W. Todd
W. Dickson	J.C. McGowan	W. Topping
W. Docherty	T. McGowan	J. Townsend
W. Easton	A. McHolm	T. Walker
W. Faithful	H. McKean	R. Wallace(1)
J. Fortune	J. McKean	R. Wallace(2)
W.G. Fraser	A. McMillan	J. Watret
R. Geddes	A. McWilliam	W.K. Watson
J .W. Geddes	J. Marshall	H. Wells
T. Geddes	D. Maxwell	J. Wells
T. Gibson	M. Maxwell	M. Wilson
W. Gibson	A.W. Meechan	A. Byers

'G' Company Maxwellton.
Captain R.A. Grierson; Lieutenant E. Grierson
Sergeants.

D. Walker	J. McKinnel	J. Moffat
W. Hope		

Corporals.

D. Ferguson	F. McMurdo	A. Duff
R. Fettes	Wm. Moffat	J. Harper
J. Henderson	R. Crosbie	J.D. Moir

Privates.

J. Affleck	J. Henderson	J. Morley
W. Aitken	R. Holden	T. Murray
W. Armstrong	J. Hughes	J. Murchie
R. Bell	J.W. Hughes	W. Nicholson
J. Brown	A. Hume	A. Raphael
H. Byers	C. Inman	J. Richardson
A. Caven	Jas. Johnstone	J. Riley
T. Coupland	J. Johnstone	J. Rorrison
J. Craig(1)	J. Kennedy	R. Rorrison
J. Craig(2)	W. Kivlichan	W. Shortt
J .W. Cravens	J. Law	J. Sloan
A. Cuncliffe	J. Leyden	J.A. Smith
J. Dewar	T. Leyden	J. Smith(1)
W. McK. Douglas	J. McCartney	J. Smith(2)
W.D. Erskine	J. McConnachie	W. Smith
C. Ferguson	A. McCourty	T.H. Stewart
W. French	J. McGowan	J. Tait
J. Glover	A. McKay	T. Templeton
J. Graham	J. A. McKenzie	J.W. Thomson
P. Gary	S. McMillan	J. Trotter
D. Grant	J. Marshall	R.B. Trotter
Bugler R. Grierson	R. Martin	D.R. Wallace
Alfred Hannay	J. Maxwell	W. White
Albert Hannay	R. Maxwell	T. Welsh
J. Hannay	P. Meechan	J. Wilkie
J. Harley	J. Millar	T. Wilson
W. Harley	G.C. Moffat	W. Young

'H' Company Dalbeattie.

Captain A.W. Anderson Lieutenant Gillies

Sergeants.

| T. Macgregor | G. Milburn | D. Mundell |
| T. Johnston | | |

Corporals.

| J. Huxtable | J. Fell | J. Townsend |
| D. Seggie | R. Crosbie | - Logan |

Privates.

Bugler C. Crosbie	J.P. Flynn	J. McKinnell
Bugler D. Mundell	W. Forteath	T. McMeeking
Bugler J. Neilson	J. Fowler	A. McWilliam
Bugler J. Seggie	W. Garmory	E. Morris
J. Affleck	P.B. Groves	W. Mundell
G.W. Agnew	R. Halliday	A. Muirhead
C. Airlie	J. Herries	John Murphy
J. Allan	W. Heughan	James Murphy
A. Bennett	S. Hood	W. A. Murphy
G. Bennett	J. Hume	J. Robertson
J. Bower	J. Huxtable	W. Roan
R. Bryce	H. Jamieson	J. Scott
W. Burnie	A.P. Logan	W. Slingsby
D. Clark	W.J. Mackie	J. Smith
J. Carlyle	J. McCaig	R. Smith
J. Carson(1)	D.M. McCall	J. Sturgeon
J. Carson(2)	F. McEwen	J. Thomson
J. Caven	R. McDonald	R. Thomson
W. Coutts	T. McGhie	W.M. Wilbur
J. Flynn	J. McGuffog	- Bonnar
- Thompson	- Hooker	- Murphy
- Wright	- Pringle	- Stenton
R. Bell	- McKinnell	W. Slingsby
- Gibson	- Laird	- Scott
W. Bell	- Riffan	- Roan
- Burnie	- Hood	- Herries
- Affleck		

Kirkcudbright Artillery Volunteers.

Quartermaster and Hon. Major R. McConchie
Captain W. Nicholson (Commanding)
Captain A. Brown

Sergeants.

J.G. Bradsahw	W. Richardson	H. Henney
E. Kimm	D.J. Davidson	W. Mackenzie
J. Slater		

Corporal.

| D. Shields | | |

Gunners.

W. McCoull	W. Hannay	T. McCoull
D.M. Haugh	John Hughan	D. McGhie
J. Anderson	R. Hughan	James McKie
J. Burns	W. Jardine	J. McLachlan (Jnr.)
D. Carnochan	D. Kenny	N.C. McMillan
R. Clacherty	R. Leckie	W. Payne
E. Dalziel	G. Little	J. Richardson
H. Fairweather	W. Maxwell	R. Strang
D. Hair	P. McCoull	

The following roll of Galloway Rifle Volunteers attended at both the Royal Reviews held at Holyrood. Edinburgh. in 1881 and again in 1905.

Colonel J.M. Kennedy, Commanding - 39 years service.

Lieutenant-Colonel John Lennox - 28 years.

Colour Sergeant J. Macgregor - 38 years.

> (Col.-Sgt. Macgregor joined the Galloway Rifles in 1867 and during his 38 years service he attended all the camps held by the Regiment, together with his attendance at the Carlisle Review of 1868, and the Royal Reviews of 1881 and 1905). - Kirkcudbright.

Private W. Paterson, Kirkcudbright - 25 years.

Quartermaster Sergeant T. Myers, Castle Douglas - 35 years.

Colour Sergeant W. Wright, Castle Douglas - 24 years.

Sergeant S. Gordon, Castle Douglas - 25 years.

Corporal J. McGaw, Castle Douglas - 32 years.

Corporal W. McGaw, Castle Douglas - 34 years.

Private J. Turner, Castle Douglas - 30 years.

Sergeant G. McHaffie, Stranraer - 30 years.

Colour-Sergeant J. Devoy, Stranraer - 31 years.

Orderly-Room Sergeant D. Johnstone, Maxwellton - 35 years.

Colour Sergeant J. Beattie, Maxwellton - 29 years.

Sergeant Bugler J. Raphael, Maxwellton - 26 years.

Private G. Carmichael, Maxwellton - 29 years.

Note. Colour Sergeant George Tuck, the ever popular and able Instructor of 'A' Company, Kirkcudbright, between the years 1890 and 1900, and who on his retirement became the landlord of the Galloway Arms, St. Cuthbert Street, Kirkcudbright, after many years of indifferent health, died on the 18th September, 1905, the same day as the Royal Review in Edinburgh.

(7) Collection of medals won or presented to, Private William McCreadie, 'D' Company - Newton Stewart, which includes three of his five Queen's Prize Badges and five gold national trophy team medals, which represented almost one third of all the national awards won by the Galloway Rifle Volunteers.

CHAPTER 9

THE GALLOWAY VOLUNTEER ASSOCIATION 1861 - 1863
AND THE GALLOWAY ARTILLERY AND RIFLE VOLUNTEER ASSOCIATION
1864 - 1907.

On Wednesday, 16th November, 1859, an influential meeting was held in the Thatched House Tavern, London, to initiate the formation of a National Rifle Association, for the encouragement of Volunteer Rifle Corps, and the promotion of rifle shooting throughout Great Britain. Lord Elcho presided, in the absence of Mr. Sidney Herbert, Secretary for War, who approved most highly of the Association, as did Prince Albert and Her Majesty Queen Victoria, who was to offer £250 annually, to be shot for in competition by the Volunteers. This was to become the 'Blue Riband' event of the National Rifle Association, the 'Queen's Prize', which was to decide the champion shot of the Volunteer Movement from throughout the U.K. Resolutions were passed conferring the Presidency of the Association on Mr. Sidney Herbert. The subscriptions were fixed at 1 guinea per year or 10 guineas for a life subscription. The annual meetings to be held at various places, at which the best shots from the several Volunteer Corps would be involved to compete for prizes according to the rules of the School of Musketry at Hythe. Prizes were also to be offered to riflemen, whether connected with a Rifle Corps or not.

The National Rifle Association was, however, to secure from the Duke of Cambridge a tract of Wimbledon Common, on long lease, suitable for their purposes and in June, 1860, it was reported that arrangements for the first National Rifle Association Meeting of the various Rifle Volunteer Corps, to be held at Wimbledon on the 2nd July, 1860, were progressing satisfactorily, with 1200 yards having been enclosed, providing six ranges, with the ground beyond that being kept by the Police.

The National Rifle Association had received from Enfield, 1000 rifles, which were sent to the Corps of those sending deputations to the meeting, along with 90 rounds of ammunition. The prizes were announced as 20 Whitworth Rifles and a gold and silver medal with £250 offered by Queen Victoria. The conditions of entry to the 'Queen's Prize, i.e. the gold medal and £250, was the successful competitors at 300, 500 and 600 yard range, alone to compete with the Whitworth Rifle over the 800, 900 and 1,000 yard range. 360 competitors were to take place in the first 'Queen's Prize' competition.

Prior to the formation of the National Rifle Association, the 'top-shot' in the United Kingdom was awarded the 'Championship Belt' which was held for 3 months, when the holder could be challenged by anyone, the challenger, however, being required to deposit a sum of £200. The institution of the 'Queen's Prize' was to bring this top accolade within the grasp of the working class but bearing in mind the imagery of the Volunteer Corps in its infancy as being very much that of a middle and upper class movement.

The rules of competition for the 'Queen's Prize', as amended, are clearly defined in the rifle competition at Wimbledon on the 14th July, 1885: - "The 1st stage consists of three ranges, using 200, 500 and 600 yards. Seven shots are fired at each range, and the 300 competitors making the highest aggregate scores become entitled to compete in the 2nd stage, whilst the 60 next below them in order of merit retire with an award of £2 each as a consolation prize.

The chosen 300 have now to fire in the 2nd stage, 10 shots at 500 yards and 15 shots at 600 yards.

The scores in the 1st and 2nd stages are added together and their position settled according to their aggregate. The top scorer receives the Silver medal and the Silver badge of the National Rifle Association.

He and the next 59 below him, in order of merit, have the right of competing in the 3rd stage, whilst the other 240 receive prizes varying from £4 to £2.

The selected 60 fire 15 shots at 800 yards and 900 yards. The scores made at these ranges are added to the points with which they have already been credited for their performance in the 1st and 2nd stages, and on the grand aggregate depends the ultimate position.

The top score obtains the Gold Medal and Badge of the Association, together with the £250 given by the Queen.

The second man takes £60, the third £40, the 4th £30 and the 5th £20.

The next ten obtain prizes of £15, the 30 below them prizes of £12 and the remaining 15, prizes of £10.

In 1885, 2,500 competitors took part in shooting for the 1st stage for the 'Queen's Prize' and it should be noted that the ultimate winner would have had to undergo a fair amount of emotion before reaching his final goal, having had to progress from his Company Competitions, to the County Competitions, before even becoming eligible to shoot in the 'Queen's Prize.'

On the 2nd July, 1860, Queen Victoria was to open the first Wimbledon Common Prize Meeting of the National Rifle Association, by firing the first shot at a target of 400 yards, from a Whitworth Rifle, the sights of which had been aligned by Mr. Whitworth himself. The Queen was to make a bullseye.

Mr. James Payne, Ironmonger, 1st Kirkcudbright Rifles (Kirkcudbright) and Mr. Robert McGuffog, 2nd Kirkcudbright Rifles (Castle Douglas) represented the Galloway Rifle Volunteers, at this first Wimbledon Meeting, there is, however, no report of their having triumphed in any of the class firing.

On the 21st September, 1860, Lord Elcho, addressed a letter to the Lord Lieutenants of Counties, urging them in the name of the Council of the National Rifle Association, to encourage the formation of County Rifle Associations, with Wimbledon at the heart and its competitions being the climax of the Company and County meetings. To assist the provincial organisations, the central body at Wimbledon, were prepared to loan targets and other range necessities and would annually offer a Bronze Medal, to be considered the 'Blue Riband' event of the County Meetings. Lord Elcho, further desired that each County Association, should furnish a special prize to be shot for by 'All Comers' at the National annual meeting at Wimbledon.

On Tuesday, 9th April, 1861, a meeting of gentlemen interested in the formation of a Rifle Association for the County of Wigtown and the Stewartry of Kirkcudbright, was held at the Galloway Rifle's Headquarters in Newton Stewart. The Earl of Selkirk presided and the following Council was elected:-

Presidents -

The Earl of Selkirk, Lord Lieutenant of the Stewartry.-
The Earl of Stair, Lord Lieutenant of the County of Wigtown.
Lieutenant-Colonel Laurie of Woodhall - ex officis.
Colonel Clark Kennedy, C.B. Hon. Member.
Captain Munro, Adjutant of the G.R.V., Valleyfield, Kirkcudbright, Hon. Member.
Captain Shand, 1st Kirkcudbright Artillery Volunteers, Oakley House, Kirkcudbright, Hon. Member.
Captain Hamilton, Barnwhinnoch, 1st Kirkcudbright Rifles (Kirkcudbright).
Captain Mackie, M.P. of Bargaly, 2nd Kirkcudbright Rifles (Castle Douglas).
Captain Maxwell of Glenlee, 3rd Kirkcudbright Rifles, (New Galloway).
Captain McKinnell, 5th Kirkcudbright Rifles, (Maxwellton).
Captain Guthrie, 2nd Wigtownshire Rifles (Stranraer).
Lieutenant Stewart, Crosbie West, 3rd Wigtownshire Rifles, (Newton Stewart)
Lieutenant Vans Agnew of Barnbarroch, 1st Wigtownshire Rifles, (Wigtown).
Lieutenant-General Johnston of Carnsalloch.
W.H. Maxwell Esq., of Munches.
Captain Clark of Dunmuir.
Lieutenant-Colonel Sir William Wallace, Bart., of Lochryan.
Adam Skirving of Croys, 2nd Kirkcudbright Rifles, (Castle Douglas).
Mr. Alex. McCutcheon, Writer, Newton Stewart, was appointed Secretary and Treasurer.

It was agreed to form a Rifle Association for the County of Wigtown and the Stewartry of Kirkcudbright, to be called the Galloway Volunteer Association, with its aim being the promotion of efficiency in the use of the rifle by the offer of cash prizes for competition to Volunteers. Annual subscription would be set at 5/- with life membership being £3-3-0d. A sub-committee was appointed to formulate plans for an Association Rifle meeting to be held in Galloway later that year and it was further agreed that these prize meetings should be held annually and alternate between the County and the Stewartry. The next meeting was to be called on the 10th August, next, to receive the report and recommendations of the Committee and resolve upon the future conduct of the Association. The Earl of Selkirk was to close the meeting with the following remarks, "Such competitions as that in which the Rifle Volunteers are about to be engaged in will do more to strengthen the movement than anything hitherto developed."

On the 10th August, 1861, a further meeting of the Galloway Volunteer Association, was held at Newton Stewart, and as is the 'want' after the initial euphoria of the formation of the Association had expired, the influential gentlemen, instrumental in its formation took a back seat, with the working committee of Lieutenant-Colonel Laurie, Captain Mackie, Lieutenant Stewart, Captain Hamilton and Captain and Adjutant Munro, organising and laying the ground rules for the first Association meeting. The following are the various competitions organised by the Association, together with the prize money and conditions subject to each event, being followed by the regulations governing such competitions.

Galloway Volunteer Association.
Presidents
The Earl of Selkirk. Viscount Dalrymple.
First Annual Competition.
The following prizes will be competed for at the forthcoming Meeting of the Association, which will be held at Castle Douglas, in the Stewartry of Kirkcudbright, upon an early day in October, 1861. (Later fixed for 9th/10th October, 1861).

I). **The Bronze Medal** of the National Rifle Association, with £10 added by the Galloway Rifle Association, either in money or plate, at the option of the winner. 2nd prize, £5 or plate of that value.

10 rounds each; 5 rounds at 600 yards and 5 rounds at 800 yards. Entry 3/- each.

This prize is open only to Effective Volunteers of the different Corps in Galloway, and each intending competitor must send, along with his entry money, a certificate from his Commanding Officer that he has attended at least eight regular Company drills during the preceding months of July, August and September.

The winner of this competition is eligible to shoot for the Prince of Wales Prize at Wimbledon, the following year.

II). **The Galloway Rifle Association Prize** being £15 given by the Association either in money, a rifle or plate, at the option of the winner. 2nd prize, £5, either in money or plate.

5 rounds at 200 yards and 5 rounds at 400 yards. Entry 3/- each.

III). **The Ladies Prize**. given by the Ladies of Galloway. 1st Prize £12, 2nd prize £5, 3rd prize £3, all prizes may be had in money or plate.

5 rounds at 150 yards - standing. Entry 3/- each.

The two prizes Nos. (I) and (II) are open to members of the different Corps in Galloway, both Effective and Honorary, and also to members of the Association.

IV). **A Breech Loading Rifle** value £15-15-0d, the gift of Lt.-Col. Laurie of the Galloway Battalion of Volunteers. To be competed for by Effective Members of that Battalion. 300 rounds of ball cartridge and caps will be given along with the rifle.

5 rounds at 300 yards. Entry money 1/- each.

V). **Ten Pounds worth of Ammunition**, given by the Association for **Volley Firing**. To be competed for by squads of 10 men belonging to any Volunteer Corps in Galloway.

5 rounds at 400 yards. Entry £1 per squad.

VI). **Ten Pounds worth of Ammunition,** given by the Association for **Skirmishing**. To be competed for by squads of 10 men belonging to any Volunteer Corps in Galloway.

5 rounds between 200 and 400 yards. Entry £1 per squad.

VII). **The All Comers Prize**. lst prize £10. 2nd prize, £5; 3rd prize £3, all prizes may be had in money or plate.

5 rounds at 300 yards, 5 rounds at 600 yards. Entry 3/- each.

Competitors may use any kind of rifle not weighing more than 10lbs.

There will also be one or more 'Aunt Sally' targets on the ground. Each days drawings, less 25% for expenses, will be divided amongst the 'Bulls-Eyes' made. 6d per shot, including ammunition.

Copies of the Regulations under which the Competitions will take place will be forwarded to the

Commanding Officer of each Corps of Volunteers, and may be had by Members of the Association on application to the Secretary.

The following are the Regulations under which the competition was to be conducted:

I). Each intending competitor must send to the Secretary, on or before Friday, the 20th September, next, a letter stating which Prize or Prizes he proposes to shoot for, mentioning his qualification for doing so, as Effective member, No......of Company; Honorary member, No.....of Company or Member of Association, and enclosing his entrance money, together with a stamped envelope with his name and address in full. No attention can be paid to any communication not complying with these instructions; and no entry will be received upon any ground whatsoever after the 20th September.

II). The Secretary in return will furnish the intending competitor with a card, stating the probable hour at which the prize will be contested, and the squad and range in which the competitor will fire.

III). Each firing squad will be placed under the charge of a Volunteer Officer, who will call the roll, keep the firing register, and be responsible for the maintenance of discipline.

IV). The Prize about to be competed for will be announced by placard at the Secretary's tent, and also by sound of Bugle; the first Bugle Call, will serve as a warning for the competitors to assemble immediately; at the second Bugle Call, which will follow the first with a quarter of an hour interval, the officers in charge of squads will call the rolls and any competitor then absent will forfeit their chance.

V). The signal to commence firing will be given by the Umpire's Bugle.

VI). All the prizes shall be competed for with rifles of the regulation gauge and size of nipple, excepting that for 'All Comers', in which any rifle not weighing more than 10 lbs. may be used. Regulation ammunition will be supplied by the Association, on the ground, free of charge, and none other will be allowed, excepting in the 'All Comers' prize.

VII). For those prizes limited to Effective Volunteers, the Hythe position must be adhered to in firing.

VIII). No telescopic sights or artificial rests may be used for any prize whatsoever.

IX). The pull of a trigger shall not be less than six pounds, excepting in that for 'All Comers' .

X). At the conclusion of each round the Officer in charge of each squad will read over the points gained by each individual; and in case of any doubt as to the marking of any particular shot, the competitor must state his case to the Officer in Command of his squad, before the commencement of the next round, and the officer will then use his discretion as to verifying the shot, or referring it to the Umpire.

XI). Immediately on the conclusion of the firing for each prize the scores will be made up and verified by the Umpire, after which the names of the winners will be announced and placarded outside the Secretary's tent.

XII). In case of ties, they will be decided at once by firing three rounds at the longest range which has been fired at for the prize in question.

XIII). The decision of the Umpire shall in all cases be final.

XIV). A fine of Ten Shillings will be imposed on any person discharging his rifle accidentally, or at any other than the appointed time and place.

An Armourer will be in attendance.

Volley and Skirmishing Practices.

I). Each party to compete for the prizes for volley firing and skirmishing shall comprise ten non-commissioned officers or men effective members of their Corps.

II). The party during the competition shall be commanded by a Commissioned Officer of the Corps.

III). Both practices will be conducted strictly in accordance with the Hythe system.

IV). These practices being intended as tests not only of marksmanship but of discipline, the Umpire will, immediately on observing any dangerous irregularity on the part of any firing party, cause it to cease fire and exclude it from the competition. An annual subscription of not less than Five Shillings constitutes anyone a member of the association, A contribution of not less than £3-3-0d constitutes a Life Member.

By Order of the Council.

ALEX. McCUTCHEON, Hon. Secretary.   Newton Stewart, 8th August, 1861.

On the 31st August, 1861, members of the Council met at Castle Douglas. Lt. Col. Laurie in the chair, when it was reported that the envisaged programme of events at the forthcoming Association meeting were in serious danger of being curtailed through the want of funds, the subscriptions were not coming as fast as had been anticipated and it was agreed that a subscription paper should be sent to each officer of the Battalion in order that additional sums over and above the nominated subscriptions might be obtained.

A letter from the Secretary was read, stating that the Government was to send 5,000 rounds of ammunition for the competition, but that the Secretary of War would not sanction the issue of Government ammunition for prizes. The meeting determined therefore, that the £10 for Volley and Skirmishing prizes should be given to the successful Corps to purchase ammunition.

A letter from the National Association was read in which the Galloway Volunteer Association was directed to offer a subscription to the National Association of a sum not exceeding £4, in order that the Bronze Medal of the National Association might be secured.

The Council then retired to the practice grounds at Caigton and found it suitable for the proposed meeting in October. A small committee consisting of the officers of the 2nd Kirkcudbright Rifles, Castle Douglas, together with Captain Clark of Dunmuir, Joseph Grierson of Breoch and James Grierson of Caigton, were appointed to attend the arrangements carried out upon the ground, relative to the erecting of butts, marking off the distances, erection of a wooden hut to accommodate members of the Council and the issuing of ammunition, and paling off the shooting ground from the spectators.

On Wednesday, 11th September, 1861, the following subscription list was received, which together with further additional subscriptions, secured the success of the 1st Meeting of the Galloway Volunteer Association.

Galloway Volunteer Association.
Presidents.
The Earl of Selkirk - Lord Lieutenant of Kirkcudbrightshire.
Viscount Dalrymple - Lord Lieutenant of Wigtownshire.

The following Subscription Lists have been received as at the 11th September, 1861:-

	Life Member.	Annual Subs.
The Earl of Selkirk	15.15. 0	
Viscount Dalrymple	10. 0. 0	
Lt. Col. Kennedy Laurie of Woodhall	10. 0. 0	
J. Carrick-Moore Esq. of Corsewall	5. 0. 0	
Wellwood Maxwell Esq. of the Grove	3. 3. 0	
A. Oswald Esq. of Auchencruive	3. 3. 0	
Sir W.W.F. Wallace Bart., of Lochryan	3. 3. 0	
J. Stark Esq., of Troqueer Holm	3. 3. 0	
W.C.S. Hamilton Esq. of Craighlaw	3. 3. 0	
W.H.M. Maxwell Esq. of Munches	3. 3. 0	
H.G. Murray Stewart Esq. of Cally	5. 0. 0	
Walter McCulloch Esq. of Ardwall	3. 3. 0	
Captain Munro, Newton Stewart		10. 6
Captain Guthrie, Rephad		5. 0
W.R. McDiarmid, Dumfries		5. 0
Samuel Adamson, Dumfries		5. 0
Captain G. Hamilton, Kirkcudbright		1. 1. 0
Lieutenant Tennant, ..		10. 6
Ensign McLellan, ..		10. 6
D. McLellan, ..		10 .6
Sergeant Williamson, ..		5. 0
W. McMillan of Chapel		5. 0
W.J. Renny of Danevale		5. 0
J. Bell of Dunjop		5. 0
J. Henderson, Castle Douglas		5. 0
Andrew Milligan, Writer, Castle Douglas		5. 0
R. C. Thomson, National Bank ..		5. 0
A. Skirving of Croys		5. 0
Dr. Gilchrist, Dumfries		1. 0. 0
Captain McKinnell, Maxwellton		1.10.0
Lieutenant Allan, ..		1.10.0
R.K. Walker, Writer, ..		5. 0
Rev. M.M. Heron of Kirrouchtree		10. 0
James Lawson, Whithorn		1. 1. 0

Lieutenant H.D. Stewart, Whithorn		10. 6
Ensign Drew, Whithorn		10. 6
Rev. T. Johnstone, Anwoth		1.10.0
Major Hannay of Kirkdale		5. 0
Ensign Ewart, Gatehouse		5. 0
John Johnston, Kirkcudbright		5. 0
William Martin, ..		5. 0
D. Jenkin, ..		5. 0
Lieutenant Watson, Drummore		1. 0. 0
Ensign Anderson, ..		10. 6
Sergeant McCulloch, ..		5 .0
Sergeant McCosh, ..		5. 0
Dr. Ross, Stoneykirk		5. 0
W. McCreadie, Clanyard		5. 0
J. Hutchesonson, Creechan		5 .0
R. Vans Agnew Esq. of Barnbarroch	3. 3. 0	
Captain Dudgeon of Cargen	5. 0. 0	
Sir Andrew Agnew Bart., M.P.	5. 5. 0	
Captain Stoddart of Carlingwark R.N.	3. 3. 0	
J.B. Neilson Esq. of Queenshill	3. 3. 0	
Sir J.C.D. Hay Bart., of Park Place	5. 5. 0	
W. Rigg, Banks, Kirkcudbright		5. 0
Captain J.W. Stuart, Dumfries Militia		10. 0
D.A. Gordon of Culvennan		5. 0
W. Affleck, Draper, Castle Douglas		5. 0
Captain A. C. Sanderson of Glenlaggan		10. 0
Captain Guthrie, Stranraer		2. 2. 0
Lieutenant Ingram, ..		10. 6
Ensign Shaw, ..		10 .6
Sergeant MacBryde, ..		5. 0
Sergeant Wallace, ..		5. 0
Sergeant Miller, ..		5. 0
Sergeant Taylor, ..		5. 0
Corporal Gourlay, ..		5. 0
Corporal Coustom, ..		5. 0
James Jones, ..		5. 0
Alex. McCulloch of Glen	3. 3. 0	
D.H. Gordon, Kirkcudbright		10. 6
Major Blair, ..		10 .6
A. McKenzie, ..		10. 6
James Payne, ..		5. 0
D. Craig, ..		5. 0
J. Muir, Lochfergus		5. 0
Richard Hewat, Writer, Castle Douglas		5 .0

Subscriptions will be received by the Subscriber
Alex. McCutcheon, Writer, Newton Stewart.
Hon. Secretary and Treasurer.   Newton Stewart 11th September, 1861.

1st Meeting of the Galloway Volunteer Association.

The first annual prize meeting of the Galloway Volunteer Association was held on Wednesday and Thursday, 9th/10th October, 1861, the meeting taking place on a ground well adapted for such a purpose. The targets were placed on the farm of Cuil, a portion on the estate of Lady Abercromby, the 'Aunt Sally' targets on the farm of Breoch, with the shooting taking place from the farm of Caigton and Corra.

From the hill on Caigton, the public had an excellent view of the whole proceedings, whilst others were to take possession of the opposite side of the field or stood on the public road. The visitors to the ground on the Wednesday were in excess of 400, together with the Volunteers, making for a crowd of over 1000 people.

Notwithstanding the unpromising state of the weather on the Monday and Tuesday, preparations were satisfactorily completed, Captain Clark of Dunmuir having been on the field from 'dawn to dewy eve', through rain and wind, superintending the preparation of the ground.

Among the honoured guests on the ground, on the Wednesday, was Lord Dalrymple; Major-General Johnson of Carnsalloch; Lt.-Col. Simpson, 1st Lanarkshire Administrative Battalion of Volunteers; Captain and Adjutant Munro of the Galloway Rifles; Captain Sanderson of Glenlaggan and family. Mr. Maxwell of

Glenlee and family. Mr. and Mrs Maxwell of Munches; Mr. Stewart of Southwick and family; Mr. and Mrs. Congreve and family, Mollance; Mr. Murray Stewart, Cally; Mr. Stewart, Cairnsmore; Mr. Gordon, Greenlaw; James Carruthers, Craig; Mr. Barlow, Dalshangan; Mr. D. McCulloch, Auchness; Mr. Grierson, Bishopton; Mr. Neilson, Queenshill; Col. Stopford-Blair, Penninghame; Mr. Picken, Barnkirk; Mr. Craik, Newton Stewart.

The programme of events issued by the Association stated the hours of which each event was to take place, but this was soon thrown into disarray, in consequence of the large numbers who were to take part in the competitions. Shortly after 9am on the Wednesday, the sound of the bugle was heard and the squads presented themselves for the opening event of the competition, the Skirmishing.

The Officers on the field in charge of their respective Companies were:-

1st K.R.V.	(Kirkcudbright) -	Capt. Hamilton, Lt. Tennant, Ensign McLellan
2nd	(Castle Douglas) -	Capt. Mackie, Lt. Bell, Ensign Renny.
3rd	(New Galloway) -	Capt. Maxwell, Ensign Dalziel.
4th	(Gatehouse) -	Ensign Ewart
5th	(Maxwellton) -	Capt. McKinnell; Lt. Allan; Ensign Stark.
1st W.R.V.	(Wigtown) -	Lt. Vans Agnew, Ensign McHaffie.
2nd	(Stranraer) -	Capt. Guthrie.
3rd	(Newton Stewart) -	Lt. V. Agnew in the absence of Capt. Stuart.
4th	(Whithorn) -	Lt. H.D. Stewart, Ensign Drew.
5th	(Drummore) -	Lt. Watson, Ensign Anderson.

The Officer in Charge was Lieutenant-Colonel Clark Kennedy, Colonel Commandant of the Military Train. Captain Noake and his men of the Dumfries Militia were in charge of the Butts and Range duties, with their Regimental Band playing at the intervals, throughout the day.
Results of the Competitions.

I). **The Bronze Medal** from the National Rifle Association.

	600yds.	800yds	Total.
J. Muir, Balmaclellan	6	3	9
Sergeant McConchie, Newton Stewart	2	7	9
Sergeant G. Robertson, Castle Douglas	5	4	9
Sergeant Payne, Kirkcudbright	4	2	6
W. Cairns, Gatehouse	5	1	6
J. Aitken, Auchlane	4	2	6
Sergeant Brown, New Galloway	5	1	6
J. Douglas, New Galloway	3	3	6
J. Henderson, Castle Douglas	4	2	6
Joseph Grierson, Breoch	3	2	5
A. Geddes, New Galloway	4	1	5
W. Craig, New Galloway	3	2	5
Corporal Tait, Maxwellton	2	3	5
A. McMillan, Maxwellton	3	1	4
W. McCulloch, Drummore	4	0	4
Stair McConnell, Newton Stewart	4	0	4
Captain Hamilton, Kirkcudbright	4	0	4
W. Lightbody, Kirkcudbright	2	2	4
J. Grierson, Kirkcudbright	2	2	4
J. W. Whinney, Breoch	4	0	4
Sergeant McCulloch, Drummore	2	2	4

There being a tie a shoot-out was arranged:- Mr. J. Muir 3 points - 1st; Sergeant McConchie 1 point - 2nd.

Only one other competition took place on the Wednesday, which was at the 'Aunt Sally' Targets. There were 762 shots fired, at 6d per shot, at a 'bulls-eye' 2½" in diameter at 130 yards distance. John Anderson, Kirkcudbright, was to win the sweepstake with 3 bulls-eyes.

On Thursday, 10th October, the competition resumed with:

II). **The Galloway Rifle Association Prize.**

W. Nivison, Dumfries, 1st Prize.	8 points.
J. Payne, Kirkcudbright 2nd Prize (after shoot-out)	7
W. McNeillie, Dumfries	7
William Cairns, Gatehouse	6
Sergeant Smith, Dumfries	6
J. Campbell, Kirkcudbright	6
W. Inglis, Stranraer	6
St. John Gore, Assoc. Member	6
J. Douglas, New Galloway	6
Corporal Aitken, Castle Douglas	6
William Keiman, New Galloway	6
John Muir, New Galloway	6
Andrew Hannay, Kirkcudbright	6
Lieutenant Tennant, Kirkcudbright	5
Thomas Sproat, London Scottish Rifles	5
G. Dunbar, Dumfries	5
D. Bell, Kirkcudbright	5
W. Smith, Dumfries Volunteers	5
T. Martin, Kirkcudbright	5
J. Grierson, Castle Douglas	5
Corporal Hellon, Dumfries	5
Corporal Grierson, Kirkcudbright	5
Peter McCosh, Drummore	5
William Kennedy, Dumfries Volunteers	5
George Moffat, Newton Stewart	5
J. Grierson, Kirkcudbright	5
W. Lightbody, Kirkcudbright	5
F.G. Brown, Kirkcudbright	5
Sergeant Kennedy, Dumfries Militia	5
J. Young, Gatehouse	5
J. Rae, Gatehouse	5

III). **The Ladies Prize.**

Sergeant Williamson, Kirkcudbright, 1st Prize	12 points.
William Kennedy 2nd Prize	12
Alex. Kirk, 3rd Prize (after shoot-out)	11
Thomas Brown	10
W. Inglis, Stranraer	10
J. Payne, Kirkcudbright	10
T. Sproat, London Scottish Volunteers	10
Corporal Aitken, Castle Douglas	10
Sergeant Kennedy, Dumfries Militia	9
John Muir, New Galloway	9
J. Grierson, Castle Douglas	9
J. Grierson, Breoch	9
R. McGuffog, Castle Douglas	9
J. Hewitson, Maxwellton	9
Sergeant Crackston, Maxwellton	9
Thomas Rae, Gatehouse	9
Lieutenant Bell, Castle Douglas	9
Sergeant Robertson, Castle Douglas	9
Sergeant McCulloch, Drummore	8
James Erskine, Newton Stewart	8
D. Niven, Kirkcudbright	8
A. Hannah, Kirkcudbright	8
W. Picken, Newton Stewart	8
G. Christison, Wigtown	8
Sergeant Spearing, Gatehouse	8
Corporal Hellon, Dumfries	8
W. Broadfoot, Castle Douglas	8
J. Hewitson, Maxwellton	7
Agnew, Newon Stewart (1)	7
A.Y. Herries, Castle Douglas	7
Captain Shand, Kirkcudbright Artillery	7
Agnew, Newton Stewart (2)	7

W. Cairns, Gatehouse	7
P. McCosh, Drummore	6
W. Lightbody, Kirkcudbright	6
Corporal W. Borland, Castle Douglas	6
J. Grierson, Wigtown	6
J. Mitchell, Castle Douglas	6
J. Hewitson, Castle Douglas	6
John Blacklock, Kirkcudbright	6
Corporal George Dunbar, Dumfries	6
James Douglas, New Galloway	6
Ensign McLellan, Kirkcudbright	6
Lieutenant Tennant, Kirkcudbright	6
D. McGeorge, Castle Douglas	6
A. Skirving, Castle Douglas	6
Captain Maxwell, New Galloway	6
Lieutenant Allan, Maxwellton	6

IV). **Breech Loading Rifle.**

Sergeant A. Brown, New Galloway - Winner	9 points.
J. McLean, Stranraer	8
Sergeant A. Skirving, Castle Douglas	7
John Muir, New Galloway	7
Joseph Grierson, Kirkcudbright	7
James Douglas, New Galloway	7
Sergeant Craig, Kirkcudbright	6
W. Lightbody, Kirkcudbright	6
George Paton, Wigtown	6
G. Moffat, Newton Stewart	6
Sergeant Grierson, New Galloway	6
W. Cairns, Gatehouse	6
Thomas Rae, Gatehouse	6
Sergeant Thomson, Castle Douglas	6
Joseph Whinnie, Castle Douglas	5
W. Kenna, New Galloway	5
J. Kelly, Wigtown	5
J. Houston, Maxwellton	5
J. Spearing, Gatehouse	5
James Hutchinson, Drummore	5
Corporal McGuffog, Castle Douglas	5
Corporal Aitken, Castle Douglas	5
Joseph Grierson, New Galloway	5

V). **Results of Skirmishing.**

Newton Stewart Squad	34 points.
Castle Douglas	29
Drummore	29
Maxwellton	23
Kirkcudbright	21
Stranraer	17

VI). **Results of Volley Firing.**

Newton Stewart Squad	54 points.
New Galloway	49
Kirkcudbright	47
Castle Douglas	43
Drummore	42
Stranraer	37
Maxwellton	32

VII). **The All Comers Prize.**

W. Cairns, Gatehouse, 1st Prize	10 points.
W. Lightbody, Kirkcudbright, 2nd Prize	7
G. Christison, Wigtown, 3rd Prize	7
J. Grierson, Wigtown	6
J. Gibb, Gatehouse	6

A. Kirk, Castle Douglas	6
Lieutenant Bell, Castle Douglas	6
R. Beattie, New Galloway	6
J. Hewitson, Castle Douglas	6
T. Brown, New Galloway	6
J. Muir, New Galloway	5
G. Whinnie, Castle Douglas	5
Lieutenant Allan, Maxwellton	5
J. Milligan, New Galloway	5
Sergeant Craig, Kirkcudbright	5

Stranraer Company laboured throughout the tournament in consequence of their range at home being limited to 300 yards and they, having no practice whatsoever, at the longer distances. Only one accident was recorded, Captain Clark, whilst attending at the butts received a ball through the tail of his coat. It was believed that the accident was caused by one of the riflemen firing at the wrong target. Everyone, however, rejoiced in the knowledge that the only damage was to the broadcloth of Captain Clark.

I was very privileged to receive from Lieutenant-Colonel Clark-Kennedy of Knockgray, the following letter written by one of his forebears, Lt.-Col. John Clark Kennedy, C.B. the Younger of Knockgray, the Colonel Commandant of the Military Train, who supervised the 1st, and many more thereafter, Galloway Volunteer Association Rifle Meetings, to his father, General Sir Alexander Kennedy, whilst visiting Drumlanrig Castle, some days after the first Association meeting, his wife being the grand-daughter of the 4th Duke of Buccleuch:

Drumlanrig Castle,
Thornhill.

13th October, 1861.
".......At Kirkcudbright we remained for the night at the Hotel, attended the County meeting the next day and we drove to Munches by the ruins of Dundrennan Abbey. Wednesday and Thursday very fine and I was occupied as Umpire and Manager of the first Rifle Meeting in Galloway. Between ourselves, the arrangements had not been well constituted and the time for shooting the various matches had been entirely miscalculated, had I not been there to recast it on the spot there would have been a mess, but all went off well. I distributed the prizes, made a short speech and was thanked by everyone which was pleasant enough in the County we come from. Made the acquaintance of many people of both Wigtown and the Stewartry, most of them whom knew me as your son and more than one of the Volunteers asked me if I was not the son of the Waterloo Officer who took the Eagle."

This reference to taking the 'Eagle' was an action of the 11th June, 1815, during the battle of Waterloo, when General Sir Alexander Kennedy, then a Captain in the Royal Dragoons, along with Corporal Francis Stiles, of the same Regiment, was responsible for the capture of the 'Eagle' of Count D'Erlons of the French 105th Regiment. Captain Kennedy was severely wounded in this action. Corporal Stiles for his part in the capture of the 'Eagle' was to receive a Commission in the 6th West India Regiment.

2nd Meeting of the Galloway Volunteer Association.

The 2nd annual competition of the Galloway Volunteer Association was to take place on the shore near Glenluce, on Tuesday, 22nd July, 1862, in the presence of a large crowd of spectators from all over the County and the Stewartry. Among those present were, The Earl of Selkirk and party; Viscount Dalrymple and party; Mr. Fife, Balkaill; Mr. Herries, younger, of Spottes; C. S. Stewart of Cairnsmore;
Mr. Henry Stuart of Crosbie; Mr. G. Maitland, younger of Kell; Mr. Grierson, Craigadam; Captain Dudgeon of Cargen; Mr. Dun Stewart of Tonderghie; Mr. Bryce Wright and Mr. Craik, both of Newton Stewart.

The entries for the various prizes were down on the previous year, the total number being approximately 170. The ground selected for the competition was well adapted for the purpose, being at the head of a small bay off the Bay of Luce, which received the water of the Pultanton Burn.

The morning of the competition broke beautifully, with the day proving to be one of the finest of the season. The spectators scattered themselves on the farm of the Mains of Park and the targets, numbering 14 in all, were placed in such a manner along the Mains of Park Shore, that the bullets passed out to sea. One target was placed on the opposite side of the Pultanton Burn, again with the bullets passing out to sea.

Colonel Clark Kennedy, Colonel Commandant of the Military Train, once again acted as umpire and at 10am he called the competitors to him reminding them of the rules of the competition but cautioned that they were about to follow the rules pursued at Hythe, now adopted by the National Rifle Association, in which every hit would count and that in the Volley firing there must be no hanging fire, they must all be bona-fide volleys or they would not count. He further cautioned them as to disputes about the size of the targets. All targets he said had been made as equal as possible and unless the complaint was made by a Company Captain he would not look at the target but he reminded them all, that although the target may not be fair to one man, he, must be prepared to sacrifice for the good of the whole. Col. Clark Kennedy was assisted by Major Walker of Crawfordton, Inspector of Musketry for the Volunteers in Scotland. Mr. A. McCutcheon, the Hon. Secretary of the Galloway Rifle Battalion was assisted by Mr. Farrish, Assistant Secretary for the Dumfries County Association. Sergeants Mitchell, Kennedy, Macreadie, Elliot, Wilson, Lowrie and Hudson and Buglers Harkness and Adams of the Galloway Rifles attended to the range duties and distribution of ammunition.

The following Company Officers were in attendance:

1st W.R.V.	(Wigtown) -	Lt. Vans Agnew. Ensign McHaffie.,
2nd	(Stranraer) -	Captain Guthrie.
3rd	(Newton Stewart) -	Lt. Henry Stuart.
4th	(Whithorn) -	Lt. H.D. Stewart.
5th	(Drummore) -	Lt. Watson; Ensign Anderson.
1st K.R.V. (Kirkcudbright) -		Captain Hamilton; Ensign Craig.
2nd	(Castle Douglas)-	Captain Mackie M.P.; Lt. Bell; Ensign Renny.
3rd	(New Galloway) -	Captain Maxwell.
4th	(Gatehouse) -	Ensign Ewart.

Results of the several competitions.

I). **The Bronze Medal** of the National Rifle Association, with £10 added by the Galloway Volunteer Association. 2nd £5.

10 rounds each, 5 at 600 yards and 5 at 800 yards. This prize open only to effective Volunteers of the Galloway Rifle Battalion, who had shot through the 2nd and 3rd Classes. Entry fee 3/-. The competitor was further required to submit a certificate from his Commanding Officer stating that he had attended at least 8 regular Company drills during the preceding 4 months. The winner of this prize was eligible to shoot for the Prince of Wales Prize at Wimbledon the following meeting.

John McClurg, Drummore, 1st Prize	23 points.
Robert Shaw, New Galloway, 2nd Prize	17
J. Muir, New Galloway, 3rd Prize (after shoot-out)	15
A. McConchie, Newton Stewart	15
Thomas Stewart, Newton Stewart	14
R. Picken, Newton Stewart	14
J. Grierson, Kirkcudbright	10

II). **The Galloway Rifle Association Prize.** 1st £10, 2nd £5.

Conditions 7 rounds at 600 yards. Entry 3/-.

S. McCulloch, Drummore, 1st Prize	21 points.
W. Nivison, Thornhill, 2nd Prize	18
Sergeant McCulloch, Drummore, 3rd Prize	18
J. Henderson, Castle Douglas	17
J. Hewitson, Newton Stewart	17
W. Picken, Newton Stewart	17
Thomas Rae, Gatehouse	17
Sergeant R. C. Thomson, Castle Douglas	16
J. Muir, New Galloway	16
R. Shaw, New Galloway	16
Sergeant Waugh, Gatehouse	16
D. Williamson, Kirkcudbright	16
James Young, Gatehouse	16
Thomas Martin, Kirkcudbright	16
J. Mitchell, 4th Edinburgh Rifle Volunteers	16
W. Anderson, Wigtown	15

III). **The Ladies Prize.** Given by the Ladies of Galloway. 1st £8; 2nd £5; 3rd £2.
     5 rounds at 200 yards. Entry 3/-.

James Grierson, Castle Douglas	16 points.
Sergeant Payne, Kirkcudbright	15
William McGaa, Drummore	15
Thomas Rae, Gatehouse	15
W. Nivison, Thornhill	14
R. McDiarmid, Barnbarroch	14
John Murdoch, Castle Douglas	14
Sergeant Robertson, Castle Douglas	14

IV). **Artillery Carbine Prize.** Given by the Association. 1st £10; 2nd £5; 5-rounds at 200 yards.
     Entry 3/-. To be shot for according to Hythe rules by Volunteers of the Galloway Artillery Corps
     and members of the Association, with carbines and ammunition issued by the Artillery Volunteer
     Corps.

Sergeant Marland, Wigtownshire Artillery	14 points.
Gunner Dornan, Wigtownshire Artillery	13
Gunner McLean, Wigtownshire Artillery	13
Sergeant Adair, Wigtownshire Artillery	12
Mr. Welsh, Kirkcudbright Artillery	10
Gunner Shaw, Wigtownshire Artillery	10
Viscount Dalrymple, Wigtownshire Artillery	9

V). **The All Comers Prize.** 1st £8; 2nd £4; 3rd £2. This competition attracted a very large entry.
    Conditions 5 rounds at 300 yards. Hits to be counted and added to points. 3/- per entry.
Competitors to use any kind of rifle, not weighing more than 10lbs. Any position to be used.

R. McDiarmid, Barnbarroch	15 points and hits.
James Mitchell, junior, 4th E.R.V.	14
R. McCulloch, Wigtown	14
J. Muir, New Galloway	14
R. Shaw, New Galloway	14
J. Henderson, Roxburgh	13
Sergeant Brown, New Galloway	13
J. Mitchell, senior, Little Knox	13
Sergeant Miller (no designation)	13
Sergeant R.C. Thomson, Castle Douglas	13

VI). **Result of the Skirmishing Competition.** Each Company represented by a squad of 10 men.
     Prize of £10 with ammunition added.

3rd W.R.V. (Newton Stewart)	38 points.
3rd K.R.V.(New Galloway)	37
2nd K.R.V. (Castle Douglas)	36
1st K.R.V. (Kirkcudbright)	33
5th W.R.V. (Drummore)	26
2nd W.R.V. (Stranraer)	23

VII). **Result of the Volley Firing.** Prize of £10 with ammunition added.

3rd K.R.V. (New Galloway)	60 points.
2nd W.R.V. (Stranraer)	54
1st W .R.V. (Wigtown)	53
3rd W.R.V. (Newton Stewart)	52
5th W.R.V. (Drummore)	52
1st K.R.V. Kirkcudbright)	43

Pool shooting was commenced with a considerable briskness owing to the late hour of starting. This
was at a distance of 200 yards, nothing but 'bulls-eyes' to count. After a deduction of 25% for working
expenses, each 'bulls-eye' scored by a competitor was worth 16/3d. The following were the successful
competitors:

	'Bulls-eyes'	
William McHarrie, Kirkcudbright	2 -	£1. 12. 6d.
D. Telfer, Kirkcudbright	2 -	..
John Anderson, Kirkcudbright	2 -	..
John Henderson, Roxburgh	2 -	..
Peter McBride, Gatehouse	1 -	16s. 3d.
Robert Maxwell, Gatehouse	1 -	..

The shooting finished at 7pm and Colonel Kennedy presented the prizes to the various winners. In giving over the Bronze Medal to Mr. McLurg, he said, he hoped to have the pleasure of seeing him at Wimbledon the following year to compete for the Prince of Wales Prize and that he hoped he would make as good an appearance as Mr. Muir had done. Colonel Kennedy said he was not going to make a speech but he hoped to see them at the Association meeting, in the Stewartry, the next year. The assembly then dispersed.

On the ground, Mr. Dempster of the Grapes Hotel, Newton Stewart, had a large tent, but the demand was much greater than the supply and many of the competitors, at the close of the competition, were disappointed in failing to obtain any refreshment. Captain Maxwell of Glenlee also had a tent on the ground for the sale of ammunition and other accoutrements.

The Castle Douglas, Dumfries and the Portpatrick Railway Companies, ran special trains for the occasion, but that from Dumfries was badly patronised. There was a considerable number from the Stewartry who arrived back at Castle Douglas at 11.30pm and Dumfries an hour later.

In 1863, the funds of the Galloway Volunteer Association were found to be very low and a successful Fete and Review was held in the grounds of Castle Kennedy, Stranraer, the home of the Viscount Dalrymple, Lord Lieutenant of Wigtownshire, to raise funds for the 3rd Annual Meeting of the Association to be held at the Bennan Farm ranges, New Galloway.

3rd Meeting of the Galloway Volunteer Association.

The 3rd Annual meeting of the County Association was held at the ranges on Bennan Farm, New Galloway, on the Portpatrick Railway line, on Saturday, 15th August, 1863. It was felt, by the Council, in view of the disappointing turnout the previous year, that New Galloway railway station and the ranges on Bennan Farm were central to the various Companies of the Galloway Rifles and it was hoped that the change of venue might attract greater crowds.

The targets and butts occupied the slope of a hill on one side of a broad ravine and the firing points were situated at the base of the opposite declivity. The arrangements were once again ably carried out and had the weather been more favourable it may have proved to have been the most successful meeting yet. The wind blew at times a perfect gale up the valley, compelling the riflemen to allow much for its effect. The rain to played its part for waterproof paletots, pocket syphonias and eglinton overcoats severely curtailed the movement required on these occasions. However, great proficiency was exhibited by several of the competitors and the rattling response that the targets gave to the volley firing told just how fatal such leaden showers could be in the face of an oncoming enemy. The shooting at the 'Aunt Sally' was brisk but the bulls-eyes were few and far between and by the end of the competition only three had been scored, making each bulls-eye worth £3, the winners being T.R. Bruce, New Galloway, Sergeant Young, Whithorn, and William Campbell, Stranraer.

The following Company Officers were in attendance:

1st K.R.V.	(Kirkcudbright). -	Captain Hamilton.
2nd	(Castle Douglas). -	Lt. Bell, Ensign Renny.
3rd	(New Galloway). -	Capt. Maxwell, Lt. Craig, Ensign Dalziel.
5th	(Maxwellton). -	Lt. Allan.
1st W.R. V.	(Wigtown). -	Lt. Vans Agnew.
2nd	(Stranraer). -	Capt. Guthrie, Ensign Taylor.
3rd	(Newton Stewart).	Lt. Henry Stuart.
5th	(Drummore). -	Lt. Watson, Ensign Anderson.

Gatehouse and Whithorn Sub-divisions were not formally represented but individual members of the Corps were present.

The numbers who competed for the various prizes was as follows: Bronze Medal - 91; Association

Prize - 34; Volley Firing - 8 squads of 14 men each - 112; All Comers - 74; Colonel Laurie's Prize - 123.

Lt. Col. Clark Kennedy C.B. Colonel Commandant of the Military Train who had once agreed to act as umpire was urgently recalled to London, with his duties being undertaken by the Commanding Officer of the Galloway Rifles, Colonel Laurie. Captain Clark of Dunmuir, Captain Maxwell of Glenlee, Convenor of the Association's committee of management, and Captain and Adjutant Munro, had charge of the general arrangements. Mr. McCutcheon, Hon. Secretary of the Association was assisted by Mr. Farish, Clerk to the Dumfries Militia and five Sergeants from the Dumfries Militia who acted as markers.

Colonel Laurie and Captain Maxwell of Glenlee had marquees on the ground in which they were able to extend their hospitality to their honoured guests and friends.

The ground was kept by the Stewartry Constabulary under the direction of Mr. Johnston, Chief Constable.

The Competition began at 10am. with the following results:-

I). **Ten Pounds Worth of Ammunition.** given by the Association for Volley firing. To be competed for by squads of 14 men belonging to any Volunteer Corps in Galloway.
5 rounds at 400 yards.

	Bulls-eyes.	Centres.	Outers.	Points.
2nd K. R. V. (Castle Douglas)	0	24	31	79
1st W.R.V.(Wigtown)	0	14	35	63
5th K.R.V. (Maxwellton)	3	14	28	62
2nd W.R.V. (Stranraer)	1	14	24	54
3rd K .R.V. (New Galloway) (1 st Section)	0	12	25	49
3rd K.R.V. (New Galloway) (2nd Section)	2	9	27	49
3rd W.R.V. (Newton Stewart)	1	9	24	44
5th W.R.V. (Drummore)	1	4	14	24

The prize was accordingly won by the Castle Douglas Company. The strength of the Company squads was altered from 14, as originally fixed, to 10, but the alteration was objected to. The 1st K.R.V. (Kirkcudbright) Company having only sent a squad of 10 men to compete were unable to take part in the Volley firing.

II). **The Bronze Medal** from the National Rifle Association, with £8 added by the Galloway Association. 2nd prize £2.
5 rounds at 400 yards and 5 rounds at 600 yards. This prize open only to effective Volunteers of the various Corps in Galloway, who have shot in the first class and have obtained a certificate from their Commanding Officer that they have attended at least eight regular company drills during the four preceding months and that they have shot through the second and third classes.

Sergeant McVane, Castle Douglas	22 hits and points.
William Fleming, Stranraer	20
James Turner, New Galloway	20
Alex. Stevenson, New Galloway	19
J. Hewitson, Newton Stewart	19
James Erskine, Newton Stewart	18
Corporal McLean, Stranraer	18
James McCulloch, Wigtown	17
Sergeant Robertson, Castle Douglas	16
Sergeant Skirving, Castle Douglas	16
Sergeant Williamson, Kirkcudbright	16
J. Grierson, Kirkcudbright	15
Corporal Hughan, Whithorn	15
J. McKelvie, New Galloway	15
William Mackie, Wigtown	14
Daniel Henderson, Wigtown	14
George Paton, Wigtown	14
W. Picken, Newton Stewart	14
Corporal Kirk, Castle Douglas	13
G. Anderson, New Galloway	13
R. Montgomery, Castle Douglas	13
Alfred Milman, New Galloway	12

A. Corrie, New Galloway	12 hits & points
J. Grierson, Castle Douglas	12
John McLurg, Drummore	12

The first prize was won by Sergeant McVane, Castle Douglas. William Fleming, Stranraer and Mr. Turner, New Galloway, having tied, shot off with the following result:-
William Fleming 3 points, Mr. Turner 0 points. William Fleming accordingly won 2nd prize.

III). **The Galloway Rifle Association Prize.** given by the Association. 1st prize £8; 2nd prize £2.
    7 rounds at 500 yards. Open to members of the different Corps in Galloway, both honorary and effective and also members of the Association.

Ensign Taylor, Stranraer	16 hits and points.
J. McLurg, Drummore	16
Sergeant McConchie, Newton Stewart	16
J. Dargie, Newton Stewart	15
R. McDiarmid, member of the Association	15
A. McConchie, Newton Stewart	14
John Campbell, Kirkcudbright	14
Sergeant Young, Whithorn	13
Daniel Henderson, Wigtown	13
Sergeant Robertson, Castle Douglas	13
J. Christison, Wigtown	13
A. Stevenson, New Galloway	12
J. Erskine, Newton Stewart	12
J. Hewitson, Newton Stewart	12
John Grierson, Maxwellton	12
Sergeant Thomson, Castle Douglas	12
G. Tait, Maxwellton	12
J. Grierson, Castle Douglas	12
J. Mitchell, Castle Douglas	12
W. Wilson, Wigtown	11
Ensign Craig, Kirkcudbright	11
Shaw, New Galloway	11
William Craig, New Galloway	10
Corporal Kirk, Castle Douglas	10
Corporal McMillan, Maxwellton	10
Sergeant Skirving, Castle Douglas	10

There being no time to shoot off the tie, Ensign Taylor and Mr. McLurg, agreed to divide the two prizes equally between them.

IV). **The Ladies Prize.** 1st prize £6; 2nd prize £3; 3rd prize £1.
    5 rounds at 200 yards. Open to members of the various Corps in Galloway, honorary, effective and members of the Association.

W. Welsh, Kirkcudbright Artillery	15 hits and points.
Lieutenant Watson, Drummore	15
John McConnell, Whithorn	14
W. McNeillie, Member of the Association	14
W. Watson, Drummore	13
Sergeant Robertson, Castle Douglas	13
Sergeant Payne, Kirkcudbright	13
Sergeant George Tait, Maxwellton	13
John Muir, New Galloway	13
Robert McCulloch, Wigtown	13
William McGaw, Drummore	12
J. Henderson, New Galloway	12
W. Heron, Wigtown	12
Sergeant Rigg, Kirkcudbright Artillery	12
J. Grierson, Castle Douglas	12
Joseph Grierson, Castle Douglas	12
Daniel Henderson, Wigtown	12
Sergeant Thomson, Castle Douglas	12

Sergeant R. McConchie, Newton Stewart	12 hits & points
J. Dargie, Newton Stewart	11
Sergeant Anderson, S tranraer	11
Joseph Jibb, Whithorn	11
A. Stevenson, New Galloway	11
W. Anderson, Wigtown	11
Sergeant Waugh, Gatehouse	11
Sergeant W. Brown, Kirkcudbright	11
Capt. Stewart, yngr. Member of Association	10
Corporal McLean, Stranraer	10
Sergeant Shank, Portpatrick Artillery	10
Thomas Campbell, Castle Douglas	10
William Lightbody , Kirkcudbright	10
Corporal McGuffog, Castle Douglas	10
R. Montgomery, Castle Douglas	10
J. Erskine, Newton Stewart	10

In the shoot-off Lt. Watson took 1st Prize, Mr. Welsh, 2nd prize and Mr. McConnell 3rd prize.

V). **The All Comers Prize**. 1st £8; 2nd £4; 3rd £2.
Conditions 5 rounds at 300 yards. Competitors may use any rifle, not weighing more than 10lbs. Any position to be used.

J. McLurg, Drummore, 1st prize	14 hits and points.
Mr. W. Cairns, Gatehouse, 2nd prize	13
J. Murray, Newton Stewart, 3rd after shoot-out	12
R. Picken, Newton Stewart	12
Captain Oxley, Member of Association	12
R. Shaw, New Galloway	12
T. R. Bruce, New Galloway	12
J. Erskine, Newton Stewart	11
Captain Stewart, Member of Association	11
G. Anderson, New Galloway	11
Sergeant Christison, Wigtown	11
Sergeant McCulloch, Drummore	10
Sergeant Rigg, Kirkcudbright Artillery	10
James Mitchell, Castle Douglas	10
A. McConchie, Newton Stewart	9
Thomas Brown, Stranraer	9
W.G. Inglis, Stranraer	9
Sergeant Williamson, Kirkcudbright	9
J. Muir, New Galloway	9
D. Henderson, Wigtown	8
J. McCulloch, Wigtown	8
Sergeant Waugh, Gatehouse	8
J. Bruce, Member of Association	8
Sergeant Payne, Kirkcudbright	8
J. Campbell, Kirkcudbright	8

VI). **The Artillery Carbine Prize**. given by the Association. 1st £8, 2nd £2. 5 rounds at 200 yards. For Volunteers of the Galloway Corps and members of the Association with carbines and ammunition issued to Artillery Corps.

J. Grierson, Kirkcudbright, 1st after shoot-out	12
Capt. Oxley, 19th Middlesex R.V. Member of Assoc. (2nd prize after shoot-out).	12
Lieutenant Robertson, Portpatrick Artillery	11
Archibald Crawford, Stranraer	11
James McCulloch, Wigtown	11
Sergeant John Muir, New Galloway	11
Sergeant Payne, Kirkcudbright	11
Corporal McLean, Stranraer	10
Captain Shand, Kirkcudbright Artillery	10
W. Welsh, Kirkcudbright Artillery	10

David Rae, Kirkcudbright Artillery	9
Sergeant Thomson, Castle Douglas	9
John Hannah, Kirkcudbright Artillery	8
Corporal Ritchie	8
J. Duff, ...	8
Sergeant Rigg, ...	8
J. Grierson, Castle Douglas.	8
John Murray, ...	8

VII). **A Field Glass**. presented by Lieutenant-Colonel Laurie, value £6 or £4 in money, at the option of the winner, as a judging distance prize; skirmishing position; 3 rounds each. Open to all effective members of the Galloway Rifle Volunteers.

W. Cairns, Gatehouse,	9 hits and points.
J. McLurg, Drummore	9
Wilson, Wigtown	8
McKie, Wigtown	8
Craig, New Galloway	7
McConchie, Newton Stewart	7
R. Grierson, Castle Douglas	7
Wemyss, Stranraer	7
Ensign Taylor, Stranraer	7
D. McGeorge, Castle Douglas	7
Murdoch, Castle Douglas	7
McKelvie, New Galloway	7
W. Picken, Newton Stewart	7
W. Lightbody, Kirkcudbright	6
Corporal Campbell, ..	6
J. McCulloch, Wigtown	6
D. Pearson, Castle Douglas	6
J. Johnstone, Drummore	6
A. Kirk, Castle Douglas	6
T.R. Bruce, New Galloway	6
T. Crackston, Maxwellton	6
John McConnell, Whithorn	5
Corrie, New Galloway	5
R. Picken, Newton Stewart	5
J. Dargie, Newton Stewart	5
D.G. Williamson, Kirkcudbright	5
J. Grierson, Castle Douglas	5
J. Murdoch, ...	5
Ensign Craig, Kirkcudbright	5
A. Skirving, Castle Douglas	5
J. Henderson, Maxwellton	5
Waugh, Gatehouse,	5
Christison, Wigtown	5

There was a tie between Messrs Cairns and McLurg at 9 points but owing to the Stranraer train being nearly due, there was no time to shoot-off the tie and they accordingly agreed to divide the value of the prize.

The competition terminated at 7.30pm and the Volunteers were assembled by a bugle call to the Secretary's tent, where they were addressed by Col. Laurie. He congratulated the competitors, notwithstanding the weather, together with those responsible for the arrangements of the competition. He presented the prizes, with three cheers being given for Sergeant McVane, 2nd K.R.V. Castle Douglas, the winner of the Bronze Medal.

Colonel Laurie then intimated that he intended to present a rifle for Battalion drill. He had written to Colonel McMurdo of the Dumfries Militia, who advised him that any four Companies meeting together, to the number of 128 men would entitle them to a Government grant. He therefore proposed to hold a Battalion drill at Castle Douglas on Saturday next, 22nd August.

Various speeches were to continue in a patriotic manner and in praise of the Volunteers culminating in three cheers for the Queen.

On the 26th November, 1863, a meeting of the Council of the Galloway Volunteer Association was held in the Douglas Arms, Castle Douglas. Those present:- Lord Selkirk; Lord Dalrymple, Presidents of the

Association; Lt. Col. Laurie, Woodhall; Col. Clark Kennedy Knockgray; Captain Shand, Oakley House, Kirkcudbright Artillery; Captain Hamilton, Barwhinnoch; Captain Mackie, M.P.; Captain Maxwell, Glenlee; Captain Howat, Mabie; Captain Guthrie, Stranraer Lt. Vans Agnew, Barnbarroch; Lt. Stuart, Corsbie West, W. H. Maxwell, Munches; Captain Clark of Dunmuir; Sir William Wallace Bart., of Lochryan; Captain and Adjutant, Munro, Valleyfield House; Ensign Renny, Danevale; Mr. Skirving of the Croys.

Amongst various matters for discussion was the title of the Association, which was considered by the Galloway Artillery Volunteers, as being unrepresentative of a united body. On an application of Captain Shand, 1st Kirkcudbright Artillery Volunteers, Kirkcudbright, strongly supported by the Earl of Selkirk and Viscount Dalrymple, the Commanding Officer of the 1st Wigtownshire Artillery Volunteers, Stranraer, the title was unanimously changed to that of the Galloway Artillery and Rifle Volunteer Association.

It was further reported at this meeting that the balance of funds of the Association were extremely low, being £5.16s.11d, and it was agreed to make an appeal to the proprietors of Galloway for additional subscriptions. It was later reported that the sum of £98.14s.0d had been raised.

4th Meeting of the Galloway Artillery and Rifle Volunteer Association.

This fourth annual gathering of the County Association took place on Tuesday, 20th June, 1864, on the same range as the previous year, the farm of Bennan, New Galloway, it being felt by the Council that this location was central to the various Volunteer Companies of Galloway and easily accessible by rail.

The ground was well suited as a rifle range, occupying about three quarters of a natural amphitheatre. The butts and targets, 7 in all besides the 'Aunt Sally' and Pool targets, were placed at their respective distances on the slopes of the curve of the hill which bounded the range on the west, commencing from south to north in the following order, No.1 550 yards - **All Comers Prize**. No.2 600 yards - **Bronze Medal**. No.3 400 yards - **Bronze Medal**. No.4 500 yards - **Silver Challenge Cup**. No. 5 300 yards - **Gold Medal**. No.6 400 yards - **Rifle** presented by Col. Laurie. No.7 200 yards - **Artillery Carbine Prize**, also used for Consolation Prize. The Pool targets, of a new construction of wood and iron plate, 4 inches square, fixed to a centre, having a bell attached, which rang loudly when struck by a bullet, but soon after firing commenced it was found not to be satisfactory, were placed to the north of the above targets, and still further on was the Skirmishing ground. Payment to the ground was 1/-. The spectators had an excellent full and close view of the proceedings all around, especially from a green knoll on which the flagstaff was placed.

The ground was once again prepared by Captain Clark of Dunmuir and Captain Maxwell of Glenlee, Convenor of the Committee of Management. Lt. Col. Clark Kennedy, C.B. Colonel Commandant of the Military Train once again acted as Umpire. The Hon. Secretaries were Messrs. R.C. Thomson, Castle Douglas and James Andrew, Stranraer.

The weather was unfavourable for testing the true skills of the Volunteers, the wind blew strongly from the west all day, notwithstanding the windscreens erected at each of the firing points. The wind came in heavy sweeping gusts accompanied by rain, forcing the spectators to suspend the firing during a good deal of the time. Towards the evening, the weather cleared up and the wind settled to a calm but it was unfortunately too late for the unlucky competitors.

The competitors numbered 150, the largest proportion coming from the Stewartry. Those from Wigtownshire were chiefly from the 1st W.R.V. Wigtown and the 3rd W.R.V. Newton Stewart. The 2nd W.R.V. Stranraer, 4th W.R.V. Whithorn and 5th W.R.V. Drummore were only represented by about 6 competitors from each. Lt. Col. Laurie and Captain and Adjutant Munro were in attendance with the following Field Officers commanding the various Companies:-

Wigtownshire.	1st W.R.V. Wigtown - Lt. Vans Agnew and Ensign McHaffie;
	2nd .. Stranraer - Lt. Taylor and Ensign Andrews;
	3rd .. Newton Stewart - Captain Stuart;
	4th .. Whithorn Ensign Drew.
	5th .. Drummore - Lt. Watson and Ensign Anderson.,
Kirkcudbrightshire.	1st K.R.V. Kirkcudbright - Captain Hamilton and Ensign Craig;
	2nd .. Castle Douglas - Lt. Bell, Ensign Renny;
	3rd .. New Galloway - Captain Maxwell and Ensign Dalziel;
	4th .. Gatehouse - No Officers;
	5th .. Maxwellton - Captain Howat and Ensign Allan.

At 10am the bugle called the Competitors to the Secretary's tent where Col. Clark Kennedy reminded them of his duties before proceedings commenced with the following results :

I). **A Silver Challenge Cup**, given by the Earl of Selkirk, Lord Lt., of the Stewartry to the Galloway Rifle Battalion of Volunteers, with £5 added by the Association. Distances between 200 and 400 yards. 9 squads of two men took part in this competition, each Corps competing having been required to shoot, previous to the meeting of the Association, on its own range a series of qualifying competitions.

	Centres	Outers	Points
1st Wigtownshire (Wigtown) - J. McCulloch, J. Christison (Winners)	2	2	7
2nd Kirkcudbright (Castle Douglas)- Sergeants Thomson and Robertson	1	4	6
3rd Kirkcudbright (New Galloway) - Privates Craig and Coskerie	0	5	5
4th Kirkcudbright (Gatehouse) - Sergeants Waugh and Cairns	0	5	5
5th Kirkcudbright (Maxwellton)- Sergeant Tait and Corporal McMillan	0	4	4
2nd Kirkcudbright (Castle Douglas) - Corporal Kirk, Mr. McGuffog	1	1	3
3rd Wigtownshire (Newton Stewart) Sergeant Hewitson, Sergeant Picken	0	2	2
1st Kirkcudbright (Kirkcudbright) - Sergeants Payne and Grierson	0	1	1
5th Kirkcudbright (Maxwellton) - Sergeants Rae and Crackston	0	1	1

II). **The Bronze Medal** from the National Rifle Association with £10 added by the Galloway Association. The winner being eligible to shoot at Wimbledon in the Prince of Wales's Prize, 2nd Prize £2.

5 rounds at 400 yards and 5 rounds at 600 yards. There were 64 entries.

Sergeant James Andrews, Stranraer (1st Prize)	25 points
Sergeant Stewart, Newton Stewart (2nd prize)	25
Sergeant Wm. Heron, Wigtown (after shoot-out)	25
Joseph Grierson, Castle Douglas	22
James Henderson, ...	22
Wm. Craig, New Galloway	21
Robert Shaw, ...	21
W. Picken, Newton Stewart	21
John McLurg, Drummore	21
Sergeant J. Thomson, Castle Douglas	20
Private Thomas Rae, Whithorn	19
Sergeant G.D. Williamson, Kirkcudbright	18
Sergeant Crackston, Maxwellton	17
John Wilson, Castle Douglas	17
William Agnew, Newton Stewart	17
John Murdoch, Castle Douglas	17
Sergeant S. McCulloch, Drummore	16
Lieutenant Watson, ..	16
Alex. Stevenson, New Galloway	16
J. McCulloch, Wigtown	16
James Grierson, Castle Douglas	16
James Erskine. Newton Stewart	15
W. Anderson, ..	15
T. R. Bruce, New Galloway	15
Corporal McGuffog, Castle Douglas	15
Corporal McMillan, Drummore	14
Corporal J. McConnell, Whithorn	13
Sergeant James Payne, Kirkcudbright	13
George Geddes, New Galloway	13
Sergeant Robertson, Castle Douglas	13
D. Henderson, Wigtown	12
W. McCulloch, Drummore	11
James Turner, New Galloway	11
Sergeant H. Hughan, Whithorn	10

III). **A Silver Challenge Cup** presented to the Galloway Rifle Battalion of Volunteers by James Mackie Esq., M.P. for the Stewartry of Kirkcudbright, with £10 added by the Association. 2nd Prize £2.   5 rounds at 500 yards. 67 Entries.

Dr. Millman, New Galloway (1st prize)	14
Private R. Shaw, ... (2nd prize)	14
Ensign Craig, Kirkcudbright	14
Sergeant McConchie, Newton Stewart	14
Joseph Grierson, Kirkcudbright	13
Sergeant Robertson, Castle Douglas	13
Sergeant John Muir, New Galloway	12
William Watson, Drummore	12
George Geddes, New Galloway	11
John McLurg, Drummore	11
James McCulloch, Wigtown	10
Adam Corrie, New Galloway	10
W. Craig, ...	10
Sergeant Hewetson, Newton Stewart	10
T. R. Bruce, New Galloway	9
J. Christison, Wigtown	9
Joseph Grierson, Castle Douglas	9
John Erskine, Newton Stewart	9
D. Henderson, Wigtown	8
James Grierson, Castle Douglas	8
John Campbell, Kirkcudbright	7
Robert McKay, New Galloway	7
G. Papple, Castle Douglas	7
Sergeant McCulloch, Newton Stewart	7
Archibald Crawford, Stranraer	7
Ensign Stroyan, Newton Stewart	6
Lieutenant Watson, Drummore	6
Sergeant McCulloch ..	6

IV). **A Rifle value 15 guineas, with ammunition,** presented to the Galloway Rifle Battalion of Volunteers, by Lieutenant-Colonel Laurie, Commanding Officer. 5 rounds at 400 yards. 79 entries.

Sergeant John Muir, New Galloway (Winner)	17
W. Anderson, Wigtown	17
James McCulloch, Wigtown	17
J. Grierson, Castle Douglas	15
D. Henderson, Wigtown	15
John Murdoch, Castle Douglas	15
James Mitchell, ...	15
Ensign Taylor, Newton Stewart	14
J. Grierson, Kirkcudbright	14
Archibald Kerr, New Galloway	13
W. Heron, Wigtown	13
Sergeant Robinson, Castle Douglas	13
Sergeant McConchie, Newton Stewart	12
Thomas Brown, New Galloway	12
Sergeant Waugh, Gatehouse	12
Corporal McGuffog, Castle Douglas	12
J. Christison, Wigtown	12
Sergeant Mackie, Newton Stewart	12
Corporal McConchie	9
Corporal Agne	9
G. Geddes, New Galloway	8
Thomas Rae, Whithorn	8
George McConnell, Whithorn	8
Sergeant Wigham Whithorn	5

V). **Gold Medal.** or £4 of money, at the option of the winner for first prize. £3 for 2nd prize. £2 for 3rd Prize. £1 for fourth prize. Presented to the Officers and Members of the Galloway Rifle Battalion of Volunteers by Captain Munro the Adjutant.
5 rounds at 300 yards, 62 entries.

Sergeant J. Wilson, New Galloway (1st)	13 points.
Sergeant Waugh, Gatehouse (2nd)	12
Sergeant R. C. Thomson, Castle Douglas (3rd)	10
Archibald Crawford, Stranraer (4th)	9
Robert McClymont, Newton Stewart	9
Corporal Dargie, ...	9
Thomas Hogg, Castle Douglas	9
Thomas Rae, Whithorn	9
James Henderson, Castle Douglas	9
Sergeant James Andrews, Stranraer	8
James Erskine, New Galloway	8
W. R. McDowall, Castle Douglas	7
J. Murdoch, ...	7
Corporal McMillan, Maxwellton	5

VI). **Carbine Sweepstake.** Prize three-quarters of entry money.
5 rounds at 200 yards.

Private T.R. Bruce, New Galloway (winner)	14 points.
Joseph Grierson, Kirkcudbright	8
Sergeant Payne, ..	8
Sergeant Thomson, Castle Douglas	4

VII). **The All Comers Prize of £10** given by the Association. 1st prize £7. 2nd prize £3.
5 rounds at 550 yards. 32 entries.

Sergeant John Muir, New Galloway (1st)	18 points.
Corporal Agnew, Newton Stewart (2nd)	18
Sergeant Hewetson, Newton Stewart	16
Corporal McConchie, Newton Stewart	15
G. Anderson, New Galloway	15
Wm. Cairns, Gatehouse	14
James Erskine, Newton Stewart	14
J. Chisholm, Slogarie	14
J. McLurg, Drummore	13
Campbell, Castle Douglas	12
D. Williamson, Kirkcudbright	11
William Picken, Newton Stewart	8
D. Telfer, Culhorn	5

(Much interest was taken in a beautiful Henry rifle used by Mr.D. Telfer, Culhorn, which was valued at £25.)

VIII). **Consolation Prize.** given by the Association. 1st £4. 2nd £1.
3 rounds at 200 yards. 53 entries.

Sergeant Robertson, Castle Douglas (1st)	10 points.
Corporal McConchie, Newton Stewart (2nd)	10
James McCulloch, Wigtown	9
John McLurg, Drummore	9
David Telfer, Culhorn	9
Sergeant W. McCulloch, Wigtown	9
Sergeant Payne , Kirkcudbright	8
Sergeant S. McCulloch, Drummore	8
Corporal Dargie, Newton Stewart	8
George Geddes, New Galloway	8
James Mitchell, Castle Douglas	8
Joseph Grierson, Castle Douglas	8
Ensign Anderson, Drummore	8
Lieutenant Watson, ..	7
William Watson, ..	7
D. B. Hannah, Kirkcudbright	7
Adam Currie, New Galloway	6

The Pool or Aunt Sally Targets, two in number were well patronised.

The total drawings at 6d each shot amounted to £8. 9s. 0d - less 25%, was divided into eight shares of 15/6d each and given to the following parties who made one or more bulls-eyes. David Telfer, Culhorn, 2 shares £1.11s.; Sergeant Cairns, Gatehouse 3 shares, £2. 6s. 6d; John Chisholm, Slogarie, 1 share 15/6d. T.W. Campbell, Walton Park, Castle Douglas, 1 share 15/6d.

The proceedings finished just before the last westbound train to Stranraer and Newton Stewart at 6.30pm when the prizes were quickly distributed.

ABSTRACT OF INCOME AND EXPENDITURE OF THE GALLOWAY ARTILLERY AND RIFLE VOLUNTEER ASSOCIATION - 1861-1864.

Year 1861 - at Castle Douglas.

Income -	£367.12s.6d	Expenditure		£277. 7s. 1d
			Balance	90. 5s. 5d
	---------------			---------------
	£367.12s.6d			£367.12s. 6d.

Year 1862 - at Glenluce.

Balance -	£90. 5s. 5d	Expenditure	£213. 13s. 6d.
Income	£123. 5s. 4d		
Balance due Treas.	2s. 9d		
	---------------		---------------
	£213. 13s. 6d		£213. 13s. 6d.

Year 1863 - at New Galloway.

Income -	£144.11s. 3d	Balance		2s. 9d
		Expenditure		£138. 11s. 7d
			Balance	£5. 16s.11d
	---------------			---------------
	£144. 11s.3d.			£144. 11s. 3d.

Year 1864 - at New Galloway.

Income.

	£. s. d.
Balance from last year's Accounts -	5. 16s. 11d
Subscription from Advertisement in *Kirkcudbrightshire Advertiser* -	98. 14s. 0d
Annual Subscriptions -	2. 10s. 6d
Entries to various competitions -	51. 10s. 6d
Pool Targets -	2. 4s. 0d
Sighting Shots -	4. 18s. 0d
Admission to ground -	1. 5s. 0d
	£166. 18s. 5d.

Expenditure.

Prizes -	40. 7s. 6d
Advertising, printing, stationery, etc. -	24. 19s. 8d
Labour for preparing range -	4. 19s. 6d
Cartage -	1. 4s. 6d
Wood, nails, paint, glue -	2. 1s.11d
Railway carriage of Iron plate targets and tents -	4. 17s. 9d
Making up registers -	5. 8s. 2d
Subscriptions to National Association -	5. 0s. 0d
Attendance of Police -	1. 8s. 6d
Markers -	6. 12s. 0d
Mr. McCutcheon for staty. and post. since last competition	2. 10s. 4d
Ammunition -	6. 0s. 0d
Honorarium to the Secretary -	3. 3s. 0d
4 full length targets and other permanent property purchase	16. 15s 7d
Unpaid Subscriptions -	3. 3s. 0d
Balance at credit of acct. with National Bank of Scotland -	38. 10s. 0d
	£166.18s. 5d.

19th September, 1864, examined and found correct, W. Kennedy Laurie, Lt. Col.

5th Meeting of the Galloway Artillery and Rifle Volunteer Association.

The 5th annual County Association meeting of the Galloway Artillery and Rifle Volunteers took place once again on the ranges at Bennan Farm, New Galloway, on Wednesday, 14th June, 1865. Colonel Clark Kennedy, C.B. acted as Umpire. No members of the 5th Kirkcudbright Rifle Volunteers (Maxwellton) were present owing to the competition having been fixed on the Dumfries Market Day.

The following was the parade state of the Company Officers:

Lt. Col. Laurie, Commanding.		
1st K.R.V.	Kirkcudbright; Captain Hamilton, Ensign Craig.	
2nd ..	Castle Douglas; Lt. Bell, Ensign Renny.	
3rd ..	New Galloway; Captain Maxwell, Ensign Dalziel.	
1st W.R.V.	Wigtown; Lt. Vans Agnew.	
2nd ..	Stranraer; Captain Guthrie, Lt. Taylor.	
3rd ..	Newton Stewart; Ensign Stroyan.	
4th ..	Whithorn; Ensign McHaffie.	

The following are the results of the several competitions:-

I) **A Silver Challenge Cup**, presented by the Earl of Selkirk to the Galloway Battalion of Rifle Volunteers for skirmishing at 200 yards. £5 added by the Association.

2nd K.R.V.	(Castle Douglas)	36 points.
3rd ..	(New Galloway)	35
3rd W.R.V.	(Newton Stewart)	24
1st ..	(Wigtown)	17

II). **A Silver Challenge Cup**, presented by Lieutenant-Colonel Laurie to the Galloway Battalion of Rifle Volunteers for Volley firing at 400 yards. £5 added by the Association.

3rd K.R.V.	(New Galloway)	80 points.
3rd W.R.V.	(Newton Stewart)	68
2nd K.R.V.	(Castle Douglas)	64
2nd W.R.V.	(Stranraer)	54
1st ..	(Wigtown)	37

III). **Bronze Medal** of the National Rifle Association with £12 added by the Association. Conditions - 5 rounds at 200yds, 500yds and 600yd.

Corporal Picken, Newton Stewart (1st - £8)	40 points.
Sergeant Cairns, Gatehouse, (2nd - £2)	38
Private James Grierson, Castle Douglas (3rd - £1)	38
William Craig, New Galloway (4th - £1)	37
Sergeant Agnew, Newton Stewart	37
Sergeant Muir, New Galloway	36
Joseph Grierson, Castle Douglas,	35
Private J. Picken, Newton Stewart	34
Sergeant Skirving, Castle Douglas	33
R. Shaw, New Galloway	33
Private A. Stevenson, New Galloway	32
Gilbert Anderson, New Galloway	32
Sergeant R. C. Thomson, Castle Douglas	31
D. Henderson, Wigtown	31
Gordon Papple, Castle Douglas	30
James Mitchell, Castle Douglas	28
Private Erskine, Newton Stewart	28

IV). **A Silver Challenge Cup** presented by James Mackie Esq., M.P. to the Galloway Battalion of Rifle Volunteers with £12 added by the Association.

5 rounds at 500 yards.

Joseph Grierson, Kirkcudbright (1st - £4)	16
Sergeant Skirving, Castle Douglas (2nd - £2)	15
Sergeant A. McConchie, Newton Stewart (3rd-£1)	15
Thomas Rae, Gatehouse (4th - £1)	15
Alex. Stevenson, New Galloway (5th - £1)	15
James Erskine, Newton Stewart (6th - £1)	15
A. Kerr, New Galloway (7th - £1)	14
H. McCrae, Stranraer (8th - 10/-)	14
R. Shaw, New Galloway (9th - 10/-)	14
Sergeant Cairns, Gatehouse	13
Sergeant Stewart, Newton Stewart	13
W. Picken, Newton Stewart	13
T.W. Campbell, Castle Douglas	12
W. Craig, New Galloway	12
W. Hamilton, New Galloway	12
Sergeant Waugh, Gatehouse	11
James Grierson, Castle Douglas	11
J. Christison, Wigtown	11
Sergeant R. C. Thomson, Castle Douglas	11
Sergeant John Muir, New Galloway	10
D. Henderson, Wigtown	10
J. A. McConnell, Gatehouse	10
J. Wilson, New Galloway	10
G. Geddes, New Galloway	10

V). **£11 given by Captain Munro**. Adjutant. to the Galloway Rifle Volunteers.

5 rounds at 200 yards. The 1st prize to be a gold medal or £3 at the option of the winner.

J. Muir, New Galloway (1st - £3 or gold medal)	16 points.
Private J. Murdoch, Castle Douglas (2nd - £2)	16
Private J. Osborne, Kirkcudbright (3rd - £1)	14
Private G. Geddes, New Galloway (4th - £1)	14
Private J. Picken, Newton Stewart (5th - £1)	14
Private J. Erskine, Newton Stewart (6th - £1)	14
Corporal Agnew, Stranraer (7th - £1)	14
Private J. Christison, Wigtown (8th - 10/-)	13
Private J. McKelvie, New Galloway (9th - 10/-)	13
Private G. Papple, Castle Douglas	13
Private R. Dickie, Gatehouse	13
Private G. McClymont, Newton Stewart	13
Private C. Kerr, Stranraer	13
Corporal Patton, Wigtown	13
Private A. Stevenson, New Galloway	13
Sergeant Skirving, Castle Douglas	12
Private Joseph Grierson, Castle Douglas	12
Private J. Grierson, Kirkcudbright	12
Private J. Mosscroft, New Galloway	12
Private J. Laird, Wigtown	12
Private John McKie, New Galloway	12
Private A. Kerr, New Galloway	12
Private W. Craig, New Galloway	12
Private D. Henderson, Wigtown	11
Private E. Brown, Wigtown	11
Captain Guthrie, Stranraer	10
Private John Gardiner, New Galloway	10
Private R. Johnstone, New Galloway	10
Sergeant Black, Stranraer	10
Private T. Farrell, Kirkcudbright	10
Private H. McCrae, Stranraer	10
Private J. McAdam, Gatehouse	10
Sergeant McCulloch, Wigtown	10
Private J. Hinds, Newton Stewart	10
Private T. Rae, Gatehouse	10

VI). **Carbine Prize of £5** given by the Association. This competition open only to Artillery Volunteers.
5 rounds at 200 yards.

Sergeant J. McDowall, Portpatrick (1 st - £3)	11 points.
Gunner W. Cairns, Kirkcudbright (2nd - £1)	10
Gunner W. Welsh, Kirkcudbright (3rd - £1)	9
Gunner T. Gray, Portpatrick	9
Gunner J. Shanks, Portpatrick	8
Gunner C. Smith, Portpatrick	8
Captain Shand, Kirkcudbright	7
Corporal Biggam, Portpatrick	7
Gunner J. Hannay, Kirkcudbright	6
Sergeant Major Haining, Portpatrick	5
Sergeant Rigg, Kirkcudbright	4

VII). **All Comers Prize of £11**, given by the Association.
5 rounds at 500 yards.

T.R. Bruce, Slogarie, New Galloway (1 st - £4)	19 points.
Sergeant J. Wilson, New Galloway (2nd - £3)	18
Private George Geddes, New Galloway (3rd - £2)	17
Sergeant W. Cairns, Gatehouse (4th - £1)	16
J. Mosscroft, Newton Stewart (5th - 10/-)	16
Sergeant R.C. Thomson, Castle Douglas (6th - 10/-)	16
Sergeant J. Muir, New Galloway	15
J. Erskine, Newton Stewart	15
J. Chisholm, New Galloway	15
James Mitchell, Castle Douglas	15
Sergeant Hewitson, Newton Stewart	15
W. Picken, Newton Stewart	14
T.W. Campbell, Castle Douglas	14
A. Anderson, New Galloway	14
Archibald Kerr, New Galloway	14
R. Shaw, New Galloway	14
Joseph Grierson, Castle Douglas	14
Sergeant W. Agnew, Newton Stewart	12
Corporal McGuffog, Castle Douglas	12
J. Stodart, New Galloway	12
J. Grierson, Castle Douglas	12
W. Turner, New Galloway	12

VIII). **Prize of £5** given by Captain Maxwell, Glenlee, for the Volunteer of the Galloway Rifles, who makes the highest aggregate score in all the prizes.

	Bronze Medal.	Members Cup.	All Comers.	Aggregate.
Corporal W .Picken, Newton Stewart (joint winner)	40	13	14	67
Sergeant Cairns, Gatehouse (joint winner)	38	13	16	67
A. Kerr, New Galloway	37	14	14	65
Sergeant R.C. Thomson, Castle Douglas	31	11	16	58
Sergeant Agnew, Newton Stewart	37	8	12	57
James Erskine, Newton Stewart	28	14	15	57
James Grierson, Castle Douglas	38	11	5	54
Sergeant J. Wilson, New Galloway	25	10	18	53
William Craig, New Galloway	37	-	14	51
George Geddes, New Galloway	24	10	17	51
Joseph Grierson, Castle Douglas	35	14	-	49
Sergeant Skirving, Castle Douglas	33	15	-	48
Joseph Grierson, Kirkcudbright	21	16	11	48
R. Shaw, New Galloway	33	14	-	47
A. Stevenson, New Galloway	32	15	-	47
T. Rae, Whithorn	24	15	-	39

No score (-) indicates that the rifleman did not compete in that event.

Unquestionably the most popular phase of the Volunteer Movement was to be that of rifle shooting, its fascination being owed largely to its competitive nature, not only was the competitor in competition with his brother Volunteer but with himself, his highest record always being that competitive object. However, while this was so, a stimulus had to be provided, in some tangible form to sustain the interest of the Volunteer.

From the inception of the Volunteer Movement, cash prizes were offered for Company competitions and with the formation of County Associations throughout the United Kingdom, cash prizes were offered, not only for the Volunteers from that particular County, but to Volunteers from outwith the region, to encourage regional competitiveness and thus increase the standard and competitive standard of the homebased Volunteer. From the performance at these competitions there was also the desire among the Volunteers to hold a meeting to decide the 'Top-Shot' in the United Kingdom and once again cash prizes were to be the mainstay of these competitions. The following advice being offered to the novice by a veteran of the Galloway Rifles in their *Regimental Gazette*;

"The first consideration of a competitor is that he should provide himself with a high-class rifle, as a few shillings extra expended in buying a superior weapon, is, as a rule, a good investment. If economy is desired, a Government quality barrel or rifle, can be got through the Commanding Officer at a very low price. Some of the rifles are excellent but they generally require to be regulated and refitted to bring out their best shooting capabilities. At Bisley, a shooter should be prepared for an expenditure of £10-£12 and should either look on this as holiday expenses or as an investment for which he may get a return in the form of prizes."

This was to become a regular occurrence for the 'top-shots' of Regiments, to travel all over the Country in search of these lucrative cash prizes, leading to jibes from the Regular Army of 'Gold Hunter' or 'Gold Diggers' and 'Pot Hunters', with no interest in the military aspect of the movement.

Sergeant McNeil of the Dumfries Volunteers was to write an article on 'hints to recruits'

"I would commence by saying to the recruit having joined the Volunteer Force and being desirous of becoming a shot, let me ask you to remember that, important as that part of your duty may be, it is only a part, drill and shooting are the two duties you are called to learn, and I would urge you on the necessity of devoting much of you spare time to both. If you take up with enthusiasm the shooting side only, you will become a miserable, 'Pot Hunter' and rob yourself of much pleasure and many of the benefits to be gained by being a good all round Volunteer."

However, in spite of Sergeant McNeil's fine words, within the Galloway Rifle battalion, and in common with the other Volunteer Regiments and Associations of the day, Company and County Associations were held not only with large cash prizes being on offer but also for the Volunteers right to represent their Regiment at Wimbledon and other Major Volunteer venues, with even more lucrative cash prizes to be won, indeed the 'Queen's Prize' offering the vast sum of £250.

The Bronze Medal of the National Rifle Association, for competition at the County meeting was issued subject to the winner attending Wimbledon to shoot in the Prince of Wales Prize, value £100.

From 1861, the West of Scotland Rifle Association meeting was held on the sands at Irvine, with qualification through Regimental and Company competitions.

In 1862, a series of Company contests were held in Galloway to pick representatives to compete in the Caledonian Challenge Shield, held in Edinburgh. This again was to become a Major, annual event.

On the 31st October, 1863, at Newton Stewart a competition took place to decide who was to have the honour of representing the battalion in the St. George's Challenge Vase, at Wimbledon,

5 rounds at 200 yards and 5 rounds at 500 yards.

1st Private J. Christison, Wigtown	31 points.
2nd J. Muir, New Galloway	27

From the outset, the 'top-shots' of the Galloway Rifle Volunteers, in common with the marksmen from the other Volunteer Regiments, travelled to all the Major competition venues and other County Association Meetings, winning the lucrative cash prizes on offer, with the culmination of the cash bonanza, being the several competitions of 'Wimbledon Week'. Members of the Galloway Rifles were frequently participating in and winning cash prizes at such events. However, it was not until the 11th July, 1865, that the Regiment was to have its first National winner at Wimbledon. Shooting in the Alexandra Prize at 500 yards, Sergeant R. C. Thomson, Castle Douglas, was to win the event, receiving a handsome silver cup and cash prize. In the same Wimbledon week, Private T.R. Bruce, Slogarie, New Galloway was ranked among the highest scores in the Enfield Association Cup, winning a substantial cash award. Sergeant Cairns, Gatehouse, was to win a cash prize in the 'Five Groove' rifle competition.

In Wimbledon week 1866, Corporal Picken, Newton Stewart, was the first successful competitor of the Galloway Rifles to win through to the final stage of the 'Queen's Prize', being presented with the 'Queen's Badge' and £12.

On the 5th July, 1872, Captain Craig, Sergeants Osborne and Campbell, Kirkcudbright, and Captain Skirving, Castle Douglas, represented their Companies at the National Rifle Association meeting of 'Wimbledon Week'.

On Thursday/Friday/Saturday, 6th/7th/8th June, 1878, at the West of Scotland Rifle Association meeting at Irvine, on the Thursday, shooting for the Championship Prize (1st stage) Corporal Hyslop, 1st Lanark and Private J. Grierson, Castle Douglas, tied for the 1st place with a score of 90 points out of a possible 105. In the shoot-off, Private Grierson was placed 2nd winning a prize of £15. At the same meeting Lieutenant Muir, Kirkcudbright, won £1, being 25th in the Ironbroker's prize and in the New Club Prize, Private J. Grierson, Castle Douglas, was again successful, winning £1, being placed 14th.

On the Friday, Colour Sergeant Osborne, Kirkcudbright, shooting for the Renfrewshire Prizes, gained £3 and £7, with a score of 87 points. Private Lawson, Maxwellton, gained £1 in the same competition with a score of 73 points. In the Military breechloader Prize, T.R. Bruce, New Galloway, was 3rd, gaining a prize of £3. Colour Sergeant Osborne was again successful in the Aggregate scores gaining 11th place and the sum of £2.

On the Saturday, 8th June, 1878, the principal competition of the West of Scotland Rifle Association meeting, which attracted most attention was the 2nd stage of the Championship Prize, a Gold Medal and £20. This was the 'Blue Riband' event of the meeting. The 20 highest scorers in the 1st stage were entitled to compete. The match was 15 rounds, with Martini-Henry rifles, issued for this purpose by the Association, who had received them from Government.

Just after mid-day gunfire, the competitors for the 2nd stage of the competition, were paraded at the 600 yard range, by Captain Lysons, the Executive Officer, and were detailed to their several targets. Scarcely had they taken their positions when the rain fell in torrents. The men continued at their posts, completing the competition amidst great discomfort. No sighting shots were allowed for this event but Private J. Grierson, Castle Douglas was fortunate to catch a bull with his first shot, he only brought out the red disc (marker) with his next shot but he kept well on the target making 5 bulls and a Magpie (outer) on his next six shots. He concluded his score with 63 points Sergeant Simpson, Edinburgh, was to come second in the event with a score of 62 points.

Private J. Grierson's score was as follows: 5 4 4 4 4 5 3 2 4 5 5 5 3 5 5 - 63 points.

After the event was decided four men seized Private Grierson and paraded him shoulder high around the ground with the band in procession playing 'See the Conquering Hero Comes'. Lieutenant Colonel Todd of the 1st Lanark presented Private Grierson with the gold medal and £20. (Private Grierson was placed 6th in the same competition the year previous.)

On Friday, 12th July, 1878, at the Wimbledon Meeting, shooting in the St. George's Challenge Vase, Corporal Agnew, Newton Stewart, scored 29 points, Sergeant Armstrong, Maxwellton, scored 27 points, Sergeant Service, Maxwellton, scored 26 points and Private Lawson, Maxwellton scored 20 points, all winning cash prizes. The winning score was 34 points. In the Alexandra Prize, the 1st prize of £50 was won by a score of 63 points, Private Lawson, Maxwellton, was again successful in this competition winning £10 with a score of 58 points.

5th Kirkcudbright Rifle Volunteers. Maxwellton.

Instead of sending men to Edinburgh to shoot for the Caledonian Shield, the Company decided to send two representatives to Wimbledon to compete for the "Queen's" and "St. George's" Prizes, and for the selection of the two members, a series of four competitions were held, with the three highest scores out of the four competitions to count, the following being the result:-

	1st	2nd	3rd	Total.
Private J. Briggs (1st)	68	68	74	210
Sergeant R. Armstrong (2nd)	73	71	65	209
Private A. Lawson	67	63	67	197
Private C. Armstrong	66	68	60	194
Sergeant D. Cameron	63	67	59	189
Sergeant D. Johnstone	70	61	52	183
Private J. Beattie	58	66	58	182
Corporal J. Taylor	65	64	47	176
Corporal A. Roberts	64	54	57	175

To improve their shooting capabilities and competitiveness in competition, the 'top-shots' of the several Companies of the Galloway Rifle Battalion, formed their own shooting clubs with membership restricted to those of a particular standard. The first of such clubs to be formed was in May, 1884, in Kirkcudbright, the club being known as the, 'A' Company, Galloway Rifle Volunteers (Kirkcudbright) Shooting Club".

Again, to improve his marksmanship, as far back as 1867, T.R. Bruce, Slogarie, New Galloway, who had no aspirations of command but who fluctuated between a Private in the Galloway Rifles and an Associate Member, and who was attached, solely to the Regiment for shooting and competition purposes, opened his own private long range on Slogarie, at 800, 900 and 1000 yards. This range was far superior to anything used by the Association and was frequently adopted by the Association and Regiment for inter-County and inter-Regimental Competitions.

In 1897, Captain Angus McPhater, 'D' Company, Newton Stewart, was to make the following observations, "The aim should be to have no less than 12 representatives each year at Bisley, so as to be able to select a team of 10 men to compete for the 'China Cup', of course 12 assisted representatives would be rather a large order, as the sum to each man should be £5. I am inclined to advocate that a number equal to each Company should be aimed at, whether these should be selected by so many shoots, or that each Company should select one by competition are points that could be arranged."

Note. **The China Cup.** was a Challenge Cup, introduced in 1864, for annual competition and was shot for by County Teams at the Wimbledon, later the Bisley meeting of the National Rifle Association.

The Elcho Shield. was a Challenge Cup, presented in 1862, by Lord Elcho.
the 10th Earl of Wemyss and March, and was the International Volunteer Trophy, shot for at Wimbledon, between England, Ireland and Scotland, and later to be joined by the Welsh Volunteers, in teams of eight.

The Scottish Twenty Club was an institution organised with the object of encouraging rifle shooting throughout Scotland and to assist the Captain of the International team in his selection.

The Society of Miniature Rifle Clubs. formed by Lord Roberts, evolved from the Working Men's Rifle Clubs formed after the Boer War to encourage Rifle shooting as a National pursuit. Writing in the January, 1905, issue of the *19th Century and After*, Lord Roberts was to say, 'Our reverses in the Boer War were largely attributable to the fact that our men were unable to shoot and had they been trained to shoot better, some of the unfortunate incidents that occurred in the late War and that of 1880-81 would not have happened.'

An interesting feature appeared in May, 1881, in connection with the 5th Kirkcudbright Rifles (Maxwellton). 'Improved rifle practice. In view of the superiority of rifle shooting shown by the Boer over the British in the current unrest in the Transvaal, it has been established that the Boer is accustomed to shooting at moving targets, whilst the British soldier practices at stationary targets. The 5th Kirkcudbright Rifles have devised a target which is the figure of a man in canvas that is moved to and fro, on wires, by means of pulleys and it is felt that this form of target will enable the men to become more effectual marksmen.'

In Wimbledon Week of July, 1899, on the 21st of that month, three members of the Galloway Rifle Battalion of Volunteers, secured places in the final stages of the 'Queen's Prize', winning the Queen's Badge and cash prizes. Cyclist Geddes' score was equal to that which had won the previous year.

	1st stage.	2nd stage.	3rd stage.	
Cyclist G. Geddes, New Galloway			800 yds.- 39	
(£12 prize money)	93	113	900 yds.- 41	
			1000 yds.- 41	
				121 =326
William McCreadie, Newton Stewart			800 yds. 40	
(£12 prize money)	99	108	900 yds. 42	
			1000 yds. 39	
				119 =326
Cyclist Ferguson, New Galloway			800 yds.39	
(£10 prize money)	94	116	900 yds.39	
			1000 yds.25	
				103 =313

On Thursday/Friday, 14th/15th September, 1899, a team of five Galloway riflemen took part in the annual prize meeting of the Ulster Rifle Association at Kinnegar, Holywood, Belfast. The team was composed of members of the Cyclist Section; Private McHaffie, Stranraer; William McCreadie, Newton Stewart; J. Ferguson, New Galloway; G. Geddes, Crossmichael; W. Law, Maxwellton. Although not winning any of the major prizes the team won over £15 in prize money, besides several prizes in kind.

These extracts of successful competitors of the Galloway Rifle Volunteers at the various national competitions are by no means comprehensive but it is hoped that they give an overall picture of the activities of some of the 'top-shots' of the Regiment, whereas the County Associations give a more overall insight into the activities of the rank and file in competition. The Company rifle meetings are dealt with as a separate issue.

The following extracts chronicle the activities of some of the more successful members of the Galloway Rifle Volunteers, but once again it is to be emphasised that it is far short of being anywhere near comprehensive:-

"The final stage of the Caledonian Shield was shot at Malleny, Edinburgh, on Friday, 8th June, 1900. In a three way tie for first place a shoot-out over 15 rounds saw Cyclist McHaffie, Galloway Rifles win with a score of 170 points, 2nd equal being Captain J.L. Thomson, a former 'Queen's Prize' winner and Armourer-Sergeant R. Chicken, 1st Perth Volunteers with a score of 168 points.

Cyclist McHaffie who is 35 years of age is a Wine and Spirit Merchant in Stranraer. He has been a Volunteer for 19 years. He tied in 1888 for the St. George's Challenge Vase at Bisley but was unsuccessful in the tie. He has been thrice in the final stage of the 'Queen's Prize' coming 4th in 1898. He has shot for 3 years for his, country in the International match at Bisley and has won 3 gold and 2 silver crosses of his district in the Scottish Twenty Club competitions in the last 5 years.

On Wednesday, 17th July, 1904, Cyclist McHaffie, performed a feat of marksmanship, never before equalled. Shooting in the 'Keystone Burgundy' competition at Bisley, at a range of 1000 yards, he put 16 successive bulls-eyes, with the service rifle, unaided by match sights."

"1897. - Sergeant William Law, 5th Kirkcudbright Rifles, Maxwellton, was born in Liverpool and in 1868, at the age of 6 years he came north, settling at the 'Brig - en' (Maxwellton). At 17 years of age he joined the 5th Kirkcudbright Rifles, and like a duck to water, he took to shooting. In his first year he carried off the 'Recruits Prize', and steadily built himself a reputation as a crack-shot. In 1881, he won the Bronze Cross and went to Edinburgh to compete for the Caledonian Shield. He was too modest to win it in his first big meeting and contented himself with being 7th in the President's prize. He has been to Wimbledon and Bisley several times, getting into the Queen's 300 thrice and into the Queen's 100 in 1891. His list of minor events in which Law has carried off the honours would be too tedious to list but his biggest win to date is the 'West of Scotland Challenge Trophy' at Darnley."

A unique event was to take place in 1897 when three brothers of 'A' Company, Kirkcudbright (Ringford Section) of the Galloway Rifle Volunteers, Cyclist W.M. Paterson; Corporal E. Paterson and Corporal D. Paterson, all qualified for the 'Queen's Prize' at Bisley, and although they had a creditable score in the competition they failed to move on to the final stages:-

	200yds.	500 yds.	600yds	Total.
Cyclist W.M. Paterson	32	29	32	93
Corporal E. Paterson	28	35	29	92
Corporal D. Paterson	31	34	26	91

The most famous marksman of the Galloway Rifles was undoubtedly Private A. Urquhart, 'G' Company, Maxwellton, but I still find it very difficult, however, to accept his achievements as being representative of the Galloway Battalion. Private A. Urquhart was born at Heatherhouse, Irvine, Ayrshire, the son of a gamekeeper, a calling to which he readily took having been brought up from an early age with a gun in his hand. He served 10 years on the Loudoun Estates and whilst employed there he joined the 2nd Ayr Rifle Volunteers and quickly became acknowledged as one of the steadiest and deadliest shots in the United Kingdom. Besides taking many minor and local prizes he represented his country eight times in the Scottish 20 and three times in the Scottish 8. He was three times Champion in his native county of Ayr and three times won the Gold Cross and once the Silver Cross of the Twenty Club district. The following are a list of some of Private Urquhart's achievements:

Won Ladies Prize, Wimbledon - 1889
Won Scottish 20 gold cross - 1892-94
Won Scottish 8 silver cross - 1893
3rd place Alexandra Prize, Bisley - 1893

Tied St. George's Challenge Vase, Bisley - 1893
Won Lady Landowne's Cup, Ayrshire - 1893
Won Glasgow Cup - 1893
2nd place Carringing Cup, Bisley - 1893
Won Elkington Cup, Bisley - 1893
Tied Faculty Prize, Darnley 1895
Won Association Cup, Darnley - 1895
3rd place Champion of Scotland - 1894
Won Champion of Scotland - 1895
5th place Champion of Scotland - 1896
5th place St. George's Challenge Vase, Bisley - 1896
3rd place Scottish Shield - 1894
Won Stewart's Prize, Darnley - 1894
Won Brown's Prize, Darnley - 1894
Won Sweepstake, Darnley - 1893-94
Won £80 and 6 'Queen's Badges' having been 6 times in the final stage of the 'Queen's Prize'.
Won 6 Grand Aggregate Bronze Crosses, 1891-96.

In 1896 had it not been for the unfortunate inner on the wrong target he would have had the honour of tieing for the 'Queen's Silver medal'.

Great honour was reflected on a Regiment by the success of its riflemen in major national competition and it was not uncommon for the officers to 'poach' top-shots by the offer of well paid employment in their area. This was to be the case of Private Urquhart, who in 1895 was brought to Dumfries and given a job as a salesman with the firm of Brewers, Archibald Arrol and Sons, Dumfries, joining with 'G' Company (Maxwellton) of the Galloway Rifle Volunteers. However, the aspirations of a 'Queen's Prize' winner in the Galloway Battalion was to be short lived, Private Urquhart was struck by an attack of typhoid fever, dying aged 38 years on the 26th September, 1898, leaving a widow and three young children. He was buried in Maxwellton Cemetery on Rood Fair Thursday, with full Military Honours.

On the night of Saturday, 2nd November, 1901, the members of 'E' Company, New Galloway, entertained Armourer-Sergeant George Geddes at a dinner on the occasion of his retirement. Armourer Sergeant Geddes was one of the oldest Volunteers in the country having completed almost 42 years service in the Volunteer Force. He was a Mineral Agent to trade and enrolled in the 3rd Kirkcudbright Rifle Volunteers, on the 21st January, 1860. In 1868 his trade took him to Glasgow where he joined with the old 19th or 1st Highland Light Infantry Volunteers. In his first year he was promoted Corporal, in the 3rd year to Sergeant and in the 4th year to Colour Sergeant. He remained in Glasgow until returning to his native New Galloway in 1879, rejoining with his first love the 3rd Kirkcudbright Rifles and where he was to remain until age necessitated his retirement. The members of his Corps presented him with a solid silver inkstand inscribed "Presented to Armourer-Sergeant Geddes by 'E' Company Galloway Rifles on his retirement after 41 years service."

Sergeant Geddes was a distinguished rifleman with a formidable pedigree:- At Wimbledon in 1874 he came 2nd in the Queen's 60 for the Silver Medal and won £20 in the Armourer's Competition.

During the years, 1874, 75, 76, 77, he won the Colonel's Prize twice and a prize presented by the Doctors of the Regiment in 1877. The same year in a Regimental Competition he won 1st prize with the highest aggregate ever made with the Snider Rifle, namely 97 points, he was also presented with a gold medal in recognition of this feat.

In 1882, at Wimbledon he won the 'Field Memorial' and tied for the 'Gregory'. In 1883, fortunes were reversed, when he won the 'Gregory' and tied for the 'Field Memorial', he also won £15 in the 'Alexandra Prize', being placed 3rd.

In 1881, at the Scottish Meeting, he gained a prize in every open meeting, coming 3rd in the grand aggregate.

With regards to his local prizes, these were considered too numerous to detail as even Sergeant Geddes himself could not remember them all. Sergeant Geddes was a member of the Scottish 20 in the years 1882, 83, 84 and in 1886, he shot into the 'Queen's 100', winning the 'Queen's Badge'.

Sergeant Geddes' son, Cyclist George Geddes jnr., joined 'E' Company, New Galloway on the 1st May, 1891, and was, himself to go on and become a well known and able marksman.

* * * *

In 1866, the 6th Meeting of the Galloway Artillery and Rifle Volunteer Association was to take place on the ranges of Bennan Farm, New Galloway, but this was to be the last time at these ranges for the next 6 years. The Association had proposed to make the New Galloway ranges the permanent site for their County Meetings, with its central location and accessibility to all the Companies of the Battalion, by rail, and had already spent some considerable money on permanent targets and other range facilities. However, Mr. McMath, the Farmer on the Bennan Farm, wanted suitable recompense for the use of his land which the Council considered extortionate and refused to pay.

In 1867, Captain Stroyan of 'D' Company, Newton Stewart, a farmer of Knockbrex Farm, some two miles from Newton Stewart, offered the use of his farm for further County Association Rifle Meetings, and on the 18th June, 1867, the 7th Annual meeting of the Galloway Artillery and Rifle Volunteer Association was to take place at Knockbrex. The Meeting was held once more at Knockbrex in 1868, before moving to the Barrhill Ranges at Newton Stewart, where they were to remain until 1872, when the meetings returned to the Bennan, it being reported in the press that the 12th Galloway Artillery and Rifle Volunteer Association meeting had returned to New Galloway Station through the kindness of Mr. McMath, farmer, Bennan, obviously the cash problems had been resolved.

The County Association meetings were to continue on the Bennan Farm, until 1882, when at the instance of Mr. T.R. Bruce, Slogarie, New Galloway, the ranges were moved to Airds Farm, New Galloway, tenanted by Mr. Webster, farmer, and owned by Major Houghton-Hughan, Airds Estate, on the south side of the railway, near to the railway station. The use of the ground was given to the Association free of charge. The Association meetings were to continue at Airds ranges until, 1895.

17th Meeting of the G.A.R.V.A.

The 17th Annual competition of the Galloway Artillery and Rifle Volunteer Association took place at the Bennan Farm ranges, New Galloway, on Tuesday, 26th June, 1877. The arrangements for the competition were under the control of Quartermaster Harper, Secretary of the Association. Quartermaster Farish of the Dumfriesshire Battalion of Rifle Volunteers officiated in the Secretary's tent.

Officers present:- Lieutenant-Colonel Maitland and Mrs. Maitland; Major and Mrs. Renny, Danevale; Major Kennedy; Captain and Adjutant, Farrer; Quartermaster Harper - Staff.

1st K.R.V.	(Kirkcudbright) -	Captain Craig and Lieutenant Muir.
2nd ..	(Castle Douglas) -	Captain Gordon.
3rd ..	(New Galloway) -	Lieutenants Millman and Craig.
5th ..	(Maxwellton) -	Lieutenant McGowan.
6th ..	(Dalbeattie) -	Captain Maxwell; Lieutenant Kerr.
3rd W.R.V.	(Newton Stewart) -	Captain Picken; Lieutenant Agnew.
1st K.A.V.	(Kirkcudbright) -	Captain McLaren.
2nd W.A.V.	(Portpatrick) -	No Officers but were taken under the command of Captain Singleton, late Adjutant of the Galloway Rifles.

A large number of honoured guests and spectators were present and besides the public refreshment tent, Colonel Maitland also had a private marquee on the ground, in which he dispensed his hospitality.

Mr. Skirving of Croys, acted as Umpire.

In former years there was a grumbling amongst competitors in regard to the increased elevation in sighting of the 500 yard range. This was caused by the firing points being placed on the level moss, while the targets were at a considerable height on the hillside. The Secretary had the range altered in order that the sighting was much the same as that of the other ranges, the change being met with a general satisfaction.

The shooting commenced at 9am with the following results:

I). **A Silver Challenge Cup** presented by the Earl of Selkirk for skirmishing, with £5 added by the Association. To be competed for between 200 and 400 yards, by squads of not less than 14 men from each Company.

2nd K.R.V.	(Castle Douglas)		49 hits.
3rd ..	(New Galloway)		47
6th ..	(Dalbeattie)		41
5th ..	(Maxwellton) -	Disqualified.	54

II). **A Silver Challenge Cup** presented by Colonel Laurie, with £5 added by the Association, for Volley firing at 400 yards, by squads of not less than 14 men from each Company.

2nd K.R.V.	(Castle Douglas)		59 hits.
3rd ..	(New Galloway)		58
6th ..	(Dalbeattie)		53
5th ..	(Maxwellton) -	Disqualified)	60

In the skirmishing and volley firing competitions a protest was lodged by Captain Gordon, of the 2nd K.R.V. (Castle Douglas), against the winner, 5th K.R.V. (Maxwellton), being allowed to take the prizes for volley firing and skirmishing on the grounds that the squad of the 5th K.R.V. was taken from the two Maxwellton Companies, whereas they should have been taken from only one. Mr. Skirving, umpire, upheld the objection and the 5th K.R.V. were disqualified in both the skirmishing and volley firing. Prize money to be returned. At the later prize giving for these two competitions, the men of the 5th K.R.V. disrupted the proceedings with booing and heckling. It was also suggested that Mr. Skirving, a former member of the 2nd K.R.V. was biased in his decision towards his former Company. This argument was to become the subject matter of letters to the press, however, the Umpires decision was to remain unaltered.

III). **The Bargaly Challenge Cup** presented by the late James Mackie, M.P., with £10 added by the Association. Open to effective members of the Galloway Battalion of Rifle Volunteers and of the Volunteer Artillery Corps in Galloway. 1st the cup and £4 ; 2nd £2; 3rd £1; 4th £1; 5th £1; 6th 10/-; 7th 10/-;

5 rounds at 200 yards. 95 entries.

Leading scores:	
Corporal John Agnew, Newton Stewart, (1st)	18 points.
Sergeant Patterson, Kirkcudbright Artillery (2nd)	18
Corporal R. McAdam, Castle Douglas (3rd)	18
Private A. Lawson, Maxwellton (4th)	18
Colour-Sergeant Osborne, Kirkcudbright (5th)	18
Private J. Grierson, Castle Douglas (6th)	17
Sergeant R. Armstrong, Maxwellton (7th)	17
Private A. Hughan, Kirkcudbright Artillery	17
Sergeant H. McCaull, Newton Stewart	17
Private J. McGaw, Castle Douglas	17
Private McDonald, Dalbeattie	17
Corporal Myers, Castle Douglas	17
Private McBain, Kirkcudbright	17
Private Millburn, Dalbeattie	17
Private Myers, Castle Douglas	17
Private Ferguson, New Galloway	17
Private Paterson, Castle Douglas	16
Gunner James McMurray, Kirkcudbright Artillery	16
Gunner Paterson, ...	16
Private James Henderson, Castle Douglas	16
Corporal H. Murdoch, Castle Douglas	16
Private J. Beattie, Maxwellton	16
Corporal C. Ritchie, Dalbeattie	16
Colour-Sergeant J. Milligan, New Galloway	16
Lance/Corporal Noren, Kirkcudbright	16
Sergeant-Major McDowall, Portpatrick Artillery	16
Private J. Coskrie, New Galloway	16
Sergeant James Agnew, Newton Stewart	16
Sergeant J. Hyslop, Castle Douglas	16
Sergeant P. Stewart, Castle Douglas	16
Corporal J. Johnstone, Dalbeattie	16
Private W.R. Murray, Kirkcudbright	16
Private R. Agnew, Newton Stewart	16
Corporal James McAdam, Castle Douglas	16

Lieutenant Campbell, Kirkcudbright Artillery, won this competition the previous year with a score of 18 points.

IV). **The Munches Cup** presented by Wellwood H. Maxwell Esq., of the Munches. Open competition with conditions as at (III). 1st the Cup and £4; 2nd £2; 3rd £1; 4th £1; 5th £1; 6th 10/-; 7th 10/- 5 rounds at 500 yards. 90 entries.

Leading scores:-

Private Lawson, Maxwellton (1st)	17 points.
Sergeant Newlands, Maxwellton (2nd)	16
Private J. McGill, New Galloway (3rd)	16
Sergeant Osborne, Kirkcudbright (4th)	16
Sergeant T. Agnew, Newton Stewart (5th)	16
Lieutenant Craig, New Galloway (6th)	16
Corporal Coutts, Dalbeattie (7th)	16
Lance/Corporal Roberts, Maxwellton	16
Private Riddick, Castle Douglas	15
Private Galleymore, Maxwellton	15
Private McSkimming, Castle Douglas	15
Private Briggs, Maxwellton	15
Corporal T. Myers, Castle Douglas	15
Private Barton, New Galloway	15
Sergeant Stewart, Stranraer	14
Sergeant P. McKinna, Castle Douglas	14
Corporal Johnstone, Dalbeattie	14
Private Sharpe, Maxwellton	14
Lieutenant Kerr, Dalbeattie	14
Lieutenant Campbell, Kirkcudbright Artillery	14
Private R. McGill, New Galloway	14
Private Anderson, New Galloway	14
Corporal Milligan, New Galloway	14

Corporal J. Agnew won this cup the previous year with a score of 19 points.

V). **The Battalion Prizes**. open to effective members of the Galloway Battalion of Rifle Volunteers only. 1st £4; 2nd £2; 3rd £1; 4th £1; 5th £1; 6th 10/-.; 7th 10/-. 5 rounds at 600 yards. 79 entries.

Leading scores:

Private J. McGaw, Castle Douglas (1st)	15 points.
Sergeant Armstrong, Maxwellton (2nd)	14
Private Hogg, New Galloway (3rd)	13
Private J. Grierson, Castle Douglas (4th)	13
Private T. Myers, Castle Douglas (5th)	13
Private Wyness, Dalbeattie(6th)	12
Private Ferguson, New Galloway (7th)	12
Sergeant Wilson, Dalbeattie	11
Sergeant McGeorge, Dalbeattie	10
Sergeant Newlands, Maxwellton	10
Sergeant Coskrie, New Galloway	10
Private Murray, Kirkcudbright	10
Private Sharpe, Maxwellton	10
Sergeant Service, Maxwellton	10

Lieutenant Kerr, Dalbeattie, won this event the previous year with a score of 17 points.

VI). **The Bronze Medal** of the National Rifle Association. The Bronze Medal with £5 added, to be given for the highest aggregate score in competitions (III), (IV), and (V), with the money part of the prize to be conditional upon the winner shooting at Wimbledon for the Prince of Wales Prize. 2nd £1.10/-; 3rd £1; 4th £1; 5th £1; 6th 10/-.

	Bargaly.	Munches.	Battalion.	Total.
Sergeant Armstrong, Maxwellton (1st)	17	13	14	44
Private T. McGaw, Castle Douglas (2nd)	17	11	15	43
Sergeant J. Osborne, Kirkcudbright (3rd)	18	16	9	43
Private A. Lawson, Maxwellton (4th)	18	17	8	43
Private J. Grierson, Castle Douglas (5th)	18	11	13	42
Private T. Myers, Castle Douglas (6th)	17	12	13	42
Sergeant Newlands, Maxwellton	15	16	10	41
Private W. Hogg, Maxwellton	16	11	13	40
Corporal R. McAdam, Castle Douglas	18	13	9	40

Corporal J. Agnew won the Bronze Medal, the previous year with a score of 48 points.

VII). **Carbine Prize** for Galloway Artillery Volunteers only. 1st £2; 2nd £l; 3rd £l; 4th 10/-; 5th 10/-
5 rounds at 200 yards. 21 entries.

Leading scores:

Sergeant Patterson, Kirkcudbright Artillery	16 points.
Gunner A. Campbell, Portpatrick Artillery	16
Sergeant-Major McDowall, Portpatrick Artillery	15
Lieutenant T. Campbell, Kirkcudbright Artillery	15
Bombardier A. Bruce, Portpatrick Artillery	15

Gunner Patterson, Kirkcudbright Artillery won the competition the previous year with a score of 17 points.

VIII). **All Comers Snider Prizes**, 1st £4; 2nd £2; 3rd £1; 4th £1; 5th £1; 6th 10/-; 7th 10/-.
5 rounds at 500 yards. 74 entries.

Leading scores:

Lieutenant W. Kerr, Dalbeattie (1st)	18 points.
Sergeant Armstrong, Maxwellton (2nd)	17
Sergeant Blackwood, 4th D.R.V. (Penpont) (3rd)	16
Mr. W. Cairns, Gatehouse (4th)	16
Private G. Anderson, New Galloway (5th)	16
Corporal R. Murdoch, Castle Douglas (6th)	16
Corporal J. Dalziel, New Galloway (7th)	16
Lieutenant Campbell, Kirkcudbright Artillery	15
Sergeant Johnston, New Galloway	15
Lance/Corporal Roberts, Maxwellton	15
Lieutenant Johnston, 105th Lanark	15
Quartermaster Harper, Staff Officer Galloway Batt.	15
Private J. Briggs, Maxwellton	15
Private T. Riddick, Castle Douglas	15
Corporal Johnston, Dalbeattie	15
Private J. Wyness, Dalbeattie	14
Corporal G. Coutts, Dalbeattie	14
Private J. Grierson, Castle Douglas	14
Corporal J. McAdam, Castle Douglas	14
Sergeant J. Service, Maxwellton	14

Corporal R. Milligan won the event the previous years with a score of 17 points.

IX). **All Comers any Rifle Prize**. 1st £6; 2nd £3; 3rd £1.
7 rounds at 800 yards. 19 entries.

Leading scores:

Private Grierson, Castle Douglas (1st)	29 points
Sergeant J. Agnew, Newton Stewart (2nd)	26
Lieutenant Campbell, Kirkcudbright Artillery (3rd)	25
Sergeant T. Agnew, Newton Stewart	25
Corporal G. Agnew, Newton Stewart	25
Sergeant Blackwood, 4th D.R.V. (Penpont)	24
Sergeant Osborne, Kirkcudbright	23
Private Fergusson, New Galloway	22
Sergeant McCaull, Newton Stewart	21
Captain Craig, Kirkcudbright	20
Quartermaster Harper, Staff Officer Galloway Batt.	20

The prizes in this competition the previous year were won by scores of 30, 29 and 26.

A protest was lodged by Lieutenant Campbell, Kirkcudbright Artillery, against Sergeant James Agnew, Sergeant Thomas Agnew and Corporal John Agnew, by their gaining prizes in the All Comers any Rifle, they having, contrary to the rules of fair competition, failed to load and fire their own rifles. The protest was not sustained, Mr. Skirving, the Umpire, stating, "The rules do not prevent this, but merely stipulate that no two men shall use the same rifle in the same squad."

XI). **Prizes for Recruits** of the Galloway Battalion, who joined the Volunteer Force, after the 1st November, 1876. 1st £1; 2nd 15/-; 3rd 10/-; 4th 10/-; 5th 5/-; 6th 5/-; 7th 5/-.
5 rounds at 200 yards. 12 entries:

Privates McKie, Dalbeattie	(1st).
J. Sowerby, Castle Douglas	(2nd).
J. Osborne, Kirkcudbright	(3rd).
G. Davies, Dalbeattie	(4th).
J. Maxwell, Kirkcudbright	(5th).
J. Belford, New Galloway	(6th).
R. Agnew, Newton Stewart	(7th).
R. Bell, New Galloway	
R. Walker, Maxwellton	
J. McMickan, Maxwellton	
J. Thomson, New Galloway	
J. Barbour, New Galloway	

XII). **Prizes for Sergeant Instructors** of the Galloway Rifle or Artillery Volunteers. 1st 15/-; 2nd 10/-; 3rd 10/-; 4th 7/6d; 5th 7/6d; 6th 5/-; 7th 5/-.
5 rounds at 200 yards. 9 entries.

Sergeant Duncan, Stranraer (1st)	18 points.
Sergeant Murdoch, Maxwellton (2nd)	18
Sergeant Miller, Dalbeattie (3rd)	17
Sergeant-Major Brown, New Galloway (4th)	15
Sergeant Gilmour, Kirkcudbright (5th)	14
Sergeant Dowdney, Castle Douglas (6th)	14
Sergeant Walsh, Newton Stewart (7th)	13

On the 29th June, 1877, the following letter by a "Maxwellton Volunteer", appeared in the *Dumfries and Galloway Standard*, with a reply the following week from, "An Old Private of the Galloway Rifles", concerning the disqualification of the Maxwellton squads in the Volley Firing and Skirmishing competitions. Both letters are reproduced in their entirety.

"Without for a moment doubting that the Umpire, Mr. Skirving of Croys, gave the decision which seemed right according to his judgement, it ought to be known that he is a member of the Corps which received the prizes that Maxwellton had fairly won and that which is certainly not usual with Umpires, he himself was a competitor for prizes that day. Is it not possible that these circumstances, especially the fact that he is a member of the Castle Douglas Company, may have unconsciously biased the judicial temper of his mind? That there was no unconscious bias, I think there can be little doubt, for while Captain Gordon's protest only applied to the volley firing, he admits so himself, Mr. Skirving's judgement included the skirmishing, he thus having gone out of his way to deliver a verdict in a case which was not before him at all.

The ground of Mr. Skirving's deliverance is that the men of the Maxwellton squad had been selected from two Companies instead of one. Now as you know, the Maxwellton Corps is the only one in the Battalion whose members approach the point at which, what is in reality the same body of men, becomes technically two Companies and if it had ever been dreamt that our squad could not be drawn from both of these, just as it can from both branches of what is known as a Company and Sub-Division, a character which a Corps acquires at the point of 130, just as the character, for it is little more than a character, of two Companies emerges when the number 200 is reached, we could easily have transferred the men from the one Company into the other before going up to New Galloway. But we felt that not necessary, for the Regulations do not say that the squad is to be drawn from one Company, but that the prize should be competed for by "Squads of not less than 14 men from Companies". We never could have thought that this "from Companies" made it necessary either that we should send up two squads, one drawn from each Company or if one squad, that they should be drawn from one Company only.

Is it not rather suggestive too that we should have been suffered to win our trophies before the protest was made? This is not the first time that our men have had reason to complain of the New Galloway decisions and while we do not yield our claim to the prizes which have been 'Umpired' to Castle Douglas but not won by them, by refusing to take repayment of our entry money, we shall take good care that there will be some reforms effected in the management of matter before we "Gang back to yon toun".

(Signed) "A Maxwellton Volunteer."

The following reply was submitted by "An Old Private of the G.R.V."

"1st. W. Skirving of Croys, Umpire of the meeting of the Galloway Rifle Association on the 26th ult. resigned as a member of the 2nd Kirkcudbright Rifles On the 28th December, 1874.

2nd. Mr. Skirving is well known in Galloway as a most upright and conscientious gentleman and at the meeting showed himself so much so that, in order to give no one the slightest pretext for supposing that the judicial temper of his mind had been biased by his, at one time being Captain of the 2nd Kirkcudbright Rifle Volunteers, he only gave his decision after very careful consideration with all the members of Council on the ground. A majority was presented, so his award was merely that of the Council of the Association. Mr. Skirving has always taken a great interest in the success of the Volunteer Movement and has been a liberal supporter of the G.A.R.V.A. He is also an enthusiastic rifle shot and enters for the two All Comers Prizes at New Galloway. He has a perfect right to do so and the attempt of, 'A Maxwellton Volunteer' to impute to Mr. Skirving's dishonourable motives in giving his award by 'being a competitor' will be met by the scorn and contempt it deserves.

3rd. Captain Gordon distinctly stated that he meant his protest, in regard to volley firing, to apply to the skirmishing as well, and I understand that was explained to Mr. Skirving before he gave his decision. At what time of the day his explanation was made is not of the slightest consequence.

4th. In previous years the Maxwellton Companies competed with two squads and the fact that they have been and are separate Companies is graven in silver on the skirmishing and volley firing cups thus:

For skirmishing - won by the 5th Kirkcudbright Rifle Volunteers Maxwellton, 'A' Company'.
For volley firing - won by the 5th Kirkcudbright Rifle Volunteers Maxwellton, 'A' Company'.

It is manifestly unfair that Companies composed of 60 or 70 men should compete with squads of equal number against a Corps of say 180 or 190 men. The Dumfriesshire Rifle Association do not allow the 1st Dumfries Corps, whose numbers exceed a Company to enter with one squad, drawn from both Companies. This is a parallel case and the Maxwellton Volunteers must have been well aware when they entered that they were acting against the general Regulations. In fact I hear that some of them acknowledged that their Dumfries Volunteer friends told them that they would be disqualified at the New Galloway meeting if they gained the prizes, and that they were partly prepared for the result. In these circumstances it was well to see the 'bitter bit' however disappointing it must be for the squad. That the best men were not transferred into one Company is the Maxwellton Corps own concern and loss.

5th. It is perfectly absurd to read the rule, "Squads of not less than 14 men from Companies" in the way a 'Maxwellton Volunteer' does, and I am convinced he knows better. It is clear that it means from each Company, else according to his interpretation of it the 2nd Kirkcudbright Rifle Volunteers might have drawn men from all the Companies of the Battalion and competed with them as a squad from the 2nd Kirkcudbright Rifle Volunteers.

6th. When the Maxwellton men learn that fair and honest dealing is the wisest policy and the surest road to success at all rifle prize meetings, I am certain they will not have the slightest cause to complain of the decision of those in authority at New Galloway. Until then they must suffer for their misdeeds.

In his silly excuse for 'No gang back tae yon toun', 'A Maxwellton Volunteer' shows little of the soldier spirit and I can only tell them that the absence of those Maxwellton Volunteers who showed such unsoldierly and ungentlemanly conduct during the delivery of the prizes by Colonel Maitland would be, 'good company'. Their sheepish boo-booings and insulting cries were more like the actings of rustic clowns at a county fair than men wearing Her Majesty's uniform of the Reserve Forces and ere their Commanding Officer Captain Barrie allows them to attend any such prize meetings or other Volunteer gatherings, he ought to teach them that the duty of the soldier is 'Obedience'.

(Signed) ' An Old Private of the G.R.V.'

22nd Meeting of the G.A.R.V.A.

The 22nd Annual competition of the Galloway Artillery and Rifle Volunteer Association took place on Tuesday, 27th June, 1882, on a new range situated on the south side of the railway, near to New Galloway Station. The change of range was made on the application of Mr. T.R. Bruce, Slogarie, who also suggested and superintended the Swiss plan of sliding canvas targets. The improvement in the marking and the assistance the new system gave to the marksmen at the firing point by showing him the exact position of his hits, was a far superior system than the previous iron targets.

The contestants and spectators enjoyed a glorious summer's day, unlike the inclement weather of former years.

The Officers present were; Colonel Gordon Maitland; Major Kennedy; Major Maxwell; Captain and Adjutant Bovill; Quartermaster Harper - Staff.

'A' Company (Kirkcudbright) - Captain Craig; Lieutenant Muir.
'E' Company (New Galloway) - Lieutenant Craig.
'F' & 'G' Companies (Maxwellton) - Captain Lennox.
'H' Company (Dalbeattie) - Lieutenant Kerr.
Colonel Mark Stewart - Ayrshire and Galloway Artillery - Staff.
Kirkcudbright Artillery - Captain Campbell.
Stranraer Artillery - Lieutenant Dunsmore; Dr. Cochrane.

The competitors found a little difficulty in the afternoon when the wind increased and the sun shone right in the eyes of the marksmen, but on the whole matters were favourable.

There were in all 14 competitions, but for the skirmishing cup, won the previous three years by Castle Douglas, there was only one entry, with only two entries for the volley firing, namely Maxwellton and Stranraer.

For the first time competitors were squadded and had to appear punctually at the firing points at the time stated on their tickets. The competition commenced at 9am with the Sergeant Instructor's Prizes. As will be seen from the prize list, all the principle prizes were gained by members of the Castle Douglas Company, they having carried off the Bargaly Cup, the Munches Cup, the first Battalion prize, the Bronze Medal, the Glenlee Cup, the first of the Sergeant Instructor's prizes, the first of the consolation sweepstake prizes and the first in the team competition.

The arrangements were admirably carried out, throughout the day, under the active superintendence of the Secretary of the Association, Quartermaster Harper, Captain Hume of the Scottish Borderers, discharged the duties of Umpire.

Colonel Maitland, as on former occasions, dispensed his bountenous from his private hospitality tent, to the officers and his visitors.

Mr. W. McKinnell, Castle Douglas, had a refreshment tent on the ground and Mr. Orr, hotel keeper, Laurieston, also supplied refreshments during the day.

The following are the results, with a comparison of the previous years scoring. It should be borne in mind that this was the first time that the kneeling position was imperative at 200 yards, previously any position could be used.

i). **A Silver Challenge Cup**, presented by the Earl of Selkirk to the Galloway Rifle Battalion for
   Skirmishing, with £5 added by the Association. To be competed for by squads of not less than
   14 men from each Company.
   5 rounds per man.

   1st Maxwellton - No competition.

   The Castle Douglas Company gained the prize the previous year with 48 hits.

ii). **A Silver Challenge Cup**, presented by Colonel Laurie to the Galloway Rifle Battalion for Volley
   Firing at 400 yards.
   5 rounds per man. Squads of not less than 14 men from each Company.

1st Maxwellton	163 points.
2nd Stranraer	155

   Maxwellton gained the Volley Firing prize the previous year with 166 points.

iii). **The Bargaly Cup**. presented by the late James Mackie Esq., M.P., with £10 added by the
   Association. Open to effective members of the Galloway Rifles and of the Volunteer Artillery
   Corps in Galloway. 1st prize, the cup and £4; 2nd £2-10/-; 3rd £1; 4th £1; 5th £1; 6th 10/-;
   7th 10/-; 8th 10/-; 9th 5/-; 10th 5/-; 11th 5/-; 12th 5/-.
   7 rounds at 200 yards.

Corporal J. McGaw, Castle Douglas (1st)	31 points.
Private Turner, Castle Douglas (2nd)	31
Gunner Carter, Kirkcudbright Artillery (3rd)	28
Corporal W. McCaw, Castle Douglas (4th)	28
Lieutenant Kerr, Dalbeattie (5th)	28

Colour-Sergeant Osborne, Kirkcudbright (6th)	28
Private J. Hogg, Kirkcudbright (7th)	28
Bombardier W. Murray, Stranraer (8th)	28
Corporal Geddes, New Galloway (9th)	27
Private Heuchan, Kirkcudbright (10th)	27
Private A. Hogg, Kirkcudbright (11th)	27
Sergeant Coutts, Dalbeattie (12th)	27
Sergeant Slater	27
Corporal Myers, Castle Douglas	27

The Bargaly Cup was won the previous year by Corporal Murdoch, Castle Douglas with a score of 34 points.

iv). **The Munches Cup**, presented by Wellwood H. Maxwell Esq., of Munches, to the Galloway Rifle Battalion. Open to efficients of the Galloway Rifles and the Volunteer Artillery Corps in Galloway. To become the property of anyone winning it three times. 1st the cup and £4; 2nd £2; 3rd £1; 4th £1; 5th £1; 6th 10/-; 7th 10/-; 8th 10/-; 9th 5/-; 10th 5/-; 11th 5/-; 12th 5/-. 7 rounds at 500 yards.

Corporal W. McCaw, Castle Douglas (1st)	31 points.
Corporal Myers, Castle Douglas (2nd)	29
Sergeant Andersen, New Galloway (3rd)	29
Corporal Patterson (4th)	29
Quartermaster Harper - Staff (5th)	28
Sergeant Coutts, Dalbeattie (6th)	28
Colour-Sergeant Johnstone, New Galloway (7th)	28
Private Turner, Castle Douglas (8th)	28
Lieutenant Muir, Kirkcudbright (9th)	28
Private Callander, Maxwellten (10th)	28
Private Bell, Stranraer (11th)	28
Private Walker, Maxwellton (12th)	27
Private Erskine, Newton Stewart	27
Private Campbell, Kirkcudbright	27
Sergeant Beatiie, Maxwellton	27

The Munches Cup was won the previous year by Gunner Hogg, Kirkcudbright Artillery, with a score of 32 points.

v). **The Battalion Prizes** Open to effective members of the Galloway Corps of Rifle Volunteers only. 1st £4; 2nd £2; 3rd £1; 4th £1; 5th £1; 6th 10/-; 7th 10/-; 8th 10/-; 9th 5/-; 10th 5/-; 11th 5/-; 12th 5/-. 7 rounds at 600 yards.

Quartermaster Sergeant Hyslop, Castle Douglas (1st)	27 points.
Corporal Murray, Kirkcudbright (2nd)	26
Sergeant T. Agnew, Newton Stewart (3rd)	25
Private Bell, Stranraer (4th)	23
Private Turner, Castle Douglas (5th)	23
Corporal Lawson, Maxwellton (6th)	23
Sergeant J. Anderson, Newton Stewart (7th)	22
Private J. Walker, Maxwellton (8th)	22
Corporal J. McGaw, Castle Douglas (9th)	21
Private Sturgeon, Dalbeattie (10th)	21
Private Harley (11th)	21
Assistant Surgeon Cochrane, Stranraer Artillery (12th)	20
Private Law, Maxwellton	20
Private A. Hogg, Kirkcudbright	20
Private Heuchan, Kirkcudbright	20

The first of the Battalion prizes was won the previous year by Colour Sergeant Osborne, Kirkcudbright, with a score of 27 points.

vi). **Aggregates. The Bronze Medal of the National Rifle Association**, with £5 added for the highest aggregate score in competitions, (iii), iv), (v). The money part of the 1st Prize to be conditional on the winner's shooting at Wimbledon for the Prince of Wales Prize. 2nd £2-10/-; 3rd £1; 4th £1; 5th £1; 6th 10/-; 7th 10/-; 8th 10/-; 9th 10/-; 10th 10/-; 11 th 5/-; 12th 5/-; 13th 5/-; 14th 5/-; 15th 5/-.

	Bargaly	Munches	Battalion	Total
Private J. Turner, Castle Douglas (1st)	31	28	23	82
Corporal J. McGaw, Castle Douglas (2nd)	31	25	21	77
Sergeant J. Agnew, Newton Stewart (3rd)	24	26	25	75
Corporal Patterson, K.A.V. (4th)	26	29	19	74
Corporal Murray , Kirkcudbright (5th)	23	24	26	73
Sergeant G. Coutts, Dalbeattie e (6th)	27	28	18	73
Private James Bell, Stranraer (7th)	21	28	23	72
Private A. Hogg, Kirkcudbright (8th)	27	25	20	72
Private R. Erskine, Newton Stewart (9th)	26	27	19	72
Private James Walker, Maxwellton(10th)	22	27	22	71
Private Heuchan, Kirkcudbright (11th)	27	24	20	71
Lieutenant Muir, Kirkcudbright (12th)	25	28	17	70
Corporal Geddes, New Galloway (13th)	27	25	17	69
Gunner H. Carter K.A.V. (14th)	28	25	16	69
Corporal Myers, Castle Douglas (15th)	27	29	13	69

The Bronze Medal was won the previous year by Sergeant Agnew, Newton Stewart with a score of 83 point.

vi). **The Glenlee Cup,** presented by George Maxwell Esq., of Glenlee.

To become the property of anyone winning it three times. Open to efficients and recruits of the Galloway Battalion of Rifle Volunteers. Efficients to have attended, during the current year, 20 drills, including one Adjutant's drill. 1st the cup and £2; 2nd £1; 3rd 15/-; 4th 10/-; 5th 10/-; 6th 5/-; 7th 5/-.

7 rounds at 200 yards standing.

Corporal Murdoch, Castle Douglas (1st)	27 points.
Private T.R. Bruce, New Galloway (2nd)	26
Corporal Geddes, New Galloway (3rd)	26
Private J. Turner, Castle Douglas (4th)	26
Corporal J. McGaw, Castle Douglas (5th)	25
Private John Hogg, Kirkcudbright (6th)	25
Sergeant G. Coutts, Dalbeattie (7th)	24

Sergeant Agnew, Newton Stewart won the Glenlee Cup the previous year with a score of 28 points.

viii). **Carbine Prize**. for members of the Galloway Artillery Corps only. 1st £3; 2nd £2; 3rd £1; 4th 10/-; 5th 10/-; 6th 5/-; 7th 5/-.

7 rounds at 200 yards.

Gunner A. Anderson (1st)	27 points.
Corporal McCoull (2nd)	26
Bombardier William Murray (3rd)	25
Sergeant Major Rae (4th)	25
Gunner Dorrance (5th)	25
Private A. Forbes (6th)	24
Sergeant Slater (7th)	24
Bombardier J. Robertson	24

The Carbine Prize was won the previous year by Gunner Slater, Kirkcudbright Artillery with 28 points.

ix). **All Comers Snider Prize**. 1st £4; 2nd £2; 3rd £1; 4th £1; 5th £1; 6th 10/-; 7th 10/-.
7 rounds at 500 yards.

Corporal J. Agnew, Newton Stewart (1st)	31 points.
Sergeant Thomas Agnew, Newton Stewart (2nd)	31
Corporal J. McGaw, Castle Douglas (3rd)	29
Private W. Law, Maxwellton (4th)	29
Corporal T. Myers, Castle Douglas (5th)	27
Quartermaster Sergeant Myers, Castle Douglas (6th)	27
Quartermaster Harper, Galloway Battalion Staff Officer	26

x). **Prizes for Recruits** of the Galloway Battalion of Rifle Volunteers and Galloway Artillery Corps who joined the Volunteer Force after 1st November of the year previous. 1st £1; 2nd 15/-; 3rd 10/-; 4th 10/-; 5th 5/-; 6th 5/-; 7th 5/-.
7 rounds at 200 yards

Privates J. Dargavel (1st)	24 points.
G. Callander (2nd)	24
James Bell (3rd)	24
J.T. Hewat (4th)	23
John Hoatson (5th)	23
R. Dyer (6th)	23
T. McLellan (7th)	21

The first of the Recruits prizes was won the previous year by Private Murray, Stranraer, with a score of 27 points.

xi). **Prizes for Sergeant Instructors**. of the Galloway Battalion of Rifle Volunteers and the Artillery Corps of Galloway. 1st 15/-; 2nd 10/-; 3rd 10/-; 4th 7/6d; 5th 7/6d; 6th 5/-; 7th 5/-.
7 rounds at 200 yards.

Sergeant Connely, Castle Douglas (1st)	25 points.
Sergeant Gilmour, Kirkcudbright (2nd)	24
Sergeant-Major Brown, New Galloway (3rd)	24
Corporal Duncan, Artillery (4th)	22
Sergeant Compton, Artillery (5th)	20
Sergeant Flynn, Dalbeattie (6th)	19
Sergeant Walsh, Newton Stewart (7th)	18

The first prize the previous year was won by Sergeant-Major Brown, New Galloway with a score of 27 points, when any position was allowed.

xii). **Consolation Sweepstake**. Prize open to those members of the Galloway Battalion of Rifle Volunteers and the Artillery Corps of Galloway, who have never won a 1st prize at any of the Association meetings or a prize to the value of £5 at any other rifle meeting.
7 rounds at 200 yards. Entry 2/- to be divided in prizes amongst competitors, less expenses of the competition.

Corporal W. McCaw, Castle Douglas (1st)	29 points.
Private J. Heuchan, Kirkcudbright (2nd)	29
Private S. Callender, Maxwellton (3rd)	28
Sergeant James Beattie, Maxwellton (4th)	28
Private J. Carruthers, Maxwellton (5th)	27
Private H. Patterson, Kirkcudbright (6th)	27
Private J. McMillan (7th)	27

The first of the consolation sweepstake prize was won the previous year by Private Erskine, Newton Stewart, with a score of 31 points, any position being then allowed.

xiii). **Team Competitions.** Open to the Companies of the Galloway Battalion of Rifle Volunteers. Teams of 5 men. Scores in the Bronze Medal competition at 200, 500 and 600 yards to count. Entry 10/- per team - to be divided in prizes, less expenses, for competition. 3 Prizes.

1st). <u>Castle Douglas.</u>

Private Turner	82 points.
Corporals J. McGaw	77
Myers	69
W. McCaw	67
Murdoch	66
	361.

2nd). <u>Newton Stewart</u>

Sergeant T. Agnew	75 points
Private R. Erskine	72
Sergeant J. Anderson	64
Private R. Agnew	62
Corporal J. Agnew	57
	330

3rd). <u>Maxwellton No. 2 Team.</u>

Sergeant Service	66 points.
Privates Callender	65
A.Walker	64
W. Law	63
Sergeant Beattie	62
	320.

4th). <u>New Galloway</u>

Corporal Geddes	69 points
Private T. R. Bruce	67
Sergeant Anderson	64
Col. Sgt. Johnstone	57
Sergeant Hogg	54
	311

5th). <u>Kirkcudbright No. 1 Team.</u>

Private Heuchan	71 points.
Lieutenant Muir	70
Col. Sergeant Osborne	66
Private Patterson	56
Private Hogg	45
	308

6th). <u>Kirkcudbright No. 2 Team</u>

Corporal Murray	73 points
Private Campbell	65
Sergeant Douglas	59
Sergeant Norren	46
Private McBean	43
	286

7th). <u>Maxwellton 1 No. Team.</u>

Corporal Lawson	65 points.
Privates Briggs	64
Henderson	57
R.J. Walker	37
Corporal Hanlon	35
	258.

There was a 'Pool Target' held during the day. The following made bulls-eyes, each worth 9/4d.

Corporal Lawson, Maxwellton	- 2
Corporal Myers, Castle Douglas	- 2
Private Byers, New Galloway	- 2
Private Badenoch, Castle Douglas	- 1
Gunner J. Robertson	- 1
Private Law, Maxwellton	- 1
Ass. Surgeon Cochrane, Stranraer Art.	- 1
Private J. Harold, Stranraer	- 1
Lieutenant Muir, Kirkcudbright	- 1

After the distribution of prizes, Colonel Maitland, impressed upon the Volunteers the importance of Volley Firing and Skirmishing. This being a skill they might some day be called upon to use in the field. The customary cheers were given for the Queen and the Officers and the meeting was brought to a close. Major Houghton-Hughan of Airds, upon whose property the Association's meeting took place, intimated his intention to give £5 for the purchase of an additional Silver Cup to be shot for the next year.

* * * *

On the 2nd March, 1888, after a useful career of 28 years on Wimbledon Common, the National Rifle Association received an intimation from the Duke of Cambridge that the Common would not in future be allowed for the purposes of the Association. The Association offered to purchase 120 acres of the Common from the Duke but he would not agree to this purpose. On the 24th May, 1889, it was reported, "what is known as the new Wimbledon Common was formally inspected by a number of pressmen and others on Saturday, 18th May, 1889. Its site is on Bisley Common. Fears are entertained that the new range will never attain to the popularity of that which it is meant to replace." 107 years on, with Bisley still going strong as the centre of rifle shooting, his fears were never realised.

The County Association Meetings were to continue annually, without incident until the close of the 27th annual competition of the Galloway Artillery and Rifle Volunteer Association, held on the 31st July, 1887, when Colonel Maitland addressed the assembled Companies and said that he was sorry he had to say words of farewell as their Commanding Officer. He regretted very much having to sever himself from the Battalion but circumstances compelled him to do so. Colonel Maitland had been dogged by ill-health all his adult life. He continued by saying that he hoped the men would continue in efficiency as well as proficiency under their new Commander, Major Kennedy.

The following letter of reply from Major Kennedy, the new Commander of the Galloway Rifle Volunteers, was to appear in the press the following week:

New Galloway.

1st August, 1887.

"When reporting the proceedings of the annual Artillery and Rifle Association, would you permit me to say in the name of my brother Officers and men of the Galloway Rifles, that we heard with feelings of the greatest regret, at the close of the competition on Saturday, (31.7.87) from Colonel Gordon Maitland, of his intention to resign the active command of the Galloway Battalion.

As Colonel Maitland remarked in the kind words he addressed to us, before distributing the prizes, he has seen many changes in the battalion since he first joined it on returning from India many years ago changes all in the right direction of order, uniformity, efficiency and better knowledge of drill.

Under Colonel Maitland's command, the Battalion, originally 'Administrative', that is composed of separate independent Corps, became 'Consolidated', very much to its advantage in every respect, and owing to his invariable fairness, tact and kind feeling, discipline has been maintained and shortcomings have been corrected without causing irritation or lessening the 'esprit de corps' which has always existed in the Regiment. Few Commanding Officers can be congratulated on such success.

We earnestly trust that the causes which have led our Colonel to send in his resignation may gradually cease to give him grounds for anxiety and we hope he will continue to remember us, as we shall always remember him with pleasure in connection with the many years we were under his command, and the many enjoyable Association meetings when he was present, occasions rendered all the more agreeable by the hospitality and kind personal interest shown to us by Mrs. Gordon Maitland."

J.M. Kennedy. Major, G.R.V.

(Colonel Maitland died on the 25th August, 1897.)

31st Meeting of the G.A.R.V.A.

The 31st annual competition, under the auspices of the Galloway Artillery and Rifle Volunteer Association took place on the New Galloway ranges on Saturday, 19th July, 1891. The entries showed an increase from the previous year. The weather though warm and dry was unfavourable for high scoring, as a strong wind prevailed, which required careful watching and necessitated a borrow of from two to seven feet at the long distances, while at times there was a changeable light. As a result of these variable conditions the scoring on the whole was under that of the previous year.
The Officers present were:- Colonel Kennedy; Major and Adjutant, Spurgin; Major Harper - Staff Officers.

Kirkcudbright Artillery - Major Campbell.

'A' Company	(Kirkcudbright) - Lieutenants Muir, Clark and Hewitt.
'B'	(Castle Douglas) - Lieutenant Dunn.
'C'	(Stranraer) - Captain Stewart, Lieutenants Watson and McLelland.
'D'	(Newton Stewart) - Captain Agnew, Lieutenant McPhater.
'E'	(New Galloway) - Captain Jamieson, Lieutenant Stewart.
'F' & 'G' Companies -	(Maxwellton) Captains Lennox and Phyn.
'H' Company	(Dalbeattie) - Major Kerr.

Among those present on the ground were Major and Mrs. Houghton-Hughan of Airds and, party. Colonel J. Gordon Maitland and Miss Gordon Maitland, Cairn Edward; Mr. James Maitland; Mrs. Lawrence and Miss Matterson, Ernespie; Mr. and Mrs. Hutchison of Balmaghie; Mr. and Miss Renny, Campdouglas; Major Murray Dunlop and Miss Murray Dunlop, Corsock; Mrs. David Maitland and Miss Maitland, Compstone; Mrs. Marsden, Parton; Mrs. Spurgin, Corbieton; Miss Duncan, Danevale, and party; Rev. Mr. and Miss Cuthill, Balmaclellan; Rev Mr. Craig, Balmaghie; Mr. Davidson, Chief Constable, etc.

The day's shooting commenced about 9.30am. The first item on the programme was the competition for the silver challenge cup presented by the late Earl of Selkirk. This cup which in former years was given for Skirmishing, was awarded to the Company which had the best 10 aggregates. It fell to the Castle Douglas Company with 770 points, being an average of 77 per man.

For the Volley Firing Cup, 8 teams competed, being the largest entry for many years. This honour was carried off by Kirkcudbright Company with 153, being 6 points less than the winning score the previous year. Castle Douglas secured the 2nd position with 3 points less.

The Bargaly Cup was won by Sergeant McHaffie, Stranraer, with a score of 32, being one point less than the winning score the previous year. For the Munches Cup, Quartermaster Sergeant Myers, Castle Douglas, put on the highest possible, and was followed by Lance Sergeant Gordon of the same Company with one point less. The Airds Cup was gained by a recruit of 1891, Private G. Geddes, New Galloway, who made the creditable score of 31 points, being the same figure which carried off the prize the previous year. Quartermaster Sergeant Myers, Castle Douglas secured the Bronze Medal - the blue riband - of the meeting with a total of 93 points out of a possible 105. This was the second occasion in which Quartermaster Sergeant Myers had won the Bronze Medal. The Glenlee Cup was carried off by Sergeant Love, Newton Stewart, with one point less than the winning score the previous year.

Two Sergeant-Instructors were to figure in the prize list and an objection was made as to their competency to participate in these events. The objection was to be overruled and the result stood.

Gunner Campbell, Kirkcudbright, gained the first of the Carbine prizes with a score of 28, the same winning figure as the previous year. There was a falling off in the shooting for the All Comers Martini Henry. Private Geddes, 8th Lanark and Sergeant Law, Maxwellton, divided the first and second prizes with scores of 32, as against 34 the previous year. There was also a falling off in the shooting for the Recruits prize, Private Halliday, Maxwellton, was the highest scorer with 26 points as compared to 27 the previous year. There was no improvement in the Consolation Sweepstake, the first prize being taken by Sergeant McCreadie, Newton Stewart, with 32 points. For the fifth year in succession representatives from the Castle Douglas Company were successful in the team competition of 5 men.

Major Spurgin, acted as Umpire and Range Officer during the day, while the duties of Secretary were discharged by Major Harper.

The refreshments were supplied by Mr. W. Seggie and Mr. William McKinnell, Castle Douglas. The Band of the Stranraer Reformatory was present during the day and played a number of popular selections.

i). **A Silver Challenge Cup.** presented by the late Earl of Selkirk to the Galloway Rifle Volunteer Corps. To be competed for by teams of 10 men from each Company. Scores in the Bronze Medal competition at 200, 500 and 600 yards to count.

    1st Castle Douglas 770 points.

ii). **A Silver Challenge Cup.** presented by Colonel Laurie to the Galloway Rifle Volunteer Corps, with £5 added by the Association, for Volley Firing at 400 yards; 2nd £2. To be competed for by squads of not less than 10 men from each Company.
    5 rounds each.

Kirkcudbright (1st)	153 points.
Castle Douglas (2nd)	150
New Galloway	147
Newton Stewart	141
Maxwellton ('G' Company)	138
Dalbeattie	119
Stranraer	101
Maxwellton ('F' Company)	88

iii). **The Bargaly Challenge Cup.** presented by the late James Mackie, Esq., M.P. with money prizes added by the Association, open to effective members of the Galloway Rifle Volunteer Corps, and of the Volunteer Artillery Corps in Galloway - 1st £2; 2nd £1-10/-; 3rd £1; 4th £1;. 5th 15/-; 6th 15/-; 7th 10/-; 8th 10/-; 9th 7/6d; 10th 7/6d; 11th 5/-; 12th 5/-; 13th 2/6d; 14th 2/6d; 15th 2/6d.
    7 rounds at 200 yards

1. Sergeant McHaffie, Stranraer	32 points.
2. Private W. McCreadie, Newton Stewart	31

3. Corporal Sturgeon, Dalbeattie	30 points
4. Corporal W. McCaw, Castle Douglas	30
5. Private E. Patterson, Kirkcudbright	30
6. Sergeant Torrance, Stranraer	30
7. Major Campbell, Kirkcudbright Artillery	30
8. Private Haining, Maxwellton	29
9. Lieutenant Muir, Kirkcudbright	29
10. Col. Sergeant Anderson, Newton Stewart	29
11. Quartermaster Sergeant Myers, Castle Douglas	29
12. Major Kerr, Dalbeattie	29
13. Sergeant R. Fergusson, New Galloway	29
14. Corporal J. McGaw, Castle Douglas	29
15. Sergeant Walker, Maxwellton	29

iv). **The Munches Cup,** presented by Wellwood H. Maxwell Esq., of Munches, to become the property of anyone winning it three times, open as in no.iii. 1st £2; 2nd £1; 3rd £1; 4th £1; 5th 15/-; 6th 15/-; 7th 10/-; 8th 10/-; 9th 7/6d; 10th 7/6d; 11th 5/-; 12th 5/-; 13th 2/6d; 14th 2/6d; 15th 2/6d. 7 rounds at 500 yards.

1. Quartermaster Sergeant Myers, Castle Douglas	35 points.
2. Lance Sergeant Gordon, Castle Douglas	34
3. Sergeant Law, Maxwellton	32
4. Corporal Murdoch, Castle Douglas	32
5. Gunner Paterson, Kirkcudbright Artillery	32
6. Major Campbell, Kirkcudbright Artillery	32
7. Sergeant Instructor Tuck, Kirkcudbright	32
8. Colour-Sergeant Craig, Dalbeattie	31
9. Corporal Agnew, Newton Stewart	31
10. Sergeant Murray, Kirkcudbright	30
11. Corporal Murchie, Newton Stewart	30
12. Private Moffat, Maxwellton	30
13. Private Cairns, Kirkcudbright	30
14. Private Drysdale, Newton Stewart	29
15. Private Hetherington, Castle Douglas	29
Sergeant Lock, Stranraer	29

v). **The Airds Cup**, presented by Major Houghton-Hughan of Airds, to become the property of anyone winning it three times, and Battalion Prizes. open to effective members of the Galloway Corps of Volunteers only. 1st £2; 2nd £1; 3rd £1; 4th £1; 5th 15/-; 6th 15/-; 7th 10/-; 8th 10/- 9th 7/6d; 10th 7/6d.; 11th 5/-; 12th 5/-; 13th 2/6d; 14th 2/6d; 15th 2/6d. 7 rounds at 600 yards.

1. Private G. Geddes, New Galloway	31
2. Corporal Sturgeon, Dalbeattie	29
3. Quartermaster Sergeant Myers, Castle Douglas	29
4. Private Millburn, Dalbeattie	28
5. Private Hetherington, Castle Douglas	28
6. Captain Lennox, Maxwellton	28
7. Private Hall, Maxwellton	27
8. Col. Sergeant Osborne, Kirkcudbright	27
9. Corporal McCaw, Castle Douglas	27
10. Major Campbell, Kirkcudbright Artillery	26
11. Lieutenant Muir, Kirkcudbright	26
12. Sergeant Wallace, Maxwellton	26
13. Gunner McHaffie, Stranraer Artillery	26
14. Sergeant-Instructor Gallacher, New Galloway	26
15. Private Patterson, Kirkcudbright	25
Col. Sergeant Craig, Dalbeattie.	25

vi). **Aggregates** viz.:- 1st the Bronze Medal of the National Rifle Association, with £4 added, for the highest aggregate score in competitions (iii), (iv) and (v), the money part of the 1st prize to be conditional on the winner's shooting at Bisley for the Prince of Wales Prize, either in the year of winning or the year following. 2nd £2-10/-; 3rd £1; 4th £1; 5th £1; 6th 10/-; 7th 10/-; 8th 10/-; 9th 10/-; 10th 10/-; 11th 5/-; 12th 5/-; 13th 5/-; 14th 5/-; 15th 5/-.

	(iii).	(iv).	(v).	Total.
1. Quartermaster Sergeant Myers, Castle Douglas	29	35	29	93
2. Major Campbell, Kirkcudbright Artillery	30	32	26	88
3. Corporal Sturgeon, Dalbeattie	30	26	29	85
4. Corporal McCaw, Castle Douglas	30	28	27	85
5. Lance Sergeant Gordon, Castle Douglas	26	34	23	83
6. Private Hetherington, Castle Douglas	25	29	28	82
7. Sergeant McHaffie, Stranraer	32	23	26	81
8. Corporal Murdoch, Castle Douglas	26	32	22	80
9. Private Cairns, Kirkcudbright	26	30	23	79
10. Private G. Geddes, New Galloway	23	24	31	78
11. Private E. Patterson, Kirkcudbright	30	23	25	78
12. Gunner Patterson, Kirkcudbright Artillery	25	32	21	78
13. Col. Sergeant Craig, Dalbeattie	21	31	25	77
14. Corporal Agnew, Newton Stewart	24	31	22	77
15. Col. Sergeant Anderson, Newton Stewart	29	23	24	76
Sergeant Instructor Gallacher, New Galloway	26	23	26	75
Sergeant Beattie, Maxwellton	24	28	23	75
Major Kerr, Dalbeattie	29	28	18	75

vii). **The Glenlee Cup**, presented by George Maxwell Esq., of Glenlee, to become the property of anyone winning it three times. Open to efficients and recruits of the Galloway Rifle Volunteers. Efficients to have attended, during the present year, five Company drills, including one Adjutant's drill. Recruits to have attended, during the present year, 20 drills, including one Adjutant's drill. 1st the Cup and £2; 2nd £1; 3rd 15/-; 4th. 10/-; 5th 10/-; 6th 5/-; 7th 5/-. 7 rounds at 200 yards, standing.

1. Sergeant Love, Newton Stewart	28 points.
2. Sergeant Instructor Gallacher, New Galloway	27
3. Colour Sergeant Osborne, Kirkcudbright	27
4. Corporal McCaw, Castle Douglas	26
5. Major Campbell, Kirkcudbright Artillery	26
6. Private Hetherington, Castle Douglas	25
7. Sergeant Instructor Campbell, Maxwellton	25
Sergeant Law, Maxwellton	25

viii). **Carbine Prizes** for Galloway Artillery Volunteers only. 1st £2; 2nd £1; 3rd 15/-; 4th 10/-; 5th 10/-; 6th 5/-; 7th 5/-. 7 rounds at 200 yards.

1. Gunners Campbell, Kirkcudbright	28 points.
2. Dorrance, Kirkcudbright	26
3. Douglas, Portpatrick	25
4. Durham, Portpatrick	25
5. Corporal Middleton, Kirkcudbright	24
6. Gunner Lees, Portpatrick	23
7. Corporal Thomson, Portpatrick	23
Major Campbell. Kirkcudbright	23
Corporal McCoull, Kirkcudbright	23
Gunner Hale, Portpatrick	23
Bombardier Torrance, Stranraer	23

ix). **All Comers' Martini-Henry Rifle Prizes**. 1st £4; 2nd £2; 3rd £1; 4th £1; 5th £1; 6th 10/-; 7th 10/-. 7 rounds at 500 yards.

1. Private J. Geddes, 8th Lanark	32 points.
2. Sergeant W. Law, Maxwellton	32
3. Private Hetherington, Castle Douglas	31
4. Corporal McCaw, Castle Douglas	31
5. Quartermaster Sergeant Myers, Castle Douglas	31
6. Sergeant Walker, Maxwellton	30
7. Private W. Patterson, Kirkcudbright	29
Sergeant Instructor Tuck, Kirkcudbright	29

x). **Prizes for Recruits** of the Galloway Rifle Volunteer Corps and Galloway Artillery, who joined the Force since 1st November last, and also open to recruits of the previous year. 1st £1; 2nd 15/-; 3rd 10/-; 4th 10/-; 5th 5/-; 6th 5/-; 7th 5/-.
7 rounds at 200 yards.

1. Private Halliday, Maxwellton	26 points.	
2. Private G. Geddes, New Galloway	25	
3. Private Elliot, Maxwellton	22	
4. Private McAdam, New Galloway	22	
5. Sergeant Anderson, Stranraer	19	
6. Private Coltart, New Galloway	18	
7. Private Flynn, Dalbeattie	16	

xi). **Consolation Sweepstake Prize**, open to those members of the Galloway Rifle Volunteers and Galloway Artillery who have never gained a first prize at the Association's meetings, or a prize to the value of £5 at any other rifle meeting.
7 rounds at 200 yards.

1. Private W. McCreadie, Newton Stewart	32 points.
2. Sergeant Instructor Gallacher, New Galloway	31
3. Private D. Haining, Maxwellton	30
4. Private W. Hetherington, Castle Douglas	29
5. Captain Stewart, Stranraer	29
Sergeant Instructor Campbell, Maxwellton	29
Sergeant MacMurray, Castle Douglas	29

XII). **Team Competition.** open to the Companies of the Galloway Volunteers. Teams of 5 men. Scores in the Bronze Medal competition at 200, 500 and 600 yards to count.
1st Castle Douglas 414 points.

Pool Targets. - 200 yards. The under mentioned made bulls-eyes, each of which was worth 5/10d. - Sergeant R. Fergusson, New Galloway (2). Captain Jamieson, New Galloway (2). The remainder scored one bulls-eye. Private McKie, New Galloway. Sergeant Gordon, Castle Douglas. Sergeant McHaffie, Stranraer. Private Douglas, Kirkcudbright. Mr. J.C. Maitland, Kenmure Castle. Captain Lennox, Maxwellton. Lieutenant Gordon, Portpatrick Artillery. Private W. Cairns, Kirkcudbright. Corporal Thomson, Portpatrick Artillery. Mr. Forsyth, Hensol. Private Fergusson, New Galloway. Mr. McAdam, Slogarie.

At the conclusion of the shooting, Colonel Kennedy, addressed a few congratulatory remarks to the competitors. "It was a matter of satisfaction to observe that they had a larger number of entries than usual, and some excellent shooting had been recorded, one man making the highest possible, whilst another competitor from the same Company had scored only one less." He concluded by introducing Mrs. Houghton-Hughan, who presented the prizes. After the presentation of the prizes three cheers were given for the Queen and the meeting dispersed.

32nd Meeting of the G.A.R.V.A.

The 32nd annual competition under the auspices of the Galloway Artillery and Rifle Volunteer Association took place on Saturday, 30th July, 1892, at the ranges of New Galloway Station. The number of entries was much the same as in former years. The weather was of the most favourable description for outdoor enjoyment, a hot temperature and a bright shining sun prevailing throughout the day. However the conditions were not favourable for good shooting, the strong sun causing a haze, which was somewhat trying from the marksman's point of view, while the wind was very changeable and required careful watching. There was however, a marked improvement in the light in the afternoon. The scoring on the whole was superior to that of the previous year.

The Officers present were:- Colonel J.M. Kennedy; Major and Adjutant, Spurgin; Major Campbell, Kirkcudbright Artillery; Major Lennox, Maxwellton; Captain Maxwell, Dalbeattie; Captain Dunn, Castle Douglas; Captain Agnew and Lieutenant McPhater, Newton Stewart; Lieutenants Muir and Clark, Kirkcudbright; Lieutenant Stewart, New Galloway; Lieutenants McLellan and Watson, Stranraer; Lieutenant Gordon, Portpatrick Artillery.

The day's shooting commenced at 9.30am with the first item on the programme being the competition for the Silver Challenge Cup, presented by the late Earl of Selkirk. This cup was now given to the Company which had the ten best aggregates. It fell to Castle Douglas Company with 787 points, being an average of 78.7 or 17 points more than the winning number the previous year, when the same Company were in the ascendant. For the Volley Firing, only eight teams competed, the honour being carried off by the Castle Douglas Company with the splendid total of 187 points, this being the highest score yet made in that event. New Galloway secured the second position with 37 points less. For the Bargaly Cup, four competitors tied with 32 points each, the following being the result of the tie break:

Sergeant Geddes	445-13 5
Private McCreadie	544-13 2
Captain Agnew	443-11
Sergeant Law	32 - retired.

Though the Munches Cup was carried off by Corporal Coupland, Maxwellton, with one point less than the top score the previous year, nothing less than 30 got a place in the prize list. As compared to the last year there was a marked improvement in the shooting for the Airds Cup, which was carried off by Sergeant Instructor Gallacher, Dalbeattie with 32 points, the lowest being 27, while 25 had been included in the prize list the previous year. Sergeant Instructor Callacher, also obtained the first of the aggregates with a score of 95, being two points more than the winning score the previous year. For the Glenlee Cup, three competitors tied with 30 points each, being two points more then the top score of the last year. The tie resulted as follows:

Sergeant Myers	435-12
Col. Sergeant Osborne	433-10
Sergeant Fergusson	02 - retired.

There was also an improvement in the shooting for the Carbine Prizes, the first of which was carried off by Gunner Lees, Portpatrick, with 29 points, being one point more than the winning score of the previous year. Lance Corporal Hetherington secured the first of the All Comers Martini-Henry prizes, with one point less than the highest possible. The shooting for the Recruits prizes showed a remarked improvement, the winning score made by Private McKenzie, Maxwellton, being 5 points in advance of the top score the previous year. For the Consolation prize, three competitors tied with 30 points each. In the team competition of five men, Newton Stewart secured the first place with a total of 404 points, being 10 points down on the previous year.

Major Spurgin acted as Umpire and Range Officer during the meeting, whilst the duties of Secretary were again discharged by Major Harper.

Refreshments were supplied by Mr. William Seggie, Victoria Restaurant, Castle Douglas.

The Dalbeattie and Kirkcudbright teams were the first to Volley fire, and after their targets had been examined, it was found that a large number of the shots had gone over the top - Kirkcudbright lodged a protest on the grounds that they had not been shooting at the proper distance of 400 yards, and upon the ground being measured it was found to be under 370 yards. As a consequence the two teams were ordered to re-shoot the tie. The time lost in this competition resulted in the meeting being brought hastily to a close at night and without the usual presentation of prizes.

The following are the results of the various competitions:

I). **A Silver Challenge Cup.** presented by the late Earl of Selkirk, to the Galloway Rifle Volunteer Corps.
   To be competed for by teams of 10 men from each Company. No entry money to be paid.
   Scores in the Bronze Medal competition at 200, 500, and 600 yards to count.

1st Castle Douglas	787 points.
Newton Stewart	773.

(ii). **A Silver Challenge Cup,** presented by Colonel Laurie to the Galloway Rifle Volunteer Corps, with £5 added by the Association, for volley-firing at 400 yards, 2nd prize £2. To be competed for by squads of not less than 10 men from each company.
   5 rounds per man:

	Bulls Eyes	Inner	Magpie	Outer	Total points	Miss
1. Castle Douglas	16	17	7	9	187	1
2. New Galloway	10	9	10	17	150	4
Maxwellton('G'.Co.)	15	5	6	13	139	11
Maxwellton('F'.Co.)	8	7	12	17	138	6
Kirkcudbright	11	4	10	15	131	10
Newton Stewart	5	9	5	26	128	5
Stranraer	8	5	6	20	118	11
Dalbeattie	6	5	8	15	104	16

(iii). **The Bargaly Cup**, presented by the late James Mackie, Esq., MP. with money prizes added by the Assoc., open to effective members of the Galloway Rifle Volunteers Corps, and of the Volunteer Artillery Corps in Galloway, 1st £2; 2nd £1; 3rd £1; 4th £1; 5th 15/-; 6th 15/-; 7th 10/-; 8th 10/-; 9th 7/6d; 10th 7/6d; 11th 5/-; 12th 5/-; 13th 2/6d; 14th 2/6d; 15th 2/6d. 7 rounds at 200 yards.

1. Sergeant Geddes, New Galloway	32 points
2. Pte. McCreadie, Newton Stewart	32
3. Sgt. Law, Maxwellton	32
4. Capt. Agnew, Newton Stewart	32
5. Q.M.Sgt. Myers, Castle Douglas	31
6. Cpl. McGaw, Castle Douglas	31
7. Sgt. Wallace, Maxwellton	31
8. Pte. McMurdoch, Maxwellton	30
9. Major Lennox, Maxwellton	30
10. Sgt. Inst. Gallagher, Dalbeattie	30
11. Pte. Hogg, Kirkcudbright	30
12. Sgt. McHaffie, Stranraer Art.	30
13. Cpl. Murdoch, Castle Douglas	30
14. Col. Sgt. Osborne, Kirkcudbright	30
15. Cpl. Moffat, Maxwellton	29
Sgt. Briggs, ..	29
Pte.G. Geddes, New Galloway	29
Cpl. Bell, ..	29
Cpl. Douglas, Kirkcudbright	29
Lt. Gordon, Portpatrick Art.	29
Sgt. Inst. Campbell, Maxwellton	29
Pte. Bowie, Kirkcudbright	29
Cpl. Haining, Maxwellton	29
Pte. Miller, Kirkcudbright	29

(iv). **The Munches Cup**, presented by Wellwood R. Maxwell, Esq., of Munches, to become the property of any one winning it three times, open as in No.iii. 1st £2; 2nd £1/10-; 3rd £1; 4th £1; 5th 15/-; 6th 15/-; 7th 10/-; 8th 10/-; 9th 7/6d; 10th 7/6d; 11th 5/-; 12th 5/-; 13th 2/6d; 14th 2/6d; 15th 2/6d. 7 rounds at 500 yards.

1. Cpl. Coupland, Maxwellton	34 points
2. Pte. Drysdale, Newton Stewart	33
3. Sgt. Inst. Gallagher, Dalbeattie	33
4. Sgt. Instr. Tuck, Kirkcudbright	32
5. Col. Sgt. Craig, Dalbeattie	32
6. Pte. Fergusson, New Galloway	31
7. Sgt. Law, Maxwellton	31
8. Sgt. Agnew, Newton Stewart	31
9. Lt. Muir, Kirkcudbright	30
10. Pte. McAdam, Castle Douglas	30
11. Sgt. Anderson, New Galloway	30
12. L/Cpl. Hetherington, Castle Douglas	30
13. Sgt. Love, Newton Stewart	30
14. Cpl. Haining, Maxwellton.	30
15. Qtr. Mstr. Sgt. Hyslop, Castle Douglas	30

(v). **The Airds Cup,** presented by Major Houghton-Hughan of Airds, to become the property of any one winning it three times, and Battalion prizes open to effective members of the Galloway Corps of Volunteers only - 1st £2; 2nd £1; 3rd £1; 4th £1; 5th 15/-; 6th 15/-; 7th 10/-; 8th 10/-; 9th 7/6d ; 10th 7/6d; 11th 5/-; 12th 5/-; 13th 2/6d; 14th 2/6; 15th 2/6d. 7 rounds at 600 yards: -

1. Sgt. Inst. Gallagher, Dalbeattie	32 points.
2. Capt. Agnew, Newton Stewart	30
3. Cpl. W. McCaw, Castle Douglas	29
4. Cpl. J. McGaw, ...	28
5. L/Cpl. Wilson, ...	28
6. Col. Sgt. Johnston, Maxwellton	28

7. Pte. Drysdale, Newton Stewart	28
8. Cpl. Coupland, Maxwellton	27
9. Pte. Miller, Kirkcudbright	27
10. Sgt. Anderson, New Galloway	27
11. Pte. Bowie, Kirkcudbright	27
12. Sgt. Inst. Tuck, Kirkcudbright	27
13. L/Cpl. Hetherington, Castle Douglas	27
14. Sgt. Gordon, ...	27
15. Sgt. Law, Maxwellton	27

(vi). **Aggregates**, viz.; 1st the Bronze Medal of the National Rifle Assoc. with £4 added for the highest aggregate scores in Competitions 3, 4, and 5, the money part of the prize to be conditional on the winner's shooting at Bisley for the Prince of Wales Prize either in the year of winning the prize or in the year following; 1st The Bronze Medal and £4; 2nd £2.10/-; 3rd £1; 4th £1; 5th £1; 6th 10/-; 7th 10/-; 8th 10/-; 9th 10/-; 10th 10/-; 11th 5/-; 12th 5/-; 13th 5/-; 14th 5/-; 15th 5/-.

	No.3.	No.4.	No.5.	Total.
1. Sgt. Inst. Gallagher, Dalbeattie	30	33	32	95
2. Sgt. Law, Maxwellton	32	31	27	90
3. Cpl. Coupland, Maxwellton	27	34	27	88
4. Capt. Agnew, Newton Stewart	32	25	30	87
5. Pte. Drysdale, Newton Stewart	26	33	28	87
6. Sgt. Inst. Tuck, Kirkcudbright	28	32	27	87
7. Sgt. Geddes, New Galloway	32	29	26	87
8. Cpl. J. McGaw, Castle Douglas	31	27	28	86
9. Col. Sgt. Johnstone, Maxwellton	27	29	28	84
10. Pte. Fergusson, New Galloway	27	31	26	84
11. Cpl. Haining, Maxwellton	29	30	25	84
12. L/Cpl. Wilson, Castle Douglas	28	27	28	83
13. L/Cpl. Hetherington	26	30	27	83
14. Pte. Bowie, Kirkcudbright.	29	27	27	83
15. Pte. Miller, Kirkcudbright	29	27	27	83
Pte. McAdam, Castle Douglas	28	30	25	83
Pte. McCreadie, Newton Stewart	32	26	25	83

(vii). **The Glenlee Cup,** presented by Geo. Maxwell Esq., of Glenlee to become the property of any one winning it three times. Open to efficients and recruits of the Galloway Rifle Volunteers. Efficients to have attended during the present year, five company drills, including one Adjt's. drill; recruits to have attended, during the present year 20 drills, including one Adjt's. drill; 1st the Cup and £2; 2nd £1; 3rd 15/-; 4th 10/-; 5th 10/-; 6th 5/-; 7th 5/-.
7 rounds at 200 yards standing.

1. Qtr. Mstr. Sgt. Myers, Castle Douglas	30 points.
2. Sgt. Fergusson, New Galloway	30
3. Col. Sgt. Osborne, Kirkcudbright	30
4. Sgt. Briggs, Maxwellton	29
5. Pte. Bowie, Kirkcudbright	28
6. Sgt. Gordon, Castle Douglas	27
7. L/Cpl. Wilson, Castle Douglas	27

(viii). **Carbine Prize** for Galloway Artillery Volunteers only.-1st £2; 2nd £1; 3rd 15/-; 4th 10/-; 5th 10/-; 6th 5/-; 7th 5/-;
7 rounds at 200 yards.

1. Gunner Lees, Portpatrick	29 points.
2. Gunner Clark, Kirkcudbright	27
3. Sergeant McHaffie, Stranraer	26
4. Gunner Hall, Portpatrick	25
5. Sgt. McQueen, ..	25
6. Gunner Middleton, Kirkcudbright	25
7. Gunner Tarbet, Portpatrick	24
Lt. Gordon, ..	24

(ix). **All-Comers Martini-Henry Rifle Prizes;** 1st £4; 2nd £2; 3rd £1; 4th £1; 5th £1; 6th 10/-; 7th 10/-.
7 rounds at 500 yards.

1. L/Cpl. Hetherington, Castle Douglas	34 points.
2. Cpl. Haining, Maxwellton.	33
3. Capt. Agnew, Newton Stewart	32
4. Sgt. Gordon, Castle Douglas	31
5. Cpl. Murchie, Newton Stewart	31
6. Col. Sgt. Craig, Dalbeattie	31
7. Sgt. Murray, Kirkcudbright	31
Cpl. Moffat, Maxwellton	31

(x). **Prizes for Recruits** of the Galloway Rifle Volunteer Corps and Galloway Artillery who have
joined the Volunteer Force since 1st November last, and also open to recruits of last year -
1st £1; 2nd 15/-; 3rd 10/-; 4th 10/-; 5th 5/-; 6th 5/-; 7th 5/-;
7 rounds at 200 yards.

1. Pte. McKenzie, Maxwellton	31 points
2. Pte. Murphy, New Galloway	29
3. Pte. Sibson, Dalbeattie	26
4. L/Cpl. Johnstone, New Galloway	25
5. Pte. McGhie, Dalbeattie	25
6. Pte. Robertson, Newton Stewart	24
7. Pte. Osborne, Kirkcudbright	24
Pte. Smith, Castle Douglas	24
Pte. Dalrymple, Kirkcudbright	24

(xi). **Consolation Sweepstake Prize,** open to those members of the Galloway Rifle Volunteer Corps
and the Galloway Artillery who have never gained a first prize at the Association's meetings,
or a prize to the value of £5 at any other rifle meeting.
7 rounds at 200 yards.

1. Cpl. Patterson, Kirkcudbright	30 points.
2. Sgt. Gordon, Castle Douglas	30
3. Pte. Smith, Newton Stewart	30
4. Sgt. Agnew, Newton Stewart	29
5. Pte. Bowie, Kirkcudbright	29
L/Cpl. Hetherington, Castle Douglas	29
Pte. Douglas, Kirkcudbright	29
Sgt. Instr. Campbell, Maxwellton	29

(xii). **Team Competition,** open to the Companies of the Galloway Volunteers.
Teams of 5 men. Companies can enter more than one team. Scores in the Bronze medal
Competition, at 200, 500 and 600 yards to count.

1. Newton Stewart	404 points.
2. Castle Douglas (No.1)	396
3. Castle Douglas (No.2).	387

Pool Targets. - 200 yards. The under mentioned made bullseyes each of which was worth about
4/1d; Sgt. Gordon, C/D; Cpl. Haining, Mxltn; Gunner Lees, Portpatrick; L/Cpl. Wilson, C/D (2); Mr. F.
Dowdney, C/D; Lt. Watson Str; Major Campbell, Kbt Art. (3) ; Mr. Lawson, Mxltn (2); Sgt. Instr.Tuck, Kbt;
Gunner Tarbet, Portpatrick; Cpl. Bell, N/G (2); Pte. Geddes, N/G (2) ; Mr. R. Coltart, N/G; Mr. Bantock, N/
G (2); Mr. Agnew, N/S; Mr. George Hutchison, Balmaghie; Qtr. Mstr. Sgt Myers, C/D; Sgt. McHaffie, Str.
- 500 yards (worth about 1/3d each - Qtr. Mstr. Sgt. Myers, C/D (3); Armoury-Sgt. Geddes, N/G (2). Sgt.
Ferguson, N/G (2) ; Sgt. Agnew N/S (2); Sgt. McHaffie, Str. Art.; Mr. Lawson, Mxltn; Cpl. W. McCaw, C/
D; Cpl. J McGaw, C/D. Sgt. Instr Tuck, Kbt; Col. Sgt Osborne, Kbt (3); Lt. Watson, Str (2); Sgt. Murray, Kbt;
Major Spurgin (2); Pte. A.D. Bowie, Kbt; Pte. W. Dalrymple. G/House; Cpl. Coupland, Mxltn; Sgt.
McGregor, Kbt; Sgt. Macmurray, C/D; Sgt. Love, N/S ; Pte. McKie, N/G; Major Campbell, Kbt Art; Sgt.
Gordon C/D; Sgt. Scott, C/D; L/Cpl. Bell, N/G; Gunner Lees, Portpatrick Art.

The Annual meetings of the Galloway Artillery and Rifle Volunteer Association, were to continue at
the Aird Farm Ranges, New Galloway Station, until 1896, when the Association fell into dire financial

difficulties. An appeal was lodged for public subscriptions, by the Council and the sum of £70 was raised, which enabled the Executive to hold a somewhat curtailed 36th annual rifle meeting, on the 'B' Company, Castle Douglas, ranges at Caigton. The central situation, proved to be most convenient for the event and popular with both spectators and competitors alike and as such entries were much in advance of previous years. The success of this event was to eventually signal the end of New Galloway as being the central location for the Association meetings.

36th Meeting of the G.A.R.V.A.

The 36th annual competition of the Galloway Artillery and Rifle Volunteer Association took place at Caigton, Castle Douglas, on Saturday, 8th August, 1896.

The Officers present were Colonel Kennedy; Colonel Maxwell; Captain and Adjutant Blake; Major Harper, Castle Douglas; Major McLellan, Kirkcudbright; Major Phyn, Maxwellton; Captain Dunn, Castle Douglas. Captain McPhater and Lieutenant Kelly Newton Stewart; Captain Maxwell, Dalbeattie; Captain Timms and Lieutenant Stewart, New Galloway; Lieutenant McLelland, Stranraer.

The day's shooting commenced shortly after 10am. The first item on the programme being the Bargaly Challenge Cup, shot for kneeling or standing at 200 yards, for which five men tied with 31 points, being two points less than the previous year. In the shoot off for the tie, Private McCreadie won. Private McCreadie also won the Munches Cup with 35 points, being one point more then the previous year. Lance Corporal Dougan, Castle Douglas, and Corporal D. Paterson, Kirkcudbright Artillery, tied for the Airds Cup, with 32 points, which was also the winning score of 1895. The following was the result of the tie:

| Lance Corporal Dougan | 544 - 13 |
| Corporal D. Paterson | 532 - 10 |

The scoring for the aggregates was similar to the previous year, Corporal E. Patterson, taking the first place with 92 points, while 84 points was the lowest that secured a place, as compared to 85 the previous year.

Captain Blake acted as Umpire and Range Officer during the day, whilst the Secretarial duties were carried out by Captain Dunn and Quartermaster Sergeant Myers, Castle Douglas. The weather though fine and dry, was not altogether favourable for high scoring, as a somewhat unsteady breeze from the left front prevailed the greater part of the day. Luncheons and refreshments were supplied by Mr. William Seggie, Victoria Hotel, Castle Douglas.

The following are the results of the various competitions:-

I). **The Bargaly Challenge Cup.** presented by the late James Mackie Esq., M.P., with money prizes added by the Association. Open to members of the Galloway Rifle Volunteer Corps and of the Volunteer Artillery Corps in Galloway. 1st £2;. 2nd £1; 3rd £1; 4th £1; 5th 15/-; 6th 15/-; 7th 10/-; 8th 10/-; 9th 7/6d; 10th 7/6d; 11th 5/-; 12th 5/- 13th 2/6d; 14th 2/6d; 15th 2/6d. 7 rounds at 200 yards.

1. Private W. McCreadie, Newton Stewart	31 points.
2. Private W. Paterson, Kirkcudbright	31
3. Private J. Fergusson, New Galloway	31
4. Private Crosbie, Maxwellton	31
5. Corporal Murchie, Newton Stewart	31
6. Corporal E. Paterson, Kirkcudbright	30
7. Private W. Law, Maxwellton	30
8. Sergeant McHaffie, Stranraer	30
9. Sergeant S. Gordon, Castle Douglas	30
10. Corporal Coupled, Maxwellton	30
11. Lieutenant McLelland, Stranraer	29
12. Private Miller, Kirkcudbright	29
13. Corporal Haining, Maxwellton	29
14. Mus. Sergeant Murdoch, Castle Douglas	29
15. Corporal J. McGaw, Castle Douglas	29
Lance Corporal Moffat, Maxwellton	29
Private A. Geddes, New Galloway	29
Private James Ireland, Castle Douglas	29
Lance Corporal Hetherington, Castle Douglas	29
Lance Corporal Malcolm, Newton Stewart	29.

II). **The Munches Cup**. presented by Wellwood H. Maxwell Esq., of Munches, to become the property of anyone winning it three times. Open as in No.(I).
1st £2; 2nd £1-10/-; 3rd £1; 4th. £1; 5th 15/-; 6th. 15/-; 7th 10/-; 8th 10/-; 9th 7/6d; 10th 7/6d; 11th 5/-; 12th 5/-; 13th 2/6d; 14th 2/6d; 15th 2/6d.
7 rounds at 500 yards.

1. Private W. McCreadie, Newton Stewart	35 points.
2. Pay-master Sergeant Osborne, Kirkcudbright	34
3. Corporal D. Paterson, Kirkcudbright Artillery	33
4. Corporal Bell, New Galloway	33
5. Sergeant Wilson, Castle Douglas	33
6. Private G. Geddes, New Galloway	32
7. Corporal E. Paterson, Kirkcudbright	32
8. Col. Sergeant Murray, Kirkcudbright	32
9. Private John Ferguson, New Galloway	31
10. Captain McPhater, Newton Stewart	31
11. Sergeant R. Ferguson, New Galloway	31
12. Corporal W. McCaw, Castle Douglas	31
13 Private Carnochan, Kirkcudbright	31
14. Private P. Ferguson, New Galloway	31
15. Corporal J. McGaw, Castle Douglas	30
Private W. Hope, Maxwellton	30
Corporal Coupland, Maxwellton	30
Private W. Paterson, Kirkcudbright	30
Corporal Todd, Castle Douglas	30

III). **The Airds Cup** presented by Major Houghton-Hughan of Airds, to become the property of anyone winning it three times, and Battalion Prizes. Open as in No.(I). 1st £2. 2nd £1-10/-; 3rd £1; 4th £1; 5th 15/-; 6th 15/-; 7th 10/-; 8th 10/-; 9th 7/6d; 10th 7/6d; 11th 5/-; 12th 5/-; 13th 2/6d; 14th 2/6d; 15th 2/6d.
7 rounds at 600 yards.

1. Lance Corporal Dougan, Castle Douglas	32 points.
2. Corporal D. Paterson, Kirkcudbright	32
3. Private Carnochan, Kirkcudbright	31
4. Private G. Geddes, New Galloway	31
5. Corporal E. Paterson, Kirkcudbright	30
6. Private A. Urquhart, Maxwellton	30
7. Private W. Law, Maxwellton	29
8. Sergeant S. Gordon, Castle Douglas	29
9. Corporal Bell, New Galloway	28
10. Corporal Coupland, Maxwellton	28
11. Sergeant Wallace, Maxwellton	28
12. Private P. Ferguson, New Galloway	28
13. Sergeant McHaffie, Stranraer	27
14. Lance Sergeant Wilson, Castle Douglas	27
15. Lieutenant McLelland, Stranraer	27
Private J. Ferguson, New Galloway	27

IV). **Aggregates**. viz.:- 1st the Bronze Medal of the National Rifle Association, worth £4 added for the highest aggregate score in competitions (I), (II), and (III). The money part of the 1st prize to be conditional on the winner's shooting at Bisley for the Prince of Wales Prize the next year. 2nd £2; 3rd £1; 4th £1; 5th £1; 6th 10/-; 7th 10/-; 8th 10/-; 9th 10/-; 10th 10/-; 11th 5/-; 12th 5/-; 13th 5/-; 14th 5/-; 15th 5/-.

	I.	II.	III.	Total.
1. Corporal E. Paterson, Kirkcudbright	30	32	30	92
2. Corporal D. Paterson, Kirkcudbright Artillery	26	33	32	91
3. Private G. Geddes, New Galloway	28	32	31	91
4. Private T. Carnochan, Kirkcudbright	28	31	31	90
5. Private William McCreadie, Newton Stewart	31	35	24	90
6. Private J. Ferguson, New Galloway	31	31	27	89
7. Private W. Law, Maxwellton	30	29	29	88
8. Corporal J. Bell, New Galloway	27	33	28	88
9. Corporal J. Coupland, Maxwellton	30	30	28	88

10. Sergeant R.W. Wilson, Castle Douglas	27	33	27	87
11. Private A. Urquhart, Maxwellton	28	28	30	86
12. Sergeant McHaffie, Stranraer	30	28	27	85
13. Private P. Ferguson, New Galloway	25	31	28	84
14. Corporal Murchie, Newton Stewart	31	27	26	84
15. Corporal W. McCaw, Castle Douglas	27	31	26	84

From an analysis of the results, it will be seen that Kirkcudbright Company were the most successful having gained £11.17s.6d. in money prizes. New Galloway came second with £7.7s.6d. Newton Stewart gained £6.7s.6d. Maxwellton £5.7s.6d. Castle Douglas £5.2s.6d. Kirkcudbright Artillery £5. Stranraer Artillery 12/6d. Stranraer 7/6d.

A Jubilee Fund. - 1897.

A meeting of those interested in the Volunteer movement was held on Monday 29th March, 1897 in the Town Hall, Castle Douglas, for the purpose of considering the propriety of raising a Jubilee Fund to put the Galloway Artillery and Rifle Volunteer Association on a better financial position. Colonel Kennedy of Knocknalling was called on to preside, and among the others present were; Mr. Skirving of Croys; Captain Harry Timms of Slogarie; Captain Dunn, Castle Douglas; Captain Wellwood Maxwell of Kirkennan; Captain and Adjutant Blake; Lieutenant Stewart, Dalry and Quartermaster Sergeant Myers, Castle Douglas. The meeting was held in private.

The Chairman was to receive the following telegram from Sir William Gordon of Earlston, dated from Ryde. "Will support fund and rifle association; Boy's Brigade successful here; think might be established in Stewartry."

The meeting was to be informed that the targets and stop butts at the rifle range at New Galloway Station, which were used by the association for their annual meeting, had fallen into such a state of disrepair that it would have to be necessary to largely increase the expenditure in the current year in order to enable the association to carry on its meetings. Mr. Skirving moved that the meeting should invite those who had generously assisted the association in previous years to increase their subscriptions for the current year to meet the extra expenditure and with the view to laying aside a fund for the future necessities of the Association that might commemorate Her Majesty's long reign. Captain Timms, seconded the motion, which was unanimously adopted.

A Committee consisting of Captain and Adjutant Blake, Captain Maxwell of Kirkennan, Captain Dunn and Quartermaster Sergeant Myers, was appointed to visit and inspect the range at New Galloway, and report to the next meeting of the Council of the Association, the repairs necessary and probable cost.

Colonel Kennedy and Mr. Skirving, intimated their intention of increasing their annual subscriptions by £5 each and hoped that this might set some sort of precedent.

The 37th Annual meeting of the Galloway Artillery and Rifle Volunteer Association was held for the last time on the ranges at Airds Farm, New Galloway Station on Saturday, 21st August, 1897, with a full complement of twelve competitions.

On the 21st February, 1898, the annual general meeting of the G.A.R.V.A., was held in the Town Hall, Castle Douglas, when there was present, Major Lennox, Maxwellton, presiding; Captain Timms, Slogarie, 'E' Company. Lieutenant Comrie, Gategill, 'A' Company'. Captain McPhater, Newton Stewart, 'D' Company'. Sergeants McGregor and Murray, Kirkcudbright; Sergeant Murdoch, Corporal W. McCaw, Corporal J. McGaw; Captain A. Dougan, Castle Douglas 'B' Company'. Captain Dunn and Quartermaster Sergeant Myers, Castle Douglas, joint Secretary and Treasurer.

A financial report which was adopted showed a credit balance of £42-4s-6d, compared with £22-0s-3d, the last year.

The Earl of Stair; Sir Mark J. McTaggart-Stewart Bart., M.P. and Mr. Maxwell of Munches, Dalbeattie, were elected Presidents of the Association, (The Earl of Selkirk, a founding member of the Association and former President died in 1885,) while the following gentlemen were elected members of the Council, Mr. Skirving, Croys; Mr. J.W. Hutchison, Laurieston Hall (formerly Woodhall home of the former Commander of the G.R.V., Colonel Laurie.) Captain Hope of St. Mary's Isle; Mr. John Mackie, Bargaly. Major Houghton-Hughan, Airds; Colonel Sanderson, Glenlaggan.

Amongst the points for discussion were the difficulties and expense attending the ranges at Airds. The old ranges at Airds were found to be unsuitable due to the high cost of maintenance. Captain Dunn reported that it cost £20 to put the targets in order at Airds, the previous year and with it only being used once a year and together with the introduction of the Lee-Metford rifle, which was much more accurate than the old

Martini-Henry over long distances, the ranges at Airds were no longer suitable. The ranges at Bisley had now been extended, the 900 yard range in the 'Queen's Prize', having been extended to 1000 yards.

One suggestion put forward was that the Association move their annual meeting to the Maxwellton ranges at Conhuith, however, whereas there was plenty of target accommodation at the Maxwellton ranges and the Association might hold its competitions there free of charge, it was considered not to be sufficiently central for the Association's purposes. The Executive of the Council therefore fixed the location of future G.A.R.V.A. meetings to be at Caigton, Castle Douglas. The Annual Rifle competitions of the Association were to continue at Caigton until the disbandment of the Galloway Rifle Volunteers, the last meeting of the Association being held in 1907.

For the 38th annual meeting of the G.A.R.V.A., held at Caigton, Castle Douglas, on Saturday, 2nd July, 1898, the range facilities were extended to a total of 17 targets. 9 were already in existence at Caigton, the ranges of 'B' Company, Castle Douglas, with a further 8 being placed on Breoch with an addition of a further 4 targets for volley firing having been sited on Cuil Hill. The targets were of the Swiss sliding principle. The National Telephone Company erected a telephone system between the butts and the firing point which facilitated the settlement of challenged shots.

39th Meeting of the G.A.R.V.A.

The 39th annual competition in connection with the Galloway Artillery and Rifle Volunteer Association, took place on Saturday, 24th June, 1899, at the Association's new ranges, at Caigton, Castle Douglas.

Favoured with excellent weather it proved to be a fine outing for the Volunteers and a most enjoyable day for the attending visitors.

The targets were again fitted upon the Swiss sliding principle, and the National Telephone Company once again put at the disposal of the Association a telephone link to the butts and firing point.

The number of entries was the largest in the history of the Association. The competition commenced at 10.30am and finished at 6pm. There were in all 12 competitions with over £60 being offered in prize money, in addition to the several valuable cups. The Volley firing competitions had up until this year been one of the items in the annual competition, but it was brought off a fortnight earlier with the result that a good deal of time was saved on the Saturday. With the exception of a slightly troublesome fish-tail wind, especially at the 200 yard range, the weather, from the competitors point of view, was all that could be desired.

There was a marked improvement in the shooting compared with former years, and the fact that no score below 91 found a place in the Aggregate prize-list was sufficient to show the high standard of efficiency that could now be attained with the Lee-Metford Rifle. The previous year, some scores as low as 82 were in the prize-list for the Aggregate Prize.

Cyclist McHaffie, Stranraer, better known as the "Old Bombardier", who distinguished himself at Bisley the previous year (1898), by coming 4th in the 'Queen's Prize', was well to the front once more. He carried off two of the cups, together with other money prizes. Cyclist J. Ferguson, New Galloway, was also conspicuous in several of the competitions, and won the Aggregate with a total of 98 points.

The first competition in the programme was the Bargaly Cup which was won by Corporal R. Todd, Castle Douglas, with a score of 33 points, which was one better than the last year. The Munches Cup, was carried off by Cyclist McHaffie, Stranraer, with the 'Possible' at 500 yards. Private J. Ferguson, New Galloway, won the Airds Cup, with a score of 34 points, the same score with which his brother won the event the previous year. The Bronze Medal was won by Corporal A. Gourlay, Kirkcudbright, with a total of 142, an increase of 9 points over the last years winner. The Glenlee Cup was won by Cyclist McHaffie, with a score of 31 points, an increase of 3 points on the previous year. Gunner T. Galloway, Portpatrick, was first in the Carbine Prize, with a score of 30 which was 2 points better than the last year. The Members Lee-Metford prize was won by Private J. Fergusson with 31 points, one point less than the winner the last year. This was the only competition in which the score was down from the previous year. The Recruits Bronze Medal was won by Private J. Coulter, Newton Stewart, with a score of 31 points, as against 29 made by the last year's winner. The Consolation Sweepstake, was carried off by Corporal McMurdo, Maxwellton, with a score of 34 points compared to 32 the last year. In the team competition, New Galloway topped the list with a score of 456 points, while Castle Douglas teams came 2nd and 3rd. The team prize was won by New Galloway, the previous year, with a score of 442 points. The Dalbeattie team, who won the Volley firing competition two weeks earlier, did not compete in the team competition.

The statistical department was in the usual charge of Major Dunn and Quartermaster Sergeant Myers, joint Secretaries of the Association, assisted by Private Connolly.

For the convenience of the Companies tents were provided, and lunch and refreshments were provided in a large Marquee, by Mr. W. Seggie of the Victoria Hotel, Castle Douglas.

Colonel Kennedy was present during the day together with the other officers of the Regiment. Lieutenant-Colonel W. J. Maxwell, yngr., of Munches; Major and Adjutant Blake; Major Dunn; Major Harper and Lieutenant Hewat, Castle Douglas; Lieutenants Watson, McClean and Machray, Stranraer; Captain Gordon, Portpatrick Artillery; Major McPhater and Captain Kelly, Newton Stewart; Captain Maxwell, Dalbeattie; Captain Comrie, Kirkcudbright; Captain Nicholson, Kirkcudbright Artillery; Captain Timms and Surgeon Captain Cowan, New Galloway. Major Lennox and Lieutenant Grierson, Maxwellton.

The following are the results of the several competitions:-

I). **The Bargaly Challenge Cup,** presented by the late James Mackie Esq., M.P. with money prizes added by the Association. Open to members of the Galloway Rifle Volunteer Corps and the Volunteer Artillery Corps in Galloway. 1st £2; 2nd £1; 3rd £1; 4th £1; 5th 15/-; 6th 15/-; 7th 10/-; 8th 10/-; 9th 7/6d; 10th 7/6d; 11 th 5/-; 12th 5/; 13th 2/6d; 14th 2/6d; 15th 2/6d. 7 rounds at 200 yards.

1. Corporal R. Todd, Castle Douglas	33 points.
2. Lieutenant J. Machray, Stranraer	32
3. Sergeant R. Fergusson, New Galloway	32
4. Sergeant E. Paterson, Kirkcudbright	32
5. Lieutenant Watson, Stranraer	32
6. Corporal Gourlay, Kirkcudbright	32
7. Private J. Blackwood, Newton Stewart	32
8. Corporal J. Moffat, Maxwellton	32
9. Corporal R. McMurdo, Maxwellton	32
10. Private W. A. Miller, Kirkcudbright	32
11. Corporal J. Bell, New Galloway	31
12. Quartermaster Sergeant Myers, Castle Douglas	31
13. Private J. Fergusson, New Galloway	31
14. Private J. Turner, Castle Douglas	31
15. Armourer Sergeant G. Geddes, New Galloway	31

II). **The Munches Cup.** presented by Wellwood H. Maxwell Esq., of Munches, to become the property of anyone winning it three times. Open as in No.(I).1st £2; 2nd £1.10/-; 3rd £1; 4th £1; 5th 15/-; 6th 15/-; 7th 10/-; 8th. 10/-; 9th 7/6d; 10th 7/6d; 11th 5/-; 12th 5/-; 13th 2/6d; 14th 2/6d; 15th 2/6d. 7 rounds at 500 yards.

1. Cyclist G. McHaffie, Stranraer	35
2. Sergeant G. Melburn, Dalbeattie	34
3. Lance Sergeant Haining, Maxwellton	34
4. Corporal Gourlay, Kirkcudbright	34
5. Private J. Fergusson, New Galloway	33
6. Private J. McKeand, Newton Stewart	33
7. Corporal R. McMurdo, Maxwellton	33
8. Private P. Priestley, Newton Stewart	33
9. Private Reid, Kirkcudbright	33
10. Sergeant Clingan, Castle Douglas	33
11. Lieutenant Watson, Stranraer	33
12. Sergeant R. Fergusson, New Galloway	33
13. Private T. McMurray, Newton Stewart	33
14. Private W.M. Paterson, Kirkcudbright	33
15. Private D. Paterson, Kirkcudbright	33
Private G. Geddes, New Galloway	33
Private J. McConchie, Newton Stewart	33

III). **The Airds Cup**. presented by Major Houghton-Hughan of Airds, to become the property of anyone winning it three times. Open as in No (I) 1st £2; 2nd £1.10/-; 3rd £1; 4th £1; 5th 15/- 6th 15/-; 7th 10/-; 8th 10/-; 9th 7/6d; 10th 7/6d; 11th 5/-; 12th 5/-; 13th 2/6d; 14th 2/6d; 15th 2/6d.

7 rounds at 600 yards.

1. Private J. Fergusson, New Galloway	34 points.
2. Lance Sergeant Kevlichan, Maxwellton	33
3. Corporal A. Gourlay, Kirkcudbright	32
4. Private Carnochan, Kirkcudbright	32
5. Corporal Hetherington, Castle Douglas	32
6. M.- Sergeant Murdoch, Castle Douglas	32
7. Private J. Ewen, Castle Douglas	32
8. Lance Corporal Bowie, Kirkcudbright	32
9. Sergeant Agnew, Newton Stewart	32
10. Corporal J. Moffat, Maxwellton	31
11. Private James Scott, Castle Douglas	31
12. Private C. Irving, Dalbeattie	31
13. Private S. Fergusson, New Galloway	31
14. Sergeant Clingan, Castle Douglas	31
15. Private W. McCreadie, Newton Stewart	31

IV). **Aggregate**. Scores made in Competition (1), (II), and (III). 1st £3; 2nd £2.10/-; 3rd £2; 4th £1.10/-; 2 of £1; 3 of 15/-; 1 of 10/-; 3 of 7/6d; 1 of 5/-; 2 of 2/6d.

	I	II.	III	Total.
1. Cyclist Fergusson, New Galloway	31	33	34	98
2. Corporal Gourlay, Kirkcudbright	32	31	32	98
3. Cyclist McHaffie, Stranraer	30	35	30	95
4. Sergeant Fergusson, New Galloway	32	33	30	95
5. Private Carnochan, Kirkcudbright	30	32	32	94
6. L/Corporal Bowie, Kirkcudbright	30	31	32	93
7. Sergeant Agnew, Newton Stewart	28	32	32	92
8. M/Sergeant Murdoch, Castle Douglas	29	31	32	92
9. Corporal Hetherington, Castle Douglas	30	30	32	92
10. Sergeant Clingan, Castle Douglas	28	33	31	92
11. Private S. Fergusson, New Galloway	29	32	31	92
12. Corporal Moffat, Maxwellton	32	29	31	92
13. Qtr. Mstr. Sergeant Myers, Castle Douglas	31	31	30	92
14. Corporal McMurdo, Maxwellton	32	33	27	92
15. Sergeant Kevlichan, Maxwellton	28	30	33	91
16. Private W. McCreadie, Newton Stewart	29	31	31	91
17. Private Scott, Castle Douglas	30	30	31	91
18. Private G. Geddes New Galloway	28	33	30	91
19. Private McConchie, Newton Stewart	28	33	30	91
20. Private P. Fergusson, New Galloway	30	32	29	91
21. Sergeant Melburn, Dalbeattie	29	34	28	91
22. Private Blackwood, Newton Stewart	32	31	28	91

V). **The Bronze Medal** Competition. The 10 highest scorers in the Aggregate, who have not already won the National Rifle Association Bronze Medal, to fire 10 rounds at 600 yards, as laid down for second stages (N.R.A.) and their places to be decided by the aggregate of the two stages. 1st the Bronze Medal of the N.R.A., with £1 added by the Association, the money part of the prize to be conditional on the winner's shooting for the Prince of Wales Prize at Bisley, either in the year of winning or the following year.

	Aggr.	600yd.	Total.
1. Corporal A. Gourlay, Kirkcudbright	98	44	142.
2. Cyclist McHaffie, Stranraer	95	45	140
3. Private S. Fergusson, New Galloway	92	47	139
4. Private T. Carnochan, Kirkcudbright	94	45	139
5. Corporal W. Hetherington, Castle Douglas	92	43	135
6. L/Cpl. A.D. Bowie, Kirkcudbright	93	42	135
7. Sergeant J.G. Clingan, Castle Douglas	92	42	134
8. Corporal R. McMurdo, Maxwellton	92	40	132
9. Corporal J. Moffat, Maxwellton	92	38	130
10. Sergeant Agnew, Newton Stewart	92	34	126

VI). **The Glenlee Cup**. presented by the late George Maxwell Esq., of Glenlee, to become the property of anyone winning it three times. Open to efficients and recruits of the Galloway Rifles only. Efficients to have attended, during the present year, five Company drills, including one Adjutant's drill. Recruits to have attended, during the present year, 20 drills, including one Adjutant's drill. 1st the Cup and £2; 2nd £1; 3rd 15/-; 4th 10/-; 5th 10/-; 6th 5/-; 7th 5/-.
7 rounds at 200 yards, standing.

1. Cyclist McHaffie, Stranraer	31 points.
2. Private W.A. Millar, Kirkcudbright	27
3. Corporal J. Henderson, Maxwellton	27
4. Private J. Fergusson, New Galloway	27
5. Private G. Caldow, New Galloway	27
6. Sergeant Haining, Maxwellton	26
7. Sergeant Agnew, Newton Stewart	26

VII). **Carbine Prizes**. for Galloway Artillery Volunteers only. 1st £2; 2nd £1; 3rd 15/-; 4th 10/-; 5th 10/-; 6th 5/-; 7th 5/-.
7 rounds at 200 yards

1. Gunner T. Galloway, Portpatrick	30 points.
2. Captain James Gordon, Portpatrick	30
3. Sergeant J. Thompson, Portpatrick	25
4. Lieutenant Machray, Stranraer	24
5. Sergeant Kimm, Kirkcudbright	23
6. Gunner G. Ross, Portpatrick	23
7. Sergeant Slater, Kirkcudbright	20
Gunner R. Herries, Sandhead	20

VIII). **Members Lee-Metford Prizes**. open to Members of the Association.
1st £2; 2nd £1.10/-; 3rd £1; 4th £1; 5th 15/-; 6th 10/-; 7th 10/-; 8th 8/-.
7 rounds at 600 yards.

1. Private J. Fergusson, New Galloway	33 points.
2. Sergeant R. Fergusson, New Galloway	33
3. Private Carnochan, Kirkcudbright	32
4. Private W. McCreadie, Newton Stewart	32
5. Private W.A. Miller, Kirkcudbright	32
6. Lieutenant Machray, Stranraer	32
7. Sergeant E. Patterson, Kirkcudbright	32
8. Sergeant Clingan, Castle Douglas	31

IX). **Recruit's Bronze Medal and Association Prizes**. Open to recruits of the Galloway Rifle Volunteer Corps and Galloway Artillery who have joined the Volunteer Force since the 1st November last, and also open to recruits of last year. 1st £1 and recruits National Rifle Association Bronze Medal. 2nd 15/-; 3rd 10/-; 4th 10/-; 5th 5/-; 6th 5/-; 7th 5/-; 8th 2/6d; 9th 2/6d; 10th 2/6d.
7 rounds at 200 yards.

1. Privates J. Coultart, Newton Stewart	31 points.
2. C. Irving, Dalbeattie	30
3. S. Fergusson, New Galloway	29
4. Thomas Craig, Dalbeattie	28
5. James Louden, Maxwellton	27
6. S. Rae, Castle Douglas	26
7. A. Sisson, Newton Stewart	26
8. R. Dickson, Maxwellton	25
9. Gunner T. Galloway, Portpatrick Artillery	25
10. Private G. Jardine, Kirkcudbright	25

Special recruit's prizes 1. Private Colin Christison, Newton Stewart 25; 2. Private W. Birrell, Newton Stewart 18; 3. Private J. Moore, Newton Stewart 15; 4. Alex. McConnell, Newton Stewart 10.

X). **Consolation Sweepstake Prize.** open to those members of the Galloway Rifle Volunteer Corps and Galloway Artillery who have never gained a first prize at the Association's meetings, or a prize to the value of £5 at any other rifle meeting.
7 rounds at 200 yards.

1. Corporal McMurdo, Maxwellton	34 points
2. Lance Sergeant D. Haining, Maxwellton	33
3. Captain James Gordon, Portpatrick Artillery	33
4. Private J. Louden, Maxwellton	32
5. Private S. Fergusson, New Galloway	32
6. Private J. Coultart, Newton Stewart	32
7. Private S. Walker, Castle Douglas	30
8. Private Lawson, New Galloway	30
9. Private J. McKeand, Newton Stewart	30
10. Private Reid, Kirkcudbright	29

XI). **Team competition.** open to the Companies of the Galloway Volunteers. Teams of 5 men. Companies may enter more than one team. Scores in the competitions (I) (II) and (III) to count.).

1. New Galloway

Private J. Fergusson	98	
Sergeant R. Fergusson	95	
Private G. Geddes	94	
Armr. Sergeant Geddes	87	
Corporal J. Bell	85	
		456.

2. Castle Douglas (No.1 team)

Q. Mstr. Sergeant Myers	92	
Sergeant Clingan	92	
Corporal Hetherington	92	
Corporal McCaw	89	
Corporal J. McGaw	84	
		449

3. Castle Douglas (No.2 team)

M. Sergeant Murdoch	92	
Sergeant S. Gordon	90	
Corporal R. Todd	90	
Private J. Turner	88	
Private S. Walker	86	
		446.

Maxwellton ('G' Company)	444.
Newton Stewart (No. 1 team)	438.
Kirkcudbright (No.1 team)	437.
Kirkcudbright (No. 2 team)	435.
Newton Stewart (No.2 team)	423.
Maxwellton ('F' Company)	421.

Major Lennox, in presenting the prizes to the successful competitors, said he had to apologise for Colonel Kennedy, who had to leave in order to catch his train. He was very sorry at having to go away so early. However, before leaving, he remarked how pleased he was with the way every thing had been done at their annual meeting. There had been no grumbling, not a single hitch had occurred, and everybody seemed pleased with the arrangements, and he desired to thank those who had carried through the work so efficiently, and those who had assisted at the targets.

The shooting had been very good. Everyone could not hope to make a score of 98 and it was a mistake for young shots not to come forward because they could not make a score as high. The only shooting which had to be improved was that at the 200 yard range, they had to be able to stand or kneel at that range. In regards to the Volley firing which had taken place a fortnight earlier, it was one of the most interesting. The figure of merit was 61%, whereas that of the winning team at Edinburgh for the General's cup was 55%, this showed the ability of the Regiment's marksmen. Captain Maxwell, New Galloway, was singled out for the way he had trained his men especially with their having been two men short but this would be mentioned in the returns.

On the motion of Captain Maxwell, three cheers were given for the Secretaries, Captain Dunn and Sergeant Myers and for the Queen when the meeting dispersed.

The following programme was issued by the Council of the Galloway Artillery and Rifle Volunteer Association, following a meeting held in February, 1900, at the Town Hall,, Castle Douglas, relative to the 40th Rifle Meeting of the Association, to be held at Caigton, Castle Douglas, on the 4th August, 1900. The programme includes, a list of Council Members, Abstract of accounts, Rules for competition, together with the prizes to be shot for at the forthcoming meeting.

Office-Bearers 1900.
Presidents;

The Earl of Stair, K.T.; (Sir Herbert Maxwell, Lord Lieutenant of the Stewartry was appointed
President on 19th March, 1904, on the death of the Earl of Stair).
Sir Mark J. McTaggart-Stewart, Bart., M.P.
W.H. Maxwell, Esq., of Munches.
Captain John Hope, R.N., of St. Mary's Isle.

Council:

Col. J.M. Kennedy, Galloway Rifle Volunteers.
Lt.-Col. W.J. Maxwell yngr. of Munches.
Adam Skirving Esq., of Croys.
J.W. Hutchison Esq., of Laurieston Hall.
Major A.C. Armitage of Kirroughtree.
Major H. Houghton-Hughan of Airds.
Major John Mackie of Bargaly.
Major and Adjutant R.W.M. Blake, Galloway Rifle Volunteers.
Major McRobert, Stranraer Artillery.
Major Lennox, Maxwellton.
Major Phyn, Maxwellton.
Captain Nicholson, Kirkcudbright Artillery.
Captain Maxwell, Dalbeattie.
Captain Timms, New Galloway.
Captain Gordon, Portpatrick Artillery.
Captain Kelly, Newton Stewart
Captain McLean, Stranraer.
Captain Comrie, Kirkcudbright.
Captain Hewat, Castle Douglas.
Colour Sergeant J. McGregor, Kirkcudbright.
Musketry-Sergeant H. Murdoch, Castle Douglas.

Joint Secretaries and Treasurers:

Major J. Dunn, Castle Douglas.
Quartermaster Sergeant T. Myers, Castle Douglas.

Committee under Rule VI.

Colonel Kennedy	Major Blake
Major Lennox	Captain Gordon
Captain Comrie	Major Dunn
Quartermaster Sergeant T. Myers	Range Officer - Major Lennox.

List of Members.

Major Mackie of Bargaly	2. 0s. 0d
Mr. Adam Skirving of Croys	2. 0s. 0d
Colonel Kennedy of Knocknalling	10. 0s. 0d.
Mrs. Kennedy of Knocknalling	2. 0s. 0d.
Mr. J.W. Hutchison of Laurieston Hall	1. 0s. 0d.
Colonel Sanderson of Glenlaggan	1. 1s. 0d.
Mr. Duncan James Kay of Drumpark	1. 1s. 0d.
Mr. John Neilson of Mollance	2. 0s. 0d.

Mr. W.H. Maxwell of Munches	2. 0s. 0d.
The Rt. Hon. the Earl of Stair K.T.	10. 0s. 0d.
Mr. B. Rigby Murray of Parton	1. 1s. 0d.
Mr. W.A. Coats of Dalskairth	2. 0s. 0d.
Mr. William Gordon of Threave	2. 2s. 0d
Mr. Jasper Young of Garroch	1. 1s. 0d.
Captain R.D. Barrie Cunninghame of Hensol	2. 0s. 0d.
Mr. H.G. Murray Stewart of Cally	1. 1s. 0d.
Mr. David Maitland of Dundrennan	1. 0s. 0d.
Colonel Mackenzie of Auchenskeoch	1. 0s. 0d.
Captain Hamilton of Craighlaw	1. 0s. 0d.
Mr. Samuel Smith of Carleton M.P.	1. 0s. 0d.
Major Houghton-Hughan of Airds	1. 1s. 0d.
Mr. J.A. Henryson-Caird of Cassencary	1. 0s. 0d.
Major A.C. Armitage of Kirroughtree	1. 1s. 0d.
Sir Mark J. M'T Stewart Bart., M.P.	3. 3s. 0d
Colonel Kennaway, Greenlaw	10s. 0d.
Mr. A.T. Herries of Spottes	1. 1s. 0d.
Mr. Robert Stewart of Culgruff	1. 0s. 0d.
Colonel Blackett of Arbigland	1. 0s. 0d.
Sir D.R. Carrick Buchanan of Corsewall	1. 0s. 0d.
Mr. W.M. Neilson of Queenshill	2. 0s. 0d.
Mrs. Maitland Gordon of Kenmure	1. 0s. 0d.
Sheriff Jameson of Ardwall	3. 0s. 0d
Captain Hope R.N. of St. Mary's Isle	5. 0s. 0d.
Dr. E.S. Forde, Dalry	1. 1s. 0d.
Proprietors of Monybuie, per T.G. Dickson Esq.	10s. 0d.
Captain Comrie of Gategill 'A' Coy.	1. 0s. 0d.
P.M. Sergeant W.R. Murray	2s 6d.
Sergeant E. Paterson	2s 6d.
Private W. A. Miller	2s 6d.
Private W.M. Paterson	2s 6d.
Private T. Carnochan	2s 6d.
Private N.M. Heughan	2s 6d.
Private D. Paterson	2s 6d.
Private G.H. Nicholson	2s 6d.
P.M. Sergeant J. Osborne	5s. 0d.
Major M. M'L Harper, Castle Douglas	5s. 0d.
Major John Dunn, Castle Douglas	5s. 0d.
Lieutenant J.T. Hewat, 'B' Coy.	5s. 0d.
Q.M. Sergeant Thomas Myers, 'B' Coy.	2s 6d.
M. Sergeant Murdoch,	2s 6d.
Sergeant S.R. Gordon,	2s 6d.
Sergeant J.G. Clingan,	2s 6d.
Corporal John McGaw,	2s 6d.
Corporal William McCaw,	2s 6d.
Corporal William Hetherington,	2s 6d.
Corporal R. Todd,	2s 6d.
Private James S. Ewen,	2s 6d.
Private John Turner,	2s 6d.
Captain McLean, 'C' Coy.	5s. 0d.
Lieutenant W. Watson,	5s. 0d.
Private G. McHaffie	2s 6d.
Miss McHaffie, Stranraer	2s 6d.
Captain Kelly 'D' Coy.	5s. 0d.
Lieutenant C. McLean	5s. 0d.
Private W.F. McCreadie	2s 6d.
Major McPhater, Newton Stewart,	5s. 0d.
Captain Timms, of Slogarie, 'E' Coy.	2. 0s. 0d.
Surg. Captain J. Cowan,	5s. 0d.
Arm. Sergeant G. Geddes,	2s 6d.
Sergeant R. Fergusson,	2s 6d.
Corporal J. Bell,	2s 6d.
Private J. Fergusson,	2s. 6d.
S. Fergusson,	2s 6d.
P. Fergusson,	2s 6d.

G. Geddes,	2s 6d.
Major Lennox, 'F' Coy.	5s. 0d.
Private John Coupland,	2s 6d.
L. Sergeant D. Haining,	2s 6d.
Lieutenant R.A. Grierson, 'G' Coy.	5s. 0d.
Private W. Law,	2s 6d.
Captain Maxwell of Kirkennan, 'H' Coy.	2. 0s. 0d.
Lieutenant Machray, Stranraer Artillery,	5s. 0d.
Captain Gordon, Portpatrick Artillery,	10s. 0d.

	£82.11s.6d.

Abstract of Accounts.
Income.

1. Balance on hand at close of last Account	21. 8s. 4d
2. Member's subscriptions received	82.11s. 6d
3. Entry money received	66.19s. 6d
4. Sighting Shots	8.11s. 0d
5. Challenged shots	5s. 0d.
6. Cartridge Cases	11s. 6d
7. Interest on Deposit Receipts	18s. 2d.

	£181. 5s. 0d.

Expenditure.

1. On Ranges		15.11s.1d
2. On Competitions		
a) Prize money paid	84.10s. 6d.	
b) Markers and Register Keepers paid	10. 2s. 6d.	
c) National Rifle Association	5. 0s. 0d.	
d) Petty outlays	3.11s. 3d.	
	---------------	
		103. 4s. 3d
3. Capital Account for Ranges		50. 0s. 0d.
4. Printing, Advertising and Stationery		6. 4s. 5d.
5. Postages, Telegrams and Bank Charges		2. 8s. 9d.
		--------------
		177. 8s. 6d.
Balance in Treasurer's hands		3.16s. 6d.

		£181. 5s. 0d.

Castle Douglas, 24th February, 1900. - The account, of which the above is an abstract, was examined on this date and found to be correctly stated and sufficiently vouched.

Wellwood Maxwell, Captain, Galloway Rifles.

Wm. Lewis Comrie, Captain Galloway Rifles.

RULES.
Title

I. The name of the Association shall be, "The Galloway Artillery and Rifle Volunteer Association."

Membership

II. Any lady or gentleman may become a member of the Association by payment of an annual donation of not less than £1; Officers, 5s; Retired Volunteers, 5s; Non-commissioned Officers and Privates, 2s 6d. Officers of the Galloway Rifle Volunteers, and of Batteries of the Ayr and Galloway Artillery situated in Galloway, may each nominate one lady for membership upon an annual payment of 5s; and Non-commissioned Officers and Privates of the Galloway Rifles or the said Batteries may each nominate one lady for membership upon an annual payment of 2s 6d.

Annual Meeting.

III. An Annual Meeting of the Members shall be held in February of each year to elect Office-bearers, examine the Accounts of the previous year, appoint six Elected Members of Council as provided for in Rule IV, and transact any other competent business.

Council

IV. The ordinary affairs of the Association shall be conducted by a Council constituted as follows:-
    (a) The Field Officers and Adjutant of the Galloway Rifle Volunteers.
    (b) The Officers commanding Companies in the Galloway Rifle Volunteers, and Officers commanding Batteries of the Ayr and Galloway Artillery situated in Galloway.
    (c) One representative appointed by each Company of Rifle Volunteers and Battery of Artillery having ten Members of the Association.
    (d) Six elected Members appointed at the Annual Meeting of the Association.

Annual Competition

V. The annual competition shall be held on a day and at a place to be fixed by the Council.

Executive Committee

VI. The Competition shall be conducted under the direction of a Committee consisting of three Members nominated by the Council, along with the Officer Commanding and the Adjutant of the Galloway Rifles, and the Secretaries of the Association. Three to be a quorum. The Committee shall choose one of their number to act as Range Officer.

Powers of Committee

VII. The decision of the Committee shall be final and binding in all matters submitted to them for their consideration, but they may at their discretion refer any question to the decision of the Council, in which case the decision of the Council on such questions shall be final.

Permanent Staff

VIII. No Member of the Permanent Staff attached to a Volunteer Corps shall be eligible to shoot for Prizes restricted to Volunteers.

Officers at Firing Points

IX. Officers will be told off to take charge of the Firing Points. They shall test rifles, and see that Regulations are adhered to.

Restrictions

X. No Officer, Non-commissioned Officer, or Private detailed for duty at the Firing Point or in the Butts during the Meeting, shall shoot either for Prizes or Practice during the time for which he is detailed for duty.

Officers Competing

XI. No Commissioned Officers shall compete for Volunteer Prizes unless a Member of the Association.

Uniform

XII. Each Volunteer must shoot in the Uniform of the Corps as worn on parade; must, before the Competition, have attended sufficient, drills to make himself efficient, and have fired his Third Class. Puggarees or Cap Covers may be worn.

Retired Volunteers

XIII. Every Retired Volunteer who competes as such must be not less than 45 years of age, must have qualified for a Volunteer Decoration or Long Service Medal with the Galloway Rifle Volunteers or Ayr and Galloway Artillery in Galloway, and be a member of this Association.

Protests

XIV. All protests or complaints must be made in writing, and if possible, must be handed at once to the Officer in charge of the Firing Point, to be, by him, sent in to the Committee tent. Should there be unnecessary delay, the Committee may decline to entertain such protest or complaint. No objection on the score of a Competitor's dress will be entertained unless it shall have been raised before he leaves the Firing Point.

XV. All Entries must be made through Officers commanding Companies and Batteries, and Entry Money paid, Nine Days before Competition. Entries after that date will be Post Entries, which must be made through the Secretaries, and, on payment of One Shilling extra for each Entry, will be taken up to the day before the Competition; but on no condition will any Entries be taken on the day of the Competition. Officers commanding Companies and Batteries must not later than the Eighth Day before the Competition transmit to the Secretaries the Entries made with them, and Entries transmitted by them later than that day will be Post Entries. No Competitor shall enter more than once for any prize.

XVI. Competitors must themselves be responsible for the Entries they may make. Should any Competitor enter for any Competition for which he is not eligible, and the Secretaries take the same, such action on the part of the Secretaries shall not give the Competitor any claim, either to shoot in such Competitions or to claim any Prizes under any scores made in such Competitions.

Squadding

XVII. Competitors must be squadded, and must be forward and ready to commence firing when their names are called by the Register-keeper. When the black board shows that the preceding Competitors have only two shots each to fire, the next men shall make all preparations to occupy the firing point without a moments loss of time. The score on any Competitor or Team may be disallowed if undue delay is made either in firing or commencing to fire. In individual Competitions such delay shall be interpreted as being one minute from the time at which the target is clear. The Range Officer shall have power to alter the squadding when necessary, so that no Target may be vacant, but the shooting for each Competition must be completed before another is begun.

Rifles

XVIII. The Lee-Metford and Lee-Enfield Rifles and any Carbine issued by the Government to Volunteers and bearing the Government Viewer's mark shall be used. Minimum pull of trigger, six pound; and the trigger of the rifle of every Competitor who has made a Score likely to win a Prize must be tested by the Officer in charge or Register-keeper.

Penalties

XIX. Each time a Competitor strikes a wrong Target, he shall pay a penalty of 2/6d. If a Competitor challenges a shot, he must deposit 2/6d, which will be repaid if he proves correct.

Ties

XX. Ties shall be decided by the N.R.A. Rules. Competitors who make 30 or higher Scores in the following Competitions will fire three additional tie shots. The Competitors concerned are responsible for calling the attention of the Officer in charge to this requirement.

Ammunition

XXI. Regulation Ammunition will be supplied on the ground free of charge on Competitors presenting Tickets, and no ammunition is to be used except that so supplied.

Sighting

XXII. In all Competitions one Sighting shot, price 3d, will be allowed, except in the Bronze Medal Competition, in which one Sighting Shot shall be allowed without payment.

XXIII. No two men in the same Squad shall shoot with the same rifle, and each Competition must be strictly confined to the Targets set apart for it.

XXIV. All Scores shall be verified by the Officer in charge, and immediately on the conclusion of the firing for each Prize, the names of the winners will be posted outside the Council tent.

XXV. The N.R.A. Rules shall be used to settle all questions not herein provided for.

PRIZE LIST
Volley Firing Competition

The Silver Cups presented by the late Earl of Selkirk and the late Colonel Kennedy Laurie have been placed at the disposal of the Officer Commanding the Galloway Rifles to be awarded, if it can be so arranged, upon the results attained in the extra course of Musketry which is to be carried through in the Brigade Camp at Melrose, so far as applies to separate Companies.

Annual Competition on 4th August. 1900.

1. **The Bargaly Challenge Cup**, presented by the late James Mackie Esq., M.P. with money prizes added by the Association. Open to members of the Galloway Rifle Volunteer Corps and the Volunteer Artillery in Galloway.
    7 rounds at 200 yards. Standing. Entry 2/-.

2. **The Munches Cup,** presented by Wellwood H. Maxwell, Esq., of Munches, to become the property of anyone winning it three times. Open as in No.1.
    7 rounds at 500 yards. Kneeling. Entry 2/-.

3. **The Airds Cup**, presented by Major Houghton-Hughan of Airds, to become the property of anyone winning it three times. Open as in No.1.
    7 rounds at 600 yards. Any Military position. Entry 2/-.

4. **Aggregate.** Scores made in Competitions 1, 2, and 3. 22 Prizes. Entry 2/6d.

5. **Bronze Medal Competition**. 10 rounds at 600 yards. Any Military position. Entry Free. The 10 Highest Scorers in the Aggregate, No.4, to fire 10 rounds at 600 yards as laid down for Second Stages (N.R.A.) and their places to be decided by the Aggregate of the two Stages. 1st The Bronze Medal of the N.R.A., with £4 added by the Association; the money part of the Prize to be conditional on the winner's shooting for the Prince of Wales' Prize at Bisley, either in the year of winning or the following year. The money shall be paid on the winner giving satisfactory guarantees that he will fulfil these conditions.

6. **The Tyro Aggregate,** open to those Members of the Galloway Rifle Volunteers and Galloway Artillery who have never gained a First Prize at the Association's previous Meetings (Recruit's Prize excepted), or a Prize of £5 at any Rifle Meeting. Scores in Competitions 1, 2, and 3 to count. Competitors must enter for Competitions 1, 2, and 3, but Recruits may enter for and count their score in Competition No.10 in place of that of No.1. Entry Free.

7. **The Glenlee Cup,** presented by the late George Maxwell Esq., of Glenlee, to become the property of anyone winning it three times. Open to Efficients and Recruits of the Galloway Rifle Volunteers only. Efficients to have attended, during the present year, five Company Drills, including one Adjutant's Drill; Recruits to have attended, during the present year, 20 Drills, including one Adjutant's Drill.
    7 rounds at 200 yards. Standing. Entry 2/6d. The Rifle to be that used in the Volunteer Force.

8. **Carbine Prizes,** for Galloway Artillery Volunteers only.
   7 rounds at 200 yards. Standing. Entry 2/-.

9. **Members' Lee-Metford Prizes**. open to Members of the Association.
   7 rounds at 600 yards. Any Military position. Entry 1/-.

10. **Recruit's Bronze Medal and Association Prizes**. Open to Recruits of the Galloway Rifle Volunteer Corps and Galloway Artillery who have joined the Volunteer Force since 1st November last, and also open to Recruits of last year.
    7 rounds at 200 yards. Standing. Entry 2/-.

11. **Team Competition**. open to the Companies of the Galloway Volunteers.
    Teams of five men. Companies can enter more than one team. Scores in Competitions 1, 2 and 3 to count. Entry 10/- per team: to be divided in prizes, less expenses of Competition.

N.B. - All teams must be entered in accordance with Rule XV, provided that, in the event of any Member of the Team being prevented from competing, another Competitor may be substituted, but such substitution must be made before 11.30am on the day of the Meeting, and the complete list of the Team posted at the Secretary's Tent at that time. Copies of this Programme of Competitions and Rules can be had on application to the Secretaries.

Joint Secretaries and Treasurers:
John Dunn, Major.
Thomas Myers, Quartermaster Sergeant.

* * * *

41st Meeting of the G.A.R.V.A.

The 41st Annual shooting competition under the auspices of the Galloway Artillery and Rifle Volunteer Association, was held on Saturday, 17th August, 1901, at the Caigton ranges, Castle Douglas. There were 9 events on the programme, for which £80 in cash, 3 Silver Cups and 3 Bronze Medals, were offered in prizes. The weather, however, was atrocious, with a drenching rain, which came over the hills and almost obscured the targets, with the result that the start of the competition was delayed by over half an hour.

The Officers present were, Colonel J.M. Kennedy, Commanding the Galloway Rifles, who during the course of the day presented long service medals to Sergeant Wright, Corporal W. Hetherington, and Lance Corporal John Scott, all of Castle Douglas; Major Lennox, acting Adjutant; Lieutenant Grierson, Maxwellton; Captain Maxwell and Lieutenant Maxwell, Dalbeattie; Captain Gordon, Portpatrick Artillery and Captain Comrie, Kirkcudbright, who acted as Range Officers; Captain Hewat and Lieutenant Biggar, Castle Douglas; Surgeon-Lieutenant Robertson, Portpatrick Artillery. Major Dunn and Quartermaster Sergeant Myers, joint Secretaries, assisted by Lance Corporal F. Connolly, all of 'B' Company, Castle Douglas, had charge of the Statistical and Clerical Department, which was no easy task deciphering some of the score cards owing to the excessive wet.

There were 78 entries for the Bargaly Cup, which was the first event of the meeting and notwithstanding the adverse conditions, Cyclist McHaffie, Stranraer, secured the trophy with a score of 32 points, only one point less than the score with which he won the same trophy the last year. This was the fourth occasion that Cyclist McHaffie had won the trophy but not in succession. However, many of the scores in the competition dropped into the teens. In the Carbine contest, 17 cards were returned, with that belonging to Surgeon Lieutenant Harper, Stranraer, being the best score with 26 points. In the Recruit's Competition, Private C. Taylor, Kirkcudbright, came top with a score of 28 points, which included three bulls-eyes. Dalbeattie Company, who had always a tradition of excelling in the Recruit's competition, did not disappoint, with four of their men entering the prize list.

On the completion of these three events the rain became so heavy that competitors and spectators alike were forced to seek the shelter of the tents. A meeting of the Executive was hastily called, and when it was reported to them, that the targets had begun to collapse with the deluge, the Executive took the decision to postpone the meeting for a week.

The following are the results of the three completed competitions:-

I). **The Bargaly Challenge Cup,** a silver cup presented by the late James Mackie, Esq., M.P. with 15 money prizes added by the Association. Open to members of the Galloway Rifle Volunteer Corps and the Volunteer Artillery Corps in Galloway.
7 rounds at 200 yards.

1. Cyclist G. McHaffie, Stranraer	32 points.
2. Corporal W. Hetherington, Castle Douglas	31
3. Sergeant R. Ferguson, New Galloway	31
4. Private T. Carnochan, Kirkcudbright	30
5. Private A. Brown, Dalbeattie	30
6. Sergeant Major Kimm, Kirkcudbright Artillery	30
7. Sergeant J. McGregor, Dalbeattie	30
8. Private W. Patterson, Kirkcudbright	30
9. Corporal Bell, New Galloway	30
10. Sergeant E. Paterson, Kirkcudbright	30
11. Qtr. Mstr. Sergeant Myers, Castle Douglas	30
12. Corporal J. McGaw, Castle Douglas	30
13. Private W. McCreadie, Newton Stewart	29
14. Private James Haugh, Castle Douglas	29
15. Private J. Ferguson, New Galloway	29
Corporal W. McCaw, Castle Douglas	29

VI). **Carbine Prizes**. Open to members of the Volunteer Artillery Corps in Galloway only.
7 rounds at 200 yards. 7 money prizes.

1. Surgeon-Lieutenant Harper, Stranraer	26 points.
2. Sergeant J. Slater, Kirkcudbright	25
3. Captain Gordon, Portpatrick	24
4. Gunner J. Baillie, Kirkcudbright	23
5. Corporal Lees, Portpatrick	23
6. Gunner McDouall, Portpatrick	22
7. Gunner McCormick, Portpatrick	21
Sergeant W. Richardson, Kirkcudbright	21
Gunner Thorburn, Portpatrick	21
Sergeant Lees, Portpatrick	21

VIII). **Recruit's Bronze Medal and Association Prizes**. Open to recruits of the Galloway Rifle Volunteers and Galloway Artillery who have joined the Volunteer Force since 1st November last and also open to recruits of the last year. 13 money prizes.
7 rounds at 200 yards.

1. Private C. Taylor, Kirkcudbright	28 points.
2. Private A. Grewar, Dalbeattie	27
3. Private A. McWilliam, Dalbeattie	26
4. Gunner McCormick, Portpatrick	26
5. Private R. Garmory, Castle Douglas	24
6. Private J. Gordon, Castle Douglas	24
7. Gunner J. Baillie, Kirkcudbright	23
8. Private W. Kirkpatrick, Kirkcudbright	22
9. Private W. Craik, Dalbeattie	21
10. Private W. Edwards, Newton Stewart	21
11. Private A. McKeand, New Galloway	21
12. Private F.H. Gallagher, Dalbeattie	20
13. Private R. Clenahan, Maxwellton	19

The 41st meeting of the G.A.R.V.A. was resumed on Saturday, 23rd August, 1901, at Caigton, amidst brilliant sunshine, a marked contract to the disastrous weather which had prevailed the previous week. The programme comprised of 9 events but with 3 events already completed, it left a somewhat shortened meeting. The adjournment was not conducive to an increase in public interest and indeed the spectators were very much conspicuous by their absence although a good many competitors did make the effort and come forward once again for the remaining events. There were a few entrants from the previous week unavoidably absent, leading to a general lack of enthusiasm in the proceedings.

The statistical and clerical departments were once again kept by Major Dunn, Quartermaster Sergeant Myers and Lance Corporal F. Connolly, but the postponement had a profound effect on the absence of Officers of the Regiment, which no doubt contributed to the lack of enthusiasm on the part of the rank and file. Those being present; Major Lennox, acting Adjutant; Captain Comrie, Range Officer; Lieutenant Maxwell, Dalbeattie and Lieutenant Biggar, Castle Douglas.

Cyclist G. McHaffie, Stranraer, was to carry on where he had left off the previous week, winning the Airds Cup, for the 2nd year in succession and topping the list in the Aggregate with a score of 98. He also won the Bronze Medal with comparative ease and although 4th in the Munches Cup he missed out by the merest margin, having hit 3 bulls in 3 shots he suddenly hit the right hand of the target which only brought him a Magpie (outer), he completed his score with another 3 successive bulls but the Magpie denied him the trophy. The eventual winner was Private W. Paterson, Kirkcudbright, who had the best score of the day with 34 points at 500 yards. Sergeant R. Ferguson, New Galloway, headed the list in the Member's Prizes with a total of 33 points as against 34, the previous year. 'B' Company, Castle Douglas, were again first in the team competition, their No.2 team having a majority of 5 points over New Galloway, who were placed 2nd.

II). **The Munches Cup**. A Silver Cup presented by the late Wellwood H. Maxwell Esq., of Munches, to become the property of anyone winning it three times, with 15 money prizes added by the Association. Open to Members of the Galloway Rifle Volunteer Corps and the Artillery Corps in Galloway. 7 rounds at 500 yards.

1. Private W. Paterson, Kirkcudbright	34 points.
2. Corporal W. Haugh, Castle Douglas	33
3. Corporal Gourlay, Kirkcudbright	33
4. Cyclist McHaffie, Stranraer	33
5. Private Hindmarsh, Maxwellton	32
6. Corporal McCaw, Castle Douglas	32
7. Sergeant J. Coupland, Maxwellton	32
8. Private T.C. Graham, Maxwellton	31
9. Sergeant J.G. Clingan, Castle Douglas	31
10. Qtr. Mstr. Sergeant Myers, Castle Douglas	31
11. Private J. Ireland, Castle Douglas	30
12. Private J. Ewen, Castle Douglas	30
13. Corporal R. McMurdo, Maxwellton	30
14. Sergeant R. Ferguson, New Galloway	30
15. Private McGowan, Kirkcudbright	30

III). **The Airds Cup**. A Silver Cup presented by Major Houghton-Hughan of Airds, to become the property of anyone winning it three times, with 15 money prizes added by the Association. Open to members of the Galloway Rifle Volunteer Corps and the Volunteer Artillery Corps in Galloway. 7 rounds at 600 yards.

1. Cyclist G. McHaffie, Stranraer	33 points.
2. Corporal R. McMurdo, Maxwellton	32
3. Private W. McCreadie, Newton Stewart	30
4. Private J. Ferguson, New Galloway	30
5. Private Dougan, Castle Douglas	30
6. Sergeant R. Ferguson, New Galloway	29
7. Sergeant E. Paterson, Kirkcudbright	29
8. Private J. Ewen, Castle Douglas	28
9. Corporal Bell, New Galloway	28
10. Private Reid, Kirkcudbright	27
11. Private Carnochan, Kirkcudbright	27
12. Corporal W. McCaw, Castle Douglas	27
13. Col. Sergeant Craig, Dalbeattie	27
14. Lance Sergeant Coulter, Newton Stewart	27
15. Corporal Hope, Maxwellton	27
Private Gray, Newton Stewart	27
Qtr. Mstr Sergeant Myers Castle Douglas	27

IV). **Aggregate.** Scores made in Competitions (I), (II) and (III). 47 money prizes.

	(I).	(II).	(III).	Total.
1. Cyclist G. McHaffie, Stranraer	32	33	33	98
2. Sergeant R. Ferguson, New Galloway	31	30	29	90
3. Corporal W. McCaw, Castle Douglas	29	32	27	88
4. Qtr. Mstr. Sergeant T. Myers, Castle Douglas	30	31	27	88
5. Corporal R. McMurdo, Maxwellton	24	30	32	86
6. Private J.S. Ewen, Castle Douglas	27	30	29	86
7. Corporal J. Bell, New Galloway	30	27	28	85
8. Private Carnochan, Kirkcudbright	30	28	27	85
9. Private W. Paterson, Kirkcudbright	30	34	21	85
10. Private Alex. Dougan, Castle Douglas	27	27	30	84
11. Col. Sergeant Craig, Dalbeattie	28	29	27	84
12. Corporal A. Gourlay, Kirkcudbright	24	33	26	83
13. Private J. Haugh, Castle Douglas	29	28	26	83
14. Sergeant E.G. Paterson, Kirkcudbright	30	23	29	82
15. Sergeant J. Coupland, Maxwellton	26	32	24	82
16. Private William McCreadie, Newton Stewart	29	22	30	81
17. Sergeant J.G. Clingan, Castle Douglas	24	31	26	81
18. Private J.G. Ireland, Castle Douglas	27	30	24	81
19. Private J. Hindmarsh, Maxwellton	27	32	22	81
20. Private W.S. Gray, Newton Stewart	27	25	27	79
21. Lance Sergeant Coulter, Newton Stewart	27	25	27	79
22. Corporal W. Haugh, Castle Douglas	22	33	24	79
23. Sergeant G. Melburn, Dalbeattie	27	29	23	79
24. Sergeant T. McGregor, Dalbeattie	30	26	23	79
25. Corporal W. Hope, Maxwellton	28	23	27	78
26. Lance Corporal Ferguson, New Galloway	27	26	25	78
27. Private J. McGowan, Kirkcudbright	26	30	22	78
28. Armr. Sergeant G. Geddes, New Galloway	25	26	26	77
29. Private T.C. Graham, Maxwellton	24	31	22	77
30. Private J. Ferguson, New Galloway	29	17	30	76
31. Private C. Irving, Dalbeattie	23	28	25	76
32. Private A. Brown, Dalbeattie	30	22	24	76
33. Corporal Todd, Castle Douglas	25	29	22	76
34. Private G. Geddes, New Galloway	22	27	26	75
35. Private J. Turner, Castle Douglas	24	28	23	75
36. Col. Sgt.-Major Kimm, Kirkcudbright Artillery	30	28	17	75
37. Private S. Ferguson, New Galloway	23	26	25	74
38. Corporal J. Bendal, Newton Stewart	25	23	24	72
39. Private W.A. Miller, Kirkcudbright	27	24	21	72
40. Corporal W. Hetherington, Castle Douglas	31	21	19	71
41. Corporal J. Moffat, Newton Stewart	23	26	21	70
42. Sergeant S.R. Gordon, Castle Douglas	24	26	20	70
43. Corporal J. Swan, Kirkcudbright	27	19	22	68
44. Private A. Reid, Kirkcudbright	21	20	27	68
45. Corporal J. McGaw, Castle Douglas	30	20	18	68
46. Lance Cpl. Henderson, Newton Stewart	27	21	15	63
47. Lance Cpl. F. Connolly, Castle Douglas	21	24	16	61

V). **Bronze Medal Competition.** The 10 highest scorers in the Aggregate, No. (IV) to fire 10 rounds at 600 yards as laid down for second stages (N.R.A.) and their places to be decided by the Aggregate of the two stages. 1st the Bronze Medal of the N.R.A. with £1 added by the Association, the money part of the prize to be conditional on the winner's shooting for the Prince of Wales Prize at Bisley either in the year of winning or the following year. The money will be paid to the winner giving a satisfactory guarantee that he will fulfil these conditions.

	Aggr.	600.	Total.
1. Cyclist G. McHaffie, Stranraer	98	42	140
2. Corporal W. McCaw, Castle Douglas	88	45	133
3. Sergeant R. Ferguson, New Galloway	90	40	130
4. Corporal R. McMurdo, Maxwellton	86	43	129
5. Qtr. Mstr. Sergeant Myers, Castle Douglas	88	41	129
6. Corporal Bell, New Galloway	85	43	128

7. Private Carnochan, Kirkcudbright	85	43	128
8. Private Ewen, Castle Douglas	86	40	126
9. Private Dougan, Castle Douglas	84	41	125
10. Private Paterson, Kirkcudbright	85	31	116

VII). **Members Prizes.** Eight money prizes, presented by the Association. Open to Members of the Association.

7 rounds at 600 yards.

1. Sergeant R. Ferguson, New Galloway	33 points.
2. Cyclist McHaffie, Stranraer	33
3. Corporal Hetherington, Castle Douglas	32
4. Sergeant E. Paterson, Kirkcudbright	31
5. Corporal Bell, New Galloway	30
6. Corporal W. McCaw, Castle Douglas	30
7. Private Carnochan, Kirkcudbright	30
8. Private W.S. Gray, Newton Stewart	29
Private Dougan, Castle Douglas	29
Private W. Paterson, Kirkcudbright	29

IX). **Team Competition.** £2-10s. in money prizes, given by the Association. Open to the Companies of the Galloway Volunteers. Teams of five men.

Scores in competitions (I), (II), and (III) to count.

1. 'B' Company, Castle Douglas (No.2 team)
2. 'E' Company, New Galloway
   'B' Company, Castle Douglas (No. 1 team)
   'G' Company, Maxwellton

At the close, Major Lennox, in calling upon Captain Comrie to present the prizes, said the shooting that day had been very good. They were only sorry that some of the competitors who had been present the previous week were unavoidably absent on the present occasion. They were hardly likely again, to take two days for their prize meeting, for a long time to come. The prizes having been presented to the successful competitors, cheers were given for the tenants who kindly granted them the use of the ground for the ranges, for the joint Secretaries and on the motion of Major Lennox, three hearty cheers were given for King Edward and his Queen.

* * * *

On Saturday, 6th May, 1905, a meeting of the Council of the Galloway Artillery and Rifle Volunteer Association, was held in the Town Hall, Castle Douglas, Colonel Kennedy of Knocknalling presiding, with the following members present, Lieutenant Colonel Lennox, Maxwellton; Major Hewat, Castle Douglas; Sergeant McHaffie, Stranraer; Lance Sergeant Bell, New Galloway; Colour Sergeant McGregor Kirkcudbright; Corporal J McGaw, Castle Douglas, with Major Dunn and Quartermaster Sergeant Myers, the joint Secretaries of the Association.

The Annual Prize Meeting - This was fixed for the 24th June, 1905.

Encouraging Young Volunteers - Mr. G.R. Murray of Parton, offered to present a prize or prizes for the encouragement of young Volunteers who had no chance in competing with the 'Old Stagers'. Subject to Mr. Murray's approval, an aggregate prize would be introduced for 200 and 500 yards, open to members who had never won £1 altogether at the Association meetings. (This was to become the Tyro-Aggregate Competition.)

Football and Volunteering - It was reported to the Chairman that the same men carried off the prizes every year and these good shots had entirely frightened off the young recruits, could something not be done in the matter? The subject was discussed with the possibility of handicapping the better shots, but while all agreed this was common practice in Company Competitions, it would be ridiculous to consider handicapping in an open Battalion Competition. Lieutenant-Colonel Lennox was to say that in any case they could not alter the conditions of the Cups. Quartermaster Myers told the meeting that what was wanted was for the young

Volunteer to put half the energy into shooting that they put into football and there would be no need for handicapping. Lt. Col. Lennox in defence of the young Volunteer was to say that they could not put in the same practice as the 'Old Stagers' with the current price of ammunition. In the old days the ammunition was free but now they had to pay for it. Quartermaster Myers was to say "They cannot pay to come and practice shooting but they can hire a special train to go and see a football match". No action was taken as to handicapping but it was agreed by the Council that in the Member's Competition they would in future double the amount of prizes without increasing the prize money.

Bronze Medal Competition - A motion was put forward that the Bronze Medal, the Blue Riband event of the Association meeting, be done away with and that they revert to the old system of the Aggregate regulating the custody of the Bronze Medal. It was considered unfair to middle class shots who could do well at 200 yards and 500 yards but fell short at the 600 yard range, and that only the best shots in the Battalion stood a chance of winning the Bronze Medal. Sergeant McHaffie, was to come out strongly against the motion saying, 'but we want to send the best men to Bisley'. He moved that the Bronze Medal be shot for in exactly the same terms as the Prince of Wales Prize at Bisley, 10 shots at 200 and 500 yards. He said it was a great honour to a Regiment when a member was successful in the St. George's or Prince of Wales Prize. The motion to merge the Bronze Medal in the Aggregate was carried.

At the conclusion of the meeting the Chairman, Colonel Kennedy, undertook to give a free lunch to all those who entered Mr. Murray's Prize, at the next Association Meeting.

****

45th Meeting of the G.A.R.V.A.

The 45th Annual prize meeting of the Galloway Artillery and Rifle Volunteer Association took place on Saturday, 24th June, 1905, at Caigton ranges, Castle Douglas, in brilliant weather. The various Companies of the Battalion were well represented as were the local Artillery Companies. There were almost 100 competitors, this being a slight increase on the previous year. As usual the programme was an attractive one with almost £80 being offered in prize money, besides the valuable Cups and Medals. There was to be a new competition this year, that of the Tyro-Aggregate, which was open to members who had not won, altogether £1 at meetings of the Association. This competition had the effect of bringing out some of the less frequent attenders, as well as some of the younger men. It was inaugurated with the object of encouraging the younger, as well as the medium shots in the Regiment.

The Officers present were Lieutenant-Colonel Lennox; Captain A. Fraser, Adjutant, who acted as Range Officer; Captain Grierson, Maxwellton; Captain Forde, New Galloway; Lieutenant Glover, Gatehouse; Lieutenant Gillies, New Abbey; Captains Brown and Nicholson, Kirkcudbright Artillery. During the course of the day excellent music was discoursed by the Regimental Pipe-Band under Pipe Major Johnstone, Dalbeattie. Quartermaster Sergeant Myers, assisted by Sergeant F. Connolly, and Sergeant W. Haugh, all of Castle Douglas, were in charge of the Statistical Department. Tea and light refreshments were Purveyed in a large Marquee, by R. Todd, Confectioner, Castle Douglas.

The weather was favourable for good shooting but the heat was oppressive and at times the sun shone so brightly that it caused a slight mirage to the competitors. Notwithstanding the fine weather there were fewer visitors to the ground than in former years. Some notable scores were registered during the day with Armourer Sergeant McHaffie, Stranraer, making a record for the Bronze Medal with a score of 101 points. The competition began with the Bargaly Cup at 200 yards, here Sergeant McHaffie put on the 'possible' of 35 and carried off the trophy. The Munches Cup was won by a promising young shot, Private H. Haugh of Castle Douglas, who tied with Sergeant R. Todd, of the same Company, both putting on the 'possible'. The Airds Cup was won by Private D.R. Paterson, Kirkcudbright, who had tied on 34 points with Colour-Sergeant Ferguson, New Galloway. In the Carbine Prizes, Sergeant Major Kimm, Kirkcudbright, came out on top with a score of 2 points more than the previous year's winner. In the Member's Prizes, Colour Sergeant Ferguson, New Galloway and Sergeant Bell, same Company, tied with a score of 34 points and agreed to share the prize The shooting. of the Recruits was down on previous occasions, the prize being won by Private Moreley, Maxwellton, with a score of 26, whereas, Private McGhie, Dalbeattie, won the event the previous year with a score of 29 points. In both the Team and the Selkirk Cup competitions, Kirkcudbright took the 1st place closely followed by Castle Douglas.

The following are the results of the several competitions:

I). **The Bargaly Challenge Cup.** A silver cup presented by the late James Mackie, Esq., M.P., with 15 money prizes added by the Association. Open to members of the Galloway Rifle Corps and the Volunteer Artillery Corps in Galloway.

7 rounds at 200 yards.

1. Armourer-Sergeant G. McHaffie, Stranraer - 5555555 -   35 points.
2. Private S. Ferguson, New Galloway   34
3. Private Miller, Kirkcudbright   33
4. Colour-Sergeant Ferguson, New Galloway   33
5. Corporal Corrie, New Galloway   33
6. Private McMillan, Stranraer   33
7. Private G. Thomson, Kirkcudbright   33
8. Private J. S. Ewen, Castle Douglas   32
9. Private Carnochan, Kirkcudbright   32
10. Qtr. Mstr. Sergeant Myers, Castle Douglas   32
11. Private J. Turner, Castle Douglas   32
12. Corporal D. Ferguson, Maxwellton   32
13. Private J. McGowan, Kirkcudbright   32
14. Sergeant E. Paterson, Kirkcudbright   32
15. Sergeant D. Haining, Maxwellton   32
(one 32 counted out).

II). **The Munches Cup.** A silver cup presented by the late Wellwood H. Maxwell, Esq., of Munches, to become the property of anyone winning it three times, with 15 money prizes added by the Association. Open to members of the Galloway Rifle Volunteer Corps and to the Volunteer Artillery Corps in Galloway.

7 rounds at 500 yards.

1. Private H. Haugh, Castle Douglas   - 5555555 -   35 points.
2. Sergeant R. Todd, Castle Douglas   - 5555555 -   35
3. Ex-Armourer-Sergeant G. Geddes, New Galloway   34
4. Armourer-Sergeant G. McHaffie, Stranraer   34
5. Lance Corporal McGeoch, Stranraer   33
6. Corporal A.D. Ried, Kirkcudbright   33
7. Private Carnochan, Kirkcudbright   33
8. Sergeant Millburn, Dalbeattie   32
9. Sergeant W. Haugh, Castle Douglas   32
10. Private S. Brodie, Castle Douglas   32
11. Piper Clunie, Kirkcudbright   32
12. Colour Sergeant Ferguson, New Galloway   32
13. Private J. Haugh, Castle Douglas   32
14. Private Miller, Kirkcudbright   32
15. Lance Corporal Seggie, Dalbeattie   31
(four 31's counted out).

III). **The Airds Cup.** A silver cup presented by the late Major Houghton Hughan of Airds, to become the property of anyone winning it three times, with 15 money prizes added by the Association. Open to members of the Galloway Rifle Volunteer Corps and the Volunteer Artillery Corps in Galloway.

7 rounds at 600 yards.

1. Private D.R. Paterson, Kirkcudbright   34 points.
2. Colour Sergeant Ferguson, New Galloway   34
3. Armourer Sergeant McHaffic, Stranraer   32
4. Private W.A. Miller, Kirkcudbright   31
5. Qtr. Mstr. Sergeant T. Myers, Castle Douglas   31
6. Lance Sergeant McGeoch, Stranraer   30
7. Sergeant Todd, Castle Douglas   30
8. Lance Corporal Duff, Maxwellton   30
9. Sergeant Millburn, Dalbeattie   29
10. Sergeant Haugh, Castle Douglas   29
11. Sergeant E. Paterson, Kirkcudbright   29
12. Sergeant Bell, New Galloway   29
13. Private McMillan, Stranraer   29
14. Ex-Armourer Sergeant G. Geddes, New Galloway   28
15. Private T. Carnochan, Kirkcudbright   28
(Two 28's counted out)

IV). **Aggregate.** The Bronze Medal of the National Rifle Association, and silver challenge cup, presented by the late Colonel Kennedy Laurie of Woodhall, with 23 money prizes added by the Association. Scores made in Competitions (I), (II), and (III).

	(I).	(II).	(III).	Total.
1. Armourer Sergeant G. McHaffie, Stranraer	35	34	32	101
2. Colour Sergeant Ferguson, New Galloway	33	32	34	99
3. Private D. Paterson, Kirkcudbright	31	31	34	96
4. Private W. A. Miller, Kirkcudbright	33	31	31	95
5. Sergeant Todd, Castle Douglas	30	35	30	95
6. Sergeant McGeoch, Stranraer	31	33	30	94
7. Sergeant Haugh, Castle Douglas	32	32	29	93
8. Private Carnochan, Kirkcudbright	32	33	28	93
9. Sergeant Paterson, Kirkcudbright	32	31	29	92
10. Ex. Armourer Sergeant Geddes, New Galloway	30	34	28	92
11. Qtr. Mstr. Sergeant T. Myers, Castle Douglas	32	27	31	90
12. Corporal Duff, Maxwellton	30	29	30	89
13. Private McMillan, Stranraer	33	27	29	89
14. Corporal D. Ferguson, Maxwellton	32	30	27	89
15. Corporal Reid, Kirkcudbright	30	33	26	89
16. Private H. Haugh, Castle Douglas	30	35	24	89
17. Sergeant Millburn, Dalbeattie	27	32	29	88
18. Private McGowan, Kirkcudbright	32	30	25	87
19. Private Turner, Castle Douglas	32	26	28	86
20. Sergeant Coupland, Maxwellton	30	30	26	86
21. Sergeant Haining, Maxwellton	32	28	26	86
22. Lance Corporal Seggie, Dalbeattie	30	31	25	86
23. Private Miller, Stranraer	30	32	24	86

(one 86 counted out).

V). **Carbine Prizes.** Open to members of the Volunteer Artillery Corps in Galloway, and to members of the Galloway Rifles armed with Carbines. 7 money prizes.
7 rounds at 200 yards.

1. Sergeant Major Kimm, Kirkcudbright — 28 points.
2. Sergeant Slater, Kirkcudbright — 26
3. Gunner McKie, Kirkcudbright — 26
4. Sergeant Davidson, Kirkcudbright — 25
5. Gunner McMillan, Kirkcudbright — 25
6. Gunner McDowall, Portpatrick — 24
7. Gunner Seggie, Kirkcudbright — 21

VI). **Member's Prizes.** Sixteen money prizes. Open to members of the Association.
7 rounds at 500 yards.

1. Colour Sergeant Ferguson, New Galloway — 34 points.
Sergeant Bell, New Galloway — 34
3. Private McGowan, Kirkcudbright — 33
4. Sergeant Haining, Maxwellton — 33
5. Private W.A. Miller, Kirkcudbright — 33
6. Private D.R. Paterson, Kirkcudbright — 32
7. Sergeant Todd, Castle Douglas — 32
8. Lance Corporal Duff, Maxwellton — 32
9. Corporal D. Ferguson, Maxwellton — 32
10. Ex. Armourer Sergeant G. Geddes, New Galloway — 32
11. Private J.S. Ewen, Castle Douglas — 31
12. Sergeant E. Paterson, Kirkcudbright — 31
13. Private S. Ferguson, New Galloway — 31
14. Armourer Sergeant McHaffie — 31
15. Private McCulloch, Stranraer — 30
16. Sergeant Haugh, Castle Douglas — 30
(Two 30's counted out).

266

VII). **Recruit's Bronze Medal and Association Prizes.** Open to Recruits of the Galloway Rifle Volunteers and Galloway Artillery, who have joined the Volunteer Force since 1st November last, and also open to recruits of last year. 13 money prizes.

7 rounds at 200 yards.

1.	Privates Murray, Maxwellton	26 points.
2.	Tweedie, Stranraer	26
3.	J. Geddes, New Galloway	25
4.	Flynn, Dalbeattie	25
5.	Blain, Newton Stewart	23
6.	R. Paterson, Kirkcudbright	23
7.	F. Stewart, New Galloway	23
8.	Hastie, Castle Douglas	23
9.	C. Loudon, Maxwellton	22
10.	Lavery, Newton Stewart	22
11.	N. McAdam, Castle Douglas	22
12.	Robertson, New Galloway	21
13.	A. Bennett, Dalbeattie	21

(One 21 counted out).

VIII). **Tyro-Aggregate Competition**. Open to members of the Volunteer Rifle and Artillery Corps in Galloway who have not won altogether £1 in the Association meetings. Scores in either No. (I) or No. (VII) and No. (II) to count. 16 money prizes by the Association.

	200.	500.	Total.
1. Private Miller, Stranraer	30	32	62
2. Piper R. Clunie, Kirkcudbright	29	32	61
3. Lance Corporal Seggie, Dalbeattie	30	31	61
4. Private McMillan, Stranraer	33	27	60
5. Private Brodie, Castle Douglas	27	32	59
6. Private Thomson, Kirkcudbright	33	26	59
7. Sergeant Murdoch, New Galloway	30	27	57
8. Sergeant Mackenzie, Kirkcudbright Artillery	28	28	56
9. Lance Corporal McCulloch, New Galloway	27	28	55
10. Private McCulloch, Stranraer	29	26	55
11. Private Hunter, Kirkcudbright	30	24	54
12. Private F. Stewart, New Galloway	23	30	53
13. Private P. Birrell, Newton Stewart	24	29	53
14. Sergeant Bendall, Maxwellton	26	26	52
15. Private T. Kirk, New Galloway	28	24	52
16. Private Robertson, New Galloway	23	27	50

IX).**Team Competition**. Open to the Companies of the Galloway Rifle Volunteers. Teams of five men, Scores in competition (I), (II), and (III).

Kirkcudbright		Castle Douglas	
Private Carnochan	93	Quartermaster Sergeant Myers	90
Sergeant E. Paterson	92	Corporal McCaw	85
Corporal A.D. Reid	89	Private Ewan	85
Private McGowan	87	Private J. Haugh	84
Private Thomson	78	Sergeant Gordon	83
	439.		427

X). **Selkirk Challenge Cup Competition.** A silver challenge cup, presented by the late Earl of Selkirk. Open to Companies of the Galloway Rifle Volunteers, and to be won by the Company having the five highest scores in the Aggregate Competition No. (IV).

Kirkcudbright		Castle Douglas	
Private D. R. Paterson	96	Sergeant Todd	95
Private T. Carnochan	93	Sergeant W. Haugh	93
Sergeant E. Paterson	92	Quartermaster Sergeant Myers	90
Corporal Reid	89	Private H. Haugh	89
Private McGowan	87	Private Turner	86
	457		453

At the close of the meeting, Lieutenant-Colonel Lennox called upon Mr. H.A. Timms of Slogarie, the former Captain of 'E' Company, New Galloway, who, in 1896, had led the Regiment to victory in the Minto Cup competition, to present the prizes, saying that it was with great regret that Colonel Kennedy's health was such that it would not allow of his attending the Association meeting. He hoped however, to see him at the forthcoming camp. Apologies were also rendered for Major Dunn and Mr. Murray of Parton, at whose instigation, the Tyro prizes had been started.

Mr. Timms in presenting the prizes said that although it gave him very great pleasure to present the prizes, the honour conferred upon him had come as somewhat of a surprise, as he had no idea when he came that he was to be so called. He continued, that it always gave him the greatest of pleasure to attend the Association meetings but he was afraid he could not come as Captain Timms any longer. A vote of thanks was given by Captain Nicholson and three hearty cheers were given by the Volunteers.

The following analysis shows the winnings of the respective Companies: Kirkcudbright, two cups and £16.15s; New Galloway, £15.15s; Stranraer, two cups, bronze medal, and £15-2s-6d; Castle Douglas, one cup and £12.12s. 6d; Kirkcudbright Artillery, £5. 7s. 6d; Maxwellton, bronze medal and £5. 5s; Dalbeattie, £3. 2s. 6d; Newton Stewart, 17/6d; Portpatrick Artillery, 5/-; - total prize money £74. 12s. 6d.

47th Meeting of the G.A.R.V.A.

The 47th and final annual prize meeting of the Galloway Artillery and Rifle Volunteer Association was to take place at Caigton ranges, Castle Douglas, on Saturday, 10th August, 1907, although this was not known, at that time by the Officers and men of the Galloway Rifle Volunteers. The decision to disband the Galloway Rifles was not to be announced by the General Officer Commanding in Scotland, until the 24th February, 1908.

In the early Saturday forenoon rain fell heavily, with a strong wind blowing across the targets, which caused the marksmen a great deal of trouble. Notwithstanding these conditions, the scoring was a good average. About 3pm, a cloud burst stopped the firing for about half an hour, but thereafter the Competitors were favoured with ideal conditions. With the exception of Maxwellton and Dalbeattie, all the Companies were well represented, with the Artillery being particularly well represented. The entries in the various competitions were, Bargaly Cup, 62; Munches Cup, 67; Airds Cup, 56; Aggregate, 55; Carbine, 18; Members, 28; Recruits, 15; Tyro-Aggregate, 26; Rapid Firing, 40. - A total of 367 as against a total of 244 the previous year. The programme was, as usual, an attractive one with approximately £80 being offered in prize money in addition to the valuable cups and medals.

The Officers present were, Lieutenant-Colonel Lennox V.D. Commanding; Major Hewat V.D.; Surgeon-Captain Lorraine and H.B. Wilkinson, Castle Douglas; Captain and Adjutant Fraser. Captain Brown, Kirkcudbright, Artillery; Captain W.L. Comrie (Range Officer), Lieutenant E.W. Paterson, Kirkcudbright; Captain E.S. Forde; Lieutenant Clark Kennedy New Galloway; Captain Anderson, Dalbeattie; Lieutenant J.M. Glover, 'G' Company, Maxwellton; Lieutenant McKinnel, 'F' Company, Maxwellton; Lieutenant Hunter, Stranraer, and for the last and final occasion, Quartermaster T. Myers and Sergeant F. Connolly, Castle Douglas, were in charge of the Statistical Department.

Tea and light refreshments were again purveyed by Mr. R. Todd, Confectioner and Sergeant in 'B' Company, Castle Douglas, in a large Marquee, with music being discoursed during the day by the Regimental Pipe Band under Pipe-Major Johnstone, Dalbeattie. In the afternoon, Colonel Lennox and the Officers, held an 'at home' in a Marquee on the ground, the purveying being in the hands of Mr. Clint, Victoria Hotel, Castle Douglas. In the unavoidable absence of Mrs. Lennox, Miss Comrie, Gategill, acted as Hostess. The guest list which contained the 'elite of the County' together with friends of the Volunteers, amounted to almost 100, among those present being, The Countess of Selkirk, Balmae; Colonel Kennedy of Knocknalling, V.D. M.V.O.; Colonel Gordon of Threave; Colonel R.E. Dudgeon of Cargen; Mr. David Lennox, Edenbank; Colonel Kennaway, Greenlaw; Sir Mark J. McTaggart Stewart, Bart., of Southwick; Colonel McKie, D.S.O. of Bargaly; Mr. L.M. Hutchison of Laurieston Hall; Colonel Laurie, Maxwellton; Sir Herbert E. Maxwell, Bart., of Monreith; Mr. George R. Murray of Parton; Major Harper, V.D.; Major Dunn V.D.; Captain Murray Dunlop of Corsock; Colonel Rainsford-Hannay of Kirkdale; Colonel Stewart of the Ayr and Galloway Artillery; Lady Woodborn, of Mouswald, and many other influential personages.

The Competition commenced at 10am with the Bargaly Cup, which was won by Corporal Moir, 'G' Company, Maxwellton, with a score of 33 points after firing off tie shots with Cyclist D.R. Paterson, Kirkcudbright. Cyclist D.R. Paterson was, however, to spring straight back from this defeat winning the next event, the Munches Cup. This was the 2nd year in succession that he had won this event. In the Airds Cup, Sergeant R. Todd, Castle Douglas, left his refreshment marquee, to win the event with a score of 34, one point more than the winner of last year, Corporal W. McCaw also of Castle Douglas. The shooting in the Airds Cup was much better than that of the previous year. The result of the Aggregate Competition, also showed a great improvement with Cyclist D.R. Paterson, Kirkcudbright, carrying off the Bronze Medal and the Silver Cup, with the excellent score of 98, as against a winning score by Private G. Geddes, New Galloway, the previous year. There was a large entry for the Carbine event, with Kirkcudbright once again dominating this competition, being won by C.S.M. Kimm, Kirkcudbright Artillery. In the competition for the Member's prize, a tie ensued between the veteran, Ex. Armourer-Sergeant G. Geddes, New Galloway, and his son Private G. Geddes, with a score of 34. On shooting off another tie resulted when it was agreed to divide the prize. Private Warren, Stranraer, won the Recruit's Bronze Medal with 31 points, being the same score as that of Gunner Ellis, Kirkcudbright, who won the event the last year. The Tyro-Aggregate went to Corporal Moir with 65, two points more than Gunner Ellis last year. There was a record entry for the Rapid Firing Competition, the winner being Cyclist D.R. Paterson, Kirkcudbright, with a score of 30 as compared with 27 the previous year. There were two sweepstake competitions for all comers at 500 and 600 yards, but unfortunately there were no entries for these competitions, nor for the team competitions. The Selkirk Challenge Cup was carried off by the Castle Douglas Company, with 457 points, Kirkcudbright being one point below.

The following are the results of the several competitions:-

I). **The Bargaly Challenge Cup.** A silver cup, presented by the late James Mackie, Esq., M.P., with 15 money prizes added by the Association. Open to members of the Galloway Rifle Volunteer Corps and the Volunteer Artillery Corps in Galloway.   7 rounds at 200 yards.

1. Corporal J.D. Moir, Maxwellton	33 points.
2. Cyclist D.R. Paterson, Kirkcudbright	33
3. Private J. Haugh, Castle Douglas	33
4. Colour Sergeant Ferguson, New Galloway	33
5. Lance Corporal Duff, Maxwellton	32
6. Private R. Wardhaugh, Castle Douglas	32
7. Corporal A. Gourlay, Kirkcudbright	32
8. Private G. Geddes, New Galloway	32
9. Sergeant D. Ferguson, Maxwellton	32
10. Private H. Haugh, Castle Douglas	31
11. Sergeant Dougan, Castle Douglas	31
12. Ex. Armourer Sergeant Geddes, New Galloway	31
13. Private G. Thomson, Kirkcudbright	31
14. Bombardier J. McKie, Kirkcudbright Artillery	31
15. Colour Sergeant E. Paterson, Kirkcudbright	31

II). **The Munches Cup**. A silver cup, presented by the late Wellwood H. Maxwell Esq., of Munches, to become the property of anyone winning it three times. Open as in No. (I). 7 rounds at 500 yards.

1. Cyclist D.R. Paterson, Kirkcudbright	33 points.
2. Lance Corporal Duff, Maxwellton	33
3. Private S. Ferguson, New Galloway	32
4. Corporal J.D. Moir, Maxwellton	32
5. Corporal W. McCaw, Castle Douglas	32
6. Private W. McCreadie, Newton Stewart	31
7. Corporal A. Gourlay, Kirkcudbright	31
8. O.R. Sergeant W. Haugh, Castle Douglas	31
9. Private J.S. Ewen, Castle Douglas	31
10. Sergeant S.R. Gordon, Castle Douglas	31
11. Private G. Geddes, New Galloway	31
12. Colour Sergeant E. Paterson, Kirkcudbright	31
13. Sergeant Dougan, Castle Douglas	31
14. Qtr. Mstr. Sergeant Myers, Castle Douglas	31
15. Colour Sergeant Ferguson, New Galloway	31.

III). **The Airds Cup**. A silver cup, presented by the later Major Houghton Hughan of Airds, to become the property of anyone winning it three times. Open as in No. (I).   7 rounds at 600 yards.

1. Sergeant R. Todd, Castle Douglas	34 points.
2. Sergeant Bell, New Galloway	32
3. Corporal Corrie, New Galloway	32
4. Qtr. Mstr. Sergeant Myers, Castle Douglas	32
5. Private S. Ferguson, New Galloway	32
6. Corporal J. McGowan, Kirkcudbright	32
7. Lance Corporal Duff, Maxwellton	32
8. Cyclist D.R. Paterson, Kirkcudbright	32
9. Private G. Geddes, New Galloway	31
10. Private J.S. Ewen, Castle Douglas	31
11. Ord. Room Sergeant W. Haugh, Castle Douglas	30
12. Private W. McCreadie, Newton Stewart	30
13. Corporal J.D. Moir, Maxwellton	30
14. Corporal A. Gourlay, Kirkcudbright	30
15. Private James Miller, Stranraer	30

IV). **Aggregate.** The Bronze Medal of the National Rifle Association and silver challenge cup, presented by the late Colonel Kennedy Laurie of Woodhall, with money prizes added by the Association. Scores made in competitions (I), (II), and (III).

	I.	II.	III.	Total.
1. Cyclist D.R. Paterson, Kirkcudbright	33	33	32	98
2. Lance Corporal Duff, Maxwellton	32	33	32	97
3. Corporal J.D. Moir, Maxwellton	33	32	30	95
4. Qtr. Mstr. Sergeant Myers, Castle Douglas	31	31	32	94
5. Private G. Geddes, New Galloway	32	31	31	94
6. Private S. Ferguson, New Galloway	29	32	32	93
7. Corporal A. Gourlay, Kirkcudbright	31	31	30	93
8. Private J.S. Ewen, Castle Douglas	30	31	31	92
9. Col. Sergeant Ferguson, New Galloway	33	31	28	92
10. Private W. McCreadie, Newton Stewart	30	31	30	91
11. Sergeant Dougan, Castle Douglas	31	31	29	91
12. Sergeant R. Todd, Castle Douglas	27	29	34	90
13. Ord. Room Sergeant W. Haugh, Castle Douglas	29	31	30	90
14. Sergeant D. Ferguson, Maxwellton	32	30	28	90
15. Corporal J. McGowan, Kirkcudbright	28	29	32	89
16. Sergeant S.R. Gordon, Castle Douglas	30	31	28	89
17. Bombardier J. McKie, Kirkcudbright	31	30	28	89
18. Corporal W. McCaw, Castle Douglas	30	32	27	89
19. Col. Sergeant E. Paterson, Kirkcudbright	31	31	27	89
20. Private J. Haugh, Castle Douglas	33	31	25	89
21. Corporal Corrie, New Galloway	30	26	32	88
22. Corporal T. Graham, Maxwellton	30	29	29	88
23. Private G. Thomson, Kirkcudbright	31	28	28	87

V). **Carbine Prizes**. Open to members of the Volunteer Artillery Corps in Galloway, and to members of the Galloway Rifles armed with Carbines.   7 rounds at 200 yards.

1. C.S.M. Kimm, Kirkcudbright Artillery	29 points.
2. Sergeant W. Mackenzie, Kirkcudbright Artillery	29
3. Bombardier J. McKie, Kirkcudbright Artillery	27
4. Corporal Torbett, Portpatrick Artillery	27
5. Sergeant Torbett, Portpatrick Artillery	27
6. Gunner W. Cruickshanks, Kirkcudbright Artillery	26
7. Lieutenant McKinnell, 'F' Coy., Maxwellton	26

VI). **Member's Prizes**. Open to members of the Association.   7 rounds at 500 yards.

1. Private G. Geddes, New Galloway (1st equal)	34 points.
Ex. Armr. Sgt. G. Geddes, New Gall. (1st equal)	34
3. Sergeant J. Coupland, Maxwellton	33
4. Col. Sergeant Ferguson, New Galloway	33
5. Corporal T. Graham, Maxwellton	31
6. Cyclist D.R. Paterson, Kirkcudbright	31
7. Private J. Haugh, Castle Douglas	31

8. Private J.S. Ewen, Castle Douglas	29
9. Sergeant F. Connolly, Castle Douglas	29
10. Sergeant Bell, New Galloway	29
11. Corporal Corrie, New Galloway	28
12. Corporal J. McGown, Kirkcudbright	27
13. Sergeant Bendall, Maxwellton	27
14. Lance Corporal Duff, Maxwellton	27
15. Corporal McCaw, Castle Douglas	27
16. Private S. Ferguson, New Galloway	27

VII). **Recruit's Bronze Medal and Association Prizes.** Open to recruits of the Galloway Rifle Volunteers and Galloway Artillery who have joined the Volunteer force since 1st November, last and also open to Recruits of last year.
7 rounds at 200 yards.

1. Private Warren, Stranraer	31 points.
2. Piper H. Henry, Kirkcudbright	30
3. Private J. Agnew, Newton Stewart	29
4. Private W. T. Tait, Maxwellton	28
5. Private G. McCandlish, Kirkcudbright	28
6. Lieutenant Glover, Maxwellton	27
7. Private Kelly, New Galloway	26
8. Private J. Baird, Castle Douglas	26
9. Gunner W. Cruickshanks, Kirkcudbright Artillery	25
10. Private R. Wardhaugh, Castle Douglas	25
11. Private R. McIlroy, Castle Douglas	23
12. Private S. Johnston, Castle Douglas	23
13. Gunner R. Laidlaw, Kirkcudbright Artillery	23

VIII). **Tyro-Aggregate Competition.** Open to members of the Volunteer Artillery Corps in Galloway and to members of the Galloway Rifles who have not, up to the present, at meetings of this Association, won a single prize of £1 or over. Scores in either No. (I) or No. (VII) and No. (II) to count.

	200.	500.	Total.
1. Corporal J.D. Moir , Maxwellton	33	32	65
2. Sergeant D. Ferguson, Maxwellton	32	30	62
3. Sergeant Bendall, Maxwellton	30	29	59
4. Private G. Thomson, Kirkcudbright	31	28	59
5. Private R. Wardhaugh, Castle Douglas	32	27	59
6. Private W.T. Tait, Maxwellton	28	30	58
7. Private J. Ferguson, Castle Douglas	31	27	58
8. Private J. Myers, Castle Douglas	28	28	56
9. Private M. Cullen, Newton Stewart	30	26	56
10. Gunner W. Cruickshanks, Kirkcudbright Art.	25	30	55
11. Private S. Brodie, Castle Douglas	28	27	55
12. Private J. Geddes, New Galloway	29	26	55
13. Private Harley, Newton Stewart	24	30	54
14. Private H. McMillan, Stranraer	26	28	54
15. Sergeant P. Henney, Kirkcudbright Art.	26	28	54
16. Lance Corporal Hunter, Kirkcudbright	30	24	54
17. Private J. Murphy, Kirkcudbright	23	30	53
18. Private J. Agnew, Newton Stewart	25	28	53
19. Private Tweedie, Stranraer	23	29	52
20 Private Stewart, New Galloway	30	22	52

IX). **Rapid Firing Competition. Sweepstake.**
7 rounds at 200 yards. Time limit 30 seconds.

1. Cyclist D.R. Paterson, Kirkcudbright	30 points.
2. Private G. Geddes, New Galloway	27
3. Private W. McCreadie, Newton Stewart	27
4. Private J. S. Ewen, Castle Douglas	26

X). **Selkirk Challenge Cup Competition**. A silver challenge cup, presented by the late Earl of Selkirk. Open to the Companies of the Galloway Rifle Volunteers, and to be won by the Company having the five highest scores in the Aggregate Competition No. (IV).

    1. Castle Douglas   457 points.
    2. Kirkcudbright   456

At the close of the proceedings, Colonel Lennox said he was extremely sorry that Colonel Kennedy, who, as former Commanding Officer of the Battalion, had been asked to present the prizes, but he had to leave early. Mrs. Phillips, Dildawn, had, however, consented to do the honours. The shooting he said had been particularly good, although he could not say so much for the weather. He saw many familiar faces at the meeting and it especially gave him great pleasure to see Colonel Farrer, the old Adjutant of the Battalion, whose first parade was also his (Colonel Lennox's) and there was also Major Harper who rendered much service to the Battalion. There was said to be many changes coming in the Volunteers. Let them not believe it! They might be made a Territorial Regiment or Terriers or whatever they liked to call it; but if Terriers, they were always good for a worry. Whatever changes did take place, he hoped and believed that the Galloway Rifles would stick together (applause). The changes were not so frightful as they at first appeared and were changes more in name that in reality. The great bogey had been compulsory camps, but he thought they were as far forward with compulsory camps as ever they would be. He then called on Mrs. Phillips to present the prizes, who at the completion of the ceremony said she would be glad to present a cup for competition. This was replied to by Colonel Lennox, who concluded by saying, "might she live long to see the cup shot for." (Alas, this was not to be, with the disbandment of the Regiment and the Galloway Artillery and Rifle Volunteer Association, unknowingly concluding their final meeting, the cup was never presented.) The meeting was brought to a close by three ringing cheers for the King.

* * * *

With the advent of the new Territorial Force, which on the 1st April, 1908, combined Dumfries and Galloway, into one Battalion, it had been hoped to merge the two County Associations under one joint Association. However, this did not come into being until the 4th September, 1909, when the 1st Annual Prize Competition, under the auspices of the 5th King's Own Scottish Borderers Rifle Association, was to take place at the Conhuith ranges, Dumfries.

*****

(8) Scenes at Bisley Rifle Meeting as appeared in the *Daily Despatch* on the 23rd July, 1901.

Schedule of the Meetings of the Galloway Volunteer Association 1861-63 and the Galloway Artillery and Rifle Volunteer Association Meetings 1864-1907

1st	(1861) Galloway Volunteer Association...........Caigton Farm. Castle Douglas.
2nd	(1862) ....Mains of Park, Glenluce.
3rd	(1863) ....Bennan Farm, New Galloway.
4th	(1864) Galloway Art. and Rifle Volunteer Ass..Bennan Farm, New Galloway.
5th	(1865) ....
6th	(1866) ....
7th	(1867) .... Knockbrex Farm, Newton Stewart
8th	(1868) ....
9th	(1869) .... Barrhill Ranges, Newton Stewart
10th	(1870) ....
11th	(1871) ....
12th	(1872) ....Bennan Farm. New Galloway
13th	(1873) ....
14th	(1874) ....
15th	(1875) ....
16th	(1876).. .. .. ..
17th	(1877) ....
18th	(1878) ....
19th	(1879) ....
20th	(1880) ....
21st	(1881) ....
22nd	(1882) ....Aird Farm, New Galloway
23rd	(1883) ....
24th	(1884) ....
25th	(1885) ....
26th	(1886) ....
27th	(1887) ....
28th	(1888) ....
29th	(1889) ....
30th	(1890) ....
31st	(1891) ....
32nd	(1892) ....
33rd	(1893) ....
34th	(1894) ....
35th	(1895) ....
36th	(1896)..Caigton Farm, Castle Douglas.
37th	(1897) ....Aird Farm. New Galloway.
38th	(1898) ....Caigton Farm, Castle Douglas.
39th	(1899) ....
40th	(1900) ....
41st	(1901) ....
42nd	(1902) ....
43rd	(1903) ....
44th	(1904) ....
45th	(1905) ....
46th	(1906) ....
47th	(1907) ....

Note. In 1886, the 26th Galloway Artillery and Rifle Volunteer Association meeting was wrongly numbered in the Press as the 24th annual meeting and thereafter, both the Press and the Council of the G.A.R.V.A., continued with the wrong consecutive number, always two years behind. In 1897 and 1898, the 37th and 38th annual meeting of the G.A.R.V.A., were once again wrongly numbered in the Press as the 35th annual meeting in both the years, 1897 and 1898. The Press and Council now three years in arrears. The only Official Programmes of the G.A.R.V.A traced after 1886, are for the years 1900-07, and these show as three years behind. i.e. the last (47th) meeting in 1907, shows in the Official Programme as the 44th annual meeting.

CHAPTER 10

CYCLING SECTION AND MAJOR TROPHY AND MEDAL ACHIEVEMENTS OF THE GALLOWAY RIFLE VOLUNTEERS - -AMBULANCE SECTION - BANDS - FOOTBALL

Cycling and major trophy and medal achievements of the Galloway Rifle Volunteers

In June, 1882, the following announcement appeared in the *Volunteer Service Gazette*. "It is proposed to form a Volunteer Battalion of Cyclists, also a Cyclist branch of Intelligence Corps and Signallers. It is expected that the members of this new branch of the service will be of great assistance in time of actual warfare, by acting as Scouts."

By 1885, Cycling detachments had become an important part of the Volunteer Movement, being seen by those in authority as a useful substitute for Cavalry Orderlies, there being somewhat of a dearth of Mounted Troops in the Volunteer Movement. The Cyclist was expected to be adept in all forms of signalling, Morse Code, Flag Signalling, Heliograph, Helistat., etc. However, it was later realised that signalling was a particular skill and selected Volunteers from each Corps were trained in and specialised in the various forms of signalling. This did not however, relieve the Cyclist's responsibility from his obligatory skill.

In 1888, Government was to sanction the formation of Cyclist Sections in each Battalion, to comprise of 1 Officer, 2 non-commissioned officers, a Bugler, with not less than 13 and not more than 21 cyclists. However, no Government grants were payable to these Sections, over and above the normal grant for efficiency, the cyclist being expected to supply and maintain his own machine, with the result that Cyclist Commanders were to experience difficulties in maintaining these sections at a respectable strength. This was not to be so in the case of the 26th Middlesex Regiment, who were to later become the only Regiment, to raise and maintain a full Company of Cyclists.

The roll of the Cyclist in War, was seen as that of (a) Despatch Carrier. (b) Road Reconnaissance. (c) Patrolling and Intelligence - It was felt that a cyclist might penetrate deeper into enemy territory, with less chance of being seen than that of a mounted cavalryman. (d) Seizing and Holding advance positions. The Volunteer Cycling Sections were to come into their own, putting these particular skills into use, on the outbreak of the Boer War, with the formation of the Scottish Company of Volunteer Cyclists, in March, 1901, when they were sent to South Africa on active service.

Although great honour was to be reflected on a Regiment, by it's Members' successes in National, International and County competitions, it could never allay the "jibes" and stigma of "Pot Hunters" or "Gold Diggers", being only interested in shooting, with no apparent skill in the other military aspects, associated with the Volunteer Movement. This was not to be so in the case of team competitions, where, although large cash prizes were still on offer, it was felt that these competitions, encompassed all the required military disciplines of marching, cycling, fitness and stamina, with the required element of shooting being still, the most important facet, but seen to be more in keeping with conditions likely to be encountered "on active service".

Over the years, the marksmen of the Galloway Rifle Volunteers, were to keep the name of their proud Battalion, well to the fore in Volunteer circles, with frequent successes at National and International events. However, it was not until 1888, when the Government was to sanction the formation of Cycling Sections, that on the 23rd June, 1888, a young energetic Solicitor from Newton Stewart, with a great passion for cycling was enlisted into 'D' Company, Newton Stewart, as a Lieutenant, and through his guidance and leadership in National Team Competitions, the Galloway Rifles were to become, throughout the 1890's, a widely acknowledged and acclaimed Volunteer Regiment.

Lieutenant Kelly was promoted Captain on the 9th September, 1898, taking command of the Newton Stewart Company on the 10th March, 1899, on the retiral of Captain McPhater. Captain Kelly was to resign his Commission on the 22nd December, 1899, on his being elected Provost of Newton Stewart, and not being able to give due attention to both his business and the Volunteer duties. However, a week later, on the 29th December, 1899, Captain Kelly, was to withdraw his resignation, stating that everyone must make that little extra effort during the war period (Boer War). With the civic demands made on Captain Kelly, he was to lead a less active role in the Volunteer Movement, and in consequence the leading role of the Galloway Rifles, in National Team competition was to diminish, with their failing to gain any further successes.

Two of the successful members of Captain Kelly's Cycling Section were Lance Corporal Robert Picken and Cyclist Thomas Murchie, both cycle engineers from Newton Stewart, who manufactured their cycles in a factory at Kirkcowan. The cycles used in the national cycling successes of the Galloway Rifles, were manufactured by Murchie and Picken, and following their successful "raid" into England, in 1897, to win the most Prestigious of all Volunteer team events, the "Wolseley Cup", at Bisley, for the 2nd time, the cycle was named the "Royal Raider". This name was to pass to the Newton Stewart 'D' Company, the centre of the Regiment's Cycling Section, who were themselves to become known as simply, "The Raiders". The following advertisement appeared in 1897, in conjunction with the success of the "Royal Raider" at Bisley.

LORD KITCHENER
OF KHARTOUM
AND
ROYAL RAIDER CYCLES

We have not had the pleasure of receiving the gallant General's opinion on our machines.

BUT WE ARE PROUD TO MAKE IT KNOWN

that Brigadier General The Earl of Minto rides a "Raider", as also the famous Galloways, in all their successes, including 100 miles Long Distance Cup, Wolseley Cup and Gamage Shield.

The type of machine above mentioned may be viewed in course of construction, or at the Depot of

MURCHIE & PICKEN,
Cycle Engineers
NEWTON STEWART, N.B.,

who will give you better prices for anything in connection with cycles, than anyone in the country.

QUOTATIONS ON RECEIPT OF POST CARD.

Swifts, Rovers, Ascots, Humbers, Raleighs, Premiers, &c., or any make at keenest cut prices.

Machine on Hire. Club Colours and Racing Costumes. The Firm will supply the Galloway Rifles with Machines for this year's competition. Golf Requisites by well known Makers.

It would be most unfair to pass up the following "Camp Crack", circulating in 1897, with obvious Newton Stewart connotations.

"At a Galloway Cattle Show a Cyclist was careering all over the field when he was interrupted by an official with, "Hi! cyclings' no alloo'ed in the field." "Who said that?" interrogated the Byke Fiend. "It says so in the rules, and you are breaking the rule now." "Oh that's all right, " cried the departing wheelman, "I'm the Chairman!"

The following is a complete history of the Galloway Rifles National Team successes throughout the 1890's, these successes having been recorded and immortalised in their "Battle Honours", culminating in the Boer War - South Africa, 1900-02, by Colour-Sergeant McGregor, 'A' Company, Kirkcudbright, in his now famous pen and ink drawings.

MILITARY RIDE 1894

The Volunteer Cyclist Infantry Challenge Cup.

The Annual competition for the £100 Volunteer Cyclist Infantry Challenge Cup, was to take place at Blackwater, Hants, on Saturday, 25th August, 1894.

The competition was a 100 mile team cycle race arranged as follows, from Blackwater as the centre - to Reading and back, 30 miles - to Basingstoke and back, 30 miles - to Farnham and back, 20 miles - and to Virginia Water and back, 20 miles. No ammunition or valise to be carried otherwise the riders were in full marching order, of rifle, bayonet, water bottle, cloak and other equipment, signifying a weight excess of 20 lbs.

15 teams were to take part in the largest field ever engaged in this event. They were extended as follows:- Galloway Rifle Volunteers - 'C' Company, 26th Middlesex (Cyclists) R.V. Chelsea - 1st V.B. The Royal Fusiliers (London), 2 teams - 17th (North) Middlesex R.V. (Camden Town), 2 teams - 3rd V.B. Queen's (Royal West Surrey Regiment) (Bermondsey) - 2nd V.B. Duke of Wellington's West Riding Regiment, (Huddersfield) - 'A' Troop 26th Middlesex (Cyclists) R.V. Chelsea - 1st V.B.Hampshire Regiment (Winchester) - 2nd V.B. Hampshire Regiment (Southampton), - 1st V.B. Welsh Regiment (Haverfordwest team and Carmarthen team) - 3rd V.B. Welsh Regiment (Cardiff) - 2nd (South) Middlesex R.V. (Walthamgreen).

The Galloway Rifle Volunteer's Team comprised of, Lieutenant W.M. Kelly, Privates Drysdale, Mercer and Morton. Newton Stewart, Private W.H. Penman, Castle Douglas, who had all spent two weeks intensive training in the Blackwater area prior to the event. Such was the prestige to be gained from winning such a National Trophy.

The race commenced at 6.30am in torrential rain which continued throughout the day. The roads were like ploughed fields, the mud clogging the unprotected chains, causing them to snap frequently. Conditions deteriorated to such an extent that accidents and mechanical failures caused the withdrawal of 13 of the competing teams. The Galloway Rifle's team was to go on however, and win the event, in time of 8 hours 31 minutes. Only one other team, the West Riding, 2nd team, was to finish, in a time of 11 hours 13 minutes.

THE WOLSELEY CUP COMPETITION- 1896

The first competition for Lord Wolseley's Challenge Cup was to take place at Bisley on Saturday, 2nd May, 1896. The Cup, a major national trophy, was open to Volunteer Battalions throughout the United Kingdom, and was probably the Galloways finest achievement, in a competition whose name was to become synonymous with that of the Galloway Rifle Volunteers.

The competition was to test the capacity of the Volunteer in musketry, after an arduous Military Ride. The essential conditions being, 10 men to ride a distance of 44 miles within 4½ hours, and afterwards any 8 of the 10 men, to fire 10 rounds Volley, at a target from 600 yards, prone position, 5 rounds Volley, at 500 yards and 5 rounds Independent fire, kneeling, making a possible score of 160 points.

The Galloway team which comprised of, William Law, John Coupland and David Haining, Maxwellton, William McCaw and William Hetherington, Castle Douglas. John Ferguson and George Geddes Jnr., New Galloway, William Drysdale, William McCreadie and John Murchie, Newton Stewart was under the command of Lieutenant Kelly, Newton Stewart with Colour-Sergeant Peattie, Newton Stewart and Sergeant Grierson, Maxwellton, accompanying the team.

Sixteen teams were to enter the competition, which was run in four sections. First section from the Angel Hotel, Thames Ditton, by Bisley and Esher to Guildford - 16 miles. The next stretch was over the "Hog's Back", a stiff incline of four miles, the total distance of this stage being 10 miles, past Aldershot and Bagshot a further 12 miles, and on to the targets at Bisley, a further 6 miles. The Galloway team were to be declared comfortable winners over the 2nd Hants. The following is the statement of results:-

	Hours	Minutes	Points for shooting.
Galloway Rifle Volunteers	4	9	117
2nd V.B. Hants.	4	10	110
13th Middlesex	4	17	88
4th V.B. Norfolk	4	37	80
4th V.B. Hants.	4	14	79
4th V.B. West Surrey	4	13	68
1st V.B. Royal Fusiliers	4	55	63
24th Middlesex	4	26	62
4th Middlesex	4	11	59
26th Middlesex (B team)	4	01	50
20th Middlesex	4	18	43
2nd V.B. Wilts.	4	05	39
17th Middlesex	4	15	34
4th Surrey - broke down.			
26th Middlesex (C team) - withdrew.			
19th Middlesex - withdrew.			

The following Regimental Order was received by Colonel J.M. Kennedy, Commanding the Galloway Rifle Volunteers:-

21st Regimental District Orders.

by Col. E.C. Browne, Commanding.

Ayr, 15th May, 1896.

The Officer Commanding 21st Regimental District has noted with much satisfaction that the Galloway Rifles have again distinguished themselves at Bisley by winning the Wolseley Cup, and he congratulates the Corps on their success.

By Order (signed) A.H. Thorburn, Capt.,

Adjt. Depot Royal Scots Fusiliers.

THE WOLSELEY CUP COMPETITION - 1897.

The second competition for Lord Wolseley's Cup was to take place on Saturday, 22nd May, 1897, in the vicinity of Staines, Middlesex. The start of the contest was at Staines Bridge and the finish at Runneymede Ranges, a distance of 42 miles, where, as before, 10 volleys were to be fired at 600 yards, prone, 5 volleys at 500 yards, kneeling, followed by 5 rounds independent fire, once again making for a possible score of 160 points.

14 teams were to take place, the Galloway Rifle team, commanded by Lieutenant Kelly, was as follows. Privates W. McCreadie, W. Murchie, P. Priestly, Newton Stewart. Privates J. Ferguson and G. Geddes, New Galloway, Corporal William McCaw, Castle Douglas. Corporals Haining and Coupland and Privates Law and Urquhart, all Maxwellton. The Galloway Rifle's team was once again to prove successful.

	Hours	Minutes	Points for shooting.
Galloway Rifle Volunteers	3	44	126
4th V.B. Hants.	3	47	123
2nd V.B. Hants	3	43	105
13th Middlesex	3	17	99
4th East Surrey	3	06	78
4th West Surrey	3	53	74
1st V.B. Hants.	3	47	66
1st V.B. Royal Fusiliers.	3	56	64
26th Middlesex.	3	30	50
17th Middlesex.	3	36	46
4th Middlesex.	3	51	44
1st V.B. Warwick. - withdrew.			
4th Norfolk - withdrew.			
2nd V.B. Middlesex - withdrew.			

THE WOLSELEY CUP COMPETITION - 1898.

The 3rd Competition for the Wolseley Volunteer Cyclist Cup, in which the Galloway Rifle Volunteers, hoped to make the cup their own, was to take place at Runneymede, Staines, on Saturday, 28th June, 1898, without the Galloway Rifles. The regulations of the contest were changed, splitting the country into the Northern and Southern Division of the Cyclist Challenge Cup. The Cup on this occasion was won by the 2nd Hants. team, with a score of 116 points.

THE WOLSELEY CUP (NORTHERN DIVISION) - 1899.

This was held on Saturday, 12th August, 1899, at the Strensall ranges, near York. The distance to be covered was 40 miles in 4 hours, with the same rules for shooting, 10 section Volleys at 600 yards, prone, 5 section Volleys at 500 yards and 5 rounds, independent firing at 500 yards, kneeling.

The Galloway Rifles team was commanded on this occasion by Sergeant Mercer, Newton Stewart, and the team comprised as follows; D. Paterson, Kirkcudbright, E. Paterson, Kirkcudbright, T. Carnochan, Ringford, G. McHaffie, Stranraer, J. Ferguson, New Galloway, G.Geddes, Jnr., Crossmichael, W. Law and John Coupland, Maxwellton.

Once again the Galloway Rifles were to prove their domination in this competition, with a fine win, over an entry of six. The result being as follows:-

Galloway Rifle Volunteers	137 points.
Border Rifles	132
1st Lincoln	119
1st Forfar (Dundee)	113
2nd York (Scarborough)	76
5th Durham	49

THE MINTO CUP COMPETITION - 1896

The first competition for the Minto Challenge Cup, presented by Brigadier-General Lord Minto, was held at Stow, near Melrose, on Friday, 31st July, 1896.

The elements of the competition, required a team of 16 men, two reserves, to march a distance of 11 miles, from 1½ miles south of Stow to the ranges at Dingleton Common, in full marching order, under the Command of an Officer and non-commissioned officer, in under 3 hours, and on completion of the march, at once to take part in Volley Firing. The two reserves, not to fire. 5 points were to be deducted for each minute over 3 hours.

The team comprised of, Captain Timms, New Galloway, Quartermaster Sergeant Myers, Castle Douglas, Privates Paterson and Carnochan, Kirkcudbright, Corporals McCaw and McGaw, Lance Corporal Hetherington, Private Ireland, Castle Dougas, Lance Corporal Love, Privates McCreadie and Priestly, Newton Stewart, Privates Ferguson and Geddes, New Galloway, Privates Derry and Tait, Dalbeattie. Reserves Privates Black and Ferguson, Maxwellton.

The 16 competing teams started at 11am, with teams arranged in details, leaving at 45 minute intervals. The day was very hot, the Doctor's dealing with several casualties. The Galloway team arrived at the ranges well within the allotted time and after inspection scored a total of 164 points, having 3 points deducted for one irregular volley, making a winning net score of 161 points. The following is the statement of results:-

		Deductions		
	Hits	Time	Drill	Net Score
Galloway Rifles	164	-	3	161
Hawick B.R.V.	152	-	-	152
Galashiels B.R.V.	139	-	3	136
Jedburgh B.R.V.	137	-	3	134
Gordon Highlanders	134	-	1	133
Black Watch, (2nd Battalion)	132	-	2	130
2nd V.B. K.O.S.B. Duns	118	-	3	115
3rd V.B. K.O.S.B.	118	-	5	113
3rd K.O.S.B. Militia	103	-	4	99
2nd V.B. K.O.B. Chirnside	98	-	3	95

3rd Highland Light Infantry	88	-	-	88
1st Q.R.V.B.R.S.	94	-	7	87
3rd Q.R.V.B.R.S.	92	-	6	86
2nd Q.R.V.B.R.S.	89	-	5	84
7th V.B.R.S. Haddington	88	15	5	68
4th Highland Light Infantry	38	-	1	37

DARNLEY - "STARLEY ROVER" - CYCLING COMPETITION - 1897.

On Saturday, 12th June, 1897, the "Starley Rover" cycling competition was to take place at Darnley, Lanark, with first prize being a Starley Rover cycle, presented by the Rover Cycle Company Ltd., of Coventry, with £5 added by the Scottish Rifle Association.

Six teams of four men were to take part in the competition, which required them to cycle from the Headquarters of the 3rd Lanark Volunteers, in Victoria Road, to the ranges at Darnley, by way of Pollockshaws Road and Thornliebank Village. They were to dismount at the 500 yard range, stack their cycles, and fire 10 Volleys at that distance. The teams were then to remount and cycle a further 200 yards to the finishing line. Forty-five minutes were allowed to complete the course, a condition being that any team not finishing in under 50 minutes and scoring less than 90 points, would be disqualified from the prize list.

The Galloway Rifle's team was under the command of Lieutenant W.M. Kelly, Newton Stewart, and comprised of Privates William Law, David Haining, and John Coupland, Maxwellton, and Private G. Geddes, New Galloway.

The Galloway team was to win comfortably, the scores as follows:-
Galloway Rifle Volunteers, 124 points; 2nd Lanark, 110 points; 4th Hants. 87 points; 2nd Renfrew, 39 points; 8th Lanark, 12 points. One team failed to fulfil the conditions of the competition and were disqualified.

THE 100 MILES VOLUNTEER CYCLE RACE - 1897.

The 100 mile Volunteer cycle race took place at Ellesmere, Shropshire, on Tuesday, 27th August, 1897. The competition was won by the 3rd Northumberland, in a time of 7 hours 18 minutes. The Galloway Rifle Volunteers were placed third, in a time of 7 hours 42 minutes.

The team was commanded by Lieutenant Kelly (centre) and comprised, Sergeant William Mercer, Newton Stewart (right); Lance Corporal Robert Picken, Newton Stewart (left); Cyclists John Forsyth and Thomas Murchie, Newton Stewart, Cyclist Peter J. Birrell, Carsluith, Cyclist William Kirk, Dalry. The interesting aspect of this photograph, taken the week before the race, is that it clearly shows, the "Royal Raider" cycles, manufactured by Messrs. Murchie and Picken, two of the team members.

The photograph on page 446 also shows the new light weight uniform, which was supplied to the members of the Galloway Rifles Cyclist Section, through Colour Sergeant Peattie, Newton Stewart, and which would be worn for the first time by Lieutenant Kelly's team at Shropshire. The uniform was made of drab khaki, with red facings and was made up in such a way as to give it a distinctive Corps flavour. The frock was of a field service pattern, black stockings with spats. Lieutenant Kelly was to remark at the time, that some people might have found the new uniform rather 'loud' but they would change their opinion if they saw the smart uniforms worn by their English counterparts.

In the Bisley meeting of 1898, held between Monday 11th and Friday 15th July, the Galloway Rifles had an exceptional week, capturing five National trophies, whilst Cyclist G. McHaffie, Stranraer was to be placed 4th in the ultimate trophy, the 'Queen's Prize'. Cyclist McHaffie, was to be welcomed home to an enthusiastic reception.

RANELAGH CUP - 1898

Only brief details now remain of this competition, which was open to 15 teams of 6 Volunteers. Eight of the teams being from Scotland. The Galloway men were to win the cup.

The Galloway team was as follows - Cyclist McHaffie, Stranraer, Cyclist Geddes, New Galloway, Cyclist McCreadie, Newton Stewart, Sergeant Haining, Maxwellton, Cyclist Law, Maxwellton, Corporal Bell, New Galloway.

SIR JAMES WHITEHEAD CUP - 1898

This trophy was open to teams of 4 Volunteers. The conditions being that competitors should at 200 yards and 500 yards fire as many shots as possible, at a target with an invisible bulls-eye, the target being exposed for one minute. The bulls-eye counted as 2 points, the rest of the target 1 point. The Galloway Rifle Volunteers, Scotland's sole representative entered three teams in this event, their enterprise being rewarded with the 1st team winning the trophy, whilst the 3rd team were 6th and the 2nd team was 9th.

No records survive of the competing teams or Regiments.

MULLENS COMPETITION - 1898

Another Surrey Common competition, held at Bisley in the week, 11th to 15th July, 1898.

21 teams entered the competition, the Galloway Rifle Volunteers entering two teams. The aggregate value of the Mullens prize was £100, being the annual sum of interest on a gratuity, presented by Mr. J. A. Mullens, to the National Rifle Association. Of that £100, £50 was to go to the Commanding Officer of the winning team, for the encouragement of this form of shooting, and £50, to the members of the team themselves. The competition was open to, up to three teams of 6 Volunteers, with an officer or a non-commissioned officer as Section Commander.

The target was in the form of a man in the act of running, the height was 6 feet, with a width across the chest of 1' 8". Proceedings began at 600 yards where two volleys were fired from the prone position. Then an advance was made at the double with arms trailed for 50 yards, then two volleys from the kneeling position were delivered. A further advance was made when the teams engaged in independent fire, delivering as many shots as they could in 30 seconds. Points up to 3 could be deducted by the Range Officer, from each volley which in his opinion were badly delivered.

The 1st prize was won by the Galloway 1st team, with the total of 63 points, a record for the competition. The team was well drilled and had no points deducted. 2nd placed was 2nd Liverpool, with a score of 59 points. The Galloway Rifles 2nd team was 15th.

The winning team was, Team Commander Captain McPhater, Cyclist W. McCreadie, Newton Stewart, Cyclists Urquhart and Law, Maxwellton, J. Ferguson and G. Geddes, New Galloway, G. McHaffie, Stranraer.

STARLEY ROVER - CYCLING COMPETITION - 1898

Won by the Galloway Rifle Volunteers but no further details are available

GAMAGE SHIELD - 1898

The 2nd Annual Military Cycling tournament was held at the Wood Green Track, London, on Saturday, 23rd July, 1898.

In the Gamage Shield, the Galloway Rifles entered a team for the 5 mile team race, by teams of 4 men, in drill order, without arms.

The race was held in heats and in the final the Galloway Rifle's team were to beat the Royal Fusiliers, in a time of 13 minutes 23 seconds.

******

In consequence of the Galloway Rifle's successful sojourn at Bisley, the following Regimental Order was issued by Colonel J.M. Kennedy, Commanding the Galloway Rifle Volunteers -

Castle Douglas
28th July, 1898

The Officer Commanding desires to record his appreciation of the superior marksmanship displayed by the members of the Regiment, in the various competitions at the National Rifle Association meeting at Bisley this year.

In the team competition for the Mullen's Cup, which they obtained with an aggregate of hits which has never before been surpassed in the competition, they have done honour to the Regiment, and the teams which competed for the Sir James Whitehead, Ranelagh, Starley and Track team competitions, also held the highest places in the various matches, while this year the Battalion has been brought to the front by the fine shooting of Private G. McHaffie, 'C' Company, who in the competition for the 'Queen's Prize', achieved the distinguished position of being only three points behind the winner, also the steady shooting of Private W. McCreadie, 'D' Company, who secured a place in the last 100, who competed for the 'Queen's Prize'. The individual shooting of all the other competitors from the Battalion was also so very satisfactory as to give promise of good records in the future.

As accurate marksmanship is now one of the chief requirements towards efficiency, the Officer Commanding, trusts that Officers Commanding Companies, will impress upon the men who do not go to Bisley, the desirability of their giving careful attention to the instruction given in class firing and in shooting, so as to become expert rifle shots.

Brigadier-General The Earl of Minto, has expressed his great satisfaction at the splendid performance of the Regiment at Bisley this year.

(Signed) Adjutant Captain Blake,
Galloway Rifle Volunteers.

******

SIR JAMES WHITEHEAD CHALLENGE CUP - 1899

This competition was held at Bisley in the week commencing, 16th July, 1899. This was a rapid firing competition, which was easily won by the Galloway men. The teams were permitted to shoot with the magazine loaded and send off as many shots as they could in one minute at 200 yards. The same at 500 yards. The four men from Galloway won with a total of 108 points, their nearest rival being the Queen's Edinburgh, with a score of 87 points. These were the only two Scottish teams entered. The Galloway Team was composed of Cyclist G. McHaffie, Stranraer, W. McCreadie, Newton Stewart, G. Geddes and J. Ferguson, New Galloway.

ROVER COMPETITION - 1899

The Rover cyclist competition, formerly the 'Starley Rover' was held at Bisley on Friday, 21st July, 1899. The competition was competed for by 15 sections of 4 men each, two of them belonging to the Galloway Rifle Volunteers. The first prize was an Imperial Rover Roadster bicycle fitted with pneumatic tyres and valued at £30, with £10 cash added by the Association.

In this competition teams were to parade dismounted, holding their machines and were then to mount and ride the machines along a course of a quarter of a mile, during which time they had to dismount and fire 10 rounds per man at 150 yards. 9 minutes was allowed to complete the course and if over 10 minutes, the team would be disqualified. The first place was won by the Galloway Rifle Volunteers.

The winning team was Commanded by Lieutenant W.M. Kelly, Newton Stewart, and was composed of as follows - Cyclists J. Ferguson and G. Geddes, New Galloway, Cyclists W.F. McCreadie, Newton Stewart and Cyclist G. McHaffie, Stranraer.

SIR JAMES WHITEHEAD CHALLENGE CUP - 1900

This Challenge Cup was won for the third time by a team from the Galloway Rifle Volunteers but no details are now available.

AMBULANCE SECTION

In 1887, authority was granted to the Volunteer Force, for the formation of a Volunteer Medical Staff Corps. Prior to 1887, Medical Officers were purely represented by their belonging to a particular Company and it was felt, by the Authorities, that these talents of both the medical and nursing profession could be better adapted, to the advantage of the Volunteer Movement.

Medical Staff Companies were authorised, to be formed of 3 Surgeons, 1 Quartermaster and 96 other ranks, with Sergeant Instructors and these might be combined into Divisions of 2 or more Companies, for which a Surgeon Commandant, Quartermaster and Adjutant were allowed. The qualification for efficiency was to be, 16 Ambulance and 80 other drills, in the 1st and 2nd years of service, with 8 Ambulance and 9 other drills in subsequent years, with 2 extra drills in each year, if absent from the Annual Inspection.

The formation of a Volunteer Medical Corps, within the Galloway Rifle Volunteers, obviously met with little response, in the first instance, with the following Editorial appearing in the local press, prior to the commencement of the Volunteer year of 1887.

"The Volunteers will soon be again taking the field and I would throw out the suggestion that another attempt be made to form an Ambulance Corps. Though the first attempt failed, I think if the matter was taken up by the Officers it would meet with success. The Medical Officer of the Corps or his Assistant would undertake to give instruction so that wherever we may be we might be able to render first aid in case of an emergency."

However, in the close season of 1888, Surgeon Captain R. Lorraine, of Maxwellton, was to hold Ambulance Classes in the Drill Hall at Laurieknowe, Maxwellton, with the idea of forming a Volunteer Medical Corps - The course included, in addition to structural drill, construction of the body, the uses of the various parts, circulation, respiration, the various methods of dressing wounds, stopping bleeding and putting up fractures, the treatment of sudden illness, burns, scalds, and those apparently drowned, together with the methods of lifting and carrying wounded, with and without appliances.

On the evening of Thursday, 17th January, 1889, Captain Lennox, 3 Sergeants, and 17 rank and file, came up for examination and all were successful in gaining certificates of proficiency. The examiner expressing himself more than satisfied with the skill displayed by the men. The men were presented with their Ambulance certificates, which carried the right of wearing the badge of the 'Geneva Cross' on the right sleeve.

This Ambulance Section tradition was to continue within the Maxwellton Companies, but unfortunately without any regularity, and again in 1895, at the annual Brigade Camp, we find that 1 Officer, 2 Sergeants and 16 men, were drawn from the Maxwellton Corps, to act in the Brigade Bearer Companies, which were being specially trained in Ambulance work and service to the sick and wounded.

Unlike the Galloway Battalion, the Dumfriesshire Battalion of Rifle Volunteers were to maintain a substantial 'Bearer' or Ambulance Section, with a total strength of 49 of all ranks, with 27 men drawn from 'A' Company, Dumfries and 22 men drawn from 'F' Company, Annan.

BANDS

Rule 6 of "Rules generally observed in the formation of a Volunteer Corps", provided:-

"Extra expenses for ornamental purposes, such as bands etc., are not to be entered on without the question having been put to the vote, unless the Commanding Officer should wish to furnish a band at his own expense; or unless the regular subscription should be sufficient to defray the cost."

From the very outset of the formation of the Administrative Battalion of Galloway Rifle Volunteers, most of the Companies were to form their own bands and as early as, September, 1860, both Newton Stewart and Stranraer, were boasting of a band. In the case of the Stranraer band this was reported as, "an assortment of band and Volunteers, made up from the Town Band." On the 1st January, 1861, however, the members of the 2nd Wigtown Rifle Volunteers, Stranraer, were invited by Officers to a breakfast at the George Inn, and afterwards returned to the Court House, where Mrs. David Guthrie, the wife of the Captain and Provost Guthrie, presented, on behalf of the ladies, the Volunteers with new flute band instruments.

This was to be the case throughout the Battalion, most Companies forming the much simpler and cheaper, Fife and Drum bands, and as was reported on the formation of the band of the 3rd Wigtown Rifle Volunteers, Newton Stewart, "Instead of marching as heretofore, like a body of men proceeding to a funeral or some such solemn occasion, they will have the enchanting, sweet spirit and stirring melodies of the band to enliven and guide them."

On the 10th September, 1860, the 4th Kirkcudbright Rifle Volunteers, Gatehouse, enjoyed an excursion to Kirkdale, the seat of Major Rainsford-Hannay, Commanding Officer of the Corps. They left Gatehouse preceded by their amateur Fife and Drum band, where they performed a few evolutions on the lawn.

On the 12th January, 1862, the 5th Wigtown Rifle Volunteers, Drumore, marched to Kirkmaiden Free Church, headed by their Fife and Drum band, for divine service, in full mourning, as ordered for the army in consequence of the death of the Prince Consort.

In many cases, however, particularly among some of the larger Companies, they were to form their own Brass Bands, no doubt many of the members of the Town's Band enlisted themselves in the Volunteer Movement, and on the 9th January, 1861, it was reported that the 2nd Kirkcudbright Rifle Volunteers, Castle Douglas, had been presented with 13 brass instruments to form their own band, by Lady Abercromby. Newton Stewart were to form their own Brass Band in the April of 1864.

The Fife and Drum bands were to adequately fulfil the needs of many Corps for a good number of years, as it was not until the 20th March, 1868, that the Volunteers of the 2nd Wigtown Rifle Volunteers, Stranraer, held a Concert in the Queen's Hall. South Strand Street, to raise funds for the formation of a Brass Band.

On the 1st July, 1868, at a meeting held in the Town Hall, New Galloway, it was resolved to form a Brass Band for the 3rd Kirkcudbright Rifle Volunteers, New Galloway. A committee was appointed for the purpose of collecting subscriptions and securing the services of a music tutor. The following subscriptions had already been received:-

Hon. Mrs. Bellamy Gordon	5-5-0
Mrs. Maxwell of Glenlee	5-0-0
Viscountess Kenmure	5-0-0
Peter Kennedy, Garroch	2-0-0
Rev. Dr. Maitland	1-1-0
Captain J.G. Maitland, 3rd K.R.V.	1-1-0
J. D. Horne Es., Overton	1-1-0
William Barbour Esq., of Barlay	1-0-0

Thomas Barbour Esq., of Dalshangan	1-0-0
Rev. S. Blair	1-0-0
Mr. John Shaw, Parkrobin	1-0-0
Mr. A. Corrie, 3rd K.R.V.	10-0
Mr. R.S. Muir, 3rd K.R.V.	10-0
Dr. Millman, 3rd K.R.V.	10-0
Rev. George Murray	10-0
The Misses McMillan of Viewfield	10-0
Mr. F. Paterson of Muirdrochwood	10-0
C.R. Saunders Esq.	10-0
J.S. Mackie	10-0
Mr. Crosbie	10-0

To be a member of a Volunteer Corps, was to be a member of a small but exclusive club, with a great deal of camaraderie amongst its members, not only from within a Company but throughout the County, however, to be a member of the Company Band, was to be even more exclusive, not only did its members join with their comrades in arms at the rifle ranges, drills and inspections, sufficient to earn their capitation grant but in addition they were required to spend many hours in practice with their fellow bandsmen, over and above the requirements of their fellow Volunteers. Nevertheless there was always a queue of Volunteers waiting to fill any band vacancy in order to become part of and participate in that small but exclusive group.

On the 30th June, 1877, the members of the Band of the 1st Kirkcudbright Rifle Volunteers, Kirkcudbright, had their annual excursion from Kirkcudbright to Dundrennan Abbey where they partook of a splendid picnic, then to Auchencairn and home by Castle Douglas, the lovely scenery through which they passed echoing to the martial strains of the party.

On Saturday, 13th August, 1892, the Band of 'H' Company, Dalbeattie, had their annual picnic to the Abbey Burnfoot, where, although the weather was not entirely favourable, the members appeared to enjoy themselves.

On the evening of Friday, 7th April, 1893, a social evening was held in the Crown Hotel, Dalbeattie by members of the band of the local Volunteers. Mr. Frank Lawson, Bandsmaster, was in the chair. Mr. Murray, the oldest member of the band proposed the toast of the evening, "Success to Dalbeattie Volunteer Band" and spoke of the different leaders of the band from its formation, paying particular tribute to Mr. Dickie, under whose leadership the band was at its best. Mr. Murray concluded by remembering that since he joined the band, over 100 bandsmen had left and gone to other parts, chiefly America, to seek work. The proceedings finished with a dance.

It would be unfair to leave this part of the story without referring to the following annual excursion of the Dalbeattie Volunteer Band, held on Saturday, 19th August, 1899, which reflects only too well those far off heady days of long, lingering, hot, lazy, summers, when life was much simpler and at a gentler and slower pace.

"They drove in brakes to New Abbey where lunch was served and a short programme of sports were carried through on the green. The band contest in which test pieces were set to different sections of the band, was won by those under the leadership of J. Morrison. R. Henderson's Company being second and J. Smith's Company third.

The 100 yards, single ladies race, was won by Miss Walker, Glasgow, and the 100 yards, married ladies race, was won by Mrs. Morrison. The girl's race, under 12 years, was won by Miss Lawson. The girl's race, over 12 years, was won by Miss Polly Ferguson. The tug of War, ladies versus gentlemen, was won by the ladies.

The next event was a rather novel one, being a competition to the lady who could beat the best time on the big drum, to the tune of "The Keel Row", played by Privates Clark and Morrison. This was won by Mrs. Clark.

The drive then resumed to Carsethorn, where a short time was spent. A five a-side competition at football, married ladies versus single ladies, was won by the spinsters, and a similar competition for the male members, was won by Captain R. Henderson's team.

Tea being enjoyed, dancing was engaged in, Mr. Lawson, supplying the music on his violin. A concert was then arranged and half an hour was pleasantly spent, songs rendered by Mr. Lawson, Miss Wark and Miss McKenzie, and Privates Henderson and Clark. Much amusement was provided in the distribution of the prizes when some of the successful competitors found that "all that glisters" is not necessarily silver.

The Volunteer Force formed an important part of the community life, providing numbers and martial dignity to solemn or joyous occasions, with their band providing the suitable musical overtones, not only did this pomp and circumstance, combined with annual Church Parades and "Feu de Joie" on important occasions, add colour to the community life, but it also drew recruits to the Movement, and as early as the 23rd May, 1861, the 1st Wigtown Rifle Volunteers, Wigtown, paraded through the Town, on the occasion of Her Majesty's Birthday, under Ensign McHaffie, accompanied by their band, where they fired a salute in the Main Street, accompanied by three cheers for the Queen. On the same day the members of the 2nd Wigtown Rifle Volunteers, Stranraer, paraded through the grounds of Castle Kennedy, headed by their flute band, played in front of the Big House and thereafter engaged in sports, songs and dances in the grounds.

On the 1st October, 1879, in aid of the Burn's Statue fund, there was a march-out, headed by the Band of the 5th Kirkcudbright Rifle Volunteers, Maxwellton, and a torchlight procession through the Town, to the dancing arena, at the Drill Hall at Laurieknowe.

On Sunday, 30th July, 1882, the Companies of the Maxwellton Corps, held their annual Church Parade.

On the 10th May, 1885, 'C' Company, Stranraer, held their annual Church Parade. They assembled at the Armoury and under the command of Major Taylor and Lieutenant Garrick, they marched to Sheuchan Church, where the service was conducted by the Honorary Chaplain, the Rev. W.M. Johnston.

On the evening of Saturday, 22nd May, 1885, the Maxwellton Corps marched, headed by their Band, to the Old Bridge, where the customary "feu de joie" was fired in honour of Her Majesty's Birthday. The Corps, afterwards, saluted whilst the Band played the National Anthem and three cheers were given fort the Queen.

The members of 'A' Company, Kirkcudbright, and the Gatehouse Section held their annual Church Parade, on Sunday, 27th August, 1905, when 80 men, under the Command of Captain Comrie and Lieutenants Glover and Wilkinson, attended the Parish Church.

Whereas these far off and heady days may have appeared to be very laid back and idyllic, they were nevertheless, times of great change and political awareness. In 1867, a split in the Liberal Party, brought the Conservatives to power, under Lord Derby and Disraeli, who put through the 2nd Grand Reform act, which gave the vote to householders who paid rates. To the masses, still denied the right to vote, these reforms did not go far enough and rallies against the Bill were held throughout the Country. One such rally was held at Dumfries on the 1st January, 1867, at which the Band of the 5th Kirkcudbright Rifle Volunteers had been engaged to play. The Commanding Officer of the Maxwellton Corps, Captain Howat, refused his Bandsmen the right to play at this rally and in consequence the members of the Band resigned en-masse.

On the 13th February, 1867, Captain Howat, assembled the members of the Maxwellton Corps for drill, in the Mechanics Hall, and whilst drill was in progress a deputation of the late members of the 5th Kirkcudbright Rifle's Band, waited on Captain Howat and requested that he should acknowledge acceptance of their resignations, tendered some weeks before, by giving them formal discharges, as required by Act of Parliament. Captain Howat said in reply that he had accepted their resignations and that there was no necessity whatsoever for having printed discharges. The deputation however, insisted on having the formality on their side and Captain Howat agreed to comply with their wishes. The deputation then withdrew. After the men had been exercised in Company drill, they were formed in line and addressed by Captain Howat.

"Volunteers it is now 4 years since I accepted the Command of the Maxwellton Volunteer Corps, I have always felt that whatever a man doeth, let him do it heartily, be it farming, as in my own case, or whatever else may be the business of his life. When, therefore, I became your Captain I determined that my Corps would be second to none, and I think we have succeeded, the Maxwellton Corps, being one of the largest and most efficient in the South of Scotland, and I may also add, one in which the most thorough harmony has hitherto existed. That the accord which had hitherto reigned amongst us seemed for a moment to receive a shock at the time of the New Year, was therefore, a source of much annoyance to me. You are well aware of the circumstances to which I allude, the band having engaged to play at the Reform demonstration on New Year's day.

The band erred in two respects, 1st in as much as we are bound to take no part, as Volunteers, in any political demonstration, and 2nd, in making any engagement to play, without my permission, knowing full well that I neither could nor would consent to their taking part, as Volunteers, in the demonstration on New Year's day. They made their arrangements without my knowledge, thus placing me in a false position and compromising the honour of the Corps. I had of course no alternative but to act as I did. It has been said that many of the Company sympathise with the feeling which led the Band to resign, many dismal prophecies reached my ears, that my Corps was disorganised. Having always felt and I trust shown, a deep interest in the Corps, I was hurt to think that at the first cloud, that came between us, all our old friendly relations towards each other were to be forgotten. I could not believe it. I trusted in your right feeling and in your sense of justice and I am happy to say my confidence was not misplaced, not one single resignation have I received. The Band resigned with the exception of two who stood firm and are still members of the Corps. I have lost no time in the formation of a new band, which I have no doubt will soon be the equal of the one departed. I know they intend to do their utmost by the time we are called upon to show ourselves next summer at the Battalion drill. It only remains therefore, to beg each and everyone of you to be diligent at drill and to use your utmost endeavours for the prosperity of the Corps. Let us give a practical proof next summer at Newton Stewart, that we are still the largest and finest Corps in the Galloway Rifles and not yet dependant upon Drums and Fifes for our music.

The speech of the Captain was frequently applauded in the course of its delivery. At its conclusion, however, Private Robert McLauchlan put several questions to Captain Howat, with reference to the constitution of the Corps, and having been answered he declared he could no longer, as a Volunteer, serve under a Government which denied to him his birthright. He immediately left the room, followed by Private Matthew Feeney, who also signified his intention of sending in his resignation.

A decade later, on the 7th December, 1877, history was once again to repeat itself, with the Band of the 5th Kirkcudbright Rifle Volunteers, Maxwellton, being refused permission, by their then Commanding Officer, Captain Barrie, from playing at a rally, being held in the Mechanics Hall, Dumfries, and in consequence, 12 of the 16 members of the Band sent in their instruments, and clothing and in a body signed a document tendering their resignations. However, the Bandmen's resignations were not to be accepted by Captain Barrie, who dismissed the 12 men and instituted proceedings against them for the less of the capitation grant which the men would fail to earn in the forthcoming year.

Over the years, the expenses involved in the upkeep of the Company Bands, led to their demise, with only the Maxwellton, Castle Douglas and Dalbeattie Brass Bands remaining, their funding coming mainly from the grants allocated to the Regiment. In consequence of this considered unnecessary expense, on Saturday, 15th December, 1900, the Officers of the Galloway Rifle Volunteers, met at Castle Douglas, resulting in the issue of the following Regimental Orders:-

i.). The band of Maxwellton detachment is to be the Regimental Band.

ii). The brass bands at Castle Douglas and Dalbeattie detachments will be dispensed with. All instruments, drums excepted, from these two stations will be returned to Headquarters at Castle Douglas by the 5th January, 1901. A note will be forwarded by all Officers Commanding Companies stating the number and kind of drums and pipes, if any, they have in their possession, and the condition they are in to the Band President. He will issue orders for any transfers from one station to another that he may consider advisable.

iii). The Officers Commanding 'B' and 'H' Companies will give the necessary notices to Bandmasters Keane and Lawson, and report the conditions of their appointments, so that they may be paid all that may be due them, either for salary or notice, at once.

iv). A Pipe Band is to be formed, 'A', 'B', 'C', 'D', 'E' and 'H' Companies will each have two pipers.

v). Every Company will be careful to train two Buglers, but one each of these at least will be trained as small drummers, and play in the Pipe of Brass Band. A large drummer, for use at Company Drills will be allowed, but only one for the Pipe Band and one for Brass Band will attend as such at Battalion Drills and Camps. The other large drummers will fall into the ranks. The Band President will make the selection.

vi). A Pipe-Major will be appointed. He will reside at such station as the Band President decides. He will instruct the Pipers and will travel to out-stations for this purpose, as will be arranged at a subsequent date.

vii). The Pipers will be dressed in kilts, etc., but the drummers and brass band will wear the ordinary regimental uniform, with the exception that both Bandmaster and Pipers will wear silver-plated badges in their caps same as the Sergeants do at present.

The issue of these Orders was met with much objection in Castle Douglas and in response to a requisition signed by a large number of ratepayers, Provost Thomson, called a Public Meeting, which was held in the Town Hall, Castle Douglas, on Friday, 21st December, 1900, the result being the passing of the following resolution:-

"That this meeting learns with great regret the decision of the Officers of the Galloway Rifle Volunteers, to abolish the band of 'B' Company and is of the opinion that such a step will most seriously injure the Volunteer Movement in the district and therefore respectfully requests the Officers to reconsider their decision and further authorises the Chairman to forward a copy of the resolution to the Colonel."

On Saturday, 11th January, 1901, a further meeting of the Officers of the Galloway Rifle Volunteers, was held in the Town Hall, Castle Douglas, Colonel Kennedy presiding. The meeting was told by Captain Hewat that in consequence of the issue of the Regimental Order disbanding the Castle Douglas Band, that it had already had a prejudicial influence against recruiting for 'B' Company, and that many of the older members of the Band were poised to leave the Company. He had no wish to suggest that the Regimental Band should be at Castle Douglas but desired an allocation to retain the Company Band.

After discussion the meeting unanimously agreed that Castle Douglas and Dalbeattie Companies should be allowed to maintain their Brass Bands, at their own expense, with a grant of one-eighth of 7½% of the Regimental capitation grant being voted to assist these Companies. In the event of either of the Companies not wishing to retain a Company Band it was resolved that the other share of the 7½% capitation grant should be paid in full to the Company resolving to maintain its Band. It was further agreed that the Company Band should maintain a strength of not less than 18 members.

The 7½% of capitation grant referred to was the allowance under the Volunteer Regulations of which a Regiment was allowed to spend for Band purposes. The reason for the allowance of one-eight of 7½% represented the share of one of the 8 Companies of the Battalion and that any further grant would have crippled the resources of the Regiment in carrying on both a Regimental Brass Band at Maxwellton and a Pipe Band divided among the remaining Companies.

Prior to the meeting of the Officers on 11th January, 1901, 'H' Company, Dalbeattie, had already resolved to dispense with their Band and on the 22nd December, 1900, a "farewell smoker" was held in the King's Arms Hotel, Dalbeattie, by members of the Dalbeattie Brass Band, presided over by their Bandmaster of some 18 years, Mr. Frank Lawson.

The full one-quarter share of the 7½% of the capitation grant was therefore to pass to 'B' Company, Castle Douglas, who were to retain their Company Band, with subscriptions coming from both Municipal and private sources, this Company Band being the only Band available to the Magistrates for ceremonial occasions.

The following six gentlemen represent the total number of Regimental Bandmasters to the Galloway Rifle Volunteers, from its inception in 1860, until its demise in 1908. The names are in date order but unfortunately some dates are unknown:-

1. Bandmaster John Grimm, Maxwellton. 1860-
2. Herr Ludwig, Dumfries.
3. Bandmaster John Slavin.
4. Bandmaster Robert Keane, Castle Douglas, Retired 8th April, 1904
5. Bandmaster Frank Lawson, Dalbeattie, April, 1904-1905
6. Bandmaster J.P. Leroy, Maxwellton, 1905-1908

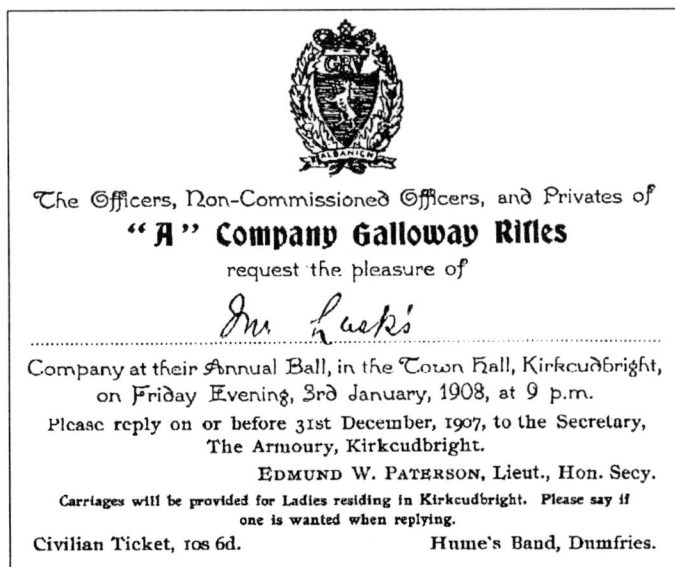

(9) Civilian ticket, in the name of Mr Lusks, (Gelston) to the Annual New Year Ball of 'A' Company - Kirkcudbright, of the Galloway Rifles, to be held in the Town Hall, Kirkcudbright, on the 3rd January, 1908

FOOTBALL

Football, in Galloway, was very much in its infancy on the advent of the Volunteer Movement, with its first ever recorded football team being that of the Kirkcudbright, "Lang Acre Team" of 1865. Jon Ritchie, Tam Whiterite, Sam Cavan, Jon Craith, Jon Seggie, Rob Chrystal, Konel McCormick, Tammie Roy, Alex Milroy, Jon Hart and Jon McGinness. Cricket, Quoiting and Bowling were very much the favoured summer pastimes, with "Curliana" taking priority over the long winter months, with league tables for these events being published weekly in the local press. Football, was not to come to prominence until after the turn of the Century.

The tale has already been told of the 15th June, 1866, when three members of the Kirkcudbright Rifle Corps, who attended a Cricket match rather than their Adjutant's drill were dismissed the service.

On the 31st July, 1872, the 2nd Kirkcudbright Rifle Volunteers, Castle Douglas, cricket Team of, Captain and adjutant Singleton, Private Barclay, Ensign Maxwell, Private Reid, Colour Sergeant Borland, Sergeant Henderson, Private S. Gordon, Private Forsyth, Ensign E. Gordon, Sergeant Dowdney and Private Myers, played a match against the civilians of Castle Douglas. The Volunteers won the match by 16 runs.

In January, 1873, a Volunteer Curling Speil, took place at Lochrutton Loch, between the Maxwellton and Lochrutton Rifle Volunteers. The conditions 4 men a-side. Sergeant Forteath was the skip of Maxwellton with Sergeant Thomson being the skip of Lochrutton. There was no recorded result.

A further recorded Curling Speil, was in the January, of 1879, when the Volunteers from Kelton played a Civilian Team from Buittle, with the losers supplying 1 Ton of coal to the poor. The Volunteers were to win by a score of 21 shots to 3. The teams were, **Kelton Volunteers:-** Private Blackwood, Private J. Grierson, Private J. Murdoch, Corporal Murdoch. **Buittle Civilians:-** Mr. Mitchell, Mr. James Gillespie, Mr. Kerr, Mr. Porter.

In 1875, it was reported that the 5th Kirkcudbright Rifles, Maxwellton, spent their winter months at their Quadrille Club.

With both the Volunteer Movement and Football growing together in popularity, it was inevitable that the Volunteers would eventually leave behind their earlier leisure pursuits and merge with and participate in this new and fast growing sport, and in due course most Rifle Corps were to be possessed of a football team.

The most prominent of these football teams was the now defunct, 3rd Lanark Rifle Volunteers - Third Lanark, of Cathkin Park fame, who were to far outlive the Volunteer Movement and pass into the modern professional ranks, their cheering from the terraces being acclaimed as the "Volunteer Roar".

Within Galloway the famous **5KRV**, who could be considered, in part the forerunners of the present **Queen of the South**, Dumfries, were formed in 1879, by members of the 5th Kirkcudbright Rifle Volunteers, Maxwellton, with their ground being that of Palmerston Park, the Drill Field of the Maxwellton Rifle Corps. Their first recorded match however, was not to be until Saturday, 13th November, 1880, when they played against **Moffat Football Club**, at Moffat, and were defeated by 2 goals to nil.

On Saturday, 20th February, 1881, a football match took place at Palmerston Park, between the Kirkcudbrightshire and the Wigtownshire Rifle Volunteers, with the object of raising funds to purchase a Challenge Cup, which would be played for annually. The Kirkcudbrightshire team won by 2 goals to 1. **Kirkcudbrightshire** Team:- goal, R. Carter 1KRV; backs, J. Creighton 5KRV, M. Paterson 1KRV; half-backs, J. Mullins 5KRV, J. Cameron 5KRV, J. Houston 1KRV; forwards, T. Harrison 1KRV, A. Sharpe 1KRV, J. Mechan 5KRV, W. Law 5KRV, J. Wallace 5KRV.

On the 20th May, 1881, the Annual General Meeting of the **5KRV** was held in their Drill Hall, with the following Office Bearers being elected. It was reported that the Club now had 70 members and although they had not won any honours, they were in a flourishing condition. Office Bearers:- Hon. President, Captain Maxwell Heron, M.P.; President, Captain Lennox; Vice President, Mr. John Raphaels; Captain, Mr. John Wallace; Captain 2nd Eleven, Mr. James Walker; Match Secretary, Mr. Robert J. Walker, Nunholm, Dumfries; Hon. Sec., Mr. James Mullins; Treasurer, Mr. John Cameron; Auditors - Messrs. Alex Steel and William Law; Committee - Messrs. D. Walker, A. Steel, W. Law, A. Queen and A. McGeorge; Match Committee - Messrs John Wallace, J. Welsh, J. Raphaels, R. Carruthers and T. Beattie.

On Saturday, 8th October, 1881, the second tie for the Football Association Cup was played at Palmerston between **5KRV** and **Queen of the South Wanderers.** The tie ended in a one all draw. An extra 30 minutes was played, with the Wanderers winning by 2 goals to 1.

On the 18th February, 1882, the **5KRV** played the **Volunteer Athletic,** Newton Stewart, at Newton Stewart, in a third round tie for the Churchill Cup, the result being a 3 all draw.

Football Hooliganism. -

Could this be the first recorded case of trouble on the terracings, now all too prevalent in the modern game. On Saturday, 3rd November, 1883, a first round tie of the Churchill Cup took place at Newton Stewart, between the **Volunteer Athletic**, Newton Stewart, and the **Vale of Fleet**, Gatehouse. The game, apparently, was an extremely exciting one, which the Vale of Fleet, in splendid form were to win by 4 goals to 2. During the course of the game, the hostility of the spectators was most objectionably displayed by hissing and hooting and opprobrious epithets applied to the **Vale of Fleet** team. The fury of the mob did not terminate on the field and on the completion of the match a large crowd pursued the Gatehouse team to their wagonette and some distance out of town, pelted them with mud, stones and other missiles. The Press was to later carry a leader offering the advice, "that Newton Stewart must learn to bear defeat gracefully, if by their play they cannot avoid it". The teams on that fateful day were.

Volunteer Athletic:- J. Kell, P. Stewart, J. E. Robertson, J. McGuigan (Captain), W.C. Gordon, M. Scobie (Girvan), A. McCreadie, T. Torrance (Stranraer), W. McBratney, T. McNaught, H.S. McLaughlin (Moffat).

Vale of Fleet:- J. McDill, R. Dalrymple (Captain), J. Biggam, T. Dalrymple, J. Henry, T. Brian, R. Brian, D. Brackenridge, J. Bailiffe, S. Leitch, J. Paterson.

At the annual general meeting of the **5KRV F.C.** held at the drill hall, Maxwellton, on the evening of Friday, 2nd May, 1884, Mr. J. Walker, Secretary, in submitting his report stated that this had been its most prosperous and successful season to date. For the Scottish Cup, they played 5 matches, winning 3 and drawing 1, losing 1; For the Churchill Cup, they played 5 matches, winning 4 and losing 1; For the Southern Counties Charity Cup, they played 2 matches, winning both and carrying off the Cup. They had played 7 Friendlies, winning 4 and losing 3. (They were to win the Churchill Cup the following season).

On the 16th January, 1885, a match took place at Castle Douglas between 'B' Company of the Rifle Volunteers, Castle Douglas, and **Oakwell F.C.**, in front of a large crowd of spectators. The game ended in a 5 all draw.

On the 4th April, 1885, **Sunderland Athletic,** the winners of the Durham Cup, played a friendly against the **5KRV**, at Palmerston Park. The Volunteers of the **5KRV** won by 2 goals to nil.

At the Annual General meeting of the **5KRV** held on the 16th April, 1886, Provost Lennox, President of the club, was to tell the meeting that they had played 22 matches, of which they had won 15 and lost 7, scoring a total of 102 goals for the loss of 66. The 2nd eleven team, had played 11 matches, winning 8, losing 2, and drawing 1, obtaining in the process 72 goals for and 21 against.

On Saturday, 8th august, 1891, **5KRV** played **Dumbarton F.C.** at Palmerston, under the patronage of the Provost and Magistrates of Dumfries. The game ended in a 3 all draw and had been quite remarkable, with the new rule of "Fisting-out" having been enforced for the first time. **5KRV** team:- goal, Mundell; back, Cherteris, McAulay; half-back, Elliott, J. Moffat and R. Moffat; forwards, Morley, Aitken, Bedford, Edgar, and Little. **Dumbarton** team:- goal, Barr; backs, Lang and Millar; half-backs, McMillan, Boyle and Kerr; forwards, R. Bell, Galbraith, Millar, McNaught, James Bell.

The **6KRV F.C.**, Dalbeattie, were in part the forerunners of the present Dalbeattie Star, and were formed prior to the Consolidation of the Battalion, on the 26th May, 1880, but their first recorded match, which was to end in disaster, was not to take place until the 5th November, 1892, when they met **St. Cuthbert Wanderers**, Kirkcudbright, at Kirkcudbright, in the first round of the Law Cup. The **6KRV** were to lose 13 goals to 3.

The teams were,

6KRV F.C.:- goal, Flynn; backs, Jack and Gourlay; half-backs, Smith, M. Hooper, E. Hooper; forwards, Gillespie, Lynch, A. Burnie, H. Burnie, T. Robertson.

St. Cuthbert Wanderers F.C.:- goal, Crossan; backs, Paterson and Douglas; half-backs, Straiton, Milligan and Wallace; forwards, T. Gourlay, Sloan, D. McMonies, Boyd, R. McMonies.

On the 17th August, 1893, at the Annual General Meeting of the **6KRV F.C.**, it was unanimously agreed to admit non-Volunteers as playing members of the **6KRV**, and in 1905, the **6KRV**, were to be merged with Dalbeattie Star, thereby ending their 25 years link to the Volunteer Movement.

New Galloway Rifle Corps were to form their own **3KRV** football club, pre 1880, but unfortunately they do not appear to have been particularly successful with no recorded matches nor any reported history. It can therefore only be assumed that their formation was to be of short duration.

On Saturday, 27th January, 1894, the **Volunteer Athletic**, Newton Stewart, and the **Vale of Fleet**, Gatehouse, were to meet once again at Holm Park, Newton Stewart, in the semi-final of the Galloway Challenge Shield. On this occasion there was to be no repeat of the previous crowd trouble with the **Vale of Fleet** coming out winners, in a high scoring game, by 6 goals to 5.

In 1897, the now defunct **1KRV** football club, Kirkcudbright, was resurrected for the Jubilee celebrations of Queen Victoria, and playing under the title of the **"Kirkcudbright Rifle (Volunteers)"**, their team being reported as; Tam Morrison, Bob Kimm, Joe Paterson, Bob Leckie, Eby Diell, Peter Henney, Jimmie Siers, Chas Finlayson, Thirdy Coull, Jimmie Blake and Johnnie Burnie.

On Saturday, 6th November, 1897, the **6KRV**, Dalbeattie were defeated 3 goals to 1 by **AYR Parkhouse**, in the 4th round of the Scottish Qualifying Cup. However, the following year, 1898, the **6KRV** were to have their most successful season in the history of the club, winning the Law Cup, the Stewartry League Cup and the Southern Counties Cup, and in a friendly match against **Carlisle City** at Maidenholm Park, Dalbeattie, on Saturday, 26th November, 1898, they were to defeat City by 5 goals to 1, the team on that occasion being; Bisset, Lindsay, and Jack; Joe Ferguson, McCartney and Henderson; R. Ferguson, McIntosh, J. Glencross, Jardine Ferguson and P.T. Ferguson.

In 1901, the **5KRV F.C.** were admitted to the Senior circles, winning in their first season the Southern Counties Charity Cup, the Potts Challenge Cup and the Annan Challenge Cup. The following season, 1902, they again won the Southern Counties Charity Cup, the Dumfries and Galloway Cup and the Wigtownshire and District Cup.

The **5KRV F.C.** were to continue in their successful role until the break up of the Volunteer Movement on the 31st March, 1908, when their team was merged to form the nucleus of a team fielded by the newly formed 5th Battalion K.O.S.B. On the 21st March, 1919, Queen of the South F.C., were formed from the leading players of Dumfries, Arrol-Johnston and the 5th K.O.S.B. Football Clubs, with their ground at Palmerston Park being, the former home of the **5KRV** and the drill field of the 5th Kirkcudbright Rifle Volunteers.

COMMITTEE.

Captain W. L. Comrie, President.	Pte. M. Coleman.
Lieut. E. W. Paterson.	„ W. M Connell.
Sergeant-Instructor A. S. Cairns.	Piper L. Murray.
Sergeant-Bugler H. Livingston.	Pte. W. G. Burns.
Sergeant J. Johnstone.	„ G. M'Candlish.
Sergeant R. Branney.	„ W. Stewart.
Corporal A. Gourlay.	„ W. Tait.
Corporal J. Murphy.	„ G. Murphy.
Corporal J. M'Gowan.	„ J. Paterson.
Pte. G. Thomson.	„ S. Wilson
„ A. Grant.	

CAPTAIN COMRIE,
LIEUTENANT PATERSON. } M.C'S.

---

(10) Reverse of Ticket on page 287, showing Officers and men who were on the Committee.

CHAPTER 11

RULES AND REGULATIONS FOR EFFICIENTS-
FORMATION OF CAMPS OF EXERCISE-
THE SOUTH OF SCOTLAND VOLUNTEER
BRIGADE, 1888 AND THE SCOTTISH
BORDER VOLUNTEER INFANTRY BRIGADE-
CAMPS OF EXERCISE ATTENDED BY MEMBERS
OF THE GALLOWAY RIFLE VOLUNTEERS IN
THE YEARS BETWEEN 1891-1907.

In consequence of the report of the Royal Commission of the 14th August, 1862, which recommended the introduction of Government grants to the Volunteers on their completion of a prescribed number of drills, Battalion drills and a course of musketry instruction, on Tuesday, 21st October, 1862, the Rifle Companies of the Stewartry paraded at the Market Hill, Castle Douglas, for their first Battalion drill, by order of their Captain and Adjutant W. Munro. They were inspected by Major Young, Volunteer Inspector of the South Western District of Scotland, who expressed himself highly satisfied with the conduct of the Companies. The parade strength was as follows:

	Officers.	Non Com. Officers	Rank & File.	Buglers.
1st Kirkcudbright	1	3	22	0
2nd Castle Douglas.	3	8	36	1
3rd New Galloway.	1	1	4	0
4th Gatehouse .	1	4	8	1
5th Maxwellton.	1	8	18	0

Total of all ranks. = 121.

On Wednesday, 22nd October, 1862, by order of Captain and Adjutant W. Munro, the Wigtownshire Companies of the Galloway Rifle Volunteers, paraded at the farm of Challoch, Glenluce, for their first Battalion drill where they were inspected by Major Young, whe expressed himself satisfied with the Stranraer and Newton Stewart Companies but he regretted that neither the drill nor the arms of the Drummore Company were such that he could approve. The Wigtown and Whithorn Companies failed to attend.
The parade strength was as follows:

> 1st Wigtown - Not represented.
>
> 2nd Stranraer - Well represented.
>
> 3rd Newton Stewart - Present.
>
> 4th Whithorn - Not represented.
>
> 5th Drummore - Represented.

On the 28th June, 1863, the following circular was issued by the War Office following the report of the Royal Commission of 14th August, 1862, and in preparation for the issue of the new Regulations to be issued on 21st July, 1863.

"It is necessary that all Corps of Volunteers which are not of sufficient strength to constitute by themselves a Regiment, Brigade or Battalion, should be either united with others to form an administrative Regiment or should be attached for administrative purposes to another Corps of the same arm, having the establishment of a Regiment, Brigade or Battalion, in order that they may partake of the sums voted by

Parliament for the Capitation Grant to Volunteers."

The Wigtownshire and Kirkcudbrightshire Companies of Rifle Volunteers had previously formed as an Administrative Battalion on the 30th June, 1860.

On the 21st July, 1863, the following Government Regulations were issued under the Volunteer Act, 1863, which recommended a grant of 20/- to every Volunteer who made himself 'efficient' by attending 9 drills in the year, of which 6, in the case of Consolidated and three in Administrative Battalion, should be Battalion drills, and who had gone through a course of musketry. A further grant of 10/- was also paid to riflemen who fired a prescribed quantity of ball cartridge in the course of a year, i.e.60 rounds in class firing and who passed out of the 3rd class. In the case of recruits, 30 drills and a short course of Musketry instruction was held as qualification. However, should the Inspecting Officer find a member non-effective his grant would be disallowed.An additional sum of 4/- per annum was given for the conveyance of effectives, the Headquarters of whose Corps was more than 5 miles from that of the Adminstrative Battalion, to which it belonged. The total cost to the Government in the implementation of this grant to the Volunteers was half a million pounds.

"On the 1st December, each year, the Adjutant of each Corps or Administrative Regiment is to issue certificates of efficiency to such Volunteers as have complied with the requirements stated.These requirements vary for light horse, artillery, engineers, mounted rifle and ordinary Rifle Volunteer Corps, but they may be summoned as requiring 18 months probation for recruits and the attendance on the prescribed drills for the 12 months preceding for Volunteers, not for recruits.

These drills in the Rifle Corps are 30 squad, Company or battalion drills and instructions in musketry for recruits and for others 9 drills of which there are to be 6 Battalion and 3 Company drills.The Volunteer must also be certified to have a competant knowledge of the various drills and to have been present at the last inspection unless absent with leave of the Commanding Officer or from sickness duly certified. This certificate is to be in force for 12 months only.

Volunteers feeling aggrieved at not obtaining a certificate may appeal to the Commanding Officer of the Corps who if he agrees with the Adjutant may either sign the certificate or concur to withholding it. The Secretary of State has the power, in the case of Rifle Volunteers, to reduce the number of Battalion drills and increase proportionately the number of Company drills and where there exist a company so situated as not to connect with any Battalion, to dispose with battalion drill altogether. The certificates will be varied accordingly.

Where the Inspecting Officer at the annual inspection reports that a Corps is not proficient in drill or instruction, to the Secretary of State, he shall have the power to direct the withholding of the certificates from all members of the Corps. The Inspecting Officer may also direct the withholding of a certificate from any Volunteer who does not appear to him to be proficient."

With the introduction of these grants the authorities were to demand the requirement of a written guarantee, from the Volunteer, that he would make himself efficient for a period of three years, the grant or capitation grant as it was to become known, being recoverable in Court of Law, should he fail to earn it. The standard of efficiency in drill, musketry, battalion drill, and annual inspection was to dramatically improve both nationally and within the Galloway Rifle Volunteers as was recruiting to the Volunteer movement. The fiasco of the 1st Wigtownshire Battalion drill in 1862, was not to be repeated and was in direct contrast to the parade state of the Galloway Rifles in their 1st full Administrative Battalion drill and Inspection, by Major Walker, Crawfordton, Inspector of Musketry, at Woodhall, Laurieston, the home of Colonel Laurie, who was in command of the Battalion, on the 24th October, 1863. Captain W. Munro, Adjutant, the Company Officers being:-

1st Kirkcudbright Rifle Volunteers.	Captain Hamilton; Ensign Craig.
2nd	Captain Mackie; Lieutenant Bell; Ensign Renny.
3rd	Captain Maxwell; Rev. George Murray of Balmaclellan, Chaplain.
4th	No Officers.
5th	Captain Howat; Lieutenant Allan; Ensign Stark.
1st Wigtownshire Rifle Volunteers.	Lieutenant Vans Agnew. Dr. Snowdon.
2nd	Captain Guthrie; Ensign Taylor.
3rd	Lieutenant Stuart.
4th	Lieutenant Stewart.
5th	Lieutenant Watson.

		Officers.	Sergeants.	Rank & File.	Total.
1st K.R.V.	Kirkcudbright	2	4	51	57
2nd	Castle Douglas	3	6	66	75
3rd	New Galloway	2	4	38	44
4th	Gatehouse	-	2	13	15
5th	Maxwellton	3	5	60	68
1st W.R.V.	Wigtown	2	-	20	22
2nd	Stranraer	2	5	66	73
3rd	Newton Stewart	1	2	20	23
4th	Whithorn	1	-	31	32
5th	Drummore	1	3	22	26

Total of all ranks.. . . . .435.

The total enrolled strength of the Galloway Rifle Volunteers for year ended 30th November, 1863, was 559.

In August, 1870, the War Office was to issue the following circular to encourage the Volunteers in camps of exercise and for the first time to authorise grants for Proficiency by Officers and Sergeants who undertook courses of instruction and a written examintion in front of their Adjutant. Captain William Agnew, then Sergeant Agnew, 3rd W.R.V. Newton Stewart, was the first man to earn the additional Proficiency grant, within the Galloway Rifle Volunteers.

"Facilities will be given to the Volunteers for the formation of camps of exercise. Application to form a camp is to be made by the Commanding Officer to the General Officer Commanding the district. The Lord Lieutenant's concurrence will be required. The Central Department will supply the camp equipage. When camps are duly authorised and last for 3 days, exclusive of the days of joining or breaking up the camp, equipage will be conveyed to and from the camp free of cost, arrangements will be made if possible for supplying rations at the Government contract rate. Allowances of 2/6d per head for average number of effectives of all ranks, shown to have been present will be made to cover the expense of cooking apparatus and other contingent outlay; the annual inspection will take place in camp. The payment of the grant will depend on the Inspecting Officer's certificate being in every respect satisfactory. The issue of Snider Rifles to the Volunteers will be first made to the Battalion which has the highest percentage of efficients. As an encouragement to acquire a thorough knowledge of their duties a special capitation grant of £2-10/- will be given to each Commissioned Officer or Sergeant of Volunteers, not including the permanent staff who attains a certificate of Proficiency by attending schools of instruction or receiving instructions from the Adjutant or Sergeant instructor of their Corps. This grant will be in addition to the 20/- or 30/- already allowed their enrolled strength in the annual returns of 1st December, 1869.

No Volunteer will be passed as efficient after 1871, unless his rifle has been inspected and found to be in good order."

In July, 1874, Government were to update the terms of efficiency with no significant change to that already issued under the 1863 Act.

On 27th July, 1877, the following Editorial was to appear in the *Dumfries Courier,*

"It is somewhat strange that though Dumfries and Galloway possess two excellent Battalions of Volunteers, neither of them has ever made an effort to gain a little experience in the most practical part of soldiering - camp life. It cannot have escaped the observation of the Officers and members of the Forces that camping out has become an annual proceeding on the part of many Volunteer Companies.

There are, or were very recently a number of Companies under canvas in Aberdeenshire and Morayshire. As to the Militia, it seems their training would not be considered complete unless they were camped out all the time in such a season as the present, the prospect of spending 8 days in tents would not be pleasant to many Volunteers but it is very seldom we have so much wet weather at Midsummer as we have had this month. Any inconvenience that might be felt would be counterbalanced by the novelty and delightful freedom of camp life. It would moreover, have many practical advantages. To be fully efficient our Volunteers should be conversant with other details of military duty than drilling and rifle shooting. The Volunteer Engineers at Chatham are at present setting their brethren in arms a very good example in this respect, they are taking part along with the Royal Engineers in making preparations for siege operations that are to be carried out there this month.

Of course the ground at Hannahfield would not be available for such a purpose but the Galloway Volunteers might pitch their camps one year at Castle Douglas and another at Newton Stewart, in the case of the Dumfriesshire Volunteers they might spend 8 days under canvas in the vicinity of Moffat, Thornhill,

Langholm and Dumfries.

A short period of training in that way would be of greater benefit to the Companies than many Battalion drills. Were they to spend 8 days each in camp before the Scottish Borderers undergo their usual training they would make a much better appearance together and when Brigaded form a far more efficient force."

On the 1st November, 1880, a further Order was issued by Government, updating the Order of July, 1874, in relation to the term 'efficient', under the Volunteer Act, 1863, once again with no major changes but for the first time dispensing with the necessity of Battalion drills should a Rifle Corps go into camp. This was to be more in keeping with the Militia, a 'Paper Regiment' for 11 months of the year, coming into being when attending their annual camp for training. Within the Volunteers, the introduction of camps was seen as a means of putting into practice the skills learned throughout their Volunteer year of drilling, shooting and other Corps Activities.

"A Volunteer shall be entitled to be deemed an efficient Volunteer only if he obtains a certificate in due form. Every certificate shall bear the date, 1st November, and shall be evidence of the efficiency of the Volunteer to the 31st October, next. Every Volunteer fulfilling the requirements shall be entitled to receive a certificate unless absent without leave or through sickness.

In the course of each year the Adjutant shall select such Volunteers as in his opinion have fulfilled the requirements and submit their names to the Commanding Officer with a view to their obtaining certificates of efficiency. If the Adjutant refuses to recommend a certificate, the Volunteer may appeal to the Commanding Officer of his Corps and if he differs from the opinion of the Adjutant, he shall refer the matter to the Officer appointed by one of Her Majesty's Principal Secretaries of State to act in that behalf, whose decision shall be final.

Similarly in the case of Rifle Corps at Battalion drills there is power to dispense with efficiency, four clear days at a camp of instruction may count specially. For weak Corps special arrangements may be made as regards proficiency. Where a Corps is by its own default not inspected during the year, or where the Officer inspecting a Volunteer Corps at the annual inspection in any year, reports that the Corps is not in perfect drill and instruction to his satisfaction, the Secretary of State shall have power to direct the withholding of certificates of efficiency at the end of the year. The inspecting Officer at the annual inspection may withhold a certificate of any Volunteer and where the situation and circumstances of an Artillery Volunteer Corps, in any particular year, creates serious obstacles to the fulfilment of the requirements of attendance at gun practice, the Secretary of State has the power to dispose with it.

Similarly there is power to dispense with Battalion drills in the case of Rifle Corps. If in any year a Volunteer is resident during the drill season of his Corps at a greater distance than 10 miles from Headquarters he may be attached, for drill purposes, to another Corps, but in this case he must wear the uniform of his own Corps."

Now that the necessity of Battalion drills had been dispensed with, should a Corps go into camp, the Secretary of State for War was to issue the following instructions. "Country Volunteer Corps who Attend Brigade Camps are debarred from receiving allowances for travelling for inspection and Battalion drills, as all drills necessary for efficiency may be performed in camp. However, Volunteers who are unable to go into camp with their Corps for 3 clear days and who attend camp purely for the purpose of performing Battalion drills or attending the annual inspection, are granted travelling allowance. In cases where Volunteers are unable to go into camp for Battalion drills they may be permitted to substitute Company for Battalion drills."

The following Regimental Order, dated 9th May, 1884, lists the Battalion drills which were to be held by the Galloway Rifle Volunteers, during the season 1884.

"31st May at Maxwellton for 'B', 'H', 'F' & 'G'; 7th June, At Newton Stewart for 'C' 'D', 'E'; 14th June, at Dalbeattie for 'A', 'B', 'F' & 'G' and 'H'; 21st June, at Stranraer for 'C' & 'D'; 28th June, at Castle Douglas for 'A', 'B' , 'H' and 'E'.

The Officer Commanding has instructed his intention of inspecting the Regiment on either the 12th or 19th July, 1884, at Castle Douglas."

On 1st March, 1886, at a meeting in the House of Commons, the House was told that there was an absolute necessity for an immediate addition of 10/- per man in order that the Volunteer Force might maintain, not only its present efficiency but its actual existence, which was seriously imperilled. The House was of the opinion that the present capitation grant of 30/- and the Proficiency grant of 50/- was totally inadequate and a Committee was appointed to consider these grants.

On the 25th February, 1887, the long awaited report was published and the recommended grant increases were to take effect from the 1st May, 1887. The actual increase of the old capitation grant was in itself not very large, being indeed only 5/- per efficient, making the new total of 35/-. This increase, in the case of Infantry Regiments, was dependent on an improved standard of musketry.

Beyond this, recognising that many Corps, especially those from the cities and other large towns had to travel by rail in order to get to target practice, the sum of 4/- was to be allowed for travelling expenses to and from the ranges. An extra 1/-, making in all an additional 6/-, was to be paid to Engineer efficients.

The Committee was to recognize the importance of the service, which it was in the power of the Volunteer Officer to give to their Corps and the country by qualifying themselves for duties superior to those of merely drilling and commanding their Regiments or Companies, for which the highest amount previously paid had been £4 per head, the same for the Sergeants. In future all Officers who passed the examination in tactics were to be given a grant of 30/-, instead of 10/-. A further grant of 30/- was to be given to Officers who passed in signalling. It was now possible for all Officers, in an ordinary way to earn the sum of £5 - 10/- per year for their Corps and in many cases, the sum of £7

The committee was also to recognise the expense in attending service with the marching columns, recommended by the Chief of Staff of the Army, and an allowance of 2/- per man was made for each day the Column was out under authority.

These increased grants were expected to add to the Army estimates of about £110,000 per year. Although allowances were to increase over the following years, the basic capitation grant was to remain static at 35/- per Volunteer until the Force ceased to exist in 1908.

These capitation grants were payable only after the completion of the Volunteer year, 31st October, once they had been earned, however, most Companies were running in debt each year until the grants and allowances had been received by the Corps and to alleviate this hardship, by Army Order 76, dated April, 1896, an additional allowance of half the ordinary Capitation grant and Proficiency allowances were paid to the Volunteer Companies to clear their outstanding debts. (Castle Douglas were labouring under a debt of £54-2-10d with Dalbeattie £33-2-8d in debt).

In November, 1896, new conditions of efficiency for Infantry Volunteers were issued by an Order in Council updating the Order of 1st November, 1880, under the Volunteer Act of 1863.

"Men who joined prior to 1st November, 1879, must do 9 drills annually, (3 of which must be Battalion). If absent from the Inspection - with leave - then two extra drills must be performed, making 11 in all.

"Men who joined after 31st October, 1879, must after their first 2 years, perform 12 drills annually, in the third and fourth years, (3 of which must be Battalion) and two extra drills making 14 in all, if absent from the Inspection. The 60 or 62 drills for the first two years have not been interfered with. "

For the year ended 31st October, 1900, the capitation grant was reported as 35/- with 2/- allowance for equipment and 1/- allowance for a great coat, if purchased. The basic requirement for the payment of this grant was reported as 9 drills (3 of which must be Battalion) and a course of musketry.

In 1889 grants for attendance at Camp, for a minimum of 3 clear days and not more than 4, were to be increased to 2/- per day, with travelling expenses being paid. This was to increase in 1890, to a maximum of 6 days in camp, with the grant of 2/- per day payable for each day spent in camp, with 4/- travelling expenses being paid for a minimum of 3 clear days attendance in camp. In the event of a Brigade camp, (All Volunteer Corps were Brigaded in August, 1888) this grant of 2/- for each clear day in camp, would be payable for a maximum of 7 days in camp, but with the added proviso that 3 Battalions with a minimum of 300 men each must be in attendance at camp.

In 1900, Britain was at War in South Africa, and by Army Order, dated 29th March, 1900, camps for Volunteers were increased to a maximum of 28 days, to train the men for Field Service with special emphasis on musketry training. To encourage the Volunteers a special grant of £2 - 2/- was instituted for the duration of the hostilities, for 14 clear days attendance in camp, with Officers and men receiving liberal inducements of Army Field Allowances (these rates are outlined on Page 374, Chapter 13). This special grant, however, was only payable if half the enrolled strength of the Battalion attended for a minimum of 14 clear days in camp.

On 20th March, 1901, by Army Order, camp allowances were once again increased, to 8/- per day, payable for a period of 6 clear days in camp. These rates were to continue until 1908.

****

Home Defence Mobilisation Scheme

In August, 1888, all Volunteer Corps were to become part of a Brigade, with the Scottish Volunteers being formed into five Brigades, under the "Home Defence Mobilisation Scheme". The largest being the Clyde Brigade, with 16,000 men, comprised of the Volunteers of (Lanark, Ayr, Renfrew, Argyll and Dumbarton). The next in strength being the Forth Brigade, with 9,000 men, comprised of the Volunteers of, (Edinburgh, Mid-Lothian, Haddington, Linlithgow, Perth, Fife, Stirling and Clackmannan). The Highland Brigade of 6,000 men, (Inverness, Ross, Sutherland, Elgin, Aberdeen and Banff). South of Scotland Volunteer Brigade, with 4,500 men, comprised of the Volunteers of, (Galloway, Roxburgh and Selkirk, Berwick, Dumfriesshire, and the two Highland Regiments, the 5th (Angus) and 2nd (Perth) Volunteer Battalion of the Black Watch. The Border Mounted Rifles were to Brigade with the South of Scotland Volunteer Brigade.) The Tay Brigade, with 3,500 men, comprised of the Volunteers of, (Dundee and Aberdeen). The efficients of the five Brigades as of 31st October, 1888, were 37, 225 men.

The South of Scotland Volunteer Brigade, under the Command of Lord Melgund was thereafter selected to form as part of the army in the field in the event of national crisis. It had been decided by the military authorities, charged with the Home Defence Scheme, that the post of Dorking, in the London, Southern Defence Line, should be held by the Highland and South of Scotland Volunteer Brigades, with the guns of the Fife, Ayr and Galloway, Aberdeen and Inverness Artillery Corps, and that no other of the Scottish Infantry Brigades should be brought into the London Scheme in the event of threatened invasion. The authorities contemplated the absorption of 90,000 Infantry Volunteers and 250 guns manned by Artillery Volunteers, into the London Scheme.

There was to be one further post on the Southern Line, beyond Dorking, at Guildford, to be held by the Home and Western Counties Brigades, with the guns of the Mid-Lothian and other Artillery Corps. The other Chief Station in the South London Line being at, Caterham, for 4 Brigades and Sevenoaks, for another 4 Brigades. There were to be 3 Chief Stations on the North Eastward Line - at Epping - Warley and Tilbury - each of 2 Brigades. The 2 Scottish Brigades Camp was to be projected behind Box Hill.

By this arrangement the Forth, Tay and Clyde Brigades were left guarding the great commercial interests of their respective regions. The position Batteries of the Edinburgh, Forfar, Renfrew and Dumbarton Brigades were left in Scotland by the scheme, together with sufficient garrison gunners of the 7 Artillery Brigades, who were also required to send moveable batteries to London, and the batteries of Banff, Argyll, Caithness and Orkney Brigades, which were purely of Garrison class.

Arrangements for the rapid transportation of the two Scottish Brigades to their Southern Line, was by the Higher Railway Officials who constituted the "Engineer and Railway Volunteer Staff Corps". It was calculated that the 2 Scottish Brigades would be in their allotted positions, around Dorking, within 4 days of the order being given for mobilisation.

The authorities were to recognise the serious inconvenience at which some Volunteers might take the field for a protracted term when apprehension of an invasion existed and to this end an important "Letter of Service" was issued in August, 1888, by the Commander-in-Chief, to Lord Stormont and Lord Melgund, the Commanders of the Highland and South of Scotland Volunteer Brigades, inviting the Brigadier-Generals, to consider what proportion of their Brigade could take the field for 2 or 3 weeks together, in the event of a threatened invasion, without serious interference to business, and how a system of reliefs could be organised which would enable that business to be attended to, and at the same time, the full strength of the Corps which would be available in the hour of need. It was pointed out by the Commander-in-Chief that timely preparation was the surest means of averting an invasion panic, and although the ultimate object of mobilising the Volunteers would be the rapid repulse and defeat of an invader, its immediate object would be by antecedent organisation to render success of an invasion improbable that it would never be attempted.

The "Letter of Service" was accompanied by a circular from Lord Wolseley emphasising the suggestions for improved efficiency and desiring that early attention be directed to equipment, the aim being the provision of everything positively indispensable for home mobilisation. The absolute minimum was laid down as arms, ammunition (70 rounds), complete accoutrements, great-coats, haversacks, water bottles and mess tins with straps for carrying towels, soap and a pair of socks to be stored in the great-coat pockets, the whole to be carried on the person of the Volunteer. Camp kettles and a small supply of entrenching tools should also be in the possession of each Corps, which should likewise assure to itself carts or waggons to transport cooking utensils, rations for 2 days, tools and 30 rounds of reserve ammunition. It was further directed to the transport, supply and medical service, which would be required to render Brigades thoroughly efficient and mobile.

In consequence of the fears of the Commanders-in-Chief and Lord Wolseley, as to how many Volunteers could take the field, fully equipped, in the event of threatened invasion, on 8th January, 1889, the War Office was to recommend that the five Scottish Brigades be assembled, during the forthcoming season into large Brigade camps, instead of the usual separate Regimental Camps, which had hitherto prevailed. (The Galloway Rifle Volunteers never held any Regimental Camps and indeed their first Brigade Camp was not to be until, 1891.)

On the 3rd May, 1889, instructions were received from the War Office, for the formation of a camp of 2,000 men of the South of Scotland Volunteer Brigade, in the neighbourhood of Hawick. The date for going into camp was fixed for the 27th June, and would be inspected by the General Commanding in Scotland on the 2nd July, 1889. The men who put in the 4 whole days at camp would draw a grant of 12/- and those putting in 3 days, a grant of 10/-, these grants being at the disposal of the Commanding Officers. The South of Scotland Brigade being one of the Volunteer Brigades selected to form part of the Army in the Field in a national crisis, the War Office emphasised that the formation of the South of Scotland Volunteer Brigade Camp was not intended for local or garrison defence but must be looked upon as an exercise in regard to the possibility of mobilisation.

The same day, 3rd May, 1889, Lord Melgund visited Castle Douglas and met with Colonel Kennedy, Major Maxwell, Major and Adjutant Douglas and other Officers of the Galloway Rifles, and afterwards addressed a few words to the men of 'B' Company impressing upon them that they belonged to the Field Brigade and were not intended for garrison defence. He continued, "there were a large number of what were called garrison brigades which were intended for local defence. The Edinburgh Volunteers were to form a garrison brigade and there were the Clyde and the Tay Brigades, all composed of Corps whose Headquarters were close together and who were easily called together. Here they were very much scattered but they ought to feel proud of being selected to act alongside the Field Army. The first thing to be done was for them to assemble at a given rendezvous, probably Hawick, where they would go into camp. They were not to look upon the camp as simply an ordinary Regimental Camp because they would have to do Brigade, Battalion and Company drills. The main object of the camp was to give the Officers and men an opportunity of assembling at a certain point and the movement was a very important experiment. He knew it was extremely difficult for the men to get away and also for the employers to do without their workmen but there was so very little known about the Brigade Scheme and Camps, that he looked upon them to make it a success."

The Brigade camp was to be formed at Hassendean, near Hawick, on the 27th June to 2nd July, 1889, but was badly attended, the fine words of Lord Melgund falling on deaf ears, with the Galloway Battalion failing to attend their first Brigade camp. Initially these Brigade camps were to take part every second year but it was not until the issue of the 'New Regulations for Volunteers', issued by Army Order 246, dated 4th November, 1901, that camps were to take place annually and for the first time attendance at these camps for both Corps and individual Volunteer was compulsory every second year.

On the 2nd December, 1890, the Commander-in-Chief issued a General Order from the War Office in which he directed that the 5th (Angus) and the 2nd (Perthshire) Battalions of the Black Watch Volunteers were to be replaced in the South of Scotland Volunteer Brigade by the transfer from the Forth Defence Brigade of the 6th (Mid-Lothian) and 7th (Haddington) Volunteer Battalions of the Royal Scots.

On the 27th June, 1895, the South of Scotland Volunteer Brigade was to be re-designated as the "Scottish Border Volunteer Infantry Brigade. "

HOME DEFENCE MOBILISATION SCHEME

Southern Defence Line –

    Guildford – Dorking – Caterham – Sevenoaks.

North Eastward Defence Line –

    Epping – Warley – Tilbury

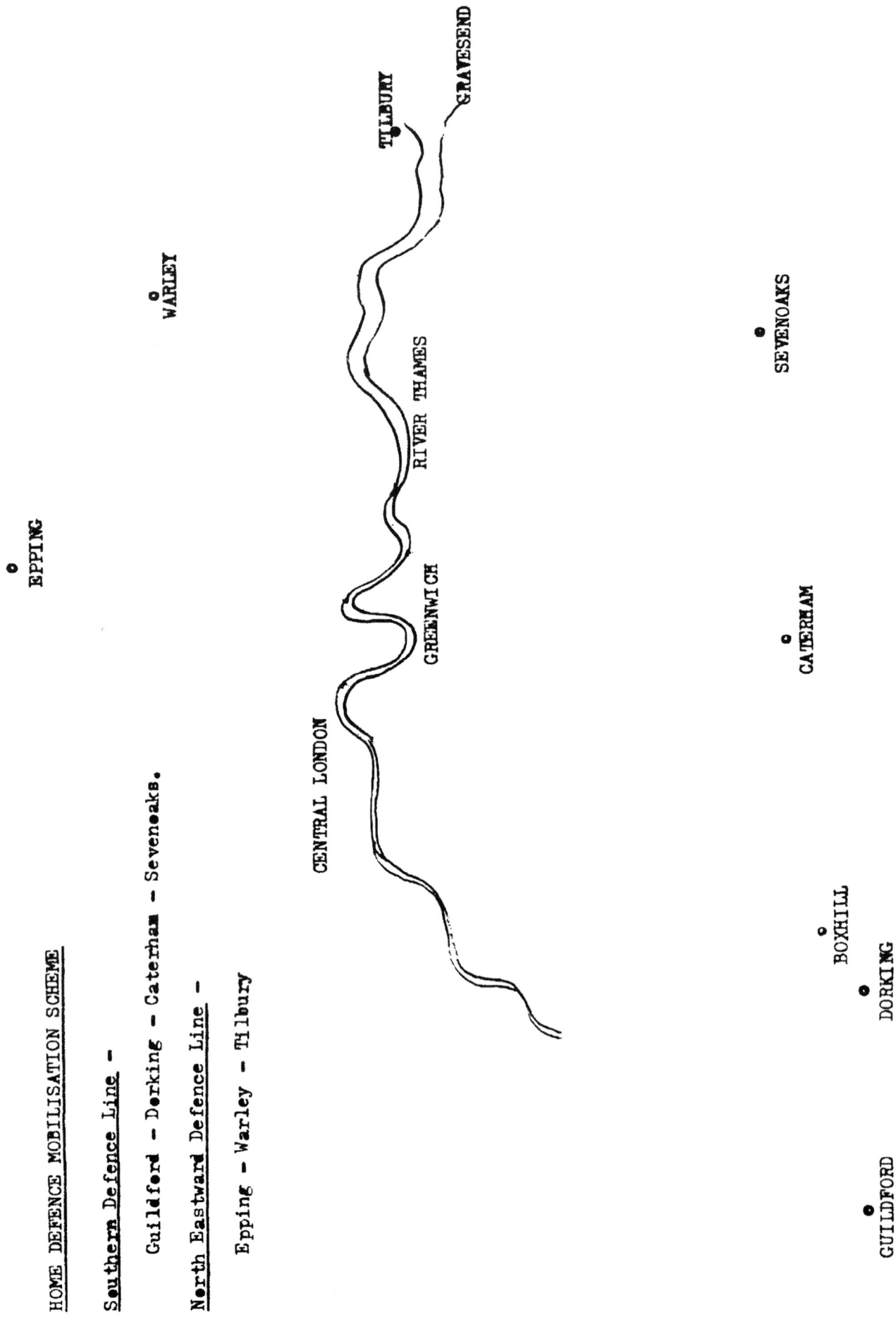

EPPING

WARLEY

TILBURY

GRAVESEND

RIVER THAMES

CENTRAL LONDON

GREENWICH

SEVENOAKS

CATERHAM

BOXHILL

DORKING

GUILDFORD

1891 Camp.

On the 3rd May, 1891, the following Brigade Orders were issued by the newly appointed Brigadier-General of the South of Scotland Volunteer Brigade, the Earl of Minto, for the formation of a Brigade Camp. This was to be the second camp held by the South of Scotland Volunteer Brigade but the first attended by the Galloway Rifle Volunteers.

(1). The Brigade Camp will be formed at Hassendean, near Hawick, from the 23rd till the 28th June, 1891. There will be four Battalions encamped, viz:- The Roxburgh and Selkirk Volunteers; the 2nd Berwickshire Volunteer Battalion; the 3rd Dumfriesshire Volunteer Battalion; and the Galloway Rifle Volunteers.

(2). An advance party from each Regiment, under the supervision of the Quarter-Masters, will proceed on the morning of the 23rd June, to pitch several camps.

(3). The main body will proceed by special train on Wednesday evening, 24th June, for 4 days and on Thursday evening, 25th June, for 3 days.

(4). The 3rd Dumfriesshire Volunteer Battalion and the Galloway Rifle Volunteers will return on Sunday evening by special trains, which will run from Hawick to Stranraer.

By Order.

The Camp was formed on the Home Farm of Minto Kaimes, Hassendean, near Hawick, owned by the Brigadier-General, the Earl of Minto. The camp was situated away from the busy township in the centre of rich pastoral country, protected at the base by the richly clad hills of Minto, while on the other side were magnificent tracts of woodland. The country to the front of the camp was of a hilly nature with several prominences crowned by fir and ash.

The fatigue parties from the four Regiments arrived on Tuesday, 23rd June, and pitched the tents, the line of which was fully a mile in extent. The camps of the Galloway, Dumfriesshire and Berwickshire Regiments were to the left of the camp site and away to the right, the camp of the Roxburgh and Selkirk - the Border Rifles, the place of honour being assigned to it as the Senior Regiment. Lord Minto provided the straw for the beds from the steading at Minto Kaimes.

Arrangements were made for the accommodation of upwards of 2,000 men of all ranks but the actual number in camp was 1,475 made up as follows; 14 Staff Officers and Sergeants, together with:

Border Rifles. 611 of all ranks, under the Command of Lt. Colonel, Sir R. J. Waldie-Griffiths Bart and Captain and Adjutant J. Hope.

Berwickshire. 218 of all ranks, under the Command of Colonel C. Hope, (brother of Captain Hope, St. Mary's Isle, Kirkcudbright) and Captain and Adjutant V.G. Tuppings.

Dumfriesshire. 386 of all ranks, under the Command of Colonel R.F. Dudgeon, and Major and Adjutant G.T.W. Hewat.

Galloway Rifles. 246 of all ranks, under the Command of Colonel J.M. Kennedy, and Major and Adjutant J.H. Spurgin.

"Reveille" each morning was sounded at 5.30am and the "Retreat" at 8pm. On Wednesday, 24th June, the Field Officer was Lt. Colonel W.J. Maxwell of the Galloway Rifles. The Brigade paraded in drill order each day at 11am and at 3.30pm. During the course of the week each of the Battalions was expected to undergo a thorough training in military manoeuvres, with the physical powers of the men being taxed in no uncompromising manner.

On the Thursday evening, 25th June, a camp fire was lit in front of the Farmhouse of Minto Kaimes, with the sloping ground leading up to the camp covered by the Volunteers. The scarlet uniform of the Dumfriesshire and Berwickshires appeared in marked contrast to the dark grey dress of the Galloway Rifles and the steel grey of the Border Rifles. An enjoyable concert of vocal and instrumental music was listened to, with the band of the Galloway Rifles playing lively selections. The Earl of Minto and the Master of Polwarth, both turned out in uniform, accompanied by a party of ladies. The gathering broke up in an orderly fashion at 10pm.

On the Friday forenoon, 26th June, the scorching sunshine of the previous two days had given way to a drenching rain, which started in the early morning and when the Volunteers began to stir, it broke the 'skin' of the tents and the water found its way inside to the great discomfort of the inmates. Brigade Orders were suspended with the hope that the 'sham' fight, due to take place in the forenoon, on Minto Crags, might come off later in the day. However, the Brigadier General was determined to carry out, as far a possible his orders and at noon the defenders consisting of the 2nd Berwickshires under Col. Hope, left the camp for Minto Crags in a perfect downpour, to take up their positions as a line of outposts, whose main body was strongly posted on the Minto Crags facing the south-west. The outpost line to be defended was between Little Law Lodge on the left and the Butterba Cottage on the right. Each man of the defending force carried fifty rounds of blank ammunition. Three scouts belonging to the Border Mounted Rifles accompanied this body. The attacking force was under the personal command of the Brigadier-General, the Earl of Minto.

As the different Regiments assembled in front of their camping grounds, the rain ceased and the air was pure and bracing. The attacking force consisted of the Galloway Rifles, the Border Rifles and the Dumfriesshire Volunteers, numbering in all over 1,000 men. It was supposed to be a Division marching from Hawick and Denholm to attack Minto Crags. The Galloway Rifles furnished an advance guard of two Companies, while all the cyclists belonging to the Brigade and two scouts of the Border Mounted Rifles, also accompanied the advance guard. Minto House, on account of its impregnable position, was not to be attacked by one or other of the forces. All the men of the attacking force carried thirty rounds of blank ammunition. Ten transport wagons under Captain Haddon and Sergeant Oliver went with the defending force, and fully forty carts and wagons went with the attacking force. The carts and wagons were not used for the purpose of warfare but turned out to make a demonstration.

The defending force lost no time in taking up its position on the Crags. In an hour after their departure, the scouts and outposts could be seen from the camp on the summits of the Minto Kaimes Hills. It was after 3pm before the 'fall-in' sounded for the attacking force, and each Regiment paraded in front of its own lines, under the command of the Brigadier-General.

The defenders who were supposed to be in possession of the position on Minto Crags, had their outposts placed in a wood near Howden, in a corner wood north of the Town Head Farm, in Town Head farm-steading and in Minto Churchyard. The churchyard was the principal position, and the defenders main body was supposed to be stationed there. The Commander of the attacking force sent forward two Companies of the Galloway Battalion, twenty miles each, under Captain Lennox, as outposts to reconnoitre the position of the enemy. At the end of the Nelson Plantations an advance party of the defenders force was discovered, and a halt was made until the main body came up. Then the Galloway Rifles were placed in the centre, with the Border Rifles to the left, the Dumfriesshire Volunteers moving to the right to force the 'enemy' from the position at Howden, only, however, to find that it had been deserted.

The Galloway Rifles dislodged the enemy from the corner wood and from Town Head Farm, while the Border Battalion marched down to Minto and the Dumfriesshire men attacked the defenders, who had possessed themselves of the ground in the churchyard, driving them out into the wood behind Minto School. Then the defenders retired into a very strong position near Minto House, where there was a deep valley, and where they set themselves the task of defending two bridges, but the Berwickshire numbers were small and had to eventually withdraw. The Dumfriesshire men were sent round by the West Lodge gate and turned them on the right. By this smart action of the attacking force the enemy was surrounded and wholly overcome. The 'cease-fire' was sounded and new formations of attack were planned, once again the defenders being defeated. A third campaign was devised with the same disastrous result for the defenders. The Brigadier-General related that the manoeuvres had been of a most practical and useful character.

On Saturday, 27th June, the weather was much improved and after the routine of the forenoon the Signalling Corps and the Ambulance Corps under Surgeon P. Kynoch, paraded and were inspected by Lord Minto. The principal event of the day, however, was the Brigade Inspection by Major General Lyttleton-Annesley.

The Inspection took place on the ground behind the camp of the Galloway Rifles and at the base of the Minto Hills. The Battalions paraded and were marched to the Brigade Parade Ground at 2.45pm where they formed in mass of columns and were deployed into lines by the Brigadier-General, the Earl of Minto. Major General Lyttleton-Annesley, Commanding the North British District, entered the Parade ground, accompanied by the Assistant Adjutant-General Colonel J. Boughey and his aide-de-camp Lieutenant C.W. Darby-Griffiths, Grenadier Guards.

The several Regimental Bands were massed behind the centre of the line, the Cyclist Section to the rear of their respective Battalions, the Brigade Ambulance Corps formed on the right of the bands and the transport of 39 carts was drawn up in line, on the right, at some distance. As the distinguished party entered the parade ground, ranks were opened and the general salute was given. The Inspecting Officer then instituted an inspection of the lines from right to left. The Brigade thereafter, formed a line of columns to the right and formed up on the saluting base and marched past in column from the front headed by the Band and Signallers, and followed by the Cycling, Ambulance and Transport Companies. The return was made in quarter column, with the Brigadier-General and his Staff leading. The Brigade again marched past in column, headed by the massed bands and signallers and disappeared from view of the thousands of spectators who lined the western side of the Parade Ground, returning to the original line and forming in mass, the Brigade advanced in Review Order, halted and gave the general salute .

The Inspecting Officer then called the Commanding Officers to the front and expressed his entire satisfaction with the appearance and drill of the troops, who he said had drilled very steadily and maintained their positions, on the rough ground, very well. He was exceedingly pleased to meet them and was especially gratified at the large turnout of the Border Rifles.

At the close of the Review the wagons were drawn up on the Parade Ground for inspection, with prizes being given for the three best turnouts, the Judges were Colonel Dudgeon of the Dumfriesshire Battalion, and Mr. Clark, Chapelhill. The first award, which consisted of a silver cup and £2 went to Mr. Cunningham, who drove a wagon belonging to the Earl of Minto, the 2nd and 3rd prizes being awarded respectively to Archibald Jackson, in the employ of Mr. Haddon, Honeyburn and Adam Hogg, in the employ of the Earl of Minto.

The purpose in establishing a transport corps, was to ascertain how far the local farmers would support the Volunteer movement by supplying vehicles and permitting their men to drive them. The experiment had been a decided success.

After the Brigade Inspection the Battalions were marched to their respective parade grounds and dismissed. Those of the Battalions who were not resident at the camp but had only come for the inspection, were marched to Hassendean and entrained for home.

The remainder of the afternoon was spent in inter-Regimental sports under the direction of the Officers. The Galloways meeting with some measure of success with Private G. Dalzell, Kirkcudbright, coming second in the 300 yards open flat race. Colour Sergeant McIlroy, Stranraer, coming second in the Sergeant Instructor's 100 yard flat race. In the tug of war competition the Border Rifles were to prove victorious over the Galloway Rifles in the final of the competition. In the evening a programme of entertainments were entered into by the Volunteers, with refreshments being supplied by an old Galloway man, Mr. Kennedy, purveyor of the Crown Hotel, Hawick, who originally hailed from Castle Douglas.

Much interest was manifested in the general bearing of the Volunteers, on account of various public correspondence which had taken place between the Parish Minister of Hawick and the Earl of Minto. It was contended by the ecclesiastic that the camp should not be held on the Sunday on which Communion took place at Hawick.

His Lordship replied that there was little choice, as the members of the Brigade were drawn from various parts of the Southern Counties and it was impossible to please everyone. Minto Kaimes was nearly 6 miles from Hawick and he could see no reason why he should change the date.

On Sunday morning, 28th June, 'Reveille' was sounded at 6am with the men en masse marching to Minto Kaimes Farm to discharge the palliasses of straw. In the forenoon a Church Service took place on the ground, attended by the different Regiments in camp. The Rev.J. Paton, Dumfries, Chaplain to the Brigade, preached from the words, 'The Law of the Lord is Perfect'.

On Sunday evening the camp broke up with the Dumfries and Galloway Battalions marching to Hassendean where they entrained for home.

1893 Camp.

The following Regimental Orders were issued on the 28th April, 1893, by Colonel J.M. Kennedy, Commanding the Galloway Rifle Volunteers.

South of Scotland Volunteer Brigade.

(1). A Brigade Camp will be formed at Minto Kaimes from the 26th June, to 3rd July, inclusive. An advance party from the different detachments will proceed fully equipped on Monday morning for Hassendean, via., Carlisle, by the trains as undermentioned; Stranraer 8.10am; Newton Stewart 9.10am; New Galloway 10am; Kirkcudbright 8.50am; Castle Douglas 10.25am; Dalbeattie 10.35am; Dumfries 11.35am. The Officers Commanding 'A', 'D' and 'E' Companies will make arrangements about tickets for any members proceeding from Wigtown, Gatehouse and Parton. Officers Commanding Companies are requested to use their utmost endeavours to get a strong advance party from their detachments to pitch camp, etc., one day's cooked rations to be taken by men in their haversacks and if possible the same men who were cooks last camp to be taken this year, with the advance party. The remainder of the Regiment will depart on Wednesday afternoon fully equipped from their stations at the hours named below:- Stranraer 3.40pm; Newton Stewart 4.41pm; New Galloway 5.33pm; Kirkcudbright 5.40pm; Castle Douglas 5.57pm; Dalbeattie 6.07pm and the whole Regiment will depart from Dumfries at an hour to be hereafter named. The same arrangements to be made by the Officers Commanding Companies, with reference to tickets for their detachments at Wigtown, Gatehouse and Parton. The Regiments will leave camp on Sunday evening 2nd July, and will leave a work party behind till Monday evening, under the charge of the Quarter-Master, to strike camp and hand over the Battalion stores to the Ordnance Store Departmental Officer

(2). The Officer Commanding Companies will be good enough to see that their non-commissioned officers and men are instructed in guard duties previous to their going to camp.

The Camp was held once again on the Home Farm of Minto Kaimes, Hassendean from the 26th June, 1893 to 3rd July, 1893, and was attended by the Battalions forming the South of Scotland Volunteer Brigade; The Roxburgh and Selkirk-Border Rifles; the 2nd Berwickshires; the 3rd Dumfriesshire; the Galloway Rifle Volunteers and the 6th and 7th Volunteer Battalions of the Royal Scots.

The Officers in Command of the Brigade were, Brigadier-General, the Rt. Hon. the Earl of Minto; Brigadier-Major, Lt. Colonel Graham; aide-de-camp Lieutenant, the Hon. W.G. Scott, Master of Polwarth. The Officers in Command of the various Regiments were as the previous camp of 1891, with the addition of 6th Royal Scots Commanded by Colonel Sir G.D. Clark Bart; and the 7th Royal Scots Commanded by Major Guild.

At the 1891 camp a certain affinity developed between the Regiments of the Border Rifles and that of the Galloway Rifles, which was to continue throughout the duration of the Brigade camps. On the Galloway Rifles march into camp on Wednesday, evening, 28th June, the Border Rifles turned out to accord the Galloways a hearty welcome, "their lusty cheers ringing out in the night air."

The Parade strength of the Galloway Rifle Volunteers was as follows:-
Staff Officers present; Colonel J.M. Kennedy, in Command; Major and Adjutant Spurgin and Major Harper. The Company Officers being; Major MCLellan, Lieutenant Clark and Surgeon Major Johnstone, Kirkcudbright: Captain Dunn and Lieutenant Surgeon Lorraine, Castle Douglas; Lieutenants Stewart and McLelland, Stranraer; Captain Agnew and Lieutenant Kelly, Newton Stewart; Captain Timms and Lieutenant Stewart, New Galloway; Captain Phyn, Captain Lennox and Surgeon Captain Rich Lorraine, Maxwellton; Captain Wellwood Maxwell, Dalbeattie.
The Parade state was as follows:-

		Officers	Sgt. Inst.	Sgts.	Band & B'gle.	R. & File.	Total.
Staff		3	-	-	-	-	3
'A'	Kbt.	3	1	4	1	24	33
'B'	C/D	2	1	7	10	32	52
'C'	Str.	2	1	2	1	34	40
'D'	N/S.	2	1	5	-	38	46
'E'	N/G.	2	1	1	-	20	24
'F'	Mxltn.	1	1	4	6	35	47
'G'	Mxltn .	2	-	-	16	31	49
'H'	Dbt.	1	1	1	11	34	50
		---	---	---	---	----	----
		18	7	26	45	248	314.

This Parade strength did not include the Cycling Sections of Newton Stewart and Dalbeattie who arrived in camp the following day, Thursday, 29th June, having cycled from their respective Company Headquarters.

The usual fatigue duties of camp life, Company, Battalion and Brigade Drills, together with Inspections, were to take place throughout the week along with the military manoeuvres 'Sham fights', shooting practice and a variety of sport's programmes. The Galloway Rifle football team of, Goal, Penman. backs, Haugh and, Macaulay; half-backs, McKean, Gourlay and Moffat; forwards; Gillespie, Sloan, Morley, Adair and Robinson, were to prove victorious in the inter-Battalion football match, with the Galloway Cyclists carrying all before them in the 'carrying and despatch' competition, the three prizes going to Newton

Stewart men; Private Morton; Private Robertson; Sergeant Agnew.

This year a Sergeant's Mess was provided for the Galloway Battalion with Quarter-Master Sergeant Hyslop in charge assisted by Privates Charteris and Wintrup. To encourage home manufacture, all the beers and liquors were brought direct from Castle Douglas.

On Saturday 1st July, Sergeant Major Wakefield of the Border Rifles and his Staff presented their compliments to the Galloway Staff and invited them to a smoking concert in their mess tent. Quarter-Master Turnbull presided and coupled the toast of 'Our Guests' with the name of Sergeant Major Ferguson, Castle Douglas, who replied, remarking that he was pleased to see the good feeling that prevailed between the Border and Galloway Rifles.

On the forenoon of Sunday, 2nd July, after Divine Service, Colonel Kennedy addressed his men and passed Lord Minto's expressions of satisfaction and thanks for their attendance at camp. Lord Minto was especially pleased with the cleanliness and neatness of the camp and in particular he paid tribute to the cooking department, Quarter-Master Sergeant Myers, Sergeant Garrett and Lance Sergeant Wilson, being singled out for praise. The, sham fight was a great success, the Galloway Rifles held the attacking party, opposed to them, in check, and the attacking party failed to take their position. The movements in close formation before the Inspecting General were exceedingly well done and the marching and wheeling were much praised. Colonel Kennedy begged to thank them for showing so much good feeling, cheerfulness and spirit in discharging their duties. 'Happy to meet', said the Colonel in conclusion, 'sorry to part. Happy to meet again.'

Captain Dunn, Castle Douglas, was so well pleased with the behaviour of his Company that, out of his own pocket, he doubled their Regimental pay of 1/- per day in camp.

There was only one case of misdemeanour, by Private Murray, Maxwellton, during the week, to come before Colonel Kennedy, the punishment for the indiscretion being confinement to camp for one day.

Camp Wit and Humour. "A sentry was on his post from 11 to 12 at night, when the Field Officer of the day went his rounds, he was promptly enough challenged by 'Halt. Who comes there?' The answer was 'Field Officer of the Day'. What was the surprise of the Officer to hear? 'Pass Field Officer of the day. What are you doing here at night?"

1895 Camp.

Once again the South of Scotland Volunteer Brigade camp was held at Minto Kaimes, Hassendean, the duration of the camp being from Tuesday, 25th to Sunday, 30th June, 1895, with the main body of the Galloway Battalion joining the Brigade late on the evening of Wednesday, 26th June. The majority of the Volunteers retired to their much needed rest with the exception of one tent of Stranraer Volunteers who were very boisterous, frequently turning on their lights, only turning to their slumbers when finally threatened with the guard-house.

The Brigade comprised the usual Battalions with the exception of the 7th Volunteer Battalion of the Royal Scots, who failed to attend and this year with the addition of a detachment of the Lothian and Berwickshire Yeomanry who joined the Brigade to assist in the Field manoeuvres.

The Parade strength of the Galloway Rifle Volunteers was:-

Staff; Colonel Kennedy in Command, Captain and Adjutant Butler, with Major Harper, Castle Douglas in charge of Battalion stores.

The Company Officers were:

Kirkcudbright	Major McLellan.
Stranraer	Lieutenants McLelland and McLean.
Newton Stewart	Lieutenants McPhater and Kelly.
New Galloway	Captain Timms.
Maxwellton	Captain Phyn and Surgeon Captain Lorraine.
Dalbeattie	Captain Maxwell and Surgeon Lieutenant Anderson.

Captain Dunn, 'B' Company, Castle Douglas, was unable to attend camp, with the command of 'B' Company, being given to the popular non-commissioned officer, Colour Sergeant Dicks.

	Officers.	Sgt. Inst.	Sgts.	Band & B'gle.	Rank & File.	Total.
Staff.	3	-	-	-	-	3
'A' Kbt.	1	1	3	1	26	32
'B' C/D.	-	1	5	8	29	43
'C' Str.	2	1	1	-	25	29

	Officers.	Sgt. Inst.	Sgts.	Band & B'gle.	Rank & File.	Total.
'D' N/S.	2	1	4	2	34	43
'E' N/G.	1	1	3	-	20	25
'F' & 'G' Mxltn .	2	1	9	13	76	101
'H' Dbt.	2	1	2	4	24	33
	---	---	---	---	----	----
	13	7	27	28	234	309.

1 Officer, 2 Sergeants and 16 men were taken from the Maxwellton Corps to act in the Brigade Bearer Company, who were to be specially trained in Ambulance work and service for the sick and wounded.

For the first time postal arrangements were complete in camp with mail being collected and delivered twice a day. The Cyclist Section was utilised for the carriage of the mail together with Brigade despatches.

On Thursday, 27th June, a Court of Inquiry was held at the Brigade hospital reporting on an injury sustained by Private T. V. Hutchison, Stranraer, whereby he broke his collar-bone whilst on duty.

Quarter-Master Hyslop, Castle Douglas, was once again in charge of the Sergeant's Mess assisted by Private Wintrup, Castle Douglas and Private Alex. Smith, Dalbeattie. Sergeant Cruickshanks was in charge of the kitchens. Private W. Haugh, Castle Douglas was Clerk in the Orderly Room with Sergeant Myers, Castle Douglas occupied in the Commissariat Department.

For the second year in succession the water supply was close to giving out but on Thursday afternoon, there was a tremendous thunderstorm which alleviated the problem.

The Brigade was inspected by Lieutenant-General Rowlands, C.B. V.C., on Saturday, 29th June, 1895.

On Sunday, 30th June, the Rev. J. Paton, Dumfries officiated at Divine Service, and for the first time the Catholics had an opportunity of having a service of their own with Father J. Duffy, Castle Douglas, officiating in camp.

The following paragraph appeared in Sunday's Orders:- "The Brigadier-General Commanding wishes to express his thanks to all ranks for the support they have afforded him during the assembly of the Brigade in camp. There has been a marked improvement in camp routine, general neatness of camps, guard mounting etc., and the Brigadier General hopes that the necessity for a thorough appreciation of camp discipline and smart performance of all duties will not be lost sight of. The Brigadier-General, would also point out that with the present year, a new system of inspection, by the General Officer Commanding, has been inaugurated. The Parade movements which were formerly alone inspected, and which, though they contributed to steadiness in drill, gave little instruction in practical work, has been abandoned and an endeavour has been made to encourage amongst the Volunteer Battalions, assembled in camp an interest in the more practical work that would be expected from them on service.. . . . ."

The camp was struck at 2pm on Sunday, 30th June, 1895, and the Galloway Rifle Volunteers entrained for home by special train. There were excellent jokes being cracked by the versatile Colour Sergeant McIlroy.

1897 Camp.

Once again the Scottish Border Volunteer Infantry Brigade held its annual camp at Minto Kaimes, Hassendean. The duration of the camp being between Tuesday, 29th June, and Sunday 4th July, 1897. The advance party of the Galloway battalion arrived on Monday, 28th June, to prepare camp.

The Camp was once more under the Command of the Brigadier General, the Earl of Minto, together with his staff, Colonel Graham, Brigade-Major, aide-de-camp, Captain Kidd. The following Battalions formed the Brigade:
Border Rifles; 2nd Berwickshire; 3rd Dumfriesshire; Galloway Rifles; 6th and 7th Volunteer Battalion of the Royal Scots.

The Galloway Rifle Parade State was: - Colonel J.M. Kennedy Commanding; Captain Blake Adjutant. Company Officer:-

Kirkcudbright -	Major McLellan, Lieutenant Comrie.
Castle Douglas -	Major Harper, Captain Dunn, Lieutenant Brand.
Stranraer -	Major Stewart, Surgeon Lieutenant Munro.
Newton Stewart -	Captain McPhater; Lieutenants W.M. Kelly and McLean.
Maxwellton -	Major Lennox, Major Phyn, Lieutenant Blacklock, Lieutenant Shortridge
Dalbeattie -	Captain Maxwell.

Captain Timms, 'E' Company, New Galloway, was unable to attend camp, with Lieutenant Comrie,

Kirkcudbright, assuming command of 'E' Company for the duration.

The total Parade state comprised; 17 Officers; 7 Sergeant Instructors; 20 Sergeants; 30 Bandsmen, Pipers and Buglers; 228 Rank and File, making in all a total of 302 all ranks.

Camp Cracks.

Quarter-Master Sergeant Hyslop, assisted by Privates B. Rae and W. Purdie, Castle Douglas, was once again in charge of the Sergeant's Mess, with Sergeant Garbett, 2nd R.S.F. Chatham, Cook Sergeant in the Galloway kitchen, ably assisted by 12 men drawn from the various Companies.

It was amazing to see some old Volunteers, but new to camp life, making their beds last night. It was evident they were unaccustomed to a 'shake down'. When they did lie down, they complained that the 'long feathers' were rather hard.

After 'lights out' inveterate smokers had to cover their heads with a blanket to hide the illicit match. The ever-verdent Sergeant Major Fergusson, was always on the alert and the shadow of a spark could not escape his watchful eye. He failed however, to detect a tent in which the merriment was too boisterous to be conducive to sleep, but who knows, he may have challenged the 'wig-wam' after all, the bland protestations of the versatile Colour Sergeant McIlroy, Stranraer, notwithstanding.

The special friendship bonded by the Officers and men of the Border and Galloway Rifles manifested itself when Colonel Sir Waldie-Griffiths, the Officers and members of the Border Rifles Sergeants Mess accepted the invitation of Colonel J.M. Kennedy, the Officers and members of the Galloway Rifles Sergeants Mess, to a smoking evening and entertainment. Sergeant-Major Fergusson opened the proceedings by proposing a toast, "To the health of the Regiment who have always been very near to us and also very dear to us since our first camp in 1891 - The Border Rifles

On Saturday, 3rd July, the Brigade was inspected by General Chapman C.B. Commanding the Scottish District, who first of all inspected the camp of each Corps, the kitchens, the supply departments and the transport section, which consisted of 16 carts sent in by the local farmers and under the command of Captain Haddon, Hawick. The Brigade Parade strength was as follows:

Border Rifles - Commander Sir Richard Waldie-Griffiths - 418 of all ranks.
2nd Berwickshire - Commander Colonel Hope - 276 of all ranks.
3rd Dumfriesshire - Commander Colonel Dudgeon - 413 of all ranks.
Galloway Rifles - Commander Colonel J.M. Kennedy - 303 of all ranks.
6th V.B. Royal Scots - Commander Sir G.D. Clark - 224 of all ranks.
7th V.B. Royal Scots - Commander Lieutenant Colonel Watson - 70 all ranks.
Supply detachment - 10 of all ranks.
Bearer Company 16 of all ranks.

The camp was to break up the following day, Sunday, 4th July, 1897.

1899 Camp.

In 1899 the Scottish Border Volunteer Infantry Brigade Camp, which was to take place in the month of July, was, for the first time to be held at Castle Moffat, North Berwick, with the Volunteers undergoing training with the Regular Forces. The Camp was however cancelled at the last minute owing to an objection from the North Berwick Town Council that, the proposed camp site was within the area of the stream which provided its Burgh water supply.

1900 Camp.

It was now 3 years since the Scottish Border Volunteer Infantry Brigade last held camp and with the Boer War raging in South Africa, camps were extended to 1 month with the Volunteers expected to put in 14 clear days attendance and shoot 60 rounds of ammunition. The Brigade had now left Hassendean and after the problems of 1899, at Castle Moffat, the authorities had secured suitable accommodation at Dingleton Common in the Eildon Hills, about ¾ mile from Melrose. A thorough course in field manoeuvres was intended with ample facilities provided for the special additional musketry course. It was to be of note that only one day in camp would be given over to ceremonial drill. For the first time the tents had wooden floors, the advantage being felt on the second day in camp, when the heavens opened, the men having to dig trenches around the tents. The Galloways were fortunate in that their tents were on the topmost line of the hillside but those of the Border Rifles, lying below them suffered from the deluge, the water running over the wooden floors.

The camp opened for the first full day on Saturday, 23rd June, 1900, the men going in 2 fortnightly batches, with the camp breaking up on the 20th July.

Battalions in camp forming the Brigade were the, Border Rifles; 2nd Berwickshire; 3rd Dumfriesshire; Galloway Rifles; and the 7th (Haddington) V.B. Royal Scots. The new Brigadier-General being Colonel A.H. Dixon, C.B. A.D.C., Commanding the 25th Regimental District. The former Brigadier-General, the Earl of Minto, resigned his command on 11th November, 1898, on taking up the appointment of Governor-General of the Dominion of Canada.

The Parade strength of the Galloway Rifles for the first fortnight in camp was; 15 Officers; 29 non-commissioned officers; and 239 rank and file, making a total of all ranks of 294, together with 3 Staff Officers. It was anticipated that over 100 men of the Galloway Rifles would attend camp for the 2nd fortnight thus securing the additional grant by there being over 50% of the total strength of the Regiment under canvas.

Camp Cracks.

"Colonel Kennedy is highly gratified with the turnout of his Galloway Lads. They had the longest distance to come of any Regiment. He shows an ever-green interest in the welfare of his Corps and as long as he can uphold it, its lustre will never be dimmed."

Lieutenant Biggar 'B' Company is an energetic and promising young Officer. He was complimented by the Colonel on Monday.

Quarter-Master Hyslop, Castle Douglas, makes an efficient Regimental Postman.
The rain on Sunday, brought home-sickness on, but it soon wore off.

Quarter-Master Sergeant Myers, Castle Douglas, is a busy man and besides acting as Regimental Paymaster, he is also in charge of stores, assisted by Corporal Hetherington, Castle Douglas. They are both old campaigners.

Pioneer Sergeant Bell, Stranraer, keeps a strict eye on the sanitary arrangements.

There had been some trouble with the kitchen trenches but by Tuesday Cook-Sergeant Kennedy of Stranraer, had the details of his department licked into shape.

Sergeant McIlroy, Stranraer, President of the Sergeant's Mess, is his usual irrepressible self.

Sergeant Major Fergusson, has Corporal W. Haugh, Castle Douglas, as clerical assistant in the Orderly Room. The years have passed since Sergeant Major Fergusson came to the Headquarters at Castle Douglas, they have been the most lustrous in the history of the Galloway Rifles.

The doings of the Regimental Cycling and shooting teams, are still fresh in the public memory. These were friendly fights but the crowning climax was the equipment and sending out of the men to 'The Front'.

Salt is a good thing, in its place, but it does not go well with tea.

The Gatehouse boys are talking in their sleep but seem to be enjoying themselves.

Pipe-Major McKinstry, Stranraer, conducts the Galloway Pipe Band while Bandmaster Sisson, Newton Stewart, is training the Buglers.

The Kirkcudbright humorist has been at it again 'Vide' circular issued by him, of which the following is a certified copy:- "Galloway Rifle Camp Variety Entertainers and Royal Orchestral Company. - All members of above corps who can play an instrument, sing a song, make a speech, or stand on his head as no other person can do, or in any way lend his assistance in the establishing of entertainments during the camp, will be good enough to show their 'phizogs' at the front door of Herr Hams' Mansion, Tent No. 5, First Row, Galloway Lines, on Tuesday night, at 9 o'clock. Any gentleman who is unable to be present, but who is willing to take part in the entertainments, will please be good enough to inform the Secretary of his capabilities, with copies of testimonials from managers of theatres, opera houses, and also how often he has appeared before Royalty, with note of fee required, which will be paid in siege soup. Amateurs please do not be afraid to give in your names although you have no diplomas. If you can sing within half a mile of tune or play Doh, we will be glad to get you. We also hope the public and the wild animals around will be the same. A committee to arrange for the evening entertainments will be appointed at said meeting. and it is hoped that all Galloways with talent and ability will show as much courage in volunteering their assistance for the entertainments as they usually do in going for their stovers, mince collops, spuds and greens. Monsieur Heughannua Pippins. Inst. Secy., Tent No 5, First Row. GRV Line.

Note. 96 years on I can crack this pseudonym, (my apologies to Grace his daughter) as being the evergreen, singer, songwriter and bugle playing Private Hugh (Pip) Livingstone of 'A' Company, Kirkcudbright, later to make Sergeant in the Rifles, rising to the dizzy heights of Lieutenant in the Volunteer Training Corps, during the depths of the 'Great War'.

A peep at the Officers Mess is most interesting, Mr. R. Oughton, of the Royal Restaurant, Dumfries, is the Caterer. The mess room, which can accommodate over 120, is beautifully fitted up. Then there are several portable buildings used as stores, kitchens etc., besides the sleeping quarters for a large staff of waiters.

Those who have yet to come to camp would do well to bring a spare pair of trousers and a change of underclothing, if the weather does not improve. (Indeed, it was to rain everyday for the first two weeks in camp, that plans had been drawn up to move the camp.) However, by contrast, the weather for the next two weeks was to improve dramatically, as one Volunteer writing home was to say, "instead of drilling in great-coats, shirt and trousers are the order o f the day".

It was during the 2nd fortnight of camp that the sad death of Private Alexander Jamieson, 'A' Company, Kirkcudbright, was reported. Private Jamieson, whose parents lived in Union Street, was among the first to enlist when the troubles broke out in South Africa. He joined with the Army Medical Corps but succumbed to Enteric fever in Pretoria.

The 2nd fortnight in camp was to consist of the same duties as those of the first detachment, with particular emphasis on Field manoeuvres and Musketry Training, together with added instruction in Field duties, for Company Officers. However, with the improvement in weather, their leisure hours were to be enjoyed in Brigade sports and football, again in direct contrast to the men of the 1st detachment, who spent the majority of their leisure hours, in their tents, sheltering from the rain .

Camp Cracks - second fortnight.

On Wednesday, the Galloways were on musketry practice at the ranges, when 6,600 rounds were expended. They have more to fire on Friday.

A splendid pavilion has been erected for the use of the Brigade. It is used nearly every night for concerts. The musical taste displayed is of a high order.

The promotion of Major Lennox and Captain Blacklock has given much satisfaction to all ranks.

The health of the camp continues excellent. The hospital staff are unemployed. (There was not to be a single case in the hospital during the whole month of the camp.) Private George Black, Maxwellton, is on duty at the Sergeant's Mess. G.B. was a champion jumper and sprinter in the 70's and early 80's but his legs have lost their suppleness.

Were any of the Galloway Lads among the stayed - away - too - late Company, who rushed the quarter-guard last night?

The reasons given by those who exceed the time of their passes are often like fairy tales. "Late trains from Gala" - and cycle breakdowns but sweethearting - never!

1902 Camp.

The South of Scotland Volunteer Infantry Brigade Camp, was to last only one week from 2nd to 8th August, 1902, owing to the Coronation of King Edward VII. The Volunteers were required for local celebrations, whereas the Senior ranking Brigade Officers were required to attend the London ceremonies. The camp was held, once again, at Dingleton Common, in the Eildon Hills, Melrose.

1903. Camp.

In 1903, the War Office secured 3,600 acres of land at Stobs, 3 miles from Hawick, to be used as a camping and training ground for both, Regular and Volunteer Forces.

On Sunday, 4th July 1903, the Galloway Rifle Volunteers, travelled to Stobs camp for their now, annual training camp, with the Scottish Border Volunteer Infantry Brigade. It was intended that the Brigade should have gone into camp the day before, 3rd July, but this had to be cancelled, by the North British Railway Company's refusal to allow the time honoured, special travelling facilities, to the Volunteers, except on a Sunday.

The Brigade now comprised of; the 1st Roxburgh and Selkirk (Border Rifles); 2nd Berwickshires; 3rd

Dumfriesshire; Galloway Rifles. The 6th (Mid-Lothian) and 7th (Haddington) V.B. Royal Scots, having been replaced by the 1st and 2nd Volunteer Battalions (Ayrshire) of the Royal Scots Fusiliers. (The 1st and 2nd V.B. of the R.S.F. did not attend this Brigade camp and were not to be Brigaded with the other Battalions of the Brigade for training until the camp of 1907).

The newly appointed Brigadier-General was Colonel Godfrey C.B. K.O.S.B.

The Parade state of the Galloway Rifle Volunteers in camp was:

Staff Officers. Colonel J.M. Kennedy, Commanding, Lt. Colonel Lennox, Captain and Adjutant Wolseley. Company Officer. Captain Comrie, Lieutenant Glover, Kirkcudbright;

Major Hewat, Lieutenant Gifford, Castle Douglas; Captain McLean, Stranraer;

Newton Stewart had no Officer present in camp; Lieutenant E.S. Forde, New Galloway; Captain Shortridge, Lieutenant R.A. Grierson, Lieutenants, E. Grierson and T.A. Charlton, Maxwellton; Lieutenant Biggar, Dalbeattie.

	Officers.	Sergeants.	Rank and File.		Total.
'A' Kirkcudbright	2	2	35	39	
'B' Castle Douglas.	5	8	42	55	
'C' Stranraer.	1	4	36	41	
'D' Newton Stewart.	0	4	64	68	
'E' New Galloway.	1	2	6	9	
'F' & 'G' Maxwellton.	4	8	62	74	
'H' Dalbeattie.	2	5	51	58	
	----	----	-----	-----	
	15	33	296	344.	

The regular forces of the 17th Lancers and the Gordon Highlanders, together with the Volunteer Battalions of the Black Watch, were encamped at Stobs, during the Brigades week in camp and assisted in the Field manoeuvres in the hills around Stobs.

Camp Cracks.

The camp was deluged by rain on Sunday and accompanied by a heavy gale on Sunday night, there was little sleep for the first nighters.

Sergeant Major Gallagher is assisted in the Orderly Room by Corporal W. Haugh, Castle Douglas.

The Cooks of the Galloways had very tidy kitchen ranges, the head of the kitchen being Cook-Sergeant McNaught, New Galloway, who recently underwent a course of instruction at Aldershot.

Pipe-Major Johnston, Dalbeattie, has been paying his usual attention to the Galloway Pipers. Bandmaster Keane, Castle Douglas, has been appointed Bugler-Major, while Privates W. Wright, G. Jamieson, and J. McLellan, Castle Douglas, had to be taken to strengthen the Regimental Brass band from Maxwellton. Brass Bands are not so much good for marching nowadays, the pace is too fast, 120 or 130 steps per minute.

Quarter-Master Sergeant Hyslop, Castle Douglas, is once again in charge of the catering of the Sergeant's Mess. Colour Sergeant McGregor, Kirkcudbright and Pioneer Sergeant Bell, Stranraer, continue the arduous duty of superintending the sanitary arrangements.

Private Macaulay, Maxwellton, is Battalion Postman.

Sergeant Birrell has charge of the Creetown Section of 'D' Company, 19 being in camp from a roll call of 22.

A Colonel asked a Corporal what his father was, "A farmer" replied he, "Pity he didn't make you follow his trade". The Corporal thereupon asked the Colonel what his father was, "A Gentleman". "Pity he didn't make you one", retorted he.

Camp was struck on Sunday, 11th July, 1903.

The following list of appointments to the Staff of the Scottish Border Volunteer Infantry Brigade, were made by Order of the 24th June, 1904:-

Officer Commanding - Officer Commanding the 25th Regimental District.

Aide-de-camp - 2nd Lieutenant W.J. Maxwell, Galloway Rifle Volunteers.

Brigade-Major - Lieutenant Colonel A.W. Pennyman, R. of O., late KOSB.

O.C.A.S.C. Company - Quartermaster and Honorary Captain J. Fulton, 2nd V.B. KOSB. (Berwickshire).

Senior Medical Officer - Brigadier-Surgeon Lt. Col. G.H. Turnbull M.B. 1st Roxburgh and Selkirk R.V.C.

1904 Camp.

For the second year in succession the Scottish Border Volunteer Infantry Brigade annual training camp was held at Stobs military training camp. The Galloway Rifles entered camp on Sunday, 17th July, 1904, an advance party of 40 men in charge of Sergeant Instructor Nelson 'E' Company, New Galloway, and Quartermaster Sergeant Myers, Castle Douglas, having attended the camp on the Friday previous to prepare the camp for the Regiments arrival. Special trains left Kirkcudbright and Stranraer where they were joined by the various Companies of the Regiment on the way to Dumfries. Camp was reached at 2pm and although rain was falling heavily it was to clear up making for a favourable week in camp.

The Battalions in camp were the 2nd Berwickshire, under the command of Col. Hope and the 3rd Dumfriesshire, under the command of Colonel Dudgeon, the former being 265 strong with the Dumfriesshires 407 strong, together with the Galloway Rifles, their Parade State being:

Staff Officers; Colonel J.M. Kennedy, Lt. Col. Lennox, Major Hewat (Acting Quartermaster), Captain and Adjutant Connell and Sergeant Major Grierson.
Company Officers; Captain Comrie and Lt. Glover, Kirkcudbright; Major Hewat, Castle Douglas; Stranraer and Newton Stewart had no Officers present; Captain Forde, New Galloway. Captain Shortridge and Lt. Grierson, Maxwellton; Captain Biggar, Dalbeattie.

	Officers.	Sgt. Inst.	Sgts.	Band.	Rank & File.	Total.
'A' Kbt .	2	1	2	4	35	44
'B' C /D .	4	1	2	-	31	38
'C' Str.	0	1	1	3	25	30
'D' N/S.	0	1	5	6	54	66
'E , N/G.	1	1	0	2	8	12
'F" & 'G' Mxltn.	2	1	6	21	72	102
'H' Dbt.	1	1	2	8	26	38
	----	----	----	-----	-----	-----
	10	7	18	44	251	330.

The time table of work for the Monday, comprised of Adjutant's parade from 7am to 8am. Commanding Officer's parade for Battalion Drill from, 10am to 11am. The afternoon was devoted to a series of movements in both attack and defence between the various Companies, on the hills overlooking Stobs camp. On their return they were dismissed for the evening.

On the Tuesday, a scheme of operation was drawn up for the forenoons work, 'A' & 'C' Companies (Kirkcudbright and Stranraer) under the charge of Captain Comrie, were told off as a defending force to take up positions on the slopes of Penchrise Pen, the idea being to prevent the enemy, represented by the remainder of the Battalion, under Col. Kennedy, from intercepting stores which were being removed from Newcastleton. Fully ½ an hour was allowed for the 2 companies to take up their positions before the remainder of the Battalion was set in motion for the attack. Captain Comrie had orders to defend his position to the last and he succeeded in repelling the attack on both flanks, although there was the possibility that the line may have been pierced in the centre. In the afternoon Brigadier-General Colonel Godfrey and his Staff inspected the Brigade lines.

The life in camp was to continue along these lines until the Brigade Inspection and Drill before the Brigadier-General on Saturday, 23rd July, 1904, with the camp being struck the following day, 24th July.

Camp Cracks.

Sergeant Major Grierson, assisted by Corporal Connelly, Castle Douglas, is in charge of the Orderly Room. Cooking arrangements are being efficiently looked after by Cook-Sergeant McNaught, New Galloway.

The Maxim Gun is in the charge of the New Galloway Camp. Col. Kennedy has very kindly presented to the Battalion a complete set of military harness for the horse drawing the gun.

The Brass Band under Bandmaster Leroy and the Pipe Band, under Pipe-Major Johnstone, have enlivened the proceedings of the camp.

The popular Quartermaster Sergeant Myers, is as usual very assiduous in attending to the wants of the men.

Colonel Gordon of Threave, is Brigadier-General of the H.L.I. Brigade, encamped on the other side of Acreknowe.

Lieutenant Glover presented a handsome money prize for the best arranged tent in the Galloway Battalion, Captain Connell being the judge. The prize was awarded to the Gatehouse Section under the charge of Lance Corporal A. Reid.

1905 Camp.

For the third year in succession, On Sunday, 9th July, 1905, the Galloway Rifle Volunteers, joined with the 2nd Berwickshire and 3rd Dumfriesshire, at Stobs Military Camp, Hawick, for a weeks training as part of the Scottish Border Volunteer Infantry Brigade. Compared to previous years the camp was somewhat deserted, the only other Regiment in camp being the 2nd Highland Light Infantry from Edinburgh Castle. The camp was therefore pitched on a fine position on a high plateau between Stob's Castle policies and the high ridge of Winnington Rig.

The Berwickshire Battalion numbered 226 of all ranks, the Dumfriesshire Battalion numbered 284 of all ranks, with a then record attendance in camp for the Galloways, the Parade state being:-

Staff. Colonel J.M. Kennedy M.V.O. V.D. Commanding; Lt. Col. Lennox;,
Major Hewat. Captain and Adjutant Fraser; Sergeant-Major Grierson.
The Company Officers:- Captain Comrie, Lt. Glover, Lt. Wilkinson, Kirkcudbright; Lt. Gifford, Castle Douglas; Once again Stranraer and Newton Stewart were without Officers; Captain Forde New Galloway; Captain R.A. Grierson, Lt. E. Grierson, Lt. Scott-Elliot, Lt. Crombie, Maxwellton; Lt. Gillies, Dalbeattie.

	Officers.	Sgt. Inst.	Sgts.	Band.	Rank & File.	Total.
'A' Kbt.	3	1	2	6	51	63
'B' C/D.	4	1	6	2	36	49
'C' Str.	0	1	4	6	32	43
'D' N/S .	0	1	2	5	39	47
'E' N/G.	1	1	2	1	1	6
'F' & 'G' Mxltn.	4	1	11	16	57	89
'H' Dbt.	1	0	7	9	37	54
	13	6	34	45	253	351.

Monday and Tuesday were devoted to Company and Battalion drills with Wednesday and Thursday given over to field manoeuvres. Friday was Company drill in the morning with the Colonel's Inspection and parade in the afternoon. Saturday forenoon was Brigade drill and inspection by Brigadier-General Colonel Godfrey, with Saturday afternoon being given over to sport and relaxation. Sunday forenoon, 16th July, 1905, was Divine Service with the camp breaking up at 2pm that afternoon.

Camp Cracks.
Kirkcudbright and Dalbeattie Companies presented a very smart appearance in their new khaki uniforms, an undoubted improvement in the old sombre uniform in which the rest of the Battalion is clothed.

On Tuesday, the new cap badges were issued to the two favoured Companies. These are similar to the old pattern but bear the words, *"S.A. 1900-02"*.

On Tuesday and Wednesday mornings the men were medically examined by Surgeon Captain Livingston, Dumfries in accordance with War Office instructions of 7th July, 1905, 'FIT-ness' of Volunteers.

Captain Fraser gave a lecture to the Officers and n.c.o's on bugle calls.

Lieutenants Scott Elliott, Gillies and Wilkinson were examined for promotion to the rank of Captain. (Lieutenant G.F.Scott-Elliott was to reach the rank of Captain, later serving with the 1/5th Battalion King's Own Scottish Borderers. He was to write the "War History of the 5th Battalion K.O.S.B.").

1906 Camp.

The Galloway Rifle Volunteers attended once again at Stobs Military Camp, Hawick, for their annual training, on Saturday, 30th June, 1906, and on detraining, marched, headed by their bands to the Scottish Border Volunteer Infantry Brigade Camp, which was on the extreme northern boundary of the Government ground, fully two miles from the 1905 camping ground. The 2nd Berwickshires occupied the lines at the top of the field, the 3rd Dumfriesshire, the centre lines and the Galloways, the bottom lines. To the right of the camp were the slopes of Colifort and to the right the Burgh lands crowned by the Vertish Hills. In front, the narrow valley of the Slitrig widened to a wooded aspect and to the rear the manoeuvring ground allotted to the Brigade stretched for some 3 miles to the slopes of Penchrise Pen.

Once again Colonel J.M. Kennedy M.V.O. V.D. was in command of the Galloway Battalion, together with:-

Staff Officers, Lt. Col. Lennox, Captain and Adjutant A.G. Fraser and Major J.T. Hewat, Castle Douglas as Quartermaster. Company Officers:- Captain W.L.Comrie, Kirkcudbright; Lt. H.B. Wilkinson, Castle Douglas; Stranraer once again no Officer. Captain R.S. Glover and Lt. Mathews, Newton Stewart; Captain E.S. Forde, New Galloway. Captain R.A. Grierson; Lt. Scott-Elliott, 'F' Company Maxwellton; Captain E. Grierson, 2nd Lts. W.F. Crombie and J.M. Glover, 'G' Company, Maxwellton; Captain A.W. Anderson, Lt. H. Gillies, Dalbeattie.

The Parade state of the Galloways was as follows:

	Officers.	Sergeants.	Buglers & Band.	Rank & File.	Total.
'A' Kbt.	1	5	4	42	52
'B' C/D.	3	7	3	32	45
'C' Str.	0	4	5	35	44
'D' N/S.	2	3	5	76	86
'E' N/G.	2	2	1	8	13
'F' Mxltn.	1	5	11	51	71
'G' Mxltn.	3	4	10	49	66
'H' Dbt.	2	6	7	41	56
	17	36	46	334	433.

Captain E.S. Forde commanded the Maxim gun detachment; Captain Glover, the Brigade Signallers and Lt. Crombie, the Cyclists.

The Orderly Room was under Sergeant-Major Grierson, assisted by Sergeant W.M. Haugh, Castle Douglas and Private Kivlichan, Maxwellton. Quartermaster Sergeant T. Myers, Castle Douglas, was in charge of stores. Sergeant F. Connelly, Castle Douglas, assisted by Private J. Ferguson and Private J. McKie, was in charge of the Sergeant's Mess. Cook-Sergeant McNaught was once again in charge of the kitchens.

The Pipe Band and Brass Band were under Sergeant Piper Johnston, Dalbeattie and Bandmaster Leroy, Maxwellton, while Sergeant-Bugler, (PIP) Livingstone was in charge of the Buglers. Private J. Law, Maxwellton was Brigade Postman.

Close to the lines were the Guild and the Y.M.C.A. tents.

The 2nd Berwickshires, numbering 220 Officers and men, were under the command of Colonel Hope of Cowdenknowes. The 3rd Dumfriesshire numbering 16 Officers and 319 men was under the command of Colonel Dudgeon. The Brigade was under the Command of Brigadier-General Colonel Trotter, who succeeded Colonel Godfrey. However, Col. Godfrey was in attendance at camp to open the permanent club and rooms of the Y.M.C.A., on Winningtonrig. This building, which comprised of reading and recreation hall, postal rooms and fully equipped kitchens, was the first permanent building of its kind erected by the Y.M.C.A. for the comfort of the Volunteers. The plan of the building was from sketches supplied by Lt.-General Leech, V.C. Officer Commanding-in-Scotland, who had given three words for the management of the institute. Rest, Refreshment and Recreation, with not too much spiritual consolation.

Camp Cracks.
Sergeant John Russell, Creetown, was presented with the Long Service Medal. Sergeant Adam Birrell, Creetown, has been promoted to Colour Sergeant.

On Wednesday, the combined Cyclists had a long outing by way of Selkirk and Melrose and home by Hawick.

On Thursday evening after the Battalion had been photographed by Private Hunter, Newton Stewart, Sergeant Instructor Fennessey, Stranraer, was presented with his good conduct medal.

The Offices at the Y.M.C.A. tent dealt with between 4,000 and 5,000 letters and postcards during the week.

The camp broke up on Saturday, 7th July, 1906, the Berwickshire and Dumfriesshire Battalions being dismissed some 3 hours before the Galloway Rifles, who did not leave camp until 7pm. This caused a great deal of dis-satisfaction on the part of the rank and file who had by far the longest distance to travel and indeed the Stranraer and Gatehouse Sections could not expect to arrive home until the Sunday morning.

1907 Camp.

From 1891, the Galloway Rifles had been encamped at Minto Kaimes, Hassendean - 4; Dingleton Common, Melrose - 2; Stobs - 4. but not, since 1897 had all the Battalions forming the Scottish Border Volunteer Infantry brigade, been Brigaded together. The 1st and 2nd V.B. Royal Scots Fusiliers (Ayrshire), who joined the brigade in 1903, had never Brigaded with their counterparts of the Volunteer Battalions of the King's Own Scottish Borderers. Steps were therefore taken to rectify this problem and a mutually agreed choice of venue was chosen, that of Irvine Moor, Ayrshire, a flat stretch of country, close to the sea and near to the Bogside Racecourse.

On Thursday, 11th July, 1907, an advance party of Captain Fraser, Captain E. Grierson, Lt. McKinnell, Quartermaster Sergeant Myers and Colour-Sergeant McIlroy, together with 61 men, attended Irvine Moor to prepare the camp. The main body of the Brigade arrived in camp on Saturday, 13th July.

The Brigade under the Command of brigadier-General Trotter of Mainshouse, Kelso, comprised of:-
1st Roxburgh and Selkirk (Border Rifles)- under the Command of Lt. Col. Haddon V.D.
2nd V.B. KOSB. (Berwickshire) - under the Command of Col. Hope.
3rd V.B. KOSB. (Dumfriesshire) - under the Command of Col. Dudgeon V.D.
Galloway Rifles - under the Command of Lt. Col. Lennox V.D.
1st V.B. Royal Scots Fusiliers (Ayrshire) - under the Command of Lt. Col. Gow.
2nd V.B. Royal Scots Fusiliers (Ayrshire) - under the Command of Captain Fulton.

The Parade State of the Galloways was as follows:
Lt. Col. Lennox V.D. Commanding. Captain A.G. Fraser, Adjutant.
Major J.T. Hewat V.D. Acting Quartermaster.

		Sergeants.	Rank and File.	Total.
'A' Co. (Kirkcudbright).	Captain Comrie	5	51	58
	Lieutenant E.W. Paterson.			
'B' Co. (Castle Douglas).	Lieutenant H.B. Wilkinson.	6	49	56
'C' Co. (Stranraer).	Lieutenant T.M. Hunter.	3	44	48
'D' Co. (Newton Stewart).	Captain R.S. Glover.	5	69	76
	Lieutenant J . Mathews.			
'E' Co. (New Galloway).	Captain E.S. Forde.	2	5	9
	Lieutenant A.K. Clark-Kennedy.			
'F' Co. (Maxwellton) .	Captain E. Grierson.			
	Lieutenant W.F. Crombie	6	51	60
	Lieutenant B. McKinnell			
'G' Co. (Maxwellton).	Captain R.A. Grierson.			
	Lieutenant Scott-Elliott.	4	56	63.
	Lieutenant J .M. Glover.			
'H' Co. (Dalbeattie).	Lieutenant H. Gillies.	4	39	44

				414.

Once again the Orderly Room was in the charge of Sergeant-Major Grierson, assisted by Orderly Room Sergeant W. Haugh and Private W.F. Kivlichan, with Private H. Haugh as Orderly.

Quartermaster Sergeant Myers, assisted by Private J. Myers was in charge of stores and rations.

The Cook-Sergeant was Sergeant D. McNaught, New Galloway, assisted by 2 Cooks drawn from each Company, whilst the Sergeant's Mess, was in the hands of Sergeant J. McCormick, late of the K.O.S.B.

Pioneer Sergeant J. Coupland, Maxwellton, was garrison Military Police Sergeant for the Brigade. Corporal McDavid, Creetown, was Regimental Postman.

A Cyclist Section consisting of Lieutenant Crombie, Sergeant J. Henderson, and 17 men, left Maxwellton on the Friday night, rested overnight at Sanquhar and reached camp on the afternoon of Saturday, 13th July.

Two Militia Battalions, the 3rd Royal Scots Fusiliers, (Prince Regent's Royal Regiment of Ayr and Wigtown) and Argyll and Sutherland Highlanders (Paisley) had been encamped on Irvine Moor for 2 months, and on Sunday, 14th July, one man of the 3rd R.S.F. (Militia), drowned whilst bathing in the River Irvine, in consequence all bathing in the river was forbidden to all.

On Monday, 15th July, the Battalion was paraded and marched through Irvine to a piece of ground on the Kilmarnock Road near Dreghorn, where they engaged in Battalion training for 5 hours, returning to camp at 3pm. The heat was oppressive and told heavily on the men who were rested for the day.

The next day, Tuesday, 16th July, dawned clear with the heat steadily becoming more oppressive as the day wore on. The brigade, together with the Militia Regiments, engaged in field manoeuvres but once again they were dismissed early in the day at 3pm owing to the continuing heat. That night a large number of men succumbed to the effects of sunstroke with one man from each of the Militia Regiments dying from the effects of the sun.

Wednesday, 17th July, a strong breeze tempered the intense heat, with the day being devoted to Battalion training, Dumfries and Galloway Battalions being utilised for the examination of Subaltern Officers of the Brigade - the Officers of the Galloway being 2nd Lieutenants, T.M. Hunter, E.W. Paterson, B. McKinnell, M.D. Mathews, A.K. Clark-Kennedy. Once again the men were dismissed early, at 2pm owing to the incessant heat, many taking advantage to attend the Bogside races. (2nd Lieutenant A.K. Clark-Kennedy was to eventually rise to the rank of Captain and while serving with the 5th Battalion K.O.S.B. on the Eastern front, he was killed at Gaza on the 19th April, 1917).

Thursday, 18th July, the duties of the day commenced at 6.30am with Battalion drill followed by Brigade Parade and Inspection by the Brigadier. Once again the afternoon was given over to the men, owing to the continuing oppressive heat. Friday, 19th was to continue in the same vein with the battalion leaving for home at 12 noon on Saturday, 20th July, 1907.

In August, 1907, the Army Council decided that each Volunteer Camp should be held, where possible, within its own Territorial area. The Scottish Border Brigade, did not from various causes profit a great deal from their recent camp at Irvine and Major Du Plat Taylor D.S.O. R.A. Brigade-Major of the Scottish Border Volunteer Infantry Brigade attended Castle Douglas on Saturday, 31st August, 1907, for the purpose of obtaining information as to any ground in Galloway which might be considered suitable for the next Border Brigade Camp. Suitable ground required a large tract of uncultivated country with broken ground, which would afford the facilities of a good water supply. It was reported that Major Taylor was favourably impressed by a site in the Castle Douglas area if the proprietors of the land were minded to give of their ground for such a purpose. Consequently between the 11th and 25th July, 1908, the newly constituted Scottish Border Brigade Camp, under the Territorial and, Reserve Forces Act, 1907, was for the first time held in Galloway, being formed at Caigton Row, Castle Douglas, under the Command of Brigadier-General Trotter, Mainshouse, Kelso. (The parade strength being fully reported on Page 392, Chapter 14.)

(12) Discharge Certificate of an Enrolled Volunteer. This Certificate relates to a Private 3554 Thomas Thorburn of 'H' Company, Langholm, of the
3rd Volunteer Battalion King's Own Scottish Borderers, Dumfriesshire.

CHAPTER 12

THE BOER WAR 11th OCTOBER, 1899 - 31st MAY, 1902

South Africa was divided into four States; Cape Colony, and Natal, being British possessions with the Orange Free State and the Transvaal being controlled by the Boer.

In 1877 control of the Transvaal was transferred to Britain, by the Boer, fearful of an attack by the natives. The natives were defeated by Britain in the Zulu Wars of 1879.

In 1880, owing to differing political persuasions, the Boer Farmer was to revolt against the British, resulting in the first Boer War. Britain was defeated with the Boer proclaiming the Transvaal, once again, a Boer homeland. Towards the end of the decade, with the discovery of large gold deposits within the Transvaal, the country was transformed from an impoverished to a very wealthy country. Britain was to covet these resources and began to meddle in the internal politics of the Transvaal, leading to the Jameson Raid of 1895, instigated by Cecil Rhodes, the then Prime Minister of Cape Colony in an effort to overthrow the legitimate Government of the Transvaal.

Over the next few years relations between Britain and the Transvaal were to deteriorate and by the May of 1899, all political dialogue between the two countries had ceased. In the September of 1899, Britain was to reinforce their standing army in South Africa and on the 9th October, 1899, the Boer demanded that these additional troops be withdrawn. Britain was given 48 hours to comply with the demand, this she refused to do and on the 11th October, 1899, Britain and the Boer were at War.

The Boer was to launch the first offensive almost immediately against Natal and over the next few weeks were to completely dominate the British, forcing their withdrawal. The Boer laid seige to Mafeking, Kimberley and Ladysmith. These defeats were seen as a major embarassment to the British Government who called for a huge Task Force of some 250,000 men to be sent to South Africa in early January, 1900, under Field Marshal Lord Roberts, Commander in Chief South Africa. To bolster the numbers, Volunteer Service Companies were to be called for from the Volunteer Battalions of the Line Regiments.

The following Regimental Order was issued by Colonel J. M. Kennedy, from the Galloway Rifles Headquarters, Castle Douglas, on the 22nd December, 1899.

"The following are the conditions under which the service of the Volunteer Force will be accepted for duty in South Africa.

(1). Every Volunteer must enlist for 1 year or for the War. In the event of the War being over in less than 1 year, he will have the option of being discharged at once or of completing his 1 years service.

(2). He must be not less than 20 years and more than 35 years of age.

(3). He must be a first class shot under Volunteer rules.

(4). He must have been returned as efficient during 1898/99.

(5). He must be of good character.

(6). He must be up to the physical standards of an infantry recruit as laid down in the Recruiting Reguations for the Army. No relaxation of standards will be allowed.

(7). He must be medically fit for active service.

(8). preference will be given to unmarried men or widowers without children. Married men will only be accepted in the event of an insufficient number of single men or widowers without children volunteering. After attestation the Volunteers will join the Regimental Depot until required for embarkation. From date of enlistment each Volunteer will receive pay and allowances of his rank as a Regular Infantry soldier, rations and clothing."

The Active Service Company of Volunteers wao drawn from all the Volunteer Battalions attached to the King's Own Scottish Borderers - the Border Rifles - the Berwickshire Volunteers the Dumfriesshire

Volunteers - and the Galloway Rifle Volunteers, in practically equal numbers. There being no shortage of Volunteers the men were regularly enlisted and placed on a reserve list, at once drawing reservist pay. The Reserve list for the Galloway Rifles was placed under the Command of Major Lennox, who had himself, volunteered for the front.

Below is a complete list of men who formed the First Service Company of the Kings Own Scottish Borderers, which left Berwick on 13th February, 1900, and sailed for Cape Town on board the S.S. Greek.

Company Officers.
Captain ANDREW HADDON, Hawick.
Lieutenant MALCOLM CRAIG-BROWN, Selkirk.
Lieutenant ROBERT STODDART, Greenlaw.
Colour Sergeant JESSE SMITH, Melrose.

Galloway Section.
Sergeant GEORGE MILLBURN, Dalbeattie.
Corporal ANDREW MURDOCH, New Galloway.
Lance-Corporal JAMES HENDERSON, Maxwellton.
Private PETER JOHN BIRRELL, Creetown.
Private ALEXANDER BROWN, Dalbeattie.
Private THOMAS BURNIE, Dalbeattie.
Private WILLIAM CALDOW, New Galloway.
Private ROBERT COCHRANE, New Galloway.
Private ROBERT CROSBIE, Maxwellton.
Private MICHAEL CROSSAN, Kirkcudbright.
Private JOHN PATTON DRYDEN, Kirkcudbright.
Private WILL IAM CURRIE HANNAH, Maxwellton.
Private ROBERT JARDINE, Maxwellton.
Private JAMES KIRK, Dalbeattie.
Private WILLIAM KIRKPATRICK, Maxwellton.
Private JOHN LOCKE, Maxwellton.
Private JOHN McKIE, New Galloway.
Private NEWALL McKINNELL, Maxwellton.
Private ARCHIBALD McLEOD, Castle Douglas.
Private ROBERT MILLIGAN, Kirkcudbright.
Private GEORGE CAMPBELL MOFFAT, Maxwellton.
Private WILLIAM NELSON, Dalbeattie.
Private DAVID McLEAN NICOLL, Maxwellton.
Private ROBERT PERCY, Maxwellton
Private WILLIAM RENNIE, Stranraer.
Private OLIVER TAYLOR, New Galloway.
Private ANGUS THOM, Maxwellton.
Private THOMAS WHITE, Maxwellton.

Dumfriesshire Section.

Sergeant ALEXANDER CUTHBERTSON, Moffat.
Corporal THOMAS McVINNE, Dumfries.
Corporal ROBERT RAE, Dumfries.
Lance-Corporal ADAM KEEN, Canonbie.
Lance-Corporal ROBERT GRAHAM ADAMSON, Lockerbie.
Drummer ALFRED KEMPSELL, Dumfries.
Private JOSEPH ADAMSON, Carronbridge .
Private ADAM CUNNINGHAM ANDERSON, Moffat.
Private ROBERT JARDINE BEATTIE, Annan.
Private THOMAS BURGESS, Moffat.
Private WILLIAM DAVIDSON, Moffat.
Private WILLIAM GARDINER, Lockerbie.
Private JOHN GRAHAM, Langholm.
Private RICHARD IRVING, Langholm.
Private JAMES JARDINE, Dumfries.
Private PETER JEFFREY, Dumfries
Private ALEXANDER LOUDON, Annan.
Private WILLIAM McCLEARY, Langholm.
Private THOMAS McGUFFOG , Annan.
Private JOHN McKIMMIE, Annan.

Private THOMAS MISKELLY, Dumfries.
Private HUGH ASHCROFT MUNRO, Dumfries.
Private HUGH MURRAY, Dumfries.
Private JAMES PAGAN, Moffat.
Private THOMAS LUCK ROBERTSON, Moffat.
Private DAVID SMITH, Dumfries .
Private JOSEPH TURNBULL, Langholm.
Private WILLIAM WATSON, Dumfries.

Border Rifle Section.

Sergeant JAMES HALL SCOTT, Melrose.
Lance-Sergeant DAVID SANDERSON, Melrose.
Lance-Corporal WILLIAM HASTIE HUME, Galashiels.
Private JAMES BALMER, Selkirk.
Private WILLIAM BELL, Selkirk.
Private JAMES RENNIE, Kelso.
Private JOHN BROWN, Melrose.
Private DAVID COUPER, Melrose.
Private FRANK CREW, Kelso.
Private THOMAS DOUGLAS, Selkirk.
Private ANDREW FALLA FAIRBAIRN, Selkirk.
Private WILLIAM HAIG, Jedburgh.
Private ADAM HENDERSON, Selkirk.
Private JOHN HINDMARSH, Hawick.
Private DAVID HOGARTH, Galashiels.
Private ROBERT HUME, Jedburgh.
Private ALEXANDE JEFFREY, Jedburgh .
Private THOMAS JOHNSTONE, Selkirk.
Private ALEXANDER LAUDER, Galashiels.
Private GEORGE LAWRIE, Selkirk.
Private RICHARD LYNN, Hawick.
Private DAVID MALCOLM, Kelso.
Private JOHN MIDDLEMASS, Hawick.
Private JAMES MILLS, Galashiels.
Private GEORGE ROBERTSON PATTERSON, Kelso.
Private THOMAS THOMPSON SMART, Melrose.
Private JOHN STORRIE, Selkirk.
Private ROBERT WALKER, Selkirk.

Berwickshire Section.

Sergeant JOHN HASTIE, Duns.
Lance-Sergeant WILLIAM HOME, Duns.
Lance-Corporal JAMES ROBERTSON HUME, Coldstream.
Drummer HUGH McTIER, Duns.
Private WILLIAM ALLAN, Duns.
Private GEORGE BOLTON, Lauder.
Private JAMES CHISHOLM, Stow.
Private THOMAS COLTART, Duns.
Private JOHN FRASER DALLAS, Chirnside.
Private GEORGE JOHNSTON ELLIOT, Duns.
Private JOHN ELLIOT, Coldstream.
Private JOHN FLINT, Duns.
Private HENRY GILLIES, Duns.
Private JOHN KIRKALDY, Duns.
Private JOHN LIVINGSTONE, Duns.
Private J OSEPH MacKENZIE LOW, Duns.
Private ROBERT MOFFAT LYALL, Greenlaw.
Private THOMAS MARSHALL, Ayton.
Private ARCHIBALD MARTIN, Duns.
Private JOHN MARTIN, Coldingham.
Private WILLIAM MIDDLEMASS, Duns.
Private HENRY WILSON MITCHELL, Earlston.
Private THOMAS PATERSON, Duns.
Private GEORGE DOUGLAS ROBERTSON, Earlston.
Private PETER ROBERTSON, Duns.

Private CHARLES MAXWELL SMITH, Earlston.
Private THOMAS WALLACE, Earlston.
Private JOHN WOOD, Coldingham.

The Following list of men formed a draft to the first Service Company of the Kings Own Scottish Borderers. Leaving Berwick on 11th May, 1900, after two weeks training and embarking on the S.S. Assaye for Cape Town. They joined with the first service company at Pretoria on the 28th August, 1900.

Lieutenant ROBERT CUNNINGHAM, Annan.
Sergeant JAMES BROWN, Duns.
Lance-Sergeant ROBERT AITKEN, Duns.
Lance Corporal JOHN DONALDSON, Galashiels.
Lance Corporal JAMES WILLIAMSON, Thornhill.
Drummer ROBERT WALDIE, Jedburgh.
Private WALTER CAIRNS, Hawick.
Private JAMES CROSSEN, Galashiels.
Private JOHN CUNNINGHAME, Sanquhar.
Private WILLIAM FERGUSON, Maxwellton.
Private ROBERT FOREMAN, Chirnside.
Private THOMAS GRAHAM, Maxwellton.
Private WILLIAM GREIG, Ayton.
Private JAMES HOGARTH, Galashiels.
Private JOHN McLEAN, Dalbeattie.
Private ADAM MacVIE, Chirnside.
Private THOMAS MAXWELL, Annan.
Private WILLIAM OLIVER, Selkirk.
Private ROBERT SHARP, Kirkcudbright.
Private JOHN SWAN WAUGH, Sanquhar .
Private ANDREW BELL WOOD, Coldstream.

Incensed by the actions of the Boer, the sieges of Mafeking, Kimberley and Ladysmith being well reported, the Volunteers for the front were hailed as heroes and feted by the inhabitants of their respective Burghs. The later 2nd and 3rd Active Service Companies were not to receive quite the same acclaim once the beseiged towns had been relieved and the Boer stronghold of Pretoria had fallen.

Lines to the Galloway Volunteers.
(On their going to the front in South Africa.

A glorious flame of patriotism
Is now shining o'er our land
And Volunteers come to the front
A loyal unselfish band;
They come, with brave, undaunted hearts
And parading now are seen
Ready in arms to join the ranks
With the Soldiers of the Queen.

And Galloway's sons the spirit show
Of the brave of Galwegian clan
Who to be free, as heroes fought
And in battle led the van.
They show the fire that in patriotic hearts
of Old, was wont to burn
Those doughty warriors Wallace wicht
And the Bruce of Bannockburn.

Leal sons of ancient Galloway
So famed in martial story
For valour, on many a battle field
That led to death or glory
Those heroes deeds you'll emulate
And untarnished keep their fame
In fighting for your country's rights
An' Scotland's honoured name.

Brave lads now leaving friends and home
And the lasses ye lo'e dear
The banks and braes O'Galloway
And its burnies running clear
To sail away to a foreign land
Sae far across the sea
Many anxious hearts will think of you
in their homes by Nith and Cree.

Brave Volunteers you've nobly done
Wha now could throw the sneer
He's only a fair weather sodger
Our handy Volunteer
And well 'tis known when in the fight
No foe will see you yield
For Queen and Country's rights you'll stand
Or die upon the field.

Brave Volunteers of Galloway
Oft with you. I've probably been
Marching in many Grand parades
And reviews before the Queen
But never did I feel so proud
As when now I see you go
Brothers in arms to Africa's shore
To lay th' oppressors low.

Brave Volunteers of Galloway
And the Borderers' sae true
Wha when in camp on Minto's knowes
Aye sae frien'ly were wi' you
As brother on the tented field
And in the bloody fray
You'll stand or fall together there
for the honours of the day.

Brave sons of Caledonia
Land of the Fair and Free
Upholding now as patriots
The cause of liberty
On Africa's sunny veldt you'll meet
A Wily treacherous foe
Sae, wary be O'Boerish traps
That hae brocht such grief and woe.

O'h may the God of battles be
In danger aye your shield
May Victory's banner o'er you wave
On every battle field
May Him, who rightly guides his arm
In life's oft weary round
Bring you all safely home again
with glory and honours armed.

Castle Douglas 25.1.1900. M. M.L.H.

(The poet in this case is believed to be ex Major Malcolm McL. Harper of the Galloway Rifle Volunteers.)

Kirkcudbright.

"Thursday, 25th January, 1900, was a red letter day in the history of the Royal Burgh of Kirkcudbright, with the departure of the three men, Privates Michael Crossan, John P. Dryden and Robert Milligan, who had volunteered for the front. The men paraded at the Armoury at 10.20am and accompanied by about 30 members of their Company, marched to the Station, headed by the band of the local Artillery Company. Before leaving the crowd gathered to considerable proportions until at the station there were upwards of 1,000 people, the platform and the approaches being literally packed and the enthusiasm of the crowd abounded. The crowd sang "Auld Lang Syne", "Rule Brittania", "Soldiers of the Queen", and on the train moving away three cheers were given for the men. The children of the Academy and the Johnstone School petitioned their teachers to allow them to go to the Station."

Dalbeattie.
"Five Volunteers from the Town, Sergeant G. Millburn, Privates, W. Nelson, T. Burnie, A. Brown, J. Kirk, were entertained at numerous entertainments the previous week and on Thursday, 25th January, at 11.45am the men paraded at the Armoury and marched to the Station, followed by the band. Hundreds of townsfolk followed the Volunteers with great enthusiasm. At the station they were addressed by Mr. Maxwell of the Munches who presented the men with a gift of money. As the train came into the station, the crowd sang "Soldiers of the Queen", and as the train steamed away cheers went up from a crowd of 1,200, who began to sing "Will Ye no come back again.""

Castle Douglas.
"On Thursday, 25th January, 1900, the Galloway Rifle Voluntcers mustered at the Armoury where Private Archibald MeLeod was presented with a purse of sovereigns. Headed by the band, with Private McLeod at the head of his Company, they marched to the station where a large crowd had assembled and the platform was crowded. The Officers present were, Major Harper, Major Dunn, Captain Hewat in Command, Lieutenant Gifford along with Provost Thomson. On the arrival of the train the enthusiasm became overwhelming and as the train pulled away the crowd began singing, "Auld Lang Syne.""

Newton Stewart.
"On Wednesday, the 24th January, 1900, comrades, and friends waited on Cyclist Private Peter John Birrell of 'D' Company and presented him with a purse of sovereigns and a bible. The presentation was made by Mr. William Shennan, Burnfoot, who wished him a speedy return.

Stranraer.
"On Thursday, 25th January, 1900, Private William Rennie, of 'C' Company was accorded an enthusiastic send off on his departure for South Africa. The Company assembled at the Drill Hall where Private Rennie was waited on by Provost McRobert, Baiilie Purdie and other members of the Town Council, who conferred the Freedom of the Burgh on Private Rennie. The Volunteers then marched to the station where they were met by hearty cheers of vast crowds lining the route. Private Rennie received numerous gifts of cash."

At Dumfries on Saturday, 27th January, 1900, Volunteers of the Galloway Rifles active service Company, under Lieutenant Shortridge, paraded at Maxwellton Drill Hall at 10.15am in full marching order, with valise, coat and mess tin. (Lieutenant Shortridge was taken ill shortly after this parade and was prevented from taking his place with the active service Company, however, on the 26th March, 1901, he was commissioned in the Scottish Company of Volunteer Cyclists, seeing service in South Africa. A letter from Lieutenant Shortridge appears later in this history.) The Officers present were Major Lennox and Major Phyn both of Maxwellton; Major Harper, Captain Hewat, Lieutenants Gifford and Biggar, all of Castle Douglas, and members of the permanent Staff. They were addressed by Provost Chicken of Maxwellton.

Headed by the massed bands of the 3rd Volunteer Brigade of the King's Own Scottish Borderers, they marched to the Dumfries Town Hall where they joined with the men of the Dumfries active service Company The procession being resumed was headed by Provost Glover, the Magistrates and the Town Council of Dumfries. The scene was memorable with the Pipe Bands now leading the Galloway Service Section. The streets were lined with crowds of cheering onlookers. The route was via Burn's statue, Academy Street, Lover's Walk to the Railway Station where a vast crowd had gathered. As the train moved off the band played the National Anthem.

The men of the active service Company proceeded to Berwick where they were to undergo two weeks training before embarking for South Africa. They left Berwick on the 13th February, 1900, and sailed for South Africa on board the S.S. "Greek".

In the meantime, on the 15th February 1900, Kimberley was relieved by General French after 124 days of seige, and on the 27th February, 1900, after fierce fighting a famous Boer General, Piet Cronje, was to surrender to Lord Roberts at Paardeberg. It was reported that in fact General Cronje was from Galloway stock, his father being a McCrone from Auchencairn and his mother a native of the Haugh of Urr. His parents moved to Sanquhar and thereafter to South Africa, where their son was born. Cronje was to adopt the Dutch rendering of his father's name, McCrone.

On the 28th February, 1900, Ladysmith was relieved after 118 days of seige.

On the 8th March, 1900, Lord Roberts marched on Bloemfontein, entering the Capital of the Orange River Colony on the 13th March. However, at Bloemfontein, the British adavance was halted by an outbreak of enteric (typhoid) fever, which by the end of April, had hospitalised upwards of 15,000 of Lord Robert's troops.

The Volunteers of the Active Service Company had meanwhile landed at Cape Town on the 9th March and were camped at Green Point. They were immediately ordered up country to guard the waterworks at Touws River Camp. The importance of this task was only later to be realised, when on the 31st March, the Boer blew up the waterworks at Bloemfontein further delaying Robert's advance by curtailing his water supply and thus increasing the enteric epidemic.

By the 3rd May, 1900, the epidemic had somewhat abated and Lord Roberts had utilised this time to assemble an army of some 44,000 troops, supported by Artillery and a huge supply column, some five miles in length, for the final offensive of the War, the march on the Transvaal Capital of Pretoria.

Our Volunteers left Touws River Camp, on the 3rd May and joined with their supply column on the 7th May, at Brandfort. They force marched with their column arriving at Kroonstad on the 13th May, where they joined with Lord Robert's column and their Line Regiment, the 1st Battalion King's Own Scottish Borderers, which had come under the 7th Division, Commanded by General Tucker. The Volunteers were attached to the Regiment as No.9 Company, under the command of Colonel Godfrey.

Lord Roberts had halted his advance at Kroonstad on the 12th May, to allow his supply columns to catch up, to rest his horses and to repair the rail lines, destroyed by the Boer retreat.

In the meantime, amid great jubilation, Mafeking was relieved on the 16th May, after 217 days seige, by General Lord Kitchener.

On the 22nd May, Lord Roberts continued his advance, crossing the Vaal river, into the Transvaal. Going back to the 13th May, Colonel Godfrey, on welcoming the Volunteers at Kroonstad had complimented the Officers and men on their fine appearance and said he would give them the chance they had come so far for by placing them in the firing line at the first opportunity. He was to keep his word and on the advance accross the Vaal river he placed the Volunteers in the front of the brigade.

On the 30th May, outside Johannesburg, there was an engagement at Doorn Kop between the Boer and Lord Robert's advance. The Volunteers, however well to the fore of the advance continued their push into Johannesburg and were the first troops to enter the City, being 16 hours in advance of any other troops in the occupation of Johannesburg. For this feat, Lord Roberts was to appoint the Volunteers of the Active Service Company, his personal bodyguard.

On the 5th June, Pretoria fell without a fight, the Boer having fled during the night under the cover of darkness. As Lord Robert's personal bodyguard, the Volunteers were given the honour of being the first Volunteer Company serving in South Africa to enter Pretoria.

Of the 44,000 troops who had set out on the great march from Bloemfontein, for varying reasons, but mainly through enteric fever, only 26,000 reached Pretoria. The actual losses in battle were relatively small with 109 men killed and 479 wounded or missing. Of the 116 men who formed the Active Service Company only 47 of all ranks reached Pretoria. Privates John Kirkcaldy, Duns, of the Berwickshire Section and Alexander Loudon, Annan, of the Dumfriesshire Section, both died from enteric fever, with another 40 suffering from enteric fever or dysentary, others had taken ill down the line, whilst others were completely done in and sent to various rest camps along the way. Private Thomas Caldow, Lauriestion, of the Galloway Section, had been accidently shot in the foot. The losses were as follows:

Border Rifles -	1 Sergeant, 1 Lance Corporal and 14 men.
Berwickshire Section -	15 men.
Dumfriesshire Section -	1 Sergeant, 2 Corporals, 1 Lance Corporal and 14 men.
Galloway Rifle Volunteers -	1 Sergeant, 1 Corporal and 18 men.

The men of the Active Service Company had covered a distance of some 380 miles in 33 days over trackless veldt, on short rations, in full kit and in the middle of the South African winter.

The following marching song was sung by the Volunteers of the Active Service Company on their long treks accross the veldt. Reminiscences by a 96 year old Kirkcudbright man, Pat Hannah, of a song taught him by his father, Private William Hannah, who was to travel to South Africa with the 3rd Active Service

Company. Full words obtained from "What a Lovely War" by Roy Palmer.

"Oh, good morning, Mr. Stevens, we've been working very hard,
Sing hurrah for the Volunteers.
We've been working very hard on the dingy pontoon hard,
Sing hurrah for the Volunteers.
Oh, you make fast, I'll make fast, make fast the dingy,
Make fast the dingy, make fast the dingy.
You make fast, I'll make fast the dingy,
Make fast the dingy tonight,
For we're marching on Pretoria, Pretoria, Pretoria,
Oh, we're marching on Pretoria,
Where they don't know sugar from
Tissue paper, tissue paper, marmalade and jam.
Oh, I saw a nigger boy sitting by a fire,
I saw a nigger boy playing with his
Hold him down while the dingy's blowing,
Hold him down till I get there.(Shout) Oh, oh, oh, oh, oh, oh, oh, oh."

After the fall of Pretoria, the Volunteers were to form part of a small garrison force left to defend the Capital, and for the next few weeks the Volunteers spent what was described as a, "Somewhat monotonous time in Pretoria, broken only by the weekly arrival of the mails." However, this monotony was to be short lived when on the 11th July, 1900, Commandant General Botha was to take up positions along the Tigerspoort Ridge, overlooking the City, with 3,000 troops, threatening to retake Pretoria. Generals French and Hamilton came to their aid and despatched the Boer but not before Kemp de la Rey, a Boer General, forced the surrender of 240 British troops at Zeticote's Nek. The Volunteers formed as part of a composite force sent to relieve the 'Lincolns and Greys' in this engagement.

On the 15th July, 1900, the Volunteers, together with their Line Regiment the 1st Battalion K.O.S.B. joined with a column under the command of General Ian Hamilton. This column was to form part of Lord Roberts advance on Botha's defensive line at Belfast, some 127 miles East of Pretoria, on the 23rd July, 1900. However, owing to the increased guerilla activity of Kemp de la Rey and another Boer General, Christian de Wet, Robert's advance was halted at Middleburg and General Hamilton's column was detailed to leave the column and go in search of de Wet's forces.

General Hamilton's column returned to Pretoria and on the 1st August, they were directed to Rustenburg to relieve and escort General Baden-Powell to Pretoria. They arrived at the Capital on the 9th August, and the following day were sent on a 130 mile trek to Potchefstroom in pursuit of de Wet. They were to continue into Krugerdorp to Johannesburg and back to Pretoria. These de Wet hunts were to continue into the Magaliesberg Mountains, 60 miles west of Pretoria, heading north, south and in every conceivable direction. Occasionaly contact was made with de Wet but after short exchanges he would take off. These hit and run tactics were to frustrate the troops who made many forced marches in pursuit, on short rations, with their clothing and boots falling to pieces. Lieutenant Home was to record. "We covered no less than 96 miles in 5 days and that over rough and difficult country. Four days later we reached Pretoria after having marched continuously for 18 days in which time we had covered 252 miles."

Meanwhile on the 7th August, 1900, Lord Roberts began his advance on Belfast. General French headed East meeting up with General Buller's Force south of Belfast on the 15th August. The Boer, some 6,000 strong had formed their defences north of Belfast awaiting Robert's advance. On the 27th August, 1900, Roberts began his final advance.

General Hamilton's column, along with the Volunteers, was to continue the hunt for de Wet until the 31st August, 1900, when he was ordered to proceed to Belfast to meet up with Lord Robert's Forces. For the next three days they force marched to Bronkhorstspruit when they learned that they were to proceed to Belfast by train, as rapidly as possible. At Belfast the Volunteers were detailed for garrison duty in the nearby Colliery Hills. These positions they held until the 24th September, 1900, when the Volunteers rejoined their Battalion, taking up positions on the Belfast to Pretoria railway line .

In the meantime, Lord Roberts had continued his advance East from Belfast, driving the Boer before him, however there was to be no final decisive action and by the 24th September, 1900, Lord Roberts had reached his objective of Koomati Poort on the Swaziland Border. He was to declare the Transvaal once again a British Colony.

On the 9th October, 1900, the Volunteers were mobilised for home, leaving Pretoria on the 15th October, as escort to 355 Boer Prisoners of War, destined for the Cape. The journey was to take 8 days and 7 nights and on arrival at Cape Town, the Volunteers, relieved of their prisoners, once again set up camp at Green Point, before finally sailing for home on the 1st November, 1900, on board the S.S. "Avondale Castle".

These few pages chronicle the overall history in the opening shots of the Boer War but the following series of letters, written by the men of Galloway to their mothers, fathers and friends, gives a greater insight into "Their War". The letters start with a great spirit of adventure but with death and disease prevailing the realities of war become all too apparent.

The following extracts are from a **letter of Cyclist Peter Birrell** of the Galloway Rifles, who was nearing the Cape on board the 'Greek'. The letter was posted in Madeira and was received by his mother at her home 'Anchorlea', Carsluith.

"We have plenty of good grub yet; that much I can say. They are feeding us well; any amount of roast beef and soups for dinner, in fact more than we can use. We get fish for breakfast - haddock or bloater herrings - plenty of bread, butter and tea.

We had a bit of physical drill on deck today, (18th February, 1900). There is any amount of fresh water to wash in but we have not had a washing day yet.

We have had a very rough passage so far but it is settling down now and the air is feeling much warmer.

I got a parcel of clothing at Berwick before we left, sent by Mrs. Dunbar of Machermore - 6 pairs of stockings, one sleeping suit, 12 towels, 1 cardigan jacket and 1 dozen hankerchiefs, so I think I am not badly off in the matter of clothing.

We had a grand night last night (19th February). Everyone seems to be recovering now from their sickness, and what with bagpipes playing' cornets and bugles and everyone singing tnere has not been much peace. The Border men and the Welshmen have been having an argument about rugby football and they finished it off in an international engagement about 2 o'clock this morning. I think we wont be long in the Cape, the majority here think we will be home by June and there are great bets being taken on it. I hope the Volunteer concert was a success."

Letter from Private David Nichol, 'F' Company, Maxwellton, Galloway Rifle Volunteers, to his father Mr. J. S. Nichol, 24, King Street, Dumfries.

S.S. Greek, 19th February, 1900.

"We are having rather a rough voyage. In the Bay of Biscay, it was something cruel, the waves lashing over the deck and coming down below. There were few who weren't sea sick, and a good many have been in the hospital. I have offered to be inoculated (not vaccinated) as a preventative against enteric fever, but I am in the best of health.

I am wearying to hear some news now, as we hear nothing about the war or anything else. We have both, English, Welsh and Scotch Volunteers on board - about 800 I think altogether and about 150 of a crew. We get plenty of meat. Those who run down the meat on the transports don't know when they are well off.

We have been watching the porpoises jumping about the ship and expect soon to be seeing sharks. I think if lots of them had known before what they have had to come through already, they would have stayed at home, as I think lots of them are as much home-sick as sea-sick. But once I am off the sea I am all right, as it is the only thing I don't care for. Some of the fellows are talking about being home by June, but I doubt they are mistaken" .

Letter from Cyclist Peter Birrell 'D' Company, Galloway Rifles to his mother at Anchorlea, Carsluith. Letter arrived 16th April, 1900;

S.S. Greek 27.2.1900.

"We arrived at Teneriffe at 8.30 in the morning, on Wednesday, 21st. Teneriffe is one of the Canary Islands. It is one of the prettiest places ever I saw, great high mountains and hollows and the sun shining on them, it looked grand.

We had no sooner dropped anchor than we were surrounded by what they call bum boats, selling all sorts of fruit, tobacco etc. They did a roaring trade.

There was a death on board that morning - a Corporal of the Northamptons. The Doctor said he would not have lasted three months ashore, and what with sea-sickness and other complaints, it soon finished him. He was buried at sea the same evening.

We had good news from the front at Teneriffe - Kimberley having been relieved by General French, who also cut the communications to Bloemfontein and captured the Boer camp.

We are having grand warm weather now - too warm in fact. On Sunday, the 25th we saw a whale. There are 2 or 3 sharks following the ship and picking up the grub that is thrown over. Any amount of Dolphins and flying fish knocking about it. It is a great difference now to what it was in the Bay of Biscay and we are steaming along grandly. We had passed no ships for three days up to last night, when there was a liner went past within a hundred yards of us. We gave her a hearty cheer. Everybody was on deck in their shirts, having turned out to have a look at her.

We have had a great day today. We crossed the line at 2 o'clock and old Father Neptune came aboard along with his men and then the fun commenced. He called his men to do their duty. The seized the first man they got and tarred him and painted him and shaved him and threw him into a big bath made of canvas that they had made for the purpose, clothes and all. I was done along with the rest but then we had our revenge for we went and collared somebody else and fetched him forward and he got the same done and so on till nearly everybody was wet through. We then turned on old Neptune and his men and gave them a sore time of it. We got the hose pipes and chased the Officers all over the ship. We caught one that wears 'specs' carried him down painted and shaved him and dipped him too. It was an awful time for about two hours and I did enjoy it.

We had sports in the evening, tug of war, obstacle races and boxing. The K.O.S.B. were second in the tug of war and I think would have won it only one of our men racked himself and they had to pull in the final with seven men. The South Wales Borderers won. I am in the final of the obstacle race. It will be run tomorrow. There were nearly 60 entries.

We have concerts on deck every evening. We get the piano out of the saloon.

I forgot to tell you about a new sort of fishing I saw at Teneriffe - three men in a boat trawling for coal, it was the greates ever I looked at.

It was a very wild night of thunder and lightning and rain last night but this morning it was lovely again."

S.S. Greek March, 7th 1900.

"We are now within 1 days sail of the Cape and we are getting our kits ready for going ashore. We have had a very pleasant voyage and I am in grand health. The Galloways are all in splendid fettle but we have no idea how the war is getting on. We have had good feeling all the voyage and plenty of it."

Sunday, 11th March, 1900.

"We arrived all right on Friday. It was very thick coming up the Bay and we did not see much but it is good weather now. Table Mountain looks grand and Cape Town is a nice place. Green Point is what they call our Camp.

Cronje's guns are here - 4 Krupp 15 pounders and 1 Maxim - Nordenfeldt. They present a very battered appearance. Cronje and his men are in ship in Simons Bay. They are building a big place for those that are sure to come.

We go up country tomorrow. I am enjoying myself fine and the food is good. I have just seen J. Brown who used to be a Mason at the Barr quarry. He gets 15/- a day here."

March 18th, Sunday, 1900

"Touws River is a Station about 150 miles from Cape Town. It is a very important one, as it supplies the water to the railways. There is a patrol of Cape Mounted Volunteers always guarding it for fear any disloyal Dutch should meddle with it. We are guarding the reservoir. If anything went wrong it would stop the railway for 300 miles.

There was a Company of Royal Artillery here but they left today. They are going to Durban. I don't think we will be shifted from here. It is not a very big place only about thirty houses. The ground that we are camped on is all sand. We get a good lot of drill. It is very warm up here but there is plenty of water to keep us cool.

There were 29 Boer prisoners at the Station today, going up to Cape Town. They are queer looking people and very dirty and hungry looking. Some of them were wounded - one in 5 places (three times through the leg) one through the body and another in his arm.

We took 14 hours to come here. It was a very slow ride. It is all mountains and plains here, never anything else. There is not much vegetation to be seen just sand and a rough sort of heather or scrub. The Railway is narrow gauge and it takes some curious turns going up the mountains. I don't know where the river is - you can only find a pool of stagnant water every here and there. There are still hundreds of troops going up the country and train loads go past everyday.

Things are very dear out here. For a tin of syrup we pay 9d, 2/- per pound of cheese, 2/6d for butter and beer 1/- a bottle, so we can't speculate largely in luxuries.

We get very rough meat now - we have tea or coffee and about 1 pound of bread for breakfast; for dinner we get beef and potatoes but it is very rough, then for supper bread and tea. We don't get any butter now. We will know what a good feed of ham and eggs is when we get them again.

We are all enjoying ourselves however. If they would send us a bit farther up we would like it better but we are at the best station in the line for a healthy place so we can't complain. We will very likely be back about the month of June or maybe sooner. There are plenty of hares in the hills here and dogs of all sorts, which stay about the camp, and when we go out for a march about 50 follow us.

All our men are well and roughing it not so bad but if we have to stay here I doubt we shall get tired of it.

I saw a fellow at the Cape called Russell. His father has a farm near Wigtown. He used to be in Davidson's the Ironmongers shop in Newton Stewart.

I see by the papers that there has been a big snow storm at home. As I am writing this letter there is a sandstorm going on enough to blind anybody.

We had a gentleman named Logan down here from Kimberley yesterday. He belongs to Hawick. He stood every man a pint of beer or a lemonade, one pound of cheese and a loaf.

Our Lieutenant is Stoddart of Berwick and he is very popular".

The following **letter from Corporal Andrew Murdoch** of the New Galloway Company of the Galloway Rifle volunteers.

Touws River Camp, 17th March, 1900.

"Dear father, mother, sister, and wee Clyde, - just a few lines to let you know that I am well, hoping this letter will find you all well. We left Cape Town on Tuesday, the 12th, about half past six in the morning, and arrived here at three in the morning. We slept in the carriages till daylight, when we marched up and pitched camp above the village. It is not a big place, and the inhabitants are nearly all black people. We are in the enemy's country now, and we are not far off them. We can hear the big guns firing every now and again. We are on the lines of communication here, and there are about two hundred Boer farmers in the neighbourhood. They have been getting news from the others that they are beating the British, and they are like to raise a disturbance. We have sentinels all round the hills, and we can see their fires at night. We are guarding the railway and go about in twos.

I enjoyed my journey very much coming here, and saw grapes and melons growing wild everywhere. We get any amount of them, and some of us have been bad with eating too many. I saw ten ostriches; big birds they were too. Every station we stopped at was crowded with people, who shouted, 'Scotchmen good fighter. Englishman not'. The meat we get here is 'bully beef' and biscuits, which are very hard. The Captain has just been telling us that Bloemfontein has been taken by the British. We hear that the Free Staters have surrendered to Lord Roberts and given up the keys. We scarcely ever see a paper.

There is a man here from Berwick who has a big store. He is a millionaire, and is going to give every man a pound of cheese and bread. He is in Bloemfontein.

There are plenty of snakes here, which are very dangerous. We killed one this morning in camp. We can also get any number of tortoises running about. The weather is very hot - 102 degrees.

I have wearied very much not getting a letter from home, and all the rest of our men getting them. It makes me think there is something wrong, as this is my third letter since leaving Southampton.

A hundred men are leaving here today for Durban. I like this place very much. We go down to the village at night to see the natives dancing. It is a funny way they do it, and I like seeing it. I am going to get a collection of flowers that grow here. We are on half rations today. We are often on that, and have to buy a lot of meat for ourselves. We are two hundred miles from Cape Town. When you write you might tell me if you have to pay anything for the letters I send to you. Some of our fellows are away on the top of a hill just now to have a look round, and I am going up also when I have finished writing to try and get a tortoise. There are a lot of them on the hill. I forgot to mention that we are expecting an order to go and reinforce our regiment. Now I think I will stop, as I have no more news.

You might give my best respects to all my old friends. Don't forget to tell John Hoyle and some more of the old people. Hoping this letter will find you all well, not forgetting wee Clyde. Tell him I am going to get a tortoise for a pet when I come home. You might tell sergeant Grierson that we all wish that he was here. Caldow has got on for military Police here. It is a fine job, and he misses every drill.

I remain yours affectionately.   Andy."

Letter from Private W. Caldow, 'E' Company Galloway Rifles, New Galloway to Captain Timms of 'E' Company.

Touws River Camp 17th March, 1900.

"I send you a few lines to let you know where we are and how we are getting on. We arrived at Cape Town on the 9th (March) and had a very good passage except in the Bay of Biscay which was pretty rough.

We camped 4 days at the Cape and then were sent on here. It is a very important Station being one of the principal water supplies in this part of the country, as the engines all draw water here and if the enemy got the pipes cut it would stop the traffic on the line for 300 miles. We guard the reservoir and railway station and a Company of mounted men guard the pipes right up to the source. There is also a battery of Cape Artillery here so we have a pretty strong camp. There are soldiers all along the line, as every bridge and station has to be guarded. This place is about 200 miles from Cape Town and over 300 miles from De Aar.

The Country is very wild and dotted all over with hills or Kopjes (as they call them here), some of them are very high and rugged. The plains are all sand and not very nice when a gust of wind comes. There are not many white people here except at the Railway Station and the Kaffirs are all against the Boers, but of course you can't talk to them as they don't know English. There are also a lot of Dutch and we have to watch them as they are not to be trusted.

We had to clean all round our camps as there are lots of Snakes and scorpions crawling about.

Cochrane is left at the Cape to look after our baggage and stores.

We hear very little of the war and seldom see a paper.

I saw the big gun they took from Cronje lying at Cape Town and there are a few thousand Boer prisoners there.

I have been put on to the Military Police here so I don't turn out to any parades. It is not a very nice job as there is a canteen in Camp and a public house not far off. No one is allowed near our Camp and the natives are not allowed to drink or mix up with the soldiers, of course it is no use speaking to them and you have just to move them about the best way you can. I don't know how long we may be here but it is thought that the war may be finished in 2 or 3 months, but of course no one knows.

It is very hot here in the day but gets cooler at night. We keep very well but are rather tired of bully beef and hard biscuits."

Letter from Corporal James Henderson, Maxwellton Company Galloway Rifle Volunteers, to his father.

Touws River Railway Station, 27th March, 1900.

"After disembarking at Capetown we were under canvas there at Green Point from the Friday to the Tuesday morning, and we were all pleased to get away from it. Sand Point Camp is the name that would suit it better, as everything was sand and everything was full of it, including our food. Coffee and dry bread for breakfast full of sand, bully beef and biscuits for dinner with sand for dessert. Black tea and dry bread for supper again full of sand. As a change we get fresh meat and soup for dinner sometimes, which was a grand change. The camp ground was very large, and can easily hold the 15,000 troops of all sorts, and acres of ground left for recreation.

From our camp here we had to walk about three quarters of a mile to get a wash. All kinds and conditions of troops were there and thousands of mules and horses. It was a sight to see the animals returning at night and going away to work in the morning. They were let loose, and then follow the leader with mounted Indian Lancers from Madras, Kaffirs and Colonials with long whips lashing them on the trot or gallop. It was a wonder none of the people in the road were hurt, or that any of the tram cars did not run into the herds.

On leaving Capetown we were supposed to be going to join our regiment, but as a matter of fact nobody knew our destination - neither our Officers nor the railway staff, not even the driver of the train - as every movement of troops is kept secret. All our kit was taken from us except those things necessary - waterproof sheet, blanket, overcoat etc. we could not even take a change of underclothing. All along the line, at bridges, crossings, stations, etc., troops were stationed. Miles from anywhere we would pass one or two sentries on a lonely sentry-go guarding a bridge or anything important, and often in the distance we caught sight of mounted men doing patrol, and often they had big guns with them. We were congratulating ourselves at being sent on past so many thousands of men doing such hard and lonely work, and were beginning to see use for the 100 rounds of ammunition that every man Jack of us carried, and with minds made up that in a short time we would be in the thick of the fighting. All in our train load - 500 men - were in the gayest of spirits. It is little wonder to me now why a little of the British Army goes a long way. All along the lines the enthusiasm was unbounded. whether regulars or Volunteers, everyone seemed determined on one point, to uphold the supremacy of the old flag. Even the quietest men in our company could not keep a hold of themselves, and to sit quietly in a corner and watch the men's faces was an experience not easily forgotten. I felt proud - indeed we all felt proud - that at last we would play a part in the large fighting machine and do something for the old country's sake. I firmly believe, from what I see, that the spirit of the British soldier is as grand today as ever it was. The men can't help themselves, it is there and must come out.

At Worcester we received our orders to detrain at this place, Touws River, about 200 miles from Capetown. There were stationed here a company of the Duke of Edinburghs' Own and two batteries of Artillery. Before pitching the tents the ground had to be cleared of the scrub and large stones. It was hard work in the sun, and all were glad when it was finished.

This is one of the most important points on the whole line. There are large water tanks here. Our camp is place alongside of them. water is brought to them as far as seven miles distant, from among the hills, and the pipe track is patrolled day and night by mounted men of the Dukes' Own. A squad of them leave camp in the morning and evening, and meet another patrol half-way, where they report to each other and then return. The patrol that leaves in the evening returns in the morning and so on. This place supplies the railway with water for 400 miles; so that will give you some idea of its importance.

Two days after we arrived here I was appointed railway station orderly corporal. It is a fair job, and certainly much more pleasant than being in camp. I have no drills or route marches to do; but I don't get much sleep at nights, so I have to make it up during the day. Some nights I don't get to sleep at all. My duties are to board all troop trains passing through, get from the officer commanding the train the number of men on board, in case of transport trains the number of horses and mules; see that the station is clear when ambulance trains pass; see that a sufficient guard is provided to keep people from speaking to Boer prisoners; to inquire where all men and animals require to be fed; and in all cases to wire information to Wellington on one side and Majestfontein on the other. I have had as many as eight troops trains, passing in a single night, and it would surprise you all if I told the exact number of officers, men, horses and mules that have passed through toward Kimberley this last week. Since I was appointed to this job fully 400 Boer prisoners have passed through my hands, you may say. Some of them are most intelligent men, but the majority look a funny crew. They are all sick of the war, and with reason, for I saw one chap lying among a crowd who had five bullets in his body. The Commanding Officer of the Scottish Rifles, who passed through this morning, said to me that Lord Roberts is to pass en route for Capetown tonight.

Most of the Officers are very nice, but there are some grumpy ones, who get up and swear at me for raising them out of their sleep. Captain Haddon tells me that probably we will strike camp on Thursday for a long march, as there are 3,000 rebels in the district. I know that there is a large body of men concentrating at Majestfontein, two hours ride from here, for the purpose of quieting the rebels. We are all hoping the news will be true.

You will be pleased to know my general health has been good Since arriving here. I was troubled lately with a bad throat and a severe cold, through sleeping out one or two nights at Green Point, but I am all right now. This job is spoiling me for any forced march we may have, as I am getting positively fat. The rest of the men are on half rations, but through the kindness of some of the people especially a Scotch woman whose husband is a guard on the railway, I have always more than sufficient. The schoolmaster Mr. Phillips, is also very kind. He gives me books to read, and tomatoes, grapes, and different things from his garden. The only things that trouble me are the mosquitoes. They are something awful down here at the station, and strange to say there is not one in the camp. I am bitten all over, face and hands especially, and have tried all kinds of tricks to prevent them, as it is only or mostly at night time they bite. My room seems full of them. I generally sleep with a pair of sox drawn over my hands and my head and face tied in a towel, but last night, Mr. Phillips, gave me some paraffin oil, which I rubbed all over my hands, arms, face and neck. It is a grand preventative, though somewhat disagreeable.

Angus Thom is in hospital with dysentery; also a few others in the company. Thom is nearly better again, and all the rest of the Dumfries and Maxwellton men are at present in good health. We hear very little about the war except from those coming down here, but I expect to be home by July.

P.S. Since writing the main part of my letter, I have it that 3,000 rebels at Calvania, have all handed in their arms, but on the day before yesterday a party 100 strong were seen on the mountains about ten miles from here."

Letter from Cyclist Peter Birrell to his brother Adam Birrell, Anchorlea, Carsluith. Received 4th June, 1900.

Brandfort, Orange Free State. 7th May, 1900.

"We are now fairly at the front. Since writing last we have had a wearisome journey but we have all kept up to it, and hope to do so till the end.

The British only occupied this place last Friday and there are still a lot of dead Boers lying unburied among the hills - at least, they say so, but as we only arrived this morning, I can't be sure as we hear so many queer things.

What I said in one of my letters about Touws River supplying the water for 300 miles was wrong, as I saw for myself that they can get it at nearly every station.

I will now give you a note of our journey here;

May 3rd.

Struck tents at 3 o'clock and all aboard the train by 4. Left Touws River at 5 and had our supper at Matjersfontein, at 8.30; then went to bed, and slept in the top berth most of the way.

May 4th.

Awoke at daybreak this morning, everybody passed a pleasant night, especially McKie of New Galloway, who slept on the floor.

We passed through a vast cloud of locusts on our way and also saw any quantity of ostriches. They go about in pairs and coveys of about fifty.

Our first important stop today was Beaufort West, about 350 miles from Cape Town. Had our breakfast there; got one pound of Bully Beef, four biscuits and some coffee, supposed to do us all day.

Grand scenery now - level ground, with big hills rising here and there, all shapes and sizes, some as level as the top of a table; others rugged and very wild looking. Beaufort West is a nice place but having been at Touws River so long perhaps makes us think so. The next stopping place was Victoria West. It is not a large place. Arrived at De Aar about 8 o'clock. Being dark we didn't see much of the place. We got some tea here and went to bed.

May 5th.

When I awoke this morning we were lying at Nauport. We arrived at Colesberg Junction about 9 o'clock. We are now fairly in the district where there has been a lot of fighting. It was here the Suffolk Regiment was cut up, 36 of them being buried close by. All the bridges we pass now have been blown up, they are still busy repairing some of them. The telegraph poles have been torn down and the wire fences along the railway are scattered all over the place. Nearly all the farmhouses are deserted, and the remains of. horses lying unburied speaks of fighting having taken place. It is now ten o'clock and no signs of breakfast. Just crossed a bridge that has got an awful smashing, parts of the old one lying all around; Masons etc., dressing stones for the new one.

Arrived at Norval's Pont and got our breakfast at 12 first meal we have got today. About half a mile north of Norval's Pont is the Orange River, the bridge across it was destroyed by the Boers, 100 yards in the centre being blown clean away. Its entire length is 480 yards. They have it nearly completed again. We crossed the river on a bridge made of sleepers, and made fast with wire ropes to the stumps of the old bridge. Further up was a pontoon lying high and dry, which I suspect would be used to convey troops across. There are a lot of workmen and soldiers engaged at the bridge.

The Orange River looked fine with trees on each side of it. The line of the Boer retreat could be traced with dead horses and broken down wire fences.

Our next stop was at Springfontein about 90 miles from Bloemfontein. It is a very busy station. We had to wait four hours for our train to start again and being nearly dark when we left, I didn't see much of the locality.

May 6th.

Arrived at Bloemfontein at one o'clock this morning. Didn't get anything to eat till 12. Lot of ambulance waggons always at the station, waiting for the sick and wounded. I saw four dead soldiers carried on a stretcher to the churchyard.

We will have to sleep in our blankets tonight in the open, for our tents are laid past in the store. Bloemfontein looks alright, but has a very deserted appearance. Troops camped for miles around it. We have to leave early in the morning for the front.

May 7th.

Paraded at 3 o'clock this morning. Had breakfast at the station, then started again, this time in a waggon truck on the top of a load of rails. Large bridge over the Modder blown away. Passed Karree siding, where the K.O.S.B. had so many killed and wounded. They are buried close to the railway. The country is all level around here, except an odd hill.

Arrived at Brandfort, which the British occupied last week and de-trained. The railway is open 10 miles farther. There are 200 Boers lying unburied in the hills. We hear the British are driving the enemy before them. They say it will not last three weeks now. I am writing in a hurry as we don't know when we start again and it may be some time before I get another chance. This is a rough life but I hope to weather it and do my bit with the rest and come home again to the old place. Give my respects to all my friends. I cannot write to many people now, for I have no time."

The following **letter written by Private W. Caldow,** Lauriston, 'E' Company, (New Galloway) Galloway Rifle Volunteers.

Brandfort, May, 8th, 1900.

"We left Touws River on Thursday last, 3rd May, arrived at Bloemfontein on Sunday morning - 60 hours ride and in open waggons, so you may guess what it was like. We came by De Aar, Colesberg and Springfontein. We crossed the Orange River at Norval's Pont, on a temporary bridge and saw the large Iron Bridge which the Boers blew up. It was a total wreck, as in fact were all the bridges right up to here, but the engineers are not long in putting them right again.

I enjoyed the journey and saw many fine sights. We saw hundreds of ostriches and went through clouds of locusts. We only stayed one day at Bloemfontein and had to lie on the ground as we have no tents, having left everything behind except what we carry on our back.

We left Bloemfontein at 3 o'clock in the morning, again in open trucks and it was very cold until the sun got up. We passed Karree battlefield where the 25th got cut up and saw lieutenant Young's grave. Crossed the Modder river on a temporary bridge at Glen, where the large bridge was wrecked. Arrived at Brandfort on Monday morning just after the fight so I may say we are really at the front now as the fighting lines are only 10 miles ahead of us. This place has been greatly damaged, but the Boers fled in all directions, leaving about 200 dead. The Argyll and Sutherland Militia had to bury them. There are lots of dead horses scattered about. We got one gun disabled which is lying here.

General French's flying column went through here today. It was a fine sight - about 10,000 cavalry, with 30 big guns, all his baggage. The column was several miles long. I saw General French a fine looking man, said to be the best cavalry General in the world.

Lord Roberts is driving everything before him now. It is said the war will be over after the next great fight at the Vaal River and I hope it will be the case as I am getting pretty well tired of it, although we have not been in action.

I have seen some of all the British Regiments now and my opinion is that the New Zealanders are the finest body of men at the front. We are to form the guard for a convoy of stores and ammunition for the front. It will be 2 or 3 miles long and will consist of large waggons each drawn by 16 fine oxen. It will be a responsible and dangerous job but we will trust in Providence and do our best.

I am keeping pretty well in health, but the food is some thing awful - nothing but bully beef and biscuits as hard as oil-cake. Don't be alarmed if you should not hear from me for a while as when on the march we have no opportunity for posting letters."

Letter from Cyclist Peter Birrell, 'D' Company Galloway Rifle Volunteers.

Kroonstad. Monday, May, 14th

"Arrived last night at Kroonstad after a very long tiresome march from Brandfort. We were guarding an ammunition supply convoy. Left Brandfort on Tuesday evening at 4 o'clock and arrived last night at 10

o'clock having covered 70 miles. The bullocks can only do about two miles an hour on an average, so you will see what sort of a march it was. We got next to no sleep - about 3 hours in the 24. Arrived at Vet River about 9 o'clock on the 8th very tired, having done about 20 miles. Vet River is a very dirty place - full of dead horses and mules. Arrived at Small Deel late. Wynberg Junction on the 9th. Lots of houses are deserted, but there is nothing left in them.

Commandeering commenced today (10th). Seeing a flock of sheep, nearly everybody went for one; we took about 20. Arrived Zaand's River at 5 and had our coffee and biscuits. The sheep we had commandeered were taken from us, so we had to go without our mutton after all.

Kroonstad should have made a good place for a stand by the Boers but they all fled on the approach of French's cavalry.

The country is level till within 3 miles of Kroonstad, then there is plenty of cover, but the Boers are said to have fled before the first gun was fired. Kroonstad is not a very big place."

Letter from Cyclist Peter Birrell, 'D' Company Galloway Rifle Volunteers .

Kroonstad. May, 17th, 1900.

"We have joined our Regiment here, and will most likely be in the next advance, but the Boers are not likely to make a stand. They had a splendid position here but fled on the approach of the British and there are lots of them laying down their arms.

The next stand will be at the Vaal River, 70 miles from here, if they do fight; but experts say that they are past fighting and that the war will be finished in a month.

They have destroyed the bridge over the river here and the whole 7th Division are busy making a new one. There is some talk of the K.O.S.B. being left here for garrison duty. Roberts, wont allow infantry to advance any nearer to an enemy's position, than 1,000 yards, he believes in doing it with artillery and cavalry.

French is the boy for them. He is away on a forced march of two days just now, so we are expecting to hear something soon. Some say it is to relieve Buller who has got into a corner, others say that he has gone to cut off the retreat of the enemy, whom Buller is driving before him. We only get three biscuits a day now, but we are getting some fresh meat and vegetables for dinner.

The convoys keep coming and going in a constant stream; but we expect the railway here next week, so we may have letters and papers again soon. I am getting tired of the war and wish it was all over, but mean to hang it out till the finish, which can't be long now.

We got a great reception when we arrived here. The pipers turned out and played us into the camp, the tune being 'Oh but you've been lang a comin' and the cheering was something grand. The Colonel then addressed us and said he had heard of our grand shooting powers and would give us a chance to show them, the first opportunity, and that if ever we saw a white flag we were to keep under cover and go for it, 'for', said he, if ever you show yourselves that's the time they go for you. Keep on firing until they come out and lay down their arms. He also advised us to look after our biscuits, for if we didn't we would soon get them stolen.

Our Regiment doesn't like the C.I.V. (City of London Imperial Volunteers) it was they that led them into a trap at Karree siding. They were out scouting and reported everything clear and when our men went forward they were fairly cut up. At Paarddeberg where they captured Cronje, the Buffs fired into them and the Lincoln's retreated in great confusion, the K.O.S.B. being the only Regiment that returned in order. They were advanced to within 400 yards of the Boer trenches without knowing it. Our men have a grand word for the Canadians and New Zealanders - they say they are the best men out here.
May 20th.

We have been busy repairing the railway all week. You have no idea how quick you can make a railway - They made one of nearly three miles last week. The Boers have made an awful hand of the bridges. We will likely make a move next week if the Boers do not give in before that."

Letter from Cyclist Peter Birrell 'D' Company Galloway Rifle Volunteers.

Johannesburg June, 2nd.

"Since writing you from Kroonstad I have seen a bit of life and what with forced marches and hunger we have been having a hard time. We were on half rations leaving Kroonstad but from the Vaal River to here we were on quarter rations and to make matters worse they served out a day's rations beforehand and, of

course, they went as soon as we got them, so we had just to starve for the remainder of the day and I can tell you it needed all our spirit to carry us through, but we are here now and getting three quarter rations.

It was a forced march from the Vaal owing to the Boers threatening to blow up the town and the Volunteers of the K.O.S.B. were the advance guard and firing line of the 7th Division, nearly all the time. At Johannesburg when we entered the Town, we were in such a hurry to get at the enemy that we left the Regiment behind, they not being able to keep up with us. We passed through the outskirts of the town and the British people nearly went mad with joy when they saw us. They gave us bread, and if we had been allowed to stop they would have given us any amount of meat and drink.

We are now General Robert's bodyguard, so you see, we are getting amongst the honours.

We had hard work on the maarch from Kroonstad. We started in the morning at 2.30am to parade for breakfast, then march at 5.15am and marched till 4pm covering about 20 miles. It was hard carrying our blankets etc., and 100 rounds of ammunition, 2 days rations and extras which we thought we needed. Lots of men fell out, and when the roll was called there were no less than 33 missing. They are awfully particular about men falling out for water, and any man caught at it generally gets 14 days fatigues.

We were on outpost duty this morning - all the Volunteers and were on till 11 o'clock, when we got orders to get ready to march through the town and past Lord Roberts. We had the honour of leading the 7th Division. It was a grand sight and the people did cheer. It made one feel that their hardships had not been in vain. The black folk fairly clapped with joy and all were shouting 'Welcome' 'God Save the Queen'. When we marched past Roberts we gave him a ringing cheer. Johannesburg is a lovely place."

Letter from Corporal James Henderson, Maxwellton company, Galloway Rifle Volunteers, to his father.

"After my last note was written at Johannesburg we left that place on the last lap of our long march on Sunday morning, 3rd June. We marched all that day, camped at night, and then off again next morning at daybreak. We marched all that day up till one o'clock; we were escort to the big guns, and came into action half and hour after they left us to take up their position on the kopjes. Our Company and 'C' Company were extended and thrown into the firing line, and advanced 200 yards over the top of the hill. We halted and were ordered to lie down, and almost directly the first bullet landed and struck the ground 10 paces directly in front of me. A good few more came over our heads. Then we advanced another 300 yards and lay down. While there we received our proper baptism of fire, and I must say the men behaved splendidly. After the first few had gone over our heads or struck the ground near us not the slightest heed was paid them, although I must confess I was expecting to be struck every minute. However, the nearest one struck within two feet of where Nichol and I were sitting, just beside his rifle. The Artillery were on our right front and left shelling the kopjes in front, and it is a long time since I have enjoyed anything like the splended practice made by our gunners. Every shell went so true and burst so splendidly that made it most enjoyable to watch. No wonder the artillery are called 'Tommy's friends', for believe me, they can clear the ground in front while the infantry are advancing. After seeing the splendid practice made by our battery that afternoon, it is hard to believe the tales of the inability of the British Artillery.

After the kopjes had been well shelled we were ordered to advance in long extended lines; but we met with no further opposition as it turned out. We climbed one kopje, then a much higher one behind it, and got on top just as it was getting dark. After a short rest, I was detailed to take 12 men on oupost duty to guard against attack, and it turned out as I expected it would, the worst night I have ever spent. We were posted behind, or rather on the face, below the skyline of the highest peak we advanced over, and facing Pretoria. The ground was devoid of any vegetation and was covered with large rough stones. No fires were allowed and we couldn't even get water, so we had to content ourselves with what biscuits we had and believe me, they were scarce, to take up our posts and watch and wait for daybreak. Our lucky star seemed to have completely deserted us that night, for it proved the coldest we have so far experienced and our greatcoats being in the baggage and it far behind, our only protection was the single blanket each man carried. After the storm came the sun. Men would do well to always keep this in mind. It would help them and comfort them in many a trouble, although I confess it is often long in rising yet, nevertheless, it is bound to sooner or later.

Well the next morning witnessed the fall of Pretoria, and the gallant K.O.S.B. had the honour of being the first full infantry regiment to enter, and our Volunteer Company the first of the Volunteers serving in South Africa. Exactly a week before we had the same honour at Johannesburg, as we were the first company of the regiment and the regiment the first of the 14th Brigade, and the Galloway Section the first section of the regiment (fitting position for the representatives of a gallant Volunteer regiment), to enter that town in the proper manner. But the truth is that our Volunteer company were the first British infantrymen to enter. This they did the night before, but it might have been a disaster instead of turning out as it did. However, 'All's well that ends well'. Yet as it turned out, Captain Haddon and his men, if he had not been stopped, would have taken one of the forts 16 hours before it came into British possession. The story is too long to write just now but it is a fact.

Since entering Pretoria we have been exceedingly hard worked, doing guard and picket. I have done 32 hours of duty at a stretch, and ill with fever (enteric) at that. I am thankful to say I am almost all right again, as it is one of the most miserable times of a man's life to be ill on active service. Further details I will leave for a longer letter I intend writing. I wish to goodness I had an idea when we will be sent home."

Letter from Peter Birrell 'D' Company Galloway Rifle Volunteers.

Pretoria. June 6th, 1900.

"Since writing from Johannesburg we have marched into the great Pretoria, over which so much blood has been shed to reach. We marched about 15 miles the first day without seeing the least trace of the Boers, but the next day about one, we came upon them, and the fun commenced. They were strongly entrenched in the hills around the town - about a mile of their position under the cover of our guns, which were now shelling them; and when the firing commenced it was simply grand - the boom of our big guns and the magnificent sight when the shells exploded on the hills; the continued pom-pom; the whirr of the Maxims and the rattle of our rifles being simply deafening.

My first impression of being under fire was just a little excitement, such as one feels at the start of a bicycle race or a football match - one wants to win, and then the excitement wears off and one gets quite cool. The bullets dropping around us kept us from dozing off.

When the first one arrived one of our fellows said 'What's that', the Colour Sergeant looked round quite cool and said 'It's a bullet, I think'. The firing kept up till 4 o'clock when the Boers left their position our fire being too hot for them. We then advanced in extended order and took the position. We were on the hill all night and with want of meat and water we were pretty well played out. When daylight broke we could see the great Pretoria. We were sure we would be in for a great fight today, but no 'Hurrah', the town had surrendered and Pretoria with all its great forts - where the Boers were going to make their grand stand was in our hands.

We marched through Pretoria past the racecourse, where our soldiers were kept prisoners. There are some of them there yet. We took up our position at the Railway Station. Our casualties in the fight were two K.O.S.B. wounded - one shot through the leg and the other through the stomach.

The town was very quiet with the exception of the Grand Hotel, where there seemed to be a lot of British Officers enjoying themselves by the amount of singing that was going on. I hear we are to stay here, they are wanting some of our fellows to join the mounted infantry, so they will be following up the Boers with mounted men.

June 8th. Pretoria.

We are now shifted from the station to the cricket ground. It is a lovely place, and we are very comfortable here, but we look a lot of queer customers - our clothes are just hanging together and no more, and some have not shaved since we left Vaal River. I hear we were the first Regiment to enter Pretoria, and the first Volunteers, so I tell you we pushed ourselves well forward. We are a lucky lot. We have been under fire, and first into Pretoria. Something for the K.O.S.B. Volunteers to boast about I think.

June 12th. Pretoria.

We are now on guard at Pretoria jail. That is where Dr. Jim and his Officers were imprisoned. There are all sorts of prisoners here, Boers, Kaffirs, etc., some are in for life. They are having a good time now. The Kaffirs are in high glee on account of the Boers getting licked. The racecourse is a large place all fenced round with barbed wire. There would be no chance of getting out of there. Such a tangle, I never saw before, 6' high and about 10 feet in width, warped this way and that, you would wonder how they get the idea to do it. We Volunteers have to do our share with the Regulars, somehow I think we do more.

June 17th. Pretoria.

I am on guard duty nearly every other day now. Was guard at Kruger's house last night. It is a very small place for a President to live in. Mrs. Kruger is there with her daughters and Mrs. Eloff. We were down as a guard of honour and our duty was to allow no one to loiter near the house, or to enter it without writing their name down. This we delivered to a servant, who in turn, delivered it to the old lady, and then she sent word whether she would receive them or not. She keeps the blinds of the house down. Once when I was on duty she ventured to have a peep out but the sight of a British Soldier was too much for her and she quickly put it down once again. The house is about 28 yards long and 10 feet high, with raised windows at either end and roofed with galvanized iron. Mrs. Kruger's bodyguard consists of six old men, veterans I think, who wander about at their leisure. They seem to be disgusted with our soldiers being here, but we only laugh at them.

I was no sooner off guard here than I was sent away to the station on fatigue duty. Whilst there I thought I saw a face I recognised in the Scots Greys (who were also there), so I spoke to him and just as I thought it was Downie of Gatehouse. The last time I saw him was at Gatehouse sports and I little thought then that the next time I saw him would be in Pretoria. He looked all right. He told me Douglas Glover of Gatehouse was also in Pretoria, he having been a prisoner, and is now on the Police Force here.

I will say nothing about the war as you will know far more about it than us here. Our principal employment when off duty is cooking and we do a lot of it. There are only 5 passes a day allowed into the town, and whoever is lucky enough to go has to bring as much back as does the whole company.

Must close now but remain your ragged but happy brother.

Peter."

Note. This was the last letter written by Private Peter John Birrell. He was struck down by the enteric (typhoid) fever at Pretoria. He was to recover but did not return home to Carsluith until the 28th January, 1901.

Letter from Corporal Henderson, Maxwellton company of the Galloway Rifle Volunteers.

Pretoria.

"Our camp is surrounded on three sides with trees. They serve the double purpose of shading us from the sun during the day and protecting us from the wind at night. In front facing the open ground, oranges and lemons were growing abundantly. I say were, because the fruit didn't last long after we had camped. An excellent supply of water runs through the wood, but it is mostly used for washing and cooking, and condensed for drinking. Yet when coming up country we used water ten times worse and right glad to get it. So you see when amidst plenty we turn up our nose at what we would have considered a great blessing a fortnight ago, and as with water so with food stuffs. While on the march our food supply was very scarce, and our fresh meat was handed to us raw, and sometimes we were served with flour. It naturally followed that we had to do our own cooking, and many's the funny dish I have seen and tasted. The food supplied to us at present would be sufficient to keep you alive - a small loaf of bread per day, generally eaten for breakfast, and for dinner meat and soup, no vegetables. So to live at all we have to buy a lot. And things are most dear here at present. Sugar 9d and 1/- per lb; rice 6d; bread, per small loaf, white, 9d and 1/-; brown, 6d and 9d; tinned milk, 1/3d to 1/6d; eggs, 5/- per dozen; jam - English, 1/6d per lb.; colonial, 1/3d per lb; tinned salmon, herring, sprats, etc., 1/6d to 2/- per lb., tin; flour very scarce and dear, mealies, 3d per lb.; tobacco cheap, the Boer kind, but English manufacture very dear. So you see poor Tommy has to spend nearly all his pay in order to live."

The following **letter**, dated 31st July,1900, from **Corporal Henderson,** Maxwellton Company of the Galloway Rifles.

Pretoria.

"Had I not honestly thought I should have returned home again before today this country would never have seen me. I am heartily 'fed up', as the soldier says, and nobody will be so thankful when we return. I am in good health. It is with thankfulness and with a greatful heart to our Heavenly Father that I still experience the same great blessing, and never before have I realised what and how much there is to be thankful for in all the blessings bestowed upon me from day to day.

We returned to Pretoria yesterday, and are resting today outside the town previous to starting again tomorrow for another march - at least so rumour says, and to all appearances its is true. Altogether we were fifteen days out and the furthest point reached by us was Balmoral, reaching and taking that place on Wednesday, 25th July. In my last letter I mentioned the peculiar way we were going, but it will be better illustrated by saying it took ten days' marching to get there, and five fairly easy days, owing to the transport animals beIng done up, to return. From the first day it was evident we had no fixed destination. Our orders appeared to move in whatever direction the enemy took. Many an oath was sworn and many a desire was expressed that our foes would stand and fight, and if they had, and the men had got at them properly, there wonld have been a deal of bloodshed. I have never known men so unanimous on a point in my life. Every man in the column is honestly tired and wearying to be home.

On Friday, the 20th, we camped in a valley after a stiff march, and generally, if I feel fit, my first road after taking off my straps is to make for firewood and water. Going along that night with one of my mates some mounted men told us about an orange grove half a mile away. Our tiredness vanished in a minute and off we went at the double, and found about twelve fine trees literally hanging with splendid fruit. I was up one of those trees in a twinkling, and soon my mates below had as many as they could carry. Very soon the place was crowded with soldiers, and there seemed to be plenty for everyone. The owner was powerless, he could only beg the men not to break the trees.

There is no doubt General Ian Hamilton has different ideas of how the disloyal Dutch should be treated than has Lord Roberts. When marching from Bloemfontein the orders against looting were so strict that one dare not even look at a garden or cultivated field, let alone enter it, even though we were practically starving on half rations, while under Hamilton the officers are nearly as bad as the men.

The same night some of our chaps found a Boer lying in the burn from where we get water, evidently sick and abandoned by his friends. He was brought into camp, and judging by his face was nearly frightened to death. A few more were brought in, and next morning they looked all right again.

On Saturday, 21st our regiment was rear guard, and the first salute we got when ready to march off was a shell whistling over our heads, quickly followed by another. I ventured the opinion that they were our guns that were firing they seemed so near, and got laughed at, but I never dreamt our outposts could allow a gun to be mounted so near the camp. The first shell struck the ground where the Argyll and Sutherland Highlanders had just left, and killed a nigger and four mules, the second going among the ambulance waggons. It was pitiful to see the poor invalids limp along to shelter, and to see what were supposed to be civilised men firing on crippled fellow-creatures. Half of the regiment (our company included) was immediately extended to cover the baggage and convoy pushing on out of danger, and the business like manner in which the heavy and clumsy vehicles, with their long span of cattle, were got along, gave one the impression that nothing unusual was going on. The Elswick Volunteer Artillery and the Canadian Artillery soon put the Boers to silence, and everything and everybody was soon out of any danger for the time being. At the first rest I had a chat with some of the Canadians, and they were greatly pleased at having at last got firing. All went well until we halted at midday. Ours was the only company with the tail end of the convoy, and without warning shell after shell came amongst us, but I believe during the whole bombardment only one shell burst. everybody escaped, but that was more owing to the nature of the ground, which being soft the enemy could not see where the shells were striking, as they all buried themselves in the ground. I tried to dig three different ones out, but could not get at them, so deep were they. Bullets are nothing in comparison with shells. All our felloes stood up excellently, never flinching, but probably, like me, were anxious to get to cover, although no one showed the slightest haste or desire. The excellent behaviour of the men only goes further to prove to my mind what I have all along said, that Volunteers under fire are as good men as the regular soldiers. There is not the slightest reason why they should not be. Although Volunteers are not so well drilled or disciplined as the regulars, that is the fault of the system and not of the men. I am certain the same applies to all Volunteers in the old Country, for if the representatives of the forces now in South Africa can behave well, why not the remainder? So you see the Volunteers are not such fireside soldiers as some would make out.

Two days later we marched into Brokerhurst Spruit, the place where the 94th regiment got cut up in 1881. It was expected we would be able to hem in Botha there, but the wily General gave us the slip. Next morning we marched to Balmoral a distance of 8 miles, and arrived there drenched to the skin. It continued raining all night, a piercing cold wind blowing all the time, and add to that half rations and you can imagine our plight. It proved to be I believe, the worst night the troops have spent in South Africa. Our regiment, being in advance that day, took possession of the railway station, the other troops being a few miles behind. Owing to the state of the roads the baggage did not come up, so picture our misery. About 10 o'clock, along with some others, I left the ground to try and obtain shelter, and stayed half the night in a large hole or drain that ran through below a store. The officers slept in a stable among the horses, and the only ones who were comfortably housed were General Lord Roberts, Hamilton and their staff. As it is always the darkest before dawn, next morning we were ordered back, French having captured Middleburg. what a sight the return journey was as far as Brokerhurst Spruit'. The road was literally covered with dead and dying horses, mules and bullocks. One conductor said they lost 300 animals during the previous day, and according to appearances he was within the number. It was an awful night. I felt like shooting every Boer in cold blood to avenge the horrible sight, for if one thing touches me more than any other it is the sufferings of dumb animals. We reached Pretoria yesterday and are off again on the march tomorrow."

Note: Several men of the column died of exposure that night at Balmoral and a large number were found the next morning to be suffering from exhaustion and exposure. One man of the K.O.S.B. apparently driven to despair, by the conditions that night, attempted to 'blow his brains out'.

Letter from Corporal Henderson, Maxwellton Company Galloway Rifle Volunteers.

Commando Nek, 6th August, 1900.

"On 11th July, we received orders to march at once from Pretoria. The reason for our quick shift was that we had to go out and relieve part of the Lincoln Regiment and Scots Greys, who were in a tight corner in a sort of pass in the range of hills or kopjes that stretch to the south west of the town and a few miles nearer the town than where we are a present bivouacked. We marched off that afternoon, going at a high rate of speed, in fact, to help us along quicker some of our baggage waggons were used, and appreciated, doubtless, by those men who were lucky enough to get a lift. The pace continued until dusk, or about two miles past Zwart Spruit, where we halted and had a rest for about an hour. While resting we learned the true cause of our journey and the effects of the disaster that had occurred. It seems - but probably you know the story better than we do that, owing to someone having blundered as usual, the men who were supposed to be holding the position were surprised by the Boers while at breakfast and literally shot down, volley after volley being poured into them. Springing to their arms, they had defended themselves as best they could (and I learn they did so right manfully) until reinforcements could be brought to cover their retirement. As we didn't arrive until dusk, darkness proved to be their friend. Peering into the gloom, we saw them coming along, and when up to us we saw by the thinned ranks the terrible effect of the Boer sharpshooters, aided by neglect, and shall I say blundering? One officer asked us for biscuits or something to eat. Some of the men had neither strap, rifle, nor helmet on; some of the Greys were walking, having lost their horses, and all we spoke to had tales to tell of the terrible time they had experienced. When all had passed we got orders to retire also and marched back to Pretoria, arriving outside the town about 2am the following morning, having covered a total distance of, I reckon, thirty miles in twelve hours, including halts.

At daybreak we were standing to our arms, and after breakfast marched to Wonderboom Fort where we bivouacked from the Thursday to the Monday.

We then started to march again round about, until Balmoral was reached. Only three Companies of the Regiment (including ours) took part in the march I have mentioned. Since that time I have had occasion to have a chat with some old soldiers and reserve men on the subject. Most of them estimate the distance at over thirty miles, and they speak of it as the stiffest march they ever had. I don't wish to brag about it, but merely to bring out the point that Volunteers can also accomplish long and trying marches, showing as much pluck and endurance as their comrades of the regulars. It is simply wonderful the amount of real hard work that a man can stand, even thriving with it. Remembering the weight each man carries, our regiment especially - generally about 40, 45 and 50 lbs. - the men desereved great credit. Yet I consider it one of the scandals that no effort is made to get the weight reduced. Of course I am aware that sometlmes the weight, or part of it, proves a blessing.

On 31st July, there was a medical inspection of all the men, and every one whom the doctor thought had reason to complain (and believe me, a man has to be real bad) was sent into the town to the rest camp.

The strength of our company has now been reduced considerably, having lost since we landed, through death, disease, and sickness, a total of 33 men. The following is the respective strength of the four sections that comprise the Company; No.1 (Border Rifles), 21 men, lost 8; No.2 (Berwickshire Rifles), 21 men, lost 7; No.3 (Dumfriesshire Volunteers), 16 men, lost 2; No.4 (Galloway Rifles), 22 men, lost 6, including Hannah of Maxwellton, who is with the Army Service Corps. All the men except 2 dead, have merely dropped out for the time being, and will all return again as soon as we mobilise for home.

Next morning, August 1st, the same column, under Ian Hamilton, again marched off, accompanied by an extra large convoy. As we had been advance guard the day we entered Pretoria on our return, we were now the rear guard. Our route was along the road we had gone to relieve the Lincolns, direct south-west. The advance guard starts at the head of the column, usually about day-break, the others according to their respective places, the rearguard about three hours after the start. It is the position least wished for, as those who form the rearguard are last to reach camp and have to march mostly during the heat of the day. That morning before we had made a start the advance guard - or rather the artillery of it - were firing away merrily with pom pom machine guns and long range guns, but firing had ceased before we got on the march. The pace was slow all day, and it was almost dark before we reached camp, which was situated exactly opposite the pass where the Lincolns got the cutting up. On arriving we learned that three of the Argyll and Sutherland Highlanders had been shot while down washing at the water. Two of the snipers were eventually caught and brought into camp, and doubtless they were treated with the utmost courtesy and respect. Heaping coals of fire on the head of your enemy is very nice, and only right and Christian-like when practised in time of peace and in civil life, but it is applicable in war time? Generally speaking then between man and man it is not, else there could be no fighting, and evidently it is left to British Generals alone to practice in its entirety that command of our master.

During the day I learned from one of our officers that the column and convoy, or the majority of it, was to go to Rustenberg, where General Baden-Powell had got fixed in a tight corner, the object being to relieve him and take food to his men. Next morning every man was up and 'standing to' their arms at daybreak, but as no move was made it was evident something was afoot. About eight o'clock the Berkshire Regiment moved off from behind us, and were extended for the attack on the pass directly infront, while half of the Argyll and Sutherland Highlanders were sent on the left, the Border Regiment (or part of it) on the right, and ourselves on the left, to protect the convoy. The position held by the Boers lay between two large hills of the range I mentioned stretching to the south-west, and though it was considerably higher than the valley where we lay, the rise was gradual and plenty of cover was to be had among trees and bushes. A good road ran over the top and along the valley beyond.

(The letter was interrupted at this point).

9th August, a few miles from Commando Nek.

Our regiment is to start south again - rumour has it that we are going to cut off De Wet. Our food rations are much better on the march and we can catch the occasional pig or fowl. Two man of the Dumfriesshire Section and one of the Galloway men are going back to Pretoria with the hospital waggon."

The following **letter** received by Captain Timm of Slogarie from **Private W. Caldow** 'E' Company, New Galloway, Galloway Rifle Volunteers.

The Camp. Crocodile River, Near Pretoria. 8th August, 1900.

"I received your letter all right some time ago, also the tobacco and I assure you it was a treat and can only thank you very much for it. I would have written sooner but the day after I got your letter we had orders to move at once to the relief of the Lincolns as they were in a right place and surrounded by Boers. We left after dinner and marched on till dark intending to go to a place called Zeticote's Nek, but we met what was left of them about a couple of miles from the place coming back, as the enemy had charged them, and they were forced to retire, after losing a good lot of men. So we came back with them, and next morning moved in another direction to a Nek about 6 miles from the Town, thinking the Boers might come that way. We lay there two days, but saw nothing of them.

Then we got put into General Hamilton's column and sent as escort with a very large convoy of forage and provisions for General French, away in the Middleburg direction. We had a lot of mounted infantry with us as scouts, and the Argylls, Berks., Border Connaughts and K.O.S.B. formed the guard, with four batteries of artillery. Altogether the convoy would be about 5 miles long. We had many a skirmish with the enemy, but the 21st July, I will never forget, as they opened on us in the morning and shelled us the whole day. We had to cross a drift with all the waggons, and it was easily seen that they had the distance measured, as their shells were landing all around us, within 20 yards. Of course we replied with our guns, but it was not easy to find out their positions as the kopjes they were on were covered with brush, but their shells were nearly all bad - I only saw two burst. We only had one Kaffir driver and 6 mules killed the whole day. It makes you feel a bit queer hearing the shells whizzing over your head. We had a short halt at Brunker's Spruit, thinking we might get a go at them but they would not stand. Then we marched to a place called Balmoral, where we handed over the convoy to Generals French and Hunter, and we started back for Pretoria, coming a different direction. Of course our move was meant to hunt them about and get them cornered. We landed back in town after a 14 days march and I was not sorry, as it is a very hard job marching in hot weather, especially on the kind of feeding we get.

We were only one day in when another convoy was got ready. and again we started, this time going in the Rustenberg direction with supplies for General Baden Powell. We had to pass the place where the Lincolns got cut up and the Boers were still there. We put our big guns on to them, and the lyddite was not long in putting them out of their trenches. Then the infantry had a go at them. Our Regiment was not in the *firing line - we were lying back as support. The Argylls and Berks., engaged them, and after about 2 hours hard fighting they put them to flight and took their positions. There were 2 killed on our side and 34 wounded. The convoy then moved on and the K.O.S.B. was left to guard this place.*

There is a bridge here crossing the Crocodile River, also a pass through the mountains and we have plenty to do as we are either on guard on the bridge or outpost on the hills. There are some kopjes pretty high. The ones we were on last night I can compare to something like the Bennan, so you will have an idea what it is like to get to the top. We are on 24 hours at a time and through the day we are building trenches, in case of any attempt to retake the position. We know very little of what is going on in the war and I don't know how long we may be here but I hope in God it will not be long till the war is finally settled. We are having it very hot in the day time but cool at night."

Letter from Corporal James Henderson 'G' Company, Maxwellton, Galloway Rifle Volunteers.

3rd October 1900

"It was not until we had joined our Regiment at Kroonstad, on May 15th (1900), and then the fact stared us plainly in the face, that owing to short rations being served to the troops we must needs look elsewhere than to the Army Service Corps for extra food, for unless a man be well fed, no matter how plain the fare, it would be impossible to stand the fatigue of the long marches it was our lot to experience. My honest opinion regarding the terrible amount of men stricken with dysentery, enteric fever, and similar ailments is that it is directly owing to the scarcity of rations and the great stress the men put their digestive organs to when the chance of extra food comes their way. Semi-starvation and then a sudden 'burst-up', to use a soldiers's expression, has killed more men during the present campaign that the bullets of the Boers.

The regulars kindly taught us how to make simi lar snacks to theirs, but very soon the pupils became the teachers, and now more individual cooking goes on among the Volunteers proportionately than among the Regulars. Why this should be it is impossible to say, but nevertheless it is true, especially in our Regiment. When the different ingredients can be secured many a very creditable and tasty dish is made and relished by the different amateur chefs. But while on the march, or in a camp situated away from any town or village, the principal extra is porridge made from mealie meal, the chief fare of the coloured natives, a quantity of which nearly every man carries. The meal is made from maize (Indian corn crushed in a mill, and of the two kinds grown in this country the white is most sought after, the yellow kind being vastly inferior and much stronger tasted.

After our arrival at Belfast, on being sent to the practically isolated post on Colliery Hill, it soon became evident to the men that some means would have to be discovered whereby our food supply could be increased, as the rations served out to us were deemed insufficient to live on, never to speak of labouring with pick and shovel digging trenches all day.

A neighbouring farmer, described by a local gentleman as a Free Stater who was frightened to fight for his skin, was interviewed one day, and he confessed to having some potatoes and maize to sell, but said he had no means of conveying them to us from his farm, seven miles from camp. The Jew who kept the shop or store at the mine suggested to me that Mr. Crockett, a Scotchman who managed the mine, might lend me his Cape Cart and horses, especially as he stood in need of potatoes for himself, so that day I acted on the hint received and my request was kindly granted. Permission of our Captain had next to be obtained, and on putting the whole matter before him, and he knowing that the men really required anything that might be got, granted what was asked, although he would not listen to only two of us going, and insisted on an escort of twenty men, so the Galloway men were told off to be 'the raiders'.

Next morning we started off, Mr. Crockett and his son, a lad of about eight years, accompanying us as far as the mounted outpost on horseback. By the way this little chap filled everyone with admiration of his horsemanship. It was a perfect treat to see him sitting astride his big mare and galloping away across the veldt as fast as the animal could go. On reaching the outpost Mr. Crockett asked me, seeing he had obliged us, to oblige him by going along to a farm in the valley to buy him some fodder for his horses, so I took one of our chaps to drive back while we left his 'black boy' to cut the stuff and await our return.

The mistress of the place appeared scared at our approach, but on seeing we intended no harm became quite talkative, and told us to get as much as we wanted. She had no fowls or eggs, as General French's men had taken them all away, and she said, her husband, who had not been fighting, as he was in bad health, had gone away into the bush veldt with what was left of their live stock, which evidently served the double purpose of keeping them comparitively safe and getting them food. If the truth had been known, however, her husband would probably have been found rifle in hand and pass in pocket - what does a Boer care for breaking an Oath? - on the kopjes among more of his kind, a mile or so further on. Our outposts could see parties of the enemy every day, but they never came within range. It may seem strange to you that I should doubt the story, especially as she seemed a most intelligent person. Probably what she said may have been true, but one soon loses what faith they might have had for the Dutch after having had dealings with them. At first I had great admiration for them, but now I simply despise them, and honestly believe the Almighty never intended them to rule such a fruitful country as this, and will prove further to be after something more effectual has been done then the mere scratching of the surface.

Having left the niggers to cut the fodder, we returned to the escort, who had stayed with the outpost, and took a road running to the left, the machine keeping the road and the escort of raiders taking a short cut through among the rocks. The driver (Cochrane of New Galloway) and I being in the machine, behind a good pair of horses, we soon outdistanced them.

On coming in sight of the farm we were somewhat startled on observing an unusual number of horsemen about it. They were evidently just arriving, and through the glasses we could see they had two waggons with them, and our surmise that they might be our own men proved correct. As soon as they halted, from out behind an outhouse there dashed a horseman at full gallop coming in our direction, and when almost within range he wheeled sharply to the left and soon disappeared behind a kopje. I am convinced that had we cut him off, as was our first intention to try, we would have discovered him to be an adventurous Boer in search for extra food like ourselves.

The road was very bad indeed, rocks, ruts and deep holes abounding and it required no little skill on my mate's part to keep the horses safe and the machine from toppling over. We pulled up at a cot house, and on making our wants known as best we could we were told that there was absolutely nothing in or about the house in so emphatic a manner that made us think for the moment that the inmates were literally starving, yet every one looked as they usually do, healthy but dirty. It was the usual tale - no husband at home, he was a prisoner of war, large wife and small family.

It is most noticable among the Dutch that their woman folk are mostly large and very fat, this being considered, I have been told, the chief point of beauty.

By this time the raiders had come within sight of the housse, and on pointing them out and telling the woman to shut up her fowls, which she asked 4/- each for, also to take the three pigs to a place of safety, thereby getting into her good grace, she produced two chunks of bread, yellow in colour, for which we paid her 1/-. This would be at the rate of 2/6d per half-loaf at home. She next brought a small ham, about eight lbs. for which she asked the startling price of £3. On scanning her face not even a blush or the slightest sign appeared on the broad surface, so apparently the price was asked in all good faith. Latterly she brought it down to 15/-, as I intended it for the officers, who had asked me to bring something. I offered her 10/- but she would not come any lower.

When the whole party was complete, we moved on to the farm and found on arriving a large body of Canadian horsemen in possession, getting foodstuffs for the Army Service Corps. Their Colonel, a French Canadian gentleman, was most kind, and asked if we were not afraid to come with so small a party, and instructed the farmer to let us have anything we wanted of what he could spare .

Eventually we came away with two large sacks of mealie (£2) and a sack of potatoes, which cost 20/-, while the men themselves by commandeering added considerably to their private store such things as meal, eggs, and nutmegs, and everything they came across. At the cot house we got some fowls, cabbages and eggs for the officers, also the ham for the 10/- on condition that the remainder of the poultry were left alone.

Leaving the escort to find their own way back, my mate and I returned with the now fairly ladened machine to the outpost, and wasn't Mr. Crockett relieved to see us back safely, as he imagined the party at the farm house to be Boers, and had concluded, seeing we were so long away, we had been taken prisoners.

After going to the house in the valley for the forage and the boy, we set off for camp, when a nasty accident occurred, that gave me a fright. The potatoes were on the back of the machine, and I was sitting holding them secure with a strap. Mr. Crockett and his little boy were some distance behind on horseback, when suddenly the little chap's horse bolted, passing the machine at a fearful rate. Mr. Crockett, being on a faster horse, started away at the gallop, evidently with the intention to lead the runaway off, when his animal came down and threw him on the ground with an awful smash. Judging by the manner he had fallen, and being a man of fifteen stone, I made sure he had broken his neck, anyway you may imagine with what gratification I found on returning that, though he was unconcious, there were no bones broken. Cochrane drove him to his house, where he soon regained consciousness and had his bruises dressed, It was a marvellous escape.

The remainder of the raiders returned to camp, bringing in with them a few sheep, which supplied a most welcome addition to the company's larder.

Two days afterwards Captain Haddon informed me that our party just escaped being fired on by the Canadians, as we approached the farm, their Commander discovering only in time who we were.

The same week four Canadians went out to the farm on the same errand as ourselves, and two of them were shot dead - murdered - we believe - one wounded severely and left for dead, and one managed to escape. It was seventeen hours after the occurrence before the bodies were found with the wounded man lying beside them. It is not always right to hallo even when you are out of the wood, but it is probably just as well the party of Canadians were at the farm the same day as us, else we might have got into a nasty corner also. However all's well that ends well, the foodstuff brought in was much appreciated by everyone in the company and lasted until we moved from Colliery Hill to a more convenient place where extras more palatable to a soldier could be bought without any risk.

Pretoria, Wednesday, 10th October, 1900.

We returned here yesterday, where all the Volunteer Companies are to mobilise before proceeding to Capetown en-route for home. I am thankful to say my health is excellent, and naturally my spirits are high, for it can't be long now, if I am spared, until I am with you again."

The following **letter was written by Private James Pagan of Moffat**, a Volunteer of the Dumfriesshire Section of the Active Service Company of the K.O.S.B. on the journey from Pretoria to Cape Town, a week prior to their embarkation for home. The letter written to his parents at Holmend, makes reference to Private Luck Robertson, Holmend, Moffat, who was killed in a train accident at Biesjis Poort, on the 21st October, 1900. Private Robertson also formed as part of the Active Service Company of the K.O.S.B.

"We have arrived from Pretoria with a hundred and sixy prisoners from Barberton, on the frontier. We have travelled in the train for a week, and we had to travel all day and night from Norval's Pont......You will be sorry to hear that Luck is killed. He fell off a wagon.

One of the Boer prisoners got him out from the rails and brought him to our wagon, and a Dumfries chap and I rolled him up in a blanket, and we brought him down to Beaufort West, where he was to be buried....While coming down past Biesjis Poort on Sunday, 21st October, at 1.30pm, I was on guard, and I went out of the wagon on to a platform of a carriage before it stopped. Anderson joined me and sat down, but the platform was only a foot broad at the place where he was sitting, and Luck came out to. We had travelled about fifty miles before the accident happened, and he was speaking to Anderson about two minutes before. He was sitting with his right heel on the edge of the platform and his left foot against the other wagon. His foot slipped and he went down between the wagons before anyhody knew what had happened. The train was not going very fast at the time, and it stopped after four wagons had gone over him. He was not much cut, but he was crushed terribly.....In the wagons, there are a lot of rods and they caused the damage."

Corporal Henderson Galloway Rifle Volunteers, writing home from Green Point Camp, Capetown, on October, 31st, 1900.

"We are to leave South Africa tomorrow (Thursday), November, 1st by the S.S. Avondale Castle. All the Company are in the highest spirits, for naturally we are all pleased at the prospect of a speedy return. For the most part all of the men who have been in the hospitals and convalesant camps in different parts of the country have re-joined the Company, some of them not having been seen for months. There are still 2 or 3 in hospital however and will not return with us but come back as soon as fit."

LIST OF CAMPING GROUNDS.

The following are a list of camping grounds north of the Orange River at which the 1st Service Company encamped. Those marked with an asterisk (*) are those at or near where they saw fighting.

May   6th Bloemfontein.
7th, 8th Brandfort.
9th Vet River.
10th Smaldeel.
11th Virginia (Zand River).

12th Geneva Siding.
13th Kroonstad.
14th Name unknown.
15th, 21st Kroonstad.
22nd Honing Spruit.
23rd Rhenoster River.
24th Name unknown.
25th Leeuwendraai.
26th Taaibosch Spruit.
27th Lindequee's Drift (Vaal River).
28th Klip River.
29th Germiston (Johannesburg, S.E.).
*30th Johannesburg
31st, 2nd June Orange Grove, (Johannesburg, N.).
3rd Leeuwenkop.
*4th Six Mile Spruit.
5th, 10th July Pretoria.
11th Daspoort Nek.
12th, 15th Wonderboom.
*16th Waterval.
*17th Haman's Kraal.
18th Walmansthal.
*19th Boekenhout's Kloof.
*20th De Wagen Drift.
*21st Name unknown.
*22nd, 23rd Rustfontein.
24th Bronkhorstspruit Station.
25th Balmoral.
26th Eloff's Bridge.
27th Bronkhorstspruit.
28th Kaalfontein.
29th Christmen Hall.
*30th, 31st Daspoort.
*1st August Mosilikatse (Nitral's) Nek.
2nd, 8th Commando Nek.
9th, 10th Groot Plaatz.
*11th Bultfontein.
*12th Zeekoehoek (Nooitgedacht).
13th Geyferfontein (Blaauwbank).
*14th Zauvfontein.

The following **letter written by Lieutenant Colonel J.W. Godfrey,**
1st King's Own Scottish Borderers, to Sir R. Waldie Griffith, commanding the Border Rifles;

Pretoria, 19th November, 1900.

Dear Sir Richard,

I must write a line to thank you and the other commanding officers for sending us such a good lot as our Volunteer Company proved themselves to be, both officers and men.

In Captain Haddon they had a very able and zealous commander, and he was well backed up by his officers, especially by Lieutenant Stoddart, of whose abilities and zeal I have formed a high opinion.

I also cannot let Sergeant Scott go away without mentioning the good work he did. I always found him most zealous and reliable in whatever position he was placed.

I am sorry to say, for the sake of the regiment, that they (the Volunteers) have left it and are now on their way home. We all wish them as hearty a 'God speed and good luck' as we did when we welcomed them.

I am sure the fact of Volunteer Companies having been sent to join the regular battalions will do a lot of good to the territorial regiment generally. It has started a comradeship which, I feel sure will be lasting, and which will bring the different battalions of the regiment closer together.

Will you kindly pass this on to the other commanding officers. I would write to each separately, but I am now Assistant Adjutant General, 7th Division, Pretoria, where my time is more than fully occupied.

Yours Sincerely

J.W. Godfrey, Lieutenant Colonel, 1st K.O.S.Borderers.

Homecoming at Dumfries .

On Thursday, 29th November, 1900, at 2pm a crowd of several thousand gathered outside Dumfries Railway Station, the platform being reserved for members of the Reception Committee. The Provosts and Town Councillors of Dumfries and Maxwellton along with Magistrates. Also present were the Galloway Rifles officers, Major Lennox, in command, Major Harper and Captain Hewat, Castle Douglas; Major Phynn, Lieutenants Blacklock, Grierson and Shortridge, Maxwellton; Captain Wellwood Maxwell, Dalbeattie; Captain Comrie, Kirkcudbright and Captain Timms, New Galloway.

The whole town and station was gay with decorations. Banners, trophies and flags were strung across the streets. The Town Hall and the Mid-Steeple were gay with Union Jacks and bunting. Over the New Bridge, leading to Galloway, was a triumphal arch bearing the words, "Welcome Home". Further along Galloway Street was another arch bearing the words, "Well Done Galloway". The afternoon was observed as a public holiday, the schools being dismissed at noon.

The Volunteers of Dumfriesshire and Galloway lined the roadway outside the station and as the train drew up at the station at 2.20pm there was a salvo of fog signals and great cheers. Provost Glover welcomed the men and a procession was formed headed by the brass bands and pipe bands of the Dumfries and Maxwellton Companies. The men, with great difficulty, owing to the seething crowds, marched to the Kings Arms Hotel, where they were treated to dinner. At 4pm the men marched to the Drill Hall, where a huge crowd had gathered. As the men entered the Dumfries Pipe Band struck up 'Native Heath' and 'Mony Musk'. The Maxwellton Band played 'Soldiers of the Queen'. The Volunteers entered the hall to great cheering and lined up in two lines on the platform, which was draped in red white and blue.

Provost Glover welcomed the men and after speeches were made the Volunteers marched to St. Michael's Church, where a brief thanksgiving service was given. At the end of the service the Galloway Rifles were marched over to Maxwellton Drill Hall, to the tune of 'See the conquering hero comes'. They were welcomed at Maxwellton Drill Hall by Provost Chicken and other local dignitories .

In the evening the Dumfriesshire and Galloway contingents were entertained to a dinner in the Mechanics Hall, at which two hundred ladies and gentlemen attended. Speeches and toasts were made into the 'Wee sma oors'. The men of the Galloway Rifles were billitted for the night at the Kings Arms and the Salutation Hotels, Maxwellton, each man being provided with a suit of clothes from the equipment fund.

Kirkcudbright.

The manner in which the Magistrates proposed to entertain their Volunteers on their return from South Africa caused a great deal of discontent in Kirkcudbright. The following invitation was sent to 70 of the 'elite' of the Town. "The Magistrates and Town Council of the Royal Burgh of Kirkcudbright, request the honour of................company in the Council Chambers on the evening of 30th November, 1900, at 7 o'clock, at a dinner to be given in honour of the Volunteers from this district recently returned from active service in South Africa." R.S.V.P.Town Clerk. The invitations were also sent to the officers of the Galloway Rifles but not to the rank and file.

The Monday prior to the Volunteers homecoming a heated public meeting was held in the Town Hall by parties wanting to attend the dinner being given to the returning Volunteers. They asked the Town Council to widen the limits of the invitations. Baillie Hogg expressed the belief that the Magistrates had not been aware that so much interest would be shown by tbe public. This remark was greeted by hissing, booing and the disruption of the meeting. On order being restored, at the suggestion of the Town Clerk, a committee, which was to include the artist, E.A. Hornel, was formed to consider the widening of the invitation list. The invitation list was not to be widened.

The Senior Magistrate at this time was Provost William McEwan a staunch temperance supporter and founder member of the Kirkcudbright Total Abstinence Society, it was he who objected, as a matter of course to the renewal of every liquor licence in the Burgh. The lines were drawn and the stage set.

It was noon on Friday, 30th November, 1900, before Kirkcudbright stirred itself for the return of the Volunteers. The buildings were ablaze with flags and bunting. Streamers spanned the streets. The barque 'Utopia' lay at anchor gaily bedecked. From the Court House flew the National Colours.

At 3pm the sound of the bugle fell upon the stillness of the town. The Rifle and Artillery Volunteers, paraded at the Drill Hall and headed by the band, marched to the Town Hall. A procession formed here, including, Provost McEwan, Baillie Hogg and other Town Council members. At the Station the Volunteers under Captain Comrie and Major McLellan formed a guard of honour. Outside the station a crowd grew to tremendous proportions. On the arrival of the train bearing the four Volunteers, Private Claude Maitland C.I.V. (City Imperial Volunteers) was also being honoured on his re turn from South Africa. There was nothing but calculated disorder, shouting and cheering. With great difficulty Provost McEwan met with the four Volunteers and bid them a hearty welcome home. Three cheers were given by a thousand voices and the band played, 'Soldiers of the Queen'.

An effort was made to form a procession, outside the station, by the Officers and Magistrates but to no avail. The rank and file were to have their 'day' to show their utter contempt for Provost McEwan and Baillie Hogg by their refusing to widen the invitation list to the dinner for the returned Volunteers. They seized the Volunteers who were borne shoulder high around the town, stopping at local hostelries where the Volunteers were plied with copious drafts of liquor. The band and townspeople followed their returned heroes, en-masse, in a disordered display of homage. Provost McEwan, who by this time was absolutely livid, retired to the Town Hall along with the other local dignitories. Later that afternoon the returned Volunteers were borne to the Drill Hall and on order being restored Provost McEwan attended to present the Burgess Tickets to, Privates M. Crossan, John P. Dryden and Robert Milligan, along with Private Claude Maitland of the C.I.V.

That evening the civic dinner to the returned Volunteers was held in the Council Chambers but was afterwards followed by a dance in the Drill Hall, attended by the returned Volunteers and the rank and file. The following song was composed and sung by the well known Kirkcudbright Poet of the day, David (Pasha) Clark, a baker from Union Street, in honour of the Volunteers homecoming.
Note. In the Great War 1914-18, David Clarke's three sons all gave their lives in the service of their country.

"Brave Lads O'Gallowa."

Brave Lads O'Gallowa
ye're welcome back brave Volunteers,
Your safe return calms a'oor fears;
We welcome you with hearty cheers
safe hame tae Gallowa.... . . . .

From Afric's battlefields you came,
Where oft you made the Transvaal hum ;
We welcome you with pipe and drum,
Brave Lads O'Gallowa............

Right well you Borderers used the steel,
and made the stubborn Boer to reel ;
Old Cronje cried 'The very deil'
Is the Lads frae Gallowa............

The Galloway Rifles far and near
are proud of you, their comrades dear;
For heroes slain, let's drop a tear
They'll ne'er return to Gallowa....

Your'e welcome back from o'oer the sea,
Back to the bonnie banks O'Dee;
Long may you live, and happy be
In Bonnie Gallowa.... . . . .

And now you've laid aside your gun,
Enjoy the feast, enjoy the fun,
And take your rest, so bravely won,
And live content in Gallowa....

Colour Sergeant McGregor who did numerous pen and brush paintings was to complete a war picture bearing the photographs of the returned Volunteers of 'A' Company, together with Queen Victoria and the following lines composed by Mr. G.G.B. Sproat, ex-Provost of Kirkcudbright;

> Ye went and ye fought our battles
> And ye did what ye could for our Queen
> And ye might have been sleeping beneath the veldt
> Instead of Whisky Jean.
> With your lives in your hands,
> like true Volunteers,
> We are proud that you crossed the main,
> We are proud that you hammered the Boer
> And we welcome you home again."

In association with other Burghs, it had been proposed by Provost McEwan and the Magistrates, to present the returned Volunteers with a local 'Tribute Medal', however, in view of what Provost McEwan considered to be scandalous conduct on the part of the Volunteers and a complete lack of respect for the Office, the Magistrates cancelled the proposed tribute and indeed took no further part in any future proceedings concerning other Volunteers bound for or returning from South Africa. The Magistrates were however committed to the issue of Burgess Tickets to all South African veterans who had seen service from the Royal Burgh and we find that the two Kirkcudbright men, Privates Adam Grant and Arthur Proctor, who formed part of the 2nd Active Service Company of the K.O.S.B. Volunteers, refused to accept their Burgess Tickets from Provost McEwan claiming it to be a 'direct insult'. Private Adam Grant was to later pay the supreme sacrifice in the Great War, 1914-18. Private Dryden was to be killed in a funfair accident in the Harbour Square, Kirkcudbright, in 1924.

Ex-Provost James Cowan, a benefactor to the town, it was he who some years earlier had presented the new Town Clock at the Tolbooth, was heartily sick at the petty mindedness of the Magistrates and he personally purchased and presented the three returned Volunteers, Privates Michael Crossan, John P. Dryden and Robert Milligan, with a local 'Tribute Medal'. This medal which was silver, 28mm in diameter was inscribed, "presented by ex-Provost Cowan to Private...... 'A' Company G.R.V. on his Volunteering for Active Service in South Africa. January, 1900." The reverse was to show a beautiful engraving of the Tolbooth. Ex-Provost Cowan died on the 19th July, 1901, and accordingly no further 'Tribute Medals' were ever awarded to future Kirkcudbright Volunteers who saw service in South Africa.

Reference is made in a book by M.G. Hibbard, 'Boer War Tribute Medals'. "It is interesting that the medal was presented by ex-Provost Cowan, rather than by the town authorities." The reason is now quite clear. M.G. Hibbard makes further reference to the medal, "There can be no doubt that the engraver of this medal was an artist with bold imagination. Its charm and quaint simplicity, make it an outstanding example of the medallists art. The complete disregard of normal convention (where one face of the clock registers time as 5.50 whereas another shows 10.20) is a sure touch of originality." The truth of the matter is that one face, 10.20am represents the time the Volunteers paraded at the Armoury on their way to War and the 5.50pm was to represent the time that the Volunteers were dismissed at the Armoury, on their return from War. Nevertheless, I would totally associate myself with the remarks of M.G. Hibbard, when he makes reference to the medals, "charm and quaint simplicity." and an "outstanding example of the medallists art."

Private Robert Sharp, who formed part of the draft to the first Active Service Company, which was sent to South Africa, was never to return to Kirkcudbright, he settled in South Africa, after the War, where he married and raised a family.

New Galloway.

The reception which was extended to the return of four of the men of 'E' Company was most enthusiastic. It had only been a year ago that 13 men of the New Galloway Rifles had offered their services for South Africa. Captain Timms at that time had been faced with a dilemma but he had resolved it by rejecting the married men. The men who had the honour of being selected were Corporal Murdoch of New Galloway; Privates W. McKie and Oliver Taylor, Dalry; Private Cochrane, Balmaclellan and Private W. Caldow of Laurieston. Private Caldow had been accidently wounded in the foot and was unable at this time to accompany his comrades home.

The men detrained at New Galloway Railway station at 3.40pm on the 30th November, 1900 and were warmly received by Captain Timms. The band of the Maxwellton Rifle Volunteers, under Bandmaster Faithful was in attendance and a procession was formed at the station. Outside they were enthusiastically greeted by a Section of 'E' Company who had formed up with Pipers. The procession travelled to New Galloway where they were greeted by Provost Cowan and members of the Town Council.

At 6pm a dinner was held for the 4 men in the Cross Keys Hotel followed by a Ball attended by Colonel Kennedy and his daughter who had travelled from London that day especially to greet the Volunteers.

On Sunday, 2nd December, a thanksgiving service was held in the Parish Church, Dalry.

Private Caldow arrived at Southampton on the 18th December, 1900, and was taken to Gosport Hospital where he was declared fit to travel. He arrived home at Laurieston on the 20th December, 1900, where he was given a hearty welcome by the villagers. It was to be noted however, that no officer or Volunteers were in attendance to receive Private Caldow on his return home. Captain Timms was to later say that this was simply a misunderstanding as to the date of Private Caldow's homecoming.

Dalbeattie.

On Friday, 30th November, 1900, a visitor to the town could not but notice some unusual stir was going on in Dalbeattie. Flags and streamers hung across the streets. Just before 3 o'clock there was a steady flow of pedestrians to the station. On its approaches people lined the streets. The Magistrates and Town Council were in attendance to welcome home the Volunteers; Sergeant George Millburn, Privates Alexander Brown, Thomas Burnie, James Kirk and William Nelson.

The Volunteer Company, headed by their band, marched to the Station and lined up in two rows at the entrance to the platform as a guard of honour.

As the train reached the station, cheers, gave vent to loud and prolonged expressions of joy. The Volunteers minus Sergeant Millburn, who was not to arrive until a later train, were marched to the platform entrance and received by the crowd. Provost Shaw addressed the men and said, Mr. Maxwell of the Munches who had seen them off was no longer with them but he was sure that if he had been present, no one would have given them a more hearty welcome. The crowd gave the 'Warriors' three cheers. Captain Maxwell of Kirkennan, in the name of 'H' Company, welcomed the men home. A procession was then made to the Armoury, amid huge crowds and revelry. The Volunteer Band played appropriate music. On reaching the Headquarters hearty cheers were given and the men dismissed. The crowd dispersed to the Cross, where the Volunteer Band continued to play.

That evening a banquet was held in the men's honour at the Town Hall, the walls of which had been hung with National Emblematic flags and portraits of Lord Roberts and other Generals of the South African campaign. The Volunteers had now been joined by Sergeant Millburn. Provost Shaw Presided over the proceedings and many speeches were made. The Chairman proposed the toast to the 'H' Company Active Service Volunteers which was replied to by Private Burnie. Mrs.Maxwell of Kirkennan pinned a gold Maltese Cross on the breast of each of the returned Volunteers. A dance followed attended by the Volunteers.

On Sunday, 2nd December, 1900, in connection with the return of the Volunteers, a Thanksgiving Service was held in the Parish Church.

Castle Douglas.

On Friday, 30th November, 1900, a large crowd accompanied the Volunteers, under Captain Hewat to the train. Major Dunn and Major Harper were also on parade. On the arrival of the train, the band played 'Rule Brittania' and a salvo of fog signals were set off. Major Harper and Captain Hewat welcomed home Private McLeod.

Outside the station a dense crowd of over 1200 had gathered and marched with the Volunteers to the Town Hall. Provost Thomson welcomed Private McLeod and a toast was drunk. Private McLeod replied and the band played him to his home at Ashtree Cottage, followed by a large crowd who gave three cheers and dispersed.

Tuesday, 12th December, 1900, was fixed as a date for celebration in Castle Douglas, as this gave the men of the Active Service Contingent time to settle down after the first wave of enthusiasm. The programme included a torch-light procession and a public dinner in the Town Hall attended by all of the Active Service Contingent of the Galloway Rifle Volunteers with the exception of Private Birrell, Newton Stewart and Private Caldow, New Galloway, who could not attend, due to illness and accidental injury by firearm. They were still at present in South Africa.

It rained all day but towards evening the rain stopped and the whole town was brilliantly lit up. At 6pm the men in khaki were met at the station and a torch-light procession was formed at the Jubilee Fountain. This was headed by the band of 'B' Company, Castle Douglas, under Bandmaster Keane. After the band came the Magistrates and Council, followed by the Active Service Contingent under Captain Hewat and Major Lennox, followed by the Oddfellows and Foresters, several of them mounted. The procession marched off under 'Rule Brittania'. The route of the march was King Street, Marle Street, Queen Street, Cotton Street, to the Town Hall, where a public dinner was held for 250. The dinner was presided over by Provost Thomson. During the evening many speeches were made to the Volunteers who aptly replied. The band played and 'Soldiers of the Queen' was sung, followed by a musical programme.

During the course of the evening Private McLeod, 'B' Company, was presented with a silver watch and chain bearing the inscription, "Presented to Private McLeod, from the people of Castle Douglas, on his return from active service in South Africa." He was also presented with a purse containing 19 sovereigns. The proceedings concluded by the singing of the National Anthem.

Stranraer

At 5. 30pm on Friday, 30th November, 1900, a large crowd assembled at the Station to greet Private William Rennie, of 'C, Company of the Galloway Rifles on his safe return from South Africa. The local Company of the Galloway Rifles lined the platform and the entrance to the station, the gates being closed to the public.

A salvo of fog signals placed along the line signalled the approach of the train and as it steamed into the station the 'Fife' band struck up 'See the Conquering Hero Comes'. The sound was however drowned out by the cheers of the crowds.

Captain McLean and the Officers of 'C' Company received the 'Lad in Khaki' and he was borne shoulder high to an open carriage. The crowds went wild, rockets were set off, blazing torches were lit, in all it was a scene of some animation. Eventually the carriage was drawn away by a contingent of the Volunteers, the procession being headed by the torch bearers and members of the Fife and Drum bands. The procession traversed the main streets on the way to Private Rennie's home in Agnew Crescent, and at some places the crowds were so dense that the entire street was blocked. Altogether the reception was worthy of the patriotic community and one befitting the occasion.

That evening Private Rennie was entertained at a Ball held in the New Town Hall. He was presented with a watch and chain. The officers present were; Major MacRobert, Captains McLean and Torrance, Lieutenants Watson, Smith and McLauchlin, Surgeon Captain Munro and the Reverend W.M. Johnstone, Chaplain of 'C' Company. Also present were members of the Town Council and officers of the Artillery Volunteers.

Just prior to the opening of the Ball a telegram was received from the War Office to the effect that Trooper Stanley Adair, a member of 'C' Company Galloway Rifle Volunteers, serving with the Imperial Yeomanry in South Africa, had been severely wounded in action at Dewetsdorp. This was to cast a shadow over the events of the evening. However, the Ball and dancing took place until 4am.

Happily Trooper Stanley Adair, whose injury consisted of a badly shattered left forearm was to return home to Stranraer on Wednesday, 26th June, 1901.

Newton Stewart

Private Peter Birrell, 'D' Company, Newton Stewart, was to return from South Africa, on the 28th January, 1901, he having been struck down with the enteric in Pretoria. On Friday, 8th February, 1901, Private Birrell was presented with a marble time-piece inscribed 'Presented to Cyclist Peter John Birrell 'D' Company, Galloway Rifle Volunteers by the inhabitants of Carsluith.' He had already been presented with a gold medal from the Town Council of Creetown.

Maxwellton.

On Thursday, 12th April, 1901, at the conclusion of the weekly drill of the Maxwellton Company of the Galloway Rifles, Provost Chicken presented gold medals to the returned 14 men of Maxwellton who formed part of the 1st Active Service Company.

The medals were gold discs, surmounted by a crown. On one side there were the arms and motto of the Burgh of Maxwellton and the legend, 'South Africa 1900', encircled by a laurel border. On the reverse was the name of the recipient and the lettering 'G.R.V., K.O.S.B. From the Burgh of Maxwellton.'

By the December of 1900, Lord Roberts had returned to Britain, the war in South Africa, to all intents and purposes, over. Lord Kitchener had assumed command of the British Forces in South Africa. However, with there having been no final, decisive action between Lord Roberts' Forces and the Boer, in the September of 1900, the Boer Army had remained pretty well intact and was now roaming the countryside at will, creating havoc, destroying convoys, attacking outposts and cutting the rail and telegraph communications.

The Boer had organised themselves into small Commandoes of 100/300 strong, coming together in large numbers as and when required. It was now feared that the Boer forces under Christian de Wet were in a position to invade Cape Colony and at the same time Louis Botha would invade Natal.

Briefly, the Boer had divided their forces as follows:

The Boer heartland of the Western Transvaal coming under the control of Kemp de la Rey, the Orange Free State, south of the Vaal River, controlled by Christian de Wet, while the Eastern Transvaal was under the control of Lord Robert's former adversory, General Louis Botha.

By the end of January, 1901, South Africa was in absolute turmoil caught up in a guerilla war being fought by the Boer Commando. Volunteers were once again called for and as in the previous year, there was to be no shortage of willing and able Volunteers, from the ranks of the Galloway Rifles, coming together with the other Volunteer Regiments of the King's Own Scottish Borderers to form as the 2nd Active Service Company.

Below is the list of men who formed as the Dumfries and Galloway Sections of the 2nd Active Service Company of the K.O.S.B., which sailed from Liverpool, bound for the Cape, on the evening of Saturday, the 14th March, 1901, on board the transport ship "Montrose."

Dumfries Section.

Corporal C.H. BOYD, Dumfries.
Lance Corporal G. JOHNSTON, Dumfries.

Private J. FAIR, Dumfries
Private J. HAINING, Dumfries.
Private J. McMURDO, Dumfries.
Private R. PATERSON, Dumfries.
Private JAMES MUNSIE, Dumfries.
Private WILLIAM HENDERSON, Dumfries.
*Private JAMES JARDINE, Dumfries.
Private W.S. BURNS, Thornhill.
Private JAMES BROWN, Thornhill.
Private W. COOK, Sanquhar.
Private G. GLENCROSS, Sanquhar.
Private J. STODDART, Sanquhar.
Private JOHN CRICHTON, Sanquhar.
Private JAMES KILPATRICK, Sanquhar.
Private ARCHIBALD McMATH, Sanquhar.
Private THOMAS SCAIFE, Ecclefechan.
*Private ROBERT J. BEATTIE, Annan.
Private JOHN McPHERSON, Annan.
Private ROBERT JOHNSTON, Moffat.
Private THOMAS IRVING, Langholm.
Private T. WINTROPE, Langholm.
Private R. BELL, Lockerbie.
Private J. GIBSON, Lockerbie.
Private WILLIAM WYLIE, Canonbie.

*Denotes previous service at the front.

Galloway Section.

Company Officer Captain JAMES BLACKLOCK, Maxwellton.
Sergeant Instructor GRIERSON, New Galloway.
Paymaster Sergeant P. DUNN, Maxwellton.
Corporal JOHN DUNKELD, Castle Douglas.
Lance Corporal T. GRIERSON, Maxwellton.
Private A. GRANT, Kirkcudbright.

Private J. SCOTT, Castle Douglas.
Private J. McKAIL, Stranraer.
Private D. WARREN, Stranraer.
Private JAMES McMILLAN, Newton Stewart.
Private JOHN McMILLAN, Wigtown.
Private THOMAS RANKINE, Newton Stewart.
Private J. JOHNSTONE, New Galloway.
Private J. CANDLISH, Maxwellton.
Private F. McKIE, Maxwellton.
Private R. DICKSON, Maxwellton.
Private R. BOYD, Maxwellton.
Private H. BROWN, Maxwellton.
Private W. SAUNDERS, Maxwellton.
Private J. RUSSELL, Maxwellton.
Private W.G. SMITH, Maxwellton.
Private A. HUME, Maxwellton.
Private W. FRASER, Maxwellton.
Private D. McQUEEN, Maxwellton.
Private J. McKINNELL, Dalbeattie.
Private J. PRESTON, Dalbeattie.
Private A. KERR, Dalbeattie.
Private G.A. COUTTS, Dalbeattie.
Private NELSON, Stranraer.
Private J. JONSTONE, Maxwellton.

Additional men who formed as a draft to the 2nd Active Service Company.

*Private A. McLEOD, Castle Douglas.
Private SIMON LUNDY, Castle Douglas. - Cycle Mechanic.
Private T.D. WILSON, Stranraer. - Telegraphist.

*Denotes previous service at the front.

On Thursday, 8th February, 1901, the Dumfries and Galloway contingent of the 2nd Active Service Company left Dumfries for Berwick by the 11.35am train. A large enthusiastic crowd had gathered at the station.

The Dumfriesshire officers present on parade were, Captain and Adjutant Campbell-Johnston, Captain Robson, Captain Kerr, Major Carruthers, Lockerbie and Lieutenant Henderson.

The Galloway Rifle officers on parade were, Major and acting Adjutant Lennox, Major Phyn, Captain Blacklock (in command of 2nd Active Service Company), Captain Comrie, Kirkcudbright, Lieutenant Shortridge and Lieutenant Grierson.

The men were addressed by Provost Glover, Dumfries, who wished the men every blessing and hoped for their safe return. The Laurieknowe school children sang "Will Ye No Come Back Again" as the Volunteers departed, Sergeant Dunn, Maxwellton, being one of the children's school masters.

On Saturday, 14th March, 1901, at 7.15pm the Transport Ship, 'Montrose', left Liverpool bound for the Cape. On board were 30 officers and 1,250 non-commissioned officers and men, consisting of Volunteers drawn from the King's Own Scottish Borderers, the Royal Scots, the Seaforth Highlanders, the Gordon Highlanders, the Border Regiment, (Carlisle), the Manchester Regiment, the West Yorkshire Regiment, the North and South Staffordshire Regiments, the Loyal North Lancashire Regiment, and the West Riding Regiment. The Ship also carried a detachment of the Royal Army Medical Corps.

The Lord Mayor of Liverpool, Mr. Arthur Crossthwaite, addressed the men from the upper deck of the ship and at the conclusion of his speech three cheers were given for the King. A large number of the Volunteers friends and relatives were present to see off the men of the Dumfries and Galloway Sections, among them, Colonel Dudgeon of Cargen, Commander of the Dumfriesshire Volunteers.

The 'Montrose' arrived at Cape Town, on the 7th April, 1901, but was unable to land, owing to, in the words of Bugler George Keane, Castle Douglas, 'Bubonic Plague'. The Ship sailed to Durban, where the Volunteers disembarked on the 12th April, 1901, and travelled by train to Pretoria, arriving on the 16th April, where they were immediately employed in the defence of Pretoria, manning the hills to the west of the Capital.

On the 4th May, 1901, the Volunteers, of the 2nd Active Service Company joined with their Line Regiment, the 1st Battalion K.O.S.B. at Krugersdorp and were attached to Brigadier-General Dixon's Column. These columns, a complete war machine in their own right, were some 5 miles in length and were designed to follow and harry the Boer, to hopefully slow down and eventually weaken his resolve to continue the War. Later, flying columns of mounted troops, carrying but the bare essentials were to operate from these columns, ensuring of more mobility in their hunt for the Boer. The Boer in turn were to harrass and snipe upon the column in a series of 'hit and run' raids, coming together when they considered the time to be right to attack the columns in large numbers.

On the 11th May, 1901, the column trecked tc Naauwpoort Nek, arriving on the 13th May, where they were engaged in garrison duties until the 20th May, 1901. They then marched to Bassfontein where General Dixon's Column was ordered into the Magaliesberg Mountain Ranges in search of de la Rey and his hidden guns. On the 28th May, 1901, the column was attacked at Vlakfontein by a large Boer Force under the command of Kemp de la Rey, who captured two of the column's 'big' guns and turned them on General Dixon's column. After fierce fighting the Boer were driven off but owing to large numbers of Boer gathering in the area Dixon was forced to withdraw under cover of darkness to Naauwpoort.

From May until July, 1901, the 2nd Active Service Company served under Brigadier-General Dixon's column and from July until the end of September they came under the command of General Kekewich who was to take over Dixon's column.

Service on these columns, in pursuit of de la Rey, which operated in the Western Transvaal was extremely arduous and entailed repeated trips of hundreds of miles, on foot, many forced marches, over rough open country, without signs of civilisation, often on short rations and relying on what they could forage to eat. These repeated trips were to take in Naauwpoort Nek - Krugersdorp Ventersdorp - Lichtenburg - into the open bush of Zeerust - and through the vast Magaliesburg mountain range.

On the 10th August, 1901, the Volunteers, operating under General Kekewich's column were in the Magaliesburg Mountains at a place near Darnhoek when the column came under heavy Boer activity. An engagement was to take place between the opposing forces and it was during the course of this engagement that Sergeant Major Grierson and 11 men of the Galloway Rifles captured Frikkie Wolmarans, a Boer Commandant - General and 30 of his armed commando. For gallantry in the field, Sergeant Major Grierson was mentioned in despatches and promoted. Lance Corporal J. McMillan, Newton Stewart and Private R. Dickson, Maxwellton, for gallantry in the disarmament of the Boer were each promoted in thc field to King's Corporals. All three men were later to be awarded the distinguished conduct medal. (L/Corporal J. McMillan, Newton Stewart, was to serve as a Sergeant with the K.O.S.B. in the Great War, making the supreme sacrifice in Egypt on the 4th August, 1916.)

In early May of 1901, in an effort to protect the railways the British devised and built a system of blockhouses which were to be later extended to cover roads and river lines. These blockhouses which were pretty well impregnable, accommodated about 6 men and were based along the particular route to be protected at approximately 1,000 yard intervals. Eventually the British were to build a massive 8,000 blockhouses, each requiring to be fully manned along an area reckoned to be in the region of 3,700 miles. These systems of blockhouses were used in association with the huge columns, sweeping through the Boer heartland and proved to be a highly successful means of dealing with the Boers guerilla tactics of 'hit and run', by cutting off his retreat.

Reference is later made in a letter by Captain Blacklock, published in the Dumfries and Galloway Standard, "Our mounted men were seen clearing out the stock and crops and burning the barns, leaving the farmhouse but bringing away the families." In conjunction with the huge columns sweeping through the Boer heartland and the blockhouses which seriously curtailed the Boer's movements, Lord Kitchener had introduced a 'scorched earth' policy whereby farms and crops were burned thus reducing the Boer's capacity for a prolonged guerilla war.

The reference to "bringing away the families". On the outbreak of war, Lord Roberts had introduced a series of concentration camps to deal with the Boer homeless. however, with the introduction of Lord Kitchener's 'scorched earth policy', the Boer homeless purposely increased and with disease rampant in South Africa an estimated 20,000 Boer women and children died in these camps, leading to calls of genocide by the influential countries of the day. Lord Kitchener was to stop this practice, banning any further intakes of homeless in December, 1901.

The Volunteers continued with General Kekewich's column until the 23rd September, 1901, when the Battalion trecked to Frederickstad, taking over the blockhouses to Naauwpoort Nek, along the Mooi River, where they were to remain until the Christmas of 1901. Life in the blockhouses was extremely monotonous for the Volunteers, miles from any form of civilisation wi th only a handful of their comrades for company 24 hours a day and with lack of exercise and unappetising food rations it was little wonder that the men became edgy and bad tempered. Many's the time an over excited Volunteer fired at a non-existant enemy, the firing reverberating along the line for some miles before it was realised they were not under attack.

The Volunteers were finally to find some relief from their mundane existence when after the Christmas of 1901, they were employed in the building of a new blockhouse system from the Mooi River to Ventersdorp. No sooner had they completed this task, than they were told to dismantle the bockhouse line and re-erect it in a completely different direction from Naauwpoort Nek to Tafel Kop. Captain Blacklock writing to Provost Glover of Dumfries was to say, "Since the end of September we have occupied, built, taken down and rebuilt blockhouses and wire fences till the very words 'barbed wire' and 'corrugated iron' stink in the nostrils. Some of the blockhouse building expeditions were not picnics but again our luck held good."

The relief from the monotony of blockhouse life was to be short lived for the Volunteers who were soon to be retrenched inside the newly built blockhouses. Up until the end of April however, the Service Company was in pretty good health, being up to strength with the exception of 4 men invalided home suffering from enteric fever, among them John Dunkeld of Castle Douglas, who returned a few months later with the 3rd Active Service Company.

Captain Blacklock, a Dumfries Solicitor by profession, and Officer Commanding the 2nd Active Service Company, was to take leave of his Company in early May of 1902, when he accepted an appointment as 3rd Member of the Special Criminal Court at Pretoria. He was replaced by Lieutenant Herbertson, who assumed command of the 2nd Active Service Company.

In the intervening year of 1901, the Boer had been constantly active meeting with some measure of success. In February, 1901, near to Klerksdorp, de la Rey had seized a British convoy, inflicting 500 casualties and taking 700 prisoners.

On the 7th March, 1901, de la Rey, attacked Lord Methuen's column at Tweebosch near to Klerksdorp, inflicting severe casualties and taking Lord Methuen captive.

In September, 1901, Louis Botha invaded Natal, killing and taking 300 prisoners from a mounted column, under General Gough. He mounted attacks on the British outposts of Mount Itola and Fort Prospect, before withdrawing, in Mid-October, to his home the Eastern Transvaal.

With the continued Boer activity, by the January, 1902, additional Volunteers were required to man the newly completed blockhouses. The 2nd Active Service Company had completed their 1 year tour of duty but this was to be further extended by an additional 6 months. Kitchener was to call for a 3rd Active Service Company to serve alongside the 2nd.

The following Regimental Order was issued by the authority of Colonel J.M. Kennedy, Commanding the Galloway Rifle Volunteers. Castle Douglas, 13th January, 1902.

(1). The War Office having called for another Volunteer company to relieve those serving in South Africa with the 1st Battalion King's Own Scottish Borderers, and this regiment having to provide a section, officers commanding companies will do all in their power to assist the authorities to obtain the men required for the Galloway continent.

(2). The conditions are as laid down in previous orders, with the addition that each Volunteer must have obtained in 1901 not less than 60 points in trained men's course of musketry, appendix vii., Volunteer Regulations.

(3). The two sections which the Galloway Rifles have already contributed having brought great credit to this regiment (the first section being the first British troops to enter Johannesburg and Pretoria, while the second section under Lieutenant Colonel Mayne captured three times their number of armed Boers) the Commanding Officer trusts to officers commanding companies to obtain as good men for the section now required as those already supplied, and so keep up the good name which has been earned for the corps.

(4). Names will be forwarded to headquarters as received.

By order, JOHN LENNOX, Major and Hon. Lt. Col.

Acting Adjutant, Galloway Rifle Volunteers.

The following members of the Galloway Rifle Volunteers were selected on the 7th February, 1902, to form as part of the 3rd Active Service Company of the King's Own Scottish Borderers.

Colour Sergeant CUMMINGS, Maxwellton.
Sergeant DONALD GRANT, Kirkcudbright.
Private WILLIAM HANNAH, Kirkcudbright.
Private JAMES MILROY, Kirkcudbright.

Corporal JAMES McPHEE, Castle Douglas.
*Lance Corporal J. DUNKELD, Castle Douglas.
Private WILLIAM PENNY, Castle Douglas.
*Corporal ANDREW MURDOCH, New Galloway.
Private JONATHAN BROWN, Dalbeattie.
Private D. SEGGIE, Dalbeattie.
Private JAMES DONNAN, Dalbeattie.
Private WILLIAM BROWN, Maxwellton.
Private GEORGE CARMICHAEL, Maxwellton.
Private ROBERT FETTESS, Maxwellton.
Private THOMAS McGEORGE, Maxwellton
Private JAMES D. McKIE, Maxwellton
*Private NEWALL McKINNEL, Maxwellton
Private JOHN RAPHAEL, Maxwellton.
Private JOSEPH TAIT, Maxwellton.
Private JAMES WALKER, Maxwellton.
*Private WILLIAM M. RENNIE, Stranraer.
Private THOMAS PIRRIE, Stranraer.
Private JOHN HANNAY, Maxwellton.
*Private JOHN LOCKE, Maxwellton.
Private JOSEPH CARTER, Maxwellton.
Private THOMAS TEMPLETON Maxwellton.
Private JAMES McKIE, Maxwellton,
Private JAMES TAIT, Maxwellton.

* Denotes previous service at the front.

It was originally expected that the 3rd Active Service Company would be as strong numerically as the 1st and 2nd which preceded it but the Berwickshire contingent failed to turn up in its entirety. Consequently the Company consisted of only one Officer, Captain James Stevenson of the Ayton Company, Berwick, and 60 men of which the largest number, 28 men were from the Galloway Rifles, proving to be the largest proportion of the 4 Volunteer Battalions in their district.

On Saturday, the 15th February, 1902, the 3rd, Dumfries and Galloway, Active Service Company, received a hearty send off when they left Dumfries for Berwick, with selections from the band of the Maxwellton Company. As the train moved off, the band struck up, 'Auld Lang Syne'.

On Friday, 13th March, 1902, the men of the 3rd Active Service Company embarked from Southampton, on board the 'Arundel Castle' bound for South Africa.

On the 15th April, the 3rd Active Service Company joined with their Regiment, the 1st Battalion K.O.S.B. and their colleagues of the 2nd Active Service Company, in the blockhouse system, operating between Naauwpoort Nek and Quaggerfontein, near to Krugersdorp, Western Transvaal, in front of de la Rey. They were to receive their baptism of fire shortly after their arrival in fierce fighting at Kaffelkop.

Once again the soldiers story, 'Their War' is graphically told in the following sequence of letters sent home to friends and loved ones.

The following **letter received from Bugler George Keane** of the Active Service Company K.O.S.B. Castle Douglas Detachment of the Galloway Rifles, on 17th May, 1901.

Sunnyside Camp, Pretoria. 15th April, 1901 .
"We arrived at Cape Town on the 7th April, 1901, but were not allowed to land owing to the prevalence of bubonic plague. We were therefore compelled to anchor in the harbour for a day and then left for Durban where we arrived on the 12th about midday. There were crowds of natives - Kaffirs, Japs, Arabians, etc., lining the pier. We went close in the following morning but did not disembark until 2 o'clock. A tram was in readiness at the station and about an hour after disembarking we moved off.

Our first stoppage was at Inchangu, where we had tea. At Pietermaritzburg, the whole of the Active Service Company (Consisting of Gordons, Royal Scots, Seaforths, West Riding, West Yorkshires, and last but not least, the K.O.S.B.s) were supplied with bandoliers, the pouches having been condemned. We then proceeded to Estcourt, travelling all night. Colenso where the big battle was fought, was the first sight that met our eyes on the morning of the 14th. We had scarcely gone a hundred yards out of the station when four graves with handsome crosses at the head of them, and covered with wreaths, were seen in a field next to the railway. The next place of interest was the Tugela River - Ladysmith - Pietershill Elandslaagte and Glencoe, where part of French's Column is in camp. At this place we saw 'Q' Battery of the above Column, which was going off to refit at Johannesburg. Every bridge along the route had been blown up by the Boers, but they are now supplanted by new ones. Farmhouses and dwellinghouses have also suffered severly, and some villages are a total wreck. Ingagane was the next station we passed. Four more graves were seen at this place and a large bridge has been erected (the old one having been blown up). We passed the 3rd L.R.V. Camp near here. At Newcastleton we met the 2nd Lancashire Fusiliers. They have been on the trail for 16 months. They said their horses were completely done up and I don't doubt it in the least, judging from the worn out appearance of the men themselves. In the evening we landed at Ingogo Station, from which place we could see Majuba Hill, in the distance. We went close past it later on, but the night being dark, we could not distinguish the monument erected upon it to the memory of General Colley and the men who fell there.

The next stoppage was Mount Prospect, near which place a tram was held up by the Boers two or three nights before our arrival there. The men were ordered to put on their bandoliers at this station and have their rifles ready in case of an attack. This precaution however proved unnecessary, as nothing ocurred to mar our progress to the next station - Volksrust - where we had something to eat in the shape of a piece of bread with the butter 'photographed' on and a little coffee in our canteens. We stopped all night at this place, as no trains are allowed to travel in the Transvaal after dark.

16th April, 1901.

As we wended our way out of the station in the morning, graves, could be seen all along the line, in some places perfect cemeteries, walled in, containing some handsome headstones and wreaths, showing the respect in which the deceased soldiers had been held.

Platrand station was next reached, at which place a number of troops were stationed. While waiting here, a wounded soldier was brought into camp on a stretcher. From information which I gleaned from one of the men stationed here, it appears that the poor fellow had been shot at while out on outpost duty. He also told me that a lot of this sort of work had been going on lately, that the enemy took the night time for their cowardly game, and that in the morning nothing could be seen or heard of them.

We had breakfast at Standerton Station at 10am. More troops stationed here. A guard of Royal Scots (Volunteers) were put on to guard the trucks, containing the guns of Frenchs' flying column (Q, Battery Artillery) which was attached to our train at Glencoe. The reason for this precaution was owing to the fact that a transport train was captured near the above mentioned station. The Name of the place is Vlaklaagte. Soldiers just heliographing here. They say there are 'bags' of Boers about this place. We have just passed the place where the train was held up. The carriages are lying on their side, and the rails are all twisted. According to what I heard further on the route regarding the capture, the Boers took all the supplies with the exception of the whisky, which they divided amongst the escort (14 men), giving them 2 bottles apiece, at the same time granting them their freedom. Further on we passed the Scottish Rifles camp at Greylingstad, also a grave on the line side with V.C. cut out on it in large letters. We landed at Elandsfontein about 7 o'clock pm and at this place we got our first 'bite' since 10 o'clock in the morning. We remained in the station all night, sleeping in our carriages. Diamond mines were to be seen as we moved out of the station at an early hour in the morning (16th). Seven men were left in hospital here, 2 suffering from enteric, one from Erysipelas (K.O.S.B.) and the rest from minor ailments.

The next stoppage was at Irene, where the Queens' Own Cameron Highlanders are stationed. There is also a large refugee camp here where hundreds of people, white and black have had to seek shelter. We met some of the Dumfries Militia going home at this place.

At last Pretoria. We had scarcely enough time to put on our equipment when we got orders to fall in outside of the station, from which place we marched to our camping ground, about 3 miles outside of the town. The heat was excessive and the dust (or sand) lying on the route of march, rose in clouds and almost choked us. The name of the camp where we are stationed is called Sunnyside Camp. It is considered a healthy place. There is a convalescent hospital on our right. We are engaged here on escort duty for transport and expect to be here for three months at the least, before joining our Regiment (the K.O.S.B.) at Eerste-Fabrieken.

17th April, 1901.

I was down in Pretoria today, having been granted a pass by Captain Blacklock. It is a beautiful place with forts all round it and should be able to keep at bay any nation in the world. I passed close to President Kruger's house. It is a gorgeous looking erection, and at the entrance a lion confronts you on each side.

18th April, 1901.

The Manchester Regiment left here last night, having had only about an hour to get ready, but no one seems to know their destination. Each man was supplied with seven days rations. The Gordons also left this morning (18th) and the West Ridings leave this afternoon. No one in camp seems to know where they are going to. They are under escort. As I sit writing, word has been brought us by our Colour Sergeant, to get our equipment together as quickly as possible, so as to be able to leave camp by one o'clock.

I am in splendid health, also J. Scott and J. Dunkeld."

The following **letter written by Private Thomas Rankine,** 'D' Company, Newton Stewart, Galloway Rifles, to his Grandmother, Mrs. Stitt, County Arms, Wigtown.

Scotch Fort, Naauwpoort Nek. 22nd May, 1901.

"When I left the convalescent camp, having been confined in hospital as the result of an accident, I was sent to Pretoria, but when I arrived I found the Regiment had shifted to Krugersdorp, which is about 20 miles beyond Johannesburg, so I had to come back to Elands fontein, and from there to General Dixon's column at Naauwpoort Nek. It is somewhere about 50 miles from Krugersdorp to Naauwpoort Nek, and it took us five days to march it, but I can say I felt very tired about the fourth day. We always started on the march about 10am and camped about 5pm. The convoy was fired on by the Boers for about four hours on the third day's march, but, as it was strongly guarded, they did little damage.

'A' and 'B' Companies of the 1st K.O.S.B.'s formed the front guard and in the centre were the Scottish Horse and three companies of Artillery, and we (the Volunteers) formed the rear guard. I may state that the convoy was five miles long.

We all arrived safe here on May, 13th, and after being two days at Naauwpoort Nek the Volunteers were sent to Scotch Fort for garrison. The nearest railway station is Mafeking, which is about 35 miles distant. We are just between Krugersdorp and Mafeking, no town or houses near us, nothing but mountains. We get very good food, fine biscuits and ham, and jam for breakfast and tea, and for dinner we have meal.

There are only 82 Volunteers here at present, all the others are in hospital ill with fever.

I have been on outpost duty nearly every other night since we came here, and you don't know the minute a Boer bullet comes whizzing past you, of course, when you hear a shot on outpost duty you have just to lie flat on the grass, and then after a little you see two or three Boers walking close past you, and you have to keep quiet as a mouse, for if you make the least move you are done for.

I have never got any letters yet, but we are expecting another convoy on Friday, the 24th May, and it is bringing two mails along with it, so perhaps some letters may come my way then. I am wearying especially for the local papers and the Weekly Mail.

25th May, 1901

General Dixon's column arrived at Naauwpoort Nek yesterday, (Friday) with convoy and English mails, so I got one letter and three papers on arrival here, General Dixon's column goes out again on the march on Monday next, so we are going along with him, and I expect we will be having it pretty hard for a bit. When his column came in yesterday they brought about 100 prisoners along with them.

We get any amount of fruit here, oranges, apples, peaches, etc. Hoping this will find you all well, as I am in the best of health myself, I am your affectionate grandson,

Thomas Rankine"

Letter to the Editor, *Kirkcudbright Advertiser*, from **Bugler George Keane,** 'B' Company, Castle Douglas, Galloway Rifle Volunteers, with the 2nd Active Service Company, K.O.S.B.

Welverdiend, near Krugersdorp. 23rd June, 1901.

"Dear Editor,

I see in some of the leading English papers, which I have read out here, a report of the Vlakfontein fight, and strange to say, the K.O.S.B.'s and the Volunteer Company are never even mentioned as having taken part in it, the highest praise imaginable being bestowed on those less worthy of it. I therefore take the opportunity of giving an account of what I saw myself and what I heard afterwards from those best qualified to judge.

The following account of the fight written though it is in simple style I dont intend to pose as a letter writer - may be of interest to readers of the Advertiser.

We were out reconnoitering on the morning of the 29th May, having with us, 'D' Company of the K.O.S.B.s', the Volunteer Company, Scottish Horse, Yeomanry, Derby Regiment (with the exception of one Company which was left in camp) and 28th Battery (four big guns and one machine gun). The Derbys' and

Yeomanry were on the left flank with two guns. The Scottish Horse in the centre and the Volunteers and 'D' Company K.O.S.B., with two big guns and one machine gun, on the right flank.

The machine gun and one Howitzer started firing at a range of about 2,000 yards, some waggons being seen amongst a clump of trees away on our front. The fire seemed to be getting too hot for those in charge of the waggons, for they speedily removed them. The only response to our fire was an occasional shot from a sniper or two. By this time the Boers had worked their way round our left flank under cover of a huge veldt fire, getting quite close to our guns without being seen. At this stage the Yeomanry are supposed to have got the order to retire, leaving the two guns in charge of the Gunners and Derbys' (who were marching into Camp in fours). The Boers getting close in on them unobserved, owing to the smoke, poured forth a heavy fire amongst them, one Company of the Derbys' being nearly annihilated. Seeing all was up, the Gunners, had the presence of mind to shoot down their horses and cut the traces, so as to prevent the enemy making off with the guns. They were however powerless to prevent the capture, by the Boers, who immediately started shelling our camp.

At this juncture, word was brought, those on the right flank ('D' Company K.O.S.B. and the Volunteer Company, with two big guns and machine gun) to advance as speedily as possible, as the Boers had captured two of their guns.

We took up our position on a kopje, on our right front. The Boers shelling us as soon as we made our appearance and the 'ping-ping' of the bullets as they whistled over our heads, was anything but sweet music. Luckily however, we were provided with splendid cover, in the shape of large boulders, giving us a chance of 'potting' our game, without affording much of a target ourselves. The Boers formed a perfect horse shoe around us, and were nearly all mounted. Three of them rode right up to where we lay concealed, doubtless thinking they were first to reach the kopje. Major Mayne as plucky a gentleman as ever sat on a horse, advanced towards them and cried out 'Hands up'. The leading Boer, however seemed to be under the impression that he had caught the Major napping and raised his rifle to his shoulder, but before he could pull the trigger a volley from 'D' Company K.O.S.B. and the Volunteers, stretched him lifeless on the veldt. The other two seeing the fate of their comrade, turned their horses heads and galloped away, but had not proceeded far, until they shared the same fate.

We then advanced over the ridge of the kopje, down into the plain, in skirmishing order. General Dixon, having given an order for every available man to turn out of camp, the remaining Company of the Derbys left there, advanced, for the purpose of recovering the guns, and under a heavy rifle fire from 'D' Company and the Volunteers (assisted by the machine gun) succeeded in getting them back, capturing three of the gunners. Before the Derbys' rushed the guns, we were exposed to a heavy rifle and shell fire and strange to say only two of 'D' Company K.O.S.B. were wounded (slightly), the Volunteers escaping without even a scratch. Luck coupled with ignorance on the part of the Boers, to manage the guns properly, was most assuredly on our side that day and every one of us had occasion to thank God for delivering us safely through so fearful an ordeal. I myself don't wish to participate in anything like it again. From information which I gleaned from one of our gunners, it seems the reason for the shells not bursting arose from the fact that the Boer gunners had forgot to take out the safety pin connecting the fuse. Lucky for us they were so negligent.

The fight started about 1 o'clock and lasted until darkness set in, after which we wended our way back to camp. The scene the next day was horrible, waggon loads of dead and wounded being brought in. Judging from the mutilated appearance of some of our dead, the explosive bullet must have been much in evidence. As near as I can learn, the number killed, would amount to between fifty and sixty. We had also about 120 wounded. The Boers must have suffered severely, as their ambulance waggons could be plainly seen roaming up and down the scene of the fight the whole of the following day. A large number of their dead were carried into our camp and buried. The Derbys' themselves admit that they would never have got their guns back had it not been for the deadly fire poured into the enemy, by 'D' Company K.O.S.B. and the Volunteers, which they say had a telling effect. Ask them what they think of the Yeomanry and Scottish Horse, and they will give you an answer directly opposite to the reports contained in some of the English papers which I have read out here, giving them praise for their gallant (?) stand! I could say a good deal more on the subject but I will refrain from doing so.

P.S. On 7th June, we had another brush with the Boers. A body of snipers gave us some trouble on our march through the valley from Naauwpoort to Oliphant's Nek, with a large convoy. The Boers were scattered along the hills on each side of the valley, and when nearing the Nek, the flank guards and rear guards were subject to heavy sniping. One Volunteer Private Young of the Berwickshires and a horse were wounded The Volunteers were on the left flank. I saw Lord Methuan, his staff and column pass through Zeerust on his way *to Mafeking. He had a lot of prisoners with him and his column would be about 4,000 strong, mostly composed of mounted troops.*

Since leaving Krugersdorp on 11th May last, we have trekked a distance of between 500 and 600 miles and are at present at Welverdiend, from which place we proceed to Krugersdorp, about three days march from here, to be refitted, our clothes and boots being completely worn out.

Private John Scott and Lance Corporal Dunkeld, are both afflicted with slow fever. The former is left at Zeerust (along with Private Hume of Maxwellton, who is somewhat similarly affected), but the latter is still with us and is undergoing treatment in the field hospital. I hope by this statement that I am not the means of causing any alarm amongst their parents or friends as I may assure them that they are all on a fair road for recovery.

I am,

Bugler George Keane.

The following **letter** which appeared in the *Dumfries and Galloway Standard* was written to friends in Dumfries by **Captain James Blacklock,** Officer Commanding the 2nd Active Service Company .

The Battle of Vlakfontein.

"We left Naauwpoort on Sunday, 26th May, (1901), with General Dixon's column. Our Regiment acted as rearguard to the column, and after a march of about twelve or fourteen miles along the veldt we encamped at a ridge called Basfontein.

Some of our guns came into action and we learned later that they did considerable execution. Our only casualties were four Imperial Yeomen, who approached a kopje without scouting and were promptly all wounded, some of them seriously. We also had a native scout killed and another wounded.

Next morning we went out to remove forage and food supplies from the surrounding farms. The district is perhaps the main Boer stonghold. It is certainly the most fertile part we have seen since we left Natal. They grow beautiful oranges and the vegetation where there has been cultivation is most luxuriant.

My company went out to hold a ridge, which commanded a fair view of operations. Our scouts found the ridge unoccupied, and we approached carefully and took possession. This was our men's first day out really, and I was afterwards asked to tell them that we had done well. Once on the ridge we had to inspect our surroundings carefully for snipers, but found none. Several Boer waggons were sighted getting away, and our guns shelled them and their escort at a range of about three or four miles. We saw all that and the bursting of the shells perfectly. Our mounted men were seen clearing out the stock and crops and burning the barns etc., leaving the farmhouses, however, but bringing away the families. In the afternoon we marched back to camp, very carefully, however, just in the reverse order to that in which we had gone out.

The following morning we trekked about five or six miles to a ridge called Vlakfontein. Our artillery came into action on the way and did some good work on a Boer convoy.

We had a little incident though. Next day (Wednesday) some more operations were to take place, and my company was marched out with three other companies of the Regiment, on the right of the expedition. After tramping a few miles I was ordered to send a section to occupy a ridge on the flank, and I sent Thomson. Then I was ordered to send half a company forward, and I took them myself, leaving Herbertson with the remaining section. Our work was to push out some scouts to our front about a mile and a half, and to advance after them in skirmishing order and occupy a hill. Meanwhile our mounted scouts had driven the enemy's fire from our right front and our Maxim guns had been peppering him, but there was not much damage done.

There were some snipers in a donga on our right as we advanced, and some men I sent up said they were fired on and replied to the fire vigourously, with what result I know not.

Our scouts having reached the downward slope on the other side of the ridge, sat down to watch. I brought the rest of the half company up and disposed of them among some clusters of rocks, and went on to the scouts to see what was doing. We were watching through glasses a Boer waggon and oxen moving off some miles away, when Mauser fire began to give out their double reports and Mauser bullets began to sing just over our heads. We lay flat, and presently we saw some Boers about 1500 or 1600 yards off. Our men fired, and the party promptly broke up and galloped off, scattering as they went, to shelter in the tree-covered dongas all around. More bullets rained in but after a while they ceased.

About one o'clock we were ordered to retire which we did in good order, and continued to march back as the flank guard on the left of the column. About two o'clock there was a tremendous fusilade on the right of our retiring force, and some bullets began to come into us from our left. The business on the left did not amount to much, and a mounted man galloped up to summons us to assist the centre. It seems that away on the right as we retired the Boers had made a desperate attack on two of our guns and captured them. Their modus operandi was ingenious. They went up the wind and fired the veldt. Under cover of the smoke they followed down behind the fire, shooting as they came along, walking with their horses, bridles over their arms. It was a game thing to do, and it came off, the guns were taken. Some companies of the Derby Regiment who were with us, along with some Imperial Yeomanry, prevented the Boers going off with the guns, but it was sometime before they were re-taken.

Meanwhile my company, which was now together, had scrambled about a mile into the centre. Bullets were whistling in all directions, and we took cover behind some clusters of rocks, and potted away for all we were worth. Just then a curious thing happened. Three Boers, one of them dressed like a trooper of the Scottish Horse, part of which body was with us, rode right up to within fifty yards of where 'D' Company of our Regiment and part of my company were, and dismounted. As they advanced it was doubtful what they were. The most probable solution was that they were two Boer prisoners in charge of a Scottish Horseman, but then they were armed. Major Mayne ran out and shouted 'Throw down your rifles' and ordered some of our fellows to fix bayonets and advance to take the Boers prisoners. The Major's servant was one of the men and the foremost Boer in a truculent way, called out, 'Put up your hands. Damn you'. At the same time he fired at Wedderburn (Maynes servant), and grazed his right arm, the bullet striking a purse he wore just at the biceps and running right round his arm. Wedderburn, who had flung himself down, got on his knee and shot the fellow through the head. Immediately a second Boer was shot through the brain, and the other, who bolted, was wounded and afterwards captured.

Shortly after this little episode we were ordered to cross a pretty wide plain towards the ridge behind which the heavy firing had been going on. We had just started our march in Indian file and extended to ten paces or so when a shell flew over our head and burst in the sand behind us. It came away from on what, now that we were turned to our front again, had become our left. The guns were located by their smoke about two miles to our left on the other side of the ridge. More shells continued to follow. Some of them struck fifty yards or so in front of us and ricochetted over our heads with an infernal row to strike again some hundred yards behind. At first we thought our own gunners were firing at the enemy, who had been peppering us from our other flank, but the sight of our remaining two 15-pounders behind us convinced us that it was they that the Boers had turned our own captured guns on. Luckily, though the beggars had the range to a nicety, they had not the trick of working the time fuses, and although a heavy shell hurtling through the air, within a few feet of you is disconcerting until you are used to it, yet its deadly effect is small if it does not burst. If a shell does happen to hit one, well, one does not remember much about it. The annoying part of it all was that we knew the Boers had no guns, so we were sure that it was part of 'P' Battery that was saluting us.

Our fellows continued to advance steadily across the plain, and when we were extended across it we were ordered to lie down. All this time several hundred horsemen, who looked like our fellows, had been occupying the ridge about two thousand yards from us. At last we got word that they were Boers, so we proceeded to give them snuff and they made off. I must say that they were game chaps and retired very prettily. If our guns or the pom-pom or the Maxim had only been at hand they could have smashed the enemy badly. Unfortunately they were elsewhere, and a magnificent opportunity was lost. When the Maxim did get started on them they cleared fast. The fight was now virtually over. We had regained the guns, but at an awful cost. Fifty-six of our men were buried together the next day, and more must die. Our total casualties were 170. The Boers lost as many dead as we, and there is reason to believe that they had quite as many wounded.

A dark stain rests on some of the Boers. I have seen great cannon-balls of cartridges for the elephant rifles used by some of them. You can imagine the kind of wound they make. Soft-nosed and expanding bullets were used against us freely, and the wounds made by them were awful. A young Sub. in the Derby's, I think it was, was wounded in the hand and while he was having the wound dressed a fiend came up and blew out his brains. One devil with a touch of the tar-brush in him was wounded in the stomach but he crawled about and killed three of our wounded who were lying helpless. He is dead now, but what punishment severe enough could be devised for such hellish work. These things can all be proved and though I would not like to slander a gallant enemy, yet it would be better to understand right away that we had to treat the Boers as savages and act accordingly. Many of our men who surrendered and held up their hands were shot down. One lot were put out in a row and told to prepare to be shot, when the arrival of a Boer officer saved them. There is no doubt they have honourable men among them, but the dark doings of the scum of their forces are horrible.

The General came up about half past four, and as we were due for outpost that night I took back half my company, leaving Herbertson with the other half. On arriving back at the camp we found everything topsy-turvy. Some shells had been sent into camp, and there had been such a packing up and preparation to move as never was. However we got some tea eventually and decided to await orders. By and bye the rest of the company came in, and as other companies had been out on piquet we remained in camp. It was bitterly cold in our bivouacs as we lay down without taking off a stitch and with our arms loaded by our hands. I slept from ten to one, and lay awake until four, when every man in camp stood to arms till daylight was well advanced. We had to wait till well in the day to allow the sun to thaw the water in our pails before we could wash, and to bath was out of the question.

Note: July 1901..

The War Office issued a report from Lord Kitchener on the conduct of the Boer at Vlakfontein, which consisted of the sworn statements of Officers and men engaged in the fight. One statement by a Lieutenant Hern, alleged that he saw a Lieutenant Spring and Sergeant Findlay shot while lying on the ground slightly wounded and that other men were like treated. The further evidence of eight men, 3 Derbyshires, three Imperial Yeomanry, a gunner of the Royal Artillery and a Private of French's Scout supported these allegations. The most prominant perpetrator from among the ranks of the Boer who committed these atrocities appeared to be a young Boer with a puggaree around his hat and who was alleged to be a German named Piet Foster. Lieutenant W.J. English of the 2nd Scottish Horse was awarded the Victoria Cross for his heroism at the battle of Vlakfontein.

The following **letter**, part published in the *Dumfries and Galloway Standard*, was written to family by **Captain James Blacklock,** Officer Commanding the 2nd Active Service Company, on Monday, 22nd July, 1901, at an undisclosed place between Ventersdorp and Krugersdorp.

Saturday. 13th July.
"We woke up at 4.45am and marched due west (from Zeerust) to Doornfontein, about 16 miles. We were then about twenty miles from Mafeking, but we were not to get to that town, much as we wanted to. The next day, 14th July, was a beastly march, the whole of the country being burnt, mainly by the Boers, so as to cut off the supply of forage between Mafeking and Zeerust. On our march we were constantly encountering whirlwinds called 'devils'. You see them a long way off like a pillar of dust, only in this case it was soot collected off the burnt veldt. They are very liesurely, and go into all the nooks and crannies in their path, industriously collecting portable material. They do not go out of their way by deep design, but they are erratic in their movements and occasionally come one's way. When that is the case the sensation is unpleasant, the wind shrieking in one's ears like a thousand fiends, and buffetting one nearly off one's feet. When it has passed you look as if you had been sweeping a chimney and feel like murdering somebody, for lo! the air is baking, and only the big black 'devil' and some others between you and the horizon remain to remind you that there is such a thing as wind.

On Monday, 15th July, we marched about twenty miles, passing through Lichtenburg, where food was very scarce, and camped three miles or so further south. That night our intelligence officer took forty men on the hunt for cattle. They got about 150, but put off time searching farms, were overtaken by the Boers next day, had the cattle re-taken, lost one Yeomanry officer, shot through the heart, and eleven prisoners. I liked the poor chap who was killed. He was captured at Lindley and again at Vlakfontein. The third time he was killed before he fell into the enemy's hands.

The next day, 16th July, we marched fifteen miles and went on outpost. The Boers were about but did not disturb us that night. The following day we marched 24 miles to Ventersdorp. On the way our mounted men recaptured forty or fifty of the cattle of the previous day. There was some shooting, but only one bullock was killed. We rested a day at Ventersdorp, which may be a nice town later on, though more likely to be a gold-mining centre.

On Saturday, the 20th we marched eighteen or twenty miles, and yesterday morning came eight or nine miles to here, where I heard a train for the first time in over ten weeks. Today we are halted and go on towards Krugersdorp tomorrow.

As I sit writing here the heat is like June at home. When the sun goes down we shall spring at once to November, and in the early morning it will be freezing for all it is worth and I shall have to take off at least an inch of ice before I can wash my face. The air is dry, and when there is no wind this high veldt is very pleasant. I am in the best of health.

James"

Letter from **Bugler George Keane** 'B' Company (Castle Douglas), Galloway Rifle Volunteers.

Boshfontein (Western Transvaal) 12th August, 1901.

"We left Krugersdorp on the 28th July, with a column under the Command of General Kekewich, Defender of Kimberley during the seige, General Dixon, having resumed sub-command of the Potchefstroom district. The usual sniping was indulged in by the Boers whilst passing through the valley leading to Oliphant's Nek, but no damage was done, our big guns soon putting a stop to their cowardly work.

We are at present engaged operating along the Magaliesberg range of mountains, in conjunction with Colonel Allanby's column, which is working in the Naauwpoort Valley, on the other side of the range from us.

On the 8th August, we came upon a body of Boers, between 300 and 400 strong, at Eland's Drift. The Volunteers and 'G' Company K.O.S.B., were advance guard, and very speedily got into action. The enemy were laagared up in the open and were taken completely by surprise. They soon recovered themselves, however, and a brisk fight was engaged in for an hour or so, until the guns began to play on them, when they made off to the hills. The Boers left one man killed and four wounded, two of whom died shortly after being taken in to our hospital. Several other Boer wounded were found by us the following day. The Boers were all mounted and are said to have carried off a lot of their dead and wounded with them. One prisoner was taken. Our loss - Scottish Horse - one killed and three wounded, One Volunteer was also slightly wounded. When the Volunteers returned to the camp, Major Mayne conveyed the congratulations of the General to them for the admirable manner in which they extended and for the alacrity they displayed in getting into action.

On the 10th August, heavy sniping was engaged in by the Boers near Eland's Kraal. Our guns shelled the place from which the sniping emanated for nearly an hour, lyddite shells being mostly used. When the shelling ceased two sections of the Volunteers - Galloway and Dumfriesshire - under Major Mayne advanced for the purpose of seeing what effect the shelling had and with the intention of trying to communicate with Colonel Allanby's column on the other side of the hill from us. In this we were successful and Major Mayne gave the order to retire, coming down the opposite side of the hill which underwent the shelling previous to our going up. Major Mayne then gave instructions to Colour Sergeant Grierson, to take some of his section through a donga (or valley) between two high hills, telling him at the same time to keep a sharp look-out; the Major going round the ridge of the hill on the left of the donga with the remaining portion of the Galloway and Dumfries Sections. Colour-Sergeant Grierson and his men (12 in number, including myself) then advanced in single file - ten paces interval being between each man - along the valley, but had not proceeded far when they sighted one horse and two mules amongst the trees, a short distance ahead. When they came up to them it was discovered that they were saddled, but no trace of the owners could be seen. The finding of the horses, however acted as an incentive for the men to advance cautiously, which they did, and had not proceeded far when the leading man discovered three Boers about thirty yards in front. The word was passed quietly along to Colour-Sergeant Grierson, who extended his men along each side of the ridge of the hill. The twelve Galloways then covered the Boers with their rifles, and with a combined shout of 'Hands Up' made the hills on each side of the valley fairly rattle, which must have had the effect of impressing the Boers that they were surrounded by a large force of men for the four of them threw down their rifles and tottered towards us with their hands extended above their heads.

They had scarcely been taken in charge when another twenty six made their appearance and advanced towards us in single file with their hands up. They had evidently been caught napping and seemed to be preparing for a nights' rest. The shout that went up from the twelve men of the 'MOSS HAGS' no doubt struck terror into the hearts of the Boers and gave them the impresssion that they were surrounded.

Our capture consisted of 30 Boers, 3 Kaffirs, 27 rifles (Lee Metford, Mausers etc.,) a large quantity of ammunition, 2 mules and one horse. Not bad work for twelve men. One of our number was despatched for Major Mayne, who soon arrived on the scene with the rest of the Galloway and Dumfriesshire Sections. We then marched our prisoners into camp, where the Volunteers got a hearty reception. General Kekewich in complimenting the men on their capture, said he did not think any other Volunteer Company in the present war had accomplished what had been done that day. He heartily thanked them for their capture, and answered them that the people of Scotland would hear tell of it."

The names of the twelve men who effected the capture are Colour-Sergeant Grierson, New Galloway; Lance Corporal J. McMillan. Newton Stewart; Private Rankine, Newton Stewart; Private Dickson, Maxwellton; Private E. McKie, Maxwellton; Private J. Johnstone, Maxwellton; Private R. Boyd, Maxwellton; Private D. McQueen, Maxwellton; Private Coutts, Dalbeattie; Private Nelson, Stranraer; Private J. Johnstone, New Galloway, Bugler, G. Keane, Castle Douglas.

Letter written to a friend in Parton, by **Colour-Sergeant Grierson** 'E' Company (New Galloway), Galloway Rifle Volunteers.

Zandfontein Commando Nek, 15th August, 1901,

"We have been here since the 13th instant and do not know when we leave or where we are likely to go, camp rumour had us away back through the valley towards Rustenburg, but the truth still finds us resting here,

We started on our travels from Krugersdorp on the 11th May for Naauwpoort Nek. where we arrived on the 13th of that month and did garrison duty there until the 20th, leaving on that date and marching to Bassfontein, where we halted the following day, a party of the column being sent out farm-burning and orange gathering. the Volunteer Company being amongst the number.

On the 28th we left for Vlakfontein and reached it about 11am We camped there for the night, and went out to dig up some ammunition, burn farms etc, Part of the Volunteer Company were early engaged with a party away on our right front, I had a bit of shooting here, the first that I had had in the country, We managed to clear the Boers out and shortly afterwards, retired to our right rear to cover a party who were down at a farm. We were a good distance away from the farm (lying watching the others at work) when a terrific fire was opened on our left front. We were at once ordered up at the double, doing my utmost, I could scarcely raise a run, However we reached the crest after having had a stiff rifle and big gun fire pouring into us. I think the rocky ridge must have saved us considerably, otherwise we must have lost heavily, On our reaching the top three Boers rode into a sort of horseshoe that the Volunteers and 'D' Company had formed and ordered us 'hands up'. They got 'hands up' quick, the poor fellows being fairly riddled with bullets. At this time we did not know that we had lost two of our guns and could not conceive where the big gun fire was coming from, We however, speedily found out when we were ordered to advance in extended order. The fire grew very heavy and the big gun fire very accurate, several of the shells striking the ground within a few yards of our Company, That they did not burst was a God-send, otherwise few of us would have been left to tell the tale, We opened fire immediately we reached the bottom of the hill, the Boers steadily retiring along the ridge until they left us in sole possession of the field. We had then a chance of seeing part of the Boer's work, the wounded lying about in all directions, Boer and British mixed. Part of the Company were ordered to camp, the remainder were detained to collect the dead and wounded, and did not reach camp until a late hour,

Our casualties were 188 all told, the Boer casualties being about the same, 41 of them being found on the field that night, dead, and a number the following day.

The Volunteer Company were next day sent on outpost duty and kept busy digging trenches and erecting barbed wire fences, until dark, I suppose this was to bluff the Boers, who were watching our every move,

About 9 o'clock that night I was ordered to collect all tools and get the men's blankets etc., together as we were marching immediately. A very short time afterwards we were on our way to Naauwpoort a distance of about 20 miles. Such a quiet march, no noise, men speaking under their breath, 20 yards away not a sound could be heard, About 4.30am we reached our destination, thoroughly done up, but a day's rest put us all in trim again. Our hospital with the wounded was left behind and they reached Krugersdorp a few days afterwards.

On the 7th June, we left on a tour round by Rustenburg, Boshhook Nek, Blackloof Railway, Roodevaal for Zeerust, reaching there on the 10th July, We had rather a good time of it up to this, plenty of oranges and sometimes any number of fowls and pigs to cook and eat.

After leaving Zeerust we marched through Ottoshoop, Lichtenburg. Ventersdorp and Welverdiend. reaching Krugersdorp on the 25th July. This was the hardest work we have encountered in the campaign, the marches being long and very fatiguing. At Ventersdorp I was about done up but managed to get through all right, and finished up decently. We were refitted at Krugersdorp and again marched for Naauwpoort, continuing on until we got near Rustenburg, the convoy being sent on with two Companies of the Derbyshire Regiment and some of the Scottish Horse. We returned to Naauwpoort rested a day and off again in the same direction as before.

On reaching a point about five miles from Oliphant's Nek, the Boers gave us the usual sniping, The guns tried to shift them, but shift they would not. They did very little damage, however, only killing one horse, We camped that night at Oliphant's Nek and resumed our journey the following morning, making for Croom River, and camping there,

The following day we occupied Breedt's Nek. and left three Companies K.O.S.B. there, another joining *them the following morning on our leaving for Ellands Drift. On our arrival at the latter place, the Boers were in position and opened fire on the Scottish Horse, who rode right into them, unaware that they (The Boers) were there. The Infantry, including ourselves at once extended and opened fire, the sight was grand. I had a splendid view of the whole affair from a small ridge, which the firing line crossed. The Boers did not stay long, but retired left and right. Our big guns and pom poms, shelling them for what they were worth. The Boer had about 12 casualties. On our side, one Scottish Horse, killed and their Doctor wounded in two places, another man was also wounded. We camped there until morning when we marched on Boschfontein, staying there for the night,*

On the following day we marched back towards Ellands Drift, as Boers were reported in numbers there. Two columns were operating together and scoured the hills in all directions. We were on the left flank, and were kept there until about 3.30pm when Major Mayne, K.O.S.B. ordered us to climb a hill where brother Boer was supposed to be. We reached the crest after a hard hour's climb but saw nothing. The Major having got communication with the column operating on the other side of the hill, ordered us to retire, taking with him the Dumfries Section and part of the Galloway Section, leaving ten Galloway men with me and ordering me to search a Donga that was on our left.

The donga was very deep and was formed in a half circle. When moving down, the men inclined to take the near-cut across the hill, but I told them to keep on the edge of the cloof. We had only gone a short distance when a saddled horse and pack mule were sighted. We went down and got a hold of them, and told some of the men to keep in the water course. We advanced a few yards further, when three Boers were espied. I ordered them 'hands up' and bagged them, then another two put in an appearance and joined the other three. More were sighted, and a shout went up from the men 'hands up'. They must have thought that we were in fair strength, as up they came with a pair of drawers as a white flag, I thought that I was never going to see the end of them. However, when they reached us, and when they saw our small numbers, they looked at one another. It was too late then. I had them trapped and disarmed and fairly in the net. We managed, by getting the other party to help us to march them to camp, and I can assure you, it was a weary wait for me, having fully half an hour to wait before the others joined us - although I had sent a messanger after them. Darkness also troubled me as the night was falling fast, and we were about three miles from camp. We arrived at the General's tent and handed them over. There were 30 Boers, 2 black boys, 28 rifles, 2 revolvers and a quantity of ammuni tion. The General gave the Company great praise and thanked me personally for my share in the affair and told the Section that the people in Scotland would know of this clever piece of work.

Amongst the prisoners were several notables, one of them being Mr. Wolmaran, the Chairman of the late Volksraad.

We reached here two days after the above date (10th August) and I expect I will leave tomorrow.
I see that 'E' Company are still keeping up to their old standard in shooting."

****

The following extract from the Army Orders, South Africa, dated 26th August, 1901.
Promotion for distinguished gallantry in the field.

The undermentioned non-commissioned officer has been brought to the notice of the General Commanding-in-Chief, for gallantry in the field:- Kings Own Scottish Borderers - Colour-Sergeant Grierson, for energy, promptness and gallantry in the capture of thirty Boers (armed) and their Commandant Wolmarans, near Darnhoek, on the 10th August, 1901.

Signed H.G.M. Amos, Captain.
Adjutant 1st K.O.S.B,

The General Commanding-in-Chief, has been pleased to sanction the promotion of the undermentioned non-commissioned officer and men, for distinguished gallantry in the field (should they be desirous of accepting it), such promotion to take effect from the date of performance of the act. They will be borne supernumary to the establishment of their unit and will be absorbed into vacancies as they occur.
K.O.S.B.

No. 7328 Lance Corporal J. McMillan; No.7330 Private R. Dixon, to be Corporals for great energy, promptness and gallantry in the capture of Commandant Wolmarans and 30 (armed) men in a deep kloof near Darnhoek on l0th August, 1901.

Signed H.G.M. Amos, Captain

Adjutant 1st K.O.S.B.

Letter to Captain Timms, Slogarie, from **Colour-Sergeant Grierson**, 'E' Company, New Galloway, Galloway Rifle Volunteers,

No.6 Blockhouse, Roodraal. 20thNovember, 1901.

"Sir,

Your letter of 7th October, to hand. I beg to thank you for your kind congratulations also for your kindness in forwarding packet of tobacco, which was duly received by me on the 17th inst.

I am sorry to inform you that we have been taken off trek and posted in blockhouses, stretching between Naauwpoort Nek and Fredrikstad,

Shortly after leaving the column it was heavily attacked by de la Rey, who was forced to retire. Our casualties, I believe were heavy. The Battalion was very sorry to hear of the mishap and would have liked a hand in the business, but had the column been up to its former strength, de la Rey, would have fought shy.

I hear today that Colonel Kekewich has caught him, but as for its truth I wont vouch.

A Boer force of 900 strong are supposed to be going near Klerksdorp, about twelve miles distant, with Colonel Hicks within striking distance. General Wilson has passed on to the above station.

We get little or no news here, only what filters through and that generally by natives, so that our news is not very reliable.

I am informed that trade about town is getting very brisk, and that a number of the mills are being opened, which leads me to believe that the war can't last much longer. At the same time there is little of this country in the Western Transvaal free from Boer, and in fact, one is not safe a mile from a blockhouse.

A short time ago news was received that a party of Boers between 100 and 200 strong were trying to reach Ventersdorp, and would try to pass through our line of blockhouses, which they did, and unfortunately it was between two of the K.O.S.B., blockhouses. Luckily they were not the Volunteer Company blockhouses.

The blockhouses, in this district, are built with corrugated iron. The one that I am in is double, the space being filled with earth and stones, making it fairly bullet proof. Close against the outside of the house is a trench, about four feet deep. The earth from it has been divided, one portion thrown up against the house, the other on the edge of the trench, making it five feet deep. Both house and parapet are loopholed. Outside the trench is a barbed wire fence four feet high, and one foot high wires are run round zig-zag, from the high to the low fence and intertwined in such a manner that the fence is about 10 feet wide, and would take a lot of cutting to get through. There is little of the blockhouse seen above the surface. We are provided with water tanks and 14 days' supplies (reserve), also apparatus for signalllng in case of attack and when wanting help. The blockhouses are distant from one another from two to three miles, the ground between having to be patrolled daily and sometimes nightly. The night work only occurs when Boers are in the vicinity. The blockhouse stands close to the Mooi River, which has a heavy flow at this point and tends to lighten our nightwork considerably, as it is impassable to man or horse at this point.

Letter from South Africa which was received by the Withorn Parish Guild.

Modderfontein, 29.1.1902.

"My Dear Sir,

I duly received your letter of 5.12.1901, and the Christmas gifts arrived two days ago and conform to your list except that there was only 23 pairs of socks instead of 24. I suppose the odd pair were extracted as a kind of ad valorem duty on imports, only payment was taken in kind. Still we were grateful for what came, like the western parson who sent round the hat amongst the crowd and got it back empty. Looking round the mob of unwashed faces, he said, "Well brithern thank God we've got back the hat."

Many of the lady members put their addresses on the things they knitted, and doubtless the recipients are gallant enough to salute as well as distances will permit, the fair givers. I have attested to the wishes of the Guild as distributing the articles, and after these were satisfied, the remainder was given to the members of the Galloway Section. which I am ashamed to say have not received the amount of attention accorded to the other Section of my Company.

"ALBANICH"

Kindly thank the Guild on my behalf, in name of No.4 Section for their useful gifts which have been highly appreciated both for their usefulness and the kind feelings at the back of them,
Yours Faithfully,
James Blacklock, Captain K.O.S.B.

Letter from **Bugler George Keane**, 'B' Company, Castle Douglas, Galloway Rifle Volunteers on active service in South Africa, to his parents.

1st May, 1902.
"That part of the blockhouse line held by our Company, viz., from Quaggafontein to Naauwpoort - was on the nights of the 29th and 30th April, respectively, subjected to an attempt, on the part of a large party of Boers, to break through, but after heavy firing on both sides the enemy was repulsed, on each occasion. The time they chose for the object they had in view was an hour or two before moon-rise. They also adopted the plan of sniping the blockhouses in the vicinity of the place where they intended escaping, for the purpose of drawing the fire of the blockhouses on the different places from which the sniping emanated, thus enabling the main body a fair chance of getting through comparitively easily, but the 2nd Service Company have been too long in the country not to be up to the artful dodges practised by Johnny Boer, and instead of paying any attention to the snipers, they directed their fire along the wire fence, (A formidable one indeed) running from blockhouse to blockhouse, which had the desired effect of causing the Boers to retire."

The Company were complimented by Major Wilkinson, the Officer Commanding the Regiment, on the sound judgement shown by them in upsetting the enemy's plans.

The war in South Africa continued until the 15th May, 1902, when it was finally accepted by the Boer Government that defeat was inevitable and hurried discussions were to take place among the Boer leaders and their British adversaries as to terms favourable for a lasting peace. On the 31st May, 1902, peace was declared in South Africa with terms favourable to the Boer, with the added assurances that no Boer would be executed for his part in the conflict and that the British would finance the ailing economies of the Transvaal and Orange Free State, in the sum of £3 million pounds. In return the Boer promised to lay down his arms and swear allegiance to King Edward VII.

The Volunteers of the 2nd Active Service Company were immediately mobilised for home and on Sunday morning the 22nd June, 1902, 89 men of that Company, under the command of Lieutenant Herbertson arrived at Berwick from Southampton, having docked at Southampton, the previous evening, on board the transport ship, 'Plassy'. They were met by the Pipes and Drums of the King's Own Scottish Borderers and marched to the Depot. They were to remain overnight at Berwick and on the 23rd June, the men of the Dumfries and Galloway contingent travelled to Dumfries, under the command of Sergeant Instructor Grierson, New Galloway.

At Dumfries the men were met by cheering crowds and members of the Town Council along with Colonel Dudgeon, Officer Commanding the Dumfriesshire Volunteers. The band played 'When Johnny Comes Marching Home.' Sergeant Grierson assembled the Volunteers and faced the assembled crowds to do them honour. The Volunteers were then escorted by detachments of the 3rd (Militia) K.O.S.B. the Galloway Rifle Volunteers and their band and marched through the principle streets of the town to Oughton's Restaurant where they were served a meal. The men thereafter departed for their respective homes.

CASTLE DOUGLAS.

Bugler Keane and Private Scott, were met by Provost Veitch, the Town Council, local inhabitants and members of 'B' Company of the Volunteers. The buildings were hung with bunting. A procession was formed and the two men were marched behind the band to the Armoury, where they were dismissed.

DALBEATTIE.

Privates A. Kerr, J. Preston, J. McKinnell, G. Coutts, were met from the train by Provost Shaw, the Town Council, and the inhabitants of Dalbeattie. A procession was formed, headed by the Pipe Band. The men marched to the Armoury, where they were dismissed. On the 11th July, 1902, at a smoking evening held in their honour, the returned Volunteers were presented with gold maltese crosses as had been presented to their comrades from the 1st Active Service Company.

KIRKCUDBRIGHT.

Privates Grant and Proctor, were met at the station by 'A' Company of the Volunteers, under Sergeant MacGregor and the band of the Artillery Volunteers. They were marched around the town and carried shoulder high. The Magistrates took no part in the proceedings, including the Officer Commanding 'A' Company, Captain Comrie, also a local Magistrate, who was reported as being unavoidably absent.

NEWTON STEWART.

Corporal McMillan and Private Rankine, two members of the local Company of Volunteers who had served in South Africa, arrived by train at Newton Stewart, along with Private Christison, Wigtown, also a member of 'D' Company, who had served in South Africa, with the Ayrshire Yeomanry. They were met by 'D' Company of Volunteers and a large crowd of townspeople who headed by the Volunteer Pipe Band marched to the Drill Hall, where the Volunteers were treated to a wine and cake banquet.

STRANRAER.

Private J. McKail, Private D. Warren and Private Nelson, were met at the railway pier by Provost Viscount Dalrymple, and members of the Town Council. The men were warmly welcomed home, a procession was formed and the men were marched to the County Buildings where they were entertained.

The members of the 3rd Active Service Company remained in South Africa to supervise the surrender of the Boer army and were mobilised for home on the 8th July, 1902. On Thursday, 1st August, 1902, the members of the 3rd Active Service Company, landed at Southampton, from South Africa, on board the S.S. 'German'. They arrived at Berwick on the 2nd August and travelled to Dumfries, arriving at 10pm.

Owing to the short notice of their arrival in Dumfries there was insufficient time to organise a reception but after hurried arrangements, the men were met by Baillies Cumming, Scott and Councillor Grierson, representing the Town Council and by, Lieutenant Colonel Lennox, Major Phynn and Lieutenant Shortridge, representing the Rifle Volunteers. After short welcoming speeches, the Volunteers were billetted in local hotels before their departure for home the following day.

There was to be little welcome for the men of the 3rd Active Service Company, with no individual reported homecomings. After the 'heady days of the 1st Active Service Company, Mafeking had been relieved, Pretoria had fallen and the war had become somewhat stagnant. To a lesser extent the returned 2nd Active Service Company received some limited adulation with peace at last being declared in South Africa during their tour of duty. Unfortunately, the men of the 3rd Active Service Company, who arrived home some 8 weeks after hostilities had ceased, had been forgotten, the public and media were now preparing for a more important occasion, the Coronation of their King, Edward VII.

EX-MEMBERS OF THE GALLOWAY RIFLE VOLUNTEERS
WHO SAW SERVICE IN SOUTH AFRICA AND RETURNED TO THE RANKS.

The patriotism that swelled the ranks of the Volunteer Regiments was also to swell the ranks of the Line Regiments, with many Volunteers enlisting in the Regular Army, as well as transferring to other Volunteer Regiments bound for South Africa. In all a total of 16 Volunteers transferred from the Galloway Rifles to the Line or other Volunteer Regiments:- Lieutenant Shortridge, 'F' Company, Maxwellton and two others to the Scottish Cyclists; Lieutenant E.S. Forde, 'E' Company, New Galloway and one other as Civil Surgeons; Private Colin Christison, 'D' Company, Wigtown, and four others to the Imperial Yeomanry; one to the South African Constabulary; Private T. McEwan, 'A' Company, Kirkcudbright, to the Gordon Highlanders; three to Fincastle's Horse. Corporal Morrison, 'D' Company, Isle of Whithorn, to the Queenstown Rifle Volunteers of the Colonial Division. The following are a short selection of four letters from the ex-members of the Galloway Rifle Volunteers who saw service in South Africa and returned to the ranks.

Private Thomas McEwan, a member of 'A' Company, Kirkcudbright, Galloway Rifle Volunteers, who enlisted in the Gordon Highlanders saw service in South Africa with 'C' Company of the 2nd Battalion Gordon Highlanders. Private McEwan was also to see service in the Great War, as a Captain with the King's Royal Rifles. In July, 1916, he was wounded, mentioned in despatches and awarded the D.C.M. The following brief history outlines the action referred to in Private McEwan's letter to his parents.

War was declared between Britain and the Boer on the 11th October, 1899, and the following day, 12th October, the Boer invaded Natal, with the intention of gaining a passage to the sea, their primary objective being the rail junction at Ladysmith. On 21st October, 1899, an action was fought against the invading Boer armies at Elandslaagte, some 10 miles from Ladysmith. This battle, won by the British, resulted in 50 British dead and 113 wounded, with 67 Boer killed and 108 wounded. This battle was one of three actions fought against a huge advancing Boer Army, culminating in the infamous seige of Ladysmith on 30th October, 1899.

The following **letter** was written by **Private Thomas McEwan,** late of 'A' Company Galloway Rifle Volunteers, Kirkcudbright, to his mother and father at 23 Townend, Kirkcudbright. His father was a Forester on St. Mary's Isle Estate, and a Sergeant with 'A' Company, Galloway Rifle Volunteers.

Ladysmith, South Africa.
October 23rd,1899

"My Dear Parents,

I am glad to be able to tell you that I have come through our first engagement all right, but I am sorry to say that we have suffered a terrible loss. God only knows how I am spared today to write this. Never will I forget the horrors of that awful day, men falling on every side, but I cannot say more to you, it would be a sacrilege to the dead. I have got a splinter in my knee, but for bullets, none touched me. Part of my kilt is riddled and there are two holes in my helmet. It was terrible I assure you.

It made me feel queer when at first the shells were landing close to us, screaming over our heads and all around us. It makes one duck your head, but after we get fairly in it you don't care a rap. The bullets were whistling like rain or hailstones, and many a good man dropped. We were coming on dead and wounded Boers all over the place. We were very good to them and gave them something to drink when we had time. We had nearly two miles to charge, under fire the whole time, so that you will have a sort of idea, for you can never know what it is like. We fought up till dark and lost most of our men at the last.

Our Captain is down wounded in two places, the Colour-Sergeant and twenty-six men. Of our three Company Officers, two are killed and the Captain wounded. So you will see that 'C' Company were well to the front. I helped to carry the Captain and the Colour-Sergeant in. It was awful carrying in the wounded, but a man was thankful that he was able to do it. Poor fellows were lying on the hillside not able to shout for assistance or to let us know where they were. I got hold of our Captain and helped carry him in. Then I got hold of the Colour-Sergeant and got him in, and the mean hounds were firing on us although they knew that we were carrying in the wounded.

The cries of the poor fellows were awful, crying for water. It was pitch dark and we could get none for them, buit I discovered a case of whisky and soon gave them some. I had a drop myself but I do not consider that I broke teetotal as I was feeling very bad and could get no water.

We have all earned our medal but we will have a bit more to do shortly as 15,000 Boers are advancing on our Company and we are getting out to meet them. I have got a bandolier full of cartridges which I took from one of the Boers. The bullet mark is on it, which carried one of his own cartridges into him. It was a splendid capture. I got a bundle of despatches and gave them to our orderly room.

Word has come in that they have fired on the party we sent out to bury the dead. So stiff as we are we must buckle up and teach them another lesson. God spare me to come through this next. After Saturday I think we can come through anything. So I will now go and get my rifle ready for the Boers again. Good Luck to the Gordon's. If I should come out safe again, I will write, if not, it can't be helped.
From your loving son, Tom."

Corporal William Morrison, from the Isle of Whithorn, was a member of Wigtown Section, 'D' Company, Newton Stewart, Galloway Rifle Volunteers, who enlisted in the Queenstown Rifle Volunteers. These Volunteers, in the main South African troops, were to form as the Colonial Division under the Command of Brigadier-General E.Y. Brabant, and on Lord Robert's great march on Pretoria, in May, 1900, they formed part of the 8th Division, under the Command of Lieutenant-General Sir H.M.L. Rundle, their task being to protect the rear of the main column. Corporal Morrison was a member of the Maxim (Machine Gun) detachment of the Queenstown Rifle Volunteers.

The following **letter** was written by **Corporal William Morrison,** Isle of Whithorn, ex-member of Wigtown Section, Galloway Rifle Volunteers, to the Secretary for the presentation to the Wigtownshire Soldiers.

Queenstown Rifle Volunteers, Queenstown, Cape Colony.
April 14th, 1901.

"Dear Sir,

In a letter from my mother, Mrs. E. Morrison, Isle of Whithorn, I am informed that she has received for transmission to me a valuable gold albert and appendage, the same being a gift from the people of Wigtownshire, and as a recognition of my services in the Boer War, as one of the Volunteers from Wigtownshire.

To yourself, committee and subscribers, I desire to tender many thanks for the valuable presentation, which I shall preserve as one of my most treasured possessions, not only for its intrinsic value, but also as a memento of the thoughtfulness of the people of my native County, towards those who volunteered for the Boer War.

A sort summary of the achievements of the regiment to which I belong may not be out of place. The Queenstown Rifle Volunteers, are an old standing corps, and have taken part in many Kaffir wars, and when, in 1899, President Kruger, proclaimed 'Oorlog' (war), the Q.R.V., true to their motto, 'Semper Paratus', were among the first in the field, and assisted to check the coastward march of the then jubilant enemy until the arrival of reinforcements from home, guarding for a few weeks the lines of communication.

We were then embodied with the Colonial Division, under General Brabant, who set the ball rolling by clearing Dordrecht, and Labuscagne's Nek of the enemy, afterwards taking part in the general advance in the Free State, assisting in the operations of the 8th Division on the Basutoland border and relief of Wepener, the advance on the Bradwater Basin, and Bothaville, the defence of Winburgh, and Helpmakaar, the capture of General Oliver, and the surrender of Prinaloo, Tabaksberg, the chase of de Wet and Krelinger, in the Colony.

A short time ago the Maxims were detached for home (Queenstown) defence, and our work now consists of tripping around any little town that is threatened by the enemy in No. 1 Area Colonial Defence, our latest trip being to Tarkasaad, where the people declared that the Q.R.V. Maxim detachment saved them a visit from the enemy.

With repeated thanks for the presentation.
I am Yours Truly, (Cpl.) William Morrison, Maxim Det.

Private Colin Christison, a member of Wigtown Section, 'D' Company, Galloway Rifle Volunteers, Newton Stewart, enlisted as a Trooper with the Ayrshire Yeomanry. He was to come under the ultimate command of Major-General W.G. Knox, (Nasty Knox), operating columns and blockhouses from as far north as Brandfort in the Orange River Colony to Dordrecht in Cape Colony. against the Forces of Christian de Wet.

In his **letter, Trooper Christison** gives an interesting insight into the newly developing methods of dealing with a guerilla war. Flying columns were now operating as 'Standing Camps and Patrols', giving of more mobility in the hunt for the Boer. 'Saving Horse Flesh'. The British Army imported tens of thousands of horses which were uncared for and driven to exhaustion by the Cavalry and Mounted Infantry. In a period of 2 years, it was reckoned that the British forces lost some 500,000 mounts. Supplies of fresh horses were drying up around the world, and a system of rest camps were devised, whereby the sick and exhausted animals were cared for until sufficiently recovered for re-deployment in the field.

Private Christison makes reference to, 'those joining the I.Y. (Imperial Yeomanry) will find they have their work cut out for them for their 5/- per day.' This divide in remuneration between Yeomanry and Infantry Volunteers was a constant source of trouble between the troops. Initially the War Office were wary of accepting the services of the Colonial Volunteers, which included Corporal Morrison's Queenstown Rifle Volunteers, as they were paid 5/- per day, whereas plain 'Tommy Atkins' was paid 1/- per day with 9d for rations. However, when the guerilla war exploded in South Africa, Yeomanry were required in large numbers, to seek out and hunt down the Boer, hence the added inducement of 5/- per day.

These Independent Yeomanry Units were formed as Troops of Imperial Yeomanry and consisted in the main of non-professionals, As in the case of Trooper Christison, a mounted infantryman, who makes reference, in his letter, last paragraph, to criticism by 'Press' and, Certain M.P.'s,' of the usefulness of the Imperial Yeomanry, as a fighting force. This paragraph relates to remarks attributed to Colonel E.H.H. Allenby, "The Yeomanry are useless. After some months in the field, they learn a bit, but by the time they are any use, they have probably been captured two or three times, presenting the Boers, on each occasion, with a horse, a rifle and 150 rounds of ammunition."

The following **letter** was written by **Trooper Colin Christison,** late of Wigtown Section, Galloway Rifle Volunteers, Newton Stewart 'D, Company, to Sergeant G. Coupland, Wigtown Section, 'D' Company, Galloway Rifle Volunteers.

22nd March, 1902.

"Landing at Cape Town on the 6th April, last year, (1901), bidding farewell to the good ship, 'Avondale Castle', we entrained for Elandsfontein, the Imperial Yeomanry headquarters in South Africa. A tedious journey of a week, which was accomplished in coal trucks, brought us to our rendezvous. A sojourn of two days at Elandsfontein sufficed, and we were despatched to Bloemfontein, where the Scottish Yeomanry were being fitted out to join Colonel Pilcher's Column. Once there I had to say farewell to my comrades for the present having as you are doubtless aware got cornered with an attack of dysentery. I was discharged from hospital on the 22nd May, and spent a month, not by any means in idleness, in the M.I. (Mounted Infantry) camp, Bloemfontein. I had to perform the tedious and monotonous work of Police duty in town, and patrolling the streets at night relieved sometimes by escorting a convoy out to Bushman's Kop or Sannas Post, in the immediate neighbourhood of that place.

It was June, 20th, that the welcome tidings came that all Pilcher's details were to join him at Brandfort. The next day we started for that place, and arrived two days later, when we were joined by Pilcher on the 26th.

At this point I propose giving you a few details of the Company's doings prior to my joining them. One portion joined Pilcher at Brand's Drift, a place not far north of Thabanchu, on 6th April. They accompanied him on his trek round Senekal and Reitz districts, and from there to Bothaville, during which they saw a considerable amount of fighting. They were reinforced by the second contingent of the Company at Bothaville in the beginning of May, who had trecked up there with Colonel Thorneycroft. After operating for a short period round Bothaville they came into Vet River Siding where farewell greetings were exchanged between the new and old Companies.

From there they went south to Brandfort, and after drawing supplies they started west or what is termed in the company as the 'Kimberley Trek', they marched to Raefontein and there Pilcher left his heavy baggage and went forth to meet the enemy as a flying column.

Not long afterwards they were heavily attacked on both rear and flank by 400 Boers under Commandant Badenhorst. The 17th Company formed the reaguard on that day. They fought bravely, but were gradually borne back in face of superior numbers until they were reinforced by some M.I.'s with guns. It did not take long when reinforcements arrived to quell the Boer onslaught. The firing was very hot for a time on both sides. Our casualties for the day were, 1 officer and 1 man killed with 2 or 3 men wounded, while the Boers had over 20 killed and wounded. The 17th had the most remarkable luck of only having one man wounded.

After the rearguard action at Orangepan the column headed off in the Kimberley direction where supplies were drawn. From Kimberley they headed east again to Brandfort. On the way an action was fought at Paardeberg, now famous in the annals of Boer history for capture and surrender of Cronje, where the 17th again figured prominently by taking a kopje from the Boers at the point of the bayonet with the loss of two men wounded. Over and above these two engagements other fighting took place on this trek which would not allow space to relate. In one of these affairs we had a Sergeant of my Company wounded.

Brandfort was reached on the 26th June, where, as I have already mentioned, I joined Pilcher. On 1st July, the whole column left Brandfort, marching east for the Korrannaberg Mountains. Nothing important happened during the first week of my trek.

On the 8th July, Pilcher moved out at 2am to attack the enemy as a flying column, leaving his ox convoy and all impediments behind in charge of the 7th M.I. and 18th and 19th Company I.Y. (Imperial Yeomanry). His fighting force consisted of the 5th M.I., 17th and 20th, and a Section of the 18th I.Y., with guns and pom-pom.

At daybreak that morning we were in touch with the enemy. Firing was pretty brisk on both flanks during the forenoon. At mid-day the 17th Company was ordered out to the right flank to reinforce the 18th Company section which had been having a lively time. After a stiff fight our flank was drawn in and we ultimately joined the main body. During the affair the 18th had three men wounded. The whole of next day the enemy were pursued and we succeeded in capturing numerous waggons and stock with one armed prisoner.

On the 3rd day we joined the ox convoy and steady headway was made for Thabauchu. After a few days at that place we left to engage in a sweeping move down the south eastern part of the O.R.C. (Orange River

Colony). A little sniping was engaged in on the first day out from Thabauchu. It was on this day that Pilcher split his column in two, one half the fifth M.I. and 20th I.Y. under Colonel Lean, the other half consisting of the 17th M.I. and 17th, 18th and 19th I.Y. under Colonel Taylor. The 14th Battery R.F.A. (Royal Field Artillery) supplied 2 guns to each column. We pushed through De Wetsdorp on the 18th July, and swept down south ultimately arriving at Bethulie capturing large herds of cattle, sheep and horses, and destroying large quantities of grain.

A four day's stay at Bethulie and we started on a movement in the south western corner of the Free State. Crossing the railway south of Springfontein we made for the Harrismith region and after operating for a short period in that district we were ordered to Jagersfontein to be in position for a sweeping move in conjunction with Dumant, Weston, Henry and Lean. Starting from the last named place at daybreak one morning the column swept over a large extent of country, every bush being searched, as the troops moved along, with the ultimate result that 40 burgers were put out of action by the various columns engaged in the movement.

Taylor then trekked north and the column lay for a week at Calabas Bridge, on the Riet or Kaffir River, near Koffyfontein, until a convoy arrived from Edenburg to replenish our exhausted stock of supplies.

During that week we were not in idleness. Patrols were out from camp daily, and we succeded in capturing seven Boers and a large amount of stock.

From Calabas Bridge we made a steady and uneventful trek on Bloemfontein. We expected a somewhat lengthy stay in the capital of the Free State, but fate was destined otherwise. We had only a stay of a night, which not a few spent in the theatre, and the day following, with one hours' warning we were entraining for some unknown destination. It was well after dark when our train got on the move, and daybreak saw us detraining at Bethulie.

The whole three companies of Yeomanry left there in the afternoon and were posted along the railway at Springfontein. We patrolled the railway, that and the following night, without coming in contact with any of the enemy. Owing to some mistake or other with the blockhouses on the railway, we had a lively time. A deadly combat went on between the blockhouses and us, and one patrol especially had all the guns of Springfontein and an armoured train pomelling them, luckily only a few horses were hit. We had two very wet and cold nights on this job, and the cold was felt more, especially as all baggage, kits and tents were left behind at Bloemfontein.

On the third night we made a night march on a place called Adam's Farm. Here we held a nek for somedays and were joined by the 7th M.I., transport and guns. After a series of operations centered round Bethulie, patrolling railways, holding neks, and blocking drifts, for the purpose, as I afterwards learned, of checking Kruitzinger, who had been driven out of Cape Colony, a three days forced march was made into Cape Colony ultimately landing at Burgersdorp.

For the greater part of the sojourn in the Colony, during September, we had a hard and trying time on account of the severity of the weather. We were under the temporary command of General French.

The column left Burgersdorp on the 10th September, for Jamestown, which we reached in five days' time. During those five days our course lay through the heart of the Stormberg mountains. Some of the passes we came through were of a very difficult nature and progress was extremely slow. Had there been 50 Boers in some of the neks they could have defied an army to pass through. My sympathy rests with poor General Gatacre after viewing the scene of his operations in the earlier phase of the campaign. From Dordrecht we escorted two or three convoys to the garrison and town of Jamestown, which had been for the last month back in a state of siege and semi-starvation.

Our next trek took us round Barkly district, where we hunted Fouche and Wessels. While in this district we still had a very difficult and mountainous district to operate on, and owing to the extreme altitude of some of the places, the cold at times was intense, nothing but snow-capped kopjes met our gaze. It reminded one of winter and the snow-topped hills of Galloway.

On October, the 3rd, we directed our footsteps for Aliwal North, where we arrived on the 5th of that month. Next day we started operations in the warm and genial clime of the Free State, under Knox, once more. For the first time for over a month I heard the plip-plot of the Mauser, but the affair amounted to nothing worse than sniping on the flank.

We wended our way along the banks of the Orange River, and then north along the Caledon River, until we came to a place called Wolvekop in the Smithfield and Rouxville district. Here we fortified our camp and started on the new scheme of operating, known as standing camps and patrols. This method is now the most satisfactory way of dealing with the enemy. The method pursued is as follows - Patrols go out with no baggage or waggons of any description. Pack mules carry rations and forage, thus ensuring a high-class standard of mobility. The enemy can thus be chased and run to earth without any hindrance or impediment in the way of transport whatever.

In this way during the months of October and November, Colonel Pilcher has accounted for more Boers than any other column, in the O.R.C. He accounted for 130 killed, wounded and prisoners. It would be needless for me to enter into a detailed account of the column's doings while at Wolvekop. All the prisoners belonged chiefly to Commandant Braunds or Brados commandoes whom we were on the hunt after. Braund had a force of between 400 to 500, and the various forces combined against him almost completely wiped out the lot.

About the middle of December the column left this district and came north of the Thabanchu Ladybrand line of blockhouses to enter into the conjunct move against De Wet and his recently concentrated forces of 1700 men with guns and pom-pom. Arriving at Thabanchu we were just in time to spend Christmas, which was celebrated by having a bean feast and sports, both on horse and foot.

Major Heath succeeded to the command of our column in room of Colonel Taylor, who said farewell for the time being to the column, having been detailed to go up with Colonel Lean to Wynburg with weak and sick horses.

This is a new plan for saving horse flesh, and ought to have been adopted long ago. Wynburg is Colonel Pilcher's temporary base depot. The method of dealing with sick horses is as follows; all weak and sick horses are sent into the depot here to be tended and rested instead of being shot. They are sent out again to the column as fresh and fit for the trek as the first day they started. They are practically speaking remounts.

Since leaving the company they have had a pretty rough time of it at the hands of 'Johnny Boer'. On each occasion a patrol of 25 under Lieutenant G.K. Anderson (Glenluce), went out and got surrounded by 150 Boers. After a gallant defence the patrol had to surrender, but not before they had killed six and wounded many of the enemy. Our fellows had one killed and seven wounded, one of them only belonged to the 17th, the remainder were 18th fellows. Lieutenant Anderson accounted for four himself. He has been recommended for the D.S.O. for his valour in the action, as well as one or two men for the D.S.M.

During various other sundry engagements in January our company had several of its members captured. The district, Major Heath is at present working in, is round Senekal and Bethlehem way. The place is simply rocking with Boers under De Wet and fighting is of daily occurrence. There has been a lot of casualties in the column during my absence. All General Knox's column are in the Senekal district. News just to hand that our column has chased a commando of the enemy into Lord Basing, who captured 50 or so of them, but I have no details of the affair. I think I have given you a fair outline of what has been going on up to date. I shall now revert my thoughts across the ocean to dear auld Scotland.

From the latest news from home I gather that the War Office has once more trusted on the patriotism of the country for part of her reinforcements in the shape of more Volunteers and Yeomanry. How are the Galloway Rifle Volunteers responding? Are there many more adventurous youths from the Wigtown section? I expect the general tendency will be to join the I.Y. with view of the increased state of remuneration. Those joining the I.Y. will find that they have their work cut out for them for their 5/- per day, whereas a Volunteer will have a comparative easy, if somewhat monotonous life, in a blockhouse.

Work on the veldt, I may say, so far as mounted troops are concerned, is harder than ever it was. Nothing but continuous night marching and incessant hard trekking is the mode now resorted to for bringing the war to a definite conclusion.

We have all completed our years service, and so far no date has been fixed, or in fact nothing has been said regarding our return home. Personally I do not expect to touch the shores of England before June at the earliest. We may hear something when all the reinforcements have arrived. Most of the fellows like the life well, and some enjoy the free roving loose sort of life. No doubt active service has its drawbacks in the shape of privatious hardships, which we have all suffered. Any soldier or Volunteer coming out here must make up his mind to these things, as active service is not always the best of sport, although at times it has a certain amount of excitement.

Speaking as the Imperial Yeomanry as a fighting force, much has been said of them at home. I think the remarks of our home press and certain M.P.'s were quite uncalled for and even unjust to those Yeomanry at present serving in South Africa. The public criticism has without a doubt cast a slur over the whole Yeomanry on account of the innefficient business. No doubt there are one or two 'bad Ones' amongst the I.Y. as there are in the best of corps, but what is something like 350 men out of 17,000 Imperial Yeomanry. Apart from the Imperial Yeomanry as a whole, and taking my Company, the 17th, itself, I can safely say there is no game dare-devil fighting men in any regular or irregular force at the present time serving in South Africa.

They all do exactly the same work as the regulars, and have often won the praise and admiration of the M.I. who fought side by side with us. Of course this is not condemning poor 'Tommy Atkins', for there is no better soldier in his country's cause than the British soldier. I hope you do not think I am boasting of the Ayrshire Yeomanry."

Lieutenant Harry Shortridge, a member of 'F' Company, Maxwellton, Galloway Rifle Volunteers, was selected as Officer in Charge of the Galloway contingent of the 1st Active Service Company, King's Own Scottish Borderers, which sailed for South Africa on the 13th February, 1900. Unfortunately, Lieutenant Shortridge, was taken ill prior to his departure and he later volunteered for and was commissioned in the Scottish Company of Volunteer Cyclists, on the 26th March, 1901.

Lieutenant Shortridge was stationed at Jagersfontein Road, in the Orange River Colony, about 80 miles south of the capital, Bloemfontein. These Cycle Companies operated in the escort of columns, and the delivery of despatches, cycling their heavy cumbersome machines over open and trackless country. All in all, however, Lieutenant Shortridge, appears to have had quite a happy war.

The following letter was written by Lieutenant Harry Shortridge, late 'F' Company, Galloway Rifle Volunteers, Maxwellton, who enlisted in the Scottish Cyclist Corps.

"Last Monday, (24th June, 1901), I had my first taste of powder. I am stationed at Jagersfontein Road, with twenty three men and that morning the Commandant sent me with a Cape Cart and sixteen men to get some furniture from a farm. We got out all right, and when about five hundred yards from the farm, on the road home, a shot came just about ten yards on the right of my bike. My men were started. There were ten Boers on our front, ten on our right and about twelve on the left. We shifted them from their first position and they dismounted and I got a grand volley into them as they were consulting together. That made them hop. They got on their horses again and in their first position started to retire. I got a grand shot at his back at about four hundred yards and bowled him right over his horse's neck. That was my first kill. We peppered away for about two hours and then Lieutenant Wisner came up with two mounted infantry and the Boers made a very wide detour to the left to try and get on to three kopjes, to cut off our retreat back to camp, but we were equal to them and got four men on to each kopje before they got round. We drew them gradually back till they came to within about 2,000 yards of our gun, and it opened fire on them. You should have seen them then. They went off like the wind. We accounted for about six of them. I have got a telegram of congratulations from General Hart, on the success of our first skirmish and hoping we will continue as we begun. I have sent the telegram home.

I am enjoying life out here, first rate. The climate is lovely.

Yesterday, with six native scouts and a man called De Koch, who is the interpreter at Jagersfontein Road, we shot six buck, ten partridges and four hares. It was fine sport."

(13) Red velvet shoulder flash worn by the men of the Galloway Rifle Volunteers, who served with the King's Own Scottish Borderers in South Africa, in 1900-02. This shoulder flash was worn by Private Robert Cochrane 'E' Company, New Galloway.

CHAPTER 13

REFORMS OF THE VOLUNTEER FORCE
THE ENROLLED STRENGTHS OF THE GALLOWAY RIFLE VOLUNTEERS,
1863 - 1908,
TOGETHER WITH THE NATIONAL ENROLLED STRENGTHS 1861 - 1908

In June, 1878, the Volunteer authorised strengths were increased to compensate for the growing unrest on the Indian Continent. It was anticipated that when the Volunteer returns for 1878 were published they would be, for the first time in excess of 200,000. Large numbers of regular troops were being mobilised and sent to the Afghanistan Border with a view to the invasion of Afghanistan. Later that year Britain was to invade Afghanistan leading to the 2nd Anglo-Afghan War.

The following figures reflect the combined strengths of the Rifle and Artillery Volunteers of the Dumfries and Galloway area for the Volunteer year ended 31st October, 1878.

	Maximum authorised Establishment	Efficients	Non-Efficients	Total Enrolled	Proficients	Officers & Sergeants
Kirkcudbrightshire	680	560	29	589	13	38
Dumfriesshire (Rifles only)	1000	688	64	752	28	49
Wigtownshire	440	353	48	401	13	19

N.B. Proficient - those who take a written military examination in front of their Adjutant and thereby earn a special capitation grant of 50/-.

The total enrolled strength of the Galloway Rifle Volunteers for the year ended 31st October, 1878 was 679 with the total enrolled strength of the Kirkcudbrightshire and Wigtownshire Artillery Volunteers being 311.

The corresponding figures for the previous year ended, 31st October, 1877, was Galloway Rifle Volunteers, total enrolled strength 671, an increase of 8 members in 1878, with Kirkcudbrightshire and Wigtownshire Artillery Volunteers being 237 members, an increase of 74 members in 1878.

With comparable increases throughout the Country, the aims of the War Office Authorities were achieved in that the Volunteer returns published on the 1st November, 1878, showed a total strength of enrolled members in the Volunteer Movement to be 203,213, of which 200,161, were efficient members.

With the unrest in Afghanistan contained, Britain was to control Afghan affairs and remain in occupation until Afghanistan gained its independence in 1919, the War Office Authorities were to use these increased Volunteer figures to institute its first reforms of the Volunteer Service, and in 1879, they were to introduce the unpopular regulations which made for the compulsory retirement of Volunteers at 50 years of age. An earlier attempt had been made by the military authorities in 1870, by the introduction of the Army Enlistment Act, to build up an additional reserve of trained men, who were more readily accessible to the authorities than those of the Volunteers, who were not subject to the same discipline, nor age and fitness requirements as those of the regular soldier. The subject of the Act was the introduction of a 12 year enlistment to the Colours, together with a further reserve of 6 years, during which time the reservist might be re-called to the Line. The introduction of this Act failed to have any great impact on the reserve forces readily available to the authorities, who were once again compelled to return to the Volunteer Force for their man-power and defence requirement. However, by the introduction of these new age requirements, the military authorities, hoped to eventually streamline the Volunteer Service , into a force more in keeping with the requirments of the Regular Army.

There was a strong resentment to the introduction of these new age regulations from within the Volunteer Movement which resulted in a climb down by the authorities who were to issue an amendment to allow existing serving Volunteers to continue their service to the age of 60 years, however, a demand that Volunteers should be allowed to continue as long as they were able was dismissed.

These new regulations were to have but little effect on the total enrolled strengths of the Galloway Rifle Volunteers:-

1879 - 686 enrolled members
1880 - 705
1881 - 715
1882 - 672

1883:-

Artillery

	Maximum Establishment	Efficient	Non Efficient	Total Enrolled	Proficients Officers & Sergeants	Present at Inspection
Ayrrshire	570	476	15	491	18	427
Kirkcudbrightshire	80	72	7	79	2	62
Wigtownshire	240	196	8	204	6	169

Rifles

Ayrshire	1516	1448	17	1465	51	1147
Dumfriesshire	1000	666	55	721	21	629
Kirkcudbrightshire	600	467	10	477	9	387
Wigtownshire	200	153	1	154	6	142

Combined total of Kirkcudbrightshire and Wigtownshire - the Galloway Rifle Volunteers, 1883 - 631.

The annual returns for the Volunteer movement in general were on the increase over this same period, no doubt as a result of the on-going Afghan War, together with the Zulu War, (1879) and the 1st Boer War (1880-81). With a total number of 209,365 enrolled Volunteers of which 202,428 were efficient, being recorded throughout the Country in 1883, this was to be the highest ever enrolled strength within the Volunteer movement from its inception in 1859. However, this slight downward trend of the Galloway Rifle Volunteers was soon to recover to match the national trend and in 1884, the total strength of the Galloway Rifles was 643 enrolled members and by 1885 had passed its 1878 figure with a total of 740 enrolled members.

It was during this period of unrest on the Indian and African Continents that Lieutenant Colonel J. G. Maitland, Officer Commanding the Galloway Rifle Volunteers was to issue the following Regimental Order, dated 2nd May, 1881.

"It is with feelings of pain and regret that the Lieutenant Colonel Commanding, records the death of Major Singleton, 92nd Highlanders, late Adjutant of this Corps. During the five years that he held the appointment he performed his duties most zealously and efficiently and his general manner, his honesty of purpose, and his many other good sterling qualities made him many friends.

His career since leaving this Corps up to the date of his much lamented death was watched with the greatest interest and anxiety.

In Afghanistan where he was promoted for conspicuous gallantry, he served in the Forces under Sir Frederick Roberts, which made a march more than famous, covering 320 miles in 24 days, and inflicting two crushing defeats on the enemy. Only a few months after this brilliant career, he received his death wounds at Majuba Hill while rallying his men. Wouded in no less that four places, and for 36 hours exposed to the most inclement weather, his state was from the first critical. On the 1st of May, he breathed his last.

Deep indeed is the sorrow of our late lamented Adjutant's friends, most sincere their sympathy with his widow and fatherless children.

As a mark of respect to the late Major Singleton the Lieutenant Colonel, desires that all Officers of this Corps, when in uniform, appear in mourning of the space of one month from this date.

By Order
(Sgd.) H. Farrer, Captain and Adjutant."

The battle of Majuba Hill, in March, 1881, was the only major battle of the 1st Boer War, fought on the Transvaal - Natal Border. This battle, won by the Boer, resulted in a peace favourable to the Transvaal, by a British Government fearful of becoming embroiled in an expensive and drawn out war.

Major L.C. Singleton served as Adjutant to the Galloway Rifle Volunteers, from the 7th November, 1871, to the 31st December, 1876. He lived near Dumfries.

Recruiting to the Volunteer movement was to continue its upward trend, no more so than in Galloway when in 1893, a total of 774 members were enrolled in the Regiment. This was to lead to a Regimental Order dated 16th January, 1894, issued by Lieutenant Colonel J.M. Kennedy, directing that in future no recruits were to be enrolled under 5'6" in height and a 35" chest measurement.

Once again this local reform was to have little or indeed no effect on recruiting, the following interesting statistics show an increase of four Volunteers, from those of 1893.

The following was the total strength of the Battalion, up to the end of the Volunteer year ended, 31st October, 1895:-

	Proficient Officers	Proficient Sergeants	Efficients	Non-Efficients	Total
'A' Company	1	5	114	3	117
'B' ..	5	7	100	1	101
'C' ..	5	4	69	1	70
'D' ..	3	5	102	2	104
'E' ..	2	6	75	-	75
'F' ..	2	7	107	-	107
'G' ..	1	4	106	-	106
'H' ..	1	5	98	-	98
	19	43	771	7	778

Ages of Enrolled Volunteers as at 1st November 1895

Under 17 years of age				9
17 years and under 18 years of age				49
18	"	19	..	61
19	"	20	..	72
20	"	21	..	68
21	"	22	..	44
22	"	23	..	38
23	"	24	..	42
24	"	25	..	39
25	"	26	..	36
26	"	27	..	29
27	"	28	..	25
28	"	29	..	28
29	"	30	..	28
30	"	35	..	82
35	"	40	..	63
40	"	45	..	30
45	"	50	..	19
50 and upwards				16
			total	778

Service of Enrolled Members as at 1st November, 1895

20 years and upwards				49
15 and under 20 years				49
10	..	15	..	80
9	..	10	..	16
8	..	9	..	22
7	..	8	..	25
6	..	7	..	36
5	..	6	..	45
4	..	5	..	59
3	..	4	..	80
2	..	3	..	96
1	..	2	..	113
Under 1 year				108
				778

In 1895 Britain was once again embroiled in the politics of the Transvaal, South Africa, bringing them into conflict with the Boer. The Boer, backed by the German Kaiser, began to re-arm, 1896-99, making the outcome of war inevitable. It was at this stage that the Volunteers (Military Service Act) 1895, was introduced in order that Volunteers could offer their services for duty which did not amount to invasion or insurrection. This was now to include service abroad and in particular South Africa, where many Volunteers were to serve under the terms of this Act (1899-1902).

In view of the threatened conflict, in October, 1897, the War Office authorities elaborated plans for extending the scope of the Volunteer Acts in such a manner as to make the whole of the Volunteer Force readily available for foreign service. The War Office could see little use, in modern warfare, for a Force whose duties were of a purely defensive nature and they believed that a re-structured Volunteer Force could be a valuable reserve for service abroad. However, the authorities were forced to admit defeat, it being reported, "the difficulty of extending the system so as to make the Volunteers more generally available has been due rather to the jealousy or conservatism of the Army than to unwillingness of the 'Citizen Army' to place itself at the disposal of the Military Authorities."

The outbreak of the Boer War in South Africa was however, to siganl the beginning of the end of the Volunteer Force as we had known it, the War Office authorities wanting to make it part of a National Army, having a well defined and determined sphere of action which would appeal to the Military authorities of the day. As such new Rules and Regulations, both of a local and national authority were issued, thereby consolidating and clearly defining the expectations of both an efficient Volunteer and Corps.

On the 17th August, 1901, Colonel J.M. Kennedy, Officer Commanding the Galloway Rifle Volunteers was to issue the following, "New Rules for the Battalion".

i). The Corps is serving under the Volunteer Act, 1863, and the members are consequently subject to the provisions of that Act, and of any other Act by which it has been or shall be amended, and to all regulations which have been or shall be issued, under the authority of the Secretary of State for War.

ii). The Corps shall consist of two classes - (1) Enrolled members, consisting of efficients and non-efficients, and of - (2) Honorary members as provided in rule xiv.

iii). Any Officer or other enrolled member who was returned in the list of non-efficients in the last annual return of the Corps, or who enlisted in the regular forces without having qualified as an efficient in the last year of, or in the year previous to, such enlistment shall on or before the 1st December next following pay to the funds of the Corps a sum equal to the amount of Government capitation grant which he failed to earn. The Officer Commanding shall have power to remit such payment in special cases. Note. This rule was enforced on the members of the Galloway Rifle Volunteers who volunteered for active service in South Africa, they being required to repay the capitation grant they failed to earn through their being absent from the Corps.

iv). The Officer Commanding will propose gentlemen for commissions as Officers, in accordance with the regulations in force for the time being.

v). The non-commissioned officers shall be appointed by the Officer Commanding.

vi). No person shall be admitted as a member unless with the approval of the Officer Commanding.

vii). Each enrolled member must be provided with uniform and accoutrements of the pattern approved by the Secretary of State for War.

viii). Each member shall be responsible for the due preservation and return in good order, when he ceases to be a member of the Corps, of all articles issued to him which are property of His Majesty's Government or of the Corps, fair wear and tear only excepted.

ix). The expression 'property of the Corps' shall include all articles which have been purchased out of the funds of the Corps or presented to the Corps.

x). Although the Officer Commanding is solely responsible for the discipline of the Corps, he is empowered by Act of Parliament to assemble at any time a Court of Inquiry to inquire into any matter relative to the Corps, excepting the conduct of a Commissioned Officer. Such Court of Inquiry when assembled, shall consist of three or five members of the Corps, one at least of whom shall be an Officer. Any inquiry in reference to a Commissioned Officer must, under Act of Parliament, be made by a Court composed of Officers of the Volunteer force within the county (i.e. A,B,E,F,G, & H Companies, Kirkcudbrightshire; C, and D, Wigtownshire) convened under due authority.

xi). The Officer Commanding shall fix the time and place for parades, drills, and rifle practice.

xii). The property of the Corps is by Act of Parliament vested in the Officer Commanding; but a Finance

Committee to aid him in the management of the finances of the Corps shall be appointed. This Committee shall consist of four members besides the Officer Commanding, and of these four the field officer appointed by the Commanding Officer and the quarter master shall always be two. The remaining two members shall hold office for one year, and shall be appointed annually, upon the first day of July by the Officer Commanding, from amongst the officers commanding Companies, in the following order:-

1st. Officers commanding 'A' and 'H' Companies.
2nd. Officers commanding 'B' and 'G' Companies.
3rd. Officers commanding 'C' and 'F' Companies.
4th. Officers commanding 'D' and 'E' Companies.

Two shall form a quorum. In the event of a vacancy occurring during the year, the Officer succeeding the Officer who has ceased to act shall take the vacant place. The meetings will be convened by the Officer Commanding.

xiii). The Officer Commanding shall cause an abstract of the accounts to be prepared annually for the information of every member of the Corps.

xiv). Honorary members shall consist of (a) Officers retired with the right to wear the uniform of the rank: (b) Non-commissioned officers and men who have been returned as efficient at least eight times in the annual return of the Corps, who are willing to re-enrol should occasion require their serives, and who, on resignation, are approved of by the Officer Commanding: (c) Commanding Officers on completion of their commands: (d) Officers, non-commissioned officers, and men retired on account of age, provided the special sanction of the Officer Commanding to their being retained has been given: (e) Officers of His Majesty's services or retired Officers of the Army, Navy, Militia, Volunteer and civil services of the United Kingdom, or of India, or Colonies, or Crown Colonies, or dependencies, on payment of five shilling per annum to the funds of the Corps: (f) Soldiers and sailors, retired, or those on leave or furlough during their residence in the neighbourhood of a rifle range by special permission of the Officer Commanding, without payment: (g) Persons who are not Volunteers or in any class above mentioned by special permission of the Officer Commanding, who will decide in such cases whether the honorary member shall pay one guinea or a less sum per annum.

(xv) Honorary members subscriptions will be treated as a private fund at the disposal of the Officer Commanding.

(xvi) Honorary members as defined in (a), (b), (c), and (d) of rule (xiv), with previous service in the Corps may wear the uniform of the Corps with the distinguishing marks prescribed by regulations. They are not to intefere in any way with the military duties of the Corps, but they may, when the Officer Commanding approves, fall in at parades other than the inspection or Adjutant's drills in uniform or plain clothes.

(xvii) Honorary members shall be permitted to use the rifle ranges when they are not required exclusively by enrolled members, under regulations to be made and altered from time to time by the Officer Commanding. Honorary members shall not be permitted to take part in any shooting competitions of the Corps, or inter-company matches, or Company competitions for prizes, excepting for any special prizes declared open to them at such competitions.

(xviii) Members will be supplied with copies of the rules of the Corps on application to the Officer Commanding their Company.

On the 4th November, 1901, by Army Order 246, the War Office were to issue the following "New Regulations for Volunteers."

(1) A Volunteer who is a member of a Corps on the 1st November in any year shall be entitled to be deemed an efficient Volunteer during the ensuing 12 months, if subject to the conditions hereinafter prescribed, he has during the preceding year, fulfilled the requirements stated in the schedule hereto.

(2) In the course of each year, ending 31st October, the Adjutant of each Corps shall select such Volunteers as in his opinion have fulfilled the requirements and possess the qualifications aforesaid, and submit their names to the Commanding Officer of their Corps, with a view to their being returned as efficients.

(3) If the Adjutant refused to return any Volunteer as efficient, and the Volunteer considers himself aggrieved thereby, the Volunteer may appeal to the Commanding Officer of his Corps.

(4) If the Commanding Officer differs from the opinion of the Adjutant, he shall refer the matter to

the Officer appointed by one of His Majesty's Principal Secretaries of State to act in that behalf, whose decision shall be final.

(5) Where the situation and circumstances of an Artillery Volunteer or Rifle Volunteer Corps, in any particular year are such, as in the opinion of one of His Majesty's Principal Secretaries of State, to create serious obstacles to the fulfillment by any of the Volunteers belonging to that Corps of the requirements of attendance at gun or musketry practice, the Secretary of State shall have power to dispense with the requirements from any of the Volunteers belonging to such Corps in such year.

(6) Where the situation and circumstances of Rifle Volunteer Corps are such as in the opinion of one of His Majesty's Principal Secretaries of State to create serious obstacles to the fulfilment by the Volunteers belonging to the Corps of the requirement of attendance at battalion parade, each number of times, within 12 months as may be prescribed. The Secretary of State shall have the power to reduce for such Corps the number of battalion parades and to increase proportionately the number of Company parades, requisite to entitle the Volunteers belonging to the Corps to be returned as efficient.

(7) Where any Corps shall have been precluded by an epidemic from complying with the requirements herein prescribed, or shall in the first year of its service have encountered exceptional difficulties in the completion of its organisation and efficiency of its members, it shall be competant to the Secretary of State to modify, so far as applies to such year of service, the stipulated conditions of efficiency of any members of such Corps.

(8) No Volunteer who is absent from the annual inspection of his Corps, except in cases of sickness, duly certified, or by leave granted in writing for special cause by the Commanding Officer, shall be entitled to be deemed efficient.

(9) Where a Corps is by its own default not inspected during the year, or where the Officer inspecting a Volunteer Corps, at the annual inspection, in any year, report that the Corps is not efficient in training and instruction to his satisfaction or that irregularities have occurred in its training and administration, then not withstanding anything hereinbefore provided, one of His Majesty's Principal Secretaries of State, shall have power to direct that none of the Volunteers belonging to the Corps shall be deemed efficient.

(10) No Corps or individual Volunteer will be exempted from attending a camp for two consecutive years.

(11) The Inspecting Officer, at the annual inspection, in any year, shall have the power to direct that a Volunteer shall be deemed non-efficient, if he considers it proper to do so, on account of the want of efficiency in training or instruction of that Volunteer, or on account of his rifle or other arm being in bad order and condition.

(12) In case any alteration in the condition for efficiency should from time to time appear expedient, one of His Majesty's Principal Secretaries of State, may make the same by regulation, so as no alteration be thereby made in the amount of the requirements and qualifications and so as none of the provisions of this order be therby altered.

(13) Terms used in this Order, or in the schedule hereto, have the same meanings as they have when used in the Volunteer Act, 1863. The term recruit used in the schedule means a Volunteer who has never served either for two months in the Royal Navy, Regular Army, Army Reserve, Royal Marines or Royal Irish Constabulary, nor has attended the preliminary drill or drill on enlistment, or annual training of a Militia unit, nor has performed one years efficient service in the Imperial Yeomanry, the Volunteers, or the permanent forces of a colony, nor in the year immediately preceding his enrolment has attended, as a member of a cadet corps or cadet battalion, sanctioned by the Secretary of State, the number of drills prescribed for recruits of the arm of the Service which he has joined.

(14) The provisions herein contained shall take effect from 1st November, 1901.

Note. The schedule referred to in these Regulations has not been traced but the varying terms relative to the making of an efficient are included throughout this history.

Much criticism was levelled by the leading Volunteers as to the introduction of these new and more stringent Regulations, the fear being that Volunteers would be unable to meet the criteria required to make themselves efficient particularly with their commitment to employers and now, even more so, with the introduction of Sction 10 which was to make attendance at camp compulsory every second year. It had only been the previous year that Colonel Kennedy had made an impassioned plea, to the employers of Galloway, through the offices of the local press, to have his men released from their labours in order that they could attend camp.

Galloway Rifle Volunteers,
Headquarters, Castle Douglas,
April 24th, 1900.

"Sir. I should consider it a great favour if you would allow me through the medium of your very widely read paper to approach the employers of labour in Galloway on behalf of the Government scheme for safeguarding the empire at this very critical time without having recourse to conscription or universal military service, which all the other nations of Europe have been obliged to adopt and to which we shall have to submit if the voluntary system fails.

The strength of our Navy has prevented attempts being made to undo all the good we have already done in India and Egypt, but it seems doubtful if we shall continue in the possession of our trade and our Colonies unless we can put into the field a much larger army than has hitherto been considered sufficient. Government hopes to do this by offering very liberal inducements to Volunteers to become more efficient and to increase their numbers.

It is hoped that the employers of labour, whose patriotism has always assisted us so much in allowing their men to go into camp, will again assist us this year when a greater sacrifice of time is asked for. We are all aware what inconvenience may be caused by granting their hands leave of absence , but steps are being taken to consult the interests of the employers. Let us hope that no apathy amongst the Volunteers themselves will land us either into conscription or national calamity.

The inducements which the Government offers to Volunteers are as follows:-

Colour Sergeants	3/- per diem, with 9d per diem for rations
Sergeants	2/4d
Lance Sergeants	2/-
Corporals	1/8d
Lance Corporals	1/3d
Privates	1/-

1/6d per diem will be added to each man from a special Government grant, and for married men separation allowance at the rate of 1/1d for the wife and 2d for each child per diem.

Take for example, the case of a Sergeant with a wife and three children. He will receive 2/4d + 1/6d + 1/1d + 6d = 5/5d per diem or 37/11d per week.

A private with a wife and three children will receive, 1/- + 1/6d + 1/1d + 6d = 4/1d per diem, or 28/7d per week.

Unmarried privates will receive 17/6d per week.

The conditions are that at least half the battalion goes into camp for not less than 14 days. Sundays included, but consecutive 14 days are not required. A volunteer may return home and go back to finish his 14 days in camp, but must pay for this extra double journey himself. The Government only takes him once to camp and back. Should a Volunteer be able to remain more than 14 days in camp he will get pay and extras on the same scale as above up to 28 days for each day in camp.

I am

J.M. Kennedy, Colonel."

With these criticisms of the new regulations very much in mind, Lord Roberts, V.C. Commander-in-Cheif South Africa, 1900-01, through the offices of the Secretary of State for War was to make the following submissions to the Volunteers. No doubt his good name and recent military fame being uppermost in the minds of the authorities.

"Lord Roberts has issued the following instructions, with the approval of the Secretary of State for War. They form an important statement of the opinion of the Commander in Chief in the utility of the Citizen Army and the standards of efficiency, in view of recent war experience, he regards as essential. Appended in the text of the Order, which will be inserted in the Regimental or Battalion Orders, of every Corps. "Volunteer Efficiency"

(1) The attention of the Volunteer force is directed to Section 7 of Volunteer Regulations respecting the conditions of efficiency for Officers and Volunteers issued by Army Order 246 of 1901, viz:- "In exceptional cases which may arise in any year when it can be shown that a Corps has made every effort to fulfil the requirements for efficiency, as laid down in the Order in Council of November, 4th 1901, but has wholly, or as regards some of its members, failed to do so, the General Officer Commanding will be kept from time to time fully informed of the facts, and any application recommended by him for exemption from the

conditions will require the special consideration of the Secretary of State.

(2) This section is intended to meet the special case of an Officer appointed or Volunteer enrolled previous to the date of issue of above Army Order, and who during the period of his present engagement with his Corps may be able to satisfy his Commanding Officer that owing to his civil occupation is prevented, wholly or partially, from attending camp in any year. Such engagement will not be held to extend beyond November 1st, 1904.

(3) Similarly, in the event of a Corps satisfying the Commander-in-Chief, on the special recommendation of the General Officer Commanding, that in consequence of its having experienced exceptional difficulties it is prevented from complying with the prescribed conditions, its case will be specially considered.

(4) Volunteers of all ranks should, however, understand that in view of the recent developments in the conditions and requirements of modern warfare, the training of troops, regular or auxilliary, must be conducted on a systematic and progressive principle, in which practice in essential duties of war is an imperative feature.

(5) For some years past the Volunteer force has constantly claimed to be seriously accepted as a reliable and organised section of the Army for home defence. It is now determined that the responsibility claimed shall be realised. Under the old regulations it was impossible for either an Officer or Volunteer, although he might become technically efficient so as to earn grants for his Corps, to attain the high standard of efficiency now requisite to enable him to take his appointed place in the Military organisation and defence of the Kingdom.

(6) It follows that the force must adapt itself to such a system of training as will admit of its members from the highest to the lowest, being exercised and inspected in actual tactical operations over suitable country or in actual works of defence. An annual camp, with which the year's training should in this manner culminate is, therefore indispensible. To facilitate such training in the case of those Corps which, in the opinion of the General Officer Commanding, are unable to train in complete units, provisional Regiments or Battalions, under Officers of the regualr forces and consisting of batteries or companies detailed from Volunteer Corps will be formed at suitable stations during certain months of the camping season. Further instructions regarding this arrangement will be issued in due course.

(7) It is fully realised that the civil occupation of some Volunteers will not admit of their complying with the minimum conditions necessary for an effective course of military training, and that, consequently, the force must ultimately lose the services of such men. It is preferable to have a somewhat smaller number of highly trained Officers and men sufficiently to meet all the demands for home defence.

(8) The State requires that a suitable standard of military training shall be secured in return for the outlay of public money, and consequently, the enrolment in future of Volunteers who are unable to afford adequate time for any military training beyond elementary barrack square drill cannot be permitted.

(9) While it is confidently expected that Officers and Volunteers will endeavour to meet the changes necessitated by the development of modern warfare, the operation of the Regulations will be carefully watched, and any amendments which experience shows are desireable will be effected."

In 1898, the total enrolled strength of the Galloway Rifle Volunteers was 749, but with the outbreak of the Boer War in 1899, maximum authorised strengths were once again increased to compensate for the Regular Army being called to South Africa. Patriotic calls to the young men of Galloway were to quickly swell the ranks of the Volunteers and in 1899, the total enrolled strength was 800. In 1900, the figures had once again increased to 817 enrolled members and by the 31st October, 1901, to a massive all time high of 830 enrolled members. However, in consequence of the implementation of these new Regulations of the 4th November, 1901, the enrolled strengths of the Galloway Rifle Volunteers were to drop dramatically, their figures being mirrored throughout the Country. The total enrolled strength of the Galloway Rifles for year ended 31st October, 1902, was 756. Bearing in mind that a Volunteer, in theory, could leave the Regiment on giving 14 days notice, in reality he had to give a written undertaking that he would make himself efficient for a period of three years or be responsible to the Company for the capitation grant he failed to earn, recoverable in Court of Law. This fact was noted by Lord Roberts who included the proviso in Secrion 2 of his Rules, "Such engagement will not be held to extend beyond November 1st, 1904." In 1903, the enrolled strength of the Galloway Rifles had dropped to 672, with the 3rd year figure of 31st October, 1904, falling to almost, an all time low of 648 enrolled members, details as follows:-

	Officers	Sergeants	Rank & File	Non-Effic.	Total
'A'	2	4	85	1	92
'B'	6	10	76	0	91
'C'	1	5	65	1	72
'D'	1	6	80	1	88
'E'	2	5	38	1	46
'F'	4	7	70	2	83
'G'	3	5	78	0	86
'H'	2	6	51	30	90
	21	48	543	36	648

The large number of non-efficients at Dalbeattie was due to the New Abbey/Beeswing section being raised on 21st October, 1904, and who had not been able to make themselves efficient in that short time. Had it not been for the raising of this Section then the enrolled strength would have been a good deal lower. However by the beginning of 1905, the enrolled strength of the Galloway Rifle Volunteers had fallen to an all time low of 584 members.

The capitation grants earned for 1904 were as follows:- 585 men at 35/- each and 27 for lower grant of 25/-, through their not having been at camp. There were two grants of 35/- each for men from Maxwellton who joined the Regular Army. The proficiency grants were 14 Officers and 41 Sergeants at 50/- and one Officer gaining a grant of 30/- for tactics.

The discovery of deficiences in the Army recently engaged in South Africa intensified the anxiety of the military authorities to establish the Volunteer Force on a much stronger basis. Much patch-work had been accomplished of recent times but one effect had been to spread dis-satisfaction amongst both Officers and men and as such, in April, 1903, a Royal Commission was appointed to enquire into the organisation, numbers, terms of service of the Militia and Volunteer Service. The Commissioners, who were also required to report whether any, and, if any, what changes were required in order to secure that these forces should be maintained in the condition of military efficiency and of adequate strength, were, the Duke of Norfolk, Chairman; the Earl of Derby; Lord Grenfel; Major-General Sir Coleridge Grove; Sir Ralph Knox; Colonel George O'Callaghan Westropp; Lieutenant Colonel E.H. Llewellyn; Lieutenant Colonel E. Satterthwaite; Lieutenant Colonal J.A. Dalmahoy; Mr. Henry Spencer Wilkinson and the Duke of Richmond and Gordon.

In June, 1904, the report, which was one of the most important drafted in relation to the Volunteer Force, could only be described as drastic and should the recommendations of the Commission have ever reached the stage of crystallisation in an Act of Parliament, the whole principle of voluntary service would have been abolished and a system of modified conscription substituted.

Militia.

The average strength of the Militia during the last ten normal years has been 113,554, the average number of men below 19 has been 35,010, and the average number of recruits annually has been 39,101. Deducting men returned as below 19, there are but 82,000 men fit, as regards age to take the field, but if, as in Continental armies, men below the age of 20 were not taken, the effective total is 69,000. The Commissioners, from the evidence received, declare that the drill and training is insufficient to fit the Militia units, at short notice, to oppose trained troops, and the average Militia Infantry Battalions would not be fit to take the field except after several months continuous embodiement. The training of the Militia Officer is inadequate to enable him perfectly to lead troops, and moreover, those Militia Officers whose purpose in joining this force is to obtain commissions in the Regular Army leave the force just as they are acquiring experience.

The Commisioners continue, We are forced in the conclusion that the Militia in its existing condition is unfit to take the field for the defence of the country. We think, however, that its defects arise from causes beyond the control of its Officers and men.

The Volunteers.

Dealing with the Volunteers, the report says that their average strength over the years 1883 to 1903, has been 223,589, the number of men below 19 being 20,000, and recruits averaging 44,000. Deducting below 20 the effective total is 165,000. After referring to the fact that the medical examination is less stringent with this force, and acknowledging the difficulties under which training is carried on, the Commissioners express the opinion that, taking the force as a whole, neither the musketry nor the tactical training of the rank and file would enable it to face with a prospect of success against a continental army.

The all-important question is the qualification of its Officers, and while many of them had an excellent military education, the majority had neither the theoretical knowledge nor the practical skill in the handling of troops which would make them competent instructors in peace or leaders in war. For these reasons, and on account of the limited training and defects of equipment and organisation, the Commissioners state that they are agreed that the Volunteer Force is not qualified to take the field against a regular army.

To increase the efficiency of these forces the Commissioners recommend increase in the period of training for the Militia particularly during the recruit stage, when a militiaman should receive not less than six month's continuous training during his first year. Commanding Officers of Battalions and a small staff of Company Officers should form part of the permanent staff, and to secure on mobilisation the requisite numbers of full age, the Militiaman should be enlisted for eight years, the last four years of obligatory training being reduced to a fortnight each year, and to keep a hold over the men the Commissioners suggest that a Militiaman should receive the present non-training bounty.

To increase the efficiency of the Volunteers, the report suggests that it should be managed from the War Office by a special department with a responsible head. The Commissioners propose certain changes in its financial administration. To obviate the undue importance Commanding Officers attach to numbers as compared with real efficiency they recommend that a portion of the State grant should take the form of an allowance per battery or company proportionate to the establishment, and that the balance only should be issued in the form of capitation grants.

The Commissioners recognise that fourteen days in camp each year is the longest period practically, and that the State should make adequate financial provision for ranges, ground of exercise, transport, tactical schools. These measures would enlarge the opportunities of Volunteers to educate themselves, and at the same time the creation of the organisation for war and the appointment of war leaders would provide the machinery for setting before the Volunteers the standards at which they must aim.

Recommendations.

(1) That as far as possible the whole able-bodied male population shall be trained to arms.

(2) That the training shall be given in a period of continuous service with the colours, not necessarily in barracks, and

(3) That the instruction shall be given by a body of specially educated and highly trained Officers.

We are convinced that only by the adoption of these principles can an army for home defence, adequate in strength and military efficiency to defeat an invader, be raised and maintained in the United Kingdom.

Thorough Training.

To make detailed recommendations under this head appears to us to be beyond the scope of the task entrusted to us, especially as the principles which we recommend cannot be adopted without producing an effect on the regular Army, but we submit the following general observations:- We believe that the necessary thorough training should be given within one year, after which only one or two annual periods of a few weeks' exercise or manoeuvres would be needed. The condition of such a short training being sufficient is that the instruction should be given by professional Officers and non-commissioned officers.

Under systems of this class the strength of the army on mobilisation depends on the numbers being taken for training each year, and upon the number of years during which liability to be called out for service in case of war remain.

Conclusion.

A home defence army capable, in the absence of the whole or the greater portion of the Regular Forces, of protecting this country against invasion can be raised and maintained only on the principle that it is the duty of every citizen of military age and sound physique to be trained for the national defence and to take part in it should emergency arise.

The report was met with a mixed reaction and elicited a great diversity of views. Volunteers accustomed to the existent status quo looked askance at the proposal to reduce the strength of their force. To some it appeared to be an act of ingratitude on the part of Government, whereas to others the object of the War Secretary, was to discourage the services of those whose aims were to play at 'Citizen Soldiers' and to encourage by every possible means the men who regarded enlistment as committing themselves to the discharge of serious obligation.

An Editorial of the *Kirkcudbrightshire Advertiser* dated, 22nd July, 1904, was to say, "It is obvious that the Volunteer who barely qualifies for efficiency cannot be so valuable, in a military sense, as the man who enters with enthusiasm into the training marked out for him. The one perfunctorily discharges his duty, the other brings it to bear on them an earnestness of purpose which commands success." It continued, "No doubt there will be some heart-searching amongst Volunteers pending the practical application of the scheme of 'Sorting Out'. Some difficulties may temporarily have to be faced but in the end the smooth working of the plan should be secured, a plan, whatever its elementary defects may be, that honestly aims at the attainment of a higher standard of efficiency, which will entitle the Volunteers still more to the respect, not only of the severe military critics, but of the country generally".

An Editorial of the same week of the *Dumfries and Galloway Standard* was to pronounce, "The inconveniences and hardships of conscription have very frequently been painted in lurid colours by those who have studied the systems on the Continent, and may consider it will be an evil day for industrial Great Britain when men have to join the colours and relegate their ordinary avocations to a secondary place. Even in time of peace militarism draws the life-blood of the nation, and however, fine conscription may be in principle in time of War it is not always infallible". It continued, "It is possible to argue of course that the threat of conscription, even in a modified form, is launched for the purpose of arresting the shrinkage of the Volunteer Force, and of stimulating enrollment, so that the lesser of the two evils may be chosen. This device, if such it be, is probably not wholly unjustifiable for the standard of the Volunteer Force has not been maintained at the desired level but in a great measure the War Office has itself to thank for the back-sliding. The pursuit of a policy of financial generosity and professional encouragement would do much to give a fillip to the Volunteer movement".

On the 7th July, 1905, the War Office was to take a step of the utmost importance which they accepted would vitally affect the Volunteer Force for the good or ill. The Army Council issued to all Officers Commanding a series of instructions, under the heading, 'The Physique of Volunteers'. It was anticipated that with the implementation of these new instructions the membership of the Volunteer Force would drop from its 1901 figure of 288,476 to a slim-lined and more effective figure of 182,000 members. The Volunteer who successfully passed through this new inquisition would be ranked as 'FIT'.

According to these new instructions, Officers Commanding, were required to have the medical Officer report on the Physique of all men under their command, with a view of seeing if they were 'FIT' to remain in the Regiment. Elaborate directions were given as to what constituted fitness. Great stress was laid upon the state of the teeth, "The Volunteer, if he is to remain in the force, must have sufficient sound teeth for proper mastication, while he must be free from all organic disease and have a first class constitution. Any defects which would prevent a man marching well or going on active service will also be fatal. Generally he must come up to the physical equivalent of 19 years, and not be over 45 years. But even if a man passes these tests satisfactorily, before he is to be counted as 'FIT' for active service, be returned as a 1st Class shot".

"Reports on these points having been completed, Officers Commanding are to inform the War Office of the number of 'FIT' and unfit under their command in the latter specifying the causes of unfitness".

"The duty is also cast in Officers Commanding, of stating whether in their judgement unfit units should be disembodied or amalgamated with more efficient Corps".

With their colours well and truly nailed to the mast, the War Office had issued some very important if not somewhat controversial instructions to the Volunteers, weeding out Volunteers who could not 'admit of their complying with the minimum conditions necessary for an effective course of military training', those considered unfit, together with the implementation of the new age Regulations. The authorities could now only sit back and await the publication of the Volunteer returns for October, 1905, to ascertain if their reforms would discourage the Volunteer or drive the nation towards compulsory military service. However, a little impetus was given in the recruitment of Volunteers, subject to the conditions of the new regulations, by the holding of a Royal Review, in the presence of His Majesty King Edward VII, at Edinburgh on, Monday, 18th September, 1905. These Reviews were generally seen by the Military authorities as a boost to morale and to encourage recruiting among both Volunteer and Regular Troops.

The authorities expectations would appear to be more than suitably founded by the report in the Press of the 8th September, 1905. "The forthcoming Royal Review has had a stimulating effect on the strength of the Galloway Rifle Volunteers, who are now 200 stronger than they were some months ago." (The actual figure was in fact, an increase of 130 Volunteers.)

The Government's introduction of the new regulations and streamlining of the Volunteer Corps was completely vindicated by the Volunteer movement, the total enrolled strength of the Galloway Rifle Volunteers as at 31st October, 1905, being 784 members. The returns as follows:-

	Officers	Sergeants	Rank & File	Total	Non-Eff.
'A' Kirkcudbright	3	7	102	112	-
'B' Castle Douglas	6	7	93	106	-
'C' Stranraer	1	6	76	83	-
'D' Newton Stewart	1	6	108	115	-
'E' New Galloway	2	5	27	34	7
'F' Maxwellton	5	9	102	116	1
'G' Maxwellton	3	5	109	117	2
'H' Dalbeattie	3	4	82	89	2
	24	49	699	772	12

Total. 784

With these enrolled strengths of the Galloway Rifles being related nationwide, on 28th November, 1905, the ex-Secretary of State for War, Mr. Arnold Forster was to pronounce, "that the Army Council had now completed their recommendations in regard to the Volunteer Force, and that they had decided that there was to be no reduction in the members of the Volunteers but that their strength should be kept up with a margin of 5% to cover any further deficiencies on the introduction of further regulations. The Council further desired to encourage better attendance at Camp and alluded in detail to the re-arrangement of grants to secure a more servicable force."

The following returns of the Galloway Rifles Volunteers for the year ended 31st October, 1906, shows an enrolled strength of 830 effective members:-

	Officers	Staff & other Sergeants	Buglers Rank & File	Total Strength	Non-Effs.
'A'	1	7	98	106	1
'B'	4	9	125	138	0
'C'	1	6	83	90	0
'D'	1	6	121	128	2
'E'	1	4	50	55	0
'F'	3	6	102	111	2
'G'	4	7	101	112	1
'H'	2	6	76	84	0
	17	51	756	824	6

Total. 830

With recruiting to the Volunteer Movement very much on the increase Government were now in a strong position to bring about their final and major reforms of the Auxilliary Forces which would in due course lead to the disbanding of the Volunteers.

The following are the total enrolled strengths of the Galloway Rifle Volunteers, 1863 - 1908, together with the national enrolled strengths, 1861 - 1908.

Year	Enrolled Strength Galloway Rifle Volunteers	National Enrolled Strength
1861	-	161,239
1862	-	157,818
1863	559	162,935
1864	673	170,544
1865	656	178,484
1866	636	181,565
1867	685	187,864
1868	770	199,194
1869	782	195,287
1870	755	193,893
1871	817	192,608
1872	777	178,279
1873	714	171,937
1874	675	175,387
1875	655	181,086
1876	680	185,501
1877	671	193,026
1878	679	203,213
1879	686	206,265
1880	705	206,537
1881	715	208,308
1882	672	207,336
1883	631	209,365
1884	643	215,015
1885	740	224,012
1886	704	226,752
1887	709	228,038
1888	685	226,469
1889	640	224,021
1890	653	221,048
1891	694	222,046
1892	738	225,423
1893	774	227,741
1894	770	231,328
1895	778	231,704
1896	804	236,059
1897	751	231,798
1898	749	230,678
1899	800	229,854
1900	817	277,628
1901	830	288,476
1902	756	268,550
1903	672	253,281
1904	648	253,909
1905	784	249,611
1906	830	255,854
1907	775	252,791
1908	847 (10.1.1908)	224,217 (up to 1.4.1908)

CHAPTER 14

THE DISBANDING OF THE GALLOWAY RIFLE VOLUNTEERS -
THE FORMATION OF THE COUNTY ASSOCIATIONS -
THE RAISING OF THE 5TH (DUMFRIES & GALLOWAY) BATTALION, KING'S
OWN SCOTTISH BORDERERS - THE 5TH (SOUTH AYRSHIRE) BATTALION,
ROYAL SCOTS FUSILIERS AND THE KIRKCUDBRIGHT BATTERY OF
ROYAL FIELD ARTILLERY-
TOGETHER WITH A SHORT RESUMÉ OF THEIR SERVICE THROUGH THE
TWO GREAT WARS

On the 4th January, 1907, the Secretary for War, Mr. Haldane, was to release his draft proposal for the creation of a National Army which would replace the whole of the Auxilliary Forces. Initially, the report was to be heavily criticised.

"Men joining the new Force would serve voluntarily for 6 years, during which period they may elect to be placed on the active service or Regular Army roll for a period not exceeding 2 years.

Special schools of instruction are to be opened in all military centres, affording opportunities for Officers to receive technical instructions and a strong reserve of Officers is to be formed from which a Staff is to be selected.

Men in the first period of their service will be subject to a period of training lasting two weeks annually. Those who pass to the 'Reserve of the Territorial Army' will not be required to attend an annual training but may be called up for an annual muster.

Those of the Reserve Army selected for special duties in war will undergo additional training".

The debate on the Territorial and Reserve Forces Bill was to take place on the 10th April, 1907. The Secretary for War, in stating his case was to say. "The scheme depended on its success, on the patriotic feeling of our fellow-citizens. That was a high ideal, the more so when it was remembered that the conditions of service in the new Territorial Force would be more onerous than in the existing Volunteer Forces. Of course it remained to be seen whether the 300,000 men would be forthcoming, but if the free and compulsory education which the nation had enjoyed for the last 30 years had been on sound and effective lines, and had developed character at all, he felt confident that there would be plenty of men to come forward and serve in this new Force.

Many men at present serving in the Volunteer Force would be unable to continue their service in the Territorial Force but on the other hand a National Army with a clear cut plan marked out for it would appeal to a great many men who hitherto had held aloof because they believed that the Volunteer Forces had never been taken seriously by the Military Authorities. Public opinion, rightly directed for the next decade, would do more to bring a Territorial Force suited to our needs into existence than any amount of compulsion".

The Bill which was to become law under the Statute, the "Territorial and Reserve Forces Act, 1907, provided the necessary constitutional authority by which the Force was to take its place as an organised Force of the Crown, commanded and trained by the military authorities, but raised and administered by County Associations.

Mr. Haldane was to remark, "We call them Associations because that is a good old term invented by Oliver Cromwell". This was a reference to the Eastern Association of Counties which maintained and equipped Cromwell's troops during the civil war, 1642-49. However, these County Associations unlike Cromwell's Eastern Association of Counties, were to be a country-wide system of Associations, similar to the old Volunteer committees, under the authority of the Lord Lieutenant, responsible for the administration of the Territorial Force.

The Act was to prescribe the conditions of enlistment, service and discharge, regulate the periods of training, and authorise, subject to the sanction of Parliament, the embodiement of the Force when the Army Reserve was called out on a permanent service.

The Territorial Force, as regard the conditions of service, was not dissimilar in its principles to those of the Volunteer Force. Enlistment was to be purely voluntary. No Territorial soldier could ever be called upon to serve outside the United Kingdom, in peace or in war against his will. He would, however, be enlisted in the same manner as the regular soldier for a period not exceeding four years, but this would not in peace time, prevent his obtaining his discharge by the payment, where it was considered just that he should recoup the Association for the expenditure upon him, a sum, the extreme limit of which was fixed at £5, and delivering up of his arms and accoutrements in good order to the County Association, to which he belonged. The Association had power to dispense wholly, or in part with these obligations.

Provisions within the Act were considered such, as would enable of a higher measure of efficiency in time of peace and a more organised force in the event of war. The Territorial Officer would be freed from the financial responsibility of the old Volunteer Officer and would in future be chosen with sole regard to his qualification for command.

The Territorial soldier was for the first time to have the opportunity of serving in an army unit or department, if he so wished of some technical branch akin to his calling in civil life, Royal Engineers, Army Service Corps, Royal Army Medical Corps., etc. The effect was to be the opening of a wider field of selection for the Volunteer and which would greatly increase the efficiency of the Force.

The organisation of the Territorial Force was to be as that of the Regular Army with less emphasis on numbers and more emphasis on its organisation and training, with recruiting to and adoption of the ancillary and back-up services, more in keeping with a modern continental army.

An important advantage, it was hoped, would result from the institution of the County Associations. These Associations were to be charged with the raising, maintainance and equipment of the Force, as well as the care of Reservists, together with discharged soldiers, thereby bringing the civil authorities, in the Counties, into close contact with the administrative questions relating to military problems and organisation. Side by side with the military authorities, responsible for command and training, the County Associations would meet to discuss all matters affecting the welfare of the Force.

The devolution of responsibility upon the County Association was to increase local interest in the units, which that particular County was to maintain and administer, with local sentiments better provided for in such a manner than would be possible in a system of centralised control.

The work of the County Association, in administering the Territorial Force, was akin to that of administering the Regular Force, and although different in degree, by its very nature was to stimulate and arouse interest in the County in order to familiarise the civil communtiy with military matters, and to obtain the best results that could accrue from a system which was to induce a wider knowledge of the Army and of the principles governing its administration, together with the general knowledge of the civilian and the technical skill of the soldier.

On the passing of the Territorial and Reserve Forces Act, the Secretary for War, Mr. Haldane expressed the desire of Government that each Lord Lieutenant be requested to accept the Presidency of the Association of his particular County, and on his acceptance of the office he would be consulted as to the constitution of the Association. On the 23rd August, 1907, Mr. Haldane issued the following communication from the War Office,

"Provision is made for constituting the Lieutenant of the County, President of the Association, and it will be a source of great satisfaction to the Government if they can count upon your services in the capacity of President of the County Association. If you are able to undertake this duty, I propose, in the first instance, to address myself to you for your advice as to personnel of the Association.

The powers and duties of an Association are 'To make itself acquainted with and conform to the plan of the Army Council for the organisation of the Territorial Force within the County, and to ascertain the military resources and capabilities of the County, and render advice and assistance to the Army Council and to such Officers as the Army Council may direct'. An Association shall have such powers and duties connected with the organisation and administration of the military Forces as may for the time being be assigned to it, but an Association shall not have any more powers of command or training over any part of the military forces. The powers thus given to the Association may include recruiting for the Territorial Force, both in peace and war, the provision and maintainance of rifle ranges, buildings etc., and sites and camps for the Territorial Force; arranging with employers of labour as to holidays for training; establishing or assisting cadet battalions of Corps; and the care of Reservists and discharged soldiers.

Haldane".

The broad principle of Mr. Haldane's scheme was to divide the Forces into two lines, the first, the expeditionary force, having its outposts in distant parts of the Empire and the second, the Territorial Force, whose primary function would be home defence. The Militia was to be utilised to supply the wastage of war, and furnish additional units for lines of communication, garrisons, etc. The Territorial Force was to be organised on the same principle as the expeditionary force, that principle extending to the defence of the Colonies. Battalions were to be about 1000 strong with no distinction between war and peace time establishments.

Grants would be available to Commanders-in-Chief for camps and training and by County Associations for maintainance and equipment. Camps would last for 15 days annually with a minimum requirement of 8 days attendance in camp. Those unable to attend for the minimum requirement would be returned as non-efficient and asked to resign.

A member of the Volunteer Force was not subject to military law and could not be made subject to it without his consent. Under the new Act, the Territorial soldier of the second line, was subject to military law as soon as he offered his services. The Territorial soldier of the second line was, as with the Volunteers, not subject to foreign service, except for the defence of the Colonies, against his will.

The Volunteer, in theory, could resign on giving 14 days notice, the Territorial soldier was expected to serve for a period of 4 years, at least. He could however, retire from the Force on giving 3 months notice, but should his term of service have been less than the period of 4 years, he could be called upon to pay a fine of £5. The payment of this fine being intended to recoup the County Association responsible for the financing of the scheme. The Associations had the power to waive these fines and to vary the terms of withdrawal of service.

Under the new system the Territorial soldier by his training and equipment was expected to demolish all artificial barriers which formerly opposed the complete fusion with the Regular Army. In his training camp the Territorial soldier would be familiarised with the concept of military law and it was hoped that the Territorial soldier of the second line would become interchangeable with their counterparts in the Regular Army.

The implementation of the new Act and the promised demise of the Volunteer Force appeared to have but little effect on the enrolled strength of the Galloway Rifle Volunteers. The returns for the year ended 31st October, 1907, was to show a decrease of some 55 members from the year previous:- 'Returns for the year ended 31st October, 1907 is now 775, this decrease is accounted for in the want of work in the district'.

	Officers	Staff and Sergeants	Band and Buglers Rank and File	Total strength
'A'	2	6	103	111
'B'	5	9	113	127
'C'	2	7	76	85
'D'	3	7	110	120
'E'	3	4	43	50
'F'	5	5	88	98
'G'	4	8	87	99
'H'	3	5	77	85
	27	51	697	775

The National figures for year ended 31st October, 1907, showed a total Force of 252,791 members, down from 255,854, for year ended 31st October, 1906. By the 1st April, 1908, the figure had dropped to 224,217 members.

On the 22nd November, 1907, the following arrangement of the new Territorial Force into Divisions was reported with the General to Command them being appointed;

Brigadier-General F. MacBean to Command the Highland Division of Scotland.

Brigadier-General H.R. Kelham to Command the Lowland Division which comprised of Corps from Edinburgh; Lanark; Linlithgow; Mid-Lothian; Haddington; Peebles; Ayr; Wigtown; Berwick Roxurgh; Selkirk; Dumfries and Kirkcudbright.

Wigtownshire

On the 31st October, 1907, a preliminary meeting to consider the formation of a County Association in Wigtownshire, under the War Secretary's Territorial Scheme was held in the McMillan Hall, Newton Stewart. Attendance was by invitation only, of the Lord Lieutenant. The Right Honourable Sir Herbert Maxwell, Bart., Lord Lieutenant of Wigtownshire presided, and among other present were; The Earl of Stair; Provost of Stranraer; Sir Andrew Agnew Bart., of Lochnaw; Sir Mark McTaggart Stewart, Bart; Major Quentin Agnew, M.V.O.; Captain Fleming Hamilton of Craighlaw; Mr. W.J.H. Maxwell of Munches (Stewartry representative); Colonel Vans Agnew of Barnbarroch; Mr. A.B. Mathews, Newton Stewart; Mr. McCaig of Challoch; Mr. W. McConnell of Glasnick; Mr. McLean, County Clerk; Mr. Cunliffe, Chief Constable; Mr. Carson, Town Clerk, Newton Stewart.

The Town Clerk thanked those in attendance and said that preliminary meetings in other Counties had been called on somewhat different principles. Lord Blythswood of Renfrewshire had issued 600 invitations, but the practice commended to them by the Army Council was to invite only those gentlemen who were likely to take an active part in the work under the Territorial and Reserve Forces Act. He had communicated with Lord Herries, Lord Lieutenant of the Stewartry, who had deputed Mr. Maxwell of the Munches to confer with them. He continued. The first step was to select probably six gentlemen who would form the civilian members of the Association. An equal number of military members would be chosen from the Officers of the Country units, by the Army Council. The duties of the Association were to raise, equip and maintain the prescribed Forces for that County. The second step was to decide upon a Secretary who would be nominated by the Association but appointed by the Army Council, and thirdly to recommend to the Army Council a Chairman and Vice-Chairman.

The Lord Lieutenant said he did not want to offer himself as Chairman but would appoint Major Quentin Agnew as Chairman of the County Association, who had a long and distinguished military career and was well acquainted with the district. The post of vice-chairman was not filled at this stage. The following gentlemen were recommended for the approval of the Army Council as the civilian members of the Association representing the different districts within the County:- The Earl of Stair; Major Quentin Agnew; Mr. John McCaig, representing the Rhins; Mr. A.B.Mathews; Captain Fleming Hamilton and Mr. P. McKeand representing the Machars.

As to the appointment of a secretary, the Secretary's duties would be no sinecure and the salary offered was exceedingly small, £40 per annum, if he was Secretary of a single County. Under the Act, the Army Council had power to appoint a joint Secretary and the proposal which the Army Council had made was a joint Secretary for the Counties of Ayr, Wigtown, Kirkcudbright and Dumfries, which would enable them to allow a salary of £200. It was the desire of the Army Council that the Secretary of an Association should be an Officer on the retired list, of field rank, and preferably experience of active service. At a later date Mr. John Symons, Clerk to the Lieutenancy, Dumfries, was appointed joint interim Secretary to the Counties, Dumfries, Kirkcudbright, and Wigtown.

There was one further point and that was the power under the Act, to appoint joint committees. When the Lord Lieutenant had the scheme put to him, he thought it desirable that Galloway should form an Association by itself but the terms of the Act did not permit of anything but separate Associations, however, there was full power to form joint committees, and he thought it desirable that Wigtownshire and the Stewartry could form as a joint committee. Mr. Maxwell of the Munches agreed to convey this request to the Stewartry Association.

Kirkcudbrightshire

On Thursday, 5th December, 1907, a largely attended and influential meeting was held in the Town Hall, Castle Douglas for the purpose of forming a County Association, for the Stewartry of Kirkcudbright. Mr. W.J.H. Maxwell of Munches, was, at the request of Lord Herries, Lord Lieutenant of the Stewartry of Kirkcudbright, appointed President of the Association. Among those present was, Lord Lucas, private secretary to Mr. Haldane, Secretary of War. After apologises had been read and the purpose of the meeting had been addressed to the company, Lord Lucas was to explain the intracacies of the new scheme;

"Under the new Act, each County was obliged to form a County Association, which was to act as the administrative authority of the Territorial Force. The Act would come into being on the 31st March, 1908.

At present, if the Auxilliary Forces were asked to take the field, it would be practically impossible to do so. They had no command of higher grade other than a Brigade; They had no subsidiary services; Practically no Field Artillery, no Army Service Corps, while the army medical Corps was far from organised. In the case of taking the field it could not do so without the assistance of the Regular Army.

The first thing to be done with the Territorial Force was re-organisation. The idea being a real army of the second line, capable of taking the field in its own right.

They had at present grouped regimental districts, Kirkcudbrightshire, belonged to the Lowland group and comprised the Lowland Counties of Scotland. Each of these grouped regimental districts was to provide a Division. The new Divsion would follow as closely in organisation as that of the Regular Army, and would consist of three Brigades of Infantry, with proper proportion of Field Artillery, Engineers, and other branches, with a properly organised medical service, army ordnance and transport. The strength and establishment was to be the same as that of war establishments of the Regular Army.

However, what was wanted in the first instance was to get the County Associations formed and afterwards a conference should be held, at which delegates from the different Associations would attend. The conference would be attended by the Millitary authorities and would decide as to the actual quota of troops which each County had to provide. It was therefore, impossible for him to tell them meantime exactly what they would have to provide.

He pointed out, as regards Artillery, there was practically no Field Artillery in the Volunteer Force. They had a large number of Garrison Artillery used for coastal defence. The committee of Imperial Defence was looking at this question and it would probably mean that a good deal of the Garrison Artillery would not be required for coast defence and they would be invited to become Field Artillery. As regards to the Infantry, there was more than could possibly be worked into the new scheme. Mr. Haldane had gone out of his way to meet this excess of Infantry in Scotland and he proposed two extra Brigades of 8 battalions of Infantry. That would save 800 Infantry which would otherwise have been dispensed with. In their regimental districts there were 24 battalions of Infantry and they required 12 for the Division and 4 for the extra Brigade. It was hoped each battalion would be 1000 strong and where a battalion was not up to strength two battalions would be combined. He could not tell them for certain if that would be the case in Galloway but he gave them fair warning of the possibility.

It was proposed under the scheme to place the command and training of the Territorial Force under the direct control of the military authorities. The General Officer Commanding in Scotland was to be responsible for this, and in order for him to carry out this work he would have under him subordinate Generals who would command two big Divisions. The Lowland Division would be under the command of General Kelham, with headquarters at Hamilton. There would be Brigadiers for each of the different branches of the service. Grants would be available to the General Officer commanding for the purpose of training. The County Associations would not have to pay for camps and for other military purposes, the military authorities would be responsible for them along with instruction in musketry, staff rides etc., the County Associations being responsible for the administration, equipment, clothing, recruiting and keeping them up to strength. To get the best possible class of men, to see that employers allowed them away for training and landowners provided ground for military manoeuvres. There was to be four grants for administration, building, clothing and equipment and travelling. All the working expenses of the association would be found for them and the transfer of financial responsibility would pass from the Commanding Officer of the Galloway Rifle Volunteers on the 31st March, 1908. It was proposed to hand over everything free of debt. The meeting was interupted by calls of "Hear - Hear" from Colonel Kennedy, ex; Commanding Officer of the Galloway Rifles, which were greeted by bursts of laughter.

Lord Lucas, continued with the constitution of the County Association and suggested that it should consist of 14 members, 7 would be military, who would be Officers who had served for 15 years in the Volunteers. The Army Council did not view with favour the appointment of Junior Officers. The County Council was entitled to representation and the Association could co-opt members for the other vacancies.

Colonel Lennox, the Commanding Officer of the Galloway Rifle Volunteers was to address the meeting. It had been hinted that Galloway was to be broken up, now, if there was a territory in Great Britian complete in itself, it was the territory of Galloway. There was no part of Great Britian that was so complete by itself as the old Pictish Kingdom of Galloway. The men were of a different race and their traditions were different and if there was to be a Territorial Army at all he did not see why Galloway should be broken up. Sir Herbert Maxwell had hinted that two Companies from Wigtownshire were to be taken and joined with Ayrshire. It was a great pity that a Regiment so strong and flourishing as the Galloway Rifles should be broken up. At present its strength was 791 and if it was not for the uncertainty of this Bill, it would be much higher.

Lord Lucas had told them that there was a possibility and a probability that battalions which maintained their strength might remain. If there was such a possibility, he was well sure Galloway could raise 1000 men.

The meeting was to continue at some length with questions being put to Lord Lucas. With regards to the £5 fine to be exacted from men who did not complete the 4 years training he said, "The Commanding Officer of the County Association, if a reasonable excuse were given could remit the whole or part of the fine. The fine was much the same as the liability of non-efficients for the capitation grant under the old regulations." On being asked if the Territorial soldier was to be equipped in the same way as the regular soldier and be given a pair of good boots he replied, "He is not to have any boots provided but will have two suits, a service dress and an undress suit."

With regards to the physique of the Territorial soldier he had to pass the same standard as the regular soldier in proportion to his age. As to the conditions of the Territorial soldier, during embodiment he might serve anywhere in the United Kingdom but no part of the Force would be carried or ordered outwith the United Kingdom without the consent of the men themselves. Every man would by way of preliminary training, during the first year of his original enlistment put in the number of drills prescribed by the Army Council, besides attending the number of drills and fulfilling the conditions prescribed for a recruit of his arm of the service. The annual training would not be less than 8 days and not more than 15 days each year. A provision had been made for men unable to put in the whole time at camp to attend either 3 or 4 weekend camps. As to embodiment they need not be frightened of this as they could only be embodied by Act of Parliament.

The meeting continued at some length coming to an end with the following being appointed to the committee of the County Association of the Stewartry of Kirkcudbright, Colonel Kennedy, M.V.O., Knocknailling; Colonel Lennox; Colonel Gordon of Threave; Colonel Rainsford-Hannay of Kirkdale; Colonel Dudgeon of Cargen; Captain W.L. Comrie of Gategill; and Captain Murray Dunlop of Corsock. Mr. John Symons, Clerk to the Lieutenancy of Dumfries, interim Secretary of the Dumfries County Association, was also appointed joint interim Secretary to the Stewartry Association.

Dumfriesshire

On the 5th December, 1907, a meeting was held in the County Buildings, Dumfries, convened by the Lord Lieutenant of Dumfriesshire, the Duke of Buccleuch. There was a large attendance of invited guests and once again Lord Lucas was to address the Dumfriesshire County Association as to the formation and administration of the new scheme. The Duke of Buccleuch as Lord Lieutenant was appointed President of the Association with Mr. Johnstone-Douglas, appointed Chairman and Colonel Dudgeon being appointed vice-chairman. Mr. John Symons, clerk to the Lieutenancy was appointed interim joint Secretary of the Association.

The implementation of the Territorial and Reserve Forces Act and the formation of the County Associations was not met with the full accord of the Volunteer and on the 13th December, 1907, the following letter appeared in the *Kirkcudbrightshire Advertiser;*

"Successive Governments have done their best to quench the military ardour of the Stewartry, and whatever we hope, there is no doubt the Stewartry will have to give way to Dumfriesshire, and the Galloway Rifles, shorn of two Companies will merge in the Dumfriesshire Battalion.

The County Associations will become, to all practical purposes a committee of the County Council. As a majority of its members, whether they term themselves military or civil members will also be members of the County Council, their duties will devolve into simply auditing the accounts. As our Volunteers appear to be, as a body very much opposed to the scheme as it affects them, the outlook is far from promising. I am yours, Ex-Volunteer."

As a result of the comments of Lord Lucas in which he hinted that Battalions which maintained their current strengths might remain and the remarks of Colonel Lennox that he was well sure Galloway could raise a battalion of 1000 men. On the 15th December 1907, Colonel Lennox, Commanding Officer, the Galloway Rifle Volunteers was to issue the following Regimental Order:-

"Colonel Lennox desires to ask the earnest assistance of Company Officers, in view of the discussion at the recent County Association meeting at Castle Douglas, it is most essential that before the promised conference of County Associations is held every effort should be made to have the Galloway Rifles as nearly at full strength as possible. This is the best means of saving the Regiment. The Officer Commanding is sure that every Company Commander will do his very utmost to attain this end. He suggests, that recruiting efforts should be gone about in as systematic way as possible. Every section commander should be asked to personally interview each member of his section, and endeavour to secure his individual assistance. This will not only ensure that all members of the Regiment will be spoken to but will induce a healthy competition between sections. Every member of the Corps should be made to feel that he can do something to preserve the position of the Regiment.

Captain R. J. Grierson, Acting Adjutant."

A similar order was also issued to Sergeant Instructors stating that the Colonel would like as much recruiting done before the 25th December, 1907, as the quarterly returns then due might be taken as the basis for allocating units under the new scheme, but it should also be continued as energetically as possible even after Christmas, as a special return of strength might be called for after that.

The irony of a situation, which was to later manifest itself, was on the 22nd December, 1907, the members of 'E' Company, New Galloway, met in the Town Hall at New Galloway with contingents from Dalry, Balmaclellan, Parton, Laurieston, Mossdale and Carsphairn, all under the command of Captain E. S. Forde, New Galloway, to discuss the new Territorial scheme and to take steps to comply with Colonel Lennox's order.

Captain Forde was to tell the Company that their present strength was 50 members, but before the Boer War it had stood at 90, he could see no reason why they could not exceed that figure and raise 100 men. On the termination of proceedings a number of recruits were enrolled and arrangements were made to hold a similar meeting and recruiting drive in Dalry.

By the 10th January, 1908, as a result of this recruiting drive by Colonel Lennox, in an effort to preserve the title of the Regiment, the enrolled strength of the Galloway Rifle Volunteers had reached an all time high of 847 effective members. However, once again, later circumstances were to prove these attempts to be futile.

There was to be much influential opposition to the suggestion that the Galloway Rifle Volunteers might be broken up and merged with other battalions. Colonel Gordon of Threave was to remark, "Supposing an amalgamated battalion was furnished by Dumfries and Galloway, what would its title be? It would be such and such a battalion of the Territorial Army, with the title of the Galloway Rifles being forever lost."

Lord Ardwell was to say, "I have already used some influence to have the Galloway Rifles retained as a seperate unit."

Colonel Kennedy, ex-Colonel, of the Galloway Rifles, was to write, "An attempt to abolish the title of the Galloway Rifle Volunteers was made many years ago, probably by some ignorant clerk in the War Office. I represented that this change of name would produce a very bad feeling throughout Galloway, with the result that we were allowed to retain our name. I suggest a petition to Mr. Haldane, stating that the change of name would produce a very bad feeling in Galloway, the whole population being united on the subject."

Mr. John H. Nicholson, Provost of Maxwellton, was to proclaim that he would do whatever was necessary to maintain the Galloway Rifles as a separate unit.

The following resolution of the 15th January, 1908, was passed by the Council of the London Galloway Association, at a meeting held in London, under the Presidency of Mr. Samuel Robinson and issued by Major Hamilton, Hon. Secretary:

"That this Council hears with concern that under the new Territorial Army scheme it is posssible that the Galloway Rifles may not be maintained as a separate unit and that the Volunteer detachments from Galloway may be divided and attended to different County units.

That the Council believes such course, if adopted, will, in view of the history of Galloway be a serious blow to recruiting in the district and respectfully urge on the Galloway County Associations the desireability of strongly resisting any such proposal. The Council also urges on its members of this Association to use their influence against any division of the Galloway units, and in support of the maintainence of the name of the Galloway Rifles as the name of one of the units of the Territorial Force."

Mr. Haldane, writing, acknowledging the receipt of a copy of the resolution was to reply in the following terms;

"It is quite recognised that the distribution over each area of the units forming the new Territorial Army Divisions is a matter to be settled only after a close study of the local circumstances and under arrangements which have been made, the quota which each County is to furnish will not be fixed until the Country through its representatives has been given the fullest opportunity of offering advice and criticism on the subject."

On the 28th January, 1908, a heated conference was held in Edinburgh between General Leach,

Commander of the Forces in Scotland, and representatives of Dumfries and Galloway and various other interested parties, forming the Lowland Group, in an attempt to defuse the situation as to the possible break-up and amalgamation of the Galloway Rifles with either, Dumfriesshire or Ayrshire. Dumfriesshire was represented by Mr. Johnstone-Douglas, Chairman of his County Association and Colonel Dudgeon, Commander of the County battalion, and vice-chairman of the County Association. The Stewartry of Kirkcudbright was represented by Mr. W.J.H. Maxwell of Munches, Colonel Hannay of Kirkdale and Colonel Lennox Commanding the Galloway Rifles. The Wigtownshire representatives were Sir Herbert Maxwell, Lord Lieutenant of the County, the Earl of Stair and Colonel Quentin Agnew, M.V.O. D.S.O.

Colonel Dudgeon was to tell the conference that after careful consideration, those representing the Dumfriesshire battalion had come to the conclusion that they could not raise their battalion to the required strength of 1000 because on the borders of Dumfries, the Galloways, recruiting outside their own area, took 150 of their men. It was impossible for them, he said, to work under those conditions. Mr. Johnstone-Douglas supported the view and asked that there should be an amalgamation of the Dumfries and Galloway to make one strong battalion.

Colonel Lennox was to fiercely challenge the statement saying, "that the question had been gone into at various times by Officers commanding Dumfries and Maxwellton detachments, and it was found that while Dumfries men went to Maxwellton, Maxwellton men went to Dumfries, so that one pretty well balanced the other out. There was a very strong feeling against the disbandment of the Galloway Rifles, who were in the Regiment of what was in some sense a separate province and he was afraid that if that happened the men would not go into the new scheme. He undertook that they would raise the Galloway Rifles to 1000 men if they were assured they would remain as a separate unit."

Major Agnew strongly supported Colonel Lennox and said that from his knowledge of the feeling in Wigtownshire there was solid opposition to any proposal to break up the Galloway battalion. The Earl of Stair and Sir Herbert Maxwell also spoke in favour of the retention of the Galloway Battalion.

Mr. Johnstone-Douglas asked that in the event of the Battalions not being amalgamated would the Galloways be prevented from taking his men from Dumfries. General Leach replied that a question of this nature had already been under consideration and that while there was not to be active recruiting outside the assigned areas, men were entitled to go to whichever Regiment they chose. General Leach intimated that representations made by both sides would receive his careful consideration.

On the 31st January, 1908, letters were received from the Army Council notifying that the following committees had been recognised as being representative of the County Associations of the Stewartry of Kirkcudbright and Wigtownshire and had been incorporated as from the 21st January, 1908.

STEWARTRY.

Mr. W.J.H. Maxwell of Munches, President; Colonel Rainsford-Hannay, Kirkdale, Chairman; Colonel Gordon of Threave, Vice-Chairman; From the 1st Ayr and Galloway Artillery, Major Nicholson and Captain Brown; From the Galloway Rifles, Colonel Lennox, Major Hewat, Major Comrie, Captain Greirson, Maxwellton, Captain Anderson, Dalbeattie; From the County Council, Provost Wallace, Kirkcudbright, Provost Vane, Castle Douglas; Co-opted members, Mr. L.M. Dinwiddie, Maxwellton, and Mr. W.N. Newall, Granite Merchant, Dalbeattie.

WIGTOWNSHIRE.

Rt. Hon. Sir H.E. Maxwell, Lord Lieutenant, President; Major Quentin Agnew, Chairman; Captain Fleming-Hamilton, Vice-Chairman; Representatives of the County Council, Messrs. John McCaig of Challoch and Archibald Crawford, Broughton Mains; Military members, the Earl of Stair, Captain Sir Andrew Agnew, Lieutenant Colonel McCaig; Lieutenant Colonel Stuart, Captain Glover and Lieutenant Hunter; Co-opted members, Lieutenant Colonel Vans Agnew and Provost McCormick.

With the County Associations now being fully incorporated by the Army Council, representatives were selected by the County Associations to attend a conference to be convened by the Officer Commanding-in-Chief, Scotland, in order that troop quotas could be proportioned to each County.

On the 15th February, 1908, at a meeting of the Wigtownshire County Association, sufficient evidence was to be released suggesting that the endeavours of Colonel Lennox and other like minded persons, to save the Galloway Rifles as a separate unit had been in vain. The efforts to raise the battalion to 1000 were now proved to be impossible especially with quotas being fixed for Galloway to provide, in addition to its infantry quota, 400 Field Artillery. The Wigtownshire County Association had then but two options open to them, they could be attached to an Ayrshire battalion or to the Dumfries and Galloway battalion. The meeting was unanimous in favour of the Wigtownshire Companies being attached to the new Dumfries and Galloway battalion.

A feature of the Secretary of War, Mr. Haldane's plan was its pure simplicity of design. Infantry Regiments of Regular battalions, 1st and 2nd would be given additional battalions, i.e. special reservists and militia, thus providing 3rd and 4th battalions, with the Territarial Force following on in numerical order. Yeomanry, who had previously enjoyed a separate independant status, would now form as a Cavalry unit within the Territorial Force.

On Monday, the 24th February, 1908, a communication was received from the General Officer Commanding in Scotland, stating that it had definitely now been fixed to have but one rifle battalion for Dumfries and Galloway. Dumfriesshire would supply four Companies, the Stewartry of Kirkcudbright three Companies and Wigtownshire one Company. The two latter Counties would also be called upon to supply, each one Battery of Field Artillery. It was also proposed that Dumfriesshire provide a squadron of Imperial Yeomanry. The headquarters of the battalion to be at Dumfries.

The various Corps belonging to the Territorial District of the King's Own Scottish Borderers, to take the consecutive numerical titles, beginning with the Regulars and winding up with the Volunteers:-

1st Battalion King's Own Scottish Borderers	-	Regulars.
2nd -	.. ..	Regulars
3rd -	.. ..	Militia
4th -	.. ..	1st Roxburgh and Selkirk and 2nd Berwickshire.
5th -	.. ..	3rd Dumfriesshire and Galloway Rifles.

On the 12th March, 1908, a joint meeting of the County Associations forming the Dumfries and Galloway, 5th Battalion, took place at Newton Stewart to discuss the questions relative to the allocation of infantry companies, a problem being, especially in Dumfriesshire where 10 Companies had to be reduced to 4. After lengthy and sometimes, heated, discussion, the following recruitment areas for the 5th battalion were defined as follows:-

'A' Company	Dumfries	formerly 'A' and 'B' Companies of the 3rd V.B. K.O.S.B. (Dumfriesshire).
'B' Company	Annan	formerly 'F' Company (Dumfriesshire).
	Canonbie	formerly 'K' Company ..
	Langholm	formerly 'H' Company ..
'C' Company	Ecclefechan	formerly 'E' Company ..
	Lockerbie	formerly 'I' Company ..
	Moffat	formerly 'G' Company ..
'D' Company	Thornhill	formerly 'C' Company ..
	Sanquhar	formerly 'D' Company ..
	Kirkconnel	formerly section of 'D' Company.
'E' Company	Maxwellton	formerly 'F' and 'G' Companies - Galloway Rifles.
'F' Company	Dalbeattie	formerly 'H' Company .. ..
'G' Company	Castle Douglas	formerly 'B' Company .. ..
'H' Company	Newton Stewart	formerly 'D' Company .. ..
	Creetown	former section of 'D' Company .. ..
	Whithorn	not previously designated.

It was agreed that 'A' Company, Kirkcudbright and 'C' Company, Stranraer, Galloway Rifle Volunteers, together with the Garrison Artillery at Kirkcudbright, Stranraer, Portpatrick and Sandhead, were all to be disbanded with their areas being given over, for recruiting purposes to the new Field Artillery units to be formed at Kirkcudbright and Stranraer. Portpatrick and Sandhead would each be required to supply a Section of 30 men to the Stranraer Battery.

With a sufficiency of recruits within the Dumfires and Galloway region, it was considered that 'E' Company, New Galloway of the Galloway Rifles, was drawn from too remote an area and it was with some reluctance that this Company was disbanded. It was to be many a long day before the men of New Galloway and the Glenkens were to forgive their home Regiment, the K.O.S.B. for their ingratitude to a Company who had produced many of the Regiments finest marksmen, two of the Regiments four Commanding Officers and their Colour Sergeant, now Sergeant Major Grierson, who had captured Commandant Wolmaran and 30 armed men in South Africa in 1901. From that date the men of the Glenkens were to offer their future services to the Cameron Highlanders.

On the advent of these new designations of title, the break up of Companies, the amalgamation of Counties, the re-organisation of Artillery, and the introduction of new regulations, it was little wonder that the average rank and file Volunteer could not comprehend the many and exacting changes and as a result the Volunteers were very reluctant to join with the new scheme. By the end of March, 1908, it was to become obvious to the authorities that the prescribed quotas of infantry and artillery for Dumfries and Galloway were not going to be met. On the 27th March, 1908, at a meeting of the joint County Association, it was reported that there had been, 304 enlisted in Dumfriesshire, about 150 in the Stewartry, with 42 having been attested for the Kirkcudbright Battery. The two Sections, Portpatrick and Sandhead had only drawn 30% of their required total and Stranraer had recruited but three men of a required 140.

As a result of this reluctance on the part of the Volunteers to join with the new Regiments, the transfer from the Volunteers to the Territorial Force was extended and senior Officers embarked on a tour of the region to explain the new scheme. Initially it was considered by the County Associations to send a circular to each Volunteer inviting him to join in the new Regiments but instead they were to release the following communication which fully outlined the scheme.

"On the 31st March, 1908, the Volunteers will cease to exist under present conditions and the Territorial Force will on the 1st April, 1908, become the organised force of the Crown. This Force will be commanded and trained by the Military authorities, on similar lines to the Volunteers. The work will be purely voluntary and no member will be required to serve outside the United Kingdom.

In the case of recruits, the enlistment will be for a period of 4 years and during times of peace any man may obtain his discharge on furnishing a reasonable excuse. The penalty, regarding which there has been so much outcry, will only be imposed in the case of men frivolously enlisting and putting the Country to unnecessary expense. Three months notice will be required on application for discharge. Men may enlist in any branch of the service applicable to his employment, such as the Army Service Corps, Royal Engineers, or other branch.

The new Force will be organised on the same basis as the Regular Army, divided into two portions; viz:- (1) the Regulars. (2) the Territorial Forces, the latter being more closely associated to the Regular Army than the Volunteers.

The duty of the County Associations is to find the number of men required within a County, maintain Drill Halls, Headquarters, ranges and stores and be responsible for all payments and outlays.

Recruits will be attested and enlisted instead of being enrolled as formerly. This will maintain a better record of service, but the rights of the Volunteer will still remain as before and under reasonable conditions the enlistment may be cancelled. The age of enlistment will be from 17 to 35 but in the case of rank and file the service might be extended from 40 to 45 years, and non-commissioned officers from 50 to 55 years. Medical examinations will be necessary for recruits but Volunteers now serving will not be required to undergo a medical examination, being already regarded as physically fit.

The present Volunteers may join the new Force or resign but the period for consideration of the scheme has now been extended to the 30th June, 1908. Volunteers joining with the new Force will be attested in the same way as recruits, but may join for any period of one to four years. If, however, changing to another branch of the Service, they will be required to enlist for the full period of four years, but Garrison Artillery Volunteers transferring to infantry or Field Artillery may do so for the period of one to four years.

Men were liable to a penalty for failing to attend the preliminary or annual training but this penalty will not be enforced for non-attendance when a satisfactory reason is given. When in Camp, training, the payments and separation allowances will be liberal.

In April, 1907, the Volunteer returns showed a strength in Stranraer, Sandhead and Portpatrick, of 8 Officers and 155 rank and file, in the Garrison Artillery, and 4 Officers and 214 rank and file in the Infantry. The new proposals are the Rhins of Wigtownshire will furnish a Field Artillery Battery of 5 Officers and 140 rank and file, with 4 guns. Stranraer is to be the local Headquarters of the Battery, with Sections at Portpatrick and Sandhead. There will be three Field Batteries in the Brigade, one each for Ayrshire, Kirkcudbrightshire, and Wigtownshire, under a Brigade Commander, with the annual training camp at Ayr. The County will also be called upon to furnish one Company of Infantry, comprising of three officers and 117 rank and file, with Newton Stewart as the Company Headquarters. Kirkcudbrightshire will furnish three Companies, with

Dumfriesshire furnishing four Companies, with Headquarters at Dumfries. It is with regret that the Stranraer, Kirkcudbright and New Galloway Rifle Companies have been disbanded but the men of Stranraer and Kirkcudbright may join with their local Field Artillery Batteries.

At the Headquarters and Section centres, the recruits will be trained by competent Instructors. The camp training will be from eight to fifteen days, with the camps being arranged at the most convenient periods between the 1st May, and the 30th September. In the first year of service, the recruits must put in 45 drills, 30 of these before the camp is held, followed by 20 drills in successive years for Artillery and 10 for Infantry.

The fault of the present Volunteer system is that it was made up of a collection of units which does not represent the branches of the Regular Army. The new organisation will form a mobile force, in complete Divisions, as in the Regular Army. A Force able to go anywhere within the United Kingdom, quickly and take up commanding positions."

The following table relates to the organisation of the Territorial Force and the allocation of units in the Counties of Galloway:-

	Officers	Rank & File
Wigtownshire.		
Artillery		
1 Field Artillery Battery (Brigade H.Q.Ayrshire)	5	140
Infantry		
1 Company (Battalion H.Q. Dumfriesshire)	3	117
	-----	-----
	8	257
Kirkcudbrightshire		
Artillery		
1 Field Artillery Battery (Brigade H.Q. Ayrshire)	5	140
Infantry		
*3 Companies (Battalion H.Q. Dumfriesshire)	10	352
	-----	-----
	15	492

*Includes 1 Major.

On Friday, 27th March, 1908, a farewell "Smoker" was held by the Company of Stranraer Rifle Volunteers, in their Drill Hall in St. Andrew Street, Stranraer, the toast being 'C' Company.

On Monday, 30th March, 1908, to mark the disbandment of 'A' Company, Kirkcudbright, a social evening was held in the Town Hall. At 6.30p.m. prior to the commencement of the social, a large muster of past and present members of the Kirkcudbright Rifle Volunteers, headed by their Pipers, marched through the Town where they were cheered by large crowds of onlookers. At the Armoury they were drawn up and dismissed for the last time by Lieutenant Paterson.

Colonel Lennox on addressing the men said that he felt as if he was going to be hanged when he came to say goodbye to so many men who had served their King, many who had gone to the front and fought for their Country, and all who had done their duty faithfully and well. Mr. Haldane practically said to that Company, they were not wanted here and they would have to join the Artillery. Colonel Lennox then read out a telegram, "Every man in 'E' Company, New Galloway, sends deepest sympathy to 'A' Company, in our great mutual sorrow." Signed Clark-Kennedy.

As in times past, the men of Galloway were slow to accept change, the introduction of the Militia Bill, 1797, was initially met with much resistance but was soon to be accepted as part of Galloway life. The restructuring of the Militia and the introduction of the Volunteer Force, 1860, once again showed the men of Galloways dislike for change and the introduction of the new Territorial Force was to be of no exception.

Initially the Wigtownshire Territorial County Association was asked to provide, from the Rhins, a Battery of Field Artillery, of 5 Officers and 140 men, and one Company of Infantry for the King's Own Scottish Borderers, of 3 Officers and 114 men, from the Machars. In the Rhins the Volunteers did not take kindly to the proposed change and by the 30th June, 1908, only 21 Volunteers had transferred to the new Regiment of Field Artillery, which along with 8 recruits, made a total of 29 men from a total of the 140 men required.

Recruiting to the Newton Stewart Infantry, 'H' Company, of the King's Own Scottish Borderers, did not proceed as briskly as was anticipated and a Section of 30 men was to be recruited from Stranraer, under the command of Lieutenant Hunter, to augument the Newton Stewart Company.

With a view to stimulating recruitment to the Stranraer and Kirkcudbright Batteries of Field Artillery, on the 1st June, 1908, a Section of the 6th Battalion of Royal Field Artillery, Maryhill Barracks, left Glsgow under canvas on a route march through the South West Counties. They camped in Stranraer on the 6th and 7th June, thereafter travelling to Kirkcudbright where they camped for a further two days on the 10th and 11th June, returning to Glasgow on the 17th June, 1908.

This visit of the Royal Field Artillery was to have but little effect on recruitment in Stranraer, it was reported that recruiting to the local battery of Field Artillery has shown some improvement but it is slight and insignificant when compared with the numbers required. The bulk of the men who served under the old regime are still sceptical about the new. They make no sign of their intentions regarding the future and as they remain cold and silent towards their Officers appeals, it is generally accepted that their taste for military service has been satisfied and that they will formally resign before the 30th June, 1908, when the extended period of grace expires.

However, by the 19th June, 1908, Kirkcudbright Battery, under the command of Major Brown, boasted a total of 90 men out of a required total of 140 men, and it was anticipated that following a recruiting drive in Gatehouse, Twynholm and Borgue, they would very soon be up to their required strength.

Between the 3rd and 18th july, 1908, the Kirkcudbright Battery of Royal Field Artillery, attended, for the first time, at their annual training camp at Buddon, Monifieth, Dundee. The reported total strength showing 5 Officers, 110 other ranks, which included Sergeant Instructors Moss and Weeks, recently appointed from 'A' Troop, St. John's Wood, London.

The following letter dated 10th August, 1908, from Mr. Haldane's Private Secretary was received by the Stewartry County Territorial Association.

"Dear Sir. It was with very great pleasure that Mr. Haldane learnt of the excellent progress which is being made in recruiting for the Kirkcudbright Battery of the Royal Field Artillery. In the past, the degree of support which has been accorded to the Volunteer Force by Kirkcudbright has been deserving of the highest praise, reflecting no little credit upon a Burgh whose inhabitants, a remarkably high percentage were members of that Force. Mr. Haldane is confident that the support of the ancient and Royal Burgh will be extended no less fully to the Territorial Force, and that, as a result, the Battery will, at no distant date be reported as up to establishment.

G.K. King. (Private Secretary)."

The total enlistment, as at the 1st May, 1908, for the 5th (Dumfries and Galloway) Battalion King's Own Scottish Borderers was as follows:-

Dumfriesshire	302 actually joined	60 promised	11 recruits.
Kirkcudbrightshire	118 actually joined	38 promised	2 recruits.
Wigtownshire	46 actually joined	17 promised	3 recruits.

Between the 11th and 25th July, 1908, the Scottish Border Brigade Camp, as constituted under the new Territorial Act, was, for the first time, formed within the borders of Galloway, at Caigton Row, Castle Douglas, the parade strength of the 5th (Dumfries and Galloway) Battalion King's Own Scottish Borderers being as follows:-

	Officers	Rank & File	Total
'A' Company Dumfries	7	104	111
'B' Company Annan	4	67	71
'C' Company Ecclefechan	2	52	54
'D' Company Thornhill	3	81	84
'E' Company Maxwellton	4	62	66
'F' Company Dalbeattie	2	7	9
'G' Company Castle Douglas	3	22	25
'H' Company Newton Stewart - (Stranraer Sect.)	2	62	64
	27	456	483

The 4th (Roxburgh, Berwick and Selkirk) Battalion King's Own Scottish Borderers, comprised 599 of all ranks.

These figures were to represent just over half the required Battalion strength.

The first annual returns of the 5th (Dumfries and Galloway) K.O.S.B. as at the 31st October, 1908, showed a strength of 31 Officers and 726 other ranks. Of the old Volunteers 382 from Dumfriesshire and 278 from Galloway had joined. For 1 years service 570 men were enrolled. For 2 years service 21 were enrolled. For 3 years service 1 was enrolled and for 4 years 78 were enrolled. The recruits numbered 56. The total strength of the Stranraer Section of 'H' Company, Newton Stewart, was 1 Officer, 3 Sergeants and 23 Rank and File. To complete the enlistment 192 more men were required - 29 from Dumfriesshire - 124 from Kirkcudbrightshire - 39 from Wigtownshire. The total national strength of the Territorial Force as at 31st October, 1908, was 188,781.

By the 31st December, 1908, it was reported that all Companies of the 5th (Dumfries and Galloway) Battalion K.O.S.B. were up to their allotted strength.

On the 7th July, 1908, at a meeting of the Wigtownshire Territorial County Association, held in the Drill Hall, Stranraer, it was reported that the War Office did not consider the Stranraer Battery of Royal Field Artillery to be non-existant, even though the extended deadline of 30th June, 1908, had now passed and the required number of men had not joined. The War Office were prepared to give the Association as much time as they required to raise the required total. However, by the 28th August, 1908, the authorities reluctantly had to admit defeat and expressed their regret that all endeavours to raise a Territorial battery of Field Artillery in Stranraer had failed.

The Wigtownshire Territorial County Association was to issue the following circular, dated 22nd October, 1908;

"In terms of a recent Army Order it has been decided to raise 2 Companies of Infantry in the Rhins District of Wigtownshire, in place of the Battery of Field Artillery.

These Companies will form part of the 5th Battalion (South Ayrshire) Royal Scots Fusiliers and are to be recruited now. All young men desirous of joining the new Companies will obtain the necessary particulars at the Drill Hall, Charlotte Street (where they may enrol any evening between 7.30p.m. and 9.30p.m.) or by letter addressed to Sergeant Stewart at the Drill hall.

Quentin Agnew, Major. (Chairman)."

This order was to be met with great satisfaction and delight by the ex-rank and file of the Volunteers who came forward in great numbers to join with their new Infantry Regiment. Many promises were made from the villages of Castle Kennedy and Portpatrick to join with the new Regiment and a decision was taken by the County Territorial Association to recruit Sections from these villages. The Headquarters of the Stranraer Companies was to be in the Artillery Hall, Bellevilla Road, Stranraer.

On the 3rd December, 1908, authority was granted to the Stranraer Section of the King's Own Scottish Borderers, attached to 'H' Company, Newton stewart to transfer to the Royal Scots Fusiliers, thereby joining with their former colleagues of the Galloway Rifles, this they did to a man.

The following circulars were issued by the Wigtownshire County Territorial Association:
"Men wanting to join the Portpatrick Section of the 5th (South Ayrshire) Battalion Royal Scots Fusiliers, will be enrolled in the Drill Hall, Portpatrick, on Thursday evening, the 3rd December, 1908, at 7.45p.m. By Order Thomas M. Hunter Lieutenant."

"Territorial Force, 5th Battalion Royal Scots Fusiliers. A Meeting will be held in the Sawmill Loft, Castle Kennedy, on Wednesday evening, 23rd December, 1908, at 7p.m. with a view to explaining the conditions of service in the Force and the further view of forming a Section for the Battalion at Castle Kennedy. The Rt. Hon. the Earl of Stair will preside. The meeting will be addressed by the Rt. Hon. Viscount Dalrymple M.P. Captain Pollock, Adjudant, R.S.F. and others. All interested are invited to attend and all desirous of joining Castle Kennedy Section will be attested at the close of the meeting. Quentin Agnew. Chairman of the Territorial Force Association."

The two allotted Infantry Companies from the Rhins were quickly formed and brought to their required strengths, their designations being, 'B' Company (Stranraer/Portpatrick) 5th (South Ayrshire) Battalion Royal Scots Fusiliers and 'D' Company (Stranraer/Castle Kennedy) 5th (South Ayrshire) Battalion Royal Scots Fusiliers.

Following the reforms of the Territorial and Reserve forces Act, 1907, the Artillery Brigades in

Scotland were stationed as follows:-

   1st Lowland Division (Edinburgh and Midlothian) stationed at Redford Barracks.
   2nd Lowland Division (Ayr and Kirkcudbright) stationed at Larbet, Stirling.
   3rd Lowland Division (Glasgow) stationed at Dunfermline.
   4th Lowland Division of Howitzers (Glasgow) stationed at Stirling.

The 2nd Lowland Division (Ayr and Kirkcudbright) comprised of Field Batteries from Ayr; Irvine; Ardrossan and Kirkcudbright. It was anticipated that Stranraer would also form a Battery of Royal Field Artillery, joining with the Division. However, on the 12th September, 1908, Ayr was to raise a second Battery of Royal Field Artillery to replace the Stranraer Battery of Royal Field Artillery which had failed to materialise. The two Ayr Batteries of Royal Field Artillery were thereafter converted to Royal Horse Artillery.

With the outbreak of the Great War, 1914-1918, the 1/2nd Lowland Division (Ayr and Kirkcudbright) were numbered as an Artillery Brigade of the 52nd (Lowland) Division and sailed for Port Said, arriving on the 20th June, 1915. In April, 1916, they were renumbered to form the 260th Brigade of the Royal Field Artillery of the 52nd (Lowland) Division. The 3rd Glasgow becoming the 261st, the 4th Glasgow (Howitzers) becoming the 262nd and the 5th Horse Artillery becoming the 263rd.

   In September, 1916, the Brigades were once again renumbered as follows:-
      260th (Ayr and Kirkcudbright) - 261st Brigade.
      261st (Glasgow) - 262nd Brigade.
      262nd (Glasgow Howitzers) - 263rd Brigade.
      263rd (Horse Artillery) - 264th Brigade.

The 261st Brigade (Ayr and Kirkcudbright) were not to serve in the Gallipoli Peninsula, with the exception of their small arms section who saw service, along with the 1st (Edinburgh) and 3rd (Glasgow).

The 261st Brigade (Ayr and Kirkcudbright) was to take part in the battles of Romani; El Arish; El Sire Ridge; 3rd Battle of Gaza, and the battles of Esdud and Katrah.

By the March of 1918 Turkish resistance had been destroyed and the 52nd (Lowland) Division Infantry were sent to France to deal with a fresh offensive by the Germans in the region of the Somme. The Artillery of the 52nd, which included the Kirkcudbright and Ayr Brigade, were transferred to the 7th Indian Division, remaining in Egypt until they returned home in the July of 1919.

A second line of Royal Field Artillery of the 2nd Lowland Division was formed at Larbert in May, 1915, being sent to England for some time before sailing for France where they served on the Western Front.

On the ceasation of hostilities the Regiment was reformed as the 79th (Lowland) Field Regiment of Royal Artillery; Ayr forming as Field Battery No.313; Irvine as Field Battery No.314; Kirkcudbright as Field Battery No.315; and Kilmarnock as Field Battery No.316.

On the outbreak of the 2nd War, Sections of the 79th formed as the 130th Field Regiment and sailed for Singapore. On the fall of Singapore the 130th had reached Durban and were re-directed to India and Burma where they served for the duration.

The 79th remained within the United Kingdom from 1939 to 1944, supplying drafts to various Brigades and first training as a Mountain Division for the possible invasion of Norway and later, in 1943, as an Airborne Division for the assault on Arnhem.

In Mid-October, 1944, the 79th as part of the 52nd (Lowland) Division, sailed for Holland where they were involved in the Scheldt estuary in the capture of the Walchern and Beveland Islands. They moved to the German border at Geilenkirchen in January, 1945, where they lauched an attack on Schundorf. In March, 1945, they moved to positions on the River Rhine, where they were involved in the crossing of the Weser and attacks at Estelsen and Baden. They reached the 52nd's objective of Bremen, which fell in April, 1945.

On the 20th April, 1946, the Headquarters of the Royal Artillery 52nd (Lowland) Division was disbanded thus signalling the end of the Kirkcudbright Battery, "The Battery" as it had become affectionately known.

The Royal Scots Fusiliers, the 21st Regiment of Foot, was raised in 1678, to deal with the menace of armed groups of Covenanters, seen as a potential threat to both Church and State. The Regiment was to receive its baptism of fire against the French, in the battle of Steenkirk, in the war of the League of Augsburg. On the Haldane reforms of 1908, the Regiment was localised in Ayr and it was to the Royal Scots Fusiliers that the former members of 'C' Company, Stranraer, of the Galloway Rifles, were attached, forming 'B' and

'D' Companies of the 5th Battalion.

The 4th/5th Royal Scots Fusiliers, together with the 4/5th King's Own Scottish Borderers formed as the South Scottish Regiment of the 2nd Lowland Division and with the outbreak of the Great War, the 1/2nd were renumbered as part of the 52nd (Lowland) Division with the South Scottish 1/4th, 1/5th Royal Scots Fusiliers and the 1/4th, 1/5th King's Own Scottish Borderers Brigaded to form the 155th Infantry Brigade; the Scottish Rifles becoming the 156th and the Highland Light Infantry, the 157th.

The 155th landed at Sedd-el-Bahr on the Gallipoli Peninsula, on the 6th June, 1915, where they were engaged in trench warfare against the Turks until the February of 1916, when they sailed to Port Said taking up positions for the defence of the Suez Canal and a railway line being laid from Egypt to Palestine. The 155th were to take part in the battle of Romani and the advance across the desert to Palestine being engaged in the 2nd and 3rd battles of Gaza before seizing key positions to Jerusalem.

After the German offensive in the Spring of 1918, the 155th sailed from Egypt with the 52nd (Lowland) Division, landing in France on the 11th April, 1918, and joined the Line at Vimy, where they took part in the advances over the Ypres-Comines Canal and the final drive through Belgium, terminating in the armistice of 11th November, 1918.

Following the armistice of 1918, the Territorial Force was to fall into abeyance being re-constituted and re-organised in 1920. In March of 1920, the allotment of units under the new Territorial Army scheme severed Stranraer - Portpatrick and Castle Kennedy's links with the Royal Scots Fusiliers, the whole of Wigtownshire now being given over to the King's Own Scottish Borderers. The County Company allocations for the Rhins and Machars of Wigtownshire was set at 240 men and 6 Officers, with half-company headquarters at Stranraer and Newton Stewart.

On the 1st October, 1921, the Territorial Force was reformed as the Territorial Army.

In 1923, the 4th and 5th Battalions of the Royal Scots Fusiliers were amalgamated as the 4/5th Battalion.

In 1939, the 5th (Dumfriesshire and Galloway) Battalion King's Own Scottish Borderers was doubled in strength and split, with the Dumfriesshire Companies forming as the 5th (Dumfriesshire) Battalion K.O.S.B. and Galloway forming as the 7th (Galloway) Battalion K.O.S.B. In 1944, the 5th (Dumfriesshire) was to see service in North West Europe, along with the 4/5th Royal Scots Fusiliers and the 79th (Lowland) Field Regiment of Artillery, as part of the 52nd (Lowland) Division, in the advance from the Scheldt Estuary in Holland to the Divisional objective of Bremen.

In 1943, the 7th (Galloway) Battalion, King's Own Scottish Borderers was converted to an Air Landing Battalion. Whilst serving with the 1st Airborne Division the 7th (Galloway) suffered such severe and heavy casualties at Arnhem that the Battalion was suspended. In 1947, the 7th (Galloway) was disbanded and reformed as the 5th (Dumfriesshire and Galloway) Battalion, K.O.S.B.

In May 1958, the Royal Scots Fusiliers were amalgamated with the Highland Light Infantry, however, the 4/5th Battalion Royal Scots Fusiliers was to continue under its own identity, uniform and traditions until, 1967. In January, 1959, the Royal Scots Fusiliers and the Highland Light Infantry formed as the Royal Highland Fusiliers (Princess Margaret's Own Glasgow and South Ayrshire Regiment) with Barracks at Redford, Edinburgh.

On the 7th March, 1961, the 5th (Dumfriesshire and Galloway) Battalion K.O.S.B. was amalgamated with the 4th Battalion to form the 4/5th Battalion K.O.S.B.

On the 31st March, 1967, the 4/5th Battalion K.O.S.B. was reduced to company strength becoming a constituent of a new Battalion of Reserve Infantry covering the Lowlands of Scotland, with the title 'C' (K.O.S.B.) Company, 52nd Lowland Volunteers (Territorial Army and Volunteer Reserve IIA). The 4/5th Battalion K.O.S.B. was also required to produce a unit consisting of Battalion Headquarters, three Headquarters Platoon (Recce, Signals, Pioneers) and two Rifle Companies to be known as 4/5th K.O.S.B. Territorials (Territorial Army and Volunteer Reserve III) these units being based at Dumfries, Stranraer and Galashiels. This A.V.R. III unit was declared to be the natural successor to the 4/5th K.O.S.B. (T.A.) who were handed the Regimental Colours, silver, funds and property.

In 1971, a 2nd Battalion of the 52nd Lowland Volunteers was raised but 'C' Company was to remain part of the original Battalion. At the same time in the 2nd Battalion a K.O.S.B. Company, No.3 Company was raised in Galashiels.

In 1979, in a further change of title of the Reserve Army in general the Territorial Army Volunteer Reserve reverted to the title of the Territorial Army.

In 1993, 'C' (K.O.S.B.) Company were transferred from 1st Battalion 52nd Lowland Volunteers to the

2nd Battalion 52nd Lowland Volunteers thus once again joining their parent Volunteer Company in Galashiels, who changed their name from No.3 (K.O.S.B.) Company to 'B' (K.O.S.B.) Company.

In June, 1995, the 2nd Battalion 52nd Lowland Volunteers became, The Lowland volunteers. The 1st Battalion 52nd lowland Volunteers, which the 'C' (K.O.S.B.) Company, had left in 1993, became the 3rd (Volunteer) Battalion The Royal Highland Fusiliers.

1996, therefore sees 'C' (K.O.S.B.) Company in Dumfries and 'B' (K.O.S.B.) Company in Galashiels under their Battalion Headquarters in Edinburgh, known as "The Lowland Volunteers".

(14) Pen & ink drawing, by Colour-Sergeant McGregor, 'A' Company, Kirkcudbright, commemorating the men of the Galloway Rifle Volunteers who attended the Royal Review, King's Park, Holyrood, Edinburgh, on 18th September, 1905. Each Company is represented by a segment of the central star, and each man's name is minutely recorded within that segment, relative to his Company.

CHAPTER 15
THE ARMOURIES AND DRILL HALLS OF THE GALLOWAY RIFLE VOLUNTEERS AND THEIR SUCCESSORS

Kirkcudbright.

The Tolbooth, High Street, Kirkcudbright, was the home of the 1st Kirkcudbright Rifle Volunteers, later to become 'A' Company of the Galloway Rifle Volunteers, being used both as an Armoury and Drill Hall, from 1860, until 1878, when the newly purpose built Drill Hall was opened in Castle Gardens, adjoining McLellan's Castle. This Drill Hall remained in use until the demise of the Galloway Rifle Volunteers in March, 1908, when it became home to the Kirkcudbright Battery of Royal Field Artillery. In June, 1908, the Drill Hall was leased for private usage and the Kirkcudbright Battery moved to their new Drill Hall in Dee Walk, which was to be formally opened in 1909. The Drill Hall at the Castle was demolished in December, 1908.

(15) The Tolbooth, High Street, Kirkcudbright.

(16) The Drill Hall, Castle Gardens, Kirkcudbright.

(17) The Drill Hall, Dee Walk, Kirkcudbright.

Castle Douglas

The Armoury and Headquarters of the 2nd Kirkcudbright Rifle Volunteers, from March until October, 1860, was the Old Town House, St. Andrew Street, Castle Douglas. The original Town House was destroyed by fire in 1892 and again in 1935. This photograph shows the 3rd Town House built on the original site.

In the October of 1860, the Armoury and Headquarters of the Castle Douglas Company removed to 136, Queen Street, where it was to remain until the demise of the Volunteers in 1908. The Tannery at 142, Queen Street doubled as a Drill Hall during inclement weather. The Volunteer Band hut of the Castle Douglas Company was at the rear of 136, Queen Street, with only its foundations now remaining.

In 1885, the Headquarters Company of the Galloway Battalion of Rifle Volunteers transferred from Newton Stewart to the Armoury at 136, Queen Street, and over the next 5 years the Volunteer Headquarters Finance Committee were to lease three properties, one at the rear of 253, King Street, one at the rear of 247, King Street, and a third property situated between these two, since demolished. These three properties were to become the Battalion Headquarters until 1904, when the Headquarters were once again transferred to the Brig'en, Maxwellton. The Headquarters at the Brig'en have long since been demolished without trace.

In 1908, Castle Douglas were to form as 'G' Company of the 5th (Dumfriesshire and Galloway) Battalion K.O.S.B. with their new Drill Hall and Armoury at Market Street, Castle Douglas. This Drill Hall was to remain in the hands of the Auxiliary Forces until the late 1960's when the Castle Douglas Company were transferred to Kirkcudbright. The former Drill Hall in Market Street was thereafter converted to the present day swimming pool.

(18) Town House, St. Andrew's Street, Castle Douglas.

(19) The Armoury, 136 Queen Street, Castle Douglas.

(20) The Tannery, 142 Queen Street, Castle Douglas.

(21) The remains of the Volunteer Band hut at the rear of 136 Queen Street, Castle Douglas.

(22) Part of the H.Q. of the Galloway Battalion of Rifle Volunteers at the rear of 253 King Street, Castle Douglas.

(23) Part of the H.Q. of the Galloway Battalion of Rifle Volunteers at the rear of 247 King Street, Castle Douglas.

(24) The Drill Hall of 'G' Company, Castle Douglas of the 5th Battalion K.O.S.B.

New Galloway

The Town Hall, New Galloway, was the Headqurters and Drill Hall of the 3rd Kirkcudbright Rifle Volunteers, later 'E' Company, from their inception in 1860, until their untimely demise in 1908. Their Armoury was an unidentified private rented store in the Burgh.

The following extracts from the Town Council Minutes gives a brief but interesting insight into the Corps use of the Hall.

November, 1875. "The 3rd Kirkcudbright Rifles subscribed £40 to the fund for the improvements of the Town Hall."

December, 1884. "It was unanimously agreed that in future the Volunteer Ball would have to be paid for according to the usual scale of charges."

November, 1891. "The Hall Committee was asked to communicate with Captain Jamieson regarding the terms proposed for the use of the Town Hall for Drills."

February, 1902. "An application by 'E' Company for the use of the Lower Hall for Morris Tube practice was approved."

(25) The Town Hall, High Street, New Galloway.

Dalry

The Headquarters of the Dalry Section of the 3rd K.R.V. ('E' Company), was a large wooden hut which was situated at Garplefoot, near to where the old bridge crosses the Garple Burn. The hut has long since disappeared.

Gatehoue of Fleet

The Cally Mill House, Ann Street, Gatehouse of Fleet, was built as a Cotton Mill in 1790, for Thomas Scott and Co., and was later to become the Cally Estate Sawmill. The Headquarters and Armoury of the 4th Kirkcudbright Rifle Volunteers - Gatehouse of Fleet, later to become a Section of 'A' Company - Kirkcudbright, were affectionately referred to in local terms as "The Barracks" and were formed within several rooms of the Mill in 1860, and continued in use until the demise of the Volunteers in 1908. The Mill has now been converted to private housing.

The "Drill Hall" commonly referred to in Gatehouse of Fleet is of much more recent origins and was the Girthon Old School building at Carney's Corner, which was the Headquarters and Drill Hall of the Gatehouse Company of Home Guard, 1939-1945, and home to the Auxillary Forces, Gatehouse until 1958, when the building was sold by them, later being purchased in 1987 by the local authority who have since converted it to residential accomodation.

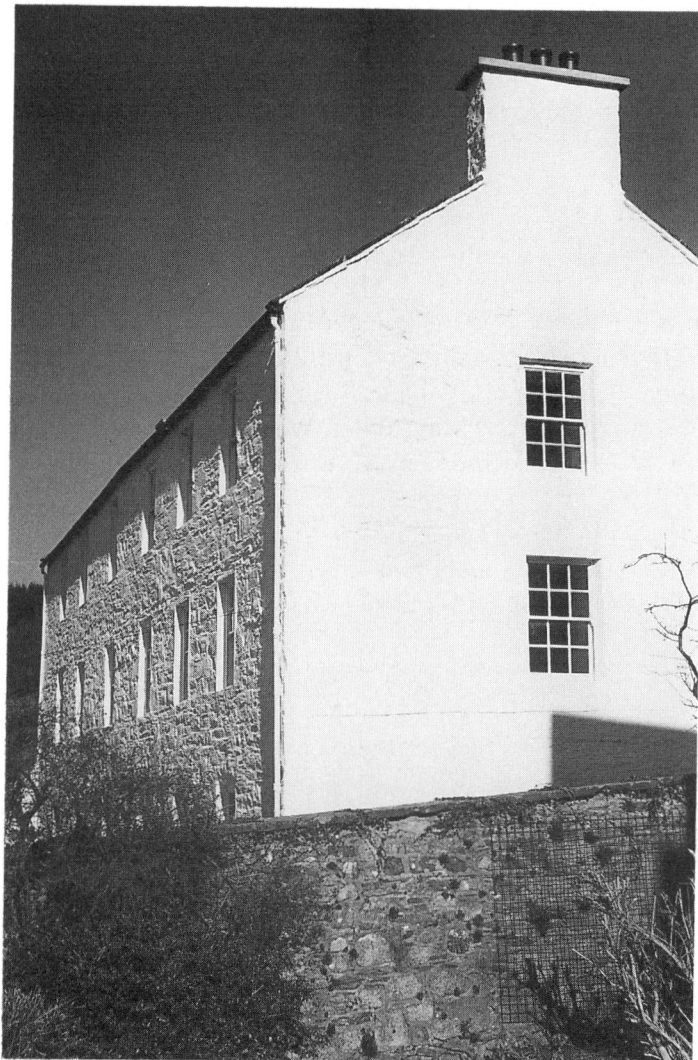

(26) The Cally Mill House, Ann Street, Gatehouse of Fleet

(27) The Girthon Old School, Carney's Corner, Gatehouse of Fleet

Maxwellton

From February to June, 1860, the Court House and Jail, which formerly stood on the corner of Glasgow Street and Haddon's place, Maxwellton, built in 1813 and demolished in 1913, was the Headquarters and Armoury of the 5th Kirkcudbright Rifle Volunteers - Maxwellton. In June, 1860, they moved their Drill Hall and Armoury to the Mechanic's Institute, Nith Place, Dumfries, where they were to remain for the next seven years. In November, 1867, they moved to their new Drill Hall and Armoury, the "Old Maxwellton West Church", at Laurieknowe, now the site occupied by "Budget Tyres", opposite the junction with the New Abbey Road. The following extracts from "Maxwellton West, the Story of a Church, 1866-1966" by A. Maclean B.S.C. A.S. and the Rev. H.E.A. Simmons M.A., chronicle its history.

"In November, 1867, the Church was leased for a period of five years to the Kirkcudbright Rifle Volunteers. One of the Court's conditions underlined was that the band must not pracice in the building.

In 1873, the Drill Hall was re-let to Captain Rennie for a period of 7 years, but in 1876, a strong letter was sent to Captain Barrie following complaints of local residents about dancing in the Drill Hall, and about noise and disturbance there.

In 1879, the Rifle Corps sought permission to have Band practice as they had taken steps to subdue the sound. It was agreed to give this a trial. In the following year a renewed lease of 10 years was sought by Captain Lennox. The Court agreed to this with sundry conditions, one of which was that no poultry be kept on the premises."

The Old Church continued as the home of the 5th Kirkcudbright Rifle ('F' and 'G' Companies) until the Regiment was disbanded in 1908. The Headquarters of the newly formed 5th (Dumfriesshire and Galloway) Battalion, K.O.S.B. was to be the Drill Hall, Newall Terrace, Dumfries, the former home of 'A' Company of the Dumfries Rifle Volunteers.

(28) The Mechanic's Institute, Nith Place, Dumfries.

(29) "The Old Maxwellton West Church", Laurieknowe, Maxwellton.

(30) The Drill Hall, Newall Terrace, Dumfries.

Dalbeattie

The Drill Hall and Armoury, Burn Street, Dalbeattie, was first built in 1812, by the Cameronians, the forerunners of the Reformed Presbyterian Church. From 1843 until 1877, it became home to the Parish Church, Dalbeattie until its move to Chaignair Street. In 1877, the building was leased to the 6th Kirkcudbright Rifle Volunteers, ('H' Company Galloway Rifle Volunteers). The Hall was to serve the Dalbeattie Company until its demise in 1908, when the Drill Hall was taken over by 'F' Company of the newly formed 5th (Dumfriesshire and Galloway) Battalion K.O.S.B. A covered miniture Rifle Range existed in the rear gardens of the Drill Hall. The Hall has now been converted to private housing.

(31) The Drill Hall, Burn Street, Dalbeattie.

Wigtown

The County Buildings, Wigtown, completed in 1863, stand on the site of an older building erected in 1756, of which the tower, faced by new stonework, and the Tolbooth beneath, still remain. This building was to be used as the Drill Hall and Armoury of the 1st Wigtown Rifle Volunteers - Wigtown, from their inception on 24th February, 1860, until their disbandment on the 20th June, 1873, and later No.4 Section - Wigtown of 'D' Company - Newton Stewart, of the Galloway Rifle Volunteers, from 9th February, 1891, until their demise on the 31st March, 1908.

(32) The County Buildings, Wigtown.

Stranraer

On the formation of the Stranraer Companies of Rifle and Artillery Volunteers, in 1860, their Armouries were situated within the small room on the 1st floor of the Old Town Hall. The Headquarters, used alternate days by the Riflemen and Artillerymen was in the "Newsroom", Castle Street, Stranraer. This Newsroom was attached to the rear of a firm of printers, who occupied the building which is now the Mains of Airies Butchers Shop, formerly "Jessons" butchers. The Newsroom was in fact a coffee shop, owned by the printer, who supplied his customers with newspapers to read, resulting in the expression, "Newsroom".

The use of the Newsroom would appear to have been of fairly short duration, with the Riflemen moving to the Old Town Hall and the Artillerymen moving to the Old Academy, Lewis Street, Stranraer.

Sometimes shortly after 1874, the Stranraer Rifle Corps were to transfer thier Headquarters and Armoury to St. Andrew's Hall, at the junction of St. Andrew's and Charlotte Street. A report of 1896, on the activities of 'C' Company - Stranraer, of the Galloway Rifle Volunteers, was to reveal, "In connection with the Armoury, there is a fair sized Recreation Room, where members of the Company gather during the winter months. The games such as, Summer Ice, Carpet Bowls, Draughts and Dominoes, are productive of much good in keeping the men together, many of whom would otherwise find the long winter months a source of weariness. To the attractions and comfort of this Recreation Room may be attributed much of the popularity, which is steadily growing in this Company."

On Thursday, 26th September, 1901, Lt. General Sir Archibald Hunter, shown in the peaked hat, opened the new Drill Hall of the Stranraer Company of Artillery Volunteers, in Bellevilla Road, Stranraer, which had been converted from the former Bellevilla United Presbyterian Church and later Good Templar's Hall, originally being built in 1782, as the Second Secession Church.

With the Haldane reforms of 1908, the Stranraer Companies of Rifle and Artillery Volunteers were disbanded. St. Andrew's Hall was returned to private use, finally being demolished in 1967. However, the Artillery Hall in Bellevilla Road was retained by the Army becoming the Headquarters of the newly formed, 'B' Company (Stranraer/Portpatrick) and 'D' Company (Stranraer/ Castle Kennedy) 5th (South Ayrshire)

Battalion Royal Scots Fusiliers. The Artillery Hall was to remain under the control of the Auxilliary Forces until 1994, when they reverted to their original use, becoming the home of the Stranraer Baptist Church.

The Headquarters of the Castle Kennedy Section of 'D' Company, 5th Royal Scots Fusiliers was the "Sawmill Loft" which was situated on the south side of the A.75, on the site occupied by the Castle Kennedy Filling Station. This loft was used for numerous social occasions and was considered to be the unofficial Town Hall.

(33) The Old Town Hall, Stranraer.

(34) The "Newsroom", Castle Street, Stranraer.

(35) The Old Academy, Lewis Street , Stranraer.

(36) St. Andrew's Hall, St. Andrew's/Charlotte Street, Stranraer.

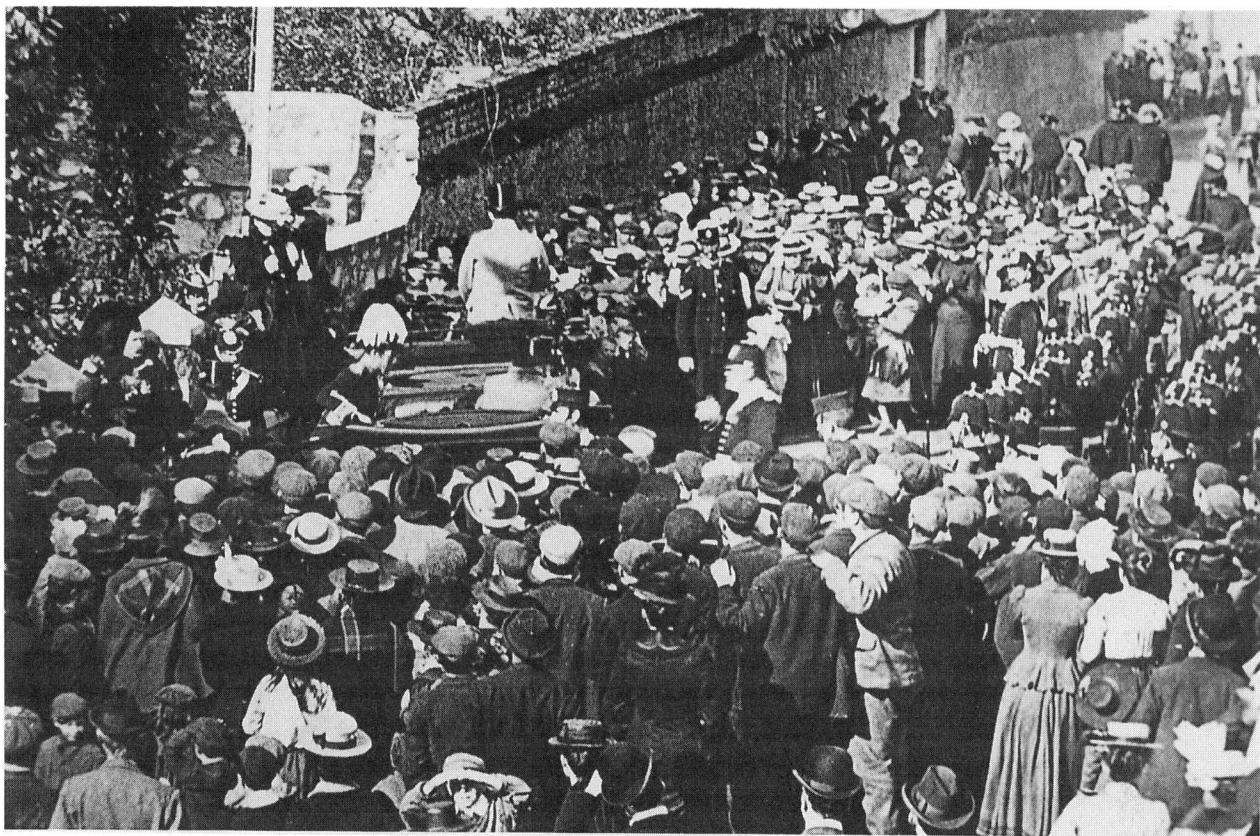

(37) Opening of the Artillery Hall, Bellevilla Road, Stranraer.

(38) The Artillery Hall, Bellevilla Road, Stranraer.

Newton Stewart

The Headquarters of the Galloway Administrative Battalion of Rifle Volunteers and the 3rd Wigtownshire Rifle Volunteers, later to become 'D' Company of the Galloway Rifle Volunteers, from 1860, was in a Hall, which is now semi-derelict and situated at the rear of No.58, Queen's Street, Newton Stewart. The Hall originally built in 1855, consisted of a large hall on the ground floor with an outside stair to the upper rooms and offices. The Hall was originally used by the Oddfellows, Rechabites and indeed for any local social occasion. The Hall was to remain the Headquarters of the Galloway Rifle Volunteers until 1885, when the Battalion Headquarters were removed to Castle Douglas. The Hall was however, to continue as the Headquarters of the Newton Stewart Company until 1896, when they removed to the Victoria Hall, Newton Stewart. The Queen Street Hall was thereafter to continue in many guises until 1960, when the outside stairs and upper rooms and offices were removed and the Hall was converted to garage a single decker bus, with large double sliding doors being fitted.

The Victoria Hall, now the Victoria Arms, 84, Victoria Street, Newton Stewart, was to become the Headquarters, Drill Hall and Armoury of 'D' Company - Newton Stewart, from 1896, until their demise in 1908, when it was to become the Headquarters of 'H' Company 5th (Dumfriesshire and Galloway) Battalion K.O.S.B. A report in 1896, referring to the Victoria Hall related, "The Newton Stewart Comapny have moved form their Headquarters in Queen Street to the Victoria Hall, which they have leased for 7 years at £18 per annum. The lower half of the Victoria Hall is used as an Armoury, Reading and Recreation rooms, Dominoes and Draughts. The upper floor is used for Drill and for further recreation purposes such as Carpet Bowling and Weight Training."

(39) Queen Street Hall, Newton Stewart.

(40) The National Reserve, Newton Stewart, outside the Victoria Hall, forming a parade in honour of King George V's Coronation Celebrations in 1911.

(41) The Victoria Hall, now the Victoria Arms, 84, Victoria Street, Newton Stewart.

Whithorn

The Old Town Hall, George Street, Whithorn, was built in 1814 to replace a Tolbooth and Steeple which previously occupied the centre of the Town. The Drill Hall and Armoury of the 4th Wigtwon Rifle Volunteers - Whithorn, from its inception on the 11th April, 1860 until its final demise on the 11th July, 1874, was formed within the Old Town Hall. A new Town Hall was built in St. John Street, in 1885.

The Drill Hall and Armoury, Drill Hall Lane, formerly referred to as the "Cameronian Entry" was built in the early 19th century by the Cameronian Church, changing in 1876 to that of the Reformed Presbyterian Church. In 1908, ownership passed to the Wigtownshire Territorial and Auxilliary Forces Association, who converted the Church to the Drill Hall and Armoury of the Whithorn Section of 'H' Company of the 5th (Dumfriesshire and Galloway) Battalion of the King's Own Scottish Borderers. The Hall remained in active possession of the Auxilliary Forces until 1958, finally being sold as a Store, to the Local Authority. The Hall, still under the ownership of the Local Authority, is at present home to a vast collection of skeletons excavated from the "Whithorn Dig" and awaiting re-interment in the local cemetary.

(42) The Old Town Hall, George Street, Whithorn.

(43) The Drill Hall and Armoury, Drill Hall Lane, Whithorn.

CHAPTER 16

PHOTOGRAPHIC HISTORY OF THE GALLOWAY RIFLE VOLUNTEERS -
INCLUDING COMMANDERS - OFFICERS - OTHER RANKS - TOGETHER
WITH A SELECTION OF MISCELLANEOUS PHOTOGRAPHS

(44) Sir William Maxwell of Monreith, Commanding Officer of the Galloway Rifles Militia until its
break-up in 1860. This pencil drawing, by D. McClise, was executed whilst Sir William was serving as a
Captain of the 14th Light Dragoons at the Dragoons' Dublin barracks in 1826.
He was later responsible for the attempts to form the Mounted Rifle Volunteer Company in 1859/60.

(45). Colonel John Gordon Maitland of Kenmure Castle, New Galloway, the second Commander of the Galloway Rifle Volunteers. He is seen here wearing the uniform of the Madras Native Infantry, prior to his leaving for India in 1856.

(46). Colonel John Murray Kennedy of Knocknalling, Dalry, the third Commander of the Galloway Rifle Volunteers. Photograph circa 1887.

(47). Lieutenant-Colonel Wellwood J. Maxwell of the Munches, Dalbeattie, second in Command of the Galloway Rifle Volunteers. He first joined the 6th (Dalbeattie) Kirkcudbright Rifle Volunteers, later to become 'H' Company of the Galloway Rifle Volunteers, as an Ensign on the 23rd June, 1869. He quickly rose through the ranks, being appointed Hon. Lieutenant Colonel of the Regiment on the 13th July, 1889. Colonel Maxwell died in 1901 whilst still serving with the Regiment.

(48). The Agnew Brothers of Newton Stewart. The eldest, Captain William Agnew joined the 3rd Wigtown Rifle Volunteers, later to become 'D' Company of the Galloway Rifle Volunteers, on its inception in 1860, serving for 23 years. In 1864, his three brothers, Major Tom Agnew, Sergeant James Agnew and Corporal John Agnew, joined the same Company. The brothers were not only among the top riflemen of the Corps, but excelled in the other sports of the day. Captain Agnew, whilst holding the rank of Sergeant, in 1864, became the first Sergeant in the Regiment to earn the extra proficiency grant for his Company. Back row, left, Major Tom Agnew, right, Corporal John Agnew ; Front row, left, Sergeant James Agnew ; right, Captain William Agnew.

(49). Captain McPhater joined the Volunteer Force as a recruit of the 3rd Lanark Rifles on the 12th November, 1874, where he served for 12 years. In 1887 Captain McPhater received a commission in the Galloway Rifle Volunteers, and in 1895, on the retirement of Major Agnew, he took command of 'D' Company, Newton Stewart. In civilian life Captain McPhater ran a successful Bakers/Confectioners in Newton Stewart. He also served theBurgh as Provost.

(50). Captain Timms of Slogarie, New Galloway, the Officer in Command of 'E' Company. He first joined the Corps on the 2nd October, 1892.

(51). Lieutenant William M. Kelly, a Solicitor from Newton Stewart. Lieutenant Kelly joined 'D, Company, Newton Stewart, of the Galloway Rifle Volunteers on the 23rd June, 1888. He was a top cyclist and led the Galloway Rifles Cycle Team to numerous national successes throughout the 1890's. He took command of 'D' Company, in 1898, on the retirement of Captain McPhater. He also served as Provost of the Burgh.

(52). Lieutenant Alex. McLelland, a Farmer of Balyett, Stranraer, joined as a Private in 'C' Company, Stranraer, of the Galloway Rifle Volunteers, in 1881 . He quickly rose through the ranks receiving his commission on the 2nd May, 1889. He emigrated to South Africa and resigned his commission on 9th September, 1898.

(53). Sergeant Major Charles Ferguson, enlisted in the Regular Army, on the 18th October, 1866, in the 2nd Battalion of the 20th Regiment. A keen gymnast, fencer and pugilist, he was appointed Sergeant in 1869, and transferred to the permanent staff of the School of Gymnastics in Dublin. In due course he was to serve with the 2nd Battalion Lancashire Fusiliers, and the Dumfries Militia, before joining the Galloway Rifle Volunteers, on the 28th September, 1887. as a Sergeant-Major, on permanent staff at Castle Douglas .

(54). Sergeant Armourer George Geddes, a Mineral Agent from New Galloway. Sergeant Geddes was the oldest and longest serving Volunteer in Scotland. He Joined the old 3rd (New Galloway) Kirkcudbright Rifle Volunteers, on the 21st January, 1860, later to become 'E' Company of the Galloway Rifle Volunteers. He served his Company for 41 years, retiring on the 2nd November, 1901. He had three sons all top shots in the Regiment, following in their father's footsteps. Sergeant Geddes' uniform and medals are to be seen on display in the Kirkcudbright Museum.

(55). Sergeant Robert Ferguson a Shepherd, from New Galloway. Sergeant Ferguson joined the 3rd (New Galloway) Kirkcudbright Rifle Volunteers, on the 29th January, 1878. He was a marksman of his Company, winning the Bronze Medal in 1895.

(56). Corporal William Hetherington, a Tailor from Castle Douglas. He first joined the 2nd (Castle Douglas) Kirkcudbright Rifle Volunteers, later to become 'B' Company of the Galloway Rifle Volunteers, on the 8th February, 1877, but left after a year re-joining on the 1st March, 1882. He was a member of the 'B', Company Band and took an active part in the Company and Battalion shooting competitions. He was responsible for the coaching of many of the young riflemen. He is pictured here having just won the 'Best Shot' in the Battalion for 1897.

(57). Private A. Urquhart, a Gamekeeper and native of Irvine, Ayrshire. He moved to Dumfries in 1894, and joined the 'G' Company, Maxwellton, of the Galloway Rifle Volunteers. He had previously served with the Ayrshire Volunteers. Private Urquhart was to become the top marksman of the Regiment. He was a yearly prize winner at Bisley and represented his Country eight times in the Scottish Twenty and three times in the Scottish eight. He was runner-up in the 'Queen's Prize' at Bisley, in 1896, this being the ultimate prize to be won by a Volunteer. Private Urquhart was struck with an attack of typhoid fever, dying on the 26th September, 1898, leaving a widow and three young sons. He was buried on Rood Fair Thursday, in Maxwellton Cemetery, with full Military honours.

(58). Sergeant William Law, Maxwellton, joined the 5th Kirkcudbright Rifle Volunteers in 1879, the same year as the formation of the famous '5KRV.' football team, of which 'Billy' was to become one of its top players. In his first year with the Regiment he won the shooting prize for recruits. He became one of the top shots of the Regiment regularly attending the Wimbledon and Bisley shoots. He is pictured here after winning the West of Scotland Challenge Trophy at Darnley in 1898.

(59). Private John Swan, a Hewer from Kirkcudbright. Private Swan enrolled in 'A' Company, Kirkcudbright, of the Galloway Rifle Volunteers, on the 11th December, 1894. He is seen here in the summer of 1895 with his young lady, not destined to be his bride.

(60). Private John Swan, 'A' Company, Kirkcudbright. circa 1900.

(61) 'C' Company, Stranraer, of the Galloway Rifle Volunteers, photographed in Ballgreen Park, Stranraer, circa 1890's. Note the Craignelder Hotel in the background .

(62). Gatehouse Section of 'A' Company Kirkcudbright, forming part of the South of Scotland Volunteer Brigade, in camp at Minto Kaimes, Hassendean, Hawick, between the 23rd and 28th June, 1891, Back Row 2nd left -. J. Adams; Back Row 3rd left - Peter Jardine. Front Row 1st left - G.H. Ferguson.

(63). Officers and non-commissioned officers of the Galloway Rifle Volunteers, forming part of the South of Scotland Volunteer Brigade in Camp at Minto Kaimes, Hassendean, Hawick, between 26th June, and the 3rd July, 1893. Fourth from left, back row, standing, Lieutenant W. Clark, 'A' Company, Kirkcudbright.

(64). Winners of the Murchie Cup, a cycling trophy confined to members of 'D' Company, Newton Stewart. Back Row - Mr. W. Mercer, Referee D. Stroyan, Esq., Judge - Mr. J. Kelly, Starter. Front Row - W. Drysdale A. Mc.C.Taylor - T. Muir. 1893

(65). The Galloway Battalion of Rifle Volunteers in Camp at Dingleton Common, circa 1900. Lieutenant-Colonel J.M. Kennedy, in Command, is seated on the horse, front centre.

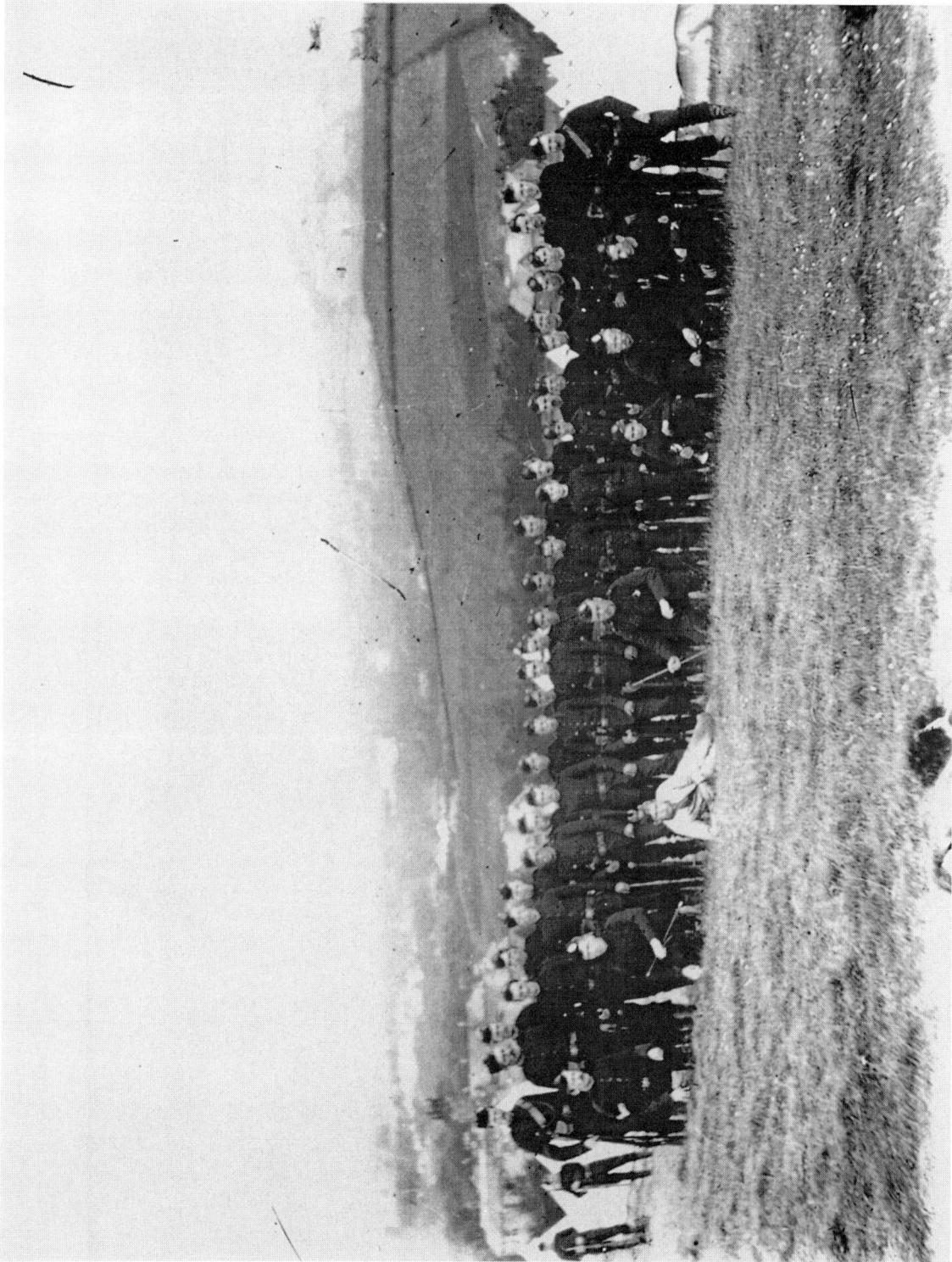

(66). 'A' Company, Kirkcudbright, in Camp at Dingleton Common, Melrose, circa 1900. Captain W. L. Comrie, front centre. Private John Swan, 3rd from right, back row.

(67) . 'A' Company, Kirkcudbright, in camp at Dingleton Common, Melrose, circa 1900. Captain W.L. Comrie, front left. Private John Swan, front centre, standing.

(68). Unknown soldier of the Galloway Rifle Volunteers, in camp at Dingleton Common, Melrose. circa 1900.

(69). 'H' Company, (No.1 Mess), Dalbeattie, in Camp, circa 1890's. Private Harry Mundell, Dalbeattie, is one of the men in this photograph but not identified.

(70) Quarter-Master Sergeant Thomas Myers, a Joiner from Castle Douglas, and Corporal W. Hetherington, a Tailor from Castle Douglas, in camp at Dingleton Common, Melrose, between the 23rd June, and the 6th July, 1900, (1st fortnight). Quarter-Master Sergeant T. Myers was the Regimental Paymaster and in charge of Stores at this camp, assisted by Corporal W. Hetherington.

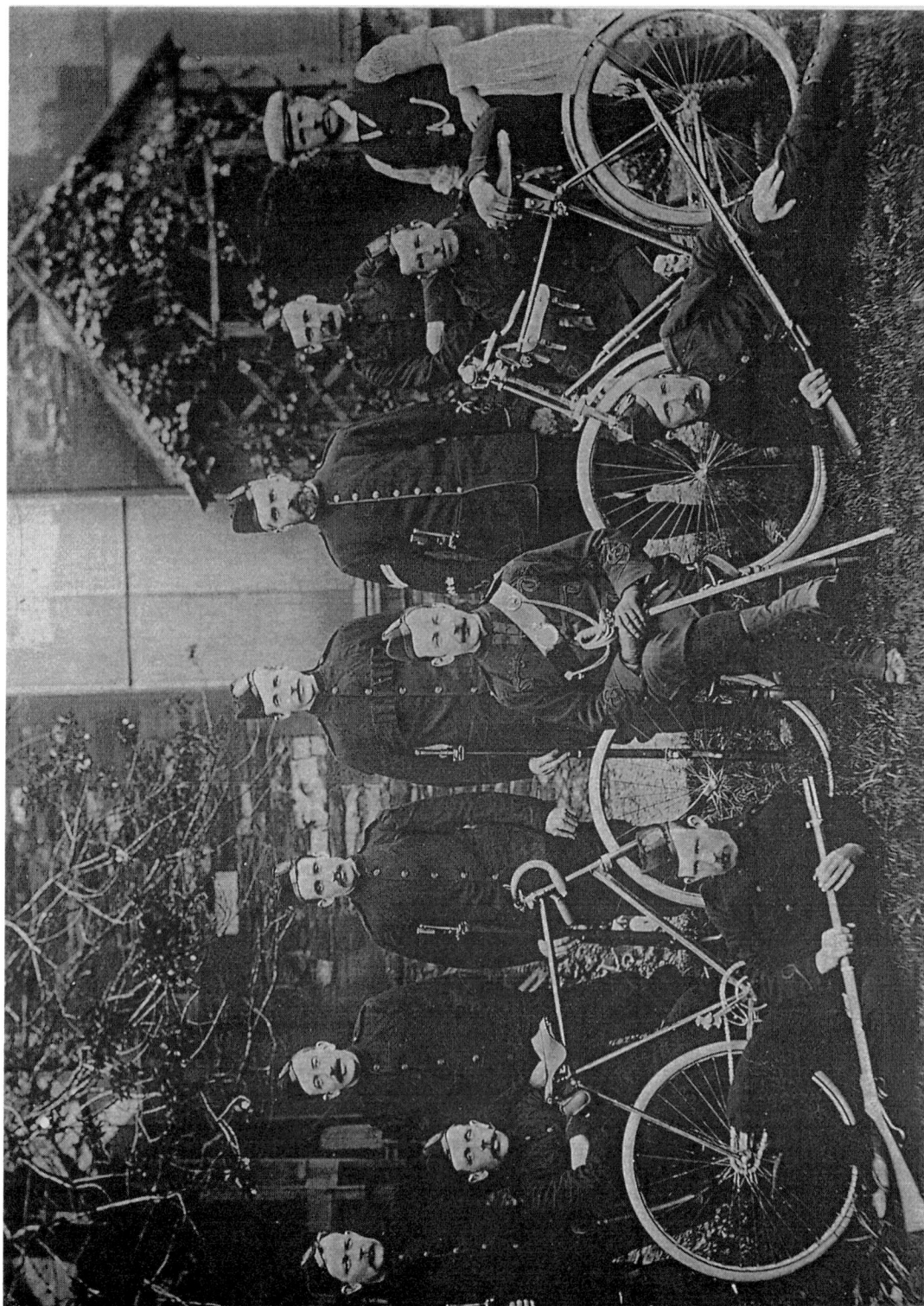

(71). The Wolseley Cup prize winning team of 1896. William Law - John Coupland - and David Haining, Maxwellton. William McCaw and William Hetherington, Castle Douglas. John Ferguson and George Geddes, Junior, New Galloway. William Drysdale - William McCreadie, (3rd left back row) and John Murchie, Newton Stewart, under the command of Lieutenant W. M. Kelly, Newton Stewart, (front centre).

(72) The Minto Cup prize winning team of 1896. Quartermaster Sergeant Myers, Castle Douglas. (3rd from left, centre). Private Paterson and Carnochan, Kirkcudbright. Corporal McCaw, (4th from right, back row), Corporal McCaw - Lance Corporal Hetherington, (2nd from right, middle row), Private Ireland, Castle Douglas. Lance Corporal Love - Privates McCreadie and Priestly, Newton Stewart. Privates Ferguson and Geddes, New Galloway. Privates Black and Ferguson, Maxwellton. Commanded by Captain Timms, New Galloway. Reserves - Privates Derry and Tait, Dalbeattie. Commanded by Captain Timms, New Galloway, (3rd from right, middle row.)

(73) Three young ladies from Kirkcudbright were photographed on the Barrhill, with three young men of the Ayr and Galloway Artillery Volunteers, circa 1900, who were encamped at the Castledykes, Kirkcudbright. The three young ladies were, back left, Jean McCoull, to become, Mrs Campbell. Jenny McCoull, back right, to become Mrs Stenhouse. Mrs Ferguson, seated on the grass was the mother of the baby in the photograph.

(74) "The 7 Angels" of 'D' Company, Newton Stewart, in camp at Dingleton Common, Melrose, circa 1900. Note inscription to this effect written on the tent, with a small Angel pinned to the canvas. The marksman in the back row, centre, is Private William McCreadie, Newton Stewart.

(75) The 100 miles Volunteer Cycle Team of 1897. The team was commanded by Lieutenant W.M. Kelly, Newton Stewart, (centre) and comprised, Sergeant William Mercer, Newton Stewart, (right). Lance Corporal Robert Picken, Newton Stewart, (left). Cyclist John Forsyth and Thomas Murchie, Newton Stewart, Cyclist Peter J. Birrell, Carsluith, Cyclist William Kirk, Dalry.

(76) Members of the Gatehouse Section of the Galloway Rifle Volunteers parading, immediately behind the Band, through the streets of Gatehouse, on the occasion of Her Majesty Queen Victoria's Diamond Jubilee Celebrations, 1897.

(77) Members of the Band of the 8th Garrison Company, Stranraer, of the 1st Ayr and Galloway Artillery Volunteers. circa 1895.

(78) Stranraer, 8th Garrison Company of the 1st Ayr and Galloway Artillery Volunteers, under the Command of Captain and Provost MacRobert, front centre, outside the former Academy in Lewis Street, Stranraer. This photograph was taken on the 22nd June, 1897, prior to the Volunteers joining the parade in Ballgreen Park, for the unveiling of the Jubilee Fountain in Stranraer.

(79) The Parade of the Stranraer Artillery Volunteers forming in Ballgreen Park, Stranraer, on the 22nd June, 1897.

(80) The unveiling ceremony of the Jubilee Fountain in George Street, Stranraer, on the 22nd June, 1897, with Stranraer Company of Artillery Volunteers in attendance, together with members of 'C' Company, Stranraer, of the Galloway Rifle Volunteers, and the Portpatrick Artillery Volunteers, under the Command of Captain Gordon. The Grand Marshal of the Parade was Major McHaffie, Stranraer, of the Ayr and Galloway Militia, who is seen here seated on the white horse, wearing the uniform of his regiment. Captain and Provost MacRobert of the Stranraer Artillery Volunteers is standing to the right of the Fountain.

(81) The famous 1898, 6th Galloway Rifle Volunteers football team, 'H' Company, Dalbeattie, forerunners of the Dalbeattie Star. This was one of the strongest teams ever fielded by Dalbeattie, winning - the Law Cup, the Stewartry League cup, and the Southern Counties cup. Back row - R. Ireland (trainer). R.Richardson, R. Murray, Joe Ferguson, A Gordon, J. Glencross, Jardine Ferguson, A. Burnie, T. Craig (assistant trainer). Middle Row- R. Wilson, (President), A. Swan, J. Brydson, J.Jack (Captain), J. Bissett, J. Thom, J. Boyle (Secretary). Front Row - G. Smith (Cassie), W. Glencross.

PORTPATRICK ARTILLERY CUP TEAM, 1899.

(82) The Portpatrick Artillery F.C. Cup Team, 1899. Back Row- Captain J. Gordon, V.A. Sergeant Major S. Munday, R.A. Team, back row- W. Monk, J. McNeil, J. Cameron, H. Best, J. Drynan, G. McNeil. Front Row- A. McColm, A.Mills, R. McNeil, J. McCracken, J. Logan.

(83) Private 7008, Michael Crossan, Kirkcudbright, of the 1st Active Service Contingent of the King's Own Scottish Borderers. He is seen here wearing his Nile expedition medal and the Khedive Star. Photograph dated 1900.

(84) Private 7009, Robert Milligan, Kirkcudbright, of the 1st Active Service Contingent, of the King's Own Scottish Borderers. Photograph dated 1900.

(85) Private 7010, John Paton Dryden, Kirkcudbright, of the 1st Active Service Contingent of the King's Own Scottish Borderers. Photograph dated 1900.

(86) Private 7306, Robert Sharp, Kirkcudbright, of the 1st Active Service Contingent of the King's Own Scottish Borderers. Photograph dated 1900.

(87) The Galloway Rifle Volunteers Section of the 1st Active Service Contingent of the King's Own Scottish Borderers, parading outside Maxwellton Railway Station, on the 26th January, 1900. Lieutenant Shortridge, front centre standing. Private R. Cochrane, New Galloway, 2nd from left back row. Private M. Crossan, 3rd from right, front row. Private R. Milligan, 7th from left back row. Private J.P. Dryden, 7th from right, back row.

(88) The Dumfries Rifle Volunteers Section of the 1st Active Service Contingent of the King's Own Scottish Borderers, with Provost Glover and his lady wife. The photograph was taken on the 27th January, 1900, outside Provost Glover's home at Hazelwood, Maxwellton, Dumfries.

(89) The combined Dumfries and Galloway Rifle Volunteers, forming as part of the 1st Active Service Contingent of the 1st Battalion of the King's Own Scottish Borderers, on Parade at Berwick H.Q., on the 30th January, 1900, having just been inspected by General C. F. Chapman, Commanding the Forces in Scotland. General Chapman recommended the Volunteers to read extracts from the 'Life of Stonewall Jackson', showing the value of discipline.

(90) Privates John Paton Dryden, extreme right, and Robert Milligan, 2nd from right, at Touws River Camp, South Africa, March/May, 1900, where they were guarding the water reservoirs which supplied Cape Town, 150 miles to the South.

The next five photographs, taken from a series of bioscope pictures, printed in 1900, features Lord Roberts and his column on their march on Pretoria, culminating in its fall on the 5th June 1900. The Galloway Rifle Volunteers formed as part of the composite force on the march to Pretoria, being Lord Robert's personal bodyguard and having the honour of being the first Volunteer Company to enter Pretoria.

(91) "On to Pretoria". - Lord Roberts Great March through the Transvaal.

(92) "Taking the heavy Naval guns across the Vet River." -
Lord Roberts' march on Pretoria, 1900.

(93) "Lord Roberts and Staff ascending the north bank of the Zand River." - On the Great March to
Pretoria, 1900.

(94) "The occupation of Pretoria, 5th June 1900. - Troops passing before Lord Roberts."

(95) "Railway station at Oom Paul's Lost Capital, 5th June 1900, the day Pretoria fell."

(96) Obverse - Kirkcudbright Boer War Tribute Medal
depicting The Tolbooth, Kirkcudbright.

(97) Reverse - Presented to Private J. P.
Dryden 'A' Company GRV.

Public Dinner

IN HONOUR OF

The Volunteers from the District recently returned
from Active Service in South Africa,

IN THE

TOWN HALL, KIRKCUDBRIGHT,

ON

30th November, 1900.

Chairman - - Provost M'EWEN.

Croupiers.

Bailies NICHOLSON and HOGG, Treasurer
SEGGIE, and Capt. COMRIE.

(98) Public Dinner invitatation card.

(99) Sergeant David James Davidson, Postman, of Castle Gardens, Kirkcudbright, and member of No.7 Garrison Artillery Company, Kirkcudbright, who volunteered for service in South Africa, with the Queen's Own Glasgow Yeomanry. Sergeant Davidson returned to the ranks on the cessation of hostilities.

(100) David Seymour Davidson, Publisher, (Father), and David James Davidson, Postman, (son), members of the Kirkcudbright Corps of Artillery Volunteers, circa 1900.

(101) 'B' Company, Castle Douglas, on parade at Queen Victoria's Funeral occasion, on Saturday, 2nd February, 1901, at the Old Town House, Castle Douglas, under the Command of Captain Hewat.

(102) The Coronation celebrations of King Edward VII, held at Kirkcudbright in August, 1902. The front of the parade formed in St. Cuthbert Street, was the Town Band, followed by the 7th (Kirkcudbright) Artillery Volunteers, under the command of Sergeant Major Kimm, and 'A' Company, Kirkcudbright Rifle Volunteers, under the command of Captain W.L. Comrie.

CREETOWN SECTION D. COY. G. R. V.

Published by J. Slevin,

(103) Creetown Section of 'D' Company, Newton Stewart. circa 1902

(104) The Galloway Battalion of Rifle Volunteers de-training at Stobbs Military Camp, Hawick, on the 9th July, 1905. Note the two distinctive uniforms. The new uniform of drab service dress was issued to 'A' and 'H' Companies, Kirkcudbright and Dalbeattie respectively, on the 19th May, 1905, but the other Companies of the Battalion did not receive the new uniform until the 22nd September, 1905.

(105) Sergeant Thomas Newlands, 5th Kirkcudbright Rifle Volunteers (Maxwellton), circa 1877. He is seen here holding the Snider conversion of the Enfield Rifled Musket.

(106) The Galloway Battalion of Rifle Volunteers marching to Stobbs Camp, 9th July, 1905.

GALLOWAY RIFLES
STOBS CAMP 1905

(107) The Galloway Battalion of Rifle Volunteers marching to Stobbs Camp, 9th July, 1905. The two uniforms are seen here quite clearly.

(108) In Camp at Stobbs, Hawick, on 9th July, 1905. Riflemen and Bandsmen of the Regimental Pipe Band.

(109) The Veterans of 'A' company, Kirkcudbright. On the 7th July, 1905, the War Office brought out new age Regulations for the Volunteers with a maximum age limit of 45 years. This photograph marks the end of an era. Back row- left to right, Paymaster Sergeant John Osborne, attached to Headquarters Staff. He was a Joiner to trade and Precentor at the Parish Church, Kirkcudbright, he was later to become the caretaker at the Sheriff Courthouse - Sergeant Adam Rain, a 'Dyker' to trade, he lived at 65, Millburn Street, Kirkcudbright - Sergeant James Livingstone, a Tailor in Kirkcudbright, he joined the Volunteers on the 27th August, 1860. He was the father of another ardent Volunteer, Hugh (Pip) Livingstone - Sergeant J. Green, a Tailor from Twynholm. Front Row, left to right - Sergeant W.R Murray, a Tailor from Ringford - Sergeant James McGregor, a Draper from Kirkcudbright. His shop premises were at 31 St Cuthbert Street. He was later to become the Truant Officer (Whipper in) for Kirkcudbright.

(110) Creetown Volunteers Football Club 1906-07. Winners of the Wigtownshire and District Cup - Galloway Shield - Tweedie Cup. Back Row - Mr. H. McDavid - C. Kevan - Wm. Oliver - R. Lupton - Mr. C. Oliver. Middle Row - Mr. R. Elliott - Private T. Goldie - Private T. O'Hara. Trainer - W. Connell - J. McNearnie - J. Kevan - Mr. S. Chisholm. Treasurer - Private M. Cullen. Front Row - Jas. Butler - Geo. Oliver - J.T. Butler - H. Vernon - W. Birrell, Captain.

(111) Galloway Battalion of Rifle Volunteers in camp at Irvine Moor, Ayrshire, July, 1907. Note the Regimental Pipe and Brass Bands, the Cycling Section and the Maxim Gun, back left of the photograph.

(112) The Officers of the Galloway Battalion of Rifle Volunteers, in Camp at Irvine Moor, Ayrshire, July, 1907. Back Row, left to right, Lieutenant J. Mathews, 'D' Company, Newton Stewart; Lieutenant E.W. Paterson, 'A' Company, Kirkcudbright; Lieutenant A.K. Clark-Kennedy, 'E' Company, New Galloway; Lieutenant Hunter, 'C' Company, Stranraer; Major Comrie, 'A' Company, Kirkcudbright; Lieutenant B. McKinnel, 'F' Company, Maxwellton; Lieutenant Glover, 'G' Company, Maxwellton; Captain R.A. Grierson, 'G' Company, Maxwellton; Lieutenant Scott-Elliott, 'G' Company, Maxwellton; Front Row, left to right- Captain R.S. Glover, 'D' Company, Newton Stewart; Lieutenant Grierson, 'F' Company, Maxwellton; Lieutenant H. Gillies, 'H' Company, Dalbeattie; Lieutenant-Colonel John Lennox, the 4th and final Commander of the Galloway Rifle Volunteers; Captain A.G. Fraser, Adjudant; Captain E.S. Forde, 'E' Company, New Galloway; Major Hewat, 'B' Company, Castle

(113) Kirkcudbright Company of 1st Ayr and Galloway Royal Garrison Artillery, Volunteers. Carbine Shooting - Winners of Sir Mark Stewart's Cup at Buddon Camp, July, 1907. Standing, left to right - W. Jardine; W. McMillan, (Bung); W.Cruikshanks; A.S. Seggie; Sergeant Major Kimm; unknown; D. Carnochan; Bob Strong. Seated, left to right - Bob Laidlaw; Sergeant Skeggs, R.A.; Major Adam Brown; Lieutenant J. Sproat; W. McKenzie; J. McKie, (Gibbie)

(114) The Parker - Jarvis Cup, 1907. Winners No. 4 Section, Wigtown.

(115) The first Camp of the newly formed 5th (Dumfriesshire and Galloway) Battalion of the King's Own Scottish Borderers, held at Caigton, Castle Douglas, in July, 1908.

(116) The newly formed Battery of Royal Field Artillery, Kirkcudbright, outside their Drill Hall at McLellan's Castle, in April/May, 1908. Major A. Brown, Commanding, is seated on the white horse. The man between Major Brown and the Policeman, is David (Pasha) Clark, a Baker from Union Street, and the well known Kirkcudbright Poet.

(117) The 50th Anniversary re-union of the members of the Galloway Rifle Volunteers, who attended the Royal (Wet Review) of Volunteers in Edinburgh, in 1881, in the presence of Her Majesty, Queen Victoria. This photograph was taken in 1931, within the Drill Hall, Dumfries. Front centre, the gentleman with the white beard, Captain William McGowan, Maxwellton, who had a Draper's Shop, next to Binns, now the Bank of Scotland, Dumfries. Front row- 4th from right, Private James Dorrance, from the Mutehill, Kirkcudbright. Centre row - 5th from right, Private J. Briggs, Maxwellton.

(118) A Royal re-union of the veterans of the Galloway rifle Volunteers, who attended the Royal (Wet Review) of Volunteers in Edinburgh in 1881. This photograph was taken in the grounds of Holyrood Park, Edinburgh, in 1949, in the presence of King George VI, and then the Princess Elizabeth. This photograph originated form Kirkcowan and it must be assumed that one of the featured veterans came from that village.

(119) Louis McGuffie, North Main Street, Wigtown, a former member of 'H' Company (Newton Stewart) 5th K.O.S.B. On the outbreak of the Great War, Private McGuffie enlisted in the 1/5th Battalion King's Own Scottish Borderers, and for most Conspicuous Bravery and Resourceful Leadership under fire near Wytschaete, Belgium, on the 28th September, 1918, he was awarded the Victoria Cross. Amongst other heroic acts he single-handed entered a number of enemy dug-outs and caused one Officer and 25 other ranks to surrender. Private McGuffie was however, to make the ultimate sacrifice, on the 4th October, 1918, being killed by an enemy shell.

APPENDIX 1

COMMANDERS OF THE GALLOWAY RIFLE VOLUNTEERS.

(1). William Kennedy Laurie, of Woodhall, (Laurieston Hall), Laurieston, held a Commission in the Duke of Brunswick's Rifle Corps, the famous 'Death's head and Cross Bones'. On the 2nd March, 1860, he was commissioned as Captain of the 1st (Kirkcudbright) Kirkcudbrightshire Rifle Volunteers, and on the 30th June, 1860, he was appointed the first Commander and Colonel of the Galloway Rifle Volunteers. He retired on the 31st July, 1871.

(2). John Gordon Maitland, of Kenmure Castle, New Galloway, the second Commander of the Galloway Rifle Volunteers. Colonel Maitland received his military training at Addiscombe and under a private tutor at St. John's Wood, London, in the days of the East India Company. In 1856, he sailed to India and joined his Regiment, the 29th Madras Native Infantry. When the East India Company was taken over by the British Government he was appointed Lieutenant, on the 8th August, 1865, in the 38th Regiment of Foot, but owing to ill health he resigned his commission on the 23rd March, 1866. On the 9th November, 1866, he was commissioned in the Galloway Rifle Volunteers and appointed Captain of the 3rd (New Galloway) Kirkcudbrightshire Rifle Volunteers. On the retiral of Colonel W. K. Laurie, he assumed command of the Regiment, being appointed Colonel on the 6th January, 1872. Colonel Maitland was dogged by ill health resulting in his early retirement on the 30th July, 1887. He died on the 25th August, 1897, aged 59 years.

(3). John Murray Kennedy, M.V.O. V.D., of Knocknalling, Dalry, the third Commander of the Galloway Rifle Volunteers. Colonel Kennedy's career was to begin with the inception of the Volunteer movement, when he joined as a Private in the London University College Company of the West Middlesex Volunteers. On the 12th November, 1860, he moved to Cambridge where he enrolled as a Private, later to be Lance Corporal, in No. 5 Company of the Trinity College Section of the Cambridge University Rifle Volunteers, until the 2nd April, 1864. On the 10th November, 1866, he was commissioned in the Galloway Rifle Volunteers and appointed Lieutenant in the 3rd (New Galloway) Kirkcudbrightshire Rifle Volunteers. On the 6th March, 1872, he was promoted Captain, and on the 17th April, 1877, promoted Major. On the retiral of Colonel Maitland on 30th July, 1887, he was appointed Commander of the Regiment and promoted to Lieutenant Colonel, being appointed Honorary Colonel on the 20th February, 1889. He retired as Colonel of the Regiment on the 31st August, 1906, under the age limit Regulations, with permission to retain the rank and wear the prescribed uniform.

(4). John Lennox, V.D., a member of the firm Messrs. D. Lennox and Sons, Dumfries, was the 4th and final Commander of the Galloway Rifle Volunteers. On the 23rd June, 1877, he was commissioned as a Sub-Lieutenant in the 5th (Maxwellton) Kirkcudbrightshire Rifle Volunteers and promoted Lieutenant on the 19th March, 1878. He was promoted Captain Commandant on the 9th July, 1879, Honorary Major on the 1st July, 1892, Major on the 21st June, 1900, Honorary Lieutenant Colonel on the 4th October, 1901, and finally appointed Lieutenant Colonel Commanding the Galloway Rifle Volunteers on the 7th September, 1906.

Colonel Lennox held the following certificates:- Certificate of proficiency (Captain) 6th August, 1877. From the School of Instruction at Wellington Barracks - Captain and Field Officer, on the 4th September, 1882, being the last Officer of the Auxilliary Forces to obtain this double certificate at the same time; Passed in tactics as laid down for Lieutenant in the Army before promotion, 4th April, 1883, also as laid down for Captain before promotion to Field rank, January, 1884; Army Ambulance certificate, 7th January, 1889; Passed in fortifications as laid down for Captain in Army before promotion, May, 1890; Passed School of Musketry, 15th January, 1890; Passed for Command of Battalion at Stobs Camp on the 19th July, 1906. From

5th March, 1890 to 21st November, 1891, he held office as Instructor of Muskery and in the years 1900-02, he acted as Adjutant to the Corps, an appointment seldom vested in Volunteers. He was rated as Captain in the Reserve of Officers (Army) from the 25th April, 1885, to the 15th January, 1905, and during the South African War he held the appointment of recruiting officer for the Army for Dumfriesshire and Kirkcudbrightshire. He was awarded the Volunteer Officers Decoration, the Volunteer Defence medal on the 31st August, 1897.

With the demise of the Galloway Rifle Volunteers on the reforms of Mr. Haldane, Secretary of State for War, on the 31st March, 1908, Colonel Lennox was forced to resign his commission, his old adversary of the Dumfriesshire Rifle Volunteers, Colonel Dudgeon, of Cargen, being appointed the new Commander of the combined 5th (Dumfries and Galloway) Battalion of the King's Own Scottish Borderers

Adjutants.

In February, 1860, Adjutants were authorised for Battalions of Rifle Volunteers, being appointed under the Queen's Commission, on the recommendation of the Lord Lieutenant. These Adjutants were men of a substantial military service and background being responsible for the instruction and military efficiency of their respective Corps. They were initially paid for by their Corps and appointed for an indefinite period, but in August, 1861, Adjutants and Drill Sergeants were paid direct by Government, the Adjutants receiving 8/- per day, changing in 1863 to 10/- per day, with 2/- per day for the upkeep of a horse and an additional payment of £4 per year for each Company forming his Battalion. The Drill Sergeants were to receive 2/4d per day if in receipt of an Army Pension, and 2/7d per day if not, with an additional 6d per day if acting as Sergeant-Major. In 1872, Adjutants were appointed from Captains of the Regular Army, for a period of 5 years only, on full or half pay.

Adjutants to the Galloway Rifle Volunteers 1860 - 1908.

(1). MAJOR W. MUNRO. - 16th July, 1860 - 31st July, 1871. Major Munro lived at Valleyfield, Ringford.

(2). CAPTAIN L.C. SINGLETON. - 92nd Regiment. 7th November, 1871 - 31st December, 1876. Lived near Dumfries. "Captain Singleton, on the completion of his 5 years service as Adjutant to the Galloway Rifles, was placed on extended leave and received half pay until a vacancy occurred in his Regiment. Mr. Wait, the Member of Parliament, raised the matter in the House of Commons, on the 22nd March, 1877, when the Secretary of War, agreed that Captain Singleton should receive his full pay during his period of extended leave. Captain later Major Singleton was mortally wounded, whilst serving with his Regiment, in the battle of Majuba Hill, in the first Boer War, dying from his injuries on the 1st May, 1881."

(3). MAJOR H. FARRER. - 27th February, 1877 - 15th April, 1882. Major Farrer lived at 22, Castle Street, Dumfries. On the 20th April, 1882, Lieutenant-Colonel Maitland, Commanding the Galloway Battalion of Rifle Volunteers, issued the following Regimental Order:
Castle Douglas. 20th April, 1882.

"Major Farrer being about to rejoin his Regiment on completion of his tour of duty as Adjutant to the Battalion, Colonel Gordon Maitland wishes to record his sense of the energy, zeal and capacity shown by this Officer in the performance of his various duties and to thank him for the ready assistance he has always offered to his Commanding Officer and to the Officers, non-commissioned officers and men of the Galloway Rifle Volunteers.

By Order.
(Signed) C.E. Bovill. Capt. and Adjt.
Galloway Rifle Volunteers"

(4). MAJOR C.E. BOVILL. - Royal Inniskilling Fusiliers. 16th April, 1882 - 2nd February, 1885. Lived near to the Railway Station, Dumfries. The following Regimental Order, relative to the service of Major C.E. Bovill, was issued by Lieutenant-Colonel Maitland:
Castle Douglas. 21st March, 1885.

"Major C.E. Bovill having been ordered to join his Regiment, on restoration to full pay, the Officer

Commanding desires to record his regret at the loss of the services of this able Officer as Adjutant of the Battalion, and to express his high opinion of the military capacity and great energy displayed by him during the 3 years he has been with the Galloway Rifle Volunteers.

By Order.
(Signed) F.W. Douglas.
Major and Adjutant. Galloway Rifle Volunteers."

(5). MAJOR FRANCIS WINGFIELD DOUGLAS. - 1st Battalion Royal Scots Fusiliers.
6th February, 1885, to 31st January, 1890. Lived in Castle Douglas. On the 4th June, 1887, Major Douglas was badly injured at Battalion Drill, by his horse falling on him, and in consequence (6). CAPTAIN CARR. - 2nd Ayrshire, acted as Temporary Adjutant until Major Douglas recovered.

(7). CAPTAIN R.W.M. BLAKE. - 1st Battalion Royal Scots Fusiliers, was selected for Adjutant in succession to Major F.W. Douglas, on the 22nd November, 1889, but on the 27th December, 1889, he resigned the appointment.

(8). MAJOR J.H. SPURGIN. - 1st Battalion Royal Scots Fusiliers. 1st February, 1890, to 25th August, 1894. Lived at Corbeton, Castle Douglas.

(9). CAPTAIN H.L. BUTLER. - 26th August, 1894 to 2nd July, 1895. Lived in Castle Douglas.

(10). MAJOR R.W.M. BLAKE. - 1st Battalion Royal Scots Fusiliers, was re-appointed Adjutant on the 3rd July, 1895 and served until 23rd August, 1900.

(11). MAJOR LENNOX. - Galloway Rifle Volunteers. Acting Adjutant. Major Lennox took over from Major R.W.M. Blake on the 23rd August, 1900, and held the position until Captain Wolseley's return from South Africa (Boer War) on the 4th July, 1902.

(12). CAPTAIN J.F. WOLSELEY. - 2nd Battalion Royal Fusiliers. Captain Wolseley was appointed Adjutant to the Galloway Rifle Volunteers, on the 23rd November, 1900, whilst serving with his Regiment in South Africa, however, with the escalation of the guerilla war in South Africa, he was ordered to remain with his Regiment until he formally took over his appointment, as Adjutant, on the 4th July, 1902. He resigned his commission the following year, in August, 1903.

(13). CAPTAIN J.C.W. CONNEL. - 1st Battalion King's Own Scottish Borderers.
Captain Connel was appointed Adjutant to the Corps on the 16th October, 1903, but rejoined his Regiment on 31st March, 1905, on the death of his wife.

(14). LIEUTENANT-COLONEL LENNOX. Galloway Rifle Volunteers. Lt.-Col. Lennox was once again appointed Acting Adjutant of the Battalion from the 31st March, 1905, until the 7th June, 1905.

(15). CAPTAIN A.G. FRASER. - 1st Battalion King's Own Scottish Borderers.
7th June, 1905, to 4th October, 1907, when he was posted to the 2nd Battalion K.O.S.B. on promotion. Captain Fraser had previously seen service in the Chitral and Tirah campaigns in India. He was on Lord Kitchener's Staff in Egypt and served in the South African War.

(16). CAPTAIN R.G. GRIERSON. - Galloway Rifle Volunteers, acted as Adjutant to the Battalion from the 4th October, 1907, until its demise on the 31st March, 1908.
On the 1st April, 1908, CAPTAIN GUNN. was appointed the 1st Adjutant to the newly formed 5th (Battalion) King's Own Scottish Borderers.

Drill Instructor Sergeants of the
Galloway Rifle Volunteers 1860 -1908.

1st Kirkcudbright Rifle Volunteers - 'A' Company - Kirkcudbright.

Drill Instructor Sergeant White -	1860 - 1866.
.. .. Sergeant Horspool -	1866 - 1870 .
.. .. Sergeant James Farries -	1870 - 1872.
.. .. Sergeant J. Gilmour -	1872 - 1882.
.. Sergeant T. Mitchell -	1882 - 1890.
.. .. Colour Sergeant George Tuck -	21.3.1890 - June, 1900.
.. .. Colour Sergeant J. Carroll -	June, 1900 - January, 1901
	(Transferred from Maxwellton)
.. .. Sergeant A. Cairns -	25.1.1901 - 31.3.1908.

2nd Kirkcudbright Rifle Volunteers - 'B' Company - Castle Douglas.

Drill Instructor Colour Sergeant William Roberts-	1860 - 1863.
.. .. Sergeant E. Dowdney -	June, 1863 - June, 1880.
.. .. Sergeant J. Connolly -	June, 1880 - 1883.
.. .. Colour Sergeant T. McIlroy -	1883 - 1886. (Transferred to Stranraer.)
.. .. Sergeant Major Fergusson -	15.9.1886 - 1901. (ex-Dumfries Militia.)
.. .. Sergeant Major Gallagher -	1901 - 4.9.1903
	(Transferred from Dalbeattie on promotion.)
	(ex-l st Battalion Royal Scots Fusiliers.)
.. .. Sergeant Major Grierson -	20.11.1903 -
	(Transferred from New Galloway) December 1904
	(Transferred to Maxwellton.)
.. .. Colour Sergeant T. McIlroy -	December, 1904 - 26.10.1907
	(Transferred from Maxwellton.)
.. .. Sergeant Gibson -	1.11.1907 - 31.3.1908. (ex-lst Battalion K.O.S.B.)

Kirkpatrick Durham/Springholm Section.

Drill Instructor Sergeant Horsley -	13.11 .1897 - 9.12.1898.

3rd Kirkcudbright Rifle Volunteers - 'E' Company - New Galloway.

Drill Instructor Sergeant Brown -	1860 - February, 1889.
.. .. Sergeant J. Gallagher -	8.2.1889 - 7.5.1892.
	(ex-l st Battalion R.S.F.) (Transferred toDalbeattie.)
.. .. Sergeant C. Farell -	7.5.1892 - 1898.
.. .. Colour Sergeant R. Grierson -	June 1898 - 1903
	(Service at Boer War 14.3.1901 - 22.6.1902
	with 2nd Sevice Co. K.O.S.B.
	Transferred to Castle Douglas on promotion.)
.. .. Colour Sergeant Cumming -	17.7.1903 - 1904
.. .. Colour Sergeant Nelson -	1904 - 31.3.1908

4th Kirkcudbright Rifle Volunteers - Gatehouse

Drill Instructor Sergeant John Spearing -	1860 - 1861
.. .. Sergeant John Wood -	1861 - 1866
	(Transferred from Newton Stewart.)
	(ex. 93rd Sutherland Highlanders.)

5th Kirkcudbright Rifle Volunteers - 'F' & 'G' Companies - Maxwellton

Drill Instructor Sergeant John Roberts -	1860 - 1861
.. .. Sergeant Murdoch -	1861 - 25.10.1889
.. .. Colour Sergeant Campbell -	1889 - 1894 (ex. RSF)
.. .. Colour Sergeant R. Grierson -	11.4.1894 - June 1898
	(Transferred to New Galloway)

Drill Instructor Colour Sergeant J. Carroll -			1898 - June 1900 (Transferred to Kirkcudbright)
..	..	Sergeant Cumming -	15.6.1900 - 17.7.1903 (ex Langholm)
			(Transferred to New Galloway)
..	..	Colour Sergeant T. McIlroy -	January 1904
			(Transferred from Stranraer) December 1904
			(Transferred to Castle Douglas)
..	..	Sergeant Major R. Grierson -	December, 1904 - 7.11.1907.
			(Transferred from Castle Douglas.)
..	..	Colour Sergeant P. Fennessey -	7.11.1907 - 31.3.1908.(ex- K.O.S.B.)
			(Transferred from Stranraer.)

6th Kirkcudbright Rifle Volunteers - 'H' Company - Dalbeattie.

Drill Instructor.		Sergeant Miller	1869 - 1880
..	..	Sergeant Flynn	1880 - 1892
..	..	Colour Sergeant J. Gallagher	4.6.1892 - 1901(ex-1st Battalion R.S.F.)
			(Transferred to Castle Douglas.)
..	..	Colour Sergeant Collard -	Temporary cover in 1901.
..	..	Colour Sergeant Anderson -	15.11.1901 - 27.2.1903
			(Transferred to 2nd V.B. K.O.S.B. Coldstream.)
..	..	Colour Sergeant J. Firth -	27.2.1903 - July, 1905.
			(ex-Border Rifles Melrose)
..	..	Colour Sergeant T. McIlroy -	July - December, 1905.
			(discharged duties at Castle Douglas and Dalbeattie.)
..	..	Colour Sergeant George Alexander -	22.12.1905.- 31.3.1908. (ex-K.O.S.B.)

1st Wigtown Rifle Volunteers. - Wigtown.

Drill Instructor Sergeant Major Ireland -			1860-1861.
			(ex-Galloway Rifles Militia) Shared with Newton Stewart.
..	..	Sergeant John Wood	1861-1862 Shared with Newton Stewart
			(ex-93rd Sutherland Highlanders) Transferred to Gatehouse.
..	..	Sergeant Lock -	July, 1862 - 20.6.1873.

2nd Wigtown Rifle Volunteers 'C' Company Stranraer.

Drill Instructor Sergeant Holding			16.3.1860 - 7.6.1860
..	..	Colour Sergeant Green	7.6.1860 - 16.1.1862 (Transferred to Dumfries.)
..	..	Sergeant George Young	16.1.1862 - 1873
			(ex- Instructor to Stranraer Juvenile Rifle Corps.)
..	..	Sergeant Major Locke	1.1.1874 - 1877. (Transferred from Whithorn.)
..	..	Sergeant Duncan	1877 - 1881.
..	..	Sergeant Harold	1881 - 1886.
..	..	Colour Sergeant T. McIlroy -	1886 (Transferred from Castle Douglas)
			January,1904 (Transferred to Maxwellton.)
..	..	Colour Sergeant P. Fennessey -	January, 1904 - 7.11.1907.
			Transferred to Maxwellton (ex- K.O.S.B.)
..	..	Sergeant James Stewart -	22.11.1907 - 31.3.1908.(ex- 2nd K.O.S.B.)

3rd Wigtown Rifle Volunteers - 'D' Company - Newton Stewart.

Drill Instructor Sergeant Major Ireland -			1860 - 1861 (Shared with Wigtown)
			(ex- Galloway Rifle Militia)
..	..	Sergeant John Wood	1861 - 1862 (Shared with Wigtown)
			(ex-93rd Sutherland Highlanders)
			(Transferred to Gatehouse.)
..	..	Sergeant James Kennedy	9.1.1862 - unknown.
			(ex- Dumfries Militia)
..	..	Sergeant Walsh.	Unknown - 1890.
..	..	Sergeant Henry Mathews	1890 - 1896.
..	..	Sergeant Milne	September, 1896 - January, 1897.
..	..	Sergeant James Axon	1897 - 1907.
..	..	Colour Sergeant Charles Johnstone	31.1.1908 - 31.3.1908 (ex- 3rd K.O.S.B.)

4th Wigtown Rifle Volunteers - Whithorn

Drill Instructor
        Sergeant Major Locke

        11.4.1860 - 1.1.1874. Transferred to Stranraer.

5th Wigtown Rifle Volunteers - Drummore.

Did not appear to have their own Drill Instructor until July, 1862, then no details are recorded. In all probability used Stranraer Sergeant Instructors until July, 1862.

Monreith Volunteer Rifle Corps.

Drill Instructor Colour-Sergeant Brown -   7.5.1860 - September, 1860 (Ex - Coldstream Guards.)

Colour-Sergeant Dowdney, Sergeant Instructor, to 2nd Kirkcudbright Rifle Volunteers. June, 1863 - June, 1880.

Colour-Sergeant Dowdney, joined the 47th Regiment of the Line, at Gosport, Portsmouth, in March, 1844, at the age of 17 years. Two years later he saw active service in Ireland, when his Regiment assisted in supressing the Smith/O'Brien insurrection. His service in Ireland was of 5 years duration, during which times he witnessed the misery which then overspread the land during the dreadful famine.

His Regiment then went to Corfu, then posessed by the British, and after a sojourn in that little island for 2 years, his Regiment repaired to Malta. A year later war was declared against Russia and the 47th was ordered to Constantinople, thence to Varna and the Crimea. Sergeant Dowdney took part at the battle of Alma, assisted in the capture of Balaclava, took part in the battle of Inkerman and the seige and capture of Sebastopol, where he was wounded. After peace was declared the 47th were ordered back to Malta and then to Gibralter, before arriving back to England in August, 1857.

In 1859, the 2nd Battalion of the 25th King's Own Borderers was raised and non-commissioned officers from various Regiments were required to fill the vacancies. Sergeant Dowdney joined his new Regiment on promotion in 1860. Sergeant Dowdney remained with the 25th until June, 1863, when he was transferred as Drill Instructor to the 2nd Kirkcudbright Rifles, Castle Douglas.

For his services in the Crimea Sergeant Dowdney received the Turkish medal, the Crimean medal, and the meritous medal for faithful service. In April, 1866, Her Majesty, Queen Victoria, upon the recommendation of the General Commander-in-Chief was graciously pleased to confer upon Sergeant Dowdney, as a reward for distinguished and meritous services in the army, an annuity of £10.

Sergeant Dowdney remained as Drill Instructor to the Castle Douglas Rifle Company, for 17 years, retiring in June, 1880, to the village of Hardgate. He died on the 10th September, 1891, aged 65 years, and was buried in Urr Churchyard, with full military honours.

APPENDIX 2

This supplement, containing the names of those men who served in the various companies of the Galloway Rifle Volunteers, is split into three Sections. The first is a full and comprehensive list of all the Officers who served in the Galloway Rifle Volunteers, 1860-1908, although in many cases their exact years with the Regiment are unknown. The second Section, is a list of all the rank and file who feature in both the completed history and who came to notice during the course of this research. It must be remembered that this Section is by no means comprehensive, in 'A' Company, (Kirkcudbright) alone, 1,240 Volunteers passed through the ranks in the years, 1860 - 1883. In the first and second Sections where the vast majority of joining dates, of the Volunteers are unknown, the year in which that particular Volunteer first came to notice has been inserted. The third Section is a wonderful, comprehensive and extremely detailed history of all members forming the various Companies of the Galloway Rifle Volunteers, as appeared in their Muster Rolls for the year, 1896.

KIRKCUDBRIGHT -

Incorporating both the 1st Kirkcudbright Rifle Volunteers, and 'A' Company of the Galloway Rifle Volunteers.

SECTION 1 - OFFICERS.

1. BLAIR; David. Assistant surgeon. 22.6.1860 - unknown
2. CLARK; W. Lieutenant. 6.12.1890 - 16.5.1894.
3. CRAIG; D. Ensign. 1860. Retired Major. 8.1.1889.
4. COMRIE; W.L. 2nd Lieutenant. 1897. Major 1907. Gategill.
5. GLOVER; R.S. Lieutenant 1902. Transferred as Officer in charge Gatehouse Section in 1904.
    1905 Transferred to Newton Stewart.
6. HAMILTON; George. Captain 1860 - Unknown.
7. HOWITT; Lieutenant. 1891. Retired Captain 1894.
8. JOHNSTONE; W. Surgeon Lieutenant. 31.5.1873. Retired Surgeon Major 16.12.1893.
9. LAURIE; William Kennedy. Captain. 2.3.1860.
    Lieutenant-Colonel Commanding the Galloway Rifle Volunteers. 30.6.1860.
10. MUIR; J. Lieutenant. 16.5.1877. Retired Captain 12.5.1894.
11. McLELLAN; T.R. Ensign. 1860 - Unknown.
12. McLELLAN; W. Ensign. 6.5.1864. Retired Major 1897/98.
13. PATERSON; E.W. Lieutenant. 1907. Joined as a Private on 7.7.1881, and was promoted from the ranks.
14. TENNANT; D. Lieutenant. 1860 - Unknown.
15. UNDERWOOD; Rev. J. Chaplain. 18.7.1860 - Unknown.
16. WILKINSON; Henry Bevis. 2nd Lieutenant 1905. Transferred to 'B' Company, Castle Douglas in 1906.

SECTION 2 - RANK AND FILE.

1. ALLAN; Private R. 1905.
2. ALLAN; Corporal J. 1905.
3. ANDERSON; Private John. 1862.
4. BECK; Private Alexander. 1860.
5. BELL; Private David. 1860.
6. BELFORD; Private James. 1860.
7. BLACKHURST: Private A. 1905.
8. BLACKLOCK; Private John. 1861.
9. BLACKLOCK; Private T. 1905.
10. BLAIR; Private Robert G. 1860.
11. BROATCH; Private Robert. 1860.
12. BROWN; Private F.G. 1861.
13. BROWN; Private Thomas. 1860.
14. BROWN; Private William. 1860. Sergeant 1863.

15. BURNIE; Private J. 1905.
16. CAIG; Private W. 1905.
17. CAIRD; Private James. 1863. Segeant 1865.
18. CAIRNS; Sergeant A. 1905.
19. CAMPBELL; Sergeant A. 1860. (1)
20. CAMPBELL; Private Alex. 1860. (2)
21. CAMPBELL; Private John. 1860. Sergeant 1876. Culcrae.
22. CAMPBELL; Private W. 1905.
23. CARTER; Private R. 1881.
24. CLARK; Private R. 1905.
25. CLARKSON; Private J. 1905.
26. CLUNIE; Piper R. 1905.
27. COLLINS; Private Peter. 1878.
28. CRAIG; Sergeant David. 1860.
29. DALRYMPLE; Private S. 1905.
30. DALZELL; Private G. 1890.
31. DAVENPORT; Private W. 1905.
32. DONALD; Private Alex. 1860.
33. DOUGLAS; Sergeant 1876.
34. FARMER; Private E. 1905.
35. FARRELL; Sergeant D.M. 1878.
36. FARRELL; Private T. 1865.
37. FERGUSON; Private John. 1860.
38. FITZPATRICK; Private E. 1905.
39. GALLAGHER; Private F. 1905.
40. GALLAGHER; Private J. 1905.
41. GILCHRIST; Private A. 1905.
42. GOODWIN; Piper R. 1902.
43. GORDON; Private David. 1860.
44. GOURLAY; Private Alex. 1860.
45. GRAHAM; Private William. 1860.
46. GRANT; Private Adam. 1901.
47. GRANT; Private Allan. 1905.
48. GRANT; Sergeant Donald. 1902.
49. GRIERSON; Corporal. 1861. Sergeant 1864. (1).
50. GRIERSON; Private James. 1860. (2)
51. GRIERSON; Private Joseph. 1861. Campbelton.
52. HALLIDAY; Private J. 1905.
53. HAMILTON; Private J. 1905.
54. HANNAH; Private Andrew. 1860.
55. HANNAH; Private D. B. 1864.
56. HANNAH; Private William. 1902.
57. HARRISON; Private T. 1881.
58. HAY; Private J. 1905.
59. HAY; Private W. 1905.
60. HENDERSON; Private D. 1865.
61. HENRY; Piper. 1907. (1)
62. HENRY; Private H. 1905. (2)
63. HERON; Private F. 1905.
64. HEUGHAN; Private A. 1880.
65. HOGG; Private A. 1880.
66. HOGG; Private John. 1880.
67. HOUSTON; Private J. 1881.
68. HOWITT; Private W.C. 1889.
69. HUGHAN; Private N.M. 1900. (1)
70. HUGHAN; Private. 1869. (2).
71. HUNTER; Private. 1905. L/Corporal. 1907.
72. JAMIESON; Private Alexander. 1900.
73. JARDINE; Private G. 1899.
74. JENKINS; Private David. 1860.
75. JOHNSTON; Private J. 1863. (1)
76. JOHNSTON; Sergeant J. 1905. (2)
77. KIRKPATRICK; Sergeant J.R. 1905.
78. KIRKPATRICK; Private W. 1901.
79. LIGHTBODY; Private William. 1860.
80. LIVINGSTONE; Private R. 1878.
81. LOGAN; Corporal. 1880.

82. MANSON; Private C. 1905.
83. MARTIN; Private Thomas. 1861.
84. MARTIN; Private William. 1860.
85. MAXWELL; Private A. 1905.
86. MAXWELL; Private J. 1877.
87. MEGGAT; Private A. 1860.
88. MIDDLETON; Private A. 1905.
89. MIDDLETON; Private J. 1905.
90. MILROY; Private John. 1905.
91. MITCHELL; Private John. 1860.
92. MURRAY; Private J.L. 1905.
93. MACKENZIE; Private Anthony. 1860.
94. MCBAIN; Private. 1877.
95. MCBEAN; Private 1882.
96. MCBURNIE; Private S. 1905.
97. MCCANDLISH; Private G. 1907.
98. MCEWAN; Private Thomas. 1899.
99. MCEWEN; Corporal J. 1905.
100. MCGAW; Private T. 1905.
101. MCGAW; Sergeant W. 1905.
102. MCHARRIE; Private William. 1862.
103. MCHARVIE; Private William. 1862.
104. MCKAY; Private D. 1905.
105. MCKENNA; Private J. 1905.
106. MCKIE; Private G. 1905.
107. MCKINNA; Private A. 1905.
108. MCLELLAN; Private David. 1860.
109. MCLURG; Private J. 1863.
110. MCMILLAN; Private A. 1905.
111. MCMURRAY; Private D. 1905.
112. MCMURRAY; Private W. 1905.
113. MCNAUGHT; Private William; 1860.
114. MCROBERT; Private. 1890.
115. MCSKIMMING; Private J. 1905.
116. NIVEN; Private David. 1860.
117. NORREN; L/Corporal. 1877. Sergeant 1882.
118. OSBORNE; Private 1892. Recruit.
119. PATTERSON; Corporal D. 1896. (1)
120. PATTERSON; Cyclist D.R. 1900 (2)
121. PATERSON; Private H. 1880.
122. PATERSON; Private R. 1905 Recruit.
123. PATERSON; Private W. 1880. Corporal 1889.
124. PAYNE; Private James. 1860. Sergeant 1861.
125. PHILLIPS; Corporal W. 1878. Bandmaster.
126. PROCTOR; Private A. 1901.
127. RAE; Private James. 1860.
128. RAE; Private D.G. 1905.
129. RAIN; Corporal Adam. 1878.
130. RAMAGE; Private W. 1878.
131. REID; Private A.D. 1899. Corporal 1905.
132. REID; Private William. 1860.
133. RODGERS; Private W. 1905.
134. ROSS; Private S. 1905.
135. SHARP; Private D. 1905.
136. SHARP; Private J. 1905.
137. SHARP; Private Robert. 1900.
138. SHARPE; Private A. 1881.
139. SPROAT; Private Andrew. 1860.
140. SPROAT; Private James. 1860.
141. STEVENS; Private A. 1905.
142. STEVENSON; Private Robert. 1860.
143. STEVENSON; Private Samuel; 1860.
144. STEVENSON; Private Thomas. 1860.
145. STEWART; Private W. 1905.
146. STRAITON; Private T. 1905.
147. TAIT; Private W. 1905.
148. TELFER; Private D. 1862.

149. THOMSON; Private Robert. 1860. (1)
150. THOMSON; Sergeant Robert. 1860. (2)
151. VEITCH; Private J. 1905.
152. WALKER; Private A. 1905.
153. WALKER; Private R. 1905.
154. WHITE; Private William. 1860.
155. WILLIAMSON; Private Alex. 1860. Sypland.
156. WILLIAMSON; Private Douglas. 1860 (1)
157. WILLIAMSON; Sergeant D.G. 1860. (2)
158. WILLIAMSON; Sergeant J. 1860.
159. WILLIAMSON; Private Samuel. 1860.
160. WILSON; Private S. 1905.
161. YOUNG; Private R. 1905.

SECTION 3 - MEMBERSHIP OF 1896.

Reg No.	Rank	No.	Name	Occupation	Address	Date of enrolment
	Cap.& Hon.					
	Major	1	McLellan, Wm	Solicitor	Kirkcudbright	6.5.1864
1534	Sgt.-Inst.	2	Tuck, G.		..	21.3.1890.
77	Col.-Sgt.	3	Murray, W.R.	Tailor	Ringford	9.1.1871
182	Sgt.	4	Green, J	Tailor	Twynholm	2.11.1866
						& 24.1.1876.
222	..	5	Livingstone, J.	Tailor	Kirkcudbright	27.8.1860
						& 1.7.1876.
885	..	6	McEwen, P.	Forester	..	6.2.1882
1048	..	7	McGregor, J.	Draper	..	22.8.1867
	Col. - Sgt.. 1905			(Truant Officer)		& 1.12.1882.
7095	Corporal	8	Belford, W.	Cabinetmaker	..	3.4.1873
						& 6.12.1892.
1326	..	9	Gourlay, A.	Plumber	..	11.4.1884
1904	L/Sgt.	10	Kirkpatrick, J.R	Draper	Gatehouse.	11.3.1873
						& 30. 5. 1888
856	Corporal	11	Paterson, E.	Hewer	Kirkcudbright	7.7.1881
1665	..	12	Swan, J.	Hewer	..	6.1.1887.
5078	L/Corporal	13	Gordon, C.	Joiner	..	2.2.1891.
7066	Bugler	14	Livingston, H.	Clerk.	..	18.4.1892.
1920	Private	15	Adams, J.	Painter	..	20.12.1888
7517	Private	16	Aitken, T.	Mason	Gatehouse	9.4.1895
7051	..	17	Baird, A.	Butter-Maker	Twynholm	16.4.1892
4038	L/Corporal	18	Bowie, A.D.	Cabinet-maker	Kirkcudbright	2.7.1890.
7263	Private	19	Branney, J.	Blacksmith	..	27.9.1893
7266	..	20	Branney, J.	Joiner	..	27.9.1893
7264	..	21	Branney, P.	Plumber	..	27.9.1893
7259	..	22	Branney, R.	Labourer	..	2.8.1893.
7329	..	23	Branney, W.	Plasterer	..	15.12.1893
337	..	24	Brown, J.	Dyker	..	17.4.1878
7711	..	25	Buchanan, H.	Plumber	Gatehouse	11.5.1896
7710	..	26	Byers, F.	Shoemaker	..	11.5.1896
889	..	27	Campbell, S.	Mason	Kirkcudbright	6.2.1882
7172	..	28	Carnochan, T.	Gamekeeper	Ringford	13.2.1893
7047	..	29	Carter, J.	Tailor	..	6.4.1892
4015	..	30	Clark, D.	Baker	Kirkcudbright	19.4.1866
						& 2.7.1890
7439	..	31	Clark, D.	Tailor	..	11.12.1894.
6035	..	32	Collins, J.	Painter	..	12.1.1892
6092	..	33	Collins, L.	Tailor	..	26.2.1892
7695	..	34	Colman, W.	Tailor	..	23.4.1896
6096	..	35	Corson, W.	Farmer	Gatehouse	1.3.1892
7644	..	36	Crossan, M.	Labourer	Kirkcudbright	31.1.1896
6034	..	37	Dalrymple, T.	Mason	Gatehouse	1.1.1892
3075	Private	38	Dalrymple, W.	Mason	Gatehouse	8.4.1890
7171	..	39	Davidson, A.	Mason	Kirkcudbright	8.12.1882
						& 13.2.1893

Reg No.	Rank	No.	Name	Occupation	Address	Date of enrolment
6026	Private	40	Dorrance, C.	Labourer	Kirkcudbright	19.2.1880& 31.12.1891
35	..	41	Douglas, W.D.	Miller	..	19.7.1866
696	..	42	Dryden, J.	Labourer	..	1.3.1881
7222	..	43	Fergusson, J.	Draper	Gatehouse	18.4.1893
7185	..	44	Fraser F. W.	Plumber	..	15.3.1893
6031	..	45	Gavigan,T.	Labourer	Kirkcudbright	7.1.1892
7573	..	46	Graham, J.	Coachbuilder	..	19.11.1895
7170	..	47	Grant, A.	Tailor	..	18.1.1893
1778	..	48	Grant, J.	Tailor	..	14.4.1887
7431	..	49	Handling, H.	Cabinetmaker	..	29.9.1894
7434	..	50	Hannah, C.	Labourer	..	26.11.1894.
7436	..	51	Hannah, G.	Labourer	..	26.11.1894
6029	..	52	Hannah, J.	Labourer	..	1.1.1892
1955	..	53	Hannah, T.	Labourer	..	19.1.1889
7050	..	54	Hannay, R.	Mineral Merchant	Tarff Station	15.4.1892
962	..	55	Hogg, J.	Wood Turner	Kirkcudbright	19.5.1882
7048	..	56	Hunter, J.	Clerk	Ringford	6.4.1892
7708	..	57	Hyslop, R	Mason	Gatehouse	7.5.1896
7096	..	58	Johnston, J.	Forester	Kirkcudbright	15.12.1892
7190	..	59	Kinna, T.	Mason	Gatehouse	15.3.1893
7605	..	60	Livingston, J.	Labourer	Kirkcudbright	24.1.1896
7381	..	61	Lees, J	Tailor	Gatehouse	28.3.1894
7542	..	62	McGregor, A	Flesher	Kirkcudbright	2.3.1877 & 6.6.1895
7572	..	63	McBurnie, G	Coachbuilder	..	19.11.1895
144	..	64	McClune, R	Slater	..	12.5.1874
7454	..	65	McClune, R	Plumber	..	17.12.1894
7563	..	66	McCormick, J	Clogger	..	23.8.1895
7049	..	67	McCormick, W	Labourer	Ringford	15.4.1892
7433	..	68	McGowan, C	Labourer	Kirkcudbright	26.11.1894
4047	..	69	McGowan, J	Labourer	..	29.11.1890
6091	..	70	McGowan, J	Labourer	Kirkcudbright	26.2.1892
7576	..	71	McKeand, J	Labourer	..	19.12.1895
7169	..	72	McKie, R	Labourer	..	18.1.1893
7709	..	73	McKie, W	Joiner	Gatehouse	11.5.1896
7331	..	74	McMillan, J	Labourer	Kirkcudbright	26.12.1893
7643	..	75	McMillan, J	Labourer	..	31.1.1896
7094	..	76	McMonies, D. G	Coachbuilder	..	2.11.1892
7079	..	77	McMonies, G	Clogger	..	13.9.1892
6027	..	78	McMonies, R	Baker	..	1.1.1892
1953	..	79	McNeillie, S	Labourer	..	18.1.1889
7706	..	80	McQuarrie, A	Gardener	Gatehouse	7.5.1896
1049	..	81	Miller, W.A	Saddler	Kirkcudbright	1.12.1882
7562	..	82	Milligan, A	Mason	..	13.7.1895
7560	..	83	Milligan, A	Joiner	..	13.7.1895
7173	..	84	Milligan, J	Tailor	..	22.2.1893
7410	..	85	Milligan, R	Labourer	..	14.8.1894
6089	..	86	Murphy, George	Tailor	..	18.1.1892
7265	..	87	Murphy, J	Letter Carrier	..	27.9.1893
7188	..	88	Neil, J	Labourer	Gatehouse	15.3.1893
7435	..	89	Neil, J	Labourer	Kirkcudbright	26.11.1894
7187	..	90	Nelson, J	Labourer	Gatehouse	15.3.1893
7737	..	91	Nicolson, G. H	Farmer	Kirkcudbright	14.9.1896
23	Paymaster-Sgt	92	Osbourne, J	Joiner	..	6.5.1864
7561	Private	93	Paterson, J	Hewer	..	13.7.1895
7378	..	94	Paterson, R	Grocer	..	15.2.1894
4037	..	95	Paterson, W.M	Hosier	Kirkcudbright	2.7.1890
7053	..	96	Pitt, S	Labourer	Ringford	16.4.1892
7701	..	97	Rae, J	Jeweller	Kirkcudbright	30.4.1896
7707	..	98	Ramsay, J.G	Draper	Gatehouse	7.5.1896
1952	..	99	Ross, A	Hewer	Kirkcudbright	18.1.1889
7330	..	100	Sharp, W	Tailor	..	26.12.1893
7077	..	101	Sheilds, J	Labourer	..	27.6.1892
1365	..	102	Smith, J	Labourer	..	11.7.1884
7440	..	103	Swan, J	Hewer	..	11.12.1894

Reg No.	Rank	No.	Name	Occupation	Address	Date of enrolment
7387	Private	104	Thomson, G	Shoemaker	Kirkcudbright	5.4.1894
4048	..	105	Thomson, J	Labourer	..	22.11.1890
7168	..	106	Tosney, J	Labourer	..	31.12.1892
7326	..	107	Tosney, S	Mason	..	14.12.1893
3077	..	108	Tweedie, W	Tailor	..	9.4.1890
864	..	109	Wilkinson, J	Labourer	..	11.7.1881

Recruits joined after the end of the financial year. 31st October, 1896

7738	Private	110	Sharp, R	Cabinetmaker	Kirkcudbright	2.11.1896
7739	..	111	Stevenson, S	Messenger	..	27.11.1896
7740	..	112	McLellan, L.P	not known	..	27.11.1896
7741	..	113	Farrell, JA	Messenger	..	27.11.1896
7742	..	114	Kirkpatrick, A	Labourer	..	27.11.1896
7743	..	115	Milroy, J	Sawyer	..	30.11.1896
7744	..	116	Broadfoot, T	Joiner	..	30.11.1896
7745	..	117	Proctor, A	Tailor	..	10.12.1896

CASTLE DOUGLAS -

Incorporating both the 2nd Kirkcudbright Rifle Volunteers, and 'B' Company of the Galloway Rifle Volunteers.

SECTION 1 - OFFICERS

1. Bell; John. Lieutenant 1860 - unknown Dunjop
2. Biggar; James Maxwell Rawlines. 2nd Lieutenant 1899-1903 promoted Captain and transferred to 'H' Company, Dalbeattie. The Grange, Kirkpatrick- Durham.
3. Brand; Lieutenant. 1897-unknown.
4. Crosbie; R. Ensign. 20.4.1868-9.2.1872.
5. Douglas; John Hannay. Surgeon Lieutenant 1899.
6. Dunn; J. Lieutenant. 17/11/1883. Captain 1891. Major 1900.
7. Gifford; P. Lieutenant 1899. Resigned his commission in December, 1907.
8. Gillespie; Rev. R.A. Chaplain 7.5.1867-22.2.1871.
9. Gordon; E. Ensign 12.3.1872. Captain 1876. Resigned his commission on 10.6.1879.
10. Harper; Malcolm McL. Lieutenant 7.6.1876. Retired Major 26.5.1899.
    Promoted from the ranks. Manager of the British Linen Bank, Castle Douglas. Author of 'Harper's Rambles in Galloway'.

11. Hewat; Joseph Train. Lieutenant 28.12.1883. Resigned his commission on 22.3.1895. Re-appointed 10.3.1899. Promoted Captain 1900. Major 1902. Quartermaster of Battalion 1905.
12. Lorraine; R.T. Surgeon Lieutenant 11.10.1890. Surgeon Captain 1896.
13. Lorraine; W. Surgeon Lieutenant 7.5.1867. Retired Surgeon Lieutenant-Colonel on 23.12.1898.
14. MacKie; James. Captain 1860. Died 1867. Member of Parliament. Bargaly.
15. Maxwell; Ensign 1872-unknown.
16. Moffat; J. Lieutenant 20.10.1877. Resigned his commission in 1879.
17. McGuffog; Robert. Lieutenant 20.4.1868.-17.4.1877. Joined as a Sergeant in 1860 and commissioned in 1868.
18. McKie; Peter L. 2nd Lieutenant 24.1.1879-16.2.1881.
19. Renny; W.J. Ensign 1860. Died on 29.1.1879 holding the rank of Major.
20. Skirving; Adam. Appointed Captain on 20.4.1868. Resigned his commission on 31.12.1874. Joined as a Sergeant in 1860. Commissioned in 1868.
21. Slesser; Rev. D.M. Chaplain 1899.
22. Walker; Rev. G. Chaplain 1877.
23. Wilkinson; Henry Bevis. Lieutenant, transferred to 'B' Company, Castle Douglas, from 'A' Company, Kirkcudbright in 1906.

*****

In December, 1867, Captain MacKie died. Adam Skirving was promoted from the ranks to Captain and placed in command of the Company, together with Robert McGuffog, also promoted from the ranks to Lieutenant and Ensign Crosbie, newly appointed. In 1875 Captain Skirving resigned his commission, when E. Gordon was appointed Captain, with Malcolm McL. Harper being promoted, soon after, from the ranks to Lieutenant. Captain Gordon resigned his commission in 1879, leaving Lieutenants Moffat and McKie in charge of the Company. Lieutenant Moffat resigned shortly after Captain Gordon, in 1879, not 1883 as reported in the Regimental Gazette, leaving the newly appointed and inexperienced, Lieutenant McKie in charge. In consequence Malcolm McL. Harper, now Captain and Regimental Quartermaster, attached to

Headquarters, was appointed Commanding Officer of the Castle Douglas Company, 'pre temp', a position he was to hold for almost the next five years, there being no Company Officers. Lieutenant McKie resigned his commission on 16th February, 1881. Lieutenants Dunn and Hewat were appointed in the November and December, of 1883. Had it not been for the endeavours of Captain Harper, this fine Company may have ceased to exist in 1881, through the lack of suitable Officers.

SECTION 2- RANK & FILE

1. Affleck; Private William. 1860
2. Aitken; Private Thomas 1860 Corporal 1861
3. Anderson; Private T. 1905
4. Anderson; Private G. 1864
5. Badenoch; Private A 1880
6. Badenoch; Private W. 1905
7. Baird; Private J. 1905 (1)
8. Baird; Corporal J.L. 1905 (2)
9. Barclay; Private 1869
10. Baxter; Private J. 1905
11. Bell; Private William 1860
12. Blackley; Sergeant J.T. 1860 Colour Sergeant 1872
13. Blackwood; Private 1878
14. Borland; Private W.D. 1860 Corporal 1861
15. Boyle; Private A 1905
16. Broadfoot; Private William 1860
17. Brodie; Private S.H. 1905
18. Burns; Private J. 1905
19. Campbell; Private Thomas W. 1860 (1)
20. Campbell; Private T. 1876 (2)
21. Clark; Private J. 1905
22. Comline; Private James 1860
23. Crosbie; Private Thomas 1860
24. Donnelly; Private 1880
25. Dougan; Private Alexander 1901 Corporal 1905
26. Ewan; Private James S. 1899
27. Ewing; Private A. 1901 Corsock Section
28. Ferguson; Private John 1893
29. Forsyth; Private 1872
30. Garmory; Private R. 1901
31. Glover; Private W.H. 1905 Kirkpatrick Durham Section
32. Gordon; Private J. 1901 (1)
33. Gordon; Private James 1860 (2)
34. Gray; Private William 1860
35. Grierson; Private James 1865
36. Grierson; Private John 1869
37. Grierson; Private Joseph 1860
38. Grierson; Private Robert 1863
39. Haggart; Private J. 1901 Corsock Section.
40. Halliday; Private John 1905 (1)
41. Halliday; Private J.W. 1905 (2)
42. Harper; Sergeant Malcolm McL 1876 Commissioned and retired Major 1899
43. Harris; Private A. 1901 Corsock Section
44. Hastie; Private R. 1905
45. Haugh; Private H. 1905
46. Haugh; Private James 1901
47. Henderson; Private George 1860
48. Henderson; Private James 1876 (1)
49. Henderson; Private James 1861 Corporal 1869 Sergeant 1872 (2)
50. Herries; Private A.Y. 1861
51. Hewitson; Private John 1860
52. Hogg; Private G. 1905
53. Hogg; Private R. 1905
54. Hogg; Private Thomas 1864
55. Hutton; Private Peter 1860
56. Hyslop; Private J 1905
57. Inglis; Private W. 1861

59. Jamieson; Private G. 1903
60. Jardine; Private David 1860
61. Johnstone; Private J. 1901 (1)
62. Johnstone; Private James 1860 (2)
63. Johnstone; Private J.M. 1905 (3)
64. Johnston; Private R. 1905
65. Johnston; Private S. 1907
66. Kay; Private D. 1905
67. Kennan; Private George 1860
68. Kennan; Private James 1860
69. Kirk; Private Alex. 1860 Corporal 1864
70. Kirk; Private T. 1880 Corporal 1893 (1)
71. Kirk; Private T. 1905 (2)
72. Landsborough; private W. 1901
73. Livingston; Private A. 1905
74. Marrine; Private J. 1901 Corsock Section
75. Mathieson; Corporal 1901
76. Mitchel; Private James 1861
77. Morgan; Private W.J. 1905
78. Muir; Private J. 1861
79. Murdoch; Private James 1860
80. Murdoch; Private John 1860
81. Myers; Private J. 1905
82. Myers; Private Thomas 1877 Quartermaster Sergeant 1891
83. McAdam; Corporal James 1876
84. McAdam; Private J. 1893
85. McAdam; Private N. 1905
86. McAdam; Corporal R. 1876 Sergeant 1880
87. McAdam; Private R. 1905
88. McClure; Private John 1860
89. McCormick; Private J 1901 Corsock Section
90. McCreath; Private 1880
91. McDonald; Private A. 1905
92. McDowall; Private W.R. 1864
93. McFegan; Private D. 1905
94. McGaw; Private R. 1905
95. McGeorge; Private David 1860
96. McGregor; Private Malcolm; 1860
97. McGuffog; Private Robert 1860 Commissioned Lieutenant 1868
98. McIlroy; Private R. 1907
99. McIlroy; Sergeant T. 1905
100. McKay; Private G. 1905
101. McKeand; Corporal J. 1901
102. McKenzie; Private William 1860
103. McKie; Private H. 1905
104. McKie; Private R. 1905
105. McKinna; Private D. 1880
106. McLearie; Private James 1860
107. McLelland; Private J. 1903
108. Mcleod; Private Archibald 1900
109. McMaster; Corporal J.R. 1860
110. McMichan; Corporal J.B. 1860
111. McNairn; Private John 1860
112. McNally; Private 1906
113. McNaught; Private John 1905
114. McPhee; Corporal James 1901 Corsock Section
115. McVane; Corporal Robert 1860 Sergeant 1863
116. Nairne; Sergeant Andrew 1860
117. O'Neil; Private Bernard 1860
118. O'Haire; Private W. 1905
119. Papple; Private Gordon 1863
120. Paterson; Private 1877.
121. Pauling; Private Samuel 1860
122. Pearson; Private D. 1863
123. Pearson; Private James 1860

126. Purdie; Private R. 1905
127. Rae; Private A. 1905
128. Rae; Private Benjamin 1860
129. Rae; Private S. 1899
130. Reid; Private 1872
131. Riddick; Private T. 1876
132. Robb; Private J. 1905
133. Roberts; Sergeant William 1860
134. Robertson; Private George 1860 Sergeant 1861
135. Robertson; Private S.E. 1905
136. Robinson; Sergeant 1864
137. Roxburgh; Private C.A. 1905
138. Roxburgh; Private J. 1905
139. Roxburgh; Private P. 1905
140. Roxburgh; Private R. 1901
141. Scott; Private G. 1905
142. Scott; Private W. 1905
143. Seaton; Private J. 1905
144. Shaw; Private John 1860
145. Skirving; Sergeant Adam 1860 Commissioned Captain 1868. Croys
146. Sloan; Corporal W. 1901
147. Smith; Private R. 1892
148. Sowerby; Private J. 1877.
149. Tait; Private J. 1905
150. Thomson; Private G. 1905
151. Thomson; Sergeant J. 1863
152. Thomson; Sergeant R.C. 1861 Manager of National Bank, Castle Douglas.
153. Trollan; Private R. 1905
154. Turner; Private John 1899
155. Turner; Private R. 1863

SECTION 3 -MEMBERSHIP OF 1896.

Reg No.	Rank	No.	Name	Occupation	Address	Date of enrolment
	Sgt. Maj.	1	Ferguson, C	Sgt. Maj.	Castle Douglas	15.9.1886
83	Qtr. Mstr Sgt	2	Myers, T	Joiner	..	31.1.1870
60	..	3	Hyslop, J	Bootmaker	..	9.2.1869
17	Colr-Serg.	4	Dick, J.	Smith	..	9.3.1864
96	Musketry-Sgt	5	Murdoch, H.	Farmer	..	7.5.1867
39	Sergeant	6	McKinnie, P	Printer	..	19.1.1870
66	..	7	McMurray,J	Painter	..	17.1.1872
421	..	8	Scott, J.	Tailor	..	25.2.1879
508	L/Sergeant	9	Gordon, S.R.	Stationer	..	6.12.1872
706	..	10	Wright, W.	Bootmaker	..	16.2.1881
1674	..	11	Wilson, R.W.	Saddler	..	10.1.1887
865	Corporal	12	Ewing, J.	Mineral Agent	..	10.7.1881
82	..	13	McCaw, William	Joiner	..	24.1.1871
110	..	14	McGaw, John	Clothier	..	14.1.1873
4057	..	15	Maxwell, G	Tailor	..	3.6.1869
1083	..	16	McNaught, J	Clerk	..	21.11.1884
1680	L/Corporal	17	Haugh, W	Clerk	..	1.2.1887
897	..	18	Hetherington, W	Tailor	..	1.3.1882
1435	..	19	Dougan, A	Tailor	..	14.1.1885
6056	..	20	Howard, R	Joiner	..	5.2.1884
2058	..	21	McGuffog, J	Coachbuilder	..	21.1.1890
1079	..	22	Murray, J.C.	Printer	..	29.1.1883
701	..	23	Scott, J	Tinsmith	..	14.2.1881
1876	..	24	Todd, R	Grocer	..	1.2.1888
7249	Bandmaster	25	Keane, R	Tailor	..	17.10.1868
7694	L/Sergeant	26	Clingan, J.G	Auctioneer	..	24.1.1887
7269	Private	27	Aitken, W	Plumber	..	1.12.1893
7182	..	28	Brown, J	Coachbuilder	..	3.3.1893
7363	..	29	Brown, T	..	..	12.3.1894
7267	..	30	Carson, J	Joiner	..	1.12.1893
6051	..	31	Colvin, Morris	Cabinetmaker	..	27.1.1892

Reg No.	Rank	No.	Name	Occupation	Address	Date of enrolment
7131	Private	32	Connolly, F	Clerk	Castle Douglas	1.2.1893
6039	..	33	Craig, D	Cabinetmaker	..	30.1.1892
7460	..	34	Conchar, R	Joiner	..	2.1.1895
1395	..	35	Crosbie, J	Clogger	..	20.12.1884
7465	..	36	Crosbie, T	Polisher	..	4.1.1895
4074	..	37	Cumming, J	Gamekeeper	Rhonehouse	6.2.1893
7452	..	38	Derby, T.B.	Engineer	Castle Douglas	26.12.1894
6017	..	39	Docherty, R	Saddler	..	21.12.1891
4064	..	40	Dougan, Archd	Tailor	..	16.1.1891
5036	..	41	Dunkeld, J	Tailor	..	4.3.1891
1393	..	42	Ferguson, Alex.	Joiner	..	6.12.1884
6055	..	43	Forsyth, E	Printer	..	2.2.1892
7179	..	44	Gaw, R	Plumber	..	6.2.1893
7457	..	45	Grierson, A.R.	Engineer	..	26.12.1894
7123	..	46	Halliday, D	Tailor	..	15.1.1893
1445	..	47	Haugh, W	Coachpainter	..	4.2.1885
4096	..	48	Hogg, W	Gardener	..	1.2.1891
6067	..	49	Howard, J	Joiner	..	2.2.1892
4077	..	50	Ireland, J	Joiner	..	26.2.1879
2063	..	51	Johnston, W	Molecatcher	..	1.2.1890
1659	..	52	Keand, J	Smith	..	17.12.1886
4071	..	53	Keane, G	Printer	..	26.1.1891
1923	..	54	Landsborough, P	Agent	..	14.12.1888
6066	..	55	Lundie, S	Smith	..	9.2.1892
6016	..	56	McCubbing, W	Joiner	..	21.12.1891
6099	..	57	McCulloch,	Baker	..	21.12.1891
6022	..	58	McCutcheon, P	Watchmaker	..	8.12.1891
7333	..	59	McGill, D	Clogger	..	1.2.1894
7468	..	60	McKnight, W	Grocer	..	4.1.1895
7533	..	61	McNaught, T	Joiner	..	13.5.1895
7595	..	62	McMillan, J	Tailor	..	29.1.1896
7600	..	63	McHattie, J	Baker	..	29.1.1896
7268	..	64	McQueen, R.S.	Decorator	..	1.12.1893
4066	..	65	McVane, R	Joiner	..	7.1.1891
7100	..	66	Maxwell, A	Moulder	..	9.1.1893
2064	..	67	Penman, W.H	Cycle-Agent	Dumfries	1.2.1890
7450	..	68	Purdie, W	Tailor	Castle Douglas	4.1.1895
7466	..	69	Rae, Benjamin	Fitter	..	4.1.1895
6062	..	70	Rae, J.G	Tailor	..	9.2.1892
6050	..	71	Robertson, W.D	Joiner	Rhonehouse	27.1.1892
6065	..	72	Scott, James	Fitter	Castle Douglas	9.2.1892
7122	..	73	Scott, J	Brewer	..	15.1.1893
6054	..	74	Smith, T	Bank Clerk	..	2.2.1892
6019	..	75	Sowerby, Leo R	Clerk	..	27.12.1891
7367	..	76	Sowerby, Nelson	Clerk	..	12.3.1894
6069	..	77	Torry, Ernest	Watchmaker	..	9.2.1892
7332	..	78	Torry, J.F	Moulder	..	1.2.1894
7541	..	79	Walker, G.W	Sanitary Insp.	Crossmichael	14.6.1891
7469	..	80	West, Alex	Coachsmith	Castle Douglas	4.1.1895
7121	..	81	Wintrup, James	Plumber	..	9.1.1893
7599	..	82	Kirk, James	Saddler	..	29.12.1890
7577	Recruits	83	Walker, S	Engineer	..	29.1.1896
7578	..	84	Wood, J	Joiner	..	29.1.1896
7579	..	85	Stewart, W	Moulder	..	29.1.1896
7580	..	86	Currie, J	Millwright	..	29.1.1896
7587	..	87	Kirkpatrick, R	Mason	..	29.1.1896
7588	..	88	Logan, R	Clogger	..	29.1.1896
7589	..	89	Duff, W	Coachbuilder	..	29.1.1896
7590	..	90	Colvin, W	Upholsterer	..	29.1.1896
7591	..	91	Stewart, J	Builder	..	29.1.1896
7592	..	92	Brown, R	Plasterer	..	29.1.1896
7593	..	93	Howard, R.W	Chemist	Castle Douglas	29.1.1896
7594	..	94	McKie, J	Painter	..	29.1.1896
7596	..	95	Priestly, T	Compositor	..	29.1.1896
7597	..	96	Craig, J	Cabinetmaker	..	29.1.1896
7598	..	97	Thompson, R	Printer	..	29.1.1896

Reg No.	Rank	No.	Name	Occupation	Address	Date of enrolment
7601	Recruits	98	Wilson, J	Printer	Castle Douglas	29.1.1896
7602	..	99	Gaw, W	Saddler	..	29.1.1896
7603	..	100	Harrison, Stephen	Joiner	..	29.1.1896
7661	..	101	Forsyth, J	Ironmonger	..	1.2.1896
7660	..	102	Cumming, J	Clerk	..	1.2.1896
7736	..	103	Ferguson, W	Not Specified	..	27.5.1896

NEW GALLOWAY -

Incorporating both the 3rd Kirkcudbright Rifle Volunteers, and 'E' Company of the Galloway Rifle Volunteers.

SECTION 1 - OFFICERS

Carruthers; James. Lieutenant 1860-unknown. Craig.

Cavan; Surgeon Lieutenant. 1896

Clark -Kennedy; A.K. 2nd Lieutenant 1907-31.3.1908

Cowan; Surgeon Lieutenant J. 2.5.1889. Surgeon Captain 1898

Craig; W.Lieutenant 6.3.1872. Retired Captain on 20.2.1889

Cuthill; Rev. 1892 Chaplain.

Dalziel; Peter. Ensign 28.3.1860. Retired Lieutenant on 29.7.1882

Forde; E.S. Lieutenant 1901. Captain 1903. A Doctor.

Jamieson; R. Lieutenant 26.7.1884. Retired Captain on 28.11.1891

Kennedy; J.M. Lieutenant 10.11.1866. Retired Lieutenant-Colonel of the Regiment 31.8.1906

Maitland; J.G. Captain 9.11.1866. Retired Lieutenant-Colonel of the Regiment on 30.7.1887

Maxwell; Wellwood. Captain 28.3.1860 - unknown Glenlee.

Millman; Alfed McKinlay R. Joined as a Surgeon Lieutenant on 8.12.1860, but later appointed Company
        Commanding Officer. Died on 19.7.1881, holding the rank of Captain of the Corps.

Murray; Rev. George Chaplain. 8.12.1860- died 22.4.1881. Balmaclellan.

Stewart; James. 2nd Lieutenant 24.8.89. Lieutenant 1892. Joined as a Private in the Corps on 22.3.1871 and was
        Commissioned in 1889

Timms; Harry A. Captain. 22.10.92 - unknown. Slogarie.

Walker; Rev. T. Chaplain. 2.6.1894.

SECTION 2 - RANK & FILE.

1. Adamson; Corporal W. 1905
2. Aitken; Private F. 1898 Recruit.
3. Anderson; Private A. 1863
4. Anderson; Private Gilbert. 1865 Sergeant 1882 (1)
5. Anderson; Private G. 1893 (2)
6. Barbour; Private J. 1877
7. Barton; Private 1876
8. Beattie; Private R. 1861
9. Belford; Private J. 1877
10. Brown; Sergeant A. 1861
11. Brown; Private D. 1887
12. Brown; Private T. 1861
13. Bruce; Private T.R. 1862 Slogarie
14. Byers - Byres; Private W. 1887
15. Caldow; Private G. 1898 Recruit Laurieston
16. Campbell; Private J. 1898 Recruit
17. Carsewell; Private 1863
18. Chisholm; Private J. 1864
19. Cochrane; Private Robert 1898 Recruit
20. Coltart; Private J. 1887
21. Coltart; Private R. 1887
22. Corrie; Private Adam 1867
23. Corrie; Corporal T. 1905
24. Coskrie; Private J. 1864
25. Craig; Private William 1861
26. Dalziel; Corporal J. 1876
27. Douglas; Private James 1861
28. Ferguson; Private S. 1898 Recruit
29. Gardiner; Private John 1865

30. Geddes; Private A. 1861
31. Geddes; Private J. 1905 Recruit
32. Gibson; Private D. 1905
33. Grierson; Sergeant 1861 Senior
34. Grierson; Private Joseph 1861 Junior
35. Hamilton; Private G. 1905
36. Hamilton; Private W. 1865
37. Harley; Private 1887
38. Henderson; Sergeant 1863 (1)
39. Henderson; Private J. 1863 (2)
40. Hewitson; Private J. 1862
41. Hogg; Private William 1876 Sergeant 1882
42. Hyslop; Private J. 1898 Recruit
43. Johnston; Private Robert 1863 Colour Sergeant 1882
44. Keiman; Private William 1861
45. Kelly; Private 1907 Recruit
46. Kenna; Private W. 1861
47. Kerr; Private Archibald 1863
48. Kirk; Private T 1905 Dalry Section
49. Kirk; Private William 1900 Dalry Section
50. Knocker; Private R 1898 Recruit
51. Lawson; Sergeant J. 1898
52. Lee; Private A. 1905
53. Martin; Private T.C. 1905
54. Milligan; Private A. 1898
55. Milligan; Private J. 1861 Colour Sergeant 1877
56. Milligan; Corporal R. 1876
57. Milroy; Private 1863
58. Moffat; Private George 1861
59. Mosscroft; Private J. 1865
60. Muir; Private James 1863
61. Muir; Private John 1861 Colour Sergeant 1869
62. Muir; Private R.S. 1867
63. Murphy; Private 1892 Recruit
64. Murray; Private William 1898
65. McCulloch; Private J. 1897
66. McGill; Private J. 1876
67. McGill; Private R. 1876
68. McGinnes; Private 1887
69. McKay; Private Robert 1864
70. McKeand; Private A. 1901
71. McKelvie; Private 1863
72. McKenzie; Private D. 1887
73. McKie; Private John 1865 (1)
74. McKie; Private John 1893 Corporal 1905 (2)
75. McKie; Private J. 1898 Recruit (3)
76. McMath; Private J 1863
77. McMillan; Private W. 1905
78. McQueen; Private F.G. 1905
79. McTurk; Private W.A. 1905
80. Nelson; Sergeant J.W. 1905
81. Robertson; Private W. 1905 Recruit
82. Shaw; Private P. 1888 Sergeant 1889
83. Shaw; Private Robert 1862
84. Spark; Private W. 1898
85. Stevenson; Private Alexander 1863
86. Stewart; Sergeant 1876
87. Stewart; Private F. 1905 Recruit
88. Stewart; Private W.T. 1905
89. Taylor; Private C. 1902
90. Taylor; Private Oliver 1900
91. Turner; Private James; 1863
92. Turner; Private William 1900
93. Watret; Private John 1865 Sergeant 1869
94. Wilson; Private J. 1863 Sergeant 1864
95. Wood; Private J 1905

SECTION 3 - MEMBERSHIP OF 1896

Reg No.	Rank	No.	Name	Occupation	Address	Date of enrolment
	Captain	1	Timms, H.A	Gentleman	Slogarie	22.10.1892
	Lieutenant	2	Stewart, J	Merchant	Dalry	22.1.1871
	Surg. Lieut.	3	Cowan, J	Medical Prac.	New Galloway	2.5.1889
	Chaplain	4	Walker, T	Minister	Dalry	2.6.1894
	Sergt.-Inst.	5	Farrell, C	Sergt.-Instr.	New Galloway	7.5.1892
61	Col. Serg.	6	Coltart, W	Tea Merchant	..	27.3.1869
1015	Sergeant	7	Bell, J	School Master	Parton	18.4.1882
297	..	8	Ferguson, R	Shepherd	Banks of Dee	29.1.1878
517	Sergeant	9	Geddes, G	Mineral Agent	New Galloway	21.1.1860
133	..	10	McCulloch, W	Labourer	Dalry	7.1.1874
1721	..	11	Turner, W	Blacksmith	New Galloway	4.1.1887
1717	Lance/Sergt.	12	Coltart, W	Labourer	..	4.1.1887
523	..	13	Dargavel, G	Labourer	..	24.1.1880
1599	..	14	McCubbing, A	Mason	..	4.1.1886
7081	Corporal	15	Finnie, A	Saddler	..	14.2.1871
1978	..	16	Wallace, J		Balmaclellan	12.2.1889
2044	..	17	Milligan, W	Postboy	Dalry	8.11.1889
1289	Bugler	18	Bell, J	Gamekeeper	Mossdale	16.1.1884
728	..	19	Corson, E	Joiner	Dalry	1.1.1865
7257	..	20	Finnie, A	Saddler	New Galloway	4.9.1893
7538	Private	21	Challis, H	Dyker	..	1.6.1895
1291	..	22	Challis, W	Labourer	..	19.5.1880
4063	..	23	Coltart, S (1)	Mason	..	16.11.1890
7659	..	24	Coltart, S (2)	Mason	..	12.2.1889
7000	..	25	Corson, G	Labourer	Dalry	1.8.1865
7296	..	26	Cumming, A	Blacksmith	Laurieston	14.11.1893
2041	..	27	Dalziel, J	Shoemaker	Dalry	8.11.1889
1723	..	28	Dalziel, R	Shoemaker	Dalry	12.1.1887
2095	..	29	Dinning, J	Farmer	New Galloway	15.1.1887
1941	..	30	Docherty, G	Joiner	..	12.1.1889
7127	..	31	Donaldson, B	Labourer	Dalry	14.1.1893
1813	..	32	Ferguson, J	Shepherd	Duchra	10.1.1888
7297	..	33	Ferguson, P	Farm Labourer	Laurieston	14.11.1893
5089	Private	34	Geddes, A	Mineral Agent	New Galloway	27.5.1872
5090	..	35	Geddes, G	Mineral Agent	Crossmichael	1.5.1891
5092	..	36	Geddes, J	Tailor	Parton	1.5.1891
7298	..	37	Haugh, J	Farm Labourer	Laurieston	14.11.1893
7459	..	38	Henderson, D.M.	Merchant	New Galloway	2.1.1895
7513	..	39	Johnston, J	Insurance Agent	Dalry	1.4.1895
5086	Lance/Corp.	40	Johnston, P	Blacksmith	Parton	1.5.1891
7300	Private	41	Kennedy, S	Ploughman	Laurieston	14.11.1893
7455	..	42	Landsburgh, S	Joiner	New Galloway	18.12.1894
7301	Lance/Corp.	43	Lawson, J	Schoolmaster	Laurieston	14.111893
5088	..	44	McAdam, J	Farm Servant	Parton	1.5.1891
7303	Private	45	McClung, J	Farmer	Airds	14.11.1893
7325	..	46	McCrone, R	Farmer	New Galloway	17.1.1894
2049	..	47	McCulloch, J	Carter	Dalry	13.11.1889
2094	..	48	McCulloch, J	Gardener	Dalry	2.1.1890
7458	..	49	McKay, J	Tailor	New Galloway	22.12.1894
7304	..	50	McKie, W	Labourer	Laurieston	26.3.1879
7514	..	51	McLauchlan,G	Labourer	Dalry	1.4.1895
7409	..	52	McNaught, D	Groom	New Galloway	26.7.1894
1980	..	53	McQueen, R	Farm Servant	..	12.2.1889
6083	..	54	McQueen, T	Butcher	..	2.2.1892
7305	..	55	Mitchell, H	Tailor	Laurieston	14.11.1893
7000	..	56	Murdoch, Andrew	Boots	New Galloway	27.2.1892
6082	..	57	Murdoch, J	Mason	New Galloway	2.2.1892
7722	..	58	Murray, H	Labourer	..	5.1.1884
7124	..	59	Peacock, J	Wood forester	Dalry	7.2.1873
5074	..	60	Pere, M.S	Quarryman	New Galloway	17.1.1879
7457	..	61	Reid, J	Merchant	New Galloway	21.12.1894
5075	..	62	Shereman, R	Labourer	..	20.1.1876
1591	..	63	Smith, W	Shepherd	Parton	20.1.1886
7395	..	64	Tait, T	Gamekeeper	New Galloway	11.5.1894

Reg No.	Rank	No.	Name	Occupation	Address	Date of enrolment
7306	Private	65	Tole-Toul-Tool H.	Ploughman	Balmaghie	14.11.1893
7456	..	66	Turner, J	Blacksmith	New Galloway	18.12.1894
7307	..	67	Walker, J	Farmer	Laurieston	14.11.1893
2047	..	68	Wilson, A	Tailor	Dalry	8.11.1889
2048	..	69	Wilson, W	Labourer	..	8.11.1889
7657	..	70	Walker, W	Labourer	..	8.11.1889
7656	Recruits	71	McKie, S	Mason	New Galloway	14.2.1896
7658	..	72	Donaldson, M	Shoemaker	Dalry	15.2.1896
7678	..	73	Caldow, William	Wood Forester	Laurieston	5.3.1896
7679	..	74	Smart, W	Labourer	..	5.3.1896
7680	..	75	Vinnie, W	Labourer	..	5.3.1896
7681	..	76	Thompson, A	Gamekeeper	..	12.3.1896

GATEHOUSE -

Incorporating the 4th Kirkcudbright Rifle Volunteers, 1860-1866, and members of 'A' Company, Gatehouse Section.

SECTION 1 - OFFICERS.

1. Ewart; David James. Ensign 1860 unknown.
2. Glover; R.S. Lieutenant. Transferred from 'A' Company, Kirkcudbright, in 1904, as Officer in Charge, Gatehouse Section. In 1905 promoted to Captain and transferred as officer in Charge of 'D' Company, Newton Stewart.
3. Rainsford-Hannay; Frederick. Lieutenant 1860-unknown.

SECTION 2 - RANK & FILE.

1. Baillie; Private J. 1883
2. Bertram; Private James. 1892
3. Biggam; Private J. 1878
4. Brackenridge; Private D. 1883
5. Brackenridge; Private R. 1878
6. Brian; Private R. 1883
7. Brian; Private T. 1883
8. Cairns; Private William. 1861 Sergeant 1865 (1)
9. Cairns; Private William. 1884 (2)
10. Campbell; Private J. 1878. Corporal 1878.
11. Carson - Corson; Private W. 1892
12. Crawford; Private W. 1892
13. Dalrymple; Private R. 1883
14. Drait; Private John. 1860
15. Ewan; Private E. 1892
16. Ewan; Private J. 1892
17. Gibb; Private J. 1861.
18. Gibson; Corporal 1864. (1)
19. Gibson; Private J. 1878. (2)
20. Glover; Private H.D. 1860.
21. Gordon; Private William. 1860
22. Hall; Private John. 1860
23. Hannay; Private. 1878
24. Haswell; Private Robert. 1862
25. Hay; Private W. 1878
26. Henry; Private J. 1883
27. Hughan; Private A. 1878
28. Hughan; Private N.M. 1899
29. Hunter; Private John. 1860.
30. Jardine; Private R. 1899
31. Kirkpatrick; Private J.R. 1879. Corporal 1892
32. Leitch; Private S. 1878
33. Maxwell; Private Robert 1862
34. Murray; Private A. 1899
35. Murray; Private W. 1899
36. Macaulay; Private 1899
37. McBride; Private Peter. 1862
38. McCourty; Private R. 1892

39. McCulloch; Private Alex. 1860
40. McDill; Private J. 1878
41. McGaw; Private W. 1899
42. McKnight; Private W. 1899
43. McLean; Private William. 1860
44. McMichael; Private J. 1878
45. McNeillie; Private C. 1878
46. Nelson; Private A. 1892
47. Patterson; Private J. 1883
48. Rae; Private J. 1861
49. Rae; Private Thomas. 1861
50. Reid; Private A.D. 1899 Corporal 1904
51. Riddick; Private J. 1878
52. Spearing; Sergeant John. 1860
53. Thomson; Private W. 1899
54. Veitch; Private D. Y. 1892
55. Veitch; Private John. 1892
56. Waugh; Sergeant Samuel. 1860
57. Welsh; Private J. 1878
58. Wood; Private John. 1860
59. Wyllie; Corporal James 1860 Sergeant 1878
60. Young; Private J. 1861

MAXWELLTON -

Incorporating the 5th Kirkcudbright Rifle Volunteers, and 'F' and 'G' Companies of the Galloway Rifle Volunteers.

SECTION 1 - OFFICERS

1. Allan; Francis S. Ensign 1860 Lieutenant 1860-unknown
2. Barrie; A.D. Surgeon Lieutenant 5.7.1867 - 25.5.1871. Rejoined as a Company Captain on 28.6.1871 - unknown.
3. Blacklock; 2nd Lieutenant James 9.9.1896. Captain 1900-unknown.
4. Campbell; Rev. J.A. Chaplain 1877
5. Carruthers; Sub-Lieutenant J. 28.4.1875-9.6.1877
6. Charlton; T.A. Lieutenant 1903
7. Crombie; W.F. 2nd Lieutenant 1905 'F' Company
8. Findlay; A.W. Lieutenant 1.1.1873-22.4.1874
9. Gibson-Starke. J; Ensign 1860 Retired Captain 13.10.1871
10. Glover; John McNaught 2nd Lieutenant 1907 'G' Company
11. Graham; Rev. William V. Chaplain 22.1.1879-unknown
12. Grierson; E. Lieutenant 1903 Captain 1906 - 'G' Company
13. Grierson; R.A. Lieutenant 1898 Captain 1903 'G' Company
14. Harkness; T.G. Ensign 5.8.1870-3.7.1872
15. Heathcote-Smith; Ensign 19.3.1873 Retired Captain 19.3.1878
16. Howat; R.K. Captain 11.2.1863-12.4.1873 of Mabie (senior)
17. Howat; Lieutenant 1864-unknown (junior)
18. Hunter; Surgeon Lieutenant 1907
19. Lennox; John Lieutenant 23.6.1877 'F' Company Lieutenant-Colonel Commanding the Galloway Rifle Volunteers 7.9.1906
20. Lorraine; Rich B. Surgeon 10.1.1885 Surgeon Captain 1891
21. Maxwell; R. Lieutenant 27.9.1866-25.5.1871
22. Murray; P Surgeon 23.6.1871-unknown
23. McFarlane; Rev. W 5.7.1867 Died during his attachment to the Rifles but date unknown
24. McGowan; Lieutenant 11.9.1873-19.5.1878
25. McKinnel; B. Lieutenant 1907 'F' Company
26. McKinnel; James Baird Affleck Captain 1860 of Macmurdiston
27. Pagan; David Lieutenant 1860
28. Phyn; C.S. Lieutenant 2.2.1882 Captain 1883 Major 1893
29. Rae; J. Lieutenant 5.7.1867-5.8.1870
30. Rennie; James Lieutenant 27.9.1866 Captain 1872 Retired Major 31.12.1874
31. Scott-Elliot; 2nd Lieutenant 1905 'F' Company
32. Shortridge; T.H. Lieutenant 1897 Captain 1903 Retired 1905
33. Slesser; Chaplain 1907
34. Symons; M.J. Lieutenant 5.4.1878 Retired Captain on 14.4.1883

SECTION 2 RANK & FILE

1. Affleck; Private J. 1905 'G' Company
2. Aitken; Private T. 1891 'F'Company
3. Aitken; Private W. 1905 'G' Company
4. Anderson; Private A. 1905 'F' Company
5. Anderson; Private 1864 Corporal 1867
6. Armstrong; Private A. 1872
7. Armstrong; Private G. 1872
8. Armstrong; Private J. 1905 'F' Company
9. Armstrong; Corporal R. 1872 Sergeant 1877 'F' Company
10. Beck; Private James 1872
11. Bendall; Private G. 1899 Sergeant 1905
12. Bedford; Private 1891
13. Bell; Private J. 1905 'F' Company
14. Bell; Private R. 1905 'G' Company (1)
15. Bell; Private R. 1905 'F' Company (2)
16. Bell; Private William 1902
17. Black; Private George 1889
18. Blackstock; Bugler 1884 Sergeant 1886
19. Blount; Private G.R. 1905 'F' Company
20. Blyth; Private Walter 1860
21. Brady; Private J. 1905 'F' Company
22. Briggs; Private John 1877 Sergeant 1886 Ambulance Sergeant 1893
23. Brown; Private 1867
24. Brown; Private H. 1901
25. Brown; Private J. 1902 'G' Company
26. Byers; Private H. 1905 'G' Company
27. Callender; Private S. 1880
28. Cameron; Sergeant 1871
29. Cameron; Private D. 1872
30. Cameron; Private J. 1881
31. Candlish; Private Peter 1880
32. Carnochan; Private W. 1905 'F' Company
33. Carson; Corporal G. 1905
34. Carter; Private Joseph 1902
35. Caskie; Private D. 1905 'F' Company
36. Chalmers; Corporal 1877 Sergeant 1880
37. Cherteris; Private 1891
38. Clenahan; Private R. 1901
39. Coltart; Sergeant 1872
40. Corrie; Private 1864
41. Coupland; Private T. 1905 'G' Company
42. Cowan; Private N. 1905 Corporal 1907 'F' Company
43. Cowan; Private W. 1905 'F' Company
44. Crackston; Sergeant A.1860
45. Crackston; Private T.E. 1860
46. Craig; Private J. 1905 'F' Comapny (1)
47. Craig; Private J. 1905 'G' Company (2)
48. Craig; Private J. 1905 'G' Company (3)
49. Cravens; Private J.W. 1905 'G' Company
50. Creighton; Private 1881
51. Crichton; Private W.D. 1905 'F' Company
52. Crossan; Private J. 1905 'F' Company
53. Cumming; Colour Sergeant 1902
54. Cuncliffe; Private A. 1905 'G' Company
55. Dalziel; Private 1889 'F' Company
56. Davidson; Corporal John 1860 (1)
57. Davidson; Private John 1860 (2)
58. Dewar; Sergeant John 1860
59. Dewar; Private J. 1905 'G' Company
60. Dickson; Private D. 1905 'F' Company
61. Dickson; Private W. 1905 'F' Company
62. Dobie; Private W. 1872
63. Docherty; Private W. 1905 'F' Company
64. Douglas; Corporal 1863
65. Douglas; Private W. McK. 1905 'G' Company

66. Duff; Lance/Corporal 1905 'G' Company
67. Easton; Private W. 1905 'F' Company
68. Erskine; Private W.D. 1905 'G' Company
69. Faithful; Private W. 1905 'F' Company
70. Feeney; Private Matthew 1867
71. Ferguson; Private C. 1905 'G' Company
72. Fettes; Private Robert 1902 Corporal 1905 'G' Company
73. Forteith; Corporal 1867 Sergeant 1873
74. Fortune; Private J. 1905 'F' Company
75. Fraser; Private W.G. 1901 'F' Company
76. French; Private W. 1905 'G' Company
77. Fryer; Private J.J. 1872
78. Galleymore; Private 1877
79. Gardiner; Private W. 1872
80. Geddes; Private Andrew. 1880
81. Geddes; Private R. 1905 'F' Company
82. Geddes; Private T. 1905 'F' Company
83. Geddes; Private W.E. 1905 'F' Company
84. Gibson; Private T. 1905 'F' Company
85. Gibson; Private W. 1905 'F' Company
86. Gillum; Sergeant 1867
87. Glover; Private James 1860 (1)
88. Glover; Private J. 1905 'F' Company (2)
89. Glover; Private Mathew 1860
90. Gordon; Private 1864
91. Gourlay; Private David 1860
92. Graham; Private J. 1905 'G' Company (1)
93. Graham; Private J.W. 1905 'F' Company (2)
94. Graham; Private W. 1905 'F' Company
95. Grant; Private D. 1905 'G' Company
96. Gray; Private P. 1905 'G' Company
97. Grierson; Private John 1860
98. Grierson; Sergeant R. 1905 'F' Company (1)
99. Grierson; Bugler R. 1905 'G' Company (2)
100. Grimm; Bandmaster John 1860
101. Grindal; Private William 1860
102. Hall; Private J. 1888 'F' Company
103. Hamilton; Private J. 1905 'F' Company
104. Handlin; Private Patrick 1860
105. Hanlon; Corporal 1880 Sergeant 1886
106. Hannah; Private John 1860
107. Hannah; Private William Currie 1900
108. Hannay; Private Albert 1905 'G' Company
109 Hannay; Private Alfred 1905 'G' Company
110. Hannay; Private John 1905 'G' Company
111. Harley; Private J. 1905 'G' Company
112. Harley; Private W. 1905 'G' Company
113. Harper; Private J. 1886 Sergeant 1905 'G' Company
114. Harrison; Private 1905 'F' Company
115. Hastings; Private Archibald 1860
116. Hastings; Private J 1905 'F' Company
117. Hastings; Private Robert 1860
118. Henderson; Private James 1899 Sergeant 1905 'G' Company (1)
119. Henderson; Private J. 1905 'G' Company (2)
120. Henderson; Corporal J. 1899 'F' Company (3)
121. Henderson; Private N. 1888
122. Henderson; Private W. 1886 Corporal 1889 'F' Company
123. Hewitson; Private Joseph 1861
124. Hill; Private John E. 1880
125. Hindmarsh; Private 1901
126. Holden; Private R. 1905 'G' Company
127. Holmes; Private 1864
128. Hope; Private James 1860
129. Houston; Private J. 1861
130. Hughes; Private J. W. 1905 'G' Company
131. Humme; Private A 1905 'G' Company
132. Inman; Private C. 1905 'G' Company

133. Irving; Private Alex C. 1860 (1)
134. Irving; Private 1887 (2)
135. Jackson; Private 1886
136. Jardine; Private W. 1872
137. Jeffs; Private William 1880
138. Johnstone; Private J. 1905 'G' Company
139. Johnstone; Private R. 1872 (1)
140. Johnstone; Private R. 1905 'F' Company (2)
141. Johnstone; Private T. 1880
142. Kennedy; Private J. 1905 'G' Company
143. Kirk; Sergeant Thomas 1860
144. Kirkpatrick; Private H. 1905 'F' Company
145. Kirkpatrick; Private J. 1905 'F' Company
146. Kirkpatrick; Private William 1900
147. Kivlichan; Private W. 1905 'G' Company
148. Lavens; Private T. 1905 'F' Company
149. Law; Private J 1905 'G' Company
150. Law; Private William 1880 Sergeant 1893 'F' Company
151. Lawson; Private 1877 Corporal 1880
152. Leyden; Private J. 1905 'G' Company
153. Leyden; Private T. 1905 'G' Company
154. Little; Private James 1872
155. Lockerby; Private W. 1872
156. Louden; Private James 1899 'G' Company
157. Louden; Private C. 1905 Recruit
158. Marshall; Private J. 1905 'G' Company (1)
159. Marshall; Private J. 1905 'F' Company (2)
160. Martin; Private R. 1905 'G' Company
161. Maxwell; Private J. 1905 'G' Company
162. Maxwell; Private R. 1905 'G' Company
163. Maxwell; Private William 1860
164. Meechan; Private A.W. 1905 'F' Company
165. Meechan; Private P. 1905 'G' Company
166. Melbourne; Private J. 1905 'F' Company
167. Millar; Private J. 1905 'F' Company (1)
168. Millar; Private J. 1905 'F' Company (2)
169. Millar; Private J. 1905 'G' Company (3)
170. Mitchell; Private 1867
171. Moffat; Private Edward 1860
172. Moffat; Private R. 1891
173. Moffat; Corporal William 1905 'G' Company
174. Moir; Private J.D. 1905 Corporal 1907 'G' Company
175. Mollins; Private J. 1881
176. Morley; Private J. 1891 'G' Company
177. Morrine; Private J. 1905 'F' Company
178. Murchie; Private J. 1905 'G' Company
179. Mundell; Private 1891
180. Murdoch; Sergeant 1860 Sergeant-Major 1886
181. Murray; Private J. 1872
182. Murray; Private T. 1891 'G' Company
183. Murray; Private W. 1872
184. McAllister; Private S. 1872
185. McAllister; Private T. 1905 'F' Company
186. McCartney; Private J. 1905 'G' Company
187. McConchie; Private James 1860
188. McConnachie; Private J. 1905 'G' Company
189. McCourty; Private A. 1905 'G' Company
190. McCourty; Private R. 1905 'F' Company
191. McGeorge; Private 1864 Sergeant 1867
192. McGeorge; Private Thomas 1902
193. McGowan; Private J. 1905 'G' Company (1)
194. McGowan; Private J.C. 1905 'F' Company (2)
195. McGowan; Private T. 1905 'F' Company
196. McHolm; Private A. 1905 'F' Company
197. McKay; Private A. 1905 'G' Company
198. McKay; Private Robert 1860
199. McKean; Private H. 1905 'F' Company

200. McKean; Private J. 1905 'F' Company
201. McKenzie; Private J. A. 1905 'G' Company
202. McKie; Private F. 1901
203. McKie; Private James D. 1902
204. McKinnell; Private J. 1905 'F' Company
205. McKnight; Private Robert 1860
206. McLauchlan; Private Robert 1867
207. McLellan; Private S. 1867
208. McLellan; Private A. 1872
209. McMechan; Private J. 1881 Corporal 1886
210. McMickan; Private J. 1877
211. McMillan; Private Anthony 1860 Corporal 1863 (1)
212. McMillan; Private A. 1905 'F' Company (2)
213. McMillan; Private John 1880
214. McMillan; Private S. 1902 'G' Company
215. McMurdo; Private F. 1905 'G' Company
216. McWilliam; Private A. 1905 'F' Company
217. Newall; Private J.1900 'F' Company
218. Newlands; Sergeant T. 1872
219. Nicholson; Private T. 1905 'F' Company
220. Nicholson; Private W. 1905 'G' Company
221. Nicoll; Private David McLean. 1900
222. Niven; Private F. 1905 'F' Company
223. Owens; Private James 1860
224. Paterson; Private John 1860 (1)
225. Paterson; Private J. 1905 'F' Company (2)
226. Potter; Private T. 1905 'F' Company
227. Pringle; Private W. 1905 'F' Company
228. Rae; Private James 1860 Sergeant 1864 (1)
229. Rae; Private James S. 1860 (2)
230. Raphael; Private A. 1905 'G' Company
231. Raphael; Private John 1905 'F' Company
232. Richardson; Private J. 1905 Corporal 1907 'G' Company
233. Richardson; Private W. 'F' Company
234. Riley; Private J. 1905 'G' Company
235. Ritchie; Corporal W. 1905 'F' Company
236. Roberts; Lance/Corporal A. 1877
237. Roberts; Sergeant John 1860
238. Rorrison; Private J. 1905 'G' Company
239. Rorrison; Private R. 1905 'G' Company
240. Russell; Private J. 1901
241. Saddler; Private T. 1905 'F' Company
242. Saunders; Private W. 1901
243. Sharpe; Private 1877
244. Short; Private W. 1905 'G' Company
245. Shortridge; Private William 1880 Corporal 1887
246. Simpson; Private D. 1896
247. Sloan; Private J. 1905 'G' Company
248. Smith; Private G.W. 1880
249. Smith; Private J. 1905 'G' Company (1)
250. Smith; Private J. 1905 'G' Company (2)
251. Smith; Private J.A. 1905 'G' Company (3)
252. Smith; Private W.G. 1905 'G' Company
253. Souter; Private 1889
254. Stewart; Private T.H. 1905 'G' Company.
255. Stewart; Private W. 1872
256. Tait; Private George 1860 Sergeant 1863
257. Tait; Private Joseph 1902
258. Tait; Private W. T. 1907 Recruit
259. Taora; Private J.1899. 'G' Company.
260. Taylor; Corporal J. 1877.
261. Telford; Private G. 1905 'F' Company.
262. Thom; Private Angus. 1900.
263. Thom; Private D. 1905 "F" Company.
264. Thomson; Sergeant1873. Lochrutton section.
265. Thomson; Private J. W. 1905. 'G' Company.
266. Todd; Private W. 1905. 'F' Company.

267. Topping; Private W. 1905. 'F' Company.
268. Townsend; Private J. 1905. 'F' Company.
269. Trotter; Private J. 1905 'G' Company.
270. Trotter; Private R.B. 1905. 'G' Company.
271. Walker; Corporal Alex 1860.
272. Walker; Private A. 1880. Sergeant 1893.
273. Walker; Private James. 1880.
274. Walker; Private R.J. 1877.
275. Wallace; Private D.R. 1905. 'G' Company.
276. Wallace; Private R. 1888. 'F' Company. (1)
277. Wallace; Private R. 1905. 'F' Company. (2)
278. Walsh; Sergeant 1889.
279. Watret; Private J. 1905. 'F' Company.
280. Watson; Corporal George 1860.
281. Watson; Private W.K. 1905. 'F' Company.
282. Waugh; Private Andrew. 1860.
283. Wells; Private H. 1905. 'F' Company.
284. Wells; Private J. 1905. 'F' Company.
285. Welsh; Private T. 1905. 'G' Company.
286. Wemyss; Private. 1867.
287. West; Private John. 1860.
288. White; Private Thomas. 1900.
289. White; Private W. 1905. 'G' Company.
290. Wilkie; Private J. 1905. 'G' Company.
291. Wilson; Private David. 1860.
292. Wilson; Private M. 1905. 'F' Company.
293. Wilson; Private T. 1905. 'G' Company.
294. Wilson; Private William. 1860.
295. Wood; Private J. 1902.
296. Wright; Private W. 1872.
297. Young; Private W. 1905. 'G' Company.

SECTION 3 MEMBERSHIP OF 1896 'F' Company

Reg No.	Rank	No.	Name	Occupation	Address	Date of enrolment
	Hon.Maj.	1	Lennox, J	Wine & Spirit Mer.	London	23.6.1877
	Ast. Chap.	2	Graham, W.V.	Minister, E.C.	Maxwellton	22.1.1879
	2nd Lieu.	3	Blacklock, J	Solicitor	..	9.9.1896
2586	Col.Ser.Inst	4	Grierson, R	Drill Instructor	..	11.4.1894
76	Ord.RoomSgt.	5	Johnstone,D	Jobbing Smith	Dumfries	4.8.1870
1990	Col.Ser.	6	Beattie,J	Foreman Tuner	Maxwellton	17.3.1889
643	Sergeant	7	Carruthers,J	Joiner	..	12.5.1880
1032	..	8	McKay,A	Plumber	..	4.4.1882
484	Bugle Major	9	Raphael,J	Billposter	Dumfries	25.6.1879
1137	Sergeant	10	Walker, D	Stocking Weaver	Maxwellton	23.1.1883
4030	..	11	Welsh, J	Fitter	Dumfries	28.8.1890
1482	Lance Sgt.	12	Coupland, J	Joiner	Maxwellton	23.1.1885
5098	..	13	Haining, David	..	..	19.5.1891
7236	..	14	Kivlichan,W	Manager	Dumfries	8.4.1893
1480	Corporal	15	Edgar,A	Warehouseman	Maxwellton	21.1.1885
1029	..	16	McGeorge,T	Blacksmith	..	2.2.1882
6008	..	17	McKenzie, Joseph	Painter	..	24.9.1891
6080	Lance/Cor.	18	Grierson,T	Joiner	..	12.2.1892
1744	..	19	Hope,W	Tailor	..	1.2.1887
7412	Bugler	20	Byers, N. McK	Labourer	Maxwellton	4.7.1894
7413	..	21	Carmichael, Geo	Implement Smith	Dumfries	4.7.1894
5057	..	22	Johnstone, J	Blacksmith	..	19.3.1891
5053	Private	23	Anderson, G	Moulder	..	19.2.1891
5052	..	24	Anderson, W	Patternmaker	..	19.2.1891
5058	..	25	Armstrong, F	Tuner	Maxwellton	19.3.1891
1861	..	26	Baxter, J	Millworker	..	2.3.1888
7372	..	27	Bell, D	Tailor	Dumfries	20.2.1894
7415	..	28	Borthwick, T	Mason	Castle Douglas	27.7.1894

Reg No.	Rank	No.	Name	Occupation	Address	Date of enrolment
7146	Private	29	Brown, J	Blacksmith	Maxwellton	5.1.1893
7399	..	30	Brown, N McD	Mason	Dumfries	11.5.1894
7414	..	31	Brown, William	Glovemaker	Maxwellton	27.7.1894
7252	..	32	Callendar, G	Engineer	..	10.8.1893
7145	..	33	Carmichael, G	Labourer	Dumfries	3.1.1893
7487	..	34	Carson, S	Joiner	Maxwellton	28.1.1895
6069	..	35	Coulon, T	Labourer	Dumfries	18.1.1895
7620	..	36	Connell, R	Plumber	..	1.4.1895
7484	..	37	Caven, A	Millworker	Maxwellton	5.2.1892
7554	..	38	Charteris, W	Manufacturer	..	13.1.1896
7320	..	39	Cowan, J	Labourer	Dumfries	11.1.1894
5059	..	40	Cowan, S	Tuner	Maxwellton	19.3.1891
7321	..	41	Crosbie, F	Millworker	Dumfries	11.1.1894
7144	..	42	Dalziel, J	Blacksmith	Maxwellton	3.1.1893
7235	..	43	Deans, T	Tweed Finisher	..	7.4.1893
1728	..	44	Docherty, H	Labourer	..	15.1.1887
7076	..	45	Docherty, T	Labourer	..	6.6.1892
7150	..	46	Edgar, J	Painter	..	16.1.1893
7421	..	47	Ferguson, D	Mason	Dumfries	5.9.1894
7309	..	48	Ferguson, S	Cabinetmaker	..	22.12.1893
7618	..	49	Ferguson, W	Designer	Maxwellton	13.1.1896
7308	..	50	Gilmour, J	Tailor	Dumfries	11.12.1893
7406	..	51	Gladstone, S	Printer	Dumfries	11.6.1894
7402	..	52	Grahams, G	Labourer	Maxwellton	8.6.1894
7417	..	53	Graham, Thomas	Cabinetmaker	Maxwellton	1.8.1894
7489	..	54	Halliday, J	Baker	..	4.2.1895
4021	..	55	Hannah, R	Saddler	..	1.9.1890
5060	..	56	Hannah, W	Baker	..	24.3.1891
5061	..	57	Hannah, W	Grocer	..	24.3.1891
7418	..	58	Harper, C	Painter	..	6.8.1894

(Killed in a shooting accident, 1901.)

Reg No.	Rank	No.	Name	Occupation	Address	Date of enrolment
7699	..	59	Inman, J	Weaver	Dumfries	1.4.1896
7700	..	60	Inman, W	Tuner	..	1.4.1896
7149	..	61	Jardine, J	Plasterer	Maxwellton	16.1.1893
7142	..	62	Kerr, C	Blacksmith	..	3.1.1893
2027	..	63	Learmont, R.K	Mason	Dumfries	14.6.1889
4023	..	64	Lennox, W	Painter	Maxwellton	1.9.1890
1931	..	65	McBurnie, T	Pattern Weaver	..	18.12.1888
748	..	66	McGeorge, R	Coachsmith	Dumfries	8.2.1881
3096	..	67	McKinnell, J	Tuner	Maxwellton	10.4.1890
7416	..	68	McLean, J.C	Plumber	Dumfries	27.7.1894
7492	..	69	McLeod, J	Ironmonger	Maxwellton	22.3.1895
7210	..	70	McQueen, R	Mason	Dumfries	10.3.1893
7419	..	71	Maxwell, D	Labourer	Maxwellton	13.8.1894
7675	..	72	Moffat, George C	Plumber	Dumfries	29.2.1896
1927	..	73	Moffat, J.D	Plumber	..	11.12.1888
3095	..	74	Morrison, J	Tuner	Maxwellton	10.4.1890
7486	..	75	Morrison, R.A	Law Apprentice	Dumfries	28.1.1895
7482	..	76	Murdoch, W	Coach Painter	Maxwellton	18.1.1895
6072	..	77	Nelson, W	Painter	Dumfries	12.2.1892
7617	..	78	Osborne, R	Warper	Maxwellton	13.1.1896
7488	..	79	Percy, R	Printer	Dumfries	4.2.1895
1346	..	80	Pool, J	Labourer	Maxwellton	4.8.1884
7493	..	81	Riddick, J	Seedsman	..	22.3.1895
7723	..	82	Ritchie, W	Stocking Knitter	..	2.5.1896
7319	..	83	Robson, G	Millworker	Dumfries	11.1.1894
7392	..	84	Rodger, J	Stocking Knitter	Maxwellton	4.5.1894
7665	..	85	Saunderson, A.K	Labourer	Dumfries	24.2.1896
7666	..	86	Scott, S	Stocking Knitter	..	24.2.1896
7490	..	87	Sharpe, A	Butcher	..	4.2.1895
445	..	88	Simpson, W	Millworker	Maxwellton	10.4.1879
4025	..	89	Smith, J	Tailor	Dumfries	15.9.1890
7724	..	90	Smith, J	Painter	Maxwellton	14.5.1896
7725	..	91	Smith, P.B	Pattern weaver	..	15.5.1896
1297	..	92	Smith, R	Blacksmith	Dumfries	17.1.1887
7619	..	93	Spence, W.B.	Manufacturer	..	13.1.1896

Reg No.	Rank	No.	Name	Occupation	Address	Date of enrolment
7420	Private	94	Templeton, Thos.	Labourer	Maxwellton	29.8.1894
7556	..	95	Turnbull, T.A	Pattern Weaver		21.5.1895
7491	..	96	Walker, W	Pattern Weaver	Dumfries	16.2.1895
7087	..	97	Welsh, R	Fitter	..	7.12.1892
7555	..	98	Wilson, C	Dyer		21.5.1895
7148	..	99	Wilson, J	Labourer	Maxwellton	16.1.1893
7553	Bearer Co.	100	Brown, A.L	Plumber	Dumfries	1.4.1895
7663	..	101	Crackston, J.E	Warehouseman	Maxwellton	3.2.1895
7546	..	102	Dunn, P	Schoolmaster	Dumfries	1.4.1895
7545	..	103	Ferguson, D	Lithographer	..	1.4.1895
7558	..	104	Gladstone, J		..	1.4.1895
7549	..	105	Goplin, A.S	Tailor	Dumfries	1.4.1895
7548	..	106	Halliday, W	Printer	Dumfries	1.4.1895
7552	..	107	McKirdy, D.G	Insp. of W&M	..	1.4.1895
7547	..	108	Rae, G	Tailor	Maxwellton	1.4.1895
7550	..	109	Rae, J	Clerk	Dumfries	1.4.1895
7664	..	110	Rae, J	Joiner	..	3.2.1896
7677	..	111	Richardson, A	Plumber	..	10.3.1896
7551	..	112	Thompson, D	Compositor	..	1.4.1895
7662	..	113	Walker, W.I	Fitter	..	31.1.1895

MEMBERSHIP OF 1896 - 'G' Company.

Reg No.	Rank	No.	Name	Occupation	Address	Date of enrolment
	Hon. Major	1	Phyn, C.S	Procurator Fiscal	Dumfries	2.2.1882
	Surgeon Cap	2	Lorraine, R.B	M.D	..	10.1.1886
93	Colour-Sgt.	3	Service, J.B	Seedsman	Maxwellton	30.10.1871
1138	Sergeant	4	Jardine, W	Joiner	Dumfries	25.1.1883
1226	..	5	McKinnell, J	Dyer	Maxwellton	29.11.1883
1021	..	6	Thompson, J	Mill Fitter	..	7.4.1882
176	..	7	Wallace, J	Wood Yardsman	..	7.7.1875
1996	Lance/Sgt	8	Crichton, J	Jobbing Smith	..	22.2.1889
338	..	9	Kerr, J	Stocking Knitter	..	23.4.1878
760	..	10	McMurdo, W	Nurseryman	..	4.2.1881
7207	Corporal	11	Crosbie, R	Joiner	..	10.2.1893
1498	..	12	Moffat, J	Painter	..	16.1.1885
1543	Lance/Cor	13	Gass, J	Weaver	Dumfries	22.5.1885
1806	..	14	Morley, W	Painter	Maxwellton	6.12.1887
6074	Bugler	15	Robison, A	Tuner	..	5.2.1892
7668	Private	16	Archibald, W	Watchmaker	..	31.1.1896
7503	..	17	Armstrong, W	Mason	Dumfries	25.2.1895
7158	..	18	Bell, C	Plasterer	Maxwellton	12.12.1892
7676	..	19	Bell, C.R	Joiner	..	10.3.1896
207	..	20	Bennett, W	Labourer	..	4.3.1876
2030	..	21	Black, G	Glovemaker	..	1.5.1889
7166	..	22	Boyd, R	Labourer	..	31.1.1893
7425	..	23	Brown, D	Clogger	Dumfries	27.7.1894
7390	..	24	Brown, G	Labourer	..	27.4.1894
1992	..	25	Brown, W	Tailor	..	15.1.1889
7400	..	26	Byers, A	Scourer	..	1.6.1894
7557	..	27	Candlish, J	Stocking Knitter	Maxwellton	1.4.1895
7161	..	28	Cochrane, W	Mason	..	6.1.1896
7238	..	29	Connelly, G	Labourer	..	3.4.1893
7670	..	30	Crosbie, R	Powerloom Turner	..	3.2.1896
7209	..	31	Cunningham, A	Stocking Knitter	Walker-on-Tyne	16.3.1893
7423	..	32	Deacon, J	Baker	Maxwellton	27.7.1894
5066	..	33	Elliot, A	Glovemaker	..	13.2.1891
1795	..	34	Gracie, A	Blacksmith	Dumfries	1.12.1887
7428	..	35	Greggan, W	Mason	Maxwellton	27.8.1894
7401	..	36	Grierson, R	Stocking Knitter	..	1.6.1894
5068	..	37	Halliday, G	Blacksmith	..	1.3.1891
5065	..	38	Halliday, H	Tweed Finisher	..	12.2.1891
7429	..	39	Hanlon, J	Pavior	Dumfries	5.5.1894
7622	..	40	Hardie, J	Stocking Knitter	..	20.1.1896
7090	..	41	Hiddleston, W	Blacksmith	..	7.12.1892

Reg No.	Rank	No.	Name	Occupation	Address	Date of enrolment
7160	Private	42	Holden, W	Labourer	Dumfries	3.1.1893
7375	..	43	Hughes, J	Millworker	..	9.2.1894
7424	..	44	Jackson, T. H	Labourer	Maxwellton	27.7.1894
7422	..	45	Jardine, Robert	Joiner	..	2.7.1894
7566	..	46	Jeffrey, W.R	Insp. of W.&Meas	Dumfries	13.8.1895
7735	..	47	Johnstone, James	French Polisher	..	28.5.1896
7623	..	48	Kennedy, T	Stocking Knitter	Maxwellton	20.1.1896
1749	..	49	Kirk, W	Mason	..	1.2.1887
3015	..	50	Kirkpatrick, W	Powerloom Turner	Dumfries	25.2.1890
410	..	51	Law, W	Joiner	Maxwellton	10.2.1879
7565	..	52	Leckie, W	Pattern Weaver	Maxwellton	10.8.1895
7568	..	53	Lillice, W	..	..	3.9.1895
7408	..	54	Lock, John	Mason	..	22.6.1894
7374	..	55	Lockerbie, J	Coach Painter	Dumfries	26.1.1894
7498	..	56	Lowe, R	Printer	..	28.1.1895
1354	..	57	Macaulay, R	Glovemaker	..	4.5.1880
7495	..	58	McKean, D	Plasterer	Maxwellton	18.1.1895
7559	..	59	McKie, E	Blacksmith	..	24.6.1895
7323	..	60	McKinnell,Newall	Plumber	..	11.1.1894
7407	..	61	McKinnon, W	Mason	..	22.6.1894
7494	..	62	McMillan, J	Apprentice Turner	Dumfries	18.1.1895
3012	..	63	McMurdo, J	Joiner	Maxwellton	4.2.1890
3018	..	64	McMurdo, R	Pattern Weaver	..	11.3.1890
7499	..	65	McQueen, D	Joiner	Dumfries	28.1.1895
7208	..	66	Milligan, J	Labourer	Maxwellton	14.3.1893
7391	..	67	Minto, P	Packman	..	29.3.1894
7007	..	68	Murray, R	Powerloom Turner	..	4.3.1892
7621	..	69	Murray, T	Stocking Knitter	..	20.1.1896
6003	..	70	Percy, A	Coachbuilder	Dumfries	5.5.1891
7098	..	71	Prentice, J	Upholsterer	..	4.5.1891
7312	..	72	Proudfoot, W	Millworker	Maxwellton	22.12.1893
7569	..	73	Rae, J.H.	Designer	..	3.9.1895
7324	..	74	Reid, A	Joiner	Dumfries	11.1.1894
1809	..	75	Russell, J	Mason	Maxwellton	6.12.1887
7241	..	76	Simpson, D	Wood Yardsman	..	8.6.1893
7504	..	77	Skilling, W	Shoemaker	Dumfries	22.3.1895
7159	..	78	Spalding, W	Stocking Knitter	Maxwellton	13.12.1892
7502	..	79	Tait, James	Mason	Dumfries	4.2.1895
6013	..	80	Taylor, N	Printer	..	17.8.1891
7734	..	81	Thom, J	Pattern Weaver	..	28.5.1896
4034	..	82	Thompson, M.B	Labourer	Maxwellton	1.9.1890
7667	..	83	Tossney, J	Plumber	..	31.1.1896
7167	..	84	Turner, A	Horseshoer	Dumfries	3.2.1893
7669	..	85	Tyson, A	Labourer	Maxwellton	3.2.1896
7501	..	86	Urquhart, A	Traveller	Dumfries	4.2.1895
6076	..	87	Walker, J	Mason	..	5.2.1892
7427	..	88	Walker, J	Painter	..	1.8.1894
3007	..	89	Walker, T	Mason	..	28.1.1890
7567	..	90	Waugh, R	Painter	..	13.8.1895
764	..	91	Wells, W	Mason	..	4.2.1881
7500	..	92	Welsh, W	Joiner	..	28.1.1895
7426	..	93	Wilson, G	Painter	Maxwellton	1.8.1894

DALBEATTIE - Incorporating the 6th Kirkcudbright Rifle Volunteers, and 'H' Company of the Galloway Rifle Volunteers.

SECTION 1 - OFFICERS.

1. Anderson; A.W. Lieutenant, 3.10.1894. Captain, 1905. A Doctor by profession.
2. Biggar; Captain. Transferred from 'B' Company, Castle Douglas to 'H' Company, Dalbeattie in 1903. Resigned his commission in 1905
3. Burnie; Lieutenant 23.6.1869 - 16.5.1871
4. Gillies; Hugh. 2nd Lieutenant. 1904 Lieutenant 1908 New Abbey Section. A Doctor by profession.
5. Grieve; James Lieutenant 23.6.1869. Died on 19.11.1876, holding the rank of Captain.
6. Hunter; Joseph. Surgeon Lieutenant M.D. 1904
7. Kerr; William, Sub-Lieutenant 20.6.1874 Captain 1884. Retired Major on 27.11.1891
8. Kirkpatrick; Rev. R.S. Chaplain. 14.8.1886. - unknown
9. Lewis; John P. Surgeon Lieutenant 24.7.1868 - 16. 5. 1878
10. MacKie; Rev. John Chaplain 24.1.1879 - 21.11.1885
11. Maxwell; Wellwood J. Ensign 23.6.1869. Hon. Lieutenant-Colonel and second in command of the Galloway Rifle Volunteers in 1889. Died in 1901. Munches.
12. Maxwell; Wellwood. Captain Late of the 1st Mid- Lothian Artillery Volunteers, (1.4.1877) assumed command of 'H' Company, Dalbeattie, on 15.1.1892. Kirkennan.
13. Maxwell; W.J. 2nd Lieutenant 1900 - unknown, but of very short duration.
14. McKercher; Ensign 21.3.1872. Resigned his Commission as Lieutenant on 8.5.1874.
15. Platt; W.W. Captain 1868-died 9.7.1869 Kirkennan.
16. Stewart; Rev. D. Chaplain 24.7.1868-16.9.1877

SECTION 2 - RANK & FILE.

1. Affleck; Private 1905 (1)
2. Affleck; Private J. 1905 (2)
3. Agnew; Private G.W 1905
4. Airlie; Private C. 1905
5. Allan; Private J. 1905
6. Bell; Private R 1905
7. Bell; Private W. 1905
8. Bennett; Private A. 1905 Recruit
9. Bennett; Private G. 1905
10. Birss; Private 1869
11. Bissett; Private 1897
12. Black; Private Theodore 1880 Recruit
13. Black; Private Thomas 1880
14. Bonnar; Private 1905
15. Bower; Private J. 1905
16. Brown; Sergeant 1877
17. Bryce; Private R 1905
18. Brydson; Private 1897
19. Burnie; Private W. 1905
20. Campbell; Private J. 1880 Recruit
21. Carlyle; Private J. 1905
22. Carson; Private J. 1880 (1)
23. Carson; Private J. 1905 (2)
24. Caven; Private J. 1905
25. Clark; Private D. 1905
26. Clark; Private G. 1880 Recruit
27. Clark; Sergeant M. 1880 Colour-Sergeant 1889
28. Coskrie; Private 1877
29. Coutts; Private 1878 Sergeant 1880
30. Coutts; Private G.A. 1901
31. Coutts; Private W. 1905
32. Craig; Private 1876 Sergeant 1880 Colour-Sergeant 1891
33. Craig; Private T. 1899
34. Craig; Private W. 1880 Recruit
35. Craik; Private W. 1901
36. Crocket; Private Ebenezer 1880 Recruit
37. Crosbie; Bugler C. 1905
38. Crosbie; Sergeant 1880 (1)
39. Crosbie; Sergeant R. 1905 (2)
40. Davies; Private C. 1877
41. Donnan; Private James 1902

42. Fell; Corporal J. 1905
43. Ferguson; Private P.T. 1897
44. Flynn; Private J. 1891 Recruit (1)
45. Flynn; Private J.P. 1905 Recruit (2)
46. Forteath; Private W. 1905
47. Fowler; Private J. 1905
48. Garmory; Private W. 1905
49. Gibson; Private 1880
50. Gilbertson; Private 1869
51. Glencross; Private 1897 (1)
52. Glencross; Private J. 1897 (2)
53. Glendinning; Private 1869
54. Goodman; Lance/Corporal W. 1899
55. Gourlay; Private S. 1880
56. Graham; Sergeant 1869
57. Graham; Private 1877
58. Grant; Private G. 1880
59. Grive; Private 1891
60. Groves; Private P.R. 1905
61. Herries; Private J. 1905
62. Heughan; Private W. 1905
63. Hood; Private S. 1905
64. Hooper; Private M. 1892
65. Hume; Sergeant 1869 (1)
66. Hume; Private 1869 (2)
67. Hume; Private J. 1899 (3)
68. Huxtable; Private J. 1905
69. Irving; Private C. 1899
70. Jamieson; Private H. 1905
71. Johnston; Sergeant T. 1905
72. Johnstone; Corporal J. 1877
73. Kimm; Corporal J. 1880
74. Kirk; Private James 1900
75. Kirk; Private R. 1880
76. Laing; Private Thomas 1888
77. Laird; Private 1905
78. Legg; Private G. 1876 Corporal 1880
79. Lindsay; Private 1898
80. Logan; Corporal 1905 (1)
81. Logan; Private A.P. 1905 (2)
82. Lynch; Private 1892
83. Marchbank; Private 1869
84. Milroy; Private S. 1880
85. Morris; Private E. 1905
86. Muirhead; Private A. 1905
87. Mundell; Bugler D. 1905
88. Mundell; Private W. 1905
89. Murphy; Private James. 1905
90. Murphy; Private John 1905
91. Murphy; Private W.A 1905
92. McCaig; Private J. 1905
93. McCall; Private D.M. 1905
94. McCartney; Private 1898
95. McDonald; Private 1877 (1)
96. McDonald; Private R. 1905 (2)
97. McEwan; Private F. 1905
98. McGhee; Private William 1888
99. McGhie; Private T. 1892
100. McGowan; Private 1880 L/Corporal 1880
101. McGregor; Corporal 1869 Sergeant 1877
102. McGregor; Sergeant J. 1901
103. McGuffog; Private J. 1905
104. McIntosh; Private 1898
105. McKenzie; Bugler John 1888
106. Mckie; Private J. 1877
107. MacKie; Private W.J 1905
108. McKinnell; Private J. 1905

109. McKnight; Private D. 1880 Recruit
110. McLachlan; Private 1869
111. McLean; Private John 1900
112. McMeeking; Private T. 1905
113. McMillan; Private J. 1880 Recruit
114. McMullen; Private 1869
115. McPhee; Sergeant 1902
116. McWilliam; Private A. 1901
117. Neilson; Bugler J. 1905
118. Nelson; Private William; 1900
119. Pringle; Private 1905
120. Rae; Corporal J. 1899. Sergeant 1903
121. Riffan; Private P. 1905
122. Riley; Private John 1888
123. Ritchie; Private C. 1869 Corporal 1877
124. Roan; Private 1905. (1)
125. Roan; Private W. 1905 (2)
126. Robertson; Corporal Charles 1888 Sergeant 1889
127. Robertson; Private J. 1905
128. Robertson; Private T. 1892
129. Robinson; Lance Corporal 1877
130. Scott; Private J. 1905
131. Seggie; Private D. 1902 Corporal 1903
132. Seggie; Bugler J. 1905
133. Shearer; Private 1869
134. Sibson; Private 1892 Recruit
135. Slingsby; Private W. 1905
136. Smith; Private R. 1905
137. Stenton; Private 1905
138.Stewart; Private J. 1880 Recruit
139. Sturgeon; Private Andrew 1880 Corporal 1889
140. Sturgeon; Private H. 1899
141. Sturgeon; Private J. 1905
142. Sturgeon; Corporal W. 1893
143. Swan; Private 1897
144. Tait; Private W. 1902
145. Thom; Private 1897
146. Thomson; Private J. 1905
147. Thomson; Private R. 1905
148. Watson; Private R. 1880 Recruit
149. Wilbur; Private W.M. 1905
150. Wilson; Private 1869. Sergeant 1877
151. Wood; Private T. 1880 Recruit
152. Wright; Private 1905
153. Wyness; Private J. 1877 Corporal 1880

SECTION 3 MEMBERSHIP OF 1896

Reg No.	Rank	No.	Name	Occupation	Address	Date of enrolment
	Captain	1	Maxwell, W	Gentleman	Kirkennan	1.4.1877& 8.1.1892
	Lieutenant	2	Anderson, A.W	Doctor	Dalbeattie	3.10.1894
	Chaplain	3	Kirkpatrick, R.S	Minister	Jedburgh	14.4.1886
1186	Serg.Instr.	4	Gallagher, J.H	Sgt. Instr.	Dalbeattie	7.2.1889
54	Col.-Serg.	5	Craig, T	Mason	..	9.7.1868
2012	Sergeant	6	Clark, J	Joiner	..	9.7.1868 &16.1.1889
241	..	7	Ferguson,W	Tailor	..	16.2.1877
2000	..	8	Gillespie, A.J	Clerk	..	7.1.1889
1768	..	9	McGregor,Thomas	Mason	..	13.1.1887
1372	Lance/Serg.	10	Clark, Michael	Mason	..	3.11.1884
7106	..	11	Mundell, D	Painter	..	1.12.1892
4011	Corporal	12	Burnie, Thomas	Mason	..	29.4.1890
1759	..	13	Flinn, J	Mason	..	13.1.1887
1827	..	14	Sturgeon, R	Mason	..	9.1.1888
1824	Lance/Corp.	15	Burnie, A	Polisher	..	9.1.1888
7072	..	16	Edgeley, T	Settmaker	..	23.4.1892

Reg No.	Rank	No.	Name	Occupation	Address	Date of enrolment
7245	Lance Corp.	17	Gray, A	Teacher	Lockerbie	23.5.1893
2007	..	18	Melburn, G	Mason	Dalbeattie	10.1.1889
7107	..	19	Morrison, J	Watchmaker	..	1.12.1892
2055	..	20	Paterson, R	Baker	..	18.12.1889
7733	Bugler	21	Gallagher, F.H		..	27.5.1896
7507	Private	22	Austin, J.M	Clerk	..	20.3.1895
7013	..	23	Blair, R	Baker	..	19.1.1892
7444	..	24	Brown, Alex.(1)	Labourer	..	10.12.1894
7634	..	25	Brown, A (2)	Mason	..	27.1.1896
7288	..	26	Brown, D	Hewer	..	8.12.1893
7526	..	27	Brown, Jonathon	Turner	..	10.4.1895
7117	..	28	Burnie, H	Settmaker	..	1.12.1892
7635	..	29	Burnie, J	Settmaker	..	27.1.1896
7508	..	30	Burnie, J.N	Clerk	..	20.3.1895
2051	..	31	Caven, S	Blacksmith	..	18.12.1889
7364	..	32	Clark, J	Mason	..	15.1.1894
4080	..	33	Clark, W	Joiner	..	29.12.1890
7463	..	34	Copland, R	Grocer	..	4.1.1895
7636	..	35	Dalziel, J	Baker	..	27.1.1896
7290	..	36	Dempster, Richard	Mason	..	8.12.1893
7445	..	37	Dempster, Robert	Mason	..	10.12.1894
7446	..	38	Derry, J	Settmaker	..	10.12.1894
7313	..	39	Dinwiddie, W	Mason	..	2.1.1894
7537	..	40	Docherty, A	Mason	..	8.5.1895
7447	..	41	Drain, J	Mason	..	10.12.1894
7138	..	42	Ferguson, Joseph	Shoemaker	..	20.1.1893
7010	..	43	Ferguson, Jardine	Mason	..	19.1.1892
7630	..	44	Ferguson, R	Polisher	..	14.1.1896
7291	..	45	Ferguson, W.J	Painter	..	18.12.1893
2009	..	46	Flinn, R	Mason	..	10.1.1889
4091	..	47	Flinn, W	Mason	..	6.1.1891
7627	..	48	Garmory, J	Mason	..	14.1.1896
7366	..	49	Gordon, A	Mason	..	18.1.1894
7522	..	50	Gordon, T	Clerk	..	25.3.1895
7033	..	51	Gourlay, A	Tailor	..	12.2.1892
7030	..	52	Grieve, W.J	Printer	..	1.2.1892
7509	..	53	Halliday, J	Watchmaker	..	20.3.1895
7019	..	54	Halliday, R	Labourer	..	19.1.1892
7510	..	55	Halliday, R.M	Clerk	..	20.3.1895
3024	..	56	Henderson, J	Wood Turner	..	20.1.1890
7228	..	57	Henderson, R	Wood Turner	..	10.4.1893
4079	..	58	Hughes, J	Mason	..	29.12.1890
7631	..	59	Hughes, W	Mason	..	14.1.1896
7035	..	60	Huxtable, J	Polisher	..	16.2.1892
7626	..	61	Jack, James	Baker	..	14.1.1896
7025	..	62	Jack, John	Baker	..	22.1.1892
4084	..	63	Jackson, H	Wood Turner	..	29.12.1890
7637	..	64	Kerr, A	Hewer	..	27.1.1896
7443	..	65	Kerr, H	Chemist	..	3.11.1894
7511	..	66	Kirkpatrick, J.W	Clerk	..	20.3.1895
7527	..	67	Laurie, R	Tailor	..	10.4.1895
1193	..	68	Lawson, Frank	Turner	..	7.5.1883
7528	..	69	Lumsden, A	Mason	..	24.4.1895
7111	..	70	MacKay, J	Grocer	..	1.12.1892
7449	..	71	McClymont, W	Blacksmith	..	10.12.1894
7638	..	72	McDonald, Neil	Mason	..	27.1.1896
7632	..	73	McGeoch, J	Mason	..	14.1.1896
7315	..	74	McGeoch, T	Mason	..	2.1.1894
7442	..	75	McMorrine, J	Labourer	..	3.12.1894
7109	..	76	McTaggart, J	Grocer	..	1.12.1892
7014	..	77	Maxwell, C	Turner	..	19.1.1892
7017	..	78	Maxwell, S	Turner	..	19.1.1892
7108	..	79	Melburn, A	Mason	..	19.1.1892
7674	..	80	Morrison, J	Painter	..	26.2.1896
1358	..	81	Murray, J	Shoemaker	..	9.4.1884
7639	..	82	Neilson, W	Mason	..	27.1.1896

Reg No.	Rank	No.	Name	Occupation	Address	Date of enrolment
7640	Private	83	Paterson, A	Mason	Dalbeattie	27.1.1896
7229	..	84	Paterson, W	Turner	..	10.4.1893
7641	..	85	Preston, J	Mason	..	27.1.1896
7292	..	86	Sloan, W	Baker	..	8.12.1893
7293	..	87	Smith, A	Mason	..	8.12.1893
7642	..	88	Smith, G	Mason	..	27.1.1896
7104	..	89	Smith, J	Mason	..	1.12.1892
7464	..	90	Smith, J.R	Draper	..	4.1.1895
7103	..	91	Smith, J	Blacksmith	..	1.12.1893
7625	..	92	Smith, W.J	Clerk	..	6.1.1896
7135	..	93	Tait, R	Builder	..	20.1.1893
7102	..	94	Thomson, H	Mason	..	1.12.1892
7673	..	95	Toon, J	Settmaker	..	24.2.1896
7450	..	96	Townsend, J	Labourer	..	10.12.1894
7633	..	97	Walker, W	Polisher	..	14.1.1896
7289	..	98	Wilson, G	Hewer	..	8.12.1893
7177	..	99	Wilson, J	Mason	..	25.1.1893
7536	..	100	Woolhouse, R	Mason	..	8.5.1895

WIGTOWN -

Incorporating the 1st Wigtown Rifle Volunteers. 1860 - 1874,

and members of the Wigtown Section of 'D' Company, Galloway Rifle Volunteers.

SECTION 1 - OFFICERS

1. Agnew; Robert Vans. Lieutenant 24.2.1860-20.8.1872
2. Hughan; Ensign. 1868-unknown
3. McHaffie; William J. Ensign. 24.2.1860-20.6.1873
4. Snowdon; Dr. Surgeon to the Corps. 1863
5. Stewart; Lieutenant. 1868-unknown

SECTION 2 - RANK & FILE

1. Agnew; Private 1862
2. Anderson; Private W 1861
3. Black; Sergeant E.S 1860
4. Boyd; Private D 1903
5. Boyd; Private W 1903
6. Brown; Private E 1865
7. Christison; Private George 1861
8. Christison; Private James 1861. Corporal 1866
9. Coupland; Sergeant 1903
10. Drynan; Private J 1903
11. Drynan; Private R 1903
12. Edwards; Private 1903
13. Gardiner; Private 1903
14. Grierson; Private J 1861
15. Henderson; Private Daniel 1863
16. Henderson; Private James 1862
17. Henry; Sergeant K 1860
18. Heron; Private W 1863
19. Kelly; Private J 1861
20. Kerr; Private 1903
21. Kevan; Corporal P.B 1860
22. Laird; Private J 1865
23. Martin; Corporal T 1860
24. MacKie; Sergeant William 1860
25. MacKie; Private William 1863
26. McAnally; Private 1863
27. McBean; Private 1863
28. McClure; Private 1903
29. McCubbin; Private 1903
30. McCulloch; Private James 1863

31. McCulloch; Private Robert 1862
32. McCulloch; Sergeant W 1863
33. McDonald; Private 1863
34. McNarney; Private 1860
35. Paton; Private George 1861 Corporal 1865
36. Russell; Corporal 1903
37. Tait; Private 1903
38. Wilson; Private W 1863 Sergeant 1866

STRANRAER -
Incorporating both the 2nd Wigtown Rifle Volunteers and 'C' Company of the Galloway Rifle Volunteers.

SECTION 1 - OFFICERS.

1. Anderson; James B. 2nd Lieutenant 15.8.1877. Lieutenant 1879 - unknown.
2. Andrews; Ensign 1864. Joined as a Sergeant in 1860. Commissioned in 1864.
3. Cochran; Surgeon 1895
4. Crawford; Archibald. Sub-Lieutenant 9.5.1874 - 3.3.1875. Joined as a Private in 1860, Commissioned in 1874
5. Easton; J. Surgeon 26.5.1871 - unknown.
6. Findlay; Lieutenant 1867
7. Fleming; Ebenezer. Hon. Surgeon 1860
8. Garrick; Lieutenant 9.1.1880. Died on 23.2.1890 holding the rank of Captain.
9. Guthrie; David. Captain. 18.3.1860 - 6.8.1870. Provost of Stranraer.
10. Hunter; T.M. Lieutenant 1907
11. Ingram; Alexander Lieutenant 1860-unknown Director of Portpatrick Railway Company.
12. Johnston; Rev. W.M. Hon. Chaplain 1864 Commissioned on 12.5.1871 Still serving in 1897
13. Kerr; C. Lieutenant 6.8.1870-11.7.1878
14. Millar; W. Lieutenant 6.8.1870-18.7.1871
15. Munro; D.D. Surgeon Lieutenant 22.6.1895. Captain 1901
16. McBryde; John Ensign 1860-unknown
17. McLachlan; Lieutenant 1900
18. McLean; J Lieutenant 6.12.1890 Captain 1900
19. McLelland; Alexander Lieutenant 2.5.1889-Emigrated to South Africa and resigned his commission on 9.9.1898 Balyett Farm.
20. Shaw; Ensign 1861-unknown
21. Stewart; P. Lieutenant 27.6.1885 Captain 1891 Major 1896 Retired 1898
22. Taylor; Ensign 16.6.1863 Captain 1870 Retired Major on 15.2.1889. Joined as a Sergeant in 1860 and commissioned in 1863
23. Watson; James Lieutenant 11.12.1867-6.8.1870
24. Watson; William W. 2nd Lieutenant 6.12.1890 Lieutenant 1895-unknown. Joined as a Private in 1866 Sergeant in 1881 commissioned in 1890

SECTION 2- RANK & FILE

1. Agnew; Corporal R. 1864
2. Anderson; Sergeant 1861
3. Andrews; Sergeant 1860 Commissioned Ensign 1864
4. Arnott; Private J 1905
5. Berry; Private J 1905
6. Biggam; Private R 1905
7. Boe; Private W 1881
8. Brown; Private Thomas 1863
9. Burns; Private F 1905
10. Byers; Private J. 1905
11. Caldwell; Private J 1881 Recruit
12. Cluckie; Sergeant Niven 1864
13. Cook; Private M 1905
14. Coustom; Corporal 1861
15. Craig; Corporal 1895 (1)
16. Craig; Private J 1905 (2)
17. Crawford; Private Archibald 1866 Commissioned Sub-Lieutenant 1874
18. Crawford; Private H 1905
19. Derry; Sergeant 1901
20. Devlin; Private W 1905

21. Devoy; Private Joseph 1905
22. Devoy; Private W 1905
23. Donnan; Private T 1881
24. Dornan; Private John 1861
25. Emmerson; Private R 1905
26. Findlay; Private A 1905
27. Fleming; Private William 1863
28. Galloway; Corporal E 1905
29. Gillon; Private 1905
30. Gillespie; Private J 1905
31. Gordon; Bugler D 1881
32. Gourlay; Private John 1861
33. Grey; Private William 1861 Corporal 1861
34. Hamilton; Private H 1905
35. Harold; Private D 1881
36. Harold; Private Joseph 1881
37. Hunter; Sergeant 1864
38. Inglis; Private W.G. 1861. Sergeant 1863
39. Irons; Corporal D 1905
40. Johnstone; Private W 1905
41. Keenan; Private J 1881 Recruit
42. Kelly; Private J 1905
43. Kerr; Private C 1865
44. Meikle; Corporal P.H 1864
45. Miller; Sergeant 1861
46. Miller; Private D 1901
47. Murray; Private D 1905
48. Murray; Private J.G 1881 Recruit
49. McBryde; Sergeant 1861
50. McCall; Private 1905
51. McCandlish; Private E 1905
52. McCandlish; Private R 1905
53. McClymont; Private 1905
54. McCrae; Private H 1861
55. McCulloch; Private J 1905
56. McCutcheon; Private H 1905
57. McDowall; Corporal W.R 1864
58. McHaffie; Private George 1899 Sergeant 1905
59. McKenzie; Private D 1905
60. McKie; Private J 1881 (1)
61. McKie; Private J 1905 (2)
62. McKie; Corporal R 1905
63. McLean; Private John 1861
64. McMurtrie; Private 1905
65. McNeill; Private W 1905
66. McQuistan; Private J 1881
67. McSkimming; Private A 1905
68. McVicar; Private D 1905
69. Nelson; Private W 1905
70. Patterson; Private W 1866
71. Pirrie; Corporal J 1905
72. Pirrie; Private Thomas 1902
73. Pirrie; Private W 1905
74. Rankine; Private James 1881
75. Rennie; Private R 1905
76. Rennie; Private William 1900
77. Stewart; Sergeant P. 1877
78. Taylor; Sergeant 1860 Commissioned Ensign 1864
79. Telfer; Private David 1864
80. Torrance; Private 1883 Sergeant 1893

81. Tweedie; Private J 1905 Recruit
82. Wallace; Sergeant 1861
83. Warren; Private D 1901 (1)

88. Watson; Private W 1866 Sergeant 1881 Commissioned Sub-Lieutenant 1890
89. Welsh; Private W 1905
90. Wemyss; Private 1863
91. Wheatley; Private L 1905
92. Williamson; Private John 1861
93. Wilson; Private T.D. 1900
94. Wingate; Private R Mann 1861
95. Wither; Private G 1866

SECTION 3 - MEMBERSHIP OF 1896

Reg No.	Rank	No.	Name	Occupation	Address	Date of enrolment
	Captain	1	Stewart, P	Gas Manager	Stranraer	27.6.1885
870	Lieutenant	2	McLelland, A	Farmer	Balyett	2.5.1889
1651	..	3	McLean, J	Farmer	Auchneil	6.12.1890
106	..	4	Watson, W	Clothier	Stranraer	6.12.1890
	Surg.Lieu.	5	Munro, D.D	Doctor	..	22.6.1895
	Chaplain	6	Johnstone, W	Minister	..	12.5.1871
812	Col. Sgt.	7	McIlroy, T	Drill Instructor	..	1.2.1889
65	..	8	McEwan, J	Tailor	..	1.12.1869
318	Pioneer-Sgt	9	Bell, J	Tele. Linesman	Kilmarnock	11.2.1878
810	Sergeant	10	Lock, H	Printer	Stranraer	22.4.1880
2033	L/Sgt	11	McCulloch, W	Tailor	..	1.2.1870
146	..	12	Devoy, J	Shoemaker	..	15.5.1874
7396	Pioneer-Cpl	13	McLauchlin, A	Joiner	..	4.6.1894
1250	Corporal	14	Stewart, T.D	Solicitor	..	1.3.1884
7529	Bugler	15	Kennedy, J	Baker	..	11.6.1895
7405	..	16	McCulloch, W	Plasterer	..	19.6.1894
7274	Private	17	Adair, R.M	Solicitor	..	11.11.1893
7534	..	18	Adair, S.W	Farmer	..	27.5.1895
7704	..	19	Berry, A	Plasterer	..	5.5.1896
7056	..	20	Bradley, J	Tailor	..	20.4.1892
5046	..	21	Brown, J	Engine Driver	Castle Kennedy	21.3.1891
7585	..	22	Caird, J	Tailor	Stranraer	14.1.1896
7276	..	23	Caldwell, N.P	Bank Clerk	..	21.11.1893
7277	..	24	Caldwell, R	Plumber	..	20.11.1893
3084	..	25	Campbell, A	Tailor	..	20.5.1890
7698	..	26	Caughie, A	Joiner	..	21.4.1896
7728	..	27	Caughie, R	Plasterer	..	29.5.1896
7671	..	28	Chalmers, W.H	School Teacher	..	18.3.1896
7582	..	29	Collins, C	Lamp Maker	..	14.1.1896
7706	..	30	Denham, W	Gardener	..	21.3.1892
7696	..	31	Devoy, J	Tailor	..	23.4.1896
7280	..	32	Douglas, A	Clerk	..	24.11.1893
7732	..	33	Douglas, A	Clerk	..	2.6.1896
7693	..	34	Douglas, L	Clerk	..	7.4.1896
7702	..	35	Easton, T.H	Clerk	..	5.5.1896
7726	..	36	Ferguson, W	Clerk	..	26.5.1896
7646	..	37	Gibb, A	Plasterer	..	10.2.1896
7718	..	38	Gibson, W	Clothier	..	18.5.1896
174	..	39	Gracie, J	Steamboat Worker	..	20.5.1875
232	..	40	Gracie, J	Plasterer	..	12.1.1877
7713	..	41	Gracie, T	Joiner	..	7.5.1896
7519	..	42	Hamilton, J	Plasterer	..	17.4.1895
7720	..	43	Hastie, J	Joiner	..	18.5.1896
7721	..	44	Higgins, R	Grocer	..	18.5.1896
7731	..	45	Higgins, W	Clerk	..	2.6.1896
7512	..	46	Hunter, T	Clerk	..	22.3.1895
7045	..	47	Irvine, W	Bricklayer	..	5.4.1892
7586	..	48	Kay, H	Engineer	..	15.1.1896
7531	..	49	Kerr, D	Tailor	..	20.5.1895
499	..	50	Kerr, J	Tailor	..	24.11.1879
7539	..	51	Kennedy, J	Labourer	..	11.6.1895
494	..	52	King, G	Baker	..	12.5.1891
6097	..					

Reg No.	Rank	No.	Name	Occupation	Address	Date of enrolment
7727	Private	55	Little, W	Joiner	Stranraer	26.5.1896
7474	..	56	Martin, W	Forester	..	20.3.1895
7583	..	57	McCracken, R	Tailor	..	14.1.1896
7581	..	58	McCormack, A	Tailor	..	10.1.1896
7697	..	59	McDowall, G	Clothier	..	20.4.1896
7715	..	60	McDowall, F	Joiner	..	12.5.1896
7281	..	61	McDowall, W	Tailor	..	27.11.1893
3072	..	62	McEwan, R	Tailor	..	13.5.1890
1696	..	63	McGeoch, H	Engineer	..	16.3.1887
2071	..	64	McGhee, J	Plasterer	..	18.4.1889
7397	..	65	McGill, J	Joiner	..	4.6.1894
7714	..	66	McKail, J	Tailor	..	8.5.1896
7712	..	67	McKail, R	Joiner	..	7.5.1896
7204	Pipe-Major	68	McKinstry, J	Schoolmaster	..	24.3.1893
7719	Private	69	McKissock, J	Clothier	..	18.5.1896
7470	..	70	McLauchlin, H	Plumber	..	20.3.1895
7521	..	71	McLauchlin, J	Joiner	..	17.4.1895
7472	..	72	McMillan, H	Labourer	..	30.3.1895
7003	..	73	McNeile, J	Farmer	..	15.3.1892
7473	..	74	Miller, James	Labourer	..	20.3.1895
7282	..	75	Miller, John	Gardener	..	28.11.1893
7729	..	76	Monie, J	Farm Servant	..	29.5.1896
7703	..	77	Murphy, J	Plasterer	..	5.5.1896
7544	..	78	Parker, J	Joiner	..	18.6.1895
7575	..	79	Reid, R	Tailor	..	20.5.1895
7717	..	80	Rennie, S	Joiner	..	18.5.1896
7543	..	81	Rodgers, J	Plasterer	..	14.6.1895
7520	..	82	Shaw, J.M.	Clerk	..	17.4.1895
7369	..	83	Shaw, W	Joiner	..	20.3.1894
7716	..	84	Toman, P	Grocer	..	15.5.1896
488	..	85	Thompson, J	Brickmaker	..	5.2.1880
2032	..	86	Thompson, R	Tailor	..	18.4.1889
7730	..	87	Thompson, W	Farm Servant	Auchneil	29.5.1896
7530	..	88	Thom, J	Tailor	Stranraer	14.5.1895
1514	..	89	Watson, J	Forester	Castle Kennedy	1.7.1885
7515	..	90	Wood, A	Cabinetmaker	Stranraer	5.4.1895
	Recruit	91	Diamond, G	Butcher	..	25.11.1896
	..	92	McLauchlin, H	Butcher	..	25.11.1896
	..	93	Spence, W	Joiner	..	25.11.1896
	..	94	Porteous, F	Clerk	..	25.11.1896

NEWTON STEWART -
Incorporating the 3rd Wigtown Rifle Volunteers, and 'D' Company of the Galloway Rifle Volunteers.

SECTION 1 - OFFICERS

1. Agnew; Thomas Lieutenant 15.12.1883- Retired Major 23.4.1895
2. Agnew; William Lieutenant 11.9.1873- Retired Captain 3.9.1883
3. Brand; Lieutenant 1898-unknown
4. Clarke; Dr. J. Surgeon 9.11.1864 - 9.8.1890
5. Douglas; Surgeon Lieutenant 1899-unknown
6. Glover; R.S. Captain 1905-1908 Transferred from 'A' Company, Gatehouse Section in 1905, to take charge of 'D' Company, Newton Stewart.
7. Inglis; Rev. J. McD 30.5.1891-unknown
8. Kelly; William M. 2nd Lieutenant 23.6.1888 Captain 1900 Resigned his commission in 1901. Provost of Newton Stewart.
9. Mathews; J Lieutenant 1907-1908
10. More; Dr. Hon. Surgeon 1860-1864
11. McKie; N.J. Surgeon Lieutenant 20.2.1892-unknown
12. McLean; C.A Lieutenant 13.1.1896 Captain 1901 Resigned his commission in 1902
13. McPhater; Angus 2nd Lieutenant 6.4.1887 Captain 1896 Resigned his commission in 1899 Provost of Newton Stewart.
14. Picken; Robert Lieutenant 18.5.1864 Captain 1873 Retired 20.5.1882 of Barnkirk.
15. Stewart; T Ensign 12.6.1868-5.6.1873
16. Stopford-Blair; Edward Ensign 1860 Resigned his Commission 1861

17. Stroyan; David Ensign 31.3.1864 A Banker with the British Linen Bank, Newton Stewart, he was sentenced to 6 years penal servitude for embezzlement, and dismissed from the service.
18. Stroyan; D Captain 8.9.1866-28.5.1873 of Knockbrex
19. Stuart; Henry Lieutenant 21.3.1860 Captain 31.3.1864-unknown
20. Taylor; Ensign 1864-unknown

After the resignation of Captain McLean in 1902, 'D' Company, Newton Stewart was without an Officer throughout the years, 1903 and 1904. In 1905, Lieutenant R.S. Glover, 'A' Company, Kirkcudbright (Gatehouse Section), who had been acting as Commanding Officer 'pro temp' of the Newton Stewart Company was promoted to the rank of Captain and transferred as Officer Commanding 'D' Company. He was to remain in charge of the Company until the demise of the Volunteer Movement in 1908.

SECTION 2 - RANK & FILE

1. Agnew; Private H 1905
2. Agnew; Private J 1907 Recruit
3. Agnew; Private J 1905
4. Agnew; Sergeant James 1876
5. Agnew; Corporal John Sergeant 1882
6. Agnew; Private R 1877 Recruit. Sergeant 1899
7. Agnew; Sergeant Thomas 1876 Commissioned in 1883
8. Agnew; Private Thomas 1888 Recruit
9. Agnew; Corporal William 1864 Sergeant 1865 Commissioned in 1873
10. Anderson; Private W 1864
11. Armstrong; Private C 1905
12. Axon; Private W.G 1905
13. Beattie; Private R 1861
14. Beattie; Private T 1903
15. Birrell; Sergeant Adam 1901 Colour-Sergeant 1906 Creetown Section
16. Birrell; Private William 1899 Recruit Creetown Section
17. Blackwood; Private 1899
18. Blain; Private J 1905 Recruit
19. Boyd; Private D.A 1905
20. Brown; Private L 1905
21. Brown; Private S 1905
22. Brown; Private W 1903
23. Bryden; Private G 1905
24. Butler; Private James 1905 Creetown Section (1)
25. Butler; Private J.T 1905 Creetown Section (2)
26. Callendar; Private A 1905
27. Carmont; Private H 1905
28. Carson; Sergeant 1860
29. Carter; Private 1888
30. Cavan; Private T.B. 1905
31. Chisholm; Private S 1906 Creetown Section
32. Christie; Private J.K. 1905
33. Christison; Private Colin 1899 Recruit Wigtown Section
34. Cochrane; Private T 1905
35. Collin; Private 1903
36. Connell; Private W 1906 Creetown Section
37. Cosker; Private O 1905
38. Coulter; Private J 1899
39. Courtney; Private W H 1905
40. Cowell; Private W 1905
41. Craik; Sergeant 1860
42. Crawford; Private S 1880
43. Cullen; Private M 1905 Creetown Section
44. Currie; Private 1888
45. Cuthbertson; Private J 1901
46. Dargie; Private James 1863 Corporal 1864
47. Dickson; Corporal 1860
48. Dodds; Private 1888
49. Dryden; Private R 1905
50. Edwards; Private W 1901 Corporal 1905 Wigtown Section
51. Elliott; Private R 1906 Creetown Section

52. Erskine; Private James 1861
53. Erskine; Private R 1880
54. Findlay; Private G 1880
55. Finningham; Private A 1905
56. Fiskin; Private S 1905
57. Garroch; Private P 1901 Creetown section
58. Garroch-Garrock-Garrick; Private J 1901 Creetown Section
59. Gardiner; Private J 1905
60. Gass; Private W 1905
61. Gibney; Private T A 1905
62. Goldie; Private T 1905 Creetwon Section
63. Gordon; Private T 1901 Creetown Section
64. Gordon; Private W.C 1883
65. Gourlay; Private John 1864 Bandmaster
66. Gray; Private W.S 1901 Sergeant 1905
67. Haining; Private W 1905
68. Hall; Private J 1903 Corporal 1905
69. Hall; Private W 1905
70. Halliday; Cyclist R 1901 Creetown Section
71. Hanlon; Private T 1899
72. Hannah; Private J.S 1905
73. Harding; Private J 1905
74. Harley; Private J 1902
75. Henderson; Lance Corporal 1901
76. Henry; Corporal William. 1901. Creetown Section
77. Heron; Private J 1905
78. Hewitson; Private Joseph 1862 Sergeant 1864 (1)
79. Hewitson; Private J 1864 Corporal 1866 (2)
80. Hinds; Private G 1880
81. Hinds; Private James 1865 Corporal 1866
82. Hodgson; Private C 1905
83. Innes; Private J 1901
84. Jardine; Private A 1905
85. Kell; Private J 1883
86. Kelly; Private W J 1905
87. Kerr; Private J 1905
88. Kevan; Private C 1906 Creetown Section
89. Kevan; Private J 1906 Creetown Section
90. Knowles; Private A 1905
91. Lavery; Private 1905 Recruit
92. Longridge; Private D J 1905
93. Longridge; Private W 1905
94. Lupton; Private R 1905 Creetown Section
95. Marshall; Private A 1905
96. Mathews; Private J M 1905
97. Millan - Milne; Sergeant J 1905
98. Moffat; Private George 1861
99. Morrison; Private William 1901 Whithorn - Wigtown Section
100. Mosscroft; Private J 1865
101. Muir; Private R E 1905
102. Muir; Private T 1893
103. Murchie; Private Thomas 1897
104. McBannister; Private T 1905
105. McBratney; Private W 1883
106. MacKie; Sergeant 1864
107. McCaull; Private H 1869. Segeant 1877
108. McCleary; Private J 1903
109. McClelland; Private 1903
110. McClure; Private A 1905
111. McClure; Private J 1905
112. McClymont; Private G 1865
113. McClymont; Private Robert 1864
114. McConchie; Private Alexander 1863
115. McConchie; Corporal Andrew 1864 Sergeant 1865
116. McConchie; Sergeant R 1860
117. McConchie; Private R 1905
118. McConchie; Private W 1905

119. McConnell; Private Alex. 1899 Recruit
120. McConnell; Private Stair 1861
121. McCulloch; Private D 1905
122. McDavid; Corporal H 1901 Creetown Section
123. McDavid; Private H 1906 Creetown Section
124. McDavid; Private W 1905
125. McDonald; Private A 1880
126. McDowall; Private D 1901
127. McDowall; Private A 1905
128. McDowall; Private R 1905
129. McFarlane; Sergeant 1880
130. McGhie; Private J 1905
131. McGhee; Private R 1905
132. McGinis; Private D 1905
133. McGinis; Private J 1905
134. McGiviran; Private W 1905
135. McGowan; Private J 1905
136. McGuffie; Private Louis V.C. 1918 Wigtown Section
137. McGuigan; Private J 1883
138. McIntyre; Private J 1902
139. McKeand; Corporal J 1899
140. McMillan; Private John 1901 Wigtown Section
141. McMurray; Private D.S 1905
142. McMurray; Corporal W 1905
143. McNair; Private J A 1905
144. McNaught; Private T 1883
145. McNearnie; Private J 1905 Creetown Section
146. McNeillie; Private G 1880
147. McWilliams; Private J F 1905
148. Nimmo; Private W.T.R. 1905
149. O'Hara; Private T 1905 Creetown Section
150. Oliver; Private C 1906 Creetown Section
151. Oliver; Private G 1906 .. ..
152. Oliver; Private W 1906 .. ..
153. Owen; Private J 1880
154. Parker; Private J 1905
155. Picken; Corporal 1860 Sergeant 1864
156. Picken; Private James 1864 Corporal 1866
157. Picken; Private R 1862 (1)
158. Picken; Private Robert 1897 (2)
159. Picken; Private W 1861 Corporal 1865
160. Rankine; Private S 1905
161. Rankine; Private Thomas 1901
162. Ravey; Private J 1905
163. Rennie; Private J 1880
164. Robertson; Private J E 1883
165. Ross; Private W 1905
166. Scott; Corporal 1860
167. Scott; Private A 1901
168. Scott; Private W 1905
169. Sloan; Private 1896
170. Smyllie; Private T 1905 (1)
171. Smyllie; Private T McD 1905 (2)
172. Stewart; Private P 1883
173. Stewart; Private Thomas 1861 Sergeant 1864
174. Stodart; Private J 1865
175. Tait; Private H 1905
176. Taylor; Private A Mc. 1893
177. Topping; Private T 1901
178. Varney; Private 1905
179. Vernon; Private H 1906
180. Watson; Corporal W 1905
181. Wilson; Private R 1901 Creetown Section

SECTION 3 - MEMBERSHIP OF 1896

Reg No.	Rank	No.	Name	Occupation	Address	Date of enrolment
1781	Captain	1	McPhater, Angus	Confectioner	Newton Stewart	6.4.1887
	Lieutenant	2	Kelly, W.M	Solicitor	..	23.6.1888
	Lieutenant	3	McLean, C A	Banker	Wigtown	13.1.1896
	Chaplain	4	Inglis, J McD	Minister	Newton Stewart	30.5.1891
68	Colour-Sgt	5	Anderson, J	Cooper	..	22.2.1870
393	..	6	Peattie, G R	Clothier	..	4.2.1879
69	Sergeant	7	Thorburn, J	Cabinetmaker	..	22.2.1870
247	..	8	Agnew, R	Joiner	..	12.2.1877
392	..	9	McDonald, Angus	Joiner	..	4.2.1879
479	..	10	Love, W	Mason	Kirkcowan	14.6.1879
1004	..	11	Malcolm, J	Weaver	Minnigaff	22.5.1882
32	Corporal	12	Agnew, J	Farmer	Barlachlin	15.3.1865
196	..	13	Campbell, W	Railway Porter	Newton Stewart	2.3.1876
248	..	14	Irving, J	Labourer	..	12.2.1877
543	..	15	Murchie, J	Mason	..	2.2.1880
1587	Corporal	16	Milroy, W	Painter	Newton Stewart	13.1.1886
5016	..	17	McAlpine, J P	Teacher	Wigtown	9.2.1891
5017	..	18	Coupland, G	Accountant	..	9.2.1891
5043	..	19	McCreadie, J P	Painter	..	3.3.1891
	..	20	Mercer, W	Plumber	Newton Stewart	2.4.1894
7357	Bugler	21	Harley, W	Tailor	..	5.2.1894
7358	..	22	McDavid, C	Joiner	..	5.2.1894
5026	Private	23	Agnew, D	Tailor	Wigtown	9.2.1891
7481	..	24	Birrell, P	Fisherman	Creetown	4.2.1895
7691	..	25	Black, P	Joiner	Wigtown	25.2.1896
7360	..	26	Brydon, J	Carter	Minnigaff	5.2.1894
7650	..	27	Callendar, G	Clerk	Newton Stewart	14.2.1896
7201	..	28	Cameron, A	Sawyer	Minnigaff	1.2.1893
7685	..	29	Campbell, R	Joiner	Kirkinner	25.2.1896
	..	30	Carmont, W	Shoemaker	Newton Stewart	25.2.1896
6044	..	31	Clanachan, J	Miller	..	21.1.1892
7652	..	32	Clanachan, W	Joiner	..	14.2.1896
	..	33	Crawford, W	Gardener	Minnigaff	1.4.1893
637	..	34	Crozier, J	Tailor	Kirkcowan	7.5.1880
7692	..	35	Cullen, J	Clerk	Wigtown	31.3.1896
1011	..	36	Davidson, J.L	Ironmonger	Newton Stewart	29.5.1882
7690	..	37	Drynan, J	Joiner	Wigtown	25.2.1896
1579	..	38	Drysdale, W	Cycle Agent	Newton Stewart	13.1.1886
7352	..	39	Erskine, W	Blacksmith	Minnigaff	5.2.1894
7339	..	40	Ewart, W	Tailor	Wigtown	27.1.1894
7475	..	41	Finninghame, W	Ironmonger	Newton Stewart	4.2.1895
7349	..	42	Forsyth, J	Bank Clerk	..	5.2.1894
7476	..	43	Forsyth, J	Ironmonger	..	4.2.1895
6088	Private	44	Forsyth, W	Joiner	Newton Stewart	15.2.1892
7654	..	45	Frazer, J	Upholsterer	..	17.2.1896
2087	..	46	Gordon, J.D	Saddler	..	5.3.1890
6046	..	47	Gouldson, G.H	Printer	..	20.1.1892
7353	..	48	Hannah, J	Saddler	..	5.2.1894
5000	..	49	Hawthorne, J	Clerk	Wigtown	9.2.1892
7686	..	50	Hope, G	Clerk	..	25.2.1896
1399	..	51	Hunter, C	Photographer	Newton Stewart	14.1.1885
6042	..	52	Hunter, W	Printer	..	21.1.1892
7571	..	53	Hyslop, R	Mechanic	Castle Douglas	5.7.1895
7611	..	54	Hyslop, T	Labourer	Newton Stewart	17.1.1896
	..	55	Irving, J	Shoemaker	Kirkcowan	13.4.1892
1841	..	56	Irving, W. C	Compositor	Newton Stewart	18.1.1888
7684	..	57	Jones, A	Carter	Whauphill	25.2.1896
7361	..	58	Kelly, J	Turner	Minnigaff	5.2.1894
7570	..	59	Kirk, W	Shepherd	Creetown	5.7.1895
7356	..	60	Laird, H	Joiner	Minnigaff	5.2.1894
7202	..	61	Lavery, W	Weaver	Newton Stewart	1.2.1893
1851	..	62	Love, J	Joiner	..	16.3.1888
471	..	63	Millar, J	Baker	Kirkcowan	14.6.1879
7651	..	64	Moffat, G	Plumber	Newton Stewart	14.2.1896

Reg No.	Rank	No.	Name	Occupation	Address	Date of enrolment
5014	Private	65	Moffat, J	Plumber	Newton Stewart	7.2.1891
5024	..	66	Moore, J	Tailor	Wigtown	9.2.1891
7336	..	67	Moore, T	Tailor	..	27.1.1894
7195	..	68	Morton, J	Miller	Newton Stewart	25.1.1893
7479	..	69	Morton, W	Druggist	..	4.2.1895
6041	..	70	Myles, W	Baker	..	20.1.1892
7653	..	71	McAllister, C	Mason	..	17.2.1896
2089	..	72	McAllister, J	Mason	..	5.3.1890
2084	..	73	McAllister, J	Labourer	..	1.2.1890
7477	..	74	McConchie, J	Clerk	..	4.2.1895
1842	..	75	McCreadie, A	Mason	..	18.1.1888
7478	..	76	McCreadie, D	Labourer	Minnigaff	4.2.1895
1104	..	77	McCreadie, W	Blacksmith	Newton Stewart	25.1.1883
716	..	78	McDavid, H	Tailor	..	3.2.1881
3093	..	79	McDavid, J	Student	..	2.4.1890
7606	..	80	McDonald, J	Mason	..	13.1.1896
7609	..	81	McDonald, W	Cabinetmaker	..	17.1.1896
7337	..	82	McKenzie,J	Coachbuilder	Wigtown	27.1.1894
5006	..	83	McKie, G	Clerk	..	7.2.1891
7615	..	84	McKie, S	Joiner	Newton Stewart	29.1.1896
7340	..	85	McKinnell, J.A	Agent	Wigtown	27.1.1894
7343	..	86	McMillan, J	Watchmaker	..	27.1.1894
7341	..	87	McMurray, J	Law Clerk	..	27.1.1894
7687	..	88	McMurray, T	Clerk	..	25.2.1896
7682	..	89	McNeil, A	Post Office	Kirkinner	24.3.1896
7612	..	90	McRae, W	Plumber	Newton Stewart	20.1.1896
7335	..	91	McTier, P. J	Law Clerk	Wigtown	27.1.1894
7683	..	92	Paton, R.C	Law Clerk	..	24.3.1896
7655	..	93	Peattie, G	Tailor	Newton Stewart	17.2.1896
	..	94	Priestley, Peter	Postman	..	1.4.1893
7194	..	95	Purdie, J	Tanner	..	25.1.1893
6087	..	96	Robertson, J	Merchant	..	21.1.1892
7608	..	97	Robertson, W	Publican	..	17.1.1896
5023	..	98	Russell, A	Farmer	Wigtown	9.2.1891
1452	..	99	Russell, J	Farmer	Kirkinner	11.3.1885
7616	..	100	Russell, R	Joiner	..	30.1.1896
2093	..	101	Scott, J	Labourer	Newton Stewart	5.3.1890
7348	..	102	Scott, J	Millwright	Minnigaff	5.2.1894
7689	..	103	Smith, J	Farm Servant	Wigtown	25.2.1896
7197	..	104	Steven, A	Watchmaker	Newton Stewart	1.2.1893
7362	..	105	Tear, P.E	Law Clerk	..	5.2.1894
7613	..	106	Thompson, J	Farm Servant	Minnigaff	20.1.1896
7688	..	107	Thompson, J	Mason	Kirkinner	25.2.1896
7480	..	108	Vernon, E	Plumber	Newton Stewart	4.2.1895
1639	..	109	Vernon, J	Upholsterer	..	14.4.1886
1845	..	110	Vernon, W	Carver	..	18.1.1888
7193	..	111	Walker, W	Saddler	..	25.1.1893
	..	112	Wallace, G	Draper	..	30.4.1894
	..	113	Wilson, H.B	Schoolmaster	Kirkinner	18.5.1892
7614	..	114	Wilson, W	Joiner	Minnigaff	20.1.1896

WHITHORN
4th Wigtown Rifle Volunteers.

SECTION 1 - OFFICERS.

1. Drew; James Ensign 11.4.1860-1870
2. Hughan; P.H. Ensign. 1870 - Until Corps disbanded in 1874
3. Stewart; Hugh D. Lieutenant 11.4.1860 - Until Corps disbanded in 1874. Tonderghie.

SECTION 2 - RANK & FILE.

1. Candlish; Sergeant 1861
2. Connel; Sergeant Stair 1862
3. Dickie-Dickey; Private H 1866
4. Dickie; Private R 1865
5. Gibb; Private J 1861
6. Halliday; Private 1866
7. Hewitson; Private 1866
8. Hughan; Private P.H. 1860. Corporal 1863. Sergeant 1864. Commissioned as Ensign in 1870.
9. Jibb; Private Joseph 1862 Corporal 1866
10. Limond; Sergeant 1861
11. Mathews; Private J 1866
12. McAdam; Private J 1866
13. McConnel; Corporal J 1861 Sergeant 1866 (1)
14. McConnel; Private J.A 1865 (2)
15. McGaa; Private William 1862
16. McNaught; Private W 1861
17. Rae; Private Thomas 1862 Corporal 1866
18. Webster; Private 1866
19. Wigham; Sergeant 1864
20. Young; Private James 1862 Sergeant 1863

DRUMMORE -
5th Wigtown Rifle Volunteers.

SECTION 1 - OFFICERS.

1. Anderson; Ensign 23.11.1860 - until the Corps disbanded in 1866
2. Watson; Lieutenant 23.11.1860 - until the Corps disbanded in 1866.

SECTION 2 - RANK & FILE.

1. Bickford; Private John 1861
2. Hutchinson; Private James 1861
3. McBride; Private John 1861
4. McClurg - McLurg; Private John 1861
5. McCosh; Sergeant 1861 (1)
6. McCosh; Private Peter 1861 (2)
7. McCulloch; Private J 1861
8. McCulloch; Sergeant S 1861 (1)
9. McCulloch; Private S 1862 (2)
10. McCulloch; Private W 1861
11. McDouall; Private 1860 House of Logan. Retired Colonel of Household Troop.
12. McGaa - McGaw; Private William 1863
13. McGavin; Private William 1863
14. McMillan; Corporal 1864
15. Watson; Private William 1863

The following is a list of Galloway Artillery Volunteers who feature in this completed history or who came to notice during the course of research:-

KIRKCUDBRIGHT-
Artillery Volunteer Corps.

OFFICERS.

1. Brown; Captain A 1905
2. Campbell; Lieutenant T 1877 Captain 1881 Major 1890
3. Grierson; Lieutenant John 1860
4. McConchie; Lieutenant Robert 1881 Quartermaster and Hon. Major 1905
5. McLaren; Captain 1877
6. Nicholson; Captain W 1905
7. Shand; Captain John 1860
8. Urquhart; Captain A. J. 1877

RANK & FILE

9. Anderson; Gunner J. 1905
10. Baillie; Gunner J. 1905
11. Bradshaw; Sergeant J. G. 1905
12. Burns; Gunner J. 1905
13. Cairns; Gunner W 1860
14. Campbell; Gunner 1891
15. Carnihan; Sergeant 1860
16. Carnochan; Gunner D. 1905
17. Carter; Bombardier 1865 (1)
18. Carter; Gunner 1882 (2)
19. Clacherty; Gunner R 1905
20. Clark; Gunner 1902
21. Connell; Gunner W 1860
22. Cruickshanks; Gunner W 1907
23. Dalziel; Gunner F 1905
24. Davidson; Sergeant D.J 1905
25. Devlin; Gunner Charles 1899
26. Dorrance; Gunner. 1891.
27.Douglas; Gunner S. 1860.
28. Duff; Gunner J. 1863.
29. Fairweather; Gunner H. 1860.
30. Fisher; Gunner R. 1860.
31. Gordon; Gunner John.1860. (1)
32. Gordon; Gunner John. 1860. (2)
33. Hair; Gunner D. 1905.
34. Hannah; Gunner John. 1863.
35. Hannay; Gunner. 1865. (1)
36. Hannay; Gunner W. 1905. (2)
37. Haugh; Gunner D.M. 1905.
38. Henney; Sergeant H. 1905.
39. Henney; Sergeant P. 1907.
40. Hughan; Gunner R. 1905.
41. Hughan; Gunner John 1905
42. Hunter; Gunner 1865
43. Jardine; Gunner W 1905
44. Kenny; Gunner D 1905
45. Kimm; Sergeant R 1902
46. Laidlaw; Gunner 1907
47. Leckie; Gunner R 1905
48. Little; Gunner G 1905
49. Little; Corporal R 1865
50. Little; Gunner W 1860
51. Maxwell; Gunner W 1905
52. Middleton; Corporal 1891
53. McCoull; Corporal 1891

54. McCoull; Sergeant 1882
55. McCoull; Gunner P 1905
56. McCoull; Gunner T 1905
57. McCoull; Gunner W 1905
58. McGhie; Gunner D 1905
59. MacKenzie; Sergeant W 1905
60. McKie; Gunner James 1905
61. McLachlan; Gunner J 1905
62. McMillan; Gunner N.C 1905
63. MacMurray; Gunner James 1877
64. McWhae; Gunner J 1860
65. Nicholson; Gunner J 1860
66. Patterson; Sergeant 1877 (1)
67. Paterson; Corporal 1882 (2)
68. Paterson; Gunner 1891 (3)
69. Payne; Gunner W 1905
70. Rae; Gunner David 1863
71. Rae; Gunner J 1860
72. Rankine; Gunner A 1860
73. Richardson; Gunner J 1905
74. Richardson; Sergeant W 1901
75. Rigg; Sergeant William 1860
76. Ritchie; Gunner J.G 1860 Corporal 1863.
77. Seggie; Gunner 1905
78. Shields; Corporal D 1905
79. Shields; Gunner M 1860
80. Sibbald; Gunner R 1860
81. Slater; Gunner J 1881 Sergeant 1899
82. Strang; Gunner R 1905
83. Stratton; Gunner A 1860
84. Stevenson; Gunner J 1860
85. Thompson; Gunner J 1860
86. Welsh; Gunner W 1862

STRANRAER -
Artillery Volunteer Corps.

OFFICERS

1. Campbell; Lieutenant John 9.2.1860
2. Dalrymple; Viscount Captain 9.2.1860
3. Dornan; Lieutenant James 1881
4. Dunsmore; Lieutenant William 1881
5. Guthrie; 2nd Lieutenant Alexander 9.2.1860
6. Harper; Surgeon Lieutenant 1901
7. Machray; Lieutenant 1899 A Doctor
8. McGibbon; Captain William 1881
9. Torrance; Lieutenant James 1881
10. Orgill; Dr. John Hon. Surgeon 9.2.1860

RANK & FILE.

11. Galloway; Gunner T 1899
12. Murray; Bombardier W 1882
13. McHaffie; Sergeant 1895 Armourer Sergeant 1905
14. Torrance; Bombardier 1891

PORTPATRICK -
Artillery Volunteer Corps

OFFICERS

1. Gordon; Lieutenant J 1892 Captain 1894
2. McClymont; Lieutenant Alexander 1881
3. Robertson; Surgeon Lieutenant 1863 Still serving in 1901

RANK & FILE

4. Best; Gunner H 1899
5. Biggam; Corporal J 1865
6. Bruce; Bombardier A 1877
7. Cameron; Gunner J 1899
8. Campbell; Gunner 1877
9. Douglas; Gunner 1891
10. Drynan; Gunner J 1899
11. Durham; Gunner 1891
12. Galloway; Gunner T 1899
13. Gray; Gunner T 1865
14. Haining; Sergeant Major 1865
15. Hale; Gunner 1891
16. Lees; Gunner 1891 Sergeant 1901
17. Logan; Gunner J 1899
18. Mills; Gunner A 1899
19. Monk; Gunner W 1899
20. Munday; Sergeant Major 1899 (Royal Artillery Instructor)
21. McColm; Gunner A 1899
22. McCormick; Gunner 1901
23. McCracken; Gunner J 1899
24. McDouall - McDowall; Sergeant J 1865 Sergeant Major 1877 (1)
25. McDouall; Gunner 1901 (2)
26. McNeil; Gunner G 1899
27. McNeil; Gunner J 1899
28. McNeil; Gunner M 1899
29. McQueen; Sergeant 1892
30. Rose; Gunner G 1899
31. Shanks; Gunner J 1865
32. Smith; Gunner G 1865
33. Thompson; Sergeant J 1899
34. Thorburn; Gunner 1901
35. Torbett; Gunner 1892 Sergeant 1907

SANDHEAD -
Artillery Volunteer Corps.

OFFICERS.

1. Cochrane - Cockran; Lieutenant William 1867
2. Frederick; 2nd Lieutenant Thomas 1867
3. Maitland; Captain John 1867
4. Milroy; Lieutenant John 1881
5. McCaig; Lieutenant 1889
6. McNeillie; Lieutenant Alex. 1881

RANK& FILE

7. Herries; Gunner R 1899.

APPENDIX 3
THE MUSTER ROLL FOR 'D' COMPANY - NEWTON STEWART 1860 -1908
WITH ADDITIONAL ENTRIES FOR 5th BATTALION KOSB UP TO 1914

During the compilation of the information contained within this book the original Muster Roll for Newton Stewart - 'D' Company was discovered. To our knowledge this is the only original roll for the Galloway Rifle Volunteers in existence. Because of the incredible amount of personal detail relating to each man, we have decided to recreate it as close to its original form as possible.

The Roll is a handwritten document. Each record extends across two pages. Unfortunately the very first page is missing which in the following transcription is indicate by ??? marks. It is evident throughout the document that several different hands have been responsible for the recording of the information. This would also account for the different styles and emphasis. For example residences and work places were sometimes recorded in great detail whilst at other times a cursory note was deemed sufficient. In 1908 the recording of the chest measurement gave way to the man's religion. Nevertheless, the amount of information is such that it can be of great use to all of those interested in military or social history.

The original document does in some instances contain other minor entries not reproduced through lack of space, the publishers have therefore agreed to make it available for closer inspection on application to their Wigtown office.

Reg No	Coy	Enrolled	Oath	Surname	Christian	Chest	Height	Age	Occupation	Residence	Remarks
1	3rd	?	?	Stewart	Heugh	?	?	?	?	Newton Stewart	Resigned
2	?	?	?	?	?	?	?	?	?	::	::
3	?	?	?	Picken	Robert	?	?	?	?	Barnkirk	Dead
4	?	?	?	?	?	?	?	?	?	::	Resigned
5	?	?	?	Howetson	Joseph	?	?	?	?	Baltersan	Res. March 1870
6	?	?	?	Stewart	Thomas	?	?	?	?	Newton Stewart	June 1873
7	?	?	?	Hinds	James	?	?	?	?	::	Jan 1872
8	?	?	?	?	?	?	?	?	?	::	::
9	?	?	?	?	?	?	?	?	?	::	::
10	?	?	?	?	?	?	?	?	?	Park	Dis. June 1868
11	?	?	?	Rae	John	?	?	?	?	Carsewalloch	Resigned
12	?	?	?	McConchie	?	?	?	?	?	Newton Stewart	::
13	?	?	?	?	?	?	?	?	?	Minigaff	::
14	?	?	?	?	?	?	?	?	?	::	::
15	?	?	?	?	?	?	?	?	?	Newton Stewart	::
16	?	?	?	?	?	?	?	?	?	Newton Stewart	Jan 1874
17	?	?	?	McConchie	?	?	?	?	?	?	::
18	?	?	?	?	?	?	?	?	?	Newton Stewart	::
19	?	?	?	Moffat	George C	?	?	?	?	::	::
20	?	?	?	?	?	?	?	?	?	::	April 1873
21	?	?	?	Picken	William	?	?	?	?	Barnkirk	::
22	?	?	?	McConchie	?	?	?	?	?	Crows	June 1870
23	?	?	?	?	?	?	?	?	?	Newton Stewart	::
24	?	?	?	?	?	?	?	?	?	Muckle Carse	Dead July '67
25	?	?	?	?	?	?	?	?	?	Newton Stewart	Resigned
26	?	?	?	?	?	?	?	?	?	::	Dead 1866
27	?	?	?	?	?	?	?	?	?	Minigaff	Resigned
28	?	?	?	?	?	?	?	?	?	Newton Stewart	Dis. July 1868
29	?	?	?	?	?	?	?	?	?	::	Resigned
30	?	?	?	Wilson	John	?	?	?	?	Kirk	April 1873
31	?	?	?	?	?	?	?	?	?	Newton Stewart	::
32	?	June '60	27/6/60	Welsh	Joseph	?	5.8"	?	Flesher	::	::
33	::	::	::	Broadfoot	Andrew	?	5.8"	?	Joiner	::	::
34	::	Sept '60	6/9/60	Blair	E. Stopford	?	5.7"	?	Gentleman	Penningham House	::
35	::	::	::	Dempster	William	?	5.10"	?	Publican	Newton Stewart	Dead 1866
36	::	::	::	Erskine	James	?	5.8"	?	Gun Maker	::	Dis. July 1868
37	::	::	::	Douglas	Robert	?	5.7"	?	Farmer	::	Resigned
38	::	::	::	Robertson	John	?	5.6"	?	Painter	::	June 1870
39	::	::	::	Allan	Thomas G.	?	5.7"	?	Merchant	::	Feb 1870
40	::	::	::	McDowall	Samuel	?	5.6"	?	Draper	::	Dead 1865

Reg No	Coy	Enrolled	Oath	Surname	Christian	Chest	Height	Age	Occupation	Residence	Remarks
41				Moffat	Andrew		5.6"	?	Plumber		Res. April 1870
42				Fraser	Alexander		5.6"	?	Clerk		
43				Cuthbertson	Alexander		5.9"	?	Carrier		July 1872
44				Patterson	George		5.6"	?	Tailor		
45				Moore	James		5.7"	?	Surgeon		Dec1885(over 50)
46				Thorburn	William		5.8"	28	Cabinetmaker		Dis. July 1868
47				McMorran	Thomas		5.8"	?	Draper		Resigned
48				McCouchie	James T.		5.9"	?	Farmer	Mains of Penningham	
49				Kennedy	Alexander		5.7"	?	Mason	Newton Stewart	
50				Thomson	John		5.8"	?	Publican		
51				McGingham	Andrew		5.9"	?	Grocer		March 1876
52		Aug '61	23/8/61	Fraser	John		5.6"	?	Clerk		
53				Muscrope	James		5.7"	?	Clerk		
54				Moore	Thomas		5.6"	?	Draper		Dead 3rd Jan 1870
55				Cuthbertson	Andrew		5.8"	?	Farmer		Resigned
56				Hinds	James		5.7"	?	Painter		
57				Reid	William		5.8"	?	Grocer		
58		July '62	20/7/62	Picken	James D.		5.8"	?	Merchant	Minigaff	Died 22nd May 1874
59				Muscrop	James		5.6"	?	Clerk	Newton Stewart	Resigned
60				Dursie?	James		5.8"	?	Clerk		
61				Milsay	Thomas		5.8"	?	Teacher		
62				Blain	Andrew		5.6"	?	Labourer		
63		Aug '61	26/8/61	Agnew	William		5.8"	18	Mason	Knockbrex	5th Sept 1883
64				Swan	John		5.8"	?	Farmer	Merton Hall	April 1869
65		Mar '64	25/3/64	Picken	Robert		5.10"	?	Farmer	Barnkirk	20th May 1882
66				Agnew	James		5.9"	?	Mason	Knockbrex	Dec 1880
67				McClymont	Gilbert		5.8"	?	Farmer	Benfield	May 1872
68				Mackie	Robert		5.8"	?	Labourer	Newton Stewart	
69				McGuffog	John		5.7"	?	Clerk		Jan 1868
70				McKenzie	John		5.8"	?	Blacksmith	Carse End	
71				McClymont	Robert		5.7"	?	Farmer	Barraer	June 1870
72				McGill	John		5.7"	?	Farmer	Boreland	March 1874
73				McConchie	James		5.7"	?	Clerk	Newton Stewart	Dec 1873
74				McMillan	Alexander		5.8"	?	Farmer	Coule	April 1876
75				McMillan	Robert		5.8"	?	Farmer		June 1869
76				Russell	James		5.7"	?	Joiner	Carse End	June 1870
77				Arthur	David		5.7"	?	Draper	Newton Stewart	June 1867
78				McCulloch	John		5.8"	?	Saddler		
79				Landers?	Charles		5.7"	?	Labourer	Mains of Penninham	
80				Erskine	Charles		5.6"	?	Blacksmith	Minigaff	March 1876

Reg No	Coy	Enrolled	Oath	Surname	Christian	Chest	Height	Age	Occupation	Residence	Remarks
81	..	..	..	Purdie	William		5.6"	?	Farmer	Newton Stewart	15th Feb 1872
82		..	..	Nelson	William		5.7"	?	Saddler		..
83		..	..	Stewart	John		5.7"	?	Gentleman	Corsby West	
84		..	..	Stroyan	David		5.10"	?	Banker	Newton Stewart	.. April 1873
85		..	..	McCreadie	William		5.8"	?	Clerk	..	Dis. Jan 1869
86		..	..	Moffat	James		5.8"	?	Plumber	..	Resigned
87		..	..	McCaull	David		5.8"	?	Saddler		Dead July 1867
88		..	..	McGeogh	James		5.6"	17	Saddler		Res 15th Feb 1883
89		..	..	Firmingham	Edward		5.6"	?	Joiner		March 1870
90		..	..	Vernon	Andrew		5.7"	?	Cabinet Maker		.. Apr 1873
91		..	..	Robertson	L. B.		5.6"	?	Merchant	..	Dis July 1868
92		..	..	Dargie	Robert		5.7"	?	Clerk		Resigned
93		..	..	McAdam	William		5.8"	?	Gardener		
94		April '64	29/4/64	Titwick?	James		5.5"	?	Painter		Dis Jan 1868
95		..	..	McCaull	Hugh		5.8"	?	Draper		Res 10th Mar 1877
96		..	..	Milligan	James		5.8"	?	Clerk	Minigaff	Dis Jan 1868
97		..	..	Gordon	John		5.7"	?	Cabinet Maker	Newton Stewart	Res April 1870
98		..	..	Nimmo	David		5.6"	?	Labourer	..	Sept 1872
99		..	..	Murray	James		5.7"	?	Farmer		Resigned
100		..	..	Taylor	Alexander		5.9"	?	Tailor		.. 10th May 1882
101		..	..	Cubbinon	James		5.6"	?	Gardener		Resigned
102		May '64	5/5/64	Irving	James		5.8"	24	Tailor		.. 1st Feb 1889
103		..	..	Sinclair	William		5.10"	?	Painter		.. Jan 1868
104		..	..	McCartney	William		5.6"	?	Farmer		.. April 1867
105		..	..	Hannah (1st)	William		5.6"	?	Grocer		.. July 1873
106		..	..	Hannah (2nd)	William		5.10"	?	Draper		.. Mar 1871
107		..	..	Dickson	James		5.7"	?	Clerk		.. Jan 1869
108		..	..	McNeillie	John		5.6"	?	Painter		Resigned
109		..	..	Bell	William		5.6"	?	Baker		..
110		..	..	Maxwell	James		5.6"	?	Gardener		..
111		Oct '64	10/10/64	Cuthbertson	George		5.10"	?	Farmer		.. Mar 1876
112		Mar '65	13/3/65	Bain	George		5.6"	?	Teacher		..
113		..	..	Wyllie	George		5.6"	?	Teacher		..
114		..	..	Wilson	Edward		5.6"	?	Cabinet Maker		.. Dec 1876
115		..	..	Galloway	Thomas		5.7"	?	Cabinet Maker		.. June 1870
116		..	..	Walsh	John		5.5"	?	Labourer		.. Jan 1879
117		Dec '64	..	Irving	John		5.7"	?	Tailor		Died 22nd Dec 1876
118		Aug '65	6/8/65	McGregor	David		5.6"	?	Brewer	Minigaff	Resigned
119		..	..	Cooke	James		5.7"	?	Clerk	Newton Stewart	
120		Sept '65	5/9/65	Grant	George		5.6"	?	Joiner		..

Reg No	Coy	Enrolled	Oath	Surname	Christian	Height	Chest	Age	Occupation	Residence	Remarks
121		Mar '65	13/3/65	Fraser	William	5.6"		?	Upholsterer	..	.. Jan 1871
122				Maxwell	William	5.7"		?	Barber	..	Dis April 1868
123		Apr '64	28/4/64	Vernon	Samuel	5.7"		?	Cabinet Maker	..	Res April 1873
124		..	..	Armstrong	William	5.8"		?	Tailor	..	April 1867
125		..	..	Milwain	Richard	5.6"		?	Coachbuilder	..	Dis 28th Sep 1871
126		..	..	Morrow	James	5.7"		?	Farmer	..	Res March 1867
127		..	..	Gordon	Edward	5.7"		?	Watchmaker	..	June 1871
128		..	..	Kendry	William	5.7"		?	Baker	..	Dis March 1869
129		Mar '65	13/3/65	Agnew	John	5.7"		18	Mason	Knock Brex	Res 2nd Sep 1897
130		Sept '65	5/9/65	Agnew	Thomas	5.7"		18	Mason	..	23rd April 1895
131		..	..	McConchie	John	5.7"		?	Clerk	Newton Stewart	Dis Feb 1868
132		..	..	McCulloch	William	5.6"		?	Saddler	..	Feb 1869
133		..	..	McLelland	Anthony	5.6"		?	Shoemaker	..	Res June 1867
134		..	..	Peacock	William	5.10"		?	Cabinetmaker	..	Oct 1875
135		..	..	Frew	William	5.6"		?	Farmer	..	Jul 1877
136		Dec '65	4/12/65	Agnew (2nd)	William	5.5"		?	Coachbuilder	..	Jul 1873
137		..	..	Henry	William	5.10"		?	Teacher	Minigaff	Aug 1876
138		..	..	Cairns	William	5.9"		?	Banker	Gatehouse	Dis June 1868
139		..	..	Bain	Robert	5.6"		?	Tailor	Newton Stewart	Mar 1869
140		..	..	Mitchell	William	5.7"		?	Farmer	..	Res 16th Feb 1872
141		..	..	McWilliam (2nd)	Robert	5.7"		?	Clerk	..	April 1870
142		..	..	Wilson	James	5.6"		?	Painter	Minigaff	Jan 1867
143		..	..	Wilson	William	5.5"		?	Weaver	..	Jan 187?
144		..	..	McAllister	James	5.6"		?	Joiner	..	Dis Dec 1866
145		..	..	McAllister	Joseph	5.6"		?	Mason	Newton Stewart	Res May 1870
146		July '66	2/7/66	Moffat	Robert	5.7"		?	Plumber	..	Mar 1868
147		Mar '66	..	McIlwraith	Peter	5.6"		?	Joiner	..	Aug 1867
148		Jun '66	..	Dickson	William	5.8"		?	Tailor	..	:
149		Mar '66	..	Paterson	George	5.6"		?	Labourer	..	:
150		..	..	Ferguson	William	5.7"		?	Labourer	..	:
151		..	..	Fulton	William	5.6"		?	Baker	..	:
152		..	..	Matthews	William	5.8"		?	Labourer	Minigaff	:
153		..	..	Martin	William	5.8"		?	Labourer	..	:
154		..	..	Martin	Samuel	5.6"		?	Brewer	..	:
155		Mar '67	6/3/67	Griffin	William	5.10"		?	Labourer	..	Dis March 1869
156		..	..	McQueen	James	5.7"		?	Farmer	Little Barr	Res July 1867
157		..	..	Hannah	Robert	5.6"		?	Joiner	Newton Stewart	March 1868
158		..	..	Jameson	Thomas	5.8"		?	Joiner	..	:
159		..	..	Mair	Thomas	5.5"		?	Tailor	..	.. May 1870
160		Apr '67	3/4/67	Gill	John	5.6"		?	Clerk	Gatehouse	.. Jan 1870

Reg No	Coy	Enrolled	Oath	Surname	Christian	Height	Chest	Age	Occupation	Residence	Remarks
161	:		10/4/67	McEwan	Lachlan	5.6"		?	Upholsterer	Newton Stewart	.. Jan 1872
162	:			Baillie	James	5.6"		?	Mason	Minigaff	Dis Feb 1868
163	:			Dunne	Mark	5.6"		?	Farmer	Merton Hall	.. Feb 1869
164	:			Byron	Stewart	5.8"		24	Shoemaker	Newton Stewart	.. ..
165 H/Staff		Nov '64	5/11/64	Clarke	James	5.8"		?	Surgeon	..	Died 9th Dec 1888
166	:	Mar '68	3/3/68	Cowper	William	5.6"		?	Mason	..	January 1873
167	:			Hough	William	5.7"		?	Labourer	Minigaff	Dis June 1868
168	:			Maxwell	Robert	5.6"		?	Labourer	..	Dead 26th June 1869
169	:			Girvan	Thomas	5.5"		?	Joiner	Newton Stewart	Res March 1871
170	:			Martin	Samuel	5.6"		?	Baker	..	Dis 28th Sep 1871
171	:			Armstrong	George	5.6"		?	Mason	..	Res Apr 1870
172	:			Hogg	Andrew	5.7"		?	Turner	Minigaff	.. Jan 1872
173	:			Wallace	James	5.8"		?	Carpenter	..	Dis 4th Feb 1870
174	:			Anderson	William	5.6"		?	Smith	..	Res Mar 1870
175	:			Baillie	Alexander	5.5"		?	Mason	..	21st July 1882
176	:			Robertson	Alwxander	5.8"		?	Labourer	Newton Stewart	Res Mar 1870
177	:			Dunlop	James	5.7"		?	Labourer	..	Dis Mar 1869
178	:			McDowall	Robert	5.7"		?	Mason	..	Res Oct 1874
179	:			McIlwraith	David	5.6"		?	Mason	..	.. Jun 1873
180	:			McKinna	James	5.9"		?	Farmer	..	Dis Jun 1869
181	:			McKie	Peter	5.8"		?	Smith	..	.. May 1869
182	:			McGeoch	Alexander	5.6"		?	Baker	..	Res May 1870
183	:			McDavid	Hugh	5.6"		?	Farmer	..	.. 16th Feb 1872
184	:			Bell	William	5.6"		17	Baker	..	.. 10th Dec 1883
185	:			Murray	Alexander	5.6"		?	Mason	..	January 1873
186	:			Bell	David	5.8"		?	Labourer	..	Res Mar 1871
187	:			McDowall	Peter	5.6"		?	Joiner	Minigaff	.. Mar 1870
188	:		21/3/68	McMillan (3rd)	Robert	5.8"		?	Farmer	Palgowan	January 1873
189	:			Dodds	Robert	5.7"		?	Schoolmaster	Bargrannon	
190	:			McMillan	Wiliam	5.7"		?	Farmer	Glen Head	April 1873
191	:			McIlwraith	Robert	5.6"		?	Farmer	Bargrannon	January 1873
192	:			McMillan	John	5.7"		?	Farmer	Glen Head	
193	:			McCutcheon	Thomas	5.7"		?	Farmer	Buchan	Res Apr 1870
194	:			Gibson	James	5.8"		?	Farmer	Barwinnock	January 1873
195	:			Findlay	William	5.7"		?	Farmer	Binie More	Res Oct 1870
196	:			Wilson (2nd)	John	5.11"		?	Labourer	Palgowan	January 1873
197	:			Murray	John	5.10"		?	Farmer	Glen Caird	Dead 3rd March 1870
198	:			Findlay	Robert	5.8"		?	Farmer	Binie More	Res Jan 1870
199	:			Blaen	James	5.9"		?	Publican	Bargrannon	.. Aug 1872
200	:			Heron	William	5.6"		?	Labourer	Buchan	Dis Jan 1869

Reg No	Coy	Enrolled	Oath	Surname	Christian	Chest	Height	Age	Occupation	Residence	Remarks
201		::	::	McCracken	William		5.9"	?	Labourer	Bargrannon	Res March 1870
202		::	::	Blaen	John		5.9"	?	Labourer	::	December 1872
203		::	::	Lourie	Hugh		5.7"	?	Cabinet Maker	Newton Stewart	Dis Jan 1869
204			3/3/68	Allison	James		5.7"	?	::	::	Res 16th Feb 1872
205		::	::	Brown	James		5.7"	?	Turner	Minigaff	.. Aug 1869
206		::	::	Agnew	Robert		5.6"	?	Labourer	Newton Stewart	.. Mar 1870
207		::	::	Robertson	James		5.7"	?	Labourer	::	January 1873
208		::	::	Hacket	John		5.6"	?	Baker	::	Res Jul 1877
209		::	::	McDavid	William		5.6"	?	Tailor		.. May 1871
210		::	::	Milroy	James		5.6"	?	Plumber		December 1878
211		::	::	McDowall	John		5.8"	?	Mason		Res Mar 1871
212		::	::	Agnew	George		5.7"	?	Mason		Died 29th June 1871
213		::	::	Hannah	John		5.7"	?	Merchant		Res May 1875
214		::	21/3/68	Bowden	Edward		5.6"	?	Saddler	::	.. Jan 1872
215		::	::	Frew	James		5.5"	?	Tailor		.. Feb 1871
216		Apr '69	6/4/69	French	John		5.7"	?	Farmer	Cordorcan	January 1873
217		::	::	Hinds	Edmund		5.6"	?	Painter	Newton Stewart	Res 14th Feb 1872
218		::	::	McGeoch	John		5.6"	?	Tailor	::	Res Jan 1872
219		Feb 1870	22/2/70	Creadie	William		5.6"	18	Cabinet Maker		.. July 1873
220		::	::	Wilson	Alexander		5.8"	18	Blacksmith	Cree Bridge	.. Apr 1872
221		::	::	Galbraith	John		5.8"	18	House Painter	Minigaff	Feb 1872
222		::	::	Hannah (2nd)	William		5.6"	20	Sadler	Machermore	.. Dec 1872
223		::	::	Nelson	George		5.6"	18	Sadler	Newton Stewart	.. Dec 1872
224		::	::	McKie (1st)	James		5.7"	19	Cabinet Maker	::	January 1874
225		::	::	Smithston	John		5.8"	22	Miner	Blackcraig	Res Apr 1875
226		::	::	Johnston	William		5.10"	18	Polisher	Newton Stewart	April 1873
227/68		::	::	Anderson	James		5.11"	19	Cooper	::	Res 1895
228		::	::	Erskine	William		5.11"	18	Blacksmith	Cree Bridge	.. April 1875
229		::	::	Hannah (4th)	William		5.10"	18	Baker	Newton Stewart	Died 3rd July 1872
230		::	::	Thorburn	James		5.6"	18	Cabinet Maker	::	Res 1895
231		::	::	McKie (2nd)	James		6.00"	24	Flesher	::	November 1874
232		Apr 1870	5/4/70	Welsh	John		5.10"	26	Labourer	Palgowan	January 1873
233		::	::	Robertson	Robert		5.6"	28	Labourer	Newton Stewart	Res June 1871
234		July 1870	9/7/70	McMorran	Alexander		5.7"	18	Draper	::	April 1873
235		::	::	Bryden	Samuel		5.5"	19	Clerk	::	Feb 1872
236		Feb 1871	2/2/71	Thomson	John		5.10"	29	Auctioneer	::	Oct 1874
237		::	::	McDowell	John		5.7"	18	Mason	Cree Bridge	.. May 1876
238		::	13/2/71	Thorburn (2nd)	William		5.6"	18	Labourer	Newton Stewart	January 1873
239		::	::	Christie	Andrew		5.8"	24	Saddler	::	Res May 1871
240		::	::	Kevan	John		5.6"	20	Draper	::	.. 12th Feb 1872

540

Reg No	Coy	Enrolled	Oath	Surname	Christian	Chest	Height	Age	Occupation	Residence	Remarks
241	..		..	Varney	William		5.9"	28	Labourer	..	July 1873
242	..		..	Rennie	William		5.7"	18	Draper	..	12th Feb 1872
243	..		..	McDowell (2nd)	Robert		5.10"	19	Draper		Dec 1874
244	..		..	Houston	Samuel		5.8"	21	Labourer	Minnigaff	Res Jan 1872
245	..		..	Moodie	James		6.1"	22	Mason	Newton Stewart	Dec 1874
246	..		..	Brown	William		5.7"	18	Clerk	..	Dec 1873
247	..		..	Ferguson	John		3.8"	18	Clerk	..	Res July/Dec 1873
248	..		..	Erskine	John		5.10"	19	Ironmonger	Cree Bridge	Feb 6th 1872
249	..		..	Wilson (3rd)	John		5.8"	18	Farmer	Garchew	January 1873
250	..		..	French	James		5.10"	18	Farmer	Cordorcan	..
251	..		..	Graham	William		5.11"	19	Farmer	Balnahoin	..
252	..	Apr 1871	4/4/71	McLaren (1st)	Duncan		5.7"	18	Farmer	House of the Hill	Res 1st June 1886
253/89	..		..	Bell (1st)	John		5.5"	17	Labourer	Newton Stewart	..
254	..		..	McKenna	Peter		5.9"	22	Carpenter	Penninghame House	Jan 1878
255	..	May 1871	2/5/71	McMillan	Thomas		5.7"	18	Clerk	Newton Stewart	December 1873
256	..	Aug 1871	2/8/71	Picken	William		5.9"	25	Farmer	Barn Kirk	Res April 1876
257	..		..	McLaren (2nd)	Duncan		5.6"	35	Farmer	Bargrennan	Jan 1873
258	..	Sep 1871	4/9/71	McDavid	Joseph		5.6"	18	Baker	Newton Stewart	Feb 1877
259/100	..	Jan 1872	22/1/72	MacKie	Robert		5.6"	18	Turner	Minnigaff	Dec 1877
260	..		..	Bell	David		5.8"	24	Labourer	Newton Stewart	Jan 1878
261	..		..	Robertson	Alexander		5.10"	25	Labourer		January 1873
262/99	..		..	Walsh	James		5.4"	18	Labourer		Res 23rd Jan 1882
263	..		..	Stewart	Peter		5.11"	18	Clerk		April 1872
264	..		..	Picken	Thomas		5.10"	18	Clerk		February 1876
265	..		..	Winton	John		5.8"	24	Watchmaker		Res May 1872
266	..	Feb 1872	26/2/72	Ferguson	Peter		5.8"	19	Shop Manager		December 1874
267	..		..	Hamilton	David		5.6"	18	Sadler		Res May 1872
268/104	..		..	McGeoch	William		5.8"	25	Baker		Dec 1880
269	..		..	McMorran	John		5.6"	18	Clerk		April 1875
270	..		..	Jack	William		5.7"	18	Draper		January 1876
271	..		..	Thomson	Neil		5.6"	18	Shoemaker		January 1873
272	..		..	Cave	John		5.5"	18	Baker		Res Mar 1872
273	..		..	Gillison	John		5.10"	18	Draper		Mar 1874
274	..		..	Adams	James		5.7"	18	Brewer		January 1873
275	..		..	Aitken	Thomas		5.8"	23	Farmer	Eldrick	Res 5th July 1878
276	..		..	Cogar	Thomas		5.9"	23	Miner	Black Craig	March 1873
277	..		..	Bell (2nd)	John		5.5"	17	Joiner	Newton Stewart	Res Oct 1873
278	..		..	Gardiner	David		5.5"	16	Cooper	..	May 1874
279	..	July 1872	3/7/72	Ferguson	David		5.10"	22	Draper	..	Jan 1874
280	..	Oct 1872	7/10/72	Ross	William A		5.9"	24	Farmer	Meikle Carse	April 1873

Reg No Coy	Enrolled	Oath	Surname	Christian	Chest	Height	Age	Occupation	Residence	Remarks
281	Feb 1873	24/2/73	Thorburn (2nd)	William		5.10"	19	Clerk	Newton Stewart	Res May 1875
282	..	..	Hannah	John		5.6"	18	Blacksmith	Cree Bridge	June 1873
283/121	May 1873	23/5/73	McNellie	George		5.8"	29	Plumber	Newton Stewart	8th March 1882
284	..	..	Martin	Samuel		5.6"	28	Baker	..	July 1877
285			Adams	James		5.9"	20	Labourer	..	Mar 1874
286	June 1873	18/6/73	Peattie	David		5.8"	23	Clerk	..	February 1880
287	..	..	McFadzean	Andrew		5.8"	17	Clerk	..	March 1876
288	July 1873	8/7/73	Wood	John		5.7"	22	Watchmaker	..	December 1873
289	..		McBratney	John		6.0"	26	Clerk	..	July 1877
290/127	Aug 1873	4/8/73	Robertson	Alexander		5.10"	29	Labourer	..	Res 5th March 1883
291	..	..	Robertson	James		5.8"	26	Clerk	..	March 1878
292	..	..	Thorburn (3rd)	William		5.6"	22	Turner	Minnigaff	March 1876
293	..	..	Cooper	William		5.10"	30	Mason	Newton Stewart	December 1878
294/128	..	..	McDavid (1st)	Hugh		5.9"	24	Skinner	..	30th April 1883
295	..	..	Hyslop	Thomas		5.8"	18	Labourer	..	Res March 1874
296	Jan 1874	29/1/74	Milroy	William		5.10"	30	Labourer	Minnigaff	November 1874
297	..	..	Milroy	Peter		5.7"	19	Ironmonger	Newton Stewart	Res June 1874
298	..	..	McMorran	James		5.10"	18	Clerk	..	November 1877
299	..	..	Hanlin	Samuel		5.6"	18	Joiner	..	Res April 1877
300	..	..	McFee	John		5.5"	17	Joiner	..	December 1878
301	..	..	McDowall	Charles		5.8"	19	Painter	Minnigaff	Res June 1875
302	..	..	Cooper	Thomas		5.9"	35	Labourer	Newton Stewart	Dec 1879
303	..	..	McKie	Joseph		5.7"	18	Joiner	Minnigaff	May 1874
304	..	..	Brown	Robert		5.6"	19	Blacksmith	Newton Stewart	July 1876
305	..	..	Walker	Samuel		5.6"	18	Upholsterer	Minnigaff	February 1876
306	..	..	McLellan	William		5.10"	18	Joiner	Newton Stewart	Res July 1877
307	..	..	Candlish	John		5.8"	17	Mason	..	Feb 1877
308	..	..	McCartney	James		5.9"	17	Farmer	..	..
309	..	..	Lockhart	George		5.6"	19	Painter	..	Oct 1875
310/134	..	..	Scott	Samuel		5.9"	22	Shoemaker	..	Dec 1880
311	..	..	Harding	Thomas		5.6"	17	Painter	..	Mar 1878
312	..	..	McCallum	John		5.7"	18	Draper	..	Jan 1876
313	..	..	McKinna	William		5.7"	19	Joiner	..	June 1874
314	..	..	Bennett	John D		5.6"	22	Printer	..	Died 30th July 1877
315	..	..	Erskine	William		5.8"	18	Grocer	Newton Stewart	July 1877
316	..	..	McDavid	Thomas		5.6"	18	Joiner	..	Res 5th June 1883
317	..	..	Erskine	Robert		5.9"	19	Blacksmith	Minnigaff	Feb 1877
318	..	..	Hannah	John		5.6"	18	Blacksmith	..	March 1876
319	..	..	Houston	Samuel		5.8"	23	Sawyer	..	Res Jan 1875
320	..	..	Broadfoot	Thomas		5.6"	22	Baker	..	June 1875

Reg No	Coy	Enrolled	Oath	Surname	Christian	Chest	Height	Age	Occupation	Residence	Remarks
321	::	::		Laurie	James		5.9"	26	Tanner	Newton Stewart	:: March 1876
322	::	::		Murray	Alexander		5.7"	27	Mason	::	:: June 1874
323	::	Feb 1875	::	Thomson	Neil		5.8"	23	Shoemaker	::	:: Dec 1877
324			15/2/75	Lyall	William		5.7"	19	Saddler	::	:: Dec 1876
325	::	::		Johnston	Henry		5.6"	18	Upholsterer	::	::
326	::	::		McGuffog	Robert		5.6"	17	Currier	::	:: March 1875
327/165	::	::		Irving	Samuel		5.8"	18	Skinner	::	:: 2nd Nov 1881
328	::	::		Gardner	David		5.6"	17	Cooper	::	:: Res Mar 1876
329	::	::		McKenzie	James		5.6"	17	Joiner	::	:: Dec 1879
330				Irving	James		5.7"	18	Skinner	::	:: December 1878
331	::	::		Wade	William		5.8"	19	Tailor	::	:: Res Dec 1877
332	::	::		Crawford	Thomas		5.9"	24	Labourer	::	:: Mar 1876
333	::	::		Stewart	William		5.8"	18	Joiner	Minnigaff	:: Apr 1877
334	::	::		Hinds	Edmund		5.10"	22	Painter	Newton Stewart	:: 12th Jan 1881
335/166				Hughes	Edward		5.10"	28	Labourer	::	:: April 1875
336				Milroy	Joseph		5.6"	18	Plumber	::	:: April 1875
337	::	April 1875	1/4/75	Wilson	David		5.6"	22	Weaver	Minnigaff	:: July 1876
338				Johnston	William		5.9"	24	Polisher	Newton Stewart	:: March 1876
339	::	Mar 1876	2/3/76	McGuffog	Robert	35"	5.7"	18	Skinner	::	Died 8th March 1879
340	::	::		Crossan	William		5.6"	19	Blacksmith	::	:: May 1876
341	::	::		Wright	William		5.7"	18	Cabinet Maker	::	:: Res Dec 1876
342	::	::		Finningham	James		5.7"	18	Flesher	::	:: Apr 1876
343	::	::		Duffie	William		5.6"	19	Labourer	::	:: Dec 1876
344	::	::		Willoughby	Alexander	34"	5.5"	17	Turner	::	:: June 1879
345/195	::	::		Stevenson	George	37"	5.5"	17	Baker	::	:: 1st Dec 1884
346	::	::		McCrindle	Robert	34"	5.7"	17	Clerk	::	:: January 1879
347	::	::		Wade	James	35"	5.7"	17	Shoemaker	::	:: Res July 1880
348	::	::		Simpson	William	35"	5.6"	18	Watchmaker	::	:: January 1879
349	::	::		Hamilton	William	34"	5.8"	17	Draper	::	:: Res Dec 1877
350/196	::	::		Campbell	William	35"	5.7"	18	Labourer	::	:: 18/3/99
351	::	::		Scott	Alexander		5.5"	17	Labourer	::	:: April 1876
352	::	::		Hinds	James	34"	5.5"	17	Painter	::	:: May 1878
353	::	::		Stevenson	John	36"	5.5"	18	Cabinet Maker	::	:: Dec 1877
354	::	::		Carmont	William	34½"	5.6"	18	Shoemaker	::	:: 3rd Nov 1881
355	::	::		Dodds	John	36"	5.7"	22	Skinner	::	:: April 1880
356	::	::		Hanlon	Alexander		5.6"	18	Baker	::	:: Res April 1876
357	::	::		McCreath (1st)	John	36"	5.9"	19	Clerk	::	:: December 1878
358	::	::		Neilson	Cumming	35"	5.6"	18	Draper	::	:: Res Dec 1877
359	::	::		Cave	John	36"	5.8"	21	Baker	::	:: Res July 1877
360	::	::		Erskine	Thomas	34½"	5.6"	18	Gunsmith	::	:: April 1879

Reg No	Coy	Enrolled	Oath	Surname	Christian	Chest	Height	Age	Occupation	Residence	Remarks
361				Martin	John	35"	5.6"	20	Labourer		January 1879
362		..	..	McCreath (2nd)	John	37"	5.7"	22	Ironmonger	..	..
363				Murray	Robert		5.9"	24	Joiner	Minnigaff	Res April 1877
364				Joseph	Robert		5.8"	18	Joiner		.. Dec 1876
365		Mar 1876	21/3/76	Donald	John		5.9½"	24	Saddler	Newton Stewart	..
366		..	..	McMillan	John	38"	5.8"	22	Ironmonger	..	December 1878
367		..	..	Erskine (2nd)	William		5.11"	26	Blacksmith	Minnigaff	Res Feb 1877
368		Feb 1877	14/3/77	Mallinson	Edward	34"	5.6"	18	B Turner?	..	Mar 1879
369/244				Hanlon	John	35"	5.6"	18	Joiner	Penninghame	20th July 1881
370				Sillars	John		5.6"	18	Draper	Minnigaff	Mar 1877
371/245				Thomson	James	33½"	5.7"	17	Baker	Newton Stewart	13th July 1882
372				Sellars	David	34½"	5.4"	17	Draper	Minnigaff	February 1880
373				McBratney	James	35"	5.5"	17	Grocer	..	Res April 1879
374				Thomson (2nd)	James		5.5"	18	Tailor	Newton Stewart	April 1877
375				Kennedy	Robert	37"	5.7"	20	Painter	..	March 1878
376				McLelland	Samuel	38"	5.6"	22	Labourer	Penninghame	May 1878
377/246				McLelland	John	36"	5.8"	19	Labourer	..	26th May 1882
378				Paterson	Robert		5.4"	17	Saddler	Newton Stewart	March 1877
379				Hannah	Alexander	34"	5.6"	21	Saddler	..	April 1880
380				Wilson	Adam		5.6"	17	Labourer	Minnigaff	Res March 1877
381/247				Agnew	Robert	35"	5.5"	17	Labourer	Queen St - Implement Works Knockbrex	Res 15/12/02
382/248			2/4/77	Irving (1st)	John	36"	5.5"	17	Labourer	70 King St, N. S. - Brewery	Dis for non-effic 15/10/97
383		April 1877		McKie	James	38"	5.6"	25	Labourer	Minnigaff	Re March 1879
384/263				Erskine	Robert	38"	5.10"	24	Blacksmith	..	26th Nov 1883
385/264				McFarlane	John	37"	5.7"	32	Upholsterer	Penninghame	15th April 1889
386		May 1877	8/5/77	McLellan	James	38"	5.10"	20	Hewer	..	Dis 17th Oct 1879
387		Feb 1878	4/2/78	Hastings	William	40"	5.10"	24	Flesher	..	Res Dec 1879
388				McDonald	James	36"	5.4"	19	Baker	..	December 1878
389				Sinclair	James	35"	5.4"	18	Painter	..	Res April 1879
390				McDeade	Samuel	36"	5.7"	19	Painter	..	June 18787
391/307				Owen	James	38"	5.9"	24	Painter	..	25th June 1884
392/309				Ferries	David	40"	5.6"	26	Publican	..	8th March 1884
393				Hackett	James	35"	5.8"	23	Tailor	..	June 1879
394/311		Jul 1878	18/7/78	McClymont	John	38"	5.9"	20	Turner	Minnigaff	14th April 1889
395				Wilson	David	40"	5.6"	25	Turner	..	December 1878
396				Gardner	David	36"	5.5"	20	Cooper	Penninghame	May 1879
397				McAllister	John	38"	5.6"	19	Painter	..	Res June 1880
398				Stewart	William	36"	5.7"	22	Cabinet Maker	..	May 1878
399/389		Feb 1879	4/2/79	McCulloch	David	37"	5.10"	18	Joiner	..	23rd Jan 1882
400/390				McAllister	George	34"	5.5"	17	Tailor	..	Dec 1880

Reg No	Coy	Enrolled	Oath	Surname	Christian	Chest	Height	Age	Occupation	Residence	Remarks
401	::	::		Milroy	Robert	35"	5.5"	18	Tailor	::	.. June 1879
402/391	::	::		McDavid	George	34"	5.5"	17	Labourer	::	.. 30th April 1883
403/392	::	::		McDonald	Angus	37"	5.6½"	30	Joiner	Penninghame	Res 20th April 1900
404/393	::	::		Peattie	George R	36"	5.6"	29	Cutter	::	:: ..
405/394	::	::		Cowan	James	34"	5.4½"	18	Joiner	::	..26th May 1883
406/395	::	::		Irving	Thomas	34"	5.5"	17	Tailor	::	2nd March 1881
407/396	::	::		Taylor	Robert	34"	5.4½"	18	Tailor	::	Res 14th Dec 1884
408/397	::	::		Hyslop	James	34½"	5.5"	18	Saddler	::	.. 1st June 1882
409	::	::		Hackett	Henry	33½"	5.6"	17	Tailor	::	.. April 1879
410/398	::	April 1879		McDavid	Samuel	36"	5.8"	19	Painter	::	.. 10th April 1882
411/435	::		2/4/89	Robinson	William	42"	6.0½"	35	Skinner	::	.. 12th July 1881
412/437	::	::		Doherty	Michael	41"	5.8"	20	Labourer	::	.. Dec 1889
413/487	::	::		Law	William	39"	5.7"	18	Carver	::	.. 1st Dec 1880
414	::	June 1879	7/6/79	Milroy	Joseph	37"	5.6"	22	Plumber	::	.. June 1880
415	::			Graham	James	41"	5.10½"	29	Miner	Minnigaff/Blackcraig	.. Dec 1879
416	::	::		Bennie	James	37"	5.10"	20	Miner	::	:: ..
417/461	::	::		McKain	William	37"	5.10½"	20	Teacher	::	.. 3rd Oct 1880
418/462	::	::		Graham	Edward	36"	5.8"	22	Miner	::	.. 14th Apr 1881
419/463	::	::		Borthwick	Hugh	37"	5.9"	22	Miner	::	.. 20th May 1882
420	::	::		Skimming	John	36"	5.9"	24	Miner	::	.. June 1880
421/464	::	::		Smith	John	39"	5.10"	20	Miner	::	.. 3rd Dec 1880
422/465	::	::		McGhie	William	35"	5.7"	19	Miner	::	.. 7th Feb 1882
423	::	::		Rice	James	37"	5.7"	29	Miner	::	.. July 1879
424	::	::		Hicks	Joseph	38"	5.7"	32	Miner	::	.. Dec 1879
425/466	::	::		Graham	Thomas	36"	5.10"	22	Miner	::	.. 26th Nov 1881
426	::	::		McKie	Robert	42"	5.7"	21	Miner	::	.. July 1879
428/467	::		14/6/79	Parker'	William	36"	5.6"	22	Turner	Penninghame	.. 3rd Dec 1884
429/471	::	::		Millar	James	36"	5.7"	26	Baker	Kirkcowan	.. 10th June 1900
430/472	::	::		Millar	John	36"	5.6½"	24	Baker	::	.. 1st Jan 1892
431	::	::		Smith	James	40"	5.7"	21	Mason	::	.. March 1880
432	::	::		Milroy	William	36"	5.6"	23	Tailor	::	.. July 1879
433/473	::	::		Sheridan	Robert	36"	5.7"	18	Tailor	::	.. 11th Dec 1880
434	::	::		Milroy	James	36"	5.8½"	29	Shoemaker	::	.. July 1879
435	::	::		McKinna	James	38"	5.5½"	42	Mason	::	:: ..
436/474	::	::		Rae	William	38"	5.7"	24	Baker	::	.. 5th Dec 1881
437/475	::	::		Chisholm	James	41"	5.7"	34	Blacksmith	::	.. 12th May 1881
438	::	::		Muswell	John	36"	5.6"	31	Postman	::	.. July 1879
439/476	::	::		Irving (2nd)	John	36"	5.9½"	22	Shoemaker	::	.. 10/7/91
440/477	::	::		McKenzie	Alex. Wm.	41"	5.10"	35	Merchant	::	.. 1st Feb 1883
441/478	::	::		Galloway	Robert	34"	5.7"	18	Tailor	::	..20th July 1882

Reg No	Coy	Enrolled	Oath	Surname	Christian	Chest	Height	Age	Occupation	Residence	Remarks
442/479				Love	William	43"	6.4"	20	Mason	..	20/4/1900
443				McWilliam	Samuel	38"	6.2"	34	Merchant	..	July 1879
444/480				Crawford	James	35"	5.7"	22	Tailor	..	15th Jan 1883
445/481				Kidd	George	36"	5.6"	21	Labourer	..	7th April 1882
446/482				Stewart	William	42"	6.0"	32	Joiner	..	9th June 1882
447/483				Girvan	James	35½"	5.4½"	17	Baker	Newton Stewart	17th May 1882
448/538		Feb 1880	2/2/80	Hamilton	David	37"	5.6½"	24	Saddler		14th Dec 1880
449/539				Findlay	Gilbert	36"	5.8"	18	Upholstrer		23rd Mar 1882
450				McLean	Andrew	39"	5.7"	23	Labourer		March 1880
451/560/540				McDavid	Hugh (2nd)	35"	5.5½"	19	Taylor		Res 15th June 1883
452/541				Walsh	Thomas		5.3"	15	Labourer		1/12/87
453/542				Hannah	John	40"	5.6"	24	Blacksmith		19th May 1882
454/543				Murchie	John	38"	5.6½"	23	Mason	Queen St, Newton Stewart	12/4/1905
455/100		Apr 1880	5/4/80	McKie	Robert	36"	5.6"	25	Turner	Minnigaff	12th Apr 1881
456/619				Rennie	James	39"	5.10"	19	Joiner	Newton Stewart	14th Apr 1882
457		May 1880	7/5/80	McCallum	Thomas	36"	6.0"	20	Teacher	Kirkcowan	June 1880
458/636				Crawford	Samuel	38"	5.7"	25	Joiner		20th Apr 1882
459/637				Crozier	John	34"	5.5"	18	Tailor		20/02/01
460/638				Erskine	James	37½"	5.10"	18	Gardner		12th May 1881
461/639				McWhinnie	Andrew	42"	5.9"	21	Labourer		16th Nov 1881
462/640				McNeil	Hugh	39"	5.8"	27	Sawyer?		9th June 1882
463/641				Loagan	James	37"	5.8"	19	Labourer		20th Apr 1882
464				McNally	William	39½"	5.7"	20	Mason		June 1880
713	4th	3/2/81	3/2/81	McKain	James	36"	5.10"	21	Labourer	Newton Stewart	12thMay 1881
714	..			McKie	James	38"	5.8"	21	Tailor		31st May 1882
715	..			Duffie	James	37"	5.6"	19	Labourer		15th Dec 1881
716	..			McDavid	Hugh (3rd)	35"	5.6"	19	Tailor	Agnew Terrace	30th Mar 1908
717	..			Stewart	Peter	39"	6.0"	18	Joiner	Newton Stewart	20th July 1881
718	..	8/2/81	8/2/81	Fairis	George	39"	5.10"	19	Gamekeeper	Minnigaff	6th Mar 1882
719	..			Erskine	Charles	36½"	5.6½"	18	Labourer	Newton Stewart	18th Apr 1881
720	..	8/3/81	8/3/81	McDowall	Anthony	39"	5.9"	18	Labourer	Minnigaff	21st July 1882
721	..	8/3/81	8/3/81	Mackie	John	38"	6.0"	19	Watch Maker	Newton Stewart	4th Apr 1882
		4/4/81		Wade	James		5.9"	22	Shoemaker		18th Apr 1881
823	..		4/4/81	McAllister	George	35"	5.8"	19	Tailor		15th May 1882
824	..			Dodds	John	36"	5.7"	27	Skinner		20th Feb 1883
825	..			Irving	James (2nd)	38"	5.7"	24	Skinner		20th July 1881
826	..	30/4/81	30/4/81	Haigh	Alex.	37"	6.0½"	35	Weaver	Kirkcowan	2nd May 1883
827	..			Brown	William	42"	6.0½"	23	Labourer		1st Apr 1895
828	..			Brown	Samuel	36"	5.6"	18	Labourer		20th Apr 1882
829	..			Crozier	Robert	36"	5.7"	17	Tailor		5th June 1883

Reg No	Coy	Enrolled	Oath	Surname	Christian	Chest	Height	Age	Occupation	Residence	Remarks
830	:	:	:	Henry	Andrew	35"	5.6"	17	Tailor	:	15th May 1882
831	:	:	:	McWilliam	William	36"	5.6"	17	Blacksmith	:	1st Dec 1886
846/1047	:	11/5/81	11/5/81	Willoughby	Alex.	39"	5.8"	22	Skinner	Newton Stewart	21st Nov 1883
905	:	2/2/82	11/2/82	McCartney	Thomas	35"	5.6"	18	Baker	:	5th Feb 1883
906	:	:	:	Law	Thomas	38"	5.6½"	18	Cabinet Maker	:	1st June 1882
907	:	:	:	Priestley	Peter	37"	5.6"	18	Mason	:	1st May 1888
908	:	10/2/82	24/3/82	McCubbin	William	35"	5.6"	17 3/12	Skinner	:	1st Dec 1887
909	:	22/3/82	24/3/82	Wade	James	36"	5.8¼"	23	Shoemaker	:	16th May 1882
985	:	17/5/82	17/5/82	Welsh	Joseph	36"	5.10"	19	Ironmonger	:	15th Mar 1885
986	:	:	:	Gordon	William	34½"	5.9¾"	19	Compositor	:	21st Feb 1884
987	:	:	:	Hunter	John	35½"	5.10¾"	19	Compositor	:	4th Dec 1884
988	:	:	:	Thomson	George	36"	5.9¼"	19	Baker	:	Died 15th Aug 1882
989	:	:	:	Byron	Hugh	41"	5.7½"	20	Blacksmith	:	Res 8th Feb 1884
990	:	:	:	Neilson	Thomas	37"	5.8½"	19	Mason	:	2nd Jan 1886
991	:	:	:	Park	John	34"	5.5"	17	Clerk	:	1st Dec 1886
992	:	19/5/82	19/5/82	Doherty	Francis	39"	5.11"	20	Mason	:	12th May 1885
993	:	:	:	Stewart	Peter	38"	6.1"	19	Joiner	:	25th Jan 1884
994	:	:	:	Dewar	Adam	34"	5.6"	18	Tailor	:	9th Mar 1883
995	:	:	:	Montomery	Peter	35"	5.5½"	18	Clerk	:	1st Dec 1884
996	:	:	:	Erskine	Charles	37"	5.10"	19	Gardener	:	1st Apr 1887
997	:	:	:	Corbett	George	35"	5.6½"	19	Tailor	Minnigaff N/S	31st May 1882
998	:	:	:	Macreadie	Andrew	36"	5.9½"	19	Joiner	Newton Stewart	20th Jan 1886
999	:	:	:	McLaughlan	Hugh	36½"	5.9"	25	Merchant	:	24th Sep 1883
1000	:	:	:	Stroyan	David	38"	5.11"	20	Law Clerk	:	5th May 1883
:	:	:	:	McGuigan	James	37"	6.0"	29	Post Driver	:	Resigned
1001	:	22/5/82	22/5/82	McKeand	James	40"	5.8½"	20	Joiner	:	8th Feb 1884
1002	:	:	:	McNaught	Robert	35"	5.5"	18	Printer	:	11th Dec 1883
1003	:	:	:	Kelly	James	37"	5.9"	17	Mason	:	8th June 1882
1004	:	:	:	Malcolm	John	39"	6.1"	18	Weaver	:	12th Dec 1902
1005	:	:	:	Gordon	James	34"	5.6½"	17	Saddler	:	1st Dec 1887
1006	:	:	:	McIlwraith	Thomas	36"	5.5½"	18	Tailor	:	5th June 1883
1007	:	:	:	Byron	James	37"	5.9"	18	Grocer	:	10th Feb 1885
1008	:	:	:	Irving	James	33"	5.7½"	17	Tailor	:	30th Feb 1886
1009	:	:	:	McCreadie	Thomas	39"	5.9"	21	Joiner	Minnigaff N/S	31st May 1882
:	:	:	:	McIlraith	William	37"	5.5½"	22	Mason	Newton Stewart	8th June 1882
1010	:	29/5/82	29/5/82	Edwards	William	34"	5.7½"	18	Tailor	:	8th June 1882
:	:	:	:	Mills	Fred	33½"	5.7½"	18	Joiner	:	15th June 1882
1011	:	:	:	Davidson	James	36"	5.6"	20	Ironmonger	:	10th Dec 1902
1012	:	:	:	Scott	Peter	35"	5.6"	17	Joiner	:	1st Dec 1888
1013	:	:	:	Vernon	James	36"	5.7"	17	Carver	:	5th June 1883

Reg No	Coy	Enrolled	Oath	Surname	Christian	Chest	Height	Age	Occupation	Residence	Remarks
1014	..			Moffat	Joseph	35"	5.5"	18 8/12	Plumber	..	..25th Jan 1884
1092	..	15/1/83	15/1/83	Rankin	Robert	38"	5.10½"	17	Joiner	..	.. 16th Apr 1883
1093	..	..	..	Maxwell	Thomas	36"	5.5½"	19	Slater		.. 2nd Dec 1885
1094	..	..	..	Cowper	John	38"	5.5"	17 6/12	Mason		.. 1st May 1889
1095	..	..	..	Welsh	John E	36"	5.8"	17	Law Clerk		..20th Mar 1886
1096	..			Macmoran	Thomas G.	33"	5.10½"	18	Banker		6th Jan 1885
1097	..			McCalla	Michael	34"	5.4"	19	Shoemaker		..20th Apr 1886
1098	..			McNairn	Samuel	37"	5.10"	18	Ironmonger		4th Dec 1884
1099	..	18/1/83	25/1/83	Morrison	Henry S.	36"	5.5½"	17	Bank Clerk		..25th Apr 1883
1100	..	22/1/83	..	Garvie	William	33"	5.5"	19	Gardener		..10th May 1884
1101	..	..	..	Shennan	Andrew	34"	5.11"	20	Painter		Discharged 1896
1102	..	25/1/83	25/1/83	McKie	Robert	35"	5.4"	25	Turner	Minnigaff	Res 1st March 1885
1103	..			McGeoch	James	35"	5.7"	18	Saddler	Newton Stewart	..20th Feb 1888
1104	..			McCreadie	William	35"	5.7"	18	Blacksmith		..30th Mar 1908
1105	..			Rennie	James	41"	5.11"	21	Joiner		..2nd Dec 1885
1175	..	2/4/83	4/4/83	Galloway	Robert	35"	5.8"	22	Tailor	Kirkcowan	..2nd June 1884
1176	..	19/4/83	19/4/83	Davidson	James	34"	5.5"	18	Tailor	Newton Stewart	..4th Dec 1884
1261	..	16/4/84	16/4/84	Guthrie	James	37½"	5.8"	17	Mason		Resigned
1262	..			Murphie	Peter	36"	5.7"	18	Baker		..1st Jan 1992
1263	..			Welsh	Alex.	33"	5.7½"	17	Labourer		..1st Dec 1888
1264	..			Blackwood	James	35"	5.6"	17	Plumber		..1st Dec 1887
				Priestly	John	34"	5.5"	17	Tailor		
1265	..	21/1/84	21/1/84	Guthrie	Alex.	35"	5.5"	17	Tailor	Minnigaff	.. 1st Aug 1887
1266	..			Jordon	John	34½"	5.5"	17	Weaver	Newton Stewart	Resigned
1267	..			Campbell	William	35½"	5.6"	17	Taylor		Died 23rd July 1884
1268	..			Kelly	James	36"	5.5"	18	Labourer		Res 2nd Dec 1885
1269	..			Robertson	John	35"	5.5"	18	Painter	Minnigaff	.. 1st Jan 1887
1270	..			Martin	William	35"	5.4"	23	Clerk	Newton Stewart	..9th Feb 1885
1271	..			McMahon	Thomas	34½"	5.5½"	19	Blacksmith		6th Jan 1885
1272	..	19/2/84		Thorburn	Samuel	36"	5.5½"	19	Grocer		..2nd Dec 1885
1273	..			Thorburn	William	35"	5.7"	18	Blacksmith	Minnigaff	1st Jan 1890
1274	..			Walker	James	34½"	5.8"	18	Draper	Newton Stewart	30th Jan 1886
1275	..			Lorimer	William	34½"	5.8½"	18	Upholsterer		16th Feb 1886
1276	..			Cowper	William	34½"	5.5"	17	Mason		1st June 1992
1277	..			McNaught	Robert	36"	5.5½"	19	Painter		2nd Dec 1885
1338	..	1/4/84		Haigh	Alex.	35"	6.0½"	38	Weaver	Kirkcowan	.. 1st May 1888
1339	..	11/4/84	11/4/84	Alexander	William	36"	5.8½"	19	Joiner	..	.. 1st Apr 1887
1340	..	14/4/84	13/4/84	Walsh	Roland	32"	4.9"	13	Labourer	Newton Stewart	.. 1st Dec 1887
1342	..	2/5/84	2/5/84	Kelly	James	38"	5.8"	18	Mason		..9th Apr 1895
1341	..	..	..	Park	William	37"	5.8"	17	Draper	..	..20th Apr 1886

Reg No	Coy	Enrolled	Oath	Surname	Christian	Chest	Height	Age	Occupation	Residence	Remarks
1343	::	::	::	McMillan	Thomas	34"	5.6"	17	Grocer	::	..16th Feb 1886
1407	::	14/1/85	14/1/85	Shedden	David	34"	5.6"	17	Saddler	::	..20th Feb 1888
1405	::	::	::	Park	David	34"	5.5"	17	Draughtsman	::	.. 1st Dec 1888
1399	::	17/1/85	17/1/85	Hunter	Charles	35"	5.9"	19	Photographer	::	..30th Mar 1908
1409	::	17/1/85	17/1/85	Wilson	James	34"	5.9"	17	Tailor	::	.. 1st Mar 1887
1406	::	::	::	Priestly	John	34"	5.7"	17	Tailor	::	.. 1st Jan 1887
1403	::	::	::	McGowan	James	41"	6.1"	22	Mason	::	.. 1st May 1889
1408	::	::	::	Wade	James	38"	5.9"	22	Shoemaker	::	.. 1st Jan 1891
1410	::	::	::	Willoughby	William	36"	5.7"	25	Farmer	::	.. 1st Jan 1890
1401	::	::	::	McCartney	James	35"	5.9"	23	Baker	::	.. 1st Feb 1887
1398	::	::	::	Craig	William	39"	5.7"	24	Sawyer	::	Resigned
1404	::	::	::	McNearnie	Hugh	37"	5.8"	20	Butcher	::	Enlisted 4th Jan 1887
1402	::	::	::	McGill	James	33"	5.4"	17	Ironmonger	::	Res 1st Jan 1887
1400	::	::	::	Irvine	Robert	33"	5.4"	18	Tailor	::	.. 1st Jan 1888
1417	::	21/1/85	21/1/85	McDowall	Anthony	39"	5.9"	23	Sawyer	::	..15th Jan 1892
1413	::	::	::	Hannah	Archibald	34"	5.8½"	17	Ironmonger	::	..20th Feb 1886
1420	::	::	::	Nicolson	Allan	35"	5.9"	17	Chemist	::	..30th Feb 1886
1418	::	::	::	McCartney	John	34"	5.5"	17	Sawyer	::	.. 1st Jan 1887
1416	::	::	::	Hislop	John	34"	5.7½"	17	Gardener	::	.. 1st Jan 1887
1422	::	::	::	Scott	Samuel	40"	5.7½"	30	Shoemaker	::	.. 1st Apr 1887
1414	::	::	::	Haswell	John	39"	5.8"	33	Gardener	::	.. 1st Jan 1887
1411	::	::	::	Gemmel	Alexander	33"	5.6½"	18	Miller	::	..20th Apr 1886
1421	::	::	::	Parker	Benjamin	33½"	5.3"	17	Farmer	::	
1419	::	::	::	McIlwraith	John	33"	5.3"	17	Plumber	::	..20th Jan 1886
1412	::	22/1/85	22/1/85	Hannah	Thomas	35"	5.10"	18	Labourer	::	
1415	::	::	::	Hyslop	John	37"	5.10"	23	Sawyer	::	..22nd Jan 1886
1423	::	27/1/85	27/1/85	Smith	John	36"	5.5½"	19	Skinner	::	..16th May 1885
1425	D	2/2/85	2/2/85	Dodds	John	36"	5.7"	30	Draper?	::	.. 1st Jan 1889
1429	::	3/2/85	3/2/85	Ross	John	36"	5.11"	39	Skinner	::	.. 3rd Feb 1887
1426	::	::	::	McDavid	Hugh	36"	5.9"	33	Draper	::	.. 1st Feb 1887
1424	::	4/2/85	4/2/85	Clark	William	33"	5.7"	17	Baker	::	.. 1st Dec 1888
1430	::	::	::	Thomson	James L.	36"	5.9"	25	Skinner	::	..10 Jan 1891
1428	::	::	::	Purdie	Ephraim	35"	5.5"	20	Printer	::	.. 1st Jan 1891
1427	::	::	::	McIlwraith	David	34"	5.4"	18	Saddler	::	..20th Feb 1886
1449	::	9/2/85	9/2/85	McGeoch	Peter G.	34"	5.6½"	21	Shoemaker	::	..20th Feb 1888
1450	::	::	::	Carmont	William	36"	5.6½"	25	Joiner	::	..10th Apr 1885
1451	::	11/3/85	11/3/85	McClean	William	39"	5.9"	30	Joiner	Causewayend Newton Stewart	.. 1st Dec 1886
1452	::	::	::	Russell	John	37"	5.7"	20	Blacksmith	Kirkinner	Dr.T.X. 12th Apr 1912
1453	::	::	::	Lynch	John	38"	5.9"	19	Police	Causewayend Newton Stewart	Res 1st Dec 1886
1536	::	8/4/85	8/4/85	McFadzean	William	40"	6.1"	23		Newton Stewart	..20th Jan 1886

Reg No	Coy	Enrolled	Oath	Surname	Christian	Chest	Height	Age	Occupation	Residence	Remarks
1537	..	29/4/85	29/4/85	Hodges	Thomas H.	36"	5.7"	20	Schoolmaster	..	.. 20th Feb 1886
1538	..	30/4/85	30/4/85	Anderson	William	36"	5.9"	27	Bookseller	..	.. 1st Jan 1892
	..	13/1/86	13/1/86	Gibson	Alexander	34"	5.7"	19	Carter	..	Resigned
	..	..	..	Hamilton	William	25"	5.10"	25	Draper	..	..
	..	13/1/86	13/1/86	McCartney	Robert	32"	5.4"	17	Printer	..	..
	..	..	..	Murphy	James	34"	5.4"	17	Skinner	..	..
	..	..	..	Paul	John	32"	5.3"	17	Tailor	..	..
1579	..	..	..	Drysdale	William	33"	5.4"	18	Blacksmith	..	Res 16th Apr 1897
	..	..	..	Scott	John	33"	5.4"	17	Sawyer	..	Resigned
	..	..	..	Saggie	William	32"	5.3"	17	Compositer	..	..
1586	..	..	..	McMillan	James	34"	5.4"	17	Tailor	..	Res 1st Jan 1892
1581	..	..	..	McCreadie	William	35"	5.9"	19	Sawyer	..	Res 1st May 1888
	..	..	..	Campbell	Andrew	33"	5.4"	17	Blacksmith	..	Resigned
	..	..	..	McConchie	Thomas	34"	5.4½"	18	Tailor	..	..
1587	..	..	..	Milroy	William	33"	5.5"	18	Painter	..	..
1575	..	20/1/86	20/1/86	Christie	Andrew	36"	5.7"	19	Sawyer	Minigaff	Res 1st Apr 1887
1591	..	..	..	Smith	Walter	34"	5.6"	17	Shepherd	..	left the district
	..	..	..	Gibson	Alexander	36"	5.7"	19	Carter	..	..
1589	..	..	..	Smith	John	37"	5.7"	21	Labourer	..	Res 16th Feb 1888
1590	..	..	..	Smith	Peter	36"	5.6"	19	Labourer	..	.. 1st Dec 1886
1583	..	22/1/86	20/1/86	McGowan	William	35"	5.8"	17	Labourer	..	.. 1st Dec 1888
	..	..	..	Ross	Hugh	37"	5.9"	29	Labourer	..	Resigned
1577	..	25/1/86	25/1/86	Crawford	David	38"	5.10"	23	Brickmaker	Carty	.. 1st Jan 1891
1576	..	..	..	Crawford	William	37"	6.0"	18	Gardener	Minnigaff	.. 1st Feb 1892
1582	..	29/1/86	29/1/86	McEwan	Duncan	37"	5.8"	22	Draper	..	.. 6th Feb 1888
1597	..	13/2/86	13/2/86	Walker	Thomas	36"	5.6"	26	Tailor	..	.. 1st Dec 1887
1592	..	..	..	Stewart	John	39"	6.1"	20	Joiner	Kirkcowan	.. 1st Jan 1887
1584	..	..	..	McWilliam	James	36"	5.8"	22	Joiner	..	.. 1st Dec 1886
1580	..	..	..	Crozier	William	35"	5.10"	18	Tailor	..	.. 1st Apr 1887
1585	..	..	..	Marshall	John	36"	5.6"	18	Joiner	..	.. 1st Apr 1889
	..	..	..	Stewart	James	36"	5.7"	20	Grocer	..	..
1593	..	..	..	Stewart	William	35"	6.1"	21	Joiner	..	Res 1st Mar 1887
1594	..	..	..	Sharpe	William	35"	5.8"	20	Weaver	..	.. 1st Dec 1894
1588	..	..	..	Holland	Thomas	38"	5.8"	26	Labourer	..	Resigned
	..	..	..	Parker	William	36"	5.6½"	28	Tanner	Newton Stewart	.. 1st Mar 1889
1574	..	..	..	Brown	James	36"	5.7"	17	Joiner	Kirkcowan	.. 1st May 1888
1595	..	..	..	Scott	John	35"	5.7"	17	Baker	..	.. 1st Feb 1887
1596	..	..	..	Wade	George	36"	5.7"	18	Labourer	..	.. 1st Feb 1887
1578	..	..	..	Crawford	William(2nd)	36"	5.8"	27	Carter	..	20th Apr 1886
	..	14/4/86	14/4/86	Thorburn	Samuel	36"	5.5½"	20	Grocer	Newton Stewart	.. 1st Jan 1887

Reg No	Coy	Enrolled	Oath	Surname	Christian	Chest	Height	Age	Occupation	Residence	Remarks
1639				Brown	James	38"	5.8½"	21	Upholsterer	:	16th Aug 1897
1705	4	13/4/86	13/4/86	McDavid	Hugh(3rd)	38"	5.6"	25	Tailor	:	1st Aug 1887
1704		19/1/87	19/1/87	Lorimer	William	34½"	5.9"	20	Upholsterer	:	1st Jan 1891
1702				Laurie	Robert	33"	5.5"	17	Tailor	:	1st Dec 1888
1716				Edgar	Thomas	33"	5.5½"	18	Baker	:	1st Dec 1887
1703				Walker	Adam	32"	5.3"	18	Gardner	Minigaff	1st Apr 1890
				Irvine	John	33"	5.4"	17	Painter	Newton Stewart	1st Jan 1888
				Baird	Peter	32"	5.3½"	18	Draper	:	1st Jan 1887
1706		24/1/87	24/1/87	McCartney	Robert	33"	5.4"	18	Compositor	:	1st Dec 1888
1712				Muir	Hugh	33"	5.6"	17	Compositor	:	Resigned
1714				Paul	John	33"	5.3"	18	Tailor	:	1st Dec 1888
1707				McCulloch	Robert	34"	5.8"	18	Druggist	:	6th Feb 1888
1715				Robson	William	35"	5.6½"	21	Tailor	:	1st Aug 1887
1698				Agnew	John	34"	5.9"	17	Tanner	Minigaff	1st Feb 1889
1713				Moffat	Andrew	33"	5.4"	18	Plumber	Newton Stewart	1st May 1890
1701				Edwards	William	33"	5.6½"	24	Tailor	:	5th Feb 1894
1699				Blair	Archibald	34"	5.4"	17	Baker	:	2nd Jan 1888
1700		11/2/87	11/2/87	Dewar	Adam	34"	5.6½"	22	Tailor	:	Died 26th Apr 1889
1711		12/3/87	12/3/87	Morland	James	36"	5.11"	19	Joiner	Kirkcowan	Res 1st Jan 1891
1710				McWilliam	John	36"	5.4½"	20	Blacksmith	:	1st Jan 1891
1709				McWilliam	William	35"	5.8½"	18	Labourer	:	Resigned
1708				McFadzean	William	40"	6.1"	24	Railway Porter	Newton Stewart	1st Jan 1890
1784		26/4/87	26/4/87	Stewart	James	36"	5.4"	20	Grocer	Kirkcowan	1st Jan 1892
1783				Drysdale	Robert	35"	5.5"	18	Tailor	:	1st Jan 1891
1781		6/4/87	6/4/87	McPhater	Angus	36"	5.8"	37	Confectioner	Newton Stewart	4th Mar 1899
1782		21/4/87	21/4/87	Connelly	James	35"	5.6"	20	Baker	Kirkcowan	1st Dec 1887
1842		18/1/88	18/1/88	McCreadie	Andrew	35"	5.6"	18	Mason	Newton Stewart	20th July 1897
1843				Malone	Alexander	34"	5.7"	17½	Labourer	:	1st Feb 1889
1841				Irving	William C	34½"	5.9"	18	Compositor	:	20th Feb 1897
1844				Seggie	William	34"	5.7"	18	Compositor	:	1st Jan 1890
1845				Vernon	William	37"	6.4"	19	Carrier	:	15th Feb 1898
1840				Carter	Martin	34½"	5.8"	18	Ironmonger	:	1st Jan 1990
1839				Campbell	John	34"	5.7"	17	Draper	:	1st Jan 1887
				Bell	David	37"	5.10"	39	Publican	:	
1846		24/1/88	24/1/88	Wade	William	36"	5.8"	18	Draper	:	24th Jan, 1889
1838		1/2/88	1/2/88	Agnew	Thomas	35"	5.9"	17	Farmer	:	1st Mar, 1889
1847				Blackmore	John	34½"	5.9"	18	Plumber	:	1st Jan. 1887
1848				McClymont	Robert	33"	5.6"	17	Draper	:	1st Dec, 1888
1849				Thorburn	William	34"	5.5½"	17	Carter	:	10th Sept, 1891
1850				Thornton	John	35"	6.1"	20	Tailor	:	1st Jan, 1890

Reg No	Coy	Enrolled	Oath	Surname	Christian	Chest	Height	Age	Occupation	Residence	Remarks
1854	..	..	..	Sellers	William	36"	5.8"	22	Tailor	..	1st Feb, 1889
1855	..	..	..	Wilson	James A.	35"	5.9"	20	Tailor	..	1st Dec, 1888
1851	..	16/3/88	16/3/88	Love	John	38"	5.7"	18	Joiner	Kirkcowan	25th Aug, 1897
1852	..	..	..	McNeil	Alexander	38"	5.9"	24	Labourer	..	1st Jan, 1890
1853	..	..	..	Curry	Thomas	34"	5.6½"	17	Draper	..	5th Feb, 1894
1908	..	31/3/88	31/3/88	Byron	James	37"	5.9"	24	Grocer	Newton Stewart	Resigned
1909	..	4/4/88	4/4/88	Paul	William	30"	5.0"	14	Labourer	..	..
1910	..	..	..	Irving	Robert	31"	5.0"	14	Tailor	..	1st Dec, 1893
1911	..	22/6/88	22/6/88	McDavid	William	32"	5.4"	17	Tailor	..	24th Apr, 1898
	..	23/6/88	23/6/88	Kelly	William M	36"	5.9"	24	Lawyer	..	15th Jan, 1907?
	..	..	..	McNearnie	Hugh	36"	5.8"	24		..	3rd Sept, 1897
	..	20/2/92	..	Mckle	Norman J	34"	5.9"	29	Doctor	..	
	..	30/5/91	..	Ingles	M D J				Chaplain	..	
1966	..	12/2/97	12/2/97	McLean	Chas. A	34½"	5.8"	35	Solicitor	Wigtown	30th Apr, 1902
1965	..	23/1/89	23/1/89	Adams	William	35½"	5.5½"	17	Tailor	Newton Stewart	11th Mar, 1895
1961	..	..	..	McCartney	William	35½"	5.6	17	Bobbin Turner		1st Jan, 1890
1962	..	..	..	Purdie	Robert	33½"	5.4"	17	Cabinet Maker		1st Jan, 1890
1963	..	27/1/89	27/1/89	Anderson	John	35"	5.8"	17	Farmer	Casmair Minnigaff	2nd Feb 1890
	..	..	..	Laird	David	36"	5.9"	20	Blacksmith	Minnigaff	
	..	..	..	McGuigan	Andrew	34"	5.6½"	19	Labourer	Newton Stewart	1st Oct, 1896
	..	..	..	Priestly	James	34"	5.9½"	18	Sawyer		Resigned
1964	..	..	..	Sheddon	Robert	34"	5.8"	17	Compositor	.	
1972	..	18/3/89	18/3/89	Callander	Gavan	34"	5.11"	17	Clerk	Minnigaff	3rd Apr, 1895
1973	..	..	..	Landers	William	36"	5.8"	22	Sawyer		2nd Feb, 1890
1971	..	..	..	Fulton	Robert	34"	5.4"	17	Mason	Newton Stewart	23rd Apr, 1895
1970	..	..	..	McConnell	William	35"	5.10"	18	Law Prentice?	..	1st Jan, 1890
1969	..	..	..	McCulloch	John R	35"	5.9"	18	Clerk	..	Resigned
1968	..	..	..	Coutts	James D	34"	5.9½"	20	Clerk	..	1st Apr, 1890
1967	..	..	..	McCrie	Kevin	33"	5.10"	17	Clerk	..	1st Dec, 1893
1976	..	..	..	Edgar	John J	35"	5.5"	17	Clerk	Kirkcowan	1st Jan, 1892
1975	..	..	..	Milroy	James	35"	5.11"	18	Clerk	..	1st Jan, 1890
1974	..	..	..	Jardon	David	34"	5.7"	18	Clerk	Newton Stewart	1st Apr, 1890
1977	..	..	..	Cowper	James	33"	5.5"	17	Clerk	..	1st Dec, 1893
	..	9/4/89	9/4/89	McNearnie	Hugh	37"	5.9"	24	Labourer	..	Resigned
	..	5/3/90	5/3/90	Williamson	Samuel	33½"	5.4"	17	Tailor	..	9th May, 1890
2093	..	..	..	Scott	John	34"	5.5"	18	Labourer	..	15th Apr, 1899
2088	..	..	..	Hughes	Peter	35½"	5.4"	20	Labourer	..	1st May, 1890
2092	..	..	..	Neillie	Oliver	35"	5.5"	23	Sawyer	..	3rd Dec, 1894
2091	..	..	..	Morton	Alex. S	36½"	5.11"	18	Farmer	..	1st Feb, 1890
2087	..	..	..	Gordon	James D	35"	5.8"	24	Saddler	..	15th Apr, 1899

Reg No	Coy	Enrolled	Oath	Surname	Christian	Chest	Height	Age	Occupation	Residence	Remarks
2089	..	..		McAllister	James	34"	5.6"	17	Mason	:	13th Jul, 1897
2090	..	..		McGowan	James	41"	6.1"	27	Mason	:	1st May, 1892
2086	..	..		Cowper	John	36"	5.6"	22	Mason	:	
2078	..	29/1/90	29/1/90	Hendrie	Bryce	36"	5.8"	17	Clerk	:	1st Jan, 1892
2076	..	..		Kelly	John	34"	5.9"	17	Clerk	:	3rd Dec, 1894
2077	..	..		Hendrie	William	36"	5.7"	19	Clerk	:	1st Jan 1892
2075	..	..		Sangster	James	36"	5.8"	18	Baker	:	1st Dec 1893
2079	..	..		Frazer	Robert	34"	5.5"	22	Watchmaker	:	1st Jan, 1891
2074	..	..		Anderson	James	33½"	5.6"	17	Ironmonger	:	1st Jan, 1892
2083	..	1/2/90	1/2/90	Muir	Thomas	33"	5.6"	17	Clerk	:	1st Dec 1893
2082	..	..		Marshall	Alick	33"	5.3"	17	Labourer	:	23rd Apr, 1895
2084	..	..		McAllister	John	34"	5.3½"	17	Labourer	Queens St, Newton Stewart	10th Jan, 1903
2081	..	..		Porter	Robert	34"	5.7"	17	Tailor	Newton Stewart	1st Dec, 1893
2085	..	..		Gordon	James	33"	5.6"	17	Saddler		1st Dec, 1893
2080	..	..		Allan	Fred. W	34"	5.7"	17	Law clerk		1st Jan 1892
3093	..	2/4/90	2/4/90	McDavid	James	34"	5.5"	17	Clerk		15th Mar, 1898
4098	..	28/1/91	28/1/91	MacGowan	William	36"	5.9"	22	Lawyer	Queens Street	
5000	..	..		Bryden	John	34"	5.7"	18	Labourer	Minnigaff	Resigned
5008	..	7/2/91	7/2/91	McFarlane	Thomas	36"	5.10"	19	Carter	Newton Stewart	
5010	..	..		Thompson	Hugh	37½"	5.9"	17	Law appren.	Wigtown…County Buildings	1st Dec, 1895
5004	..	..		Firmie	Matthew	39"	5.8½"	39	Coach builder	Bladnoch	1st Jan, 1892
5012	..	..		Bell	William	38½"	6.0	26	Coach builder		1st Dec 1893
5013	..	..		Tait	James	38½"	5.6"	28	Labourer	Wigtown	23rd Mar, 1894
	..	..		Haugh	Nathan	36"	5.6"	26	Joiner		Resigned
5005	..	..		Skimming	James	36½"	6.2"	20	Labourer		1st Jan, 1892
5009	..	..		Frazer	Gordon	35"	5.8"	117	Clerk		1st May, 1892
5007	..	..		Smith	George	37"	5.10"	23	Painter		23rd Mar, 1894
5006	..	..		McKie	George	34½"	5.7½"	19	Clerk		10th Aug, 1897
5011	..	..		Turner	William	36"	5.8½"	21	Blacksmith		
5014	..	..		Moffat	Joseph	35"	5.6"	28	Plumber	Newton Stewart	10th June, 1902
5020	..	9/2/91	9/2/91	Hawthorn	John	35"	5.8"	24	Clerk	Wigtown	10th Apr, 1899
5022	..	..		Stenhouse	David	36"	6.0"	22	Teacher		
5021	..	..		Nelson	Alexander	35"	5.8"	20	Clerk		1896
5018	..	..		Carroll	John	35"	5.10"	20	Dealer		15th Jan, 1895
5019	..	..		McMurray	John	34½"	5.8"	17	Clerk		3rd Dec, '894
5030	..	..		Dickie	Nathaniel	36"	5.6"	40	Tinsmith		1st May, 1892
5029	..	..		Fitzsimmons	Andrew	35"	5.7½"	35	Labourer		1st Dec 1893
5024	..	..		Moore	John	37"	5.7½"	28	Tailor		12th Feb, 1897
5025	..	..		Park	William	36"	5.8"	30	Tailor		19th Mar, 1894
5026	..	..		Agnew	David	35"	5.6"	32	Tailor		24th May 1899

Reg No	Coy	Enrolled	Oath	Surname	Christian	Chest	Height	Age	Occupation	Residence	Remarks
5014				McKeand	James	39"	5,8½"	29	Joiner	Newton Stewart	1st May 1892
5027				McGinn	Peter	34"	5.7"	22	Carter	Wigtown	19th Mar, 1894
5028				Park	Samuel	36"	5.9"	29	Tailor		15th Feb, 1899
5016				McAlpine	John P	36"	5.10"	23	Teacher		15th Dec 1903
5017				Coupland	Gavin	35"	5.8"	23	Accountant		15th Dec, 1907
5023				Russell	Andrew	35"	5.7"	18	Farmer		
5044		2/3/91	2/3/91	Milroy	William	35"	5.7"	22	Painter	Newton Stewart..10 Princes St.	18th Jan, 1904
5043		3/3/91	3/3/91	McCreadie	John P	37"	5.6"	34	Painter	Wigtown	20th Apr, 1900
5076		8/4/91	8/4/91	Wallace	Robert K	36"	6.0"	24	Grocer	Newton Stewart	1st Jan, 1902
1813		10/1/88	10/1/88	Ferguson	John				Farmer	New Galloway	Transferred to E Coy
6048		28/1/92	28/1/92	Fulton	John	34"	5.6½"	18	Printer	Newton Stewart	Res. 1st Dec, 1893
6046				Gouldson	George H	33"	5.6½"	17	Printer		15th Nov, 1902
6047				Blackwood	Robert	34"	5.7½"	17	Mason		…
6041				Myles	William	35"	5.6"	19	Baker		14th Aug, 1897
6045				McAllister 2Nd	John	35"	5.11"	19	Mason		
6049				Priestly	James	34"	5.10"	21	Labourer		
6043				Taylor	Alexander	32"	5.5"	17	Tailor		22nd Apr, 1895
6087		21/1/92	21/1/92	Robertson	John	35"	5.7"	23	Merchant		
6042		20/1/92	20/1/92	Hunter	William	33"	5.5"	19	Printer	Trans. To Border Rifles Penrith 31st Mar, 1907	
6044		1/2/92	1/2/92	Clanachan	James	34"	5.4"	19	Saw Miller	Creebridge	Res. 20th Sept, 1897
6086		15/2/92	15/2/92	Nicholson	Alan	36"	5.11"	23	Chimnist	Newton Stewart	23rd Apr, 1895
6088		13/4/92	13/4/92	Forsyth	William	36"	5.8"	18	Joiner	Upper Barr	15th Mar, 1898
7057		18/5/92	18/5/92	Irving	John	36"	5.9½"	33	Shoemaker	Kirkcowan	22nd Sept, 1897
7058		25/1/93	25/1/93	Wilson	Hugh Baird	38"	5.8½"	29	Schoolmadter	Kirkinner	4th Jun, 1897
7195				Morton	John	37"	5.10"	18	Merchant	N/Stewart Dismissed for non-efficiency 15th Oct, 1897	
7194				Purdie	John	34"	5.5"	18	Tanner		Res. 2nd June 1897
7193				Walker	William	35"	5.7"	18	Saddler		
7196				Russell	Alexander	35"	5.10"	18	Ironmonger		22nd Apr, 1895
7200		1/2/93	1/2/93	Murphie	Peter	36"	5.8"	27	Baker		20TH Mar, 1894
7198				McCulloch	William	35"	6.0	19	Clerk		15th Mar 1895
7197				Stevens	Amos	34"	5.7"	17	Watchmaker		20th Apr, 1898
7199				Johnston	John	36"	5.9"	18	Clerk		1st Dec 1893
7202				Lavery	William	36"	5.8"	17	?	Minnigaff	2nd Jun 1897
7201				Cameron	Alan	36"	5.9"	18	Sawyer		
7243		1/4/93	1/4/93	Priestley	Peter	36"	5.9"	27	Mason	Penninghame	15th Jun 1903
7242				Crawford	William	37"	5.11	23	Gardener	Minnigaff	15th Dec 1900
		1/6/93	1/6/93	Kelly	James M				Clerk	Penninghame	5th Dec, 1894
7344		27/1/94	27/1/94	Ewart	James	35"	5.7½"	18	Coach turner	Wigtown	Resigned
7345				Fraser	Gordon	35"	5.6"	17	Law Clerk		26th Feb, 1897
7343				McMillan	John	38"	5.11"	28	Watchmaker		Vol. Service Co. S.A.

Reg No	Coy	Enrolled	Oath	Surname	Christian	Chest	Height	Age	Occupation	Residence	Remarks
7342	..	..		Black	Andrew	38"	5.11"	18	Coachbuilder	Bladnoch	Res 11th Mar, 1895
7341	..	..		McMurray	James	37"	5.10"	17	Bank Clerk	Wigtown	10th Aug, 1897
7340	..	..		McKinnell	John	36"	5.9"	28	Commission Agent	..	Dismissed for non-efficiency 15th Oct, 1897
7336	..	..		Moore	Thomas	36"	5.9"	17	Tailor	..	Res. 12th Feb, 1897
7335	..	..		Mactier	Patrick J	36"	5.9"	17	Law Clerk	..	
7339	..	..		Ewart	William	36"	5.8"	20	Tailor		
7334	..	..		Gardener	Samuel	37"	5.9"	18	Tailor		.. 9th Mar, 1897
7338	..	..		McLueen	Robert	36"	5.6½"	18	Law Clerk		.. 13th Mar, 18956
7337	..	5/2/94		Mackenzie	James	39"	5.9"	22	Cabinet Maker		.. 15th Jul, 1897
7348	..	5/2/94		Scott	John	36"	5.7"	18	Millwright	Newton Stewart	.. 11th Aug, 1897
7347	..	..		Wilson	Ronald	37"	5.9"	18	Turner	Minnigaff – Newton Stewart	.. 17th Mar, 1895
7346	..	..		McCreadie	James	35"	5.6"	19	Fitter	..	.. 15th Jul, 1897
7354	..	..		Duff	George	38"	5.6"	26	Carter	..	Resigned
7351	..	..		McGuigan	James	36"	5.10"	18	Driver	Newton Stewart	
7356	..	..		Laird	Hugh	36"	5.7"	20	Joiner	Minnigaff	Trans. L.R.V. 8/2/97
7352	..	..		Erskine	William	36"	5.7"	19	Blacksmith	..	Res. 15th Jan. 1900
7355	..	..		Harley	James	35"	5.6"	18	Fitter	Newton Stewart	.. 18th May, 1895
7353	..	..		Hannah	James	37"	5.8"	18	Saddler	..	.. 20th Sept, 1897
7350	..	..		McKinna	Robert	36"	5.7"	17	Joiner	..	.. 20th Apr, 1895
7349	..	..		Forsyth	James	35"	5.8½"	17	Bank Clerk	Upper Barr – Newton Stewart	.. 28th Feb. 1899
7357	..	..		Harley	William	33"	5.4"	15	—	Newton Stewart	.. 20th May 1897
7358	..	..		McDavid	Chas. W.	32"	5.4½"	15	—	..	.. 2nd June 1897
7359	..	..		McFarlane	Joseph	37"	5.8"	17½	Baker	,,	Resigned
7362	..	..		Lear	Peter	38"	5.10"	18	Law Clerk	..	.. 20th Jan 1898
7361	..	..		Kelly	John	35"	5.10"	18	Turner?	Minnigaff	.. 15th Mar. 1898
7360	..	..		Bryden	John	38"	5.8"	19	Sawyer		.. 20th Mar 1899
7394	..	2/4/94	2/4/94	Mercer	William	40"	5.11"	38	Planer	Newton Stewart	.. 15th Feb 1901
	..	30/5/94	30/5/94	Wallace	George	38"	5.8"	32	Draper		??
7481	..	4/2/95	6/3/95	Berrell	Peter	36"	5.6"	24	Fisherman	Carsluith – Creetown	
7475	..	..		Finningham	William	36"	5.9"	24	Ironmonger	Queen St. – Victoria St	.. 15th Mar. 1898
7476	..	..		Forsyth	John	37"	5.9½"	24	Ironmonger	Victoria St – Victoria St	10th Nov 1900
7477	..	..		McConchie	John	36"	5.7"	18	Clerk	Creebridge – Gazette Office	Trans E Coy 31/3/09
7478	..	..		McCredie	David	36"	5.8"	17½	Labourer	Minnigaff – Kirroughtree	Dismissed 15/10/97
7479	..	..		Morton	William	36"	5.9"	18	Miller	Victoria St. – Victoria St.	Res 15th Dec 1898
7480	..	..		Vernon	Ernest	35"	5.6"	18	Plumber	Ivey Place – Victoria St	.. 15th Mar 1902
7570	..	5/7/95	5/7/95	Kirk	W.	—	—	—	—	—	Trans E Coy 18/11/98
7607	..	13/1/96	13/1/96	Cole	Thomas	36"	5.11"	20	Clerk	85 Queen St – 85 Queen St	Res 16th Apr 1897
7571	..	5/7/95	5/7/95	Hyslop	Robert	—	—	—	—	—	.. 20th Sep 1898
7606	..	13/1/96	13/1/96	McDonald	John	36"	5.6"	18	Mason	Dashwood Sq – Dashwood Square	.. 15th Mar 1899
7610	..	17/1/96	17/1/96	Milne	Alfred	38"	5.5"	20	Cycle Mechanic	Victoria St – Victoria St	

Reg No	Coy	Enrolled	Oath	Surname	Christian	Height	Chest	Age	Occupation	Residence	Remarks
7609	..	..	..	McDonald	William	5.6"	36"	17	Cabinet Maker	..	20th Apr 1899
7611	..	..	..	Hyslop	Thomas	5.6"	35"	20	Labourer	11 Princes St - 11 Princes St	26th Aug 1897
7608	..	20/1/96	..	Robertson	William	5.7"	37"	21	Publican	2 Victoria St - 2 Victoria St	20th Sept 1897
7614	..	20/1/96	20/1/96	Wilson	William	5.6"	36"	18	Joiner	Sawmills - Saw Mills	15th Jan 1898
7613	..	..	..	Thompson	John	5.6"	36"	18	Farm Servant	Machermore - Machermore	15th May 1900
7612	..	..	..	McRae	William	5.9"	39"	24	Plumber	Station Rd - Mr Mercer	15th Dec 1903
7615	..	29/1/96	29/1/96	McKie	Samuel	5.11"	40"	22	Joiner	Kirroughtree	20th Mar 1899
7616	..	30/1/96	30/1/96	Russell	Robert	5.7"	36"	19	Joiner	Clauchrie - Kirkinner	12th Feb 1897
	..	3/2/96	3/2/96	McCulloch	James	5.8"	—	24	Gardener	Cumloden - Cumloden	
7648	..	..	..	Byrne	John	5.8"	—	22	Upholsterer	Station Road - Victoria St	20th May 1897
7649	..	..	..	Sloan	John	5.7"	—	22	Caninet Maker	Station Road - Victoria St	24th Mar 1899
7652	..	14/2/96	14/2/96	Clanachan	William	5.10"	38"	21	Joiner	12 King Street - Victoria St	15th Dec 1898
7651	..	..	..	Moffat	George	5.8"	37"	18	Plumber	Victoria St - Victoria St	28th Jan 1897
7650	..	17/2/96	17/2/96	Callander	Gavin	5.7"	36"	22	Clerk	Railway Station - Railway Station	20th Mar 1900
7655	..	..	..	Peattie	George	5.7"	35"	19	Tailor	Victoria St - Victoria St	Non Eff 15/10/97
7654	..	..	..	Fraser	John	5.9"	36"	19	Upholsterer	Arthur St - Arthur St	Res 20th Apr 1898
7653	..	..	..	McAllister	Charles	5.8"	38"	19	Mason	Mr Olney's	31st Mar 1908
7647	..	22/2/96	22/2/96	Carmont	William	5.7"	40"	36	Shoemaker	65 Arthur St - Victoria St	Non Eff 15/10/97
7691	..	25/2/96	25/2/96	Black	Peter	5.9"	38"	27	Joiner	Wigtown - Mr Smillie, Kirkinner	Res 20th Jan 1900
7690	..	..	..	Dryman	John	5.11"	39"	20	Joiner	Kirkinner	28th May 1896
7689	..	..	..	Smith	James	5.9"	36"	18	Farm Servant	Barglass	15th Jun 1900
7687	..	..	..	McMurray	Thomas	5.10"	36"	16	Clerk	Wigtown - Mr McClean	20th May 1897
7688	..	..	..	Thompson	John	5.7"	35"	17	Mason	Kirkinner - Garlieston	9th Mar 1897
7686	..	..	..	Hope	George	5.8"	36"	20	Clerk	Bank Office - Wigtown	20th Dec 1898
7685	..	..	..	Campbell	Robert	5.11"	38"	29	Joiner	Kirkinner - Saw Mill, Kirkinner	Non Eff 15/10/97
7684	..	..	..	Jones	Andrew	5.9"	38"	20	Carter	Whauphill - Barnbarroch	Res 15th Apr 1899
7682	..	24/3/96	24/3/96	McNeill	Alexander	5.8"	36"	20	Postal	Kirkinner - Kirkinner	
7683	..	..	..	Paton	Robert C	5.7"	36"	18	Lawyer	Wigtown - Wigtown	Join Reg Force 29/10/97
7692	..	31/3/96	31/3/96	Cullen	James	5.9"	37"	19	—	Wigtown - Wigtown	Trans Highlanders 31/1/07
7763	..	1/11/96	1/11/96	Murchie	Thomas	5.7½"	37"	25	Labourer	Borland, Kirkcowan - Mr Smith, Road Survey. Wigtown	Res 15th Jun 1903
7765	..	20/1/97	20/1/97	Agnew	William	5.11"	34"	18	Compositor	34 Arthur St - Gall. Gazette	—
7764	..	..	..	Baird	John	5.5½"	33"	19	Clogger	Birkwood - Mr Baird's, Birkwood	15th Mar 1902
7769	..	..	..	Harley	John	5.5"	33½"	18½	Joiner	Mitchell Tce - Hillside N.S.	15th Mar 1899
7768	..	..	..	McKeand	John P	5.7½	37"	19	Dyer	Cumloden Mill - Minnigaff	15th Apr 1901
7766	..	..	..	Mair	Charles	5.5"	32"	18	Watchmaker	Thornbank - 40 Albert Street	10th Mar 1901
7767	..	..	..	Vernon	Charles	5.6"	34½"	20	Compositor	11 Dashwood Sq - Gall. Gazette	3rd Nov 1902
7770	..	..	..	Duffield	William A.	5.8"	33"	19	Blacksmith	43/96 Queen St - Hillside Station Rd	15th May 1900
7771	..	..	..	McCreadie	Samuel	5.7½"	34"	19	Blacksmith	43 Queen St - 43 Queen Street	15th Apr. 1901
7772	..	..	..	McDonald	Robert	5.7"	34"	17	Mason	16 Princes Street - Mr Agnew's Dashwood Sq	Res 20/11/00

Reg No	Coy	Enrolled	Oath	Surname	Christian	Chest	Height	Age	Occupation	Residence	Remarks
7837	..	3/2/97	12/2/97	Sproat	John N	38"	5.10½"	18½	Law Clerk	Baldoon - Nat. Bank of Scot. Wigtown	15th Jan 1908
7841	..	..	..	Smith	Herbert	34"	5.5"	17	Bank Clerk	Wigtown - ..	15th Jul 1902
7853	..	..	..	O'Neil	James	38"	5.6"	18	Labourer	Wigtown - Wigtown	15th Jan 1898
7840	..	..	..	Cullen	Alfred Wm.	35"	5.9"	18	Law Clerk	Wigtown - Mr Black's, Wigtown	20th Apr 1898
7838	..	..	..	Hanlin	Thomas	38½"	5.8¾"	32½	Dairyman	Torhouskie - Mr Ross, Wigtown	10th Nov 1900
7839	..	..	..	Coulter	William	36"	5.5"	27	Farmer	Torhouskie - Mr Coulter's, Wigtown	20th Apr 1898
7595	..	29/1/96	29/1/96	McMullen	James	37"	5.7½"	28	Tailor	Victoria Street	2nd Apr 1897
7861	..	10/2/97	10/2/97	Muir	Andrew	34"	5.6½"	17	Printer	63 Arthur Street - Gall. Gazette	20th Dec 1898
7854	..	12/4/97	12/4/97	Picken	Robert	35"	5.8"	21	Cycle Agent	Brewery House - 2 Arthur St	12th Jan 1900
7862	..	12/2/97	12/2/97	McDowall	David	35"	5.5"	20	Stone Mason	36 Queen St - 36 Queen St	15th Nov 1903
7856	..	20/5/97	20/5/97	Smith	John	35"	5.7"	31	Postman	47 Arthur St - Post Office	Deceased 20/5/98
7857	..	2/5/97	2/5/97	Blackwood	James	35"	5.7"	29	Plumber	Victoria St - Vuictoria St	Res 15th May 1900
7855	..	19/4/97	19/4/97	McKenna	Robert	37"	5.6"	20	Joiner	Beechwood Cott. Church St.	20th Apr 1899
7858	..	28/6/97	28/6/97	McDavid	Chas. W	35½"	5.7"	19	Cabinet Maker	5 Queen St - 5 Queen St	25th Apr 1898
Lieut.	..	12/4/97	12/4/97	Brand	James	41"	5.5"	38	Civil Engineer	Grovehill, Minnigaff - N.S	30th Apr 1902
6812	..	1/1/97		Akom??	John	40"	5.19"	37	Sgt. Instructor	Windsor Tce. - Armoury GRV	
7978	..	10/1/98	10/1/98	Murray	Wm. M	33"	5.9"	17	Joiner	Rowntree Cott. Minnigaff - same	10th Feb 1902
7979	..	..	..	McKeand	Wm. A	34"	5.9"	17	Weaver	Cumloden Mill, Minnigaff - same	15th Nov 1905
7981	..	..	..	Borland	Thomas	33"	5.6½"	17	Law Clerk	42 Victoria St - Mr Kelly's Office	15th Dec 1901
7977	..	..	..	McClumpha	John	36"	5.7½"	23	Labourer	Roadfoot Minn. - Captain Dunbar's	15th Apr 1899
7980	..	..	..	Harding	John	32"	5.5½"	17	Postman	34 Arthur St - Post Office	Discharged Termination of engagement - 31st March 1910
	..	12/1/98	12/1/98	McNally	John	—	—	17	Tailor	35 Arthur St - 66 Victoria St	Struck Off - 15/2/98 did not attend after being enrolled.
7982	..	..	..	Johnstone	Benjamin	33"	5.6"	25	Clerk	38 Queen St - Public Health Office	Res 30th Apr 1902
	..	..	..	McKie	Andrew J	32½"	5.6"	20	Groom	Machermore Castle - same	20th Apr 1898
8010	..	17/1/98	17/1/98	Bell	James	34"	5.7"	10	Clerk	7 Arthur St - Post Office	10th Mar 1901
8000	..	22/1/98	22/1/98	McCubbin	Robert	34"	5.6"	17	Tailor	12 Jubilee Rd - 3 Queen St	10th May 1900
	..	..	..	Gibson	George	—	—	17	Miller	Kirroughtree Lodge - Grain Mill	Struck off - 15/2/98 did not attend after being enrolled.
7999	..	31/1/98	31/1/98	Clement	Robert	32½"	5.5½"	18	Plumber	96 Queen St - Mr Blackwood's,	Res 15th May 1900
7998	..	..	..	McDowall	James	34"	5.7"	19	Telegraph Clerk	77 Victoria St - Railway Station	15th Mar 1899
8004	..	1/2/98	1/2/98	McClelland	Thomas	33"	5.7½"	18	Clerk	Fordbank, Wigtown - Bladnoch	10th May 1899
8002	..	..	..	McQueen	Wm. N	33"	5.6"	19	Clerk	4 Bank St, Wigtown - same	15th Apr 1901
8003	..	..	..	Rankine	Thomas	32½"	5.5½"	17	Law Clerk	1 Bank St, Wigtown - same	Joined Regular Army 3/11/1902
8001	..	..	..	McCredie	James	34"	5.6"	17	Painter	31 N. Main St, Wigtown - same	Res 10th Dec 1901
	..	..	..	Smith	John	—	—	20	Hostler	6 Low Vennel, Wigtown - same	Struck Off 15/2/98 - did not put in any attendance.
8005	..	..	..	Moore	Joseph	34"	5.7½"	18	Tailor	17 High St, Wigtown - Mr Morris	Res 15th May, 1903

Reg No	Coy	Enrolled	Oath	Surname	Christian	Chest	Height	Age	Occupation	Residence	Remarks
7984	::	7/2/98	7/2/98	Milroy	John	32½"	5.5"	20	Gardener	Old Schoolhouse, Minnigaff	..15th Feb, 1900
8006	::	::	::	Weddington	Robert W.	38"	5.10"	22	Gardener	21 Queens St – Penninghame House	..10th Mar, 1901
8011	::	8/2/98	8/2/98	Christie	Thomas	34"	5.6"	18	Blacksmith	Kirkinner – same	..20th Jan 1900
8012	::	15/2/98	15/2/98	Kennedy	James	32½"	5.5½"	17	Tailor	8 N. Main St, Wigtown – Wigtown	..10th May 1900
8013	::	16/2/98	16/2/98	McGowan	Joseph	37"	5.7"	37	Labourer	32 Windsor Rd – same	..31st Jan 1908
7986	::	3/3/98	3/3/98	Priestly	Edward	34"	5.4½"	19	painter	42 King Street – same	..15th May 1902
7985	::	::	::	Ferries	Andrew	34"	5.7"	21	Carter	Reed Tce – Mr Morton's Victoria St	..26th May 1905
8015	::	::	::	Kerr	James	33"	5.8"	18	Farmer	Machermore – same	..10th May 1899
7987	::	7/3/98	7/3/98	Fitzsimmons	Wm F.	40"	5.9½"	21	Groom	Machermore – Cornwall Park	..10th Apr 1899
7988	::	::	::	Tait	Wm. J.	33"	5.00"	19	Groom	48 Queen St – Doonhill, N.S.	..20th May 1899
7989	::	::	::	Groves	Peter Bruce	35"	5.10"	22	Carter	Cree Bridge, Minn. – Victoria St	..15th May 1901
8007	::	::	::	Litterick	John	33"	5.7½"	17	Clerk	68 Arthur St – Brit. Linen Bank	..10th Feb 1902
8008	::	::	::	Nimmo	James	32"	5.3"	18	Tailor	Agnew Tce. – 3 Queen St, N.S.	..15th April 1899
8009	::	::	::	Scott	Alexander	32"	5.3½"	18	Tailor	69 Arthur \St – 66 Victoria St, N.S.	..20th June 1899
8014	::	21/4/98	21/4/98	Coulter	John	37"	5.7½"	28	Insurance Agent	74 Queen St, N.S. – same	..15th Dec 1903
8022	::	24/5/98	24/5/98	O'Neill	James	37"	5.4"	19	Groom	9 Low Vennel, Wigtown – same	..15th Feb, 1900
8118	::	16/1/99	16/1/99	Beattie	William	35"	5.8"	21	Sett Maker	Carsluith – same	..15th June 1905
8119	::	::	::	Birrell	William	34"	5.7"	25	Fisherman	::	Disch. 11th July 1913
											Employment Unsuitable
8120	::	::	::	Carter	Samuel B	36"	5.10½"	21	Stone Cutter	High Rd Creetown – same	Res 20th Feb 1901
8121	::	::	::	Garroch	Peter	36"	5.9½"	18	Miller	Carsluith – Mr McGuffie's	..12th May 1903
8122	::	::	::	Gordon	Thomas	36"	5.10½"	26	Gardener	The Hollow – Miss Grant, Barholm	..15th May 1900
8123	::	::	::	Henry	William	36"	5.11"	34	Farmer	Chapelton, Creetown – same	..15th Nov 1905
8124	::	::	::	Hyslop	Peter	34"	5.4"	19	Fisherman	Carsluith – Messrs Birrell & Sons	..15th June 1901
8125	::	::	::	Irving	Robert J.	36"	5.6"	22	Gardener	St John St – Mr Caird's Creetown	..15th Mar 1902
8126	::	::	::	McConnell	Alexander	35"	5.10"	20	Law Clerk	The Hollow – Mr. McCormick's N.S.	..20th Dec 1904
8127	::	::	::	McDavid	Henry	37"	5.10"	19	Chemist's Ass.	St John St – Mr J Stark's Creetown	..10th Nov 1904
8128	::	::	::	MacDonald	Alexander	35"	5.9"	34	School Teacher	Norris St – Mr Robertson's Creetown	..10th May 1903
8129	::	::	::	McDowall	David	37"	5.8"	28	Fisherman	Carsluith – same	..10th June 1903
8130	::	::	::	McDowall	John	35"	5.10"	24	Fisherman	Carsluith – Birks, Creetown	..15th June 1900
8131	::	::	::	McMillan	John F.	40"	5.8"	21	Labourer	SpitaL Farm – Bowman Quarries	..20th May 1899
8132	::	::	::	O'Hara	Robert L.	38"	5.6"	28	Stone Cutter	Duke St – Wilson Quarry, Creetown	..15th May 1901
8133	::	::	::	Scott	John	38"	5.8"	24	Fisherman	Carsluith – same	..20th Nov 1900
8134	::	::	::	Scott	Adam	37"	5.8"	22	Sett Maker	Carsluith – Constable's Creetown	..15th Jan 1903
8135	::	::	::	Smith	James	32"	5.7"	17	Carter	Harbour St. – Mr Smith, Harbour st	..15th Feb 1900
8136	::	20/1/99	20/1/99	McGowan	James	38½"	5.11"	20	Carter	St John St. – Mr Turner St John St	..15th June 1900
8137	::	::	::	McGowan	Thomas	37½"	5.10"	23	Assurance Agent	Harbour St – Prudential Ass Co	..15th June 1900
8138	::	::	::	Gass	Archibald	36"	5.8"	30	Blacksmith	:: – The Quarries	..20th Feb 1901
8139	::	::	::	McGuffie	Alexander	35"	5.11"	19	Labourer	Silver St – Mr McQueen's, Creetown	..15th Mar 1902
8140	::	::	::	Birrell	Adam	35"	5.8"	30	Fisherman	Burnfoot Creetown – same	

Reg No	Coy	Enrolled	Oath	Surname	Christian	Chest	Height	Age	Occupation	Residence	Remarks
8141	..	..	..	Dodds	William	37"	5.9"	26	Blacksmith	Harbour St - The Quarries, Creetown ..	15th Apr 1901
8142	..	..	..	Davitt	Patrick	39"	5.9"	39	Labourer	New Buildings - Mr Sutcliffe, Quarry ..	20th Feb 1907
8143	..	..	..	Innes	John	38"	5.8"	37	Quarryman	Harbour St - The Corporation ..	31st Mar 1908
8144	'..	..	..	Smith	William	36"	5.7½"	21	Carter	Old St - W. Smith, Old St Creetown ..	12th Jan 1900
8145	..	..	..	Topping	Patrick	39"	5.7½"	25	Quarryman	Victoria Villa - Mr Wilson's ..	11th Nov 1902
8146	..	..	..	Cutherbertson	James	37"	5.9"	26	..	Harbour St - Liverpool Corporation. To Canada 18/6/10	
8147	..	..	..	Sproat	John N	39"	5.11"	20	Farmer	Baldoon, Wigtown - same	Res 10th Dec 1901
8148	..	..	..	McNeill	Wallace	36"	5.7"	21	Clerk	3 N. Main St Wigtown - McNeill's ..	15th Dec 1901
8149	..	..	..	Dryman	Robert	37"	5.10"	19	Joiner	Kirkinner - Wm Mains Kirkinner ..	15th Mar 1905
8150	..	..	..	McClure	Andrew	35"	5.8"	21	Mole Catcher	Kirkinner - same ..	12th Apr 1905
	..	..	..	Templeton	James	35"	5.5½"	32	Labourer	N. Bank St Wigtown - Mr Kie's	Struck off 15/2/99 (Put in no attendance)
8167	..	3/2/99	3/2/99	Wallace	George	35"	5.7"	37	Draper	41 Victoria St N.S. - same	Res 15th Apr 1901
8167	..	..	..	Session	Aaron	41"	5.10½"	41	Hotel Keeper	Queen St - Queens Arms N.S. ..	15th Mar 1901
8151	..	10/2/99	10/2/99	Finnigan	Archibald	35"	5.6½"	19	Tailor	15 Harbour Rd - 3 Agnew Cres Wgtn ..	10th Dec 1901
8152	..	..	..	Christison	Colin	34"	5.6"	18	Law Clerk	Barglass, Kirkinner - same ..	20th May 1903
8153	..	..	..	Innes	James	35"	5.7½"	17	Painter	17 N. Back St - Agnew Cres, Wigtown .. 15th Nov 1900	
8169	..	16/2/99	16/2/99	Yellowlees	Robert	36"	5.6"	21	Printer	6 Albert St - Gazette Office N.S. .. 10th Nov 1900	
8154	..	17/2/99	17/2/99	Copland	William M	34"	5.6"	19	Joiner	N. Back St - New Road Wigtown	15th Nov 1900
8155	..	1/4/99	1/4/99	Irving	John	36"	5.6"	39	Maltsman	30 King St - S.W. Brewery. N.S. ..	15th Mar 1901
8156	..	..	..	McDonald	Donald	35"	5.7"	22	Upholsterer	Gertrude Cott - 59 Victoria St N.S. ..	15th Feb 1901
8173	..	..	..	Robertson	Donald	39"	6.2"	39	Mason	46 Queen St N.S. - same ..	10th Mar 1901
8170	..	..	..	McDonald	George	31"	5.3"	16	Apprentice	Gertrude Cott - 59 Victoria St ..	15th May 1903
8172	..	..	..	Irving	Peter	30"	5.2"	14	..	30 King St - McCreadie's Printers ..	15th Apr 1901
8171	..	..	..	Robertson	William	29"	4.8"	13	Nil	46 Queen St N.S. - same ..	10th Nov 1905
8209	..	3/5/99	3/5/99	Taylor	Alex. M.	35½"	5.7½"	22	Clerk	70 Arthur St - S.W. Brewery N.S.	Transferred to 'j' Coy, Rothesay. A&S Highlanders, 30th April 1902.
8210	..	15/5/99	15/5/99	Milroy	Alex. M	33"	5.6"	17	Dyer	Old Schoolhouse, Minnigaff - same Res 20th Nov 1900	
8211	..	..	..	Kelly	William	32"	5.4½"	18	Tailor	40 King St - Mr McDavid Victoria St .. 10th May 1900	
8212	..	22/5/99	22/5/99	Dunn	Robert	32"	5.5"	17	Draper	70 Arthur St - 66 Victoria St N.S. ..	15th Mar 1901
8213	..	7/6/99	7/6/99	Morton	John	38½"	5.11"	25	Grain Merchant	13 Victoria St.N.S. - same ..	10th Jun 1902
8214	..	..	..	Campbell	William	38"	5.7½"	40	Railway Porter	Arthur St - Railway Station N.S ..	15th Nov 1902
	..	1/7/99	1/7/99	Douglas	John H	36"	5.11"	24	MBCM	St Ninians Whithorn - same ..	30th Apr 1902
8368	..	26/2/00	26/2/00	Crosbie	David	35"	5.5½"	20	Baker	69 Arthur St - Mr Bryson, Dashwood Sq .. 10th Nov 1900	
8369	..	..	..	McClelland	Robert	35"	5.9"	19	Clerk	Sunnybrae Minn. - Gazette Office ..	10th Mar 1901
8370	..	12/3/00	12/3/00	McKie	John	34"	5.9"	25	Rly Signaller	Challoch Croft - Railway Sation ..	15th Mar 1901
8371	..	..	..	Agnew	Henry	33"	5.5"	18	Brewer	Milburn Cott - S.W. Brewery ..	15th Nov 1906
8372	..	..	..	Haining	William	34"	5.9"	19	Postman	9 Princes St - Post Office N.S. ..	30th Mar 1908
8373	..	..	..	McMillan	James	34"	5.9"	17	Clerk	7 Victoria St - Clydesdale Bank N.S... 10th Nov 1902	
8374	..	22/3/00	22/3/00	Finninghame	Alexander	33"	5.5"	23	Joiner	37 Victoria St N.S. - same	Disch. 11/7/1911

Reg No	Coy	Enrolled	Oath	Surname	Christian	Chest	Height	Age	Occupation	Residence	Remarks
8375	..	6/4/00	6/4/00	Lees	Thomas	34"	5.9"	21	Clerk	High St Wigtown - same	Res 15th Feb 1902
8376	..	..	..	Hodgson	Charles	33"	5.6"	19	Labourer	High Vennel - Creamery, Wigtown ..	10th May 1901
8377	..	..	..	Yates	Samuel	37"	5.10"	29	Dairyman	.. : ..	15th Dec 1900
8378	..	..	..	Edwards	William	38"	5.11"	31	Labourer	Bladnoch -	
8379	..	..	..	Tait	Hugh	36"	5.8"	27	Labourer	25 High St - Distillery, Bladnoch ..21st Apr 1905	
8380	..	..	..	Smith	Andrew D	36"	5.11"	20	Clerk	Jubilee Cott. Kirkinner - 42 Vict. St NS .. 10thNov 1901	
8381	..	..	..	Dewar	John	34"	5.5"	22	Draper	Bladnoch - J. McClumpha's Bladnoch .. 15th Apr 1901	
8382	..	7/4/00	7/4/00	Heron	Peter	35"	5.10"	28	Labourer	Harbour St. - Sutcliffe's Quarries ..	15th Mar 1901
8383	..	20/4/00	20/4/00	Wallace	John A	33"	5.5"	17	Clerk	Claycrop Kirk. - John Black's Wigtown .. 15th Mar 1902	
8384	..	..	..	Young	Robert	35"	5.11"	22	Farmer	Corwar Sorbie - W. Young Kirkinner .. 15th June 1903	
8385	..	..	..	McClelland	William	33"	5.6"	17	Clerk	Bladnoch - A. S. Walker's Wigtown .. 10th Dec 1901	
8386	..	..	..	Smith	James	34"	5.6"	20	Farm Servant	Kirkinner - A Smith's Kirkinner ..	15th Jul 1902
8387	..	2/5/00	2/5/00	Purdie	John	35"	5.6"	25	Tanner	Albert St N.S. - same ..	15th Nov 1902
8388	..	..	..	Cullen	Alfred W	34"	5.7"	21	Law Clerk	Wigtown - same	Transferred to Highlanders, Edinburgh. 13th Dec 1900
8389	..	..	..	Harley	John	34"	5.7½"	22	Joiner	Mitchell Tce. - Mr McClelland's N.S Dis. TX	
8390	..	..	..	McIntyre	John	34"	5.7½"	35	Labourer	41 Arthur St - Mr T Agnew's N.S. Res 12th Apr 1905	
8391	..	..	..	McKenna	Robert	35"	5.8"	21	Joiner	Wigtown - same ..	15th Mar 1902
8392	..	12/6/00	12/6/00	McDonald	William	34"	5.7½"	21	Cabinet Maker	Gertrude Cott. - Victoria St N.S. ..	10th Mar 1902
8393	..	..	..	Turner	James	33"	5.6"	18	Labourer	Queen St N.S. - same ..	15th Apr 1901
8394	..	..	..	McDowell	David	33"	5.5"	17	Labourer	Queen St N.S. - same ..	15th Apr 1901
8395	..	20/2/01	20/2/01	McCaull	James	35"	5.8"	18	App. Joiner	Arthur St - Mr Finninghame's N.S ..	15th Mar 1902
8396	..	..	..	Hanlin	John	34"	5.7"	17	App. Timber Merch.	Minnigaff - Saw mills ..	15th Mar 1903
8397	..	..	..	Nelson	Alexander	34"	5.5"	19	App. Painter	36 Arthur St - Mr Hinds' N.S. ..	30th Jan 1904
8516	..	..	..	Mair	David	34"	5.4½"	17	Tailor	75 Queen St N.S. - same ..	16th May 1904
8517	..	..	..	Young	John	35"	5.9"	17	Bank Clerk	46 King St - Clydesdale Bank ..	15th Nov 1903
8518	..	..	..	Parker	James	38"	5.8½"	18	Skinner	11 Queen St - W. Purdie, Victoria Lane, N.S.	
8519	..	..	..	Fulton	Andrew	36"	5.5"	21	Mason	13 Princes St - Mr McGaw, Church Lane ..15th June 1901	
8520	..	..	..	Varney	Stanley	33"	5.4½"	18	Labourer	80 King St - Mr Callander, Sawmill Resigned	
8523	..	..	..	Gregg	Edgar	37"	5.10"	22	Labourer	Mossvale, Minn..- ..	10th Nov 1905
8524	..	15/3/01	15/3/01	Stewart	James	36"	5.10"	17	Plasterer	Station Rd - Mr McGaw, Church Lane ..23rd Mar 1904	
8525	..	..	..	McKeachie	John	38"	5.9½"	25	Draper	Kirkinner - same ..	20th Jul 1902
8526	..	..	..	Muir	Peter	36"	5.7"	21	Blacksmith	Braehead - Kirkinner ..	15th May 1902
8527	..	..	..	Harrison	Samuel	37"	5.8½"	20	Mason	Sloehabbert, Whauphill - same ..	10th May 1904
8528	..	..	..	Orr	David	38"	5.10"	31	Farmer	Smallmuir, Whauphill - same ..	15th June 1904
8529	..	..	..	Boyd	William	37"	5.8"	22	Stone Builder	Capenoch, Whauphill - same	Term. of engagement
8530	..	..	..	Smith	William	36"	5.7"	18	App. Blacksmith	Kirkinner - Mr Christie's Kirkinner Res 20th Apr 1902	
8531	..	..	..	Garrity	Charles	37"	5.9"	18	App. Joiner	North Balfern - Skimming's Kirk. ..	15th Apr 1903
8532	..	..	..	Galloway	John	37"	5.4½"	20	Farm Servant	Capenoch - W Galloway's Whauphill .. 10th June 1904	
8533	..	..	..	Brown	William	37"	5.11"	18	Farm Servant	Kildarroch, Whauphill - same	Resigned

Reg No	Coy	Enrolled	Oath	Surname	Christian	Chest	Height	Age	Occupation	Residence	Remarks
8534	..	..	..	McClurg	James	38"	5.8½"	23	Farm Manager	South Balfern, Kirkinner - same	30th Dec 1902
8535	..	..	..	Wallace	George	36"	5.7½"	17	Labourer	N. Back St, Wigtown - Wigtown	15th June 1903
8536	..	..	..	Wallace	Andrew	33"	5.9½"	19	Law Clerk	Claycrop, Kirkinner - Mr McLean's	10th July 1902
8537	..	..	19/3/01	Boyd	James	35"	5.7½"	18	App. Joiner	Baldoon - W J McKie's, Wigtown	15th June 1903
8538	..	19/3/01	19/3/01	Wilson	Robert	42"	6.4"	19	Farm Labourer	Cairnholy - T. Wilson's Creetown	10th Nov 1903
8539	..	1/4/01	1/4/01	Smylie	Thomas	35"	5.7½"	42	Joiner	Kirkinner - same	31st Mar 1908
8540	..	..	..	Boyd	David	38"	5.10"	23	Creamery	Baldoon - Bladnoch	10th Nov 1904
8541	..	..	..	Kerr	James	38"	5.7"	27	Labourer	Maidland, Wigtown - Mr McClelland Time Exp. 1/4/1912	
8521	..	20/2/01	20/2/01	Moffatt	George	36"	5.6"	24	Plumber	53 Victoria St. N.S. - same	Discharged TX
8522	..	..	..	Gordon	Thomas	37"	5.9"	28	Stone Cutter	Hollow - Fellhill Granite Co Creetown Res 15th June 1905	
8542	..	1/4/01	1/4/01	Wallace	John	39½"	5.9"	30	Labourer	Bladnoch - Mr McClelland's	10th Jan 1903
8543	..	8/4/01	8/4/01	Gray	William	39"	5.7½"	28	Teacher	32 Queen St. N.S. - same	27th May 1909
8544	..	16/4/01	16/4/01	Scott	Adam	37"	5.6"	25	Carter	Carsluith - same	10th June 1903
8545	..	..	..	Garroch	James	36"	5.7"	29	Quarryman	Carsluith - Carsluith Quarries Co	
8546	..	1/4/01	1/4/01	Christie	Thomas	35"	5.7"	21	Blacksmith	Kirkinner - Bladnoch	10th Feb 1902
8547	..	..	..	Copland	William M	35"	5.6"	21	Joiner	North Back St - Wigtown	10th Feb 1902
8594	..	14/6/01	14/6/01	Innes	James	35"	5.7½"	19	Painter	17 N. Back St - Wigtown	15th Mar 1902
8595	..	..	..	Drynan	John	37"	5.11"	25	Joiner	Causewayend, N.S. - same	15th Mar 1905
8663	..	8/2/02	8/2/02	McCaull	William	33"	5.8"	18	Draper	47 Arthur St - Mr Brown's Victoria St .. 10th Nov 1902	
8664	..	..	..	Law	Fred. Wm.	33"	5.4½"	17	Harness Maker	38 Queen St - Mr Nelson, Saddler	15th Mar 1905
8665	..	..	..	Hall	Edwin	33"	5.5½"	17	Painter	92 Queen St - Mr Hinds', Painter	25th May 1905
8666	..	..	..	Rankin	Samuel	33"	5.6"	17	Painter	Mitchell Tce. - ..	22nd Dec 1904
8667	..	..	..	Brown	Leo	33"	5.5½"	17	Cycle Engineer	Mitchell Tce. - Mr McEwan, Vict. St...31st Mar 1908	
8668	..	..	..	Milne	Adam	34	5.5½"	17	Drover?	Ellangowan Hotel - Creetown	12th May 1903
8669	..	..	..	Brown	Samuel	33"	5.6"	19	Farm Labourer	Mill St - Creetown	31st Mar 1908
8670	..	..	..	McNearnie	John	36"	5.9"	18	Blacksmith	St John St, Creetown - same	Dis TX 12/4/1912
8671	..	..	..	Wilson	William	35"	5.8"	17	Gardener	St John St. - Creetown	Res 15th Nov 1903
8672	..	..	..	Gemmel	Robert	37"	5.7½"	23	Labourer	St John St, Creetown - same	15th June 1902
8673	..	..	..	Diamond	John L	35"	5.10"	17	Joiner	Creebridge N.S. - same	14th Nov 1903
8674	..	..	..	Butler?	James	34"	5.6"	17	Stone Cutter	Park Cresc. Creetown - Granite Quarry .. 15th June 1902	
8675	..	8/3/02	8/3/02	Cook	Ernest	34"	5.7"	17	Game keeper	Minnigaff - same	20th Jan 1904
8676	..	18/3/02	18/3/02	Lupton	Robert	35"	5.6½"	18	Fisherman	Mill St Creetown - same	Dis TX
8677	..	..	..	Hunter	William	36"	5.7"	29	Insurance Agent	12 Church St N.S. - Gazette Office	Res 21st Mar 1904
8678	..	21/3/02	21/3/02	Murdoch	Thomas	35"	5.7"	22	Baker	Arthur St N.S. - Mr Kay's Baker	10th Apr 1904
8735	..	29/4/02	29/4/02	O'Hara	Robert L	36"	5.6"	29	Stone Cutter	Duck St, Creetown - Quarries	10th Mar 1904
8736	..	23/5/02	23/5/02	Hodgson	Charles	35"	5.6"	21	Labourer	High Vennel Wigtown - Wigtown	15th Dec 1906
8737	..	18/6/02	18/6/02	Murray	William M	36"	5.8"	19	Joiner	Minnigaff - same TSR Engagement 12/4/1910	
8738	..	..	..	Bryden	John	37"	5.8"	24	Sawyer	Minnigaff - Callander's Sawmill	.Res 10th Apr 1906
8810	..	..	..	Beattie	Thomas	34"	5.10"	17	Blacksmith	Weir Cott. Carsluith - Carsluith	15th May 1906
8811	..	2/3/03	2/3/03	Cullen	Murray	35"	5.6"	18	Stone Cutter	Woodford Cott. Creetown - Quarries Term Engag. 31/3/09	

Reg No	Coy	Enrolled	Oath	Surname	Christian	Chest	Height	Age	Occupation	Residence	Remarks
8812	..	..	..	Dunlop	James	37”	5.9½”	22	Labourer	60 Arthur St N.S. - same	Res 15th Nov 1904
8813	..	..	..	Gray	John	33”	5.4½”	17	Groom	Machermore N.S. - Mr Dunbar’s	Joined Regular Army
8814	..	..	..	Hall	John	35”	5.4½”	17	Sett Maker	Duke St Creetown - Quarries	Res 15th Nov 1906
8815	..	..	..	McCleary	John	34”	5.4”	18	Stone Cutter	Rainbank Cott. Creetown - Quarries	
8816	..	..	..	McConchie	Robert	35”	5.7”	28	Shepherd	Risk, Minnigaff - Mr S McConchie’s	.. 31st Mar 1908
8817	..	..	..	McLauchlan	John	34”	5.6”	21	Law Apprentice	38 Albert St N.S. - 60 Victoria St	.. 21 Dec 1904
8818	..	..	..	Watson	William	36”	5.7”	28	Telegraphist	32 Queen St N.S. - Post Office	Ter. Engage.31/3/09
8879	..	3/4/03	3/4/03	McClelland	John	36”	5.5”	17	Law Clerk	Glenturk Wigtown - Mr McClure’s	Res 10th June 1904
8880	..	..	..	McMurray	David	36”	5.8”	17	Bank Clerk	County Build. Wigtown - B. L. Bank	Disch. Left district
8881	..	..	..	McWilliam	John	34”	5.6”	18	Law Clerk	Clydesdale Bank, Wigtown.	Res 13th June 1907
8882	..	10/4/03	10/4/03	Gardiner	John	37”	5.10”	19	Labourer	Bladnoch - Creamery	.. 15th Mar 1905
8883	..	..	..	McCubbin	William	36”	5.10”	18	Labourer	Bladnoch - Creamery	.. 21st Mar 1905
8884	..	15/4/03	15/4/03	McAulay	Archibald	37”	5.10”	23	Draper	Victoria St N.S. - same	.. 20th Dec 1904
8885	..	..	..	Kelly	William	33”	5.5”	21	Tailor	40 King St N.S - Victoria St	.. 10th Apr 1904
8886	..	26/5/03	26/5/03	Courtney	William	34”	5.7½”	20	Postman	5 Ivy Place N.S.- Post Office	.. 31st Mar 1908
8887	..	3/6/03	3/6/03	Malcolm	John	42”	6.2”	39	Weaver	Minnigaff - Cumloden Mill	.. April 1908
8888	..	..	..	McDavid	William	36”	5.5½”	32	Tailor	Albert St N.S.- Mr Dixon Tailor	.. 31st Mar 1908
7019	..	19/1/92	19/1/92	Halliday	Robert	38½”	5.10”	17	Engineer	St Crispins St. Creetown - Sc. Granite	Transferred to ‘H’ Coy. 1st May 1905
8944	..	22/3/04	22/3/04	Butler	James	35”	5.8”	19	Stone Cutter	Park Cresc. Creetown - Quarries	Dis. 24th Feb 1910
8945	..	..	..	Goldie	Thomas	33”	5.5”	17	Stone Cutter	St John St. Creetown - Quarries	Dis. TX 10/4/1912
8946	..	..	..	Vernon	James D	33”	5.5”	17	Stone Cutter	Duke St. Creetown - Quarries	Res 15th May 1906
8947	..	..	..	McConchie	William	33”	5.4½”	17	Farmer	The Risk, Minnigaff - same	.. 31st Mar 1908
8948	..	..	..	McNair	J Anderson	33”	5.4½”	17	Telegraphist	Queen St. N.S. - Post Office	.. 31st Mar 1908
9011	..	4/4/04	4/4/04	McKie	William	33½”	5.7½”	21	Builder	Challoch Croft - Mr McGaw’s N.S.	.... 10th Apr 1906
9012	..	8/4/04	8/4/04	Blain	William	35”	5.6”	18	Driver	High St. Wigtown - Commercial Hotel	.. 10th Nov 1905
9013	..	..	..	Muir	Robert E	37”	5.10”	20	Driver	High St. Wigtown - Commercial Hotel	Dis. 18th July 1911
9014	..	..	..	Jardine	Alexander	36”	5.5”	20	Tailor	High St. Wigtown - Mr McClumpha’s	Res 15th Sep 1906
9015	..	..	..	Little	Robt. James	38”	5.9”	19	Insurance Agent	28 North Back St. Wigtown - same	..15th Nov 1904
9016	..	..	..	McClure	James	35”	5.7”	17	App. Blacksmith	Kilwhirren Hse - Mr McNeillie’s	.. 15th Dec 1906
9017	..	12/4/04	12/4/04	McKay	John	35”	5.5”	18	Labourer	St Ninians Cott. N.S. - same	.. 21st Dec 1904
9018	..	26/4/04	26/4/04	McDowell	David	37”	5.8”	33	Fisherman	Carsluith - same	Dismissed for misconduct, 20th July 1904
9019	..	3/5/04	3/5/04	McGinis	Daniel	35”	5.6”	21	Stone Cutter	Norris St. Creetown - Quarries	Res 4th June 1907
9020	..	17/5/04	17/5/04	Cochrane	Thomas	36”	5.7”	17	Labourer	Harbour St. Creetown - Quarries	Ter. Engage. 31/3/09
9021	..	20/6/04	20/6/04	Axon	Wm Chas	32”	5.7”	15	Schoolboy	Windsor Terrace N.S.	Res 15th Nov 1905
9022	..	..	..	Carmont	Herbert	30”	5.2”	14	Apprentice	Arthur St - Mr Vernon’s Albert St	.. 31st Mar 1908
9130	..	31/5/05	31/5/05	Armstrong	Charles	36”	5.4½”	24	Labourer	St John St. Creetown - Quarries	Ter. Eng. 31/3/09
9131	..	..	..	Butler	John Thos	33½”	5.7”	17	Stone Cutter	Park Cresc. Creetown - Quarries	.. .. ..
9132	..	..	..	Hall	William	34”	5.6”	18	Sett Maker	Duke St. Creetown - Quarries	.. .. ..

Reg No	Coy	Enrolled	Oath	Surname	Christian	Chest	Height	Age	Occupation	Residence	Remarks
9133	::	::	::	Heron	James	35"	5.10"	20	Stone Cutter	Norris St. Creetown - Quarries	Res 15th May 1906
9134	::	::	::	McCleary	Peter	34½"	5.4½"	30	Sett Maker	Hazelwood, Creetown - Quarries	.. 4th Apr 1905
9135	::	::	::	McDowell	Archibald	36"	5.8"	21	Sett Maker	Norris St Creetown - Quarries	Ter. Eng. 31/3/09
9136	::	::	::	McGinis	James	35"	5.7"	21	Stone Cutter	Norris St Creetown - Quarries	Res 31st Mar 1908
9137	::	::	::	O'Hara	Thomas	35"	5.9"	38	Sett Maker	Victoria Villa Creetown - Quarries	Ter. Eng. 31/3/09
9138	::	7/2/05	7/2/05	Callander	Alxander	39"	5.9"	20	Farmer	Lenies Creetown - same	Res 11th June 1907
9139	::	::	::	Gordon	William	342	5.8"	19	Shepherd	Barholm Dairy Creetown - same	Dis T.X. 2/4/1914
9140	::	21/2/05	21/2/05	Blain	John	35"	5.8"	24	Grocer	St John St Creetown - same	T.X. 2/4/1912
9141	::	2/3/05	2/3/05	Lavery	James L	40"	5.7½"	22	Brick layer	Park Cres. Creetown - Grimshaw's	Res 15th Nov 1905
9142	::	16/3/05	16/3/05	Agnew	John	34"	5.7"	17	Apprentice	Tait Cott. Minn. - Minnigaff	..31st April 1908
9143	::	::	::	Bryden	Samuel	35"	5.8"	18	Apprentice	47 Arthur St N.S. - 37 Victoria St	..15th Oct 1909
9144	::	::	::	McDowell	Robert	35"	5.7"	20	Dairyman	Challoch N.S. - Mr McGill's	..31st Mar 1908
9145	::	::	::	Ravey	James	33"	5.5½"	19	Labourer	78 King St N.S. - Morton's Minn.	..31st Mar 1908
9170	::	30/5/05	30/5/05	McDavid	Henry	40"	5.10"	25	Chemist Asst.	St John St Creetown - same	Dis T.X.
9278	::	7/8/05	7/8/05	Bannister	Thomas M	37½"	5.6"	24	Labourer	Woodside Minnigaff - Minnigaff	Res 15th Nov 1906
9279	::	::	::	Lavery	James	37"	5.4½"	21	Baker	Old Minnigaff - Mr Kay Arthur St	..31st Mar 1908
9280	::	::	::	Fiskin	Thomas	36"	5.8"	20	Plumber	Windsor Rd N.S - 28 Albert St	T.X
9281	::	::	::	Hannah	James	35½"	5.6½"	17	Shoemaker	59 Arthur St N.S. - 4 Dashwood Sq	Res 31st Mar 1908
9282	::	::	::	Nimmo	Wm. Thos.	37"	5.5"	21	Tailor	17 King St N.S. - Victoria St	..15th June 1907
9283	::	::	::	Matthew	James	34"	5.8"	20	Bank Clerk	Brit. Linen Bank - same	Promoted to 2nd Lieutenant 27th Sept 1905. Res. 6th March 1908
9284	::	::	::	McGhie	James	37½"	5.11"	18	Labourer	46 Arthur St N.S. - Morton's Minn.	Res 15th June 1907
9285	::	15/8/05	15/8/05	Rankine	Samuel	33½"	5.7"	21	Painter	Mitchell Tce N.S. - Arthur St	..31st March 1908
9286	::	::	::	Caven	Thomas B	36"	5.10"	21	Stone Cutter	Church St Creetown - Quarries	..10th Dec 1906
9287	::	::	::	Gass	William	33½"	5.6"	17	Stone Cutter	Poulton Tce Creetown - Quarries	Ter. Engage.
9288	::	::	::	McCulloch	David	39½"	5.10"	20	Gardener	Cassenary Stables - Mr Caird's	Res 10th Feb 1906
9289	::	::	::	Longridge	William	34½"	5.8"	18	Labourer	Duke St Creetown - Mr Stark	Ter Engage.
9290	::	::	::	Longridge	David J	35½"	5.5"	19	Stone Cutter	- W. Scott's	Transferred to Regular Army 6th Jan 1906
9291	::	::	::	McGiveran	William	35½"	5.5"	20	Post Office	St John St Creetown - Mr Sloan	Res 31st Mar 1908
9301	::	::	::	Scott	William	34"	5.8"	18	Labourer	Poulton Tce Creetown - Sutton's	Join Militia 10/12/06
9292	::	::	::	Cowell	William	35½"	5.6"	18	Stone Cutter	St John St Creetown - Sutton's	Dis 24th Feb 1910
9302	::	::	::	Kirkpatrick	William	33½"	5.5"	17	Stone Cutter	.. ..	Dis T.X
9293	::	::	::	Gordon	Thomas	34"	5.10"	33	Roadman	Barholm St Creetown - Council	Res 10th Dec 1906
9294	::	::	::	Smiley	Thomas	34"	5.4"	20	Joiner	Kirkinner - Same	Res 31st Mar 1908
9295	::	::	::	Marshall	Alexander	34"	5.10½"	18	Joiner	Kirkinner - Mr Skimming	..6th June 1907
9296	::	::	::	Christie	John K	34"	5.5"	18	Blacksmith	Kirkinner - same	..31st March 1908
9297	::	::	::	McGibney	Thomas A	34"	5.9"	19	Bank Clerk	Kirkinner - Clydesdale Wigtown	..31st Marh 1908
9298	::	::	::	McGhie	Robert	35"	5.8"	19	Carter	Kirkinner - Mr Robb, Wigtown	..31st March 1908
9303	::	::	::	Kelly	William J	36"	5.8½"	17	Labourer	16 Bank St Wigtown - Mr Waddell	Join Militia 3/11/06

Reg No	Coy	Enrolled	Oath	Surname	Christian	Chest	Height	Age	Occupation	Residence	Remarks
9304	..	..	..	Drynen	Robert	36"	5.11"	25	Joiner	Causwayend - same	Res 15th Nov 1906
9299	..	..	..	Gardiner	John	38"	5.10"	22	Dairyman	Bladnoch - Mr Green's	.. 15th Nov 1906
9305	..	..	..	Boyd	David	40"	5.10"	27	Creamery	Bladnoch - Creamery	.. 31st March 1908
9300	..	..	..	McClure	Andrew	35"	5.9"	27	Mole Catcher	Kirkinner - Mr McClure's	.. 31st March 1908
9306	..	..	..	Cosker	Owen	37"	5.8"	43	Labourer	Wigtown - Mr Green's	.. 31st March 1908
9307	..	..	..	Knowles	Alexander	35"	5.6"	19	Tailor	Bladnoch - Mr McClumpha's	.. 31st march 1908
9308	..	..	..	Ross	William	40"	5.10"	35	Postman	25 High St Wigtown - Post Office	Dis 11/7/1911
9309	..	..	..	Thomson	Robert K	36"	5.7"	17	Photographer	Bank St Wigtown - same	Join Militia 3/11/06
9310	..	2/2/06	..	Tait	Hugh	39"	5.8"	32	Labourer	25 High St Wigtown -J. McClelland	Res 31st March 1908
9390	..	2/2/06	2/2/06	Cairney	Thomas	40"	5.8"	24	Cab Driver	Mill St Creetown - Mr Waddington	.. 31st March 1908
9391	..	..	..	Hamilton	Alexander	37"	5.8½"	24	Sett Maker	Loveside Creetown - same	18th June 1907
9392	..	..	..	Innes	William	39"	5.6"	30	Labourer	Carswalloch Creetown -same	.. 31st March 1908
9393	..	..	..	Kirkpatrick	James	33"	5.5½"	17	Joiner	St John St Creetown - same	
9394	..	..	..	McManus	James	37"	5.7½"	23	Quarryman	Creetown - same	.. 15th Sept 1906
9395	..	..	..	O'Hara	John	35"	5.8"	19	Sett Maker	Poulton Tce Creetown	.. 31st March 1908
9396	..	..	..	Oliver	George	33½"	5.6½"	26	Sett Maker	Duke St Creetown	.. 31st March 1908
9397	..	..	..	Oliver	William	33½"	5.7"	18	Sett Maker	Adamson Sq Creetown	.. 31st March 1908
9398	..	..	..	Stevenson	Andrew	33½"	5.8"	18	Stone Cutter	..	Transferred to A&S Highlanders 6th April 1911
9399	..	..	..	Templeton	Peter W	35"	5.6½"	33	Sett Maker	Carsluith - Same	T.X 8th June 1910
9400	..	28/2/06	28/2/06	Dunlop	Peter	35½"	5.8"	17	Labourer	70 King St N.S. - Cumloden Mill	Res 31st March 1908
9401	..	..	..	Grierson	Thomas	33½"	5.7½"	18	Law Clerk	Eskdale Cott. N.S. - Mr McCormick's	.. 31st March 1908
9402	..	..	..	Thomson	Robert	33½"	5.6"	17	Farm Servant	66 Arthur St N.S. - Knockstocks	.. April 1908
9403	..	21/3/06	21/3/06	White	Thomas	34½"	5.9"	18	App. Joiner	Institute Place N.S. -59 Victoria St	.. 31st March 1909
9479	..	..	..	Crosbie	Daniel	34"	5.7"	18	Factory Worker	15 Harbour Rd Wigtown	.. 15th Sept 1906
9480	..	..	..	Ferguson	Robert	37½"	5.9"	18	Builder	Barrachan Wigtown - same	Ter. Engage. 31/3/09
9481	..	..	..	McGarva	John	35"	5.5½"	26	Bookkeeper	Wigtown - Creamery, Bladnoch	Res 31st March 1908
9482	..	..	..	McGaw	William	36"	5.5"	18	Factory Worker	Bladnoch - same	
9483	..	..	..	McNeil	Thomas	39½"	5.11"	21	Dairyman	Wigtown - Creamery Bladnoch	.. 31st March 1908
9484	..	..	..	Riddick	William	35"	5.7½"	20	Builder	Barrachan Wigtown	.. 31st March 1908
9485	..	..	..	Yuill	Alex. F	37"	5.11"	21	Clerk	18 Harbour Rd Wigtown - Creamery	.. 31st March 1908
9486	..	30/3/06	30/3/06	McGuffie	John	35"	5.7"	19	Boots	28 Sth Main St Wigtown - Mr Grant's	.. 13th June 1907
9487	..	..	..	Copland	Robert	38"	5.4½"	18	Tailor	8 Nth Main St Wigtown - McClumpha's	.. 6th June 1907
9488	..	..	..	Anderson	James	39"	5.8"	39	Postman	20 Harbour Rd Wigtown - Post Office	.. 31st March 1908
9489	..	7/4/06	7/4/06	Beattie	William	37"	5.7"	29	Sett Maker	Carsluith - Carsluith Granite Co	Dismissed for misconduct 25th May 1907
9490	..	9/5/06	9/5/06	Agnew	John	38"	5.10"	18	Farmer	Barlachlon N.S. - same	Dis T.X
9491	..	..	..	McGeoch	James	34½"	5.9"	19	Farmer	Barmean? N.S. - same	Res 31st Mar 1908
9492	..	4/6/06	..	Laird	Alfred	35½"	5.9"	19	Farmer's son	Torhouse, Wigtown - same	.. 31st Mar 1908

Reg No	Coy	Enrolled	Oath	Surname	Christian	Chest	Height	Age	Occupation	Residence	Remarks
9493	..	13/6/06	13/6/06	Axon	William	33½"	5.11"	17	Apprentice Telegraph Office	1 Windsor Tce N.S.	.. 31st Mar 1908
9494	..	..	..	Priestly	John	33"	5.4"	16	Telegraph Office	Sunnybrae Cott. Minn. - Post Office	Left dist. 10/9/1910
9496	..	28/7/06	28/7/06	Fraser	Andrew	37"	5.4"	17	Stone Cutter	St John St Creetown - Quarries	T.X 2/4/1912
..	..	4/4/03	4/4/03	Glover	R. S.	38"	5.7½"	26	Solicitor	Gatehouse - same	Promoted Captain and transferred from 'A' Coy. 1st Nov 1905
9523	..	25/2/07	25/2/07	Dounan	James	38"	5.8"	25	Upholsterer	6 Arthur St N.S.	Dis T.X 12/4/1912
9524	..	..	..	McGeoch	James	'35"	5.5½"	21	Saddler	64 Victoria St N.S.	Dis T.X. 12/4/1912
9525	..	..	..	Griffin	Robert	38"	5.11½"	17	Mason	27 Princess St N.S.	Res 31st March 1908
9526	..	..	..	Baird	Peter	37"	5.4½"	18	Mason	6 Princess St N.S.	Join Regular Army?
9529	..	6/3/07	6/3/07	Scott	James	38½"	5.4"	18	Grocer	63 Arthur St N.S.	Res 31st March 1908
9527	..	5/3/07	5/3/07	Beattie	Robert	37"	5.8"	23	Fisherman	Carsluith - Creetown	.. 31st March 1908
9528	..	..	..	McWilliam	James	34½"	5.6½"	19	Labourer	High St Creetown -Quarry	.. 31st March 1908
9597	..	28/3/07	28/3/07	Brown	William	36"	5.11½"	19	Bank Clerk	Drumskeog Mochrum - B.L.Bank	.. 31st March 1908
9598	..	..	..	Hannah	James	38"	5.5½"	19	Farm Labourer	Carsduchan - Landberrick	Ter. Engage. 30/3/09
9599	..	18/4/07	18/4/07	Drysdale	Thomas	37"	5.7"	19	Butcher	Port William - same	Res 31st Mar 1908
9415	..	7/2/06	7/2/06	Donnan	William	36"	5.7"	19	Upholsterer	6 Arthur St N.S.	31st March 1910
9629	..	25/6/07	25/6/07	Elliott	Robert K	33"	5.5"	17	Labourer	St John St Creetown	Left Dist. 23/4/10
9699	..	23/12/07	23/12/07	Blaen	James		5.8"	25	Miller	Creetown - Barony Mill, Creetown	
9700	..	..	..	Longridge	James			18	Stone Cutter	Creetown - Fell Hill Quarry	31st March 1910
9701	..	..	..	McDavid	Joseph I		5.8"	17	Draper	St John St Creetown - same	T.X 2nd April 1912
..	..	..	..	Smith	Wm B			17	Sett Maker	Woodfall Cott Creetown - Quarries	Failed Medical Test
9703	..	28/12/07	28/12/07	Black	Alexander	35"	5.9"	17	Farm Servant	Ravenshall Cott Creetown - Scott's	Dis 24/2/1910
3401	..	23/1/08	16/10/89	Johnson	Charles		5.7"	34	Sergeant Inst.	Windsor Tce. N.S. - Armoury N.S.	Promoted to Sergeant Major, transferred to Dumfries H.Q.
9719	..	2/3/08	2/3/08	McCleary	David	P	5.2½"	21	Farm Servant	Black Craig - same	
9721	..	9/3/08	9/3/08	McClymont	James	P	5.5½"	17	Carter	Black Craig - same	
5th King's Own Scottish Borderers											
6028	H	13/4/08	13/4/08	Topping	John		5.5"	19	Carter	Lodge Penningham - Arthur St	Dis T.X. 12/4/12
6027	..	..	..	Smith	William			18	Sett Maker	Woodfall Cott Creetown - Quarries	Dis 24/2/10
6079	..	20/4/08	20/4/08	Allan	David		5.6"	26	Printer	44 Arthur St N.S. - Gazette	Struck Off 31/8/08
6264	..	..	..	Blair	William		5.5"	22	Labourer	High St Wigtown - Comm. Hotel	Dis 24/2/1910
6217	..	30/4/08	30/4/08	McGaw	Alexander		5.10½"	18	Clerk	Bladnoch - Creamery	Dis T.X.
6260	..	2/6/08	2/6/08	Shaw	James		5.2½"	20	Blacksmith	Duke St Creetown - Mersey Dock Co	Transferred to A&S Highlanders 13th April 1909
6261	..	..	..	Ross	Robert		5.7"	22	Sett Maker	Waterloo Carsluith - ...	Dis 24.2.1910
6262	..	3/6/08	3/56/08	Evans	John		5.6"	29	Farm Servant	Old Hall N.S. - same	Trans.To RSF 1/3/09
6282	..	11/6/08	11/6/08	Hannah	Alex. J		5.10"	18	Bank Clerk	c/o Mr Maclean Wigtown	Dis 29/6/1911
4102	..	21/8/08	21/8/08	McCaskie	Thomas		5.7"	18	Clerk	4 High Vennel - Sc. Wholesale Soc	
4163	..	9/10/08	9/10/08	Templeton	David		5.7"	18	Farm Servant	12 King St N.S.	Left dist. Dis 24/5/10

Reg No	Coy	Enrolled	Oath	Surname	Christian	Chest	Height	Age	Occupation	Residence	Remarks
4113	::	30/11/08	30/11/08	Thomson	William		5.5"	17	Printer	52 King St N.S - Gazette	Dis T.X
4112	::	::	::	McKenzie	James	P	5.4"	17	Printer	6 Ivy Place NS - Gazette	Dis T.X 29/11/13
4114	::	::	::	Little	James		5.4"	21	Tailor	Windsor Rd N.S. - Victoria St	Left dis 6/4/1917
4111	::	23/11/08	23/11/08	McMaster	Archibald		5.9"	34	Postman	Main St Kirkcowan - Post Office	dis T.X
4014	::	::	::	McNeil	Patrick		5.7½"	33	Labourer	::	Dis T.X.
4105	::	::	::	Morrison	David P		5.8"	19	Tweed Designer	Lencuan Kirkcowan - Armstrong's	Dis left dis. 11/5/11
4106	::	::	::	Irvine	Samuel		5.4½"	17	Tailor	Newton Stewart Rd Kirkcowan	Dis T.X
4107	::	::	::	McCulloch	Alexander		5.10½"	21	Farmer	West Croshrie Kirkcowan?	Dis 9/3/1911
4108	::	::	::	Nicholson	Thomas		5.4"	19	Tailor	Main St Kirkcowan - Mr Caldwell	Dis T.X.
4109	::	::	::	Nicholson	James		5.4"	30	Cabinet Maker	::	Dis T.X
4110	::	::	::	Clerke	John		5.4"	30	Mill Worker	Tarff Row Kirkcowan - Milroy's	Dis T.X
4116	::	4/12/08	4/12/08	Barry	William		5.9"	18	Labourer	Main St Kirkcowan	Join Regular Army 11/10/09
4115	::	::	::	Jardine	Alexander		4.6"	17	Grocer	Kirkland Cott Kirkcowan	Res 19/11/1909
4117	::	17/12/08	17/12/08	Stewart	Robert		5.4"	17	Postman	Minnigaff - Post Office	Dis 24th Feb 1910
4118	::	28/1/09	28/1/09	Watt	Harry		5.5"	18	Hairdresser	Gilmour Tce N.S.	Dis to America 12/4/11
4121	::	12/12/08	12/12/08	McNeill	Alexander	P	5.7½"	18	Gentleman	Shennanton Kirkcowan	2nd Lieut. 12/12/08
4120	::	1/2/09	1/2/09	Robertson	Alexander		5.8"	21	Farm Servant	Annabaglish - same	Dis 24th Aug 1910
4119	::	::	::	Scanlon	Michael		5.9"	20	Farm Servant	Shennanton - same	Dis 24th Aug 1910
4122	::	10/2/09	10/2/09	Taylor	James		5.11½"	17	Labourer	St Couans Tce - Mr Galloway's	Res 19/6/1909
4123	::	17/2/09	17/2/09	Stroyan	John		5.9"	20	Fishmonger	Queen St N.S. - Mr Stewart's	Dis 9/3/11
4124	::	19/2/09	19/2/09	Stewart	William		5.9½"	18	Post Clerk	Post Office	Trans 'E' 14/1/11
4125	::	26/2/09	26/2/09	Clark	William		5.4"	22	Butcher	21 Botany Wigtown	Dis 4/6/1912
4126	::	::	::	Kennedy	Francis W	RC	5.6"	23	Joiner	11 Low Vennel Wigtown	Dis T.X
4127	::	4/3/09	4/3/09	McCreadie	Arthur		5.8½"	25	Painter	21 North Main St Wigtown	Dis left dis. 25/3/11
4140	::	9/3/09	9/3/09	McKie	John		6.1"	23	Ploughman	Black Craig - same	res 17/5/09
4128	::	::	::	Jamieson	William		5.6½"	18	Gardener	Norris St Creetown - The Hill	medical unfit 6/4/12
4129	::	10/3/09	10/3/09	Stewart	James	P	5.6"	17	Postman	Harbour St Creetown - Post Office	Dis24/2/1910
4138	::	::	::	Robertson	James		5.6"	19	Mason	46 Queen St N.S. - McMaster's	T.X. 9/3/1913
4130	::	::	::	Campbell	Robert		5.10½"	17	Schoolteacher	Woodlea - Kirkmabreck School	Dis left dis 1/12/10
4131	::	17/3/09	17/3/09	Boreland	James	P	5.6½"	17	Compositor	35 Arthur St N.S. - Gazette	Dis T.X
4139	::	22/3/09	22/3/09	Hughes	Thomas		5.7"	25	Labourer	Main St - Mrs Galloway's	Dis 24/2/1910
4132	::	23/3/09	23/3/09	Lupton	Jeffrey	P	5.6"	18	Quarryman	St John St - Creetown Quarries	Dis left district
4133	::	24/3/09	24/309	Elliot	Magnus		5.6"	17	Clerk	St Couans Rd N.S - Creetown	Left district
4135	::	::	::	Robertson	William		5.5"	17	Clerk	St Couans Rd N.S. - P.P.&W Railway	Left Distric 1/4/1910
4134	::	31/3/09	31/3/09	Hunter	William		5.9½"	17	Law Clerk	93 George St Whithorn - … / 81 Victoria St - Bank N.S	To Canada 5/6/1911 / Res 9th Feb 1910
4136	::	::	::	McKeana	Wallis		5.6"	20	Law Clerk	Clydesdale Bank N.S.	Dis left dis 6/7/1912
4142	::	29/3/09	29/3/09	McClelland	William		5.8"	17	Baker	St Couans Tce - Kirkcowan	Joined Reg Army
4141	::	1/4/09	1/4/10	Boyd	Robert		5.7½"	26	Buttermaker	Baldoon - Creamery Bladnoch	T.X
	::	::	::	Ewing	William	P	5.10"	18	Cooper	Police Office - …	Dis to Police Force 24/5/11

Reg No	Coy	Enrolled	Oath	Surname	Christian	Chest	Height	Age	Occupation	Residence	Remarks
4137	..	18/3/09	18/3/09	Hacker	Thomas		5.6"	18	Saddler	c/o Hendry N. Main St Wigtown	Dis T.X 11/3/1914
4143	..	7/4/09	7/4/09	Harding	James	P	5.6"	23	Postman	3 Victoria St N.S - GPO	Dis T.X
4144	..	6/4/09	6/4/09	Lupton	Peter	P	5.9"	23	Fisherman	St John St Creetown - same	Dis T.X.
4147	..	8/04/09	8/4/09	Christie	John		5.7"	20	Blacksmith	Kirkinner - same	Dis 24/2/1910
4146	..	..	:	Smylie	Thomas		5.7"	24	Joiner	Kirkinner - same	Dis 26/3/1910
4145	..	..	:	Edwards	John	P	5.8½"	19	Moletrapper	Harbour Rd Wigtown - same	T.X 1/4/1914
4154	..	7/4/09	7/4/09	Hackett	Andrew		5.8"	21	Postman	2 High St Whithorn - Post Office	Tran to 8th Batt 13/7/09
4167	..	..	:	Fraser	James		5.6"	20	Tailor	St John St Whithorn - Brown's	Dis Left dis 1/3/1910
4165	..	..	:	Cosh	Andrew		5.9"	22	Farm Servant	Drummaston Whithorn	To Canada 18/6/1910
4150	..	..	:	Martin	Edmonstone		5.4"	18	Ironmonger	Temperance Hotel Whithorn	Left dis 25/3/1911
4151	..	..	:	Henderson	John	P	5.7"	28	Mason	78 George St Whithorn	Trans to Res Batt. Dumfries
4149	..	..	:	Robertson	Robert	P	5.5½"	21	Baker	93 George St Whithorn	T.X 6/4/1913
4150	..	..	:	Johnstone	Robert	P	5.11"	31	Forester	43 High St Whithorn - Capt Stewart	T.X 6/4/1913
4164	..	..	:	Rennie	William	P	5.10"	18	Shoemaker	2 Bruce St Whithorn	T.X 6/4/1913
4163	..	..	:	Douglas	David S	P	6.00"	21	Butcher	70 St John St Whithorn - Douglas'	Dis Med Unfit 7/8/1914
4162	..	..	:	McBride	Vans	P	5.11"	21	Joiner	Bruce St Whithorn - A McAdam	Dis left dis 30/3/1911
4148	..	..	:	Scott	William	P	5.9"	23	Farm Servant	Kings Road Whithorn - E. Chapelton	.. 18/6/1910
4161	..	..	:	McBratney	Thomas	P	5.11"	21	Blacksmith	12 High St Whithorn - same	To Canada 24/5/1910
4160	..	..	:	Court	Thomson	P	5.11½"	19	Gardener	Castlewigg - same	Res 18th Nov 1909
4159	..	..	:	Stewart	Matthew	P	5.10"	24	Draper	High Mains - J. Horner Kings Rd	Dis to Canada 24/5/11
4158	..	..	:	Donnan	John A	P	5.9"	20	Postman	76 George St Whithorn - Post Office	Dis left dis 27/9/12
4157	..	..	:	McMeechan	Alex.		5.8"	20	Farm Servant	21 Kings Rd - Mr Milligan	Dis left dis 30/3/11
4156	..	..	:	McKie	John M		5.9"	17	Farm Servant	Isle Of Whithorn - Culroach	Left dis 25/3/11
4155	..	..	:	Whannell	Thomas	P	5.8½"	24	Grocer	117 George St Whithorn - G.K. Muir	T.X. 6/4/13
4153	..	..	:	Caine	Henry		5.10"	19	Draper	Castle Hill - Hawthorn George St	Trans to London Scottish
4169	..	28.4/09	28/4/09	Varney	Stanley		5.4"	26	Labourer	Kings St N.S. - Major Armitage	To Canada 25/3/1911
4168	..	..	:	Ravey	James	P	5.4"	23	Labourer	Dashwood Sq - McCreath Skaithe	Trans to Reserve Battalion Dumfries
4170	..	..	:	McGeogh	John		5.6"	18	Farmer	Barnane N.S. - same	To Ayrshire Yeomanry 6/4/1912
4171	..	30/4/09	30/4/09	Thompson	Robert		5.6"	19	Labourer	Tahall Cott Kirkinner - Milldriggan	Dis Canada 24/6/12
4172	..	..	:	Milroy	Gordon		5.7½"	19	Grocer	Kirkinner - same	Dis Canada 12/4/11
4173	..	24/408	24/4/08	McChesney	David		5.8"	26	Joiner	Whithorn	Tran GRSF 12/4/1910
4174	..	10/5/09	10/5/09	Garrick	Peter	P	5.6½"	30	Labourer	Kings Rd - Whithorn	
4175	..	12/5/09	12/5/09	McGinn	Hugh	P	5.4½"	17	Labourer	St John St - Whithorn	
4176	..	10/5/09	10/5/09	Steel	Christopher P		5.7½"	22	Labourer	11 Isle St - Whithorn	T.X. 9/5/1913
4177	..	..	:	Cain	James A	P	5.7½"	22	Blacksmith	Castle Hill - Whithorn	
4178	..	12/5/09	12/5/09	Cain	Andrew		5.7"	21	Blacksmith	St John St - Whithorn	Dis Canada 24/5/11

Reg No	Coy	Enrolled	Oath	Surname	Christian	Chest	Height	Age	Occupation	Residence	Remarks
4179	::	::	::	Cain	William		5.8"	22	Saddler	Ballgreen Wigtown - Whithorn	Dis left dis 4/6/12
4180	::	::	::	Walker	Henry	P	5.11"	23	Farmer	High Skeog Wigtown - Whithorn	Dis 11/7/13 Employment unsuitable
4181	::	::	::	Christie	Tom		5.10"	19	Clerk	113 George - Whithorn	To Canada 6/4/12
4182	::	::	::	Coid	Alex.	P	6.00"	26	Baker	5 Glasserton St - Whithorn	T.X. 9/5/1913
4183	::	::	::	Steel	George		5.5½"	17	Tailor	22 High St - Whithorn	Joined Regular Army 10/10/1910
4184	::	::	::	McCredie	William	P	5.2½"	26	Labourer	6 Park Lane - Whithorn	Transferred to Reserve Battalion Dumfries
4185	::	::	::	Wickie	John		5.4½"	24	Shoemaker	12 Glasserton St - Whithorn	Left dis 1/3/1912
4186	::	::	::	Arnott	Arthur G	P	5.3½"	19	Watchmaker	14 George St - Whithorn	
4187	::	::	::	Hughan	John		5.8½"	24	Grocer	St John St - Whithorn	To Canada 18/6/1910
4188	::	::	::	Allison	William		5.11½"	28	Cabinet Maker	Bladnoch - Whithorn	Dis Emp Unsuitable 27/9/1912
4189	::	::	::	Lofts	William R		5.8"	19	Game Keeper	Caslewigg Whithorn	Dis left dis 30/3/11
4190	::	::	::	Martin	Henry		5.4½"	17	Draper	Temperance Hotel - Whithorn	Left dis 1/3/1912
4191	::	::	::	Hawthorne	W			22		Join Regular Army, Royal Engineers 19/8/09	
4192	::	::	::	Finlay	William	P	5.8"	19	Joiner	Glasserton - Whithorn	T.X. 9/5/1913
4193	::	::	::	Doughty	Langlands	P	5.11½"	21	Game Dealer	George St - Whithorn	Dis T.X. 9/5/1914
4194	::	::	::	Douglas	William	P	5.10"	22	Farmer	St John St - Whithorn	::
4195	::	::	::	McMeechan	Andrew	P	5.8"	23	Labourer	Kings Rd - Whithorn	
4196	::	27/5/09	27/5/09	Watt	James C	P	5.10"	19	Gardener	The Hill Creetown - same	T.X. 26/5/1913
4197	::	8/6/09	8/6/09	Lillerich	William		5.7½"	19	Farm Servant	McClymont Whithorn - same	Dis 24/2/1910
4198	::	2/6/09	2/6/09	Cain	James		5.92	22	Blacksmith	Isle of Whithorn - same	Left dis 1/12/1910
4199	::			Stewart	John		5.7"	17	Farmservant	Mains Whithorn	To Canada 6/4/1912
4200	::	1/6/09	1/5/09	Arnott	Sidney		5.2½"	17	Grocer	123 George St - 14 George St	Left dis 19/6/1912
4203	::	31/3/10	31/3/10	Adams	William		5.3½"	18	Painter	25 Queen St N.S.	Joined Regular Army Royal Scots Fusiliers 16/3/1911
4202	::	::	::	Dunlop	Peter		5.7"	21	Mill Worker	52 King St - Newton Stewart	Dis left dis 30/3/11
4201	::	28/3/10	28/3/10	McGhie	William		5.4"	20	Postman	Harbour St Creetown - Post Office	Dis at own request 7/5/1910
4205	::	5/4/10	5/4/10	Scott	Andrew		5.4"	19	Engineer	18 King St - Newton Stewart	Left dis 1/3/1912
4204	::	7/4/10	7/4/10	McDonald	James	P	5.7"	18	Manufacturer	Gertrude Cott N.S	Dis left dis
4212	::	1/4/10	1/4/10	McBratney	William	P	5.8"	17	Labourer	High St - Whithorn	Dis to Canada 2/6/13
4211	::			Martin	William	P	5.4"	20	Labourer	George St - Whithorn	Dis left dis
4208	::			Heron	Stewart	P	5.9"	22	Grocer	Kings Rd - Whithorn	Deceased 13/9/1912
4207	::			Hannah	Oswald		5.10"	17	Clerk	Whithorn - Cutyaws	Dis left dis 30/3/1911
4206	::			Boyce	Alexander		5.8½"	20	Farm Servant	Kings Rd - Balcray Whithorn	::
4213	::			Scott	Thomas		5.9"	25	Labourer	Kings Road - Whithorn	::
4209	::			Mallet	William	P	5.7"	22	Tailor	High St - Whithorn	.. left district

Reg No	Coy	Enrolled	Oath	Surname	Christian	Chest	Height	Age	Occupation	Residence	Remarks
4210	..	..	..	Loan	Eswin		5.8"	17	Draper	Bruce St - Whithorn	.. 11/5/12
4218	..	18/4/10	18/4/10	Kiltie	Thomas		5.8"	21	Labourer	Craiglemine - Whithorn	Dis to Canada 12/6/12
4216	..	9/4/10	9/4/10	Smith	Robert		5.3"	17	Student	Culderry Row Garlieston	Dis 9/3/1911
4215	..	1/4/10	1/4/10	McCulloch	Thomas		5.9"	17	Labourer	High Row Garlieston	Joined Reg Army 29/12/10
4214	..	..	..	McCulloch	David		5.7"	21	Tailor	St John St - Whithorn	To Canada 5/6/1911
4220	..	9/4/10	9/4/10	Belcomb	Robert		5.3"	17	Miller	High Row Garlieston	left dis 1/3/12
4217	..	..	..	Malone	John		5.3"	17	Labourer	Church St Garlieston	.. 1/12/10
4219	..	16/4/10	16/4/10	Ronnie	Robert	P	5.8"	19	Dairyman	Garrarie Whithorn- same	Dis emp. Unsuitable
4221	..	30/4/10	30/4/10	McKeand	John		5.7"	19	Ironmonger	Mansefield N.S.	Left dis 1/3/12
4222	..	28/2/11	28/2/11	Arnott	James		5.7"				Dis left dis 1/3/12
812	..	23/3/11	23/3/11	McDonald	Andrew	P	5.5"	18	Farm Servant	Woodside - The Risk Minnigaff	Dis left dis
779	..	27/2/11	27/2/11	Whitton	Harold		5.8½"	17	Labourer	High St - Whithorn	Joined Regular Army
										Special Reserve Royal Scots Fusiliers 31st March 1911	
775	..	..	..	McKeachie	James		5.7"	18	Labourer	Railway Crossing - Outon, Whithorn	Left dis 1/3/12
776	..	..	..	Garrick	Alexander	P	5.5"	18	Labourer	Kings Rd - Outon Whithorn	
778	..	28/2/11	28/2/11	Smith	John	RC	5.4"	18	Joiner	Green Larne - Whithorn	
777	..	..	..	Flannigan	John	P	5.5½"	17	Grocer	9 Glasserton St - St John St, Whit.	.. 1/3/12
772	..	21/2/11	21/2/11	Milligan	Robert	P	5.6"	17	Grocer	George St - Whithorn	..
774	..	25/2/11	25/2/11	Laurie	William	P	5.8½"	17	Clerk	Cutyaws - Whithorn	..
773	..	21/2/11	21/2/11	Milroy	John	P	5.3"	17	Draper	113 George St - Whithorn	
783	..	3/3/11	3/3/11	Anderson	Robert		5.8"	17	Blacksmith	Mochrum - Whithorn	.. 1/3/12
782	..	2/3/11	2/3/11	McGinn	Peter	P	5.10"	17	Labourer	George St Whithorn	
781	..	..	..	McKeachie	John	P	5.6"	17	Shoemaker	St John St - Whithorn	.. 4/7/13
780	..	..	..	Kiltie	William	P	5.4"	18	Labourer	Craiglemine - same	.. To Canada 28/4/14
814	..	7/3/11	7/3/11	Kirkpatrick	Thomas A	P	5.2"	19	Shoemaker	St John St - Creetown	
813	..	..	..	McDowall	Robert	P	5.4½"	18	Blacksmith	St John St - Scottish Granite Creetown	
818	..	20/3/11	20/3/11	Turner	Thomas	P	5.7½"	18	Labourer	Craiglemine - same	Trans to Reserve Batt Dumfries
4049	..	..	..	McHaffie	George				Publican	Stranraer	Dis T.X. 31/3/12
821	..	1/4/11	1/4/11	Boyce	Hugh	P	5.10	20	Labourer	Glasserton - Glasserton	Trans to Reserve Batt Dumfries
823	..	..	..	Bryden	John	P	5.7½"	19	Tailor	Kings Rd - George St Whithorn	Deceased 9/11/13
822	..	..	..	Hughes	William	RC	5.8½"	18	Dealer	George St - Whithorn	Dis left dis 12/12/13
851	..	31/5/11	31/5/11	Johnston	Thomas	P	5.2"	17	Labourer	Dunbar House Newton Stewart	.. 9/2/14
871	..	24/10/11	24/10/11	Irving	Hugh	P	5.10"	18	Labourer	Waterloo Tce - Sc. Granite Creetown	Transferred to Reserve Battalion, Dumfries
882	..	21/12/11	21/12/11	Curran	William	P	5.7"	17	Clerk	Barterslow - Comm. Bank N.S.	
883	..	..	..	McWhiston	George	P	5.8"	19	Clerk	Perartree Cott - Br. Linen Bank N.S. Dis to Canada	
881	..	..	..	McDowall	David	P	5.8"	19	Clerk	35 Arthur St - National Bank N.S.	Dis left dist
884	..	..	..	Milligan	Alexander	P	5.7½"	21	Farm Servant	Graddock	Dis Med.Unfit 2/7/14
885	..	..	..	Gibson	William		5.2"	17	Labourer	Minnigaff	*Para 15b (9)* TFR 1/3/12
880	..	27/12/11	28/12/11	McKeand	Samuel	P	5.8"	18	Draper	Arthur St - Newton Stewart	

Reg No	Coy	Enrolled	Oath	Surname	Christian	Chest	Height	Age	Occupation	Residence	Remarks
886	..	28/12/11	..	Lamb	David	P	5.10"	19	Water Bailiff	Cumloden Lodge	Dis to Canada
904	..	24/1/12	24/1/12	Gibson	Alexander	P	5.7"	20	Farm Servant	82 Queen St Newton Stewart	
903	..	..	..	Clement	Thomas	P	5.2"	17	Barber	82 QueenSt Newton Stewart	
905	..	..	..	Owen	Robert	P	5.7"	18	Plumber	Queen St Newton Stewart	
906	..	..	..	Parker	John	P	5.4"	17	Butcher	11 Queen St Newton Stewart	
907	..	..	..	Diamond	John	P	5.11"	28	Surfaceman	Princess St N.S.	
908	..	26/1/12	26/1/12	Nelson	Alexander		5.8"	18	Saddler	10 Victoria St Newton Stewart	Dis left dist11/5/12
910	..	27/1/12	27/1/12	McGuigan	James	RC	5.6½"	17	Labourer	Creebridge N.S	Dis to Canada
909	..	..	..	McClymont	Robert	P	5.8"	17	Labourer	Blackcraig	
932	..	..	..	Stewart	Luke	P	5.11"	18	Labourer	Mains Whithorn	Dis to Canada 2/.6/13
933	..	..	..	McCutcheon	James	P	5.5"	18	Blacksmith	Glasserton St Whithorn	Trans to Res Battalion Dumfries
934	..	..	..	Jolly	William	P	5.8"	20	Labourer	High St Whithorn	
926	..	24/1/12	24/1/12	Donnan	Stewart	P	5.5"	18	Van Man	St John St Whithorn	..
928	..	..	..	Bodle	Robert	P	5.4½"	18	Labourer	Carleton Whithorn	Dis left dist 12/12/13
929	..	..	..	McCleary	John		5.8"	17	Farm Servant	Ravenstone Mains	*Dis Para 15b-9-TFR 18/4/12*
931	..	25/1/12	25/1/12	Henderson	John	P	5.7½"	17	Draper	2 George St Whithorn	To Canada 28/4/14
937	..	..	..	Ambrose	Thomas	P	5.6"	27	Labourer	Kings Rd Whithorn	Dis Med Unfit
927	..	24/1/12	24/1/12	Scott	Thomas	P	5.9"	27	Labourer	Kings Road Whithorn	Trans to Res Battalion Dumfries
930	..	..	..	Woods	Donald	P	5.8½"	18	Labourer	Isle St Whithorn	
925	..	..	..	Woods	John	P	5.6½"	18	Farm Servant	Craiglemine Whithorn	Dis left dist 12/12/13
924	..	23/1/12	23/1/12	McCulloch	William	P	5.11½"	25	Labourer	High Row, Garlieston	..
923	..	..	..	Gulline	Sam	P	5.6"	33	Labourer	Church St. Garlieston	Trans. To Res. Batt. Dumfries.
922	..	..	..	McKie	John	P	5.8½"	24	Postman	Culderry Row, Garlieston	Disch to Canada
921	..	..	..	Thomson	Robert	P	5.8½"	23	Labourer	Church St. Garlieston	Trans to Res Battalion Dumfries
920	..	..	..	Kennedy	John	P	5.7"	23	Labourer	Queen St Newton Stewart	Dis. Emp. unsuit. 28/4/14
919	..	..	..	McConnell	Thomas	P	5.6½"	17	Forester	Kilsture, Sorbie	
918	..	..	..	Orr	Robert	P	5.6½"	25	Insurance Agent	South St, Garlieston	Dis. To Canada
917	..	..	..	McGarva	James	P	5.4½"	17	Labourer	Home Farm, Galloway House	
916	..	..	..	Lofts	William	P	5.8½"	23	Carter	Extreme Point, Garlieston	
915	..	..	..	Gulline	James	P	5.4½"	30	Labourer	Church St, Garlieston	Trans. To Res. Batt. Dumfries
914	..	..	..	Latimer	James	P	5.8"	17	Labourer	Old Town Crossing, Sorbie	
913	..	..	..	Donnan	James	P	5½"	17	Labourer	Glenmalloch Lodge, Cumloden	Dis. 11/1/14 Joined Regular Army
912	..	..	..	Leabody	William	P	5.7"	17	Blacksmith	Church St, Garlieston	
911	..	..	..	Dalrymple	George	P	5.5"	24	Labourer	High Row, Garlieston	Dis. To Canada
938	..	10/2/12	10/2/12	McCallum	Robert	P	5.10"	17	Labourer	Galloway Hse, Gardens	Dis. Left district
940	..	..	..	Orr	James	P	5.10"	21	Gardener	South St, Garlieston	Dis. Left dis. 9/2/14
939	..	7/2/12	6/3/12	Gulline	John	P	5.5"	17	Drainer??	Church St, Garlieston	Trans. To Res. Batt. Dumfries
949	..	7/2/12	..	Orr	Thomas	P	5.7"	27	Gardener	Glenmalloch Lodge, Cumloden	Dis. Left dis. 9/2/14
948	..	28/2/12	28/2/12	Cron	Alexander	P	5.7½"	23	Forester	Newton Cott. Kirkinner	Dis to Canada 6/5/13

Reg No	Coy	Enrolled	Oath	Surname	Christian	Chest	Height	Age	Occupation	Residence	Remarks
946	::	17/2/12	17/2/12	Ambrose	John	P	5.9"	18	Labourer	High St, Whithorn	Dis to Canada
947	::	20/2/12	20/2/12	Fraser	John	P		25	Gardener	Galloway Hse. Gardens	Served in 1st Vol. Battalion Cameronian Highlanders. 4th R.S.F. for one year.
975	::	14/3/12	14/3/12	McAdam	Andrew	P	5.8"	24	Labourer	Bladnoch	
976	::	::	::	Paterson	John	P	5.9"	20	Farm Servant	Boreland, Whauphill	To Canada 28/4/14
974	::		::	Barr	Alexander		5.11½"	18	Blacksmith	13 High St, Wigtown	Dis. Left dis. 11/5/12
988	::	26/3/12	26/3/12	Cowan	David	P	5.10"	19	Farm Servant	Greenburn, Creetown	Dis To Canada 6/5/13
993	::	21/3/12	21/3/12	McNeil	James	P	5.7"	18	Motor Assistant	10 North Main St, Wigtown	
994	::		::	Gilmour	James D	RC	5.4"	19	Factory Worker	8 North Back St. Wigtown	
1008	::	18/4/12	18/4/12	Fitzsimmons	Walter	P	5.5"	23	Labourer	Low Vennell, Wigtown	Dis. Left dis 16/7/14
1013	::	26/4/12	26/4/12	Stevenson	Andrew R	P	5.9"	25	Stone Cutter	Grinshawe St, Creetown	Dis emp. Unsuitable
1026	::	1/5/12	1/5/12	Craig	James	P	5.4"	19	Woodcutter	69 Arthur St, Newton Stewart	Dis. To Canada
1024	::	2/5/12	2/5/12	Hall	Edward	P	5.8½"	17	Labourer	Bladnoch	Dis. Left dis 16/7/14
1025	::		::	Knowles	Robert	P	5.6"	17	Labourer	North Back St, Wigtown	,, .. 9/2/14
1036	::	27/4/12	27/4/12	Briggs	James	P	5.6"	20	Labourer	Extreme Point, Garlieston	
1047	::	20/5/12	20/5/12	Stitt	Robert	P	5.11½"	30	Forester	Whithorn Lodge	Dis To Canada 2/6/13
1061	::	28/5/12	28/5/12	Heron	John	P	5.6½"	20	Labourer	Ladysmith	Dis Med. Unfit 7/3/14
1062	::	6/6/12	6/6/12	Kerr	James	p	5.7½"	39	Labourer	Main St. Wigtown	
1221	::	21/2/13	21/2/13	McBratney	Alexander	P	5.6"	18	Blacksmith	Glasserton	
1224	::	::	::	Ross	William	P	5.11"	17	Ironmonger	St. John St, Whithorn	To Canada 28/4/14
1225	::	::	::	Ross	David	P	6.11"	17	Draper	St John St, Whithorn	
1220	::	::	::	McKeachie	Alexander	P	5.11½"	21	Grocer	St. John St, Whithorn	
1226	::		::	Flannigan	James	RC	5.10"	24	Labourer	Glasserton St, Whithorn	Trans to Res. Batt. Dumries
1223	::	25/2/13	25/2/13	Saunders	Andrew	P	5.8"	17	Labourer	Bailliewhir, Whithorn	
1222	::	27/2/13	27/2/13	McCutcheon	Hugh	P	5.7"	17	Keeper	Castlewigg, Whithorn	Tran to Res.Batt. Dumfries
1270	::	18/3/13	18/3/13	Lupton	John	P	5.6"	19	Quarryman	St. John St, Creetown	
1271	::		::	Vernon	Peter	P	5.4"	20	..	Barholm St, Creetown	Dis Left dis 28/4/14
1273	::	24/3/13	24/3/13	Carr	James	P	5.11"	17	Gardener	Galloway Hse. Gardens	Dis Left district
1272	::	::	::	Muir	George	P	5.8"	22	Gamekeeper	Church St, Garlieston	Dis empl unsuitable 28/4/14
1291	::	29/3/13	29/3/13	Rattary	William	P	5.6½"	21	Gardener	Galloway Hse. Gardens	Dis Left district
1290	::		::	Fingland	Alexander	P	5.8"	17	Forester	Whitehills, Sorbie	
1294	::	3/4/13	3/4/13	McCleary	Peter J	P	5.2½"	18	Farm Servant	Barnkirk, Newton Stewart	
1306	::	19/4/13	19/4/13	McRobert	William	P	5.4½"	17	Blacksmith	13 High St, Whithorn	
1305	::		::	Litterick	Robert	P	5.4½"	17	Farm Servant	Barlae, Kirkinner	Enlisted Regular Army, A&S Highlanders, 29/5/14
1307	::	22/4/13	22/4/13	McDavid	James C M	P	5.9½"	18	Tailor	St John St. Creetown	
1308	::		::	McCleary	Alexander	P	5.6½"	20	Postman	Main St. Kirkcowan	Dis. Left dis 28/4/14
1318	::	17/4/13	17/4/13	Martin	Matthew	P	5.8"	30	Labourer	George St, Whithorn	Trans to Res. Batt. Dumfries
1334	::	14/5/13	14/5/13	Wallace	William	RC	5.6½"	25	Carter	31 Arthur St, N.S.	
1335	::		::	Topping	John	P	5.5½"	24	Porter	43 Princes St, N.S.	Dis Med. Unfit 7/8/14

Reg No	Coy	Enrolled	Oath	Surname	Christian	Chest	Height	Age	Occupation	Residence	Remarks
1336	..	13/5/13	13/5/13	Harvey	Daniel	RC	5.5"	19	Labourer	21 Harbour Rd, Wigtown	Dis to Canada 21/6/13
1355	..	24/5/13	24/5/13	Crawford	Peter	P	5.8"	17	Blacksmith	Glaisnick Smithy, Kirkcowan	
1354	..	27/5/13	27/5/13	Stevenson	Andrew	P	5.9"	26	Stone Cutter	Adamson Sq. Creetown	Dis Left dis 28/4/14
1353	..	..	..	McClelland	John A	P	5.8"	22	Clerk	Barnkirk, N.S. - Valuation Office	
1356	..	21/5/13		Edgar	James	P	5.11½"	20	Clerk	32 Queen St. N.S. - ..	Dis Left dis 28/4/14
1357	..	21/5/13	21/5/13	Clarke	John	P	5.6"	34	Labourer	Tarff Row, Kirkcowan	
1358	..	..	..	McMaster	Archibald	P	5.9"	34	Postman	Post Office, Kirkcowan	Trans to Res. Batt. 11/1/15
1366	..	2/6/13	2/6/13	Irving	Samuel	P	5.6"	22	Tailor	Shannanton Croft, Kirkcowan	
1367	..	19/6/13	19/6/13	Nicholson	James	P	5.4"	34	Cabinet Maker	Main St. Kirkcowan	Dis Med. Unfit 7/3/14
1385	..	4/9/13	4/9/13	Edwards	John	P	5.8"	24	Mole Trapper	Harbour Rd. Wigtown	
1432	..	5/11/13	5/11/13	Martin	William	P	5.8"	24	Labourer	123 George St, Whithorn	Trans to Res. Batt. 19/11/14
1433	..	..	..	Martin	Robert	P	5.8½"	17	Gardener	86 George St, Whithorn	..
1434	..	..	..	Gordon	John	P	5.7½"	17	Postman	2 George St, Whithorn	..
1435	..	10/11/13	10/11/13	McCallie	Robert	P	5.3"	24	Mason	Kings Rd. Whithorn	Trans to Res. Batt. Dumfries
1431	..			Boyce	John	P	5.7"	26	Roadman	115 George St, Whithorn	..
1447	..	20/11/13	20/11/13	McCallie	Andrew	P	5.7½"	26	Labourer	St. John St. Whithorn	..
1451	..	9/12/13/	9/12/13	Elder	William	P	5.7"	22	Motorman	Bladnoch	Trans to Res. Batt. 5/1/15
1452	..	17/12/13	17/12/13	Murchie	Alexander	P	5.10½"	22	Joiner	44 Queen St. N.S.	30/1/14
1472	..	15/1/14	15/1/14	Ballantyne	John	RC	5.7"	29	Dealer	124 George St, Whithorn	..
1473	..	..	..	Black	Wwilliam	P	5.4"	22	Vanman	22 High St, Whithorn	..
1479	..	24/1/14	24/1/14	Edgar	John	P	5.6½"	17	Joiner	Extreme Point, Garlieston	Trans to Res Batt. 9/1/15
1478	..			Hughes	Alexander	P	5.6½"	17	Blacksmith	Church St. Garlieston	..
1474	..	21/1/14	21/1/14	Gulline	Peter	P	5.6"	17	Miller	..	30/1/14
1476	..			Richardson	William	P	5.7"	18	Labourer	Whithills, Sorbie	Trans to Res. Batt. Dumfries
1477	..	..	..	Watt	Peter	P	5.9"	21	Gardener	Galloway Hse. Gardens	..
1475	..			Hawkins	John	P	5.8"	18	Labourer	Church St. Garlieston	To Canada 28/4/14
1480	..	31/1/14	31/1/14	Simpson	Wlm. Mc	P	5.7½"	18	Clerk	37 Princes St, N.S.	
1487	..	4/2/14	4/2/14	McGowan	William	P	5.7"	19	Baker	32 Arthur St. N.S.	
1485	..	27/1/14	27/1/14	Edgar	William B	P	5.7½"	19	Postman	Extreme Point, Garlieston	
1486	..	28/1/14	28/1/14	Keith	James	P	5.9"	22	Postman	Kings Rd. Whithorn	
1491	..	12/2/14	12/2/14	Scott	Walter	CofE	5.5"	17	Clerk	63 Arthur St, N.S.	
1501	..	19/2/14	19/2/14	McAllister	George	CofE	5.6"	17	Tailor	17 Arthur St. N.S.	
1505	..	..	..	Kennedy	Robert	P	5.9"	21	Labourer	Church St, Garlieston	
1525	..	4/3/14	4/3/14	Hunter	John	P	5.3"	17	Clerk	4 Queen St. N.S.	
1533	..	7/3/14	7/3/14	Walsh	Charles	CofE	5.5½"	17	Clerk	16 Queen St, N.S.	To Canada 2/7/14
1529	..			Kerr	James E W	P	5.5"	18	Motor Assistant	Kilwhirn Rd. Wigtown	
1534	..	12/3/14	12/3/14	Bolt	William H	P	5.3"	18	Labourer	Albert Place, N.S.	
1536	..	14/3/14	14/3/14	Findlay	Thomas	P	5.7"	32	Railway Porter	32 Arthur St. N.S.	
1535	..	..		Ferries	Alexander	P	5.9"	24	Joiner	45 Princes St. N.S.	Trans to Res. Batt. Dum-fries

Reg No	Coy	Enrolled	Oath	Surname	Christian	Chest	Height	Age	Occupation	Residence	Remarks
1538	..	..	..	Thompson	Matthew	P	5.7"	17	Labourer	131 George St, Whithorn	:: :: ::
1545	..	19/3/14	19/3/14	Lockhart	William	P	5.4½"	17	Butcher	57 Queen St. N.S.	
1548	..	..	..	McNaught	John	P	5.7"	18	Sawyer	21 Arthur St. N.S.	
1546	..	20/3/14	20/3/14	Mackie	John	P	5.4½"	21	Baker	11 Dashwood Sq. N.S.	
1547	..	..	..	Maginess	Henry J	P	5.5"	28	Labourer	39 Arthur St. N.S.	
1549	..	..	..	Ross	Robert	P	5.6"	26	Painter	71 Arthur St. N.S.	
1550	..	..	..	Scott	William	CofE	5.4½"	19	Draper	63 Arthur St. N.S.	
1553	..	25/3/14	25/3/14	Hamilton	James	P	5.5½"	33	Plasterer	87 King St. N.S.	
1560	..	27/3/14	27/3/14	Baillie	James	P	5.5"	17	Blacksmith	Albert Place. N.S.	
1561	..	25/3/14	25/3/14	Agnew	John Wm	P	6.0"	26	Farmer	Barlachlan. N.S.	
1577	..	11/4/14	11/4/14	Steele	Christopher	P	5.9"	26	Gardener	Isle St. Whithorn	Dis Med. Unfit 7/8/14
1578	..	14/4/14	14/4/14	Cochrane	Thomas	RC	5.8"	27	Roadman	Woodfall, Creetown	
1579	..	15/4/14	15/4/14	Griffin	Wm John	P	5.7½"	20	Lorryman	13 Station Rd. N.S.	
1580	..	..	..	Hawthorn	Aleander	P	5.7"	22	Clerk	Barnkirk, N.S.	Dis Left dis 16/7/14
1581	..	16/4/14	16/4/14	Hogg	Thomas	P	5.3"	18	Farm Labourer	Landberrick, Mochrum	
1582	..	20/4/14	20/4/14	Thomsom	Robert	P	5.8½"	25	Creamery Worker	6 Bank St. Wigtown	
1607	..	6/5/14	6/5/14	Carson	Robert	P	5.6"	18	Cheesemaker	Appleby, Whithorn	
1608	..	16/5/14	16/5/14	Dodds	Peter	p	5.6"	29	Labourer	Isle St. Whithorn	
1620	..	15/6/14	15/6/14	Logan	James	P	5.6"	28	Postman	Bridgeend, Creetown	
1616	..	11/3/13	11/3/13	Cochrane	Frank	RC	5.7"	18	Labourer	Norris St. Creetown	(Trans from Ayrshire Yeomanry 11/6/14)
1676	..	5/8/14	5/8/14	Boyd	James	P	5.7½"	20	Gardener	Slate Row, N.S.	
1667	..	..	..	Boyd	William	CofE	5.5"	22	Drover	Roadfoot, N.S.	
1672	..	..	..	Gibson	Robert	P	5.11"	29	??	Creebridge, N.S.	
1673	..	..	..	Hill	John	P	5.4"	21	Painter	32 Queen St. N.S.	
1668	..	..	..	Maginess	John	P	5.9½"	26	Grocer	71 King Str. N.S.	
1669	..	..	..	Murdoch	Andew	P	5.10"	22	Clerk	15 Station Road. N.S.	
1674	..	..	..	Sharpe	John	P	5.5"	21	Coach Painter	54 King St. N.S.	
1671	..	..	..	Shennan	John	CofE	5.6½"	19	Coach Painter	Queen St. N.S.	
1675	..	..	..	Gilbert	Robert	P	5.9½"	17	Joiner	Creebridge, N.S.	
1670	..	..	..	Murchie	Thomas	P	5.9½"	21	Builder	44 Queen St, N.S.	
1666	..	..	..	McLean	William	P	5.4"	20	Bottler	16 King St. N.S.	
1663	..	6/8/14	6/8/14	Hogg	Thomas	P	5.3"	18	Farm Labourer	Mabie, Dumfries	
1665	..	..	..	McMeeken	Alexander	P	5.7½"	25	Dairyman	Kings Rd. Whithorn	
1664	..	..	..	McKie	Herbert M	P	5.6"	19	Chauffeur	17 Princes St. N.S.	
1811	..	7/8/14	7/8/14	Ross	William	P	5.8"	20	Ironmonger	Dunfermline	
1807	..	9/8/14	9/8/14	Boyd	David A	P			Creamery Worker	Agnew Cresc. Wigtown	
1808	..	..	..	Cameron	Donald	P			Postman	Minnigaff	Tran to Res Batt. 30/1/14
1810	..	..	..	Matheson	Andrew	P			W. B. Officer	George St. Whithorn	
1809	..	..	..	McRae	William	P			Borough Superintendant	Princes St. N.S.	

Reg No	Coy	Enrolled	Oath	Surname	Christian	Chest	Height	Age	Occupation	Residence	Remarks
1907	:	5/9/14	5/9/14	McEacharn	Neil B W	P			Gentleman	Galloway House, Garlieston	Tran to Res. Batt. Dumfries
1908	:	26/9/14	26/9/14	McDavid	William	P				51 Arthur St. N.S.	
1920	:	:	:	Milligan	Andrew	P				Graddock Mill, Palnure	
1964	:	29/9/14		Kirkby	Michael	RC				Dumfries	
1980	:	30/9/14		Maginess	Walter	P				King St, N.S.	
2002	:	5/10/14		Gibson	Alexander	P					
2255	:	6/10/14		Milligan	Robert	P					
2287	:			McGuffie	L						
2047	:			McGowan	S						
				Thomson	W						
				McGeoch	W						

574

BIBLIOGRAPHY
Main Sources.

(1) *Dumfries and Galloway Standard,* 1859-1908.

(2) *Galloway Gazette,* 1870-1908.

(3) *Kirkcudbrightshire Advertiser* (*Galloway News*), 1859-1908.

(4) *Wigtown Free Press,* 1859-1908.

Additional Sources.

(5) *A History of the Scottish Borderers Militia.-* Rev. Robert W. Weir, M.A.

(6) *All the Blue Bonnets. The History of the K.O.S.B.* - Robert Woollcombe.

(7) *Auld Lang Syne in the Rhins of Galloway-* Professor Charles McNeil.

(8) *Dumfries and Galloway Courier.* (Selected years).

(9) *Dumfries Weekly Journal.* (Selected years).

(10) *Edinburgh Courant,* 1803-1816.

(11) *Encyclopedia Brittanica.*

(12) *Maxwellton West. The Story of a Church. 1866-1966.* - A. Maclean B.S.C. I.A.S. (Retd.) and
      Rev. H.G.A. Simmons, M.A.

(13) *On To Pretoria* - Hume.

(14) *Record of the Scottish Volunteer Force 1859-1908.* - Lt. General Sir James Moncrieff-Grierson, K.C.B.
      C.V.O. C.M.G. A.D.C. Also produced in facsimile by Frederick Muller Ltd., 1972.

(15) *Regimental Gazettes of the Galloway Rifle Volunteers.* Volumes 1 and 2 dated 1897 and 1899.

(16) *Rifleman Form. A Study of the Rifle Volunteer Movement 1859 - 1908.* I. F. W. Beckett.

(17) *The American Civil War.* A. H. Allt.

(18) *The Boer War, Concise Campaigns.* Eversley Belfield.

(19) *The History of Headquarters Royal Artillery 52nd (Lowland) Division. During the German War
      1939-1945.* The Staff of the Divisional Artillery Headquarters 52nd (Lowland) Division
      British Army on the Rhine 1945.

(20) *The Illustrated Encyclopaedia of Firearms.* Ian V. Hogg.

(21) *The Scottish Regiments. A Pictorial History 1633 - 1987.* P. J. R. Milejam.

(22) *The Volunteer Force. A Social and Political History 1859 - 1908.* Hugh Cunningham.

(23) *The World's Great Guns.* Frederick Wilkinson.

(23) *War History of the 5th Battalion King's Own Scottish Borderers.* G. F. Scott-Elliott.

"No longer do the Defence Committee anticipate that we have to reckon with invasion by a large body of troops, but in the case of a Great War, we do not think that the Country would feel comfortable if solely dependent on the Navy for its protection, as raids might do incalculable mischief unless immediately checked by Defensive Troops."

1st December, 1905.

Joseph Chamberlain, 1836 - 11914.